GRAN COCINA
LATINA

GRAN COCINA
LATINA

The Food of Latin America

MARICEL E. PRESILLA

Photographs by Gentl & Hyers/Edge
Prop Styling by Andrea Gentl
Drawings by Julio Figueroa

W. W. NORTON & COMPANY
NEW YORK · LONDON

For information about permission to reproduce selections from
this book, write to Permissions, W. W. Norton & Company, Inc.,
500 Fifth Avenue, New York, NY 10110

For information about special discounts for bulk purchases,
please contact W. W. Norton Special Sales
at specialsales@wwnorton.com or 800-233-4830

Manufacturing by Courier Kendallville
Book design by Beth Tondreau
Cartography by Adrian Kitzinger
Production manager: Anna Oler

Library of Congress Cataloging-in-Publication Data

Presilla, Maricel E.

    Gran cocina latina : the food of Latin America / Maricel E.
Presilla ; photography by Gentl & Hyers/Edge ; illustrations by
Julio Figueroa. — 1st ed.

       p. cm.

Includes index.

    ISBN 978-0-393-05069-1 (hardcover)

    1. Cooking, Latin American. 2. Cooking, Caribbean. 3. Cooking,
Mexican. I. Title.

TX716.AIP746   2012

641.5972—dc23

                        2012017701

W. W. Norton & Company, Inc.
500 Fifth Avenue, New York, N.Y. 10110
www.wwnorton.com

W. W. Norton & Company Ltd.
Castle House, 75/76 Wells Street, London W1T 3QT

2 3 4 5 6 7 8 9 0

To my husband, Alejandro Presilla, my North Star in all weather, for
believing in this life-changing journey.

With gratitude to my parents, Angélica Parladé and Ismael Espinosa, for feeding my curiousity and
making me believe even someone born on an island could eat the world.

To the taxi drivers of Latin America, the best culinary tour guides in the world.

CONTENTS

GRAN COCINA
LATINA

JOURNEY OF THE
SAPOARA

Every year at the end of July, when the fierce summer rains swell the Orinoco River, the spiny silver fish called *sapoara* leave the lagoons where they hatched in quiet seclusion and swim upstream. It is their time to escape and live dangerously.

Most of the year, the people of Ciudad Bolívar, a Venezuelan town on the banks of the Orinoco, move in a slow, predictable rhythm. When the *sapoara* come, they rouse from their tropical languor and rush to join a frenzy of fishing and eating. At the water's edge, fishermen cast their nets into the engorged current. Nearby, on the side of the road, women make deep cuts across the wriggling fish from head to tail and fry them until golden in enormous cauldrons set over a wood fire for the hungry crowd.

One day in July, I happened to be in Ciudad Bolívar for the coming of the *sapoara*. At sundown, I fought my way down the crowded Rio Orinoco Boulevard to watch hundreds of local people wrestling the silver fish out of the swift, muddy waters with their nets. Pairs of seasoned fishermen paddled slender dugout canoes to the center of the river, where the current is the strongest and where the biggest fish swim. One man maneuvered the boat in a zigzag pattern to keep it miraculously steady while the other one flung his net into the water. Against the dying Guayana sun, the chocolate-brown river reverberated with specks of light, the reflection of thousands of fish jumping in and out of the water to fight the strong current. The fishermen's nets shone like golden spiderwebs.

In Ciudad Bolívar, there is a saying: If you eat the head of the *sapoara*, you, like the silver fish, will always come back. In writing this book, I became the returning *sapoara*, caught in a net of my own doing. This association stayed with me as a symbol of my longing to return to the landscape of my memory by immersing myself vicariously in the cultures that I experienced in my journeys.

This book first took shape as a map of memories patched together from the stories of friends who, like me, fondly recalled their homes in Latin America. My dear friend the late Felipe Rojas-Lombardi, the Peruvian chef with whom I first trained in Manhattan, used to describe the beloved stews his mother, Judith, made, the long, narrow kitchen of his grandmother, with whom he lived during most of his childhood, and the hours he spent daydreaming on the roof beside his grandfather's pigeon coops. Retracing Felipe's steps in Lima, I found his grandmother's house turned into a pottery studio, the coops now ravaged by time. Yet when his elderly mother cooked for me, Felipe and his memories of the sensuous tastes of a Lima kitchen suddenly came to life.

I had lived a settled and fruitful life in the United States for many years. I could not have known that embarking on a Latin American cookbook and traveling time and again to more than twenty countries that were not Cuba, my homeland, would cause me to experience one flashback after another.

When I started my journey, I thought I was not only doing something apolitical but heading out into a vast free continent in the opposite direction from the Cuba of all my conflicted loyalties. Not so. Again and again, I was forced to remember that food is always deeply political. Sharing meals with people for whom putting food on the table is a constant struggle brought back my teenage years of ration cards and endless queues. Knowing that for me such hardships were a thing of the past and that worse deprivations are daily reality for others in many Latin countries saddened me and often made me feel awkward. But people's unfailing generosity, the joy with which food is always shared in Latin America, also made me realize that the love of food transcends even the most bitter of realities. Deprivation does not deny us our pleasures; it whets our appetites, lets us dream and talk of all the foods we yearn for.

The tastes and smells that greeted me from cooking pots across the Americas also made me realize how much I missed the sense of belonging that for all of us is forever associated with the foods of our childhood.

The rhythm of Latin America—the conviviality and long lunch hours, the impromptu get-togethers, the fact that much of life revolves around food—suits me. At the same time, the things I treasure are also fast disappearing. Many times I have traveled to Lake Pátzcuaro in Michoacán, Mexico, to eat the legendary white fish, a fish so transparent that you can see its delicate bones. But today the neighboring mountains, once thickly forested with pine trees and eucalyptus, are barren, and heavy rains wash soil into the lake. The traditional fishing nets shaped like butterfly wings only flutter to entertain tourists.

With such complicated and ambivalent emotions, I traveled from village to village, from country to country, absorbing, allowing each place to leave its mark on me, as I did on it. Many of these destinations became my home for some precious interval of time—perhaps all the more intensely felt because I have no native homeland to return to.

I will always belong to the places where I tried my hand at local dishes, cooked with the ingredients that I bought at a local market, fed my friends, and left my sweaty imprint on a frying pan.

UNITED STATES

Atlantic Ocean

Rio Grande

MEXICO

Gulf of Mexico

BAHAMAS

Mexico City

BELIZE

Havana

CUBA

GREATER ANTILLES

HAITI

DOMINICAN REPUBLIC

JAMAICA

Kingston

Puerto Rico

San Juan

LESSER ANTILLES

Belize City

Santo Domingo

Port-au-Prince

Guatemala City

Tegucigalpa

HONDURAS

Caribbean Sea

GUATEMALA

San Salvador

Managua

NICARAGUA

Port of Spain

TRINIDAD & TOBAGO

EL SALVADOR

San José

Panama City

Caracas

VENEZUELA

GUYANA

SURINAME

COSTA RICA

PANAMA

ORINOCO BASIN

Orinoco

Georgetown

Paramaribo

Guyane (French Guiana)

Cayenne

Bogotá

COLOMBIA

EQUATOR

Quito

ECUADOR

Galapagos Is.

Amazon

A N D E S

AMAZON

BASIN

BRAZIL

PERU

Lima

BOLIVIA

La Paz

Brasilia

Pacific Ocean

PARAGUAY

Rio de Janeiro

São Paulo

Asunción

URUGUAY

M O U N T A I N S

Santiago

Buenos Aires

Montevideo

CHILE

ARGENTINA

N

Falkland Is. (Malvinas)

South Georgia I.

Latin America

N

UNITED STATES

NEW MEXICO

ARIZONA

SONORA

Ciudad Juárez

Moctezuma

CHIHUAHUA

TEXAS

Rio Grande

COAHUILA

Gulf of California

DURANGO

NUEVO LEÓN

SINALOA

MEXICO

ZACATECAS

Gulf of Mexico

SAN LUIS POTOSÍ

TAMAULIPAS

Tropic of Cancer

NAYARIT

AGUASCALIENTES

Huasteca

JALISCO

Guadalajara

Tlaquepaque

Lake Chapala

Guanajuato

Ojo del Agua

Celaya

Querétaro

San Martín

CUBA

Lake Pátzcuaro

Quiroga

HIDALGO

Papantla

Tzintzuntzan

Morelia

COLIMA

Pátzcuaro

Erongaricuaro

MICHOACÁN

Toluca

MEXICO CITY

TLAXCALA

Tecolutla

Mérida

Tixkokob

YUCATÁN

Cuautla

Tlaxcala

Xalapa

Veracruz

Campeche

Valladolid

Huexca

Popocatepetl (volcano)

Puebla

PUEBLA

Orizaba

Tlacotalpan

VERACRUZ

Los Tuxtlas

Catemaco

CAMPECHE

QUINTANA ROO

GUERRERO

Acapulco

TABASCO

Oaxaca

Santa Maria el Tule

BELIZE

Caribbean Sea

Guila Naquitz Cave, Mitla

OAXACA

CHIAPAS

Alta Verapaz

Soconusco

Colotenango

Livingston

GUATEMALA

Tela

San Pedro Sula

Sololá

Lake Atitlán

Antigua

Guatemala City

San Salvador

HONDURAS

Pacific Ocean

Antiguo Cuscatlán

La Libertad

EL SALVADOR

NICARAGUA

Managua

Lake Managua

Granada

Lake Nicaragua

Masaya (volcano)

COSTA RICA

Limón

San José

Cartago

San Blas Islands

Panama City

PANAMA

Kilometers

0   100   200   300   400   500   600

Miles

0   100   200   300   400

Mexico & Central America

Atlantic Ocean

UNITED STATES

Gulf of Mexico

Miami

THE BAHAMAS

N

Tropic of Cancer

HAVANA
Pinar del Rio
Las Martinas
CUBA
Trinidad
Sierra de la Cubitas
Gibara
Sagua   Baracoa
CAYMAN ISLANDS   Sierra Maestra   Gran Piedra   Maisí
Santiago de Cuba

TURKS AND CAICOS

HAITI   DOMINICAN REPUBLIC
Cibao Mountains   Santiago de los Caballeros
JAMAICA
HISPANIOLA   SANTO DOMINGO
Cabo Rojo
Cayo Caracoles   Phosphorescent Bay

PUERTO RICO   Luquillo
La Parquera   VIRGIN ISLANDS   ANGUILLA
ST. MARTIN   BARBUDA
MONTSERRAT   ANTIGUA
GUADELOUPE
DOMINICA
MARTINIQUE
ST. LUCIA
ST. VINCENT
GRENADA   BARBADOS
MARGARITA
TRINIDAD & TOBAGO

HONDURAS

NICARAGUA

Caribbean Sea

ARUBA
CURAÇAO
BONAIRE

RICA
PANAMA

Pacific
Ocean

COLOMBIA

VENEZUELA

GUYANA

ECUADOR

PERU

BRAZIL

Kilometers
0 100 200 300 400 500 600

Miles
0   100   200   300   400

The
Caribbean
Islands

Atlantic Ocean

Caribbean Sea

Guajira Peninsula
Los Roques Islands
Margarita Island
Cumarebo
Paria Peninsula
Valedupar
Churuguara
Valencia
Yaguaraparo
TRINIDAD & TOBAGO
Barranquilla
Macaraibo
Carora
CARACAS
Cartagena
Barquisimeto
VENEZUELA
Guanare
Puerto Ordaz
Barinas
GEORGETOWN
Antioquia
Bucaramanga
PARAMAIBO
Medellin
Orinoco
Cayenne
Boyaca
Sierra Pacaraima
GUYANA
SURINAME
Madrid
Guyane (French Guiana)
BOGOTA
COLOMBIA
O R I N O C O   B A S I N
Cali
EQUATOR
Cauca
Magdalena

QUITO
Sangolqui
Ilha Marajó
MANABI
Latacunga
Belém
ECUADOR
Guayaquil
A M A Z O N
Cuenca

Maranon
BRAZIL
Catacaos
Piura
LAMBAYEQUE
CEARA
Chiclayo
Reque
PERNAMBUCO
Huanchaco
Trujillo

Caral
PERU
Tarma
Supe
Huancayo
LIMA
Pucusana
Lurin
Ayacucho
Cusco
BAHIA
Ica
Salvador da Bahia
Nazca
Lake Titicaca
Illampu (mountain)
BOLIVIA
BRASILIA
LA PAZ
Illimani (mountain)
Goiás
Arequipa
Cochabamba
GOIAS
Tacna
Potosí
MINAS GERAIS
Belo Horizonte
ESPIRITO SANTO
Tarija
Espírito Santo
PARAGUAY
São Joao
Tiradentes
São Paulo
Rio de
ASUNCIÓN
Janeiro
Salta
Villeta
Ciudad del Este

Tucuman
Copiapó
Santiago del Estero
ARGENTINA
Freirina
ENTRE RIOS
La Serena
URUGUAY
San Juan
Córdoba
Mendoza
Valparaiso
Isla Negra
SANTIAGO
Marchigüe
BUENOS AIRES
MONTEVIDEO
Carico
Rio de la Plata
Chillan

Traiguén
Cholchol
Temuco
Valdivia
Corral

Chiloé Island

N

Pacific Ocean

Kilometers
0 100   300   600

Miles
0   100 200 300 400

South
America

CHAPTER 1

WHAT IS LATIN AMERICA?

When I came to the United States, I gave up one citizenship and gained two. As I became an American, I began to discover that I was also a Latin American. In one way or another, all of us Spanish-speaking Latin Americans living in the United States are refugees, but with deep New World roots. Forced together by our needs, we live in the same neighborhoods, shop in the same markets, and work in the same factories, offices, and restaurant kitchens. We can't help learning from each other.

For many years, I never thought of writing about this process of discovery because I was too busy experiencing it. Transplanted to the United States, a nation that is proud to live in the present, I chose to explore the past. I went to New York University to get my doctorate in medieval history, working under the guidance of a great historian, Norman Cantor, who encouraged me to explore history from every angle. My research took me to Castile in Spain, where I had lived for several years after leaving Cuba in 1970, and I combed through documents and badly lit archives, explored crypts, and visited cemeteries. I became absorbed in understanding how Arabs, Jews, and Christians each contributed to the development of the Spanish character, culture, and cuisine. Gradually I began to see that what had made Latin America the world's first and greatest laboratory of intercontinental culinary "fusion" was the arrival of Iberian cooks carrying a complex legacy.

But I missed the seductive smells and flavors of a living, boiling cooking pot, its hidden potential to reveal the past, present, and future. So I found myself leaving the classroom behind and boarding a plane for Latin America. It may appear a wild leap to move from the thirteenth-century court of King Alfonso X to a pan–Latin American cookbook. Or

perhaps not. In many ways my research was eerily relevant to what I would find myself doing after I stumbled into working in Latin kitchens and musing about how different peoples have contributed to Latin food.

Back in our original countries, we saw ourselves as essentially Cuban, Mexican, Brazilian. We jealously guarded our differences. This was especially true of our cooking. We treated our kitchens as bastions of national identity, and we often sealed off our pots from culinary intrusions.

But in this country, maintaining a well-defended Latin American national cuisine is nearly impossible. Even if you have never before smelled an aromatic Peruvian *adobo* or *seco*, you will be drawn to your neighbor's kitchen and find yourself sticking a spoon in her pot. "My kitchen" becomes "our kitchen" before you know what is happening.

Writing this book is a way of acknowledging my expanding personal identity and the way I cook now. In some ways, it's easier to re-create Latin American cooking in this country than it has ever been. Yet I believe that there are many false paths that remain. The cooking of many Latins in the United States was shaped by a similar moment of adaptation—when people reached for substitutions that became standards but are no longer necessary, when traditional cooks embraced shortcuts out of need or because they were dazzled by a slew of convenience foods. I realized that in order to learn everything I wanted to know, I would have to go back to the geographical Latin America and talk to the men and women who guard the ancestral pots. Only then could I answer the question, "What is Latin America?"

Geographically speaking, the Latin America that concerns this book—the Spanish and Portuguese-speaking countries that emerged from the disintegration of Iberian colonial power—begins at the Rio Grande, the frontier between Mexico and the United States. It spreads east across the Caribbean to the three islands of the Hispanic Caribbean: Cuba, Puerto Rico, and the Dominican Republic. It continues from Mexico south through Central America—except for English-speaking Belize—hops across the Panama Canal to South America, and incorporates every country there except the English-, French-, and Dutch-speaking Guianas.

The people we have come to call Latin Americans have been thrust together by a common history. All of them, from the Yanomami Indians in Amazonia to the Italian immigrants of Buenos Aires, have been touched and shaped, sometimes reluctantly, by the powerful force of Iberian colonialism.

First the Spanish went to the lush, humid islands of the Caribbean, after Columbus's first trip of discovery in 1492. Then they voyaged to the arid Yucatán peninsula, next to Veracruz, and then to the central valleys of Mexico, down through Central America to the Caribbean coast of Venezuela, and through the high ridges of the Andes. At roughly the same time, Portuguese explorers had made forays into the Atlantic coast of South America, discovering what would become Brazil. In all these areas, Iberian explorers encountered different climatic zones, as well as indigenous peoples who ranged from hunter-gatherers to sedentary farmers, from loosely organized tribal societies to highly stratified, politically unified empires. And everywhere the Spaniards went, they applied the models of economic and political organization they had learned during the *reconquista*, their centuries-long struggle to make one Christian Spain out of the medieval Muslim-Christian patchwork.

Transcending the regional particulars of each Latin American country, there is something higher that links us, a shared heritage of the Old World: foods and cooking techniques, Catholicism, Roman law, Iberian rhythms. There was a time in the colonial period when we were all (even Brazilians for a short period) citizens of the same empire.

Though the wars of liberation that led to the present twenty Latin American nations were themselves the outcome of a pan-American spirit born of colonialism, inevitably they resulted in a balkanization of the big colonial construct. The fragmentation is especially visible in the Andean regions, where the empire founded by the Incas and continued by the Spanish was completely broken down by petty national concerns.

We have a word to describe the civilization that came into being here from the amalgam of native and Iberian cultures and influences from Africa and elsewhere: *criollo* (meaning "of the land"). You may have seen it on the window signs of Latin restaurants in the United States that advertise "*Comidas Criollas*," a term that I translate as "the foods of the land." We make a distinction between *cocina criolla* and *cocina española* (Spanish cuisine). *Criollo* is our word to define what is ours as Latin Americans.

The word *criollo*, like the French *creole*, comes from the Portuguese *crioulo*, which referred to black slaves born in Brazil rather than Africa. In Brazil, *crioulo* retains its original meaning and refers to people or elements of culture that have an African component. Initially the word *criollo* was used in this context in the Spanish colonies, but gradually it came to be applied to people of European descent born in the American colonies. Several centuries later, *criollo* is now a proud banner pointing to the uniqueness of José Martí's "Our America." *Criollo* encompasses all the elements of our culture, from food to music, that are the unique products of the mingling among Indians, Africans, and Europeans in the New World. Those of us born and raised in Latin America are joined together by a feeling of being *criollo*, of being of this land.

This "creolization" did not create one homogeneous Latin America. Even today sizable groups of people in many countries speak languages (against growing disruption) and follow ways of life that existed long before the Europeans came. Pre-Hispanic food skills live on virtually intact in some parts of Latin America—Inca or Aymara descendants freeze-dry their potatoes to this day on the cold windswept Andean *altiplano*. Fierce ethnic messages are also part of the political and cultural dialogue, from Mexico to Paraguay. And yet the overwhelming majority of those born and raised in Latin America are joined together by the sense of being *criollo*, even if they do not accept this semantic label.

Yet for all the things that we have in common, food remains a touchy subject. The Latin brand of kitchen chauvinism is very strong. Latin "fusion" food is not welcomed by those who eat and cook within tightly defined national and regional borders. A Venezuelan salivates thinking of his land's corn cakes, *arepas*, but to a Cuban or Dominican, *arepas* can seem as tasteless as cardboard. Coconut milk, the key ingredient in Colombian coastal cuisine, is dismissed as "*cosa de africanos*" (that African thing) in the inland cities of Medellín and Bogotá. People in Lima consider the cebiches of Guayaquil, in coastal Ecuador, with their liberal doses of tomato sauce, to be abominable. For many Hispanic Caribbeans, born and raised eating yuca,

Brazilian *farinha* (prepared from the same root) is more like sawdust than food.

I understand the instinct that makes someone defend his or her region's red rice and beans against one of its many siblings, but I know enough about the roots of Spanish food and have had enough opportunity to compare Latin flavors from cuisine to cuisine to see another story. These treasured regional and national dishes are themselves hybrids born out of centuries of colonial mixing. The above-mentioned dish, for example, features Old World rice, New World red beans, the African way of combining rice and legumes, and the very old Iberian way of deepening flavor through a *sofrito*, the crucial cooking-sauce foundation that I will discuss again and again under different local names.

As I began to piece together a connected understanding of what I was tasting, I was amazed at the centrality of what were essentially medieval cooking techniques brought from the Iberian peninsula that got a new lease on life in Latin America. In fact, no matter how far I traveled to find Latin dishes, I kept finding medieval Spain—sometimes in techniques that have died out in Spain itself. Listening to Latin friends in this and that region disparage the foods of other regions and extol their own, I saw similarities they were unaware of.

For a farewell dinner on one of my visits to Lima in 1996, my eighty-year-old hostess, Judith Lombardi de Rojas, prepared *tajadón*, a special dessert, which she described as a traditional specialty unique to Lima. As I helped her, I began to see a familiar pattern. First we beat an unfathomable number of egg yolks until fluffy and creamy for a spongy egg cake, then soaked it in an aromatic syrup. With the first bite, I was transported to Mérida in Mexico, where I had eaten a similar dessert called *huevos reales*, and to Guatemala City, where I had eaten an identical dessert known as *huevos chimbos*. In all three, I knew I was tasting the flavor of a family of sweets perfected in medieval Spanish and Portuguese convents. The *tajadón–huevos reales–huevos chimbos* complex is just one in the large list of Iberian-inspired desserts that were granted green cards in different parts of Latin America.

In the *escabeches* of Veracruz, I detected the complex Old World spice blends and love of vinegar that characterized medieval Islamic cooking. The better I understood Mexican *moles*, the more I saw the marriage of two cultures devoted to intricate flavoring—the Aztec empire and medieval Spain. The theme of medieval survival is one you will find repeatedly in this book.

An equally important motif is the influence of Africa, from the Caribbean islands far south and west. I was always aware of this in my homeland's cooking. When you look at an *ajiaco*, the big soup that is the Cuban national dish, you see primary evidence of Africa becoming amalgamated with pre-Columbian America and Old Spain—plantains and yams brought by slaves along with New World tropical tubers, tomatoes, and peppers and age-old Iberian elements like pork, olive oil, and even cilantro (which most of modern Spain has forgotten about). When I visit Brazil, I enjoy the gracious Old World hospitality of friends in São Paulo but also react viscerally to other aspects of the culture that harmonize with many of my early island memories, both in the foods of Salvador da Bahia in the northeast of Brazil and in the sounds of Candomblé rituals and the elusive chants praising the Yoruba Orixas (deities) Oxum and Xango. It's the same Iberian matrix intermingled with powerful Indian and African influences.

My travels have enlarged my understanding of people with whom I share much more than a language. I doubt there has ever been a better moment to extend the same understanding to other cooks in the United States, the new meeting place of all Latin cultures.

One factor is the flood of "new" foods that weren't available in this country ten, or just three, years ago. Now many of these are even being grown in the United States for the huge market that is developing here. In south Florida, fields of yuca and malanga, two important New World tubers, stretch to the horizon. Quinoa and multicolored Andean potatoes thrive in Colorado. Mexican chiles add a fiery splash of color to the fields of Texas and New Mexico. And what cannot be grown here is now being imported. But even as new vistas open up here, the past is fast disappearing in Latin America. While we refugees from "Our America" are learning to know each other in the process of adapting to life in the United States, the lands we left behind are going through numerous social and economic dislocations. When I was researching this book, I realized that it could be my last chance—but not only mine—to learn from a diminishing generation of Latin cooks.

Two inspirations lie at the heart of this book: to celebrate the wonderful present moment of mixing that is creating a Latin American identity without boundaries in the United States, and to search diligently for what can be preserved of traditional or sometimes even ancient practices. The strange beauty of Latin America is that these two seemingly opposite truths—change and the lingering value of old ways—continually crisscross. Gifted cooks are searching for ways of cooking that are no compromises but novel, imaginative creations that give new life to tradition without losing its essence.

So I am able to offer two kinds of recipes in this book: authentic recipes (both traditional and innovative ones) collected from talented cooks all over Latin America, and my own very personal interpretations. Sometimes it's important to be faithful to the original context, even to the point of strictly following the regional names for certain foods or dishes (*ají* for hot pepper in the Andes, *chile* in Central America; *sofrito* for the archetypal Spanish-derived sauce in Cuba, *aderezo* or *ahogado* for its close cousins in Peru and Ecuador). But sometimes it's appropriate to turn tradition on its head, because that's what many Latin cooks do on an everyday basis.

My table is a pan-American table. The appetizer might start in Juárez, Mexico, and the dessert end in the Caribbean. A scorching-hot Venezuelan *ají* plays the devil's advocate to liven up a Colombian tamal from Valle del Cauca. I mix when I see great possibilities, playing on the subtle links that unify seemingly different foods.

The road from the Latin American kitchen to the North American table is filled with potholes, and border crossing takes a lot of little adjustments. Many of the recipes I have collected were originally meant for large gatherings, and I have adapted them for a smaller number of guests while keeping them generous. For the most part, I use less salt and fat in my cooking than is common in Latin America. But my aim is always the same: to adapt and transform the elemental beauty and tastes of Latin American cooking to the modern kitchen while respecting the food's primary flavors, and to create earthy, intensely flavored dishes that keep you reaching for more.

CHAPTER 2

THE LATIN KITCHEN

IN THIS CHAPTER

A MAGIC SPACE

I learned to cook in my grandfather's old colonial-style kitchen in Santiago de Cuba, a long room with a tiled charcoal-burning stove that ran the length of the wall, holding many separate fireboxes. At the age of seven, I made a dish of *congrí*, the traditional rice and red kidney beans of the Oriente region. I was so small that Inés, the family cook, who had taken me under her wing, had to help me climb on a stool to see the inside of the pot. It was Inés who taught me the trick of placing an oiled brown paper bag on the surface of the rice to make it fluffy, which I still do occasionally. Serving my first meal to a waiting family who ate every grain of my rice and beans and applauded my effort christened me as a cook.

In the late 1950s, my cousins Jaime and Carlos wanted to give my aunt Anita a gift of an electric stove to modernize the family kitchen. My aunt gracefully accepted the electric stove, but she kept the old one too. She would never have discarded such a cherished part of her heritage or the practiced rhythms of cooking that had fed our family's bodies and spirits since the stove was built. The Latin cook's frame of thinking, his or her basic understanding of food, always dictates the type of kitchen he or she runs. No other room of the Latin house is so shaped by history.

The Mapuche Indians of southern Chile spend most of their time in a circular hut called a *ruka* that doubles as kitchen and living space. In the center of the *ruka*, there is a wood fire. Four stones support the cooking pots. At baking time, fresh flatbreads called *tortillas al rescoldo* (from the word for cinder, *rescoldo*) are buried in the dying embers and ashes. High above the fire, baskets of food hang from the rafters—corn, wheat, garlic, onions, *ristras* (garlands) of scarlet *cacho de cabra* ("goat's horn") peppers. The kitchen also serves as chicken coop. Hens lay their eggs in low baskets suspended in a nook of the *ruka*.

A *ruka* has no chimney or windows, just a small opening in the roof to let the smoke from the hearth escape. Yet it might as well be closed—*rukas* are always smoky. Smoke fills every corner of the hut; it stains pots and baskets, lingers on people's clothes, permeates and flavors the food. You could not put walls around the activity of the hearth without destroying the integrity of the home.

At the opposite extreme—but not really so opposite—are kitchens that are freestanding structures, not attached to the house. This was the norm for colonial haciendas, especially in tropical countries, where the masters didn't want to be near the heat and bustling activity of the kitchen.

In many parts of the Americas, rambling colonial homes were built with at least three distinct clusters of living spaces, each opening to a separate courtyard or patio. The kitchen, where the Indian or black servants worked and the white mistress commanded, was relegated to the third patio area. The reason for this was partly practical: many kitchen chores were—and still are—done in the patio itself. This separation also underlined the hierarchy of colonial plantation societies. This is the type of kitchen one can still find in places like Cartagena, Colombia; Antigua, Guatemala; and Querétaro, Mexico—as well as wherever colonial homes have been preserved and passed down through generations.

A separate kitchen is by no means always a sign of wealth or exclusivity. Cooking spaces were located beyond the walls of the house in some pre-Columbian societies—and still are today. In the Mexican town of Uricho, near Lake Pátzcuaro, my Tarascan Indian friend Francisca de la Luz Cortés cooks in a one-room adobe structure with a cavernous oven built into the wall. From the outside, the smooth protruding rounded shape of the oven looks like the apse of an abandoned Romanesque church. Found all over Latin America, these distinctive ovens date back to the time of the Romans and were built everywhere Spaniards settled. In Villeta, a town built by squatters on the Paraguay River, the Caballero family bakes *chipá*, a cornmeal and yuca starch bread, in a beehive adobe oven called a *tatacuá*. The *tatacuá* is essential for baking *chipá*, but it also serves to roast river fish like the giant *surubí* and the tasty *pacú*.

Rain or shine, at Francisca's home in Uricho, every meal starts with her crossing the yard from the house to the kitchen. Dominating the space is a large *comal*, a slightly concave clay grill fueled by wood. Next to the *comal* sits a huge *metate*, a grinding stone of volcanic rock, a wedding gift from her mother. For cooking beans or stews and frying, there is a stove of three stones, over which she bends to tend the pots.

On the plains of Barinas, Venezuela, the rural kitchens are the essence of simplicity. They are one-room cabins with walls made of thin horizontal wooden slats, to allow for air circulation, and thatched roofs. At the center of the structure sits the reason for the separation from the ranch house: a huge grill for cooking meat over a wood fire, supervised by old women who stoke the smoky air with their straw fans.

You would not improve anything by connecting these freestanding kitchens with the house, any more than you would by shutting off the Mapuche hearth from the rest of the hut. Cooking traditions have a way of asserting their own needs when people try to squeeze them into the wrong kinds of kitchens.

There is some flexibility built in. Throughout Latin America, the more laborious, messy cooking is often done outside of the kitchen. This is easy, for most kitchens open up onto a yard or interior courtyard. Even in homes with electric or gas stoves, there is always an *anafre*, a type of portable charcoal hibachi. It's on this portable stove that cooks will set the large cast-iron pot to make pork cracklings or to char chiles for a *mole* sauce, letting the smoke billow into the air (the acrid fumes from the chiles can be like something from a small war).

Sitting Down: The Zen of the Latin Kitchen

Those of us who work in modern kitchens often take the spatial arrangements for granted—a place for everything, with virtually all the cutting and preparation done on waist-high countertops. We forget that even in America such arrangements are fairly recent, going back at most to the early twentieth century. Kitchens were bigger then, and most preparations were done on tables. The same was true of the middle-class Latin kitchen then, and it is still so today. Not everybody has the means or the desire to turn a kitchen into a state-of-the-art showcase. Latin kitchens are as varied in their contours as Latin women, but the space is usually welcoming, good to stay in while you go through detailed tasks at an unhurried pace.

The floor used to be the chief work space, and it still is in rural or very simple kitchens. Francisca de la Luz Cortés is unusual in having her *metate* and *comal* set up at waist height for grinding corn and cooking tortillas. Most of her neighbors do those jobs kneeling on the floor. Elsewhere, it is more likely to be a table than a counter. There is seldom a chopping block to stand over, because the traditional Latin woman sits as she works—on the floor, on a low stool, or in a chair. The classic posture is the one I've seen used by a Mapuche Indian in Patagonia, a middle-class woman in a posh Santiago home, the wife of a famous winemaker in Mendoza, Argentina, and a cook in Salvador da Bahia—all sitting down to cut onions for a cooking sauce in the same comfortable way. In the left hand they hold half an onion, in the right a cheap kitchen knife. A little at a time, they score a fine crisscross pattern in the cut surface of the onion and deftly pare it off, achieving dice finer than I would ever dream of producing with conventional chopping techniques. I have seen tomatoes, bunched-up parsley or cilantro, and rolled-up leaves of kale shaved into incredibly fine bits by women casually sitting and talking as they work. They cradle the work in their laps along with a bowl, as much at ease as a mother with a child.

This feeling of being comfortable with cooking can be seen even in restaurant kitchens where women are the workforce. In Cartagena, Colombia, I visited a popular restaurant in Getsemani that serves hundred of complicated meals a day, and I found the women cooks sitting around a large table at their ease, chatting away while they grated coconuts in astronomical quantities to make coconut milk. In Cuenca, Ecuador, I was fascinated by a group of women who make *empanadas de viento* (a kind of empanada that puffs up dramatically in frying) on the streets. They sit on small stools and tend to a pot of bubbling oil while rolling out the dough and filling the empanadas on a wooden board balanced

on their knees. Similar scenes of leisured efficiency can be found in every corner of Latin America.

My editor, Maria Guarnaschelli, likes to sit at her dining room table when she peels apples for a pie. It's the same thing I do at my home and even at my restaurant when tackling a repetitive chore such as grating corn for tamales.

It can be argued that this easygoing way of cooking is not only a vestige of the past or a survival of rural habits rooted in necessity, but also an efficient and realistic way of coping with the time-consuming demands of artisanal Latin cuisines. Sitting down is the Zen of the Latin kitchen.

To me, the Indians of the Orinoco and Amazon Basins have achieved the ideal cooking setup: many times I have seen a cook swinging gently in her hammock as she stirs a pot over a warm, cozy fire.

TOOLS OF THE TRADE

I've always been fond of adventure stories like *Robinson Crusoe*, where castaways scratch out an existence, and even achieve an enviable level of comfort, with just a few objects salvaged from the wreck of their ships. I cheered when the characters in Jules Verne's *The Mysterious Island* opened two barrels that seemed to have come from a shipwreck (their actual provenance being the key to the story) and found a trove of useful items, among them "one iron pot, six galvanized copper saucepans, three iron plates, ten aluminum table settings, two kettles, one small portable stove, and six table knives," which the castaway Ned covered with kisses.

I know which cooking utensils I would take

to a desert island. No galvanized copper saucepans, to be sure, but the time-tested utensils of the traditional Latin kitchen: a sturdy mortar and pestle, a box grater, and the cast-aluminum cauldron we call a *caldero*.

With these simple implements—plus a sturdy chef's knife to defend myself and to cut open green coconuts and oysters—I would be in business. I could cook delicious dishes with whatever ingredients I found, just as Latin women have long created wondrous worlds of flavor in places as devoid of creature comforts as any isle that Daniel Defoe or Jules Verne imagined.

Mortar and Pestle

In the Hispanic Caribbean, a wooden mortar and pestle are essential to mash garlic for the citrusy marinades called *adobos* and the zesty sauce called *mojo*, the favorite seasoning for boiled yuca and twice-fried green plantains. I don't remember ever chopping garlic until I began cooking professionally in the United States. Like everyone else in my family, I mashed garlic to a pulp with a mortar and pestle.

Through trial and error, I learned that chopping garlic with a knife has its place, particularly when you don't want its flavor to overwhelm the food. Still, the first thing I do when preparing a garlicky marinade is to reach for my trusted olive wood mortar and pestle. Not only do I love the pungent aroma that fills the room, but I cherish the power of taming an ingredient with a rudimentary tool as old as mankind.

That is not just a figure of speech. The first Stone Age mortars were large rocks, the pestles smaller ones. Later people graduated to smooth, concave rock slabs and rounded grinding stones. In Peru, the Spanish found people grinding food with huge slabs and stones, which they christened with the Spanish name *batán*, from the large mallets used to beat cloth. To me these are the archetypal Latin grinders. They remind me of monumental pieces of sculpture. Some of the slabs are as large as three or four feet across, and the half-moon-shaped stones can weigh up to ten pounds. The sixteenth-century Peruvian chronicler Garcilaso de la Vega describes Indian women grinding foods by rocking the top stone over the slab, not by pounding, in his *Comentarios reales de los Incas* (*Royal Commentaries of the Incas*).

Every Latin American country has its version of the mortar and pestle. My friend Isabel Aguilar from Mérida in Mexico showed me a black stone she had found on a beach in Campeche fifty years ago. That's what she uses to grind the spices for her *recado*. Isabel joked that she would have to name an heir for this stone, or her daughters would fight over who gets it!

The three-legged volcanic stone mortar called a *molcajete* fitted with a pestle (*tejolote* from the Nahuatl in Mexico; *mano*—hand—in Spanish) of the same material is one of Mexico's greatest contributions to the world kitchen. Unlike wooden pestles, which are used with a pounding motion, the *tejolote* is pressed and rotated to grind the food against the rough surface of the *molcajete*. The ingredients are bruised, not pureed, releasing their essential oils and leaving them with enough texture to make a difference. There is nothing like a *salsa cruda* or tomatillo sauce prepared this way.

Box Graters

A box grater is also extremely useful—the four-sided kind with two grating surfaces (fine and coarse), a shredding surface, and one with slits for slicing. I own three food processors of different sizes, but nothing beats my grater for processing fresh corn for tamales. Although it is far speedier, the processor bruises the corn, while the grater yields a thicker, earthier texture that translates into a richer flavor.

I have also found, to my surprise, that the fine side of the grater produces richer, thicker milk from fresh coconuts than the, again, immensely faster food processor. On the Caribbean coast of Colombia, where coconut milk is a favorite ingredient, you will often find women comfortably seated at a kitchen table grating tons of coconuts on large metal graters. And in both Cartagena and Barranquilla, the most important towns of this region, cooking sauces similar to *sofritos* are prepared by grating onions, tomatoes, carrots, and even green and red bell peppers.

The most beautiful graters I have seen are the ones made by some Orinoco Basin tribes, like the Panare of Venezuela. The Panare yuca grater, or *rallo*, is a long, narrow wooden board embedded with quartz teeth and painted with symbolic geometric patterns. When a *rallo* gets old, the Panare sell it or trade it to collectors and other tribes such as the Yanomami. If you are ever in Caracas, take a drive to the nearby town of El Hatillo and visit Hansi, a store specializing in native crafts. They often sell old Panare *rallos*. The Garífunas of Honduras and neighboring Belize grate yuca to make *casabe* on similar graters.

The *Caldero*

Every Latin American kitchen is also stocked with a core of essential pots that vary according to region. Everywhere I traveled, I found plain, flimsy aluminum pots and pans and the heavier cast-aluminum cauldrons called *calderos*, or cast-iron pans stained pitch-black. Newer refinements such as pressure cookers and blenders may be there as well, but even the fanciest house always has a big old-fashioned pot that sits on the stove, bubbling with delicious soups and stews. In the Ecuadorian sierra, where soups are important sources of body heat as well as nourishment, one can always find a collection of wooden spoons presided over by the trusty "mother spoon," or *cucharamama*—an oversized spoon for stirring the pot of soup.

As for the *caldero*, it is the ideal all-purpose pot. Its cast-aluminum composition makes it a good diffuser of heat, its slightly flared shape means less liquid is needed to cook a rice dish or stew, and its two handles come in handy when making large batches. It is perfect not only for stovetop cooking, from braising to frying, but also for finishing dishes in the oven, and even for cooking outdoors over a wood fire. Like many Latin women I know, I have a special *caldero*, blackened with use, that I use exclusively for rice. It is my lucky pot, the one I choose when I want my white rice to come out dry and fluffy, with separate grains.

The closer people live to nature in Latin America, the larger and heavier the mortar and pestle, the grinding stones, the graters—all utilitarian items that tame and transform raw ingredients into manageable pieces. More and more, though, these old-fashioned tools, some as personal as Isabel's prized beach stone, are being replaced by machine-made utensils, since in Latin America, anything modern is looked on with respect. Among the Yanomami, the traditional hand-coiled clay pots are being replaced with aluminum ones, since they are lighter and less breakable. Everywhere the precious implements that can be traced to pre-Columbian times—beautiful handwoven baskets, simple but elegant clay bowls, solid stone graters like the *batán*—are fast becoming artifacts of the past.

Yet in every Latin community in the United States, you will be able to find some version of the mortar and pestle, the grater, and the all-purpose cast-aluminum *caldero* in neighborhood markets or hardware stores. They are surprisingly inexpensive, immensely useful, and totally reliable. They will not only save your life if you are ever stranded on a desert island, but allow you to capture the artisanal spirit of the traditional Latin kitchen in your own home.

THE LATIN COOK

Cucharamama: The Kitchen as a Source of Liberation

My aunt Belén, an accomplished pianist and composer, used to say, "Never tell anyone you are good at the piano! Every time a party is held, you will have to play while everyone else dances." You might be tempted to say the same of being a good cook. Whenever there's a gathering of family or friends, you'll be stuck in the kitchen while everyone else is having a good time. But who can resist the call of the kitchen when there is so much power invested in the woman who cooks in Latin America? That's why the view of the kitchen as a jail for women just doesn't fit in Latin America. Very often food and cooking are the sole means a woman has to empower herself and to achieve a measure of self-control.

In houses big and small throughout Latin America, kitchen matriarchs rule with their pots. They are *huarmi-mandanas*, a Quechua and Spanish composite term used in highland Ecuador to describe "the women who rule." Their cooking is the magnet that draws the family together and brings them home again and again. These grandmothers and mothers are skilled at making the special comfort foods—the laborious, painstaking dishes that take hours to make and everyone loves. I call these women the *cucharamamas* of Latin America because they remind me of the mother spoons that stir the thick soups of the Ecuadorian sierra.

Sometimes a man takes on this role. For my father, cooking began as a hobby. He started making special dishes like land-crab stew (*enchilado de cangrejos*)—anything messy, larger than life. Now he is the official cook of the family and he gets everybody's attention. Arturo Rubio, the owner of several successful restaurants in Lima, is the one who orchestrates every party at his home, pampering friends as if they were family. Miro Popiç, a Chilean-born food journalist friend who lives in Venezuela, is also a fabulous cook. His Sunday lunches are legendary, as family and friends gather around to enjoy his elaborate meals. Miro also makes the nurturing gestures of the *cucharamama*, waking up his guests in bed with a cup of strong coffee that he offers like a cup of new life. But essentially it is the women who rule through cooking, even if a man appears to wear the toque.

I often think of Delia, a tiny, bronze-skinned native Guayanese, the mother-in-law of Ercole D'Addazio, a formidable Italian who owns a very successful restaurant in Puerto Ordaz, Venezuela. The last time I saw her she was very old and fragile, but when she was younger, she was a sweet but formidable force of nature. While Ercole ran a first-rate Mediterranean restaurant downstairs with Old World patrician dignity and flair, Delia presided over a *criollo* kitchen upstairs that takes up a third of Ercole's elegant modern penthouse. With a mischievous laugh, she boasted of the gradual "creolization" of her son-in-law. "When we first got mixed up with the Italian race, I learned to make all the pastas he liked, but then little by little I started feeding him Guayanese food," she recalled at our first meeting, in 1994. "First came the *guarapo* [light coffee] with *casabe* [yuca bread] for lunch." She cackled. "Then I made *hallacas* for Christmas. And now he has even accepted my *pastel de morrocoy*" (a pie made with land turtle, a Guayanese favorite). Delia, like so many of the *cucharamamas* I met during my trips, wielded prestige and power through her value to the family.

Marisa Guiulfo, a prominent caterer in Lima, Peru, is a modern-day *cucharamama*. Every weekend during the summer, she plays mother and cook for throngs of friends who flock to her home in the fishing port of Pucusana, on a tiny island. Though she has kitchen help, she does most of the cooking, often elaborate dishes that take hours to prepare, and she takes the time to set every table lovingly with whimsical touches to make the food shine.

But cooking holds another kind of importance for Latin women. For many of them, it is the only way to earn a living, a lesson I learned through my own experience as a chef and restaurateur. Cooking to support oneself goes back to colonial times and before. Making desserts and special sweets was historically a respected tradition belonging to women. Although professional bakeries now compete with skilled home craftswomen, wedding cakes are often entrusted only to a famous local homemaker known for her elaborate, fantastical creations. The ones I remember from Cuba were elegant, covered in ivory icing, and decorated with chains of tiny meringue flowers.

Cloistered nuns have been turning special confections into paying concerns for centuries. Several years ago, I met a group of nuns who had happily supported themselves in their monastery in Orizaba, in the cool highlands of Veracruz, making exquisite, delicately shaped marzipan out of pumpkin seeds. But then the industrious nuns were transferred to a more tropical climate in Santiago Tuxtla, where their marzipan spoiled. They became desperate for money, washing clothes and selling tortillas and tamales on feast days to earn their keep. That's how I got to know them, and it broke my heart. I was touched when my friend Raquel Torres, herself a woman empowered by the restaurant business, tried to take the nuns under her wing, dispensing advice on how to turn their monastery corridors into a venue for other profitable food ventures.

As the economy has worsened in Latin America, many professional women have gone into catering and baking. The kitchen has allowed them to keep themselves and their families going. But there is a long history of small food businesses run by women in Latin America. Throughout the Caribbean, you can see signs of female entrepreneurial drive at tiny roadside stands, street carts, and marketplace stalls. Lined up along Luquillo, a famous beach in Puerto Rico, are small concrete kiosks selling fried snacks, all of them run by women. There can be great art in the simple productions of these businesswomen, particularly in Mexico. In Querétaro, in front of fabulous baroque churches, women sell cups of strips of jícama and fruits arranged like magnificent still lifes.

But what I love most are the little roadside restaurants that are really extensions of women's homes. In Rinconada, on the road from Veracruz to Xalapa, you will find such restaurants that specialize in *garnachas* (tortillas doused in chile sauce), and you cannot help but notice the homey touches—the tablecloths, the food served straight from the stove at a long family-style table. It is as if you were sitting in someone's kitchen.

On the road from Oaxaca to the ancient ruins of Mitla, in Santa María el Tule, right across the street from a gigantic Montezuma cypress, there is a roadside restaurant where hefty women serve fresh tortillas and quesadillas filled with squash blossoms and cheese. The food goes straight from the smoky *comal* to the table where you are sitting just a few feet away. To me this is the ultimate luxury, to see food being cooked in front of my eyes, to be served by the woman who cooks the meal.

COOKING IN THE KITCHEN OF LOVE

Every instinct tells me that the Latin American attitude toward cooking a meal is connected with the sense of life-giving nurture. There is a bond between those who cook and those who eat.

In Latin America, the important feast dishes are the ones on which women have always lavished endless care, for as long as their children and grandchildren can remember. The great traditional dishes like the Brazilian *feijoada*, Mexican *moles*, all kinds of tamales, the tripe stew called *mondongo*, and spoon desserts such as the Hispanic Caribbean *majarete* or the well-traveled trifle *bienmesabe* not only reveal deep culinary sophistication, they are truly monu-

ments to love—love translated into skill, delicacy, and intelligence. I am offended when I hear such dishes patronizingly pigeonholed as "hearty peasant food." True, these foods are close to the land. But that only means that their flavors are all the more vivid and all the more care is invested in their making. The work that goes into them is stupendous, and honored. To cook this food is to help knit the fabric of the family.

I will never forget the lesson of Nair, a fabulous Bahian cook who used to travel back and forth between Brazil and New York to be with members of her large family. She would say that her family had spilled all over the world "like a sack of beans" and that her role in life was to keep those beans together with her cooking. While in New York, she made some money cooking for a few well-to-do Brazilian families and busy single working people, such as my film producer friend Mara Mourão, whom Nair adopted as a member of her own extended family. Nair would go to Mara's loft and cook up a storm, leaving the refrigerator stocked with a remarkable array of dishes for every day of the coming week—everything neatly stored and labeled. I could not believe that a single woman as trim as Mara could eat such substantial meals, but she did. Nair's food, Mara explained, was what kept her sane and emotionally tied to Brazil. Like spilled beans everywhere, she needed to be gathered up and restored by the embrace of the cooking pot.

Even in the poorest of Latin American households, Christmas tables groan under the weight of feast foods. For the filling of the Venezuelan Christmas tamal (*hallaca*), pork and chicken are delicately cut into small even-sized bits and artfully arranged over the *masa*, together with raisins, olives, and bell pepper strips. All that work to make a colorful still life that just gets covered with another layer of dough! Yet every bite of steaming *hallaca* shared with family and friends redeems woman-hours—or days—that are consumed in its making. Every carefully folded plantain package is the ultimate Christmas gift, for it contains a golden, edible treasure that speaks only of love. For those who struggle all year to put every morsel of food on the table, a well-filled Christmas *hallaca* is a horn of plenty; a golden brown suckling pig is an anthem to hope. I know of many families who would rather eat less throughout the year than forgo the pleasure of a holiday meal.

But other, more subtle acts of love are enacted every day in the Latin kitchen. Because pollution and disease have ravaged the Americas, cooking requires not only time but scrupulous attention to potential health hazards. However fresh fish, meat, or vegetables may look in the market, chances are that they are contaminated with some form of bacteria. Latin women often scrub vegetables with chlorinated water or boil the cooking water. Near Lake Pátzcuaro, in Michoacán, Francisca de la Luz Cortés goes so far as to boil the water she uses to wash her *nixtamal* for tortillas. During hurricane season in the Hispanic Caribbean, women are always prepared to pull together a meal without water or a working stove. Behind every meal, there are countless acts that speak of women's concern for the health of their families and others.

These habits remind me of my aunts in Cuba, who had to scavenge for food to put on the table for our extended family during the civil strife in the 1950s and then later after the revolution. Despite extraordinarily difficult circumstances—food shortages, water problems, electricity outages—they managed to keep a spotless working kitchen. At the time, I took their efforts for granted, having

no idea of the labor those efforts required. Now I understand how all that hard work was an expression of their love.

Sometimes love is expressed in the smallest details. From the Iberian peninsula, Latin America inherited a passion for tablecloths. Even the poorest table will be covered with a tablecloth. It may be brightly colored plastic adorned with a centerpiece of artificial flowers, but someone has made a conscious effort to create grace and beauty out of humble elements. For a special meal, all over the Americas, those who can afford it cover their tables with white linen cloths trimmed with lace or crocheted borders, *manteles largos*.

Dressing the table is the last step in a carefully choreographed dance that starts with the first whistle of the beans in the pressure cooker; it's a ritual that makes the distinction between the trivial and the important. The table may be set with fine heirloom silver or porcelain or special pieces showing local Indian influences, or with cheap enameled plates made in China. But always the tablecloth anchors Latin food, giving recognition to the effort that's gone into the cooking.

THE LATIN COOK AND THE MARKET

The traditional Latin kitchen is an earthy one, where from an early age children are given intimate exposure to the food their families cook and learn how the food gets to the table. They are asked to help with kitchen chores such as peeling plantains, cleaning nixtamalized corn for *pozole*, and slicing okra. They run errands to the market. Even in urban households, children see chickens and pigs slaughtered. Everyone in Latin America believes that the chicken or pig that is slaughtered at home tastes better.

The Latin American kitchen is changing rapidly, especially in upwardly mobile households. Some Latin supermarkets now put American ones to shame. In Rio, I once went to a market at the Barra with 180 cash registers—a place so large that employees moved from place to place on roller skates. But even with the rise of convenience foods and packaged meats (economy packs, I'm convinced, were meant for Latins), most home cooks can still easily kill a living fowl, buy whole chickens and cut them to their taste, clean large fish and seafood, and even butcher large cuts of meat. This knowledge comes in particularly handy in the United States if you cannot find a butcher who will cut the meat according to the style of your country.

Although larger Latin companies are cleverly catering to the busy Latin housewife by selling convenience items like grated yuca to make bread or empanadas, plantains ready to fry into *tostones*, frozen cooking sauces (*sofritos* and *recados*), and dozens of spice blends, people with some time and fresh memories of artisanal cooking prefer to start from scratch—and the place to do it is in the market.

In Latin America, food shopping is taken very seriously and markets brim with wonderful produce artfully displayed. In the Andes, you find stacks of brilliant red and yellow hot peppers, corn partly husked to reveal the flowerlike hues (ivory, burnt orange, deep purple, pink, rainbow) within, and multicolored mountains of potatoes. In Oaxaca, rich-toned *mole* pastes from black to crimson glisten in great earthenware *cazuelas*. In Ciudad Bolívar on the Orinoco, rounds of *casabe* a yard across are piled in stacks taller than I am next to towering mounds of brown-skinned yuca and bright green plantains.

The frontier towns in the Brazilian Amazon have the most stunning markets. Ver-o-Peso in Belém, on the river's edge, is by far the most splendid and exotic, a tropical souk where the inevitable conveniences of modern life—plastics, dried pastas, Coca-Cola, and blaring radios—share space with shimmering huge fish, jungle animals, turtle eggs, mounds of shredded yuca leaves, and bottled *tucupí* (a yuca vinegar).

This chaos and bounty reminds you of the wildness within the not-so-distant jungle, and not only in the Amazon. The traditional Latin American market is also a thrilling border between the wild and the domestic. The women who buy there are frontier fighters, conquering nature for their kitchens. Some markets, especially the large central ones, are not for the tame of stomach. Shoppers must wend their way down narrow, labyrinthine corridors, fighting crowds and dodging fresh merchandise as it is trundled past. Vegetables still have clumps of dirt clinging to their skins, and bloody cow's feet hang in the butchers' stalls, showing shredded skin. In some markets, such as Sangolquí in Ecuador, you can watch as heads of bulls are split open and tripe is washed in huge stone sinks.

In the stunningly beautiful fish market of Puerto Libertad in El Salvador, boats are winched right out of the water onto the piers, where the fishermen sell their multihued catch from silvery metal buckets, each daubed with a special mark. Everywhere you can see fishermen busy gutting fish and smell the overpowering odor of fish drying in the sun.

Why would a middle-class woman who has access to a modern North American–style supermarket go out of her way to venture into these smelly, intense dens of bloody meats, unwashed vegetables, and still-flapping fish? What brings the women to these sometimes grisly arenas is the Latin esteem for food straight from the land or the water. Latin cooks are obsessed with free-range chickens—*gallinas de patio, gallinas criollas*, or *gallinas indias*, as they are variously known—and their eggs. My maternal grandfather, Santiago Parladé, would eat raw eggs while they were still warm from the hen. My friend Nela Ortiz in Cuenca, Ecuador, will only buy bona fide *huevos runa*. These are country eggs from free-range hens that are highly prized for their intense flavor and deep yellow yolks. The term *runa* comes from a Quechua word for "man," which the Spaniards adopted as a pejorative term for non-Spaniards. Gradually it was applied to anything from the countryside raised by Indians, particularly food items like live fowls and freshly laid eggs. When Nela buys these eggs, she grills the vendor: "Are you sure that these are fresh *huevos runa*? If I go home and find that these are not, I will bring them back to you, and I will never buy from you again."

Rather than brave the huge central markets on an everyday basis, most cooks do their daily shopping at neighborhood markets, to which they are fiercely loyal. An elderly woman I know from Mérida still goes back to Santiago, her old neighborhood, to buy special items, even though she moved away years ago. One day I accompanied her to the central market in Mérida, where she sneered at the mounds of orange *recado*, the seasoning paste that is a staple of Yucatán cooking: "Look, it smells of vinegar, because they didn't use enough spices. I'll take you to my neighborhood market in Santiago. There I know a place where you can get a pretty *recado* with all the right spices." She took me to the Santiago market, where she bought her *recado*. But when we got home, I found her crushing allspice berries and garlic to add to it. "Didn't you tell me that was the only place where you get a *recado* with all the right ingredients?" I asked. "You can never be sure," she replied.

When a cook becomes the client of a particular vendor, their relationship is a kind of holy (if cantankerous) covenant. The vendor demands total loyalty and will not tolerate clandestine buying from a next-door competitor. The clients, on the other hand, feel free not only to ask for special favors and hard-to-get ingredients, but also to chastise the merchant when they don't get the best quality for the best prices. Daily the two parties enact a familiar ritual: vendors fawn over their special clients, who, in turn, stay aloof and skeptical, sniffing and poking at the food offered them. Both know their roles, and both know the limits of those roles. But pity the poor vendor who breaks the pact!

On a trip to Quito, Ecuador, I joined Berta and Elisa Peña, two savvy sisters who had elevated food shopping to a fine art. Every Saturday, they drove to Sangolquí to buy food for Sunday, when their whole family got together for a splendid late lunch. They marched straight to the stalls of their favorite *placeras*, as female vendors are called in Ecuador, resisting the siren calls of those who want to snatch away their business. Like most Ecuadorians from the highlands, the sisters were polite to a fault, exchanging greetings with other shoppers in old-fashioned Spanish and addressing the *placeras* with the respectful "*usted*." Yet when a *placera* took advantage of their trust and tried to sell them *gato por liebre* (a cat instead of a rabbit) their smiles turned to stern frowns. The formal treatment vanished, and the polite "*usted*" was haughtily replaced by a peremptory, harsh "*vos*."

One week the sisters requested a specially tender and clean cut of meat from their favorite *placera*. When they arrived to pick it up the next week, however, the vendor handed them a sad-looking piece of meat, mottled with fat and fiber. The sisters were incensed. They had already planned the Sunday lunch menu around this meat! After touching and sniffing the meat, they took turns chastising the *placera*. "What you sell is good for nothing—what you have given me, you can keep. From now on, I'm not buying from you, and I'll tell all my friends not to buy from you anymore. In this market, there's plenty to choose from," one of the sisters said, waving her finger angrily. The *placera*, who had expected this reaction, offered a humble, and well-rehearsed, apology: "But, *patronitas* (ladies), don't get mad. Let me see if I have what you want. Look, see if you like this. Don't go."

Knowing that this was the moment to extract a bargain, the sisters pretended to leave, one waving an angry finger at the *placera* one last time and tossing a final rebuke over her shoulder: "Since you have tried to sell me the worst that you have, and you won't give me a good price, I will not take it." Once the sisters had put the *placera* in her place, the confrontation ended, and the exchange returned to the original respectful *"usted."* Had the sisters pushed too far, they would have gotten more than they bargained for: Ecuadorian *placeras* are famous for their foul language and will lash back with all their ample and colorful repertoire of invective. That day, however, everyone was happy. The *placera* kept two faithful customers, and the sisters went home with excellent meat at the lowest possible price.

But the preoccupation with freshness that arms shoppers for combative rituals with suppliers also makes the suppliers willing to go the extra mile to please. It is not uncommon to see merchants filling in the time between customers by performing little culinary tasks just as they would be done at home—separating heads of garlic neatly into cloves, for example, or slicing the kernels from ears of fresh corn in full view of everyone, to show off the freshness of their wares. In the same spirit, women go to the Andean marketplaces to sell sacks full of hot, freshly boiled *mote* (kernels of lime-treated dried corn), fresh corn, Andean lupins (*chochos*), and shelled fava beans, or to cook the same things on the spot, replenishing the pot as each batch is sold out. In this way, shoppers have all the advantages of convenience food without swapping home-cooked quality for the impersonality of mass-produced food.

Because of the intimate, cherished relationship between vendor and customer in Latin America, what may be considered everyday drudgery is elevated to a special, personalized status. This does not always spill over into North American Latin stores. In the twenty-five years that I have lived in one of New Jersey's largest Hispanic communities, I have seen both an increasing array of Latin products and what strikes me as an increasing indifference to quality, especially in fresh produce, which is so beautiful in Latin America.

I confess that I am a spoiled, fastidious shopper who demands special treatment. In Union City, one of my favorite vegetable vendors used to be a man who looked just like a cowboy, with a huge ten-gallon hat and a knife strapped to his waist. This man would cut open any item, from a twelve-pound pumpkin to a giant yuca root, for my appraisal. He is no longer there wielding his knife, but I still expect the same from my huge local Latin supermarket,

Bandera—I astonish the other shoppers when I ask to see the stock from the back room. And I rely heavily on the excellent farmers' markets in and around New York City, where seasonal tomatoes, corn, squashes, and even hot peppers can't be beat for freshness.

THE SUPERSTITIONS AND LORE OF THE LATIN COOK

Considering the resources and cunning that Latin cooks employ in getting their hands on the raw materials, it is hardly surprising that even today they often think of foods as people, susceptible to the elements and even to emotional or physical influences from those in the kitchen.

Throughout Latin America, beliefs from three superstitious cultures—pre-Columbian, Iberian Catholic, and African—converged to create a rich body of cooking myths that always manage to swim to the surface like the foam on a pot of soup. Traditional cooks firmly believe that food can be affected by malicious intentions or jinxes, and they have little rituals to ward off harm. I cannot forget my aunt's injunction never to stir or taste anything with a knife, a symbol of strife. A gaucho, who cooks and eats with his knife, would laugh at this, but it's one taboo I would never dare violate.

To prevent their delicate, sometimes temperamental *dulce de leche cortada* (sweetened milk very lightly curdled with lime juice) from ending up too runny or too toughened through someone's ill will, old Cuban cooks always pour the lime juice on the surface of the milk in the shape of the cross. Cooks in Veracruz use the same universal sign of blessing when sprinkling salt into a cooking pot.

Many cooks believe that foods can fall apart under a fierce gaze or profit from a gentle one. While learning to make conch soup in Tela, Honduras, I discovered the importance of the *buen ojo*, or good eye. The essential ingredient for Honduran conch soup is coconut milk. But, my teacher, Mary Kawas, explained, some people are banned from her kitchen when she cooks it, since one look from them will curdle the soup. "I'm not talking about the evil eye," Mary said. "It is just that their eyesight is too strong." Ahhh! I said to myself, this explains the Cuban saying "There are looks that knock down coconuts." I made sure to give the cooking pot as gentle a look as I could muster. To my relief, Mary's soup was a triumph. The coconut milk turned the ivory color of conch, blending with the ingredients without a single dreaded lump, to make a velvety cushion for the earthy tropical vegetables.

Corn, the preeminent Latin grain, is the subject of innumerable superstitions. The accounts of Aztec kitchen lore that the Spanish friar Bernardino de Sahagún collected from elderly Mexicans in the sixteenth century show people observing taboos and precepts that still strike a chord today. Sahagún was told that corn that was spilled on the floor and not picked up would complain to the corn deity; "Lord, punish him who saw me spilled and did not pick me up, or give him hunger." He also records an obsession with the hazards of tamal making that has been a constant to this day. Sahagún reports that a pot of tamales would never cook right if a twin even looked at it—the Aztecs believed that twins had dangerous powers—and some modern cooks preoccupied with a fear of the evil eye paint crosses on their *tamaleras* (tamal steamers). I thought my friend Raquel Torres in Veracruz State, an anthropologist turned restaurateur, had added the crosses on hers as a decorative folk touch, but she was dead serious. "Tamales are delicate foods," she explained. "Anything can go wrong, and they need all the help they can get."

One of Sahagún's descriptions provides a strong clue to the attitudes behind what we call old wives' tales. He talks about cooks breathing over corn "as if giving it courage, so it will not be afraid of the cooking." It's as if the cook really empathized with the food's feelings. A cook I met in Veracruz claimed that cold water "scares" the food. "*La comida se espasma*," she argued ("The food suffers a spasm" would be the literal translation). So you try to avoid this trauma unless working with a tough customer like yuca root, which sometimes has cold water added during cooking *para asustarla* ("to scare it"). Scared yuca softens faster, our family cook, Inés, explained.

These beliefs mirror the entire way of approaching ingredients in traditional Latin cooking as opposed to the depersonalized modern kitchen. It's like the difference between a stainless steel spoon and a big wooden *cucharamama* used to stir soup: one goes back and forth without becoming a part of the world inside the pot, the other coaxes and reassures everything it touches. The point is that if you think ingredients are inanimate objects, to be impersonally manipulated, you can cook a Latin dish efficiently enough, but you won't be inside the right frame of reference unless you can imagine that the food is alive, listening and feeling in your company.

COOKING LATIN AMERICAN FOOD IN THE UNITED STATES: THE WELL-STOCKED KITCHEN

The traditional Latin American kitchen is not cluttered with hundreds of gadgets that remain unused, collecting dust in drawers or cabinets. Cooks prepare their regional specialties with a handful of carefully selected utensils. Such simplicity is not just a sign of spartan frugality or lack of sophistication. Even in the humblest of rural households, you will find a tool or a pot for every specific use (see page 32), or objects of everyday life imaginatively transformed into kitchen equipment—a bottle used as a rolling pin, an empty tin turned into a mold for baking cakes and flans, a tall, well-scrubbed kerosene can used to boil a hundred tamales over a wood fire.

On the other hand, the higher the social and economic status of the Latin cook, the more his or her kitchen will resemble an American or a European one. There was a time when only the wealthy and the well-traveled had access to superior French cooking tools or American appliances. But now that millions of Latins have found a home in the United States, you will see them at airports loaded with boxes containing home and kitchen appliances, or even with refrigerators, when they go back for a visit to their families. Second only to the demand for computer equipment and television sets is that for domestic appliances in the busiest free port city of Latin America, Ciudad del Este, on the border between Paraguay and Brazil. So it is not surprising to see a Japanese hibachi rice cooker in a humble Guaraní (native Paraguayan) kitchen.

Yet if you look closely at a modern Latin kitchen stocked with a blender, food processor, and sophisticated pots and pans, you will always find the well-used traditional piece of equipment too. Food writer Miro Popiç, who lives in Caracas, owns a professional Viking stove and has a huge array of copper pots and pans collected on his trips to France and New York. But next to the stove hangs a large metal grater he uses for yuca, and sitting on one of the burners is a cast-iron *budare* (a traditional griddle, or *comal*) to make *arepas*, the Venezuelan corn patties. In São Paulo, my friend Gina Nogueira has a collection of French baking pans for every baking need and the whole line of heavy Le Creuset pots. Yet for cooking *carne seca* (dried beef), she will use a blackened clay casserole from Espiritu Santo. And when she decides to make a bean paste from Minas Gerais, she will use the sturdy stoneware typical of Minas.

This mixture of elements is not only endearing but practical. When you work with Latin American food, you find that the most professional-looking, imposing cookware and appliances can have amazing limitations. They work miracles but then fail to do something simple as it should be done. A food processor doesn't begin to approach the efficiency of a hand grater or a mortar and pestle when you want a particular texture. Rice absorbs the cooking liquid more perfectly in my cheap cast-aluminum *caldero* than in any of the beautifully crafted French pots that also live in my kitchen. The supple basket sieve of the Amazon and Orinoco Basins can't be surpassed for sifting the flour for *casabe*, the traditional yuca bread. Unfortunately, the traditional cooking implements are rapidly losing ground to all that saves time and glitters and is attached to an electric cord. But cooks who value perfect results continue to reach for some

"primitive" tool even in otherwise up-to-the-minute kitchens—a good lesson for cooks trying to capture the soul of the Latin kitchen far from its geographical boundaries.

You do not need to rush to a Latin market to buy a Mexican *comal* or a cast-aluminum *caldero* to cook Latin food, but if you want to be a part of the Latin experience, you need to experience it at every level. When I arrive in a Latin country—or anywhere else I travel—I do not even bother opening my suitcase before I head for the markets and the hardware store, where I know I will find the true, time-tested tools of traditional cooking. Like my Latin friends, I am always loaded with kitchen gadgets for gifts when I travel to Latin America, but when I return I am always hunched over, burdened like the mule of a Brazilian *tropeiro* (as my exasperated husband would say), with heavy mortars, *comales*, *calderos*, graters, and every traditional piece of equipment I can get my hands on. Cooking with them gives me the vicarious pleasure of foreign travel in the comfort of my own kitchen.

In the United States, most kitchens are already stocked with such necessities as mixing bowls, ladles, spatulas, butcher's twine, rolling pins, vegetable peelers, measuring cups and spoons, and pots, saucepans, and skillets of many sizes. What I list below is a selection of kitchen tools I have found especially useful when cooking recipes from this book in my own American home. Some will be familiar to the average cook; others are little known or almost forgotten in kitchens here.

Utensils, Hand Tools, and Other Basics

Batería de Cocina

ESSENTIAL

Scales: I own a couple of digital scales that register both ounces and grams and are good for amounts up to five pounds. For larger amounts, I prefer an old-fashioned beam scale with a large removable pan for holding the food.

Straight-sided **box grater**, preferably a four-sided model with two grating surfaces (fine and coarse), a shredding surface, and a side with slits for slicing.

Large array of **wooden spoons.**

Several **slotted spoons,** to lift out meats and vegetables from cooking liquids or frying oil.

Four-sided box grater

Skimming ladles, to skim broths and to lift foods from frying oil.

Long-handled tongs, for turning roasting chiles and grilled meats.

Several **whisks,** for everything from emulsifying sauces to making meringues.

Hand juicer for citrus fruits.

Hand-cranked **pasta machine,** for rolling out pasta or Cuban bread.

DESIRABLE

Medium-sized river or beach **stones,** to use as weights. They are also good grinding and cracking tools.

Wooden **mallet** and stainless steel **meat pounder,** to pound chops and steak.

Panela (brown loaf sugar) **cutter.**

Wooden *tostón* press (*tostonera*)

Wooden *tostón* press for stuffed *tostones*

Tostonera, for pressing plantain slices. There are two types, one for flat and the other for cup-shaped *tostones.*

Mandoline or similar slicer.

Molinillo (Mexican wooden chocolate mill).

Spray bottle, for making bread.

Pots, Pans, and Cooking Surfaces

To start, I suggest sturdy heavy-bottomed saucepans and skillets in assorted sizes with well-fitting lids and a stockpot or a Dutch oven big enough to be used as a stockpot (10- to 12-quart capacity). Beyond this, I recommend:

ESSENTIAL

A heavy-gauge rectangular or round metal **griddle** or a metal *comal,* at least 11 inches wide, or a large cast-iron **skillet** for griddle-roast-

Comal

ing vegetables. Clay *comales* are cheaper and more traditional but are very short-lived; they also need to be cured with a lime solution after every use.

Tamalera (tamal steamer) or an improvised steaming arrangement large enough to hold a large batch of tamales. You can use a fancy double steamer or a Chinese wok and bamboo steamers.

At least one large heavy-gauge **roasting pan.**

If you own a professional gas stove, buy a couple of heavy-gauge cast-aluminum **rimmed baking sheets.** They are perfect for roasting a whole suckling pig or baby lamb.

DESIRABLE

Several lidded cast-aluminum *calderos* (Dutch oven–like cauldrons, found in many Latin houseware stores and groceries). They come in many sizes, from 4-gallon giants to 1-cup babies. These are great for making fresh corn *arepas* (page 399).

Caldero

Clay *cazuelas* and *ollas* (casseroles and pots). These are excellent for baking vegetables or cooking rice. The deep ones are perfect for making fermented drinks like *chicha*, fruit vinegars, cheese, and creams. You can find them in Spanish and Hispanic Caribbean markets as well as in Portuguese or Brazilian stores.

Large (16-inch) hammered-iron or steel **paella pan** (good for *empanadas*).

Large (11- to 12-inch) deep, heavy **sauté pan.**

At least one large (8-quart) tinned **copper pot** (I like the feel and look of the copper and the way it conducts heat).

Tools for Grinding

ESSENTIAL

Several sturdy heavy-duty **mortars and pestles** in different sizes and preferably of different materials (e.g., wood and stoneware). Two purchases you will never

Wooden mortar and pestle

regret are a large olive wood mortar for pounding garlic and a Mexican three-legged volcanic-stone *molcajete* (mortar) with a pestle (*tejolote*) of the same material. Anyone who travels in Latin America should keep an eye out for special regional mortars and pestles, such as the Andean *batán* (except it is so heavy you would need the *Queen Mary* to bring it back home to America). I bought several stone and granite mortars by a British designer a few years ago at the Japanese store Takashimaya in New York. Similar in shape to Thai stone mortars, they are superb for grinding nuts.

Molcajete

Batán (Peruvian grinding stone)

Meat grinder, either the tinned cast-iron type that clamps to a table or the meat-grinding attachment of a machine such as a Moulinex or KitchenAid standing mixer.

Tinned cast-iron **plate mill** with table clamp, for grinding corn (such as a Corona brand *molino para granos* from Colombia).

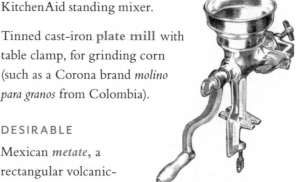

Plate mill (Corona brand)

DESIRABLE

Mexican *metate*, a rectangular volcanic-stone grinding slab on three legs, with a *mano* (pestle) of the same material.

Metate

Tools for Cutting and Chopping

Latin American cooks do not place a high priority on fancy heavy-duty knives to cut up or mince ingredients. By all means, use an arsenal of good knives if you have them (I do), but remember that grinding, grating, and the scoring-and-paring techniques described on page 19 are often more authentic Latin ways to deal with peppers, onions, and other vegetables for basic sauces.

For cutting tough sugarcane, there is nothing like a **machete,** available in Hispanic-Caribbean hardware stores. Also, for cutting bones, a heavy **Chinese cleaver** is very useful.

Tools for Straining

ESSENTIAL
Mesh strainers in various degrees of fineness.

Cheesecloth.

Food mill.

DESIRABLE
Drum sieve.

Electric Appliances

ESSENTIAL
Heavy-duty **blender.**

Food processor (preferably a large professional one with a large feed tube and slicing disks of various sizes).

Electric coffee or spice **mill.**

DESIRABLE
KitchenAid **standing mixer** or (less useful) a handheld mixer or hand blender.

Ice cream maker.

Electric juicer.

Miscellaneous

ESSENTIAL
A large collection of **jars** and storage **containers.**

Timer.

Thermometers: instant-read, oven, candy, and deep-frying.

18-inch **ruler.**

DESIRABLE
Cafetera (espresso pot, preferably Bialetti brand).

Achiotera (a metal container with a spout for dispensing and storing achiote-infused oil).

Mate **gourds and straws** (one for every guest, since you will find that Americans resist sharing a single *mate* and straw).

Mate gourd with *bombilla* (silver straw)

A small battery-operated **frother** (sold in Cuban hardware stores; look for Crema de Café by Vandel) to cream sugar and coffee to make the famous foam on a cup of Cuban coffee.

Caja China, a portable contraption to roast a whole pig.

CHAPTER 3

THE
LAYERS
OF
LATIN FLAVOR

IN THIS CHAPTER

When I see people eating Latin American food in this country, I can tell with one glance whether they are Latins or Anglos. Non-Latins fill their plates by putting the meat with a little sauce in one corner, the rice in another, and the beans and different vegetables in their own places. Even salad-like garnishes such as sliced onions and avocado will probably receive their own places. If there are table salsas, Anglos carefully put a little in this food or that. They bring neat forkfuls of different things in turn to their mouths, trying to taste the elements of the meal one at a time.

Latins, meanwhile, will shovel the meat over the rice with lakes of sauce and make mixtures of beans and onions and vegetables, combining everything into everything else and trying to crowd as many components of the meal as possible onto each forkful. No, this is not chaos. Most of our cooking is highly structured, even when we are not following written recipes. But the way many of us eat complete meals on a single plate shows that for Latin diners, the experience of eating is not complete unless they are perceiving lively juxtapositions of varied tastes and textures from the first bite. They want lots of different tastes going on at once, so they can sense different layers of flavor above and beneath and beside each other.

This effect of dimension begins in the kitchen with each dish, as the cook creates layers of seasoning. Even if a cook seems to put together a dish spontaneously, there is an inner structure of flavoring any good Latin cook understands even when combining the simplest ingredients.

A Latin cook might start a stew by seasoning meats in a marinade puckery with the tang of bitter oranges and sharp with the bite of fresh garlic. Then she (or he) prepares a cooking sauce by sautéing garlic, onion, sweet and hot peppers, aromatic spices and herbs, and a bit of tomato or coconut milk. She adds the meat and its marinade to the cooking sauce, and the stew slowly simmers, the meat absorbs the rich flavor of the seasonings from both the marinade and the cooking sauce. At the same time, the meat exudes its juices, which blend with and enrich the other flavors. Finally, the stew will receive yet another layer of flavor at the table. The cook might set out a bowl of a crunchy *salsa cruda*, a pitcher of silky ripened cream, or a bottle of *manteiga de garrafa* (a warm clarified butter with a strong taste of fermented whey) and invite guests to spoon or drizzle some over the dish.

You will find these flavoring principles surfacing again and again with different names throughout the countries of Latin America, always with the same underlying purposes: depth of taste, contrast of flavors. The effect is the basic code that identifies each country's cuisine. I ask you to think about how this is achieved as you explore the recipes in this chapter. Almost without knowing it, you will begin to sense some common factors at work even in the simplest, and seemingly unrelated, preparations.

Our way of playing off the flavor elements against each other is a lesson inherited from the European Middle Ages, a legacy that was, to some extent at least, forgotten in most of the Old World—France, for example. When I studied the basics of French cooking at the French Culinary Institute (now the International Culinary Center) in New York, the veteran chef assisting one of my teachers used to taste my food and say, "There goes Madame Prrresilla again," rolling his eyes. "Oh, you Spaniarrrds," he said, "always adding vinegar and lemon juice to food." The chef never did quite grasp that I was Cuban, but otherwise he was right! For us "Spaniarrrds" of the New World, the medieval instinct to animate the flavors of a sauce with a sour accent still endures. Nor have we lost the medieval sense of sweetness as an intrinsic element of savory dishes or of salt as a partner with sugar in desserts. We would find these tastes one-dimensional without each other. (By the way, the chef always came back to my work station for seconds.)

I could list many specific features of medieval Iberian cuisine and pre-Columbian cooking that triumphantly survive in modern Latin America—in fact, I do just that in every chapter of this book. But the broad culinary principles handed down from the past that I want to identify here begin with playing sour, sweet, salty, and sometimes hot and savory flavors against each other fully and flexibly. There are several techniques for achieving this, and they are not necessarily dependent on a lot of exotic ingredients (though you certainly do need to recognize the flavor profile of some strategic ingredients that have no substitute). The two most fundamental of these techniques date back to the Spanish Middle Ages.

The one you will be using the most is *sofreír*, or what might be called "modulated frying." Have you ever started a dish by sautéing some sliced onions and garlic in oil, knowing that later on in the cooking they will not only lend flavor to a simple unthickened sauce but also help give it body? Then you have been making a Spanish *sofrito* without knowing it.

Broadly speaking, a *sofrito* is a flavor enrichment of sautéed onions and/or garlic, with or without a few other common additions, that is either the jumping-off point for a dish (for example, a soup or stew) or added to it at some point during cooking. The term can be stretched to include any sauce made by the *sofrito* principle. The versatile cooked tomato sauce on page 48 is an example of a *sofrito* in this sense. So is the famous sauce for fish *a la veracru-* zana (page 48). So are many other flavor-enhancing mixtures or sauces that you will be introduced to under such widely different regional names that Latins from one country may not know what Latins from another mean by them.

You will learn much by looking for the basic *sofrito* in any recipe, simple or complex. Does a recipe begin with onions and garlic cooked in oil or lard or rendered bacon fat? Then it begins with a *sofrito*, and it starts with a delicate foretaste of the sweetness (from the natural sugar in the onions) that is one of our pivotal balancing flavors. (As you will see, the sugar we use in cooking is very rarely plain refined sugar, and so it has depth of flavor besides sweetness). When a Mexican or Peruvian cook grinds hot peppers and sautés them in sizzling lard or oil, she is preparing the base of a *sofrito* that will later be enriched with other seasoning ingredients.

Almost equally important is the technique we call *adobar*. The term resists brief translation, but if you have ever rubbed steaks or chops with a mixture of garlic, seasonings, and lemon juice before you put them in the pan, or used a similar flavor mixture as the main seasoning for a meat stew, you know more about *adobos* than you think you do.

An *adobo* can be either a marinade for meats or a liquid for braising them that contains the key elements of hotness and sourness tempered with other flavors. In Old Spain, the hot and sour players would have been black pepper and vinegar. Here in the New World, native hot peppers got in on the *adobo* act, and in some regions (for example, the Yucatán) they are often combined with citrus juices, a lot of garlic, and various herbs and spices. I use the term *adobo* mostly to refer either to hot-sour-garlicky mixtures, some thick enough to be rubs and some thin enough to be basting sauces, or to stews or soup-stews where the meat is cooked in a sauce (thick or thin) that provides a foundation of acidity and heat that still endures.

This chapter lets you in on the pleasure of layered flavoring by giving many national and regional variations for each technique: making *adobos* and *sofritos* as well as coloring with achiote, adding sweetness or sourness, playing with texture, and adding finishing flourishes. Think of this chapter as the flavor foundation of the whole book. Here you'll find basic recipes for marinades and seasoning pastes, homemade vinegars, cooking sauces, and spice blends that will help you build your Latin pantry. Having these flavorings at hand means that you can quickly whip up a complex meal with Latin flavors without having to start from scratch (or sacrifice flavor by using shortcuts).

Latin seasoning mixes are versatile and can be used creatively in all types of cooking. Learn to improvise, reaching into the vast storehouse of Latin flavor with a sense of adventure. Use the Chilean smoked spice mix *merkén* as a dry rub for grilled chicken. Stir a spoonful of the uncooked Puerto Rican seasoning mix called *recado* into a pot of beans for an instant boost of flavor. Ladle a Cuban *sofrito* over plain grilled chicken, and you'll be giving it a superb flavor patina.

THE *ADOBO*: THE FIRST LAYER

The first thing I think of when I think of *adobo* is how I, a Cuban born and bred, behave when I return from the market with some fresh meat, poultry, or fish. I immediately reach for garlic, allspice, cumin, and bitter, or Seville, oranges, to start preparing a quick marinade. People from my tradition can hardly imagine starting to cook without having already converted the unseasoned into the seasoned. For us, what distinguishes a civilized from an uncivilized kitchen is not the Lévi-Straussian distinction between the raw and the cooked but the difference between the unseasoned and the seasoned. In this sense, the *adobo* is of profound importance.

To make my *adobo*, I crush a blend of seasonings, mostly allspice and garlic, in a mortar with a pestle and add the juice of bitter oranges for moisture and tang. I season everything with this paste: steaks, stew meats, pork leg, chicken breasts, red snapper fillets, the huge holiday turkey, even a whole pig. I especially like to rub a small amount of it all over the thin sirloin top steak Cubans call *palomilla*, then let it rest for 20 to 30 minutes—just enough time to infuse the meat with terrific garlicky flavor.

When I prepare a large fresh ham for roasting, I make a more liquid marinade and, for maximum flavor, let the meat sit in it for at least a day. As the meat roasts, I add some oil, melted lard, and the pan juices to the leftover marinade and baste the meat with it, giving the roast yet another layer of seasoning.

My recipe for *adobo* is just one of many you will find throughout Latin America—a tangy mixture of seasonings combined with an acidic liquid, most commonly citrus juice or vinegar. Some are wet pastes, others are more liquid. Some are very simple, just crushed garlic and salt combined with citrus juice; others are more complex, glistening pastes, cooked or raw, made with roasted dried chiles and half a dozen spices.

In Puerto Rico and the Dominican Republic, *adobos* are similar to my version, generally composed of garlic mashed to a paste and an acidic medium, either citrus juice (bitter orange or lime) or vinegar. In Cuba, aromatic spices such as cumin, oregano, and allspice tame the tart edge of the citrus and the pungency of the garlic, rounding out the flavors. Oregano plays a more prominent role in the *adobos* of the Dominican Republic and Puerto Rico.

In Brazil, *adobos* are called *temperos* (a generic word for a mixture of seasonings) or *vinha-d'alhos*, which can be loosely translated as "garlic wine." A *vinha-d'alhos* is an acidic liquid marinade made with crushed garlic, vinegar or wine, black pepper, bay leaf or cilantro, and salt, spiked with devilish *malagueta* pepper. In Bahia, no seafood touches the pot before being marinated in a mixture of lime juice, salt, and garlic.

In the *adobos* of coastal Colombia, garlic is also omnipresent, but other seasoning ingredients that Latins usually reserve for cooking enter into the mix, such as onions and tomatoes, grated on a traditional box grater. In Guatemala, tomatoes often join forces with acidy tomatillos in *adobos* for meat. In El Salvador, a complex spice blend called *relajo*, which contains at least a dozen ingredients, including aromatic spices and dried hot chiles, is ground to a paste with assertive yellow mustard to season chicken and red meat.

Peruvian marinades from the highlands are spicy and deeply herbal. Two intensely perfumed Andean herbs, *chinche* and *huacatay*, are combined with the local hot peppers (*ají mirasol* or *ají panca*), cumin, and oregano in *adobos*, or *aderezos*, to marinate meats to be stewed, roasted, or grilled. In the north of Peru, a fermented drink made from sprouted corn, called *chicha de jora*, gives acidity with backbone to most *adobos*. In southern Ecuador, these marinades are often called *aliños*. *Cuy* (guinea pig), which is feast food all over the Andes, is marinated with garlic, cumin, and salt, all mashed to a paste on a grinding stone or with a mortar and pestle.

The Latin obsession with seasoning foods with fragrant pastes and marinades before cooking them illustrates the force of long-lasting Spanish traditions that found a fertile soil throughout Latin America. The modern Spanish verb *adobar* (to marinate) comes from the Old French *adouber*, "to dub," one of whose meanings refers to arming a knight with the equipment of his office, like sword and spurs. Like the momentous tapping of the lord's sword on the shoulder of the knight, an *adobo* arms, or equips, Latin food with marvelous flavor.

Gonzalo de Berceo, a prolific twelfth-century Castilian writer whose work is the standard source for the study of medieval Spanish, described *adobo* as marinated pork, a usage that survives to this day in many parts of Spain, particularly in Galicia. Galician marinades for pork are very intense and garlicky, serving not only to flavor the meat but also to cure, tenderize, and preserve it—preserving being one of the reasons meats were marinated in the first place. By the fifteenth century, on the eve of the discovery of America by the Spanish, the word *adobo* had taken on related meanings; for instance, it was also used to describe a type of stew in which meats were cooked in their marinade with some broth or were seasoned in the pot with a mixture of vinegar and spices.

There are, of course, exceptions to every rule. Not everybody in Latin America subscribes to the theory that everything needs to be seasoned before cooking. Though Argentinean and Uruguayan cooks often season chicken and lamb with some lime or lemon juice, white wine, salt, pepper, a bit of oregano, and a bit of chopped parsley, they grill their beef with almost no seasoning, sometimes only a sprinkling of salt. But at the table they smother the meat with a delicious table sauce called *chimichurri*, made with garlic, spices, fresh herbs like parsley, crushed dried hot peppers, and vinegar. You could argue that the puckery chimichurri in effect doubles as an *adobo*, infusing the cooked meat with flavor and aroma.

Exceptions aside, in all its incarnations, the *adobo* is a distinctively Latin American seasoning tool, a first gilding of flavor that helps make Latin dishes truly spectacular.

Cuban *Adobo* for a Large Fresh Ham

Adobo Cubano para Pierna de Puerco

While other Latin American cuisines use *adobos* in moderation, Cubans are obsessed with them. The fragrance of garlic hovers over Cuban pork or turkey dishes like a spirited national banner. No piece of meat, fish, or poultry reaches a skillet or grill without first being marinated in a garlicky *adobo*.

In every home, there is an *adobo* maker. Back in Cuba, my uncle Oscar assumed this important role, which included roasting the Christmas Eve pig. I can still picture him pounding prodigious amounts of garlic, allspice, cumin, and oregano in a well-worn wooden mortar and calling out to his wife, "Carolina, squeeze more bitter orange!"

Now I am the *adobo* maker in my family. Like Oscar, I take pride in the special flavor of my *adobos*, smearing the fragrant paste over the holiday pig like a precious ointment, relishing the continuation of this family tradition. This recipe has the distinct allspice aroma of my hometown, Santiago de Cuba, the only part of Cuba where this complex spice is used in cooking.

MAKES ABOUT 1 CUP, ENOUGH TO MARINATE A 12-POUND FRESH HAM (LEG OF PORK)

- 1 head garlic, separated into cloves and peeled
- 2 teaspoons black peppercorns
- 2 teaspoons ground cumin
- 2 teaspoons allspice berries or ground allspice
- 2 teaspoons dried oregano
- 1 tablespoon salt
- ¾ cup fresh bitter orange juice (from about 6 oranges), or equal parts lime juice and orange juice
- 1 tablespoon freshly rendered lard (page 82; optional)

▶ Place the garlic, peppercorns, cumin, allspice, oregano, and salt in a large mortar and pound to a paste with the pestle. Stir in the bitter orange juice. Or puree these ingredients in a blender or food processor.

If using, heat the lard in a small saucepan over high heat until it sizzles. Pour in the *adobo* and immediately remove from the fire. To use for a leg of pork, rub the meat all over with marinade, reserving a few tablespoons. Halfway through the roasting time, brush with the reserved *adobo*.

Storing: Place in a glass or plastic container and refrigerate, tightly covered, until ready to use; this will keep for 2 to 3 days.

Uses: Use to marinate a large fresh ham or a whole fish or chicken or turkey. Double the recipe to season a 20-pound pig.

Garlic "Wine" to Season Fish

Vinha-d'Alhos

When Brazilians marinate meats, poultry, or fish before cooking, they follow careful rules of seasoning—for instance, bay leaf and cilantro are reserved for fish marinades, such as this one. They have other seasoning sauces, the *temperos*, that bring together a number of spices (also confusingly called *temperos*).

Vinha-d'alhos is often made in advance and refrigerated until needed. This recipe was given to me by the Nogueira family, who have roots in the city of Minas Gerais. It is great for fish, but it is so good that I break with tradition and use it to marinate meats and even, mixed with some extra-virgin olive oil, as a dressing for tomato and watercress salad.

MAKES ABOUT 1 CUP, ENOUGH FOR 8 POUNDS FISH

- 6 garlic cloves
- 2 pickled *malagueta* peppers (see Cook's Note page 144) or 1 pickled jalapeño
- 2 cilantro sprigs
- 1 teaspoon salt
- 1 teaspoon freshly ground black pepper
- 1 bay leaf, crushed
- ¼ teaspoon ground cumin
- ½ cup distilled white vinegar

▶ Place all ingredients in a food processor or blender and process to a rough-textured puree (not too fine).

Storing: Store in a tightly sealed glass jar, in the refrigerator. This will keep for months.

Uses: Use for grouper, red snapper, and tuna; do not marinate the fish for more than 10 minutes, or the marinade will coagulate the fish's protein, as in cebiche.

Yucatecan Red Seasoning Paste for Pit-Roasted Pig

Recado o Adobo Rojo para Cochinita Pibil

When I visited the central market of Mérida, in the Yucatán, I saw mounds of the bright-colored seasoning paste called *recado rojo*, a marvelous alliance between the Old and the New World sealed with the golden blood of the tropics, the seeds of a shrub or small tree called achiote.

From Mayan chronicles and the accounts of the Spanish bishop Diego de Landa, who wrote extensively about the Yucatán on the eve of the Spanish conquest, we know that the achiote tree was known to the Maya, who always kept one growing next to their huts. Its widespread cultivation in the Yucatán was promoted by the Spaniards, who used the seeds as a substitute for saffron. Achiote gives this marinade not only a stunning intense orange-red color but also the distinctive flavor of the seed—nutty, smoky, and faintly resinous.

In the Yucatán today, the hard seeds of achiote are ground to a paste in special artisanal mills together with other seasonings, among them garlic, cloves, cinnamon, oregano, and bitter orange juice or vinegar. Allspice has the last word in this Yucatecan *recado*, its intense complex scent bringing together the essence of the other spices. A good *recado* must be rich in aroma; that's why savvy Yucatecan cooks always doctor up market-bought *recados* at home by adding more garlic and spices.

This versatile condiment finds its best use as a seasoning for the famous Yucatecan pit-roasted pig (*cochinita pibil*, page 725) or for the meats used to fill the *mucbipollo*, the huge tamal that is a Days of the Dead specialty. In the Yucatán, these dishes are cooked in stone-lined pits (*pibs*), but I have had great success in reproducing them through oven-roasting or grilling. The *recado rojo* carries the essential taste of the *pib*.

MAKES ABOUT 1½ CUPS, ENOUGH FOR 7 TO 8 POUNDS MEAT

- 2 heads garlic
- 1 tablespoon black peppercorns
- 1 tablespoon allspice berries or ground allspice
- 1 tablespoon cumin seeds or ground cumin
- 1 tablespoon dried oregano
- 1 teaspoon cloves
- 1 teaspoon ground cinnamon
- 5 tablespoons ground achiote, store-bought or home-ground (page 89)
- 1 cup bitter orange juice (from about 7 oranges) or equal parts lime juice and orange juice
- 1 tablespoon salt

▶ Separate 1 head of garlic into cloves, peel, and reserve. Roast the other whole head of garlic on a *comal* or heavy griddle or in a cast-iron skillet over medium heat, turning occasionally, until lightly charred on all sides, 3 to 5 minutes. Peel and reserve.

Add the peppercorns, allspice, cumin, oregano, cloves, and cinnamon, and toast over medium-low heat, stirring constantly, for 1 minute. Transfer to an electric spice mill or coffee grinder and grind to a fine powder.

Place the spice mixture, roasted garlic, raw garlic, ground achiote, orange juice, and salt in a food processor or blender and blend to a thick paste.

Cook's Note: This recipe is tame. To make the sauce deliciously spicy, lightly roast 1 stemmed and seeded habanero chile on a *comal* or in a heavy-bottomed skillet, and add to the blender or food processor along with the rest of the ingredients.

Storing: The *recado* will keep well for months, refrigerated and tightly covered, if you omit the orange juice when you make it and add ½ cup distilled white vinegar. When you are ready to use the *recado*, loosen it up with ½ cup bitter orange juice (or one of the alternatives listed in the ingredients).

Uses: This wonderful sauce is a godsend when trying to put a meal together in a hurry. One of my favorite ways to use it is as a marinade for chicken before roasting. With just 1 cup, you can season two 3½-pound chickens. Cut the chickens into 8 serving pieces each (see instructions on page 659), place in a bowl, and season with salt and pepper. Then rub the *recado* all over the chicken. If you have time, let stand for at least 30 minutes in the refrigerator, tightly covered with plastic wrap. Place the chicken in a baking pan and roast in a preheated 350°F oven for 1 hour, turning with a spoon halfway through cooking. You will never go wrong!

Guatemalan *Adobo*

Adobo Guatemalteco Simple

In Guatemala, cooks often pair tomatoes and green tomatillos—called *miltomates* there—in marinades. The result is a flavorful *adobo* with the body and complexity of a cooking sauce. I also like to use this tangy, fruity marinade as a sauce for grilled or broiled meats or chicken.

12 large tomatillos (about 1¼ pounds), husks removed, cooked in boiling water for 8 minutes

3 plum tomatoes (about 9 ounces), peeled and seeded

8 garlic cloves, peeled

2 teaspoons salt

1 teaspoon store-bought achiote paste

1 teaspoon black peppercorns

½ teaspoon dried oregano

½ teaspoon ground cumin

¼ cup distilled white vinegar

▶ Place all the ingredients in a blender or food processor and process to a fine puree. To use, rub pork, beef, or poultry all over. Let marinate, tightly covered, for at least 2 hours, or up to 12 hours in the refrigerator.

Storing: Refrigerate in a plastic or glass container, tightly covered, until ready to use.

Uses: Use to marinate meat or poultry before roasting or stewing, or serve as a sauce for grilled or broiled meat or chicken.

Salvadorian Spice Mix

Relajo Salvadoreño

Relajo is a Salvadorian spice mix used to season tamales and turkey. You usually buy it at the market, as a made-to-order mixture of whole dried spices, and take it home to toast and grind as needed. *Relajo*

can be bought premixed but not ground in plastic packets in some Hispanic markets. Here is the *relajo* I learned in El Salvador several years ago from Ofelia Ramírez, the chef of the restaurant Mar y Tierra in Antiguo Cuscatlán, not far from Puerto Libertad, and from a *relajo* vendor at the municipal market, which is right across from the restaurant.

MAKES ½ CUP

1 *guaque* chile or dried guajillo chile, stemmed and seeded

1 *ciruela* chile or ancho chile, stemmed and seeded

1 tablespoon black peppercorns

1 teaspoon cloves

1 bay leaf

2 tablespoons sesame seeds

2 tablespoons hulled pumpkin seeds

2 tablespoons unsalted peanuts

1 teaspoon dried oregano or marjoram

1 teaspoon dried thyme

1 tablespoon ground achiote, store-bought or home-ground (page 89)

▶ Most often the ingredients of a *relajo* are simply mixed together and stored in a glass jar to be toasted and ground as needed. But there is a problem with this approach—the *relajo* will be much better if the ingredients are roasted separately before they are mixed, so that each is given its own time to develop flavor. I suggest this sequence: Heat a *comal*, griddle, or heavy skillet over medium-high heat. Place the chiles on the *comal* and roast for 2 to 3 minutes, turning once or twice. Remove and set aside. Proceed with the peppercorns, cloves, and then the bay leaf, roasting them for only 1 minute or less and shaking the pan to prevent scorching. Finally, roast the sesame seeds, pumpkin seeds, and then the peanuts for about 2 minutes, or until golden, shaking the pan. Let cool slightly.

With a sharp knife, chop the roasted chiles into fine bits. Crumble the bay leaf into small pieces. Combine all the roasted ingredients with the dried herbs and achiote and grind to a powder in an electric coffee grinder or spice mill.

Storing: Stored tightly covered in a glass jar, this will keep its fragrance for 1 to 2 months.

Uses: Use as a dry rub for turkey and chicken or add to any cooking sauce for a boost of flavor. Or mix 1 tablespoon with 2 tablespoons of yellow or Dijon mustard to season jack and mackerel before pan-frying or roasting, as is done in Puerto Libertad.

THE *SOFRITO*: THE SECOND LAYER

The purest, most unvarnished, most ancient Spanish *sofrito* would be a flavor base of onions cooked in olive oil long enough to bring out their depth and sweetness. Garlic might join the onions or replace them. In some regions, scallions are nearly as common as onions; in others (though not often), leeks or chives may enter the picture instead. Once the Old World–New World exchanges of foods began, *sofritos* moved to the Americas and peppers (sweet and/or hot, fresh and/or dried) and tomatoes frequently formed part of the *sofrito* base in both hemispheres.

A very early recipe for *sofrito* appeared in the fourteenth-century Catalan cookbook *Libre de Sent Soví*, by an anonymous author. It instructs the cook to sauté onions, garlic, and leeks in bacon fat or olive oil for a base to flavor soups or stews. The *sofrito* as we know it today in Latin America is not so different: a few vegetables, most often onions and garlic, sautéed in lard, oil, or fat rendered from bacon or salt-cured fatback. This simple sauté is the first stage in making a cooking sauce that will gain flavor from peppers, tomatoes, herbs, coconut milk, spirits, fermented liquids such as vinegar, and/or cheese.

Latin Americans do not make semantic distinctions between the different stages of a *sofrito*. For the Latin cook, *sofrito* is a broad term that means both a simple sauté and the final cooking sauce. Since this blurring of meanings seems to be the source of endless confusion for my non-Latin students, in this book I refer to the first stage of the *sofrito*, the sautéing of onions and garlic, as a flavoring base. I call the sauce that results from adding other ingredients and preparations to the base a cooking sauce. A cooking sauce can be as simple as an Ecuadorian *ahogado*, where just cumin and cilantro are added to the flavoring base, or as complex as a lush Puerto Rican *sofrito* enriched with a *recado*—an uncooked puree of cilantro, broad-leaf *culantro*, and the aromatic pepper *ají dulce*—and half a dozen other ingredients, including capers, olives, and tomato sauce.

The method by which the ingredients for the cooking sauce are prepared is determined by the equipment a cook has at hand. Some things that we take for granted in our own kitchens—like chopping boards and counters—are completely unknown to the great majority of Latin cooks. In some traditional kitchens, cooks score the onion and slice it while holding it in the palm of one hand. Sometimes onions, tomatoes, and even peppers are not chopped or minced but instead are grated on a metal grater (*guayo* or *rallo*). Most cooks prefer to crush garlic to a paste with a mortar and pestle or a stone grinder.

In Mexico and Central America, as well as in Andean countries such as Bolivia and Peru, onions and peppers are often roasted before being cut or ground. However, the flavoring ingredients for a cooking sauce—whether raw, toasted or roasted, chopped, minced, or ground to a paste—are always sautéed in some type of fat to release maximum flavor. In Latin America, good cooks pay attention to the flavor and temperature of the fat, though they may have different opinions about the order in which the ingredients are added, as well as their texture. They heat the fat over brisk heat until it ripples. Then they add the flavoring ingredients, all together or in a well-orchestrated sequence, so they will fry, not steam in their own juices—which would happen if the fat were not hot enough. With high heat, the pungent flavor and the aroma of the seasonings burst forth vividly.

The Many Names of *Sofrito*

Although *sofrito* is the preferred term in the familiar Hispanic Caribbean—Cuba, Puerto Rico, the Dominican Republic—not everyone in Latin America calls their cooking sauce *sofrito*. You may be talking about *sofrito* to a person from Santiago del Estero, in northwestern Argentina, who seems uncomprehending at first, but then pipes up, "Ah, you mean the *salsita* (the little sauce)!" When the Spaniards brought the concept of *sofrito* to Latin America, it acquired new names (some based on different ways of saying *sofrito* in different parts of Spain itself). Here are some of the most important regional names and definitions:

Aderezo: In Peru, *sofrito* is often known as *aderezo*, which literally means adornment or dressing—a perfectly accurate description of what this marvelous cooking sauce does to food.

Ahogado: The word *ahogado* is used for *sofritos* in parts of Colombia, Venezuela, Ecuador, and Bolivia. Other popular variations include *hogo* and *ajogao* (the *j* pronounced as a prominent *h*). The citizens of Cuenca, Ecuador, pride themselves on pronouncing all four syllables of *ahogado*.

Rehogado: In parts of Peru, *ahogado* resurfaces as *rehogado*.

Refogado: In Portuguese, a Romance language closely related to medieval Castilian and Galician-Portuguese, the *f* of vulgar Latin (the corrupt Latin spoken in the former provinces of the Roman Empire) never became a silent *h*, as in Castilian. So *refogado*, the Brazilian *sofrito*, is an archaic linguistic cousin of the Castilian *rehogado*.

Refrito: *Refrito* literally means "refried"; it is often used interchangeably with *aderezo* or *ahogado* to refer to *sofrito*.

Guiso: In Barranquilla, Colombia, a *sofrito* is considered a *guiso*, which is loosely translated as a type of braise or stew.

The Sequence of the *Sofrito*

When it comes time to cook a *sofrito*, everyone can agree on the first technique: sautéing. However, the order in which ingredients are added to the pan and whether they go in in stages, one by one, or all at once vary from country to country and from cook to cook. For example, cooks who are afraid of burning the garlic always add the onion first and cook it until translucent or golden brown before adding other ingredients.

In Mexico and parts of Central America, peppers, onions, tomatoes, garlic, and even spices are often roasted and then ground to a paste in a *molcajete* or blender. This seasoning paste is poured into the hot lard or oil and cooked until it thickens and the sauce separates from the oil, which begins to sizzle again, in effect giving the sauce a second frying and thereby deepening its flavor. In Cuba, cooks like to add the flavoring ingredients in stages. They usually begin by rendering the flavorful fat from smoked bacon, salt-cured fatback, fatty ham, or chorizo in some lard or oil to build a strong flavor foundation from the start, then add minced garlic and quickly sauté it until golden before adding other flavoring ingredients.

The cooking sauces of Puerto Rico and the Dominican Republic are enriched with a fresh uncooked seasoning mix called a *recado*, or *recaíto*, which is composed of cilantro, broad-leaf *culantro*, and the tiny lantern-shaped sweet pepper called *ají dulce*. These aromatic ingredients are chopped or pureed in a blender and are often mixed with vinegar and other seasonings. Cooks keep this heady puree in hand, refrigerated or frozen, and when ready to make a *sofrito*, they swirl a spoonful or two into the flavoring base of sautéed onion and garlic for an instant boost of flavor.

3 tablespoons extra-virgin olive oil
2 garlic cloves, coarsely chopped
1 medium yellow onion (about 8 ounces), coarsely chopped (about 1½ cups)
7 or 8 ripe medium plum tomatoes (about 1¼ pounds), cored and quartered, or drained canned tomatoes
2 flat-leaf parsley sprigs
4 thyme sprigs or ⅛ teaspoon dried thyme
½ teaspoon salt, or to taste
¼ teaspoon freshly ground black pepper, or to taste

▶ Heat the oil in a large (12-inch) skillet or sauté pan over medium heat until it ripples. Add the garlic and onion and sauté, stirring, for 2 minutes. Add the tomatoes, herbs, salt, and pepper, reduce the heat, and simmer, covered, for 20 minutes. Taste for seasoning.

Pass the sauce through a food mill. The food mill will render a smooth, seedless, full-bodied sauce.

Storing: This will keep well, tightly covered, for 1 week in the refrigerator.

Uses: Use in lieu of commercial tomato sauce in *sofritos*, rice dishes, and stews. For a dipping sauce, add ¼ cup finely chopped fresh cilantro and 2 jalapeños, seeded and finely chopped, to the cooled sauce.

Light Tomato Sauce

Salsa de Tomate Ligera

This versatile sauce only takes minutes to put together whenever I find ripe, good-tasting tomatoes at the market.

MAKES ABOUT 1½ CUPS

Veracruz Tomato Sauce for Fish

Salsa para Pescado a la Veracruzana

From the day in the sixteenth century on which Hernán Cortés landed near what is today Veracruz, the cuisine of this Mexican state has been influenced by Spain. Trade between New Spain and the mother country was done through the fleet system—the ships first visited Havana and then Veracruz before setting sail for the port of Cádiz in Andalusia, Spain.

Perfectly at home (except for the heat of the pickled jalapeño, revealing its Mexican origin) in Andalusia and Havana, this tangy, light tomato sauce is traditionally spooned over red snapper (*huachinango*) and snook (*róbalo*, a brackish-water fish), the two most popular fishes of Veracruz.

This cooking sauce follows all the steps of a classic Andalusian *sofrito*, with finely chopped garlic and onion added first to the hot fat, followed in sequence by the other ingredients. When Mexican cooks refer to sautéing the ingredients, they do not use the verb *sofreír* (to sauté) but the distinctly Mexican term *acitronar*, which means to cook the onions until they become translucent—like candied citron.

MAKES ABOUT 4 CUPS

- ¼ cup extra-virgin olive oil
- 6 garlic cloves, finely chopped
- 1 large white onion (about 12 ounces), finely chopped (about 2 cups)
- 12 medium plum tomatoes (about 2 pounds), cored and finely chopped, or canned tomatoes with some juice
- ¼ cup capers in brine, drained, or salt-packed capers, rinsed
- 25 pimiento-stuffed olives, left whole or halved crosswise
- 2 bay leaves
- ½ teaspoon dried oregano
- ¼ teaspoon dried marjoram
- 3 pickled jalapeños, cut into thin strips
- ½ teaspoon salt
- ¼ cup water

▶ Heat the oil in a large (12-inch) heavy skillet or sauté pan. Add the garlic and sauté until golden. Add the onion and cook, stirring, until translucent, 3 to 4 minutes. Add the tomatoes and cook, stirring, for 5 minutes. Add all the remaining ingredients, lower the heat, cover the pan, and cook at a lively simmer for 10 minutes. Taste for seasoning. The sauce should have a pleasant tang and a delicate aroma.

Storing: Covered tightly and refrigerated, this sauce will keep well for 1 week.

Uses: Heat the sauce in a skillet until warm. Add fish steaks, shrimp, or shredded reconstituted salt cod. Cook very briefly, just 3 to 5 minutes.

Variations: The Mediterranean herbs and spices that flavor this sauce are compatible with other seasonings such as cumin and cilantro. A touch of beer (¼ to ½ cup) will turn this sauce into a tasty *sofrito* for My Father's Very Soupy Rice and Chicken (page 317).

Coconut Milk
Leche de Coco

Fresh coconut milk appears in countless Latin American dishes. In savory preparations, it replaces tomato sauce or mingles with it in a cooking sauce. Walk into any restaurant in Cartagena, Colombia, early in the morning, and you will see cooks grating dozens of coconuts and squeezing out the liquid into huge containers. Coconut milk is as important in the cuisine of coastal Colombia as the choicest homemade broth.

Although extracting milk from fresh coconuts is a way of life for the cooks of tropical America, for North Americans it is a time-consuming process requiring patience. But the results are well worth the effort: just compare the smell of the best canned coconut milk you can find with the fragrance of fresh, creamy coconut milk.

HOW TO CRACK OPEN A COCONUT

Coconut

After struggling for years with the mighty coconut—smashing my knuckles with a hammer, almost slicing off a finger with my father's machete—I finally stumbled upon an efficient method for dealing with this stubborn fruit. With a screwdriver, I pierce through the three "eyes" of the nut and shake out all the water. Then I place the coconut on top of a gas burner turned to medium-high and fearlessly scorch it, turning it from time to time with tongs, until it begins to crack in several places. I remove it from the flame and wrap it in a kitchen towel. After two or three blows with a hammer, the nut cracks open readily. Removing the meat from the outer hard shell is easy, since the heat has done the work for you. With the help of a table knife, the meaty flesh will practically fall out of the shell. If you do not have a gas stove, place the coconut in a preheated 400°F oven (once you have pierced the eyes and removed the water) and bake for 20 minutes, then follow the procedure outlined above.

If you have the time, grate the coconut pieces very fine with a box grater and you will be rewarded with the creamiest possible coconut milk. If you are in a hurry, cut the coconut meat into very small pieces and process in a food processor until very finely ground. A large coconut (about 1¾ pounds before the water is drained) will yield about 4 cups grated meat.

THE FIRST AND SECOND MILKS OF THE COCONUT

Many Latin recipes call for "the first milk" or "the second milk" of the coconut. The "first milk" is obtained by soaking the grated coconut in just a little warm water and then squeezing out the creamy liquid. This is the coconut milk that is boiled down to extract the coconut oil used to fry Cartagena's famous coconut rice (see page 300). The "second milk" is obtained by soaking the squeezed-out grated coconut a second time in a few cups of water to extract whatever juices remain, then squeezing out the liquid. This thinner milk is commonly added to stews or soups together with the creamy "first" milk to build up coconut flavor in a dish. Here is how you can make these two ingredients at home.

Creamy ("First") Coconut Milk

MAKES 1½ CUPS

4 cups grated coconut meat
1 cup warm (115°F) water

▶ Place the grated coconut in a large bowl and pour the warm water over it. Allow to sit for 2 to 3 minutes. Line another large bowl with a double layer of cheesecloth and pour in the liquid and the grated coconut. Pick up the edges of the cheesecloth, bring them together, and twist. Squeeze tightly in your hands to extract the maximum amount of liquid (Cartageneros use just their hands, no cheesecloth for this process). Reserve the coconut for the "second" milk, if desired. The milk will separate on standing; just stir to recombine before using.

Light ("Second") Coconut Milk

MAKES 4 CUPS

Grated coconut used for "first" coconut milk

4 cups warm (115°F) water

▶ Place the squeezed-out coconut in a bowl and pour the water over it. Allow to sit for 5 minutes. Pour the mixture into a fine-mesh strainer set over a bowl and press with the back of a spoon to release all of the liquid remaining in the coconut pulp. Discard the coconut.

Storing: Coconut milk will keep well refrigerated in a tightly covered glass or stainless steel container for 1 to 2 weeks. Stir well to recombine before using.

Uses: Coconut milk can be used in lieu of or combined with tomato sauce in a cooking sauce. After you have sautéed the seasoning vegetables (onions and garlic), add the milk and cook briefly, over low heat to avoid curdling. Coconut milk gives a silky finish to cream soups or stews if added just at the end of cooking.

Valle del Cauca Cooking Sauce

Ahogao Vallecaucano

Saffron lends an elegant touch to this flavorful tomato cooking sauce from the Valle del Cauca region in Colombia, but it is an everyday preparation used to season a wide array of traditional dishes. Its name, which resembles the Spanish word for "drowned"

(*ahogado*), might seem to indicate that its flavoring ingredients are drowned—in fat. But the word *ahogao* actually is derived from the Latin *focus*, meaning fireplace or hearth, and was used in medieval Spain to describe the act of sautéing the seasoning ingredients of a dish—in short, it is another word for *sofrito*.

MAKES ABOUT 1¼ CUPS

3 tablespoons achiote-infused corn oil (page 89)

3 garlic cloves, finely chopped

12 scallions, white and 3 inches of green parts, finely chopped

6 medium plum tomatoes (about 1 pound), peeled, seeded, and finely chopped, or canned tomatoes, drained and finely chopped

1 teaspoon saffron threads, softened in 1 tablespoon warm water

1 teaspoon salt, or to taste

¼ teaspoon ground cumin

▶ Heat the achiote oil in a medium (9-inch) skillet over medium heat until fragrant, about 1 minute. Add the garlic and sauté until golden, about 1 minute. Stir in the scallions and sauté for 3 minutes. Add the tomatoes and cook, stirring, for 5 minutes. Add the saffron with its liquid, salt, and cumin. Cook for 2 more minutes. Taste for salt and remove from the heat.

Storing: The sauce can be stored in a tightly covered glass or plastic container in the refrigerator for 3 to 4 days.

Uses: In Valle del Cauca, this is used for everything from cooking meats to flavoring empanada fillings. I like to spoon it over boiled potatoes or Colombian Tamales with Potato and Peanut Hash (page 470).

Bogotá Cheese Cooking Sauce

Hogo Bogotano

Santa Fé de Bogotá, the capital of Colombia, is a highland town. As in other parts of the Andes (the Ecuadorian sierra, for example), cooks add liberal amounts of fresh white cheese to their cooking sauces, or *hogos*—the local word for *sofritos*. This creamy sauce is poured over boiled potatoes to make *papas chorreadas* (page 204), the classic accompaniment to a roasted rolled flank steak (*sobrebarriga*). Traditional cooks prepare the sauce with the layer of thick cream that forms on the surface of unhomogenized milk, but a mixture of butter and heavy cream produces the same effect.

Working Ahead ▶ Remove the sauce from the heat when the tomatoes are cooked and let cool; store, covered, in the refrigerator for 3 to 4 days. When ready to use, heat through over medium heat and add the cream and cheese.

MAKES ABOUT 1½ CUPS

  1 tablespoon butter
  8 scallions, white and 3 inches of green parts, finely chopped
  6 medium plum tomatoes (about 1 pound), peeled, seeded, and finely chopped, or canned tomatoes, drained and finely chopped
  1 teaspoon salt, or to taste
  ¼ cup heavy cream
  4 ounces fresh cheese (*queso blanco*), crumbled or coarsely grated (about 1 cup)

▶ Heat the butter in a medium (9-inch) skillet over medium heat until it starts to bubble. Add the scallions and sauté, stirring occasionally, for 3 minutes, or until lightly wilted. Add the tomatoes and salt and cook, stirring, for about 7 minutes, until thickened. Stir in the cream and cheese and cook, stirring, for 2 to 3 minutes. This is supposed to be a chunky, coarse sauce, with the cheese not entirely melted.

Storing: The sauce base, without the cream and cheese, can be stored, tightly covered, in the refrigerator for 3 to 4 days.

Uses: Spoon over boiled potatoes or any other boiled starchy tubers, such as yuca. This is also a delicious table sauce for Colombian Tamales with Potato and Peanut Hash (page 470).

Ecuadorian Golden Cooking Sauce

Ahogado Serrano

In the cold, windswept highlands of southern Ecuador, cooking sauces (*ahogados*) are simple, flavorful, and rich in ground cumin, the most important spice in the region. When making soups, cooks always begin with this golden sauce. Pale soups, no matter how tasty, are shunned—the achiote-infused oil adds the crucial yellow color Ecuadorians admire.

Cook's Note: For meat or poultry stews, this sauce can be enriched with a ripe tomato, green pepper (locally called *pimiento verde*), and chopped parsley. A few sprigs of cilantro may also be added to the pot but should be taken out before serving. Ecuadorian cooks have a saying: *"Bueno es culantro pero no tanto* (Cilantro is good, but not too much of it)."

MAKES ABOUT ½ CUP

2 tablespoons achiote-infused corn oil (page 89)

3–4 garlic cloves, finely chopped

1 small white onion (about 5 ounces), finely chopped (about 1 cup)

½ teaspoon ground cumin

½ teaspoon salt, or to taste

¼ teaspoon freshly ground black pepper

▶ Heat the oil in a small saucepan or skillet over medium heat. Add the garlic and sauté until golden, about 45 seconds. Add the onion and sauté until translucent, 2 to 3 minutes. Stir in the cumin, salt and pepper, and cook for 1 more minute.

Storing: The *ahogado* will keep well in the refrigerator for a week.

Uses: Use for building stews or vegetable soups.

Peruvian *Ají Mirasol* Cooking Sauce

Aderezo de Ají Mirasol

The mounds of brightly colored *ajíes amarillos* stacked high in every Peruvian market always capture my attention. I am simply in love with this marvelous fleshy, orangy-yellow pepper and would like nothing more than to buy it by the kilo to bring back home. If I were given a choice, I would prefer to cook with the fresh *ají amarillo*. Nothing beats its bright color, aroma, and flavor. Unfortunately, the pepper is seldom available fresh in this country, though you can find it frozen whole in select Latin American markets, or jarred, already ground into a paste. But it is always easier to find the whole dried *ají mirasol*, which is also terrific.

I learned to appreciate the goodness of *ají amarillo* in all its forms through Ana María Rojas-Lombardi, a fabulous cook and the sister of my dear friend Felipe Rojas-Lombardi, the late chef of the Ballroom restaurant in Manhattan. Ana María leads a busy life in her native Lima, yet she manages to cook two complete meals a day for her husband and two finicky, demanding sons. They are grown men now but even when they were kids, they preferred to take an hour bus ride from school to have lunch at home, where they expected nothing but the best from their mother's kitchen. The best still comes to the table brightly seasoned with a cooking sauce made primarily with the fresh *ají amarillo* or its dried incarnation, *ají mirasol*.

Keeping a batch of an *ají mirasol* cooking sauce in the refrigerator is like having a Peruvian kitchen ally always at the ready. This is a basic recipe that can be enriched to taste with a number of spices, such as cumin and oregano. Stir a few tablespoons into a white bean soup along with some cumin and cilantro, and in minutes you will have a Peruvian *menestra* simmering on your stove. Combine some of the paste with a bit of vinegar in a bowl and use as a marinade for chicken, pork, or fish. The pepper will permeate the meats, giving them a coppery gilding and heady aroma.

MAKES ABOUT 1 CUP

3 dried *mirasol* peppers (about ½ ounce), stemmed and seeded

3 tablespoons vegetable oil or lard

4 garlic cloves, mashed to a paste with a mortar and pestle or finely chopped and mashed

1 medium red onion (about 8 ounces), coarsely chopped (about 1½ cups)

½ teaspoon salt, or to taste

▶ Making the *Ají Mirasol* Paste: Place the peppers in a small bowl and soak in 2 cups hot water until plump, about 30 minutes. Alternatively, combine with 2 cups water in a small saucepan and boil for 15 minutes, or until soft.

Drain the chiles, reserving ¼ cup of the liquid. Add to a blender or a small food processor, with the reserved liquid, and puree. (The puree can be kept refrigerated for about 1 week; makes about ¼ cup.)

Preparing the Cooking Sauce ▶ Heat the oil in a small skillet until it ripples. Add the garlic and sauté until golden. Add the onion, pureed peppers, and salt and cook, stirring, for 10 minutes, until the vegetables begin exuding oil. Let cool.

Storing: Refrigerated in a tightly closed glass jar, this will keep well for up to 3 weeks.

Uses: Use to season Peruvian Shrimp *Chupe* (page 532), Creamy Peruvian Chicken Stew (page 671), and rice dishes.

Ground Andean Peppers

Ají Molido

Many Peruvian and Bolivian recipes call for a fine powder of *mirasol* pepper (dried *ají amarillo*) called *ají molido*. The pepper is ground by machine, so the powder is usually very fine. Several Peruvian companies in the United States import *ají molido*, but I prefer to grind my own so I can be assured of its freshness.

MAKES 1 CUP

24 dried *mirasol* peppers (about 6 ounces), stemmed and seeded

▶ If the peppers are still pliable and a bit fresh, spread on a cookie sheet and dry in a 200°F oven for 1 to 2 hours, or until brittle. Let cool completely.

Chop the peppers with a knife, or crush to small bits between two pieces of wax paper using a rolling pin or a mallet, or with mortar and pestle. The smaller the bits, the easier they will be to grind. Grind to a powder in a spice mill. I like a coarse texture. Grind twice or longer if you want to obtain a very fine powder.

Storing: Keep in a tightly covered container in a cool, dark place.

Uses: Stir into soups or stews or sprinkle on finished dishes for instant heat and color.

Variation: For ground *panca* peppers, *ají panca molido*: Substitute 5 ounces dried *ají panca* peppers (about 24 peppers).

Junín's *Ají Panca* Cooking Sauce

Aderezo Colorado de Junín

Junín, a town in Peru's central highlands, is famous for its lively pre-Lenten carnival (Mardi Gras) and its pork dishes. The secret of Junín's flavorful food is this simple but brilliant cooking sauce made with the spicy dried hot red pepper *ají panca*.

MAKES ABOUT 1 CUP

6 dried *panca* peppers (about 1½ ounces), stemmed and seeded

8 garlic cloves

1 medium red onion (about 8 ounces), coarsely chopped (about 1½ cups)

3 cilantro sprigs, coarsely chopped

2 tablespoons fresh mint leaves

1 teaspoon red wine vinegar

1 teaspoon achiote-infused vegetable oil (page 89)

▶ Soak the peppers in 2 cups hot water for 30 minutes, or until plump. Alternatively, combine with 2 cups water in a medium saucepan and boil for 15 minutes, or until softened. Drain well.

Place the peppers and all the other ingredients except the oil in a blender or food processor and process to a coarse puree.

Heat the oil in a small saucepan or skillet over medium heat until it ripples. Stir in the puree and sauté, stirring occasionally, for about 8 minutes, until it thickens.

Storing: The *aderezo* will keep well refrigerated in a tightly covered glass or stainless steel container for a couple of weeks.

Uses: In Junín, large chunks of pork or pork cracklings are stewed in this rich bright red *aderezo* and served with steamed white rice as a main course. You can also use it as a seasoning base for beef or chicken stews.

Three-Step Mexican Chile Cooking Sauce

Salsa Mexicana en Tres Pasos

This cooking sauce is a Mexican classic, a type of *sofrito* made with dried peppers that involves a three-step cooking process: First you roast the chiles, then you puree them in a blender, and last you fry them. This is what I call the easy three-step Mexican kitchen dance that turns any dried chile into a dazzling and versatile cooking sauce.

MAKES ABOUT ¾ CUP

4 dried ancho chiles (about 1¾ ounces), stemmed and seeded

8 ripe medium plum tomatoes (about 1½ pounds)

1 small white onion (about 6 ounces), not peeled

3 garlic cloves, not peeled

2 tablespoons finely chopped cilantro

½ teaspoon ground cumin

¼ teaspoon dried oregano

1¼ teaspoons salt, or to taste

2 tablespoons sunflower, peanut, or corn oil

▶ Heat an ungreased *comal*, griddle, or heavy skillet over medium heat. Add the peppers and roast for about 1 minute, pressing them against the hot surface of the pan with tongs. Turn over and roast for 1 more minute. Place the chiles in a large bowl with 4 cups hot water and let soak for about 20 minutes, or until softened. Alternatively, combine with 4 cups water in a medium saucepan and boil for 12 to 15 minutes, or until soft and plump. Drain the chiles, reserving ⅓ cup of the liquid.

In the meantime, roast the tomatoes, onion, and garlic in the same pan, or under a preheated broiler about 4 inches from the heat source, turning occasionally with tongs, until they look lightly charred all over, about 10 minutes. Remove from the heat.

Peel the onion and garlic, and remove any patches of tomato skin that seem too burned. Place the chiles and reserved soaking liquid, the roasted vegetables, and the cilantro, cumin, oregano, and salt in a blender or food processor and blend to a smooth paste. Strain into a bowl, pushing the paste through a sieve with the back of a spoon.

Heat the oil in a 9-inch heavy skillet over medium heat. When it is very hot, add the chile paste (stand back, it will splatter). Cook, stirring, for 15 minutes, or until the sauce thickens. Add water a tablespoon or two at a time if the sauce becomes too dry.

Storing: Stored tightly sealed in a glass or plastic container in the refrigerator, this will keep well for about 2 weeks.

Uses: Use as a cooking sauce for all types of boiled meats, to season taco fillings and to sauce enchiladas. I love this as a marinade for chicken. Rub the sauce all over chicken pieces and refrigerate for 20 to 30 minutes, then bake in a preheated 350°F oven for about 1 hour. Easy and delicious!

THE HISPANIC CARIBBEAN: *THE RECADO*

In Puerto Rico and the Dominican Republic, cooks make an uncooked seasoning paste called a *recado* that gives their food a distinct herbal pungency. The main ingredients are most commonly cilantro, broad-leaf *culantro*, and the tiny lantern-shaped sweet pepper *ají dulce*. It is an essential preparation that Puerto Ricans and Dominicans always have in their refrigerators or freezers to add to the sauté base of their *sofritos*.

To complicate things, for many island cooks, the term *recado* may refer specifically to the three most important ingredients of the *sofrito* or just to aromatic cilantro or *culantro*, which is also called *recao* in the islands and the Mediterranean cilantro, *recadito* or *recaíto*.

Dominican Traveling *Sazón*

Sazón o Recado Dominicano

Blackouts are a way of life in the Dominican Republic. If one occurs while you are at the airport waiting for a flight, chances are that you will stay there for a long time or have to go back to your hotel to spend the night. That happened to me years ago in Santo Domingo. Minutes before I was to board a New York–bound flight, the lights blinked off and the blackout descended. Hundreds of passengers crowded the waiting area, scrambling to find places to sit on the floor. After a while, the sounds of passengers cursing and stomping around gave way to the distinctive trill and tap-tap beat of merengue, as people tapped the floor, their chair arms, any nearby hard surface.

Luckily, I happened to be sitting next to two lively Dominican women, Inés Estevez and Altagracia Genoveva Quesada, who talked to me all night about Dominican cooking. Inés, a handsome woman of about sixty dressed in her best clothes and surrounded by full shopping bags, told me that she had lived her whole life in Santiago de

Los Caballeros, a colonial city in the mountains of Cibao, and was traveling to New York to visit her son and family. Then she flourished a plastic bag and pulled out a large jar filled with a thick greenish liquid. "This is homemade *sazón*. I am taking it to my daughter-in-law."

Since all the ingredients for *sazón* (another word for *recado*) can be found in any Hispanic market in New York, I wondered why she bothered to carry a heavy jar filled with sauce on the plane. She stared at me in disbelief, then opened the lid and handed it to me. "Smell," she ordered.

I sniffed, and a sharp, intense scent billowed out of the jar. Now I understood. Like the trill and the beat of merengue pulsing beneath this frustrating vigil, Inés's *sazón* bore the distinctive essence of her region: the concentrated flavors of home-grown Caribbean sweet peppers and broad-leaf *culantro*, the powerful scent of wild Dominican oregano, the distinctive stamp of her *buen punto*, her very own seasoning touch. This is her recipe.

MAKES ABOUT 1¾ CUPS

- 13 garlic cloves
- 1 medium yellow onion (about 8 ounces), quartered
- 1 medium bell pepper (about 6 ounces), or 2 cubanelle peppers, cored, seeded, deveined, and quartered
- 12 Caribbean sweet peppers (*ajíes dulces*), seeded
- 6 fresh broad-leaf *culantro* leaves
- ¼ teaspoon crumbled dried Dominican or Mexican oregano
- 2 teaspoons salt
- 1 teaspoon freshly ground black pepper
- 1 tablespoon distilled white vinegar
- ¼ cup extra-virgin olive oil (omit if keeping for less than 2 days)

▶ Place all the ingredients in a blender or a food processor and blend to a coarse paste.

Storing: Refrigerated in a tightly sealed glass or stainless steel container, this will keep well for 2 to 3 weeks.

Uses: Use as a flavor base for Dominican and Puerto Rican dishes. I like to turn the *sazón* into a vinaigrette for avocado salad or a dipping sauce for all kinds of fritters. It is also terrific as a marinade for red snapper or chicken.

Dominican *Sofrito*

Sofrito Dominicano

Dominican food is among the tastiest in the Caribbean. The secret of such good flavor begins with the uncooked pureed seasoning called *sazón* or *recado* and ends with the cooking sauce, *sofrito*.

MAKES ABOUT 2 CUPS

- ¼ cup achiote-infused lard or corn oil (page 89)
- ¼ pound bacon or Smithfield ham, cut into ¼-inch dice
- 1 cup Dominican Traveling *Sazón* (page 56)
- 1 cup Light Tomato Sauce (page 48) or store-bought tomato sauce
- 2 teaspoons salt, or to taste

▶ Heat the lard in a medium (9-inch) skillet or sauté pan over medium heat until it begins to ripple. Add the bacon and cook until golden brown, about 8 minutes. Stir in the *sazón* and tomato sauce and cook, stirring occasionally, for 10 minutes, or until the oil separates from the sauce.

Storing: Refrigerated in a tightly covered glass jar or stainless steel container, this keeps well for 2 to 3 days.

Uses: This *sofrito* adds a marvelous flavor to red and pink bean stews and rice and vegetable dishes.

Charito's Puerto Rican Seasoning Mix

Recado Puertorriqueño de Charito

Thirty-four years ago, I was literally brought back to life through my first taste of Puerto Rican cooking. This happened in an unlikely place—the town of Valladolid, in the heart of Castile, Spain, where my husband was studying medicine. The night we arrived there, the town was bustling with visitors, since it was the feast day of Saint Gregory, the town's patron. After hours of fruitless searching for a decent hotel, we landed in a shabby, dirty *pensión* near the train station. One taste of their food nearly killed me: I spent two days racked with a high fever, pitifully calling for my mother.

Not knowing what to do, my husband phoned a fellow medical student, Edgar Silvestri, and his wife, Charito, who were born in Cabo Rojo, at the eastern end of Puerto Rico. Before I knew it, Edgar and Charito were pulling me out of bed and taking me to their home, where I remained for nearly three weeks, nurtured by Charito's cooking. Slowly I regained my strength, graduating from her tasty but subtly seasoned soups to more succulent Puerto Rican fare.

Like my Dominican friend Inés, Charito believed in the magic of the traveling *recado*. Everyone who came from Puerto Rico to visit her knew they had a single important duty to fulfill: to bring her large jars of frozen *recado*. Without *recado*, there is no Puerto Rican *sofrito*, and therefore no Puerto Rican cooking. Here is her recipe, straight from beautiful Cabo Rojo—the *recado* that traveled to Spain.

MAKES ABOUT 2¼ CUPS

1 medium cubanelle pepper (about 5 ounces) or 1 small green bell pepper (about 5 ounces), cored and seeded

12 Caribbean sweet peppers (*ajíes dulces*) or 2 more cubanelle peppers, seeded

1 medium plum tomato (about 3 ounces), cored, seeded, and coarsely chopped

1 medium yellow onion (about 8 ounces), quartered

12 cilantro sprigs

4 fresh broad-leaf *culantro* leaves

2 teaspoons dried oregano

1 tablespoon cider vinegar or distilled white vinegar

1 teaspoon salt, or to taste

¼ teaspoon freshly ground black pepper

▶ Place the ingredients in a food processor or blender and process to a thick paste. Use within 1 day. If storing for longer than 1 day or if freezing the mix, omit the tomatoes when you make it, then process them into the (thawed) mixture.

Storing: Stored in a freezer bag or tightly sealed plastic container in the freezer, this will keep well for about 1 month.

Uses: This is the building block of the Puerto Rican *sofrito*. It also makes a delicious dipping sauce for Caribbean-style fritters and a flavorful marinade for chicken and fish. Or spoon it over My Fresh Corn Tamales Cuban Style (page 455) or Puerto Rican *Pasteles* (page 474).

Puerto Rican *Sofrito*

Sofrito Puertorriqueño

The herbal taste of the tiny Caribbean cooking pepper *ají dulce* combined with the musky perfume of cilantro and broad-leaf *culantro* adds complexity to the simple cooking base of sautéed garlic, onions, and milder cubanelle peppers.

MAKES ABOUT 1 CUP

- 2 tablespoons achiote-infused lard, corn oil, or olive oil (page 89)
- 3 ounces salted fatback or pancetta, cut into ¼-inch dice
- 4 ounces ham, preferably cooking ham (*jamón de cocinar*) or Smithfield ham, cut into ¼-inch dice
- 4 large garlic cloves, finely chopped
- 1 cup Charito's Puerto Rican Seasoning Mix (page 58)
- 2 teaspoons salt, or to taste
- ½ teaspoon freshly ground black pepper, or to taste

▶ Heat the lard in a 9-inch skillet over medium heat until it begins to ripple. Add the fatback and sauté until golden brown, about 2 minutes. Add the ham and cook until golden, about 2 minutes. Add the garlic and cook, stirring, until golden, then stir in the seasoning mix. Cook, stirring occasionally, for 10 minutes, or until it thickens. Add the salt and pepper.

Storing: Refrigerated in a tightly covered glass jar or stainless steel container, this keeps well for 2 to 3 days.

Uses: This *sofrito* adds marvelous flavor to red and pink bean stews and rice and vegetable mixes. I also like to add a couple of spoonfuls of it to Puerto Rican *Pasteles* (page 474) or use it as a marinade for fish.

FLAVOR FROM PEPPERS

Latin American *sofritos* and *adobos* would be impossible without peppers, which grow from Mexico to Patagonia and offer unimaginable variations of shape, color, flavor, and degree of heat or pungency. Old World cooks arriving in the New World found that peppers marry miraculously with all kinds of other ingredients, from humble onions to aromatic cinnamon, giving heat or sweetness, brightness or depth to some of our iconic dishes. We love our many peppers, from the sweetest to the hottest. We dry them, smoke them, roast them, grind them into pastes and powders, chop them to stir into marinades and sauces.

Our part of the world is the cradle of all peppers belonging to the genus Capsicum. Five major Capsicum species were domesticated by prehistoric American peoples. This mere handful—*C. annuum, C. baccatum, C. chinense, C. frutescens,* and *C. pubescens*—gave rise to hundreds of cultivars used today for a broad range of culinary effects. Tiny, devastatingly hot wild peppers (chiefly *C. frutescens*) also survive in many places and are gathered for cooking purposes.

The substance responsible for the sting of hot peppers is an alkaloid called capsaicin that is chiefly concentrated in the inner ribs or veins. The seeds can pick up some of the capsaicin fire, too. Of course, there are many varieties without a trace of heat.

A great confusion of names surrounds the vast tangle of New World peppers. The Spanish carried them back to the mother country as "pimientos," after *"pimienta,"* the Spanish word for the black peppercorns Columbus thought he would find in the "Indies." In Brazil, peppers are still generically called *"pimenta."* The name by which the Taínos and

Arawaks introduced the invaders to the strange plant was "*ají*," still the common term everywhere but Central America and Mexico. Quechua-speaking Andean farmers called their local kinds "*uchu*," though "*ají*" has come to be more common among Spanish speakers. But the word most familiar to U.S. cooks is "chile," from the Nahuatl (Aztec) "*chili*."

Broadly speaking, most of the Mexican and Central American peppers belong to the *annuum* group, which probably embraces more different varieties than any other species and has made more intricately nuanced contributions to cooking. The Amazonian-Caribbean-Orinoco regions boast several *chinense* offshoots like the familiar habanero and Scotch bonnet, along with another *chinense* subspecies called "*ají dulce*" that contains all the floral notes of these incendiary peppers but none of their heat. The Andean nations are home to the uniquely fruity, deep-flavored golden *baccatum* pepper known as "*ají amarillo*," as well as the ferocious scarlet "*rocoto*," a representative of the *C. pubescens* species.

Any kind of pepper could theoretically be eaten either fresh or dried, but most are best suited to one or the other state. Some (both fresh and dried) respond brilliantly to techniques like griddle roasting or fire roasting, some are best sautéed with no preliminaries. Dried peppers usually go through a soaking stage to reconstitute the flesh and bring out the flavor. As you explore the recipes in this book, you will begin to develop a feeling for working with peppers and understanding their special affinities.

I hope that you will also be inspired to grow your own *ajíes* and chiles. Most are very adaptable, forgiving plants, and every year more varieties are available as seedlings to be transplanted to home gardens.

Peppers: A Short Glossary

FRESH PEPPERS

Ají Amarillo or *Ají Escabeche*: A beautiful golden or apricot-colored Andean pepper with meaty texture, complex sweetness, and mild to moderate heat. Available frozen in many Latin American stores and fresh from a few specialty growers. For the dried form, see **ají mirasol** (page 64). *C. baccatum.*

Ají amarillo

Ají Caballero or **Puerto Rican Jellybean**: A small hot pepper chiefly grown in Puerto Rico, where it is usually pickled in vinegar with a few other seasonings to make a condiment called "*pique*." *C. baccatum.*

Ají Colorado or **Ecuadorian Ají**: A popular, versatile cultivar that carries moderate heat; this slim little red pepper is the star of the ubiquitous Ecuadorian table sauces also called "*ajíes*." *C. baccatum.*

Ají Cristal: Dubbed the "glass pepper" for its almost translucent lemony green skin when unripe, this pepper plays the role of the jalapeño or serrano pepper in Chilean cooking and is used in favorite table salsas like the *pebre* (a type of chimichurri) and the curiously christened *Ají cristal* *chancho en piedra* (literally "pig on a stone"), a mixture of tomatoes, onions, cilantro, and fresh hot peppers crushed in a stone mortar. *C. baccatum.*

Ají Dulce: A workhorse of the Hispanic Caribbean kitchen from Cuba and Central America to Colombia and Venezuela. These small lantern-shaped peppers (some bonnet-shaped) have a fresh, flowery quality indispensable in several national cuisines. It is actually a close cousin of habaneros and similar firebomb peppers, easy to mistake for them at a quick

Ají cachucha

glance, but with its own delicate charm. Peppers of this overall type are also called *ají cachucha* (Cuba) and *ajicito dulce* (Puerto Rico). *C. chinense.*

Ají Rocoto (Peru), *Locoto* (Bolivia): The square, blocky shape and glistening deep red skin of this Andean favorite conceal a savage punch of capsaicin. It's best to remove the inner veins and black seeds before proceeding with any recipe. Available frozen in many Latin American stores, fresh from a few specialty growers. For its Central American relative the **chile manzano**, see page 62. *C. pubescens.*

Ají rocoto or locoto

Bell Pepper or Sweet Pepper: Also locally known when ripe as "*pimiento morrón*" or "*chile morrón*," "*ají*" or "*pimiento verde*" (in the green state). Its thick skin and fleshy walls help it stand up to many cooking purposes.

Latin American cooks have a soft spot for it when it is fully ripened to a harmonious, meaty succulence and a vivid red color. Large red cultivars found their way to Spain, where they eventually became staples for fire roasting and preserving or the making of *pimentón* (ground paprika); both techniques concentrate the natural sweetness and richness of ripe red peppers. Jarred or canned red pimientos then came back to the Hispanic Caribbean and parts of South America. In Cuban *ropa vieja* or an Argentinean chicken stuffing, they are the edible trace of a Spanish-dominated culture that valued sweetness and color over heat. More recently, preserved fire-roasted *piquillo* peppers imported from Navarra in northern Spain have acquired a following among U.S. food-lovers. Sold in gourmet shops everywhere, these smaller, triangular peppers are ideal for stuffing. *C. annuum.*

Pimiento de piquillo

Cayenne Pepper: The name originally referred to Cayenne, the capital of French Guiana, but came to be applied to a small, slender red (sometimes yellow) pepper that packs blinding heat. Various peppers of similar appearance are also called "cayenne pepper," and today "cayenne" is a generic label for dried ground red pepper that may contain a mixture of cultivars. *C. annuum.*

Chiltepín, Chiltecpín, Chiltepe, or *Chile Piquín:* This searingly hot little pepper, often no bigger than a large pea, grows wild in Central America and the northern Mexican desert, and figures in both cooking sauces and table condiments. It is also widely used in dried form. *C. annuum.*

Chiltepín

Chile Habanero: In the United States, the most popular *C. chinense* cultivar, known for sparkling heat along with aromatic complexity. It can be red, orange, yellow, or grass-green (when mature but not fully ripe). The Scotch bonnet; *ají chombo* (Panama); Congo pepper (Trinidad); and *dátil* pepper, grown in St. Augustine, Florida, are near cousins. *C. chinense.*

Chile habanero

Scotch bonnet pepper

Chile Jalapeño: Named for the city of Xalapa in Veracruz state, Mexico, this was the first Mexican hot fresh pepper to gain popularity with mainstream U.S. cooks, and is still the only one many people reach for. Whether used green or red, it is a safe choice for any sauce where you want moderate, lightly flavorful heat without any other overpowering flavor. An excellent pepper for pickling, it is widely sold bottled *en escabeche*. For the dried form, see **chile chipotle** (page 65). *C. annuum.*

Chile jalapeño

Chile Manzano (Mexico), *Siete Caldos* (Guatemala): A red or golden Central American relative of the Andean **ají rocoto** (page 61). It thrives in cooler regions of Guatemala like the western highlands and Alta Verapaz. *C. pubescens.*

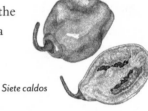

Siete caldos

Chile Poblano: Thinner-skinned and more flavorful than the bell pepper, this is equally good for stuffing and also is the favorite pepper of Mexican cooks for *rajas* (sautéed pepper strips). Poblanos are notably unpredictable in hotness, and also occur in a range of colors from glossy deep green to dark brown. For the dried forms, see **chile ancho** (page 64) and **chile mulato** (page 65). *C. annuum.*

Chile poblano

Chile Serrano: Smaller and stubbier than jalapeños, with slightly more penetrating, clean flavor. Mexican cooks tend to prefer this versatile pepper over the jalapeño for most fresh salsas. The name means "mountain chile." *C. annuum.*

Chile serrano

Cubanelle Pepper or Italian Frying Pepper: For most cooking purposes, Hispanic Caribbean cooks greatly prefer this slender, apple-green type to green bell peppers. (My family resorted to the latter only when cubanelles were unavailable.) It has a musky, herbaceous taste reminiscent of *ajíes dulces*, and blends beautifully into the *sofritos* of Puerto Rico, Cuba, and the Dominican Republic. Its low water content makes it ideal for frying purposes. *C. annuum.*

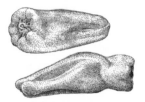

Cubanelle pepper

New Mexican Pepper: Developed at a New Mexico horticultural research center by the Chihuahua-born agronomist Fabian García, this long, graceful chile has become a boon to the state's economy. Many cultivars are now grown everywhere in the state. It's probably best known in its dried form, but has a lovely sweetness, along with mild to strong heat, when eaten fresh (either green or red). The "Anaheim" chile pepper from California is a close relative. Many people in New Mexico are loyal to a cousin called the "*chimayo*" pepper that originated near the town of Chimayo, a little northwest of Santa Fe, and is recognized as a separate "land race" (locally adapted strain) of the type that became García's "New Mexican" chile. *C. annuum.*

Pimenta Cumari: A round Brazilian cultivar in colors ranging from gold to salmon, it has the same flavor and heat profile as the fiery *ají charapita*, a lantern-shaped pepper from the Peruvian Amazon region. Available pickled in Latin markets. *C. chinense.*

Pimenta de Cheiro: Small peppers with the "bonnet" or "lantern" shape of the related habaneros, these Brazilian favorites have an aroma that reminds me of apricots or newly mown grass. Perhaps this accounts for the name (literally, "odorous" pepper).

They are usually pickled in vinegar and added to table sauces. *C. chinense.*

Pimenta Malagueta: This small, aggressively biting cultivar is the most popular of all hot peppers in Brazil. In the United States it is found only bottled in vinegar, to be added to table sauces. Lovers of African food should know that it crossed the Atlantic to become the explosive piri-piri of one-time Portuguese colonies like Mozambique and Angola. *C. frutescens.*

Pimiento del Padrón: In the last ten or fifteen years these small, thin-skinned green peppers from Galicia near the Portuguese border of northwestern Spain have taken U.S. kitchens by storm. They're now being grown in California,

Pimiento del padrón

and are sometimes available at farmers' markets in other states. *Padrón* peppers are notorious for unpredictable variations in heat level. *C. annuum.*

Tabasco Pepper: Named for the state of Tabasco in southeastern Mexico, this fierce, skinny little pepper is now best known as the chief ingredient in Tabasco sauce, the fiery condiment made by the McIlhenny Company of Louisiana. *C. frutescens.*

DRIED PEPPERS

Mild, sweet pepper varieties are seldom subjected to any drying process, except to make sweet *pimentón*, the Spanish version of paprika. Hot peppers are another story. When dried, they change dramatically, turning different shades of russet-red, deep or light brown, copper, or old gold. At the same time, their flavor deepens. Any heat that was present in the fresh state is usually intensified. So are any original sweetness and fruitiness. If smoke is part of the process, it contributes still more complexities.

Pre-Hispanic cooks achieved great skill in understanding the varying flavor and color effects produced by drying and reconstituting different kinds of hot peppers. For Mexican and other Central American cooks especially, choosing the right variety or combination of varieties to use in a *mole* or *pepián* is an art.

Before reconstituting dried peppers, Mexican cooks and their neighbors in Guatemala, Honduras, Nicaragua, and Salvador commonly bring out the flavor even more by roasting them on a hot *comal*. (This is seldom done in other parts of Latin America.) You can think of roasting as the beginning of a three-step dance that is second nature in Mexico and parts of Central America. For a description of the process, see page 744.

Ají Cacho de Cabra: The most important dried pepper used in Chile. Thin-skinned and bright red when fresh, it dries to a maroon color. The name, literally meaning "goat's horn pepper," refers to its curved shape. It is often smoked, or simply dried. Combined with other spices, it is the backbone of the delicious paprika-like condiment *merkén* (page 74). It is not imported into the United States, but Mexican guajillos or *puyas* are a good substitute. *C. annuum.*

Ají cacho de cabra

Ají Mirasol: This is the dried form of **ají amarillo** (page 60). The color of old copper, it has a lovely sweetness and fruitiness with winey, slightly smoky notes. You can buy it pre-ground to a powder. I

Ají mirasol

usually prefer to do this myself at home in a spice mill, or to reconstitute it through soaking or brief boiling before blending it to a golden ochre paste. *C. baccatum.*

Ají Panca: In Peru and Bolivia this is a meaty, thick-fleshed, all-purpose hot pepper. In drying, it darkens from red to a deep wine color, and gives a lovely deep cherry or plum color and rich, fruity flavor to sauces made with it. *Pancas* should be boiled or soaked to reconstitute, then ground in a blender and strained into a smooth paste. *C. baccatum.*

Chile Ancho: The dried version of the **chile poblano** (page 62), reddish black before soaking and somewhat wrinkly. It is one of the most versatile dried chiles of Mexico and Central America. On soaking it turns a rich mahogany red, contributing an attractive color to the many sauces in which it figures along with meaty body and grassy notes of green bell pepper. *C. annuum.*

Chile ancho

Chile Cascabel: A moderately hot Mexican pepper that when dried both looks and sounds like a child's rattle (the meaning of the name). Dried *cascabeles* are a very dark reddish-brown and give rich tannic notes to table and cooking sauces. *C. annuum.*

Chile Chilhuacle: A highly prized pepper chiefly grown in the Mexican state of Oaxaca. The shape recalls a small, tapered bell pepper, but the fruit has the peculiarity of ripening to a number of different shades from nearly black to yellow or red, each plant contrasting with its neighbors. On drying, it develops very complex, plumlike flavors with moderate heat. Dried *chilhuacles* are crucial players in several classic Oaxacan dishes, including the famous *mole negro* (page 778). *C. annuum.*

Chile Chipotle, Chile Meco, Chile Ahumado, Chile Seco: The smoke-dried form of ripe red jalapeños, the most internationally popular of all Mexican dried chiles. A chubby purplish type is known as *chile morita*. Smoking transforms the comparatively simple flavors of the fresh pepper into something deep, complex, and adventurous. Canned chipotles in a spicy, bright-colored tomato *adobo* are widely available in Latin American groceries and U.S. gourmet shops. But the dried chile itself makes a gorgeous, glistening brick red paste. *C. annuum.*

Chile meco

Chile morita

Chile Cobán, Chile Cobanero, Ululte, Tolita: A tiny and very hot pepper from the Alta Verapaz region of Guatemala, often smoke-dried, used in the turkey soup-stew called *sac-ic* (page 674). It has similarities to chipotle in flavor and makes an incendiary, smoky salsa of an orange

Chile cobán

brown color. In Guatemalan markets you will likely find dried *cobán* resembling tiny wrinkled berries and a larger oval pepper about an inch long, of less intense smokiness and a redder color. *C. annuum.*

Chile Costeño: A moderately hot pepper with a narrow, tapered shape and bright orange-red color. *C. annuum.*

Chile de Árbol: One of the best-known Mexican dried hot peppers, with sharp, clean flavors and bright red color that work well in many sauces and soups. *C. annuum.*

Chile de árbol

Chile Guajillo, Guaque (Guatemala): A long, thin, maroon-colored pepper with thin but sturdy smooth skin that contributes sharp, bright, and tangy flavors to sauces without being overwhelming. The closely related *chile puya* is a good substitute. *C. annuum.*

Chile guajillo

Chile Mulato: A dried form of poblano, similar to anchos but darker-skinned and milder in flavor. *C. annuum.*

Chile Pasilla: The dark, wrinkled skin gives this its Spanish name ("little raisin"). It is the dried form of a pepper called *chilaca* in the fresh state. With green bell pepper notes toned down by a tannic edge, it is lovely cut crosswise into thin slivers and tossed into a quick stir-fry dish. *C. annuum.*

Chile pasilla

Chile Pasilla de Oaxaca: With a wider shape than the regular pasilla, this smoke-dried chile has densely wrinkled reddish skin and a strong, smoky heat. A great favorite for stuffing and frying in Oaxaca, it also figures in some Oaxacan *moles*. *C. annuum.*

Chile Seco de Yucatán: Though "*chile seco*" can refer to any dried pepper, the kind used in the Yucatán is a small yellow-orange chile that is not just toasted but actually burnt before being ground and added to the famous Yucatecan black *recados* (page 676). *C. annuum.*

Chiltepín, Chiltecpín, Chiltepe, Chile Piquín: These tiny wild chiles are not only used fresh but also added to various sauce mixtures in dried form. *C. annuum.*

New Mexican Pepper: Probably the best loved of all dried hot peppers in the southwest United States, and widely available either whole, flaked, or finely ground. It is an excellent substitute for either *cacho de cabra* or guajillo chiles. *C. annuum.*

Cooking with Peppers

DRIED PEPPERS

Selecting and Storing: Inspect either loose or packaged dried peppers as carefully as you can, avoiding anything that looks dusty, crumbled, or moth-eaten. Peppers should be firm, slightly supple and flexible (not desiccated and brittle), with dis-

tinct colors. They will keep for months stored in tightly sealed plastic bags in a dry spot. But check at intervals for signs of insect infestation, since occasionally a batch will prove to harbor small bugs. For more information on preparing dried hot peppers, see page 744 in the Hot Pepper Pots chapter.

FRESH OR FROZEN PEPPERS

Selecting and Storing: No matter what kind of pepper you are buying, look for plump, firm-stemmed, glossy-skinned fruit without discolored or soft spots. Jalapeños should have no cracks (although some Mexicans prefer specimens with some "corki-ness," or small brownish striations). With batches of the tiny *ajíes dulces*, carefully inspect them one by one to avoid any with brown or moldy spots.

For best flavor, keep fresh peppers at room temperature no more than two or three days before using. I prefer to store them in good old paper bags. If you need to keep them longer, refrigerate, but don't place them in tightly closed plastic bags where they will sweat and spoil. It is best to use paper bags or the perforated plastic bags sometimes used for vegetables; you will need to change the former often to keep the peppers dry.

When buying the frozen Andean *ajíes rocotos* or *ajíes amarillos*, choose packages without any buildup of ice crystals indicating prior thawing and refreezing. Defrost at room temperature, rinse under cold running water as soon as possible before using, and pat dry.

PREPARING PEPPERS FOR COOKING

Coring, Seeding, and Deveining: Many of my recipes call for seeding fresh peppers before cooking. If they are hot, wearing protective gloves is a good precaution. First rinse the peppers under cold running water. If they are to be left whole for stuffing, either cut all the way around the stem to detach it (best for large, deep-shouldered peppers) or slice about ¼ inch off the top (preferable for long, skinny, or odd-shaped peppers) before trimming away the core and seeds. If you want to leave the stem (it looks pretty in a stuffed poblano), make a lengthwise slit alongside the pepper and scrape out the seeds with a spoon or small knife. Otherwise, halve the peppers lengthwise and scrape out the seeds. For hot peppers, carefully cut away as much as you can of the inner membranes and veins, which are the chief source of heat.

Pre-Cooking: The layering of flavors that Latin American cooks seek to accomplish through *sofritos* and other related cooking sauces often depends on pre-cooking peppers before marrying them with other ingredients in the pot. In some regions they are briefly boiled. Or, as directed in some of my recipes, they may be baked, or plunged into hot fat until blistered and fragrant. But the most common techniques for whole peppers are roasting or broiling. These intense dry-heat methods help caramelize sugars and concentrate flavors, lending a certain mellowness and maturity to the natural flavor of the peppers. The sweetness will be more noticeable with fully ripened red or yellow peppers.

Roasting may be done using a *comal* or heavy skillet, or in the open flame of a gas burner.

For the first method (griddle-roasting), heat the *comal* or skillet over medium-high heat until a drop of water sizzles on contact. Place the whole peppers on the hot surface and roast, turning occasionally with tongs, until they are blackened on all sides. This may take 2 to 3 minutes for small peppers; 5 minutes for long, thin peppers; and up to 15 minutes for bell peppers. Remove from the heat and place in a paper or plastic bag to "sweat" for a few minutes (this helps loosen the skin).

Flame-roasting gives the most intense, smoky flavor. Working with one at a time, hold the whole peppers with tongs over the flame of a gas burner or grill. Turn often to char all sides evenly. If you have no gas burner or grill, you can broil the peppers. Place them on a baking sheet at a distance of 4 inches from the heat source and broil, turning occasionally, until they are blistered and charred on all sides. The time will depend on the size and shape of the peppers. Place the flame-roasted or broiled peppers in a bag to "sweat" as described above.

When they are slightly cooled, peel the charred skin from the roasted flesh. Some people do the job under running water, but this washes away the wonderful caramelized juices that add so much to the flavor. It is better to scrape and pick off the black bits a little at a time. Core and seed the peppers before proceeding with the recipe.

FLAVOR FROM TOMATOES, COCONUT MILK, AND SPIRITS

Fresh tomatoes or tomato sauces are integral ingredients in many cooking sauces (*sofritos*), particularly in the Hispanic Caribbean, where the acid tang of the tomato is considered essential for the final balance of a dish. In some regions, people routinely use globe tomatoes like ours. In others, the meatier and more compact plum tomato is preferred. And in some places, such as rural eastern Cuba, the favorite is cherry tomatoes, which in this country are mainly viewed as a salad vegetable or a garnish. They have a concentrated sweetness and acidity that is considered the secret of many sauces. Although people don't talk about heirloom tomatoes, the varieties that they raise in their home gardens have as much flavor as the ones we pay a premium for in grocery stores and at farmers' markets.

In many Latin countries, such as those of the Hispanic Caribbean, canned tomato sauce has partially displaced fresh ripe tomatoes in cooking. I dislike this trend and in my cooking use either fresh tomatoes or homemade tomato sauce (page 48). The tomatoes (fresh or in a sauce) are added to the pot after the vegetables in the flavoring base have been sautéed. In Mexico and Central America, tomatillos are often added along with tomatoes or by themselves to a *sofrito*. In Peru, Ecuador, and Bolivia, some sauces use tamarillos, or tree tomatoes, for that much-needed touch of acidity.

In some countries, coconut milk or spirits such as beer, wine, or *vino seco*—an inexpensive salted cooking wine very popular in the Hispanic Caribbean—are poured into the pan once all the ingredients of the *sofrito* look well blended and the oil is sizzling and beginning to separate from the sauce.

FLAVOR FROM SPICES AND HERBS

You cannot think of any Latin cuisine without thinking of spices. Their fragrance invades the kitchen and tells you where you are. In Cuba, when you smell the musky aroma of cumin, dried oregano, and fresh garlic, you know the cook is preparing an *adobo* (marinade) for pork. In the Yucatán, the scent of allspice, that most complex and beguiling of spices, tells you that a *recado* (marinade) is in progress. In southern Peru, when the marigold smell of the herb called *huacatay* fills the air, you know a cook is marinating a goat or lamb for the barbecue (*pachamanca*). If a Veracruzan cook is making a *mole*, you will be intoxicated by a cache of marvelous Old World spices—anise, cloves, cinnamon—releasing different fragrances as the sauce slowly cooks.

Latins excel at combining spices, often putting them through different stages of cooking so they acquire depth and dimension. For example, the spices for the Veracruzan *mole* are lightly toasted before being ground or pounded together with nuts and aromatic vegetables, and then the *mole* paste is fried. The caress of hot lard or oil brings the flavors of all the spices together. In a good *mole*, no single spice plays a starring role—all surrender their individuality to the harmonious interplay of flavors of the cooking pot.

Spice Blends

Like medieval Spanish cooking or the cuisines of modern India, many Latin American recipes rely on the careful orchestration of spice blends. These can consist of only two or three spices or more than a dozen. They might be added to a dish in separate pinches—as in the essential duo of dried oregano and cumin that makes Cuban black bean soup taste Cuban—or ground together in specific proportions, as in the smoky hot pepper and spice blend *merkén* or the Salvadorian spice mix *relajo*.

The *relajo* beautifully exemplifies all the features of medieval cuisine that were grafted onto pre-Columbian techniques and ingredients. Here we find aromas from Old World cloves, peppercorn, bay leaf, dried oregano, and thyme combined with the heat

pher what people are actually talking about when they refer to cilantro or *culantro*. For this book, I use "cilantro" to refer to the Old World plant and "broad-leaf *culantro*" for the New World plant. While cilantro now can be found everywhere in the United States, from ethnic markets to mainstream supermarkets, broad-leaf *culantro* has not yet achieved such widespread distribution. You may see a few leaves of it tied in bundles in Hispanic Caribbean markets, usually next to the *ají dulce* and the cilantro. You are also likely to find it in your local Chinatown. The Vietnamese use it in their cooking, particularly in pho, the popular noodle dish. They call *culantro* sawtooth herb, or *ngo gai*. But if you can't find it, do not despair. Cilantro and *culantro* can be used interchangeably.

New World oreganos: A cluster of aromatic herbs generically called oregano, though they are not related to European oreganos (*Origanum vulgare*).

Orégano de altura (Hedeoma mandoniana): In a stew, just a few leaves of this Andean herb will infuse the meat with a marvelous fragrance.

Mexican, Puerto Rican, and Dominican oreganos (Lippia graveolens): These uniquely scented New World oreganos are actually members of the verbena clan. You can find dried Mexican oregano and Dominican oregano in Latin markets across the United States.

You can also purchase seeds from specialized herb farms and grow your own herbs. Because these oreganos have more stalk portions than Mediterranean oregano, you need to crush the dried herbs in a mortar or sift them before using. Store away from light and heat in a tightly closed glass container.

Huacatay (Tagetes graveolens): An Andean plant of the marigold genus, huacatay has small, serrated green leaves with a strong medicinal flavor, which becomes almost overpowering when they are dried and powdered. In the cooking of the Peruvian and Bolivian highlands, this potent herb takes the place of cilantro. It adds a particular flavor and aroma as well as a greenish color to marinades (*aderezos*) for pork, lamb, and goat. Andean people use *huacatay* generously, because they know that cooking tames its assertive flavor.

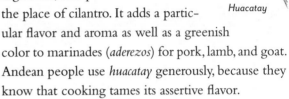

Huacatay

Huacatay is sold in powdered form or as frozen fresh leaves in Hispanic markets specializing in Andean foods. I use frozen *huacatay*. Use as you would cilantro to season Andean dishes like the meats for the pit barbecue (*pachamanca*) or to make Peruvian and Bolivan marinades.

Other names: *Aymara, chijchipa; Quechua, wacataya; Spain, mastranzo; Bolivia, suico.*

Guasca (Galinsoga parviflora): An Andean herb used in the departments of Cundinamarca and Boyacá in the central highlands of Colombia to season potato dishes like the famous *ajiaco bogotano*, a rich, creamy potato and chicken soup, *guasca* adds a delicate herbal flavor. Dried *guasca* is sold in small packages in Hispanic markets. Use sparingly as you would use oregano to season creamy soups or potato dishes. Store in a tightly closed container away from heat or light.

Epazote (Chenopodium ambrosioides): The classic Mexican seasoning for beans, epazote has a powerful aroma that reminds most people of turpentine, yet I have seen skillful Mexican cooks plunge several bunches into their soups with marvelous consequences—epazote magically loses its harshness in cooking. Called wormseed in English, epazote grows wild throughout the United States from summer to fall. You'll find it in parks and growing between the cracks of sidewalks. Epazote is available fresh and dried in most Hispanic markets. Dried epazote has none of the complex flavor of the fresh herb, but it does a decent job if fresh epazote is not available. Fresh epazote keeps well in the refrigerator for several days, wrapped in a damp towel. Use generously to season beans and other Mexican and Central American dishes, such as the sauce for green and red enchiladas and Oaxacan and Veracruzan dishes.

Other names: *apazote, epasote, paico.*

EPAZOTE

By the beginning of August, my New Jersey garden loses its orderliness and becomes as unkempt as a vacant lot. Blame it onepazote, a tenacious cooking herb that invades every nook and cranny.

Epazote is the hobo of the herb world, a sturdy tropical American plant that has become naturalized even in the cold Northeast, forgoing fertile garden beds to live between paving bricks and in sidewalk cracks, wherever it can sink its strong roots into a smidgen of soil. There is no doubt epazote is a fighter, but I suspect its intense aroma—something between turpentine and skunk—is also key to its survival. It even repels insects!

In the marvelously expressive language of the ancient Aztecs, this upright herb with serrated leaves is called *epazotl*, from the words for skunk (*epatl*) and dirt (*tzotl*). Its botanical name is *Chenopodium ambrosioides* or *foetidum* (smelly).

Epazote

It is precisely its aroma that makes epazote so special in cooking. It gives food a kind of umami, the savory fifth taste that is not easily described. It comes on strong but morphs into a more subtle green backbone that adds immense character to soups, stews, and sauces.

Its culinary merits and brave, bullish behavior have won epazote a place in my garden. Years ago, I found a little seedling growing next to a lamp post and transplanted it to a generous, well-fertilized bed in my garden. I let the plant grow strong and go to seed that year, the next, and the next, winding up with more epazote than I had bargained for, and in places I had not wanted it. Now I let the annual invasion go unchecked until the beginning of August, when the plants are strong enough to be transplanted into pots and yet tender enough to be used in cooking at home and in my restaurants.

I did not grow up loving epazote. In my native Cuba, where it is often called *apasote*, it is strictly a vermifuge, an herbal remedy for intestinal worms and a footnote in Celia Cruz's famous song "El Yerberito": *Tengo apazote para los brotes* (I have epazote for rashes).

In Mexico and all over tropical America, epazote is considered a medicinal plant, used to treat maladies from asthma to rashes, but it is also used in cooking. In Peru, where it is called *paico*, cooks layer whole bunches on top of the meats and vegetables cooked underground in the *pachamanca*, or earth oven, or they grind the herb together with their bright orange *ají escabeche* to make a spicy table sauce.

I fell in love with epazote's intense, wild-animal smell while doing research around Catemaco, a mysterious lagoon in the Mexican state of Veracruz, where I met a cook named Sara Hervís, who used epazote as deftly as an Italian cook might use flat-leaf parsley. For her soups, she would plunge a whole jungle of fresh epazote, stems and all, into the pot, and come in with the most flavorful broth I had ever tasted.

Though I have experimented with epazote in all sorts of dishes, the herb is at its best in time-tested Mexican classics like guajillo-flavored chicken soup, the Veracruzan *huatelpe de camarones* (shrimp in a green broth thickened with corn masa), and Oaxacan dishes such as pork in green *mole* and melted cheese sauces.

I once ate a fabulous creamy sauce made with fresh cow's milk cheese, strips of fire-roasted poblano peppers, and fresh epazote leaves at a vanilla farm in Papantla, in northern Veracruz. The cook kept making small, fresh corn tortillas on a large *comal* propped under the trees for us to top with the savory sauce and roll into tacos. The amazing transformation of the epazote tamed by the chiles and cheese is still etched in my mind.

Cook with epazote. Perhaps it will convince you to open the doors of your garden to this stinky, stupendous New World original. ◆

Quillquiña (Porophyllum ruderale Cass): *Quillquiña* (also spelled *Kilkiñe*) grows practically wild in the Bolivian Andes and parts of Peru. Just three small leaves will perfume a large salad or carry the tune in the Bolivian salsa called *llajkwa*. It can be found near Cochabamba, which explains why it is used to flavor the region's favorite corn and cheese salad, *soltero* (the bachelor).

Quillquiña

In markets all over Bolivia, *quillquiña* is sold tied in bundles next to the parsley, cilantro, and *huacatay*. The stems are light purple and the leaves narrow, elongated, and dark green. *Quillquiña* is not sold in Hispanic markets here, but you can buy seeds through mail-order from Horizon Herbs in Oregon, an herb farm specializing in medicinal plants (*quillquiña* reputedly lowers blood pressure).

The best substitute for this herb is its Mexican relative *papaloquelite* (*Porophyllum seemannii*), an herb of the Apiaceae family that has small leaves shaped like butterfly wings. I have found this highly aromatic herb in farmers' markets on the West Coast and in New York City. Only a couple of leaves are needed to add intense aroma to sauces, salads, and fortifying Andean soups like *chupes*.

Ishpingo

Ishpingo: In the Amazonian region of Ecuador the Spaniards found the Indians using a tree called *ishpingo* (*Ocotea quixos*) to obtain a delicate cinnamon-like seasoning. The bark and woody calyxes—shaped much like the caps of acorns—were used by the Indians as a traditional flavoring for *chicha*. *Ishpingo*, which the conquistadores prized for its lovely fragrance as much as they did true Ceylon cinnamon, was one of the lures that prompted them to explore the Amazon region, leading to Francisco de Orellana's navigation of the entire Amazon River in 1542. *Ishpingo* calyxes range in size from 1 to 2 inches. When you are able to find them, use as you would cinnamon in any recipe.

Cinnamon *(canela)*: While cassia cinnamon is preferred in the United States, the softer, more complex true Ceylon cinnamon is the flavor of tradition for Mexicans and most Latin Americans. Ceylon cinnamon grows in Mexico, where it is known as *canela*.

When grinding cinnamon, do not try substituting the product called cinnamon in the supermarket. It is hard cassia bark, and it will break your spice mill. Look in Hispanic markets for Mexican *canela*, also called soft-stick cinnamon.

MERKÉN: CHILEAN SMOKED PEPPER AND SPICE BLENDS

If I could take only one spice blend to a desert island, it would be this one: a coarse, brick-colored blend of smoked hot pepper and spices. *Merkén* is a perfect sum of contrasting flavors, the smoky hot pepper giving a subtle background heat to a harmonious blend of sweetly aromatic spices such as cumin, coriander seeds, and oregano. I use *merkén* in the same way as smoked paprika. Yet because it offers so much more flavor than paprika, I also find myself using it for a variety of other seasoning purposes—mixed with fresh onions and garlic in *sofritos*, as a dry rub for meats and poultry, in table sauces like Chilean *pebre*, as a seasoning for sautéed shrimp.

Merkén is a specialty of the Mapuche Indians, who live in Chilean Patagonia. At the heart of *merkén* is a dried hot red pepper known as *cacho de cabra*, or "goat's horn," because of its shape.

Crushed *cacho de cabra* is found in most Chilean hot sauces. Unlike the Mexican *chile de árbol* or guajillo, which immediately sets your mouth ablaze, *cacho de cabra* performs like a fireworks effect that takes time to blossom in the sky. At first you feel a suggestion of heat, which then intensifies and fills your mouth.

The Mapuches hang garlands of *cacho de cabra* from the rafts of their straw-thatched huts over the hearth. Days of exposure to the sultry smoke of the ill-ventilated wood fire that heats the house both dry the peppers to perfection and impregnate them with smoke and the smell of countless Mapuche meals.

Most of the other spices used in a *merkén* have endured a similar smoky fate, since they are also kept near the fire. The peppers and the spices—cumin, oregano, coriander seeds, and sometimes others—are ground together with salt to a powder in a wooden mortar with a stone pestle. This results in a slightly coarse, uneven texture that is one of *merkén*'s charms. Homemade *merkén* is stored in an earthenware container called a *monka* and covered with a piece of cloth. Mapuche women also use electric spice mills to grind *merkén* in bulk for sale in the markets.

Merkén from Chillán

Merkén de Chillán

Each *merkén* has its own distinctive taste. The *merkén* from Chillán, a town in southern Chile, is rich with the aroma of cumin, bay leaf, garlic, oregano, and coriander seeds. For years, every time I went to Chile I bought as much as I could from a Mapuche family I know, invariably causing a stir when U.S. customs officials checked my bags, suspiciously heavy with spices.

One November day, I bought two large *ristras* of Anaheim-type peppers at the central market in Juárez, right across the border from El Paso, Texas. Come Christmastime, I hung them all around the fireplace as decoration. On a chilly morning, the chimney got blocked and the living room filled with smoke. As I saw billows of smoke enveloping the peppers, I had an epiphany. Having seen the Mapuche Indians dry their *cacho de cabra* peppers over open hearths, I devised a contraption that allowed my *ristras* to be exposed to the fireplace smoke without burning up.

As a result of my experiment, that winter my living room was as warm and as aromatic as my busy kitchen. I lighted a fire as often as I could to get my peppers really smoky. After one month of constant fireplace use, I ground the peppers, adding the spices that I know the Mapuches in Chillán use for *merkén*. To my delight, it tasted very close to the authentic *merkén de Chillán*, which I had always greedily stocked up on in southern Chile. The smoke treatment paid off. Now I could make my *merkén* at home.

If you don't want to turn your house into a smoky hut to get a few ounces of a seasoning mix, use a professional smoker or add a couple of teaspoons of the best smoked paprika you can find to the mix.

Cook's Note: In Chile, *merkén* is made by grinding the smoked dried peppers and spices in a stone mortar. You can use a Mexican *molcajete* or, better still, a *metate* (see page 34); a wooden mortar with a stone pestle will also do the job. Do not try to get an extra-fine powder—traditional homemade *merkén* is always coarse.

MAKES ⅓ CUP

6 dried New Mexican chiles, preferably smoked (see headnote)

2 teaspoons coriander seeds

2 teaspoons cumin seeds

1 teaspoon dried *piquín* chiles

1 bay leaf

1 teaspoon salt

1 teaspoon garlic powder

2 teaspoons hot *pimentón* (Spanish smoked paprika), if the chiles have not been smoked

▶ Wipe the peppers clean with a wet towel. Stem and cut them open; do not remove the seeds. Heat a *comal*, griddle, or heavy skillet over high heat. Lower the heat to medium and place the peppers flat on the *comal*, skin side down. Carefully toast them on both sides, without burning them, pressing down with a metal spatula; the idea is to dry the peppers and char just slightly, so they get the delicious smoky flavor so characteristic of traditional *comal*-roasted peppers. Alternatively, roast the peppers in the oven: Place the prepared peppers in a single layer on a baking sheet and bake at 200°F until completely dry and brittle, 1 to 2 hours.

In either case, it is important that the peppers dry completely, because if they still retain any moisture, they will not grind easily. Crumble the peppers or coarsely chop. Reserve.

Briefly roast the coriander seeds, cumin seeds, dried *piquín*, and bay leaf in the same pan over medium heat until fragrant. Let cool.

Combine the spices, peppers, salt, and garlic powder in an electric spice or coffee grinder and grind to a coarse powder. If the first grind is too coarse, repeat the process.

Storing: Store in a tightly sealed jar in a cool, dark place. The *merkén* will keep its aroma for 1 to 2 months.

Uses: Use as you would smoked paprika. Add to table sauces or stir it into cooking sauces for a touch of smoky heat.

Coriander-Flavored *Merkén* from Temuco

Merkén de Temuco

At the main market in Temuco, a delightful but perennially humid city in southern Chile, I asked the vendor to let me taste some of his *merkén*. I noticed that it was light-colored and as finely ground as commercial paprika, not coarsely ground like the *merkén* from Chillán. The spice blend was a traditional one, made with dried *cacho de cabra* peppers, coriander seeds, and salt, the vendor explained, but it was not homemade—it came from a small factory in Temuco. Yet it was so tasty I bought some and used it to season many recipes from the Temuco area, such as *cazuela de ave con chuchoca*, a soupy chicken casserole with corn flour ground from sweet corn (page 521). This is my version of what I bought in the market.

MAKES ABOUT ⅓ CUP

- 6 Chilean *cacho de cabra* peppers or 6 dried New Mexican or Anaheim chiles
- 1 tablespoon coriander seeds
- 1 teaspoon *pimentón* (Spanish smoked paprika, hot or sweet)
- 1 teaspoon salt

▶ Preheat the oven to 200°F. Wipe the peppers clean with a damp towel. Stem them and cut them open. Do not remove the seeds. Place the peppers in a single layer on a baking sheet and roast until completely dry and brittle, 1 hour or more, depending how thoroughly dried they are to begin with. Turn them after 30 minutes so they dry evenly.

Crumble the peppers or coarsely chop. Reserve.

Briefly roast the coriander seeds on a *comal*, griddle, or heavy skillet over medium heat until fragrant, about 2 minutes.

Place all the ingredients in an electric coffee or spice grinder and grind to a fine powder.

Storing: Stored in a tightly sealed jar in a cool dark place, the *merkén* will keep its aroma for 1 to 2 months.

Uses: Use as you would paprika. Add to table sauces or stir into cooking sauces for a touch of smoky heat.

Maya Cacao and Chile Balls

Bolas de Cacao y Chile Ululte de la Alta Verapaz

The great Mesoamerican threesome of cacao, chiles, and turkey has been keeping company for probably millennia before the invention of *mole poblano*. In Copán, Honduras, a center of Classic Maya civilization, archaeologists found a vessel containing turkey bones. Chemical analysis of the vessel's other residues by Jeffrey Hurst of Hershey showed traces of theobromine and capsaicin, the chemical markers of cacao and chiles, respectively.

Cacao, chiles, and turkey still keep this ancient connection among the Kekchi Maya of Alta Verapaz. One of their favorite condiments for turkey and other celebratory foods is a combination of little wild chiles of the *piquín* type (called "*ululte*") with roasted cacao beans ground to a paste and shaped into small balls. To use, grate as much as you want over the food.

Cook's Note: A mini–food processor is essential for grinding the cacao and chile.

MAKES TWELVE ½-OUNCE BALLS

3 ounces cacao nibs (about ⅔ cup)

3 ounces *chiles de árbol* or *piquín* chiles

1 teaspoon salt

▶ Heat a *comal*, griddle, or cast-iron skillet over medium-high heat. Toast the cacao nibs and chiles for 2 to 3 minutes.

Stem the chiles and grind finely in an electric spice or coffee mill. Place in a food processor with the cacao nibs and salt and grind until the cacao becomes a paste. Shape into small (½-ounce) balls and place on a piece of parchment paper to dry.

Storing: Store in a tightly covered jar in a cool, dark place.

Uses: Finely grate and sprinkle over Alta Verapaz Turkey Stew (page 674), Smoky Pureed Pumpkin and Cacao Soup (page 527), or any food that might benefit from heat and extra flavor.

THE COOKING MEDIUM

The Pig and the Olive: The Fate of Two Fats

It is a commonplace that the soul of a cuisine lies in its favorite cooking fat, but distinctions like the ones food lovers like to make about France's butter, lard, and olive oil regions do not apply to Latin America. Though many studies claim that pork fat has traditionally been dearest to the Latin heart, it is only a small fragment of a complex story that began in old Iberia.

From ancient times, peoples who settled in the Iberian Peninsula planted olive trees and treasured the making of olive oil. The Syrians, Arabs, and Berbers who invaded and settled in Spain starting in A.D. 711 came from lands where the cultivation of olives and the production of olive oil was a way of life. They planted olive groves all over Andalusia and even in the northeast, in Catalonia and Aragon, areas where there hadn't been any olive trees.

However, although the Muslims of southern Spain cooked with olive oil, the Christians who contested with them for control of the peninsula for eight hundred years did not all come from olive-producing regions. The original settlers of Old Castile migrated from humid northern Spain, where olives do not grow. They used pork fat in their cooking. The hearty soups of northern Spain were originally enriched with fat rendered from pork products like bacon and salted fatback. The earthy lamb and suckling pig roasts of Castile owed their golden crust to a generous basting with melted lard.

Along with the *reconquista*, the piecemeal Christian "reconquest" of Islamic Spain that occurred between 711 and 1492, came a "dialogue" between the pork fat that dominated the cooking of the northern (and most Christian) provinces and the olive oil beloved of the south, where Muslims ruled longest. As the Christian pork eaters moved south, they added olive groves to their possessions, olive oil to their culinary storehouse. As a result, one legacy in some parts of Spain was a characteristic fondness for cooking with both olive oil and lard—rendering the fat from fresh or cured pork by cooking cut-up bits in olive oil and putting the magical alloy to work as a sautéing fat. However, as the Christian kingdoms continued to expand southward, the use of olive oil increased. Starting in the mid-thirteenth century, when conquered Islamic lands were divided up among Christian peasants and soldiers from the north, smallholders would receive a house in town as well as vineyards and olive groves. In Jaén, Seville, and Cordova, large estates turned over to aristocrats and the church by the Crown were blanketed with olive groves and produced massive amounts of olive oil for export. These estates were to exert a strong influence on Spain's economic policies toward its colonies.

In the dark, cramped hold of every ship that sailed from Spain to the Americas after Columbus's first voyage were sacks of wheat flour, barrels of salted pork, capers, spices, and olives, and glazed clay urns brimming with precious olive oil. Along with the staples of the Old World came the collective memory of the Iberian kitchen and the promise that the New World would be transformed not just by the force of the sword but by the flavors and the aromas of the cooking pot.

Like a beloved old blanket, soft and familiar, the foods of the Old World brought the Spanish conquistadores closer to the world they had left behind. Olive oil, the culinary insignia of the Mediterranean Basin, spoke an ancient but intimate language. Every golden drop conjured up the delights of tart *escabeches*, the aromas of freshly baked wheat bread, the pungency of sautéed onions and garlic, the fragrance of the *adobo*, and the hissing sound of tasty fish being fried in a busy Sevillan marketplace. For those first Spanish immigrants in the New World, cloaked in the armor of soldiers, olive oil was both promise and memory.

The promise was never truly fulfilled. With their warm winters, fertile soil, and violent storms, which usually come during the harvest season, the subtropical Caribbean islands did not welcome Mediterranean crops. Francisco López de Gómara wrote in 1551 that the very richness of the soil made "olive trees sterile." Neither grapevines, nor wheat, nor olives fared well.

The Spanish did have their hopes for growing olives realized in the cooler central valleys of Mexico. The trees that twelve Franciscan missionaries led by Martín Valencia planted in 1524 flourished and bore abundant fruit. But the olive quickly fell afoul of colonial politics. Like those of France and England, the Spanish monarchy had turned to thoughts of lucrative monopolies, as olive oil was one of Spain's biggest exports. The colonists' petitions to grow olives in places like Atlixco, Puebla, were sternly rejected, and many of the existing groves were destroyed. Here and there in Mexico some limited production of olive oil to be used in the Catholic liturgy was permitted, but the oil was not allowed to take root in popular cooking.

While the Spanish Crown could police Mexico, the wilder Andean provinces—a region of great potential for olives—defeated its vigilance. In 1560, a royal official named Antonio de Rivera managed to plant three olive saplings from Seville (the only survivors of a cargo of one hundred) in Lima. Despite round-the-clock security measures involving a hundred black slaves and thirty guard dogs, one of the three was kidnapped and taken to Chile. By the seventeenth century, olive groves stretched from Santiago, Chile, to Quito, Ecuador.

But nowhere in the Americas did olive oil become the popular cooking medium it was in the Mediterranean. Though the protectionist policy of the Spanish government could not wipe out olives everywhere, it did help relegate olive oil to certain social circles and certain culinary uses. The groves planted in Peru, Chile, Ecuador, and eventually western Argentina produced wonderful table olives but were almost never used to make oil.

Meanwhile, the pig was transforming the diets of the Native Americans. Introduced to Hispaniola perhaps as early as the first voyage of Columbus, pigs ate their way from the subtropical jungles of the Caribbean islands to the chilly, rugged wilds of the Andes. Nearly all the new environments proved to be pig heaven. By the sixteenth century the animals were a roving menace, gobbling up settlers' *conucos* (little cultivated patches) in the jungles and foraging in the potato fields of Peru. Not surprisingly, lard became the everyday cooking medium in a hemisphere that had never known any form of frying fat.

Pre-Columbian Americans boiled, steamed, or roasted their food. In the land of the Maya, pumpkin seed oil was used as a garnish for elaborate dishes like the *papadzules*, and ancient Peruvians added llama fat to stews and soups almost as a seasoning. For these people, who had no collective memory of cooking fats, richly unctuous lard would become the flavor of tradition—the only right fat for the earthy and flavorful tamales of the Yucatán, the sumptuous *moles* of Puebla and Oaxaca, and hundreds of much humbler dishes, especially in relatively isolated areas not often reached by Spanish ships. Pork and pork lard quickly became a mainstay of poor people in the countryside. The enormous influx of African slaves to the sugar plantations accentuated this proclivity for pork fat—it was lard that they turned to in the absence of palm oil, notably in Cuba during the nineteenth century.

As a cheap and self-reliant livestock animal, the pig was ideally suited to being kept under fairly casual conditions in poor households. In the highlands of Peru and Bolivia, you still see women and children taking their pigs to the fields to forage along with the family's llamas, sheep, and ubiquitous single cow. It's a funny sight—the pigs in single file following the llamas. Before sunset, they are all brought back to the family compound to sleep together in the same corral. When I was growing up in the 1950s, in middle-class Cuban households that had yards you could often find a pigpen where a couple of unsuspecting pigs lived happily eating tasty leftovers from the table. They were fattened for lard or to sacrifice for the holiday feasts. After the revolution, it was not uncommon for urban families to keep a pig anywhere—on a rooftop, even in a bathtub, although the government implemented periodic sanitary inspections of private homes to curb the custom.

In the early colonial period, the Spanish, the native peoples, and the Africans all found that tropical root crops like yuca blossomed if fried or otherwise cooked in the fat that was one of the by-products of slaughtering a pig. Until recently, *la matanza*—the killing of the pig, with the careful cutting up and cooking of every part and the rendering of the lard—was a familiar ritual all over Latin America. The lime-treated corn of Mexico had the same wonderful affinity for lard as did the tropical root vegetables. So did the potatoes and other tubers of the Andes. From northern Mexico far into South America, lard rapidly became the trusted cooking medium of the people—finding stiff competition only in Argentina, where beef fat (suet), commonly known as *pella*, had been enthroned since the early colonial period, a time when cows were more abundant than people.

It is not too much to say that you cannot enter into the spirit of popular Latin cooking without relishing the flavor of good fresh lard. However, olive oil, contributed a spirit of its own. Early on, the Spanish succeeded in making it into an expensive commodity, the cooking fat of the upper classes. The use of Spanish olive oil became a culinary pledge of allegiance to the mother country, an indication of class, income, and ethnicity. The use of olive oil generally stood in an exactly inverse relationship to the size of an area's black or Indian population. In postcolonial times, newer migrations from Spain and southern Europe continued to renew the love of something that is liquid memory—a link with the ancient but intimate flavor code of the Mediterranean.

Eventually olive oil carved out several important niches for itself in the Latin kitchen. Like lard, it turned out to be a glorious vehicle for many New World ingredients, though a vehicle destined to make scattered regional stops and starts rather than a comprehensive circuit of all Latin America. The dishes most often made with olive oil are of fish or seafood, a culinary association going back to twelfth-century Muslim Andalusia, later reinforced by the traditional Spanish codfish dishes eaten on the eve of feast days, including Christmas. The combination of vinegar and olive oil in *escabeches* (pickling sauces), used to flavor and preserve many different ingredients from fish to vegetables, is another very old survivor. Today in Spain an *escabeche* tends to be pared down to a few basic elements, but the fascinating blends of herbs and spices that perfumed it in medieval Spain can be glimpsed in some of its modern Latin guises—for example, an escabeche of *róbalo* (snook) from Xalapa in Veracruz that explodes with the Old World flavors of thyme, marjoram, cloves, black pepper, cumin, and cinnamon.

In Brazil, with its large multicultural population, the picture was complicated by the introduction of *dendê* oil from the African palm, prized not only for its strong, distinctive flavor but also for its attractive reddish color. People in Brazil choose cooking fats with the same kinds of flavor discriminations that would be applied to herbs. In the northeast, especially the state of Bahia, lard coexists with *dendê* oil. Canola and other vegetable oils are used for everyday cooking, but lard is preferred for the earthy dishes of Minas Gerais. In most of Brazil, olive oil is employed for salads, some of the table sauces (*molhos*), certain seafood dishes, and Portuguese classics.

In Cuba, olive oil moved into middle-class kitchens in the twentieth century, bestowing a Hispanicized bourgeois baptism on foods like black bean soup, boiled yuca—which was often served with a Cuban *mojo* made of garlic, bitter orange juice, and olive oil—and even the *fufú* (plantain mash) that slave cooks brought into urban kitchens. While lard remained the only fat available to the Cuban *guajiro* (peasant), who managed to render it himself, in the urban centers a creative compromise was reached between lard, together with other pork products such as salt fatback and smoked slab bacon, and olive oil. Each retained particular, though sometimes overlapping, niches in Cuban cooking. This peaceful coexistence mirrors the dialogue between olive oil and lard in medieval Spain and defines the flavor of Cuban cooking. By 1956, Cuba was the largest importer in the world of Spanish olive oil—quite remarkable for such a tiny nation. While Cubans in exile are among the largest Latin consumers of Spanish olive oil in the United States, olive oil has become a precious commodity in contemporary Cuba, a black-market luxury that can be purchased only on rare occasions.

Argentina, which today has the largest olive groves of South America and a sizable European population, mostly of Spanish or Italian descent, is something of an anomaly. It might be expected that olive oil would have replaced beef fat and lard as the favorite cooking medium. Yet, as food journalist Elizabeth Checa explained to me when I interviewed her in Buenos Aires, during the last century, the producers of vegetable oils (sunflower, soy, and cotton) waged war against both the national olive oil industry and imported olive oil. They extolled the health-giving benefits of their neutral-tasting fats over the flavorful olive oil, which they lumped together with lard as an evil fat. The results can still be seen today. A housewife from San Juan in the northeast might make her empanadas with beef fat or margarine, but her *carbonadas* and *sofritos* are cooked with vegetable oil, not olive oil. Taste any of the many types of chimichurri sauce served in Argentinean *parrilladas* (steakhouses), and you will know they are made with vegetable oil.

Yet although olive oil never fulfilled the promise seen by the first Spanish colonists in New Spain and the neighboring colonies, it continued to furnish a vital link with the mother country, not just for those loyalists who went on using imported oil but also for people who were applying classic Iberian techniques to new ingredients. The most basic kitchen technique brought over by the colonists consisted of lovingly cooking onions and garlic in olive oil to use as a foundation of flavor and body in most cooked dishes—the *sofrito* described earlier in this chapter. Wherever Iberian cooks went, some version of *sofrito* went with them. It might be made with a combination of olive oil and salt pork or bacon, thus continuing the lively Spanish conversation between the olive and the pig. It might be transformed with New World tomatoes and peppers, an idea soon carried back to the whole Mediterranean Basin. Or a *sofrito* christened with some new name might literally take on a different complexion if the red seeds of achiote were infused in the olive oil—or lard—or, later, vegetable oils like corn, sunflower, and soy. But in all cases, anyone who knows Iberian cooking will discern a key phrase of a culinary language first spoken in medieval Spain by way of olive oil.

Though olive oil didn't become a major Latin American commodity, the sight of the groves that furnished table olives in favorable climates was bound to inspire twentieth-century immigrants from olive oil territory. In the Chilean valley of Curicó, a little south of Santiago, an Italian family of winemakers who arrived in the 1930s started producing oil in commercial quantities from a grove in Sagrada Familia. At around the same time, a few hundred miles to the north, the Croatian-born Roko Popiç was supplying his household with oil he pressed himself, using olives bought from a relative and taken to the Russian immigrant who ran the one small mill in La Serena. Now his son, food writer Miro Popiç, is giving his own children in Caracas—a place not known for the use of olive oil—the same loyalty to the oil, enjoyed Croatian style with fresh peasant bread and home-cured ham.

The Chilean producer Eduardo Iriarte—who started out in the 1960s crushing home-grown Ligurian olives in a meat grinder and still had only a primitive mill when I met him fifteen years ago—was finding local markets for his olive oil infused with cumin seeds (one of the most important Chilean seasonings).

It's a swiftly changing scene. Latin America was slow to overcome the handicaps imposed by colonial era interdictions on olive growing. Not only did the colonies lag behind Europe in olive oil production, but many Latin American cooks long remained less comfortable with olive oil than with any other cooking fat. People found the flavors overpowering and complained about the expense. This is still true to an extent. But attitudes have been changing along with the dietary repute of olive oil—not to mention the spread of an olive oil connoisseurship in foodie circles.

Today every Latin American country where olives still grow is seeking to cash in on the new-found popularity of olive oil. Chile and Argentina have taken the lead experimenting with boutique single-origin and single-variety oil production. Winemakers will often diversify by adding an olive oil line to their wine offerings—natural enough since olive trees and grapevines flourished together in the Mediterranean since before the dawn of history. Most of the new oils are designed for export rather than domestic use. But already I see far greater interest in olive oil on the part of Latin American cooks. The signs are clear that Latin Americans are at last reclaiming olive oil as part of their heritage.

Freshly Rendered Lard and Its Reward: Pork Cracklings

Chicharrones y Manteca de Chicharrón al Estilo Cubano

When I was growing up in Cuba in the fifties, I remember rushing to buy lard (*manteca*) for my aunts at our nearest convenience store, a roadside wooden shack built under a huge mango tree. Nicolás Oliva, the owner, scooped out a large slab of solidified lard from a big wooden barrel and deftly wrapped it in brown paper, like an empanada. The transaction was completed with a piece of candy, or *ñapa*. That's why I always volunteered for this errand.

In fancier stores with refrigerated sections and in butcher shops, you could find 1- to 2-pound packages of imported American Swift or Armour lard—the kind my aunts reserved for making pies and empanadas because they thought it produced finer pastry. For frying savory foods, they used either vegetable oil or Nicolás's lard. Imported Spanish oil, such as Sensat, Sansó, or Ibarra brand, was a must for salads, fish, and sautéing in general. But for special treats when a traditional flavor was paramount, such as a garlicky *mojo* for tubers or the *sofrito* to flavor our local fresh corn tamales, or frying eggs for breakfast, my aunts always kept a bottle of lard they had made themselves. It was kept warm near the stove, so the lard, golden and liquid, was always ready to pour. There was nothing comparable to the marvelous nutty, earthy flavor of this *mantequita* ("little darling lard"), as we affectionately called it.

Like most suburban Cuban families with large backyards, my aunts always kept a well-fattened pig. Come slaughtering time, every part of the animal was put to use, but for many people: the most anticipated moment of the ritual was the making of lard. To me, however, lard was of secondary importance—I was more interested in the pork cracklings. Several times a year, my family slaughtered and cooked a pig, as was done all over the countryside. My uncle would cut the pig's belly into huge chunks containing rind, meat, and fat and put them in a huge cast-iron cauldron to cook for hours over a wood fire. Because the pieces were so large, it took hours for those whitish chunks of fat and meat to turn golden and crunchy. I can still hear the burbling music of the pot, the sudden splatter of sizzling fat when my aunts stirred the pot with a large spoon, and the beckoning aroma and hissing sound of the voluptuous piping-hot cracklings, *chicharrones*, as they were fished out of the oil and drizzled lightly with some bitter orange or lime juice. I've always thought of *chicharrones* as the just rewards for so many hours of hard work and anxious waiting.

We gobbled up the *chicharrones* in minutes, but the lard was judiciously and selectively used, so that it would last for months. When the supply was getting low, my aunts would make small batches of *chicharrones* from store-bought pork belly on the stovetop to obtain a few cups of lard to get them by between pigs. Those were smaller *chicharrones*, the meat scored neatly into four lobes. I loved them just as much as the big ones.

This simple recipe will produce delicious *manteca* and dainty *chicharrones*—small, easy-to-eat cracklings that can be served as an appetizer. To find the special pork cut you need for *chicharrones*, seek out a Hispanic Caribbean, Hungarian, or Latin butcher or ask your own butcher to special-order a large sheet of fatty pig's belly with the rind and some meat attached. If you go to a Cuban butcher, ask for *barrigada* (pig's belly) to make lard and meaty

chicharrones. He will ask you how would you like your *chicharrones* cut. In most Hispanic Caribbean butcher shops, *barrigada* has the rind and some meat attached. When buying from a Dominican, Puerto Rican, or Colombian butcher, if you are not specific and just casually say that you want to make *chicharrones*, you might get the front portion of the pig's belly with pieces of rib with fat and rind on. You will get delicious *chicharrones* but very little lard. If buying from an Ecuadorian or Peruvian butcher, spell out every detail: in Ecuador, lard is rendered from skinless slabs of pork belly fat called *lonja* (see page 85); the rind is sold separately.

MAKES 3 CUPS LARD AND 5 CUPS PORK CRACKLINGS

> 4   pounds fresh pork belly (*barrigada*) with rind and
>   some meat attached
> 1   tablespoon salt
>   Juice of 1 medium bitter orange (about ¼ cup),
>   strained

▶ Cut the meat into 2-inch squares, leaving the skin on. With a sharp knife, score a cross about ¼ inch deep on the fat side of each square. As they fry, each *chicharrón* will open up into four lobes. Place the meat in a large bowl and toss with the salt, then transfer to a large heavy-bottomed pot, a cast-aluminum *caldero*, if possible. Do not use a flimsy lightweight pan, or the *chicharrones* might scorch. Cook uncovered over medium heat, stirring gently, for 10 minutes. At this point, the pork will have released only some of its fat and so may stick to the bottom of the pot. Cover and cook, stirring occasionally, for 20 more minutes. Uncover and continue cooking until the pork pieces turn golden brown. Do not expect the *chicharrones* to become completely crispy while on the heat—if they crisp too much during cooking, they will be stiff as cardboard when they cool and give an off taste to the lard. The total cooking time will depend on how meaty your *chicharrones* are. Very meaty *chicharrones* with pieces of rib bone from the front of the pig's belly may take from 1 hour to 1 hour and 15 minutes, less meaty *chicharrones* 35 to 45 minutes.

With a slotted spoon, remove the *chicharrones* from the fat and place on a plate lined with paper towels to drain. Sprinkle with the bitter orange juice when still hot. Allow the *chicharrones* to stand for at least 15 minutes to crisp up before eating.

Storing and Using Lard: Although the amount of lard obtained from *chicharrones* will vary, this recipe will render approximately 3 cups; expect less if the *chicharrones* are exceptionally meaty. Let the lard cool, then strain it into a tightly covered glass or metal container. Do not discard the solid residue of fried pork bits that remain in the bottom of the pot and in the strainer. They are great to season beans or Ecuadorian Toasted Corn (page 154). Traditionally lard is kept at room temperature (I like to store the lard in a covered earthenware jar, as is done in rural Spain), but feel free to refrigerate it.

Lard can be used interchangeably with other fats in frying, but I advise you to use it selectively and in small amounts, almost like a spice or a wonderful imported butter, to give a special traditional flavor to *sofritos*, *mojos*, and especially tamales.

Serving and Cooking with *Chicharrones*: Warm *chicharrones* in a low oven (200°F), and drizzle with a couple of tablespoons of Cuban *Mojo* (page 140) for a stupendous contrast, just before serving as an appetizer with cocktails. A couple of cracklings added to a red kidney bean stew will impart the special earthy flavor of fresh homemade lard.

Storing: A word of caution—if you are making pork cracklings intended for future use, make sure there are no Cubans around. Pork cracklings, as you know, are addictive. If you can manage to keep the Cubans at bay, place them in a double paper bag and keep at room temperature and out of reach (the most important point) for 2 to 3 days. Or, for longer storage, keep in the refrigerator. They will become soft but retain their wonderful flavor.

Uses: Add a few pieces of cracklings to any favorite bean dish and allow to cook until very soft. Use the lard to prepare the cooking sauce for My Fresh Corn Tamales Cuban Style (page 455) or Chicken Tamales from Lima (page 472). Stir a hot spoonful into a Cuban *Adobo* (page 42). In short, use as you would vegetable oil in all sorts of traditional Latin preparations.

Pork Cracklings in the Style of Minas Gerais

Torresmos

These small cracklings with blistery skin and no meat are popular in Minas Gerais, Brazil. I find them as addictive as the meaty kind. There is no better complement for beans than *torresmos* fresh from the pot. They add a crunchy texture as well as salty flavor to the soft beans. The ones I remember from São Paulo and Minas are light and crunchy like the Mexican *chicharrones de viento* but bite-sized. They are essential for Mineiro cooking.

Cook's Note: Feel free to use *torresmos* in any recipe calling for light cracklings without meat.

2 pounds pork belly, skin and some fat only

½ teaspoon salt

3½ ounces (about 6 tablespoons) lard, preferably freshly rendered (page 82)

The First Frying ▶ With a sharp knife, cut the pork into 1-inch cubes. Sprinkle with salt. Place the lard in a 4-quart saucepan or cast-aluminum *caldero*, at least 10 inches wide, and melt over medium-low heat. Add the pork and cook, stirring occasionally, until the pork is golden and the skin begins to blister. Immediately lift out of the pot and place on paper towels to drain.

The Second Frying ▶ The cracklings now look golden and the skin shows some blisters. They are perfectly delicious, but in Minas and other parts of Latin America people like them still more crunchy and blistered. They usually fry the cracklings again, once they are cold, in another batch of hot lard. If the lard in which you first cooked the cracklings has not darkened too much, heat it over medium-high until shimmering. Add the cracklings and cook just enough to blister the skin. Do not overbrown, or the cracklings will taste bitter. Lift out with a skimmer and place on paper towels. If not using immediately, let cool and store in a tightly covered container.

Ecuadorian Black Lard and Cracklings

Manteca Negra (Mapahuira) y Chicharrones Ecuatorianos

When you visit an Ecuadorian market, you may notice two kinds of lard: *manteca blanca* and *manteca negra*, white and black. The distinction is based not on quality but on flavor. The first is pure lard that has been strained carefully to remove any bits of solid matter, while the latter is a flavorful unstrained lard with tiny bits of toasted pork fat that look like miniature *chicharrones*. *Manteca negra* is used as a flavoring more than a cooking medium.

In Ecuador, lard is rendered from *lonja*, a slab of pork fat with rind and just traces of meat. The *lonja* is cut into small cubes, about ½ inch across, and seasoned with salt, garlic, and onion. It is cooked in a heavy-bottomed pot and stirred occasionally until it releases most of its fat and the pieces look well browned and shriveled. When you render lard from *lonja*, do not strain it—leave all the dark, shriveled pieces. Store as you would regular lard, and use in dishes that call for the extra special flavor of cracklings.

If you find an Ecuadorian butcher, he will know what you mean when you ask for *lonja*, or *gordo del chancho*, the rindless, practically meatless layer of pork belly fat. But just in case, be very specific. Most Hispanic butchers can accommodate your order and be willing to prepare it according to your specifications. The worst-case scenario is that they will ask you to pay for both the meat and the rind.

MAKES ABOUT 3 CUPS FAT AND 2 CUPS *CHICHARRONES*

2½ pounds *lonja* (rindless, meatless pork belly fat), cut into 1-inch pieces

1 teaspoon salt

6 scallions, white and 3 inches of green parts

½ head garlic, cut crosswise in half

▶ Rub salt on the *lonja* and place it in a large heavy-bottomed pot, a cast-aluminum *caldero* (see page 33), if possible, and cook uncovered over medium heat until it has rendered much of its fat, about 20 minutes. Add the scallions and garlic and allow them to brown, about 8 minutes, stirring occasionally. Remove from the pot and discard. Continue cooking until the pieces of *lonja* are golden brown and shriveled and have released most of their fat, approximately 10 more minutes. Do not overcook, or the lard will taste bitter.

Remove the pot from the heat and lift the *chicharrones* from the fat with a slotted spoon. Set aside on a plate lined with paper towels to drain. Use to season beans or Andean hominy (*mote*).

Stir the fat, then pour it into a clay pot or other container, including the brown particles on the bottom of the *caldero*. As it cools, the black lard, with tiny bits of fat and meat, will sink to the bottom and a paler layer of fat will solidify on the surface. Scoop it out and store separately if you wish.

Cumin-Scented Olive Oil

Aceite Condimentado con Comino

Although Chile now has a flourishing olive oil industry, it used to be difficult for many rural Chileans to buy favorite national brands, such as Canepa. They had to resort to ingenious local producers. Thirty years ago, Eduardo Eriarte and his wife, who live in Freirina, a small town in the valley of Copiapó in northern Chile, crushed their home-grown olives in meat grinders. Ten years ago their mill was still primitive, and it worked well only with the tiny, oily Italian Ligurian olives that grow in Copiapó. These olives must be fully tree-ripened and then sun-dried until dehydrated before they can be pressed.

Eduardo had added spices to his extra-virgin olive oil to bolster sales. Cumin is one of the most important ingredients in Chilean cooking, and toasted cumin seeds give a special earthy flavor to this infused olive oil. Use it for cooking fresh cranberry beans (page 265) or drizzle over roasted vegetables or grilled meat.

MAKES 2 CUPS

- 2 cups extra-virgin olive oil
- 2 tablespoons cumin seeds, lightly toasted
- 2 teaspoons dried oregano
- 20 black peppercorns
- 2 bay leaves
- 3 dried Chilean *cacho de cabra* peppers (about ¼ ounce) or cayenne peppers
- 2 garlic cloves, peeled

▶ Pour the oil into a small heavy saucepan and heat very gently over medium-low heat. Add the rest of the ingredients and immediately remove from the heat. Allow the oil to cool, then store in a glass container in a dark, cool place until ready to use. Keeps about three months.

Tropical Oils: Palm Oil and Coconut Oil

PALM OIL

When you fly from the Caribbean coast of Honduras to the inland city of San Pedro Sula, it's difficult to distinguish the plantain fields from the African palm groves. When Californian agronomist Wilson Popenoe introduced the African palm to Lancetilla, the experimental botanical garden created by the United Fruit Company near Tela in the 1920s, he probably had no idea of how successfully this new arrival would adapt or what it would do to Central American cooking. He saw the benefits of a new cash crop for an impoverished nation, but he never envisioned palm oil cropping up in every market in its hydrogenated incarnation, commercial palm oil margarine sold as vegetable lard (*manteca vegetal*).

The African palm (*Elaeis guineensis*) is an imposing plant, with fruits growing in gigantic clusters like pinecones. If you scratch the surface of a palm fruit, which looks like a small coconut, your hands will be stained a deep orange—the color of the unrefined palm oil used in northern Brazilian cooking, *azeite de dendê*.

I don't see the point of cooking with solid hydrogenated palm oil margarine, since it is a highly saturated fat with none of the fine flavor of freshly rendered lard (which has less saturated fat). *Dendê* oil, however, should be used where it belongs, in the sultry dishes of black Bahia such as *vatapá*, *carurú*, and *xinxim de galinha*. I use a mixture of oils when making Bahian dishes. For frying, I mix corn oil and *dendê* oil, and for sautéing, I use an achiote-infused sunflower or corn oil, adding a smaller amount of *dendê* oil, carefully, as a seasoning.

Fresh Coconut Oil

When passing by the saffron-colored mansions of Old Cartagena, Colombia, at noontime, you can smell the aroma of fried fish and hear the sizzling hiss of coconut milk as it cooks into a fragrant oil. These are the same seductive aromas and sounds encountered along the Caribbean coast of Central America from Tela in Honduras to Livingston in Guatemala and Limón in Costa Rica—all places with a strong Afro-Caribbean presence and a penchant for cooking with both coconut milk and the oil made from the milk. Both are used in the famous coconut rice from Cartagena (page 300).

While proportions and ingredients vary from cook to cook, everyone agrees that there is no better coconut rice than that sautéed in a few tablespoons of freshly rendered coconut oil (*titote*), to give it a golden brown color and a slightly chewy texture.

MAKES ½ CUP COCONUT OIL

4 cups Creamy ("First") Coconut Milk (page 50)

▶ Pour the creamy coconut milk into a heavy-bottomed pot and bring to a boil over moderate heat. Begin stirring with a wooden spoon as soon as the coconut milk begins to separate into its two components, oil and a solid residue. Strain through a fine sieve and store in a glass or stainless steel container in a cool place or in the refrigerator. It will solidify very rapidly and keep well for several weeks.

Storing: Stored in a glass or stainless steel container in a cool place or in the refrigerator (where it will solidify), the oil will keep well for several weeks.

A PENCHANT FOR COLOR

Latin Americans are obsessed with imbuing their foods with intense colors. Everywhere you go in the tropical Americas, rice, marinades, stews, soups, desserts such as rice pudding, and even some chocolate drinks are tinted a reddish orange-gold with achiote (annatto), the tiny seeds of a small tropical bush whose botanical name is *Bixa orellana*. This reddish gold should be the official color of the Latin kitchen. Paprika-infused oil and *dendê* oil from Brazil are beloved for this same reason, but nothing surpasses the popularity of achiote for imparting a magical hue.

Achiote is a medium-sized shrub or small tree with wide branches whose delicate flowers grow in clusters and turn into hairy pods, the *bixa* fruit. When ripe, these spiny capsules open up, showing rows of tiny seeds surrounded by a waxy orange substance called bixin. Both the bixin and the seeds are used to imbue food with a deep golden orange color.

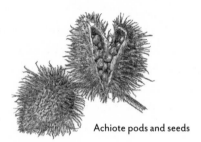

Achiote pods and seeds

One of my fondest memories of Nicaragua is of my stay at the achiote farm of my friends Elías and Gloria Cuadras in the town of Ticuantepe, halfway between Managua and Granada. At night you can see the menacing glow of the Masaya volcano from the farm, as red and luminous as the mounds of achiote seeds the Cuadrases harvest once a year. By October, the pods have turned from bright red to dark brown and are beginning to open. This first early harvest commands the highest prices in the market, since Nicaraguans covet fresh achiote. The peak of the harvest takes place between November and December. Workers inspect the plants on a weekly basis and collect the ripe opened pods by hand. The pods are placed on sheets of canvas to be sun-dried for a couple of days, then they are crushed to liberate the tiny red seeds. The seeds are placed on sheets of canvas to dry for a couple of days in the sun, and then are passed through a sieve. At Elías and Gloria's farm, a final cleaning is done with the help of a large fan that Gloria brings to the backyard

to blow away any debris still attached to the seeds. Then they are bagged and sold in the market, to be used for achiote paste or infused in lard or oil for cooking. Gloria, a savvy businesswoman, always reserves a portion of the last crop to sell when prices rise again in the spring.

For her personal use, Gloria makes a flavorful achiote paste. She soaks the seeds in water briefly and then sends them to a local mill to be ground with her own blend of garlic and spices. This paste is very much like the Yucatecan *recado* (page 43), with the distinctive nutty and resinous aroma and flavor of the achiote seed kernel.

In many Latin American countries, though, cooks prefer to extract the milder-tasting waxy bixin rather than crush the strongly flavored achiote seeds. Guatemalans free the bixin from the seeds by boiling them, then use the deep orange sediment that forms a thick paste at the bottom of the pot. The fresher the achiote, the more paste you will collect. The larger the amount, the easier it is to get a good layer of this sediment. If you boil just a few ounces of achiote, the result is so paltry that most of the sediment will simply coat the bottom of the pot.

Guatemalans make a distinction in quality and price between the fine achiote (*achiote fino*) obtained through sedimentation and the more assertively flavored "second-class" achiote (*achiote de segunda clase*), the paste obtained by grinding soaked whole achiote seeds. Guatemalans and other Central Americans store achiote paste in small packages made of corn husks.

In Cuba, traditionally achiote seeds were lightly crushed, then allowed to ferment in large vats of water. Once the bixin precipitated and formed a sediment in the bottom of the vats, the water was carefully poured off and the resulting paste allowed to dry. Then it was kneaded into blocks and wrapped in plantain leaves to be sold at the market. This process is somewhat similar to that for the Guatemalan fine achiote.

My Cuban relatives the Ferrer family, who live in secluded farms high in the mountains of the Oriente region, not far from Maisí, Cuba's easternmost point, wrap handfuls of achiote seeds in small pieces of fabric and steep them like tea bags in cooking liquids such as broth and coconut milk, to extract the achiote's golden color. They also place achiote seeds in a contraption full of tiny holes that they immerse in the foods they want to color. This is a method I suspect Cuban peasants learned centuries ago from the primitive inhabitants of the island, the Arawak (Taíno) Indians.

Whole achiote seeds are sold in most Hispanic markets. Choose only bright-colored seeds that will stain your fingers red when touched. Dark brown seeds have lost their capacity to color and are often bitter-tasting. Store the seeds in a tightly sealed container away from heat or light, and discard them if they turn brown.

One day someone had the bright idea to grind achiote into a powder and to sell it in small packages under the name of *bijol*. For decades, rather than laboring with achiote seeds, Cubans and other Latin Americans have used this packaged achiote powder, which they've grown so used to they have forgotten that the coloring comes from a plant. Not surprisingly, *bijol* manufacturers have no qualms about adulterating the natural, healthful achiote with artificial dyes and other additives. If buying a powdered achiote, or prepared achiote paste, read the label carefully. If you see a list of artificial additives, choose another brand—or buy fresh achiote seeds and infuse them in the fat of your choice or water.

Home-Ground Achiote

If you want pure ground achiote without additives, you will usually have to grind it yourself.

MAKES ⅓ CUP

½ cup achiote seeds (about 3 ounces)

▶ Place in a spice mill, and grind, in batches as necessary, to a fine powder. Store in a tightly covered jar, preferably in a cool, dark place to best maintain the color and flavor.

Achiote-Infused Oil or Lard

Aceite o Manteca de Color

Cuban *achiotera* from Jaca, with whole achiote seeds

In Latin America, achiote-colored lard or achiote-infused oil is part of any well-stocked pantry, traditionally stored in an *achiotera*, a special metal container with a spout. My friend and mentor Felipe Rojas-Lombardi, the brilliant Peruvian-born chef and author who created the Ballroom restaurant in Manhattan, loved the sunny color and subtle smoky flavor of achiote-infused olive oil. He used it for everything from marinating the luscious suckling pigs that he proudly displayed at the counter of his tapas bar to enhancing the color of his spicy mayonnaise to giving his lamb empanadas a gilded look. This recipe gives you both a seasoning and a coloring.

MAKES 2 CUPS

- 2 cups corn oil, extra-virgin olive oil, or freshly rendered lard (page 82)
- ½ cup achiote seeds (about 3 ounces)

▶ Place the oil and achiote in a small saucepan and heat over medium heat until beginning to bubble. Remove from the heat and allow to cool. Strain and discard the seeds.

Storing: Stored in a cool, dark place, the oil will keep well for 1 to 2 months.

Paprika: The Other Latin Color

In the cupboard of any Latin cook from Juárez to Punta Arenas, you will find a little can of *pimentón* (paprika). Derived from fleshy peppers of *Capsicum annuum*, the same species as bell peppers, this condiment is used not only in Spanish-inspired dishes like bean stews but also in traditional *criollo* dishes such as Argentine empanadas and Peruvian *jamón del país*, a cured ham.

There are national brands of paprika in all the pepper-producing countries of Latin America, and some regions, such as northern Peru, are emerging as important sources of paprika for the export market, but finicky Latin cooks still prefer imported brands from Spain. Though peppers are New World plants, the best paprika comes from Spain and Hungary, the two European countries that perfected the cultivation of *Capsicum annuum* varieties suited to its production.

I never liked *pimentón* and consciously broke with tradition by omitting it from my cooking until I tasted the smoked *pimentón* from La Vera in Extremadura, a region in the interior of Spain encompassing the provinces of Cáceres and Badajoz. Decades ago, Irma Alfonso, a Cuban friend who lives in Madrid, introduced me to its wonders. A fearless motorist, she drove me through the mountains and valleys of the Sierra de Gredos at nerve-racking speed. We caught our breath at the monastery of Yuste, where Charles V died in 1558 and where the monks are said to have popularized the production of paprika in this region. In La Vera, Extremadura's premier paprika-producing area, I was stunned by the beauty of the fields: long fire-engine-red peppers, ready to be harvested, hung so heavily they seemed to be pulling the plants down to the ground.

The peppers are harvested in October and dried over oakwood fires for a week or two. The smoke sets their color and intensifies their flavor, which is what makes this *pimentón* truly special. Once dried, the peppers are ground at large commercial mills, not once but several times, to obtain the finest possible powder. The degree of piquancy is determined by the cultivar and by the amount of seeds left in the pods.

In Spain and Latin America, paprika is an essential condiment for beans and chickpeas. Because of its antioxidant qualities (it helps prevent fats from turning rancid), paprika is crucial for producing cured meats, lending its reddish hue to the delicious fat that oozes from fried chorizo. A judicious dash of paprika added at any stage of cooking does wonders for seafood, pork, and bean dishes. Paprika lends backbone and meaty richness to food, giving it an umami-like fifth taste that rounds and intensifies all other flavors. Like any other spice, paprika should be bought fresh and stored in a cool place away from heat and light.

Argentinean Fried Paprika

Grasita Colorada Argentina

Around Salta, a town in northwestern Argentina, thousands of pounds of peppers are dried in the sun to make paprika, turning the earth bright red for miles at a stretch. It is a breathtaking sight. A favorite way to add color to food in this region is with "fried" paprika, which is known by the funny name *grasita colorada*, "little red fat." Wait until you taste this incredibly rich coloring and seasoning—you won't believe what your mouth will tell you: *grasita* tastes like freshly rendered pork lard.

MAKES 1⅔ CUPS INFUSED OIL AND ¼ CUP *GRASITA COLORADA*

- 2 cups corn oil or light extra-virgin olive oil
- ¼ cup (2 ounces) smoked hot or sweet *pimentón*, (preferably Spanish), to taste

▶ Combine the oil and paprika in a small saucepan and heat over medium heat for 5 minutes, or until hot but not sizzling. Remove from the heat and add 2 tablespoons cold water. The paprika will settle to the bottom. Carefully strain the oil from the paprika sediment, and pour into a storage container (such as a stainless steel vessel with a spout), leaving the paprika sediment behind. If you use a glass container, be sure to store it in a dark place. The sediment is the *grasita colorada*—spoon it into a small container and store in the refrigerator or a cool, dark place. Use it to flavor potatoes or the thick Andean potato soup called *locro* (page 522).

Chilean Paprika-Infused Oil or Lard

Color Chileno

Paprika and cumin are seldom missing in Chilean food, and paprika-infused oil is referred to as *color chileno*, "Chilean coloring." This infused oil is used to season and color beans and vegetable dishes.

MAKES ABOUT 2 CUPS

- 2 cups corn oil or freshly rendered lard (page 82)
- 4 garlic cloves, peeled
- 1 tablespoon *pimentón* (Spanish smoked paprika, hot or sweet), to taste

▶ Heat the oil in a saucepan over medium heat. Add the garlic and cook until golden brown. Remove the pan from the heat. Remove the garlic with a slotted spoon and discard. Stir in the paprika, and pour the oil into a glass or other nonreactive container. Store in a cool, dark place until ready to use.

Cacho de Cabra–Infused Oil

Ají de Color Chileno

The Mapuche Indians from southern Chile make a spicy flavoring and coloring by simmering smoked hot *cacho de cabra* peppers in lard or oil.

2   cups corn oil or freshly rendered lard (page 82)

6   *cacho de cabra* peppers (about 1¼ ounces) or New Mexican, Anaheim, or medium guajillo chiles, stemmed and cut into 3 pieces each

½   teaspoon salt

▶ Combine the oil, peppers, and salt in a small saucepan and bring to a gentle simmer over medium-low heat. Cook for 10 minutes. Let cool, then strain.

Storing: Store in a tightly sealed glass or stainless steel container until ready to use, for up to one month.

Uses: Use the infused oil to sauté seasoning vegetables and to add color and heat to Chilean dishes such as Cranberry Beans with Squash, Corn, and Green Beans (page 266).

BALANCING ACT: SOUR, SALTY, AND SWEET FLAVORINGS

Dona Flor, the heroine of Jorge Amado's novel *Dona Flor and Her Two Husbands* "had been born with a gift for seasoning" and grew up "sure-handed in her use of salt and sugar." Like the dash of acidity in my sauces that jolted the palate of Monsieur X, a seasoned assistant cook at the French Culinary Institute, those are the magic balancing tools that make things happen in our cooking, sometimes to the surprise of cooks from other traditions.

A good Latin cook knows that salt and sugar work together and instinctively uses a little salt to bring out the sweetness and full flavor of any dessert. In fact, a Latin woman who has just eaten one of your desserts might comment; "*Le falta un poquito de sal, verdad?* (It needs a bit of salt, right?)," rather than the expected "It needs more sugar." Sugar is one-dimensional without salt. Sweetness and sourness deepen each other in the same way.

Sweet-and-Sour Zing: Raisins, Capers, and Olives

The ingredients that Latins reach for when balancing sweet and sour are carefully chosen. In dishes with a strong Spanish influence, raisins are often the source of sweetness while pickled foods like capers and olives lend the critical note of tangy sharpness. From childhood on, Latins love pickled green olives. The distinctive sweet-and-sour zing of this beloved pairing is one you will become familiar with in many dishes, notably empanadas—when you bite into a traditional Latin empanada, whether it comes from an adobe oven in Chile or the northeast of Argentina or a frying pan in Cuba, you will always be jolted by the bright note of the olive-raisin combination.

Today olives are grown in Mexico, the highlands of Colombia in Villa de Leyva, the dry valleys of Peru, and the north of Chile, with groves as far south as Santiago, and across the Andes, in Córdoba and Mendoza. South American olives are gaining an international reputation and are now being imported into the United States. I am very fond of Peruvian Alfonso olives. Sold as *aceitunas de botija*, they are purple like Kalamata olives but much larger and softer. Spanish olives stuffed with pimientos are still an all-important ingredient for Latin American cooking sauces and are also widely used as a garnish.

Citrus Juices

Citrus juices, especially lime and Seville or bitter orange, are deeply fixed in the pantheon of Latin flavors.

SEVILLE OR BITTER ORANGE (*CITRUS AURANTIUM*)

For half a millennium, this native of Southeast Asia reigned supreme in European orchards, before being displaced by the sweet orange. Introduced into Spain by the Arabs in the eighth to tenth centuries and brought to Hispaniola by Columbus on his second voyage (1493), the Seville orange, *naranja agria*, was the first orange to become naturalized in the New World. The bitter orange is used throughout Latin America in desserts and as a seasoning, particularly in the Hispanic Caribbean and the Yucatán, where it is added to most *adobos* and *recados* (marinades). In Peru and Ecuador, it was the original acid medium for cebiches. Less sweet than the juice of ordinary oranges and less acidic than the juice of the Mexican lime, bitter orange juice adds balanced acidity and an incomparable flavor to any marinade.

The bitter orange is a forgiving fruit—when overripe, it becomes hollow and sickly looking, yet you can still use its juice in marinades. However, if you can find them, your best bet is to buy firm, slightly greenish Seville oranges (available year-round) and juice them when they are at their prime; the juice keeps well for about a week in the refrigerator.

The unique flavor of the aromatic juice is hard to duplicate. The rough, warty skin of the fruit is filled with oil glands while the pith of the fruit is deeply bitter. Some of the fragrant oil as well as some bitterness find their way into the juice. I find that the only close substitute is a careful blend of lime, grapefruit, and orange juice plus a small amount of grapefruit or sweet lime (*lima*) zest. When time is of the essence, you can use a mixture of lime and sweet orange juice in equal amounts.

LIME (*CITRUS AURANTIFOLIA, C. LATIFOLIA*)

Two kinds of lime are important in Latin American cooking. One is *Citrus aurantifolia*, the small, slightly pebble-skinned fruit commonly known as "Key lime" in the United States. In some parts of Latin America, it is often called *limón mexicano* or "Mexican lime" (*limón sutil* in Peru; *limón de Pica* in Chile), though it was originally an Indo-Malayan native brought to Hispaniola by the Spaniards on Columbus's second voyage. The color is greenish-yellow, lightening to yellow-green as the fruit matures.

More commercially important in this country is the larger, smoother, evenly green-skinned *C. latifolia*, which goes by several names, including "Persian lime" or "Tahitian lime." It lacks the intense aroma, bright acidity, and complex flavor that make the Mexican lime so highly appreciated in classical Latin drinks such as the daiquiri and *caipirinha*, and for other uses including cebiches or simply squeezing over fried fish, grilled foods, and soups as a table condiment. But the Persian lime is still excellent in its own right, and almost always to be preferred to lemon as the citrus note in most Latin American recipes. Unless otherwise noted, Persian lime is what is meant by "lime" in my recipes.

Vinegars

In the Latin kitchen, vinegar is the soul of many marinades, or *adobos*, such as that for *anticuchos*, the beef heart kebabs Peruvians like to grill over a charcoal fire, as well as of certain Peruvian stews that are also called *adobos*. It is an essential ingredient in escabeches, pickles (*encurtidos*), many spicy table sauces, and other savory dishes, and the classic seasoning for Central American chicken stews, of which *gallo en chicha* is the best known.

Open the cupboard in any Latin kitchen and you will probably find one or two commercial bottled vinegars: distilled white vinegar and cider or red wine vinegar. But if you look closely, you will inevitably come across a glass jar or clay pot in a warm spot on the kitchen counter or in a corner of the room, covered with a kitchen towel and filled with a cloudy liquid. Sniff and you will smell vinegar-in-process, put together from local ingredients: such as plantains or bananas (for Ecuadorian *vinagre de Guineo*, a specialty of the Manabí province), apples, or pineapple, or corn beer (*chicha*), or perhaps the juice extracted from yuca roots. Some of these vinegars are a bit crude, but they all have something in common. Fruity and full of flavor, they not only give foods a welcome touch of acidity but also help identify regional and national cuisines.

Salvadorian Pineapple Vinegar

Vinagre de Piña

Pineapple vinegar is a mild, sweet, and perfumed vinegar that adds an intense fruity flavor to the Salvadorian chicken stew called *gallo en chicha* (page 663). Salvadorians leave the mildly fermented pineapple drink called *chicha de piña* (page 337) in the pot for about 2 months to turn it into vinegar.

MAKES 2 CUPS (IF ALLOWED TO FERMENT FOR THE FULL 2 MONTHS)

- 3 pounds pineapple peel (from 2 medium pineapples of about 4 pounds each), well rinsed under cold running water
- 2 quarts water, or as needed
- 1 pound grated brown loaf sugar (preferably light *panela* or Salvadorian *dulce de atado*; see page 100) or dark Muscovado sugar, or to taste

▶ Place the pineapple peel and water in a 3-quart crock or glass jar. Cover with a clean cloth or kitchen towel, set in a moderately warm spot, and let ferment for 3 days. Once a day, skim off and discard the foam that forms on top of the liquid.

After 3 days, add the sugar and stir with a wooden spoon until completely dissolved. Cover again and let ferment undisturbed for 2 weeks.

Remove the cloth and taste the liquid. If you think it is too acidic, add more sugar as necessary. If some of the water has evaporated, replenish to the original level. Cover again and leave to continue fermenting. Ideally the vinegar should ferment for about 6 weeks longer (a total of 2 months), but it will be good enough to cook with after 2 more weeks.

When ready to use the vinegar, strain it though a double layer of cheesecloth.

Storing: Stored in a tightly sealed glass container in the refrigerator, the vinegar will keep for 1 to 2 months.

Uses: Use as you would cider vinegar.

Peruvian Sprouted-Corn Beer

Chicha de Jora

Several Andean nations—Ecuador, Bolivia, and Peru—make corn into a mildly alcoholic fermented drink called *chicha* that can be further fermented into a vinegar or left to mature for several years until it tastes like cherries (*chicha de año*). The basic ingredient for this ancient pre-Columbian brew that has remained popular until the present is corn kernels from dent corn. Cooks allow them to sprout, then dry them and grind them into a coarse meal. The dried sprouted corn is called *jora* or *maíz de jora*. *Chicha de jora* is one of the most versatile condiments I know, giving character to a number of fabulous northern Peruvian stews, or *adobos* and *secos*.

I fell in love with the distinctive molasses flavor of this drink when I visited northern Peru. When I returned to New Jersey, I missed it as much as a native Peruvian away from home. My local supermarket now sells dried *jora*, both whole and ground, so I started making my own *chicha*, far better than the kind that comes in a bottle. It is easy to make and keeps for months in the refrigerator. It is an essential condiment if you want to make authentic-tasting Peruvian dishes like Pork *Adobo* Cusco Style (page 749).

Cook's Notes: If you can only find whole *maíz de jora*, grind it to the consistency of a coarse meal in your food processor.

Reserve the sediment that remains in the bottom of the pot after straining the *chicha*. You can use it to make a sourdough starter for bread.

MAKES 9 CUPS

14 ounces (about 2 cups) ground *maíz de jora* (available in Hispanic markets)
  About 6 quarts water
9 ounces grated brown loaf sugar (preferably *chancaca* or *panela*), or about 1¼ cups packed dark Muscovado sugar or dark brown sugar

▶ Place the *maíz de jora* and 4 quarts of the water in a large heavy-bottomed pot and bring to a boil over medium-high heat. Reduce the heat to medium-low and simmer uncovered, stirring occasionally, for about 1½ hours. Replenish the pot with boiling water as it boils away.

Remove from the heat, add the sugar, and stir until completely dissolved. Strain into a 3-quart clay pot or glass jar. Cover with a clean towel and allow to ferment for 5 days in a moderately warm spot in your kitchen.

At the end of the fermentation period, strain the liquid through a fine strainer. The *chicha* is now ready to be drunk or to be used for cooking.

Storing: Stored tightly covered in the refrigerator, the *chicha* will keep for several months.

Uses: In Peru, *chicha de jora* is used as the essential cooking sauce for spicy stews (*secos*), for marinating meats, and to season Peruvian Rice with Duck (page 322).

OF PERUVIAN *CHICHA* AND LIZARDS

For years I have been fascinated by the expressive pottery of the Moche, a pre-Inca people who lived and thrived in northern Peru between A.D. 200 and 800. My first opportunity to learn more about their culture came in 2003, when I was invited to go to Huanchaco, a quaint fishing village not far from Trujillo, to learn about the Moche Foodways Archaeological Project led by Dr. George Gumerman IV, an archaeologist and the chair of the anthropology department at Northern Arizona University in Flagstaff.

At the time, Gumerman and his team were classifying the remains of daily life excavated earlier at various archaeological sites in the Moche and Chicama Valleys, the heartland of the Moche. Under their microscopes, I could see minuscule seeds, broken corncobs, fish and animal bones, pieces of seaweed, shell fragments, and paper-thin peanut shells—the stuff ancient people had discarded after their cooking, found in pre-Columbian garbage dumps, gravesites, and kitchens. Gumerman handled these seemingly insignificant objects like precious jewels.

Later, as I began to explore archaeological areas like El Brujo, which are still under excavation, I saw the remains of a Moche kitchen excavated by Gumerman, with big hearths and storage jars, not far from a large adobe-brick pyramid (*huaca*). The abundance of tiny corncobs all around it as well as the telling pottery fragments revealed that one of its functions was the making of *chicha* for the religious ceremonies performed at the *huaca*. This fizzy fermented brew was not only a staple drink and condiment for food, but a sacred libation for the dead.

Archaeologists view the size and complexity of pre-Colombian *chicha* kitchens (and food remains) as indicators of social and political organization. Highland *chicha* kitchens of the Inca period were huge industrial facilities to supply the needs of a politically centralized society. The Inca distributed *chicha* to the general population and to their armies as food. The smaller size of Moche kitchens and hearths and the more modest storage facilities for corn and *chicha* show that these communities were politically decentralized, with self-sufficient households enjoying a great level of independence.

The memory of the ancient kitchen I saw at El Brujo was alive in my mind the day I went lizard hunting at the tail end of my trip. Archaeologist César Gálvez, who has researched the history of reptile consumption in the region, took me to San Pedro de Lloc, in the province of Pacasmayo to the north, to meet Alfonso Tapia, a restaurateur of sorts who makes a living hunting lizards (*cañanes*) and cooking them for scores of devoted wild meat aficionados. I had visions of a lithe native hunter armed with a sling, but when I showed up at his house at the crack of dawn, I found a muscular *criollo* Rambo, dressed in camouflage fatigues and holding a scary rifle. We drove to a place called Las Ruinas and stopped our truck on the edge of a rice field. We continued on foot to reach an acacia grove where lizards live and feed on the trees' sweet pods. I knew we were near a *huaca*. Crunching beneath my feet were human bones and pottery shards, seashells, and minuscule corncobs dug out by looters.

As I knelt to examine the corn, a couple of *cañanes* scurried over the hot sand, seeking shelter under a spiny bush. Tapia got his rifle ready. With a single shot to the head, he killed one of the animals. He kept shooting lizards for our lunch, and I walked toward an earth mound nearby. On my way, I saw hundreds of tiny desiccated corncobs and large pieces of thick pottery blackened by fire, and I immediately knew these were the remains of a kitchen producing *chicha* to serve the ritual needs of a ceremonial center. Vicariously, I had become an archaeologist. ◆

Spicy Yuca Cooking Sauce

Tucupí

Tucupí is a vinegary condiment made out of fermented yuca juice used to season two traditional dishes from the state of Pará in the Brazilian Amazon, a duck dish called *pato no tucupí* and the soup *tacaçá*. *Tucupí* is the by-product of *farinha de mandioca*, a coarse yuca flour often used in Brazilian cooking. The recipe calls for a yellow variety of bitter yuca that contains a high percentage of poisonous hydrocyanic acid. To purge the yuca of this toxin, the tubers are grated and the pulp is packed into a long flexible reed cylinder called a *tipiti*, which is then twisted to extract the juice. The poison-free pulp is then spread out to dry on flat baskets or plantain leaves to be toasted into yuca flour (*farinha*; see page 152); the pale yellowish juice is poured into a pot and allowed to stand until a thick white sediment settles on the bottom. The sediment is tapioca (*polvilho azedo* in Brazil). The liquid is strained into another pot and boiled for several hours, until every trace of hydrocyanic acid has evaporated. Then the purified liquid is allowed to ferment lightly for 2 to 3 days, and the result is *tucupí*.

Since *tucupí* is difficult, if not impossible, to come by in the United States, I have been making my own version from the fresh nonpoisonous sweet yuca sold here in Caribbean markets. It renders a less flavorful juice, but it makes a good substitute for bitter yuca, which is not imported. To dye the juice the subtle yellow of the original, I doctor it up with a teaspoon of achiote. Learning to make it brought me closer to the elemental flavors of the jungle and heightened my respect for the versatile yuca. The spicy sauce is very good as a table sauce for fried fish and can be used in marinades and cooking sauces as you would vinegar.

MAKES 2½ CUPS

10 pounds yuca
  Pinch of salt
 1 teaspoon achiote seeds
 5 pickled Brazilian hot peppers (*pimentas de cheiro* or *cumari*, available in Brazilian markets) or 2 habaneros or Scotch bonnet peppers (see uses, below)

▶ Peel the yuca according to the directions on page 166 (it should yield a little less than 8½ pounds peeled). Cut into 1-inch chunks. Working in manageable batches, place in a food processor and pulse until finely ground, like a mush.

Cut two 16-inch squares of doubled cheesecloth. Place one-quarter of the grated yuca on the cheesecloth, fold the cloth over, and tie the ends tightly. Squeeze as much juice as you can from the grated yuca into a bowl. Repeat with the rest of the yuca, one-quarter at a time (if necessary, work with smaller batches to make it easier on your hands).

You can use the drained solids to make the flatbread called *casabe*. Pour the yuca juice into a 2-quart plastic or (more traditionally) earthenware container. Cover with a cloth and let stand overnight at room temperature.

The next day, you will see a white sediment in the bottom of the container—it is tapioca. Carefully, a little at a time, pour or spoon the liquid into a nonreactive saucepan, being sure not to disturb the tapioca. (The tapioca can be saved for baking or thickening custard. Remove it with a spoon and spread on a shallow dish to dry, then scrape into a small jar when completely dry.) Stir the salt and achiote seeds into the liquid, bring to a gentle boil, and cook, uncovered, until reduced by half. Strain the liquid through cheesecloth into a 1-quart container, preferably earthenware, and discard the achiote seeds.

Cover the container with plastic wrap or a kitchen towel and let the strained liquid stand overnight to ferment. You will see bubbles beginning to form on the surface of the liquid and it will be noticeably acidic (in Brazil, fermentation is carried on longer, but I prefer to stop at this stage).

Strain the liquid through a double layer of cheesecloth into a glass container. Stir in the peppers and refrigerate until ready to use. In a few hours, the peppers will start to do their fiery job. Taste the *tucupí* to judge the heat, and discard the peppers when the liquid has reached the level of hotness you like.

Storing: Store in the refrigerator for up to three weeks.

Uses: The amount of hot peppers can be adjusted according to taste and the intended use. *Tucupí* made with 5 pickled *pimentas de cheiro* is a very hot sauce even if the peppers are very small. It can be used sparingly to flavor stews and soups or as an unusual table sauce for freshwater fish.

STONES OF HONEY: BROWN LOAF SUGAR

Whenever I heard the Cuban singer Celia Cruz shout out "¡*Azúcar!*" I believed she was pulling from a substance that has deeper meaning in Latin America than the bags of Dixie Crystals and boxes of Domino cubes mourners carried in homage to her in New York when she died. For me, her "*azúcar*" meant sweetness with backbone, a deep sweetness that comes from within, qualities that define the large family of unrefined brown sugars that Latin Americans love so much: *piloncillo, panela, papelón, chancaca,* all the golden brown color of Celia's skin.

These brown sugars have more flavor and depth than the cloyingly sweet refined white sugar. In particular, the rustic, blistery solid blocks that look like fossils or meteorites offer sweetness with personality.

Their uses go beyond sweetening a morning cup of coffee or a flan. Brown loaf sugar is the Latin cook's secret weapon, the ingredient that gives our food, both savory and sweet, an elusive quality that keeps people guessing. In my kitchen, you will always find several types of these complex sugars—some are winey or spicy or deeply fruity; others taste like molasses. I use them to make limeades and syrups, to prepare fermented drinks, and to sweeten and flavor desserts. More often I cook with them as if they were spices to add depth, color, and texture to dishes as diverse as Caracan black beans, Colombian pot roast, and Venezuelan chicken and rice.

Adding sugar to savories as a seasoning is a technique that harks back to colonial cooking, and even farther back to medieval Spanish cooking. Because of its rarity, medieval cooks often considered sugar a spice. Even a cursory reading of fourteenth- to sixteenth-century Spanish cookbooks reveals numerous recipes for meat and chicken calling for sugar together with aromatic spices such as saffron, cloves, and cinnamon.

When the Spanish colonies in the Americas began to produce abundant sugar, starting in the sixteenth century, the use of sugar as a condiment began to wane in Europe—not so in the Americas. Unrefined brown sugar, a relic of the time before large industrialized sugar mills devoured the tropical lowlands, is still very much a part of Latin cooking, particularly in Venezuela, Colombia, and Mexico. Even today, Latin countries keep alive an artisanal sugar-making technology that the world's big sugar companies discarded more than a century ago. The tastiest of the brown loaf sugars of Latin America, the ones with a distinct fruity flavor, dark color, and coarse texture, are produced the old-fashioned way. Years ago, I spent days looking for artisanal *papelón* in western Venezuela. I found it almost by chance on a secluded farm high in the Venezuelan Andes, not far from Mérida. The column of smoke that rose behind the sugarcane field and the distinctive smell of sugarcane juice (*guarapo*) being boiled down over a wood fire drew me in. Under a palm-thatched roof, horses turned a rudimentary mill (*trapiche*) that crushed the sugarcane to extract its juice. Sweaty, weathered workers tended several burbling cauldrons nearby, and an old man seated on a tree stump unmolded dark cones of *papelón* that glistened under the sun.

The steps of turning sugarcane juice into sugar are more or less the same in all the producing regions. The unrefined sugarcane juice goes into a series of kettles for reduction through repeated boiling over a wood or coal fire. The molten sweet gold that emerges from the last boiling is beaten by hand until barely crystallized, then poured into molds called *panelas* or *papelones* to harden. When it has cooled, workers wrap the blocks of sugar, ranging in color from amber to dark muddy brown, in plantain leaves or husks.

However, not all versions have the same flavor. The manufacturing of brown loaf sugar has not been standardized, and consequently the sugars sold in Latin markets can look and taste very different, like local variations in some types of cheese. If you can, compare several kinds and brands. I find some popular light-colored Colombian *panela* sugars as flavorless for cooking as U.S. brown sugar (which is really refined white sugar dyed with some molasses). The authentic artisanal sugar jolts your palate with a deep molasses flavor that verges on a fruity acidity, but it is not at all bitter or harsh.

In recent visits to the Latin markets of my area, I have found several brands of grated light brown loaf sugar from Colombia and Brazil (where it is called *rapadura*). When I can't get the Latin stuff, I often use granulated dark Muscovado sugar from Mauritius, an island in the Indian Ocean, because I like its deep molasses flavor. For a lighter color and a less emphatic taste, I turn to Demerara sugar from Mauritius, which reminds me of Cuban granulated brown sugar (*azúcar parda*).

It is true that ordinary brown sugar is convenient and nonthreatening, while some unrefined sugars sold as solid blocks, particularly the large cylinders packaged like mummy bundles in corn husks, may inspire more fear than confidence. But try to see past their exterior, and experiment with them. Their layers of flavor will seduce you.

I have seen *panela* disks that come already

quartered, but cooking with brown loaf sugar usually involves the adventure of breaking up the hard loaf in order to measure the amount called for. If a recipe gives a cup measurement, the simplest thing is to grate the sugar on the fine side of a straight-sided grater (hence the name *raspadura*, or "filings"). If a certain weight is called for and you know the weight of the loaf you bought, you can chop it up with a cleaver or whack it into pieces with a hammer and make a "guesstimate" at the correct fraction (a little more or less usually won't matter

much). Or buy a *partidor de panela*, an inexpensive guillotine-like contraption available in Hispanic markets. In some cases, you may be able to sidestep the problem by simply dissolving a whole cake of sugar in a given amount of boiling water to make a simple syrup; this will keep well in the refrigerator for several weeks. At my restaurant Zafra, I always have both a simple brown loaf sugar syrup and a more complex, aromatic syrup we call *melado de panela* (page 101) to serve with yuca *churros*, sweet fritters, ice cream, and cheese.

LATIN LOAF SUGARS

These are some of the names under which Latin loaf sugar is sold. The color and flavor vary with the optional addition of a bleaching agent such as lime, the amount of impurities left in the reduced juice, and the type of sugarcane (purple varieties produce a darker product).

Panela: Panela is the most common term in Latin countries. The color may be tan, amber, or dark muddy brown. Most varieties of *panela* are molded in thickish disk shapes about 6 inches across, rounded on top and flat on the bottom, weighing about 1 pound (though there is no single standard). In this country, *panela* is usually sold wrapped in plastic. Rectangular or square blocks of unrefined brown sugar cut from larger rectan-

gular loaves are also called *panela*; they come wrapped in plastic wrap, plantain leaves, or corn husks or in cardboard packages.

Panela

Piloncillo (little pylon): In Mexico, *piloncillo* (little pylon) is the name for the cone-shaped sugar loaves called *panela* in many other countries. (In most of Mexico, *panela* refers to a kind of cheese). Two important producing areas are Veracruz and Oaxaca. The sugar is commonly sold in approximately half-pound cones or smaller ones about the size of a fat thumb. *Piloncillo* lends complex flavor and a dark color to Mexican favorites such as the pig-shaped cookies known as *marranitos*, *café de olla* (coffee boiled in a pot with cinnamon), and many *moles*.

Piloncillo

Panela

of guajillo chile and the fruitiness of ancho chile, both from the New World. Nuts and seeds give the mix body as well as round off the flavors. Individual cooks may vary the proportions slightly or choose another spice from the same basic palette, but every Salvadorian knows what to expect from a *relajo*.

When Latin cooks prepare a spice blend, the overriding consideration is that the spices reinforce each other harmoniously in the finished dish. Together they are more than the sum of their parts. You cannot indiscriminately replace any one spice with something else you happen to fancy, because you might destroy the balance. Like *adobos* and *sofritos*, spice blends carry the flavor code of a particular Latin cuisine.

Spices: A Little History

The quest for the spices of the Far East was one of the forces that fueled the great European voyages of discovery during the fifteenth century and ultimately drove Spaniards to the New World. Ironically, Spaniards were disappointed to discover few spices in the New World, though they recognized that the ones they found all have a penetrating quality that makes them stand out in any company of spices.

A sure way to date a Latin American dish is to look at the number of sweet spices in its composition. The older the dish, the heavier in spices, the headier and sweeter the aroma. During the colonial period, massive amounts of cloves, anise, saffron, cinnamon, black pepper, and cumin were imported from Spain. To this day, two areas of Latin America still exhibit a marvelous devotion to the Old World perfumed cooking (*cocina de perfume*): Mexico and Guatemala in Central America, and Peru in South America. But in many other areas, such as the Hispanic Caribbean, the nineteenth-century wars of independence and the influx of throngs of northern Spaniards, who used fewer spices in their cooking, caused the range of spices in savory dishes to decline and relegated sweet spices to the realm of desserts. Some of the sauces and marinades were gradually pared down to a few clusters of seasonings, like oregano and cumin.

New World Spices and Herbs

Allspice (*Pimenta dioica*): Allspice comes from a tropical tree related to myrtle that grows in the West Indies and Central America. The bark, leaves, and berries of the tree have a high content of fragrant pimento oil and are all used in cooking. The name allspice is expressive: allspice seems to bring together in one pinch the taste of cloves, cinnamon, nutmeg, and black pepper.

Allspice was first found by Columbus in Hispaniola (today the Dominican Republic and Haiti). Because the dried immature berries are small, round, and dark brown, the Spaniards confused them with black peppercorns and hence called the berry *pimienta* (pimiento). In parts of the Hispanic Caribbean, allspice is called the fat pepper (*pimienta gorda*). Because its aroma is so intense and complex, allspice was a favorite of colonial Mexican cooks, who called it *pimienta de Chiapas*. When I visited Peru, I heard cooks refer to it the same way, a usage that harks back to the seventeenth century.

Jamaica is the world's largest producer of allspice. Though Jamaican allspice berries are smaller than Mexican and Central American berries, they are highly prized for their more pronounced aroma.

Allspice is sold both ground and whole. Whenever possible, buy small amounts of whole, preferably Jamaican, berries and crush them to a powder in a mortar with a pestle or in an electric spice mill or coffee grinder just before you are ready to cook to capture their full aroma. Substitute allspice for black pepper in marinades (*adobos*) and cooking sauces (*sofritos*) for an interesting variation and greater complexity of flavor. When I want the taste of a cluster of aromatic spices from just one berry, I add a few whole allspice berries to soups and broths or infuse them in hot milk to make custards, flans, and hot chocolate. Since colonial times, allspice has been the flavoring of choice for hot chocolate in both the New World and Spain.

Store allspice in a tightly closed glass container away from heat or light. Discard once the berries lose their pronounced complex aroma.

Other names: *Yucatán and Guatemala, pimienta de Chiapas; Ecuador, pimienta de dulce; Venezuela, pimienta guayabita.*

Broad-leaf *culantro* (*Eryngium foetidum*) and cilantro (*Coriandrum sativum*): Cilantro is the only ingredient of Mediterranean origin that can stand up to the pungency of the New World hot pepper in a *sofrito*, *adobo*, or other sauce. Its New World relative, broad-leaf *culantro*, is equally assertive. These two herbs smell and taste similar but are not members of the same genus; they do not even look alike. *Culantro* has broad serrated leaves and grows wild in damp places throughout tropical America. Its taste is somewhat stronger than that of cilantro, and it has a coarser texture. Because it does not darken with prolonged heat as cilantro does, it is an ideal seasoning for soups and stews—dishes that require long cooking.

Culantro

Cilantro was brought to Spain by the Muslims and became very popular. In medieval Spanish cookbooks such as the fourteenth-century *Libre de Sent Soví*, there are sauce recipes that call for large amounts of fresh cilantro combined with saffron, black pepper, and vinegar. As the flavors of Spanish cuisine became tamer, however, probably through Italian or French influence, the strong-flavored cilantro gradually disappeared from the culinary lexicon. In fact, it is unusual to find cilantro in mainstream Iberian cooking today, except in the Canary Islands, some parts of Andalusia, and Portugal. However, cilantro flourished in the Spanish colonies of the New World precisely because colonial cuisine, an offshoot of Spanish medieval cooking, was also very strongly flavored.

Cilantro

Throughout Latin America, and often even in a single country, people use many terms for these two plants, sometimes interchangeably. Cilantro (*Coriandrum sativum*) is also called *cilantrillo, cilantrico, recado, recaíto, recadito, culantro de Cartagena,* and *culantrillo.* In Peru and Ecuador, it is always called *culantro,* as it was in medieval Spain. The broad-leaf *Eryngium foetidum* is also known as *culantrico, cilantro, cilantro ancho, recao, recado, acopate, hierba del sapo* (toad's herb), *cilantro sabanero,* and *chillangua* (in Ecuador's Esmeraldas province).

I am always on the lookout for mistaken identities, but I am often misled when trying to deci-

Papelón: Once so prized it was used as currency, the Venezuelan *papelón* is, in my opinion, the most flavorful of all unrefined brown sugars. It is not yet imported into the United States—but it is almost worth a trip to Venezuela. From the day I first tasted *papelón* in a Carúpano market on the Paria Peninsula, I have been a collector of this rare and precious sugar. *Papelón* is produced as a fine craft throughout the country, using an old-fashioned process. First the sugarcane is crushed in a rudimentary mill, the millstone often turned by horses or cattle, and then the juice is boiled in a series of five different kettles, each bearing its own name: *la tacha, la propia, la antorcha, el guarapo,* and *la balatería.* After the last boiling, the molten sugar traditionally was poured into large, beautiful clay or wooden molds that look like rusted old bells. They emerged as cones of sugar that resemble sparkling granite, with a deep, rich, winey molasses scent. Today *papelón* is

Papelón

more commonly found in square blocks. Because some people don't like the dark color, the sugar artisans often add lime to the last cauldron, which makes a lighter, honey-colored sugar.

Dulce de atado

Dulce de atado: *Dulce de atado* is a Salvadorian variety of unrefined sugar that is sold as stubby cylinders weighing about 1¾ pounds, tied up in corn husks.

Chancaca: *Chancaca* is the dark brown loaf sugar of Peru, Bolivia, and Chile. Like *panela*, it can be round or square. A dark molasseslike syrup made from *chancaca* is called *miel de chancaca* and is served like maple syrup for pillowy fritters such as the Chilean pumpkin *sopaipillas* and the doughnut-shaped Peruvian *picarones*. ◈

Simple Brown Loaf Sugar Syrup

Miel (Melado) de Panela

In brown loaf sugar territory, cooks always keep some of this syrup on hand for various cooking uses.

MAKES 1 CUP

- 8 ounces *panela*, chopped or broken into small pieces
- 1 cup water

▶ Combine the *panela* and water in a small saucepan and bring to a gentle simmer over medium heat. Cook, stirring occasionally, for about 15 minutes, until the syrup coats the back of a spoon. Allow to cool, then pour into a glass or plastic container. Store, tightly covered, in the refrigerator.

COOKING WITH CHEESE

Latins love cheese, as a snack, in sandwiches, to round off flavors, and to crumble into soups or over beans. They also love to cook with cheese. In some countries, a sharp cheese garnish completes the flavoring of a savory dish. For instance, Mexicans grate hard aged *cotija* (an aged cow's-milk cheese) over black beans, creating a contrast between tangy cheese and earthy beans. In Mexico, there are also a number of dishes in which softer melting cheeses are more substantial players, as in *enchiladas suizas*. In Mexico and Central America, vegetables such as breadfruit, chayotes, potatoes, and yuca are often cooked with rich white sauces and melting cheeses.

In the Hispanic Caribbean, salty fresh cheese, *queso blanco* (literally, white cheese), is eaten alone as a snack or as a complement to sweet fruit desserts such as guava and orange shells in syrup. In Peru, you find fresh cheese used in savory dishes. Both the *ocopa arequipeña* and *ají de gallina* (pages 379 and 671) involve sauces made with *queso fresco* (fresh cheese) and thickened with bread and nuts.

Paraguay has two popular cheeses: *queso menonita* (Mennonite cheese) and *queso paraguay* (also spelled *paraguai*). *Queso menonita* is more expensive and has the texture and flavor of Muenster. It is usually eaten sliced as an accompaniment to very sweet fruits cooked in syrup. *Queso paraguay* is the country's quintessential cooking cheese and is used in large amounts to make the yuca flour breads called *chipas*, as well as the famous local corn bread, *sopa paraguaya*.

In Brazil, Minas Gerais produces European-style cheeses of good quality and also makes its own queijo mineiro, a delicious white cheese. Aged dry *queijo mineiro*, which tastes a bit like Parmesan, is used in the *pão de queijo*, a delightful cheese and yuca bread.

My favorite Latin cow's-milk cheeses are the Venezuelan ones: the intense cured *queso llanero* (cheese of the plains), which I love to sprinkle over black beans, and *queso de mano*, from the Orinoco Basin, near Puerto Ordaz, which has to be eaten fresh. This soft and creamy cheese is artisanally made with *cuajo*, calf's rennet. The soft curd is heated like mozzarella, skillfully stretched by hand into a thin film, folded into layers, and punched down to shape. There's nothing like a slice of *queso de mano* sandwiched in a hot *cachapa*, the Venezuelan fresh corn griddle cake.

All over Latin America you also find soft, sweet-tasting, fresh homemade cheese. Straight from rural Spain, where it is called *requesón* or *requeixon*, this cheese is made with no fuss. For setting the cheese, people use earthenware pots, which provide a friendly environment for bacteria, and add some fresh *cuajo* or store-bought rennet to the milk. In the Ecuadorian sierra, homemade cow's-milk cheese curdled this way is called *quesillo* and is liberally added to soups such as potato *locro* and every vegetable dish. You find the same uses of fresh cheese in Peru and Bolivia. Costa Ricans call their version *cuajada* (curd), and they eat it for breakfast together with the rice and bean mix known as *gallo pinto*. *Cuajada* is also the name in Colombia, where the same dish is a specialty of the province of Cundinamarca.

In the Hispanic Caribbean and parts of Mexico, many cheeses are curdled not with rennet but with a combination of acid and heat—the same principle as for Indian paneer—and the cheese is then pressed to make it firmer. This method produces a cheese that does not appeal to North American cheese lovers because it often verges on the rubbery and has little taste. However, it is much appreciated in Cuba, Puerto Rico, and the Dominican Republic. In this country, you will find innumerable versions under the name of *queso blanco* or *queso fresco*. Unlike cheeses coagulated by the dual action of bacteria and rennet, they remain firm in cooking instead of melting when heated, which, to aficionados, is part of their appeal. A low-moisture type of *queso blanco* known as *queso de freír*, is used for panfrying.

The Andean versions of *queso blanco* and *queso fresco* are another story. Unlike their Caribbean counterparts, they are full of flavor and texture, and they melt into sauces. I have not found them for sale in this country, but after much experimentation have decided that the best substitute is sheep's-milk feta from France; other fetas are too salty.

Besides the "home-grown" cheeses, certain European cheeses play a crucial role in Latin cuisines, precisely because these do melt in cooking: Emmenthal, Gruyère, Roquefort, Parmigiano-Reggiano, Muenster, and taste-alikes such as Monterey Jack. In my own cooking, I have come to prefer the complex, nutty-flavored French Comté in most dishes that call for Emmenthal or Gruyère. Domestic versions of the major European cheeses are also made in many Latin countries, especially Argentina. They are usually blander and less interesting than the originals, but they are popular because of their relatively low price.

Dutch cheeses such as Gouda and Edam occupy a special place in Latin cooking. They have been perennial favorites throughout the Caribbean Basin since colonial times. Like year-round Christmas ornaments with their red wax coating and festive cellophane wrapping, wheels of Gouda and melon-shaped Edam cheeses brighten the sparse cheese sections of Latin markets in the United States. These classic cheeses have as much a right to be there as the craggy slabs of *queso blanco* and the handful of other European cheeses we have adopted.

True, Gouda and Edam are not the most complex or flavorful of European cheeses. But Latins love them precisely for their straightforward "cheesiness," for their saltiness and subtle tangy notes, and for the easy way they blend with our sweet fruit confections and heavily seasoned savory foods. Most of all, we love them because they have been with us for so long. The two cheeses first made their way to Latin America on Spanish ships when Spain, under the Hapsburgs, controlled parts of the Low Countries (today's Belgium and the Netherlands), from the sixteenth to the early eighteenth centuries. In the early seventeenth century, the Dutch established their own commercial outposts in the Caribbean and carried on a lively illegal trade with lands under Spanish control, from Venezuela to the Yucatán. In those areas today, you will find recipes for stuffed Edam or Gouda in which the cheese is hollowed out, filled with a savory stuffing of pork, seafood, chicken, or pasta, and steamed or roasted until it softens. The typical Venezuelan stuffing is made with pork seasoned with *ají dulce*, Worcestershire sauce, and the sweet-and-sour counterpoint of brown loaf sugar, raisins, and olives. At home, I prepare a pared-down version similar to a gratin, and I always try to get my hands on a raw-milk Gouda (Boerenkaas) or a blend of young Gouda and an aged one for it. Gouda aged three or four years has superb flavor with winey notes and nutty sweetness, and it also forms a delicious crust when broiled. Gouda Parrano is also worth exploring. Relatively new on the U.S. market, this cheese has the creaminess of a traditional young Gouda and the nutty, cooked-milk flavor of Parmigiano. While supermarket Gouda may seem good enough when drowned in the syrup of canned guava shells, it is a step forward in our growth as cooks when we seek out greater complexity in the foods we love.

In today's Latin markets, all things Spanish seem to have acquired a particular cachet. You now find fine Spanish cheeses such as the sheep's-milk Manchego and the cow's-milk *tetilla*, from Galicia. When buying Manchego, to be sure you are getting the real thing, look beyond the traditional herringbone pattern on the rind, and search for the numbered commercial seal of approval of the Consejo Regulador de la Denominación de Origen Queso Manchego (which every true Manchego cheese must bear) and a seal stating that the cheese is made with Manchega ewe's milk. Young Manchego, with a minimum of sixty days ripening, is labeled *fresco*. Manchego aged for about six months is *semicurado* (semicured), and that aged from six months to one year is *curado*. Older cheeses, aged for more than sixteen months, are called *añejo* (aged).

Like a well-structured wine that has been aged to reach its full potential, an *añejo* Manchego is usually the most complex, with a drier texture and a more emphatic brininess and pungency. At any age, however, the cheese is a pleaser. When young or semicured, it is terrific in sandwiches and in filling for croquettes. An aged Manchego comes close in pungency to a good Parmigiano-Reggiano and it is delicious by itself as a tapa with some crusty bread. Aged Manchego is also a versatile cooking cheese. At my restaurant Zafra, we sprinkle it over *piquillo* peppers in a vanilla chipotle sauce and run them under the broiler to make a flavorful crust. At Cucharamama, I top our serrano ham pizzas and flatbreads with a mixture of grated aged Manchego and Parmigiano-Reggiano, spiced with ground Andean peppers. There is no more luxurious seasoning for bread.

No discussion of Latin American cheese preferences is complete without a mention of that great Latin cheese Filadelfia. That's right—Philadelphia cream cheese. People eat the American version when they can get it, but knockoffs are manufactured in many parts of Latin America. Cream cheese has a hundred uses: it is a sandwich spread, a mixer for dips, a flavoring and thickener for flans, and a filling for empanadas and even chickpea tamales in Peru. But its favorite use is in pairings with tropical fruits cooked in syrup and fruit pastes such as *pasta de guayaba* (guava paste).

Madrid's Fresh Cheese

Cuajada de Madrid

In the town of Madrid in the Colombian highlands, fresh cheese is sold in bakeries by the pound. People take it home to eat drizzled with honey or *miel* (*melado*) *de panela* (page 101), a thick syrup made with Colombian brown loaf sugar and water, or to crumble into soups.

Many people keep a special earthenware pot in which they make this cheese over and over until it is impregnated with the right bacteria. Then the cheese will coagulate from the natural bacteria in the pot without the help of any starter.

Here I follow a more reliable method, which involves heating the milk and adding some rennet. You stir the rennet into the milk, leave the pot in a warm place where the temperature remains constant, and go to sleep, and the next morning you have a sweet-tasting, delicate cheese with no hint of sourness. Serve this fresh cheese for dessert, as the people from Madrid do, or crumble it over a steamy Andean soup (page 522).

Cook's Note: I recommend Junket brand rennet because it is standardized and widely available. You can also use this recipe as the starting point for the ubiquitous *suero blanco* of the Manabí province in Ecuador (page 147).

MAKES 1 POUND

- ¼ tablet plain Junket brand rennet, crushed to a powder
- ¼ cup water or whole milk
- 1 gallon whole milk
- ½ teaspoon salt, or to taste

▶ Dissolve the rennet in the ¼ cup water or milk; set aside. Pour the gallon of milk into a pot and heat gently to a temperature of 80°F to 85°F. Remove from the heat and immediately stir in the dissolved rennet.

Pour the milk into a 5-quart earthenware pot (mine is 6 inches tall and 9 inches in diameter) or a Spanish earthenware *cazuela* or other nonreactive container. Cover with cheesecloth and let sit completely undisturbed overnight in a place with a constant temperature (I always put my pot on top of a kitchen bookcase, where the temperature remains at 77°F). Twenty-four hours later, the cheese should be coagulated, looking like a very thick yogurt.

Place a colander over a large bowl and line with a double layer of cheesecloth. Very gently ladle the curd into the cheesecloth, and let drain for 2 to 3 hours.

Gather up the edges of the cheesecloth and bring together to make a bag, and twist the gathered edges lightly to squeeze out more of the whey; reserve the whey for spicy sauces or to make Ecuadorian *suero blanco*. If you are interested in getting the last drop of whey—I always am—tie the cheesecloth bag up with kitchen twine and suspend it from the kitchen faucet over another bowl; let drain for another hour or two.

When the cheese is firm enough to be molded, turn it into a bowl and work in the salt with your hands or a wooden spoon.

To shape the cheese, line a round 6- to 8-inch earthenware *cazuela* with a large square of sterilized cheesecloth. Pack the cheese into it, then bring the edges of the cloth up over to cover the cheese. Refrigerate for a couple of hours. (You can also shape the cheese into a thick log—which makes slicing easier—and wrap it tightly in cheesecloth until set, or you can mold the cheese in a soufflé or baking dish.)

To serve, unwrap the cheese and invert the *cazuela* onto a plate, or simply gather up the edges of the cheesecloth and lift the cheese out of the bowl and onto a serving plate.

Storing: A fresh cheese that is not heavily salted should be used within 2 or 3 days. Store it in the refrigerator, loosely covered with plastic wrap.

Uses: Crumble into Quito's Potato and Cheese Soup (page 522) or stir into Shrimp in Spicy Peruvian Pepper Sauce (page 760) or Peruvian Walnut–Mirasol Pepper Sauce (page 128).

LATIN UMAMI

In the last few years, cooks from every corner of the earth have begun exploring the concept of umami—the fifth essence or flavoring principle embodied in such foods as Japanese dried bonito flakes, some seaweeds and mushrooms, and various kinds of fermented products. (It is also what is behind the flavoring effect of monosodium glutamate.) *Umami* refers to a savory taste sensation that lends depth to a dish. Wherever you have certain kinds of protein breakdown, umami is the result, and it is now known that our tongue has specialized receptors to detect it.

This savory sensation has always been highly valued in Latin America. Today Latin Americans often resort to the MSG bottle (Ajinomoto brand) to achieve it, but there are many other sources in traditional Latin cooking. Ingredients such as dried or smoked shrimp and dried salted fish of many varieties, such as mackerel and salt cod, carry umami. So do several fermented products. Some—for example, aged cheeses, hams, and other cured meats—are not uniquely Latin, but they feature strongly in the family of Latin flavorings. Others are of true pre-Columbian ancestry, such as the *chicha* brewed from sprouted corn and used widely as a seasoning in the Andean region, or the vinegary *tucupí* from the Brazilian Amazon. I believe that the nixtamalized corn of Mexico and Andean freeze-dried potatoes also possess this quality.

Now that I understand how crucial umami is to Latin cooking, my attitude toward seasoning has become more complex. I recognize that ingredients I once used only as light footnotes deserve more prominence. Thus I no longer try to make dried shrimp more delicate by removing the heads or to play down its importance by listing it as an optional ingredient. There are times where an ingredient that might be disconcerting at first as too strong, fishy, or overly ripe must be allowed to play its proper part in the dance of flavors of the Latin kitchen.

CHAPTER 4

TABLE CONDIMENTS

IN THIS CHAPTER

At the Latin table, condiments are the flourishes that add the final layer of taste to a cook's creation. These are not optional accouterments but things as basic to Latin eating as soy sauce is to certain Asian cuisines. A squirt of biting-hot Venezuelan milk and pepper sauce over a plate of fried river fish or a dollop of silky cultured cream stirred into black beans or spooned over an *arepa* hot from the griddle elevates the dish from tasty to the sublime. A similar thing happens with many Latin foods that might seem bland if eaten alone. When yuca is given a jolt with Cuban garlic-citrus sauce, it comes alive. When the combination of Ecuadorian hominy (*mote*), morsels of fried pork, and a golden potato patty is topped with a refreshing salsa of onion, tomatoes, and crisp lettuce, the humble boiled hominy is transformed into a star playing to the full range of the palate. These table condiments add zest and variety to the experience of a meal, allowing the diner to adjust textures and turn the heat up or down with a sprinkling of this, a spoonful of that. Latins are great improvisers, believers in seat-of-the-pants adjustments that allow for spontaneity and individual preference. What this also shows is again the Latin penchant for building layers of flavor instead of trying to fuse various flavors into an indivisible whole.

Some finishing touches are already on the serving plates with the cooked dishes. Diners might combine a bite of grilled steak with shredded lettuce, raw slices of onion, and chunks of avocado. If a diner feels a touch of acidity is missing, he'll reach for the lime wedge on the plate. Such raw garnishes are never just window dressing. They are classic accompaniments that provide textural contrast, aromatic lift, and/or tartness. In this category, we also can include acidified vegetables such as cabbage slaws and hot peppers pickled in vinegar.

Latins also love to add starchy condiments as a last touch, some of which may come as a surprise: popcorn, for example. A bowl of popped *canguil* (the name of a particularly valued strain of corn) is the traditional accompaniment to Ecuadorian cebiches. It's a perfect instance of the Latin fondness for juxtaposing contrasting textures. Perhaps the most unusual of the starchy condiments is the *farofa* of Brazil, made from yuca. The meal or flour (*farinha*) that results when grated yuca is thoroughly dried, crumbled, and sifted is used as a topping or binder, not unlike roasted ground rice in Thailand or Cambodia or toasted breadcrumbs in parts of Italy. For use as a table condiment, the flour is usually toasted (commercially or at home) to bring out its flavor, and it may also be briefly cooked in butter or *dendê* oil (the reddish oil from an African palm), or with any manner of seasonings. After such treatments, *farinha* acquires the name *farofa*, ready to be sprinkled on food.

Unexpected to some people is the Latin taste for sour cream—not the U.S. supermarket kind, but a variety of rich cultured cream that add a beautiful touch of smoothness and subtle acidity. Mexicans serve their cultured cream with all kinds of dishes, from enchiladas to refried beans, while other Central Americans put similar creams on fried plantains or grilled beef. Venezuelans have a light version, *suero*, made from whole milk—traditionally ripened in a gourd—that is both a popular drink and a multipurpose topping or sauce base, as well as one called *nata* that is more or less identical to Mexican cultured cream. In this country, Latin markets sell commercial versions of Mexican cream (*crema mexicana*) and Central American cream (*crema centroamericana*), but making them yourself will give you a fresh and delicious cream without the chemical stabilizers and preservatives that go into most of the commercial products.

Other essential and familiar Latin condiments are the table sauces, particularly the hot pepper–laced salsas of Mexico, Central America, and South America. But before you turn to the recipes, I would like to caution you that I often see North Americans reaching for the hot sauce when, frankly, it's not appropriate for the food. Our table sauces, a subject big enough for a whole book in their own right, are one of the real glories of Latin cuisine, but they aren't all intended to turn up the heat. In fact, they're as varied as the people who make them, not just variations on the hit tune of salsa.

Everyone in North America knows the word "salsa," but I think understanding may lag behind its popularity. Let me explain: salsa is actually the Spanish term for any kind of sauce, from béchamel to mayonnaise to bottled Worcestershire (salsa inglesa) to pico de gallo. When Americans started using the word in the 1980s, they generally thought that it referred only to the slightly chunky table sauces served in Southwestern and Mexican restaurants. Although this isn't the whole of the Latin table sauce story, it is actually a good place to start exploring the subject—as long as you realize that the salsa craze in this county has produced some creations totally unrelated to anything a Latin cook would bring to the table for any purpose.

The best known of the Latin table sauces is the Mexican and Central American salsa cruda, or pico de gallo, a simple uncooked mix of chopped tomatoes, onion, cilantro, fresh hot chiles, salt, an acid such as lime juice or vinegar, and perhaps a little oil, served at room temperature. To me this kind of salsa almost resembles a little garnish of fresh salad, recalling that the words "sauce" and "salad" (in Spanish, salsa and ensalada) are really cousins; both go back to the Latin sal, meaning "salt" in the extended sense of something lending relish or zest.

A fresh Mexican salsa like this is also a beautiful example of how American ingredients went through a period of acculturation in Spain and came back to these shores with a Mediterranean accent. A late-seventeenth-century recipe for Spanish-style tomato sauce in Antonio Latini's Lo scalco alla moderna (The Modern Steward), published in Naples (which was then ruled by Spain), sounds amazingly like a modern salsa cruda. There are a few deviations, but most of them, like roasting the tomatoes in embers, are actually found in some of today's Mexican versions. Many of the simple Latin table sauces and salsitas ("little sauces," which are usually very hot and served in a bottle) still have a hint or more of Mediterranean origins.

Americans' enthusiasm for fiery salsas tends to blind them to the fact that a table sauce doesn't even have to be called a salsa. Many go by other names. In Central America and parts of Mexico, there is a family of sauces called chirmoles, whose name comes from the same word as "chile." In the same way, the ajíes of the Andes and parts of the Caribbean are called by the local name for hot peppers. They can be thin and light, like the excellent Venezuelan milk ají, or rich and creamy from a thickening of pureed nuts, cheese, or bread. Going south, we encounter the Chilean pebres (the name comes from the black pepper that was used to spice medieval sauces in Spain) and the mildly spicy chimichurris of Argentina and Uruguay, with their powerfully Mediterranean combinations of oil, vinegar, parsley, and garlic. In and around the Caribbean, the dominant table sauces are the mojos, best known in this country through Cuban versions fragrant with garlic and bitter orange juice.

These splendid condiments certainly don't exhaust the list of important Latin table sauces and dips. Today everyone knows guacamole, the Mexican mashed avocado sauce, but few Americans have discovered *guasacaca*, the Venezuelan cousin made with the more delicate-textured West Indian avocado. And sauces of the mayonnaise type are not only a favorite dressing for some kinds of salad but also a popular form of dip or table condiment.

Latin American table sauces are usually based on a fairly narrow, though vivid, palette of flavors. Their natural ability to wake up other foods usually starts with a combination of heat and acidity. There are important sauces that have neither, but in the ones closest to native originals, heat (from hot peppers) and acidity (from tomatoes, tomatillos, tart fruits, or the juices from fermented starchy vegetables) predominate. The Spanish conquerors eventually added other forms of heat (black pepper) and acidity (vinegar or citrus juice), along with different garlic-onion relatives, making more nuances possible. Herbs both native (*huacatay, quillquiña, culantro*) and Mediterranean (cilantro, parsley, oregano) allow even richer, more subtle interplays. But today's table salsas still tend to be strong, simple, and direct blends of a few basic elements.

While table salsas belong on the table, as the crowning touch that will be added according to each person's taste, they are also invaluable cooking resources that belong in your pantry or refrigerator as you learn the Latin art of improvisation. I always have jars of several table sauces on hand in my home kitchen and at my restaurants; I find Chilean *pebre* and the Cuban garlic-citrus *mojo* to be the most versatile. Start experimenting and you will be forever grateful, because they are incredibly full of flavoring potential for all kinds of cooking. To take just one example, a little Chilean *pebre* can be rubbed over chicken cutlets for a great quick marinade, brushed on grilled meats as a basting sauce, stirred into a pot of beans for a sudden flavor transformation, or used as a dressing on vegetable salads and side dishes. Having an assortment of such sauces on hand means an advance start on that complex layering of flavors, that instinctive adjustment of delicate balances between salt-sweet-acid-heat-spice that is so central to Latin American cooking.

In this chapter, you will find the full range of Latin American condiments, organized into broad categories: table sauces, relishes, and condiments such as toasted corn. I have divided each category into families that share common elements or are known by a common name in several regions of Latin America: for example, the chile-spiked salsas and *chirmoles* of Mexico and Central America; the *ajíes* of Ecuador, Colombia, and Venezuela; the creamy sauces of the Andes; the Mediterranean-inspired *pebres* and chimichurris of Argentina and Chile; the *mojos* of the Hispanic Caribbean; and the ripened creams of Mexico, Central America, and Venezuela.

SPICY HOT PEPPER SALSAS AND *CHIRMOLES*

The first settlers in New Spain (Mexico) learned how to cook with tomatoes from the Aztecs, who used them abundantly in stews and sauces. With the constant movement of people and foods from Spain to its colonies and back, tomatoes found their way to Spain, but it took Spaniards more than two centuries to lose their fear of being poisoned by them. When the Old World cooks discovered the tomato's goodness and versatility, they developed recipes for it using onions, vinegar, parsley, and olive oil. The recipes then traveled back to Mexico and other parts of the Americas, where they were enriched with the addition of hot pepper and became the basis of the different sauces that are typical of Latin American cooking.

Chunky Tomato Salsa, or "Rooster's Beak"

Salsa Cruda, o "Pico de Gallo"

Some version of this simple sauce appears on every table in Mexico and in most of Central America. Learn to make it and you will always have a fast all-purpose condiment to set off all kinds of dishes. It is also a great teaching device for showing how just a few basic elements affect each other, a mini-lesson in how Latins can vary and play with just a few flavors. The rock-bottom ingredients are ripe tomatoes, onion, fresh chile peppers, and cilantro. First make the sauce using just these. Then see how it tastes as you add other ingredients one at a time—vinegar or orange juice, oil, oregano, cumin. It will be equally good but slightly different at every stage.

MAKES ABOUT 1 CUP

 2 very ripe medium globe tomatoes (about 13 ounces)
 1 small white onion (about 5 ounces), peeled
 2–3 jalapeños, or to taste, seeded if desired
 10–12 cilantro sprigs, leaves stripped from stems (about ⅓ cup)
 ⅓ cup distilled white vinegar or ¼ cup fresh orange juice, or to taste
 ¼ cup extra-virgin olive oil, or to taste
 About 1 teaspoon dried oregano
 Pinch of ground cumin
 Salt to taste

▶ With a large sharp knife, finely chop the tomatoes. Scoop them and their juices into a bowl. (Do not try making the salsa in a blender or food processor—the hand-chopped texture is what you want.) Finely chop the onion, chiles, and cilantro and add to the tomatoes. Taste the salsa and begin adding the other ingredients, one at a time and a little at a time, mixing well and tasting often to register the different balances of acid, heat, herbal quality, and oil. Feel free to vary the proportions as you discover what you like. Serve as soon as possible (do not refrigerate). The fresh aromatic quality of the salsa lasts only a few hours.

Green Tomatillo-Chile Salsa

Salsa Verde

Two large tomatillos and a *tomatillo de milpa*

There is nothing like a green tomatillo and chile salsa or tomato salsa prepared in a *molcajete* (see page 33). The ingredients are bruised, not pureed, releasing their essential oils but leaving them with enough texture to make a difference.

This recipe is the quintessential green tomatillo salsa, the peerless condiment that gives a jolt of fragrant acidity and heat to any Mexican dish. One taste of this salsa made in a *molcajete* turned me into a convert. If you must use a blender or food processor, process the ingredients with quick pulses. Just make sure to leave the sauce with some texture.

Cook's Note: The tomatillo, or *miltomate* (*Physalis ixocarpa*), is as important as the tomato in the cooking of some Central American regions. As sold in markets and supermarkets, tomatillos are covered with a waxy green or papery husk, under which they look just like green tomatoes. Tomatillos go by many names, and are prized for a herbal acidity that brightens the flavor of many sauces while lending them body. In Guatemala, many cooks prefer *P. philadelphica*, a tiny and very sharp-flavored cousin, often wild and with a purplish hue, which they call *tomate de milpa* or *tomatillo de milpa; milpa* being the name for a small plot of ground planted with an intricate polyculture of corn and other vegetables.

MAKES 1½ CUPS

6 medium tomatillos (about 9 ounces), husked and rinsed

2 serrano chiles, stemmed

2 large garlic cloves

¾ teaspoon salt

¼ cup cilantro leaves

¼ cup water

▶ Heat a *comal*, griddle, or heavy skillet over medium-high heat until a few drops of water sprinkled onto the hot surface of the pan seem to dance before evaporating. Add the tomatillos and roast for 7 minutes, turning occasionally with tongs. Add the serranos and roast, turning occasionally, until both the tomatillos and the chiles are lightly charred, about 3 more minutes. Lift the tomatillos and serranos onto a plate and set aside.

Place the garlic and salt in the *molcajete* and mash the garlic to a pulp, using a grinding motion. Add the cilantro and serranos and grind to a coarse pulp. Cut the tomatillos into quarters, add to the *molcajete* in 2 batches, and grind to a coarse pulp. Add the water and stir to combine. The salsa is best served on the same day, but it can be kept covered tightly and refrigerated for 2 to 3 days. Serve straight from the *molcajete*.

Tomato and Serrano Chile Salsa

Salsa Roja de Molcajete (o de Jitomate)

This zesty *salsa roja de molcajete*, as many Mexicans call this fresh tomato salsa spiced up with serrano chiles, is a favorite for tacos. As with any salsa prepared in a *molcajete*, it has an appealing chunky texture. It also makes a wonderful cooking sauce for scrambled eggs. If you must use a blender or food processor, process the ingredients with quick pulses. Make sure to leave the sauce with texture.

MAKES 1¾ CUPS

> 4 very ripe medium plum tomatoes (about 12 ounces)
> 2 serrano chiles, stemmed
> 2 large garlic cloves
> ½ teaspoon salt
> 1 tablespoon cilantro leaves
> ¼–½ cup water

▶ Heat a *comal*, griddle, or heavy skillet over medium-high heat until a few drops of water sprinkled onto the hot surface of the pan seem to dance before evaporating. Add the tomatoes and roast for 10 minutes, turning occasionally with tongs. Add the serranos and roast, turning occasionally, until both the tomatoes and the chiles are lightly charred, about 3 more minutes. Lift the tomatoes and serranos out of the pan and set aside.

Place the garlic and salt in the *molcajete* and mash the garlic to a pulp, using a grinding motion. Add the cilantro and serranos and grind to a pulp. Cut the tomatoes into eighths, add to the *molcajete* in 2 or 3 batches, and grind to a coarse pulp. Add the water and stir to combine. Serve directly from the *molcajete*. It is best used on the same day.

"Tree Garlic" Salsa

Salsa de Guaje

This simple green salsa is made with *guaje*, the seeds of a tree native to Mexico and Central America. The small seeds, which are soft and green with a subtle garlicky taste, are encapsulated in long, flat pods. On a visit to the small town of Huexca, in the state of Morelos, I found *guaje* trees growing wild in the fields around town and stacks of *guaje* pods tied in bundles in every market.

Mexicans often eat *guaje* seeds raw as a snack or a fresh accompaniment to tacos, but they also add them to such foods as the tasty *huasmole* of Puebla, a kind of stew, or make them into salsas such as this one.

Cook's Notes: *Guaje* is available year-round in Latin markets catering to Mexicans. When buying it, select fresh-looking, unblemished reddish green or green pods. As *guaje* dries out, the seeds begin to harden and lose their garlicky flavor and spring green color.

If not using a *molcajete*, make sure to grind the ingredients coarsely.

MAKES 1½ CUPS

> 2 serrano chiles
> 1 pound fresh *guaje* (about 80 pods), shelled (about 1¼ cups seeds)
> ½ teaspoon salt, or to taste
> 1 cup water

▶ Heat a *comal*, griddle, or heavy skillet over medium-high heat until a few drops of water sprinkled onto the hot surface of the pan seem to dance before evaporating. Add the chiles and roast, turning occasionally with tongs, until lightly charred all over, about 3 minutes. Transfer to a plate and set aside.

Place ¼ cup of the *guaje* seeds in a *molcajete* and mash to a coarse pulp, using a grinding motion. Add the serrano peppers, salt, and another ¼ cup of the *guaje* seeds and grind the seeds and chiles into a coarse paste. Repeat the process, adding the rest of the *guaje* seeds in small batches. Add the water and stir to combine. Taste for salt, and serve straight from the *molcajete* or in a rustic bowl. It is best eaten right away.

"Finger Sauce"

Salsa de Dedo

On my first trip to Guadalajara in Mexico, I was given the royal treatment by the family of my friend Lourdes (Lulu) Verea. One of the highlights of the visit was a surprise *taquisa* (taco party) prepared by cooks hired from a nearby *taquería*. They brought dozens of appetizing sauces with them, but none compared with the one Lulu made with a generous bunch of devilish *árbol* chiles. It's a family recipe that Lulu learned from her uncle Conrado Ceballo, an elegant gentleman with mischief in his eyes. The family calls it *salsa de dedo* because of his matchless technique of crushing the cooked tomatoes and tomatillos with his thumb.

In Lulu's experienced opinion, nothing but *chile de árbol*—the tiny, very hot but flavorful dried pepper that Mexicans also call *chile bravo*, for its "bravado"—will do for this salsa. (I have trimmed the handful of peppers to just seven.) I use it as an all-purpose condiment for grilled chicken or fish, tamales, and empanadas. A small dollop will add heat and flavor to any soup.

Cook's Note: At my restaurant Zafra I developed a version of this sauce without tomatillos and with fire-roasted red bell peppers. We call it "Lulu Sauce." It is terrific with My Fresh Corn Tamales Cuban Style (page 455).

MAKES 5 CUPS

- 7 dried *chiles de árbol* (reduce to 1–2 if you fear for your life)
- 1 pound large tomatillos (about 6), husked and rinsed
- 6 medium plum tomatoes (about 18 ounces)
- 1 small white onion (about 5 ounces), coarsely chopped (about 1 cup)
- 3 garlic cloves
- ¼ cup distilled white vinegar
- ¼ cup finely chopped cilantro
- ¼ teaspoon dried oregano
- ¼ teaspoon ground cumin
- 1½ teaspoons salt, or to taste

▶ Place the chiles in a small saucepan, cover with 2 inches of water, and bring to a boil over high heat. Lower the heat to medium and simmer until the chiles are softened, 10 to 12 minutes. Drain and stem the chiles; set aside.

Meanwhile, combine the tomatillos and 4 cups water in a medium saucepan and bring to a boil over high heat. Lower the heat to medium and simmer for 5 minutes, or until barely soft. Drain and set aside.

Heat a *comal*, a griddle, or skillet over medium-high heat until a few drops of water sprinkled into the hot surface seem to dance before evaporating. Add the tomatoes and roast, turning occasionally with tongs, for 10 minutes, or until dark and blistered on all sides. Remove to a plate or bowl. When the tomatoes are cool enough to handle, scrape off any burned patches of skin. Set aside.

Place the chiles, onion, garlic, and vinegar in a food processor or blender and pulse to a coarse puree. Add the roasted tomatoes, tomatillos, cilantro, oregano, cumin, and salt and pulse for about 30 seconds to obtain a fluid but coarsely textured sauce. If the salsa looks too thick, stir in a little cold water 1 to 2 tablespoons at a time. Serve at room temperature. It will keep well in the refrigerator for 3 to 4 days.

Spicy Bolivian Table Sauce

Uchu Llajwa o Jallpa Huayka

This sauce is as ubiquitous in Bolivia as *salsa cruda* is in Mexico. Bolivians spoon it freely over just about anything from boiled potatoes to grilled meats. *Uchu llajwa* is a Quechua name from the words for hot pepper (*uchu*) and liking (*llajwa*); *jallpa huayka*, the Aymara-language name, means the same thing.

As you can see, the ingredients are very similar to those of the Mexican *salsa cruda*, but here the preferred herb is the Andean *quillquiña* (see page 73), which imparts an incomparable musky perfume reminiscent of that of its relative the Mexican herb *papaloquelite*. The hot pepper is the kind called *rocoto* in Peru and *locoto* in Bolivia, fiercer and more colorful than a jalapeño. Some specialized North American farmers have begun experimenting with Andean peppers, but chances are that you will not find fresh *locotos* in our markets. Luckily, they are available frozen in many Latin supermarkets. Just defrost and proceed with the recipe. You can substitute any fresh hot red pepper, such as cayenne or jalapeño, for the *locoto*. It will not be as Andean-tasting, but it will still give that marvelous jolt of heat.

Cook's Note: In the Andes, this salsa is traditionally made on the grinding stone called *batán* (page 33), which functions much like a *molcajete*, but nowadays most urban Bolivian cooks use the blender.

MAKES 2 CUPS

1 fresh-frozen Bolivian *locoto* (see headnote) or 2–3 jalapeños, or to taste, stemmed, seeded (do not devein), and coarsely chopped

6 medium plum tomatoes (about 18 ounces), peeled, seeded, and coarsely chopped
3 cilantro sprigs, leaves only
¼–½ cup water
1 small white onion (about 5 ounces), coarsely chopped (about 1 cup)
2 tablespoons finely shredded *quillquiña*, *papaloquelite*, or mint leaves
1 teaspoon salt, or to taste

▶ Place the chile(s), tomatoes, and cilantro leaves in a blender or food processor and pulse to chop coarsely. Add the water and pulse to obtain a fluid salsa. Add a little more water if the salsa seems too thick. Pour into a bowl and stir in the onion, herbs, and salt. It is best eaten right away.

Antillean Three-Pepper Sauce

Salsa Antillana

Before Columbus, European cartographers thought there were islands in the uncharted Atlantic to the west of Europe. They called these mythical lands Antilia. After Columbus reached the Americas, the islands of the Caribbean were dubbed "las Antillas" (Antilles) and divided by size into the Greater and Lesser Antilles. The large Spanish-speaking islands of Cuba, Hispaniola, and Puerto Rico are all part of the Greater Antilles. Anything pertaining to these Spanish islands, from music to food, is often generically described as Antillean (*antillano* or *antillana*), a term I often prefer to "Caribbean" because of its musical sound and historical meaning.

This Antillean sauce began as an experiment: what would I get if I took one of the Dominican or Puerto Rican cooking sauce bases that go by the name of *recado*, which I adore for their pleasant acidity and heady mix of cilantro, garlic, tomatoes, and mild sweet peppers, injected a bit of heat, and deepened the flavor by roasting some of the vegetables? What I got was a sauce with the sweet note of the bell pepper, the herbal aroma of the elegant little *ají dulce*, and a lively but not overpowering kick from the third pepper in the blend, the fiery Scotch bonnet. It is a perfect table condiment for boiled or roasted root vegetables, empanadas, and tamales. I like to add a couple of spoonfuls to red beans, and it is also a wonderful marinade for fish or chicken.

MAKES ABOUT 3 CUPS

- 2 ripe medium globe tomatoes (about 13 ounces)
- 1 medium green bell pepper (about 6 ounces)
- 10 large Caribbean sweet peppers (*ajíes dulces*) or 1 cubanelle pepper
- ½ Scotch bonnet or habanero pepper or 3 Puerto Rican hot peppers (*ajíes caballero*), seeded and finely chopped
- 7 garlic cloves
- 1 teaspoon capers, drained
- 1 cup cilantro leaves
- ½ teaspoon dried oregano
- ¼ teaspoon ground cumin
- ½ cup extra-virgin olive oil
- ⅓ cup tomato puree
- ¼ cup balsamic vinegar
- 1 teaspoon salt, or to taste

▶ Heat a *comal*, griddle, or heavy skillet over medium heat. Add the tomatoes and bell pepper and roast, turning occasionally with tongs, until dark and blistered on all sides. Transfer to a plate and let cool slightly.

Scrape the blackened bits of skin from the tomatoes and coarsely chop. Peel, core, and seed the pepper. Place the tomatoes and pepper in a food processor or blender along with the rest of the ingredients and process to a smooth puree.

Storing: Refrigerate in a tightly covered glass jar. The salsa will keep well for 3 to 4 days.

Veracruzan Chipotle Table Sauce

Salsa de Chile Seco Veracruzana

I was traveling in the old vanilla-farming country of Gulf Coast Mexico in northern Veracruz when I stopped for a cold beer at El Mirador, a cliffside restaurant with a view of an imposing Golden Gate Bridge look-alike spanning the Tecolutla River. The beer came with corn chips, mayonnaise, and a wonderful dense, mahogany-colored sauce that had me asking for seconds and thirds as the waiters regaled us with stories of a forest spirit called Kiwikgolo dwelling in the caves of the cliff just below the restaurant.

The sauce was a Veracruzan classic made with the local chipotle chile, which people there call just *chile seco* (dried chile) and which permeates many aspects of the cuisine. At its simplest, a *salsa de chile seco* isn't much more than chipotles and garlic sautéed in some oil, but with its deep smoky aroma and flavorful heat, it is unforgettable. It is a fine dipping sauce for tropical vegetable chips (such as yuca and plantain; pages 168 and 181) or corn chips. Like most salsas, it also makes a splendid addition to many stews and soups.

25 small or 15 large dried *morita* chipotles (about 4 ounces)

3 garlic cloves

¾ cup light olive oil, sunflower oil, or corn oil

▶ Stem and seed the chipotles. Heat a *comal*, griddle, or heavy skillet over medium heat. Add half the chiles and roast, stirring and flattening them against the surface of the pan with a metal spatula. Scoop into a bowl and repeat with the remaining chiles. Cover with 2 cups warm water and let stand until softened, about 20 minutes.

Drain the chiles, reserving ⅓ cup of the soaking liquid. Place the chiles, garlic, and reserved liquid in a blender or food processor and blend to a coarse paste.

In a small skillet, heat the oil over medium heat until very hot but not quite smoking. Stir in the chile paste and cook, stirring constantly, for 15 minutes, or until the oil begins to separate. Remove from the heat.

Storing: The salsa will keep for several days in the refrigerator well wrapped in plastic wrap.

Variation: Chipotle and Vanilla Table Sauce (Salsa de Chipotle y Vanilla)

When I got home from Veracruz, I had an impulse to try adding vanilla to the Veracruzan chipotle salsa. The combination is wonderful! It takes a few minutes for the vanilla to start coming through after you add it, but in the end the fruity perfume expands to lend the assertive sauce subtle and complex dimensions. I think the vanilla gives it a special affinity for seafood—try it with grilled or poached shrimp, passing a bowl of homemade mayonnaise separately.

▶ Cut 2 moist, plump vanilla beans (preferably Mexican; see page 802) into 1-inch pieces. Grind to the texture of fine bread crumbs in a small food processor or a coffee or spice mill; you should have about 1 tablespoon. Prepare the salsa as directed, stir in the ground vanilla, and serve at once.

Guatemalan Hot Sauce

Chirmol de Chiltepe

Combine the words for chile pepper, *chilli*, and sauce, *molli*, in the Nahuatl (Aztec) language and you have *chilmolli*, the name of a pre-Hispanic family of sauces using crushed chiles and tomatoes. The word still survives in different spellings in parts of southern Mexico as well as Guatemala, Honduras, and El Salvador. There are *chilmoles* in the Yucatán that are cooking sauces for hot pepper stews of pork and chicken, but in Guatemala and El Salvador *chirmoler*, *chirimol* or *chirmole*, refers generically to a chile-tomato table sauce, cooked or uncooked.

This simple hot red sauce is made with roasted tomatoes and dried *piquín* chiles (see page 66). The roasted tomatoes add sweetness and a smoky edge and the ground chile gives the sauce a lovely rust color and powerful heat. This sauce is a great sidekick for grilled meats, poultry, and shrimp.

MAKES 2½ CUPS

2 teaspoons dried *piquín* chiles

6 medium plum tomatoes (about 18 ounces)

1 small red onion (about 5 ounces), finely chopped (about 1 cup)

1 teaspoon salt

½ cup boiling water

▶ Grind the chiles to a coarse powder in a spice or coffee grinder; set aside.

Heat a *comal*, griddle, or heavy skillet over medium heat. Add the tomatoes and roast, turning occasionally, until blistered all over, about 12 minutes. Transfer to a bowl and let cool slightly. Peel and coarsely mash the tomatoes with a large mortar and pestle. Combine with the onion, ground chiles, and salt in a medium bowl. Stir in the boiling water.

Storing: The salsa will keep for a couple of days in the refrigerator, tightly covered with plastic wrap. Bring to room temperature before serving.

Guatemalan Dried Shrimp Sauce

Chirmol de Camarón Seco

In parts of Latin America—Mexico, Central America, the Caribbean, and Brazil—tiny dried shrimp play a role somewhat like that of fish sauce in southeast Asian cuisines. They are a salty, pungent accent that intensifies other flavors, adding depth and character to a range of dishes and the savory sensation known as umami. In spicy sauces like this Guatemalan *chirmol*, the dried shrimp surrender some of their aggressive brininess and take on a mellow edge. Guatemalan cooks roast the shrimp briefly to soften them before grinding them. This salsa is excellent with grilled meats and poultry and adds a fine flavor boost when spooned over boiled vegetables.

- 2 ounces dried shrimp (about 1½ cups; available in Hispanic and Asian markets)
- 2 tablespoons corn oil
- 1 small red onion (about 5 ounces), finely chopped (about ¾ cup)
- 4 garlic cloves, finely chopped
- 6 medium plum tomatoes (about 18 ounces), finely chopped
- 4 scallions, white and pale green parts, finely chopped
- 1 tablespoon dried whole *piquín* chiles
- ¼ teaspoon salt, or to taste

▶ Heat a *comal*, griddle, or heavy skillet over medium heat until hot. Add the shrimp and roast, stirring, for 4 minutes. Transfer to a food processor or blender and pulse to grind; set aside.

Heat the oil in a medium skillet over medium-high heat. Add the onion and garlic and sauté until golden, about 5 minutes. Add the tomatoes, scallions, and chiles and cook for about 5 minutes, stirring occasionally. Stir in the ground shrimp. Taste for salt.

Storing: The sauce will keep for 2 to 3 days in the refrigerator, tightly covered. Serve at room temperature.

Salvadorian *Salsa Cruda*

Chirmol Salvadoreño

A dollop of this refreshing sauce, redolent of cilantro and mint, adds a final layer of flavor to a number of Salvadorian dishes. Try it with grilled poultry or corn *pupusas* (page 401). It also makes a vivid foil for Salvadorian Red Silk Bean and Short Rib Soup-Stew (page 510).

MAKES ABOUT 3 CUPS

> 6 medium plum tomatoes (about 18 ounces), peeled, seeded, and cut into small cubes (about 1½ cups)
>
> 1 medium white onion (about 8 ounces), finely chopped (about 1 cup)
>
> 1 small green bell pepper (about 5 ounces), cored, seeded, deveined, and finely chopped (about ½ cup)
>
> 1 jalapeño, seeded and finely chopped
>
> 2 teaspoons finely chopped cilantro
>
> 2 teaspoons finely chopped mint
>
> Juice of 2 medium bitter oranges (about ½ cup), strained, or equal parts lime juice and orange juice
>
> 1 teaspoon salt

▶ Combine all the ingredients in a small bowl. Serve at room temperature or chilled. It is best served the day it is made, but it will keep well in the refrigerator for 2 to 4 days, tightly covered.

AJÍES

If you are confused by the word *ají*, you have good reason. It is the Arawak-derived name for three different but related things in parts of Latin America: the peppers that Mexican and Central Americans know better as chiles; a family of hot pepper stews from the Andes; and, finally, a cluster of table sauces that are usually flavored with hot peppers. These last are chiefly found along the Andes-Pacific culinary axis that includes Bolivia, Ecuador, and Peru, but they also turn up in the Orinoco Basin and its area of influence in Colombia and Venezuela. Venezuelans even have a name for *ají* containers: *ajiceros*, which may be heirloom glass cruets or recycled soda bottles.

As mentioned earlier, one of the purposes of table sauces in all Latin American countries is to enable diners to adjust the amount of heat in any dish to their individual taste. This is true even in regions where much of the food is fairly hot to begin with, but it takes on more importance in places like Ecuador, where people prefer to cook most dishes without the hot stuff and add it only at table, from bowls or bottles of sauce or relish. Cooks don't usually temper the sauce by increasing or decreasing the number of peppers; it is up to the diner to spoon more or less over a dish to adjust heat, flavor, and texture to his or her liking.

The *ajíes* of Ecuador are especially fascinating. They add wonderful nuances of flavor to simple foods like boiled hominy (page 251) or potato soup (page 522) that might otherwise be considered bland and monotonous. They run the gamut from thin, liquid condiments spiked with a handful of fierce little peppers to creamy sauces containing nuts, potatoes, or pumpkin seeds. I have also encountered wonderfully exotic *ajíes* in Venezuela, often made with the tiny, incredibly hot peppers that can be found in many regions and are generically known as *ajíes chireles* (*chirel* means immature fruit). Unfortunately, some of these call for ingredients that are not available here, such as agave flower buds or roasted ants. However, I have been able to reproduce the splendid milk-based *ají* of the Orinoco Basin. It has become a regular presence in my refrigerator and in my South American restaurant, Cucharamama, where I serve it with tamales.

In this section you will find recipes for unusual *ajíes* made with milk and whey from Venezuela and Ecuador, respectively; a delicious Colombian *ají* that resembles an Argentinean chimichurri; and a peanut *ají* that isn't in the least hot and uses black pepper instead of Andean *ají* peppers.

Spicy Milk Sauce from Ciudad Bolívar

Ají de Leche

I first tasted this fiery milk sauce on a smoldering hot, sticky day in Ciudad Bolívar, Venezuela, at a rustic restaurant with a palm-thatched roof overlooking the Orinoco River. To accompany my pan-fried *lau lau* steaks (a local catfish), the waiter brought a large Pepsi bottle with holes punched in the cap, filled with a thick white liquid of amazing sinus-cleansing powers. It was plain milk laced with the wild peppers of the region called *ajíes chireles* and a few other seasonings.

Since these tiny but potent peppers are not available here, I replicate the sauce using Scotch bonnet peppers, which are a relative of the Venezuelan hot peppers. When I gave some of the *ají* to my friend Harold McGee, the food science authority, after it had been sitting in my refrigerator for two weeks, he was amazed that it tasted so fresh. It was still fresh-tasting and delicious after more than two months in the refrigerator.

This milk *ají* is superb as I first sampled it, with fried fish. It is also a brilliant condiment for empanadas and tamales, particularly Puerto Rican *Pasteles* (page 474), Colombian Tamales with Potato and Peanut Hash (page 470), and Chilean Fresh Corn Tamales Flavored with Basil (page 459). It's an amazing flavor picker-upper—I stirred some into a fish chowder, and Wow!

MAKES ABOUT 3 CUPS

- 3 cups whole milk
- 4 habanero or Scotch bonnet peppers, stemmed
- 2 scallions, white part only, coarsely chopped
- 2 garlic cloves
- ¼ cup coarsely chopped cilantro
- 2 teaspoons salt, or to taste

▶ Place all the ingredients in a blender or food processor and blend well to a puree. With a wooden spoon or pusher, force the sauce through a medium sieve into a bowl, pressing against the solids to extract as much of the liquid as possible.

Storing: The sauce will keep surprisingly well for about a month—but if you want to err on the cautious side, 10 to 12 days—if refrigerated and tightly covered.

Ecuadorian *Ají*

Salsa de Ají

This is an all-purpose Ecuadorian table sauce, a kind of *salsa cruda* that brightens up any food with a kick of heat and the tang of lime juice and fresh tomatoes. There are more onions than hot peppers in this *salsa cruda*, but still people in Ecuador use it to add some heat to their meals and it is therefore a *salsa de ají* (pepper), the generic name for hot pepper sauces in many Latin American countries.

MAKES ABOUT 1 CUP

- 1 large red onion (about 12 ounces), cut in half lengthwise and thinly slivered
- 1 tablespoon salt, plus more to taste
- 2 ripe medium globe tomatoes (about 6 ounces each), seeded and coarsely chopped
- 2 Ecuadorian hot peppers, fresh cayenne peppers, or serrano chiles, seeded and minced
- ½ cup fresh lime juice
- ¼ cup finely chopped cilantro

▶ In a medium bowl, toss the onions with 1 tablespoon salt and let stand for 5 minutes. Add 3 cups hot tap water and let stand for 10 minutes longer. Pour the onions into a colander, rinse under cold running water, drain well, and pat dry.

Wipe out the bowl with paper towels and return the onions to it. Stir in the tomatoes, chiles, lime juice, and cilantro and season with salt to taste. If not using immediately, cover with plastic wrap and refrigerate. It is best used fresh.

Ecuadorian Whey Hot Pepper Sauce

Ají de Suero Serrano

In the Ecuadorian highlands, this sharply peppery *ají* is made with the whey (*suero*) left from making the fresh cheese called *quesillo*. Like many other peoples with household cheese-making traditions, highland Ecuadorians make good use of whey both for cooking and for feeding livestock. This table sauce seasons the starchy staple foods of the region—potatoes and *mote*, the Andean hominy. In this country, *ají de suero* can be successfully replicated with buttermilk, though it will have a tarter flavor. Be sure that the buttermilk contains live cultures. If you make the creamy cultured milk of Venezuela (page 146)—which also confusingly goes by the name *suero*—or try your hand at the fresh cheese on page 104, save the drained whey to make this pungent *ají*.

MAKES ABOUT 2¼ CUPS

- 2 cups cultured buttermilk or whey
- ¼ teaspoon salt
- 3 serrano peppers or other small hot peppers, seeded and very thinly sliced

▶ Combine the buttermilk and salt in a small saucepan and bring to a boil over medium heat. Add the peppers and cook for 1 minute. Scoop out the peppers and set aside; let the buttermilk cool. Pour the cooled buttermilk into a jar and add the peppers.

Storing: The *ají* will keep for 2 to 3 weeks, refrigerated.

Colombian Hot Sauce

Ají Pique Vallecaucano

This sauce, also called simply *pique*, looks like an Argentinean chimichurri, but with lots more onion rather than garlic and a strong note of sweetness. The *pique* is what gives a jolt of heat to the famous white corn tamales (see page 470) of the Valle del Cauca region in southwestern Colombia. In that part of the country, *pique* is made with a hot pepper called *ají chivato*, but Vallecaucanos living in the United States substitute fresh cayenne peppers or any other fresh Mexican chiles.

MAKES 2 CUPS

- 6 serrano chiles, cayenne peppers, small Asian hot peppers, or other small hot peppers, finely chopped
- ⅓ cup distilled white vinegar
  Juice of 1 medium bitter orange (about ¼ cup), strained, or equal parts lime juice and orange juice
- ¼ cup corn oil or light olive oil
- 3 scallions, white and most of the green parts, finely chopped (about ½ cup)
- 1 medium yellow onion (about 7 ounces), finely chopped (about 1¼ cups)
- ⅓ cup finely chopped cilantro
- 1 tablespoon grated brown loaf sugar, preferably *panela*, or dark brown sugar
- 1 teaspoon salt
- ½ teaspoon freshly ground black pepper

▶ *To make the sauce in the Valle del Cauca style*, combine the chopped peppers, vinegar, orange juice, and oil in a medium bowl. Let stand for at least several hours, or overnight.

Strain the liquid through a fine strainer, and discard the peppers. Return the liquid to the bowl, and whisk in all the remaining ingredients.

▶ *For a hotter version*, simply combine all ingredients (do not strain out the peppers).

Storing: Tightly covered and refrigerated, the sauce will keep for several weeks.

Andean Yellow Pepper and Epazote Sauce

Salsa de Ají Escabeche y Paico

Dora Asmat Holguín is the enterprising cook who keeps the archaeologists and service staff at Huaca de la Luna (Pyramid of the Moon) in Moche, northern Peru, well fed. She and her brother run a little restaurant called Don Merce on the outskirts of town, in the shadow of the imposing Huaca del Sol (Pyramid of the Sun), the largest pre-Columbian adobe pyramid in the Americas. It is open only for lunch, and the menu is simple and limited to a few local favorites.

Dora cooks outdoors, and the main feature of her kitchen is a gigantic stone mortar (*batán*) she inherited from her grandmother. Growing beside it is epazote, an herb more closely associated with Mexican cooking. In Peru it is called *paico* and is used both in cooking and as a medicinal herb. Dora likes to make a spicy sauce for potatoes by grinding fresh *ají amarillo* (also called *ají escabeche*) and a few *paico* leaves in her huge *batán*. The greenish sauce could not be simpler or more delicious, a true pre-Columbian sauce that only needs some salt to add flavor to the area's starchy yellow potatoes or to yuca. To finish it, however, Dora mixes in some vegetable oil and a few drops of lime juice, two obvious concessions to Spanish cooking. At home, I make the sauce in a blender to achieve the smooth texture obtained with the *batán*.

MAKES ¾ CUP

8 fresh or frozen yellow Andean peppers (*ají amarillo*)

14 large fresh epazote leaves

2 tablespoons vegetable oil or mild olive oil

1 teaspoon fresh lime juice

½ to 1 teaspoon salt, or to taste

▶ If using frozen peppers, place in a colander and thaw under running lukewarm water. Seed and devein the peppers and coarsely chop them. Combine all the ingredients in a blender and process to a smooth puree. Serve at room temperature.

ANDEAN CREAMY NUT, SEED, AND CHEESE SAUCES

I never fully understood the enormous importance of the peanut as a staple food in the Americas until I stared at a magnificent Moche necklace made of gold and silver beads realistically shaped like peanut shells at the American Museum of Natural History in New York. The piece was part of the touring exhibit of the Lord of Sipán's burial treasure, a finding that revolutionized our understanding of the Moche, the pre-Inca civilization that flourished between A.D. 200 and 800 along the northern coast of Peru.

In 1987, a group of tomb raiders (*huaqueros*) desecrated a Moche burial at Huaca Quebrada, an archaeological site in northern Peru. Under the cover of night, they managed to remove thirty-three objects from the site before being detained by local police, who confiscated some of their loot. Among the booty, the police found magnificent gold objects, including a stunning mask with lapis lazuli eyes and large beads shaped like peanut shells.

Archaeologist Dr. Walter Alva, who was called to examine these objects, realized they were part of a much larger cache and decided to excavate the area. After months of arduous work hindered by limited funds and the continuous threat of *huaqueros* and townspeople trying to loot the site, Dr. Alva and his small team reached the untouched burial chamber of the Lord of Sipán, a Moche warrior-priest from the period around A.D. 200. Dubbed the Tutankhamen of the New World, this powerful lord had been laid to rest with a veritable treasure trove. Under several layers of other ornaments, Dr. Alva found a stunning necklace close to the body wrought of ten gold and ten silver peanut-shaped beads similar to the ones confiscated by the police.

That a skillful Moche goldsmith had used the humble peanut as a model for a stunning gold and silver necklace is surprising. That a powerful Moche lord had deemed it worthy of his elaborate burial attire is even more startling—and reveals the peanut's importance. Together with corn, beans, and peppers, peanuts were a nutritious, protein-packed staple for the people of coastal Peru. Moche cooks probably roasted them for a snack or ground them to add flavor and texture to spicy sauces and nourishing soups and stews, as Peruvians and other Latin Americans do today.

In the same way that the peanut crossed the Andes from its ancestral home in the forests of Brazil to reach the Peruvian coast in pre-Columbian times, it traveled north to Mesoamerica and the Caribbean islands, where Columbus encountered it for the first time under the Taíno (Arawak) name *maní*.

As with so many other New World foods that the Spaniards first encountered in Hispaniola and other Caribbean islands, the Arawak name stuck in most of Spain's American colonies. Only in Mexico was the peanut called by a name close to its native Nahuatl roots, *cacahuate*.

It seems that the first Spanish settlers of the Caribbean in the sixteenth century were not bowled over by its flavor, however. Chronicler Gonzalo Fernández de Oviedo caustically remarked that though the native Arawaks grew it abundantly, it was a food of low sustenance and mediocre flavor more suitable for low-class Spanish men, slaves, young people, or people "who would eat anything" (*que no perdona su gusto a cosa alguna*). A more enthusiastic report comes from the Inca Garcilaso, a mixed-blood Peruvian writer of the same period, who compares the peanut with the almond and praises its good flavor when roasted or mixed with honey in nougat.

Perhaps some of the prejudices of the first settlers of the Caribbean rubbed off on their descendants. In Cuba, peanuts were always considered a street food, a snack, or an ingredient for popular confections, not fine desserts. But for many Latin Americans, the peanut evokes much more complex associations. Say *amendoin* (peanut) to a Brazilian from Bahia, and she will reminisce about sultry seafood casseroles colored with African palm oil and the peanut brittle sold by street vendors. Say *maní* to a Bolivian from the highlands, and his mouth will water thinking of fabulous heart kebabs (*anticuchos*) served with a spicy peanut sauce. Whisper the same to a Peruvian or an Ecuadorian, and you may spend hours listening to descriptions of pig's feet braised in a peanut-laden sauce, of boiled potatoes smothered in creamy peanut sauces enriched with the pungent Andean herb *huacatay*, of thick, nourishing quinoa and peanut soups that ward off the cold in the windswept highlands.

Colombian Hot Peanut Sauce

Ají de Pipián

This nutty, savory peanut sauce, typical of the Valle del Cauca region of southwest Colombia, is an essential accompaniment to the region's tasty *tamales de pipián* (page 470) and crunchy corn *empanadas de pipián vallecaucana* (page 433), both filled with a potato–peanut mixture. I like to pass this *ají* in a sauceboat. Its texture and taste are similar to the Ecuadorian creamy pumpkin seed sauce called *salsa de pepa de zambo* (page 129), only hotter. The peppers in Colombia are the small, sharp *ajíes pique*, for which Colombians in this country substitute fresh Mexican chiles or fresh hot peppers of the cayenne type.

2½ ounces unsalted roasted peanuts (about ½ cup)

8 serrano or cayenne peppers, finely chopped

2 medium plum tomatoes (about 6 ounces), peeled, seeded, and finely chopped

3 scallions, white and pale green parts, finely chopped

1 hard-boiled egg, finely chopped

¼ cup finely chopped cilantro

½ cup chicken broth

Juice of 1 lime (about 2 tablespoons)

¼ teaspoon salt, or to taste

▶ Grind the peanuts to a coarse paste with a mortar and pestle or in a food processor. They should still have some texture. Scoop into a bowl and stir in all the remaining ingredients.

Storing: The sauce will keep for 2 to 3 days, tightly covered, in the refrigerator.

Peruvian Peanut–*Mirasol* Pepper Sauce

Salsa de Ocopa Arequipeña

This classic table sauce from southern Peru features dried *mirasol* peppers (*ajíes mirasol*), fresh cheese, nuts (usually peanuts, sometimes walnuts), and the pungent herb *huacatay*. Traditionally served over boiled potatoes, it is a versatile sauce that will do wonders for fried yuca (page 168) or steamed fish or shellfish. In this country, my preferred substitute for Peruvian fresh cheese is French sheep's milk feta.

6 dried *mirasol* peppers (about 2 ounces), stemmed and seeded

½ cup mild extra-virgin olive oil

4 large garlic cloves, finely chopped

1 small red onion (about 5 ounces), coarsely chopped (about 1 cup)

1 tablespoon chopped fresh-frozen *huacatay* or ground dried *huacatay* (both available in Hispanic markets catering to Peruvians) or chopped cilantro, or to taste

1¼ cups (about 6 ounces) unsalted roasted peanuts

8 ounces French sheep's milk feta cheese, crumbled (about ¼ cup)

¾ cup evaporated milk

½ teaspoon salt, or to taste

½ teaspoon freshly ground black pepper

▶ Heat a *comal*, griddle, or heavy skillet over medium-high heat until hot. Add the peppers and roast, turning once, until lightly charred, about 30 seconds on each side. Place in a small bowl, cover with 2 cups hot water, and let soak until the peppers are softened, at least 30 minutes. Alternatively, place the peppers in a small saucepan with 2 cups water, bring to a boil over medium heat, and simmer until soft, about 15 minutes.

Drain the peppers, reserving ½ cup of the cooking liquid. Coarsely chop the peppers and set aside.

Heat 2 tablespoons of the oil in a medium skillet over medium heat. Add the garlic and sauté until light gold, about 30 seconds. Add the onion and peppers and sauté, stirring occasionally, until the onion is soft, about 5 minutes. Remove from the heat and let cool.

Transfer the onion-pepper mixture to a blender or food processor and add the *huacatay*, peanuts, cheese, milk, and reserved ½ cup cooking liquid. Process into a smooth puree while adding the remaining oil in a stream. Season with salt and pepper. To serve, spoon over hot boiled potatoes. Garnish with lettuce, Peruvian purple olives or Kalamata olives, and hard-boiled eggs.

Peruvian Walnut–*Mirasol* Pepper Sauce

Salsa Huancaína

This is my interpretation of the sauce that is a classic accompaniment for boiled potatoes all over Peru. Similar to the creamy *ocopa arequipeña* sauce on page 127, it is made with fresh cheese, walnuts, and *mirasol* peppers and is a favorite of both Peruvian and Bolivian cooks. Peruvian home cooks often use fillers like crackers to give body to the sauce (a way of using less cheese, which is expensive) and lots of evaporated milk to keep it fluid. I like my sauce on the thick side and feel that the taste of the evaporated milk masks the flavor of the hot peppers. I strain it over boiled starchy vegetables like potatoes (page 378), yuca, *ulloco*, and *oca*. I even smear it on hot toast instead of butter.

MAKES 1½ CUPS

- 2 dried *mirasol* peppers, or more to taste, stemmed and seeded
- ¼ cup walnuts or hazelnuts, plus about 2 tablespoons chopped nuts for garnish
- 3 garlic cloves

- 8 ounces creamy French sheep's milk feta cheese, crumbled
- ⅓ cup achiote-infused oil (page 89)

▶ Place the peppers in a small bowl, cover with 2 cups warm water and let soak until softened, at least 30 minutes. Alternatively, place the peppers in a small saucepan, cover with water, bring to a boil over medium heat, and simmer until soft.

Drain the peppers, reserving ¼ cup of the soaking liquid. Place the peppers, reserved liquid, walnuts, and garlic in a blender or food processor and pulse until the walnuts are well combined. Add the feta cheese and process for 1 minute. With the motor running, add the achiote oil in a thin stream and process to the consistency of a thick mayonnaise. Transfer to a serving bowl, sprinkle the chopped nuts over the sauce, and serve at once.

Storing: The sauce (without the garnish) can be refrigerated, tightly covered, for up to 1 week; bring to room temperature and sprinkle on some of the chopped nuts before serving.

Ecuadorian Peanut and Milk Sauce

Ají de Maní

A spoonful of this creamy peanut sauce is the final flourish for any number of soups and stews in coastal Ecuador and a favorite condiment for the country's golden potato cakes, *llapingachos* (page 395). This *ají* is unusual in that it does not contain hot peppers, but it is an example of eclectic taste when it comes to salsas. Here the heat and flavor come from black pepper and onions sautéed in reddish achiote oil with cumin, a favorite spice in Ecuador.

MAKES ABOUT 1⅔ CUPS

- 3 ounces unsalted roasted peanuts (about ¾ cup)
- 3 tablespoons achiote-infused corn oil or light olive oil (page 89)
- 1 medium white onion (about 8 ounces), finely chopped (about 1½ cups)
- ¼ cup finely chopped cilantro
- ¼ teaspoon ground cumin
- ½ cup whole milk
- 1 teaspoon salt, or to taste
- ½ teaspoon freshly ground black pepper

▶ Grind the peanuts to a coarse paste with a mortar and pestle or food processor. Set aside.

Heat the oil in a medium skillet over medium heat. Add the onion and sauté until lightly golden, about 5 minutes. Add the cilantro, cumin, peanut paste, milk, salt, and pepper. Cook, stirring, until the mixture is well blended, about 2 minutes. Serve at room temperature.

Storing: The sauce can be refrigerated, tightly covered, for 3 to 4 days. Bring to room temperature before serving and thin slightly with some milk.

Ecuadorian Pumpkin Seed Sauce

Salsa de Pepa de Zambo

In the cold Ecuadorian highlands, this simple, creamy sauce lends substance and spice to many dishes. Pass a bowl of it with Andean Hominy (page 251) or "Crazy Potatoes" (potatoes cooked with pork rind, page 207), or potato soups like *locro* (page 522). In Ecuador it is made with the seeds of the white-fleshed squash called *zambo* in the Andes and *chilacayote* in Mexico; cooks in the United States substitute pumpkin seeds to good effect.

MAKES ABOUT 1⅔ CUPS

- 1 cup (about 4 ounces) *zambo* seeds or hulled pumpkin seeds, lightly roasted
- 1¾ cups whole milk
- 2 tablespoons achiote-infused corn oil or lard (page 89)
- 4 garlic cloves, finely chopped
- 3 scallions, white and pale green parts, finely chopped
- 2 teaspoons ground dried *chile de árbol* or ground cayenne
- 1 tablespoon heavy cream
- 1 teaspoon salt, or to taste

▶ Combine *zambo* seeds and milk in a blender and process to a coarse puree.

Heat the oil in a medium skillet over medium heat. Add the garlic and sauté until pale golden, about 45 seconds. Add the scallions and sauté for 1 minute. Stir in the ground chile and the milk mixture and bring to a simmer. Reduce the heat to low, stir in the cream and heat through. Season with the salt. Serve either hot or at room temperature.

Storing: The sauce can be refrigerated, tightly covered, for 2 to 3 days. Let come to room temperature, or reheat gently before serving; thin lightly with milk.

Bolivian Peanut Sauce

Ají de Maní Paceño

Anticuchos, the much-loved Peruvian Grilled Beef Heart Kebabs (page 389), are served in the Bolivian capital, La Paz, with this spicy golden peanut sauce. The heat of the *mirasol* peppers and the acidity of the tomatoes provide a vivid counterpoint to the earthy peanuts. The sauce is delicious and versatile—try it with grilled meats and chicken, or even fish.

MAKES ABOUT 1½ CUPS

- 10 dried *mirasol* peppers (about 2½ ounces), stemmed and seeded
- 6 medium plum tomatoes (about 18 ounces), peeled and seeded
- ½ teaspoon salt
- 2½ ounces unsalted roasted peanuts (about ½ cup)

▶ Heat a *comal*, griddle, or heavy skillet over high heat. Add the peppers and roast for about 2 minutes, flattening them with a spatula and turning once.

Combine the peppers and 2 cups water in a small saucepan and bring to a boil over medium heat. Reduce the heat slightly and simmer until the peppers are softened, about 10 minutes. Drain, reserving ½ cup of the cooking liquid.

Place the drained peppers, reserved cooking liquid, tomatoes, salt, and peanuts in a blender or food processor and process to a coarse puree.

Storing: The sauce can be refrigerated, tightly covered, for several days. Bring to room temperature before serving; thin lightly with some warm water.

PEBRES AND CHIMICHURRIS

The word *pebre*—infrequently used in modern Latin America outside of Chile, where it usually refers to a table sauce based on oil and vinegar with lots of hot pepper—is derived from the Latin *piper*, meaning black pepper, one of the few piquant spices known to Europeans before the arrival of hot peppers from the New World. Its Iberian history can be traced to the medieval Catalan *pebrada*, a bread-enriched sweet-and-sour sauce for game or fish made with black pepper, honey or sugar, and other spices such as ginger, and to a large cluster of sauces called *pebres*, whose only common feature is black pepper.

By the eighteenth century, *pebre* also referred to a garlicky pork stew seasoned with black pepper, described by Juan de Altamiras in his *New Art of Cooking* (*Nuevo arte de cozina*), an important Spanish cookbook. The late-nineteenth-century Mexican cooking encyclopedia *The New Mexican Cook in Dictionary Form* (*Nuevo cocinero mexicano en forma de diccionario*) makes a connection between *pebre* and the French term *poivrade*, and it also describes *pebres* as a family of soups or stews using black pepper and spices like cloves and saffron.

Modern Chilean *pebres* are more like an Argentinean chimichurri than any of these, though chimichurris are generally less hot. Both the *pebre* and the chimichurri probably hark back to some medieval Spanish oil, vinegar, and pepper forebears. Most versions of *pebre* start with a simple hot-pepper-oil-vinegar sauce called *ají chileno*, then add aromatics like onion and garlic.

Chilean Hot Pepper Sauce

Ají Chileno

This blend of hot peppers, oil, and vinegar is as ubiquitous in casual restaurants throughout Chile as Tabasco in American diners. Chileans reach for the red plastic bottle labeled "*ají chileno*" and squirt a few drops of the thick red sauce on anything that might need a little heat and flavor. Bottled commercial versions can be found in some Latin markets in the United States, but it is so easy to make your own. *Ají chileno* is the flavor base for the traditional Chilean "Goat's Horn" *Pebre* (recipe follows), a more complex table sauce. In Chile, this sauce is made with the peppers called *cacho de cabra* (goat's horn). If you can't find these, dried Mexican guajillo or *puya* chiles are a good replacement. Use this as you would Tabasco.

MAKES ABOUT ¾ CUP

> 5 dried *cacho de cabra* peppers or *puya* or guajillo chiles (about ½ ounce), stemmed and seeded
> ½ cup extra-virgin olive oil or sunflower oil
> ½ cup red wine vinegar
> ¼ to ½ teaspoon salt

▶ Place the peppers in a small saucepan, cover with 2 cups water, and bring to a boil over high heat. Reduce the heat to medium and simmer until the peppers are softened, about 15 minutes.

Drain the peppers and transfer to a blender or food processor. Add the oil and vinegar and process to a puree. Season with salt to taste.

Storing: The sauce can be refrigerated, tightly covered, for several months. Serve at room temperature.

Chilean "Goat's Horn" *Pebre*

Pebre de Ají Cacho de Cabra

The *pebres* of Chile play the same role at the table as chimichurris in Argentina and Uruguay. Essentially, they consist of an oil-and-vinegar dressing with hot peppers (usually some version *of ají chileno*) combined with finely chopped herbs and aromatics such as cilantro, parsley, onion, and garlic, sometimes even tomatoes. You can put *pebre* on anything from eggs to grilled steak to roast chicken. It has become one of my favorite condiments for Cuban Fried Beef Empanadas (page 426). It also miraculously doubles as a quick marinade for meats and a splendid salad dressing. Feel free to vary the proportions to your taste.

MAKES ABOUT 1½ CUPS

> ½ cup Chilean Hot Pepper Sauce (recipe above)
> 1 small red onion (about 5 ounces), finely chopped (about 1 cup)
> 1 head garlic, separated into cloves, peeled, and finely minced
> ¼ cup finely chopped cilantro or flat-leaf parsley
> 1 teaspoon ground cumin
> 1 teaspoon salt

▶ Combine all ingredients in a small bowl. The sauce will keep in the refrigerator, tightly covered, up to a month. Serve at room temperature.

Chilean Hot Sauce

Pebre Chileno

This wonderful Chilean salsa is a fine complement to soups, stews, and grilled meats. It also makes a quick marinade for chicken, pork, or grilled vegetables.

MAKES 2 CUPS

  1   medium yellow onion (about 8 ounces), coarsely chopped (about 1½ cups)
  ¼   cup coarsely chopped cilantro
  3   medium plum tomatoes (about 9 ounces), peeled, seeded, and coarsely chopped
  ½   cup extra-virgin olive oil
  ¼   cup red wine vinegar
  1½ teaspoons hot *pimentón* (Spanish smoked paprika)
      Coarse salt to taste

▶ In a food processor, pulse the onion with the cilantro until finely chopped. Add the tomatoes and pulse until finely chopped. Add the olive oil, red wine vinegar, and *pimentón* and pulse just until blended. Transfer the salsa to a bowl and season with salt. The salsa can be refrigerated for up to 2 days.

Patagonian *Pebre* Sauce with *Merkén*

Pebre con Merkén

The secret of this wonderful little sauce is *merkén*, the sultry smoked paprika and spice mix made by the Mapuche Indians in southern Chile. Like Argentinean chimichurri, it does wonders for anything from stews and soups, such as the hearty chicken stew with dried fresh cornmeal (page 521), to grilled skirt steak or lamb chops and pan-seared shrimp. It also makes a good marinade and a lovely salad dressing for sturdy salad greens like romaine and endive.

MAKES ABOUT 2 CUPS

  3   medium plum tomatoes (about 9 ounces), peeled, seeded, and very finely chopped
  1   small yellow onion (about 5 ounces), very finely chopped (about 1 cup)
  ¼   cup finely chopped cilantro
  ½   cup extra-virgin olive oil
  ¼   cup red wine vinegar
  2   teaspoons *Merkén* from Chillán (page 74) or 1½ teaspoons *pimentón* (Spanish smoked paprika, hot or sweet) plus ½ teaspoon ground cayenne if using sweet paprika

▶ Mix all the ingredients in a bowl. The sauce will keep in the refrigerator, tightly covered, for up to a week. Serve at room temperature.

Argentinean Chimichurri "La Porteña"

One summer day many years ago I trekked from Manhattan to Queens with food writer Cara de Silva to introduce a group of food writers to Argentinean cooking at a neighborhood restaurant called La Porteña. The hits of the occasion were the *asado* (mixed grill) of sausages, tripe, ribs, and beef and the chimichurri sauce that came with it, which the waiters replenished, bowl after bowl. Not content with slathering the sauce on all the meats in sight, some writers took to dunking their bread in it, and I even caught one Southerner spooning it over his Russian salad of potatoes, carrots, and mayonnaise.

That is how food lovers behave when they discover chimichurri, the infinitely adaptable sauce that Argentineans and Uruguayans serve with their grilled specialties. After many years, I am still infatuated with it. It should be the salsa of the new millennium. It is exotic-sounding but actually very Mediterranean, and it is at home with almost every kind of food.

I always have a batch on hand in my refrigerator for quick impromptu cooking. I like to use it as a table sauce for *churrasco* (grilled Argentinean skirt steak) and *palomilla* (a thin Cuban steak) and as a marinade for pork, chicken, and lamb. I also like to toss penne or linguine with a couple of spoonfuls of chimichurri, or serve it hot or cold with grilled chicken.

Cook's Note: There are many versions of chimichurri. Some call for lots of dried herbs, such as oregano, and are reddish from the addition of red pepper flakes. Parsley, not cilantro, has always been the traditional ingredient in chimichurri, but nowadays many cooks have begun using cilantro instead.

MAKES ABOUT 1¼ CUPS

- 1 bunch flat-leaf parsley, leaves only, finely chopped (about ½ cup)
- 1 large head garlic, separated into cloves, peeled, and finely minced
- 1 tablespoon dried oregano, lightly crushed
- 1 teaspoon crushed red pepper flakes
- ½ cup distilled white vinegar
- ½ cup safflower oil or extra-virgin olive oil (La Porteña uses soy oil)

- 1 teaspoon salt, or to taste
- 1 teaspoon freshly ground black pepper

▶ Mix all the ingredients in a small bowl, or combine in a food processor and pulse to a coarse puree.

Storing: Argentineans often don't bother to refrigerate chimichurri, and it certainly will come to no harm in a couple of days. Refrigerated, tightly covered, it will keep for 2 to 3 weeks. Whisk well before serving. Serve at room temperature.

Variation: Uruguayan Chimichurri
Though Uruguayans insist that their version of chimichurri is totally different from that of Argentina, the two are in fact very similar. Call this Freud's "narcissism of small differences"—the need to differentiate yourself from that which is most similar to you. For 1 bunch parsley, use 1 head garlic, 1 teaspoon dried oregano, 1 teaspoon ground cumin, 1 tablespoon crushed pepper red flakes, ½ cup red wine vinegar, 1 cup corn oil or light olive oil, 2 teaspoons salt, or to taste, and 1 teaspoon white pepper.

Red Chimichurri

Chimichurri Rojo

A blend of Spanish smoked paprika (*pimentón*) and hot ground pepper gives this chimichurri a sultry reddish hue. I also love how the onion and cilantro work together with these seasonings to make a deeper sauce that adds more than acidity and a garlicky touch to grilled meats.

MAKES ABOUT 2 CUPS

½ cup fresh cilantro, finely chopped
1 large head garlic (about 12 large cloves), peeled and finely minced
1 small yellow onion (about 5 ounces), finely chopped (about 1 cup)
1 tablespoon dried oregano, lightly crushed
1 tablespoon *pimentón* (Spanish smoked paprika, hot or sweet)
1 tablespoon crushed hot red pepper flakes or Argentinean *ají molido* (ground red pepper)
½ cup red wine vinegar
½ cup extra-virgin olive oil
1 teaspoon freshly ground black pepper
   Salt to taste

▶ Mix all the ingredients by hand in a small bowl, whisking to blend well, or mix in a food processor by pulsing until the ingredients are finely chopped but not pureed. Serve at room temperature. It will keep in the refrigerator, in a well-sealed glass container, for 2 to 3 weeks.

Passion Fruit and Ginger Sauce

Salsa de Granadilla y Jengibre

Passion fruit

This sauce was inspired by my love for its main components: passion fruit, garlic, and fresh ginger.

It has the floral aroma and the sweet-and-sour tang of some Southeast Asian dipping sauces. Either purple or yellow passion fruit works well here. I like to pair this with fish and shellfish. It is terrific spooned over pan-seared monkfish, snapper, or tuna. It is also good on scallops, lobster, and shrimp. At a dinner party, you could serve the sauce in the passion fruit shells.

Cook's Notes: Passion fruits are members of a large family of climbing vines native to the New World tropics. Though the name carries a whiff of aphrodisia, it actually refers to the Passion of Christ. The flowers of all the species have dramatic-looking pistils and filaments that were seen as symbols of the nails with which Christ was crucified and his crown of thorns.

The fruits vary in color and size, but all have hard seeds embedded in translucent sacs. Rapid pulsing in the blender releases the juice from these sacs. Perfumed and intense, with a hint of guava and jasmine, passion fruit juice is the ambrosia of the American tropics. It is available frozen in most Hispanic markets and many ethnic food stores.

To make 1½ cups of juice yourself, you will need at least 15 fresh fruits. Cut the fruits in half and scoop out the pulp with a spoon. Place the pulp in a blender, add ¼ cup water, and pulse until the small dark seeds are freed from the pulp. Strain the juice through a fine-mesh strainer, pushing against the seeds with a wooden spoon to extract as much juice as possible. You should have 1½ cups.

MAKES ABOUT 1¼ CUPS

1½ cups fresh or thawed frozen passion fruit juice (see Cook's Notes)
¼ cup sugar
4 garlic cloves, peeled

2 teaspoons grated fresh ginger

½ Scotch bonnet pepper, seeded

2 tablespoons finely chopped chives

2 tablespoons finely chopped red bell pepper

3 tablespoons Salvadorian Pineapple Vinegar (page 94) or cider vinegar

¼ teaspoon ground cumin

Salt to taste

▶ Combine the passion fruit juice and sugar in a small saucepan and bring to a boil over medium heat, stirring to dissolve the sugar. Reduce the heat to low and simmer, stirring, until the syrup thickens enough to coat the back of a spoon, about 20 minutes.

Transfer the syrup to a blender or food processor, and combine with the garlic, ginger, and Scotch bonnet pepper. Pour the sauce into a small bowl and add the chives, bell pepper, vinegar, and cumin. Whisk to combine, and season with salt to taste.

Storing: The sauce will keep in the refrigerator, tightly covered, for 5 to 6 days. Serve at room temperature.

MAYONNAISE AND FAMILY

Latin Americans have an inordinate fondness for mayonnaise. This amazingly versatile emulsion of egg yolks and olive oil that we inherited from Spain serves as a dressing for the Mexican Christmas beet and fruit salad and the Uruguayan classic potato and pea salad, as a spread for Chilean chicken sandwiches, as a glaze for the baroque molded rice and chicken "imperial" of Cuba, and as a table condiment for breaded chicken or beef cutlets (*milanesas*) in Argentina. In Veracruz, it even makes it to the table with a bowl of chipotle chile sauce as a dip for chips.

Although U.S. brands like Hellman's and Kraft have been readily available in Latin markets since the middle of the twentieth century, most Latins prefer homemade mayonnaise, preferably flavored with garlic. For us it is a delicacy.

Garlic Mayonnaise

Allioli Criollo

I learned to make homemade mayonnaise when my aunt Anita pierced a fat clove of garlic with a fork and handed it to me, saying, "With this you beat the yolks while pouring the olive oil as if you were shedding tears." From my aunt's one-clove-scented mayonnaise, I graduated to a more intense version that uses 8 cloves of garlic, conveniently emulsified in the food processor. I use it as a dip for Puerto Rican Salt Cod Fritters (page 383), spoon it lightly over paella, rice, or chicken, and often stir it into a seafood soup. The effect is magical.

MAKES 2¾ CUPS

8 large garlic cloves, peeled

2 large eggs

½ teaspoon salt

2 cups extra-virgin olive oil

Juice of 1 lime (about 2 tablespoons)

▶ Place the garlic, eggs, and salt in a blender or food processor and pulse to blend. With the motor running, pour in the olive oil in a thin stream. Turn off the machine, add the lime juice, and process briefly to blend. The puree should be thicker than a jarred mayonnaise, with some texture remaining from the garlic.

Storing: The mayonnaise keeps well in the refrigerator, tightly covered, for at least 3 days.

Variation: Guajillo Allioli

In a blender or food processor, combine the garlic mayonnaise with 2 guajillo chiles, seeded, soaked, and drained (see page 744). Process until smooth. The sauce will have a nice pinkish color.

Mirasol Mayonnaise

Mayonesa de Ají Mirasol

This golden mayonnaise packs a flavor punch belied by its sunny appearance. *Mirasol* peppers give it heat but also a warm mellowness and richness. It goes divinely with omelets like the Spanish tortilla, Brazilian Salt Cod and Potato Balls (*bolinhos de bacalhao*, page 381), and as a "frosting" for the Lima-Style Mashed Potato Terrine (*causa limeña*, page 206).

MAKES 1⅓ CUPS

- 4 dried *mirasol* peppers (about 1¼ ounces), seeded
- 1 cup mayonnaise, homemade (page 135) or store-bought
- 2 garlic cloves, peeled
- ¼ teaspoon ground cumin
- 2 teaspoons freshly squeezed lime juice
- ½ teaspoon salt or to taste

▶ Place the peppers in a small bowl and cover with 3 cups hot water; let soak until soft, about 20 minutes. Alternatively, place in a small saucepan with 3 cups water and bring to a boil over medium heat. Simmer until soft, about 15 minutes. Drain and place in a blender or food processor with the remaining ingredients; process into a smooth puree. Spoon into a bowl and serve. It will keep refrigerated, tightly covered, for up to 2 weeks.

Creamy Cilantro Sauce Presilla

Salsa de Cilantro a la Presilla

Yuca comes to life when drenched in tart sauces. It was in my search for the perfect sauce for my yuca fries that I stumbled upon the idea for this recipe. Indian cilantro chutney had caught my imagination on a trip to India, but I decided to turn it into a mayonnaise flavored with cilantro and my favorite spices, and of course garlic. The day I tried the "Yuca Fries with Cilantro Sauce a la Presilla," as I started to call the pairing, on Cuban and Indian friends, they applauded the sauce and almost drank it from the bowl. That was my "Aha!" moment. For the first time in my newly embraced culinary career, I felt I had created something delicious and useful out of simple ingredients.

As often happens with tasty foods, my idea was widely imitated. The pairing of yuca fingers and cilantro has now become a Cuban classic.

MAKES 2 CUPS

- 2 cups mayonnaise, homemade (page 135) or store-bought (Hellmann's or Kraft)
- 4 garlic cloves, peeled

½ cup (well-packed) cilantro leaves, washed and dried

1 serrano or jalapeño pepper, seeded, deveined, and coarsely chopped

1 teaspoon ground cumin

¼ teaspoon ground allspice

½ teaspoon dried oregano

Juice of 1 lime (about 2 tablespoons)

Salt to taste

▶ Place the mayonnaise in a blender or food processor. Add the garlic, cilantro, hot pepper, cumin, allspice, and oregano. Process until smooth and velvety. Season with the lime juice and salt to taste. If using a jarred mayonnaise, you might not need either since some brands are already tart and salty. If using Hellmann's, add 1 teaspoon salt and the full amount of lime juice indicated in the recipe. Place in a bowl and serve with Yuca Fingers (page 386).

Storing: Keep in the refrigerator, covered with plastic film, for a couple of days. Bring to room temperature when serving with the yuca fingers or any other hot tidbit.

Venezuelan Chunky Avocado Sauce

Guasacaca

Venezuelans accompany their tasty grilled meats with an avocado sauce that resembles guacamole. The West Indian avocado that local cooks use gives the sauce a lighter texture and fresher flavor than one made with the oil-rich avocados from Mexico.

Some people like *guasacaca* smoothly pureed. I prefer it a bit chunky, because that was how I was taught to make it at the Finca San Joaquín, a cacao farm in the western Venezuelan plains of Barinas (it has since been destroyed), far away from a blender or food processor. Agronomist Beatriz Escobar, a great cook, chopped all the ingredients by hand and coarsely mashed them in a gourd with a fork. Serve as an accompaniment to barbecued and roasted beef or chicken, or use as a dip for toasted yuca bread (*casabe*, page 573) or *arepas* (page 586). Or simply serve with chips, as you would guacamole.

MAKES ABOUT 5 CUPS

1 large (2 to 2¼-pound) ripe West Indian avocado

5 ripe medium plum tomatoes (about 13–14 ounces), finely chopped

4 scallions, white pale and green parts, finely chopped

1 small green bell pepper (about 5 ounces), cored, seeded, deveined, and finely chopped (about ½ cup)

1 medium red bell pepper (6–7 ounces), cored, seeded, deveined, and finely chopped (about ¾ cup)

¼ cup finely chopped flat-leaf parsley

6 tiny Caribbean sweet peppers (*ajíes dulces*), finely chopped

1 habanero or Scotch bonnet chile, seeded and finely chopped

½ cup extra-virgin olive oil

¼ cup distilled white vinegar or fresh lime juice

Salt to taste

▶ Cut the avocado in half lengthwise. Remove and reserve the pit. Peel the skin from the flesh, cut each half lengthwise in two, and cut into large dice.

Place the avocado in a bowl with the tomatoes, scallions, bell peppers, parsley, and hot peppers. Coarsely mash with a fork. Beat in the olive oil, vinegar, and salt.

Storing: If not using immediately, cover and refrigerate for up to 3 hours. (To prevent the sauce from turning dark, the Venezuelan food writer Armando Scannone recommends putting the pit in the bowl of guasacaca. It works.)

FRUIT

Ecuadorian Spicy Onion and Tamarillo Salsa

Ají de Tomate de Árbol

Tamarillo (tree tomato)

Ecuadorian highlanders make table sauces and cebiches with the yellow tamarillo, an Andean fruit they call *tomate de árbol*, or tree tomato. They usually reserve the red variety, which reaches them from Colombia, for dessert. In Cuenca, the sauce is called *ají* (pepper), but it is understood by everyone that

the central interest comes from the tamarillo, which lends body and a pleasant tart edge that is never overpowering.

I did not really understand this sauce until I talked to my friend Santiago Peralta, founder of Pacari, Ecuador's leading chocolate maker, who adores tamarillos and grows them in his garden in Quito. He had plenty to say about the *ají*, since he makes it himself to eat with everything, but he also directed me to his mother, Susana Polo Eljuri, to get a more complete account. Susana is an energetic businesswoman from Cuenca who projects a thoroughly modern image, but when she talks about food she becomes the daughter and granddaughter of traditional Cuenca cooks. She promptly corrected me on the way onions should be cut. I had been slivering the onion very finely as if for cebiche. According to Susana, they should be good and thick, a style popularized in Cuenca by a woman who owned a successful shop called La Gorda de los Sandwiches (The Fat Woman of the Sandwiches). When I told her that I had made a version of the *ají* with a blend of tomatoes and tamarillos, she said "Why?" in a puzzled voice, and proceeded to set me straight. Later I realized that the tomato only distracts from the perfectly balanced aroma and flavor of the tamarillo itself.

MAKES 4 CUPS

- 4 fresh or frozen tamarillos (about 1 pound), preferably yellow
- 1 large red onion (12 ounces), halved and cut lengthwise into ¼- to ½-inch slices
- 1 tablespoon salt
   Juice of 2–3 large limes (about ½ cup)
- 2 tablespoons vegetable oil, preferably extra-virgin olive oil

2 Ecuadorian hot peppers, or serrano or cayenne peppers, seeded, deveined, and finely chopped

¼ cup finely chopped cilantro

Salt to taste

▶ Cut a small cross on the tip of each tamarillo. In a medium saucepan, bring 1 quart water to a boil. Add the tamarillos and cook for 1 minute for fresh tamarillos, 10 minutes for frozen. Drain. Peel the tamarillos and coarsely mash with a fork. You should have about 1¼ cups. Set aside.

Place the onion and salt in a medium bowl. Add tap water to cover, stir, and allow the onion to stand for 10 minutes, stirring occasionally with your hands.

Place the onion in a colander, rinse under cold running water, and drain thoroughly. Place in a medium bowl, toss with the lime juice, and let stand for 5 minutes. Stir in the tamarillo pulp, along with the rest of the ingredients. Serve at room temperature.

Serving: This is a perfect accompaniment to a Cuenca Pork Sandwich (page 590) or to an Ecuadorian *fritada* (page 394).

Zoila's Tamarillo Jam

Salsa Dulce de Tomate de Árbol al Estilo de Zoila Eljuri

Sweet sauces for savories are not the norm in Azuay province in southern Ecuador, where people reach for a combination of salt and acid to give extra flavor to meats and starchy staples. But you find exceptions among old cooks from Cuenca like Susana Polo Eljuri's mother, Zoila Eljuri Chica, a descendant of the Lebanese immigrants who settled in Azuay province at the turn of the nineteenth century. She made this silky sauce as a complement to a roast leg of pork (*pernil*). This minimalist yet sophisticated sauce is almost a savory marmalade, playing on the fruity, complex flavor of the tamarillo. It goes well with any fatty roast meat or poultry.

MAKES ABOUT 1⅓ CUPS

12 fresh or frozen tamarillos (about 2 pounds), preferably yellow

5 whole cloves

5 allspice berries

½ teaspoon salt

½ cup sugar

▶ Cut a shallow cross on the tip of each tamarillo. Place the tamarillos in a medium saucepan with water to cover, bring to a boil over medium heat, and cook until soft, about 20 minutes. Drain the tamarillos and peel. Force the pulp through a medium-mesh strainer into a bowl, pressing with a wooden spoon to extract as much pulp as possible.

Place the puree in a small saucepan or skillet with the cloves, allspice, salt, and sugar. Stir to mix well; simmer over medium-low heat until the sauce is as thick as jam, about 10 minutes. Serve warm.

Storing: The sauce will keep well in the refrigerator, tightly covered, for up to 2 weeks.

MOJOS

Mojo is a generic term for a number of very simple Latin American sauces that usually call for lots of garlic and an acidic medium such as citrus juice or vinegar. The word is thought to derive from the Spanish *mojar*, to moisten. This is plausible, since the role of the *mojo* is to moisten the food it is paired with while endowing it with flavor. But this etymology does not explain why the word *mojo* does not appear in Spanish cookbooks. The *Dictionary of the Royal Academy of the Spanish Language* lists *moje*, not *mojo*, as a generic word for the sauce of any stew. You can find *mojo* only in Andalusia, the Canary Islands, and parts of the New World. The emblematic Canary Islands *mojo* is a spicy cilantro sauce that bears a resemblance to the Puerto Rican *ajilimójili* and the Venezuelan *mojo de cilantro*.

Why were table sauces called *mojos* in the Canary Islands and not *pebres* or *salsas*, as in the rest of the peninsula? My assumption is that Canary Islanders, who had important commercial relations with Portugal from an early period (the islands were formally ceded to Spain during the reign of Ferdinand and Isabella), adopted the Portuguese word *molho*, which is a broad term that designates any kind of sauce, from béchamel to vinaigrette. And it was the Canary Islanders who popularized the word *mojo* in the regions of the New World where they settled in large numbers, such as Cuba, Puerto Rico, and Venezuela.

It was through trade with the Canary Islands and the steady flow of Canary Islands immigrants from the sixteenth century until late into the twentieth century that the Hispanic islands, Colombia, and Venezuela borrowed the variants of Andalusian Spanish and Portuguese that had crystallized there. *Sancocho* (big soup), *mojo*, and *mojito isleño* are all examples of such linguistic and culinary borrowings.

Simple Cuban *Mojo* for Boiled Root Vegetables

Mojo Cubano

This garlicky sauce is the traditional accompaniment to the starchy root vegetables of the Hispanic Caribbean, especially Cuba. The acidic medium is usually Seville, or bitter, orange juice, though lime juice or white vinegar can be substituted. The *mojo* is at its best spooned or brushed over piping-hot boiled yuca, plantains, or other starchy tropical vegetables.

MAKES ABOUT ¾ CUP

12 garlic cloves
  Juice of 1 medium bitter orange (about ¼ cup), lime juice, or distilled white vinegar
½ cup extra-virgin olive oil
1½ teaspoons ground cumin
  Salt and freshly ground black pepper to taste

▶ There are several different ways of combining the ingredients. The most traditional is to pound the garlic to a paste using a mortar and pestle, then to stir in the remaining ingredients. Modern cooks may do the whole thing in a blender or a food processor, but they are careful to leave the sauce a bit coarse. The sauce can also be served hot. Pound or mash the garlic to a paste. Heat the oil in a small saucepan. Add the garlic paste and sauté briefly, then stir in all the other ingredients and serve at once.

Storing: The sauce will keep in the refrigerator, tightly covered, for up to 3 days.

Puerto Rican Cooked Tomato *Mojo*

Mojito Puertorriqueño

The ingredients of this old Puerto Rican *mojo* are the same as those of a simple Spanish *sofrito*. Instead of sautéing these ingredients, however, cooks just boil them together to create a red sauce for fish. Both the sauce and the finished fish dish are called *mojito isleño*, which means, literally, "little island *mojo*."

The technique of boiling together a number of seasoning ingredients similar to those in this Puerto Rican *mojo* is found in several old Spanish and Portuguese recipes for *escabeche*. A popular Brazilian *molho de escabeche*, for instance, calls for boiling onions, vinegar, bay leaves, tomatoes, salt, and black pepper together. The mix is then combined with olive oil and serves as a sauce for fish.

This Puerto Rican *mojito* is delicious over pan-fried or steamed fish or boiled tubers and starchy vegetables.

MAKES ABOUT 5 CUPS

- 1 medium red bell pepper (about 6 ounces), roasted (see page 67), peeled, cored, seeded, and cut into ½-inch-wide strips
- 1 medium onion (about 8 ounces), cut into ⅛-inch slices
- 8 medium plum tomatoes (about 1½ pounds), peeled, seeded, and diced
- 5 garlic cloves, finely chopped
- 1 cup extra-virgin olive oil
- 1 cup water
- 12 Manzanilla (Spanish) olives, with pits
- ¼ cup capers, drained
- 2 tablespoons minced flat-leaf parsley
- 2 bay leaves
- 1 teaspoon salt
- ½ teaspoon freshly ground black pepper

▶ Combine all the ingredients in a medium saucepan and bring to a boil over medium heat. Reduce the heat to medium-low, cover, and cook, stirring occasionally, until the liquid has reduced and the vegetables are melded in a rich sauce, about 40 minutes. Serve hot.

Storing: The sauce will keep in the refrigerator, tightly covered, for up to a week.

Canary Islands Cilantro *Mojo*

El Mojo Isleño de Erótida Cáceres

This version of the traditional Canary Islands cilantro sauce comes from Erótida Cáceres, the mother of Abel Hernández, who founded the Union City, New Jersey, market Mi Bandera (now called Bandera after Abel sold it to one of his partners), for many years the largest, most complete Latin emporium in the Northeast. Abel's mother was born in the Canary Islands and, after marriage, went to live in central Cuba with her farmer husband. She later moved to Miami, where she continued to preside over a hybrid Cuban–Canary Islands kitchen. Periodically she would send Abel huge plastic containers filled with her thick, perfumed green cilantro *mojo*.

The first time I tasted Erótida's *mojo* was as a table sauce for a fabulous, hearty Cuban big soup (*ajiaco*; page 502) that Abel's late wife, Rosita, made for us. I thought the combination was marvelous; the *mojo* was a godsent addition to the thick peasant soup.

MAKES ABOUT 1½ CUPS

1 bunch cilantro, leaves and tender stems

1 head garlic, separated into cloves and peeled

1 medium green bell pepper (about 6 ounces), cored, seeded, deveined, and coarsely chopped

½ cup extra-virgin olive oil

¼ cup distilled white vinegar

1 teaspoon salt

¼ teaspoon ground cumin

▶ Place all the ingredients in a blender or food processor and process to a coarse puree. Serve at room temperature.

Storing: The sauce will keep in the refrigerator, tightly covered, for several weeks.

Venezuelan Yuca *Mojo*

Mojo de Yuca

Venezuela is a land of *mojos*, no doubt because of the many Canary Islanders who settled in the country at different times in its history. You can find true replicas of the popular Canary Islands Cilantro *Mojo* (page 141) and more tropical versions containing avocados and starchy root vegetables such as yuca. This version from the Andes, with yuca, *ají dulce*, and avocado, is a favorite of mine, and I use it in many ways—for example, with Argentinean skirt or rib-eye steaks in lieu of chimichurri, or spooned over creamy seafood soups as a garnish. It is so filling that it can even double as a vegetable side dish.

MAKES ABOUT 5 CUPS

1½ pounds peeled fresh yuca (see page 166) or frozen yuca chunks

12 Caribbean sweet peppers (*ajíes dulces*), seeded and finely chopped

1 medium green bell pepper (about 6 ounces), cored, seeded, deveined, and finely chopped (about ¾ cup)

1½ habanero or Scotch bonnet chile

4 garlic cloves

½ cup extra-virgin olive oil

½ cup cider vinegar or distilled white vinegar

2 teaspoons salt, or to taste

¼ teaspoon ground cumin

1 yellow onion, finely chopped

2 tablespoons finely chopped flat-leaf parsley or cilantro

1 medium West Indian avocado or 2 Hass avocados, pitted, peeled, and cut into ½-inch dice

Cooking the Yuca ▶ Place the yuca in a 4-quart pot, cover with 2 quarts water, and bring to a boil over high heat. Boil until the yuca is fork-tender but still keeps its shape, about 25 minutes. Drain. When the yuca is cool enough to handle, cut into ½-inch dice (you will have about 5 cups).

Making the *Mojo* ▶ Combine the Caribbean peppers, bell pepper, chile, garlic, oil, vinegar, salt, and cumin in a food processor or blender and process to a puree. Place the diced yuca in a bowl and toss with the puree, chopped onion, and parsley. Add the avocado and serve.

Storing: The yuca-pepper mixture will keep in the refrigerator, tightly covered with plastic wrap, for about 2 days; bring to room temperature and add the avocado just before serving.

Puerto Rican–Style
Ají Dulce Sauce

Ajilimójili

Ajilimójili (ah-*hee*-lee-MOH-hee-lee) is the wonderful whimsical name for this Puerto Rican–inspired sauce. How to translate this tongue-twister? It seems that it is a composite of the words *ajo* (garlic) and *moje* (sauce), but much more can be drawn from it. In Cuba and the Mexican state of Tabasco, *ajilimójili* is a colloquialism for the Castilian Spanish *intríngulis*, a hidden reason that is suddenly revealed, or the workings necessary to pull something off, or the key to making a difficult feat look simple. Why was this sauce called *ajilimójili*? Perhaps because it has its own *ajilimójili*—the "inner workings" to make any food it touches splendid. Serve with Puerto Rican *Pasteles* (page 474) or My Fresh Corn Tamales Cuban Style (page 455).

MAKES ABOUT 2¼ CUPS

- 12 Caribbean sweet peppers (*ajíes dulces*)
- 1 cubanelle pepper, seeded and coarsely chopped
- ½ Scotch Bonnet or habanero chile, seeded
- 7 garlic cloves, peeled
- 1 small yellow onion (about 5 ounces), coarsely chopped (about 1 cup)
- 1 cup extra-virgin olive oil
- ⅓ cup distilled white vinegar
- 1 bunch cilantro, leaves stripped from stems (about 2 cups)
- 1¼ teaspoons salt, or to taste
- ½ teaspoon dried oregano
- ¼ teaspoon ground cumin

▶ Combine all the ingredients in a food processor or blender and process to a coarse emerald-green sauce. The sauce will keep in the refrigerator, tightly covered, for 2 to 3 days.

Brazilian Sauce for Grilled Meats

Molho de Campanha

In Brazilian steakhouses, the frillier counterparts of the more rugged Argentinean *parrilladas*, or grilled meats, come to the table with a simple vinegary sauce called *molho de campanha*, which translates as country sauce. It is not as fragrant as chimichurri, but it gives a welcome tart kick to the grilled meats. I like to add some garlic, which is not in the original version.

MAKES 2½ CUPS

- 2 medium plum tomatoes (about 6 ounces), peeled, seeded, and finely chopped
- 1 medium green bell pepper (about 6 ounces), cored, seeded, deveined, and coarsely chopped (about ¾ cup)
- 1 medium white onion (about 8 ounces), coarsely chopped (about 1½ cups)
- 2 garlic cloves, finely chopped (optional)
- ½ cup white wine vinegar or distilled white vinegar
- ¼ cup water
- 2 tablespoons extra-virgin olive oil or sunflower oil
- 1 teaspoon salt
- ½ teaspoon freshly ground black pepper

▶ Mix all the ingredients together in a bowl and let sit for at least 10 minutes. Serve at room temperature. This is best made and served on the same day.

Cacique's Spicy *Malagueta* Pepper Table Sauce

Molho de Pimenta "Lambão"

While staying in a rented house in San Antonio, a residential neighborhood in Salvador's Cidade Alta, I cooked and experienced daily life like a Bahian. For instance, I learned that Bahian food is not inherently hot. Diners often add a spoonful of a spicy table sauce (*molho de pimenta*) to their food to taste, and they have clear ideas about what table sauce is the best complement for each specific food. A combination of small *malagueta* peppers, *dendê* oil, ground dried shrimp, onion, and cilantro is the preferred *molho* for *acarajé*, the black-eyed pea fritters everyone loves in Bahia. For some fish dishes, people like an aromatic and very hot *molho* prepared with *pimenta de cheiro* (a *Capsicum chinense*, the Brazilian counterpart to the habanero chile and Scotch bonnet pepper), scallions, and cilantro.

My friend Jurici Martins da Silva (aka Cacique), my driver and cooking teacher when I visit Salvador, made an all-purpose sauce that I found delicious with all the dishes we cooked at home. He calls it *molho de pimenta lambão*, which basically means, "the hot-pepper table sauce that makes you lick your plate." I have found recipes for this calling for thinly sliced cooked okra, but Cacique's version is simpler, like a *pico de gallo*, with tomatoes, onion, peppers, yellow onion, and cilantro, all finely chopped and mixed together with lime juice and olive oil. The people of Salvador love Portuguese olive oil (*azeite de oliva*), which they call *azeite doce* (sweet oil).

On every visit to the central market with Cacique, we bought hot peppers by the kilo—*pimentas de cheiro* in tones of salmon, red, and yellow; tiny fiery red and green *malagueta* peppers; yellow and purplish *cumari* peppers; finger-length *dedos de moça*. I wanted to experiment with them in my cooking, and also use them as decoration, beautifully displayed on the woven-straw square sieves I had bought by the dozen at the market. I whirled the peppers without ceremony into a number of table sauces I created to accompany our everyday food, but Cacique was more particular about which one to use for each particular *molho*. For his *molho de pimenta lambão*, he used only the tiny *malagueta*. He was looking for a clean flavor and straightforward heat without the herbaceous quality and heady aroma of the *pimenta de cheiro*.

Cook's Note: *Malagueta* is a *Capsicum frutescens* somewhat similar in shape and taste to Tabasco pepper. I have grown *malagueta* in my garden, but I have not found it fresh in my local markets. You can use the pickled *malagueta* pepper sold in bottles in Brazilian markets, but I find it too vinegary (it needs a rinsing). It is better to use a fresh pepper like those sold as hot finger peppers in Hispanic markets, which are a bit longer (about 2 inches long) and thicker than *malagueta*, but have a similar clean taste. Fresh cayenne (preferably red), serrano chiles, and better still the tiny Asian bird pepper or bird's-eye pepper (which is pretty similar to *malagueta*) will also work well for this recipe.

MAKES 1½ CUPS

20 *malagueta* peppers (red and some green), fresh or pickled, stemmed (see suggested substitutions in Cook's Note)

1 teaspoon salt
   Juice of 2 limes (about ¼ cup)

1 ripe medium tomato (about 7 ounces), finely chopped (about 1 cup)

¼ (about 2¼ ounces) of a medium yellow onion, finely chopped

2–3 tablespoons cilantro, finely chopped

⅓ cup extra-virgin olive oil or to taste (a bit less will also work)

▶ Chop the peppers coarsely and crush with the salt with a mortar and pestle or chop finely. Add to a bowl and mix with the lime juice, tomato, onion, cilantro, and olive oil. Stir to mix and serve as a table sauce. This hot *molho* is best when freshly made but it can be refrigerated for a couple of days. It tastes best at room temperature.

Brazilian Hot Pepper and Lime Sauce

Molho de Pimenta e Limão

The tang of fresh limes and the heat of fiery *malagueta* peppers in this simple table sauce give a much needed jolt of brightness to the dark, earthy flavors of a *feijoada*.

MAKES 1½ CUPS

16 pickled *malagueta* or *cumari* peppers, lightly crushed with the side of a knife

1 small yellow onion (about 4 ounces), very finely chopped (about ½ cup)

6 garlic cloves, finely chopped

2 scallions, white part only, finely chopped (about 2 tablespoons)

½ cup extra-virgin olive oil

2 tablespoons distilled white vinegar
Juice of 4–5 large limes (about ½ cup)

2 teaspoons salt or to taste

▶ Place all ingredients in a small glass bowl and mix to blend. Let rest for a few minutes before serving to let all flavors meld. The sauce can be prepared the day before and refrigerated, covered with plastic film. Bring to room temperature before serving as a table sauce for the *feijoada completa* (page 512).

CULTURED CREAM AND MILK

SUERO, CREMA, Y NATA

Among the great European legacies in Latin America are the dairy herds brought by the Spanish, which today give us our many good cheeses and their by-products. No other part of the world has better versions of soured cream and milk. You must remember that milk and cream curdle very quickly in tropical countries. One preservation method is canning; another important one is letting the lactic acid bacteria do their work and eating the results in the form of lightly fermented products resembling sour cream, crème fraîche, or yogurt, but with flavors all their own. These are among our favorite finishing touches, almost like instant little sauces. We also use them to some extent in cooking, though some will break down with too much heat. Latin cooks and diners well know that like other milk products, these have a wonderful ability to soften the sting of hot chiles—the reason that yogurt is often eaten or drunk with hot dishes in India.

Mexican cookbooks used to recommend U.S. supermarket sour cream for everything from refried bean toppings to enchilada fillings, but the flavor was never quite right. Today Latin markets in this country carry bottled versions of *crema mexicana* that are much closer to the *crema* sold in Mexico. Go into any Latin store and ask for *crema*, and everyone will know that you mean cultured rather then fresh cream. A similar thing happened when large numbers of immigrants from El Salvador and other Central American nations started looking for their own forms of ripened cream here. You can now find products labeled *crema salvadoreña* or *crema centroamericana* next to the *crema mexicana* in many Latin American groceries. Do not try to substitute the Mexican kind, much less ordinary sour cream, for Salvadorian or Central American *crema*; the real thing is saltier and riper-tasting.

Although it is convenient to have these products in U.S. markets, the labels of the commercial versions usually list so many dubious additives that I am happier making my own. If you have ever made crème fraîche, the formula is the same. If you are new to homemade cultured cream, *crema mexicana* (page 148) is good to begin with because it is so simple. All you do is mix a little buttermilk or sour cream into heavy cream and leave the mixture in a warm place for 18 to 24 hours before refrigerating. Check the label to be sure that the buttermilk or sour cream contains active cultures and that the cream has not been ultrapasteurized. This smooth, silky cream is interchangeable with a Venezuelan counterpart that goes by the name of *nata*.

Venezuelan Ripened Milk

Suero Venezolano

Among my favorite Latin cultured dairy products is a kind of sour milk from northern Venezuela that I have never seen in this country. It is called *suero*, which is the word for whey in Spanish. The Venezuelan *suero*, however, is unrelated to what we usually call whey. On its home turf—especially the town of Carora in Lara state—people make it by pouring milk into a dried gourd that has been prepared like an old-fashioned artisanal cheese culture; successive batches of milk are added to the gourd, then discarded and replaced until the right combinations of lactic-acid bacteria have set up shop.

I have made *suero* following the instructions of a Carora-born restaurateur I met in Barquisimeto, the capital of Lara. I tried to get him to sell me one of his already cured gourds, but he wouldn't part with it. So I bought one at a nearby roadside stand and had it up and running a few days after I got back to my own kitchen. I have also made *suero* by the simpler method of adding a buttermilk or sour cream starter to whole milk. It is worth doing both for its own sake and because when you drain the liquid to concentrate it, it makes a fine stand-in for *crema centroamericana* (page 147). Serve *suero* as an accompaniment to Venezuelan Pan-Fried Shredded Beef (page 715), or Venezuelan *arepas* (pages 586 and 587).

MAKES 1 QUART

- 4 cups whole milk
- 2 tablespoons buttermilk or sour cream (not low-fat) with active cultures
- ¼ teaspoon salt, or to taste

▶ Place the milk in a medium saucepan and gently warm it to 82°F. Remove from the heat and stir in the buttermilk and salt. Pour into a large nonreactive container (stainless steel, glass, enamel, or glazed earthenware). Cover with a cloth and place in a warm spot where the temperature will remain fairly constant at around 77°F. Do not move or jostle the bowl, and allow to sit for about 24 hours.

When the milk has reached the consistency of a very runny yogurt, transfer to a tightly covered glass jar and refrigerate. The *suero* will thicken a bit but will remain fluid.

Storing: The sauce will keep, refrigerated, for 2 weeks.

Ecuadorian Curd and Whey

Suero Blanco

This soupy dish of curd and whey is beloved in Ecuador's Manabí province, where people eat it like a soup, with fire-roasted plantains and one of two closely related condiments: the *maní quebrado* described on page 155, or a similarly seasoned blend of toasted peanuts and dried corn called *salprieta* (dark salt). I plan my trips to cacao farms in the region in time for breakfast just to savor this addictive combination that is never missing at a farmer's table. It is also a condiment of sorts, not unlike Central American cream or Mexican *crema*, as it is spooned over roasted plantain and even rice to enhance their flavor. *Suero blanco* grows on you, like cereal or oatmeal in the morning.

SERVES 4

2 recipes Madrid's Fresh Cheese (page 104)
½ teaspoon salt or to taste

▶ To make *suero blanco*, follow the recipe for Madrid's Fresh Cheese through the stage of draining the curd in a cheesecloth-lined colander. This time set the colander over a deep bowl or medium saucepan to catch all the whey. Let drain for about 2 hours; the curd should still remain somewhat moist.

Divide the curd into equal parts. Place one in a blender with the drained whey and the salt and process to the consistency of a creamy soup. Season the remaining curd with more salt to taste and loosely shape into four equal-sized balls. Place a ball of curd in each of four soup plates, as is traditional in Manabí, and spoon the creamy *suero* around it.

Serving: In Manabí, *suero blanco* is served for breakfast with roasted ripe or green plantains and a side of rice. I simply love it with Ember-Roasted Plantains (page 184) sprinkled with Manabí Golden Crushed Peanuts (page 155).

Central American Ripened Cream

Crema Centroamericana

The ripened cream eaten by Salvadorians, Hondurans, and other Central Americans is much like the Mexican version (page 148), but the few differences are crucial. Mexican cream has a very pure taste just barely offset by a subtle acidity. Central American cream, *crema centroamericana* or *crema salvadoreña*, has a saltier tang and more of a fermented taste. You cannot substitute one for the other without altering the balance of flavors in a dish.

I have experimented with recipes for homemade *crema centroamericana*, and the closest I have come to the original is to prepare Venezuelan *suero*, then drain off some of the whey until it is about as thick as kefir. It is finished with either a discreet touch (my preference) or a generous dose of salt (the Salvadorian way). The combination of tartness, saltiness, and creaminess makes the *crema* ideal for folding into beans, topping ripe plantains, or as a side for Salvadorian Grilled Sirloin Tip Steak (page 704).

MAKES ABOUT 2 CUPS

> A double recipe of Venezuelan Ripened Milk (*suero*; page 146)
>
> ½ teaspoon salt, or to taste

▶ Line a colander with a double layer of cheesecloth and set it over a large bowl. Ladle the *suero* into the cheesecloth and let it drain for 2 to 3 hours.

Pour off the whey and reserve for another use if desired, such as Ecuadorian Whey Hot Pepper Sauce (page 123). Gather up the edges of the cheesecloth, tie into a knot, and continue to drain over the bowl until no liquid is dripping, about 4 hours. Alternatively, gather up the edges of the cloth and twist to squeeze out the excess whey (this is faster but might result in some loss of the curd).

Place the drained curd in a bowl and stir in the salt a little at a time with a wooden spoon). Transfer to a glass jar and refrigerate, tightly covered.

Storing: The *crema* will keep well in the refrigerator for about 2 weeks.

Variation: Central American Dip
This version of *crema* makes a great dip for empanadas and tamales when blended with garlic, scallions, and peppers, both sweet and hot. For 1 cup of the cream, I usually use 2 garlic cloves, 1 scallion (white and pale green part), 4 to 6 tiny fresh Caribbean peppers (*ajíes dulces*), stemmed and seeded, and 1 habanero chile, stemmed and seeded; but the proportions can be varied to taste. Coarsely chop the seasonings, combine in a food processor with the cream, and puree.

Mexican or Venezuelan Ripened Cream
Crema Mexicana o Nata Venezolana

Crema, a slightly tart fermented cream very similar to the French *crème fraîche*, has a soothing finish that softens the edge of many fiery Latin dishes. Milk, cultured creams, and yogurt help neutralize capsaicin (the alkaloid that makes hot peppers hot) and cool your burning mouth. But even if you don't need to put out a fire, this recipe provides a satiny and sensuous complement to many Mexican foods. Nowadays you can buy commercial U.S.–made versions labeled *crema mexicana*, but none is as delicious as one you make yourself. The Venezuelan ripened cream called *nata* is made the same way.

MAKES ABOUT 2 CUPS

> 2 cups heavy cream (not ultrapasteurized)
> 6 tablespoons buttermilk or sour cream (not low-fat) with active cultures

▶ Pour the cream and buttermilk into a glass jar, seal tightly, and shake to combine thoroughly. Set in a warm place where the temperature will remain fairly constant at about 77°F. Let sit for 18 to 24 hours without disturbing or jostling.

When the *crema* has thickened to the consistency of a slightly runny yogurt, refrigerate, tightly covered. It will continue to thicken as it chills.

Storing: The *crema* will keep for about 2 weeks.

BRAZILIAN CLARIFIED BUTTER
Manteiga de Garrafa

In northeastern Brazil, particularly in Pernambuco, you will find a bottle filled with a warm amber liquid on restaurant tables. This is *manteiga de garrafa*, a clarified butter made from whey rich in butterfat.

At first I found the idea of drizzling melted butter over a plate of air-dried beef (*carne seca*), yuca, and beans a bit strange, but after trying it once, I was hooked. *Manteiga de garrafa* is no ordinary fat. It is a flavoring that combines the pungent, musky, tart taste of *queijo mineiro curado* (a popular aged cow's milk cheese from Minas) and the soothing qualities of butter—a perfect complement to the slightly dry, salty, earthy dishes of the Brazilian northeast. The best *manteiga de garrafa* I've had came from the Ilha de Marajó in the delta of the Amazon River, and it was made from buffalo milk whey.

Marajó, which is the size of Switzerland, is the world's largest alluvial island. Periodically the swollen waters of the Amazon inundate the island's lowlands, creating an ideal habitat for water buffalo. On Marajó and in other parts of South America, such as the Paria peninsula in Venezuela, where water buffalo have been introduced, cheeses are often made without adding rennet. Artisanal cheese makers place the mass of curds in square containers and weight them with large stones or cement blocks to separate the curds from the whey, which is rich in butterfat—ideal for *manteiga de garrafa*. Buffalo milk is rich in fat, with almost 8 percent butter compared to the 3 to 4 percent in cow's milk. If you are unable to find *manteiga de garrafa* in Brazilian markets, use clarified butter or Indian ghee to add a silky touch to boiled yuca, beans, and Brazilian dried beef dishes. ◆

RELISHES AND PICKLES

ENCURTIDOS

Yucatecan Red Onions Pickled in Bitter Orange Juice

Salsa de Cebolla

This cooling and pungent relish made with red onions and bitter orange juice is the obligatory accompaniment for *cochinita pibil*, the pit-barbecued pig of the Yucatán. I love how the thinly sliced onions turn a beautiful light purple when drenched in the bright citrus juice.

MAKES ABOUT 4 CUPS

1 large red onion (about 12 ounces), cut lengthwise in half and thinly slivered
   Juice of about 8 bitter oranges (about 2 cups) or equal parts lime juice and orange juice
¼ cup finely chopped cilantro
1 habanero chile, seeded and finely chopped

▶ Treat the onion according to the instructions on page 139. Combine the onion with the remaining ingredients in a bowl, tossing to distribute well. Any leftover juices can be used to make a refreshing vinaigrette.

Storing: The onions will keep in the refrigerator, covered, for about 2 days.

Peruvian Onion and Yellow Pepper Relish

Salsa Criolla Peruana

This simple onion sauce, found on every Peruvian table, imparts a welcome freshness and crunch along with a wonderful jolt of heat and acidity that rounds out the flavors of any hearty Peruvian dish, from home-cured ham (page 727) to tamales (page 472).

MAKES ABOUT 2½ CUPS

- 1 large red onion (about 10 ounces) cut lengthwise in half and thinly slivered
- 1 fresh-frozen yellow Andean pepper (*ají amarillo*), thawed, seeded, and cut into thin 2-inch-long strips (or substitute a hot Hungarian wax or banana pepper)
- 1 teaspoon salt
- ½ cup fresh lime juice

▶ Treat the onion according to the instructions on page 139. Toss the onion in a small bowl with the remaining ingredients and let stand for at least 30 minutes before serving. This is best served the same day it is made.

Guatemalan Red Cabbage Slaw/Relish

Col Morada Encurtida Guatemalteca

This is a classic, a flavorful, intensely purple-red cabbage slaw/relish that Guatemalans dollop freely over tamales and enchiladas. They also eat it with grilled beef. Raquel Mazariego, who has a catering business in Guatemala City, taught me the recipe. To obtain a deeper purple color, she adds some beet juice to the dressing; I have made it optional.

MAKES ABOUT 7 CUPS

- 1 medium red cabbage, cored and finely shredded
- 2 medium red onions (about 8 ounces each), cut lengthwise in half and thinly sliced
- 1 large carrot, shredded
- 1 jalapeño, seeded and minced
- 1 cup red wine vinegar
- ¼ cup grated brown loaf sugar (*piloncillo* or *panela*) or Muscovado sugar, or dark brown sugar (about 5 tablespoons)
- 1 cup extra-virgin olive oil
- ¼ cup beet juice (optional)
- ¼ cup fresh lime juice
  Grated zest of 1 bitter orange or regular orange
- ¼ cup finely chopped cilantro
- 2 bay leaves
- ⅛ teaspoon ground allspice
  Salt and freshly ground black pepper to taste

▶ Bring a large pot of salted water to a boil. Add the cabbage and blanch for 2 minutes. Drain well in a colander.

Turn the cabbage out into a large bowl and add the onion, carrot, and chile. Toss well. Add the remaining ingredients and toss well.

Storing: The relish will keep in the refrigerator, tightly covered, for 2 to 3 days.

Honduran Pickled Jalapeños

Curtido de Jalapeños

Many years ago on my first trip to Honduras, I stayed at the Gran Hotel Sula in San Pedro Sula. I was impressed by the buffet: the selection was terrific, and I especially loved a beautiful large dish brimming with onions, bay leaves, and ripe jalapeño peppers, which guests ate as a relish. The chef, Hernando Moreno, who was Colombian, not only gave me this and other recipes but became my informal guide to San Pedro Sula, taking me to markets and private homes, always comparing the foods of Honduras with those of Colombia, which I had just visited. In this way, Colombia became a handle that eased my way into the Honduran kitchen.

To duplicate the dish I so admired, use a combination of ripe red and green jalapeño peppers. If red ones are not available, you can get the same spicy kick using only green chiles, though the relish will not be as colorful.

MAKES ABOUT 4 CUPS

 1 cup extra-virgin olive oil
 2 medium white onions (about 8 ounces each), cut
   into ½-inch dice
 12 garlic cloves, peeled
 24 jalapeños, preferably a combination of red and
   green
 10 bay leaves
   Salt to taste
 1 teaspoon dried oregano
 1 teaspoon black peppercorns
 1 cup distilled white vinegar

▶ Heat the oil in a large skillet over medium heat until hot. Add the onions, garlic, chiles, and bay leaves and fry, stirring, for 5 minutes, until the chiles are soft. Add salt. Add the oregano and black peppercorns and cook for 1 minute, stirring. Add the vinegar and cook for 2 minutes longer. Remove from the heat and let cool to room temperature.

Transfer the relish to a glass container and refrigerate, tightly covered, for 2 to 3 days before serving.

Storing: The relish will keep well for about 2 weeks.

Salvadorian *Pupusa* Relish

Curtido Salvadoreño

The street vendors who make *pupusas*, Salvadorian filled tortillas (page 401), prepare this simple relish every day. For them, the relish is as important as making the dough and the filling for the *pupusas*. Very early in the morning, you see women grating cabbage and carrots with box graters, packing them into large glass jars, and adding distilled white vinegar diluted with some water. That's how simple the classic *curtido* is. By midafternoon, the first batch is practically gone, and they have to start again.

MAKES ABOUT 6 CUPS

 1 medium white cabbage (1½ pounds), cored
 1 large carrot (about 8 ounces), peeled
 1 cup distilled white vinegar
 ¼ cup water
 1½ teaspoons salt
 1 teaspoon dried oregano

▶ Shred the cabbage and carrot on the large holes of a box grater. Place in a large bowl, add the remaining ingredients, and toss to combine well. Use within 1 day.

Storing: To keep the relish for longer than 1 day, pack it into a sterile glass jar and add enough vinegar to cover. Cover tightly and refrigerate for up to 4 days.

TABLE CONDIMENTS FOR FLAVOR AND TEXTURE

That bowl you find on the table in any Brazilian restaurant is filled not with sawdust, as it might appear at first glance, but with a coarse meal called *farinha*, from the endlessly useful yuca plant, also called *mandioca* in Brazil. It takes time to get used to sprinkling this enrichment on your Brazilian stews and dried beef (*carne seca*), but it will start to grow on you, and you will begin to understand its place in a Brazilian meal. For one thing, it adds crunchy texture. For another, it rounds out the other flavors of the meal with its earthy taste—and it binds the fat of any sauce or stew with the other ingredients, making it taste less greasy.

Farinha is a coarse flour made from bitter yuca after grinding and squeezing the grated pulp to extract its poisonous juice. In the Orinoco Basin and other parts of tropical America, the flour is mostly used for a flatbread called *casabe*, but in Brazil it is also toasted to make the flavorful *farinha torrada*. *Farinha* is the ultimate movable food of Brazil, deeply connected to its advancing frontier—muleteers would make a mixture of *farinha* and beef, which nourished them as they rode into the interior. *Farinha* later became the food of the slaves, and from their kitchens, it moved into the kitchens of every Brazilian to become the crowning table condiment at every meal.

At any market in Brazil, from the sleek European-style Central Market of São Paulo (one of the cleanest of Latin America) to the labyrinths of Ver-o-Peso in Bélem, in the Amazon, you can find a bewildering array of *farinhas*: yellow and coarse; grayish white or toasted to a light tan hue; very coarse and granular; or labeled with the names from different regions of the country. On a recent visit, I started buying every type I could find and did my own private tasting. In each one, I could taste the unmistakable flavor of yuca, yet they were all distinctive. It is not surprising to see that these *farinhas* all have different uses. Some are fried with *dendê oil*, or with olive oil or butter. Others are used as an ingredient, mixed with kale or beans, as in the black bean dish (*feijoao tropeiro*) of Minas Gerais, or with dried beef in *paçoca*, a specialty of the Brazilian northeast. And still others are turned into thick porridges called *pirão* by cooking them in flavorful broth.

In Brazilian markets, you will always find raw and toasted *farinha*, labeled respectively *farinha crua* and *farinha torrada*. Brazilian recipes are specific as to which one should be used.

The following are Brazil's most popular *farinhas*:

Farinha torrada: In São Paulo, this golden-brown fine-grained *farinha* is the usual accompaniment to *feijoada* (page 512). This coarse yuca flour is toasted (*torrada*) on a *comal*-like flat clay griddle or in a special pot.

Farinha d'agua: This *farinha* has large, hard, pale yellow granules. It is made with bitter yellow yuca that is processed in a special way. Before grating the tubers, the indigenous people of Pará state soak them in water for several days, almost to the point of fermentation, then peel and grate the softened yuca. The pulp is squeezed in the traditional *tipiti*, a cone made of palm fibers, then sun-dried and passed though a sieve. This *farinha* is eaten raw. It is a favorite in the north of the country.

Simple Buttered *Farofa*

Farofa de Manteiga

When yuca flour, *farinha*, is cooked in fat (olive oil, palm oil, or butter), or enriched with flavoring ingredients, or mixed with eggs or kale, it is rechristened *farofa*. Brazilian cooks have created hundreds of different versions taking advantage of the chameleon-like ability of starchy *farinha* to absorb flavors. In this simple recipe from Minas Gerais, the *farinha* is sautéed in butter and seasoned with a traditional *tempero*, a mixture of pureed aromatics. It can accompany any Brazilian dish, but it is tailor-made for saucy ones.

Cook's Note: When making any *farofa*, remember to sauté the *farinha* briefly and keep it on the dry side, especially if working with raw (*crua*) *farinha*. If you cook it with too much liquid or too long, it will clump.

MAKES ABOUT 2½ CUPS (ENOUGH FOR 6 SERVINGS)

½ small white onion (about 5 ounces), quartered
1 scallion, trimmed
2 garlic cloves, peeled
2 flat-leaf parsley sprigs
3 tablespoons butter
2 cups *farinha crua* or *farinha torrada* (available in Brazilian and Portuguese markets)
¼ teaspoon salt

▶ Place the onion, scallion, garlic, and parsley in a blender or food processor and process to a fine puree.

Heat the butter in a medium skillet over medium heat until it foams. Add the puree and sauté for 2 minutes, or until the moisture evaporates. Stir in the *farinha* and cook, stirring, for 1 minute to mix well. Turn out into a bowl and serve at once.

Scrambled Egg *Farofa*

Farofa de Ovo

Farofa de ovo is one of the many accompaniments that go with a full-scale Brazilian *Feijoada*, or *feijoada completa* (page 512). Some recipes call for hard-boiled eggs. I much prefer the flavor of this scrambled egg version.

SERVES 4

1 small white onion (about 5 ounces)
3 tablespoons olive oil or butter
5 eggs, lightly beaten
1 cup *farinha torrada*
¼ teaspoon salt, or to taste

▶ Grate the onion on the fine side of a box grater. Heat the oil in a medium skillet over medium heat until it ripples. Add the onion and cook, stirring, for 2 to 3 minutes, until the moisture evaporates. Stir in the eggs and cook, stirring with a fork, until they just start to thicken and set. Stir in the *farinha* and salt and cook until the eggs are set. Serve at once.

Ecuadorian Toasted Corn

Tostado

There is a round and fleshy corn, similar to the grain of the Lucanas, that the Spaniards eat as a toasted tidbit, and it has a better taste than roasted garbanzos.
—JOSÉ DE ACOSTA,
Historia natural y moral de las Indias (Natural and Moral History of the Indes), sixteenth century

Toasted corn is one of the pleasures of Ecuadorian and Peruvian kitchens. Eaten with cebiche, it provides a nutty, crunchy complement to the tart citrusy seafood that is never forgotten once tasted. It is just about obligatory with boiled *chochos* (Andean lupins) and the tasty fried pork morsels called *fritada* (page 394). It also makes a great snack by itself.

Ecuadorians refer to toasted corn simply as *tostado*. The variety most used is a yellowish dent corn called *chulpi*. In the province of Azuay, in southern Ecuador, people prefer a white corn called *huarmi-blanco*. Ecuadorians have a way with toasted corn. They flavor it with lard left over from making the *fritada*, full of wonderful garlic and cumin flavor; the dark lard extracted from pork fat (see page 82); or lard infused with scallions and garlic.

In the highlands, it is not unusual to find a bowl of hominy and a bowl of *tostado* waiting on any restaurant table, the way you would find bread in the United States.

Latin markets in the United States sell dried corn for toasting from both Peru and Ecuador. The Peruvian corn is usually labeled *cancha*. It is easy to recognize, with large white kernels. Ecuadorian dent corn has smaller, pointy kernels, but you will also find brands with larger kernels similar to the Peruvian kind. They will all work well for this recipe.

MAKES 3 CUPS

- 14 ounces Ecuadorian or Peruvian corn for toasting
- 2 tablespoons freshly rendered lard (page 82)
- 1 garlic clove, peeled
- Salt to taste

▶ Combine the corn and 2 quarts water in a medium saucepan and bring to a boil over high heat. Lower the heat to medium, cover, and cook for 20 minutes. Remove from the heat and let stand for 1 hour.

Drain the corn, pat dry with towels, and spread on a cookie sheet to dry thoroughly, preferably overnight.

Heat the lard in a large heavy pot over medium heat. Stir in the corn and cook, uncovered, until golden brown and crunchy. The corn will jump like missiles once it begins to toast, in about 2 minutes. As soon as this happens, clap on the lid, leaving just enough of an opening for a wooden spoon. Stir from time to time, until all the kernels are golden brown but not burned, about 15 minutes. Add the garlic close to the end of the cooking time, stirring so it flavors all the kernels.

Remove the corn from the heat, discard garlic, stir in the salt, and turn out into a serving dish.

Ecuadorian Tiny Popcorn

Canguil

In Ecuador, a variety of corn with very small pointy kernels called *canguil* is used to make popcorn. This treat makes it to the table as one of the companions of cebiche or of fried morsels of pork, *fritada*. In the Ecuadorian highlands, a bowl of *canguil* comes to the table in lieu of the otherwise ubiquitous hominy, proof that *canguil* is considered not only a snack or a side dish but a food in its own right. People like to toss it with their cebiches or *fritadas* or to dip it in spicy hot pepper sauce.

Cook's Note: In El Salvador, I found a tiny round popcorn called *maicillo* that is used for both popping and chicken feed. It is very similar to *canguil*, and the kernels open like miniature rosettes that are delightful to eat. But if you can't find these Lilliputian wonders, use regular popcorn.

MAKES 4 CUPS

- 2 tablespoons corn oil
- 4 ounces popcorn (about 1 cup)
  Salt to taste

▶ Heat the oil over low heat in a large heavy-bottomed pot with two stout handles and a well-fitting lid. Lower the heat to medium. Add the corn and cover the pot. In less than 20 seconds, the corn will begin to pop. Using kitchen towels or mitts, grab the pot by the handles, anchoring the lid with your thumbs, and shake the pot. Repeat every 20 seconds or so; the corn will be ready in about 2 minutes. Season with salt to taste and serve.

Manabí Golden Crushed Peanuts

Maní Quebrado de Manabí

Nowhere else in Ecuador or in any other country of Latin America are peanuts more lavishly used than in Manabí, a beautiful coastal region along the Pacific, birthplace of the legendary Panama hat and with a reputation as the best dining destination in the country. Perhaps Manabí's peanut addiction is a legacy of its pre-Columbian past. The Manteño culture, which flourished in this region between A.D. 850–1535, is one of the seminal civilizations of South America. The Manteños were skilled farmers and eager travelers who sailed in large rafts south and north along the Pacific coast, as far as Central America, in search of colorful Spondylus shells. It is just beginning to be known that they were also accomplished city builders. The settlement at Jaboncillo, a hill not far from Manta, the capital of the province, has been likened in scope by archaeologists to ten Machu Picchus.

It was after a trip to Jaboncillo, still impressed by the Manteños' elaborate irrigation works and terraced fields, that I tasted peanuts in dozens of forms—in soups, sauces, braises—at El Tomate, a roadside restaurant in Puerto Viejo, not far from the archaeological site. I had been directed there earlier by my Manta-born friends Rosalía Cevallos Savando and Lourdes Delgado, who insisted this was the best place in the region to taste traditional food. On my first visit I had been smitten by an unusual combination of ripe plantains roasted in an outdoor tandoor-like oven at the back of the restaurant and served with a dish of curd and whey in wide soup plates, accompanied by a table condiment of crunchy toasted and crushed peanuts seasoned with onions sautéed in achiote-infused oil and mixed with chopped cilantro (often called *yerbita*, "little herb," in Manabí). The chef and owner of the place, an enterprising woman named Aidee Rodríguez Molina, came to our table apologizing because she could not serve us *salprieta*, another iconic condiment of the region, a blend of toasted peanuts and corn ground to a fine powder seasoned like the cracked peanuts. I told her not to worry; I had simply fallen in love with her *maní quebrado*.

On a visit to Bahía de Caráquez, an important port in the northern part of the province, I had the fortune to meet María Dolores Gutiérrez, a gifted cook, at the lovely bayside hotel El Ceibo. She gave me an unforgettable cooking lesson that to my delight started with making the ubiquitous soupy curd and whey dish I had enjoyed at El Tomate (and on every cacao farm I visited in the region in time for breakfast) with the crunchy peanut sidekick I had so admired at El Tomate. Aidee explained that she preferred it to *salprieta* and gave me a few pounds to take home.

When I returned to New Jersey, I adapted the peanut seasoning and now serve it at my restaurant Cucharamama with ripe plantains roasted in our wood-burning oven. It is a wonderful and versatile seasoning that can be spooned over soups, salads, and just about anything that needs some crunch.

MAKES 2 CUPS

- 2 cups shelled toasted peanuts (about 4½ ounces)
- 2½ tablespoons achiote-infused corn oil (page 89)
- 1 small yellow onion (about 5 ounces), finely chopped (about 1 cup)
- 2 tablespoons finely chopped cilantro
- ¾ teaspoon salt or to taste

▶ Heat a dry, heavy-bottomed medium skillet over medium heat. Add the peanuts and toast, stirring, until a deeper golden brown. Scoop out of the skillet and let cool a little. Place in the bowl of a food processor and pulse only until the peanuts are coarsely chopped. Place in a small bowl. Add the oil to the skillet and heat over medium heat. Add the onion and sauté, stirring, until soft, about 3 minutes. Pour over the peanuts, add the cilantro and salt, and toss to mix. Cover with plastic film and store in the refrigerator if not using immediately. Bring to room temperature before using. Use as a table condiment with coastal dishes like Ember-Roasted Plantains (page 184) and Ecuadorian Curd and Whey (page 147).

CHAPTER 5

TROPICAL ROOTS AND STARCHY VEGETABLES

IN THIS CHAPTER

In June, when nightly frost covers the fields in the Bolivian highland plains (*altiplano*) and farmers gather around to sort their freeze-dried potatoes, they tell the story of Atojj and the parrots. Atojj, a greedy, hungry fox, climbed up to heaven to eat his fill of all the wonderful vegetables and fruits that did not then exist on earth. His hunger satiated, he was starting to climb back down on a rope when a flock of parrots fluttered close enough to annoy him. The fox began jeering at them: "Hear me, you with the hooked noses, you dirty little beasts." Angered, the parrots flapped their wings, cawed, and protested, threatening to cut the rope if he did not take back his words. The cunning fox asked for forgiveness, but the moment the parrots flew off, he was back to his old tricks, mocking the colorful birds. They returned again, demanding that he stop his nasty mutterings. Once more the crafty fox obliged and apologized, but as soon as he thought the birds were far away, he resumed his abusive catcalling. This time the furious parrots swooped down and gnawed at the fox's rope with their beaks until it was severed. The fox plunged to earth, crying, "Please spread a blanket for me!" But to no avail. When he hit the ground, his belly split open, and the seeds of the plants he had eaten in heaven went scattering over the earth.

Tales like this can be found all over the Americas, and they follow a similar pattern. Invariably they involve some wily, ambitious figure who raids the fruits of heaven and fails to get away with it—but his fall brings about the miracle of food on earth.

These fertility myths drive home the intense connection that the first people of the Americas felt with their staple plants. The tale of the greedy Atojj can also be seen as an apt metaphor for the colli-sion we call colonization. Like Atojj, the Iberian conquistadores were driven by curiosity and greed to plunder another realm's wealth. Their bloody conquest of native populations in the Americas brought about the destruction of civilizations and massive disruption of ecosystems. But the impact of the crash was worldwide and scattered the riches of the plundered lands across oceans and continents to Europe, Asia, and Africa: potatoes to Spain and Ireland, sweet potatoes to Japan, corn and yuca to tropical Africa. Conversely, some of today's Latin staple plants came here from the other side of the globe. This fact has long been forgotten, and the "new" arrivals (plantains, taro, African yams, fava beans, chickpeas, and many others) are regarded today as purely Latin foods.

There is much that we don't know about these exchanges. What we do know is that several Old World imports quickly and effortlessly fitted into the agricultural system developed centuries earlier in the American tropics. Rice, however, required new skills and special conditions, as did the grains that Europeans tried to introduce to the New World. Wheat called for farming techniques and systems of land organization that would irrevocably change those areas where cultivation succeeded (parts of Mexico, the Andean high plains, and the temperate regions of South America). Both wheat and rice had to be planted and tended as monocultures, a concept that came easily to Europeans but was quite alien to the Taíno (Arawak), Aztec, Inca, and Amazon and Orinoco Indian way of seeing the land.

Plant culture was the backbone of every civilization the Europeans encountered in the Americas. Though puzzled by the scant use of meat in many societies they encountered and by the absence of fields tilled in the recognizable European manner, nearly everywhere they stood in awe of the indigenous farmers and their skills, which left far fewer people hungry or starving than in Europe.

The plants I introduce in this chapter are tropical natives or adoptees that still come close to being the staff of life in different parts of Latin America. But I must clear up a misconception. People from European, North American, and even Asian food traditions almost automatically equate staple plants with monocultures, such as wheat or rice fields. In all parts of Latin America, from the lowland tropics to the Andean *altiplano*, the real staff-of-life plants have traditionally been grown as a complex of many different kinds, densely interplanted on tiny plots of land lovingly tended by peasant families usually right next to their homes.

Such crowded polycultures have persisted to this day, in spite of the progressive industrialization of agriculture everywhere in Latin America, because they are an incredibly resourceful, efficient use of space, labor, and soil. It is a triumph of the human spirit that people who were herded together on great plantations and forced to work monocultures of cash crops such as sugar, cacao, and coffee for European and North American consumption continued to grow their own food as much as possible by this ancient, sustainable system.

The core dishes of each region of Latin America are the direct reflection of what has traditionally been grown in these small fields next to people's homes. During my travels through stretches of the Latin American countryside where the old ways still prevail, I could instantly discern the foundation of the regional cuisine just by looking at what these tiny plots produced.

In Mexico and other Central American countries, the traditional mixed-use patches of land are called *milpas*, from the Nahuatl *milli* (seedbed). Corn, beans, and squash—the three plants that fed Mesoamericans for millennia before Cortés—are the backbone of these small plots of land. Other flavorful vegetables, such as peppers, tomatoes, and tomatillos, are planted around the intertwined trio of staples. In the Andean countries and western Amazonia, the local plots are called *chacras*. This was the Quechua name for potato fields in the middle reaches of the Andes, which the Spaniards later applied to all vegetable farms. In every region of the Andes, there are groups of plants that normally grow together. In Peru, for instance, at altitudes between 7,500 feet and 11,500 feet, the sturdy corn, beans, and squash grow with potatoes of different kinds and a number of nutritious roots like *arracacha* and *yacón*. At higher altitudes, between 11,500 feet and 13,500 feet, where corn does not prosper, some types of potatoes are planted with root vegetables such as *oca*, *ulluco*, and *mashua*, legumes like the lupin *tarwi*, and quinoa (it looks like a cereal grain but doesn't belong to the same botanical family) and its relative *kañigua* (also spelled *kañiwa*). At the extreme heights of the *puna*, between 13,500 and 15,700 feet above sea level, frost-resistant potatoes destined for freeze-drying grow with some lupins and the tuber *maca*. Down on the Amazonian side of the Andes, farmers grow yuca and many of the starchy plants we find in the Caribbean.

The agricultural tradition I identify with most strongly is that of the Hispanic Caribbean and the Orinoco Basin. There the small farms scattered throughout the countryside are called *conucos*, and they are built on a combination of the incredibly adaptable corn-bean-squash threesome and tropical lowland root vegetables. Yuca is the most important of these, and it is usually found along with *malanga* and sweet potato, also American natives, and the Old World true yam and often taro (also an import), which is better suited for waterlogged soils. Typical *conucos* also boast assorted garden vegetables like tomatoes, cooking herbs like broad-leaf *culantro*, achiote for coloring foods, and plantains, which came from Africa and became part of the Afro-Caribbean tradition.

My paternal grandmother's family, who still live in the forested mountains along the Jauco River in eastern Cuba, have been able to endure decades of hardship on ration cards because they can cook what they grow in their *conucos*. Their small vegetable gardens are prodigiously fertile, producing yuca, *malanga*, plantains, true yams, sweet potatoes, tiny *cachucha* peppers, leeks, seasonings like broad-leaf *culantro* and chives, and achiote. Next to their fields, tall coconut palms, whose fruit they use in cooking, give shade to coffee and cacao.

I found a similar busy polyculture on the edge of the Orinoco in Venezuela, on a boat trip I took to the river delta years ago. I saw *conucos* with plantain trees weighed down by heavy clusters of ripening fruit; yuca, with its slender stems and splayed leaves; the tendrils of *auyama* (Caribbean pumpkin) entangled with the delicate vines of the white yam (*ñame*). When we stopped in Warao Indian villages, where palm-thatched houses are built on stilts in the water, I found women cooking big soups with all the vegetables I had seen in the *conucos*. The ones who were married to Venezuelan *criollos* were flavoring their soups with onion, garlic, cilantro, and scallions, as most non-Indian Guayanese do. I felt like eating a gourdful, so familiar and tempting was the aroma. In contrast, the pure Warao households in the same village ate a spartan diet of river fish, grilled or boiled in soups with tubers and plantains

and no seasoning other than salt. There and everywhere in the delta, I was mesmerized by the way the women built fires in hollowed-out logs on the wooden floors of their huts—wood on wood, but somehow not burning the house down.

As I got closer to the delta, I noticed that the mix of plants in the *conucos* changed, because yuca does not tolerate waterlogged conditions. In the mixed fields (*daukabas*) of the more sedentary Warao villages I visited, yuca's place was filled by the more water-tolerant taro (*ure* in Warao), an Asian import, and by the *moriche* palm, an Orinoco native that supplies the Warao with fruit, a nutritious starch (*yuruma*) that they use for bread, and wood and fiber.

I believe that you need to understand the *milpa/chacra/conuco* mentality and how much it means to us, even when we live in cities and buy rather than grow our food, to appreciate Latin food. Though yuca, corn, potatoes, and plantains might be grown today as cash crops in large fields that bear little resemblance to the plots of small farmers, they still remain close and dear to us. They evoke personal memories of the countryside and the labor of our own hands—or at least of our parents' and grandparents' hands.

I always keep a basket full of yuca, plantains, the hardy squash we know as *calabaza*, sweet potatoes, and other root vegetables on my kitchen counter. This bounty gives me a feeling of security, the sense that I can never go hungry, because in a way I am eating the earth. In his book *Las comidas profundas* (*Deep Meals*), Cuban writer Antonio José Ponte describes our penchant for roots as "a boundless appetite for the earth." For Cubans, he writes, "to eat is . . . to excavate roots, foundations, wooden poles." Even to other people who regard root vegetables such as potatoes as a staple, the tropical obsession for vegetables that look like the trunks of small trees often seems peculiar.

Our most basic craving is for what brings us closer to home. Sitting in front of a plate of boiled yuca or sweet potato with just a sprinkling of hot olive oil or lard and some salt is enough to give us a sense of communal rootedness. The starchy vegetables and roots that are the staff of tropical Latin cooking are more than vegetables—they are a way of life—and that is why I am devoting an entire chapter to them.

I have chosen to begin with what is least familiar to most United States cooks but most dear to me: yuca and the other tropical New World tubers. They are true wonder plants wrested from the jungle, an example of New World peoples' genius at nurturing the plants that would nurture them. Following these are the African yams and plantains that so quickly became indispensable wherever the American tropical roots were eaten—which also happens to be wherever African slaves had their biggest impact on the emerging *criollo* culture. Then I introduce the versatile starchy fruit of the peach palm, and from here we explore the realm of Andean tubers. They are a very different bunch from the starchy tubers of the hot, moist lowland tropics. The most famous root crop of the Andes is the potato, but it is only one among a nourishing cornucopia from one of the richest areas of plant domestication in the Americas, the Bolivian and Peruvian highlands.

The recipes in this chapter are deliberately simple. I have chosen not to showcase all the wonderful things a culinary virtuoso might do with yuca, plantains, and the rest, but rather to present the basic approaches that a Latin cook would learn as soon as she/he was able to walk, with a few flourishes here and there. (Be assured that you will find a large range of both innovative and traditional recipes using all of these amazingly versatile vegetables in the other chapters of this book.) Here I provide a brief introduction to the everyday uses of our major life-giving tubers and starchy vegetables, with instructions on selecting, handling, and basic cooking methods.

THE STARCHY VEGETABLES OF THE TROPICAL LOWLANDS: ROOTS AND PLANTAINS

To people from the low-lying, humid tropical regions defined by the Caribbean, the Orinoco and Amazon Basins, and parts of the northern Pacific coast down to Peru, starchy roots and vegetables are almost synonymous with food. In fact, Cubans call them *viandas* (viands, as in meats) and Colombians *vituallas* (provisions), because these were the foodstuffs that sustained settlers as they moved from place to place. No matter where I traveled in these regions, I found that people literally live on these gifts of the earth—piping-hot boiled yuca piled high, sprinkled with some lard or olive oil, for example, or large chunks of African yam complementing the saltiness of almost fossil-like foods resurrected by boiling, such as salt cod, dried river fish, or beef jerky.

Although we also loosely identify plantains, the dense-fleshed Caribbean *calabaza* (a type of squash), and even corn as *viandas* or *vituallas*, the usual suspects are roots: yuca, *malanga*, taro, true yam, and sweet potato. Regular potatoes definitely belong to the complex too, but their real home and highest point of development and use is the Andean countries.

Outsiders often have trouble telling one tropical lowland tuber from another, and indeed they can be confusingly similar. All are brown, gray-brown, or reddish brown, and look like tree trunks, mineral deposits, or fossilized bones pulled from the ground. For the uninitiated, they all taste somewhat alike, but beneath their comforting, familiar blandness are subtle nuances of flavor, nutty accents and textures that we treasure.

Tubers are also extremely versatile. They can be cooked as a vegetable or turned into flour to make bread. The starchiest ones are ideal for making doughs for pies and empanadas. They can be deep-fried, or enjoyed simply boiled and doused with vivid sauces like a garlicky *mojo*, or turned into silky purees.

Latin cooks revel in the subtle differences between these delicious roots and often serve more than one at the same meal, or even in the same dish, as a complement to meat, poultry, or seafood. My father's favorite food is a combination of chunks of true yam and *malanga* and slices of half-ripe plantains (*plátanos pintones*) drizzled with a hot table sauce of garlic sautéed in extra-virgin olive oil. Years ago, his physician put him on a strict low-carbohydrate diet and warned him not to eat tubers or plantains. My father, who has a taste for the theatrical, told the doctor he would rather die.

That same afternoon, he sat in my kitchen and stared at the large basket filled with tubers, plantains, chayotes, and yams sitting on my kitchen counter. Then he went out to the garage, got out a huge canvas, and with charcoal, drew my basket

on a dramatic red background. The painting now hangs in my restaurant Cucharamama.

Yuca

Yuca

For the sake of simplicity, *yuca* (pronounced "YOO-ka") is the name I use for the plant also known in English as manioc or cassava and in Brazilian Portuguese as *mandioca* or *aipim*. (Do not call it yucca, which is a totally unrelated desert plant in the agave family.)

By any name, yuca is the great food plant of the New World lowland regions lying between about 20 degrees north and south of the equator. Like corn, it is put to every possible use in the area where it originated. It was at the heart of belief for the first peoples the Spanish encountered in the islands, along the Caribbean coast, and in the Orinoco Basin. Even today, when the Makiritare people living along the upper Orinoco in Venezuela celebrate the first harvest of a new *conuco* (farming plot), they tell a creation myth that begins with a lone hero, the Watunna, climbing from a barren, starved earth to heaven to raid a giant yuca plant that will become the mother of all plants. At the end of the story, the people are taught how to feed themselves: the men by clearing the soil for small plots, the women by planting and tending yuca. In Cuba and the Hispanic Caribbean, yuca was the staple crop of the Taíno (Arawak) Indians and it is still both a daily staple and a feast food, as indispensable a companion to our Christmas Eve pork as rice and beans.

Yuca is a spindly perennial shrub, often six feet tall or more. It has lovely slender leaves shaped a little like marijuana leaves. In the tropics, particularly in Brazil, these are called *maniva* and are often cooked like spinach in a dish known as *maniçoba*, a type of *feijoada* with sausages and pork products. But the most important edible part of the plant is a cluster of swollen roots covered with a slightly shiny, barklike brown or pinkish brown skin and containing pale yellow or dazzling white flesh. In terms of harvest per acre, yuca is the highest-yielding of all tuber crops. It also has the advantage that the roots of some varieties can remain in the ground for as long as two or three years before harvesting, gaining in starch content.

Yuca roots have a major genetic variable, their concentration of poisonous, bitter-tasting hydrocyanic acid. At one time, botanists actually classified the plant into two different species, *Manihot utilissima* and *Manihot dulcis*, in the belief that one was poisonous and the other was not. Now it is thought that there is a range of possibilities in what is one and the same species, rechristened *M. esculenta*. The bitterest (most poisonous) varieties keep longest in the ground.

The Spaniards found the Taíno women of Cuba and Hispaniola patiently grating yuca pulp against rough granite stones (*guariquetén*), or stones covered with the coarse skin of the fish called *libuza*, or wooden graters. They packed the grated pulp into long, flexible woven containers looking something like windsocks, made from palm fronds and called *cibucán*, which they twisted to let the poisonous juices drip out until only the drained meal and a fine powdery starch were left. The women knew that the poison had evaporated during cooking, and when the juice was boiled down to a syrupy consistency (as is still done for West Indian *cassareep* and Brazilian *tucupí*), no trace remained.

The women would spread the pulp with a circular motion over a flat griddle made of clay, which rested on three or four river stones, and cook it on both sides until golden. The resulting flatbread (*casabe*) was allowed to dry under the sun for a few hours. *Casabe* was not only the basis of the Taíno diet but the ritual food offered by women to one of the most important deities of the Taíno pantheon, the god Yúcahua. So central was yuca to Taíno culture that their *cemis* (idols representing their deities) had a conical shape like the earth mounds where cassava was planted.

The Spanish tasted and soon adopted *casabe*. Experimenting further with the fine starch extracted from the pulp, European cooks came up with what we now call tapioca; the word is derived from the Brazilian Tupi Guaraní language, meaning the fine starch left from squeezing yuca. In Latin America today, yuca meal and starch, prepared by different methods and christened with various names, are used in numberless ways to make everything from breads and rolls to cakes, pastry and tamal doughs, porridges, and fritters. In Brazil, the local version of yuca meal (*farinha de mandioca*) is elevated to the status of a table condiment and is always served as an accompaniment to soups and soupy stews or sprinkled over bean dishes like the *feijoao tropeiro* from Minas Gerais (page 278).

"Sweet" (free or nearly free of cyanide) and "bitter" strains of yuca have always coexisted in the Latin tropics, but the "sweet" kinds have become progressively more predominant with modern selection through breeding. The disadvantage is that they are often more watery-textured and more subject to rot both before and after harvesting than the bitter roots.

More often than not—and always in the United States—the yuca cooked as a vegetable is "sweet." No other kind is offered for sale in this country. Much of the yuca in our markets comes from Costa Rica and usually has a wax coating that is meant to retard spoilage—unfortunately, not a foolproof measure. For variety, I seek out either Florida-grown yuca, unwaxed and usually of excellent quality, or the small, stubby, thin-skinned tubers from the Dominican Republic. No matter where it comes from, you must buy a larger amount than a recipe calls for in order to allow for bad spots.

SELECTING

The yuca you will see in markets catering to Latin clienteles here looks like an irregularly shaped club, usually about 2 inches in diameter and 8 to 12 inches long. (In Paraguay I've seen yuca the size of softball bats.) Do not be shy about asking people in the produce department to help you choose good specimens. The roots should be firm and even-colored, without soft, moldy patches. Ask someone to cut one open: the flesh should be dense and bright white or light yellow, with no blotches, purplish veins, or grayish rings. Even with these precautions, you can expect to get only between 3 and 4 pounds of trimmed flesh for every 5 pounds of whole yuca.

KEEPING AND PREPARING

At home, keep the uncooked roots in a cool spot like a garage or basement (not the refrigerator) for up to 2 weeks. After that, yuca may start to become mushy (or moldy) and spoiled, or shrivel up like a mummy. It must be peeled before cooking. The skin of different cultivars varies in thickness, and the kinds we get here can be troublesome. (I never ceased to marvel in Paraguay at how easily cooks removed the thin skin of the huge local kind with just a potato peeler.)

Begin by cutting a root into 3- to 4-inch sections with a sharp heavy knife. With most varieties, you will see two layers of rind: the rough, dark outer bark and an underskin that is pink on the outside, white on the inside. With the tip of a small sharp knife, make several cuts down the length of each section, deep enough to go through the underskin. Work in the knife tip under this inner layer to detach it from the flesh until you can remove an entire piece. Pare away any stubborn bits, as they will be as tough as leather even after long cooking. Split each chunk lengthwise down the middle and cut off the thin woody spindle in the center—or simply pull it out after boiling the tubers. As you work, drop the peeled chunks into a large bowl of cold water to keep them from discoloring. (This is necessary with most of the starchy *viandas*.) Well covered with water, the prepared chunks will hold for a few hours at room temperature or about 2 days in the refrigerator. They also freeze well, stored in tightly sealed bags, for up to 3 months. If freezing, remove the central spindle in advance.

Many Latin American cooks in this country buy frozen peeled yuca chunks from Florida, Costa Rica, the Dominican Republic, Ecuador, and, most recently, Peru (which supplies a yellow-fleshed kind). While the frozen is not as flavorful as the fresh, I recommend it, not only for the sake of convenience but also because the densely starchy vegetable benefits from freezing; this also saves you from guessing about the quality of the whole roots. In 2005, canned yuca made its debut in Miami markets, becoming an instant success because of its good flavor and convenience. Use as you would boiled yuca.

Boiled Yuca

Yuca Hervida

Boiled yuca is a small miracle. I can hardly think of another vegetable so transformed just by simple boiling. The impenetrable tuber, which starts out fibrous and as hard as the tusk of an elephant, becomes a creamy and supple vegetable. Boiled yuca is also the stuff with which many other preparations start, and you will come back to it time and again.

There is no single rule that will help you figure out how much time it will take to cook fresh yuca until fork-tender. A general estimate is 30 minutes, but it might take less time or much longer, depending on the type of yuca. Start testing the vegetable with a fork 15 minutes after the water comes to a boil and continue to test until you reach the desired texture. Usually I prefer to remove the central spindle after rather than before cooking. It takes some force to whack through it when you're cutting the raw yuca into chunks, but it is much easier to detach the spindle from cooked yuca. Serve the yuca with a sauce of your choice or with just a sprinkling of olive oil and some salt.

Cook's Note: Follow this procedure in any recipe that calls for boiled yuca, allowing about 4 cups of water per pound of trimmed yuca. The beautiful buttery texture becomes congealed if the yuca is allowed to cool or even chill. This is a plus for certain applications, like pan-frying. Boiled yuca should be allowed to cool at room temperature or in the refrigerator before frying.

SERVES 4

3 pounds fresh yuca, peeled as described on page 166 and cut into 3-inch sections (about 2 pounds trimmed weight), or 2 pounds frozen yuca
1 tablespoon salt

▶ Place the yuca, 3 quarts water, and salt in a 4-quart saucepan and bring to a boil over high heat. Reduce the heat to medium and cook at a gentle boil until either fork-tender (Paraguayan style), about 25 minutes, or very tender (Cuban style), 30 to 40 minutes. Drain, quickly removing the spindles, and serve at once; or keep warm in the cooking water over very low heat until ready to serve. Douse with a table sauce if you wish, and serve piping hot.

Storing: Leftover boiled yuca will keep well in the refrigerator for about 1 week. If you will be pan-frying or deep-frying the yuca, place on a baking sheet lined with parchment paper and cover loosely with plastic wrap, to prevent weeping.

Pan-Fried Yuca

Yuca Frita al Sartén

As with potatoes, to pan-fry or deep-fry yuca, you need to boil the woody tuber first. In either case, the outside forms a crust, a pleasurable barrier to the soft and appealing inside.

To serve as an appetizer, I trim the traditional chunky fried yuca to thin, elegant fingers before deep-frying (page 386). For a side dish, I cut the yuca into larger chunks and pan-fry it until it develops a thin golden brown crust that contrasts with the meltingly rich interior. I love sprinkling a savory sauce like a green *mojo* from the Canary Islands over it.

Working Ahead ▶ Boil the yuca the day before frying it and refrigerate. That way it will be crispy outside and tender inside.

SERVES 4 TO 6

3 tablespoons extra-virgin olive oil
1 recipe Canary Islands Cilantro *Mojo* (page 141)
1 recipe Boiled Yuca (page 167), prepared and cooled

▶ Heat the oil in a medium skillet over medium heat until it ripples. Add the yuca and cook until it develops a crunchy golden crust on the first side, about 10 minutes. Turn over with a spatula and cook until golden on the second side.

Serving: Place on a serving platter and drizzle with Canary Islands Cilantro *Mojo*. Pour any remaining *mojo* into a sauce boat and pass at the table. Serve as a side dish for Grilled Skirt Steak (page 704), Puerto Rican Pan-Fried Yellowtail Snapper (page 631), or Santiago de Cuba's Roast Pork (page 721).

Yuca Chips

Mariquitas de Yuca

Deep-frying concentrates the sweetness of yuca. Of all the chips made from tropical tubers, yuca chips most reveal the raw tuber, with its grain and its concentric circles.

MAKES ABOUT 6 CUPS

2 pounds fresh yuca
Corn oil for deep-frying (about 4 cups)
Salt to taste

▶ Peel the yuca according to the instructions on page 166. Cut it into 3-inch or 6-inch sections, depending on whether you want shorter or longer chips. To slice in a food processor, use the 2-millimeter slicing blade and trim the chunks of yuca to fit the feed tube. Traditional cooks use the slicing side of a box grater; or you can use a mandoline or other vegetable slicer to cut the thin slices.

Heat the oil in a 2-quart saucepan over medium heat to 350°F. Fry the yuca in batches: Add the yuca slices to the oil, then turn after about 30 seconds with a slotted spoon. The chips will be golden brown in 1 to 2 minutes. Lift them out of the oil as soon as they look golden; do not overbrown, or they will taste bitter. Drain on paper towels and serve hot, sprinkled with salt and a dipping sauce of your choice, as a cocktail appetizer, a side for sandwiches, or a garnish for main courses.

Mashed Yuca with Peruvian Seasonings

Majado de Yuca Rinconcito Cataquense

There isn't much to see in the parched and dusty gray town of Catacaos in northern Peru, but step into the Rinconcito Cataquense, one of its many *picanterías* (popular restaurants serving spicy foods), and you will discover a luscious oasis of flavors. Their *majado de yuca* is a pungent, full-bodied surprise—a coarse yuca puree panfried until crusty in a rich Peruvian cooking sauce spiked with hot Peruvian yellow pepper and enriched with small chunks of pork.

Cook's Note: You can skip the pork for a vegetarian yuca mash. In that case, use 2 tablespoons oil to prepare the cooking sauce.

What to Drink: If serving as a main course for lunch, pair with a Lucas Chardonnay from Mendoza, Argentina.

SERVES 6

- 4 pounds fresh yuca (about 3 pounds trimmed weight), or 3 pounds frozen
  Salt
- 1 pound pork butt with some fat, cut into ½-inch cubes, or meaty slab bacon, cut into ¼-inch dice
- 1 tablespoon corn oil or mild extra-virgin olive oil, preferably made from Arbequina olives (optional)
- 12 garlic cloves, mashed to a paste with a mortar and pestle or the flat of a chef's knife blade, or finely chopped and mashed
- 1 medium red onion (8 ounces), finely chopped (about 1½ cups)
- 1 fresh or frozen Andean yellow pepper (*ají amarillo*) or fresh jalapeño, seeded and finely chopped
- ½ teaspoon ground cumin
- ⅛ teaspoon freshly ground black pepper
- 1 tablespoon cider vinegar

▶ If using fresh yuca, peel it according to the instructions on page 166. Cut it into 3-inch sections. Place the fresh or frozen yuca in a 6-quart pot, add 4 quarts cold water and 1 tablespoon salt, and bring to a boil over medium heat. Cook, uncovered, until fork-tender, 20 to 30 minutes.

Drain the yuca and, working quickly, split the chunks lengthwise in half and remove the central fiber. While it is still hot, mash it coarsely with a fork or, working in small batches, with a large mortar and pestle.

While the yuca cooks, place the pork in a large skillet and cook, stirring frequently, over medium heat until it has browned and rendered its fat, about 20 minutes.

Stir in the 1 tablespoon oil if the pork has not released enough fat to sauté the seasonings. Add the garlic and sauté until golden, about 40 seconds. Add the onion and cook, stirring, until golden, about 8 minutes. Add the yellow pepper, cumin, and black pepper and cook, stirring, for about 1 minute. Add the vinegar and season with salt to taste.

Add the yuca and cook, stirring, until the yuca crusts a little. Serve hot.

Serving: In Catacaos, *majado* is served as a side dish for meats together with the usual rice and Stewed Peruvian Canary Beans (page 511). Here at home, I like to serve it with a simple Avocado, Watercress, and Pineapple Salad (page 548) as a main course for lunch.

Colombian Yuca and Coconut Torte

Enyucado

This yuca cake comes from Cartagena, a lovely city on the Caribbean coast of Colombia. It is traditionally cooked in a skillet and turned to brown on both sides, like a Spanish tortilla. The result is a dense, chewy pancake that is cut into wedges and served as a side dish for savory foods or eaten as a dessert. I like to bake it in the oven, which is easier than the skillet method. The baked *enyucado* looks like a flat torte, with a crunchy golden top and a chewy, coconutty interior.

SERVES 6

3	pounds fresh yuca, peeled (see page 166) and finely grated on the fine side of a box grater or in the food processor (about 3 cups)
1½	cups coarsely grated fresh cow's-milk cheese, preferably a soft *queso blanco* or Monterey Jack cheese (about 7½ ounces)
¾	cup plus 2 tablespoons finely grated fresh coconut (from 1 small coconut; see page 50) or frozen grated, unsweetened coconut
¾	cup unsweetened coconut milk
¾	cup plus 2 tablespoons sugar
2	teaspoons anise seeds, lightly crushed
¼–½	teaspoon salt (depending on the saltiness of the cheese)
2	tablespoons butter, melted

▶ Preheat the oven to 350°F. Butter a 10-by-2-inch round cake pan and line it with parchment paper.

In a large bowl, mix the yuca with the cheese, coconut, coconut milk, sugar, anise seeds, salt, and melted butter. Let stand for 15 minutes.

Pour the yuca mixture into the prepared pan. Bake until the cake is golden brown and pulls away from the sides of the pan, about 2 hours. Transfer to a wire rack and let cool in the pan for about 10 minutes.

Run a knife around the side of the pan to release the cake and invert it onto the rack. Peel off the parchment paper and invert the cake onto a platter.

Serving: Cut into wedges and serve as a side dish for Pot Roasted Stuffed Eye of Round Cartagena Style (page 707).

Storing: The cake can be stored at room temperature or refrigerated for up to 3 days. Reheat in 325°F oven before serving.

Sweet Potato

Boniato (Cuban sweet potato)

In Latin America, sweet potatoes are appreciated as a nutritious, versatile, savory vegetable. Instead of wanting sweet potatoes that are dense and very sweet, Latin cooks often prefer varieties with a drier, mealier texture and more subtle, chestnutty flavor. Cubans love the knobby sweet potato called *boniato*, with thin, patchy red skin and only mildly sweet ivory-white flesh that darkens to a delicate blue-gray in cooking. In some other parts of the Hispanic Caribbean, including Colombia, the same type is called *batata*. In most Latin countries, the general name for all sweet potatoes is *camote* (it's *batata doce* in Brazil). The flesh may be off-white, pale yellow, or even purplish; the deep orange kind that North Americans mistakenly call yam is not common—and not appropriate for some Latin American dishes.

The oldest authenticated remains of the sweet potato were found in coastal Peru. Though primarily a lowland vegetable, sweet potatoes are more tolerant of altitude than other lowland tuber crops. The Spanish found them throughout the American tropics and subtropics, from the Pacific and the valleys of the Andes to the Caribbean and Central America.

Latin Americans use sweet potatoes in many guises. Almost every traditional Peruvian cebiche is garnished with large chunks of boiled *camote*, every Puerto Rican and Dominican *sancocho* calls for *batata*, and every Cuban salt cod salad or panfried beef jerky (*tasajo*) comes with a side of steaming boiled *boniato*.

SELECTING

Buy only sweet potatoes that feel heavy and firm, with no soft or moldy spots. Florida-grown *boniatos*, which are generally superb, often come to market with bruised skin that looks a bit dried out; as long as the *boniato* feels heavy for its size, it is fine for cooking. Always buy more *boniatos* than your recipe calls for, as some specimens may have sections of discolored flesh that you need to cut off.

KEEPING AND PREPARING

Store sweet potatoes in a cool, dark place, but not the refrigerator. Use as soon as possible, though the tubers will last well for about a week. Peel with a sharp paring knife, making sure to cut off any dried patches of skin or dark, soft spots. Place in a bowl and cover with water if not using immediately. Sweet potatoes can be boiled, steamed, or baked. For baking, I prefer the moist-fleshed, orange sweet potatoes we usually call yams in this country.

Boiled Sweet Potatoes
Camotes Hervidos

A thick slice of boiled sweet potato (*camote* in Peru) adds a subtle touch of sweetness to a variety of Latin dishes, from Cuban beef jerky to the cebiches of northern Peru. At my restaurant Zafra, I serve marinated chicken kebabs skewered with big chunks of boiled sweet potato.

Cook's Note: The mealier Caribbean *boniatos* and Mexican *camotes* are preferred for boiling. North American yams are better wrapped in aluminum foil and roasted.

SERVES 4 TO 6 AS A SIDE DISH

  2 large sweet potatoes (about 3½ pounds), peeled and cut into ½-inch rounds
  2 teaspoons salt
  2 teaspoons sugar, if using *boniatos* (optional)

▶ Place the sweet potatoes, salt, sugar, if using, and 2 quarts water in a medium pot and bring to a boil over high heat. Lower the heat to medium and boil until the potatoes are easily pierced with a fork. Drain and serve, or remove from the heat and keep in the cooking water until ready to serve, up to 30 minutes.

Caribbean Sweet Potato Fries

Boniaticos Fritos

These sweet potato fries are dense and mealy. Unlike yuca, which has to be boiled before frying, the grayish blue *boniatos* will cook through easily without previous boiling, developing a delicious, lightly sweet, crunchy crust.

MAKES 4 SERVINGS

- 1 large (about 1¾ pounds) *boniato* (Caribbean sweet potato)
- 4 cups corn oil for deep-frying
  Coarse sea salt or kosher salt
  Sugar

▶ Peel the *boniato* and cut it into sticks 3 inches long by ½ inch thick; don't worry about getting perfectly even pieces.

Heat the oil in a 3-quart saucepan or deep fryer to 325°F. Add the *boniato* in small batches and cook, stirring occasionally, until lightly golden, about 10 minutes; keep the temperature between 275°F and 300°F. Lift the fries out of the oil with a slotted spoon and drain on paper towels. Season with coarse salt and sugar and serve hot.

Variation: Oven-Fried Sweet Potatoes
Place the sweet potato sticks in a bowl and toss with a little olive oil and coarse salt. Spread on a baking sheet in a single layer and bake in a preheated 375°F oven for about 35 minutes. Turn with a spatula halfway through baking.

Warm *Boniato* and Fresh Cheese with Creamy Paprika Dressing

Boniato con Queso Blanco y Aliño Cremoso de Pimentón

Both at home and in my restaurants I love tossing cubes of boiled Caribbean sweet potato with tangy sauces such as this creamy paprika dressing, which complements the tuber's subtle sweetness. Because of its mealy texture, *boniato* benefits from the creaminess of fresh cheese. This simple dish is a step up from the simple chunks of boiled sweet potato that are brought to our tables on a large platter as a side for many of our traditional foods. It is lovely with grilled meats, chicken or turkey, and panfried fish.

SERVES 6

- 4 medium sweet potatoes (about 4 pounds), preferably *boniatos* (Caribbean sweet potatoes; about 3½ pounds), peeled and cut into ¼-inch cubes (about 5 cups)
- ½ cup extra-virgin olive oil
- 1 tablespoon cider vinegar
- ¼ cup Mexican *crema*, store-bought or homemade (page 148), or crème fraîche
- ¼ cup cultured buttermilk
- 4 garlic cloves
- 1 teaspoon hot *pimentón* (Spanish smoked paprika) or *Merkén* from Chillán (page 74)
- ½ pound fresh cheese, preferably lightly salted homemade *cuajada* (page 104), or *queso blanco*, cut into ¼-inch cubes

▶ Bring a medium saucepan of water to a boil over medium-high heat. Add the sweet potatoes, cover, and cook until tender, 12 to 15 minutes. Drain, reserving ¼ cup of the cooking water. Set the potatoes aside.

Combine the oil, vinegar, *crema*, buttermilk, garlic, paprika, and reserved cooking liquid in a blender or food processor and process until creamy.

Place the sweet potatoes and cheese in a bowl and toss with the dressing.

Malanga

Malanga

Shaped like a small crookneck squash, *malanga* is covered with wiry brown hairs and patches of dark and tan skin. Cut the tuber open and it is wet and sticky, crunchy as a water chestnut, and with a similar nuttiness. Its earthy aroma faintly recalls truffles or porcini mushrooms. By looking at the smooth patches of skin, you can often tell the color of the pulp—it ranges from pure or creamy white to light gray to opalescent purple.

For many people in the Hispanic Caribbean, *malanga* does not have the "feast food" status of yuca. It is comfort food, especially in Cuba, where it is given to people suffering from colds, upset stomachs, and other ailments requiring a little pampering. Any Cuban with ulcers is put on a diet of *malanga* and milk.

There are several theories about the origin of the word *malanga*, but all point to Africa. It is most commonly believed that the word comes from the Kikongo *ma-lànga*, meaning a plant with edible tubers and leaves. American shoppers not familiar with tropical vegetables can have trouble figuring out what *malanga* is in a Latin American market. It doesn't help that in Puerto Rico and the Dominican Republic it's called by the Taíno name *yautía*, and that in parts of the West Indies it turns up as *tannia*, *cocoyam*, or *taro* (a misnomer). Venezuelans call it *ocumo*.

True malanga is the small brown or tan corm of *Xanthosoma sagittifolium* and several other *Xanthosomas*, tropical arums with enormous glossy leaves similar to those of elephant ears, a distantly related plant. It's hard to believe that these huge, luxuriant leaves are attached to such odd-looking little roots.

Different *malanga* species vary somewhat in appearance. White *malanga* (*X. sagittifolium*), the most important in this country, has skinny corms about 5 to 10 inches long, round at one end and tapered at the other. The shaggy brown skin, which grows in more or less pronounced crosswise scaly ridges, may have a scattering of wiry brown hairs and is thin enough in patches to show the whitish flesh. When cut open, it reveals dense, moist, and crunchy flesh. Yellow *malanga* (*X. atrovirens*) is about the same length but has a stockier, more compact shape and is firmer and drier when cooked. Both kinds can be eaten as a vegetable or made into doughs for various purposes.

Cubans are more likely to treat white *malanga* as a vegetable to be eaten boiled, mashed, or fried in chips or fritters and to reserve the yellow kind for special uses like our sweet *buñuelos* (fritters in the shape of a figure eight). Puerto Ricans, however, often use the white kind for the dough of *pasteles* and the meat-filled fritters known as *alcapurrias*. Less important in this country is the pale purple or lilac *malanga* (*X. violaceum*), which is similar in shape and texture to white *malanga*. Its grayish purple hue is too faint to give it the exotic box-office appeal of vivid purple potatoes. It is prepared and cooked just like white *malanga*. All varieties are wonderful in soups, practically melting into the liquid and giving it body along with marvelous flavor. With its trufflelike earthy aroma, *malanga* is simply delicious for purees.

SELECTING

Look for sound roots with crisp, juicy flesh: Heft them in your hands—they should feel heavy for their size. Lightly pierce the skin with a fingernail to be sure the fresh is firm and dense, not soft or shriveled.

KEEPING AND PREPARING

Store *malanga* in a cool place for up to 4 days. Though it is not as subject to mold and soft spots as yuca, it tends to shrivel when held too long. *Malanga* is easy to peel with a small paring knife or potato peeler. Be sure to cut out any dark, soft bits. Rinse each root under cold running water as you finish it and drop it into a bowl of cold water. The roots can be held, well covered with water, for a few hours at room temperature or up to 1 day in the refrigerator. Frozen *malanga* is available in Latin markets, but fresh *malanga* is so easy to peel that I don't see the need to use it frozen.

Boiled *Malanga*

Malanga Hervida

A plate of hot *malanga* drizzled lightly with some olive oil can make anyone born in the Hispanic Caribbean happy. Here is a basic recipe that can also be the starting point for more complex preparations, such as purees.

SERVES 4 AS A SIDE DISH

- 4 large *malangas* (about 3 pounds, 2½ pounds trimmed weight)
- 1 teaspoon salt, or to taste
  Extra-virgin olive oil or melted butter

▶ Peel the *malangas*, cut into 2-inch chunks, and place in a bowl or colander and rinse under cold running water. Place in a medium pot, add 4 quarts water and the salt, and bring to a boil over medium heat. Cook until tender, about 20 minutes. Drain and serve hot drizzled with olive oil or melted butter. Malanga is also delicious doused in a Cuban *mojo* (page 140).

African Yam

Dig up a true African white yam (*Dioscorea alata*), and you may feel as if you've stumbled upon an elephant, hunched in the dirt taking a mud bath. These tubers can be enormous, with cracked, scaly brown hides. But some are tiny, like the Puerto Rican *mapuey*, which is a New World cultivar the size of a *malanga*.

African white yam (*ñame blanco*)

I grew up eating oversized home-grown white yams. Every year my father would spend weeks building up large mounds of compost near a fence in our backyard to plant the corms. Soon the yams developed tendrils that climbed the fence and anything else they could use as support. Nourished by the compost, our yams were so gigantic, as large as 2 to 3 feet long, that we often cut them into pieces to give away to our relatives and neighbors.

Large or small, these tubers are greatly appreciated throughout tropical America, especially in areas with a strong African presence, where cooks have found myriad ways to prepare them. Please don't mistake the true yam for the orange-fleshed sweet potatoes that North Americans usually call yams. This confusion of names is not limited to the United States, and it goes back a long way. Apparently as early as the Portuguese voyages of discovery before Columbus, the West African term *nyami* (true yams) was being generically used by the Portuguese, as *inhame*, for any similar-looking root crop. Columbus seems to have garbled this into *mame*, with an equally loose meaning; in modern Spanish, it is *ñame* (pronounced "NYAH-may"). And if you think the English usage is confusing, the Spanish is even more so; in the Puerto Rican countryside, farmers call other popular root vegetables *ñame de yautía* (*malanga* yam) or *ñame de batata* (sweet potato yam).

Luckily, the vegetable itself is much easier to recognize than some of its names. There are dozens of different true yam species, nearly all native to the Old World. Some may have originated in tropical Asia, some in Africa. One or two are plants of the New World tropics. The largest can weigh well over a hundred pounds, and when dug up they look like something primeval.

For cooking purposes, yams have some resemblance to yuca and *malanga*, though they are a bit grainy. They are very starchy and appear to perfect advantage in the same guises as the other *viandas* or *vituallas*, primarily boiled or mashed. In Cuba we call the big ones with white or purple flesh *ñame blanco* (white yam) or *ñame de agua* (water yam). They are often eaten as a boiled vegetable by themselves, just sprinkled with salt, or with salt and some olive oil or fresh lard, or they may be doused in a lusty, tangy table sauce like Puerto Rican Cooked Tomato *Mojo* (page 141).

The small club-shaped *mapuey*, a New World species also called cushcush yam in the West Indies, is good for soups and purees. It is very popular in Puerto Rico. The big African *D. rotundata* (with white or yellow flesh) and the very similar African *D. cayenensis* (yellow-fleshed, also called Guinea yam) become denser and stickier when cooked. Either by themselves or combined with another starch, such as plantains, these are classically pounded with a heavy pestle and made into dense-textured mashes or dumplings, both generically called *fufú*. Other yams do not have enough body to produce the same result.

SELECTING

Like yuca, yams can look sound but have blemished portions. Look for smooth skin and feel them to be sure they are firm, with no soft spots. Larger yams are often sold cut open; the cut flesh should look clean and even in color.

KEEPING AND PREPARING

Store yams in a cool spot, unrefrigerated and uncovered. They will keep for weeks, even months. Despite their formidable-looking skin, they are easy to peel with a small sharp knife. The grainy flesh, which comes in many colors—yellow, pale pink, purple, light gray, and white—will sweat a sticky substance. If you have a very large chunk or a whole yam, you can peel and cut off as much as you need, then set the rest aside; the cut surface will heal itself at once and no covering is necessary. The flesh of a good *ñame* should be juicy and even-colored. After you peel them, keep the yams in cold water until ready to use—for up to a few hours at room temperature, or refrigerated, covered with plastic wrap, for up to 24 hours. The large yellow kind, the so-called Guinea yams, need different handling, because they oxidize quickly on exposure to air and will turn a rusty brown. For these, have the cooking water at a rolling boil before you peel and cut them, so you can drop them in at once.

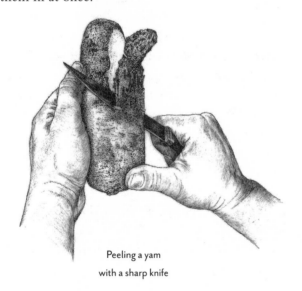

Peeling a yam
with a sharp knife

Simple White Yam Puree in the Style of Barranquilla

Puré de Ñame Barranquillero

In coastal Colombia, boiled white yams are coarsely mashed with a fork and seasoned with finely chopped red onions, milk, and butter. This hearty puree showcases the yam's pleasant grainy texture. In Latin America, tuber and vegetable purees are served as side dishes with meat, poultry, or fish. In Barranquilla, this yam puree is not the only starch on the plate—it shares space with white rice, and everything is heaped on the plate together in authentic tropical Latin style.

SERVES 4 TO 6

- 1 large or 2 smaller white yams (about 4 pounds, about 3½ pounds trimmed weight)
- 1 tablespoon salt, or to taste
- 1 large red onion (about 12 ounces), finely chopped (about 2 cups)
- 1 cup hot whole milk
- 2 tablespoons butter

▶ Peel the yam according to the instructions on page 166. Place in a bowl and rinse under cold running water. Place in a large pot, add 2½ quarts water and the salt, and bring to a boil over high heat. Lower the heat and simmer, covered, until fork-tender, 20 to 30 minutes.

Drain the yam and place in a medium bowl. Coarsely mash with a fork or potato masher. Add the onion, hot milk, and butter and beat with a wooden spoon to combine. Taste for salt. Transfer to a bowl or serving platter and serve hot as you would mashed potatoes.

Silky White Yam Puree

Muselina de Ñame

Once you have mastered the basics of boiling yams, you can go a step further and create a refined, silky puree. I love to serve this white puree with other tropical vegetable purees that offer a contrast of flavor, texture, and color—for example, a sweet greenish gold ripe plantain puree (page 185) or a complex light yellow *arracacha* puree (page 216). Do not think of this as an embarrassment of riches. In tropical Latin America, where starchy vegetables grow in abundance, locals like to serve several of the vegetables together, either by themselves or as side dishes.

SERVES 4 TO 6

- 1 large or 2 smaller white yams (about 4 pounds, about 3½ pounds trimmed weight)
- 1 tablespoon salt, or to taste
- 2 cups heavy cream or half-and-half
- 2 tablespoons butter
- 12 scallions, white part only, coarsely chopped
- 1 shallot, coarsely chopped
- 6 small Caribbean sweet peppers (*ajíes dulces*) coarsely chopped, or 1 cubanelle pepper, seeded and finely chopped

▶ Peel the yams (see page 166) and rinse under cold running water. Place in a large pot, add 2½ quarts water and the salt, and bring to a boil. Lower the heat and simmer, covered, until fork-tender, 20 to 30 minutes; drain when ready to use.

While the yams are cooking, combine the cream, butter, scallions, shallot, and peppers in a small saucepan and bring just to a simmer. Reduce the heat to low and simmer, uncovered, until the cream is reduced by half, about 30 minutes. Force the cream through a fine-mesh strainer, pressing against solids with a spoon. Keep warm in a double boiler until ready to use.

While the yams are still hot, put them through a food mill into a medium bowl. Stir in the reduced cream mixture and season with salt to taste.

Serving: Serve with your Thanksgiving turkey or as a side for grilled or roast lamb, pork, and saucy stews.

Yellow Yam and Plantain Dumplings in Tomato Sauce with Sesame

Albóndigas de Ñame Amarillo y Plátano Pintón con Ajonjolí

I simply adore these hearty dumplings. They are so rich in flavor and substance that they seem almost meaty. The half-ripe plantain adds a subtle sweetness. You can eat the dumplings by themselves as a vegetarian main course for lunch, but they are also a terrific side for Cuban-Style Pot-Roasted Chicken (page 670) or any grilled or pan-fried meat or seafood.

Cook's Note: To toast sesame seeds, heat a small heavy skillet or Mexican *comal* over high heat. Add the sesame seeds and toast, stirring constantly, until golden, about 3 minutes. Transfer to a plate to cool.

SERVES 4

For the Dumplings

- 1 tablespoon fresh lime juice
- 1 teaspoon salt
- 1½ pounds (1 pound trimmed weight) yellow Guinea yam (do not substitute another yam), peeled and cut into 2-inch chunks
- 1 half-ripe plantain (about 11 ounces), unpeeled, cut into 3 sections
- 4 garlic cloves, mashed to a paste with a mortar and pestle or the flat of a chef's knife blade
- 2 tablespoons extra-virgin olive oil
  Salt and freshly ground black pepper to taste

For the Tomato Sauce

- 3 tablespoons extra-virgin olive oil
- 4 garlic cloves, mashed to a paste with a mortar and pestle or finely chopped and mashed
- 1 small onion (about 5 ounces), finely chopped (about ½ cup)
- 1 small green bell pepper (4–5 ounces), or 2 cubanelle peppers, cored, seeded, deveined, and finely chopped
- 6 medium plum tomatoes (about 18 ounces), peeled, seeded, and coarsely chopped, or one 16-ounce can plum tomatoes, drained and coarsely chopped
- 1 teaspoon salt
- ¼ teaspoon ground allspice
- 2 cups chicken broth, homemade (page 538) or store-bought

- 2 tablespoons toasted sesame seeds (see Cook's Note), for garnish

Preparing the Dumplings ▶ Place 2½ quarts water, the lime juice, and 1 teaspoon salt in a large pot and bring to a boil over high heat. Add the yam and cook for about 30 minutes on high heat.

Meanwhile, cover the plantain with water and bring to a boil. Boil for about 20 minutes or until fork-tender. Peel.

While they are still warm, drain the yam and plantain and mash them in small batches into a coarse puree, using a mortar and pestle or a potato masher. Place in a medium bowl, add the garlic, olive oil, salt, and pepper, and mix well with a wooden spoon or potato masher. Shape into 12 balls (about 2 ounces each). Set aside.

Making the Tomato Sauce ▶ Heat the olive oil in a 12-inch skillet over medium heat. Add the garlic and sauté until golden, about 40 seconds. Add the onion and sauté, stirring, for about 4 minutes, until soft. Add the green pepper and sauté for 1 minute. Add the chopped tomatoes, salt, and allspice and cook, stirring frequently, for 5 minutes. Add the chicken broth and bring to a boil.

Lower the heat to medium and add the dumplings, shaking the skillet to moisten the dumplings evenly. Heat them through, for about 3 minutes. Sprinkle with the toasted sesame seeds and serve.

Plantain

Walk inside the thatched-roof home and into the *sokkaka* (kitchen) of any of the Kuna people of Panama's San Blas Islands and you will see a huge mound of plantains. It's a sobering sight in some ways—at one time, this native tribe probably subsisted on root vegetables and corn. But the Kuna, like many other native groups, couldn't resist the African plantain, which took the New World by storm.

Like many of the yams eaten in Latin America today, plantains and their close botanical cousins, bananas (*Musa* spp.), are an import from the Old World that flourished here wherever Africans settled. Portuguese traders brought them to the Canary Islands from the Guinea coast of Africa at the start of the fifteenth century, and in 1516 the Spanish Dominican friar Tomás de Berlanga brought plantains and bananas to Hispaniola, where so many Old World food plants were introduced. They rapidly spread throughout the islands and along the coasts of Central and South America, and for centuries plantation workers and people in the countryside grew bananas and plantains in little plots (*conucos*) along with the native staple crops. Bananas eventually became a plantation crop destined for North American and European tables.

In Cuba, we use the plantain, a foreign crop that quickly became native in tropical America, as a symbol for assimilation. When Spaniards and their descendants started acting and thinking like New World *criollos*, we said that they had become *aplatanados*—native like the plantain.

The plantain fit readily into the system of sustainable agriculture created by tropical lowland peoples, yet because of its resilience and productivity, it became the dominant crop in the system of monoculture sponsored by the United Fruit Company at the turn of the nineteenth century. Even before United Fruit banana plantations devoured huge areas of Central America, the plantain had become as ubiquitous as yuca. For their feasts, the Yanomami Indians of Venezuela and Brazil make gallons of plantain soup, as do the Kuna Indians— and as does my family in Miami, adding crunchy deep-fried green plantains for texture. The soup might be served in a china bowl, a gourd, or a hand-coiled clay vessel, but the cooking technique is the same.

To understand what is special about plantains, you have to realize that unlike the starchy root vegetables, they can be used at any stage after the fruit reaches its full growth. Plantains from Colombia have the reputation of being harvested at their optimal degree of maturity—*llenos* (full), as a Dominican cook who used to work for me said. If the country of origin is specified, I choose these. Plantains also come from Honduras and other Central American countries, Ecuador, Hawaii, and Florida. At each stage of ripeness—green (*verde*), half-ripe (*pintón*), ripe (*amarillo*), and black-ripe (*maduro*)—they are suitable for different purposes. Always note the stage of ripeness called for in a recipe, because they are not necessarily interchangeable.

For the recipes in this book, I call for a plantain we call *platáno macho*, which is long, full, and relatively narrow, with flavorful firm flesh. Occasionally you find stocky, shorter cultivars with softer flesh sold as *plátanos burros* and even fatter ones with very light flesh labeled Hawaiian plantains. If you like deep-fried plantain rounds (*tostones*) that are very soft in the center, choose these, but for better flavor, stick to the *plátano macho*.

GREEN PLANTAINS

Firm and dense, green plantains have a marvelous nutty flavor with no hint of sweetness. They are used much like yuca, *malanga*, and the other starchy vegetables—boiled in soups or as a side dish, grated to thicken soups, mashed with flavorful fats and seasonings, deep-fried, or turned into dumplings or pastry or tamal dough. The most popular versions of fried green plantains are chips, like the Ecuadorian *chifles*, and the twice-cooked, lightly flattened crunchy rounds or ovals called *tostones* or *patacones*.

HALF-RIPE PLANTAINS

At the half-ripe stage plantains become yellower and will start to blacken in spots. They now have

A green plantain

A half-ripe (half-green) plantain

A ripe plantain

several places first or make a shallow longitudinal cut down one of the ridges before roasting. Ripe plantains are also delicious roasted directly in the embers of a fire and are ideal for slicing and deep-frying. The flesh exudes a slightly fermented juice that gives them a delectable caramelized exterior on frying, and the inside is as sweet as a banana but firmer. People sometimes pair pan-fried plantains with cream cheese or another mild fresh cheese to cut the sweetness, as they do with guava paste. Cultured Central American cream (*crema*) is another wonderful partner. Ripe and black-ripe plantains are excellent for sautéing in butter, stewing, or combining with other fruits in certain Mexican and Guatemalan *moles*. They go into baked dishes both savory and sweet; ripe plantains sometimes figure in the borderline savory/sweet preparations that Latin Americans treat as side dishes but that would work perfectly well as desserts (for example *plátanos guisados borrachos*, page 190, or Venezuelan *torta de plátano*, page 190).

Please note that the cooking time for plantains decreases with advancing maturity, though timing also depends on the cooking method. Green plantains boiled in the skin may take 40 minutes to cook through, while peeled superripe plantains deep-fry to perfection in 1 to 2 minutes.

a little more sweetness and a slightly softer texture that is still good for boiling and mashing. For more gentrified Cuban versions of the classical African *fufú*, cooks often use half-ripe plantains, or a combination of green and ripe.

RIPE AND BLACK-RIPE PLANTAINS

When they reach the color of overripe bananas, plantains become fairly soft (though they may be still a little starchy at the core) and develop a delicate sweetness, which becomes even more pronounced when they have turned almost solid black and lost the last trace of starch. At that stage, plantains are ideal for baking or grilling, wrapped in aluminum foil or not. Always puncture the plantain skin in

SELECTING

All plantains are harvested green. How fast they ripen depends on their subsequent handling. They arrive at the market either fully green or just beginning to turn yellow, and are then separated according to the stage at which they are to be sold. The ones to be kept green are stored at a cooler temperature than the others, which are then sorted by color as they go from one stage to the next. Green plantains should be solid green and unblemished and feel full in their skins and firm to the touch. Look for the larger plantains. The smaller ones are from the bottom of the bunch. Half-ripe plantains should still be firm, but with the color changing to yellow-green. Ripe plantains should be yellow with large brown and black splotches and yield slightly to the touch. When superripe, plantains are all but solid black and soft to the touch. Avoid plantains that feel stiff or shriveled or moldy.

KEEPING AND PREPARING

Plantains will go on ripening, though slowly, after you bring them home. Keep an eye on them, because ripe ones can't be used in the same ways as green ones. Green plantains stored in a cool room will usually keep for about 1 week before starting to change color (a bit longer in the refrigerator). They will become yellow-green (half-ripe) in 3 days and yellow-brown-black in 2 to 3 days after that. Once they are thoroughly black, use as soon as possible.

Unlike bananas, plantains can be difficult to peel. The green ones are especially stubborn. Some recipes for green or half-ripe plantains call for them to be boiled in the skin, usually with the tips cut off, until tender before peeling (about 40 minutes for green, 20 to 30 minutes for half-ripe ones). To peel them before cooking, cut off the tips with a small sharp knife. Leave the plantains whole or cut crosswise into 2 or 3 chunks. Make 2 or 3 lengthwise incisions in each, following the ridges that run down the fruit. Trying to bruise the flesh as little as possible, pull the skin away from the flesh with a table knife or even the handle of a spoon, then work it free with your fingertips. Trim off any stubborn underskin with a small sharp knife (it becomes bitter in cooking). Ripe and black-ripe plantains can be peeled the same way as a banana, though you should still begin by cutting off the tips.

Green and half-ripe plantains will darken once peeled. If you are not planning to cook them at once, place them in a bowl of cold water; they will keep for several hours at room temperature or 1 to 2 days in the refrigerator. Be sure to blot thoroughly dry before deep-frying.

Note: Plantains are never eaten raw.

Plantain Chips

Mariquitas, Platanutres, Trompetas, Chifles

The people of tropical America—so diverse ethnically and historically—are united by their love for crunchy plantain chips. In Cuba, they are known as *mariquitas* and are consumed with relish as a snack or appetizer. Puerto Ricans and Dominicans call them *platanutres* and *trompetas*, and Ecuadorians call them *chifles*.

I grew up eating round plantain chips, but the minute I got hold of a meat slicer at Victor's Café, when I started working there as a food consultant in the 1980s, I began to experiment and sliced the whole plantain lengthwise into long, elegant slices that we served in nontraditional Cuban fashion with spicy sauces. This very simple idea was soon widely imitated and has now become the norm in most Latin restaurants.

SERVES 4 TO 6

3 very large, firm green plantains (about 2½ pounds)
4 cups corn oil for frying
  Salt to taste

Peeling and Slicing the Plantains ▶ Peel the plantains according to the instructions on page 181. If not using immediately, place in cold water to avoid discoloration. If using a meat slicer, slice the whole plantain lengthwise into very thin chips, about 1/16 inch (1 to 2 millimeters). If using a mandoline, you might want to cut the plantain in half crosswise for easier handling. You can also use a food processor with a large feed tube fitted with a 2-millimeter slicing disk. Trim the plantain to fit the tube.

Frying the Chips ▶ Heat the oil in a medium saucepan to 375°F. Add the plantain slices a few at a time and fry, moving gently with a slotted spoon to keep the slices from curling or sticking to one another, until they are golden and barely beginning to brown. Lift them out of the hot oil with a perforated ladle and place on paper towels to drain. Place in a basket lined with a napkin or a decorative bowl. Sprinkle with salt to taste and serve with a spicy sauce of your choice such as Venezuelan Chunky Avocado Sauce (page 137), "*pico de gallo*" (page 113), Peruvian *salsa* "*huancaína*" (page 128), or "Finger Sauce" (page 116).

Fried Green Plantains

Tostones o Patacones

Green plantains are fried twice to make the delicious and addictive fritters known as *tostones* in the Hispanic Caribbean and *patacones* in Colombia and Ecuador. First the plantain is cut crosswise into sections—the thickness is a matter of personal taste. The sections are deep-fried in hot oil over medium-low heat to cook them through, then they are scooped out of the oil and flattened with a mallet, punched down with a fist, or pressed flat between the hinged wooden (or plastic) sides of a contraption known as a *tostonera* (see page 32). The flattened pieces are plunged back into the hot oil to crisp the outside. It seems simple, but not every Latin cook is capable of making extraordinary *tostones*. If you follow this recipe, chances are that you will become a great *tostón* maker.

Some Hispanic Caribbean cooks I know slice their green plantains for frying on an angle. That's how Colombians make their *patacones*—literally, "shoe soles." I belong to the round *tostón* school. When you fry a plantain round, mash it out flat, and then fry it again, you can suddenly see the fruit's hidden contours, its delicate veins and necklace of seeds. The results of the process are golden medals, pinwheels encased in a crunchy armor. I prefer them as is—with just a touch of salt and garlic—but many of my American guests like them dipped in a sauce, so I usually put out a spicy sauce or *mojo*.

MAKES 16 *TOSTONES* **(SERVES 4)**

- 4 cups corn oil, light olive oil, or, for a more traditional flavor, freshly rendered lard (page 82) for deep-frying
- 4 green plantains (about 2½ pounds)
- 1 cup water
- 1 tablespoon salt
- 1 garlic clove, lightly smashed

▶ Heat the oil for deep-frying in a medium heavy-bottomed saucepan to about 325°F. Meanwhile, peel the plantains according to the instructions on page 181. Cut them into 2-inch rounds. Combine the water, salt, and garlic clove in a small bowl and stir to dissolve the salt; set aside.

Add the plantain slices to the hot oil, about 4 at

CLOCKWISE FROM TOP LEFT: Venezuelan Chunky
Avocado Sauce (*page 137*); Chunky Tomato Salsa,
or "Rooster's Beak" (*page 113*); Plantain Chips
(*page 181*) and *malanga* chips; Peruvian Walnut–
Mirasol Pepper Sauce (*page 128*)

Salvadorian Corn on the Cob with
Mustard, Mayonnaise, and Ketchup *(page 238)*

My Father's Very Soupy Rice and Chicken *(page 317)*

Jicama Sticks with
Chile and Lime *(page 375)*, with and without cilantro

Yuca Fingers with Cilantro Sauce Presilla *(page 386)*,
served with Zafra's One-Lime Limeade *(page 346)*

FROM TOP: "Dirty *mote*," Ecuadorian-style spareribs, and a serving of Ecuadorian-Style Spareribs with "Dirty *Mote*" (*page 394*) and a simple tomato salsa (*page 395*)

COCKTAIL HOUR IN CENTRAL AMERICA:
Costa Rican Small Corn Tortillas *(page 403)*
with, FROM TOP, "Finger Sauce" *(page 116)*;
Veracruzan Refried Bean Dip *(page 277)*;
Costa Rican Chayote, Fresh Corn, and Beef
Hash *(page 230)*; Green Tomatillo-Chile
Salsa *(page 114)*; and Salvadorian *Pupusa*

Galician Empanada with
Tuna Hash (*page 412*)

a time (the temperature will drop to about 300°F), and fry until just golden brown; the slices will float when they are cooked through, in 3 to 4 minutes. Remove from the oil with a slotted spoon and drain on paper towels. As you lift the plantains from the hot oil, plunge the rounds one at a time into the salted water and remove immediately. (I was taught this method by my aunts in Cuba—it salts the plantains and makes them crisp better when fried again.)

To flatten the slices, place the rounds between two brown paper bags and punch them down with your fist or the heel of your hand; you can also use a wooden mallet. The trick is to control the thickness of the plantains. If you flatten them too much, the *tostones* will taste good and have a lot of crunch but will dry out quickly. A 2-inch piece that is 1 to 1½ inches in diameter (the usual size) should be flattened to about 2½ inches in diameter. That way the *tostones* will be crispy outside and tender inside.

For the second frying, increase the heat of the oil to about 375°F. Return the plantain rounds to the oil, a few at a time, and deep-fry, turning with a slotted spoon, until evenly golden brown and crispy. Drain on paper towels, sprinkle with salt, and serve hot. They lose their marvelous crispy texture as they cool.

Fried Ripe Plantains

Platanitos Maduros Fritos (Tajadas)

I have never encountered a Latin American who does not like fried ripe plantains. Who can resist their fruity, seductive caramel taste? In the Hispanic Caribbean, we call fried ripe plantains *plátanos maduros fritos*, or simply *maduros*. Like many Cubans, I call them by their diminutive, *platanitos fritos*. In Colombia, Venezuela, and parts of Central America, they are called *tajadas* (slices).

As a child, I would not eat my dinner—not even my soup—if I did not have at least one slice of fried ripe plantain. My aunt Belén—who had the patience of Job because she loved me—tried every trick in the book to make me eat a thick red bean soup I particularly disliked. The only one that worked was to add tiny bits of *platanitos* to the soup and tell me they were the golden sardines of the Russian Prince Sadko, my favorite fairy-tale character. With every spoonful came a few bits of plantain, their sweetness overpowering the mealy taste of the beans. When I had eaten them all, I refused to eat any more. As a grownup, I now eat many more bean soups than fried plantains—unless I can find perfectly ripe plantains in my market. Then I rush to the frying pan.

Frying plantains well does not require much technical skill. You just need plantains at the proper degree of ripeness. The best plantains for frying are very soft, with dark skins that have begun to ooze some juice. They will fry to perfection, with no hint of astringency, developing a lovely thin crust and exuding a ripe fruit aroma.

Cook's Notes: There are several ways to cut ripe plantains for frying. Many traditional cooks like to cut the plantains lengthwise into ¼-inch-thick slices. Others cut the plantain at an angle into shorter, thicker (½-inch) slices. Although I was raised eating ripe plantains cut into long thin slices, I prefer the thicker ones cut at an angle. Thick slices do not burn as easily as thin ones.

If you are stuck with half-ripe plantains that are still yellow and firm to the touch, resist the temptation to cut them into thin rounds or slices. They will remain starchy and unyielding when fried. Instead, cut them into 1-inch rounds and fry them twice, following the procedure for Fried Green Plantains on page 182 but pressing the plantain rounds to a ¼-inch thickness before frying them the second time. They will not be as deliciously sweet as ripe plantains, but they will not be hard with an astringent aftertaste.

SERVES 6

4 very ripe plantains (about 2 pounds)
2 cups corn oil

▶ Trim the tips of the plantains and peel them. Cut them into ½-inch-thick slices on an angle—you should get about 6 slices from each plantain.

Heat the oil in a medium heavy-bottomed saucepan or a deep skillet over medium heat until barely rippling, about 350°F. Add the plantain slices in batches and fry until golden brown, about 1 to 2 minutes on each side. Remove from the skillet with a slotted spoon and place on paper towels to drain. Serve immediately as a side dish for any Hispanic Caribbean, Venezuelan, Colombian, Ecuadorian, or Brazilian meal.

EMBER-ROASTED PLANTAINS
Plátanos Asados

A central fire burns in the center of the *sokkaka*, the kitchen of the Kuna, an indigenous people who live on tiny islands off the Caribbean coast of Panama. The men go to the mainland to search for firewood. When they return home, they place four large thick logs in a cross pattern on the dirt, and the women push them in as they burn. Cooking pots are placed on grills resting on three stones over the fire. This grill is where ripe plantains are often roasted until they burst. But to the Kuna women, the easiest way of cooking ripe plantains is to bury them in the warm ashes and dying embers. In less than twenty minutes, the skin will look charred and blistered, but the inside will be juicy and tender, ready to eat, with the seductive orange color and smoky flavor that only direct contact with a wood fire can provide.

At home you can do as the Kuna do. At the end of any barbecue, when the coals have died down, bury the plantains in the ashes and cook for 10 minutes. Peel and serve. I like to use these cinder-roasted plantains in salads with a tart vinaigrette (see page 559) or add them to a lobster soup flavored with coconut milk and *ají chombo*, a Panamanian relative of the Scotch bonnet pepper.

A similar method is used in the province of Manabí on the Pacific coast of Ecuador, where plantains are the main staple and used in every conceivable dish. Cooks there use a special tandoor-like wood- or charcoal-burning oven to roast plantains at all stages of ripeness and almost in direct contact with the fire. The plantains are eaten with fresh cheese or *suero blanco* (page 147), a mixture of curd and whey, and an omnipresent table condiment called *salprieta* made with toasted corn and peanuts seasoned with onions sautéed in achiote-infused oil and scattered with cilantro. ◆

Sweet Ripe Plantain Puree

Puré de Plátano Maduro

This puree has the gutsy flavor of the Afro-Cuban mash *fufú*, the silky texture of a refined mousseline, and the rounding influence of the *sofrito* (cooking sauce). It's the next step up from the earthy green plantain puree that is a staple in tropical America.

MAKES 3½ CUPS PUREE (SERVES 6)

- 5 ripe or soft half-ripe plantains (yellow, beginning to blacken in spots; about 3 pounds)
- 2 Ceylon cinnamon sticks (*canela*)
- 1 teaspoon salt
- 2 tablespoons extra-virgin olive oil
- 4 ounces slab bacon, finely diced
- 1 small yellow onion (about 5 ounces), finely chopped (about 1 cup)
- 6 garlic cloves, mashed to a paste in a mortar and pestle or finely chopped and mashed
- ¼–½ cup chicken broth, preferably homemade (page 538)

▶ Cut the unpeeled plantains into 3 pieces each. Place in a 3-quart saucepan with the cinnamon sticks, salt, and 2 quarts water. Bring to a boil and cook for 10 to 15 minutes, until the softened plantains begin to burst out of their skins. Drain and let sit until cool enough to handle, then peel them.

Meanwhile, heat the oil in a medium skillet over medium heat. Add the diced bacon and cook, stirring, until it is golden brown. Stir in the onion and salt to taste and cook, stirring, until the onion is translucent, about 5 minutes. Add the garlic and cook very briefly, for about 10 seconds. Remove from the heat.

Pass the plantains through a food mill into a bowl. (Do not use a food processor or the plantains will be gluey.) Add to the onion and garlic mixture and stir to combine. Gradually stir in enough of the broth to lighten the texture.

Serving: Serve as a side dish for meat, poultry, or fish. I love to use this puree in timbales like the following recipe, or put a few spoonfuls over hearty stews and soups as a flavorful garnish.

Ripe Plantain–Swiss Chard Timbale

Tambor de Plátano Maduro y Acelga

Typical of middle-class Latin cooking are recipes for pies and timbales using tubers and corn as a savory crust. In Cuba, timbales are called *tambores* (drums). Every starchy tuber of our *conucos*, plantains, and corn are often turned into a crusty dough to enclose a filling. Fillings range from salt cod to beef jerky (*tasajo*), and they are always seasoned with a tasty *sofrito*. One of my favorites is a *tambor* made with ripe plantains and Swiss chard.

I always make extra ripe plantain puree when I prepare the preceding recipe. Here I first cook the Swiss chard with a simple *sofrito* of tomato and onion flavored with nutmeg, then bind it together with the plantain puree and a creamy, cheesy custard base. The combination is marvelous—an ideal side dish for the Thanksgiving turkey or capon, roast ham, or chicken.

Working Ahead ▶ The assembled timbales can be covered with plastic wrap and refrigerated for a day before baking.

Cook's Note: Cut each tomato in half and press against the medium-sized openings of a four-sided grater, and grate until you're left with only the skin of the tomato.

SERVES 8

- ¼ cup extra-virgin olive oil
- 4 garlic cloves, finely chopped
- 1 medium yellow onion (about 8 ounces), finely chopped (about 1½ cups)
- 4 medium plum tomatoes (about 12 ounces), peeled, seeded, and finely chopped, or grated (see Cook's Note)
- ½ teaspoon salt
- ½ teaspoon freshly ground black pepper
- ½ teaspoon ground cayenne
- ¼ teaspoon ground nutmeg
- ⅛ teaspoon ground allspice
- 1 bunch Swiss chard (about 1½ pounds), trimmed, rinsed, and coarsely chopped (about 9 cups)
- 4 ounces *queso fresco* (about 1½ cups) or feta cheese (preferably French), crumbled (about ¾ cup)
- ½ cup heavy cream or half-and-half
- 1 large egg yolk, lightly beaten
- 1½ cups Sweet Ripe Plantain Puree (page 185)
- 1 cup Cuban *sofrito* (page 257), warmed

Cooking the Chard ▶ Heat the oil in a large skillet over medium-high heat until rippling. Add the garlic and sauté until golden, about 20 seconds. Stir in the onion and cook until golden, about 4 minutes. Stir in the tomatoes, salt and pepper, cayenne, nut-meg, and allspice and cook for 5 more minutes. Add the chard and cook, stirring, until it wilts. Remove from the heat and let cool.

In a large bowl, whisk together the cheese, cream, and egg with a whisk. Add the chard mixture.

Preheat the oven to 350°F. Lightly butter eight ½–cup ramekins.

Assembling the Timbales ▶ Spoon in ¼ cup ripe plantain puree and even out with a spoon. Top with ¼ cup chard mixture and smooth out with a spoon.

Set the ramekins in a large baking pan and add enough hot water to come halfway up the sides of the ramekins. Bake for 1 hour, or until the timbales are set and golden brown.

Run a knife around the edges of each ramekin and unmold. Serve atop a pool of hot Cuban *sofrito* (page 257).

Cuban Green Plantain Mash with Garlic and Olive Oil

Fufú Cubano

Wherever Africans were brought to the New World, one can find variations of this plantain mash. In Africa, *fufú* meant any vegetable or tuber mash—the West African favorite was and is still made with the true yam, the type we call in Spanish *ñame blanco*, or with yellow yam. In Cuba, *fufú* means a coarse, hearty plantain mash, often flavored with garlic, a touch of melted lard or olive oil, and lots of pork cracklings. When I don't have time to make fresh pork cracklings, I use a mixture of olive oil and bacon bits (a combination well known in Spain and in the Hispanic Caribbean) to flavor the mash.

Plantain mashes similar to the Afro-Cuban *fufú* can be found on the other Hispanic Caribbean islands. Puerto Ricans call their version, made by pounding green fried plantains to a coarse puree, *mofongo* (page 188). The Dominicans call theirs *mangú* (page 187).

SERVES 6

4–5 green plantains (about 3 pounds)
  1 ripe plantain (about 8 ounces)
  2 teaspoons salt
  ¼ cup extra-virgin olive oil, plus more for drizzling
  6 ounces slab bacon, coarsely chopped
6–8 garlic cloves, mashed to a paste with a mortar and pestle or finely chopped and mashed
    Juice of 1 large lime (about 1 tablespoon)
    Salt and freshly ground black pepper to taste

▶ Peel the green plantains according to the instructions on page 181. Trim the tips of the ripe plantain and peel it. Place the peeled plantains in a medium saucepan, add 3 quarts water and the salt, and bring to a rolling boil over high heat. Cover and cook until soft, 15 to 20 minutes.

While the plantains cook, heat 2 tablespoons of the olive oil in a small skillet over medium heat. Add the bacon and sauté until golden. Drain the bacon, reserving the fat.

Drain the plantains, reserving ¼ cup of the cooking water. Using a mortar (or large bowl) and working in batches as necessary, mash the plantains to a coarse puree with a large pestle or potato masher. (You can use a food mill if necessary, but you will not achieve the rough texture of traditional *fufú*.) Place the plantain mash in a bowl, add the garlic, the reserved cooking liquid, the bacon and bacon fat, and the remaining olive oil, and mix well. Add a little hot water if the mixture is too dry. Season with the lime juice and salt and pepper.

Serving: Serve instead of any vegetable puree, drizzling on a little extra virgin olive oil at the table. *Fufú* is particularly delicious alongside spicy grilled and roasted meats. I love to add a spoonful or two to oxtail stew (page 711) or to a hearty red bean soup (pages 509 and 510).

Dominican Green Plantain Puree

Mangú

The plantain is one of the stars of Dominican cooking. People eat it boiled as a side dish or cooked with a constellation of other starchy vegetables in *sancocho*, the Dominican big soup; twice-fried into golden *tostones*; or coarsely mashed into the hearty puree called *mangú*. Dominicans even eat plantains for breakfast. At the poshest hotels in Santo Domingo, where American- or European-style menus rule, an exception is made for the *criollo* breakfast of fried eggs, sausages, fried fresh cheese (*queso blanco frito*), and *mangú*.

If you like grits for breakfast, *mangú* is for you. I adapted this recipe from Ligia de Bornia's classic *La cocina dominicana* (*The Dominican Kitchen*). Mrs. Bornia, who died a few years ago, was the grande dame of Dominican cooking. Her *mangú* is a simple but flavorful plantain mash that you just can't stop eating.

SERVES 6

> 4 green plantains (about 3 pounds)
> 2 teaspoons salt
> 4 scallions, white and 3 inches of green parts, finely chopped
> 1 tablespoon distilled white vinegar
> ¼ cup corn oil or light olive oil

▶ Peel the plantains according to the instructions on page 181 and cut each into 3 sections. Place the plantains, 1 teaspoon salt, and 2 quarts water in a large pot and bring to a boil over high heat. Lower the heat to medium-low and simmer until the plantains are fork-tender, about 30 minutes. Drain, reserving ½ cup of the cooking liquid.

Working in small batches, mash the plantains to a coarse puree with a mortar and pestle or a potato masher. Transfer to a bowl and set aside.

Place the chopped scallions and vinegar in a small bowl; let stand for 2 to 3 minutes. Heat the oil in a 12-inch skillet over medium heat. Add the scallions with the vinegar and sauté until lightly golden, about 2 minutes. Add the mashed plantains, the remaining 1 teaspoon salt, and the reserved cooking liquid and cook, stirring, until the puree is heated through, about 5 minutes.

Puerto Rican *Mofongo*

Mofongo Puertorriqueño

Mofongo, a coarse plantain mash with pork cracklings, is as popular in Puerto Rico as Christmas *pasteles* (the national version of tamales), but it is eaten year-round and at all hours of the day. Stores at shopping centers have been known to create gargantuan *mofongos* weighing 4 tons and feeding thousands to break records and attract customers. Young chefs gentrify it and dress it to the nines. They stuff it with seafood, chicken, or pork and serve it from cute little mortars. Nowhere has a rustic plantain mash received more attention. Here is a plain traditional recipe that you can dress up any way you want with different fillings or table sauces.

The word *mofongo* is of African origin. Curiously, in some parts of eastern Cuba *plátano mofongo*, or *fongot*, refers to the stocky variety of plantain we call *plátano burro*.

SERVES 4

> 4 large green plantains (about 3 pounds)
> 4 cups corn oil, light olive oil, or, for a more traditional flavor, freshly rendered lard (page 82) for deep-frying
> Salt
> 6 garlic cloves, mashed to a paste with a mortar and pestle or finely chopped and mashed
> 8 ounces prepared pork cracklings (preferably crunchy and blistered, without meat; page 82)
> 3 tablespoons extra-virgin olive oil, or as needed

▶ Peel the plantains according to the instructions on page 181, cut into 2-inch rounds, and deep-fry once according to the instructions for *tostones* on page 182. Drain on paper towels and sprinkle with salt to taste.

While the *tostones* are hot, pound them one by one with a pestle together with a little of the crushed garlic, a few of the cracklings, some olive oil, and salt. (If you don't have a mortar and pestle, use a sturdy bowl set on a damp kitchen towel to keep it steady and smash the plantains with a meat mallet.) Pound until the plantains are coarsely mashed and the ingredients are well integrated into a rough-textured puree. If you feel that the puree is too dry, add 1 more tablespoon olive oil. Divide into 4 portions and mold into balls.

Serving: Serve as a first course with some broth (chicken or beef) on the side to moisten the plantain, or as a side for any red meat, pork, or fish.

Esmeraldas Plantain Balls with Pork Cracklings

Bolones de Verde con Chicharrones de Esmeraldas

The warm Pacific coast of Ecuador is a world apart from the highland regions. While highlanders prefer hominy (*mote*) to any other vegetable, the plantain is central to the coastal diet. The green plantain (*plátano verde*, commonly known simply as *verde*), is served fried, boiled, pureed, or formed into balls.

A *bolón de verde* is a large green plantain ball flavored with pork cracklings, cheese, or peanuts, amazingly similar to *mofongo*. The resemblance is not simply fortuitous. The northern Ecuadorian province of Esmeraldas near the Colombian border is home to a sizable black population—hence the popularity of *bolones*, which are a version of the African *fufú* and its siblings in the Hispanic Caribbean.

In Ecuador I have eaten *bolones* of all sizes. Some are as large as oranges, and just one is a meal in itself, often breakfast. The recipe is almost identical to that of Puerto Rican *mofongo*. My favorite *bolones* are from a street vendor in Atacames, a beach town in Esmeraldas, who makes them to order while you watch and loads them with crunchy pork cracklings.

MAKES FOUR *BOLONES*

1 recipe Puerto Rican *Mofongo* (page 188)

▶ Follow the recipe for Puerto Rican *Mofongo*, but use lard or corn oil and a bit of broth if needed to shape the balls.

Serving: Serve *bolones* with slices of fresh cheese and an egg for breakfast.

Drunken Stewed Plantains

Plátanos Guisados Borrachos

Stewed ripe plantains in a rich wine glaze are a savory side dish in Cuba, although a look at the list of ingredients might make you expect dessert. My mother loved to make them for lunch, which was our most important meal. Sometimes she would finish the plantains with some rum and set them alight, like cherries jubilee. But no, this was not dessert—we liked to eat it with braised eye of round and red kidney beans and white rice.

In Cuba, the dish is also known as *plátanos en tentación* (something like "plantain temptation"). It can be made with red wine, port, sherry, or even the dry salted cooking wine we call *vino seco*. I have often made it with dark aged Bacardi or Venezuelan Santa Teresa rum, and the result is delicious. The advantage of the red wine is that it gives the plantains a lovely garnet color on the outside while the inside remains golden yellow, a pretty contrast.

In Cartagena, a Colombian city on the Caribbean, a similar dish is called *plátanos pícaros*. This version is made by simmering the plantain in a syrup of brown loaf sugar flavored with spices like cloves and cinnamon, without the wine.

Cook's Note: It is very important to use plantains that have ripened to the black stage and are very soft.

SERVES 4

- 4 very ripe, very large plantains (about 3½ pounds)
- 4 tablespoons (½ stick) butter
- ½ cup packed dark brown sugar (about 4 ounces)
- 1½ cups fruity red wine (preferably Malbec), port, sweet sherry, or aged rum
- 2 Ceylon cinnamon sticks (*canela*)
- 3 star anise pods
- 2 whole cloves
- Salt

▶ Peel the plantains according to the instructions on page 181. Cut into 3-inch pieces.

Place the butter in a medium skillet and heat over medium heat until bubbly. Add the plantains and brown on all sides. Add the brown sugar and cook, stirring occasionally, until the sugar dissolves and begins to caramelize. Stir in the wine, cinnamon, star anise, cloves, and a pinch of salt, cover, and let simmer until the sauce thickens into a rich glaze, about 20 minutes.

Serving: Serve immediately as a side dish for Stuffed Eye of Round Pot Roast Cartagena Style (page 707). The plantains will harden as they cool.

Venezuelan Plantain and Cheese Torte

Torta de Plátano

While walking through the enchanting gardens of my Venezuelan friend Nelly Galavís's sprawling family compound in Los Chorros, Caracas, we smelled the familiar aroma of frying ripe plantains wafting from one of the kitchens. To me this is a siren's call.

We marched into the kitchen hoping to snatch a slice or two from the cook, but she had other plans. She was making a *torta de plátanos*, a traditional Venezuelan torte made with layers of fried ripe plantain slices brushed with a syrup made with the prized Venezuelan brown loaf sugar, *papelón*, and sprinkled with grated cheese. We pleaded for just one slice each, but she was firm. She needed every one to assemble the torte. Nelly and I looked at each other, grabbed our slices, and ran out of the kitchen like a couple of children.

SERVES 8 TO 12

For the Plantains

8 very ripe plantains (about 4½ pounds)

2 cups corn oil

For the Syrup

9 ounces Latin American brown loaf sugar, preferably *papelón* or *panela*, or Demerara sugar, or packed brown sugar (about 1 cup)

2 Ceylon cinnamon sticks (*canela*)

1 star anise pod

4 whole cloves

5 allspice berries

1 teaspoon fresh lime juice

2 cups water

2 tablespoons dark rum, preferably aged Venezuelan Santa Teresa or Bacardi Black

For the Torte

1 teaspoon mild extra-virgin olive oil or butter

1 pound *queso blanco*, grated (about 3 cups)

3 large eggs

½ teaspoon salt

Freshly ground black pepper to taste

Frying the Plantains ▶ Peel the plantains according to the instruction on page 181 and cut lengthwise

into slices about ¼ inch thick. You should get about 4 slices from each plantain.

Heat the oil in a large wide skillet to 350°F. Add the slices in batches and fry until golden, about 1 minute on each side. Drain on paper towels.

Making the Syrup ▶ If using a large chunk of loaf sugar, cut it with a heavy knife into 2- or 3-inch pieces, or break into chunks with a hammer. Place the sugar in a medium saucepan with the spices, lime juice, and water and bring to a boil. Reduce the heat and simmer until the syrup thickens, about 15 minutes.

Add the rum and simmer for 1 or 2 minutes more, to the consistency of maple syrup. Strain the syrup and keep warm.

Assembling the Torte ▶ Preheat the oven to 350°F. Grease an 8-inch square glass baking dish with the olive oil or butter.

Place a layer of plantain slices side by side in the bottom of the dish—select the best-looking slices for this layer if you are planning to unmold the torte. Brush the plantains generously with syrup and sprinkle with 1 cup of grated cheese. Cover with another layer of plantains and repeat the process, until you have 4 layers in all.

Beat the eggs lightly with the salt and pepper, and pour over the torte. Top with any remaining cheese.

Bake for 20 minutes, or until golden brown.

Serving: Most people bring the *torta* to the table in the baking dish. (That is why Pyrex is so popular in Latin America.) I prefer to unmold the *torta* onto a pretty platter. Although the top of the *torta* looks rather nice with its thick golden crust, I like to see the clean design of the plantain slices in the bottom layer with their caramel color and tiny black seeds. In either case, cut the *torta* into long thin slices, following the contour of the plantain slices, or into squares. Serve hot as a side dish with roast meats like Venezuelan Short Ribs in Black Sauce (page 713).

Plantain-Eggplant Puree from Barranquilla

Boronía Barranquillera

The Colombian *boronía* is a coarse ripe plantain and eggplant puree seasoned with the local cooking sauce, called *guiso*. It is a simple dish that surprises with its deft combination of flavors and textures, the peppery, unctuous, somewhat slippery eggplant playing to the creamy, sweet plantain, the whole being given a welcome kick by the acidity of the tomatoes and the pungency of the onions and garlic in the cooking sauce. *Queso costeño*, the hard cow's milk cheese typical of the Caribbean coast of Colombia, rounds out the flavors.

The name *boronía* is a sign of this dish's ancient pedigree. An eggplant dish called *al-buraniyya* was served at the wedding banquet of the Muslim caliph al-Mamun to honor his bride, Buran. From an Islamic royal banquet hall to the kitchens of Christian Andalusia to the kitchens of the New World, *al-buraniyya* changed names and became *alboronía* or *boronía*, picking up a few tasty companions along the way: pumpkin, peppers, tomatoes, and even the tropical chayote and plantain.

Cook's Note: If you can't find *queso costeño* in your local Hispanic supermarket, use aged Mexican *cotija* or hard Salvadorian aged cow's-milk cheese, or even aged ricotta salata, an Italian cheese with a salty flavor and grainy texture similar to *queso costeño*.

SERVES 6

- 4 ripe large plantains (about 2½ pounds)
- 2 large purple eggplants (about 2 pounds)
- 1 medium red onion (about 8 ounces), peeled
- 2 small plum tomatoes (about 6 ounces), halved
- ¼ cup extra-virgin olive oil
- 1 head garlic, separated into cloves, peeled, and mashed to a coarse paste with a mortar and pestle
- 1 medium red bell pepper (about 6 ounces), cored, seeded, deveined, and finely chopped (about ¾ cup)
- 4 ounces (about 1 cup) Colombian hard cow's-milk cheese (*queso costeño*), grated (for serving)

▶ Cut the plantains crosswise in half, without peeling. Cut the eggplant lengthwise into quarters, leaving the quarters barely attached at the stem.

Place the vegetables in an 8-quart pot, cover with 3 quarts water, and bring to a boil over high heat. Lower the heat to medium, cover, and cook for about 20 minutes. Check for doneness. The plantains will probably be fork-tender; if so, remove from the water and set aside. The eggplants may still be a bit hard; if so, put back into the pot, cover, and cook for 5 to 8 minutes longer. When they are done, remove from the pot and let cool slightly.

Cut the stems off the eggplants and peel them. Peel the plantains. Working in small batches, mash the plantains and eggplant with a fork into a coarse puree. Set aside.

Grate the onion and then the tomatoes into a bowl, using the medium-hole side of a box grater. Set aside.

Heat 3 tablespoons of the oil in a 12-inch skillet over medium heat until it ripples. Add the garlic and sauté for a few seconds, until golden. Add the onion, tomatoes, and bell pepper and cook, stirring, for 10 minutes. Add the plantain-eggplant puree and mix well with a wooden spoon. Add the remaining 1 tablespoon oil and beat into the puree, then continue to cook until heated through. Transfer to a serving bowl.

Serving: To finish, sprinkle with grated cheese at the table or pass the cheese in a small bowl. In Barranquilla, *boronía* is served with white rice as a side dish to accompany red meats, poultry, or fish. For an unusual appetizer dip, mound the *boronía* on a colorful plate, sprinkle with the grated cheese, and surround with long golden Plantain Chips (page 181). At my restaurant Cucharamama, *boronía* is the side dish for the organic half chicken we roast in our wood-burning oven.

Peach Palm Fruit

Chontaduro or pejibaye (peach palm)

For the inhabitants of humid rain forests across the Americas, several palm species play a pivotal role in daily life, both providing wood and fiber and competing in importance with the yuca or plantain as a staple food. Tropical palms were "a new tree of life" to Joseph Gumilla, a Valencian Jesuit who explored the Orinoco Basin in Venezuela during the early eighteenth century and wrote about his experiences in a book called *El Orinoco ilustrado* (*The Illustrated Orinoco*). More significant than the manna that sustained the ancient Hebrews in the desert, Gumilla writes, the palm tree is a "miracle of nature's Supreme Creator," the giver of bread, food, drink, clothing, housing, and canoes for the natives of this region.

Three centuries later, the Warao Indians of the Orinoco Delta still depend on the native *moriche* palm for wood for their stilt homes and canoes; fiber for nets, baskets, and hammocks; fruit; and a nutritious starch (*yuruma*) extracted from its pith to make their most basic food, a flatbread that they eat with fish.

From Central America to Brazil, the African palm is an important source of the *dendê* oil used in Afro-Brazilian cooking, while the genus *Euterpe* is the main source of the coveted heart of palm (*palmito*), the ivory-colored inner core of the tree's terminal bud.

The tall, slender *Guilielma gasipaes* or *Bactris gasipaes*, another important source of heart of palm, is even more prized for its edible fruit. Known as *pejibaye* in Costa Rica, *chontaduro* and *cachipay* in Colombia, and *chonta* in Bolivia and Peru, the peach palm fruit (its common English name) grows in large, beautiful clusters, like a cross between miniature coconuts and persimmons, in shades of orange, yellow, and green. The flesh is deep orange and mealy like a Caribbean sweet potato, but more fibrous. Because of its high starch content, it seems more like a tuber or a green plantain, with very little sweetness.

In some areas of Central and South America, the peach palm fruit plays the part of corn, rice, or starchy vegetables like yuca and plantain. Some say the taste resembles chestnuts, sweet potatoes, or corn. I find that it tastes like a blend of different tubers like sweet potatoes, yuca, and malanga. The fruits are always boiled or roasted in embers and then peeled before being eaten cut into chunks or as an earthy puree.

In Chocó, a rainy area on the Pacific coast of Colombia, cooks mix the boiled and mashed fruits with milk and sugar to make a nourishing porridge. They also use the fruit for a type of buttery torte called *torta de chontaduro*. In some indigenous South American communities, the pulp is ground into flour, then dissolved in water and fermented to make a mildly alcoholic drink called *masato* or *chicha*.

Though not as nutritious as legumes, peach palm fruit are a good source of protein, beta-carotene, and other carotenes. Because the fruits tend to ferment quickly after harvest, they are cooked and packed in brine for export. In most pan-Latin markets, you will find large jars of them in brine, looking like miniature orange coconuts, labeled *pejibaye* or *chontaduro*.

SELECTING AND PREPARING

Peach palm fruits come to Hispanic markets in the United States already cooked, packed in jars of brine. To use, drain and rinse under cold water. Because they are usually hard and fibrous, the canned fruits need to be cooked further before using. Place in a large pot, cover with 3 inches of water, and bring to a boil over medium heat. Cook, covered, until the fruit feels soft when pierced with a fork, 40 minutes to 1 hour. Let cool, then halve lengthwise. Scoop out the seeds, peel the fruit, and proceed according to the recipe directions.

Simple Peach Palm Fruit Puree

Puré de Chontaduro

The stunning saffron yellow color of the peach palm, known as *chontaduro* in parts of Colombia, makes this puree a marvelous accompaniment for any roast. Boiling and pureeing is one of the simplest ways to prepare this dense fruit. It is important to take the trouble of passing the puree through a food mill or wire-mesh strainer to remove the fruit's fibers. Garnish it, if you like, with sprigs of purple basil, a popular herb on the Pacific coast of Colombia.

SERVES 6

Two 27-ounce jars peach palm fruit (labeled *chontaduro* or *pejibaye*), drained
1 cup whole milk
4 tablespoons (½ stick) butter
¼ teaspoon freshly grated nutmeg
½ teaspoon salt, or to taste
½ teaspoon freshly ground black pepper
Basil sprigs, for garnish

▶ Prepare the peach palm fruits as directed above. Place the fruits and milk in a food processor or blender and puree. Pass through a food mill or a coarse strainer to remove fibers. You should have about 2½ cups of puree.

Place the puree in a small saucepan, add the butter, nutmeg, salt, and pepper, and heat over low heat, stirring, until hot. Serve garnished with basil sprigs.

Peach Palm Timbales

Tortas de Chontaduro Chocanas

In the Pacific region of Colombia, particularly in the departments of Valle del Cauca and rainy Chocó, cooks make sweet or savory tortes out of starchy vegetables and tubers such as *arracacha* and peach palm fruits. Because of their dense, mealy texture, these fruits lend themselves beautifully to such rich puddinglike dishes. This recipe is my lighter version of a traditional savory *torta de chontaduro* from Chocó, cooked in individual ramekins.

SERVES 6

- 1 cup Simple Peach Palm Fruit Puree (page 194)
- 2 tablespoons butter
- 3 scallions, white part only, finely chopped
- 2 large eggs
- 1 cup heavy cream or whole milk
- 4 ounces *queso blanco* or Monterey Jack cheese, grated (about ⅔ cup)
- ½ teaspoon salt, or to taste

▶ Preheat the oven to 350°F. Butter six ½-cup ramekins.

Place the puree in a medium bowl. Melt the butter in a small skillet. Add the scallions and sauté for about 2 minutes, stirring. Stir into the puree.

In a small bowl, whisk together the eggs, cream, cheese, and salt. Pour into the puree and stir to mix well. Pour the mixture into the ramekins, filling them two-thirds full.

Place the ramekins in a large baking pan and add enough hot water to come halfway up the sides of the ramekins. Bake for 30 to 45 minutes, until the custard is golden brown and firm to the touch.

Remove the ramekins from the water. Run a knife around the edges of each timbale, invert onto a plate, and then invert again to serve with the browned crust on top.

Serving: Serve with Colombian "Sweated" Chicken Stew (page 669), Colombian Corn Rice (page 254), or Braised Chicken in Coconut Sauce in the Style of Cartagena (page 668).

Peach Palm Salad with Citrus, Mint, and Purple Basil Dressing

Ensalada de Chontaduro

I often serve peach palm fruit with fish or chicken or in salads at my restaurant Cucharamama. In this salad, it is flavored with lime and orange juice, mint, and fresh purple basil, the traditional seasonings of Colombia's Chocó region, where it is a staple. Nestled on a bed of peppery watercress, the deep orange fruit looks stunning. Serve this colorful salad as a light main course for lunch or as a side dish for grilled chicken or fish.

What to Drink: If serving as a main course for lunch, pair with a floral and citrusy Alamos Viognier from high-altitude vineyards in Mendoza, Argentina, which will complement the sweet aromas of basil and mint in the salad.

Two 27-ounce jars peach palm fruit, preferably
Colombian, drained

5 scallions, white and 3 inches of green parts, finely
chopped

1 medium red onion (about 8 ounces), cut into
lengthwise slivers

1 medium red bell pepper (about 6 ounces), cored,
seeded, deveined, and thinly slivered

¼ cup extra-virgin olive oil

¼ cup fresh orange juice

¼ cup fresh lime juice

2 garlic cloves, finely chopped

1 teaspoon salt

6 or 7 purple or green basil leaves, finely shredded
(about 1 tablespoon)

12 mint leaves, finely chopped (about 1 tablespoon)

1 bunch watercress, rinsed, stemmed, and dried

▶ Cook the peach palm fruit until soft, as directed
on page 194. Peel, halve lengthwise, scoop out the
seeds, and cut into quarters. Place in a bowl with
the scallions, onion, and bell pepper.

In a small bowl, whisk the oil with the orange
and lime juices, garlic, and salt.

Pour the dressing over the salad and toss to
coat. Add the basil and mint and toss again. Arrange
the salad on a bed of watercress and serve at once.

Storing: The salad will keep well in the refrigerator for 2 to
3 days, well covered with plastic wrap.

THE STARCHY VEGETABLES OF THE TROPICAL HIGHLANDS

Some parts of the world have been cradles of genetic
diversity. The Fertile Crescent of the Middle East,
for instance, was the prehistoric gene bank for not
just one but most of the world's great domesticated
grain crops—several species of wheat, along with
oats, rye, and barley. In the same way, the western
part of the South American tropics was the birthplace of not one but many potato species, along with
eight or nine other important root vegetables that
were domesticated by pre-Columbian peoples. But
the parallel is not perfect.

The early Middle Eastern farmers did not
have to deal with environmental extremes. The
first peoples of tropical South America between
the eastern part of the Andes and the Pacific, just
south of the equator, faced a multitude of contrasting environmental conditions. Their land went from
humid, stiflingly hot Amazonian jungle in Colombia,
Ecuador, Bolivia, and Peru through coastal deserts,
where it sometimes doesn't rain for a generation,
up through low and high mountain valleys to the
bitter, freezing, and seemingly plantless reaches of
the *altiplano* (the high plateau lying in Peru, Bolivia,
and northern Chile) and some lesser Andean slopes.
It was this last, nearly uninhabitable area, which
barely satisfies the minimum oxygen requirements
of human hearts and lungs, that has been the point
of origin for more different kinds of edible root
vegetables than any other region of the planet.

Without the highland root vegetables, the Inca empire as the Spanish found it could not have existed. When the Inca rulers unified the Andean region, only about a century before the Europeans arrived, they also brought all of its food resources into one interlinked system, building great storehouses to hold the different crops from every corner of the realm and keeping complex records of what was to be distributed at certain times and places. As a result, the half-Incan and half-Spanish chronicler El Inca Garcilaso related to Spanish readers in the sixteenth century, "No one ever begged for alms in Peru" (meaning the Inca empire). No member of the Spanish invading force could have failed to recognize that this was not the case in Europe.

The highland root vegetables made the Inca food system possible because they grew where nothing else would. Long before the Incas, the Andean peoples of what is now Peru had learned to cultivate the land at increasing altitudes with progressively decreasing temperatures. At sea level in desert-like coastal areas, they created irrigation systems to grow some of the lowland root vegetables like yuca, along with corn, beans, peppers, and squash. Farther inland, at higher elevations with little rainfall, they built astonishing networks of irrigation canals to supply water to raised beds and carried loads of landfill to carved-out mountainside terraces (*andenes*). On much of this "made" land, they were able to grow corn, beans, some cold-loving peppers like the *rocoto*, and squash. Some of the canal and raised-bed infrastructure is still visible, though the Spaniards destroyed much of it.

In the highest habitable levels of the Andes, Europeans found people tilling the soil under conditions they could scarcely believe. They had created useful crops out of the only plants that could be made to live under conditions of fierce cold, fierce sun, and alternating rainy and dry seasons: the most stubbornly cold-tolerant varieties of potatoes and other native root vegetables. It was a stunning achievement to make some of these foods edible, much less delicious. All the high-altitude, cold-tolerant strains of Andean root vegetables tend to be the most bitter of their kind, at least as they come fresh from the soil. But thousands of years ago, people realized that the June and July daily cycle—freezing temperatures over a slightly longer than twelve-hour night, followed by a shorter interval of intense tropical sunshine—could be used as a preservation method that improved the flavor of the least likely roots. It was the first freeze-drying of foods in human history.

The Spanish conquerors were in awe of the complex and productive husbandry lavished on root vegetables like the potato. Today we can see that the long-keeping underground vegetables were actually the most efficient Andean crops. Not only do they yield more usable food (in calories) per acre than other plants of the region, but the habit of planting and often cooking combinations of several root vegetables together produced a source of high-protein, high-carbohydrate, vitamin-rich, and deeply satisfying sustenance not matched by any other category of plant food in the tropical highlands.

Potatoes filled a central role in Andean cooking, similar to that of wheat in the ancient Middle East. But though grains like rye and barley successfully accompanied wheat on many of its prehistoric travels throughout Europe and Asia, Andean root vegetables, with the exception of some of the potatoes, generally failed to get beyond the Andes.

Among the non-potato root vegetables that are still eaten today in Peru, Bolivia, Ecuador, and northern Chile are the nasturtium relative called *añu* and *mashua* in the Andean languages; *maca*, a garden cress cousin with a certain reputation as an aphrodisiac; *ulluco* or *melloco*, which comes in a spectrum of colors from purplish to pink, orange, and white; the delicately waxy, also multicolored *oca*; and the subtle but luscious *arracacha*. Only the last three show up here (generally frozen) in Latin American markets, and even they are barely known compared to the modern commercial potato. But the situation is changing fast, thanks to swelling numbers of Latin American immigrants and the heirloom vegetable movement among American gourmets.

Potatoes

I have watched potatoes being planted in Peru with a simple wooden foot plow called a *chaquitaclla* that harks back to Inca times. I spent time with a Cusco family and their neighbors during harvest, but no experience in my many travels for this book has been more amazing than standing on a mass of pebble-sized potatoes close to the shore of Lake Titicaca in Bolivia with an Andean woman who was preparing the freeze-dried potatoes that people have been making for millennia on the chilled but sun-baked *altiplano*. The two of us, barefooted, trod up and down on the bumpy carpet of potatoes, which had already frozen several times in the sharp *altiplano* nights and been thawed under a layer of straw during the day before. With our feet, we rubbed off the skins, already loosened by the freeze/thaw operation, to start breaking down the cell structure of the potatoes and allow their moisture to leach out. When we were finished, I waded into the frigid waters of the lake to help her pull out sacks of previously harvested potatoes that lay soaking in the water. Later we savored hot, fortifying dishes made from potatoes that had received the same treatment the previous year, which were piled like dry stones in her kitchen. In this part of Bolivia, people practically live on boiled potatoes and thick gruel-like soups made with freeze-dried potatoes and bits of freeze-dried lamb (*chalona*).

How potatoes got to the Andean highlands is the stuff of ancient legends, such as the Bolivian Aymara tale of Mallku the condor. One day, the story goes, Mallku flew from the Illampu mountain to the pampas, flat lands dotted with stones (*illas*) that the people considered sacred. An old woman saw the condor land in the pampa called Wiplaspay and decided to venture closer. She saw that Mallku carried a beautiful white flower on one of his wings, and that his head was crowned with a purple flower. Frightened, she threw a stone at him. When he didn't move, she picked a bigger stone. "You!" she shouted. "Who are you?"

The condor began to move its wings like a whirlwind. The beating of the wings grew so intense that the old woman was thrown to the ground. When she was able to see clearly, she saw that the stones, the *illas*, had become different-colored potatoes that at once began to speak. One announced, "I am the black girl," while another one said, "I am the red girl" (the name of two important cultivars). The old woman took them home as delicious potatoes. The condor, meanwhile, turned into potato vines, and its eggs became potatoes.

The soil of the Andean *altiplano* does seem as if it would need supernatural aid to bring forth anything edible, yet it proved to be a rich food basket. Among the highland root crops, the potato was queen. But I have to point out that "potato" means something different to botanists and Andean farmers than to the rest of us. The kind eaten around the world today is *Solanum tuberosum*, a nightshade relative that produces the starchy tubers we turn into French fries and purees. But many other tuber-yielding and mountain-loving members of the *Solanum* genus are also potatoes. Nature scattered more than 200 different species in the Americas, each with its own qualities. There is a cluster of species in the southwestern mountains of North America and a larger, more important one in the Andes. Many are tiny (some only the size of large peas) and extremely bitter when freshly harvested, or even poisonous.

The many different Andean *Solanums* crossed and recrossed repeatedly in the wild, as they still do today. By 4000 B.C., or perhaps several millennia earlier, the pre-Inca peoples of the region had already created domesticated varieties descended from at least a dozen wild species. How the different kinds are related is unclear even to botanists, who are still threshing out competing ideas about where particular species, subspecies, and traditional cultivars belong on the family tree.

Our U.S. commercial potatoes represent only a tiny percentage of this diversity. *Solanum tuberosum* was the only potato species to successfully make the passage from the Andes to Europe and eventually to the rest of the inhabited world. For some reason, this species (some call it a subspecies, *S. tuberosum ssp. tuberosum*) was able to weather the drastic shifts in altitude, latitude, and intensity of solar radiation that kept other potatoes—and the rest of the Andean

tubers—from crossing the equator and traveling to temperate European and North American regions. Even today it is difficult for plant breeders to produce versions of traditional Andean potatoes and other root crops of the region that will grow under alien conditions.

Before the Spanish conquest, *S. tuberosum*, or something quite close to it, had already become very popular everywhere on the Pacific side of South America because of its pleasant texture and flavor as well as its convenient large size and good yields. But farmers at the highest altitudes either didn't plant it at all or cultivated it as only one among many varieties belonging to several species—many of them filled with bitter glycoalkaloids. Almost inedibly acrid when harvested, these potatoes were always put through some version of the freeze-drying cycle that I saw in progress at Lake Titicaca. The bitterness leaches out with the juices, leaving what look like potato fossils. Since pre-Inca times, these freeze-dried potatoes have been the mainstay for the peoples of the *altiplano* and an article of trade with other, lower-lying communities.

Do not think, however, that "regular," nonbitter potatoes have been unimportant in the Andean countries. Bitter potatoes for *chuño* always predominated at the highest inhabited levels, but most of the *altiplano* has traditionally enjoyed a huge spectrum of traditional varieties eaten fresh that are even more delicious than the best kinds we can get in the United States. They come in a good number of different shapes (round, skinny, twisty, knobby, knotty), colors (white, yellow-white, deep golden, pale pink, red, purple, blue-black), textures (all degrees from *harinosa*, or mealy, to compact and waxy), and taste (from deeply earthy to sweet and mild). But today this millennia-old "enemy of hunger," as Pablo Neruda called the potato, is threatened as never before. I find it ironic that unusual or "heirloom" potatoes have achieved gourmet status in the United States just at the time when people in the Andean towns and cities are eating fewer and fewer varieties. Not long ago, a Peruvian or Bolivian farmer might have had 100 or more different kinds as insurance against any one failing through some caprice of nature. Now that practice is dying out except in the more isolated, self-sufficient communities of the highlands.

SELECTING

The increasing number of different potato varieties in U.S. farmers' markets and produce stores is a wonderful thing. It brings cooks here in touch with some of the best potatoes grown in other parts of the world. I encourage you to try as many different kinds as possible. But in the Andean highlands, one quality takes precedence over all others in cooking with nonbitter potatoes—the more *harinosa* (floury), the better, no matter what the size, shape, or color. Elsewhere in Latin America, people favor waxy potatoes for salads and even for frying, but these are seldom used for the traditional potato dishes of Bolivia, Peru, Ecuador, and the highlands of Colombia.

I suggest that you do some experimenting with the selection in your local market and learn the names of reliably mealy kinds. That said, I have to point out that unless a certain size or color is desired, most of the time plain old russets will beat all the fancy competition for that crucial Andean mealiness. Starchy potatoes like purple potatoes are also terrific, when color is not an issue, in most Andean

dishes. Medium-starchy varieties like Yukon Gold and Yellow Finn are acceptable, though not ideal, for these purposes.

Whatever kinds you choose, look for very hard, unblemished potatoes, without sprouts and free of the green tinge that develops on exposure to light and that signals a concentration of poisonous solanine.

KEEPING AND PREPARING

Potatoes last best when stored in dark, cool, airy conditions (never the refrigerator). If you haul them out of a storage place and find that they are green-skinned or starting to sprout a little, all is not lost, although the quality will be slightly compromised. You will just have to peel and trim them very thoroughly. For potatoes that are to be cooked in the skin, first scrub them well with a vegetable brush. If they are peeled before cooking, drop them into a bowl of cold water as you work.

THE INTERNATIONAL POTATO CENTER (CIP)

Forty minutes from downtown Lima, researchers from 25 countries hold in their hands the genetic past and future of the potato. Spread out over about 40 acres in the residential district of La Molina, the Centro Internacional de la Papa (CIP) is both a scientific research hub and an outreach institution that supports sustainable agriculture throughout the Andes and elsewhere.

Visitors touring the facilities, a core of six squat buildings (no taller than two stories high), greenhouses, and agricultural plots, start at the communications building, with a permanent exhibit of photographs and live potato and other Andean tuber specimens and a well-stocked bookstore. The heart of the CIP is the world's most comprehensive potato germplasm bank, housing more than 150 wild potato species and 4,049 varieties of 8 species of cultivated potatoes. In total, between research material, improved clones, and wild species, there are over 11,000 plants in vitro at CIP, collected by Peru's leading potato expert, the late Dr. Carlos Ochoa, and a team of resident scientists. The center maintains experimental fields at La Molina and across the Andes. In Huancayo, at an altitude of 10,695 feet above sea level, more than 5,000 potato varieties are planted every year for research and conservation in vitro and as seed.

The CIP's work grows in urgency every year, as most potato farmers now grow only two or three varieties of "improved" mealy potatoes with profitable yields or disease resistance. Only in isolated Andean communities do a few farmers keep to the old practice, planting close to a hundred varieties on tiny plots of ground to safeguard the crops against disease through diversity. In these *chacras*, the harvest, a motley assortment of odd shapes and rainbow colors, is classified according to flavor, texture, and flesh color. The bitter potatoes are spread on the ground to freeze-dry, a process that takes weeks. The sweeter, mealy varieties are used fresh in hearty soups and stews or steamed in underground ovens or taken to market.

A few years ago, I examined a rainbow-colored collection of freshly harvested specimens at the CIP. Some I had seen in Peruvian markets: *huairo rojo*, a handsome red-and-yellow-spotted potato; the long, cream-colored *huamantanga*; and *peruanita*, a lovely, roundish red potato sporting cream stripes. The rest were mostly odd-shaped potatoes raised by highland farmers for private consumption. I was bowled over by the gorgeous, pinecone-shaped *llunchuy waccachi*, with deep-set eyes that reminded me of a pineapple. Its Quechua name means "the torture of the daughter-in-law," a reference to the difficulty of peeling this bumpy potato. Other varieties look like inanimate objects, exotic flowers, or animals, with resounding native names perfectly descriptive of their startling appearance. Take the potato called *puma maki*. As the Quechua name indicates, this black-skinned beauty with cream flesh has an uncanny resemblance to a puma's paw. Then there are purple-skinned potatoes shaped like coiled snakes (*kewillu*), and pink ones resembling succulent roses.

Just as startling as their outward appearance is the color of their flesh. On another visit to the CIP, I watched researchers make potato chips from native varieties. When they were deep-fried, the carotenoids and anthocyanins that color the flesh burst out in rippled patterns of purple, blue, lavender, yellow, ochre, pink, or red, like the luminous rings of distant planets. The chip making was a test run in an ongoing project to develop small-scale, sustainable industries in Peru's potato-farming communities. As with other native crops, most farmers need incentives and outlets to continue cultivating heirloom varieties rather than concentrating on a few commercial types. The scientists of the center call the farmers who continue planting native potatoes "conservationists" and salute them as partners in a mission. ◆

Andean Dried Potatoes

In regions from the Andes to the Pacific, the dry season is incredibly dry—the perfect conditions for dehydrating food for long storage. Since ancient times people have taken advantage of the climate to preserve potatoes and other root vegetables through several drying methods.

At high altitudes, the most important technique is freeze-drying through repeated exposure to night frosts and brilliant daytime sun. It is used on the bitter potatoes that thrive at this height, where other kinds do not prosper. In one such process, the potatoes are alternately frozen and thawed (under a straw covering) for 4 to 6 days and are stomped on during the thawing phase to crush out the bitter juices. After a final sun-drying, they look like a cross between blackish-brown dried mushrooms and dark pebbles and are known as *chuño negro* (or just plain *chuño*). *Chuño blanco*, also called *tunta* or *moraya*, undergo a more complicated process to make them more delicate. After the initial freezing/thawing cycle, the potatoes are loaded into sacks and submerged in the cold waters of a running stream or lake. After about 4 weeks they are pulled out, given a night's freezing, and stomped on to expel water and partly detach the skins. They are then exposed to the sun for another 10 to 14 days, until bone-dry, and given a final rubbing to remove the last remnants of skin. The finished potatoes are as white as chalk.

Chuño made by either method will keep in Andean households for many months, though the white type is the longer lasting.

It is exported to North America in dried form in 1-pound packages, or pre-softened and precooked in cans. I use canned *chuño* only if I can't find dried.

Like dried salt cod, *chuño* is reconstituted just before cooking. Black *chuño* should first be well rinsed under running water to remove some of the detritus that clings to the surface. Neither form of *chuño* tastes exactly like boiled fresh potatoes. They have a stronger, earthier flavor, especially the black kind. I believe that *chuño* contains umami and adds an unusual savory depth to other foods. The texture—spongy and a little clayey—is also unique.

The third member of the Andean dried potato trio, *papa seca*, is not nearly so exotic as *chuño negro* or *blanco*. *Papa seca* is made by cooking and dicing regular potatoes—that is, nonbitter kinds that need no special processing to get rid of glycoalkaloids—before setting them to dry in the sun. Today there are also industrial drying techniques (the packaged versions available in this country are all factory produced). Potatoes prepared by this method take on an interesting nutty flavor and have a chewy but appealing texture when cooked.

Basic Boiled *Chuño*

1 pound Andean freeze-dried potatoes
  (*chuño* or *tunta*)

▶ Place the potatoes in a large bowl, cover them with 2 quarts cold water, and let stand overnight for 8 hours if using *tunta*, or 12 hours for the coarser *chuño negro*.

Drain the potatoes and squeeze them firmly between your hands to force out excess moisture. Cover them again with lukewarm water and let stand for a couple of hours, then drain once more and squeeze. *Chuño negro* may crumble a little, but that won't affect the results.

To cook, place the potatoes in a 3-quart saucepan with 2 quarts cold water and bring to a boil over high heat. Reduce the heat to medium and cook, uncovered, for 40 minutes to 1 hour. Cooking time depends on how the potatoes are going to be used; for a dish like *locro* (a thick potato soup) where there is further cooking, limit the initial cooking time to 20 minutes.

Freeze-Dried Potatoes with Scrambled Eggs and Fresh Cheese

Chuño Phasi

This simple preparation for *chuño* with scrambled eggs belongs to the large family of popular Andean vegetable and egg dishes flavored with fresh cheese and some version of a garlic–onion–hot pepper *sofrito*. In Bolivia the dish is known as *chuño pfati*. This recipe comes from Huancavelica in Peru. It's ideal for Sunday brunch or a hearty lunch.

Cook's Note: When using feta as a substitute for Andean *queso fresco*, I suggest using French sheep's milk feta, which is creamy and only moderately salty. In many parts of the United States, you will be able to find only saltier feta from other countries. Taste it before using—if it is very salty, soak it in fresh cold water for a few hours to take out some of the salt. This is crucial! In many parts of the world where brined white cheese is used, from Egypt to Afghanistan, people routinely soak it as needed.

SERVES 6

1 pound Andean freeze-dried potatoes (*chuño* or *tunta*)

2 dried *mirasol* peppers, stemmed and seeded

3 garlic cloves

2 tablespoons corn or sunflower oil or olive oil

1 medium red onion (about 8 ounces), finely chopped (about 1½ cups)
Salt to taste

6 large eggs, lightly beaten

4 ounces *queso fresco* or feta cheese (see Cook's Note), crumbled (about ⅔ cup)

▶ Prepare the potatoes according to the instructions on page 202; drain.

Meanwhile, place the peppers in a small bowl, cover with 2 cups hot water, and let soak until soft, about 20 minutes. Or boil in 2 cups water until soft, about 10 minutes. Drain, reserving ¼ cup of the soaking liquid. Place the peppers, garlic, and the reserved ¼ cup liquid in a blender or food processor and process to a smooth puree; set aside. With a large heavy knife, coarsely chop the drained potatoes; set aside.

Heat the oil in a 10-inch skillet over medium heat. Add the onion and sauté until golden, 8 to 10 minutes. Pour in the chile puree and sauté for 2 to 3 minutes. Season with salt. Add the potatoes and stir well, then add the beaten eggs and cook, stirring, until set. Serve sprinkled with the crumbled cheese.

Fresh Potatoes

Ecuadorian Golden Potatoes

Papas Doradas

Throughout the Andean countries, one finds various versions of this dish, whose name means gilded potatoes. In Ecuador, the potatoes are cooked in a sauce with lots of garlic and cheese; the golden color comes from achiote-infused lard or oil. In some parts of southern Ecuador, cooks use early-maturing potatoes, or *chauchas* (from the Quechua word for precocious, a highland potato belonging to the *chaucha* species), which they cook whole in their jackets. Elsewhere the dish is closer to this version from Cuenca, which uses quartered mealy potatoes and is a traditional accompaniment to roast guinea pig (*cuy*). The potatoes should practically dissolve into the sauce during cooking. A whole head of garlic is not too much to season the dish, but use your discretion.

SERVES 6

¼ cup achiote-infused corn oil (page 89)

6–10 garlic cloves, or to taste, finely chopped

1 medium white onion (about 8 ounces), finely chopped (about 1½ cups)

6 medium russet potatoes (about 2½ pounds), peeled and quartered

¼ teaspoon salt

3 ounces fresh cow's-milk cheese, preferably a soft *queso blanco* or homemade *cuajada* (page 823), crumbled, or Monterey Jack cheese, coarsely grated (about ½ cup)

▶ Heat the oil to rippling over high heat in a wide heavy medium saucepan. Add the garlic and sauté until golden, about 2 minutes. Add the onion and sauté for another 2 minutes, until soft. Add the potatoes, salt, and 1 quart lukewarm water, reduce the heat to medium, and cook, covered, for 20 minutes. Uncover the pan and cook for another 10 minutes or so, stirring occasionally, until the water almost completely evaporates, leaving the potatoes cooking in the golden fat (do not let them scorch). Stir in the cheese and serve at once.

Boiled Potatoes with Colombian Tomato-Cheese Sauce

Papas Chorreadas

Papas chorreadas, potatoes "doused" in sauce, is traditionally made by boiling peeled mealy potatoes until very soft and blanketing them with the cheese-enriched tomato sauce called *hogo bogotano*. I have also had good results with small Yukon Golds, cooked whole in their jackets. This is a good side dish for roast meat or chicken, the traditional Colombian skirt steak called *sobrebarriga*, or an Argentinean-style skirt steak.

SERVES 6

5 medium russet potatoes (about 2 pounds), peeled

2 teaspoons salt

1½ cups Bogotá Cheese Cooking Sauce (page 52), warm

▶ Place the potatoes in a medium saucepan, add 2 quarts water and the salt, and bring to a boil over high heat. Lower the heat to medium and cook, covered, until tender, about 20 minutes.

Drain the potatoes and arrange on a serving platter or dish. Serve blanketed with the sauce.

Peruvian Warm Purple Potato and Squash Salad with Olive Oil and Paprika Dressing

Ensalada Tibia de Papas Moradas y Calabaza con Aceite de Oliva y Pimentón

I first made this terrific salad on a day when my friend Harold McGee, the food science writer, came to visit bearing a jar of olive oil from northern California. It was a first-press oil from green Mission olives, so fresh and peppery that its producer had named it "two-cough oil," for the result when people tasted it. We invented a dressing on the spot, blending peppery oil with sharp smoked paprika and aromatic spices, and we tossed it with Peruvian purple potatoes and deep yellow, mealy *calabaza*. The result was a triumph. You won't get the "two-cough" effect unless you have a very rambunctious young olive oil, but it will still be wonderful.

Cook's Note: I am a great fan of the blue and purple potatoes that have begun reaching farmers' markets and specialty produce stores in this country. Usually they cook up to a beautifully mealy texture that is wonderful in many Andean dishes. Use them in any soup-stew calling for potatoes, or—better still—any of the Peruvian *adobos* in the Hot Pepper Pots chapter; they

will generally be tender but still retain their shape if added 15 to 20 minutes before the end of the cooking time. Purple potatoes are also lovely when simply boiled and tossed while hot with one of the sumptuous Andean creamy sauces, such as Peruvian Peanut–*Mirasol* Pepper Sauce (page 127) or Peruvian Walnut-*Mirasol* Pepper Sauce (page 128).

When peeled, some types of purple potato lose the stunning deep color that seduced you into buying them and look mottled and unhealthy. But do not discard them; cooked, the interiors will turn a uniform and lovely lighter shade of purple.

Working Ahead ▶ For best results, toss the dressing with the still-warm vegetables and serve at once, but if need be, you can prepare the salad up to 2 hours ahead and hold it at room temperature.

SERVES 6

- 2 pounds purple potatoes, peeled and cut into 1-inch cubes
- 2 pounds *calabaza* (West Indian pumpkin) or Hubbard, kabocha, or butternut squash, peeled, seeded, and cut into 1-inch cubes
  Salt
- ½ cup extra-virgin olive oil, preferably peppery and young
- ¼ cup balsamic vinegar
- 1 tablespoon hot *pimentón* (Spanish smoked paprika)
- ¼ teaspoon ground cumin
- ⅛ teaspoon ground allspice
- 1 small red onion (about 5 ounces), finely chopped (about 1 cup)

▶ Place the potatoes and squash in separate saucepans, cover each with about 2 inches of water, and add 1 teaspoon salt to each pan. Bring to a boil over medium heat and cook, covered, until tender but not mushy, 15 to 20 minutes. Drain.

Meanwhile, to prepare the dressing, whisk together all the remaining ingredients in a small bowl. Add salt to taste and whisk again.

Combine the warm pumpkin and potatoes in a serving bowl. Toss gently with the dressing, and serve at once.

Serving: Serve as a side for Grilled Skirt Steak with Argentinean Chimichurri (page 704) and Peruvian Grilled Beef Heart Kebabs (page 389).

Lima-Style Mashed Potato Terrine

Causa Limeña

Causa limeña is a classic example of Peru's *criollo* cuisine, with European and pre-Hispanic elements intermingled. The name comes from the Quechua *kausaq*, which means "that which gives life"—a very appropriate translation for the delicious and nourishing dish. The idea is simple: boiled potatoes mashed into a rich, velvety spiced puree, complemented with other textures and flavors. Usually, though not always, the mashed potato mixture encloses a filling—a well-seasoned meat mixture, a rainbow-hued vegetable mélange, poached shrimp, anchovies, tuna, poached or braised chicken, or what you will. The dish may be served almost bare of decoration or surrounded by all manner of garnishes, from cut sections of Andean corn on the cob to purple Alfonso olives. At the minimum, scatter some small cheese cubes and olives around the platter.

My interpretation of this endlessly versatile standby uses a simple but colorful filling of hard-boiled eggs, tomatoes, anchovy fillets, and red pepper strips. I love to finish it off with a "frosting" of a garlicky homemade mayonnaise laced with hot, full-flavored Andean *mirasol* peppers. But the *causa* is still very good without that, or with just a small amount of regular mayonnaise spread over the filling ingredients. Ideally, the mashed potato mixture should be gilded with a brilliant achiote-tinged oil, since it is made with white russets, not the lovely yellow potatoes used in Peru.

SERVES 6 AS A FIRST COURSE OR SIDE DISH

For the Potato Mixture

- 10 medium russet potatoes (about 4 pounds), peeled and quartered
- 2–3 teaspoons salt
- ½ cup achiote-infused olive oil (page 89) or plain extra-virgin olive oil
- 1 tablespoon ground dried *mirasol* pepper, store-bought or homemade (see page 54)
  Juice of 1 lime (about 2 tablespoons)

For the Filling and Assembly

- 2–3 tablespoons achiote-infused olive oil or extra-virgin olive oil
- 1 cup *Mirasol* Mayonnaise (page 136) or regular mayonnaise
- 2 hard-boiled eggs, cut into even slices
- 9 canned anchovy fillets, drained (6 ounces)
- 2 ripe but firm medium plum tomatoes, cut into even slices
- ½ medium red bell pepper (about 4 ounces), cored, seeded, deveined, and cut into thin strips
- ½ medium red onion (about 4 ounces), thinly sliced
- ¼ cup minced flat-leaf parsley

For the Garnish

- 4 ounces *queso blanco* or French sheep's milk feta cheese, cut into small cubes (about ½ cup)
- 24 Peruvian purple olives or Kalamata olives
- 4 chunks Boiled Yuca (page 167; optional)
- 4 chunks Boiled Sweet Potatoes (page 171; optional)
- 4 sections boiled corn on the cob (optional)
- 2 hard-boiled eggs, cut into 8 wedges (optional)
- 1 pound cooked medium shrimp (optional)

Making the Potato Mixture ▶ Place the potatoes in a large saucepan, add 1½ quarts water and 2 teaspoons salt, and bring to a boil over high heat. Reduce the heat to medium and cook, covered, until fork-tender, 15 to 20 minutes.

Drain the potatoes well and pass through a food mill or potato ricer into a large bowl, or mash thoroughly with a potato masher. Beat in the oil, ground *mirasol* pepper, and lime juice. Taste for seasoning, and add up to 1 teaspoon more salt if desired. Set aside.

Making the Filling and Assembling the Terrine ▶ Line an 8-inch square glass baking dish with several pieces of heavy-duty plastic wrap, allowing about 6 inches of overhang on all sides. Brush the surface with the oil (this will make unmolding easier). Spread half of the potato mixture over the bottom of the dish, then spread ¼ cup of the mayonnaise over the potato mixture. Arrange the filling ingredients over the potatoes: Begin with the sliced hard-boiled eggs, leaving at least a ½-inch border on all sides. Place the anchovy fillets over the eggs, then the sliced tomatoes and red pepper. Scatter the onion and parsley over the top. Carefully spread the rest of the potato mixture over the filling, smoothing the top with a spatula. Refrigerate for up to 2 hours to firm up for easier cutting.

Serving: Carefully unmold the terrine onto a serving platter and peel off the plastic wrap. Spread ½ cup of the remaining mayonnaise over the top and sides, like frosting. Arrange the cheese, olives, and any other chosen garnishes around the edges of the platter. Spoon the remaining ¼ cup mayonnaise into a small bowl and serve on the side.

Cuenca-Style "Crazy Potatoes"

Papas Locas Cuencanas

The 10 de Agosto Market in the Corazón de Jesús barrio of Cuenca is a great place to eat *papas locas*, one of the most popular dishes of southern Ecuador. Early in the morning, you see peasant women coming to town leading donkeys loaded with clay pots and heavy cauldrons of food. In appointed sections of the market, they park themselves on the floor in front of their braziers and ladle out helpings of steaming food like *mote* (Andean hominy), rice, *tallarines* (spaghetti), and "crazy potatoes." Why "crazy"? I don't know, but they sell like crazy.

The succulence of the dish comes from pork rind cooked until tender. Ecuadorian cooks are very inventive at using every conceivable part of the pig, and most pork dishes are cooked without the skin, which is reserved for special purposes like toasted cracklings or—as in this case—giving a melting, gelatinous richness to a cooking sauce. The sauce is a robust-textured Andean pumpkin seed sauce enriched with a savory *ahogado*, the Ecuadorian version of the classic pan-Latin *sofrito*.

SERVES 4 TO 6

1½ pounds pork rind (without fat attached, available in Latin and Italian butcher shops), cut into 1½-inch squares

3 tablespoons achiote-infused corn oil (page 89)

8 garlic cloves, finely chopped

1 medium red onion (about 8 ounces), finely chopped (about 1½ cups)

2 cups Ecuadorian Pumpkin Seed Sauce (page 129)

½ teaspoon ground cumin

¼ teaspoon freshly ground black pepper

½ teaspoon dried oregano

2 teaspoons salt

12 medium russet potatoes (about 4½ pounds), peeled

▶ Place the pork rind in a medium saucepan with 3 quarts water and bring to a boil over high heat. Reduce the heat to medium and cook, covered, until tender when pierced with a knife, about 1½ hours. Drain, reserving the cooking liquid. In a medium saucepan over medium heat, heat the oil to rippling. Add the garlic and sauté until golden, about 2 minutes. Add the onion and cook, stirring, until translucent, another 2 to 3 minutes. Add the pumpkin seed sauce, along with the cumin, pepper, oregano, and salt. Stir in the reserved cooking liquid and pork rind. Bring to a boil, add the potatoes, and cook, covered, 18 to 20 minutes, or until the potatoes are tender. It will be somewhat soupy.

Serving: Serve with Ecuadorian-Style Rice (page 295) and Ecuadorian *Ají* (page 123).

OTHER ANDEAN ROOT VEGETABLES

Thousands of years before Pizarro set foot in Peru, the ancient farmers of the Andean uplands had domesticated the largest known constellation of the world's edible root vegetables. Part of their survival strategy was sowing an array of different kinds together, to boost the vegetables' resistance to disease or adverse conditions. Where the climate permitted, they also rotated the root vegetables with other staples that ripened at different seasons (roots generally are harvested at the onset of winter). Today crop experts and adventurous eaters everywhere in the world are curious about the potential of the historic Andean foods.

Although few have been successfully transplanted and grown beyond the highland tropics, it is encouraging that at least a handful are now reaching Latin markets here in frozen form. Some canned versions are also imported, but I find most of these inferior. The principal three are *oca*, *ulluco*, and *arracacha*.

Oca

Oca

Next to potatoes, this relative of ornamental oxalis (wood sorrel) is the most important of the Andean root crops. It's a little hard to describe, since its qualities have not been commercially standardized. *Oca* tubers are shaped roughly like fingerling potatoes, though they are more bulbous. The smooth, waxy-looking surface is punctuated by distinctive bulges and grooves. What's most striking is the spectrum of possible colors, from off-white to purple-black, with many different reds and pinks. The pink ones are especially beautiful. I remember the baked earth of fields around Lake Titicaca covered with dabs of hot pink shining in the sun, and mountains of hot pink *oca* at the Gertrudis Bocanegra market in Pátzcuaro, Michoacán, in Mexico.

This valuable crop goes by many different names in South America, including *apilla* or *apiña* in Aymara-speaking Bolivia, *ibia* or *iribia* in Colombia, and *ciuba* or *ciuva* in Venezuela, as well as *oca* among Quechua-speakers. From its first home somewhere in Peru or Bolivia, *oca* eventually spread as far as Colombia and Chile. Over the centuries, people have tried transplanting it to other parts of the world, usually without success—the best-tasting kinds tend to prefer equatorial day/night ratios. But *oca* has become well established in central Mexico (where people call it *papa roja*, red potato) and New Zealand (where against all logic it's known as New Zealand yam).

I hope that *oca* does find a commercial future in North America, because it can be a delicious vegetable. The problem is a wide variation in the sugar and acid content, especially of the harsh-tasting oxalic acid. On Andean farms it is standard practice to spread out the newly harvested crop in direct sunlight for at least a week; in Bolivia the process is called *kawichar* (*cauichar* is another spelling). This intensely concentrates the sugars and slightly reduces the acid content. But some *ocas* are just too bitter to eat without special processing. These are freeze-dried and soaked in water like *chuño blanco* (see page 202). *Oca* treated in this fashion is known as *caya*. Yet other *ocas* have just a little edge of sourness, and still others are subtle and delightful.

SELECTING

Unfortunately, most U.S. shoppers cannot go to a market and select fresh tubers from a pile of *oca*. But the fresh tuber is imported seasonally (July–October) from New Zealand by specialty fruit and vegetable distributors like Frieda's. It is also available frozen in plastic bags in Latin markets, imported from Peru.

KEEPING AND PREPARING

If you buy frozen *oca*, keep it frozen and cook without thawing.

Bolivian Oven-Roasted *Oca*
Oca (Apilla) al Horno al Estilo Boliviano

For special occasions Julia Arias, who lives in El Alto, a city adjacent to La Paz, the capital of Bolivia, makes a whole pig in a bread oven she has installed in her kitchen. The pig looks very much like the Ecuadorian *hornado*, with a crisp skin full of blisters. Julia garnishes it with purple potatoes (*papas negras*), plantains, and *oca*. She parboils the tubers first and adds them to the roasting pan at the last minute. Though I absolutely loved the pig, I was even more interested in the *oca*. It was sweet and succulent, suffused with the delicious fat and juices from the pan. Next time you are roasting a leg of pork or a pork loin or any rich meat like lamb, parboil a few *ocas* and add them to the pan about 20 minutes before the end of cooking.

Glazed Oca

Oca (Apilla) Glaseada con Chancaca

This recipe was inspired by *thaya*, a type of artisanal ice cream from Potosí, Bolivia (one of the highest cities in the world), made with pureed *oca* left to freeze overnight outdoors in the frigid nights of the *altiplano*. The flavorings—brown loaf sugar and a few aromatic spices—work just as well for *oca* as a hot side dish.

SERVES 4 AS A SIDE DISH

- 1 pound *oca*, fresh or frozen (thawed)
- 2 teaspoons salt, plus more to taste
- 2 tablespoons butter
- 3 cloves
- One 1-inch Ceylon cinnamon stick (*canela*)
- ¼ cup grated brown loaf sugar (*panela* or Peruvian *chancaca*) or Muscovado sugar
- ½ cup freshly squeezed orange or fresh pineapple juice

▶ Place the *oca* in a medium saucepan and cover with 2 quarts water; season with 2 teaspoons salt. Bring to a boil over medium-high heat. Reduce the heat to medium and simmer until the tubers are almost soft, about 10 minutes. Drain and set aside. Melt the butter in a medium skillet with the cloves and cinnamon. Add the *oca* and sauté until golden. Add the sugar and cook, stirring, until it dissolves and coats the tubers. Stir in the fruit juice and let the sauce simmer for a few minutes, until lightly thickened. Season with salt to taste.

Serving: Serve hot as a side dish for grilled duck, pork, or lamb chops.

Ulluco

This ancient staple of the *altiplano* comes in about as vivid an array of colors as *oca* and probably has even more names—of which *ulluco* (also spelled *ullucu* or *olloco*) and *melloco*, as it is known in Ecuador, are almost interchangeable throughout the old Inca empire, while *papa lisa* (smooth potato, from the thinness of their skins) is understood everywhere from Venezuela to Argentina. Like potatoes, *ullucos* can be any shape from round to fingerlike, even sickle-shaped. You see them the size of thumbs, mini-croissants, walnuts, or medium potatoes. The flesh can be white, yellow, or orange.

Ulluco (or melloco)

Ullucos vary widely in texture. Some have a lot of sticky mucilaginous starch, and even in Andean countries some people therefore turn up their noses at all *ulluco* as being *baboso* (slimy). Others say it's hard to digest; Bolivians often cook it with mint, which is believed to aid in digestion.

The basic way of cooking *ulluco* is boiling. The vegetable is often used along with (or instead of) potatoes and other root vegetables in hearty soups or stews. The boiled tubers are also eaten in salads (with a tart dressing) or with hot savory sauces, often enriched in the Andean manner with milk and cheese. For some stews, they are paired with dried meat.

In the Andean countries, *ulluco* comes to market in different lots that people can sort through to choose ones of uniform size and color. Here, where it is available only frozen or canned, you haven't much choice in the matter. Usually a package or can will contain either all fingerling type or all round tubers.

Ecuadorian *Ullucos* in Cheese Sauce

Mellocos con Quesillo y Leche

This is a typical peasant dish of the southern Ecuadorian highlands, where the humblest vegetable becomes an excellent meal when simmered in one of the ubiquitous Latin onion-and-garlic-based sauces enriched with milk and fresh unripened cheese. *Melloco* is the usual local name. Ecuadorian children, who tend to regard the *ulluco* with less enthusiasm than either the sauce or the cheese, usually beg for more of both to mix in with the rice or Andean hominy (*mote*) that usually accompanies this dish. The fresh cheese should not melt but form cheesy bits.

Cook's Note: I have recently found wonderful Ecuadorian fresh cheeses that are perfect for Andean recipes calling for soft fresh cow's-milk cheese. Two brands I like are Queso Fresco San Fernando from Azuay and Santa Cruz Queso Crema from Cuenca. The Colombian *quesito* under the Zarzal brand, which is soft and crumbly, is also a good choice. They can be found in all stores catering to an Ecuadorian clientele.

SERVES 4 AS MAIN DISH, 6 AS SIDE DISH

- 1 pound frozen *ullucos* (*mellocos*), not thawed
- 1½ teaspoons salt
- 2 tablespoons achiote-infused corn oil (page 89)
- 3 garlic cloves, mashed to a paste with a mortar and pestle or finely chopped and mashed
- 1 small red onion (about 5 ounces), finely chopped (about ¾ cup)
- 1 teaspoon ground cumin
  Freshly ground black pepper, to taste
- ¼ cup whole milk
- 4 ounces fresh cow's-milk cheese, preferably a soft Ecuadorian cheese or homemade Colombian *cuajada* (page 823), or farmer's cheese, crumbled (about ⅔ cup)

▶ Place the *ullucos* in a saucepan, add 1 quart water and 1 teaspoon of the salt, and bring to a boil over high heat. Reduce the heat to medium and cook, covered, until tender: for small finger-shaped tubers or round ones smaller than 1½ inches in diameter, 10 to 12 minutes; slightly longer for larger round ones. Drain well.

It is not necessary to peel *ulluco* after cooking, since the skin is very thin. Cut larger potato-sized ones into halves or thirds; leave smaller ones whole. Set aside.

In a medium skillet, heat the oil over medium heat until fragrant. Add the garlic and cook, stirring, until golden, about 40 seconds. Add the onion and cook until translucent, about 3 minutes. Add the cumin, pepper, and the remaining ½ teaspoon salt, then stir in the milk and cheese. Add the *ullucos* and cook over medium-low heat just until heated through, about 3 minutes.

Serving: Serve hot with Ecuadorian-Style Rice (page 295) or Andean Hominy (page 251). In the countryside, this is a main course; city people serve it as a side dish.

Ulluco Salad

Ensalada de Melloco

In the highlands of southern Ecuador, people like to eat *ulluco* in salads, with other vegetables and a simple vinaigrette. I especially like it with peppery radishes, which magnify *ulluco*'s pronounced earthy flavor.

SERVES 6

- 1 pound fresh or frozen *ullucos*, preferably La Cholita brand
- ½ cup olive oil
  Juice of 2½ medium limes (about ¼ cup)
- 1 bunch radishes, thinly sliced (about 1½ cups)
- 1 small red onion (about 5 ounces), thinly julienned
- 1½ teaspoons salt

▶ In a 4-quart pot, bring 2 quarts water to a boil over high heat. Add the *ullucos* and cook until tender, about 18 minutes. Drain and cut into ¼-inch slices. Set aside.

Whisk together the olive oil, lime juice, and salt in a small bowl.

Combine the *ullucos*, radishes, and onion in a bowl and toss with the dressing.

Arracacha

Andean *arracacha*

Though *arracacha* is a native of the Andean lands, it does not grow at the same extreme heights as potatoes and *oca*. In fact, it has been able to take root outside the Andes, winning a following in parts of the Caribbean, Central America, the Orinoco and Amazon Basins, and Brazil. And small wonder—it is among the world's most appealing root crops. You may fall in love with it at first bite.

It really defies description. Try to imagine the best qualities of yuca, plantain, sweet potato, parsnip, and fresh coconut all wrapped up in one fragrant, lusciously starchy whole. Its story is complicated by the fact that at least two parts of the plant can be eaten. *Arracacha* is a perennial with green shoots branching out of a knobby, thickened central root stem that extends above the ground. From the same stem, many long lateral roots like parsnips branch off underground. These are what people prefer in the Andes, where the plant most often goes by names derived from the Quechua *rakkacha* or Aymara *lakachu*. In Venezuela and the islands, however, the usual names are spin-offs of *apio* (celery)—*apio criollo* or *apio amarillo*, or simply *apio*—and the part that is eaten is the gnarled, wrinkled, yellow-brown central stem, which does indeed look enough like celery root to justify the name.

Apio amarillo (Caribbean *arracacha*)

In eastern Cuba, where I come from, *arracacha* is called *afió* and used in fritters. The roots are the part eaten in Brazil, where the most common name is *mandioquinha* (little yuca) or *mandioquinha-salsa*. On a recent trip to Salvador da Bahia, I ate delicious gnocchi made with *mandioquinha* and dried beef at the swank Trapiche Adelaida restaurant. I had ordered them mistakenly, thinking of yuca gnocchi, which I adore, but I wasn't sorry—they were terrific too. To add to the confusion, some English-language sources have christened the vegetable "white carrot," though it really doesn't taste anything like carrots.

The branching roots and the knobby root stem have somewhat similar flavor, though the roots are more tender. In this country, stems grown in the Dominican Republic are sold fresh as *apio* in Latin markets; the much more perishable roots reach us only in frozen form. With both, the color of the flesh can be anything from pale to bright yellow-white (the stems are a scruffy tan on the outside).

I am used to cooking with knobby stems of fresh *arracacha*, which is what I can get in my local markets, but they are not a pleasure to peel; be prepared to buy at least 2 pounds more than your recipe suggests. The frozen roots from Peru, Ecuador, or Colombia are much more convenient, though a little less flavorful and aromatic.

The stems and roots are partly interchangeable in cooking.

Both the roots and the stem are most often boiled. You can eat plain boiled chunks with a garlicky *mojo*, a savory fresh cheese sauce, a dollop of butter, or anything that you'd put on other starchy vegetables. Or you can slice it thin, boil it, and dress it with tangy vinaigrettes for a luscious salad or relish. More often, however, boiled *arracacha* is roughly mashed or finely pureed with seasonings, or made into a creamy pureed soup. Like yuca and the other starchy lowland tubers, it is best eaten piping hot, but it loses less in texture than the rest as it cools, and it reheats very well. As it becomes better known in this country, I would predict a happy love affair between U.S. cooks and this marvelous vegetable.

SELECTING

Only the gnarled tan-yellow stems (*apio amarillo*) are sold fresh in Latin produce markets here. Look for ones that are firm and feel heavy for their size, not limp and shrunken.

KEEPING AND PREPARING

Store stem-type *arracacha* in a cool, airy place for up to 3 days; after that it gets moldy, flabby, or dried out. Before using it in a recipe, trim away the gnarled surface to expose the flesh beneath. Be thorough about this—you don't want any of the elephantlike hide in your silky puree. Rinse well, then use at once.

Pan-Fried *Arracacha*

Arracacha Salteada

Did I tell you that cooked *arracacha* is very pretty? Cut into cubes, it boils to a sunny yellow. I often serve it simply boiled, with a drizzle of olive oil and a sprinkling of coarse salt, but it tastes even better pan-fried with butter, garlic, and onion and sprinkled at the table with good Parmigiano-Reggiano, which gives it a lovely tang. Try serving it on dark plates to accentuate the golden color.

SERVES 4

- 3 pounds fresh *arracacha* stems (about 2 pounds trimmed weight), or 2 pounds frozen roots
- 1 tablespoon salt
- 1 tablespoon sugar
- 4 tablespoons (½ stick) butter
- 2 garlic cloves, finely chopped
- 1 small white onion (about 5 ounces), finely chopped (about 1 cup)
- ¼ cup chicken broth, homemade (page 538) or store-bought, or reserved *arracacha* cooking liquid
- 2 tablespoons freshly grated Parmigiano-Reggiano cheese

▶ If using fresh *arracacha* stems, peel and trim very thoroughly with a sharp heavy knife, removing every vestige of skin. Cut into 1-inch rounds and then cut into rough 1-inch cubes. Rinse thoroughly under cold running water.

Place the *arracacha* in a 6-quart pot, add 3 quarts water, salt, and sugar, and bring to a boil over high heat. (If using frozen *arracacha* roots, bring the water and seasonings to a boil, then add them.) Reduce the heat to medium and cook, covered, until fork-tender, 15 to 20 minutes (10 to 15 minutes for frozen). Drain, reserving ¼ cup of the cooking liquid, if using, and let cool.

Heat the butter in an 11-inch skillet over medium heat. Add the garlic and sauté for 10 seconds, or until barely gold. Add the onion and cook until soft, about 5 minutes. Add the *arracacha* and cook, stirring gently (make sure not to mash the *arracacha*) for a couple of minutes. Stir in the broth or reserved cooking liquid, increase the heat to medium-high, and cook, stirring occasionally, until the *arracacha* is lightly browned in spots, about 5 minutes. Remove from the heat and turn onto a serving platter. Sprinkle with cheese and top with a dollop of butter.

Serving: Serve with Fish Fillets in Tropical Juice *Adobo* Cooked in Plantain Leaves (page 628), Grilled "Leaping Frog" Chicken (page 665), or Cuban-Style Pot-Roasted Chicken (page 670).

Arracacha Salad

Ensalada de Arracacha

"Luminous" and "post-modern" are some of the adjectives my guests have used to describe this unusual, colorful salad, inspired by the relishes that Central Americans eat with all sorts of corn *masa* dishes like *pupusas* and enchiladas. The creamy yellow *arracacha*, cut into thin, odd-shaped slabs, looks stunning when paired with bright orange carrot slices (preferably thick ones with a creamy yellow aureole). For a contrasting edge of bitterness, I add a little *pacaya*, the long blossoms of a Central American palm that resemble fluorescent ivory octopus tentacles.

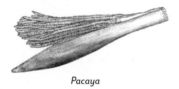

Pacaya

Cook's Notes: Frozen *arracacha* is not suitable for this dish.

Pacaya canned in brine is available in Hispanic markets catering to Central Americans. It is a prized ingredient for relishes in Guatemala, El Salvador, Honduras, and Costa Rica.

SERVES 6

- 3 pounds *arracacha* stems (about 2 pounds trimmed weight)
- 1 tablespoon plus 2 teaspoons salt
- 2 celery stalks, cut into 2-inch sections and slivered
- 1 large fat carrot (about 5 ounces), peeled and cut into ¼-inch rounds
- 8 ounces cauliflower, separated into tiny florets
- 2 canned *pacaya* fronds, rinsed and drained (strings only, no stems)
- 6 tablespoons extra-virgin olive oil
- 5 tablespoons distilled white vinegar
- 1 jalapeño, seeded, deveined, and cut into very fine slivers

▶ Peel the *arracacha*, rinse it, and trim very thoroughly with a sharp heavy knife, removing every vestige of skin. Cut into ¼-inch-thick slabs about 2 inches square.

In a large saucepan, bring 3 quarts of water to a boil with 1 tablespoon salt. Add the *arracacha*, celery, carrot, cauliflower, and *pacaya*, reduce the heat, and simmer until the carrot and *arracacha* are barely tender, 5 to 7 minutes. Drain and place in a bowl.

Make the vinaigrette by whisking together the oil, vinegar, jalapeño, and 2 teaspoons salt. Pour over the vegetables, tossing to coat. Let stand at least 1 hour before serving.

Variation: *Arracacha* Relish (*Curtido de Arracacha*)

Transfer the cooled salad to a glass jar and add enough distilled white vinegar to cover completely. Cover tightly and store in the refrigerator. It will keep for several weeks.

Spiced *Arracacha* Puree

Muselina de Arracacha

This is a more lavish take on the theme of pureed *arracacha*, perfumed with both sweet spices and savory aromatics and enriched with a good chicken broth reduction. It makes a terrific side dish for just about any main course.

SERVES 4 TO 6

- 6 pounds fresh *arracacha* stems (about 5 pounds trimmed weight) or 5 pounds frozen roots
- 1 Ceylon cinnamon stick (*canela*)
- 4 whole cloves
- 1 star anise pod
- 1 tablespoon grated brown loaf sugar or dark brown sugar
- 1–2 teaspoons salt
- 2 cups chicken broth, preferably homemade (page 538)
- 12 scallions, white part only, coarsely chopped
- 1 shallot, coarsely chopped
- 8 Caribbean sweet peppers (*ajíes dulces*) or 1 cubanelle pepper, coarsely chopped
- 5 allspice berries
- 2 broad-leaf *culantro* leaves or 3 cilantro sprigs
- 1 tablespoon extra-virgin olive oil or butter

▶ If using fresh *arracacha* stems, peel and trim very thoroughly with a sharp heavy knife, removing every vestige of the skin (it is easier to do this if you first cut it into 3-inch chunks.) Rinse thoroughly under cold running water.

Place the *arracacha* in a large saucepan, add 2 quarts water, the cinnamon, cloves, star anise, sugar, and 1 teaspoon salt, and bring to a boil over high heat. (If using frozen *arracacha* roots, bring the water and seasonings to a boil before adding them.) Reduce the heat to medium and cook, covered, until fork-tender, 15 to 20 minutes (10 to 15 minutes for frozen).

While the *arracacha* is cooking, combine the broth, scallions, shallot, peppers, allspice, and *culantro* or cilantro in a small saucepan and bring to a boil over medium-high heat. Boil, uncovered, until reduced by half, about 15 minutes. Strain the broth through a fine-mesh strainer, pushing on the solids with a wooden spoon to extract as much liquid as possible. If the *arracacha* is not ready, keep the broth warm over very low heat (use a Flame Tamer or other heat diffuser if necessary).

When the *arracacha* is done, drain thoroughly, pick out the whole spices, and immediately pass through a potato ricer or food mill into a bowl; or mash with a potato masher. Beat in the reduced broth and oil or butter. Taste for seasoning, and add up to 1 teaspoon more salt if desired. Serve at once.

CHAPTER 6

SQUASHES, CORN, QUINOA, AND BEANS

Many of the great Latin American food plants often clung to their own native soil and refused to grow elsewhere. Not so with squash, corn, and beans. Defying all ecological odds, centuries before Columbus, people managed to establish all three in latitudes from Canada to southern Chile. This threesome is at home in the mixed fields of farmers living in the cool highlands of Mexico and Central America and in the sweltering heat of the lowland tropics, where they grow together with yuca and plantains in people's small vegetable plots. They also share space with potatoes, other Andean tubers, and even quinoa on small parcels of land at different altitudes throughout the Andes.

Their natural biological coexistence is reflected in the way Latin Americans eat: this trio appears together, in the company of other staple plants, in many of our emblematic dishes. Take *charquicán*, a Chilean classic. It is a mixture of fresh corn kernels and the South American squash known as *zapallo*, with potatoes, green beans, and meat seasoned with peppers and tomatoes. On Hispanic Caribbean plates, where several foods share space, braised or pureed squash can be a side for a beef and potato stew together with white rice and either black or red kidney beans. Chunks of boiled corn, yuca, and sweet potatoes are the starchy counterpoint to tangy cebiches from Peru's northern coast. The small, tender summer squash called *calabacitas* are braised with pork, corn, and ripe plantains in Oaxaca, Mexico.

Corn in the form of tortillas is present at any Mexican and Central American meal. In parts of Guatemala, corn tortillas can be a meal in themselves with some beans and boiled *ayotes* (a squash with filaments like spaghetti squash) or the squash relative *güisquil* (chayote). Or they can be served with lusty plates of meat, rice, refried beans, and perhaps a stew of *calabacitas* in popular Mexico City restaurants.

This alliance of Latin staples on the plate is as old as agriculture in the Americas. Scientists are constantly reassessing the dates of earliest domestication for these plants, establishing, for instance, that squashes predate corn. But in ancient archaeological sites from the highlands of Mexico to the arid coast of northern Peru, squash seeds are often found together with pepper seeds, desiccated corncobs, and beans, demonstrating that once these plants were domesticated, people chose to grow and eat them together.

SQUASHES AND THEIR COUSINS

Purely from a visual standpoint, squash may be the most astonishing of all the American food crops. If you were to assemble all the members of the family Cucurbitaceae (aka cucurbits) grown in the New World, you would have a still life breathtaking in its range of shapes, sizes, and colors—with most of the diversity coming from south of the U.S. border.

There are various Old World cucurbits, too, from cucumbers to watermelons. But when you look at the Central and South American branches of the clan, you marvel at what the pre-Columbian gardeners were able to call forth: minute tender-fleshed squashes the size and color of green peapods; near relatives, covered with green-on-green freckles, that a single man couldn't lift; bottle-shaped squashes with smooth, creamy tan skins; cousins looking like mottled green-and-white basketballs, or like heavy yellow clubs, or like flattened spheres, sectioned into lobes by deep-set ridges; and still others in strange blue-gray or greenish black hues, with bulbous shapes and as many warts as an alligator.

Botanists are still sorting out the relationships of these and many other colorful members of the notoriously confusing cucurbit family. Some apparently originated in what is now Mexico, and others in central or northern South America, earlier than both corn and beans. Archaeologists have found 10,000-year-old squash remains in Ecuador.

Probably the first attempts to domesticate squash focused on the seeds rather than the flesh. To this day, squash seeds play a major part in Latin American cuisine. In Mexico, for example, ground *pepitas* (pumpkin seeds) give body to the stews called *pepianes*. In Ecuador, the seeds of *zambo* squash are ground and used in delicious table sauces.

There are five cultivated squash species, of which four come into our story, along with two more distant relatives, chayote and *caigua*, which belong to other genera within the Cucurbitaceae family. These last two are quite distinctive, but be aware that squashes can fool you. You can't always tell one species from another simply by looking, or necessarily by tasting.

The squashes most familiar to North Americans belong to *Cucurbita pepo*, which was first domesticated in Mexico before 7,000 B.C. Remains of *C. pepo* found in the Guila Naquitz Cave in Oaxaca are said to be 10,000 years old. Apparently, though, the species did not spread south of Central America in pre-Columbian times. Members of this species, like most others, come in all colors, sizes,

and shapes: the kinds that we call summer squash—tender, quick-cooking, thin-skinned squashes like the various zucchini—all belong to *C. pepo*. The species also includes some of the winter squashes, the larger, more mature vegetables with yellow or orange flesh and harder seeds. Pumpkins of most North American jack-o'-lantern types also belong to this species. ("Pumpkin" basically describes any round winter squash that somebody wants to call a pumpkin.) By and large, the *C. pepo* winter squashes are watery, dull-flavored, and not suitable for use in Latin American recipes. But new breeding experiments appear all the time, and some cultivars are better than others.

More important in most of Latin America are winter squashes belonging to the species *C. maxima* and *C. moschata*. The two species were domesticated in both Central and South America in prehistoric times, with *C. maxima* predominating on the Pacific side of South America and *C. moschata* found from the Amazon-Orinoco region to the Caribbean. Both types are commonly eaten at maturity.

In South America, *C. maxima* includes the world's largest naturally grown squashes, usually called *zapallos*—not bulked up with water like the huge pumpkins that win state-fair prizes in this country, but dense and solid. Usually they are round, but you also see thick oval or stubby teardrop shapes. Many, though not all, are deeply ridged. There are smooth-skinned and grotesquely warty ones, in colors ranging from fierce orange to slate blue, as well as striped or mottled specimens. The flesh is medium to deep orange. One of my favorite South American squashes is the *zapallo loche*. Intensely aromatic, with meaty bright orange flesh, it is a favorite in the north of Peru, where it is cooked with other vegetables in thick soup called *locros*. Also popular is the *zapallo macre*, which reaches a great size. It is used for *picarones*, delicious sweet fritters made with a leavened squash dough that are cooked and sold by women as street food. In this country, Hubbard is the best-known *maxima* squash.

Zapallo loche
from northern Peru

The *moschatas* also grow quite large in Latin America. They too come in many shapes and colors—crook-necked and uniform tan all over, melon-shaped and covered with green-on-green or green-on-orange blotches, along with dozens of other variations. The flesh is usually a very intense deep orange. The North American butternut squash and cheese pumpkin are both *moschatas*. So are the large, speckled green squashes lumped together as "West Indian pumpkins" in Latin markets—usually grown in South Florida or Tennessee from Cuban seeds.

Botanists distinguish between *moschatas* and *maximas* (and other species) by factors such as the shapes of stem and leaf, which aren't much help for most shoppers. Luckily, the two are interchangeable in cooking. Both have dry, firm-textured flesh, starchier and meatier to the bite than most of the pumpkins we see in North America. Indeed, they can be starchy enough to be grouped with staple roots and vegetables in places where people eat yuca and plantains. The dense, not-too-sweet orange flesh is as satisfying as a good potato.

Because of their size, they are more often used a piece at a time than cooked whole, and it is customary to buy them by the chunk.

C. ficifolia, the last of the major Latin American squash species, is a very different creature. Whereas the others can thrive in torrid-zone heat, it usually prefers cooler, mid-level mountain habitats. It may have originated in the Mexican highlands and found its way to the lower Andean valleys—or perhaps vice versa, according to recent research. It is a blocky round to oblong squash that can range from a few pounds to more than twenty. Usually it has mottled dark- and pale-green skin, though it can be off-white or dark green streaked with white. The seeds are white in younger specimens, later darkening to tan or black. The flesh is more tender than starchy. As the squash matures, it develops a mass of interior filaments like those in a spaghetti squash (though they aren't the same vegetable—spaghetti squash belongs to *C. pepo*).

Matching these botanical species with all the common names for squashes in different parts of Latin America can be a guessing game for U.S. shoppers. In Cuba, *calabaza* unmistakably refers to *moschata* squashes which I remember as wonderfully varied and delicious, from the long, cylindrical *calabaza de Castilla* (Castile squash) and the turban-like *calabaza de bonete* (bonnet squash) to the snake-shaped *calabaza serpiente* and a small, highly prized one called *yema de huevo* (egg yolk). But elsewhere you may find that *calabaza* or another local name just means winter squashes in general.

Here is a highly incomplete guide and recipe selection that isn't guaranteed to produce instant understanding in all Latin markets or groceries but covers the important bases.

Cucurbita Pepo

C. pepo squashes of the summer squash type are most often known as *calabacita* in Mexico and Central America, or *zapallito* on the Pacific coast of South America. In some places people often just add the word *tierno* (tender) to any local name for winter squash. The Brazilian name is *aboborinha*.

Small, round summer squash (*calabacita*)

SELECTING

Calabacitas have begun to crop up in Latin markets catering to Mexicans and Central Americans. According to Elizabeth Schneider, in her encyclopedic vegetable guide *Vegetables from Amaranth to Zucchini*, tatume and Korean zucchini, the round and egg-shaped cultivars with dense flesh that you can now find in Asian markets in North America, are similar to the Mexican *calabacita*. Pick squashes with taut, shiny skin that feel firm to the touch, without any dark spots.

KEEPING AND PREPARING

These squashes are best kept refrigerated, as they spoil easily. Because their skin is tender and their seeds soft, they don't need to be peeled or seeded, only stemmed. Peel and seed them, however, when you want firm, even dice.

Summer Squash in Tomato Broth with Almond, Sesame, and *Chile de Árbol* Sauce

Calabacitas en Caldillo de Jitomate con Salsa de Almendra, Ajonjolí, y Chile de Árbol

With more than fourteen cookbooks to her credit, Patricia Quintana is Mexico's most visible and influential culinary star. She has been a restaurant consultant, cooking teacher, media personality, and, more recently, the chef and owner of Izote, a charming restaurant in the elegant Polanco district of Mexico City. Some of her dishes are inspired by Mexican everyday cooking, such as this brightly seasoned summer squash, which she refines by serving it with an elegant almond sauce.

SERVES 4 AS A SIDE, 8 AS AN APPETIZER

For the Squash

- 1 large white onion (12 ounces), finely chopped (about 2 cups)
- 8 medium plum tomatoes (about 1½ pounds), seeded and coarsely chopped
- 3 garlic cloves
- ⅓ cup corn oil or mild extra-virgin olive oil, preferably from Arbequina olives
- 2 tablespoons butter
- 2½ pounds small to medium zucchini (regular or round-shaped) or other summer squash, peeled, seeded, and cut into ¼-inch dice
  Salt to taste
- 1–2 jalapeños, cut lengthwise in half
- 6 cilantro sprigs

For the Almond Sauce

- 4–6 dried *chiles de árbol*
- ¼ cup sesame seeds (1½ ounces)
- 1 cup blanched almonds (any form)
- 1 small unpeeled onion (about 5 ounces)
- 3 garlic cloves, not peeled
- 1½ cups warm chicken broth, preferably homemade (page 538), or more to taste
- Salt to taste

Cilantro or epazote sprigs, for garnish

Cooking the *Calabacitas* ▶ Combine half the onion, the tomatoes, and the garlic in a blender or food processor and process to a fine puree; set aside.

Heat the oil and butter in a 12-inch skillet over medium heat. Add the rest of the onion and sauté until soft, about 5 minutes. Add the squash and cook, stirring, for 1 minute. Pour in the onion and tomato mixture, add the jalapeños and cilantro, and bring to a simmer. Add salt to taste. Cook until the liquid is reduced and thickens a bit, about 8 minutes.

Preparing the Almond Sauce ▶ Heat a *comal*, griddle, or heavy skillet over medium-high heat. Add the *árbol* chiles and roast, turning once or twice with tongs, until fragrant and lightly toasted, about 40 seconds. Set aside. Add the sesame seeds and toast lightly. Transfer to a small bowl.

Add the almonds to the pan and toast, stirring, about 2 minutes, until lightly golden. Transfer to the bowl with the sesame seeds. Toast the onion and garlic, turning occasionally, until lightly blistered and soft, about 8 minutes. Let cool slightly, then peel. Combine the onion, garlic, toasted chiles, almonds, sesame seeds, and warm broth in a blender or food processor and process to a smooth puree. Season with salt.

Serving: Serve the squash as a side dish with a dollop of the almond sauce. Or serve as a vegetarian first course garnished with cilantro or epazote sprigs. Pour the almond sauce into a sauceboat and bring to the table with fresh corn tortillas.

Cucurbita Moschata and *Cucurbita Maxima*

Calabaza (West Indian pumpkin)

The most frequent names for *moschata* squashes are *calabaza* (Cuba), *auyama* (Venezuela and the Dominican Republic), *abobora* (Brazil), and *ayote* (Central America). In Paraguay they go by the Guaraní name *andaí*. Generally speaking, *maximas* predominate from most of Ecuador south to Chile and are called *zapallos* throughout the region, from the Quechua word *zapallu*. But their range partly overlaps that of *moschatas*, so that in parts of Colombia and Ecuador, *zapallo* can refer to either of these winter squashes.

The Spaniards were amazed at the gigantic size of the South American *zapallos*. The sixteenth-century chronicler Oviedo reports that some of them were so huge that a man could carry only one of them at a time. Researchers have found *zapallo* seeds in some of the oldest archaeological sites along the Peruvian coast.

Andean *zapallo*

In Ecuador, you will find huge *zapallos* in Loja, in the south of the country, as well as smaller ones called *zapallos limeños* (squashes from Lima) or *zapallos castellanos* (Castilian squashes) with dark green skin and white stripes. The same squash is found in Chile, where it is called *zapallo de guarda*. In Chile, sturdy squashes that can be kept during the winter months are called *de guarda*, which means "for keeping"; it is the equivalent of the label winter squashes. Here in the United States, Ecuadorians buy kabocha squash (which can be either *C. maxima* or *C. moschata*) as a substitute for *zapallo*. Other good substitutes are Hubbard, butternut, or buttercup squash.

SELECTING

Select firm squashes with no soft spots or blemishes. A proper winter squash should be *panudo* (literally, bready), with toothsome quality. Depending on the size and how much you need for a recipe, you may want to buy a whole *calabaza*; in that case, ask the produce man to cut it open first for your inspection. Otherwise, buy a chunk of an already cut one. It should have sound orange flesh with no sign of softness or wateriness. There will be some loss in trimming; count on buying about 2 pounds to obtain 1 pound trimmed and seeded flesh.

KEEPING AND PREPARING

Store whole squashes in a cool, dry place, not the refrigerator. They will keep for a long time. Most winter squashes keep well for several days after being cut, even if you leave them out of the refrigerator uncovered. But it's best to keep cut squash refrigerated, covered with plastic wrap.

Because of the hard shell, you need a large knife to cut open a large squash like *calabaza*. To prepare for cooking, peel off the hard skin and scrape out the inner fibers and seeds (some people prefer to cook the squash first and then peel it).

Grandmother Paquita's Chunky *Calabaza* Puree

Yurumú de Calabaza

I was a skinny teenager, which was a source of worry to my paternal grandmother, Paquita. If I visited when she was making *yurumú*, she would heap lots of the chunky *sofrito*-scented squash puree onto my plate, saying that it was good for fattening my thighs (*pantorrillas*). If you are having second thoughts about eating *yurumú* on this account, don't—my grandmother's cooking never got my *pantorrillas* the way she had envisioned. It took other meals in other countries to do the job.

Not many Cubans know about *yurumú de calabaza* unless they came from the Oriente region, in the eastern part of the country. As for the meaning of *yurumú*, I always assumed that it was an African word, since the cooking of my hometown is heavily influenced by black cooking, but I have not found the equivalent in any Congo or Yoruba dictionaries. However, I have eaten a dish closely resembling *yurumú* in Martinique, where it is called *giraumonade*, after *giraumon*, the word for pumpkin. Oriente, which is near Haiti and Jamaica, was much more open to immigrants from the Lesser Antilles than any other part of Cuba. One of the best cooks ever to grace my grandfather's house was from Martinique—so perhaps there was a connection.

SERVES 6 TO 8

- 3 tablespoons extra-virgin olive oil
- 6 ounces slab bacon, cut into small dice
- 6 garlic cloves, finely chopped
- 1 medium yellow onion (about 8 ounces), finely chopped (about 1½ cups)
- 1 medium green bell pepper (about 6 ounces), cored, seeded, deveined, and finely chopped (about ¾ cup)
- 4 medium plum tomatoes (about 12 ounces), peeled, seeded, and cut into small dice, or 4 canned plum tomatoes, drained, seeded, and cut into small dice
- ¼ teaspoon ground cumin
- ⅛ teaspoon ground allspice
- 1 teaspoon thyme leaves
- 1 bay leaf
- 3 pounds *calabaza* (West Indian pumpkin), peeled, seeded, and cut into 1-inch cubes

▶ In a heavy 12-inch skillet, heat the oil over medium heat. Add the bacon and sauté until golden, about 5 minutes. Add the garlic and sauté until golden, about 40 seconds. Add the onion and sauté, stirring, until soft, about 5 minutes. Add the bell pepper and cook for 2 minutes. Add the tomatoes, cumin, allspice, thyme, and bay leaf and cook for 1 more minute. Season with salt and pepper to taste.

Stir in the pumpkin, lower the heat, and simmer, covered, for 20 minutes. (Because *calabaza* can be watery, chances are it will not stick to the pan, but keep your nose on the alert for the slightest sign of burning.) Stir for 1 minute, cover again, and cook for 10 minutes. Continue cooking, stirring every 10 minutes, until the *calabaza* is fork-tender. Then continue cooking over low heat, pressing on the *calabaza* with the back of a wooden spoon, until it practically melts into a puree. The whole process will take about 50 minutes.

Serving: Remove the bay leaf and serve hot as a side for any stew or braised meat. I also love it as a side for Lamb *Adobo* Tarma Style (page 748) or Grilled Skirt Steak (page 704).

Paraguayan Polenta with Winter Squash

Kiveve

In Paraguay and neighboring parts of Argentina and Brazil, there are several winter squash dishes called *kiveve*. The Brazilian and Argentinean versions are based on pureed squash alone, but in Paraguay people make a *kiveve* with *andaí*, a local squash of the *C. moschata* family, and cornmeal. I read an old Paraguayan cookbook that describes this as the only Paraguayan dish without onions and the country's only sweet-and-sour dish. I have taken a few liberties, including adding onions and cheese, as in a version from Corrientes, Argentina, because I think they give the polenta a terrific flavor. I use Muenster cheese, which is similar to Paraguayan Mennonite cheese (see page 102). Omit the onions and cheese for a more authentically Paraguayan version.

SERVES 6

2½ pounds butternut or kabocha squash or *calabaza* (West Indian pumpkin), peeled, seeded, and cut into 2-inch chunks (about 2 pounds peeled)
2 tablespoons sugar
2½ teaspoons salt
4 cups whole milk
2 tablespoons corn oil
1 medium yellow onion (about 8 ounces), finely chopped (about 1½ cups)
1 cup finely ground cornmeal
6 ounces Muenster cheese, grated (about 1½ cups)

Cooking the Squash ▶ Place the squash, sugar, salt, and 2 quarts water in a medium pot, and bring to a boil over high heat. Lower the heat to medium-high and cook until the squash is tender, 15 to 20 minutes.

Drain the squash and transfer to a blender or a food processor. Add the milk and process to a smooth puree.

Making the *Kiveve* ▶ Heat the oil in a 4-quart saucepan over medium heat. Add the onion and sauté until soft, about 5 minutes. Pour in the pureed squash and cook, stirring constantly, while adding the cornmeal in a drizzle. Simmer for about 8 minutes. Stir in the cheese and continue cooking, stirring, until the cheese is melted and the mixture is rich and creamy like polenta, about 5 more minutes.

Cucurbita Ficifolia

Chilacayote (zambo squash)

C. ficifolia has its own array of labels. Among English-speakers, it has somehow acquired the names Malabar gourd and fig-leaf gourd. In Mexico, it is most often *chilacayote*, from the Nahuatl *tzilacayote* (*tzilac*, smooth, and *ayotli*, squash). Many other countries use versions of the same word, like *lacayote*, *alcayote*, *cayote*, *ayote*, and so forth. In Costa Rica it is *chiverre*. In the Andean countries, where people call it *zambo*, it is a very important vegetable.

You can often substitute spaghetti squash for *C. ficifolia*, but in summer, the real thing is starting to turn up here at farmers' markets as well as in Mexican groceries. Frozen chunks of good-quality squash reach Latin markets from the Andes all year-round.

SELECTING

If you find fresh *zambo* or *chilacayote* in your farmers' market or an ethnic grocery, look for a firm, dense specimen with no soft spots.

KEEPING AND PREPARING

Zambo usually comes to Hispanic markets quartered and frozen in packages of approximately 1½ pounds. Defrost in the package at room temperature or in a bowl of warm water. You might expect it to be a bit soft from freezing, but when you cook it you will be amazed at how well the squash keeps its shape and wonderful crunchy texture.

When preparing *zambo*, discard only the thick center part that contains most of the seeds. The tender seeds embedded in the flesh do not need to be removed. They are sweet and have a pleasant soft texture.

Ecuadorian-Style Squash and Potatoes in Peanut Sauce

Ensalada de Zambo

Though Ecuadorians from the highlands call this dish *ensalada*, it belongs to that special Andean category more resembling warm side dishes. In this example, lightly cooked *zambo* is mixed with boiled potatoes and flavored with an *ahogado*, the golden local version of the universal Latin American *sofrito*, or cooking sauce.

In the northern highlands, the vegetables are flavored with both peanuts ground with milk to form a thick puree and *nata*, the thick layer of cream that forms at the top of unhomogenized boiled milk. In Azuay province in the south, where *zambo* is also very popular, it is cooked with just milk and crumbled fresh cheese. My adaptation combines the peanut puree and the cheese.

SERVES 6

    3 pounds fresh or thawed frozen *zambo*
   2¾ teaspoons salt
    4 medium russet or other mealy potatoes (about 1½
       pounds), peeled and cut into 1-inch dice
    1 cup whole milk
    ¼ cup unsalted roasted peanuts (about 1¼ ounces)
    2 tablespoon achiote-infused corn oil (page 89)
    6 garlic cloves, finely chopped
    1 medium red onion (about 8 ounces), finely
       chopped (about 1½ cups)
    ½ teaspoon ground cumin
    ¼ teaspoon freshly ground black pepper, or to taste
    4 ounces fresh cow's-milk cheese, preferably a soft
       Ecuadorian fresh cheese of homemade *cuajada*

(page 823), or a very soft *queso blanco*, crumbled, or pot cheese or farmer's cheese, crumbled (about ⅔ cup)

1 tablespoon finely chopped cilantro

Preparing the Zambo ▶ Peel the *zambo* and cut into ½-inch slices. Place in a 4-quart saucepan, add 4 cups water and 2 teaspoons salt, and bring to a boil. Cook for about 15 minutes. Drain and set aside.

Cooking the Potatoes ▶ While the *zambo* cooks, place the potatoes in a 3-quart saucepan with 2 cups water and ½ teaspoon salt. Bring to a boil over high heat. Lower the heat to medium and cook until soft, about 15 minutes. Drain and set aside.

Preparing the Peanut Puree ▶ Combine the milk and peanuts in a blender or food processor and process to a smooth puree. Set aside.

Preparing the Cooking Sauce ▶ Heat the oil in a medium skillet over medium heat until it shimmers. Add the garlic and sauté until golden, about 40 seconds. Add the onion and sauté until soft, about 5 minutes. Stir in the cumin, ¼ teaspoon salt, the black pepper, and the peanut puree and cook, stirring, until the sauce comes to a boil. Stir in the cheese. Taste and add salt and pepper if necessary. Add the *zambo* and potatoes and cook for 10 more minutes, stirring occasionally to keep the cheese from sticking to the pan, until the potatoes crumble.

Serving: Serve warm as a side dish. In southern Ecuador, *zambo* salad is served alongside white rice. In the northern highlands, it comes to the table with toasted corn (*tostado*, page 154).

Chayote (*Sechium Edule*)

A perennial vine native to the American tropics, chayote (*Sechium edule*) gets its modern name from the Nahuatl *chayutli* or *chayotl*, meaning a fruit shaped like a small pumpkin. It was probably first domesticated in southern Mexico and neighboring areas of Central America, where every part of the plant, from fruit to tendrils to starchy roots (*ichintal* in Guatemala), was and still is used in cooking. Like cucumbers and squashes, chayote is a member of the rambunctious Cucurbitaceae family, a botanical group of enormous range in shape, size, color, and geographic distribution.

It is grown commercially in many parts of the United States, Central America, the Caribbean, and South America, and even as far afield as New Zealand and China. But Costa Rica and Veracruz remain the main suppliers for the North American market. Throughout Central America you see it growing in backyards, propped on rusty fences. But in Costa Rica's Orosí Valley, I gazed in astonishment at mile after mile of chayote fields, the vines trained on simple wooden trellises and enveloped at dawn in fog that descends from the mountains and slips through the lush foliage to leave a coating of dew, almost as if the plants had been freshly watered.

North American shoppers can easily buy light green and ivory-white chayotes in supermarkets and produce stores. In Hispanic markets you can find darker green cultivars with smooth skin and others like hedgehogs, covered with ferocious-looking spines—handle these with care! The white ones are usually large and meaty, particularly the ones with spines, but they tend to bruise easily or develop dark soft spots. I find that the dark green chayote, with or without spines, keeps better. It has a darker-colored flesh and a dense texture which makes it ideal for grilling.

Guatemalans, who have a special penchant for chayotes, have given particular names to each type: the denser-fleshed dark green with smooth skin is referred to as *güisquil*, the one with spines is the *güisquil criollo*, and any type with varying shades of white is a *perulero*. All these are preferred over the more watery light green cultivars. They can be used as vegetables in stews and soups; boiled and cut into thick slices that sandwich slices of cheese and some cooking sauce (*chirmol*) and then are fried in an egg batter (*chilaquiles de güisquil*); hollowed out and stuffed with a sweet bread filling and baked in the oven (*chancletas*, page 822); grilled; or pan-fried.

Dark green chayote (*güisquil*)

Light green chayote

Spiny chayote (*güisquil criollo*)

White chayote (*perulero*)

SELECTING

Select plump and crisp-looking green or white chayotes with no soft or dark spots.

KEEPING AND PREPARING

Store chayotes in the vegetable section of the refrigerator. They will keep well for a couple of weeks.

Even when the fruit has begun to germinate, it remains good for cooking. You can boil or bake chayotes unpeeled for stuffing and other uses. If your recipe calls for peeling, use a sharp paring knife. When peeling uncooked green chayotes, you might occasionally find that your hands get covered with an uncomfortably sticky substance that dries like glue; just wash your hands under warm running water. Once it is peeled, halve the chayote lengthwise, scoop out the soft whitish seed with a spoon, and then slice or dice the vegetable according to your recipe.

Costa Rican Chayote, Fresh Corn, and Beef Hash
Picadillo de Chayote, Elote, y Carne Costarricense

Chayote is the most popular vegetable in Costa Rica and a common ingredient in picadillo, a type of hash. Costa Rican picadillos make clever use of staples like green plantains, *arracacha*, green beans (*vainicas*), and green papaya as well as combinations of vegetables like chayote and fresh corn. These are often, as in this recipe, mixed with beef, which almost acts as a seasoning for the mild chayote.

Cook's Note: In Costa Rica, the beef is "sweated" (braised) first before chopping. Here I use ground beef, so there is no need for precooking it. Worcestershire sauce is a beloved condiment in Costa Rica, in its national incarnation as Salsa Lizano.

SERVES 4 TO 6

3 medium light green chayotes (about 2 pounds 4 ounces)

2 teaspoons salt

¼ cup achiote-infused vegetable oil (page 89) or mild extra-virgin olive oil

1 small white onion (about 5 ounces), finely chopped (about 1 cup)

4 garlic cloves, finely chopped

1 small green bell pepper (about 4 ounces), cored, seeded, deveined, and coarsely chopped (about ¾ cup)

8 ounces coarsely ground beef (chuck or top round)

1 cup fresh yellow corn kernels (from 1 medium ear) or thawed frozen kernels

2 tablespoons finely chopped cilantro

½ cup chicken or beef broth, preferably homemade (pages 538 and 540)

3 tablespoons Worcestershire sauce

½ teaspoon freshly ground black pepper

▶ Split the chayotes lengthwise. Place in a 4-quart saucepan, add 2 quarts water and the salt, and bring to a gentle boil over medium heat. Reduce the heat slightly and simmer until the chayotes are tender yet firm, about 15 minutes. Drain.

Scoop out and discard the soft seeds in the center of the chayotes, and peel them. Place each chayote half on a cutting board, cut side down. Cut into ¼-inch slices, then cut at right angles into ¼-inch pieces. Set aside.

Heat the oil in a 12-inch skillet over medium heat. Add the onion, garlic, and bell pepper and cook, stirring, until soft, about 6 minutes. Add the beef and cook, stirring and breaking up any lumps with the back of the spoon, until the meat is cooked through but still juicy, about 10 minutes. Add the chayote, corn, cilantro, broth, Worcestershire sauce, salt to taste, and pepper, stir, and reduce the heat to medium-low. Cook, covered, for about 15 minutes to blend the flavors.

Serving: Serve hot as a light main course with rice or as a topping for Costa Rican *gallitos surtidos* (page 403).

Chayote Gratin

Chayotes Gratinados

This is one of my favorite gratins for company, a terrific first course or a savory side for red meat, poultry, or fish. Comté is a French cousin of Swiss Gruyère, which can be substituted.

SERVES 6 TO 8

8–9 medium light green, dark green, or white chayotes (about 6 pounds)

Salt

4 tablespoons unsalted butter

8 ounces slab bacon, cut into ¼-inch dice

3 tablespoons all-purpose flour

2 cups whole milk, heated, or 1 cup hot milk plus 1 cup hot chicken broth (preferably homemade)

1 cup finely grated Comté or Swiss Gruyère cheese (about 4 ounces)

1 large egg yolk

Dash of grated nutmeg

Freshly ground black pepper

½ cup freshly grated Parmigiano-Reggiano cheese

Preparing the Chayotes ▶ Split the chayotes lengthwise. Place in a medium pot, cover with water, add salt to taste, and bring to a gentle boil. Reduce the heat slightly and simmer until the chayotes are tender yet firm, about 15 minutes. Drain.

Scoop out and discard the soft seeds in the center of the chayotes, and peel them. Cut each piece in half lengthwise before cutting crosswise into 1-inch-wide slices; set aside.

Preparing the Cheese Sauce ▶ Melt 2 tablespoons of the butter in a small skillet over medium heat. Add the bacon and sauté until golden brown. Transfer to a plate and reserve. Add the remaining butter to the fat in the pan, then whisk in the flour and cook until it froths. Pour in the hot milk, whisking constantly. Cook, stirring, until the sauce thickens, then remove from the heat and stir in the cheese until melted. Let cool.

Beat the egg yolk into the sauce; season with the nutmeg and salt and pepper to taste. Set aside.

Preparing the Gratin ▶ Preheat the oven to 350°F. Butter a shallow baking dish.

Arrange half the chayote slices over the bottom of the baking dish. Sprinkle with half of the bacon. Cover with another layer of the remaining chayote slices and sprinkle with the rest of the bacon. Pour the cheese sauce evenly over the top.

Bake for 15 to 20 minutes, until golden and bubbly. Remove the chayote from the oven and heat the broiler. Sprinkle the Parmigiano-Reggiano cheese over the gratin and place under the broiler, about 4 inches from the heat source, until golden brown, about 10 minutes. Serve immediately.

Caigua or Achocha

Caigua, an Andean vegetable of the squash clan, looks like something from *Jack and the Beanstalk*, a light green bean pod swollen to gigantic size. The fruit of a climbing vine, like chayote, it is often grown in people's backyards in Ecuador, Peru, and Bolivia. *Caigua* does well at different altitudes, flourishing both in the warm, dry weather of the northern Peruvian coast, where it is highly prized

Caigua

as a vegetable, and at higher altitudes under cooler, more humid conditions. The hollow fruit, which measures about 6 inches in length, is gently curved, wider at the center and tapered at both ends. It holds a few odd flat black seeds that need to be removed. They are rectangular with one straight side and a crenellated top edge. To me, the seeds look something like the merlons of an Islamic defensive wall—an esoteric association that could only occur to someone who once taught a course on medieval castles. But that's not all that's strangely symbolic about them; on each side of the flat seed there is a cross-shaped indentation.

My fascination with the shape of the *caigua* seed came in handy in northern Peru. I was watching a group of archaeologists examine a cache of ancient seeds excavated from sites of the Moche civilization (A.D. 200–800) under the microscope. Even from a certain distance, I could tell that the sample contained *caigua* seeds.

SELECTING

Caiguas are imported frozen from Ecuador (where they are called *achochas*) and Peru and sold in Hispanic markets. Keep in mind that they shrink considerably during cooking.

Braised Tender *Caiguas* with Colombian Cheese Sauce

Pepinos Tiernos con Hogo Bogotano

In Bogotá, Colombia, a friend once served me a simple dish of very small, tender *caiguas* (locally called *pepinos*, or "cucumbers") flavored with left-over Bogotan *hogo*, the wonderful cheese-enriched cooking sauce, that she had used the day before to dress boiled potatoes (*papas chorreadas*, page 204). It was a delicious pairing. The texture and herbal flavor of the *caiguas* reminded me of green bell peppers, only more tender.

Cook's Note: I prefer La Cholita brand frozen *caiguas*.

SERVES 4

- 1 teaspoon salt
- 2 pounds (about 20) frozen *caiguas* (*achochas*) from Ecuador, not thawed
- 1 teaspoon butter
- 1½ cups Bogotá Cheese Cooking Sauce (page 52)

▶ Place 2 quarts water and the salt in a medium saucepan and bring to a boil over high heat. Add the *caiguas* and cook for about 10 minutes until tender. Drain.

Peel the *caiguas* if you wish, then seed and devein. Cut them lengthwise into 1-inch-wide strips.

Melt the butter in a medium skillet over medium heat. Add the *caiguas* and sauté for 1 to 2 minutes. Reduce the heat to low, stir in the sauce, and cook until heated through, 1 to 2 minutes.

Serving: Serve hot as a side dish for Grilled Skirt Steak with Argentinean Chimichurri (page 704).

CORN

When the Spaniards pushed on from Cuba to Mexico and the Yucatán in search of gold, they encountered a different kind of nugget: corn (*Zea mays*). They found it as malleable as gold in its many uses. The native peoples of the Americas ate it toasted or popped as a crunchy snack; turned it into porridges and nourishing beverages; ground it into flour and dough for bread; steamed it or cooked it over ashes for tamales; and ate it boiled on the cob.

All the peoples of Mesoamerica, from the Maya to the Aztecs, placed corn at the center of their culture and cuisine. Utensils for processing corn—the round-bellied clay pot used to boil corn with lime for softening the skins, the *metate* for grinding, the *comal* for cooking tortillas—were ubiquitous in any household from central Mexico to Costa Rica. Among the most striking objects found by archaeologists on the coast of Costa Rica are *metates* and corn-grinding stones. The *metates* are not the simple three-legged kind you find today in Mexico, but sculptural pieces with elaborate, astonishingly beautiful designs suggesting a wealth of ceremonial meanings.

The cultures of Mesoamerica were steeped in lore about this essential crop. Every people had its corn myth. The Popol Vuh, the sacred book of the Quiche Maya of Guatemala, tells this myth of creation: When the forefathers of the world, Tepeu and Gucumatz, were finished with their work of creation, they decided it was time to make man, who would in turn nourish and sustain them. So they held a council in the darkness of night to figure out what might be eaten by humans. Just before the sun, the moon, and the stars appeared, there came a procession of animals from the lands called Paxil and Cayalá—the *yac* (mountain cat), the *utiu* (coyote), the *quel* (small parrot), and the *hoh* (crow)—carrying ears of yellow and white corn. These animals showed the gods the road that led to the abundant land of Paxil, where there was golden and white corn, along with honey, cacao, and other fruits. By grinding the corn, the Creators made nine drinks and created the muscles and strength of man; out of cornmeal dough, they made the arms and legs of man; and in this way, they created the first fathers of humankind.

This myth strikingly illuminates the main uses of corn for Mesoamerican societies: drinks to give strength and doughs to make staple dishes like tortillas and tamales. In the Guatemalan highlands, where the Popol Vuh was created, farmers still eat corn three times a day in different forms. In the village of Colotenango, where soils are poor and hunting and fishing are scarce, the core of the diet is almost entirely corn gruel (*atole*), tortillas, and, on occasion tamales. The ethnographer León A. Valladares found in 1957 that the only substantial additions to this austere ancient regimen were wild herbs, a few vegetables such as *güisquil* (chayote), and the chile sauce called *chirmol*. Today the people of Colotenango consider yellow corn a "hot" food, according to the same system of medical beliefs the Spanish brought from medieval Europe. Especially in the cold climate of the highlands, hot foods are supposed to be strengthening. So are chiles, which are always eaten with tortillas.

As the Spanish advanced through Mexico and down through Central and South America, they found many varieties of corn. Accustomed to the small kernels of field corn in the island of Hispan-

iola, Mexico, and Central America, they were surprised at the size of kernels grown in what are today Ecuador, Bolivia, and Peru. In Cusco, they found corn with kernels as large as a toenail. That is only the beginning of the profound variations between strains of *Zea mays*. The kinds of corn that people grow from place to place are as different as breeds of dogs. There is red corn, black corn, purple corn, speckled corn, white corn, yellow corn. There are kinds with kernels almost as tiny as barley grains and others bigger than lima beans. Some are as tender as new peas, other dense and chewy.

Native Americans knew from experience what modern chemists would later confirm: that corn kernels vary in their composition to the point that one may be absolutely useless for a purpose another fills brilliantly. Some types of corn are best eaten fresh, others only release their full potential when dried. The kernels may contain varying amounts of protein, sugar, and different starches. Some types when dried are literally as hard as flint, hence the name "flint corn." Others, the so-called flour corns and dent corns (named for the characteristic indentation of the kernels), contain an abundance of floury starch that makes them perfect for versatile doughs. Some are so sweet that you taste almost nothing but sugar. There are other strains that respond to high heat by expanding with a sudden pop, turning into miniature ivory roses.

With sprouted corn of various types and colors, Andean people made fermented drinks, *chichas*, that served as ritual libations; everyday drinks; and condiments. In the highlands of the Andes, where food storage was extremely important during the winter months, farmers developed special strains of corn that could be dried for a crucial staple. One type with a soft pericarp (fibrous skin), known as *chulpi* in

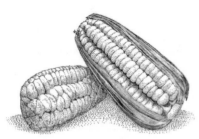

Andean corn

Ecuador, was dried on the cob and toasted to make a parched corn called *tostado* in Spanish and *cancha* in Quechua, which the Inca armies carried with them on military expeditions; it is eaten as a snack today. But even more important were the strains of starchy, mealy dent corn. The huge kernels were dried and further treated with a lime solution to remove the tough hulls, then dried again for storage until their final cooking, when they would plump and burst open. In Ecuador, Bolivia, and Peru, this skinless dried corn is called *mote*, and to this day, it is used more often than fresh corn as the basis for everything from side dishes to soups and tamales.

Believed to have descended from a wild grass (*teosinte*) from southern Mexico, corn went through many transformations over the millennia (the oldest remains of corn found in the Guilá Naquitz Cave in Oaxaca, Mexico are 6,250 years old). In the Andes, I have seen desiccated remains of Moche corn in sites from around A.D. 200 to 800, fairly recent dates in the long evolutionary history of corn, but the cobs were tiny, no longer than an index finger, with minute kernels.

In this same area today, the favorite strains are corn with large cobs and tight rows of yellow kernels or Andean corn with stocky, shorter cobs and huge white kernels, all the result of man's tinkering.

Unlike other grain crops, whose seeds can be propagated without human intervention, the very nature of corn, with its tight rows of kernels containing the vegetative life of the plant enclosed in a protective bundle of leaves, makes human manipulation necessary for propagation. Therefore, it is man, not natural selection, who created the many forms of corn that we know today.

In this section, I introduce you to the rich corn cuisine of Latin America. It would require several volumes to do justice to the wonderful corn dishes Latins cook from Juárez to Patagonia, but here you will find selected examples of the major categories of corn preparations. I start with everyone's favorites, simple boiled corn on the cob and creamy corn stews. Then I move on to dried corn and cornmeal, with nourishing porridges and hearty braises. Key to this section is corn treated with lime, a staple in Mexico and in the Andean region, where hominy (*mote*) has the same importance as bread. Dried corn in all its forms has the greatest significance in Latin American life and cooking. In many rural communities today, time is measured by the cluster of activities necessary to process it, from the drying of the ears of corn to the cracking of the kernels in large mortars or their treatment with lime to remove the skins, to the making and kneading of corn dough and its shaping and cooking to make daily bread.

Fresh Corn

In Michoacán in central Mexico, farmers celebrate the harvest of fresh corn ears (*elotes*) right in the cornfields, with a joyful feast called the *elotado*. While part of the first crop is reserved for the fresh corn tamales called *uchepos*, women also set big pots over wood fires to boil some of the *elotes* on the spot.

In my hometown, Santiago de Cuba, the corn harvest, which coincided with carnival in July, was also a time for feasting. We loved eating fresh corn on the cob the same way it is prepared in the United States, with some butter and salt, and we also made luscious fresh corn tamales called *ayacas*. In Chile, summer is the time for *humitas*, fresh corn tamales seasoned with basil, and rich vegetable stews such as *porotos granados con mazamorra* (cranberry beans cooked with grated fresh corn) and *charquicán*, which joins together meat, squash, potatoes, and corn. In Brazil, June is time for the sweet fresh corn tamales called *pamonhas*.

All over Latin America, we wait eagerly for the coming of fresh corn to make this delicious food under wraps. But if you looked closely into our kitchens, you would also see fresh corn cooked like a vegetable, cut into chunks and simmering in big soups and stews. In our markets, beside the mountains of corn fresh from the field, women cut the kernels from the cob and grind them to sell as a convenience food to cooks who do not want the hassle of grating corn at home for various uses, such as polenta or fritters. Amble down our streets, and your nose will guide you to the stands where people wait in line to buy corn on the cob from street vendors who boil the ears of corn on makeshift stoves or grill them over charcoal. Everyone loves the earthy warmth of freshly cooked corn.

SELECTING

The qualities that Latin Americans appreciate in corn are not necessarily the ones American farmers look for when creating new corn hybrids. Here in the United States, sweet corn with almost no starch is prized. In Latin America, we are used to mealier corn with much less sweetness, though we are rapidly learning to enjoy the sweeter American corn, primarily for corn on the cob slathered with butter.

When you buy corn from a supermarket, it is impossible to know if you are buying corn with regular sweetness, the so-called "normal sugary" (SU); corn with medium sweetness, the "sugary enhanced" (SE); or "supersweet" (Sh2)—the three types of hybrid corn most American farmers grow today. Supersweet hybrids are not recommended for Latin cooking, not just because of their excessive sweetness, but also because they lack creaminess and the kernels have tougher skins. If you want both corn picked at its peak and information about varieties, go to a farmers' market. Select corn that feels heavy for its size, in tight green husks without any dry spots, which are signs of aging. Pull the top leaves back a little to see if the cob within looks healthy, with succulent kernels and no signs of dryness or rot. The kernels should be plump and burst with milky juice when punctured with your nail. I have had good results with the early maturing yellow hybrid Seneca Horizon, the white hybrid Silver Queen, and the bicolored Sugar & Gold, all with normal levels of sweetness.

Andean corn from Ecuador and Peru, which has stocky cobs and very large white kernels, is available frozen in Latin markets. Look for packages that show no signs of ice, the telltale indication that they have been thawed and frozen again. For most recipes, thaw corn in its package at room temperature or in warm water before cooking. Andean corn is very starchy and has no sweetness at all.

Cooks in this country often ask whether they can substitute frozen corn kernels for whole ears or kernels freshly stripped from the ears. The answer is "Sometimes." I have indicated the substitution in recipes, where appropriate.

KEEPING AND PREPARING

For recipes where sweetness is important, cook fresh corn as soon as you get it. It begins losing sugar very rapidly after harvesting, particularly at warm temperatures. Store, unrefrigerated, for 2 to 3 days if you want the corn to be starchier—for instance, to make some Latin tamales. Otherwise, store in the refrigerator, unhusked, for 2 to 3 days. When ready to cook, husk and remove the silk.

Corn on the Cob on a Stick, Mexican Street Vendor Style

Elotes con Crema y Queso Plaza de San Francisco

Elotes are one of the few instances in which Mexicans eat corn fresh as a vegetable. In Mexico, preparing corn on the cob is a street art that brings out much that is whimsical and inventive. The *elotes* sold by the charming vendors in the square of San Francisco, in the heart of colonial Querétaro, taste better than those from anywhere else. The tender ears are boiled in large aluminum containers, smothered with melted butter and ripened *crema*, and sprinkled with grated aged fresh cheese. A final squirt of lime and dusting of chile powder transforms the corn into an appetizing snack.

Cook's Note: At both my restaurants, we boil the corn without removing the husk or silk, because we believe the husk is a flavoring. When the corn is done to our taste, in about 10 minutes, we peel the husks back and remove the silk. We tie the peeled-back husks together with a thin strip of husk for a decorative effect. When ready to serve it, we brush the corn with butter and grill it briefly or roast it in our wood-burning oven and proceed as instructed below. The husks, charred in spots by the fire, look beautiful and serve as a handle for the ear of corn. For a tapa-style dish, we cut the corn into chunks for easy eating but fit the pieces back together as if they were a single ear.

SERVES 6

- 6 medium ears tender fresh corn
- 1 teaspoon salt, plus more for serving
- 2 tablespoons butter, at room temperature
- 2 tablespoons Mexican *crema* (page 148) or crème fraîche, slightly warmed, or mayonnaise
- 1 cup grated sharp aged *cotija* cheese, ricotta salata, or Parmigiano-Reggiano cheese (about 4 ounces)
- 2 teaspoons ground *piquín* chiles or cayenne
- 4 limes, halved
- 6 sturdy wooden skewers

▶ Husk the corn and remove the silk. Place in a medium pot with the salt and cover with 2 quarts water. Bring to a boil over high heat and cook until tender, about 15 minutes; drain.

Quickly spread 1 teaspoon butter and 1 teaspoon *crema* over each ear of corn. Spread the cheese on a shallow dinner plate and roll the corn in it to coat thoroughly. Sprinkle with salt, ground chile, and lime juice to taste. Stick each ear on a sturdy wooden skewer and serve immediately. If the idea of eating a whole ear on a skewer seems too difficult, cut each cob into 2-inch sections and serve.

Salvadorian Corn on the Cob with Mustard, Mayonnaise, and Ketchup

Elote Loco

A few years ago, I was in the Planes del Rendero, a popular gathering place high on a hill in the outskirts of San Salvador. Everywhere I turned, there were women selling food: *pupusas*, *riguas* (fresh corn tortillas), and *elote loco*, corn on the cob seasoned with mustard and mayonnaise. I asked a woman why it was called *elote loco*, which translates as "crazy corn." She shrugged her shoulders and said, "Who knows?" But Manuel López, a bystander who was listening intently to the conversation, said, "How does corn on the cob get into a party? By pretending he is crazy, 'loco.' That's how he always manages to sneak in."

Loco or not, boiled or grilled corn on the cob with mayo and mustard is a must at any popular Salvadorian fair or street celebration. And many Salvadorians love to give it a final gilding with a sprinkling of ketchup. These days they also like to finish it off with a squirt of a black sauce resembling a thicker, sweeter Worcestershire.

Follow the recipe for Mexican-style corn on page 237 but instead of the *crema*, use 1 tablespoon mustard and 1 tablespoon mayonnaise. Omit the lime and chile, roll the ears of corn in the cheese, and finish with a squirt of ketchup if you like. You can peel back the husk to use as a handle or you can skewer each ear on a wooden stick as is done in El Salvador.

Dominican-Style Corn Stew ("Parrot's Crop")

Buche de Perico

This Dominican dish owes its name to the noisy, shrieking Hispaniola parrots (*pericos*) that teem in the forests of the island. They are very colorful, the undersides of their bright green wings streaked with blue, yellow, and red feathers. Peasants catch them to keep as pets or to sell in town. Beloved pets that they are, they eat what their owners eat: corn, green peppers, and red tomatoes—precisely the ingredients of this dish. Serve as a side dish or for brunch or lunch topped with fried or scrambled eggs.

SERVES 4 TO 6

- 4 cups fresh yellow corn kernels (from 5 medium ears) or thawed frozen kernels
- 2 teaspoons salt, plus more to taste
- 3 tablespoons extra-virgin olive oil or butter
- 8 ounces smoked ham or slab bacon, finely diced, or Spanish chorizo or Dominican sausages (*longaniza*), cut into ¼-inch dice
- 4 garlic cloves, finely chopped
- 1 medium onion (about 8 ounces), finely chopped (about 1½ cups)
- 1 medium red bell pepper (about 6 ounces), cored, seeded, deveined, and finely chopped (about ¾ cup)
- 1 medium green bell pepper (about 6 ounces), cored, seeded, deveined, and finely chopped (about ¾ cup)
- ½ cup Light Tomato Sauce (page 48) or prepared tomato sauce
- ⅓ cup water or chicken broth, preferably homemade Freshly ground black pepper
- 2 tablespoons finely chopped cilantro

► Place the corn in a medium saucepan, add 1 quart water and the salt, and bring to a boil over high heat. Cook for 5 minutes. Drain and set aside.

In a large skillet, heat the oil or butter over medium heat. Add the diced ham, bacon, or sausage and cook, stirring, until browned. Add the garlic, onion, and peppers, and cook until the onion is translucent, about 5 minutes. Add the tomato sauce and the ⅓ cup water or broth and cook, stirring, for 5 minutes, until slightly thickened.

Add the corn, salt and pepper to taste, and the cilantro. Cook, stirring, until heated through.

Panamanian Baked Fresh Corn Ring

Rueda de Maíz Nuevo Panameño

This is a simple but succulent savory corn pudding that Panamanians often eat for breakfast. It comes to the table with a plate of hot shredded smoked pork, which in Panama is called *tasajo*, and another of sliced fresh cheese (*queso blanco*). The recipe is simple, but every family seems to give it its own twist. My friend Patricia Gallo, a food writer, makes it without cheese. My Panamanian relative Marcela Wright prepares it in Miami with cheese and condensed milk, and uses cornstarch to help thicken the corn. I prefer evaporated milk.

In Panama, the corn is very starchy and requires only two eggs and no additional cornmeal or starch. The corn mixture sets perfectly and unmolds like a flan, without falling flat. You will find similar dishes in several regions of Latin America.

SERVES 8

5½ cups fresh yellow corn kernels (from 5–7 medium ears) or thawed frozen kernels

One 12-ounce can evaporated milk

3 large eggs, beaten

4 tablespoons (½ stick) butter, melted

2 tablespoons cornstarch

¼ cup sugar

1 teaspoon salt, or to taste

1½ pounds fresh cow's-milk cheese (preferably a very soft Ecuadorian fresh cheese, *queso blanco*, Monterey Jack, or Muenster cheese), ½ pound grated for the corn ring and 1 pound sliced to use as a garnish

► Preheat the oven to 350°F. Butter a 9-inch Bundt or tube pan.

Place the corn in a blender, in 2 or 3 batches, and process into a smooth puree. You should have about 4 cups ground corn.

Press the corn through a medium-mesh sieve into a medium bowl, pushing on the solids to force through as much as possible; discard the residue. Add the milk, eggs, butter, cornstarch, sugar, salt, and cheese and mix well. Pour into the prepared pan. Cover with foil and place in a baking pan filled with 2 inches water. Set the arrangement in the oven and bake until the mixture feels set like a flan and a toothpick comes out clean when inserted in the middle, about 1 hour. Let stand for about 10 minutes before serving.

Unmold onto a round platter at least 12 inches wide. Arrange the sliced fresh cheese around the edge or serve on a separate platter.

Cuban Fresh Corn Polenta

Tamal en Cazuela

Don't let the word "tamal" confuse you into picturing hot corn-husk bundles moistly emerging from a cloud of steam, for not all tamales are wrapped. Instead, imagine a creamy-textured polenta or a soft Southern spoon bread made with buttery fresh corn and flavored with a garlicky tomato *sofrito* embracing chunks of braised pork.

This Cuban classic belongs to the large family of rustic corn porridges born on slave plantations and refined in urban colonial kitchens. Some cooks took the trouble to smooth out its rough edges by grating the corn kernels and straining the resulting thick puree to extract only the corn milk. That is what I do here. The result is one of the silkiest Latin American corn porridges that I've eaten.

In my family's house in Cuba, the tamal was served in wide soup plates, like a stew. In popular restaurants, it was dumped unceremoniously onto flat dinner plates, where it spread like a sticky flood, and was eaten with rice and a little lettuce and tomato salad.

Cook's Note: Because Cuban corn is exceptionally starchy, in Cuba there was no need to add cornmeal, for the mixture thickened itself rather rapidly. To come close to the texture of Cuban corn, I have added a small amount of cornmeal.

What to Drink: Pair with a Benmarco Malbec from Mendoza, Argentina.

SERVES 6 AS A MAIN COURSE, 8 AS AN APPETIZER

For the Pork *Adobo*

- 6 garlic cloves
  Juice of ½ lime (about 1 tablespoon)
- 1 pound boneless pork shoulder with some fat, cut into 1-inch pieces

For the Tamal

- 8 cups fresh yellow corn kernels (from about 12 medium ears) or thawed frozen kernels
- 3 cups whole milk
- 1 tablespoon sugar, or to taste
- 1 tablespoon salt, or to taste
- 4–5 tablespoons mild extra-virgin olive oil, preferably from Arbequina olives
- 4 garlic cloves, finely chopped
- 1 small yellow onion (about 5 ounces), finely chopped (about 1 cup)
- 1 small green bell pepper (4–5 ounces), cored, seeded, deveined, and finely chopped (about ½ cup)
- 1 small jalapeño, seeded and finely chopped
- 2 cups Light Tomato Sauce (page 48) or prepared tomato sauce
- ¾ cup (about 4 ounces) fine yellow cornmeal
- 2 tablespoons butter

Preparing the *Adobo* ▶ With a mortar and pestle, crush the garlic to a paste. Alternatively, mince the garlic with a knife and then mash it to a paste by spreading and crushing it with the side of the knife blade on the cutting board, repeating the process until you have a smooth paste. Place the garlic paste in a small bowl, add the lime juice and the pork, and rub the garlic mixture all over the meat. Cover with plastic wrap and marinate for 1 hour at room temperature or refrigerate for up to 12 hours.

Preparing the Corn ▶ Place half the corn kernels in a blender or food processor. Add half the milk and puree until smooth. Strain the mixture through a medium-mesh sieve into a bowl, pressing on the solids with a wooden spoon or spatula to extract as much liquid as possible. Discard the skins in the strainer, and repeat the process with the remaining corn and milk. You should have 5 to 6 cups corn milk. Stir in the sugar and salt and set aside.

Preparing the Cooking Sauce ▶ Scrape the marinade off the pork and reserve it. Dry the pieces with paper towels.

Heat the oil in a 12-inch heavy skillet or a 3-quart sauce pan over medium-low heat. Add the pork and sauté, stirring often, until the pork is golden brown and has rendered most of its fat, about 8 minutes. Add the garlic and cook, stirring, until golden, about 40 seconds. Add the onion, green pepper, jalapeño, and reserved marinade and cook, stirring occasionally, until the liquid has nearly evaporated, 5 to 7 minutes.

Stir in the tomato sauce and cook, uncovered, until the pork is fork-tender, about 1 hour. Stir in a little water if the mixture dries out during cooking. Taste for salt.

Finishing the Tamal ▶ Add the reserved corn milk mixture to the pan. Raise the heat to medium and cook, stirring, for 5 minutes.

Gradually add the cornmeal in a thin stream, stirring constantly, until smooth. Add the butter and stir to melt. Cook, stirring frequently, over medium-low heat, until the tamal is thick and creamy, like soft polenta, 45 to 50 minutes. Add sugar and/or salt to taste if necessary.

Serving: Serve in shallow soup bowls as a main course or in small bowls as an appetizer, topped with a spicy sauce like Antillean Three-Pepper Sauce (page 117) for a nontraditional touch of freshness and a kick of heat and spice.

Fresh Corn Polenta in the Style of Lambayeque

Espesado de Choclo

Nicolás Carranzo Suyón is a man of few words, but he does not need to speak much—his cooking does all the talking. He was born in Salas, a small town in the north of Peru not far from Lambayeque, and even after many years of living and working as a chef in Lima, his cooking bears the unmistakable flavoring of his home region.

One night he heard me telling his wife of my love for the thick polentas of Cuba and Brazil. The following day, for lunch, he surprised me with this fresh corn porridge from northern Peru. The word *espesado* means thickened, which is very appropriate—the Andean corn used in this dish is very mealy and starchy and thickens rapidly when cooked.

What follows is Nicolás's recipe with one change. He cooked several chicken thighs to make a rich broth for cooking the corn. When the *espesado* was done, he turned it into a main dish by serving it together with the cooked chicken topped with the cooking sauce. I use chicken broth but let you choose what to serve it with as a side dish.

Cook's Note: Andean corn is key to the recipe if you are seeking authenticity. If you make it with American sweet corn, it will still be delicious but have an untraditional sweetness. If using American corn, reduce the amount of broth to 2 cups.

SERVES 8

For the *Espesado*

6 frozen ears Andean white corn (Ecuadorian or Peruvian; see page 154), thawed, or 7 ears medium sweet white corn

3 fresh-frozen yellow Andean peppers (*ajíes amarillos*), thawed and seeded

1 small red onion (about 5 ounces), coarsely chopped (about 1 cup)

4 garlic cloves

4 cilantro sprigs

6 cups chicken broth, preferably homemade (page 538), if using Andean corn; 2 cups if using fresh sweet corn

1 cup whole milk

3 tablespoons corn, safflower, or canola oil

1 teaspoon salt

For the Cooking Sauce

2 tablespoons corn oil

1 medium red onion (about 8 ounces), cut lengthwise in half and thinly sliced

4 medium plum tomatoes (about 12 ounces), peeled, seeded, and finely chopped

1 teaspoon cider vinegar

1 bay leaf

½ teaspoon salt, or more to taste

Making the *Espesado* ▶ Scrape the kernels from the corncobs with a sharp knife. Place in a blender or food processor, add the peppers, onion, garlic, cilantro, 1 cup of the broth, and the milk, and process to a smooth puree.

Heat the oil in a heavy 12-inch skillet or 6-quart pot over medium heat until it shimmers. Pour in the corn puree and cook, stirring, for about 2 minutes. Add the remaining broth (5 cups if using Andean corn, 1 cup if using sweet corn) and the salt and cook over low heat, stirring occasionally, for about 20 minutes. The mixture should look like a thick polenta.

Making the Cooking Sauce ▶ Meanwhile, heat the oil in a small skillet over medium heat until it shimmers. Add the onion and sauté until golden, about 4 minutes. Add the tomatoes, vinegar, bay leaf, and salt and cook, stirring, until the tomatoes are soft, about 6 minutes. Remove from the heat and discard the bay leaf.

Pour the *espesado* into a serving bowl and top with the cooking sauce.

Savory Corn Bread with *Rajas* and Cheese

Budín de Maíz con Rajas y Queso

This recipe was inspired by the puddinglike corn breads flavored with strips of roasted chiles you find all over Mexico. With its mixture of fresh corn and cheese, my corn bread is spongy, moist, and succulent—and a lifesaver when you are entertaining. It is easy to make and you may even have leftovers for breakfast. The roasted poblanos give it a welcome kick without overpowering the subtle taste of corn, and a pinch of cinnamon adds an elusive note of flavor. This corn bread is a marvelous side dish for stews and saucy dishes.

2 cups fresh yellow or white corn kernels (from about 4 medium ears) or thawed frozen kernels

1 cup heavy cream

2 tablespoons sugar

2 teaspoons salt, or to taste

½ teaspoon freshly ground black pepper

⅛ teaspoon ground cinnamon

2 cups (about 11 ounces) fine yellow cornmeal

2 teaspoons baking powder

5 poblano peppers, roasted (see page 67), peeled, seeded, and cut into ¼-inch-wide strips

4 ounces Monterey Jack cheese or fresh cow's-milk cheese (preferably a soft *queso blanco*), grated (about ⅔ cup)

2 tablespoons butter, melted

1 medium white onion (about 8 ounces), finely chopped (about 1½ cups)

▶ Preheat the oven to 375°F. Butter an 8-inch square baking dish. Place the corn, cream, sugar, salt, black pepper, and cinnamon in a food processor or blender and process to a coarse puree; do not overprocess. Pour the mixture into a bowl. Add the cornmeal and baking powder and stir to mix. Add the roasted poblano strips, cheese, butter, and onion.

Pour into the buttered baking dish. Bake for 40 minutes, or until golden and set.

Unmold onto a serving platter, or cut into squares in the baking dish and use a spatula to serve.

Paraguayan Corn Bread

Sopa Paraguaya

Paraguayans are lovers of breads made from dried ground corn and yuca. One of the most popular corn-based examples is a dense corn bread enriched with cheese. With the misleading name of "Paraguayan soup," this is the country's favorite Good Friday food and a must at any wedding. Instead of asking, "When are you getting married?" people will often ask, "When are we going to eat the *sopa*?" At weddings, a plate of *sopa paraguaya* cut into squares is placed on every table, together with beer and a bottle of whiskey.

Paraguayans living in the United States often use butter and fresh corn in their recipes, but the classic Paraguayan corn bread is made with lard or oil and only cornmeal. In many traditional recipes, the onion is boiled, not sautéed. At first I resisted this technique and sautéed the onions. But later, after traveling to other parts of South America such as Mendoza, Argentina, where onions are boiled before they are added to the beef filling for empanadas, I understood that in a way, the cooks were treating the onion as a vegetable, using it for moisture rather than its pungency.

This dish is said to have originated in the kitchen of the Paraguayan president Carlos Antonio López, an enlightened dictator who ruled between 1844 and 1862. He was fond of soups thickened with cornmeal. One day his cook slipped up and added too much cornmeal. The president christened the new recipe *sopa paraguaya*.

SERVES 6

2 cups fine yellow cornmeal, plus extra for dusting

2 large yellow onions (about 11 ounces each), finely chopped (about 4 cups)

2 teaspoons salt

½ cup freshly rendered lard (page 82) or 8 tablespoons (1 stick) butter, at room temperature

4 large egg yolks

12 ounces fresh cow's-milk cheese, preferably farmer's cheese, crumbled (about 2 cups)

12 ounces Muenster cheese, grated (about 3 cups)

2 cups fresh corn kernels (from 2 medium ears) or thawed frozen kernels (optional)

2 cups whole milk

▶ Preheat the oven to 400°F. Butter an 8-inch square baking dish and dust lightly with cornmeal.

Place the onions in a small saucepan, add 3 cups water and the salt, and bring to a boil over medium heat. Cook until soft. Turn off the heat and let the onions cool in the liquid, then drain. Set aside.

Place the lard or butter in the bowl of a standing mixer (or use a handheld mixer and a large bowl) and beat with the paddle attachment at high speed until fluffy. Lower the speed to medium and add the egg yolks one by one, beating well after each addition. Continue beating until creamy and light-colored. Beating at low speed, add the cheeses, corn kernels, and milk, and then the cornmeal in a fine stream, mixing well.

Pour the butter into the prepared baking dish. Bake for 45 minutes to 1 hour, until a toothpick inserted in the middle of the cornbread comes out clean.

Serving: Cut into squares and serve as a side for grilled red meats and soups.

Chilean Sweet Yellow Cornmeal

Chuchoca

The Mapuche people of southern Chile thicken and flavor their soups and stews with *chuchoca*, a coarse flour made from dried sweet corn. By drying the corn when it is fresh, the Mapuche preserve its sweetness and intensify its flavor.

When the Mapuche harvest the first sweet corn, they blanch the ears in boiling water and put them to dry on the straw roofs of their *rukas* (huts) or hang them over the hearth if it is raining—which it usually is. Once the ears have dried, they cut off the kernels and grind them into a coarse or fine flour, which can be stored until ready to use.

I always bring back *chuchoca* from my trips to Chile, but when I run out, I make it at home, which is lots of fun. I learned to dry the corn in the oven, not from a Mapuche friend but from cookbook author and vegetable expert Elizabeth Schneider, who experimented with drying sweet corn in the indispensable book *Better than Store-Bought* (written with Helen Witty). After drying, the kernels are crunchy and can be eaten as a snack or added as an unusual garnish for salads. When ground, the corn becomes a tasty thickener for braises and soups such as Chicken and Sweet Cornmeal Stew in the Style of Chol Chol (page 521). Once you have made *chuchoca*, be sure to put the finished product out of sight, or it will disappear before you have a chance to use it—it can become addictive.

Chuchoca is also known in other parts of the Andes. In fact, the word *chuchoca* comes from the Quechua *chuchucca*, meaning cooked and dried sweet corn. In parts of the Peruvian Andes, cooks make tamales with *chuchoca*.

MAKES 3½ CUPS DRIED CORN OR ABOUT 2 CUPS COARSELY GROUND CORNMEAL

12 medium ears sweet yellow corn

▶ Husk the corn and remove the silk. Bring 3 quarts water to a boil in a large pot. Working in 2 batches, blanch the ears of corn in the boiling water for 2 minutes. Lift out of the water with tongs, drain, and dry between kitchen towels, then let cool to room temperature.

With a sharp knife, cut off the kernels very close to the cob, to keep them as whole as possible (you will have about 12 cups kernels). Spread in 1 or at most 2 layers on two large baking sheets (if you have a small oven, three smaller baking sheets might fit better).

Preheat the oven to warm. Set the baking sheets on the bottom and top racks and leave the corn in the oven for 8 to 10 hours, until it is totally dried and the kernels feel light in weight and crunchy. Change the position of the trays periodically, stirring the corn and spreading it out evenly again each time. To make sure no moisture remains in the corn, leave it overnight in a turned-off gas oven with a pilot light. If you have an electric oven or a gas oven without a pilot light, you might want to use a dehydrator.

Let the corn cool completely and store in a glass jar with an airtight lid. To use as a thickener for Chilean soups, grind the kernels to a coarse meal in a food processor, pulsing on and off, or grind in batches in an electric coffee grinder or spice mill. *Chuchoca* keeps well for 3 months.

Cuitlacoche (Huitlacoche)

Cuitlacoche

Mexicans, who believe that no food should ever go to waste, use every conceivable part of the corn plant: the fresh ears bursting with milky juice for corn on the cob and delicate tamales; the dried kernels to grind into doughs for tortillas, tamales, and a plethora of corn tidbits such as tacos, *gorditas*, and *garnachas*; and the husks to wrap tamales. They even eat the fungus called *cuitlacoche* (also known as *huitlacoche*) that grows on ears of tender corn, making the kernels eventually swell and darken into a dense inky mass.

Known even to the ancient Aztecs as a food, *cuitlacoche* is a specialty of the cooler central highlands of Mexico. During the harvest season between July and August, you find it in markets everywhere, ears of corn showing monstrous silvery gray excrescences piled high for people to buy, or the fungus scraped off from the cobs and sold in plastic bags.

Scientists refer to *cuitlacoche* as galls and U.S. farmers know it by the unpleasant name "corn smut." *Cuitlacoche* is a Nahuatl word that perfectly describes the corn's eerie look—it comes from *cuitlacochin*, which means bad ear of corn. *Cuitla* means excrement or tumor—not a very appetizing descriptor for a food that is both delicate and complex in flavor and utterly addictive.

The fungus that causes such odd changes to ears of corn is *Ustilago maydis*. Botanists classify it as a basidiomycete, a division of the fungi kingdom (including mushrooms such as shiitakes) that produces spores from a club-shaped structure called a basidium. Left to their own devices, the spores will attack corn through any openings in the leaves, but they primarily penetrate the ear of corn through the channel, the top part of the ear from which the silk sprouts. Once inside, the spores stimulate the corn tissue, which begins to grow and divide unchecked to form edible galls that contain both fungal and corn tissue—that's why *cuitlacoche* has the sweetness and flavor of corn. In natural conditions, corn is susceptible to fungal attack from the time the ears begin developing silk until the silk begins to age. But there is a perfect time for inoculation, which farmers who cultivate *cuitlacoche* commercially know is optimal for high yields. A few days after the corn develops silk, farmers armed with large syringes go from plant to plant injecting a culture of *cuitlacoche* into each ear of corn through the silk channel. (This reminds me of the painstaking work of pollinating vanilla flowers.) Another important variable is the type of corn to grow and its time of maturity. For some farmers, a late-harvest corn of medium sweetness is best.

SELECTING

Some U.S. farmers sell fresh *cuitlacoche* at harvest time in the summer. In Florida, where there are two corn harvests a year, fresh *cuitlacoche* is available from July to August and again in November. *Cuitlacoche* can be purchased frozen year-round from select farmers in several states and in cans at Mexican markets. Select only plump whole kernels of either the fresh or frozen *cuitlacoche*.

KEEPING AND PREPARING

Fresh *cuitlacoche* should be used at once or refrigerated; it will keep well for 2 to 3 days. Otherwise, freeze it in tightly sealed freezer bags, where it will keep very well for about 3 months. Thaw before using. If using the canned product, drain it.

Cuitlacoche and Jalapeño Quesadillas
Quesadillas de Cuitlacoche y Rajas

Mexicans love *cuitlacoche* in quesadillas. The fillings are simple, usually including sautéed garlic and onion and an herb like epazote, cilantro, or the perfumed *pepicha* or its relative *pápalo*.

Working Ahead ▶ You can prepare the filling a day ahead; cool, then refrigerate, well covered with plastic wrap. The quesadillas can be assembled a few hours ahead and kept, covered with plastic wrap, in the refrigerator until ready to fry.

MAKES 8

The Filling

- 6 ounces fresh, frozen, or canned *cuitlacoche*, thawed if frozen
- 2 tablespoons mild extra-virgin olive oil or safflower oil
- 4 garlic cloves, finely chopped
- 1 large white onion (about 12 ounces), cut into thin lengthwise slivers
- 4 jalapeños, seeded and thinly sliced
- ¼ cup chicken broth, homemade (page 538) or store-bought

2 tablespoons finely shredded epazote (about 22 leaves)

Salt to taste

½ recipe dough for Mexican Corn Tortillas (page 579)

4 ounces Muenster or Monterey Jack cheese or *queso fresco*, finely shredded (about 1 cup)

2 cups corn oil for frying

Preparing the Filling ▶ If using canned *cuitlacoche*, drain well. Heat the oil in a 10-inch skillet over medium heat. Add the garlic and sauté until light golden, about 40 seconds. Add the onion and jalapeños and sauté until the onion is soft and light golden, 6 to 7 minutes. Add the *cuitlacoche* and sauté for about 1 minute. Add the chicken broth, stir, and let simmer to evaporate, about 1½ minutes. Add the epazote, stir, and cook until fragrant. Remove from the heat and taste for salt. Let cool.

Assembling the Quesadilla ▶ Divide the tortilla dough into 8 equal portions. One at a time, flatten the pieces of dough into tortillas about 6 inches in diameter (see page 579), but fill each tortilla before removing it from the bottom round of plastic: Place 1 heaping tablespoon of the filling in the center of the tortilla. Top with 1 tablespoon of the shredded cheese. Grab the opposite edges of the liner and fold into a semicircle. With the heel of your hand, press the edges together to make a 1-inch-wide flat border. (If assembling them ahead, use a separate plastic liner for each quesadilla and keep them wrapped until ready to cook, to prevent from drying out.)

Frying the Quesadillas ▶ Heat the oil in a medium saucepan or deep skillet to 375°F. Add one quesa-dilla to the hot oil. Almost immediately the quesadilla will bob, float to the surface of the oil, and puff a little. Turn over with a slotted spoon and fry until golden, about 2 minutes longer. Transfer to paper towels to drain, and repeat with the remaining quesadillas.

Serve hot; drizzle with *salsa verde* (page 114), then dollop with Mexican *crema* (page 148).

Dried Corn Treated with Lime

Just as revolutionary as the domestication of corn for prehistoric Mesoamerican and Andean societies was the development of a sophisticated technique for treating the dried kernels with a lime solution or ashes to make the grain more digestible, known as nixtamalization.

Native Americans realized the nutritional importance of grains like corn and made efforts to make corn more digestible by removing its fibrous skin, or pericarp. Through trial and error, they discovered that boiling dried corn in an alkali such as slaked lime (*cal*) or ashes dissolved in water helped get rid of the skins easily without the losses incurred by pounding the corn in a mortar. The Aztecs called the treated corn *nixtamal*, from the Nahuatl *nextli*, ashes, and *tamal*. When the treated kernels are cooked further until soft, they open up like cottony flowers. Then they are known as *pozole*, a name that comes from the Nahuatl *pozolli* (loosely, soft as foam), the word for the soft cotton sandals used by merchants in pre-Columbian Mexico. *Pozole* is also the name of the stew made with the boiled treated corn kernels. In the American South, where the settlers learned the alkalizing techniques from native Americans, the local equivalent of *nixtamal* or *pozole* is hominy, which is probably the name most familiar in this country.

The alkalizing process, nixtamalization, almost completely dissolves the skins and also changes the flavor of the corn by transforming the structure and chemical composition of the kernels. Nixtamalization improves the quality of some digestible proteins, though it makes others more difficult to metabolize. It also reduces the amount of niacin, which is concentrated in the skin, but the transformation improves the bioavailability of the remaining forms of niacin. The grain is more digestible and less likely to interfere with the absorption of nutrients from other foods that are eaten together with corn. When poor Europeans and the North American descendants of European immigrants adapted their own versions of a corn diet without the crucial alkali treatment, they invariably developed pellagra.

Much of the corn consumed in Mexico today, even some varieties of popcorn (*maíz reventador*), is nixtamalized before cooking, and much of the nixtamalized corn is ground into a coarse flour that is then kneaded with water to make the dough called *masa*. The flour processed from dried *masa* and sold commercially under brands like Maseca or Quaker Masa Harina is a product of modern industrial technology. Until recently, Mexican cooks used "true" *masa*—ground either at home or at a small-scale neighborhood *molino* (milling facility)—for a host of dishes. It was the source of corn tortillas, tamales, and the thick drinks called *atoles*.

We tend to associate the nixtamalization process only with Mexico, but it is found in many corn-producing regions of Latin America, from Mesoamerica to the Caribbean, from Brazil to the Andes. On All Saint's Day, practitioners of Cuban *santería*, a cult that fuses popular Catholicism and the Yoruba religion, traditionally offered a plate of *pozole*, called *maíz finado*, accompanied by a glass of water, to the spirits of the dead. This was also the traditional food served in most Havana homes on the Days of the Dead from the colonial period up to the mid-twentieth century. The dried corn was soaked overnight in a mixture of water and ashes, then rinsed carefully to remove the skins, trimmed, and boiled again until soft. Finally the cooked corn was sautéed with onion, aniseed, and lard until very soft.

In the Andean highlands, the dried corn is skinned by soaking it in a solution of ashes or quicklime and boiled to make the staple called *mote* (from the Quechua word *umuti*, meaning cooked corn), or *maíz pelado* (Spanish for hulled corn). Large amounts of corn are cooked to make *mote*—7 or 8 pounds of dried corn at a time. The preferred strains of corn in the Ecuadorian highlands for this purpose are starchy types like the mealy *maíz blanco*, *zhima*, and *morocho*. *Zhima*, a dent corn with large white, soft kernels, is everyone's favorite. *Morocho*, a flint corn with smaller hard, translucent kernels, is used mostly in poor rural areas. The treated kernels are soaked and dried as described on page 250 without the bother of trimming the germ as for Mexican *pozole*.

There are two other important differences between Andean *mote* and Mexican *nixtamal*. One is that after the tough hulls are dissolved, the kernels for *mote* are soaked further in several changes of cold water for a day or two. The other is that the treated corn is most often eaten whole and simply boiled. It is ground into *masa* only to make certain tamales and porridges.

After the alkali-softened soaked kernels have

been drained, they are spread out on straw mats and dried in the sun. It is this twice-dried whole corn, called *mote pelado*, that is cooked in a large range of dishes. You may find it in Latin American markets as *mote pelado* or *maíz pelado*. For their final cooking, the kernels may be boiled either to the al dente stage (when the corn is described as *motecauca* in Ecuador) or until very soft (*motepatashca*).

Very few cooks prepare *mote* from scratch nowadays. Even in rural towns, it is a convenience staple that you can buy already processed and even cooked. In the 10 de Agosto Market in Cuenca, Ecuador, there is a special section for the *mote* vendors, or *moteras*. There, women set up shop under tents and sell hot cooked *mote* from huge baskets. They process most of the *mote* at home, but they also cook some at the market. Here in the United States we don't have the convenience of *mote* vendors, but we can buy *mote pelado* in Hispanic markets. On a recent visit to my local market in northern New Jersey, I was stunned by the large stack of packaged *mote* next to bags of Mexican precooked *masa* for tortillas and tamales. Twenty years ago when I started buying groceries in Latin markets along Bergenline Avenue in Union City, the only dried corn I could find was cracked yellow corn and cornmeal of the type used in Caribbean cooking. Obviously, the new wave of immigrants from other parts of Latin America, particularly Mexico, Central America, and the Andean region, has created a demand for lime-treated corn. Noticeable among the brands of *mote* was Goya, which has started to sell this Andean staple in sixteen-ounce packages and large family packs. All you need to do is soak the corn and cook it for a couple of hours until soft.

Goya has also started to sell canned cooked nixtamalized corn as corn for *pozole*, or hominy. The alkali-treated corn from Ecuador, Peru, and other Andean regions should not be used interchangeably with the Mexican version or with the American hominy corn—they do not taste the same, nor do they have the same texture. It is a matter both of different technologies and the differences between the preferred strains of corn. Mexican immigrants, however, are turning increasingly to Andean lime-treated corn (*mote*) because of the large kernels and convenience.

You can buy dried Mexican-type nixtamalized corn, labeled as *maíz para pozole* (corn for pozole), in Mexican and some specialty food stores in the United States. It usually comes in small packages, and all you need to do is boil the corn until it opens up like a rose. But I give directions for making Mexican-style nixtamalized corn from scratch here because it is a process that illustrates an ancient technique that is at the heart of our corn culture. If you are truly interested in getting to know the cuisines of the Americas from the inside, this recipe can open a window of understanding on a daily chore performed by Mesoamerican women through the centuries. The treatment of corn with lime is still the daily ritual that marks time for many rural communities in Mexico and Central America.

But don't let my musings stop you from buying the dried nixtamalized corn or opening a can of Mexican *pozole* if time and convenience are of the essence.

Basic Mexican *Pozole*

When I nixtamalize corn for any dish—but particularly for *pozole*, the rich soup/stew—I view it as something very special. It is a process that requires care. Not only is any Mexican cook worth her salt familiar with the changes the corn goes through in cooking, but she is willing to cut off the germ end of every single kernel of corn in order to eliminate the slight bitterness of the germ and make the kernels flower when cooked again. For this effort you must have your mind fixed on a high and shining purpose, great texture, and good looks, not just fifteen minutes of table fame.

I have seen recipes telling you to use a can of Southern hominy for *pozole*. Please—no! Whether it is the lye used for hominy (not the same as the calcium hydroxide for treating Mexican corn) or the effect of the can, the flavor just seems horrible to me. Make *pozole* from scratch even once and you will know the right taste. This recipe will come in handy if you want enough treated corn for a large pot of *pozole*. True *nixtamal* is perishable because it is not dried before the final cooking.

MAKES 1½ POUNDS *POZOLE*

- 1 pound dried white field corn (see page 248) or dried corn for *pozole* (sometimes called "white hominy" corn, available in Mexican markets and specialty stores)
- 1 tablespoon slaked lime (available in Mexican markets as *cal* or in some pharmacies as calcium hydroxide; see page 247)

▶ Place the corn in a bowl and rinse under cold running water; drain. Place in a medium saucepan, add 3 quarts water, and set over medium heat. Dissolve the lime in ½ cup water, add to the corn, and stir. Almost immediately the corn will turn bright yellow and you will start smelling the unmistakable musky aroma of fresh tortillas. Bring to a boil, then reduce the heat to a simmer and cook for 20 to 30 minutes, or until the skins of the corn begin to loosen. Drain.

Place the corn in a deep bowl and rinse it under cold running water, rubbing it between the palms of your hands to loosen all the skins, which will have practically dissolved during cooking. Continue to rinse and rub the grains until the water runs clear and the corn no longer feels slippery.

At this point, the kernels will look white and the hard base of the kernel, popularly known in Mexico as the *cabeza* (head), will still be a deep yellow. With a sharp knife, cut out the *cabeza* from each kernel—a tedious and fastidious job that will pay off during further cooking, when the hominy opens up like an unblemished popcorn rosette. (For *masa* for tamales and tortillas, it is not necessary to cut out the germ end of each kernel.)

Put the nixtamalized corn in a clean medium pot with 4 quarts water and bring to a boil over high heat. Reduce the heat to medium and cook, covered, for 2 hours, or until the kernels are soft and fully open. Remove from the heat, drain, and proceed with the recipe of your choice. See page 518 for the soup called Oaxacan Chicken *Pozole* and pages 579, 460, and 461 for recipes for *masa* for tortillas and tamales. (*Pozole* will keep for 2 days, no more, refrigerated and covered with plastic wrap.)

Andean Hominy

Mote Pelado

In areas of the Andes under former Inca domination, very starchy strains of corn have been developed to a high degree of perfection. The corn is eaten fresh as *choclo* (from the Quechua word *chucllu*, meaning tender ear of corn) and in dried alkalized form as *mote* or *maíz pelado*.

You cannot understand the cooking of the Andean highlands without *mote*. In southern Ecuador and parts of Peru, *mote* is as important as bread, perhaps even more so.

During a visit to Cuenca, Ecuador, I was invited to the birthday party of a very important man, a local politician and writer. The table was beautifully set with a lace tablecloth and shining silverware. Placed in the center was a basket of seductive, beautifully shaped, anise-scented egg rolls and a large platter filled with steaming *mote*. The *mote* circulated briskly around the table and was replenished time and again, but no one touched the rolls, which looked so inviting. Finally I reached out to grab one and was struck with a piercing look from my hostess. The rolls, as one of my friends explained later, were meant as a sign of status—they were simply there as decoration. What people really coveted was the humble *mote*.

On every table, rich or poor, you will always find a plate of hot *mote*, the lush, plump ivory kernels soft and steamy. People serve *mote* simply, just boiled, or sautéed in a flavorful dark lard with tiny bits of pork cracklings. At the table, *mote* is given a kick of freshness with a spicy sauce that is spooned over the corn by diners according to taste.

Eaten alone, *mote* might seem bland, but when you sauté it in rich flavorful fats and douse it with spicy Andean sauces, it will grow on you and you will begin to understand its place in Andean cooking. *Mote* absorbs flavors beautifully, and it has a musky taste combined with a mealy richness that I find appealing.

Here is a simple recipe that only calls for boiling corn until it is soft. Lucky for us, the hard work of treating the corn with lime to peel it has already been done.

MAKES 6 CUPS

One 16-ounce package Andean corn for *mote* (sold as *maíz pelado* or *mote pelado* under many brand names, including Goya)

▶ Place the corn in a large bowl and cover with cold water. Let soak overnight. Drain the corn and place in a heavy 8-quart pot. Add 4 quarts of water and bring to a boil over high heat. Lower the heat to medium and cook, covered, until soft, 1½ to 2 hours. To determine when the *mote* is cooked properly, take a couple of kernels out of the water and split them open. If the interior looks whitish and mealy, it is not done—properly cooked *mote* is translucent. (Cooked Andean *mote* does not burst open like a cotton ball, as does Mexican *pozole*, which has been specially trimmed to remove the germ tip.) Drain the *mote* and proceed with any recipe. (Stored covered in the refrigerator, *mote* will keep for about 2 days.)

Ecuadorian Scrambled Eggs with *Mote*

Motepillo

When a Cuenca man is suffering a bad hangover (*chuchaqui*) from a night of partying and drinking potent Zhumir *aguardiente*, he will plaintively ask his mother or, worse, his wife to pamper him a little and cook him a *motepillo* to soothe his "wounded" stomach.

This scrambled egg and cooked *mote* dish is not just for *chuchaquis*; it is everyone's favorite comfort food in southern Ecuador. At midmorning, the women who have been shopping at the 10 de Agosto Market in Cuenca come home loaded with groceries and their daily bag full of steaming boiled *mote*. They are hungry and need a pick-me-up while they prepare lunch, so they say to each other, "Let's make a *motepillo*." The name comes from *mote* and the Quechua word *pillu* ("wrapped"), referring to the prized black lard, *manteca negra* or *mapahuira*, that is used to cook the dish. The *mote* and eggs are enveloped by the *manteca negra*.

My friend Inés Mantilla in Quito had warned me about the *mote* diet that would be imposed on me in Cuenca. At first I resisted, but *mote* eventually grew on me to the point that I always asked for *motepillo* for breakfast. You can use bacon fat or achiote-infused oil instead of the black lard.

SERVES 4 TO 6

- 2 tablespoons *manteca negra* (page 85), bacon fat, or achiote-infused lard or olive oil (page 89)
- 3 garlic cloves, finely minced
- 5 scallions, white and 3 inches of green parts, finely chopped (about ½ cup)
- 2 cups Andean Hominy (*mote*; page 251)
- 4 large eggs
- ¼ teaspoon salt
- ¼ teaspoon freshly ground black pepper

▶ Heat the lard, bacon fat, or oil in a medium skillet over medium heat. Add the garlic and scallions and sauté for about 2 minutes, until heated through. Add the *mote* and sauté for 2 minutes.

Meanwhile, crack the eggs into a bowl, season with the salt and pepper, and beat lightly. Pour into the skillet and cook, stirring, for about 2 minutes, or until the eggs are set but still moist and creamy.

Serving: Serve for breakfast or brunch. It is delicious with Ecuadorian *Ají* (page 123).

Ecuadorian "Dirty Mote"

Mote Sucio

This *mote* dish is called *sucio* ("dirty") because it is coated with black lard (*manteca negra* or *mapahuira*), the flavorful fat with tasty brown bits that remains in the pot after making pork cracklings or braising the seasoned pork ribs called *fritada* (page 394). There is no more delicious fat to add luster to any boiled grain or legume. The boiled *mote* is added to the pot and stirred until it glistens with the pan drippings and is speckled with the browned bits of pork fat and meat. But it is not difficult to make *mote sucio* by itself without the *fritada*. In that case, cooks buy *mapahuira* in the market or make their own. In the Ecuadorian highlands, *mote sucio* is a popular side for almost any main dish, as well as *fritada*.

Cook's Note: If you cannot make or buy *manteca negra*, you can use bacon renderings instead. Coarsely chop 6 slices fatty bacon and cook in a small skillet over medium heat until very brown; use the fat and some of the bacon bits to replace *manteca negra*.

SERVES 4 TO 6

- 2 tablespoons *manteca negra* (page 85)
- 2 garlic cloves, mashed to a paste with a mortar and pestle or finely chopped and mashed
- 4 scallions, about 3 inches of green included, finely chopped (about ⅓ cup)
- 2 cups cooked Andean Hominy (*mote*; page 251)
  Salt and freshly ground black pepper (optional)

▶ Heat the lard in a medium skillet over medium heat. Add the garlic and scallions and sauté until the garlic is fragrant and lightly golden, about 2 minutes. Stir in the *mote* and cook, stirring, over medium-low heat for about 10 minutes, so the corn absorbs the flavor of the lard. Taste for seasoning and add a little salt and pepper if you think the dish needs it. Serve hot.

Cracked Dried Corn and Cornmeal

The taste of nixtamalized corn is not universally liked throughout Latin America. Many regions use untreated dried corn kernels as a staple, ground into a flour for breads such as Colombian and Venezuelan *arepas* or the dough for some kinds of tamales. But even where the preference is for plain dried corn, people understand the need to eliminate the fibrous hulls of the kernels. In Colombia and Venezuela, the dried kernels are traditionally peeled by pounding the corn in large wooden mortars called *pilones*. It's a painstaking job requiring much stamina—that's why it has always been performed by women!

In rural areas, women still crack and peel their corn this way, but the process has also been industrialized in much the same way as nixtamalization in most parts of Mexico and Central America. In Venezuela, for instance, the corn is stored in large silos that can hold close to 56 million kilos. It is fumigated and aerated, then cleaned of any foreign matter and sent to gigantic hydraulic mortars, where it is hulled and cracked. The corn is winnowed, precooked under steam, and pressed into thin flakes that are cooled and ground to a flour for *arepas* and tamales, or *hallacas* (the Venezuelan tamal). This is the corn flour that is sold in Latin markets as precooked corn flour for *arepas* (*harina de maíz precocida para arepas*).

Colombians and Venezuelans prefer the brand P.A.N., which is widely available in the United States. This company, owned by the giant Polar Corporation from Venezuela, has made a great effort to improve the productivity of local Venezuelan corn in recent years, yet a large percentage of the corn processed there for precooked corn flour is white corn imported from the southern part of the United States or from South Africa.

Dried whole and cracked corn (white or yellow), often sold as *maíz trillado*, and cornmeals of varying fineness have long been a staple all over Latin America and can be found in any Latin market. These products run the gamut from cracked corn to the large dried Cusco corn sold to be toasted. If you take inventory of the many Latin dishes that are made with cornmeal and cracked corn, from Cuba down to the Andes, you will find that the preparations are very similar. Dried corn is cooked in sweets with milk and aromatic spices, or in savory porridges that range from the spartan *angú* from Minas Gerais (page 256) to the brightly seasoned Cuban *harina* (page 256).

Colombian Corn Rice

Arroz de Maíz Chocano

"Even when there is no rice, there are always *vituallas*," said the Chocó cook who gave me this recipe. In rainy Chocó, on the Pacific coast of Colombia, local people lump corn together with yuca, plantain, squashes, and even rice, as one of their staple *viandas* or *vituallas* (provisions). In this inventive recipe, cracked corn is cooked as yellow rice is with the typical Pacific coast cooking sauce called *ahogao*. The result is unexpectedly appetizing, a substantial side dish that harmonizes with any red meat, fish, or poultry the way rice does.

SERVES 4

- 8 ounces yellow or white cracked corn (sold as *maíz trillado* in Latin markets)
- 2 tablespoons achiote-infused corn oil (page 89)
- 6 garlic cloves, mashed to a paste with a mortar and pestle or finely chopped and mashed
- 6 scallions, white and 3 inches of green parts, finely chopped
- 4 medium plum tomatoes (about 12 ounces), seeded and finely chopped, or 4 canned plum tomatoes, drained, seeded, and finely chopped
- 3 ounces finely grated aged cow's-milk cheese (*queso añejo duro*), Mexican *cotija*, or ricotta salata (about ½ cup)
  Basil sprigs, preferably purple basil, for garnish

▶ Place the corn in a bowl and rinse in several changes of cold water until the water runs clear. Cover with fresh cold water and let soak overnight; drain.

In a medium saucepan or, preferably, a Latin American cast-aluminum *caldero* (see page 33), heat the oil over medium heat until it shimmers. Add the garlic and cook, stirring, until golden, about 20 seconds. Add the scallions and sauté for about 2 minutes. Stir in the tomatoes and cook for 3 minutes. Add the drained corn. Increase the heat to high and add water to cover. Lower the heat to medium and cook, uncovered, until bubbles and then craters appear on the surface of the corn. Add the cheese and fluff with a fork. Lower the heat and cook, covered, for about 10 more minutes—the corn should be soft but with some bite. Serve garnished with basil sprigs (purple basil is a favorite herb in Chocó).

Cracked Yellow Corn and Spareribs Braised in the Style of Minas Gerais

Canjiquinha con Costelinha de Porco

One of the many gutsy dishes of the Brazilian state of Minas Gerais is *canjiquinha*, a stew of cracked yellow corn cooked slowly with meaty spareribs (*costelinha de porco*). The ribs are first browned in their own fat, and the braise is seasoned with a simple Brazilian *sofrito*, or cooking sauce, called *refogado*, made with garlic, onions, bay leaves, and a touch of fiery *malagueta* peppers. It harks back to colonial days, when Minas was a rough frontier region and the local people had to invent ways to add flavor to staples such as dried corn.

Dona Lucinha, the owner and chef of her two eponymous restaurants in Belo Horizonte, the capital of Minas Gerais, and São Paulo, graciously parted with the recipe for her homespun version of the savory *canjiquinha* that she serves in big clay pots at lavish buffets. This is a substantial party dish that can be done in stages, then finished shortly before serving.

Canjiquinha, or *canjica*, is also the name of a popular Brazilian dessert made with white cracked dried corn (in the north of the country it is called *mungunzá*, an African word from the Bantu; see page 813). And the confusion does not end here. According to Maria Stella Libânio Christo, author of an important Mineiro cookbook, *Fogao de lenha* (The Savory Dish), *canjiquinha* is known as *péla-égua* in parts of Minas and *quirera de milho com suâ* in the interior of neighboring São Paulo.

Cook's Note: Dona Lucinha's seasonings are fairly spartan—garlic, onion, and bay leaf—as she wants to showcase the earthy flavor of the corn and the succulent ribs. For a variation, add 3 tomatoes and a couple of scallions, pureed in the blender, to the *refogado*.

SERVES 6 TO 8

8 ounces cracked yellow corn (sold as *canjiquinha amarela de milho* or *canjica de milho* in Brazilian markets and as *maíz trillado* in Hispanic markets)

2 pounds meaty spareribs, cut into 2-inch sections across the bone

¼ cup Brazilian *cachaça* or any other unflavored *aguardiente* or grappa
Juice of 1 lime (about 2 tablespoons)

1 teaspoon salt

For the Cooking Sauce (*Refogado*)

1 tablespoon achiote-infused lard or vegetable oil (page 89)

5 garlic cloves, mashed to a paste with a mortar and pestle or finely chopped and mashed

1 large yellow onion (about 12 ounces), coarsely shredded on a box grater

2 bay leaves

2–3 pickled *malagueta* peppers (see Cook's Note, page 144) or pickled cayenne peppers, or ¼–½ teaspoon of the pickling vinegar

▶ Place the corn in a bowl and rinse in several changes of water until the water runs clear. Cover with fresh cold water and let stand for at least 30 minutes before cooking.

Place the spareribs in a large bowl. Combine the *cachaça*, lime juice, and salt and pour over the ribs, tossing to coat. Let marinate for 10 to 15 minutes.

Place the ribs in a heavy 4-quart pot or a deep flameproof earthenware *cazuela* and add water to cover (about 2 cups). Bring to a boil over high heat, then lower the heat to medium-low and cook until the water evaporates and the ribs are nearly tender and are beginning to render their fat, 20 to 25 minutes.

Add the lard or oil and increase the heat to medium. Sear the ribs for 10 to 15 minutes, until browned on all sides. Lift out of the pot and set aside on a platter in a warm place.

Pour off all but 2 tablespoons of the rendered fat and return the pot to medium-high heat. Add the garlic and sauté until golden, about 40 seconds. Add the onion and bay leaves and cook for 3 minutes. Drain the soaked corn and add to the pot along with 2 cups water. Cook, covered, over medium heat for about 20 minutes, adding a little warm water if the corn seems to be sticking. The corn should be just slightly chewy.

Add the ribs, ½ cup warm water, and the pickled peppers or pickling vinegar. Do not go overboard with the peppers—you will have the chance to spice up the dish at the table with a fiery table sauce. Reduce the heat to medium-low, cover, and cook for about 25 more minutes, stirring occasionally to keep the corn from sticking. The ribs should be very tender, practically falling off the bone, and the corn tender but not turned to mush. As Lucinha would say, "*Deixe cozinhar ati fica bom*" (cook for as long as it needs to be good)." Remove the bay leaves before serving.

Serving: Dona Lucinha recommends serving *cajinquinha* with white rice, shredded and sautéed kale (page 516), black-eyed peas (page 271), and pork cracklings (page 82). I would also suggest a tangy Brazilian table sauce like Cacique's Spicy *Malagueta* Pepper Table Sauce (page 144) or Brazilian Hot Pepper and Lime Sauce (page 145).

Simple Cornmeal Polenta

Angú a Moda Escrava

When you taste the thick polenta that accompanies many of the emblematic dishes of Minas Gerais, such as *galinha com quiabo* (chicken with okra), you might be surprised to find it bland and unseasoned, without a drop of salt. There is nothing wrong with the cook. It is *angú*, made in the fashion of the *senzala*, the slave house.

In the early days after the discovery of gold in Minas, salt had to be brought by boat and then mule to the mines and was sold at a premium. It is understandable, then, that a staple food like *angú*, which was made in enormous amounts to feed the workers, would be unsalted. The tradition did not die with slavery. Today everyone makes unsalted *angú* as an accompaniment to saucy, well-seasoned dishes. The cornmeal is a starchy *tabula rasa* that absorbs the flavors of the sauce.

SERVES 6 TO 8

2½ cups (about 1 pound) fine yellow cornmeal, preferably stone-ground (*fubá de moinho de pedra or fubá mimoso* in Brazilian markets)

2 quarts water

▶ Mix the cornmeal with the water in a large pot. Cook over medium-low heat, stirring constantly, until it thickens, about 20 minutes. Pour onto a deep serving platter.

Serving: Serve as a side dish for saucy stews from Minas Gerais (pages 254 and 278).

Cuban Cornmeal Polenta with *Sofrito*

Harina de Maíz Guisada

As in Minas Gerais (see preceding recipe), cornmeal cooked with water to a mush was one of the main staples of the African slave diet on the sugarcane plantations of Cuba. Cheap and filling, it was what the plantation owners fed to their slaves along with salt cod and beef jerky (*tasajo*). In Cuba and in many parts of tropical Latin America with plantation economies fueled by slave labor, the dish was known as *harina* (cornmeal) or *funche*. The word *funche*, which is widely used along the coast of Venezuela, comes from the Angolan Kikongo word *nfungi or nfundi*, which means porridge. Traditional *funche* was as austere as the *angú*, seasoned simply with lard and some salt. It also became an important part of the diets of the Cuban free peasants and the urban poor.

Gradually *funche* lost its austerity, as cooks enriched it with tasty *sofritos* and other more complex flavorings. Today it is an intrinsic part of Cuban cooking, and you might find it cooked with pork, chicken, blue crab, or even the luscious stone crab, which is abundant in the western region of the island.

SERVES 6 TO 8

For the Cooking Sauce (*Sofrito*)

3 tablespoons freshly rendered lard (page 82) or extra-virgin olive oil

6 garlic cloves, mashed to a paste with a mortar and pestle or finely chopped and mashed

1 medium yellow onion (about 8 ounces), finely chopped (about 1½ cups)

4 medium plum tomatoes (about 12 ounces), peeled, seeded, and finely chopped

1 teaspoon salt

For the Polenta

1 teaspoon salt, or to taste

2½ cups (about 1 pound) coarse yellow cornmeal

2 quarts water

Making the Cooking Sauce (*Sofrito*) ▶ Heat the lard or oil in a medium skillet over medium heat until it shimmers. Add the garlic and sauté until light golden, about 20 seconds. Add the onion and sauté until golden, about 8 minutes. Stir in the tomatoes and 1 teaspoon salt and cook, stirring, for 10 minutes, or until the tomatoes are soft and the fat is separating from the solids and starts sizzling again. Remove from the heat and set aside.

Cooking the Polenta ▶ Place the cornmeal and the remaining 1 teaspoon salt in a large pot and stir in the water. Cook over medium-low heat, stirring constantly, for 10 minutes, until the polenta has thickened. Stir in the reserved *sofrito* and continue to cook, stirring, for 10 to 15 minutes. Taste to see if all the flavors have come together. Add more salt if needed.

Serving: Pour into a deep platter or shallow bowl and serve immediately as a side for stewed or braised beef, pork, or seafood.

Variations: In Cuba we would not add cheese to the *harina*, but I love the way it tastes with some grated Parmesan or aged *cotija* or ricotta salata.

QUINOA

As you drive through the small communities along the Bolivian side of Lake Titicaca in June, you will see farmers sorting their freeze-dried potatoes and spreading hulled quinoa on large woolen blankets on the naked fields. The mounds of quinoa I saw seemed small, just enough to feed a family during the winter months, with little left for selling or bartering.

Quinoa (*quinua* in Spanish) is an important Andean crop, grown since pre-Columbian times throughout the highlands from Colombia to Chile. This is the area that corresponds to the limits of the great Inca Empire in the heyday of its power in the fifteenth century, and it is possible that it was the Incas who disseminated this plant (commonly known as a grain, though botanically it is a fruit) throughout the Andes from its birthplace, the highlands of today's Bolivia.

Quinoa is now enjoying a renaissance after decades of neglect and competition from grains such as wheat. This nutritious member of the goosefoot family is now grown from Bolivian seeds in high, cold regions of the United States such as parts of Montana, the San Luis Valley in southern Colorado, and around Phoenix, Arizona, where it thrives during winter. It is starting to be bred in different-colored versions.

SELECTING

U.S.-grown quinoa comes to the market quite clean. Imported quinoa from Ecuador and Peru, however, needs to be carefully picked over for stones and other foreign objects before cooking.

KEEPING AND PREPARING

Quinoa will keep well in its package or in a tightly closed container for several months. Older strains of quinoa were covered with a layer of bitter compounds called saponins. Today both U.S.-grown and imported quinoa have usually been subjected to a process that removes part of the saponin layer, but just to be sure, I like to wash it in several changes of water, until the water runs crystal-clear. Place the quinoa in a large bowl under the kitchen faucet with the tap running slowly, and rub the grains between your hands until the water runs clear. (In Peru, they wash it in seven changes of water.) Then drain and proceed according to the recipe.

Simple Boiled Quinoa
Quinua Hervida Simple

Here is a basic recipe for cooking quinoa, which can then be used in any preparation.

MAKES ABOUT 6 CUPS

- 1 pound (about 2½ cups) quinoa, rinsed as directed above
- 2 teaspoons salt

▶ Combine the quinoa, salt to taste, and 2½ quarts of cold water in a large saucepan and bring to a boil over medium heat, stirring occasionally. Lower the heat and simmer for about 10 minutes, or until the quinoa is just barely cooked—all the grains should have turned translucent. Remove from the heat and drain well; do not rinse. When I will be using the quinoa for stir-frying or sautéing and I want a loose consistency without lumps, I spread the quinoa on a baking sheet and let it sit to allow the excess moisture to evaporate.

Storing: The quinoa can be refrigerated for a couple of days, tightly covered.

Sautéed Quinoa with Swiss Chard
Quinua Salteada con Acelga

Near Cusco, in Peru, I once tasted boiled quinoa flavored with the sautéed leaves of the quinoa plant. For centuries, highland people in Peru and Bolivia have used quinoa leaves (*lliccha*) as a vegetable. Although quinoa is grown in the United States, I have not been able to find the leaves here, so I use Swiss chard or spinach instead. It's a marvelous combination. At my restaurant Cucharamama, this lovely quinoa sauté is a side for our braised short ribs; the pairing is stupendous.

SERVES 8

- 7 ounces slab bacon, finely diced
- 4 garlic cloves, finely minced (about 1 tablespoon)
- 1 medium yellow onion (about 8 ounces), finely chopped (about 1½ cups)
- 2 fresh yellow Andean peppers (*ajíes amarillos*), seeded and coarsely minced
- ½ bunch Swiss chard, leaves coarsely chopped, stems halved lengthwise and then cut into ¼-inch slices
  Freshly ground black pepper to taste
- 4 cups Simple Boiled Quinoa (page 258)
- 1 tablespoon extra-virgin olive oil
  Salt to taste

▶ Cook the bacon in a large skillet over medium heat, stirring occasionally, until it is lightly browned and has rendered its fat, about 8 minutes. Add the garlic and sauté until golden, about 40 seconds. Add the onion and chiles and cook until the onion is light golden, about 6 minutes. Add the Swiss chard stems and cook until tender, about 7 minutes. Add the black pepper and stir for 1 minute. Add the chopped chard leaves and cook, stirring, until they wilt, about 1 minute. Remove from the heat and stir in the cooked quinoa and olive oil. Cook to heat through. Season with salt if necessary.

Serving: Serve as you would rice with any braised meat, like Short Ribs in Black Sauce (page 713) or the Pot-Roasted Stuffed Eye of Round Cartagena Style (page 707). This is also delicious as a side for Grilled Duck Breast with Tamarillo and Pink Peppercorn Sauce (page 680).

Stewed Quinoa with Dried Shrimp

Quinua Atamalada con Camaroncitos Secos

When a dish has the consistency of a soft polenta, Peruvians describe it as *atamalado*, like a tamal. There are several recipes for *quinoa atamalada*. Some are made with pork, others with chicken or a combination of ingredients. I like them all, but I find this creamy shrimp quinoa with potatoes very elegant and a welcome change from the many Peruvian dishes that call for pork.

SERVES 6 TO 8

- 8 dried *panca* or dried guajillo chiles (about 2 ounces), stemmed and seeded
- 1 pound quinoa (about 2 cups), rinsed as directed on page 258
- 2 large russet potatoes (about 14 ounces), peeled and quartered
- ⅓ pound dried shrimp
- 4 cups homemade chicken broth (page 538)
- 2 tablespoons achiote-infused olive oil (page 89)
- 4 large garlic cloves, finely minced
- 1 medium red onion (about 8 ounces), finely chopped (about 1½ cups)
- 1 teaspoon *pimentón* (Spanish smoked paprika, hot or sweet)
- 10 ounces feta cheese, preferably French sheep's milk feta, crumbled (about 2 cups)
- ¼ cup roasted peanuts (about 1½ ounces; optional)

▶ Soak the *panca* peppers in 1 quart hot water until plump, about 30 minutes. Drain, reserving ¼ cup of the liquid. Alternatively, boil in 1 quart water for 15 minutes, or until soft. Drain, reserving ¼ cup of the liquid.

Combine the chiles and the reserved liquid in a blender or small food processor and process to a puree. You should have about ¼ cup.

Combine the quinoa, potatoes, dried shrimp, and 2 cups of the chicken broth in a large saucepan and bring to a simmer over medium heat. Cook, adding more broth a little at a time as the liquid is absorbed (not unlike cooking risotto) and stirring occasionally with a kitchen fork, taking care not to mash the potatoes, until all the liquid is absorbed, the potatoes are tender, and the quinoa is cooked, about 30 minutes. The quinoa should be dry and fluffy.

Five to 10 minutes before the quinoa is done, heat the achiote oil in a medium skillet over medium heat. Add the garlic and sauté until golden, about 40 seconds. Add the onion and sauté, stirring, for 5 minutes, until softened. Add the *pimentón* and pureed chiles and cook, stirring, for 2 minutes. Remove from the heat.

When the quinoa is cooked, stir in the onion mixture and the crumbled cheese. If desired, stir in the peanuts for a crunchier texture. Pack the quinoa into oiled individual ramekins and unmold onto serving plates, or mound in a decorative bowl.

Serving: Serve as a side dish for a poultry or meat course such as Quail in Almond Sauce (page 684).

Mountain Quinoa

Quinua Serrana

Various versions of this dish are found in the high-lands of Peru and Bolivia, where it is often called *peske*. The use of milk and a salty fresh cow's-milk cheese resembling feta is as typical of the region as are the potatoes and *mirasol* peppers.

MAKES 6 TO 8 SERVINGS

- 3 dried *mirasol* peppers, stemmed and seeded
- 3 tablespoons olive oil
- 8 garlic cloves, mashed to a paste with a mortar and pestle or finely chopped and mashed
- 1 small red onion (about 5 ounces), finely chopped (about 1 cup)
- 2 ounces feta cheese, preferably French sheep's milk feta, crumbled (about ⅓ cup)
- ½ teaspoon ground cumin
- 1 teaspoon salt
- 2 medium russet or other mealy potatoes (10–12 ounces), peeled and cut into 1-inch dice
- 8 ounces quinoa (about 1 cup), cooked according to the instructions on page 258 and drained
- ½ cup whole milk

▶ Place the dried chiles in a small saucepan, add 2 cups water, and bring to a boil. Reduce the heat and simmer gently until soft, about 15 minutes. Or soak the chiles in 2 cups hot water for 20 minutes. Drain, reserving ¼ cup of the cooking water.

Combine the chiles and the reserved liquid in a blender or small food processor and process to a puree. Set aside.

Heat the oil in a medium saucepan over medium heat. Add the garlic and sauté until golden, about 40 seconds. Add the onion and sauté for 5 minutes. Stir in half of the crumbled cheese and cook, stirring, for 30 seconds. Pour in the chile puree and cook for 1 minute. Add the cumin and salt, stir in the potatoes, and cook for 30 seconds. Stir in the quinoa, then the remaining cheese, and mix. Add 1 cup water and cook, stirring occasionally, for 12 minutes, or until the potatoes are tender and all the water has evaporated. Stir in the milk, mixing well, bring to a boil, and cook for 1 minute. Remove from the heat.

Serving: In some parts of the *altiplano,* this dish is served as a thick, porridge-like main-dish soup. It is also served together with a meat course and rice in affluent Peruvian households.

BEANS

In many Latin households from Mexico to Brazil, a meal would scarcely be recognized as a meal without beans: beans simply boiled and drained, in hearty soups, in light soups seasoned with herbs, refried in flavorful cooking fats, in a hundred other guises. Beans appear in pairings with the other great staple foods of the lowland tropics (yuca and company) or the highland tropics (potatoes and cousins), or the entire New World (squash and corn); and, perhaps most memorably, they are served in every possible way together with the eagerly adopted Old World staple, rice. No food is more emblematic of the relationship between the peoples of Latin America and the land itself.

It is hard to believe that in Europe, until the voyages of Columbus, the word "bean" referred almost exclusively to one kind, the fava bean (*Vicia faba*), although people did eat other legumes, including lentils, chickpeas, and field peas. The Americas held most of the world's bean varieties. The indigenous peoples and the conquerors at once recognized the value of each other's staple legumes. Beans from the New World were rapidly planted in gardens throughout Europe, while the peoples of the Americas quickly adopted lentils, fava beans, chickpeas, and, most likely field peas as their own. To complete the picture, during the years of the slave trade black-eyed peas and pigeon peas (*gandules*) were brought from Africa.

Nonetheless, today, Latin Americans—especially in the Andes—still grow and eat a profusion of beans as yet little known in the rest of the world. Most belong to the so-called common bean species, *Phaseolus vulgaris.* (The Spanish and Portuguese names, *frijol* and *feijão,* are derived from the same root as *Phaseolus.*) Navy beans, black beans, kidney beans, cannellini, and most of the other kinds familiar in the United States belong to the common bean clan, all native to the New World. The lima bean (*Phaseolus lunatus*), or *pallar,* as it is called in Peru, is an Andean native of great antiquity and importance in pre-Columbian times that spread from there to Central America and Europe. In Spain the dried lima bean, called *garrafón,* is an indispensable ingredient for an authentic Valencian paella.

Andean markets sell common beans in a dazzling range of colors and markings—bright red, deep purple-black, tan, yellow, speckled, piebald.

Among other surprises you will find beans called *ñuñas* that pop like popcorn when heated and are eaten as a snack. In northern Peru, you can buy them from street vendors who also sell toasted corn and other grains.

In Mesoamerica the Spanish discovered what is actually a highly sophisticated food pairing: corn and beans. Corn lacks two essential amino acids, but combined with beans, it makes a complete protein. This was something the pre-Columbian civilizations of Mesoamerica seem to have instinctively understood. Mesoamerican cooks prepared beans in imaginative ways, turning them into soups or mashing them into a paste to fold into corn tamales or to eat wrapped in hot tortillas. To this day, refried beans and tortillas are the first thing that comes to mind when many people think about Mexican food. Remnants of Maya cooking techniques for beans can be found in Guatemala, where black beans are mashed and molded into shiny log-shaped cylinders under the name *frijoles volteados*. In El Salvador, Nicaragua, and Costa Rica, thick refried beans are served even alongside these countries' feast dish, rice and chicken.

Throughout Latin America, you will find different ways of treating beans and deeply entrenched preferences. Latin cooks are fond of immature fresh beans in the pod, like our green beans, and they use shell beans—fava beans, cranberry beans, lima beans, green pigeon peas—either quite young and fresh or dried. In Peru, where beans are more often consumed in thick soups, or potages, that people ladle over rice, cooks also make a dish, *tacu tacu*, that calls for a mixture of cooked rice and beans molded into a log shape. In the Hispanic Caribbean as well, beans are mainly cooked into thick potages with rice. Beans are seldom mashed into a paste and refried as in Mexico, with the exception of the Cuban dish *muñeta*, lightly mashed white beans flavored with sausages (traditional Catalan *butifarras*) or a *sofrito*.

Chileans are exceedingly fond of cranberry beans, which are known by the Hispanicized Quechua name *porotos*. They prepare them in stews, braises, and thick soups. In the highlands of Ecuador, Bolivia, and Peru, the Old World fava bean (*haba*) reigns supreme. In Cuenca, in southern Ecuador, people eat mountains of shelled fava beans simply boiled in their skins. They enjoy taking their time, peeling them one by one. In northern Ecuador, people like their fava beans toasted. They munch on them as a snack, not seeming to mind that they are almost as hard as pebbles. An Ecuadorian dentist friend of mine used to say that *haba* noshers had very strong teeth—very difficult to extract.

Together with toasted *habas*, northern Ecuadorians are fond of the bitter Andean lupin (*Lupinus mutabilis*), which they call *chocho*. This New World relative of the Spanish *altramuz* and the Italian *lupini* bean (*L. albus*) is one of the most nutritious beans in the world, containing an estimated 46 percent lysine-rich protein. However, if you bite into a freshly boiled *chocho*, an innocent-looking roundish ivory-colored bean, it seems as if you have bitten into an aspirin. Its bitterness is caused by water-soluble alkaloids. *Chochos* need prolonged soaking before they are edible. Peasant women wrap them in large burlap or woolen bags and leave them to soak, tied with a cord to a tree or a rock, in the running water of mountain streams. But you can always find presoaked *chochos*, already free of bitterness, in any market throughout the Andes.

Andean lupins grow from Venezuela to Colombia to Peru. In Peru, you will often find *chochos* with a brownish aureole. That explains the name *chocho*, which comes from the Quechua *chuchu*, referring to a woman's nipple. With the leaves of the *chocho* plant ancient Peruvians made *kanchiyuyu*, a type of soup. Bolivians call *chochos* by the Aymara word *tarhui* (also spelled *tarwi*). In Bolivian markets, it is common to find the boiled legumes labeled *mote de tarhui*.

While in Peru *chochos* have been associated with feast days since pre-Columbian times, northern Ecuadorians eat them at any time: they cook them in soups or eat them simply boiled and enlivened with onion relish and *tostado*, the Ecuadorian version of toasted corn. Toasted *chochos* and fava beans are often combined with fresh corn and *mote* as snacks, seasoned with the ever-present Ecuadorian onion relish (*salsa* or *ají de cebolla*), and are the most nutritious of fast foods. In the streets and markets, one sees women with braided hair standing in front of piping-hot containers of legumes and corn, scooping them into paper bags.

Green Beans

Green beans are as popular in Latin America as in Europe and North America. But throughout Latin America, green beans are normally flavored with the local version of *sofrito* and often enriched with milk, cream, cheese, and/or pork products like bacon or sausages. In the Brazilian *sertão*, the interior dry lands in the northeast of the country, cooks prepare them with the area's clarified butter, *manteiga de garrafa*. Everywhere green beans are eaten as a simple side dish, but they also figure in big soups, braises, and stews, and even in some soupy Mexican moles and *pepianes*.

SELECTING

Though green beans (and yellow wax beans, which are somewhat less common in Latin America) can be bought here year-round, they are best in early summer, when you can find them at their freshest at farmers' markets. Select crisp, firm beans that are a nice green without blemishes and that snap cleanly when broken.

KEEPING AND PREPARING

Fresh green beans will keep for a few days refrigerated but are best cooked as soon as possible. To prepare for cooking, snap off the tips. These days in the United States it is usually no longer necessary to remove any fibrous strings, though traditional strains of Latin American beans still have them. If a recipe calls for cooked beans, you can either blanch them briefly in a generous amount of boiling salted water (3 quarts or more per pound) and refresh them in ice-cold water to stop the cooking, or steam them over boiling water. The first method results in crisper, greener beans.

Colombian-Style Green Beans Cooked in Milk

Habichuelas Guisadas al Estilo de la Costa

Angélica Laperira, who was born in 1905 in the small town of Remolino, about half an hour inland from Colombia's Caribbean coast, cooked for her family every day of her long life. I met her when she was in her early eighties and was impressed by how careful she was in cooking even the simplest dishes, like these green beans braised in a tomato *sofrito* enriched with milk. Unlike many traditional Latin cooks, who cook green beans until they turn the color of army fatigues, she blanched the beans briefly, just enough to soften them, then immediately cooled them in cold water, a method that she had learned as a young girl from her mother—and what every contemporary chef does to keep the green beans at their brightest color. The milk does wonders for the simple sauce, giving the beans succulence.

SERVES 4

- 3 teaspoons salt
- 1 pound green beans, trimmed
- 4 garlic cloves
- 3 tablespoons extra-virgin olive oil
- 1 small white onion (about 5 ounces), finely chopped (about 1 cup)
- 2 scallions, white and some green parts, finely chopped
- ½ cup whole milk

▶ Bring 3 quarts water to a boil in a large pot. Add 2 teaspoons salt, then add the beans and cook for 2 to 3 minutes. Drain and plunge into a bowl of ice water to cool, then drain again and set aside.

Crush the garlic and remaining 1 teaspoon salt to a paste with a mortar and pestle; set aside.

Heat the oil in a 12-inch skillet over medium heat. Add the onion and scallions and sauté until soft, about 5 minutes. Add the garlic and sauté for about 2 minutes.

Stir in the green beans and milk, bring to a boil over high heat, and cook until the sauce thickens, about 2 minutes. Transfer to a serving bowl and bring to the table immediately.

Serving: In Colombia, the beans are served as a side dish for beef dishes with rice or mashed potatoes, Fried Green Plantains (page 182), and a simple salad.

Green Beans with Bacon

Habichuelas Guisadas con Tocino

I was inspired by recipes for green beans in old Cuban cookbooks calling for bacon, parsley, and nutmeg. There is nothing like bacon to turn green beans into a substantial dish.

SERVES 4

- 3 teaspoons salt
- 1 pound green beans, trimmed and cut into 3 pieces each
- 1 tablespoon extra-virgin olive oil
- 8 ounces slab bacon, cut into ¼-inch dice
- 3 garlic cloves, finely chopped
- 1 small yellow onion (about 5 ounces), finely chopped (about 1 cup)
- 3 medium plum tomatoes (about 9 ounces), peeled, seeded, and coarsely chopped
- 1 tablespoon finely chopped flat-leaf parsley
- ¼ teaspoon freshly ground black pepper
- ⅛ teaspoon freshly grated nutmeg

▶ Bring 3 quarts water to a boil in a large pot. Add 2 teaspoons salt, then add the beans and cook for 2 to 3 minutes. Drain and plunge in a bowl of ice water to stop the cooking, then drain again and set aside.

Heat the oil in a 12-inch skillet over medium heat. Add the bacon and sauté until lightly browned, about 5 minutes. Add the garlic and sauté until golden, about 40 seconds. Add the onion and sauté until soft, about 5 minutes. Add the tomatoes and parsley, the remaining 1 teaspoon salt, pepper, and nutmeg, and cook until the tomatoes are soft, about 3 minutes.

Stir in the green beans and cook, stirring once or twice, for 3 minutes. Taste for salt and pepper, transfer to a serving bowl, and serve immediately.

Cranberry Beans (*Porotos*)

Cranberry beans are common New World beans. When fresh and tender, they are cream-colored with pretty rosy specks, though these cook to a drab beige. The creamy and lightly sweet beans are a favorite in Chile, where fresh cranberry beans spell summer, and they are served in many guises—in salads, with seafood, and with squash and fresh polenta, often flavored with some basil.

SELECTING

Look for fresh cranberry beans at farmers' markets. Choose beans that look plump and full throughout, with flexible pods that still have some green in them.

KEEPING AND PREPARING

Shell the beans as soon as possible; cover and refrigerate them for no longer than 2 days. Simmer in gently boiling water until tender. The cooking time depends on the age of the beans. Very fresh young beans will cook in less than 15 minutes; older beans may take 25 to 30 minutes.

Cranberry Beans with Fresh Corn Polenta

Porotos Granados con Mazamorra

Fresh cranberry beans braised with soft fresh corn polenta are a summer treat in Chile, as eagerly awaited as fresh corn and the delicate basil-scented tamales Chileans call *humitas*.

SERVES 6 AS A MAIN COURSE; 8 AS AN APPETIZER

- 4 medium ears yellow corn, husked
- 3 tablespoons extra-virgin olive oil
- 8 ounces slab bacon, coarsely chopped
- 4 garlic cloves, finely chopped
- 1 small white onion (about 5 ounces), finely chopped (about 1 cup)
- 1 small green bell pepper (about 5 ounces), cored, seeded, deveined, and finely chopped (about ½ cup)
- 1 *ají cristal*, Hungarian wax pepper, or jalapeño, seeded and finely chopped
- 1 tablespoon salt
- 2 teaspoons ground cumin
- 1 teaspoon freshly ground black pepper
- 1 teaspoon dried oregano
- 4 plum tomatoes (about 12 ounces), finely chopped
- 3½ pounds fresh cranberry beans, shelled (about 6 cups)
- 1 cup chicken broth, preferably homemade (page 538)
- 2 tablespoons basil leaves, rolled up tightly and thinly slivered

▶ Grate the corn on the small holes of a box grater. Alternatively, slice the kernels from the ears and process in a blender to a coarse puree. You should have about 2 cups. Set aside.

Heat the oil in a 12-inch skillet over medium heat. Add the bacon and sauté until golden brown, about 8 minutes. Add the garlic and sauté until golden, about 40 seconds. Add the onion, bell pepper, *ají*, salt, cumin, black pepper, and oregano and sauté, stirring, until the onion is soft, about 5 minutes. Add the tomatoes and cook for 2 minutes. Stir in the beans. Add the broth and bring to a simmer, then reduce the heat to medium-low, cover, and simmer gently until the beans are tender, about 25 minutes.

Add the corn and basil and cook, stirring, until the corn is very tender, about 15 minutes.

Serving: Serve as an appetizer, or as a main course with Chilean White Rolls (page 590), Chilean Tomato Salad (page 549), and Chilean "Goat's Horn" *Pebre* (page 131).

Cranberry Beans with Squash, Corn, and Green Beans

Porotos Granados

This is one of the most popular summer foods of Chile, a delicious example of the coexistence of squash, corn, and beans in Latin cooking.

SERVES 6

1½ pounds fresh cranberry beans, shelled (about 3 cups)

2 teaspoons salt

3 tablespoons vegetable oil or extra-virgin olive oil

1 medium yellow onion (about 8 ounces), finely chopped (about 1½ cups)

2 teaspoons *Merkén* from Chillán (page 74) or hot *pimentón* (Spanish smoked paprika)

¼ teaspoon ground cumin

5 medium plum tomatoes (about 1 pound), peeled, seeded, and chopped

2 pounds meaty winter squash (kabocha, Hubbard, or buttercup), peeled, seeded, and cut into 1-inch dice (about 4 cups)

½ teaspoon freshly ground black pepper

1 cup fresh corn kernels (from 1 to 2 ears) or thawed frozen kernels

½ teaspoon dried oregano

1 tablespoon thinly slivered basil leaves

▶ Place the beans in a 4-quart pot, add 2½ quarts water, and bring to a boil over medium heat. Lower the heat to medium-low and simmer, partially covered, 25 minutes or until the beans are tender; when they are almost soft, season with 1 teaspoon salt. Drain the beans in a colander set over a bowl, reserving 4 cups of the cooking liquid; set aside.

Heat the oil in a 12-inch skillet over medium heat until it shimmers. Add the onion and sauté, stirring, until soft, about 5 minutes. Add the *merkén* or paprika and cumin and cook, stirring, for 1 minute. Add the tomatoes and sauté until soft, about 5 minutes. Add the squash, the reserved cooking liquid, the remaining salt, and the pepper and stir to mix. Cover and cook until the squash is soft, about 20 minutes.

Add the corn, beans, and oregano and cook, stirring, for 5 more minutes, until heated through. Stir in the basil, and serve.

Serving: I like to serve this in earthenware bowls as an appetizer. Or serve as a vegetarian main course with Chilean Tomato Salad (page 549), Chilean "Goat's Horn" *Pebre* (page 131), and Chilean White Rolls (page 590).

Fava Beans

Of all shell beans, new young fava beans are my favorite. Snuggled in their fuzzy, woolly pods, they look like curled-up tiny infants, waiting to be freed from their protective waxy inner skin to show off their apple-green color, a sign of freshness that heralds spring. Thanks to our various weather zones, we can start getting fava beans from southern California as early as March. I buy them by the case from my neighborhood Italian grocer, who keeps me well supplied during their growing season—which is never long enough to make me happy.

An Old World crop of great antiquity, beloved by the Egyptians and the Romans and later firmly established in all Mediterranean cuisines from Spain to the Middle East, fava beans found their way to the temperate regions of the Americas with the Spaniards. A cold-tolerant plant, the legume found a welcoming home in the cool, windswept Andean highlands, where it joined shell beans like the native *pallar* (lima bean) in the cooking pot.

I learned to cook fresh fava beans during my student days in Spain. The Aragonese like to sauté the shelled beans with serrano ham in freshly rendered lard. In Andalusia, cooks sauté them in olive oil or lard with bacon or salt cod and vegetables such as artichokes, fresh peas, potatoes, or chard and season them simply with onions and garlic, a pinch of saffron, or a little fresh mint for delicious first courses. Similar dishes, plus more complex fava bean stews and soups, crop up all over the Andean region, often enriched with native aromatic herbs and fresh cheese or spiced with pungent hot peppers. But paradoxically, for people who are obsessed with bold flavors, Andeans love fava beans best in their purest form, and that often means just boiled.

I once ate at a popular restaurant in Cuenca, Ecuador, where the main attraction was fava beans and *mote* (hominy made from large kernels of Andean corn) boiled by the metric ton by robust women under a makeshift roof at the entrance of the restaurant. After a short wait, a waiter brought to my table a mountain of fava beans and *mote* enveloped in a thick cloud of steam. The beans came with their tough skins intact, and I burned my fingers trying to slip them off while everybody else around me was doing this with no effort at all or not bothering to peel them. This is also how Bolivians enjoy their fava beans at street-food stands, where beans are combined with boiled potatoes in their skins and fat Andean corn on the cob to make *plato paceño*, the country's most popular snack.

SELECTING

Look for firm green pods without blemishes and soft spots, and always buy more than your recipe calls for. Even a perfect-looking pod might contain only a single bean or some discolored ones that need to be discarded. A good estimate is to expect about ½ pound (about 1 cup) shelled favas from 1 pound beans in the pod.

KEEPING AND PREPARING

Keep in a cool place or in the refrigerator and use as soon as you can. Shelling the beans is easy: just split the pods with your fingers. Blanch the beans briefly in boiling salted water. Timing is of the essence to keep their color bright green—the longer they cook, the more color they will lose. Drain and strip off their skins with your fingers.

Andean-Style Boiled Fava Beans

Habas Hervidas al Estilo Andino

Even at their simplest, boiled in salted water, there is something deliciously luxurious about fava beans. Their short growing season and the time-consuming job of freeing them from their pods and painstakingly stripping away their inner skins make us covet them. Get fresh fava beans while you can, and don't fuss too much with them. Boil them in salted water just enough to loosen the skin, and eat them in all their green, meaty glory by the load, as Andean people do. The chore of peeling the fava beans is left to the diners, but it is worth the trouble.

SERVES 4

    1 tablespoon salt
    6 pounds fresh fava beans, shelled (about 6 cups)

▶ Bring 3 quarts water to a boil in a large pot over high heat. Add the salt and fava beans and cook for 1 to 2 minutes. Drain, pile on a serving plate, and bring to the table with a salt cellar. Then show your guests how to peel the beans.

Fava Bean, Corn, and Fresh Cheese Salad/Relish

Solterito Arequipeño

From the old recipe notebook of my late friend Judith Lombardi de Rojas, a gifted cook who taught me the basics of Peruvian cooking, comes this lovely recipe for a salad of fava beans, corn, slivered red onions, and fresh cheese. *Solterito* (the name means bachelor) is a traditional dish from Arequipa, an important highland town in the southern part of the country. Judith's version calls for a garnish of boiled potatoes and purple Peruvian Alfonso olives. I often add a couple tablespoons of finely chopped cilantro or a few leaves of the Andean herb *quillquiña* to the *solterito* to bring it closer to the Bolivian version, *soltero* (page 561).

At my restaurant Cucharamama, we spoon a couple of tablespoons of *solterito* onto many dishes, from oven-roasted chicken to red snapper, as a relish or garnish.

Cook's Note: I enjoy the pungent bite of the Andean *rocoto* pepper in this dish, but be warned that the veins and black seeds are phenomenally hot.

SERVES 4 AS A MAIN COURSE SALAD

    1 large red onion (about 12 ounces), cut into thin
       lengthwise slivers
    2 cups red wine vinegar
    4 pounds fresh fava beans, shelled (about 4 cups),
       cooked and drained according to the instructions
       above, and peeled (about 3½ cups)
    2 cups frozen Andean corn kernels (from about 2
       ears), thawed

1   pound fresh cow's-milk cheese, preferably a soft
    queso blanco or French sheep's milk feta, cut into
    ¼-inch dice (about 2⅔ cups)

3   medium plum tomatoes (about 9 ounces),
    seeded and cut into ¼-inch dice

1   red *rocoto* pepper or 2 red jalapeños, seeded and
    finely chopped

¼   cup extra-virgin olive oil

2   tablespoons red wine vinegar or distilled white
    vinegar

1–2 teaspoons salt

4   boiled medium russet potatoes, peeled and cut
    into ¼-inch slices, for garnish

½   cup purple Peruvian Alfonso or Kalamata olives,
    for garnish

▶ Combine the onion with the vinegar in a medium bowl and let stand. Drain. If not using immediately, refrigerate, tightly covered.

Combine the fava beans, corn, cheese, tomatoes, and *rocoto* in a large bowl and toss with the onions. Drizzle with the oil and vinegar, season with the salt, and toss to combine well.

Serving: To serve as a salad, mound on a platter and surround with slices of boiled potato and the olives. For an appetizer, garnish each serving with 1 slice of boiled potato and a couple of olives.

Dried Beans

Like many staple foods, most legumes are more useful and versatile dried than fresh. Not only will they keep for months or years if stored properly, but their flavor and texture blossom when they are gently softened by simmering in a liquid. Then they can be eaten on their own, used in soups and potages, added to braised dishes, or turned into flavorful purees—of which Mexican refried beans are the most familiar in this country.

When the Europeans arrived in the New World, they recognized that the native peoples were applying many of the same cooking methods to beans that they used in their own countries. There was subsequently culinary cross-fertilization in both directions, with New World beans becoming one of the most successful transplants in Europe and Old World legumes such as chickpeas becoming completely acclimated to this side of the Atlantic.

Throughout Latin America, markets brim with an amazing spectrum of dried beans and other legumes in all shapes and colors. Some are already available in this country, like Peruvian Canary beans and the silk beans of El Salvador, and more are making their way to North American markets every year. By and large, the handling of all varieties is the same. Feel free to experiment with new types as you see them, but keep in mind that they may have been harvested, transported, and stored under very different conditions. This translates into great unpredictability in cooking times.

My recipes are based on legumes that are now widely available in the United States. You can substitute other, less familiar kinds as long as you are willing to stand by the stove testing for doneness and adding more water if necessary.

SELECTING

The ideal would be beans that have been recently harvested and dried. They take less time to cook than older beans. But that is exactly the information that you are not going to find on labels in this country, though it is standard in Spain, where fine beans from particular regions have achieved gourmet status. I would state, however, as a general rule that with familiar types such as black beans and red kidney beans, the U.S.-grown product cooks faster and more reliably than counterparts imported from Latin America.

Since most beans come in packages so you have little opportunity to examine the contents, it is a good idea to become familiar with a few brands that you can depend on (though even then there may be variations).

KEEPING AND PREPARING

Beans are very forgiving of different storage conditions, though you should avoid temperature and humidity extremes. Store in the original package or transfer to an airtight container. Although packaged U.S.-grown beans are usually quite clean, some Latin American brands tend to have more debris and small stones that must be picked out before using.

To soak or not to soak, that is the dried bean question. Anyone born in Latin America has been taught that legumes must be soaked for twenty-four hours before cooking. But in Latin America, legumes and grains often are much tougher than those grown in the United States. They frequently have a higher mineral content, which tends to slow the cooking process. Try cooking Salvadorian silk beans without a pressure cooker and you may find yourself despairing after 4 to 5 hours.

When using legumes grown in the United States, I tend not to soak them. With tough-skinned legumes such as chickpeas (many of which are imported), I find that soaking usually saves at least an hour of stovetop cooking. But never, ever soak black beans, or they will lose the stunning color that makes them so appealing. When I cook black beans for Moors and Christians (page 310), I always use about half a pound more beans than are called for in the recipe, so I will have plenty of inky water to stain my rice deep black. You will find instructions as to whether the beans need to be soaked or not in the individual recipes.

BOILING

Boiling is the basic way of cooking dried legumes all over. People were probably doing it in the Stone Age. Even today, it's the first step you need to take when preparing any dried legume. In Mexico and Central America and virtually every place where indigenous culinary legacies are still very much alive, people adore beans simply boiled in plain water with at most an herb or two, such as epazote. There is a purity about these minimalist beans. Eating them, you remember that for centuries a bowl of beans with corn tortillas was many people's main meal—and sometimes still is. You can enjoy the following two recipes as stand-alone dishes, or you can use these basic preparations as the foundation for many more complex bean dishes I present.

I normally start cooking my beans in cold unsalted water, slowly bringing it to a boil and then simmering the beans gently so they will keep their shape. For most beans, I use no less than 3 quarts water per pound of dried beans. When cooking white beans such as Great Northern or navy beans, however, I start with just enough water to cover the beans, then add cold water as the beans dry out, a trick I learned from a Catalan friend. Though it takes a bit longer, this method ensures luscious whole beans that are tender and creamy inside. I never add salt until the beans are soft. I've been taught since childhood that salt added to beans at the beginning of cooking toughens them—a legend of the Latin kitchen I haven't challenged yet.

Mexican-Style Boiled Black Beans

Frijoles Hervidos

This is a basic recipe for boiled beans, as prepared in kitchens throughout Mexico. If you will be using these boiled beans to make refried beans you don't need to season them with any salt. But reserve some of the liquid to make pureeing the beans easier. Or for added flavor to serve the beans with tortillas, increase the water by 2 cups and season the beans with 1 tablespoon freshly rendered lard or oil, added at the beginning of cooking. Do not add the salt until the beans are soft.

MAKES 6 CUPS

- 1 pound dried black beans, picked over and rinsed (about 2 cups)
- 1 white onion, halved
- 4–6 cilantro or epazote sprigs
- 2 teaspoons salt (omit if you are cooking the beans for refried beans)

▶ Place the beans in a 4-quart heavy pot, add 2½ quarts water and the onion and cilantro, and bring to a boil over high heat. Reduce the heat to low and simmer until the beans are soft, about 2 hours. Add the salt and simmer another 10 minutes.

Drain the beans, reserving 2 cups of the liquid if you will be making refried beans; discard the onion and cilantro. Serve at once.

If you are pureeing the beans: Working in two batches, place the beans in a blender or food processor with the reserved liquid and process until smooth. (Makes about 4 cups puree.)

Simple Boiled Black-Eyed Peas

Feijão Fradinho Cozido

In Brazil, the black-eyed pea (*feijão fradinho*) is a popular bean with many uses. In Salvador da Bahia, the capital of Bahia State in the northeast of the country, cooks use it soaked and skinned, without prior cooking, to make delicious fritters (*acarajé*). They also eat the boiled peas in salads and in a dish called *arrumadinho* (page 272), where the peas are served along with different sautéed meats (sundried beef, sausages); a type of *salsa cruda* of diced tomatoes, onions, and peppers seasoned with oil and lime juice; and a dusting of yuca flour (*farinha de mandioca*).

MAKES 4¼ CUPS BOILED PEAS

- 1½ cups (about 11 ounces) dried black-eyed peas
- 2 scallions, white and 3 inches of green parts
- 3 cilantro sprigs
- 1 small onion (about 5 ounces), peeled and halved

Cleaning the Peas ▶ Place the peas in a bowl and cover with cold water. Swish them around with your hands. Pour out the water, holding your hand over the peas so that they don't wash away. Repeat until the water runs clear.

Cooking the Peas ▶ Place the peas with 6 cups water and the scallions, onion, and cilantro in a 4-quart pot. Bring to a boil over high heat. Lower the heat to low, cover, leaving the lid a bit ajar, and simmer gently until the peas are soft but whole, about 45 minutes to 1 hour. Drain; cover with plastic wrap and refrigerate if using at a later time. The peas will keep well for a couple of days. Use in salads with a simple olive oil and vinegar dressing or to make the following Bahian *arrumadinho*.

Bahian Black-Eyed Pea
Arrumadinho

Arrumadinho Baiano

In Brazilian Portuguese, *arrumadinho* means gussied up, tidied up, or well put together. That is the perfect description of a dish made from humble ingredients cooked separately but served beautifully arranged, each component alongside the others, giving each other warmth and reinforcing each other's flavors. If this idea does not whet your appetite and make you run to the kitchen, think of the players and it will do the trick: black-eyed peas cooked until tender but perfectly whole, next to golden morsels of smoky Brazilian Calabrese sausages or salty sun-dried beef, brightened up by a simple little salad or *salsa cruda* of ripe tomatoes, green bell peppers, and onion, with just enough lime juice to give the tomatoes a tart kick, some olive oil to mellow the whole, and a dusting of *farinha* to bring it all together.

I first learned to love *arrumadinho* at the Cruz do Pascoal, a bar near my rented townhouse in Santo Antonio in Salvador de Bahia. My husband and I spent many an afternoon sitting on the terrace looking at the splendid Bahia de Todos os Santos and eating every version of the *arrumadinho* on the bar's limited menu; with *carne-de-sol* (or *carne seca*, a type of salted sun-cured beef jerky typical of the northeast of Brazil), with smoky Calabrese sausages or *linguiça*, or with bacon. But when I came back home, I tried what I had learned on a few of my friends, and they all invariably went for the Calabrese sausages. It is now one of my favorite party dishes, and I like to serve it family-style in a beautiful earthenware bowl.

In 2009, when I cooked for 400 guests at the White House for Fiesta Latina, I did a vegetarian version enriched with vegetables that I picked from the White House garden: fennel, little sweet orange tomatoes, and hot peppers. Cristeta Comerford, the executive chef, served the *arrumadinho* in small, delicate white dishes that she placed on tiered silver trays and nestled on a bed of yellow *farinha*, a thoughtful touch that forever endeared her to me.

SERVES 4

For the Peas

About 4 cups Simple Boiled Black-Eyed Peas (page 271)

For the Salad

6 medium plum tomatoes (about 1 pound), diced
1 medium yellow onion (about 8 ounces), peeled and finely chopped (about 1 cup)
1 medium green bell pepper (about 6 ounces), stemmed, seeded, cored, and finely chopped (about ½ cup)
3 tablespoons extra-virgin olive oil
2 teaspoons freshly squeezed lime juice
1½ teaspoons salt

For the Sausages

3 tablespoons extra-virgin olive oil
1 pound Brazilian-style Calabrese sausages (6 sausages), Polish kielbasa, or any similar cooked smoked sausage (preferably with skin removed), cut into ½ inch slices

For Garnish

1 cup Brazilian toasted yuca flour (*farinha de mandioca torrada*, see page 152)

Making the Peas ▶ Prepare the peas according to the recipe on page 271 and keep them warm.

Preparing the Salad ▶ Place the tomatoes, onion, and pepper in a small bowl and toss with the olive oil, lime juice, and salt. Taste for seasoning and set aside.

Preparing the Sausages ▶ Add the oil to a medium skillet and heat over medium heat. Add the sausages and brown lightly, 4 to 5 minutes. Lift out with a slotted spoon and place on a plate.

Serving ▶ Choose a handsome shallow bowl or deep platter large enough to hold all the ingredients. Arrange the warm black-eyed peas in the center. Place the tomato salad along one edge of the dish (lift out with a slotted spoon to let excess dressing drain off), flanking the peas. Arrange the sausage slices along the other edge. Dust all ingredients with a little of the toasted yuca flour, and place the rest of the flour on the platter in a small bowl with a spoon for guests to help themselves.

Refried Ayocote Beans

Ayocotes Refritos

Ayocotes are large, mealy scarlet runner beans that come in many shades of red and purple. They are a favorite in the Mexican state of Puebla and neighboring Morelos, where cooks prepare them for weddings and other special occasions. Most people like refried *ayocotes*. Prepared in this fashion, the beans become almost a condiment, to be smeared over hot tortillas or eaten with rice and different meats. The same type of bean is called *piloy* in the Guatemalan highlands, where it is found in many different colors.

A few years ago, I spent several days working with a Mexican woman named María Santibáñez while she and her relatives prepared the food for the *quinceañera* (fifteenth birthday party) of her niece in Huexca, a small town in Morelos. The day before the party, the women spent hours picking over a huge amount of *ayocote* beans. The following morning, they boiled them, with only salt as seasoning, in large clay pots set over a wood fire. When the beans were tender, a couple of the women mashed them into a thick puree, using large wooden spoons, while another sautéed onion slices in vegetable oil in another clay pot. Then they lifted the browned onions out of the pot, leaving behind the oil, poured the mashed beans into the onion-flavored oil, and sautéed the beans for a while. As a final touch, they stirred in a strained puree of avocado leaves plucked early in the morning from a nearby tree. The avocado leaves gave the beans a subtle anise flavor and aroma.

The food for the party was dished up all together on individual plates at an assembly line set up behind María's kitchen and taken in trays to the guests who waited under a canopy. The beans, along with rice, were the perfect sides for the pork and beef.

MAKES 7 CUPS, SERVES 6 AS A SIDE DISH

- 1 pound dried *ayocote* beans (available in some Mexican markets; or substitute pinto or red kidney beans and start tasting for doneness after 1 hour), picked over and rinsed
- 1 tablespoon salt
- ½ cup canola oil
- 1 large white onion, (about 12 ounces), cut into thick slices
- 40 fresh or dried Mexican avocado leaves (about 2 cups; sold in Mexican markets)

▶ Place the beans in a large bowl, cover with 1½ quarts water, and let soak overnight.

Place the beans in a heavy 8-quart pot along with the soaking water, and add 2½ quarts more water. Bring to a boil over high heat, then lower the heat and simmer gently, uncovered, until the beans are tender, about 3½ hours. Add more hot water if the beans dry out as they cook.

Working in batches, place the beans and salt in a food processor or blender and process to a fine puree. Pass through a fine-mesh strainer into a bowl, pushing the puree through with a ladle or a wooden spoon. Set aside.

Heat the oil in a heavy 6-quart pot or 12-inch sauté pan over medium-high heat. Add the sliced onion and sauté until deeply browned, about 12 minutes. With a slotted spoon, remove the onion from the oil. Pour in the beans and cook, stirring, for 10 minutes.

Meanwhile, make the avocado leaf puree: Place the leaves and ½ cup water in a blender or food processor and process to a puree.

Strain the puree through a medium sieve into the beans and cook, stirring, until the beans are thick and begin to "plop."

The beans can be made ahead. Let cool, cover, and refrigerate for up to 5 days.

Guatemalan Molded Refried Black Beans

Frijoles Volteados

Frijoles volteados is a log made from pureed and refried black beans that is served as a side dish in Guatemala, primarily for breakfast with eggs and usually accompanied by fried ripe plantains with ripened cream. I am always amazed at how perfectly shaped and black the log is. It is the result of patient cooking and hand-shaping with a spoon.

SERVES 4

8   ounces dried black beans (about 1 cup), picked over and rinsed, or 3 cups freshly cooked or canned beans, with 1 cup of their liquid
1   small white onion (about 6 ounces), cut in half (omit if using cooked or canned beans)
6   garlic cloves
2   teaspoons salt
¼   cup vegetable oil or extra-virgin olive oil
1   small white onion (about 6 ounces), cut into thick slices

▶ Cook the dried beans with the onion halves according to the directions on page 271, using 2 quarts water and omitting the salt. Drain, reserving 1 cup of the cooking liquid.

To refry the beans, place the beans, garlic, and salt in a blender or food processor, add the reserved bean liquid, and process to a smooth puree. Strain through a fine-mesh sieve into a small bowl, pushing on the puree with a ladle or the back of a spoon.

Heat the oil in a nonstick or well-seasoned skillet over medium heat. Add the onion slices and sauté until golden, about 10 minutes.

Remove the onion with a slotted spoon, leaving behind the onion-flavored oil. Add the bean puree and cook, stirring with a rubber spatula or a wooden spoon, until hot. Then mold the puree into a log shape, using the spatula or spoon and tilting the pan to help you work. Turn out onto a platter.

Serving: Serve hot, accompanied by Central American Ripened Cream (page 147), *chirmol* (page 119), Fried Ripe Plantains (page 183), and Mexican Corn Tortillas (page 579). Or for an interesting appetizer, let the log cool, cut into ½-inch rounds, and serve with guacamole and fresh corn tortillas.

Canary Bean and Rice Log

Tacu Tacu

A specialty of northern Peru, *tacu tacu* is a delicious and ingenious way to use leftover rice and beans. The rice and Canary beans, the preferred beans for this dish, are sautéed together in a skillet and then gradually shaped into a tapered log with the help of a wooden spoon.

Food historians believe that *tacu tacu* was created by Afro-Peruvians on the northern coast, where great landed estates with slave labor flourished throughout the colonial period. Today, *tacu tacu* is eaten everywhere in Peru. It is usually served with a panfried thin steak so wide that it practically covers the whole plate, or with slices of beef tenderloin sautéed with onions and tomatoes (*lomo saltado*). A fried egg crowns the ensemble, adding a splash of sunshine to this earthy dish. Each region of Peru has its particular version, made with different

beans, but I love the beautiful golden color of the Canary beans of Piura.

Many years ago, I tasted a marvelous *tacu tacu* at the *cebichería* Punta Sal in Lima, where the owner breaks with tradition by serving it with a rich array of fresh seafood lightly sautéed in butter and the traditional northern Peruvian cooking sauce from Piura. Nowadays the top chefs of Lima are experimenting with the humble *tacu tacu*. In modern restaurants, *tacu tacu* is usually smaller than the versions you find in popular restaurants and is stuffed with delicious seafood fillings.

SERVES 4 TO 6

1 pound dried Canary beans, picked over and rinsed

2 medium red onions (about 1 pound)

5 dried *mirasol* peppers (about 1½ ounces), stemmed and seeded

¼ cup corn oil or extra-virgin olive oil

4 garlic cloves, minced

1 teaspoon ground cumin

2 teaspoons salt

2 cups cooked white rice (see page 292)

1 tablespoon finely chopped cilantro

▶ Place the beans in a large pot, add 1 onion, halved, and 3 quarts water, and bring to a boil over high heat. Reduce the heat to low and cook, covered, until tender, about 2 hours.

Meanwhile, make the cooking sauce. Place the dried peppers in a small saucepan with 2 cups water and bring to a boil over high heat, then lower the heat to medium and simmer, covered, until soft, about 20 minutes.

Drain the chiles, reserving the cooking liquid. Combine the chiles and ½ cup of the cooking liquid in a food processor or blender and process to a puree (reserve the remaining cooking liquid). Force the puree through a fine-mesh sieve into a small bowl, pushing with a wooden spoon against the solids. Set aside.

Heat 3 tablespoons of the oil in a medium skillet over medium heat. Add the garlic and sauté until golden, about 40 seconds. Finely mince the remaining onion and cook, stirring, for 2 minutes. Stir in the cumin and salt, pour in the chile puree, and cook for 2 minutes. Remove from the heat and set aside.

When the beans are tender, add the onion mixture and 1 cup of the reserved pepper liquid, cover, and cook for 20 minutes. Then uncover the pot and let the beans cook at a gentle simmer until they have the consistency of a fairly thick bean soup. Remove from the heat and let cool. (The beans can be made ahead and refrigerated, covered, overnight.)

To make the *tacu tacu*, combine the beans and rice in a large bowl, mixing thoroughly. Heat the remaining 1 tablespoon oil in a large skillet, preferably nonstick or well-seasoned. Add the bean and rice mixture and cook, stirring, until the mixture thickens and develops a thin crust on the bottom. If you are using a nonstick skillet, scrape up the crust with a rubber spatula. Tilt the skillet to roll the mixture into a log-shaped cylinder, using a heat-proof spatula to help you shape the log. This takes practice, but with a little coaxing of the spatula, even an inexperienced cook can turn the rice and bean mixture into a fairly handsome log. Turn it out onto a plate and garnish with the chopped cilantro.

Yucatecan Refried Beans with Epazote and Habanero

Frijoles Colados Yucatecos

A few sprigs of epazote and the musky hot habanero chile lend delicious flavor, heat, and backbone to this simple Yucatecan dish. In this part of Mexico, cooks are fastidious and are very careful to strain the puree before refrying it, for a velvety texture.

MAKES 4 CUPS

> Mexican-Style Boiled Black Beans (page 271), with 2 cups reserved cooking liquid
> 1 habanero or Scotch bonnet chile
> 2 tablespoons freshly rendered lard (page 82) or corn oil
> 5 epazote sprigs
> 1 teaspoon salt, or to taste

▶ Working in 2 batches, place the beans and the reserved cooking liquid in a blender or food processor and process to a smooth puree. Force through a fine-mesh strainer into a small bowl, pushing against the puree with the back of a wooden spoon. Set aside.

Heat a *comal*, griddle, or heavy skillet over medium-high heat. When it is hot, add the chile and roast, turning with tongs, until charred on all sides, about 2 minutes. In a medium skillet, heat the lard or oil over medium-high heat. Stir in the pureed beans, habanero, and salt, and cook until the beans thicken, about 3 minutes. Season with the salt and remove from the heat.

Serving: Serve as a side dish with any Mexican-style meat or poultry, but especially with *cochinita pibil* (page 725) and Yucatecan Saffron Rice (page 301).

Veracruzan Refried Bean Dip

Frijoles Refritos Veracruzanos

Black beans become silky and intensely flavorful when they are pureed and then sautéed with garlic and tomatoes. At the now-defunct Churrería del Recuerdo, a Xalapa restaurant that specialized in the tasty fare that Mexicans like to eat in the late afternoon, such as tamales and all sorts of *botanas* (tidbits), accompanied by hot chocolate or *horchata*, these refried beans were used in *pambazos* (a kind of sandwich) or *gorditas*, and as a topping for *picaditas*, thick tortillas seasoned with beef and salsa.

I like to keep these refried beans on hand in my refrigerator for instant *taquitos*, to fill Venezuelan *empanadas*, or to use as a dip for corn and plantain chips.

MAKES 3 CUPS

- ½ recipe Mexican-Style Boiled Black Beans (page 271) with 1 cup reserved liquid
- 1 medium white onion (about 6 ounces), coarsely chopped
- 2 garlic cloves
- 2 tablespoons olive oil
- 3 medium plum tomatoes (about 6 ounces), coarsely chopped
- 1 teaspoon salt, or to taste

▶ Place the beans in a blender or food processor and process to a fine puree. Transfer to a bowl. Rinse the blender or processor. Add the onion, garlic, and tomatoes and process to a smooth puree.

Heat the lard or oil in a medium skillet over medium heat. Pour in the tomato puree and sauté, stirring, for 5 minutes. Stir in the bean puree and sauté, stirring, until it thickens and begins to "plop," about 5 minutes. Season with the salt, and remove from the heat.

Serving: Use as a savory dip with corn chips or use to smear over *garnachas* (page 399) and to fill *taquitos* (page 394).

Brazilian Bean Puree with Yuca Flour

Tutu à Mineira

A small plate of pork cracklings (*torresmos*) is brought to your table when you order your first fabulous *caipirinha* at the restaurant Dona Lucinha in Jardins, an elegant neighborhood in São Paulo. They also reappear as a garnish for hearty *tutu à mineira*, a traditional stick-to-the-ribs bean puree thickened with yuca flour. The dish is emblematic of Minas's *cozinha tropeira*, the cooking of the itinerant muleteers who once brought provisions to this region.

This is Dona Lucinha's recipe, with very little embellishment from my own kitchen. To make this dish, it is always best to use leftover beans from a *feijoada* or even from a bean soup, since the beans are full of flavor. But you can also cook a simple pot of beans until very soft specially for this dish.

Cook's Note: The *torresmos* of Minas Gerais (page 84) are cracklings without meat. They are made by frying small pieces of pork belly until they are golden and their skin is crunchy and blistered. They are essential to traditional *mineiro* cooking, but you can use cubed slab bacon sautéed until golden instead.

SERVES 4 AS A SIDE DISH

8 ounces dried black beans (about 1 cup), picked over and rinsed, or 3 cups freshly cooked or canned black beans or leftover beans with 1 cup of their liquid

4 scallions, white and 3 inches of green parts (if using dried beans)

4 cilantro sprigs (if using dried beans)

2 teaspoons salt (if using dried beans, 1 teaspoon if using freshly cooked or canned)

1 teaspoon freshly rendered lard (page 82) or bacon fat

8 ounces slab bacon, cut into small dice

4 garlic cloves, mashed to a paste in a mortar and pestle or finely chopped and mashed

1 small yellow or white onion (about 5 ounces), coarsely shredded on a box grater

1 bay leaf

¼ cup raw yuca flour (*farinha de mandioca crua*; see page 152)

▶ If starting with dried beans, cook them, with the scallions and cilantro, in a 4-quart pot with 2 quarts water as directed on page 271. Add 1 teaspoon salt just before they are done. Drain, reserving 1 cup of the cooking liquid.

Place the beans in a blender or a food processor with the reserved liquid and puree.

Heat the lard in a 10-inch skillet over medium heat. Add the bacon and cook for about 6 minutes, until golden brown. Add the garlic and sauté until golden, about 20 seconds. Add the onion and 1 teaspoon salt and cook, stirring, until the onion is golden, about 8 minutes. Add the bean puree and cook over high heat, stirring constantly, for about 5 minutes, until it thickens. Add the bay leaf. Add the yuca flour little by little, stirring constantly with a

wooden spoon. Reduce the heat to low and cook, stirring occasionally, for 10 minutes, or until the puree is very thick. Remove the bay leaf and serve hot. Makes about 2½ cups.

Serving: *Tutu à mineira* is traditionally accompanied by white rice sautéed with some garlic (page 298), Pork Cracklings in the Style of Minas Gerais (page 84), and a spicy table sauce like Cacique's Spicy *Malagueta* Pepper Table Sauce (page 144).

"Muleteer's" Beans with Bacon and Yuca Flour

Feijão Tropeiro

From the land of gutsy bean dishes, Minas Gerais, comes this hearty dish of small pinto or pink beans, golden brown bacon, and yuca flour. As its name indicates, this was the food of the muleteers, the men who carried supplies to Minas Gerais when the region was a mining outpost. This energy-rich dish kept them going in their long journeys, and it has now become a Brazilian classic that everyone loves. I first learned to appreciate this dish with my friends María Lúcia Clementino Nuñes (Dona Lucinha) and her daughter Elsinha, two busy restaurateurs from Minas Gerais. I like the simplicity of Dona Lucinha's recipe and her touches such as frying the eggs in the bacon fat rather than boiling them, so they have more flavor.

Cook's Note: The sautéed diced bacon in this recipe gives flavor to the beans and is a substitute for the luscious pork cracklings in the original. If you happen to have about 8 ounces of Pork Cracklings in the Style of Minas Gerais (page 84) on hand, do not use the reserved bacon. Instead, add the cracklings to the beans before serving.

SERVES 8 AS AN APPETIZER, 4 TO 6 AS A MAIN COURSE

- 8 ounces (about 1 cup) pinto, pink, or Roma beans, picked over and rinsed or canned
- 1 small white onion (about 5 ounces), peeled
- 2 scallions, white and 3 inches of green parts
- ¼ cup vegetable oil or freshly rendered lard (page 82)
- 8 ounces slab bacon, cut into ¼-inch dice
- 2 large eggs
- 4 garlic cloves, mashed to a paste with a mortar and pestle or finely chopped and mashed
- 1 medium white or yellow onion (about 7 ounces), finely chopped (about 1½ cups)
- 8 ounces pork cracklings, preferably Pork Cracklings in the Style of Minas Gerais (page 84), optional
- 5 scallions, white and 3 inches of green parts, finely chopped
- 1 tablespoon finely chopped flat-leaf parsley
  About ¼ cup yuca flour (*farinha de mandioca*; see page 165)

▶ Cook the beans with the small onion and 2 scallions in a 4-quart pot with 2 quarts water, as directed on page 271. Cook for 1 hour, until tender. Drain and discard the seasonings.

Heat the oil or lard in a 10-inch skillet over medium heat. Add the bacon and sauté, stirring, until golden brown, about 6 minutes. Lift out of the pan with a slotted spoon and place on a plate; set aside.

Crack each egg into the pan and fry, spooning the hot fat over the yolks, until the eggs are set and the yolks are cooked to your taste. Using a slotted spatula, transfer to a cutting board and set aside.

Add the garlic to the pan and sauté, stirring, for 10 seconds. Add the chopped onion and cook until light gold, about 7 minutes.

Meanwhile, coarsely chop the eggs.

Add the beans to the pan and cook, stirring, for about 2 minutes, pushing down on the beans to crush just a little. Add the chopped egg, the reserved bacon or the pork cracklings, and the chopped scallions. Sprinkle with parsley and yuca flour to taste.

Serving: Some cooks like to serve this dish with sausages or pork. I find it so rich and delicious by itself that I like to eat it as an appetizer with a Brazilian sauce (*molho*, pages 143 and 145) or as a main course with Kale in the Style of Minas Gerais (page 516), and Brazilian-Style Simple Pilaf (page 298).

Chickpea Polenta in the Style of América Sánchez

Pepián de Garbanzos

América Sánchez's house in Magdalena de Cao, a town in La Libertad department in northern Peru, is a restaurant and hostel of sorts for the archaeologists working at El Brujo, a nearby archaeological site. On their way to work, they stop by América's to let her know they will be coming for lunch and to discuss the menu. It is a friendly ritual that works for everyone. The archaeologists get to eat the foods they want and América gets paid to buy the ingredients and cook. I learned to trust the dining habits of the archaeologists the first time I had lunch with them at América's house, in 2003. Following protocol, I dutifully visited América early in the morning to select a menu. I was surprised when she agreed to cook almost a dozen dishes for me on such short notice, including braised *cuy*, goat stew, and *pepián de garbanzos*, which she described as delicious.

I never imagined that this polenta–like dish, made with raw chickpeas ground to a fine paste in América's imposing stone mortar (*batán*), could be so memorable. On a second visit to América's place 3 years later, I asked her not only to make it again but to teach me how to make it. I learned that it takes time and patience to peel each chickpea by hand, but it is a necessary step that can't be skipped. America's stone *batán*, which sits like a monument in her backyard, right next to her kitchen, does a marvelous job of grinding the skinned chickpeas to a very smooth paste. My food processor does a fine job too, but I wish I could use a *batán* for a silkier texture.

América serves the *pepián* as a side dish with beef, lamb, or goat stews. Throughout La Libertad and in traditional restaurants, you can eat *caiguas* stuffed with a savory beef hash nestled on a pool of *pepián de garbanzos*.

Chickpeas have a wonderful flavor and don't need much help, but América and other local cooks I met often make a flavored oil with ground dried *panca* peppers to add to the *pepián* at the table. I also substituted *mirasol* peppers, and it's also a perfect finish.

Cook's Note: I have recently found dried skinned chickpeas at my local Turkish grocery store. They are not as tasty as the ones with skin but they are a time-saver.

SERVES 4

- 8 ounces dried chickpeas (about 1¼ cups)
- ½ cup vegetable oil or light extra-virgin olive oil
- 4 garlic cloves, finely chopped
- 1 small onion (about 5 ounces), very finely chopped (about 1 cup)
- 3 medium plum tomatoes (about 9 ounces), seeded, peeled, and finely chopped (about 1 cup)
- 2 teaspoons salt, or to taste
- 2 teaspoons ground dried *mirasol* or *panca* pepper or 2 whole *mirasol* or *panca* peppers, soaked in hot water until soft or boiled for 10 minutes, and pureed to a paste with 1 tablespoon boiling water

▶ Place the chickpeas in a medium bowl, cover with 2 quarts cold water, and soak overnight; drain.

Peel the chickpeas: There are two ways of doing this. Pinch the germ tip of each chickpea with your thumb and index finger and pull back the membrane. Alternatively, place a kitchen towel on your kitchen counter. Working in small batches, place a few chickpeas on the towel and hit them lightly with your closed fist or a mallet to loosen the skin. If you smash the chickpeas, picking up the pieces is not fun—so be gentle. This is an excruciating task that is absolutely essential for the success of the final dish.

When you are finished, rinse the chickpeas to make sure no skins are clinging to them. Place half of the chickpeas in a food processor with ¼ cup water and process to a very smooth paste. Transfer to a bowl and repeat with the second batch. Set aside.

Heat ¼ cup oil in a wide (about 9-inch) saucepan over medium heat. Add the garlic and sauté, stirring, for 10 seconds. Add the onion and sauté for 6 minutes, until it is soft and light gold. Add the tomatoes and cook, stirring, until they are soft and reduced almost to a pulp, 5 to 6 minutes. Add the chickpea paste and the salt. Cook, stirring, for 1 to 2 minutes. Stir in 1 quart hot water and whisk until smooth. Reduce the heat to low and cook, stirring occasionally, until the puree thickens and turns satiny, about 45 minutes. Pour or ladle the chickpea polenta into a deep bowl. It will set nicely.

Heat the remaining ¼ cup oil in a small skillet over medium heat. Add the ground pepper or pepper puree and salt to taste and cook, stirring, for a few seconds. Pour over the polenta.

Dried Lima Bean Puree with Parmigiano

Puré de Pallar

The idea for this terrific lima bean puree comes from Jorge (Coque) Ossio, a Lima chef and the son of Marisa Guiulfo, Peru's most exciting caterer. Coque contributed the recipe to Tony Custer's *The Art of Peruvian Cuisine*, which contains many wonderful recipes from the Guiulfo family. The original calls for cream, but I prefer to use milk. You will love the richness and creaminess of this puree. The use of Parmigiano-Reggiano should not surprise anyone who has visited Lima. Italians have lived and worked in Peru since at least the nineteenth century, and their cooking has had enormous impact on Peruvian food.

Cook's Note: The dried beans must be peeled after they are soaked. To do this job, I sit at my kitchen table or on a stool by my kitchen counter and work slowly, with pleasure. When you see the thickness of the skin and how much you are discarding, you will understand why Peruvians want to get rid of it: from 8 ounces of dried lima beans, you lose about 2 ounces of skins.

SERVES 6

1 pound (about 2 cups) dried large lima beans
1 small onion (about 6 ounces), cut in half
Salt
½ cup whole milk
4 tablespoons (½ stick) butter
⅔ cup finely grated Parmigiano-Reggiano cheese

▶ Place the beans in a large bowl and cover with 3 quarts water. Let soak for at least 12 hours, or overnight.

Drain the beans and cover again with cold water. Soaking will have started to loosen the thick skins of the beans. By rubbing the beans gently with your hands, you can speed up the process. Otherwise, pinch the skin gently and pull it off. As you stir the beans with your hands, the skins will float. Every so often, drain off the water and the floating skins and add more water.

When all the beans are peeled, place them in a 6-quart saucepan, add the onion and 3 quarts water, and bring to a gentle boil. Reduce the heat and simmer, uncovered, until the beans are tender, 45 minutes to 1 hour. Skim the beans often—they will foam a lot. Fifteen minutes before the beans are done, stir in salt to taste. Drain, discarding the onion.

Transfer the beans to a blender or food processor and process to a fine puree. Pour into a medium saucepan, add the milk, and heat over medium heat, stirring, until hot. Add the butter, stirring until it melts. Stir in the Parmigiano and add salt to taste. Pour into a serving bowl and serve hot.

Serving: Serve as a side dish for Peruvian hot pepper stews (pages 753–58). I also love serving a couple of turkey or beef meatballs (pages 676 and 697) over a few spoonfuls of this puree for a first course.

Peruvian-Style Seasoned Lima Bean Puree

Causa de Pallares

Josie Sisson Porras de la Guerra is a Lima institution, the heiress of a notable family and a socialite of sorts who happens to cook very well. Her book *El Perú y sus manjares* (The Delicious Foods of Peru) is a treasure trove of classical recipes spiced by the personal touch of its many contributors, all friends and acquaintances of Ms. Sisson Porras. The book is as baroque and complex as its author, and every time I read it, I find some wonderful recipe I haven't noticed before, like a *causa* made with a puree of lima beans. In Lima, a *causa* is normally a terrine of brightly seasoned potato puree with layers of various fillings. The *causa de pallares*, however, is just a puree seasoned, like the terrine, with lime juice, garlic, and some ground hot pepper. It is garnished with Peruvian olives and hard-boiled eggs and topped with an onion relish. Here is my version.

SERVES 4

- 1 pound (about 2 cups) dried large lima beans
- 1 small onion (about 5 ounces), cut in half
- 1 fresh or frozen yellow Andean pepper (*ají amarillo*), or 1–2 hot yellow peppers, such as Hungarian wax or banana, or 1 jalapeño, seeded and deveined
- 2 tablespoons achiote-infused olive oil (page 89)
  Juice of 1 lime
- ½ teaspoon salt
- ½ cup Peruvian purple Alfonso olives or Kalamata olives, for garnish
- 8 ounces fresh cow's-milk cheese, preferably a soft *queso fresco*, or French sheep's milk feta cheese, cut into 1-inch dice (about ⅔ cup), for garnish
- ½ cup Peruvian Onion and Yellow Pepper Slaw-Relish (page 150), for garnish

▶ Soak, skin, and cook the beans with the onion as directed on page 282. Place the cooked beans in a blender or food processor and process to a smooth puree.

Pour the puree into a medium saucepan. Put the hot pepper, olive oil, lime juice, and salt in the blender and process to a smooth puree. Scrape into the bean puree and cook, stirring, over medium heat until hot. Serve garnished with the purple olives and diced cheese and topped with the onion relish.

Serving: Serve as a first course or as a side for Peruvian hot pepper stews (pages 753–58). I also like to serve a spoonful or two of the *causa* next to Coque Ossio's Dried Lima Bean Puree with Parmigiano (page 281), for contrast as a side for Grilled Duck Breast with Tamarillo and Pink Peppercorn Sauce (page 680) or grilled red meat, or alongside shrimp or chicken kebabs.

Boiled Lupins

Chochos Hervidos

Chochos (Andean lupins)

In Ecuador, you might find women retrieving sacks full of cooked lupins (locally called *chochos*) from mountain streams to take to market. This ancient legume, an important source of protein for highland people, is bitter when freshly cooked and needs prolonged soaking to get rid of the unpleasant flavor. In the north of the country, particularly around Quito, where *chochos* are very popular, restaurants always have a large batch of *chochos* soaking.

The first time I tried cooking with *chochos* at home, I could only find jarred Italian lupins in American markets, and these do not taste like the ones from the Andes. So I got into the habit of cooking a large batch of *chochos* and going through all the necessary steps to get rid of their bitterness just the way I had seen it done in Ecuador. Though lengthy, it is an easy and doable process.

MAKES ABOUT 6 CUPS

14 ounces dried *chochos*, preferably La Cholita brand from Ecuador (available in Latin markets)

▶ Place the beans in a large bowl and rinse well under cold running water. Drain, then cover with 2 quarts cold water and soak overnight.

Drain the beans, place in a 6-quart pot, and add 4 quarts water. Bring to a simmer over medium heat, then reduce the heat and simmer gently for 1 hour. Drain the beans, cover with fresh cold water, and cook for another hour. Drain and repeat the process, cooking the beans for about 1½ hours longer.

These beans are inordinately resilient. After 3½ hours of cooking, they should be soft but still feel a bit al dente and retain their shape (and bitterness).

Drain the *chochos*, place in a large bowl, and cover with about 3 quarts water. Soak for about 1 week, changing the water twice a day. Taste the beans daily to see if they have lost their bitterness. For the last 3 days of soaking, it's best to place the beans in the refrigerator to prevent fermentation. When the beans are no longer bitter, drain and refrigerate until using.

Lupins with Toasted Corn

Chochos con Tostado

Tossed with a bright table sauce of sliced onions and diced red tomatoes flavored with cilantro and garnished with toasted *chulpi* corn, lupins (*chochos*) make a refreshing salad. This is a midmorning repast throughout Andean Ecuador, especially in the northern highlands. The minute I tasted this unusual combination of flavors in Quito, I knew I had to try duplicating it at home.

Cook's Note: Fortunately for those who hesitate to undertake the long soaking process for boiled *chochos*, you can now find prepared Ecuadorian *chochos* in a jar at any Latin market (if you want to try the process at home, see page 283). Some brands come seasoned with hot pepper and packed in vinegar like a relish. For this recipe, buy *chochos* packed in brine (*chochos en salmuera*).

MAKES 6 SMALL SERVINGS

  4 cups Boiled Lupins (page 283) or two 14-ounce jars *chochos* in brine, drained
     Ecuadorian *Ají* (page 123)
  2 cups Ecuadorian Toasted Corn (page 154)

▶ Divide the *chochos* among six individual salad plates and top each serving with some of the salsa and 1 or 2 tablespoons toasted corn. Or serve in a bowl topped with the sauce, with the toasted corn in a separate bowl alongside.

RICE

If the way people put food on their plates can be a guide to their hearts, then the plates of Latin Americans reveal a love affair with rice matched only by that of Asians. We pile rice on our plates by the heap, the hill, the mountain range. We judge the quality of a meal by whether there is enough rice for everyone to fill each plate again and again, and by whether the rice is properly cooked. Yet this absolutely indispensable part of the tropical Latin diet is a relative newcomer to the Americas. How did it come to join native staples like corn, yuca, and potatoes on our tables, sometimes even replacing them?

Rice was brought to Hispaniola by Columbus on his second voyage, in 1493, probably as both provision and seed for cultivation. It seems that rice mattered deeply to the early settlers, since in 1495 we find them complaining to the Spanish Crown that they have not been adequately supplied with honey, sugar, almonds, raisins, and rice—in other words, grouping rice with some of the main ingredients of the Spanish Mediterranean diet. The early Spanish colonists, eager to re-create the world they left behind, brought to the island seeds or cuttings of most of the food plants that grew in the peninsula, including such important commercial crops as olives, grapes, and rice. Their agricultural experiments in small farms and in the island's budding plantations met with varying degrees of success. While sugarcane spread out like a weed, producing more concentrated juice than in the Mediterranean Basin, grapevines and olive trees grew vigorously but failed to bear fruit. Spanish chronicles do not dwell on the fortunes of rice in Hispaniola. It seems that the rice brought by Columbus on his second voyage did not germinate. But there are indications that later experiments, beginning around 1515, were not a failure. By the seventeenth century, Spanish settlers and their descendants, as well as African slaves and Indians, were growing rice on all the islands of the Hispanic Caribbean, in the swampy lands on the coast of Panama, in Veracruz, Mexico, on the Caribbean coast of Colombia near Santa Marta, and along the north coast of Peru.

Less perishable than tropical tubers, rice (*Oryza sativa*) was a rich source of carbohydrates, an important consideration for plantation societies based on slave labor. Together with tubers, beans, and, to a lesser extent, salt cod and beef jerky, rice became one of the most important foods in the diet of the African slaves. Gradually rice was embraced by everyone, master and slave alike. Even the potato-eating Indian farmers of the Andean regions succumbed to the lure of rice.

Despite the evidence that rice was part of the Spanish settlement in the New World from at least 1515, trying to connect the dots between that epoch and the rich rice cuisine of today's Latin America is very difficult. Scholars aren't certain what type of rice the Spaniards brought to Hispaniola, the early experiment station of Spanish agriculture in the New World. My guess is that the first seeds the Spaniards planted were of the medium-grain *japonica* subspecies from Valencia and Murcia, the two great rice-growing regions of Spain. If so, *japonica*, which is best suited to temperate climates, came to be supplanted by strains of long-grain *indica* rice, which thrived in warm tropical climates. These probably reached the Spanish colonies via the galleon trade with the Philippines or were obtained from Dutch and Portuguese traders who had long-established contacts with the rice-growing regions of Asia and the Indian Ocean. Another, later possible source was the American South, where a rice culture based on long-grain rice was nurtured by African slave labor from the end of the seventeenth century.

As in South Carolina's Low Country, the people who first actually did the hard labor of planting and cultivating the grain in Latin America were African slaves. As it happened, the rice species they had known in West Africa was better suited to the Caribbean climate than *Oryza sativa*. A body of evidence is starting to emerge suggesting that the slaves brought not only seeds of their well-loved *Oryza glaberrima* for their own use but an ingrained knowledge of rice cultivation in West Africa, which resembled the climate and terrain they found in the rice-growing regions of Latin America. Like the peoples of the Far East, they had evolved a distinctive, sophisticated rice culture based on centuries of experience. They also had a preference for a style of cooked rice with cleanly separated grains that I see reflected in most of today's Latin American rice-eating regions, as well as the nutritional wisdom to mix rice with legumes in a nearly ideal combination of protein and carbohydrate.

Unfortunately, Latin America did not long remain self-sufficient as a rice producer. As plantation crops like sugar and cacao came to dominate tropical economies, and as the population of the colonies grew, most regions were forced to begin importing rice. Most of it came from the Philippines, originating either there or in southern China, and was of the long-grain *indica* type.

But the Asian rice culture, and Asian techniques for steaming rice, never made the journey along with the grain. People in Latin America went on cooking their rice according to African or Mediterranean tastes. What they wanted was nicely separated grains, not the kind of lightly clumped rice produced by favored Chinese methods. The two most popular approaches to cooking rice today remain the African-inspired method (in which the rice is cooked in a large pot of boiling water, then drained and often left on or near a low fire to form a delicious crust on the bottom of the pot) and a version of the pilaf method common around the Mediterranean (in which the rice is first sautéed in fat, then simmered in a carefully measured amount of liquid until it completely absorbs the liquid).

Today the Latin regions with the strongest rice traditions are the ones with the biggest African or Spanish presence. Both influences are powerful in the islands of the Hispanic Caribbean, where rice is present at every meal. You will find it sharing space on the plate with other filling, starchy foods like yuca and plantains, as well as with beans. This pattern also holds on the Caribbean coasts of southern Mexico, Central America, Colombia, and Venezuela (which has made great advances in rice cultivation in the state of Portuguesa). It is equally powerful in Ecuador, Bolivia, Peru (which has rice fields in the north coast and the Amazon region), and especially Brazil, one of the world capitals of rice cooking.

Brazil is now the largest producer of rice in Latin America. Peru produces its own rice for domestic consumption, while Ecuador is able to export rice to neighboring Colombia and Venezuela. Most Latin American countries, however, still import rice, though there are many commercial plantings of strains developed at rice research centers like the Philippine-based International Center for Rice Cultivation (IRRI). For special recipes such as rice and chicken, *asopao*, and paella-like dishes, a medium-grain rice (often imported Valencia rice from Spain) is generally preferred. But the kind that people heap on their plates every day is long-grain rice, some of it from the United States. In fact, rice from this country has been going to Latin America since at least the nineteenth century.

Cuban cooks used to look for Carolina rice, which was the name for rice from South Carolina before it became a brand name. We also took joy in parboiled rice—Uncle Ben's is the label everyone knows—which always cooks up into nice separated grains. People who consider that some sort of heresy should know that parboiling rice is an ancient technique developed separately in both India and Africa, and that today African-descended blacks and other cooks in Latin America swear by Uncle Ben's.

In most of tropical Latin America, rice is most often the binding starch for a meal, which is why it's difficult to judge the merits of a rice dish on its own. What might seem bland and uninspiring can become stupendous when paired with a stew, beans, sweet fried ripe plantains, a slice of creamy avocado, or a simple tomato salad. Not even complex rice dishes like paella or its New World offshoots like the *arroz con mariscos* (seafood rice) are allowed to shine on their own. To me, the countless dishes in which rice is cooked with vegetables, meats and seafood, or even fruit testify to the innate Latin need to blend all the elements of a dish before eating it. In these cases, though, the blending is done not on the plate but in the pot.

The recipes in this chapter cannot do justice to the richness of the Latin rice kitchen, but I have chosen them to illustrate several major categories of rice cooking, from basic white rice to the wonderful combinations that use rice as a backdrop to all kinds of other foods. I call these compound rice dishes. Perhaps the most important of these are the rice and legume dishes, the living legacy of the Africans who were the first rice cooks of the Americas.

All my life, I have found rice to be an indispensable element of party menus. From a practical standpoint, it can be made in big amounts without ruining your budget, and it can be conveniently prepared ahead of time and reheated. For me it is the anchor of a menu, often the first thing I decide on when planning what to cook. For Sunday lunch with family nothing matches a generous pot of *arroz con pollo* (rice and chicken). Baked rice with cheese and strips of poblano peppers, or with hearts of palm, is an effortless, foolproof recipe for a fancier dinner for eight. Yellow rice brimming with legumes and grains and seasoned with Spanish chorizo is a crowd pleaser for a buffet lunch or brunch that can be served with fried eggs or turned into a salad. In fact, all the recipes in this chapter can be flexibly paired with main courses and side dishes from throughout the book to create complete meals for a small family or for a group of eight to twelve people.

A RICE PRIMER

Types of Rice and Recommended Brands

The types of rice used in Latin cooking vary not only from country to country but also according to the dish. Cubans prefer medium- or short-grain rice for paellas and rice and chicken cooked soupy style (*a la chorrera*), and reserve long-grain rice (particularly Uncle Ben's) for rice and bean combinations. Puerto Ricans use medium-grain rice in all kinds of dishes. Latin Americans call medium-grain rice "Spanish rice" or "Valencia-type rice," generic terms encompassing a number of *japonica* rices that grow along the Mediterranean seaboard of Spain and in other parts of the world, including the United States. Technically speaking, they are all medium-grain rices capable of absorbing lots of liquid while keeping their shape (the rounder true short-grain rices tend to clump together). They are ideal for paellas and soupy rice dishes.

Valencia rices are grown mostly in the Albufera, a marshland area not far from the city of Valencia. I prefer the Bomba rice grown in Calasparra, in the mountains of Murcia, farther south. This is a premium medium-grain rice that is capable of absorbing more liquid than most Valencia types. Unlike Arborio, the Italian risotto rice, which turns creamy with prolonged cooking, Bomba swells up but retains a firm, slightly dry quality. For my soupy-style rice and chicken, I add 6 cups of liquid to 1½ cups of rice and in the end get a pot of rice with moist grains that have not lost their shape or bite. Made with another rice, the same dish would require substantially less liquid.

Latin Americans also classify rice according to quality and price. Not everyone is able to afford premium grades of rice. When you go grocery shopping at a *tienda de abarrotes* (a convenience store specializing in nonperishables) in Ecuador, you'll find several different grades of short-grain and long-grain rice. Long-grain rice ranges in color from yellowish brown to bright white. The least expensive is usually broken-up long-grain rice, followed by rices in shades of yellow—normally bought only by those on very tight budgets. Most cooks feel this yellowish rice has an odd aftertaste, or *tujo*. Those who care about rice and can afford a better quality prefer long-grain rice with very white, perfectly formed grains.

Fortunately, most of the rice available in supermarkets across the United States is of pretty good quality. One of my rules of thumb is to avoid any brand that I've found to have broken or yellowish grains (except, of course, for "converted" rice, which normally has a yellowish tinge that comes from the process of parboiling and does not affect taste). The recipes calling for long-grain rice in this book were tested for the most part with either Canilla (a brand distributed by Goya) or Carolina rice. I found no difference in cooking quality between them. There is no reason not to use any good long-grain rice sold in your area, but I do suggest that you become familiar with one brand and don't try switching to another without making a few test batches. There are subtle variations in absorptive quality that can be disastrous if you're not aware of them. This is even truer of medium-grain rice.

My recipes for dishes with medium-grain rice were tested mostly with imported Arroz Unio and Arroz Montsia Extra from the Ebro River region and Bomba rice from Calasparra in Spain. I highly recommend these three, which are available in Spanish markets and upscale North American specialty food stores and by mail-order. In a pinch, I have used Goya Valencia rice or supermarket brands of American medium-grain rice. You can do the same, but the amounts of liquid in the recipes may need adjusting. Count on using less liquid for soupy rice made with brands other than the Spanish Bomba.

Choosing a Pot

People who cook rice all the time are very particular about the pot they use. You can have good results with different materials or types of pots, but you must keep three things in mind for basic cooked rice: The pot must have a tight-fitting lid, so that steam can build up. The pot must be heavy, so the water doesn't evaporate before the rice is cooked. And, for the same reason, it should not be too wide in relation to its depth: the shape of the pot will affect the rate of evaporation. Expert rice cookers often say that the depth of the water or other liquid (how many inches above the surface of the rice it is when cooking starts) is more important than the particular amount. I've seen cooks stick a spoon into the rice to see whether it stands up by itself—meaning the amount of water is right—or falls over—a sign of too much liquid. Some people check things by sticking a finger in the pot to see whether the water above the rice covers the tip up to the first joint; this is usually a good guide. I must emphasize that even a slight difference in the dimensions of a pot will make a big difference in the timing and success of the rice. For this reason, I give what I consider the optimum pot capacity and dimensions for cooking specific amounts.

I know most of my readers will be using ordinary American saucepans, and these can be fine if they don't differ too widely from the suggested size. The ideal rice pots, in my opinion, are Latin American cast-aluminum *calderos*, described on page 33 (be sure to season any *caldero* well before using it for rice). The material is a good diffuser of heat; the pots have a slightly flared shape, which means it takes less liquid to cover the rice to the right depth; and they have two handles, which comes in handy when cooking a large batch of rice. Any heavy stainless steel saucepan that fits this general description is appropriate for rice cooking. I also like straight-sided casseroles with handles. I own a 5-quart straight-sided lidded copper casserole, 11 inches wide and about 3½ inches deep, that cooks 2 cups rice with vegetables, chicken, pork, and seafood just as well as my favorite *caldero*. For more elaborate soupy-style rice and seafood dishes, you need a taller pan, even for 2 cups of rice, because you will be using more liquid and shellfish takes up a lot of space.

No self-respecting Latin American cook would make less than 2 cups of uncooked rice, even to feed just two people. Nor would she make the mistake of simply doubling or halving a rice recipe to feed more or fewer people. Rice is one of those foods that can't be cooked by an unvarying ratio. In deference to North American prejudices, I am giving formulas for both 1-cup and 2-cup batches, but please don't try anything smaller.

BAKING DISHES

Any ovenproof casserole that can withstand direct heat will be fine for baked rice dishes, but I have to say that for soupy or risotto-like dishes using short-grain or medium-grain rice, nothing is as good as a clay *cazuela*. Not only does it go from stovetop or oven to tabletop more elegantly than anything else, I think that it imparts a wonderful earthy flavor to the rice.

THE PAELLA PAN

To be called paella, the rice must be cooked in the flat, two-handled pan called *paella*, from which the dish took its name. The antecedent of today's paella pan is the Roman *patera*, a ceremonial vessel used in religious and funerary ceremonies as well as in cooking. In its contemporary incarnation, a paella pan is designed to cook rice over an open fire. The shape is so wide that the rice can be spread in one layer with the minimum of water. The wide surface means that it absorbs the aroma of the wood fire.

These qualities are not as relevant when you have to use the stovetop, but the pan can work. However, you have to compensate for the quicker evaporation of moisture by covering the pan with aluminum foil or any lid that fits. Nowadays you can find paella pans made from stainless steel, with lids, imported from Spain. All-Clad, among other American companies, makes a 4-quart paella pan, about 13 inches wide and 2½ inches deep, that works very well. A 12-inch sauté pan or a large skillet fitted with a lid is quite suitable for paella-style dishes.

Working Ahead ▶ Preparing a rice dish for dinner parties and holiday get-togethers does not have to be a labor-intensive proposition if you prepare some of its components ahead of time. You can make *sofritos* and cooking sauces 2 to 3 days ahead and store them in the refrigerator. Poultry and meat can be marinated and partially cooked (to keep it juicy) a few hours before beginning the rice. Then all you need to do is add these to the pot in the order indicated in your recipe.

Storing and Reheating Rice

For me, one of the great blessings of rice is that it can be cooked ahead and stored in the refrigerator for 2 to 3 days. It also freezes well. Let it cool completely and store in freezer bags or plastic containers for up to 3 months. Let it partly thaw before reheating. Rice loses moisture and becomes hard in the refrigerator or freezer, but if you add about 2 tablespoons water per cup of rice when you reheat it, the rice will regain its original moisture.

The microwave is the fastest way of reheating cooked rice. Place the rice in a microwaveproof container and stir in the water. Microwave for 2 to 3 minutes at high power, until the rice is moist and heated through.

To reheat the rice on the stovetop, place it in a pot large enough to let it expand slightly, stir in the water, and heat over the lowest possible heat, tightly covered, for 20 minutes.

I use leftover rice to make croquettes or rice salads or to whip up an impromptu little meal when someone comes to visit out of the blue. But it will be flinty in texture unless you reheat it, even if you then need to let it cool to room temperature before using it.

SEARCHING FOR THE PERFECT FORMULA FOR PLAIN WHITE RICE

Everyone in Latin America agrees that a broad range of textures and degrees of moistness is acceptable in a compound rice dish—a rice and chicken dish can be dry or soupy, an *arroz atollado* (a type of seafood paella from Chocó in Colombia) somewhat lumpy. Where Latins become truly fastidious and opinionated is in the definition of what constitutes perfect plain white rice.

For some, the ideal rice is fluffy and dry, with soft, well-opened grains, and shiny. In Ecuador and coastal Colombia, where rice is often cooked with a 1 to 1½ ratio of water to rice, it is slightly al dente.

In Cuba, a hostess will often ask guests whether they want their rice with or without crust (*raspa*). In coastal Colombia, perfect rice must have well-separated grains, but it is slightly chewy, often with a bottom crust, called *cucayo*. The *cucayo* is not burned, but a delectable, toasted brown layer that comes off the pot easily and that people fight over.

When my Colombian friend Rita Ruíz was very young, she was a Latin bombshell. Every time she went for a stroll with her friends in downtown Barranquilla, she would be accosted by admiring men who brazenly sized her up with their eyes and showered her with *piropos* (suggestive compliments). One day a tall, good-looking young man said to her, "*Si cocinas como caminas, me como hasta el cucayo*" (If you cook the way you walk, I'd eat down to the crust of the rice). Who does not love to eat *cucayo* in Colombia?

To make crusty white rice, *arroz con cucayo*, Rita adds 1 to 2 tablespoons of oil per cup of water to the pot, and when all the water has been absorbed, she lets the rice steam, tightly covered, over low heat for about 20 minutes longer and then increases the heat to medium-low for 10 minutes so it can develop a bottom crust. As for Rita's *cucayo*, the young man who called out the *piropo* came to stick around for forty years of marriage.

To anyone who loves the well-separated rice of Latin America, the sight of lumpy, gummy white rice with broken grains is disgusting, the sign of a bad cook. In Ecuador, lumpy rice is disdainfully called *api*, from the Quechua word for porridge. That's why when Latins go to a Chinese restaurant, they will always order *arroz chaufa* or *arroz frito*, fried rice, instead of the plain Chinese white rice, which they find sticky and flavorless. Every Latin American country has a *criollo* version of fried rice. But every rule has its exceptions, and there are people in Latin America who actually like their rice gummy—the Kuna Indians of Panama, for instance, who husk their own rice with a mortar and pestle. While I was doing research among the Kuna for a book on *molas*, the decorated fabric panels on women's blouses, I had to endure countless meals with rice so gummy that it stuck to the roof of my mouth.

As with bread, all you need to make white rice are elemental ingredients: rice, water or another liquid, and salt. Most cooks also use fat. The proportion of rice, liquid, and fat is the key to the texture.

With long-grain rice, a 1:1 ratio of water to rice will render an al dente rice with well-separated grains. When you add a little more water, let's say 1½ to 1¾ cups water per cup of rice, the grains will have enough moisture to swell but will remain whole and a bit firm. A 2:1 ratio, which is popular in some circles because it helps the rice stretch further, is adequate for some types of short-grain rice, but it may make long-grain rice clump.

If 1 tablespoon fat is added per cup of rice at the start and the rice is cooked over medium-low heat after 20 minutes of undisturbed steaming at very low heat, it will begin to stick to the pot and sometimes to fry. This produces the tasty brown crust that some people fight over. It's another example of how Latin kitchens saw a merging of preferences from Spain and Africa, both of which have a tradition of preparing rice with a crust.

Following are five basic methods of preparing plain white rice, from Cuba, Ecuador, West Africa, and Brazil. They illustrate the most popular methods of cooking white rice all over Latin America, with important variations that affect both texture and flavor.

When testing these recipes, I opted to work with a minimum of 2 cups of raw rice. My aim was to obtain about 4 cups of cooked white rice with separate whole grains to feed 4 to 6 people comfortably as a side dish for most of the plentifully sauced dishes and thick bean soups I offer in this book. My decision was based on my experience feeding Americans both at home and at my restaurant Zafra. To me, about 1 heaping cup of cooked rice per person has always been a safe amount; your guests will be able to mix the rice with the sauce of a stew or a *mole* and mingle it with the other foods of the plate in true Latin style, and to have seconds if they wish.

My editor, however, thought I should reduce the minimum amount of raw rice to 1 cup. She argued that no North American home cook was going to cook that much rice. After much discussion, we settled for the original recipe, along with precise instructions on how to halve it.

All these methods for basic cooked rice involve a cooking period of 20 minutes (after the rice is added to the water and given a brief initial cooking), during which the pot must be tightly covered and the rice left completely undisturbed. Do not lift the lid to look at it, and do not stir it during this period. (I've seen children slapped and adults scolded for taking a peek inside the pot during this sacrosanct time.) The heat must be as low as possible. Just a little too much heat, and the rice will burn. If you have trouble adjusting your burner to an absolute minimum, use a heat deflector such as a Flame Tamer. If you don't have one, improvise with a griddle. On my gas stove, I sometimes raise the pot by putting it on one burner stacked on top of another, to make sure that the flame does not lick the bottom of the pot.

Cuban-Style Rice, One-Step Boiling Method I (Basic Absorption Method)

My aunt Anita, who presided over a genuine rice kitchen back at my grandfather's house in Cuba, added rice to a pot of boiling water seasoned with salt and some lard or oil, cooked it uncovered until most of the liquid was absorbed, and then left it to cook undisturbed, tightly covered, for another 20 minutes. This is a classic Old World technique that probably evolved in Persia and later in India for more elaborate rice dishes such as *pullao*. With the proper ratio of rice to water, it invariably produces fluffy rice with separate grains. I have found this to be one of the preferred cooking techniques for rice in medieval Spanish cookbooks, though the cooking liquid would probably have been well-seasoned, fatty beef broth rather than water, and the rice would have been short-grain.

Recommended Pots: For full recipe—2½- to 3-quart heavy-bottomed 10-inch pot, at least 2 to 3 inches deep, or 3-quart 9-inch cast-aluminum *caldero*, 3 inches deep. For half-recipe—1½- to 2-quart heavy-bottomed 7- to 8-inch pot, at least 2 to 3 inches deep, or 3-quart 9-inch cast-aluminum *caldero*, 3 inches deep.

SERVES 4 TO 6 (MAKES 4 TO 5 CUPS)	
2	cups (about 13 ounces) long-grain rice
3	cups water for firm rice with separate grains (3½ cups water for soft, fluffy rice)
2	tablespoons vegetable oil or lard
1¼	teaspoons salt, or to taste
1	large garlic clove, peeled

SERVES 2 TO 4 (MAKES ABOUT 3 TO 3½ CUPS)	
1	cup (about 6½ ounces) long-grain rice
1¾	cups water
1	tablespoon vegetable oil or lard
¾	teaspoon salt, or to taste
1	large garlic clove, peeled

▶ Place the rice in a medium bowl, cover with cold tap water, and swirl the rice, then drain while holding the rice in place with one hand. Repeat the process as many times as necessary until the water runs clear. Drain well in a sieve or strainer.

Place the water, oil, salt, and garlic in the pot and bring to a rolling boil over high heat. Add the rice, reduce the heat to medium, and simmer, uncovered, until most of the water is absorbed and small craters form on the surface of the rice. Cover tightly and cook over very low heat for 20 minutes. Remove from the heat, uncover, and fluff with a fork. Let rest, covered, for 10 minutes before serving.

Ecuadorian-Style Rice, One-Step Boiling Method II

In Ecuador, from the highlands to the coast, rice is the obligatory accompaniment for stews and thick bean soups (*menestras*) and just about everything, even stewed potatoes and other tubers. The foolproof Ecuadorian ratio for long-grain rice with cleanly separated grains is 1½ cups of water per cup of rice. My friend Mirza Ortíz, who is from Cuenca, puts the rice, cold water, salt, and fat in a pot and brings it all to a boil. When all the liquid is absorbed, she covers the pot and waits for the obligatory 20 minutes of undisturbed cooking before taking an anxious peek inside. I tell her not to worry. She has never cooked a pot of rice by this simple technique that has not come out just perfect.

Recommended Pots: For full recipe—2½- to 3-quart heavy-bottomed 10-inch pot, at least 3 inches deep, or 3-quart 9-inch cast-aluminum *caldero*, 3 inches deep. For half-recipe—1½- to 2-quart heavy-bottomed 7- to 8-inch pot, at least 2 to 3 inches deep, or 1½-quart 7-inch cast-aluminum *caldero*, 3 inches deep.

SERVES 4 TO 6 (5 TO 6 CUPS)	
2	cups (about 13 ounces) long-grain rice
3	cups water for firm rice with separate grains (3½ cups water for soft, fluffy rice)
1½	teaspoons salt, or to taste
2	tablespoons corn oil or vegetable oil

SERVES 2 TO 4 (2 TO 5 CUPS)	
1	cup (about 6½ ounces) long-grain rice
1¾	cups water
	Scant 1 teaspoon salt, or to taste
1	tablespoon corn oil or vegetable oil

▶ Place the rice in a medium bowl, cover with cold tap water, and swirl the rice, then drain while holding the rice in place with one hand. Repeat the process as many times as necessary until the water runs clear. Drain well in a sieve or strainer.

Place the rice, water, salt, and oil in the pot and stir well. Bring to a rolling boil over medium heat and cook, uncovered, for 5 minutes. When most of the water is absorbed and tiny craters form on the surface of the rice, reduce the heat as low as possible, and cover tightly. Cook for 20 minutes undisturbed. Remove from the heat, uncover the pot, fluff with a fork, and cover again. Let rest for 10 minutes before serving.

West African-Style Rice, Two-Step Boiling Method

The West African way of cooking rice involves a two-step method. First the rice is boiled in a large amount of water until it is practically cooked but still whole. Then the rice is drained, returned to the pot, and cooked over a very low fire (originally a spent fire) until all the moisture is absorbed and the grains are separate and firm. Many Latin Americans still cook rice this way, not aware of its African origin, but they almost invariably add some fat when they return the drained rice to the pot. This addition greatly enhances the flavor of the rice and gives it a lovely sheen.

Recommended Pots: For full recipe—2½- to 3-quart heavy-bottomed 10-inch pot, at least 3 inches deep, or 3-quart 9-inch cast-aluminum *caldero*, 3 inches deep. For half-recipe—1½- to 2-quart heavy-bottomed 7- to 8-inch pot, at least 2 inches deep, or 3-quart 9-inch cast-aluminum *caldero*, 3 inches deep.

SERVES 4 TO 6 (MAKES ABOUT 6 CUPS)

- 2 cups (about 13 ounces) long-grain rice
- 2½ quarts water
- 1 tablespoon salt
- 2 tablespoons vegetable oil, lard, or mild olive oil

SERVES 2 TO 4 (MAKES ABOUT 3 CUPS)

- 1 cup (about 6½ ounces) long-grain rice
- 2 quarts water
- 2 teaspoons salt
- 1 tablespoon vegetable oil, lard, or mild olive oil

▶ Place the rice in a medium bowl, cover with cold tap water, and swirl the rice, then drain while holding the rice in place with one hand. Repeat the process as many times as necessary until the water runs clear. Drain well in a sieve or strainer.

Place the water and salt in the pot and bring to a rolling boil over high heat. Lower the heat to medium, stir in the rice, and simmer, uncovered, for about 12 minutes. At once drain the rice in a sieve. Return the rice to the pot, add the fat, and stir with a fork. Cover tightly and cook over the absolute lowest heat, undisturbed, for 20 minutes. Remove from the heat and fluff the rice with a fork. Cover the pot again and let sit for 10 minutes before serving.

Cuban-Style Simple Pilaf, Method I

Plain white rice is a Cuban favorite, served along-side thick bean soups and stews. It is also frequently topped with a fried egg (my favorite way of eating rice). Though I loved my aunt Anita's rice, I thought the white rice made by Inés, one of our cooks, was much more flavorful. Inés (unknowingly) made a pilaf, first sautéing the rice in fat with a couple of garlic cloves until well coated. Then she added the water and let it be totally absorbed before lowering the heat, covering the pot, and cooking the rice for 20 minutes longer. Along the Caribbean coast of Colombia, cooks use a similar ratio of water and rice and follow the same cooking method, but they seldom use garlic. This style of rice cooking was brought by the Muslims to Spain and coexisted there with other ways of cooking rice.

Recommended Pots: For full recipe—2½- to 3-quart heavy-bottomed 10-inch pot, at least 3 inches deep, or 3-quart 9-inch cast-aluminum *caldero*, 3 inches deep. For half-recipe—1½- to 2-quart heavy-bottomed 7- to 8-inch pot, at least 2 to 3 inches deep, or 3-quart 9-inch cast-aluminum *caldero*, 3 inches deep.

SERVES 4 TO 6 (MAKES 4 TO 5 CUPS)

- 2 cups (about 13 ounces) long-grain rice
- 2 tablespoons mild olive oil, corn oil, or lard
- 2 large garlic cloves, lightly crushed
- 3 cups water for firm rice with separate grains (3½ cups water for soft, fluffy rice)
- 1¼ tablespoon salt

SERVES 2 TO 4 (MAKES ABOUT 3 CUPS)

- 1 cup (about 6½ ounces) long-grain rice
- 1 tablespoon light olive oil, corn oil, or lard
- 1 large garlic clove, lightly crushed
- 1¾ cups water
- ¾ teaspoon salt

▶ Place the rice in a medium bowl, cover with cold tap water, and swirl the rice, and then drain while holding the rice in place with one hand. Repeat the process as many times as necessary until the water runs clear. Drain well in a sieve or strainer.

Heat the oil in the pot. Add garlic and sauté for 10 seconds. Add the rice and cook, stirring, until all the grains are coated, about 1 minute. Stir in the water and bring to a rolling boil. Cook over medium heat until most of the water is absorbed and small craters form on the surface of the rice, about 12 minutes. Cover and cook over very low heat for 20 minutes. Remove from the heat and fluff the rice with a fork. Cover and let sit for 10 minutes.

Brazilian-Style Simple Pilaf, Method II

Brazilians adore rice. In some parts of the country where Africans had an impact, as in Salvador da Bahia, you might find women cooking the rice by the African method. But wherever there is a Portuguese influence, you will not find bland plain white rice. Though the rice is meant to be paired with flavorful saucy foods, many Brazilians prefer their white rice to have a flavor of its own, so they follow the pilaf method of sautéing it first in some fat with garlic, onion, and other seasonings, such as scallions and even bay leaf. This is typical of Minas Gerais.

Recommended Pots: For full recipe—2½- to 3-quart heavy-bottomed 10-inch pot, at least 2 to 3 inches deep, or 3-quart 9-inch cast-aluminum *caldero*, 3 inches deep. For half-recipe—1½- to 2-quart heavy-bottomed 7- to 8-inch pot, at least 2 to 3 inches deep, or 3-quart 9-inch cast-aluminum *caldero*, 3 inches deep.

SERVES 4 TO 6 (MAKES ABOUT 4¼ CUPS)	
2	cups (about 13 ounces) long-grain rice
2	tablespoons corn oil or lard
½	small yellow onion, finely chopped
2	large garlic cloves, lightly crushed
1	bay leaf
3	cups water
1¼	tablespoon salt

SERVES 2 TO 4 (MAKES ABOUT 3 CUPS)	
1	cup (about 6½ ounces) long-grain rice
1	tablespoon corn oil or lard
½	small yellow onion, finely chopped
1	large garlic clove, lightly crushed
1	bay leaf
1¾	cups water
½	teaspoon salt plus a pinch

▶ Place the rice in a medium bowl, cover with cold tap water, and swirl the rice, then drain while holding the rice in place with one hand. Repeat the process as many times as necessary until the water runs clear. Drain well in a sieve or strainer.

Heat the oil in the pot over medium heat. Add the onion and garlic and sauté, stirring, until the onion is translucent. Add the rice and bay leaf and sauté, stirring, until all the grains are well coated in the fat; do not brown. Stir in the water and salt and bring to a rolling boil. Cook over medium heat for 12 to 15 minutes, or until the water evaporates and small craters form on the surface of the rice. Cover and cook, undisturbed, over very low heat for 20 minutes. Remove from the heat and fluff the rice with a fork. Cover and let sit for 10 minutes. Remove the bay leaf before serving.

COLORED AND FLAVORED RICE

A simple pot of rice colored gold with achiote-infused oil or saffron, or olive green with cilantro and peppers, or brick red with tomatoes, paprika, or ground dried hot red peppers, is the cook's best friend. With little effort, the rice is dressed up a notch in color and flavor, offering much more than a tabula rasa for other foods on the plate.

For many colored rices, you don't even need a recipe. You can simply put one together by starting with 2 cups of rice, one of the prepared cooking sauces in "The Layers of Latin Flavor" chapter, and some broth, canned for convenience or homemade for pure, unadulterated flavor (see the basic broth recipes in the soup chapter), or even water. Start by heating at least ¼ cup of the cooking sauce in an appropriate pot (see "Choosing a Pot," page 290) and adding the raw rice. Cook, stirring, to coat the rice with the sauce, then stir in the broth or water. If using long-grain rice, use the proportions indicated in Brazilian-Style Simple Pilaf, Method I, page 294. Taste for salt and follow the usual technique of boiling the rice until craters appear. Then stir the rice carefully with a fork, reduce the heat to very low, cover, and cook the rice undisturbed for 20 minutes.

Starting with this basic method, you can get creative and add vegetables and legumes (freshly cooked or canned), sautéed ham, bacon, and/or sausage (or anything that tickles your fancy) to the rice. Here are a few suggestions for quick colored rices.

For yellow rice: Use 2 to 3 tablespoons achiote-infused olive oil (page 89) for plain yellow rice, Ecuadorian Golden Cooking Sauce (page 52) for fuller flavor, or Peruvian *Ají Mirasol* Cooking Sauce (page 53) for color and spicy flavor.

For reddish rice: Use Light Tomato Sauce (page 48), Veracruz Tomato Sauce for Fish (page 48), or Valle del Cauca Cooking Sauce (page 51). Or use Bogotá Cheese Cooking Sauce (page 52), holding the cheese and stirring it into the rice at the end of cooking; Three-Step Mexican Chile Cooking Sauce (page 55) for color and heat; or Dominican *Sofrito* (page 57) or Puerto Rican *Sofrito* (page 59) for color, the musky flavor of the tiny Caribbean pepper (*ají dulce*), and the aroma of cilantro.

For deep red rice: Boil a few beets (preferibly sliced to extract more color) and use the intense red cooking liquid instead of broth.

For greenish rice: Use Dominican Traveling *Sazón* (page 56) or Charito's Puerto Rican Seasoning Mix (page 58) for color and the aroma of the tiny Caribbean sweet pepper (*ají dulce*) and cilantro.

Colored Rice Starting with Cooked Plain White Rice

This is a quick way of coloring and flavoring cooked rice that is popular in some Latin restaurants. Heat a small amount of oil in a well-seasoned wok or nonstick skillet over medium heat until shimmering, and stir in the cooked rice and the cooking sauce of your choice. Pour in some broth as you stir for more flavor and to add moisture to the cooked rice. Lower the heat and let the rice absorb the flavors of the sauce.

This is the basic technique, believe it or not, for many of the compound rice dishes served in restaurants, from rice and chicken to paella and *gallo pinto*, the traditional rice and legume mix of Central America (page 313). It saves the customer waiting time, though few diners suspect that their paella, which comes to the table in an authentic paella pan, has actually been stir-fried.

Fried Coconut Rice with Raisins from Cartagena

Arroz Titoté (Frito) con Coco y Pasas Cartagenero

The cuisine of Cartagena is tinted with the colors and flavors of the Caribbean. Anywhere one walks in "the little stone corral" (*corralito de piedra*), as Colombians endearingly call this small but majestic fortified city, you glimpse slivers of the blue Caribbean shimmering through the windows in the massive city walls. Walking past saffron-colored mansions at noontime, you smell the aroma of fried fish and hear the sizzling hiss of coconut milk as it turns into fragrant oil in heavy iron pots. This scent and sound indicate a strong Afro-Caribbean presence even in this most Spanish city of Colombia.

Coconut milk is the key ingredient of Cartagena's famed coconut rice. While proportions and ingredients vary from cook to cook, everyone agrees that there are two distinct ways of preparing it: boiled (*hervido*) or fried (*titoté*). The first is a simple dish of rice boiled in the coconut milk. The "fried" coconut rice is a richer, more flavorful version, speckled with flecks of brown coconut. The rice is not really fried but sautéed in a few tablespoons of freshly rendered coconut oil to give it a golden brown color and a slightly chewy texture. The subtle sweetness and delicious aroma the coconut milk imparts to this dish make it an excellent complement to other local specialties, such as clove-scented baked plantains (*plátanos pícaros*) and roast beef tongue.

Cook's Note: This dish calls for fresh coconut milk, both a creamy one and a lighter one. If you follow the instructions on page 50, you will find that the process of extracting these two types of coconut milk is a bit lengthy but not difficult at all. I tried using canned coconut milk instead of fresh here, only to find that there is no substitute for the fresh stuff.

Recommended Pots: 3-quart heavy-bottomed 10- to 12-inch pot, at least 3 inches deep, or 3-quart 10- to 11-inch cast-aluminum *caldero*, 3 inches deep.

SERVES 8 (MAKES ABOUT 9 CUPS)

- 2½ cups (about 1 pound) long-grain rice
- 1½ cups Creamy ("First") Coconut Milk (page 50)
- 2 tablespoons grated brown loaf sugar (preferably Colombian *panela*), Demerara sugar, or light brown sugar
- 1½ cups (about 9 ounces) dark raisins
- 4 cups Light ("Second") Coconut Milk (page 51)
- 1½ teaspoons salt

▶ Place the rice in a medium bowl, cover with cold tap water, and swirl the rice, then drain while holding the rice in place with one hand. Repeat the process as many times as necessary until the water runs clear. Drain well in a sieve or strainer.

Pour the creamy coconut milk into the pot and bring to a boil over medium heat. As soon as the coconut milk begins to separate into thick solid particles and a clear oil, start stirring constantly with a wooden spoon. In about 10 minutes, the solids will become a crusty light brown mass and the oil will have separated completely from the solids. This oil will be used to sauté the rest of the ingredients.

Add the sugar, stir well until dissolved, and then add the raisins. Add the rice and sauté, stirring, for 5 minutes, or until the grains are a light gold and well coated in the coconut oil. Add the light coconut milk and salt, stir to combine, and cook over medium heat until most of the liquid is absorbed.

Reduce the heat to the lowest possible setting, cover tightly, and cook for 20 minutes. Remove from the heat, uncover, and fluff the rice with a fork. The aroma of coconut will rise from the pot and the rice will be a lovely golden color with bits of brown coconut. Let sit for at least 10 minutes, covered, before serving.

Serving: Serve with Pot-Roasted Stuffed Eye of Round Cartagena Style (page 707) and Drunken Stewed Plantains (page 190).

Yucatecan Saffron Rice

Arroz Yucateco Azafranado

In Yucatán, remnants of Maya cuisine coexist with marvelous Old World recipes that hark back to the colonial period, such as this lush saffron rice. This is one of my favorite dishes for company and holiday entertaining, and an ideal foil for the quintessential Yucatecan pork dish, *cochinita pibil* (page 725).

Recommended Pots: 4-quart 10- to 12-inch heavy-bottomed pot, at least 3 inches deep, or 4-quart 11-inch cast-aluminum *caldero*, 3 inches deep.

SERVES 6

2 cups (about 13 ounces) long-grain rice
1 teaspoon saffron threads
3 cups chicken broth, homemade (page 538) or store-bought, or the *salpimentado* from Yucatecan *Lima* Soup (page 536)
3 tablespoons corn oil or extra-virgin olive oil
8 medium plum tomatoes (about 1½ pounds), peeled, seeded, and finely chopped
1 medium white onion (about 8 ounces), finely chopped (about 1¼ cups)
1 medium green bell pepper (6–7 ounces), cored, seeded, deveined, and finely chopped (about 1 cup)
1 to 1½ teaspoons salt, or to taste

▶ Place the rice in a medium bowl, cover with cold tap water, and swirl the rice, then drain while holding the rice in place with one hand. Repeat the process as many times as necessary until the water runs clear. Drain well in a sieve or strainer.

In a small cup, soak the saffron in a little of the broth.

Heat the oil in the pot over medium heat. Add the rice and sauté until light gold, about 5 minutes. Stir in the tomatoes, onion, green pepper, and saffron and sauté for 10 minutes. Stir in the broth and salt and bring to a boil, then cook over medium-high heat until most of the water has been absorbed and small bubbly craters begin to form on the surface of the rice, about 15 minutes. Reduce the heat to very low, cover tightly, and cook for 20 minutes.

Fluff the rice with a fork and let sit for 10 minutes, uncovered, before serving.

Serving: Serve as a side dish for *cochinita pibil* or Yucatecan Refried Beans (page 276), with a bowl of Yucatecan Red Onions Pickled in Bitter Orange Juice (page 149).

Mexican Rice

Sopa Seca de Arroz Mexicana

Rice was introduced to Mexico by the Spaniards and was quickly embraced as a staple side dish. The term *sopa seca* (literally, dry soup) is difficult for non-Mexicans to understand, since they don't see how a soup could be dry. The idea is simply that the rice is cooked in abundant liquid like a soup but that it is all absorbed. On colonial Mexican menus, *sopa seca* used to follow a "soupy soup," or *sopa caldosa*—a real soup.

The key to making perfect Mexican rice is to sauté it in fat until the color changes to a golden beige. Then add onion, garlic, tomatoes (in many versions, pureed), and broth and cook until the rice absorbs all the lovely flavors. In Mexico, I have seen restaurant cooks sautéing the rice in lots of oil until golden brown, then draining and discarding the fat before proceeding with the dish.

I learned this recipe from the family cooks at the house of Juan Castillo, a dairy farmer in the town of Huexca in Morelos State. This was the rice dish served to a thousand guests on the occasion of the fifteenth birthday of his niece Marisol Pérez. I was in awe of the cooks' skill as they turned out pot after pot of perfectly cooked rice without a single lump.

Recommended Pots: 3½-quart heavy-bottomed 10- to 11-inch pot, at least 3 inches deep, or 3½-quart 10-inch cast-aluminum *caldero*, 3 inches deep.

SERVES 4 TO 6

- 2 cups (about 13 ounces) long-grain rice
- 4 medium plum tomatoes (about 12 ounces), seeded and quartered
- 1 medium white onion (about 8 ounces), coarsely chopped (about 1½ cups)
- 2 large garlic cloves, peeled
- 4 tablespoons safflower or canola oil or mild olive oil
- 3 cups chicken broth, homemade (page 538) or store-bought, or water
- 1¼ teaspoons salt, only if using store-bought low-sodium broth or water

▶ Place the rice in a medium bowl, cover with cold tap water, and swirl the rice, then drain while holding the rice in place with one hand. Repeat the process as many times as necessary until the water runs clear. Drain well in a sieve or strainer.

Place the tomatoes, onion, and garlic in a food processor and process to a fine puree. Transfer to a medium bowl and set aside.

Heat the oil in the pot over medium heat. Add the rice and sauté, stirring, until light gold, 5 to 7 minutes. Add the tomato-onion puree and cook, stirring often, until the mixture becomes bright orange, about 3 minutes. Stir in the broth and add the salt, if using. Bring to a boil and cook, undisturbed, until most of the liquid has been absorbed and craters appear on the surface of the rice, 8 to 10 minutes. Reduce the heat to very low, cover, and steam until the rice is tender, about 20 minutes. Remove the pot from the heat and let sit, undisturbed, for 10 minutes, then fluff the rice with a fork.

Serving: Serve as a side dish for *barbacoa* (page 698), *moles* (pages 771–85), *pepianes* (pages 764 and 765), or any Mexican-style entrée.

RICE WITH VEGETABLES AND CHEESE

Colombian-Style Rice with Caribbean Pumpkin

Arroz con Auyama

In my travels along the Caribbean coast of Colombia, particularly the towns of Barranquilla, Sabana la Larga, and Soledad, I found delicious rice dishes. One of my favorites, which I learned from Hilda Lapeira de García in Barranquilla, is this rice with *auyama*, the Caribbean name for West Indian pumpkin. The pumpkin is cut into small pieces and practically melts into the rice as it cooks, coloring it a lovely orange hue.

Recommended Pots: 2½- to 3-quart heavy-bottomed 10- to 11-inch pot, at least 3 inches deep, or 3-quart 9- to 10-inch cast-aluminum *caldero*, 3 inches deep.

SERVES 6

- 2 cups (about 13 ounces) long-grain rice
- 3 tablespoons extra-virgin olive oil
- 4 garlic cloves, mashed to a paste with a mortar and pestle or finely chopped and mashed
- 1 medium yellow onion (about 8 ounces), finely chopped (about 1½ cups)
- 1 small red bell pepper (about 5 ounces), cored, seeded, deveined, and finely chopped (about ½ cup)
- 1 pound *calabaza* (West Indian pumpkin) or Hubbard, butternut, or kabocha squash, peeled, seeded, and cut into ½-inch cubes (3½–4 cups)
- 3 cups chicken broth, homemade (page 538) or store-bought, or water
- 1 bay leaf
- 1¼ teaspoons salt, only if using water or low-sodium broth
- 2 tablespoons finely chopped cilantro (optional)

▶ Place the rice in a medium bowl, cover with cold tap water, and swirl the rice, and then drain while holding the rice in place with one hand. Repeat the process as many times as necessary until the water runs clear. Drain well in a sieve or strainer.

Heat the oil in the pot over medium heat. Add the garlic and cook for 20 seconds. Add the onion and red bell pepper and sauté for about 5 minutes. Add the rice and cook, stirring, for 2 minutes. Add the pumpkin, broth, bay leaf, and salt, bring to a boil, and cook over medium heat until most of the liquid is absorbed and small craters appear, about 15 minutes.

Stir in the chopped cilantro, if using, lower the heat to the lowest possible setting, cover tightly, and cook for 20 minutes. Remove from the heat and fluff the rice with a fork. Cover again and let sit for 10 minutes. Remove the bay leaf before serving.

Serving: I like to play with this rice once it is cooked, mixing it with chopped scallions and grated sharp or creamy fresh cheese, or sometimes diced fresh cheese.

Colombian Rice with Cheese

Arroz con Queso Blanco o Costeño

Tangy, lightly salted fresh cheese is used in savory dishes and sweets all over Colombia. I first ate this simple white rice flavored with grated cheese in the town of Santa Marta, on the Caribbean coast, where it usually accompanies stews, breaded steaks, fried ripe plantains, and simple tomato and avocado salads. It is considered a *plato de diario*, an everyday dish, one way of transforming the ever-present white rice into something a bit fancier.

Cook's Note: I also often stir-fry plain cooked rice with about ½ cup Bogotá Cheese Cooking Sauce (page 52) and finish it with grated sharp cheese like Mexican *cotija*.

Recommended Pots: 2½- to 3-quart heavy-bottomed 10-inch pot, at least 3 inches deep, or 3-quart 9-inch cast-aluminum *caldero*, 3 inches deep.

SERVES 4 TO 6

2 cups (about 13 ounces) long-grain rice

3 cups water

¼ teaspoon salt if using a salty cheese, or more to taste if using a milder cheese

2 tablespoons corn oil

2 cups finely grated fresh cow's-milk cheese (a soft *queso blanco* or an aged *queso costeño*, similar to Mexican *cotija* or ricotta salata) or Monterey Jack cheese (about 8 ounces)

▶ Place the rice in a medium bowl, cover with cold tap water, and swirl the rice, then drain while holding the rice in place with one hand. Repeat the process as many times as necessary until the water runs clear. Drain well in a sieve or strainer.

Place the rice, water, and salt in the pot and bring to a boil over medium heat. Boil until the water is almost all absorbed, about 12 minutes. Stir in the oil and cheese, reduce the heat to low, and cook, tightly covered, for 20 minutes.

Remove from the heat, fluff the rice with a fork, and let sit, covered, for 10 minutes before serving.

Rice with Corn, Chickpeas, Green Beans, and Chorizo

Arroz con Maíz, Garbanzos, Habichuelas, y Chorizo

When I was a student at Miami Dade College in the 1970s, my English teacher, Piedad Robertson, a Cuban-American woman whom I admired for her panache and terrific cooking (very French, à la Julia Child, in those days), threw a party for the faculty and students of the Modern Languages Department.

She was known for her elaborate fêtes, and I was expecting no less than caviar. But Piedad made a simple but flavorful rice with vegetables, a Cuban beef hash, and a salad, and I watched how everyone, Anglos and Latinos, went back for seconds, cleaning their plates. The party was declared a success, and I was left with a valuable lesson: good flavor rules.

From that day, I have not hesitated to create menus around a pot of rice cooked with vegetables. In Latin American and Caribbean cooking, it is common to find rice combined with grains, legumes, and starchy vegetables and seasoned with slab bacon or chorizo. Every country and cook has developed many permutations of this theme. Here the pungent and richly colored Spanish sausage cured with paprika will not only impart flavor but tint the rice. Sometimes I omit the chorizo, though I love it, and cook the rice with vegetable broth or water. It saves me the trouble of preparing something special for a vegetarian friend.

Recommended Pots: 5-quart heavy-bottomed 11-inch pot, at least 3 inches deep; or 4- to 5-quart 10- to 11-inch cast-aluminum *caldero*, 3 inches deep.

SERVES 4 TO 6

- 2 cups (about 13 ounces) long-grain rice
- 3 tablespoons achiote-infused olive oil (page 89)
- 6 ounces Spanish chorizo (about three 3½-inch sausages or one and a half 7-inch sausages), cut into ¼-inch dice or ¼-inch rounds
- 3 large garlic cloves, finely chopped
- 1 medium yellow onion (about 8 ounces), finely chopped (about 1½ cups)
- 1 medium green bell pepper (about 7 ounces), cored, seeded, deveined, and finely chopped (about 1 cup)
- 4 medium plum tomatoes (about 12 ounces), peeled and finely chopped, or 4 canned tomatoes, drained and finely chopped
- 1 cup fresh or frozen corn kernels
- One 15-ounce can chickpeas, drained and rinsed, or 2 cups plain cooked chickpeas
- 4 ounces Green Beans with Bacon (page 264)
- 3½ cups chicken broth, homemade (page 538), or store-bought, or water

▶ Place the rice in a medium bowl, cover with cold tap water, and swirl the rice, then drain while holding the rice in place with one hand. Repeat the process as many times as necessary until the water runs clear. Drain well in a sieve or strainer.

Heat the oil in the pot over medium heat. Add the chorizo and sauté until golden brown, about 5 minutes. Add the garlic, onion, and green pepper and sauté until the onion is translucent, about 5 minutes. Add the tomatoes and cook until soft, about 5 minutes. Add the corn, chickpeas, green beans, rice, and broth and bring to a boil over high heat. Lower the heat to medium and simmer, uncovered, until most of the liquid is absorbed and small craters form. Fluff the rice lightly with a fork, cover tightly, and cook over the lowest possible heat for about 20 minutes. Remove from the heat and let sit, covered, for about 10 minutes; fluff again before serving.

Serving: Serve as a side dish for any type of meat or fish. This is also delicious with fried eggs and a Chilean Tomato Salad (page 549) or a Cuban Avocado, Watercress, and Pineapple Salad (page 548).

Baked Rice with Pumpkin, Poblanos, and Cilantro

Arroz con Calabaza, Rajas de Poblano, y Cilantro

Most cooks have at least one favorite dish that always makes them look good when company appears out of the blue. This is my life-saving rice—a simple but elegant casserole with time-honored flavors that still seduce. Like most rice casseroles, it can be made ahead of time and reheated before serving.

Recommended Pots: 2½- to 3-quart heavy-bottomed 10-inch pot, at least 3 inches deep, or 3-quart 9- to 10-inch cast-aluminum *caldero*, 3 inches deep.

SERVES 6 TO 8

- 3 cups (about 1 pound 3 ounces) long-grain rice
- 2 tablespoons extra-virgin olive oil
- 2 large garlic cloves, finely chopped
- 6 scallions, white and pale green parts, finely chopped (about ⅓ cup)
- 1 tablespoon Muscovado sugar or dark brown sugar
- ¼ teaspoon ground cumin
- ¼ teaspoon ground cinnamon
- 5 cups chicken broth, homemade (page 538) or store-bought
- 1 tablespoon cider vinegar
- 1 teaspoon salt, or to taste
- 1 pound *calabaza* (West Indian pumpkin) or Hubbard, butternut, or kabocha squash, peeled, seeded, and cut into ½-inch dice (3½–4 cups)
- 1 cup grated fresh cow's milk cheese, preferably a soft *queso fresco*, Monterey Jack, or Muenster (about 3 ounces)
- ½ cup Mexican *crema* (page 148), or crème fraîche
- 6 poblano chiles (about 1¾ pounds) roasted (see page 67), stemmed, seeded, and cut into ¼-inch-wide strips
- ¼ cup finely chopped cilantro

▶ Place the rice in a medium bowl, cover with cold tap water, and swirl the rice, then drain while holding the rice in place with one hand. Repeat the process as many times as necessary until the water runs clear. Drain well in a sieve or strainer.

Heat the oil in the pot over medium heat. Add the garlic and sauté until golden, about 40 seconds. Add the scallions and sauté for 1 minute. Add the rice, sugar, cumin, and cinnamon and sauté, stirring to coat the grains of rice, for 2 minutes. Add the broth, vinegar, and salt, bring to a boil over medium heat, and cook until almost all the liquid is absorbed. Stir in the pumpkin, reduce the heat to the lowest possible setting, and cook, tightly covered, for 20 minutes. Preheat the oven to 350°F. Butter an 8-by-10-inch glass baking dish. Remove the rice from the heat and stir in the cheese, *crema*, roasted chile strips, and cilantro. Firmly pack the rice into the buttered baking dish. Bake for 20 minutes. Unmold onto a serving platter.

Variations: The rice mixture also makes an excellent stuffing for poblano chiles, red bell peppers, and Spanish *piquillo* peppers.

Soupy Skillet Rice with Vegetables and Legumes

Arroz Caldoso con Vegetales y Legumbres

I decided long ago that the only paella worth its salt is not the surf-and-turf version combining a plethora of seafood with chicken and pork or the seafood extravaganza you find in most touristy restaurants in Spain and Latin America. True Valencian paella is rather austere, combining vegetables in season such as artichokes and the broad white beans known as *garrofón* (the Valencian name for dried lima beans) with rabbit, chicken, or snails.

I like to prepare paella-like rice dishes such as this in a flared heavy nonstick skillet with a lid. It is much easier to clean than a traditional paella pan, and it gives me the advantage of a broad surface for even cooking.

The recipe calls for fresh artichokes (which grow beautifully in Peru's coastal valley), meaty mushrooms, and three South American favorites, fresh cranberry beans, dried lima beans (*pallares*), and fava beans, flavored with a savory Latin-inspired tomato and onion *sofrito* colored gold with achiote-infused oil. Like most Latin Americans, I prefer the dish to be a bit soupy and the rice not as firm as in Spain. The skillet and other New World liberties aside, a judicious pinch of saffron softened in some wine anchors it firmly in the centuries-old rice cuisine of Mediterranean Spain.

Cook's Notes: My recipe calls for fresh vegetables, but feel free to use canned or jarred artichokes and canned beans instead of the cranberry beans.

What to Drink: A fruity and fresh Bodegas Lurton Pinot Gris from Mendoza, Argentina

SERVES 4

For the Vegetables
- 1 pound fresh cranberry beans, shelled (about 1 cup)
- 4 medium artichokes (about 2 pounds)
- 1 lime, halved
- 1 pound fresh fava beans, shelled (about 1 cup) and peeled
- 4 ounces chanterelle, oyster, or shiitake mushrooms
- ½ cup dried lima beans, soaked and simmered according to the directions on page 282

For the Rice
- 1 generous pinch of saffron
- ¼ cup dry white wine
- 1 cup medium-grain Valencia-style rice, preferably Montsia Extra or Unio from the Ebro region or Bomba from Calasparra
- ¼ cup achiote-infused extra-virgin olive oil (page 89)
- 4 garlic cloves, finely minced
- 1 medium yellow onion (about 8 ounces), finely chopped (about 1 cup)
- 1 small red bell pepper (about 4 ounces), cored, seeded, deveined, and finely chopped (about ⅔ cup)
- 1 small green bell pepper (about 4 ounces), cored, seeded, deveined, and finely chopped (about ½ cup)
- 4 medium plum tomatoes (about 12 ounces), peeled, seeded, and finely chopped, or 4 canned tomatoes, drained, seeded, and finely chopped
- 1 teaspoon freshly ground black pepper
- 1 teaspoon sweet *pimentón* (Spanish smoked paprika)
- ½ teaspoon ground cumin
  Salt
- 4 cups chicken broth, homemade (page 538) or store-bought, or vegetable broth

- 2 medium red bell peppers (about 8 ounces each), roasted (see page 67), peeled, cored, seeded, and cut into ½-inch-wide strips, or 12 jarred *piquillo* peppers, drained and cut into 1-inch-wide strips

Preparing the Vegetables ▶ Place the cranberry beans in a medium pot, cover with 1 quart water, and bring to boil over medium-high heat. Lower the heat to medium and simmer for 20 minutes, or until tender. Drain and set aside.

Meanwhile, rinse the artichokes under running warm water. One at a time, holding each by the stem, trim by first bending and then pulling off the tougher green leaves. Slice off the pale green inner core of leaves to expose the choke. Remove the choke by cutting at an angle with a paring knife or scoop it out with a serrated or pointed spoon. As you work, rub the cut portions with lime juice to prevent discoloration. Cut off and discard the stems and trim off any dark green parts. Place the hearts in a medium bowl of cold water as you prepare them, then squeeze in the rest of the lime juice. Set aside.

Place the fava beans in a small saucepan with 3 cups water and ½ teaspoon salt and bring to a boil over medium heat, then reduce the heat and simmer for 3 minutes. Drain, let cool, and peel. Set aside.

Rinse the mushrooms and pat dry. Cut into halves or quarters, depending on their size. Discard stems if using shiitakes. Set aside. Drain well in a sieve or strainer.

Preparing the Rice ▶ Lightly toast the saffron in a hot skillet for a few seconds. Combine with the wine in a small cup and let soak until ready to use.

Place the rice in a medium bowl, cover with cold tap water, and swirl the rice, then drain while holding the rice in place with one hand. Repeat until the water runs clear. Set aside. Drain well in a sieve or strainer.

Heat the oil in a 12-inch nonstick or well-seasoned skillet over high heat. Add the garlic and sauté until fragrant, about 30 seconds. Add the onion and sauté for 5 minutes. Stir in the bell peppers and sauté for 3 minutes. Add the mushrooms and sauté for about 3 minutes. Add the tomatoes and sauté for about 5 minutes, until the excess juices evaporate. Stir in the black pepper, paprika, cumin, and salt to taste (about 2 teaspoons) and sauté for 1 minute. Add the rice and sauté, stirring to coat the grains thoroughly, for 1 minute. Pour in the broth, bring to a boil over medium-high heat, and cook for 10 minutes.

Stir in the artichokes and cranberry beans, cover with a lid or aluminum foil, lower the heat to the lowest possible setting, and cook for 20 minutes, or until the rice is tender and still a bit soupy.

Stir in the fava and lima beans and warm through; transfer to a *cazuela* or decorative serving platter. Garnish with the strips of roasted bell pepper or *piquillo* pepper.

Serving: Serve as a vegetarian main course or as a side dish for grilled fish, seafood, or chicken. Bring to the table with a bowl of pungent *allioli* (page 135), the traditional accompaniment for some rice dishes in Alicante.

Baked Rice with Hearts of Palm

Arroz con Palmitos

In countries where hearts of palm are a staple, such as Costa Rica and Brazil, there are numerous rice and *palmito* dishes. This is my own version, an easy-to-assemble casserole of salmon-colored rice and *palmitos* enriched by a light tomato sauce and a creamy cheese mixture.

SERVES 8

- 5 cups cooked white rice (about 1 recipe Brazilian-Style Simple Pilaf, Method II, page 298)
- 4 scallions, white and pale green parts, finely chopped (about ½ cup)
- 1½ cups Light Tomato Sauce (page 48), or canned tomato sauce
- ½ cup Mexican *crema* (page 148) or crème fraîche
- 1 cup grated Monterey Jack cheese (about 4 ounces)
- ¼ cup plus 1 tablespoon freshly grated Parmigiano-Reggiano cheese
- Two 14-ounce cans hearts of palm, drained and cut into ¼-inch rounds (about 3½ cups)
- 2 tablespoons butter

▶ Preheat the oven to 350°F. Butter an 8-by-10-inch glass baking dish.

In a large bowl, combine the rice, scallions, tomato sauce, *crema*, Monterey Jack cheese, and ¼ cup of the Parmigiano. Gently mix in the hearts of palm, taking care not to break them. Spoon the rice mixture into the baking dish. Dot with the butter and sprinkle with the remaining Parmigiano.

Bake for 20 minutes. Unmold onto a decorative platter and serve.

RICE AND BEANS

Historically, rice and beans were the food of the coastal plains of tropical America, from Mexico down to Brazil on the Atlantic and Peru on the Pacific—plantation lands where slaves survived on just a few staples. The idea of cooking rice with legumes is very old. It came to the Americas with the Spaniards and with the Africans as well, becoming a favorite combination for everyone, *criollos*, Africans, and Indians alike.

There is no mystery to the numerous regional variations on the theme. Rice and bean cookery follows the unwritten rules of seasoning that distinguish each region or country of the Americas. In Puerto Rico and the Dominican Republic, for instance, rice and green pigeon peas are seasoned with a *recado*. In eastern Cuba, cooks often flavor their rice and red kidney bean combinations with thyme and allspice, as in nearby Jamaica. Along the Caribbean coast of Central America as well as in coastal Colombia, rich coconut milk enters the pot. In Costa Rica, rice and beans are sautéed in a skillet and seasoned with the country's cooking sauce enriched with a dash of Worcestershire sauce to make a dish called *gallo pinto* (page 313).

When I was staying at the farm of my friend Gloria Cuadras in Ticuantepe, Nicaragua, I was invariably awakened at the crack of dawn by the mooing of Gloria's cows and the aroma of her *gallo pinto*. As in Costa Rica, *gallo pinto* is breakfast food. Leftover rice and beans are mixed together with a rich tomato *sofrito*, but whatever the cook wants, even spaghetti, also goes into the pot.

In Miami, where hardworking Nicaraguans

have left their mark on the restaurant scene, *gallo pinto* is served with all meals. At the popular steakhouse Los Ranchos in Sweetwater, a waiter carries a large platter of *gallo pinto* surrounded by fried ripe plantains and plantain chips from table to table, replenishing the diners' plates.

Moors and Christians

Moros y Cristianos

For seven centuries, Moors and Christians fought one another in Spain, but in the guise of black beans and rice they surrendered to each other's charms within the all-embracing New World pot. Like the hybrid culture that flourished in medieval Spain, the rice dish known as *moros y cristianos* is an exemplar of exchange between civilizations.

It is feast food in Cuba, where you'll find it in the western provinces. Considering that there is a Veracruzan version of this dish and that Cuba always imported black beans from Mexico, we are left in doubt as to which version came first. Regardless of its place of birth, it is one of the most felicitous rice and bean combinations I have ever tasted. The flavors of all the other ingredients are absorbed seamlessly by the rice, the vinegar providing point and counterpoint to the mealy beans, the aroma of cumin and oregano a subtle backdrop for the meaty smoked bacon, which in turn joins forces with the olive oil to add aroma and sheen to the rice. And then the color, a dark brown or hybrid of white and black.

Cook's Note: For this recipe the beans do not need to be soaked. The standard procedure is to use the same amount of cooked beans as raw rice, but that ratio can be adjusted to taste. However, if the beans are slightly overcooked, reduce the amount to avoid turning the rice mushy. Cubans have always used Uncle Ben's converted rice because of its low starch content.

Working Ahead ▶ The beans may be cooked up to 2 days ahead. Drain them, reserving the cooking liquid, and refrigerate the beans and liquid separately. For a quick fix, this recipe may be prepared with 2 cups canned beans (one 15-ounce can). Drain in a colander set over a bowl, and use the bean broth as part of the liquid called for in the recipe.

Recommended Pots: 4- to 5-quart 10- to 12-inch heavy-bottomed pot, at least 3½ inches deep, or 4- to 5-quart 10- to 12-inch cast-aluminum *caldero*.

SERVES 8

For the Beans

- 8 ounces dried black beans
- 1 medium yellow onion (about 8 ounces), peeled
- 1 medium green bell pepper (about 7 ounces), cored, seeded, and halved
- 6 Caribbean sweet peppers (*ajíes dulces*) or 1 cubanelle pepper
- 1 ham hock (optional)

For the Dish

- 2 cups (about 13 ounces) long-grain rice or Uncle Ben's converted rice
- 2 tablespoons extra-virgin olive oil
- 4 ounces slab bacon, diced
- 1 medium yellow onion, finely chopped (about 1¼ cups)
- 1 medium green bell pepper (about 7 ounces), cored, seeded, deveined, and finely chopped (about 1 cup)
- 1 teaspoon ground cumin

1 teaspoon dried oregano

1 bay leaf

1 tablespoon distilled white vinegar, or to taste

1 tablespoon dry sherry, or to taste

2 teaspoons salt, or to taste

Cooking the Beans ▶ Rinse and pick over the beans. Place in a medium heavy-bottomed pot with 2½ quarts water, the onion, bell pepper, *ajíes* or cubanelle pepper, and the ham hock, if using, and bring to a boil over high heat. Lower the heat to medium and simmer, uncovered, until the beans are tender but still retain their shape, about 2 hours. Drain, reserving 4 cups of the cooking liquid. Discard the vegetables and ham hock; you should have 2 cups cooked beans.

Finishing the Dish ▶ Place the rice in a medium bowl, cover with cold tap water, and swirl the rice, then drain, holding the rice in place with one hand. Repeat the process as many times as necessary until the water runs clear. Drain well in a sieve or strainer. Heat the oil in the heavy-bottomed pot over medium heat. Add the diced bacon and sauté until golden, about 3 minutes. Add the onion, green pepper, cumin, oregano, and bay leaf and sauté until the onion is soft, about 5 minutes.

Add the rice and stir to coat thoroughly. Add the beans and the reserved bean cooking liquid, then add the vinegar, sherry, and salt. Mix well and taste for seasoning; add a dash more of sherry, vinegar, and/or spices if needed. The cooking liquid should be flavorful. Cook, uncovered, until most of the liquid is absorbed and small craters have formed on the surface of the rice. Fluff the rice slightly with a kitchen fork, reduce the heat to the lowest possible setting, and cook, tightly covered, for 20 minutes.

Remove from the heat and let stand, uncovered, for at least 10 minutes before serving.

Garífuna Rice and Beans with Coconut Milk

The Garífuna are Latin Americans of both black and Carib Indian ancestry. In their communities along the Caribbean coasts of Honduras, Guatemala, and Costa Rica, the English term "rice and beans" is part of the people's language—you never hear it in Spanish translation. It belongs to the culinary culture of the Garífunas and *criollos* alike.

The way rice and beans is cooked in these black communities has more to do with Jamaica—where red beans and rice, often cooked in coconut milk, are a favorite—than with the cooking of Central America, with its strong Indian culture. This is an earthy dish with fluffy reddish rice; the coconut milk softens the tang of the tomato cooking sauce and adds a distinct aroma and sheen to the rice.

Working Ahead ▶ The beans can be cooked up to 2 days ahead. Drain, reserving the cooking liquid, and refrigerate separately. For a quick fix, this recipe can be prepared with 2 cups canned beans. Drain the beans in a colander set over a bowl, and use the bean broth as part of the liquid called for in the recipe.

Recommended Pots: 4-quart 10- to 12-inch heavy-bottomed pot, at least 3 inches deep, or 4-quart 10-inch cast-aluminum *caldero*.

SERVES 6

For the Beans

- 1¼ cups (about 8 ounces) dried kidney beans
- 1 small yellow onion (about 5 ounces)
- 2 broad-leaf *culantro* leaves or 4 cilantro sprigs
- 2 thyme sprigs

For the Dish

- 2 cups (about 13 ounces) long-grain rice
- 1 teaspoon corn oil
- 4 ounces slab bacon, finely diced
- 1 small yellow onion (about 5 ounces), finely chopped (about ⅔ cup)
- ½ cup Light Tomato Sauce (page 48) or canned tomato sauce
- 2 cups Creamy ("First") Coconut Milk (page 50) or canned unsweetened coconut milk
- 1¼ teaspoons salt
- 1 teaspoon dried thyme or 2 teaspoons chopped fresh thyme

Cooking the Beans ▶ Rinse and pick over the beans. Place in a medium heavy-bottomed pot with 3 quarts water, the onion, *culantro* or cilantro, and thyme and bring to a boil over high heat. Lower the heat to medium and simmer, uncovered, until the beans are tender but still retain their shape, about 2 hours. Drain, reserving 3 cups of the cooking liquid. Discard the onion and herbs; you should have 2 cups cooked beans.

Finishing the Dish ▶ Place the rice in a medium bowl, cover with cold tap water, and swirl the rice, then drain while holding the rice in place with one hand. Repeat the process as many times as necessary until the water runs clear. Drain well in a sieve or strainer.

Heat the oil in the heavy-bottomed pot over medium heat. Add the bacon and sauté until golden, about 3 minutes. Stir in the onion and sauté until

soft, about 5 minutes. Add the tomato sauce and let simmer briefly. Add the coconut milk, salt, and thyme and cook, stirring, for 3 minutes. Stir in the rice and beans. Bring to a boil over moderate heat and cook, uncovered, until the liquid is absorbed, about 12 minutes.

Fluff the rice with a fork, reduce the heat to very low, cover, and cook for 25 minutes. Remove from the heat, fluff with a fork, cover, and let sit for 10 minutes before serving.

Puerto Rican Rice and Green Pigeon Peas
Arroz con Gandules

The dishes served at the Christmas table are often an indication of a country's favorite foods. This hearty rice and green pigeon pea mix is never missing from the Puerto Rican holiday table, as a side for roast pork and *pasteles*, the earthy tamales made with plantain and *malanga*.

Green pigeon peas (*Cajanus indicus*), called *gandules* in Puerto Rico, were first domesticated in India and made their way into the Caribbean through the African slave trade. Earthy and mealy, they are usually eaten fresh, flavored with the tangy Puerto Rican *sofrito*, in soups or with rice. I love cooking fresh pigeon peas and using the cooking water to prepare the rice. It communicates an especially gutsy flavor to this Puerto Rican classic.

Cook's Notes: In the United States, green pigeon peas can be found frozen or canned, and occasionally fresh. Hispanic brands such as Goya include acceptable canned pigeon peas. If you use them, drain and reserve the liquid to use as part of the total liquid in the recipe. Defrost frozen peas under cold running water and drain well before using. If you do find fresh peas, boil them in 1 quart water until tender yet still whole, and reserve the water to cook the rice.

The standard 20 minutes of covered cooking time that is used for long-grain rice does not necessarily apply to medium-grain rice. The Valencia type sold by Goya, found in most Hispanic markets and some supermarkets, needs about 35 minutes cooking over very low heat.

Recommended Pots: 4-quart 10- to 12-inch heavy-bottomed pot, at least 3 inches deep, or 4-quart 10-inch cast-aluminum *caldero*.

SERVES 6 TO 8

- 2 cups medium-grain rice, preferably Goya
- 1 pound fresh or frozen green pigeon peas, or one 15-ounce can Goya green pigeon peas
- 1 tablespoon achiote-infused corn oil or extra-virgin olive oil (page 89)
- 4 ounces slab bacon, finely diced
- 4 ounces baked or boiled Virginia ham, finely diced
- 4 large garlic cloves, finely chopped
- 1 teaspoon ground cumin
- ½ teaspoon dried oregano
- 1 cup Puerto Rican *Sofrito* (page 59)
- ¼ cup store-bought tomato sauce
- 1 quart water; chicken broth, homemade (page 538) or store-bought; or water from cooking fresh pigeon peas

▶ Place the rice in a medium bowl, cover with cold tap water, and swirl the rice, then drain while holding the rice in place with one hand. Repeat the process as many times as necessary until the water runs clear. Drain well in a sieve or strainer.

If using fresh pigeon peas, cook them as directed above, reserving 1 quart of the cooking liquid. If using frozen peas, thaw them (see Cook's Notes). If using canned peas, drain them, reserving the liquid to use in the recipe.

Heat the oil in the pot over medium heat. Add the bacon and sauté until golden, 3 to 4 minutes. Add the ham and sauté until golden brown, about 5 minutes. Stir in the garlic and cook until golden, about 40 seconds. Stir in the cumin and oregano, add the *sofrito*, and cook, stirring, for 5 minutes. Pour in the tomato sauce and cook, stirring, for 3 minutes. Stir in the rice, water or other liquid, and pigeon peas, mixing well, and bring to a gentle boil over medium heat. Simmer, uncovered, until almost all the water is absorbed, about 13 minutes.

Fluff the rice with a fork, cover, and cook over very low heat for 30 to 35 minutes, or until the rice is soft but not mushy. Serve hot.

Serving: This goes well with many meat dishes such as Drunken Braised Meat and Potatoes (page 707). As part of a Puerto Rican Christmas dinner, it is dished up on plates with roast pork, Puerto Rican *Pasteles* (page 474), Fried Ripe Plantains (page 183), and Avocado and Onion Salad (page 547).

"Speckled Rooster" Central American Rice and Beans

Gallo Pinto

The names of some Latin foods are as colorful as the foods themselves. A *gallo pinto* is a speckled, brown-feathered rooster, but in Costa Rica and Nicaragua, it is also the name of a tasty mélange of leftover rice and beans bound by a simple *sofrito* and served for breakfast or lunch. This Costa Rican recipe calls for black beans, the country's favorite, spiced with a touch of Salsa Lizano—the national version of Worcestershire sauce. Go to any Costa Rican restaurant or home and you will find a bottle of this condiment on the table or in the pantry.

Working Ahead ▶ The beans can be cooked up to 2 days ahead. Drain, reserving some of the cooking liquid, and refrigerate the beans and liquid separately. For a quick fix, this recipe can be prepared with 3 cups canned beans. Drain in a colander set over a bowl, and use 1 cup of the bean broth in place of the liquid from freshly cooked beans.

SERVES 6

- 1 tablespoon extra-virgin olive oil or corn oil
- 4 ounces slab bacon, cut into small dice
- 2 large garlic cloves, finely chopped
- 1 small yellow onion (about 8 ounces), finely chopped (about ⅔ cup)
- 1 medium green bell pepper (about 7 ounces), cored, seeded, deveined, and finely chopped (about 1 cup)
- ⅓ cup store-bought tomato sauce
- 2 tablespoons Worcestershire sauce or Costa Rican Salsa Lizano
- ½ teaspoon dried oregano
- 1 teaspoon salt, or to taste
- 1 teaspoon freshly ground black pepper
- 4 cups cooked long-grain rice, cooked using any recipe from pages 294–98
- 3 cups black beans, cooked according to the directions for Mexican-Style Boiled Black Beans (page 271)
- 1 cup bean cooking liquid
- ¼ cup finely chopped cilantro
- ½ teaspoon salt

▶ Heat the oil in a 12-inch skillet over medium heat. Add the bacon and sauté until golden brown and crispy, about 5 minutes. Add the garlic, onion,

and green pepper and sauté, stirring, until the onion is translucent, about 6 minutes. Add the tomato sauce and cook for 5 minutes. Stir in the Worcestershire sauce, oregano, salt, and black pepper, mixing well. Stir in the rice and cook for 3 minutes. Stir in the black beans, the reserved cooking liquid, and the cilantro, lower the heat, cover, and cook for 5 minutes. Serve hot.

Serving: Serve as a side dish for Costa Rican Chayote, Fresh Corn, and Beef Hash (page 230), with grilled beef or chicken, or with fried eggs for breakfast or lunch.

Ciudad Bolívar Rice and Beans
Palo a Pique

A *palo a pique* is a makeshift home put together out of any materials one can find. True to its name, *palo a pique*, a popular rice dish in Guayana and the plains of Venezuela, is made with whatever ingredients a cook can find in her pantry: beans, rice, tubers, dried beef, salt pork.

I learned this dish in the town of Guanare, in the state of Portuguesa, from Consuelo Escobar, a tall, strong woman and the best cook I met in the Venezuelan plains. When Consuelo announced that she was making *palo a pique* for dinner, I imagined a much simpler dish put together in a hurry. Watching her cook it, I was surprised by the sophistication of the dish, and by how beautifully the starchy vegetables like yuca and squash and white beans blended in with the rice.

At the charming restaurant Ña María in Ciudad Bolívar, I later learned the Orinoco version of *palo a pique*, which I liked as much as Consuelo's.

The restaurant is in La Sapoara Market, on the shore of the Orinoco River. The owners, Ana Farfán and her mother, María Lourdes Rojas, a genial Guayanese who proudly wears shiny 24-karat gold jewelry earned by her success, are old friends. I met them on my first visit to the city for the coming of the *sapoara* (see page 1), and on every subsequent trip to the region I made a point of stopping by their restaurant to eat María Lourdes's delicious *palo a pique* with fried *sapoara* and other river fish.

One day I managed to steer an old boat against the swollen river current and dock it right next to her restaurant. I felt like Rosie in The *African Queen*. María Lourdes and Ana welcomed me and my Venezuelan friends with open arms. We gulped down ice-cold Polar beer and ordered the house's specialty, a lovely, aromatic fish *sancocho*, brimming with chunks of *morocoto* (a river fish) and tropical tubers. After that we had crisp fried fillets of *laulau* (another river fish) served with a mound of steaming *palo a pique*. I felt I was visiting family; the taste of their food was dear and welcoming. At her restaurant, María Lourdes cooks *palo a pique* with black beans and without any meat, but at home, she cooks it with red beans and can't bear to eat it without a bit of bacon or smoked pork chop.

Working Ahead ▶ The beans can be cooked up to 2 days ahead. (I use Goya dried *frijoles colorados*.) Drain, reserving the cooking liquid, and refrigerate the beans and liquid separately. (You will need only 1 cup of the beans for this recipe; use the rest for another dish). For a quick fix, this recipe may be prepared with 1 cup canned kidney beans that have been drained in a sieve and rinsed under cold water.

Recommended Pots: 4- to 5-quart, 10- to 12-inch heavy-bottomed pot, at least 3 inches deep, or 4- to 5-quart, 10- to 12-inch cast-aluminum *caldero*.

SERVES 6 TO 8

For the Beans

   8 ounces small dried red beans

For the Rice and Cooking Sauce

   2 cups (about 13 ounces) long-grain rice
  ¼ cup extra-virgin olive oil
   4 ounces slab bacon, salt fatback, or boned smoked pork chop, finely diced (optional)
   8 garlic cloves, finely chopped
   1 small yellow onion (about 5 ounces), finely chopped (1 cup)
   1 small green or red bell pepper (about 5 ounces), cored, seeded, deveined, and finely chopped (about 1 cup)
 12 Caribbean sweet peppers (*ajíes dulces*) or 1 cubanelle pepper, seeded and finely chopped
   4 scallions, white and pale green parts, finely chopped
  ½ leek, split lengthwise, rinsed, and finely chopped
   1 celery stalk with leaves, finely chopped
   1 tablespoon finely chopped cilantro
   2 teaspoons finely chopped flat-leaf parsley
   3 broad-leaf *culantro* leaves
   1 teaspoon salt or to taste

Cooking the Beans ▶ Rinse the beans under cold water and pick over. Place in a medium heavy-bottomed pot, add 3½ quarts water, and bring to a boil over high heat. Reduce the heat to medium and simmer, uncovered, until the beans are tender but still retain their shape, about 1½ hours. Drain the beans, reserving 4 cups of the cooking liquid. Set aside 1 cup of the cooked beans for this recipe, and reserve the remaining beans for another use.

Preparing the Rice and Cooking Sauce ▶ Place the rice in a medium bowl, cover with cold tap water, and swirl the rice, then drain while holding the rice in place with one hand. Repeat the process as many times as necessary until the water runs clear. Drain well in a sieve or strainer.

Heat the oil in the pot over medium heat. Add the bacon or pork and sauté until golden brown, about 5 minutes. Stir in the garlic and sauté until golden, about 40 seconds. Add the onion, bell pepper, *ajíes*, scallions, leek, celery, cilantro, and parsley and sauté until the vegetables are soft, about 5 minutes. Add the 1 cup cooked beans and sauté briefly, about 2 minutes.

Add the rice, stirring to coat well. Add the reserved cooking liquid, salt, and *culantro* and stir to combine. Bring to a rolling boil over high heat, then reduce the heat to medium-low and simmer until most of the liquid has been absorbed and small craters appear on the surface of the rice, about 6 minutes. Fluff the rice with a fork, reduce the heat to very low, cover, and cook for 25 minutes. Remove from the heat, again fluff the rice with a fork, and serve.

RICE AND POULTRY

Of all the combinations of rice and other ingredients found in Latin cooking, everyone's favorite is *arroz con pollo*, rice and chicken. There is something deeply satisfying about this one-pot meal, the golden rice bursting with flavor, the succulent chicken juices giving moisture and backbone to the rice. Everywhere in Latin America, this is the food that anchors Sunday lunch when extended families get together, and that is served to a special guest as a gesture of appreciation.

Rice and chicken is a food charged with memory and longing, and it is hard for people to recognize the merits of other people's versions—everyone gravitates to the recipe he or she grew up eating at home. But in writing this book and sharing *arroz con pollo* with people I love across the Americas, I have come to appreciate its many permutations: Costa Rican chef Arlene Lutz's rice and chicken flavored with *sofrito* and vegetables; the opulent rice and chicken of the Peruvian-Cuban grandmother of Lima chef Pedro Miguel Schiaffino; the spartan rice and chicken flavored simply with saffron and cloves that I ate for lunch at the house of winemaker Nicolás Catena in Mendoza, Argentina, after a bumpy ride in a buggy pulled by two handsome but slightly nervous Percheron horses. Through conversations with older cooks from eastern Mendoza, I discovered that *arroz con pollo* is an old Spanish dish that probably harks back to colonial times. Nicolás adores it because it tastes exactly the way his grandmother Nicasia used to make it. When Irene, the cook, came to work at La Vendimia, Nicasia ruled the kitchen, and that's how Irene learned the recipe.

Chef and television personality Arlene Lutz, who used to own a French restaurant in a posh residential neighborhood in San José, went native every Sunday at the restaurant, serving Costa Rican *arroz con pollo* on traditional, brightly decorated enameled plates—humble tableware imported since the nineteenth century from China and used by many Costa Ricans as their good china. Her version was loaded with fresh vegetables—corn, string beans, and carrots—and served with a side of refried black beans and a refreshing cabbage-carrot salad, all on the same plate.

The day Pedro Miguel Schiaffino invited my business partner Clara and me for Sunday lunch at his parents' beach house near Lima, he was secretive about the menu, but after much prodding, he let out that his grandmother was preparing Cuban food in our honor. When in Rome I usually do what the Romans do, and so I would have much preferred Peruvian food. To my delight, then, the *piqueo* (hors d'oeuvre) was Peruvian, and so was the sublime pisco sour Pedro Miguel's father mixed for us. But then I smelled something endearing, familiar, coming from the grandmother's kitchen. Clara and I looked at each other and in unison said, "*Arroz con pollo.*"

We rushed to the kitchen to find Pedro Miguel's grandmother lifting the lid of an enormous pot of rice, plumes of fragrant steam wafting into the air. The chicken was beautifully arranged over the rice, together with the familiar garnishes of peas and pimiento strips. We dug our spoons into the mountain of rice and began eating right in the kitchen. Later we helped the grandmother carry the pot to a long table set on the porch where the whole family waited. We ate next to the Pacific Ocean, with waves lapping against the porch sending spray into the air—a most peculiar place to be eating the food of my childhood. Just from the smell, we knew it was authentic Cuban rice and chicken, as delicious as I remembered it.

My Father's Very Soupy Rice and Chicken

Arroz con Pollo a la Chorrera

When I was growing up in Cuba in the 1950s, there were two main versions of *arroz con pollo*. One was a fluffy, dry dish made with long-grain rice, the other a soupy one made with a short-grain rice generically called Valencia (regardless of its actual origin). In both, the rice and the chicken were cooked together and garnished with canned asparagus, peas, and pimientos, the last two a classic duo that you will find garnishing *arroz con pollo* all over Latin America.

At my grandparents' house in Santiago de Cuba, my aunts, who were in charge of Sunday lunch, alternated between the dry and the soupy styles, but in Miami, my father, who rules the kitchen, is partial to the soupy version. I often tease him about the canned asparagus and green peas that crown his rice, but the joking stops when he hands me a bowl of his soupy rice, fresh from the pot, the chicken pieces nestled in the glistening, moist golden rice, spirals of aromatic smoke tickling my nostrils.

Here is my version, integrating techniques and ideas of my own, such as using Bomba rice from Calasparra or Montsia Extra from the Ebro Delta in Cataluña (my dad is not choosy—he uses the ingredients he can find easily). The idea of adding bacon to the *sofrito* comes from my sister-in-law Virginia Valdor, raised in Puerto Rico where ham flavors *arroz con pollo*.

What to Drink: A Pilsener beer like Corona, Peruvian Pilsen Callao, or Argentinean Quilmes Imperial; or a fresh and tangy Montes Sauvignon Blanc from Casablanca Valley, Chile; or a Spanish tempranillo such as San Vicente or Emilio Moro Malleolus from the Ribera del Duero

Recommended Pots: 5- to 6-quart 11- to 12-inch heavy-bottomed pot, at least 3½ inches deep, or 5-quart 11-inch cast-aluminum *caldero*.

SERVES 6 TO 8

6 whole chicken legs (thighs and drumsticks; about 4½ pounds), skin removed

For the Seasoning Paste

6 large garlic cloves
1 teaspoon ground cumin
¼ teaspoon dried oregano
¼ teaspoon ground allspice
  Juice of 1 bitter orange (about ¼ cup) or 2 tablespoons fresh lime juice
1 teaspoon salt

For the Dish

1½ cups (about 10½ ounces) Valencia-style medium-grain rice (preferably Bomba or Montsia Extra)
¼ cup achiote-infused extra-virgin olive oil (page 89)
3 ounces slab bacon or Virginia ham, cut into ¼-inch to ½-inch dice (about ½ cup)
8 large garlic cloves, finely chopped
1 medium yellow onion (about 8 ounces), finely chopped (about 1½ cups)
1 medium green bell pepper (about 6 ounces), cored, seeded, deveined, and finely chopped (about ⅔ cup)
2 teaspoons ground cumin
1 teaspoon dried oregano
1 bay leaf
¼ teaspoon freshly ground black pepper, or to taste
1 cup Light Tomato Sauce (page 48) or canned tomato sauce
1 cup lager beer
1 quart chicken broth, homemade (page 538) or canned
1 cup green olives, such as Manzanilla (about 35), pitted
¼ cup capers, drained

½ cup water
2½ teaspoons salt, or to taste (depending on the saltiness of the broth)
6 fat white or green asparagus spears, trimmed, peeled, halved crosswise on the bias, and blanched, or 6 canned white or green asparagus spears, halved crosswise on the bias
½ cup fresh or thawed frozen peas
One 8-ounce can pimientos or 1 large red bell pepper (about 12 ounces), roasted (see page 67), peeled, cored, seeded, and cut into ¼-inch-wide strips

Seasoning the Chicken ▶ Rinse the chicken pieces and pat dry with paper towels. Put in a large bowl.

Using a mortar and pestle or a food processor, grind or process the garlic, cumin, oregano, allspice, orange juice, and salt to a paste. Rub the chicken pieces all over with the paste. Let sit for 2 hours at room temperature or for up to 24 hours in the refrigerator, tightly covered with plastic wrap.

Preparing the Rice and Chicken ▶ Place the rice in a medium bowl, cover with cold tap water, and swirl. Drain while holding the rice in place with one hand. Repeat the process as many times as necessary until the water runs clear. Drain well in a sieve or strainer.

Heat the oil in the chosen pot over medium heat. Add the bacon or ham and sauté until lightly golden, about 3 minutes. Scrape the seasoning paste from the chicken pieces and reserve it. Working in batches, add the chicken pieces to the pot and sauté until golden, turning occasionally with tongs, about 5 minutes on each side. Remove to a platter. Leave the bacon or ham pieces in the pot.

Add the garlic to the fat remaining in the pot and sauté until golden, about 20 seconds. Add the onion and sauté until light golden, about 6 minutes. Add the bell pepper, cumin, oregano, bay leaf, and black pepper and cook, stirring, for 5 minutes. Stir in the tomato sauce and reserved seasoning paste and simmer for 8 minutes. Add the rice and cook, stirring to coat well, for 2 minutes. Add the beer and continue simmering for 2 minutes.

Add the chicken broth, olives, and capers and let simmer in the sauce to absorb flavors for about 5 minutes. Pour in the water and salt, and mix well. Taste for salt. Bring to a boil over medium heat, then lower the heat to medium-low and simmer, covered, for 15 to 20 minutes. The liquid will not be fully absorbed.

Stir gently with a kitchen fork to fluff the rice and mix all ingredients. Reduce the heat as low as possible and cook, tightly covered, for 15 minutes. If using fresh asparagus, place on top of the rice before covering. If using canned, add to heat through at the end of cooking, 1 to 2 minutes. Add the peas and the pimientos or roasted peppers and fluff the rice with a fork. Let rest for 5 to 10 minutes before serving. The texture of the rice should be creamy yet with grains that still have some bite. Remove from the heat and spoon the rice and chicken onto a platter. Garnish with the asparagus and pimiento.

Serving: Serve accompanied by Cuban Avocado, Watercress, and Pineapple Salad (page 548) and Fried Green Plantains (page 182) or Fried Ripe Plantains (page 183). I like to add a couple of dollops of *allioli* (page 135) to my rice.

Variation: Cubans prepare a version of this dish called *arroz imperial* (imperial rice) that is molded and glazed with a garlicky *allioli* sauce. Here is how we do it. Once the dish is finished, remove the chicken pieces, remove the meat from the bones, and cut the meat into ½-inch cubes. Preheat the oven to 350°F. Butter a deep rectangular baking dish. Place a layer of rice on the bottom and cover with a layer of chicken. Repeat the process, finishing with a layer of rice. Sprinkle with Parmigiano-Reggiano and bake for 20 minutes. Turn out onto a serving platter and spread a layer of *allioli* (page 135) all over the top and sides with a spatula. Serve garnished with pimientos, asparagus, and parsley.

FINAL TOUCHES: *PETITS POIS*

Back in the 1980s, a famous food critic blasted a New York Cuban restaurant of some renown for garnishing *arroz con pollo* with canned asparagus and peas. Adding the drab, limp vegetables to a dish of traditional credentials must have seemed an abomination to the reviewer. Say that to Cuban home cooks, however, and they will laugh in your face. To them, canned asparagus and peas are indispensable staples, time-honored finishing touches that make favorite foods like rice and chicken truly special. For many Latin Americans, canned green peas above all are like the cherry on a sundae. Their use is a long-established culinary practice that reached its peak in the mid-twentieth century.

Clearly influenced by Spanish cooking, Cuban cookbooks from the late nineteenth and early twentieth centuries call for fresh green peas in soups (*potajes*), egg dishes, salads, and stews. The peas were called *chícharos frescos*, the Galician term, or *albejas* (sometimes *arbejas*), from the Castilian *arveja*, a synonym for *guisante*, the more common word for green peas in parts of Spain and in Argentina and Chile. Since the 1940s, *chícharos* has been understood to mean dried split peas, and most recipes call for tiny canned green peas by the fancier French name of *petits pois*.

From Ana Dolores Gómez, the first great doyenne of Cuban cooking, to the more practical Nitza Villapol, the author of the widely influential *Cocina al Minuto*, to "The Three Guys from Miami," Cuban recipe writers have used a *latica* (small can) of *petits pois* as a key final ingredient in party salads and elaborate rice dishes meant for company. Every Cuban remembers last-minute preparations for a large Sunday lunch and the cook's frantic call from the kitchen: "I am out of *petits pois*—someone please, please, rush to the store to get me a *latica*."

Although the can might have come from Spain, France, or the United States, the words *petits pois* on the label proclaimed its Frenchness. Perceived to be a cut above other vegetables because of this lofty association, *petits pois* were considered a delicacy, as important a garnish for the Cuban home cook as microgreens are for the contemporary Nuevo Latino chef.

For those of us weaned on Cuban chicken salad studded with peas the color of boiled lettuce, it is hard to let go; *petits pois* are the flavor of nostalgia. But it is time to consider the alternative: fresh green peas. In season, the slightly curved pods are swollen with juicy, sweet, spring-green peas, ready for the picking. All you need to do is pinch the stem and pull off the fibrous thread that runs down one side of the pod to free the peas. As with most sugar-rich crops, timing is of the essence. Fresh peas are at their best and sweetest when cooked right after picking and shelling.

Frozen new peas are also an infinitely better choice than canned. Flash-freezing preserves both the bright green color and the sweetness of the peas. They'll still add a retro touch to your Cuban favorites, but with a lot more color and texture than canned *petits pois*. ◆

Orinoco Chicken and Rice *Pelao*

Pelao de Gallina

I've eaten some of the best food in Venezuela at Ercole, my Italian friend Ercole D'Addazio's restaurant in Puerto Ordaz, a thriving industrial town on the middle course of the Orinoco River. On one visit, I found Ercole, then in his seventies, preparing the traditional Orinoco rice and chicken dish known as *pelao de gallina* for his wife and his mother-in-law, Delia. A few years before, I had seen Delia, then a formidable woman, tending to Ercole with *criollo* and Italianized Guayanese food (see page 22).

When she became too old and fragile to cook, it was Ercole's turn to take care of her, giving an Italian twist to Venezuelan food. He was treating the *pelao* like risotto, using short-grain rice and adding the broth in stages. He respected the authentic flavor of the dish, but I felt the risotto treatment was an enlightened way to showcase what was special about *pelao*: the seductive mellow sweetness of the brown loaf sugar that is used to glaze the chicken. I found it so delicate and delicious, I was immediately inspired to try his version, adapting it to my way of cooking short- and medium-grain rice.

What makes this dish distinctively Venezuelan is its pronounced sweet-and-sour flavor. The chicken pieces are browned in the delicious unrefined brown sugar Venezuelans call *papelón*, and gherkins and capers add a sour counterbalance to the sweetness of the soup. At my restaurant Zafra, I have come up with a Cuban version of the *pelao* by marinating the chicken in bitter orange juice with lots of garlic.

Cook's Notes: To prepare this dish like Ercole's risotto, heat the chicken broth or water and then add it to the rice and chicken mixture in two or three stages, allowing the liquid to be absorbed by the rice before adding more.

I prefer to remove the skin from our fatty American chickens before cooking.

What to Drink: Susana Balbo Torrontes from Mendoza, Argentina

Recommended Pots: 6- to 8-quart, 11- to 12-inch heavy-bottomed pot, at least 4 inches deep, or 6- to 8-quart 11- to 12-inch cast-aluminum *caldero*.

SERVES 8

One 3½-pound chicken, cut into 12 serving pieces (see page 659)

For the Seasoning Paste

1 medium head garlic, separated into cloves and peeled
1 tablespoon ground cumin
1 teaspoon freshly ground black pepper
1 teaspoon salt
½ cup bitter orange juice or 6 tablespoons fresh regular orange juice plus 2 tablespoons fresh lime juice

For the Cooking Sauce

5 tablespoons achiote-infused corn oil or mild olive oil (page 89)
¼ cup (1¼ ounces) grated brown loaf sugar (preferably *papelón* or *panela*), or packed dark brown sugar
1 large yellow onion (about 12 ounces), finely chopped (about 2 cups)
5 scallions, white and pale green parts, finely chopped (about ⅓ cup)
1 medium green bell pepper (about 6 ounces), cored, seeded, deveined, and finely chopped (about ¾ cup)
12 Caribbean sweet peppers (*ajíes dulces*), stemmed and coarsely chopped, or 1 cubanelle pepper
5 medium plum tomatoes (about 1 pound), peeled, seeded, and finely chopped (about 1½ cups), or 5 canned plum tomatoes, drained, peeled, and finely chopped
1 teaspoon ground cumin
1 teaspoon freshly ground black pepper
½ teaspoon salt

For the Rice

2 cups Valencia-style medium-grain rice, preferably Montsia Extra, Unio, or Bomba
8 ounces gherkins or cornichons, thinly sliced
¼ cup small capers, drained
2 quarts chicken broth, homemade (page 538) or store-bought, or water
1 tablespoon salt, or to taste

Marinating the Chicken ▶ Rinse the chicken and pat dry. Put the pieces in a baking dish. Using a mortar and pestle, crush the garlic with the cumin, black pepper, and salt to make a thick paste. Stir in the orange juice. Rub the chicken pieces all over with this paste. Let sit for 2 hours at room temperature or for up to 24 hours in the refrigerator, tightly covered with plastic wrap.

Preparing the Cooking Sauce ▶ Heat the oil in the pot over medium heat. Add the brown sugar and cook, stirring, until the sugar dissolves, about 2 minutes. If using loaf sugar, it will look gummy and stringy at first, but it will eventually dissolve. Lift the chicken from the marinade, letting the excess drain back into the dish, add to the pot, and brown on all sides, turning occasionally, about 10 minutes. Do this in batches. The dissolved sugar in the oil will coat the chicken pieces nicely like a glaze, giving them a lovely golden color. Take the chicken pieces out of the pot with a slotted spoon and set aside.

Add the onion and scallions to the pot and sauté until soft, about 5 minutes. Add the bell pepper and *ajíes* and sauté for 5 minutes, stirring occasionally. Add the tomatoes and sauté until soft, about 4 minutes. Add the reserved marinade and the cumin, black pepper, and salt and cook, stirring, for 2 more minutes.

Meanwhile, place the rice in a medium bowl, cover with cold tap water and swirl the rice, then drain while holding the rice in place with one hand. Repeat the process as many times as necessary until the water runs clear. Drain well in a sieve or strainer.

Preparing the Rice and Chicken ▶ Add the rice to the pot and cook for 2 minutes, stirring to coat. Add the browned chicken, along with the gherkins and capers, then stir in the chicken broth or water. Bring to a rolling boil over high heat and boil for 10 minutes. Reduce the heat as low as possible, cover

the pot, and simmer for 20 minutes. The rice should be soft and creamy but retain its shape. The dish should be almost like a soupy risotto.

Serving: Serve with Fried Green Plantains (page 182) and Avocado and Onion Salad (page 547).

Peruvian Rice with Duck

Arroz con Pato Chiclayano

In Peru, even the simplest dish is flavored with a potent cooking sauce, or *aderezo*, that carries the unmistakable signature of its region of origin. I have tasted rice in combination with duck all over northern Peru, where this dish is regarded with great esteem, but nowhere did I have a version more delicious than that of Chiclayo, with its subtle aroma of cumin and cilantro. The rice, with whole separate grains dyed a brownish olive green, is just as flavorful as the duck itself.

I had made several variations of this dish, always with the goal of showcasing the duck, not the rice (duck is one of my favorite foods). But I succeeded in coming close to the traditional recipes I had tried in Peru only after it dawned on me that the duck is simply a flavoring for the rice—no wonder the dish is called rice with duck, and not duck with rice.

Cook's Note: For this dish, I suggest using a Muscovy duck, not only because it is a meaty, muscular bird that flourishes with long cooking, becoming tender and succulent, but because it is native to Peru. Northern Peru, where rice and duck is immensely popular, is the land of the Moche, the pre-Inca civilization that first domesticated the Muscovy duck. When visiting Moche sites near Trujillo, I was enchanted by vividly painted murals depicting the hunting of Muscovy ducks.

What to Drink: Peruvian Cuzqueña or Pilsen Callao beer or a red Callet Anima Negra from Mallorca

Recommended Pots: 5-quart 10- to 12-inch heavy-bottomed pot, at least 3 inches deep, or 4- to 5-quart 10- to 11-inch cast-aluminum *caldero*.

SERVES 12

One   5-pound Muscovy duck, cut into 8 serving pieces, or 5 pounds duck legs and thighs

For the Cooking Sauce

3   dried *panca* peppers or 3 dried guajillo chiles (about 1 ounce)
1   teaspoon red wine vinegar
6   large garlic cloves, finely chopped
1   medium red onion (about 8 ounces), finely chopped (about 1¼ cups)
1   medium green bell pepper (about 6 ounces), cored, seeded, deveined, and finely chopped (about 1 cup)
1   teaspoon ground cumin
½   teaspoon salt
1   teaspoon freshly ground black pepper
½   cup pisco, grappa, or very dry white wine
2½   quarts water

For the Cilantro Puree

1   cup chopped cilantro
¼   cup broth from cooking the duck

For the Rice

3   cups (about 1¼ pounds) long-grain rice
1   tablespoon salt

Cooking the Duck ▶ Heat the pot over medium heat. Add the duck pieces, skin side down, and cook to brown and render excess fat, turning with tongs to brown evenly. Remove the duck to a platter. Pour off the fat and reserve ¼ cup.

Preparing the Cooking Sauce ▶ Stem and seed the dried peppers. Rinse under running water. Place in a small saucepan with 2 cups water, bring to a boil over medium heat, and cook until soft, about 15 minutes. Drain, reserving ¼ cup of the cooking liquid. Place the peppers, the reserved cooking liquid, and the vinegar in a blender or food processor and puree. Set aside.

Heat half of the reserved duck fat in the same pot. Add the garlic and sauté until golden, about 40 seconds. Add the onion and sauté until golden. Add the green pepper, cumin, salt, and black pepper and cook for 1 minute. Stir in the chile puree and cook for 2 minutes. Add the pisco, grappa, or wine and simmer for about 3 minutes.

Add the duck and water and bring to a boil over high heat. Lower the heat to medium and simmer, uncovered, until the duck is almost fork-tender and the liquid is reduced to 1 quart, about 40 minutes.

Making the Cilantro Puree ▶ Place the cilantro and reserved duck broth in a blender or food processor and process to a smooth puree. Set aside.

Preparing the Rice ▶ Place the rice in a medium bowl, cover with cold tap water, and swirl the rice, then drain while holding the rice in place with one hand. Repeat the process as many times as necessary until the water runs clear. Drain well in a sieve or strainer.

In a large skillet, heat the rest of the duck fat over medium heat. Add the rice and sauté until light gold, about 5 minutes. Remove from the heat and set aside.

Finishing the Dish ▶ When the duck is almost fork-tender, add the rice and the cilantro puree and stir to mix. Bring to a boil over medium heat and cook until the liquid is almost all absorbed, about 12 minutes. Fluff the rice with a fork, lower the heat to the lowest possible setting, cover, and cook for 20 minutes. Let rest for 10 minutes, covered, and fluff again before serving.

Serving: Serve with a bowl of Peruvian Onion and Yellow Pepper Slaw/Relish (page 150).

DRINKS

In Latin America, what we drink is as important as what we eat. You will not understand the food unless you understand our intense emotional connection to our unique drinks—those we think are special in childhood and the ones that puzzle North Americans by being a peculiar hybrid of drink and food.

The category is broad, often defying any preconceptions. Some of our beverages, like wine, are Eurocentric enough to match North American preferences; others are deeply rooted in cultures that were already ancient when Columbus was young. Many mark the passage of time, anchoring beloved feasts like Christmas and the solemn Days of the Dead.

The Spanish and other explorers discovered the native peoples consuming a variety of beverages, some of which they thought were bizarre. In the lowland tropics, they tasted a sort of beer brewed from cut-up yuca roots using a technique that was also applied to other starchy tubers as well as to grains: the women would take a mouthful at a time of the boiled yuca or other food and chew it for a long time, until it became sweet. Saliva contains the enzyme ptyalin, which breaks down starch into simple carbohydrates like maltose and finally glucose, which can be fermented into alcohol.

Like beer, this enzyme-engendered brew was nourishing and mildly alcoholic. Today preparations based on the same basic principle are generically called *chicha* (a word of unclear origin, most likely from the language of the Aztecs) in most parts of Latin America, though the original chewing technique is now rare except in isolated communities of the Andes and the Orinoco and Amazon Basins.

Pre-Hispanic *chichas* were also made from corn. In Peru, the seventeenth-century missionary Bernabé Cobo saw *chicha* being brewed by various methods from various foods, including an unchewed kind based on malted (that is, partially sprouted) corn, which is still popular in the highlands of Ecuador and Peru. The kernels of corn were buried until they began to sprout (today the kernels may be kept moist between layers of plantain leaves), releasing the enzyme amylase, which triggered the chemical breakdown of starch to fermentable sugars. The malted corn was then dried (at which point it was called *jora*), boiled down with spices, and set aside in large clay jars to ferment into *chicha* (or, if left long enough, a tasty vinegar).

Some *chichas* were stronger than others, the determining factor being the amount of sugar available for fermentation. The most highly alcoholic drink of this type is probably the sticky, milky Mexican beer called *pulque*, made from the sweet sap (*aguamiel* in Spanish) of the *maguey* plant (*Agave* spp.). *Pulque* is still consumed in areas of Mexico with large indigenous populations, such as Oaxaca.

Other, milder *chichas* are made by fermenting fruits such as apples or pineapple skins. In Ceará, Brazil, they make a lovely *chicha* with the fermented juice of the cashew apple fruit, called *mocororó*. These refreshing bubbly fruit drinks are my favorites, since fermentation adds a new layer of flavor to simple juices and infusions.

In Mexico, the conquerors also found a large number of nourishing drinks called *atoles* that were thickened with corn *masa* to a consistency somewhere between spoonable and drinkable. *Atoles* were made with a variety of flavorings—sweet, sour, fragrant, or spicy. Drinks of this kind were often made with chocolate, which in pre-Hispanic Central America, and possibly northern South America, was almost entirely reserved for beverages.

This type of drink would not have been strange in medieval Europe, where nourishing cereal porridges and gruels existed in great variety. These thick porridgelike drinks eventually vanished from most European cuisines, but they have remained popular in Central America and in parts of the Andean countries that make use of cereal grains.

CHOCOLATE

Most of the native drinks of the Americas were meant for nourishment, even if they were also intended to stimulate and energize, like chocolate, or intoxicate, like *chicha*. Both of these startled European explorers: chocolate for the sophisticated techniques involved in its making (fermentation, roasting, spicing, thickening), *chicha* for the sheer physicality of its making, the direct hands-on, or, better put, mouth-on, effort that was often involved in its preparation.

Of the two, it is not surprising that chocolate was the one to make a successful crossover. The Iberian conquistadores showed a voracious appetite when it came to sex and survival. When hungry, they would eat anything that crawled, flew, or ran. Yet it is hard to imagine Andalusian or Castilian women back home chewing tubers and spitting mush back into a pot to make a fermented drink. From the sixteenth century, it was chocolate that captured the imagination and the taste buds of polite European society. And cacao, not yuca or corn, was the first tropical crop of the New World to be valued almost as much as gold by the Europeans. For many food lovers, this product of the slender evergreen cacao tree (*Theobroma cacao*) is the New World's most dazzling gift.

Chocolate is made from the cacao seeds, or "beans," enclosed in colorful thick-skinned pods sprouting from both trunk and branches of the tree in the shaded understory of tropical forests. When you cut open a pod, you find a sweet litchi-flavored mucilaginous pulp that anyone can appreciate. Not so the beans attached to their central "placenta." Bitter and astringent in raw form, they taste nothing like chocolate until they have been fermented, dried, roasted, and ground.

We used to distinguish three types of domesticated cacao: *criollo, forastero,* and *trinitario,* a hybrid of the first two—a convenient, easily remembered scheme simplistically pitting the fine flavor of *criollo* cacao (white cotyledons, nutty flavor, great complexity) against the harsher *forastero* (dark cotyledons, bitter edge, astringency). But this durable paradigm has recently been shattered. A seminal study in 2008 by Venezuelan geneticist Juan Carlos Motomayor, who works for both the USDA and the Mars Company, showed a more complex picture. Motomayor first reported that the species *Theobroma cacao* is composed of ten genetic clusters, each native to South America and more specifically to individual areas of Amazonia close to the Andes (which has been proven to be the center of genetic diversity for cacao as well as its birthplace). Three more clusters were added in 2012, thanks to a joint expedition of USDA and Peruvian scientists in the Peruvian Amazon.

From primeval, humid South American forest habitats, cacao traveled north to Mesoamerica, where it was domesticated more than four millennia ago and made the great leap to chocolate. It was probably Mesoamerican women, especially women of the Maya peoples, who first saw past cacao as a fruit to unlock the complexities of chocolate. In only the last ten years, scientists have pushed back the date of chocolate's arrival on the Mesoamerican culinary stage to about 1900 B.C. by examining the residue from ancient pottery at the Paso de la

Amada site in Mexico's Chiapas state, as well as vessels from other sites like the Ulúa River Valley in today's Honduras. In the laboratories of the Hershey Company, biochemist Jeffrey Hurst has found traces of theobromine and caffeine (the chemical markers of cacao) in the Paso de la Amada remains. Some archaeologists argue that they could have contained a kind of mildly fermented cacao *chicha* rather than a full-fledged chocolate drink from roasted and ground cacao beans. Not everyone agrees, but what is clear is that cacao had been domesticated by Mesoamerican farmers and processed into drinks predating both the Olmecs and the Maya.

Mesoamerican chocolate was not made into the smooth, glossy chocolate bars we know today. Pre-Columbian chocolate, as well as the chocolate adopted by the conquerors and eventually taken up everywhere in Europe, was dull-colored, crumbly, and coarse—best for making nourishing beverages. In most cases, it did not even achieve a dried solid stage, since women ground it to a paste on grinding stones and dissolved it immediately in hot or cold water, or used it in thick gruels of nixtamalized corn *masa* (page 444), generically called *atole* (Mexico) or *atol* (Guatemala).

On pottery and in mural paintings, the ruling aristocracy of the classic Maya is often shown drinking foamy chocolate drinks while seated on low platforms. At arm's length there is usually a dish of tamales, often shown with a dark sauce that I interpret as a type of proto-*mole* enriched with chiles and cacao. Glyphs adorning vases meant for drinking chocolate also tell us about the many ways in which Maya women prepared the drinks: colored red with achiote seeds, sweetened with honey, thickened with corn *masa*, flavored with dried "ear flower" (*orejuela*, the most coveted flavoring for chocolate among the Maya), and fresh, as in the juice from the cacao pulp. In all its forms, for the Maya and later for the Aztecs of Mexico's central highlands, chocolate drinks were imbued with sacred meaning and consumed in ritual or medicinal contexts.

Already in pre-Columbian times, the peoples of Mesoamerica had learned to cultivate a particularly fine strain of cacao originally native to a region of Venezuela between Lake Maracaibo and the Andes that had arrived there in prehistoric times. What the Maya, the Aztecs, and the Spanish colonizers all recognized was the superiority of the cacao that came to be called *criollo*. Especially in the rich, well-watered volcanic Maya lands stretching along the Pacific coastal plain, the coveted *criollo* was valuable enough to make fortunes both before and after the Spanish conquest.

Its long reign in Mesoamerica, however, began to crumble as early as the sixteenth century, when boom-and-bust cycles shifted the production of cacao destined for Spain and chocolate-hungry capitals like Mexico City from Soconusco in present day Chiapas state to Suchitepéquez in Guatemala, then to Izalco in El Salvador. Outbreaks of disease and lack of labor took further tolls in these old lands of cacao. Eventually the main cacao-exporting scene moved to Venezuela and Ecuador. Artisanal chocolate-making, however, never completely died out. Wherever I travel in cacao-growing regions of Guatemala and Southern Mexico, I find women still roasting and grinding beans and making complexly flavored drinks featuring many ingredients that have survived as elements of drinking chocolate since pre-Columbian times.

In Suchitepéquez, women make artisanal chocolate in many guises. Some still use the traditional grinding stone; many more rely on mechanized mills to grind heavy loads of home-roasted cacao—the cacao relative *pataxte* (*Theobroma bicolor*), prized for its white cotyledons—toasted corn, spices, and lots of sugar, which are blended in various proportions for different purposes. With these ingredients and a handful of spices like achiote for coloring, the women make local drinking chocolate specialties such as *tixte* (a blend of cacao, *pataxte*, rice, and achiote); *pinol* (toasted cacao, *pataxte*, corn, and cumin); or *panecito* (toasted cacao, *pataxte*, corn, cloves, cumin, and the ancient Maya ear flower). When the price of cacao is favorable, *panecito* made with a higher proportion of cacao is often shaped into small loaves (hence its Spanish name, meaning "little loaf").

Every Guatemalan community also has a particular style of making and shaping plain chocolate heavily flavored with sugar. In Samayac, some women press the warm, freshly milled cacao mass into large plastic containers. Later they cut the massive unmolded chocolate blocks into long, narrow strips and roll them into cylinders, which they cut into disks. These are cupped in one hand and rolled on the smooth surface of a work table to round the edges and give the chocolate a satiny shine. The sound of making chocolate in Samayac reminds me of old Cuban men playing dominos in Miami's Little Havana.

Of greater historic importance are the chocolate specialties of particular towns like San Bernardino, a small town between San Antonio Suchitepéquez and Mazatenango. There every important feast day is celebrated with *pozunke*. At its simplest, this is an unsweetened corn and rice *atol* flavored with chocolate. What makes it truly special and a relic of ancient Maya tradition is that it requires a doughy mixture of peeled unroasted and roasted cacao beans, *pataxte*, and a blend of corn *masa* and soaked broken-up corn tortillas. A handful of old women in town still grind the cacao mixture using the traditional grinding stone. The trickiest

and most difficult task, however, is kneading the cacao mass while adding warm *atol* and cold water (or even ice cubes) to bring the cacao fat and the corn to the surface in the form of a lumpy foam with the texture of whipped cream—the crowning glory of the *pozunke*, as it was for ancient Maya and Aztec chocolate drinks. The women usually skim and set aside the foam, then blend the mixture with separately cooked boiling *atol*. They pour the liquid mixture from one vessel to the other to blend and aerate it and to create more foam, a technique probably as ancient as chocolate itself. The coveted reserved thick foam is carefully apportioned to each serving. This is the drink of choice for the long vigils of Good Friday and communal cooking gatherings for the Days of the Dead.

A similarly fascinating drink is the *atol de súchil* of nearby Samayac. It starts as a thick, dark paste composed of a blend of toasted cacao and corn flavored with the seed of the *mamey sapote*, which is practically carbonized by toasting, and ear flower (both taste like black pepper). Women stir this flavor base into a plain unsweetened *atol* of corn *masa* and rice, which is eagerly consumed for breakfast and sold at the town's main market.

In markets in Oaxaca you can taste *tejate*, a delicious cold drink of cacao, calcified *pataxte*, and corn closely related to the Guatemalan *pozunke* but more assertively flavored with a flower known in Oaxaca as *rosita de cacao*. This is the tiny white blossom of an understory tree in the kapok family (*Quararibea funebris*, dubbed *cacahuaxochitl* by the Aztecs). You will be seduced by the maple flavor imparted by the *rosita* and the heavy layer of creamy froth crowning the big earthenware *cazuelas* from which the drink is ladled into the traditional painted red drinking gourds.

I am not the only observer to think these traditions deserve rediscovering. Today some

North American microbatch chocolate makers are experimenting with flavorings so old that they seem new again. For ethnobotanist Nat Bletter of Madre Chocolate, a go-for-broke microbatch chocolate maker with an ad hoc budget and a fearless palate working in a 600-square-foot factory on Oahu, Hawaii, there is no better way to preserve and spread the iconic flavors of Mesoamerica's rich chocolate drink traditions than to give them new life in a shiny chocolate bar. Pick up a bar of his Rosita de Cacao 70%, unwrap it, and bring it to your nose. You will be enveloped by a heady aroma of fresh curry leaves and toasted fenugreek. Take a bite and you will detect the familiar effect of maple syrup over freshly made pancakes, then the bright tang of red fruits punctuated by nuts, the whole held together by a mild tannic astringency. Here combined in a single bite are the signature scents of an ancient Aztec chocolate drink flavored with *cacahuaxochitl*, together with the flavors of Soconusco cacao—the finest to be had among the Maya—from today's Chiapas state in Mexico. In this thoughtful blend of flower and cacao, Maya and Aztec, Bletter is satisfying his own deeply cherished hope that with use and demand, farmers in the lands that were once the cradle of chocolate in Mesoamerica will have the incentive to hold on to their cacao as well as the plants that give it fragrance and substance.

Though the female-dominated traditions of home-scale or artisanal chocolate making have never waned in the old lands of cacao, twenty years ago I would have said that the old Mesoamerican strongholds of fine cacao were doomed. In Guatemala, for example, the once-coveted *criollo* had been replaced by hardier, less flavorful cultivars of the *amelonado* type (a genetic strain from the lower Amazon that became the foundation of the West African cacao industry) and sturdy productive hybrids. Even these have been endangered by the cumulative effect of centuries-long neglect and a preference for easier crops like sugarcane. In Honduras, fine cacao has all but disappeared, and El Salvador has so little cacao that it has to import it from its neighbors, primarily Nicaragua. I couldn't have guessed that the cacao scene would ever change for the better.

But today we seem to be on the threshold of a new golden age for cacao and chocolate in every aspect, and not only in Mesoamerica. The pioneers of the movement have been North American and European chocolate makers willing to seek out the best cacao strains and respect the superior flavor of well-handled beans from Latin American plantations. But in many ways, the biggest beneficiaries of their vision have been growers and manufacturers in Latin America. The pioneer was the Venezuelan company El Rey, which since 1994 has been exporting world-class single-origin chocolates to the United States, followed by markets in Europe and Japan. There was a gap of several years before other Latin American countries began following El Rey's example. But good cacao is suddenly back in style. In every region of Latin America where cacao grows, ecologically sustainable farming practices are being deployed to raise fine cacao strains that had been in danger of disappearing. In El Salvador, a group of farmers associated in the cooperative Es-Cacao, led by the former coffee grower Rafael Trigueros, is bent on revitalizing the famed *criollo* from Izalco. By chance, Rafael stumbled upon a strange cacao growing on one of his farms. During a conference in Suchitepéquez, he showed me the pictures and I gasped. It had the telltale signs of a *criollo*: a pronounced tip and gigantic, round beans sporting lovely ivory-colored cotyledons. A sample of leaves sent to USDA scientists in Virginia for genetic analysis confirmed our hunch—Rafael

Trigueros had found an old *criollo*. Cuttings from this tree and other *criollos* that have been identified throughout El Salvador are now being grafted on the farms of the members of Es-Cacao and interplanted with valuable hybrids with strong *criollo* blood. This year I had the honor of helping choose a name for this cacao, "Gran Maya Blanco de Izalco," and now I can't wait to taste the first chocolate made from its beans.

Even big industry players like the Colombian firm of Luker are starting to manufacture single-origin chocolates based on the output of individual plantations. The famed "Nacional" cacao strain of Ecuador, long recognized to be something exquisite but not well understood in its relation to other cacaos and often condescendingly labeled a "good *forastero*," is being cultivated with new understanding of its nature and needs. The Ecuadorian firm of Pacari, founded in the first years of the twenty-first century by the husband-and-wife team Santiago Peralta and Carla Barboto, started making organic chocolates several years ago and now produces the world's only biodynamic chocolate. In Bolivia, long a neglected stepchild of the cacao-and-chocolate enterprise, the cacao cooperative El Ceibo is sending cacao harvested in the lowland region of Alto Beni to its plant in La Paz—the highest chocolate factory in the world, at 12,000 feet.

Cacao as a way of life is undergoing a resurgence, with exciting consequences for forest ecologies and local economies. Take the Kallari growers' co-op in the Napo River region of Ecuador, where hundreds of indigenous people are now working together to grow cacao on sustainable farms and collecting the resources to build their own factory using their own cacao. Or look at Brazil, where an industry once devastated by outbreaks of the fungal disease "witches' broom" as a result of shortsighted

growing priorities is now rebounding with delicious single-origin chocolates like Amma.

In all this I see the seeds for the growth of new culinary traditions: desserts that break away from the old reliance on European models, using excellent chocolates made in the country of origin and enhanced with Latin American seasonings; dazzlingly flavorful drinks based on a full range of Latin American chocolates, from stone-ground rustic cacao balls to industrially produced bars, that capture the full complexity of regional Latin American cacaos without the besetting Latin sins of excessive sugar and poor hygienic manufacturing conditions. In short: I believe that the future of chocolate once again belongs to Latin America.

YERBA MATE

In South America, Europeans found *yerba mate*, a tealike stimulant brewed from the leaves and twigs of a native holly species. Perhaps the caffeine level (higher than that of chocolate) helped spread its adoption by the invaders. In any case, *mate* (pronounced "MAH-tay") rapidly developed a devoted colonial following. (If you want to be a stickler, *mate* actually refers to the gourd into which *yerba mate*, or herb *mate*, is packed before brewing, but in the United States, the word *yerba* is usually dropped.)

As cattle ranching took over the pampas of Argentina, Paraguay, and Uruguay and nearby areas of Brazil and Bolivia, *yerba mate* became the South American cowboy coffee. In South American art and literature, gauchos are usually depicted either on horseback, chasing and lassoing a bull or a *ñandú*, the Patagonian ostrich, or hunkered around the fire sipping *mate* from a gourd with a silver straw, passing it around from hand to hand. In *mate*-drinking countries, traditional *mate* paraphernalia—silver-chased gourds that replaced the simple ones first used by the Guaraní Indians, ornate silver straws—mirror the ornate silver-studded clothing of the gauchos and their similarly decorated riding gear. A gaucho never mounted his horse without packing his silver gourd and straw. These were just as important as his knife, which he used to cut and eat grilled meats.

DRINKS FROM THE OLD WORLD: COFFEE AND OTHER NONALCOHOLIC DRINKS

Within a few decades of the conquest of the New World by the Spanish and the Portuguese, both cacao and *yerba mate* became cash crops, followed in the eighteenth century by coffee, a stimulant that had just begun to capture the interest of European society. Less than two centuries after the conquest, coffee plantations had sprouted all over tropical America from Mexico to the Caribbean to Brazil, and coffee had become more important as a drink than the native chocolate and *yerba mate*.

Coffee arrived in the Americas shrouded in mystique and intrigue. It is believed that a Frenchman named Gabriel Mathieu de Clieu managed to sneak away a coffee plant that had been given as a gift to Louis XIV by the Dutch in 1723. The plant had been jealously guarded at the Jardin des Plantes, a botanical garden in Paris. After a perilous rough crossing, de Clieu brought it to Martinique, where it became the source of the island's coffee planta-

tions. From Martinique, coffee spread to other French colonies in the New World and to Jamaica, Puerto Rico, and Cuba. And not only did it become a major plantation crop in Central America, the Caribbean, and parts of South America, but it also became woven into the fabric of the lives of Latin Americans.

I have vivid images inspired by coffee. As I sip my morning coffee in my backyard, I remember misty mornings on an abandoned eighteenth-century coffee plantation on the windswept Gran Piedra mountains near my Cuban hometown, or the fruity-acid smell of whole pulp-covered berries in a water tub at the start of the post-harvest process on a Colombian farm, or at my great-grandfather's house in San Pedro surrounded by rows of coffee trees and gardenias. When I grind freshly roasted coffee beans at my restaurants, I can see the callused hands of my grandmother Paquita or my aunt Carolina stirring a big smoking pot of roasting beans over a charcoal fire. When I go to a Miami cafeteria and drink a tiny cup of superpotent espresso, I recall the coffee bars of downtown Santiago de Chile where miniskirted waitresses coquettishly dispense Brazilian coffee to politicians and businessmen.

Coffee reached us accompanied by two other European imports, sugar and milk from dairy cows or goats. For Cubans, the three are still inseparable. "You want a *café con leche*?" is our first question to a friend or relative needing a little nurturing. Even today, when my coffee fix has to be decaffeinated, I can't go to sleep without my reassuring cup of coffee and its warm frothy milk.

Sugarcane probably played an even bigger role than coffee in the story of Latin drinks. Sugar transformed most of the native beverages it came in contact with. It was used to create many kinds of sweet *atoles* and similar thickened drinks. Perhaps no other plant has made its way into more Latin American beverages in more different forms than this archetypal slave-plantation crop. Nowadays, of course, it figures in many popular Latin soft drinks, some of which are worth exploring if you live near a pan-Latin market—Guaraná, Inka Kola, Materva.

Equally popular in Latin America is freshly crushed sugarcane juice, *guarapo*, enjoyed by Latins old and young everywhere the plant grows. This delightful beverage is, curiously, not cloyingly sweet but herbal and refreshing. In Cuban luncheonettes and cafeterias and in restaurants in Florida and even New Jersey (including my restaurant Zafra, named after the sugarcane harvest), the sugarcane is crushed in heavy-duty juicers that resemble miniature sugar mills to extract its juice.

Both as refined white sugar and in the form of rich-flavored brown loaf sugar, this successful transplant from the Old World to the New World makes dozens of heavenly marriages with fruits from both hemispheres. Tropical and other fruits are crushed or pulped and combined with sugar and water to create wonderful, thirst-quenching fruitades called *aguas frescas*—a beautiful name meaning "fresh waters"—or *refrescos*.

Other sweetened cold drinks that refresh body and spirit hark back to the Spanish *horchatas*, based on the "milk" of ground chufa nuts or almonds. There are lovely Latin *horchatas* made from melon seeds, rice, and coconut milk. Even more plentiful are the drinks that combine fresh fruits—often the same ones used for *aguas frescas*—with sugar and milk (sometimes part or all canned) to produce a rainbow of milk shakes known as *batidos* (Puerto Rico has similar drinks called *champolas*). With an instinct for combining food and drink into one filling, nourishing whole, Latins may make the best milk shakes in the world. In Brazil, where the shakes are often spiked with rum or *cachaça*, they are called *batidas*.

Milk was unknown in the cooking of the pre-Hispanic peoples, and once cows and goats were brought to the New World, it must have been a strange addition to the diet. But in regions where dairy animals thrived, both highland and lowland, people began using fresh or soured milk thriftily and ingeniously, doing wonderful things with by-products such as whey and buttermilk. I love the cultured milk *kumis*—one of several preparations resembling drinkable yogurt or sour milk, probably introduced by Middle Eastern immigrants—that Colombians of the Valle del Cauca sweetened with brown loaf sugar and pureed fruit. Ecuadorians make a sort of spiced drinking porridge (thickened with dried corn ground to a fine flour consistency) with the whey from cheese making. In high windswept regions of the Andean nations, where food is painstakingly wrung from the earth, milk has been a blessing to be carefully exploited in all possible ways.

ALCOHOL-FUELED CHANGE

The Spanish brought their own alcoholic drinks—wine, sherry, beer, brandy—to the peoples of *pulque* and *chicha*. But it was sugarcane, brought in by the conquistadors early in the sixteenth century, that changed the making of traditional brews like *chicha*, because adding sugar to the pot of fermenting yuca and corn sped up the process and produced a beverage with higher alcohol content as well as more sweetness, acidity, and fizz. Today all kinds of *chicha* are routinely made with sugar. To make *chicha*, people generally use brown loaf sugar, which adds more mellowness and depth than white sugar. There are sugar-fermented drinks, however, in which the cleaner and more neutral effect of refined sugar is what you want: for example, the so-called sorrel wine of red hibiscus made in Puerto Limón, Costa Rica (page 339).

The Spanish also introduced wine making to the temperate regions of the Americas. One of the pillars of Mediterranean civilization, wine followed the Spaniards across the Atlantic, along with recipes that called for wine. Though grapes of the genus *Vitis* did grow wild in North America, Central America, and the Caribbean, the native people did not use them for making wine. Everywhere the Spanish settled, they planted cuttings of the European *Vitis vinifera*—even in the hot, humid islands of the Hispanic Caribbean, where the vines grew but failed to bear enough fruit to support wine making.

Vineyards also sprang up wherever there were monks or missionaries, because wine was a cornerstone of the Catholic mass. As in Europe, in fact, monastic institutions were the great disseminators of a wine culture. Naturally, wine making on a large scale was possible only in the temperate regions of Latin America. The first vineyards and wineries of the Americas were established in New Spain (Mexico). Within a few decades after the conquest, grapevines were growing in Coahuila, Puebla, and Querétaro, and later in Sonora and in the temperate valleys of today's Baja California. But it was in South America, particularly in Peru and then in Chile and Argentina, that vineyards and wine making really flourished.

At first the Spanish colonial government encouraged grapevine planting in their New World colonies, and the availability of local wines must have been a blessing for the early Spanish settlers and their descendants. By 1630, Spanish and Peruvian-born merchants were transporting 200,000 *botijas* (earthen jars) of wine produced in the Andean coastal valleys of Ica and Nazca to Lima. However, Andalusian wine makers, who had been doing a brisk business selling their wines to Spain's New World colonies, began to worry about competition and mounted an aggressive campaign to curtail wine production in the New World. In the first half of the seventeenth century, when wine production in Peru had reached a record high and Peruvian wines were even being exported to Mexico, the Spanish Crown enacted protectionist laws forbidding the wine merchants from sending wines up to Panama and Guatemala and banning new vineyards. These widespread controls enabled the Spanish wine imports, which had always commanded higher prices, to share the market with the local wines. These, however, were still preferred to any import for cooking and drinking purposes. Even today, in Mendoza, the most important wine-producing region in Argentina, where grapevines were planted in the sixteenth century, the cooking wine of choice remains a brash local one poured from a 5-liter container called a *damajuana*.

Although the Spanish had introduced some beer brewing, large-scale commercial brewing had to wait until German immigrants arrived all over Latin America in the nineteenth century. Today, some of the world's best commercial beers are brewed in Latin America—not only standard lagers and dark beers like the many labels belonging to the giant Mexican Moctezuma brewing empire but also lesser known boutique brews from regions not known for their beers, like the highlands of Panama's Chiriquí province.

Far more powerful in its eventual economic effects was the alcohol distillation process introduced by the Spanish a few decades into the colonial era, when some sixteenth-century genius discovered that the already lucrative sugarcane crop could be used to produce rum. This translated in effect into an open invitation to England, the Netherlands, France, and Spain to expand the slave trade. The Caribbean islands were the most drastically affected, but other New World sugar-raising areas also felt the reverberations. Rum became one of the glories of the islands and Caribbean Venezuela. While in the French islands, particularly Haiti, Martinique, and Guadeloupe, rum is distilled from sugarcane juice (*rhum agricole*), in the Spanish-speaking world it is almost always made from one or another of the molasses-extraction stages in the refining process. The lovely, characteristic warmth and richness of the rum comes from the caramelized sugars in the molasses.

Rum is the best known of the New World sugarcane liquors, but wherever sugar went, someone eventually started distilling it. The production of most cane liquors other than rum remained largely local enterprises until fairly recently. Every region had its own version, usually called *aguardiente* (firewater) or *caña* (cane). In Brazil, the local cane liquor is familiarly known as *cachaça*, a term for booze (*pinga* is the more dignified name). Most *aguardientes* live up to the name, being fiery and often throat-burning, but their flavors are neutral, though the very fine Guatemalan El Venado brand, one of my favorites, is quite aromatic. There are, however, certain regional preferences. Colombians, for instance, like their *aguardiente* flavored with anise.

Following the introduction of wine grapes and the distilling process, Latin-produced grape brandy established a few local footholds in scattered regions of Latin America. In the Andean countries, primarily Peru and Chile, the brandy of choice is pisco, a fiery spirit somewhat like grappa. The more aromatic pisco comes from Peru.

European distilling and Mexican *maguey* sap—the clear, sweet *aguamiel* that is still the source of *pulque*—united in the production of the strong, stinging liquor called mezcal and the more elegant tequila. Tequila distilling probably dates back to the seventeenth century in Jalisco, where several distilleries seem to have been well established by the eighteenth century. Tequila differs from mezcal in that it is made only from blue *maguey* (*Agave tequilana Weber*) rather than any of several lesser species, and can be as refined as great cognac or rum.

WHAT LATIN AMERICANS CRAVE IN A DRINK

Years after coming to Latin America, Cuban-born writer Oscar Hijuelos learned that the mysterious bedtime drink he'd tasted for so long in memory—"so Cuban, so delicious"—was nothing more than milk and Hershey's syrup. Like Hijuelos, I too had to discover the prosaic ingredients of a long-cherished childhood drink that my father always made when we played with our friends in Santa María, in the mountains outside Santiago de Cuba. Ice-cold, with hints of citrus, his ruby-red drink had that perfect balance between sweet and sour that children of the tropics love so much. One luminous morning in 1958, during the revolution, as my brother and I played on stilts in our front garden, my father came out of the house stirring a pitcher and poured us each a glass. Before we could take a sip, an army plane flew low. We looked up and started waving. Unexpectedly, bullets started raining down a few feet from the garden, just like in the movies. Shocked, I threw my glass in the air and ran for my life into the house, to find refuge in the special bunker that all Cuban houses were equipped with at that time. Against the rat-a-tat-tat noise of bullets and the frightful drone of the plane, my parents counted noses and realized that Ismar, my brother, was missing. My mother, pregnant at the time with my younger brother, Marco Alejandro, almost had a miscarriage on the spot. We didn't know that at the first sound of bullets, Ismar had run to the next-door neighbor's house, clutching his magic drink for dear life. He was still hugging it to his chest when we found him an hour later. When I was an adult, I found out that this drink my brother risked his life over was nothing more than limeade colored with strawberry Jell-O.

You never know what flavors are encoded in someone's enchanted memory. In both these cases, though, I'd say it was sweetness—or rather, a perfect balance between sweetness and something else, the tartness of lemonade or the slight bitterness of chocolate. As children of the sugar-growing tropics, millions of Latin Americans, including me, like drinks with a balance of sweetness and spicy bite, fragrance, creaminess, the kick of coffee, the sturdy taste of rum, or the many notes of fruit.

Our love for sweetness extends to alcoholic drinks. For most Latins, a perfect cocktail is one that begins with something fruity, like citrus juice or often fresh fruit, and adds a good dose of spirits, often a flavorful and aromatic liqueur, and a judicious amount of sugar.

This chapter is a grand tour of the drink traditions of Latin America. It begins with fermented drinks, including a *chicha* from the tropical lowlands made from pineapple peel, a fruity Andean *chicha* made with purple corn, and a mildly fermented ruby-colored hibiscus drink from Costa Rica. Next is a broad selection of nourishing nonalcoholic drinks, ranging from chocolate to the fruit

milk shakes of the Hispanic Caribbean. Here you'll find a perfumed chocolate inspired by seventeenth- and eighteenth-century recipes; filling concoctions thickened with grains from Mexico, Central America, and Ecuador; my favorite aromatic hot chocolate from Guaraparo, a small town in Venezuela; and milk shake made with the delectable *mamey* fruit. Lighter drinks combining fruit or nuts with water follow—a *horchata* and a cooling limeade.

Stimulating drinks like coffee and *yerba mate* cannot be missing from a Latin American cookbook, and here are recipes from Argentina, Paraguay, and Cuba, where coffee is king. Equally important are alcoholic drinks. In this broad category are egg- and-milk-enriched drinks that are Christmas favorites, such as the Venezuelan *ponche crema* and Puerto Rican *coquito*, and cocktails that have traveled the world over, like the Cuban daiquiri and mojito, the potent Brazilian *caipirinha*, and the seductive pisco sours of Peru and Chile.

FERMENTED DRINKS

Fermented Pineapple Drink
Chicha de Piña

In my grandfather's kitchen, there was always a large cloth-covered glass container filled with thick chunks of ripe pineapple peel and water. The changes in the pot fascinated and scared me: the bubbles and foam crackled on the surface of the liquid, the golden pineapple darkened, and a vinegary yet perfumed smell invaded the kitchen. Then came the pleasurable surprise. My grandfather strained the ominous-looking brew, and it was transformed into an amber-colored tropical champagne that made our noses tingle.

You will always find pineapple *chicha* in most tropical countries—it is a clever form of kitchen recycling. In the tropical kitchen, there are always plenty of pineapple peels. In Veracruz, pineapple *chicha* is called *tepache* and is sweetened with *piloncillo*, Mexican brown loaf sugar. In the Churrería del Recuerdo in Xalapa, *tepache* used to be made in huge containers, which were constantly being replenished as the fermented brew was poured out into clear glass jugs.

MAKES 3 QUARTS

    2 ripe large pineapples (about 5 pounds each)
    3 quarts spring water
 1–2 cups sugar

▶ Peel the pineapples, cutting deeply and leaving some flesh attached; reserve the remaining fruit for another purpose. Place the peels (about 2 ½ pounds) and water in a 5-quart earthenware pot or glass jar. Cover with a double layer of cheesecloth and set aside to ferment in a warm place for 3 days.

Stir sugar to taste into the pineapple mixture and let sit for 2 more days.

Strain the liquid through a double layer of cheesecloth and refrigerate until chilled. It will keep well in the refrigerator for about 1 week. Serve chilled over ice.

Variations: In Veracruz, the drink called *tepache* is made by the same process but sweetened with Mexican brown loaf sugar (*piloncillo*) instead of white sugar. Use 2½ cups grated brown loaf sugar or packed regular brown sugar. Some cooks add cinnamon, cloves, and allspice berries to the brew. There are also versions that call for the addition of beer.

Peruvian Purple Corn Punch
Chicha Morada

This refreshing and aromatic purple drink flavored with spices and fruits is not technically a *chicha* because it is not fermented, but everyone calls it *chicha morada*. Peruvians love it at all times, but it is mostly drunk during the October feast of the Cristo Morado, the "Purple Christ," in Lima because its deep color matches the color of mourning of the religious season.

MAKES 7½ CUPS (ABOUT EIGHT 7-OUNCE SERVINGS)

    8 ears dried Peruvian purple corn (about 2 pounds)
    1 teaspoon whole cloves, or to taste
    4 Ceylon cinnamon sticks (*canela*)
       Peel of one 4-pound pineapple (about 1 pound, with some flesh attached)
    1 cup dried cherries (about 6 ounces)
    5 quarts water
   12 ounces *chancaca* (Peruvian brown loaf sugar) or any other Latin American brown loaf sugar, grated (2¾ cups), or 2¾ cups Muscovado sugar or packed brown sugar
   ¾ cup fresh lime juice (from about 6 small limes)

▶ Rinse the ears of corn under cold water and place in a large stockpot. Add the cloves, cinnamon sticks, pineapple peel, dried cherries, and water and bring to a boil over high heat. Reduce the heat to medium-low and simmer, uncovered, for 1 hour.

Strain the punch though a layer of cheesecloth into a bowl or other container. Add the brown sugar and lime juice. Stir to dissolve the sugar and taste for sweetness. Let cool to room temperature, then refrigerate until chilled. Serve cold over ice.

Variations: Stir in cut-up fresh fruit and 1 cup pisco for a refreshing Andean sangría. Or for a refreshing and mildly alcoholic drink, place the *chicha* in an earthenware pot or glass jar, cover with two layers of cheesecloth or a loose lid, and allow to ferment at room temperature for 3 days.

Costa Rican Hibiscus Wine

Vino de Flor de Jamaica

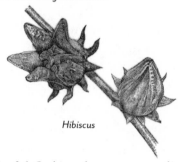

Hibiscus

The colorful fleshy calyxes surrounding the seed pods of the shrub *Hibiscus sabdariffa* are dried and made into tart ruby-red drinks in Mexico, Central America, and the Caribbean. They are called sorrel or roselle by local English speakers; in Spanish it is *flor de jamaica*. Something deeper lies beneath the pretty hue—a grassy taste that is not so innocuous. I call it backbone.

In Costa Rica and all the black communities of Central America, particularly among the Garífuna, this sweetened hibiscus drink is fermented into a mildly alcoholic, tingly beverage that looks like red wine. My Garífuna friend Sinford Mejías was toasted with hibiscus punch on the day of her wedding in Honduras.

MAKES 2 QUARTS (ABOUT EIGHT 8-OUNCE SERVINGS)

4 ounces (about 3¼ cups) dried hibiscus flowers (*flor de jamaica*)

2½ quarts water

2 cups sugar, or to taste

2 star anise pods

2-inch piece of fresh ginger (about 1 ounce), peeled

2 Ceylon cinnamon sticks (*canela*)

5 whole cloves

▶ Place all the ingredients in a 6-quart pot and bring to a boil over medium-high heat. Reduce the heat to medium-low and simmer for 15 minutes.

Strain the mixture through a fine-mesh strainer into a large heatproof glass jar and let cool to room temperature. Cover with a double layer of cheesecloth or a loose lid and set aside to ferment at room temperature for about 3 days for a mildly fermented drink. Or, for a more alcoholic drink, allow it to ferment for 21 days as is done in Costa Rica. Serve chilled in rock glasses.

DRINKS AS FOOD

Hot Chocolate *"Agasajo"*

Chocolate Caliente para Agasajos

Cacao was first brought to the Iberian Peninsula from the Americas in 1520. What followed was a love affair between Spaniards and chocolate that has lasted until today, but in no other period of Spanish history was chocolate more appreciated and sought after than in the seventeenth century. On every street there were stands that ground processed cacao mixtures and sold hot chocolate. And every afternoon in bourgeois and aristocratic households, chocolate reigned supreme. Elegant afternoon soirees called *agasajos* centered on the drinking of chocolate, which was served along with marzipan, nougats, and cold drinks to female guests seated on low stools. The hot chocolate was frothy and heavily spiced with rosebuds, saffron or achiote, and even hot peppers, strongly reminiscent of the heady cacao concoctions enjoyed by the con- quistadores in the Americas.

MAKES 8 CUPS (ABOUT TEN 6-OUNCE SERVINGS)

- 2 quarts whole milk
- ¼ ounce dried unsprayed rosebuds (sold as *rosa de Castilla* in Hispanic markets; also available at Middle Eastern shops)
- 2 teaspoons saffron threads, lightly crushed
- 4 Ceylon cinnamon sticks (*canela*)
- 1 dried *chile de árbol* or 2–3 *piquín* chiles, or to taste
- ¼ cup sugar
- 2 vanilla beans, preferably Mexican
- 7 ounces bittersweet chocolate such as El Rey Gran Samán (70%), Pacari Los Ríos (72%), or Cluizel Los Ancones (67%), coarsely chopped

▶ Place the milk, rosebuds, saffron, cinnamon sticks, chile, and sugar in a medium nonreactive pot and bring to a boil over medium heat.

Split the vanilla beans in half, scrape out the seeds with a paring knife, and add both seeds and beans to the milk. Reduce the heat to medium-low and simmer for 10 minutes. Remove from the heat and let sit, covered, for 10 minutes.

Strain the mixture into a large saucepan and set over medium heat. Stir in the chocolate and beat vigorously with a wire whisk or Mexican *molinillo* until you have a good froth. Serve hot.

Variation: For a richer, more full-bodied drink, use 10 ounces chocolate.

Spiced Venezuelan Hot Chocolate

Chocolate en Taza Yaguaraparo

The cacao balls made by Ana Rodríguez in Yaguaraparo, a small village in Paria Peninsula, Venezuela, are scented with half a dozen spices. They are living relics of the time before chocolate bars. A glance at the ingredients she uses and the painstaking manual labor that is required to make them reveals a great deal of sophistication and inge- nuity. To approximate the flavor of the hot choco- late made with Ana Rodríguez's chocolate balls, you need to use a high-quality dark chocolate and her special spice blend.

Cook's Note: If you happen to have a *mamey sapote* seed on hand from making a *batido* (page 344) or *mamey* flan (page 831), crack it open and grate about a quarter of the fleshy interior into the sugar instead of the almond extract. Another traditional ingredient of the Paria chocolate mixture, the tonka beans from an Amazonian tree native to southern Venezuela and Brazil (*Dipteryx punctata*), have an aroma reminiscent of vanilla beans, which I use here.

MAKES 8 CUPS (ABOUT EIGHT 8-OUNCE SERVINGS)

- ½ cup sugar
- 1 tablespoon ground Ceylon cinnamon (*canela*)
- 6 star anise pods
- 4 whole cloves
- 1 teaspoon coarsely chopped peeled fresh ginger
- 1 teaspoon almond extract

2 vanilla beans, preferably Mexican, coarsely chopped

2 quarts whole milk

7 ounces bittersweet chocolate such as El Rey Gran Samán (70%), Amano Chuao (70%), or Cluizel Concepción (66%), extra bitter, coarsely chopped

▶ Combine the sugar, cinnamon, star anise, cloves, ginger, almond extract, and vanilla beans in a mini-food processor and grind to a fine powder. Alternatively, you can grind the dry spices in a spice mill and then process them with the sugar, ginger, and almond extract.

In a large saucepan, combine the spice mixture with the milk. Heat to just under a boil over medium heat, stirring constantly. Reduce the heat to medium-low and simmer for 10 minutes. Remove from the heat and let sit, covered, for 10 minutes to allow the spices to infuse the milk.

Strain the milk into another large saucepan, place over medium heat, and add the chocolate. Beat vigorously with a wire whisk or Mexican *molinillo* until you have a good froth. Serve at once.

Variation: For a thicker, creamier texture, increase the chocolate to 10 ounces.

THE GRAN NACIONAL

Ecuador stood poised to replace Mesoamerica as an important exporter of cacao starting in the late sixteenth and early seventeenth centuries when Spanish planters began to exploit the luxuriant groves of cacao they had discovered along coastal rivers, particularly the Guayas, in what is today the province of Los Ríos. This become the home of the *grandes cacaos* of Ecuador, powerful cacao growers who made great fortunes, just as their brethren in Venezuela did with their fine *criollo*, satisfying the appetite for cacao all over Latin America and Spain. The cacao of the coastal regions of Ecuador crossed the Andes from the Amazonian region in prehistoric times. It came to be known as *Arriba*, a name that simply means "from upriver," because it grew more abundantly upriver along the Guayas.

Until very recently, this fine aromatic cacao was listed as a good *forastero*, but now geneticists have proven that it belongs to a particular cluster, Nacional. Ecuadorian Nacional has undergone a very intense process of hybridization because cacaos from other regions of the Americas were introduced into Ecuador at various points in time starting in the late nineteenth century, and particularly from the 1930s to the 1950s as a result of spells of disease. The resulting mix, in synergy with the distinct regional *terroirs* of the country, particularly along the coast, has given rise to a delicate and flavorful type of cacao that has now been labeled as "Nacional Complex by Trinitario." Feminine and sophisticated, Ecuadorian cacao has distinct herbal and woody notes that often recall a pine forest or recently mowed grass with bright notes of red fruit reminiscent of Andean blackberries. At its purest, Nacional can be intensely floral with the aroma of orange blossoms (*azahar*). Though it has suffered setbacks due to competition with more robust hybrids in recent years, it is currently undergoing a revival through the work of scientists at INIAP (Ecuador's National Institute of Agricultural and Livestock Research) who have developed flavorful, productive, and disease-resistant clones from cacaos with strong Nacional blood. In an even more promising development, they have also collected pure Nacional cacaos in the Ecuadorian Amazon, which in a few years will be ready to revitalize the country's commercial cacao bloodstream. ◆

Ecuadorian Barley-Thickened Hot Chocolate

Chocolate con Máchica

In the Ecuadorian highlands, *máchica*, or toasted barley flour, often thickens drinks in much the same way as corn in other parts of Latin America. This robust version of hot chocolate uses a chocolate made from Ecuadorian beans and a mixture of *máchica* with brown loaf sugar and cinnamon to sweeten and bind the liquid. I usually make up the mixture in a 1-cup batch. You can store any excess in a cool place, in a tightly covered jar.

MAKES 1 SERVING

- 1 cup whole milk
- 1 ounce dark chocolate, preferably Pacari Manabí (65%), Guittard Quevedo (65%), or Pacari Los Ríos (72%, for a more intense taste), coarsely chopped
- 2 tablespoons Spiced *Máchica* Mix (recipe follows)
  Pinch of salt

▶ Bring the milk barely to a boil in a small saucepan over medium heat. Add the chocolate and stir with a wooden spoon to dissolve it, about 1 minute. Stir in the *máchica* mix and salt. Cook, stirring, until the mixture thickens to the consistency of a light porridge, about 2 minutes. Strain through a mesh sieve and serve at once.

Spiced *Máchica* Mix

MAKES ABOUT 1 CUP

- Two 3-inch Ceylon cinnamon sticks (*canela*)
- ½ cup finely grated brown loaf sugar (preferably *panela* or *piloncillo*), Muscovado sugar, or firmly packed dark brown sugar
- 1 cup *máchica* (Ecuadorian toasted barley flour)

▶ Grind together the cinnamon and sugar in a spice mill until very fine. Combine thoroughly with the *máchica*.

Ecuadorian Purple Colada

Colada Morada

Ecuadorian *coladas* are thick, nourishing drinks made with grains and fruits and served warm. This delicious *colada* made of purple corn and fresh fruits is served all over Ecuador on November 2, All Souls' Day, because of its intense purple hue, the color of mourning. Ecuadorians use a type of local berry, *mortiño*, for its deep purple color, but here in the United States I substitute blackberries or blueberries. In Cuenca, the *colada* is accompanied by a dark-crusted, anise-flavored bread called *costra*.

MAKES 3 QUARTS (16 SERVINGS)

- 2¾ quarts water
- 8 ounces purple corn flour (available in Hispanic markets)
- 8 ounces brown loaf sugar (*piloncillo* or *panela*), coarsely chopped, or 1½ cups packed brown sugar
- 7 ounces frozen *naranjilla* puree or the juice of 6 fresh or frozen *naranjillas*, available in Hispanic markets (also known as *lulo*)

2 Ceylon cinnamon sticks (*canela*)
1 teaspoon whole cloves
1 teaspoon allspice berries
4 orange leaves (optional)
1 ripe small pineapple (about 3 pounds), peeled, cored, and diced
1 cup blueberries or hulled blackberries

▶ Pour 2 quarts of the water into a large saucepan and bring to a simmer over medium heat. Add the corn flour, stirring to mix. Add the *naranjilla* puree and half the brown sugar and cook, stirring, until the sugar dissolves.

Pour the mixture into an enameled or an earthenware pot, cover with a double layer of cheesecloth, and set aside to ferment for 2 days.

Stir the mixture and strain through two layers of cheesecloth into a large nonreactive pot. Bring barely to a boil, then reduce the heat to medium-low and simmer, stirring, until it thickens, about 10 minutes. Add the rest of the sugar and stir to dissolve.

While the corn flour mixture is cooking, place the cinnamon, cloves, allspice berries, and orange leaves, if using, in a small saucepan with the remaining 3 cups water, bring just to a boil, and simmer over low heat until fragrant, about 5 minutes.

Strain the infused water into the corn mixture (discard the spices) and continue simmering until the *colada* has the consistency of a pourable yogurt, about 15 minutes.

Stir in the diced pineapple and blackberries. The colada will look ominously dark purple, but do not fear—it will be delicious. Serve hot or cold, with any sweet bread.

Colombian Fruit and Corn Punch

Champú

This is one of the most delicious and refreshing Andean drinks I know, aromatic, chock-full of fruits, and lightly thickened with pureed white corn. It is my choice for an outdoor buffet party. The traditional recipe calls for *naranjilla* juice, but I have found passion fruit juice equally delicious. My recipe also calls for less corn than traditional versions. In any case, it will thicken a bit in the refrigerator.

This makes a generous amount, but do not be tempted to cut the recipe in half, because your guests are sure to ask for more.

MAKES ABOUT 4 QUARTS (8 SERVINGS)

8 ounces cracked white corn, such as Goya white hominy corn (*maíz trillado blanco*; see page 445)
3 quarts water
1 pound grated brown loaf sugar (*panela* or *piloncillo*), or 3¼ cups Muscovado sugar or packed dark brown sugar
 Peel of 1 orange
8 whole cloves
4 Ceylon cinnamon sticks (*canela*)
4 orange leaves (optional)
1 ripe 5-pound pineapple, peeled, cored, and cut into ¼-inch cubes (about 5 cups)
2 cups *naranjilla* juice (sold frozen in Hispanic markets; also called *lulo*) or passion fruit juice
5 cups crushed ice

▶ Place the corn and 2½ quarts water in a 4-quart heavy pot and bring to a boil over high heat. Lower the heat to medium and simmer until the corn is tender, about 1½ hours.

Scoop out 1½ cups of the corn and ½ cup of the cooking liquid, transfer to a blender or food processor, and process into a smooth puree. Pour the puree back into the pot, stir to mix well, and set aside.

Meanwhile, prepare the brown sugar syrup. Place the brown sugar, remaining 2 cups water, orange peel, cloves, cinnamon sticks, and orange leaves, if using, in a small saucepan and bring to a boil over high heat. Reduce the heat to medium-low and simmer for about 25 minutes, until lightly thickened and aromatic. Strain into a heatproof bowl and let cool.

Add the syrup, pineapple cubes, and *naranjilla* or passion fruit juice to the cooked corn, mixing well. Pour the *champú* into a decorative pitcher and stir in the crushed ice. Mix well and serve in tall glasses with long spoons. Be sure to stir the mixture well as you serve the punch, as the corn has a tendency to sink to the bottom of the pitcher.

Storing: Any leftover punch will keep for 2 to 3 days in the refrigerator.

Mamey Sapote Milk Shake

Batido de Mamey

At any Latin American market, neighborhood eatery, or cafeteria, people will be quenching their thirst with all kinds of delicious *batidos*—milk shakes based on the best local fruit. I am partial to *batidos* made with *mamey sapote*. In Cuba, we call this luscious tropical fruit *mamey*, and it is often sold under that name in this country. Technically, however, the name *mamey* belongs to another tropical species, *Mammea americana*, and our Cuban *mamey* is really

Pouteria sapote. Several cultivars are regularly found in U.S. markets; the large Magaña and the smaller Pantín are the most familiar.

This drink takes me back to the 1960s, when the bite of rationing had begun to take a toll on the simple pleasures Cubans cherished, like tropical milk shakes or juices with a hot Cuban sandwich as a morning pick-me-up, for the *merienda* (the afternoon meal), or at night after going to the movies. When I was in high school, I looked forward to our brief midmorning break so I could rush to a nearby cafeteria with dozens of other students, hoping to be the first in line for a *batido de zapote* (as we called it in Santiago, my hometown). Because I knew that the milk shake could be gone forever tomorrow, I drank every drop with enormous pleasure. I loved the cool, creamy sensation of the thick shake gliding down my throat, my hunger as satiated as if I had eaten a nourishing porridge.

Cook's Note: You can find frozen *mamey* pulp in any Hispanic Caribbean market. Usually I wait to buy the fresh *mameyes* grown in south Florida. Save the shiny black seed—it has a wonderful almond flavor that is irresistible in Spiced Venezuelan Hot Chocolate (page 340) and Rice *Horchata* (page 345).

MAKES 2 QUARTS (ABOUT SIX 12-OUNCE SERVINGS)

- 2 pounds *mamey sapote* (1 medium Magaña or 2 Pantín) or about 4 cups (1 pound 3 ounces) thawed frozen *mamey* pulp
- 1 quart milk
- ½ cup sugar, or to taste
- ⅛ teaspoon salt
- 4 cups crushed ice

▶ Cut the fruit lengthwise in half and remove the seed. Cut each half into 2 or 3 long slices and peel off the skin. Cut into 1- to 2-inch chunks. You should have about 4 cups.

Working in 2 batches, place the *mamey* pulp, milk, sugar, salt, and ice in a blender and process until frothy. Serve at once in tall glasses.

Variations: Almost any fresh fruit can be used to make a *batido* with this formula. The only variation will be in the amount of sugar needed. The frozen pulp of many kinds of tropical fruit is available year-round in Latin markets, and it is convenient when fresh fruit isn't in season or of good quality.

To Die While Dreaming

Morir Soñando

The name of this Dominican favorite literally means "to die while dreaming." Dominicans adore this blend of fresh orange juice and sweetened milk, which thickens lightly as you stir it. Don't try it with pasteurized orange juice. You want the best oranges you can get.

SERVES 1

> Juice of 1 medium orange (about ½ cup)
> ¼ cup whole milk
> 2 tablespoons sweetened condensed milk, or to taste
> 1 cup ice cubes

▶ Pour the orange juice into a 12-ounce tall glass. Add the whole milk and condensed milk, stirring. The mixture will thicken to a light creamy consistency. Add the ice cubes and stir well. Serve cold.

HORCHATA AND LIMEADE

Rice *Horchata*

Horchata de Arroz

To wash down hearty and highly seasoned Yucatecan dishes like *cochinita pibil*, there is nothing better than a rice *horchata*, a drink descended from the *horchata de arroz* popular in rice-growing areas of Spain. The Yucatecan version calls for an unusual flavoring ingredient, the seed of the *mamey sapote*.

When you cut open a football-shaped *mamey sapote*, you find a single large seed nestled in the center of the salmon-colored pulp. You need to crack open the hard, shiny black shell to get to the fleshy interior. I first tasted the seed as a curious child in Cuba and was told not to swallow it because it was toxic. Yes, the *mamey* seed is laden with cyanide—hence its intense bitter almond flavor. Yet in small amounts it is not dangerous. Ground with the rice, *mamey sapote* adds a subtle bitter almond aroma and flavor to this refreshing Yucatecan drink.

MAKES 12 CUPS (EIGHT 12-OUNCE SERVINGS)

> 2 cups (13 ounces) long-grain rice, rinsed
> 1 cup (about 4 ounces) blanched whole almonds
> 2 Ceylon cinnamon sticks (*canela*), cut into 1-inch pieces
> ¼-inch chunk of a *mamey sapote* seed or 1 teaspoon almond extract
> 1 cup sugar, or to taste
> ⅛ teaspoon salt

▶ Place the rice and almonds in a large bowl, cover generously with 3 quarts of water, and let soak overnight.

Drain the rice and almonds, reserving 2 quarts of the soaking water. In a large food processor or blender, working in 3 batches, combine the rice, almonds, and mamey sapote seed, if using, with the reserved water and grind to a mush. Put the ground rice and nuts back in the bowl, add the sugar, salt, and almond extract, if not using the *mamey sapote* seed, and stir well. Strain through a fine-mesh strainer, pour into a pitcher, and refrigerate until chilled. The *horchata* will keep well refrigerated for about a week. Stir before serving, and serve over ice cubes if desired.

Zafra's One-Lime Limeade

Limonada de Zafra

This delicious limeade was inspired by a drink from the hot and sticky port of Guayaquil, in Ecuador. The beauty of it is that all you need is 1 whole lime, peel and all, water, and sugar. At my restaurant Zafra, I have refined the process to get lots of flavor from the peel without excess bitterness. It has become one of our signature drinks.

SERVES 1

    1 large unpeeled lime, cut into chunks
  1⅓ cups water
    3 tablespoons sugar
    1 cup ice cubes
    1 lime slice, for garnish

▶ Place the lime chunks and water in a blender and process at high speed until the lime is chopped to minuscule bits. Strain through a coarse strainer. Pour back into the blender, add the sugar and ice cubes, and process until frothy. Serve at once in a tall glass garnished with the lime slice.

STIMULANTS: *YERBA MATE* AND COFFEE

Yerba Mate

In testosterone country, the rough Argentinean pampas, drinking *yerba mate*, a tealike stimulant, is a concession to the womanly roundness of the kettle. One might be taken aback by the bonding intimacy of a drink that is passed around in a single gourd, the *mate*, and drunk from the same silver straw, the *bombilla*. The passing of the *mate* is an act of solidarity that only those who are born to it can fully understand.

I experienced once what it meant to share the *mate*. It was not even in Argentina or Paraguay, but in the fjords of southern Chile, aboard a small fishing boat. It was damp and terribly cold, and the sea was unexpectedly choppy. There was a small stove on the boat, with a simmering kettle set upon it. The hot *mate* was passed around, and without even thinking I sipped it from the *bombilla*. It was comforting. At the time, it seemed natural; it was only later, when I reached my comfort zone, that I recoiled, thinking of such intimate sharing.

The tea I sipped was made from the leaves of a South American holly (*Ilex paraguarensis*) generically called *yerba*, grass. Because the tea is drunk from a gourd, *mate*, the plant is also known as *yerba mate*. Because *yerba* does not grow in Chile, the brands used there are imported from Argentina. They are not of a very high quality, but the people of southern Chile are used to it. Enter the *ruka* (hut) of a Mapuche Indian or the kitchen of any fisherman in Chiloé, and you may find a group of people sitting around the fire where a kettle simmers, drinking *mate*.

The finest grade of *yerba mate* is a mixture of dark green leaves that look like oolong tea leaves and twigs. Cheaper *mate* is practically pulverized into a powder. The flavor is indescribable, but it is something like green tea with a grassier and smoky taste. The *yerba mate* ritual in which the brewing vessel also serves as drinking vessel is so much fun that I would never consider serving hot *mate* any other way, but there is no reason not to experiment with it using your teapot and small cups (for example, handleless Japanese teacups). Large cups are not appropriate, both because *mate* has a fair amount of caffeine and because it is meant to be drunk a sip at a time.

Paraguayan Herbal Iced *Yerba Mate*

Tereré

In Paraguay, this cold drink is served in bull's horns—or in rock glasses. The preparation is simple. A pitcher of ice-cold water is infused with a mixture of fresh herbs, called *yuyos*. The infusion is then added gradually to the *yerba mate*, the pitcher with the cold infusion is passed around the room, and people sip the liquid from a *bombilla* or silver straw. Serve this in rock glasses, or in the traditional small gourds—with silver *bombillas*, if you have them.

SERVES 6

- 6 cups water
  Zest of 1 small orange
- ½ bunch mint, leaves and stems coarsely crushed with a mortar and pestle
- 3–4 fresh or dried lemon verbena sprigs (optional)
- 1 lime, cut into very thin slices
- 2 cups crushed ice
- 3 cups *yerba mate* (with stems; sold in Hispanic markets as *yerba mate con palo*)
- 6 tablespoons sugar
- 6 lime slices, for garnish
- 6 mint sprigs, for garnish

▶ Place the water, orange zest, mint, lemon verbena, if using, and lime slices in a large bowl or pitcher. Let infuse for at least 4 hours. Just before serving, stir in the ice.

In a small bowl, mix the *yerba mate* and sugar; set aside.

Place 1 lime slice and 1 mint sprig in each of 6 tall rock glasses so that they will remain visible after you add the *yerba mate*. Tilt each glass at a steep angle and add about ½ cup of the *yerba mate*–sugar mixture, leaving one side clear enough to accommodate a straw without obstruction; place a straw along the side of each glass. Moisten each portion of *yerba mate* with 2 tablespoons of the cold infusion, then let your guests top up their glasses with more of the infusion.

THE *YERBA MATE* TEA CEREMONY

The essence of the ceremony is to sip and savor the fragrant, invigorating *yerba mate* as it infuses in a small gourd. People also use ceramic, metal, or wooden vessels in the shape of gourds, but the real thing is inexpensive in Hispanic markets. Small gourds, which I consider the best size, hold about 6 ounces. An opening in the top of the gourd accommodates the silver *bombilla*, a straw fitted at one end with a perforated or basketwork strainer.

I will not try to decide for you the question of whether to follow custom by using a single gourd and straw or individual ones for everyone. (A compromise might be to let couples share one.) One person traditionally acts as the *matero*, or master of the *mate* ceremony. Provide the chosen one with the gourd(s) and straw(s), a supply of good-quality *yerba mate*, and a kettle with plenty of hot—never boiling—water. Scalding-hot water burns the leaves, which gives them a bitter flavor.

First, warm the gourd by filling it with hot water. Pour out the water and pack the gourd a little more than half full with the tea leaves and stems. (For a 6-ounce gourd, use about 6 tablespoons.) You can add sugar at this point—some people regularly do so, while others regard sugar in *mate* with horror and insist on drinking the tea unsweetened. Tilt the gourd to let the contents settle to one side, not quite spilling over the edge. Moisten the *mate* with a small amount of water (3 to 4 tablespoons), either warm or cold. Let it stand for a few minutes—this begins the action of softening and absorbing. Rinse the *bombilla* with hot water and place it in the gourd. Traditionalists make the sign of the cross with the *bombilla* before placing it in the gourd. Carefully pour a few ounces of hot water over the leaves in the gourd and wait for it to be absorbed before adding a few more. Keep adding hot water, a little at a time, until the gourd is nearly full. (A real hair-on-the-chest *matero* would at this point take two sips of the infusion and spit out one over his left shoulder and one over his right.)

Now the passing of the gourd begins. When a single gourd is used, each participant in the ceremony drinks as much or as little as he or she wants and hands the gourd to the next person. At some point, the *matero* replenishes the water. Even if your party is using individual gourds, the *matero* should still keep hot water at the ready; a conscientious *matero* makes sure to ask whether anyone needs more water and refills the gourd while trying not to move the *bombilla* and stir up the leaves and twigs of the *yerba* (stirring ruins the flavor). This replenishing is called *cebar*—literally, to fatten, or to prime.

From time to time, when new leaves seem to be called for, the *matero* removes a small handful of the steeped *yerba* from the gourd and adds a bit more while trying not to disturb the contents of the gourd. The longer the *matero* can stretch out the sipping-and-replenishing process for everybody, the more satisfying the ceremony.

In the *yerba mate* regions of South America, people drink this brew at all hours of the day, as they would coffee. Argentineans love *yerba mate* for breakfast and in the afternoon when they gather to eat the small pastries called *facturas*. It is not uncommon to see construction workers sipping *mate* as they work or people driving fancy cars holding their gourds. ◆

Coffee

In 1748, a Cuban plantation owner named José Gelabert planted a few coffee beans he had obtained in Saint Domingue (today's Haiti) on his farm in Wajay, near Havana. This was the humble beginning of Cuba's obsession with coffee. For centuries, the drink of choice for both Cubans and Spaniards living on the island had been chocolate. But as soon as coffee groves began to spring up in the cool Sierra Maestra mountains and the Sagua-Baracoa mountain range, spurred by the arrival of French refugees from Saint Domingue who created model plantations, coffee replaced chocolate in people's affections.

Curiously, the first recorded Cuban recipe for coffee, dating from 1791, calls for the ground coffee to be boiled in water and then placed in a chocolate pot fitted with a *molinillo* (a whipping device) to stir the brew before passing it through a filter. In the Cuban countryside, it was not uncommon to find a sweetened unfiltered coffee known as *café carretero* (muleteers' coffee), not unlike the spiced *café de olla* (pot coffee) of Mexico and its close relative, the *café guarulo* of the Colombian plains.

The quality of most coffee now available for domestic consumption on the island is dismal. The beans are usually of the robusta (*Coffea canephora*) type, a hardy, sturdy species with little flavor and aroma. Yet I have found areas in the countryside where excellent, aromatic arabica coffee (*Coffea arabica*) still grows. Though most of this arabica coffee is exported, the people who grow it can keep a small amount of the harvest for themselves. They usually roast the coffee beans in a big pot on the stove and grind them with a mortar and pestle.

On a trip to Cuba, I visited my grandmother's family farm in time for the winter coffee harvest in December. The farm is located in Cañas, in the forested mountains of the upper Jauco River, not far from Maisí, the southeastern tip of the island. In Cañas, patches of cultivated land have been carved out of the forested hills on both sides of the river, where cacao and arabica coffee trees and bushes coexist under the shade of royal palms, coconut trees, and ancient ceibas (kapok trees).

The "cherries" (the fresh coffee fruit) mature from August till February, and they need to be picked by hand, a painstaking task that requires several visits to the same tree, as the cherries do not ripen all at once. One morning, I joined the women of the family for the harvest. The coffee bushes were heavy with red cherries, and the women expertly picked them by hand and placed them in large plastic bags hanging from their shoulders.

In every part of the world where coffee grows, it is processed by either a dry or a wet method. The latter, which produces a milder, more delicately flavored bean, consists of removing the fruit's pulp by machine and then soaking the cherries in large tanks filled with water. After a short fermentation period, the cherries are drained and spread out to dry. At that point, they can be called beans. Colombian and Costa Rican coffees owe their fine flavor and premium prices to this process. In Cañas, as in many places around the world, the beans are processed by the simpler dry method. After the harvest, the cherries are spread out to sun-dry. As is done with cacao, workers rake the beans periodically for even drying. In some parts of Latin America, however, the cherries are allowed to dry in the tree, which imparts a special flavor to the coffee.

In Cañas, everyone has a small concrete yard for drying the coffee beans that are not sold to the local cooperative. One early afternoon, I experienced a jolt of recognition that took me back to the Cuba of my childhood. I could see clouds of smoke spiraling from the kitchen and pervading the whole house with the unmistakable aroma of freshly roasted coffee. Ulda, the wife of my father's cousin Evelio, was roasting a large batch of coffee beans in a blackened pot called a *caldero* set over a wood fire. Beads of sweat rolled from her face as she stirred the beans vigorously with a wooden paddle until they were perfectly roasted. Her work finished, she sat in the shade, away from drafts, to cool off—Cubans believe they can catch a cold or suffer facial paralysis if they go outdoors too soon after roasting coffee. Later on, I heard a muted thump coming from the yard. It was Evelio, shirtless, crushing the roasted beans to a powder with a heavy *guayacán* (lignum vitae) pestle in a huge mortar.

To me, drinking this dark coffee was the ultimate luxury; home-grown, hand-roasted, ground with mortar and pestle, and brewed in a cloth cone filter, a method that produces a taste more refined than the ink-black coffee one gets from an espresso machine.

Cuban Espresso Coffee

Cafecito Cubano

I am a notorious coffee drinker. No matter how it is brewed, in a cone made out of fabric, boiled with spices, made in an espresso machine, coffee is liquid memory, my divine obsession. When I think of Cuban coffee, I see my grandmother Paquita or my aunt Carolina vigorously stirring a cauldron of beans over a fire with a long wooden spoon. Even today, many Cuban families still roast their coffee beans in a big pot on the stove and grind them with a mortar and pestle. The favorite methods for brewing coffee were with a kind of drip filter (*colador*) made of cotton cloth or in a Moka pot, the same kind of stovetop espresso pot used in many Italian homes. We call these pots *cafeteras*. They were the home equivalent of the steam-operating espresso machines used in old-fashioned Cuban *cafeterías* (coffee bars), where people sipped tiny cups of potent, ultrasweet espresso topped with a head of foam produced by whipping sugar and a tiny bit of brewed coffee to a creamy froth.

At home nowadays, I use a Moka pot and freshly ground espresso beans, and prepare the froth topping with my own battery-operated mill. You can find these mills (*molinillos eléctricos para café*) in Hispanic markets. The following recipe calls for a 3½-cup Moka pot; if using a 6-cup or 9-cup model, adjust the amounts accordingly.

MAKES 3 CUPS (12 DEMITASSE SERVINGS)

About 3½ cups cold water

8 level tablespoons (½ cup) or 4 approved coffee measures (ACM) dark roast coffee for Cuban espresso, preferably Pilón or Bustelo brand

4–6 tablespoons sugar, or to taste

▶ Fill the bottom of a 3½-cup Moka pot with the water; the water should reach just below the safety valve. Put the metal filter in place and fill loosely with the coffee. Close the pot and heat over medium heat. When the pot begins to fizz, lower the heat to medium-low and wait until the upper coffee receiver is full. Remove from the heat and serve.

To make a head of foam, pour about a tablespoon of coffee into the cup, add sugar to taste, and beat vigorously with a spoon until the sugar is dissolved (or use a battery-operated mill). Then fill the cup with the coffee; the foam should rise to the top.

Cuban Coffee and Milk

Café con Leche

Cubans always sweeten their espresso coffee heavily with brown or white sugar and accompany it with milk. In Cuban *cafeterías*, *café con leche* was usually mixed at the table. A waiter would bring the hot coffee and the frothy, steaming milk, and the customer would do the mixing to taste.

Cook's Note: For a less potent *café con leche*, use slightly more milk than freshly brewed coffee.

If beginning with unsweetened coffee, add sugar to taste.

MAKES ONE ⅔-CUP SERVING

- 6 tablespoons (about ⅓ cup) freshly brewed Cuban Espresso Coffee (page 350)
- 6 tablespoons (about ⅓ cup) hot whole milk

▶ Combine the coffee and milk in a coffee cup and stir to mix. Serve piping hot.

Colombian Sweet Spiced Coffee

Café Guarulo

Many Latin regions have a traditional version of coffee made with brown loaf sugar and spices. In Mexico, *café de olla* ("pot coffee") is often brewed just by boiling the sugar and flavorings in a pot of water, then adding the ground coffee, letting it settle, and pouring the coffee into cups. *Guarulo*, a related coffee of the *llanos* (plains) of Colombia, is a fairly light, thin brew prepared by making a boiled solution of chunks of brown loaf sugar and cinnamon sticks, then pouring it through a funnel-shaped cloth filter that holds the coffee. People drink it out of cheap, colorful enameled steel mugs made in China; you can find these in Chinese markets here.

MAKES 3 CUPS (EIGHT 3-OUNCE SERVINGS)

- 4 tablespoons light-roast Colombian coffee (2 approved coffee measures)
- 3 cups water
- ⅓ cup grated brown loaf sugar, preferably *panela*, or packed dark brown sugar
- 1 Ceylon cinnamon stick (*canela*)
- ⅛ teaspoon salt

▶ Place the coffee in a filter cone lined with a filter and set over a drip pot. Combine the water, sugar, cinnamon stick, and salt in a saucepan and bring to a boil over medium heat, stirring to dissolve the sugar. Pour the mixture through the filter and let drip, then serve.

CHRISTMAS DRINKS

In Latin America, a variety of creamy eggnog-like drinks are inextricably connected to the Christmas season. They go by many names: *crème de vie* in Cuba, *ponche crema* in Venezuela, *coquito* in Puerto Rico, *rompope* in Mexico, *Biblia* in Peru. Though they are all egg punches (*ponches de huevo*), variations in the type of milk (fresh or canned) and alcohol (from rum to cognac, sherry to pisco) give them distinct personalities.

Connoisseurs are as sensitive to any deviation as the princess to the pea. While testing the recipes for this section, I unthinkingly gave a Venezuelan guest, Saúl Galavís, a glass of Mexican *rompope,* an eggnog drink. He took one sniff and announced, "I don't know where you got this recipe, but this is not *ponche crema.*"

For Latins, these drinks are badges of identity that connect us to our infant selves, to those who first fed our Christmas memories, and to people across the Americas who share our language and culture. No wonder we idealize and romanticize them, especially if we have moved away from the places of our birth.

Just a sip of the *crème de vie* transports me to the late 1950s, to a cool December morning in my grandfather's house in Cuabitas, a quaint neighborhood perched in the blue mountains around Santiago de Cuba. I can see my Tía Anita clearly, her thin gray hair bundled into a loose chignon, standing by the coal-burning stove stirring a pot of sugar syrup while her sisters, Elena and Belén, sterilized empty bottles and opened cans of condensed milk.

I rushed to the backyard with my grandfather, Santiago, to search for freshly laid eggs in the two-story garage. There they were, brown and white, nestled among wood chips, straw, and dirt beneath a craggy set of wooden stairs. When I handed my cache of still-warm eggs to Tía Anita, she cracked them open, whipped the yolks into a thick, lemony cream, and mixed in the cooled syrup and condensed milk. Then she stirred in a generous amount of white rum and funneled the thick elixir into the bottles—but not before pouring a small amount into a tin cup and handing it to me. The drink slid down my throat. I thought it was sheer perfection, smooth and nurturing like *café con leche,* but with a grown-up edge that cut through the sweetness of the sugar and made the condensed milk aromatic and even more delicious.

All through December, and even after Three Kings Day (*Día de Reyes*) on January 6, my aunts served family and guests thimble-sized cups of this potent liquor. For company, they poured it into a crystal decanter and brought it to the living room, where Belén played the piano and everyone joined in the singing. On Nochebuena (Christmas Eve) and Navidad (Christmas), *crème de vie* was brought to the table at the end of the meal with the sweet treats typical of the season. I drank it in small sips, savoring every drop.

During my travels through Latin America, I have found many people who share my deep emotional attachment to the rich, eggy drinks of Christmas. Saúl Galavis's octogenarian father got misty-eyed remembering how his mother and his three aunts would sit on the porch of their hacienda near the Venezuelan town of San Estebán and drink *ponche crema* in small cups accompanied by delicate cookies as the holidays approached. The respected Venezuelan food historian José Rafael Lovera recalls his first taste of the Christmas drink as a kind of initiation. "*Ponche crema* was given to children to introduce them gently to the taste of alcohol," he explains. "In the fifties, when I became an adolescent, the boys and girls of my age would graduate to a *ponche crema* cocktail flavored with grenadine"—a pink drink called *tetero,* a kind of creamy, mildly alcoholic Shirley Temple that is still popular in Venezuela.

These creamy Christmas drinks are powerful stuff. Take the Peruvian *Biblia* and the Puerto Rican *coquito.* The first is a potent mixture of raw egg yolks and evaporated milk spiked with three liquors: pisco, port wine, and crème de cacao. It goes down easily, filling you immediately with a warm sensation. You will want seconds—but beware, *Biblia* can get you tipsy faster than a few straight shots of pisco. The same with *coquito*. Disguised as a tropical milk shake, this terrific cocktail, a mixture of coconut milk and condensed and evaporated milk, enriched with raw egg yolks and a generous amount of Puerto Rican white rum, can get you in a singing mood with a few sips. *Coquito* is traditionally offered to groups of carolers who serenade friends and neighbors during the holiday season. (Such musical forays are called *asaltos*, assaults, because the singers come without warning.)

The commercial evolution of a few Latin American Christmas drinks has been documented. The popular *rompope*, now sold bottled all over Mexico, harks back to colonial times; it has been attributed to the nuns of the convent of Santa Clara in the city of Puebla. The leading Mexican etymological dictionary states that the name comes from the English *rum* and *pop*, probably because of the sound made by the cork being drawn from the bottle. Today, when Venezuelans drink *ponche crema* for Christmas, they are more likely to pour it from a bottle bearing the name of Eliodoro González P. than to prepare it from scratch in their kitchens. And though nothing compares with the freshness and flavor of homemade, the bottled version has at least kept the tradition alive and accessible in Venezuela.

The Christmas drinks of Latin America are going the way of homemade eggnog in North America: slowly moving into oblivion. They have an inescapable air of the past, belonging to a time when raw eggs and creamy, sugary milk drinks were considered nutritious and health-giving. But with some modifications—cooking the egg yolks, toning down the sugar—these tasty relics can still have an important place on our holiday tables, giving us pleasure and connecting us with the spirits of our Christmases past.

Ponche Crema

As happens with many traditional recipes, there are many versions of the Venezuelan *ponche crema*, some with rum, others with brandy or cognac. This is my adaptation of a recipe contributed by Venezuelan food historian Dr. José Rafael Lovera. He developed it at CEGA, his institute of gastronomic research in Caracas, to replicate the taste he remembers from the *ponche crema* of his childhood. Like the bottled version originally created by Eliodoro González P., it calls for cognac, a choice of liquor that Lovera ascribes to the strong French influence on Venezuelan tastes during the late nineteenth and early twentieth centuries. A splash of Angostura bitters, a flavoring originally created by an army doctor in Ciudad Bolívar (once known as Angostura) around 1824, gives it a distinct Venezuelan character.

I cook the milk down to give it a creamier consistency and a nuttier taste, and I have reduced the sugar content. Venezuelans have a very sweet tooth!

MAKES ABOUT 6 CUPS (TWELVE 4-OUNCE SERVINGS)

6	cups whole milk
18	large egg yolks
1½	cups sugar
1	tablespoon vanilla extract
	Peel of 1 lime
1½	cups cognac
1	teaspoon Angostura bitters

▶ Pour the milk into a heavy 6-quart pot and bring to a boil over medium-high heat. Lower the heat to medium-low and simmer, stirring occasionally, until it reduces to 4 cups, about 30 minutes. Remove from the heat and let cool for a few minutes.

Place the egg yolks and sugar in a medium bowl and lightly beat with a wire whisk. Add the reduced milk while whisking constantly. Strain the mixture back into the pot. Simmer, stirring constantly, over medium low heat until the mixture thickens to the consistency of a thick custard, about 20 minutes. Remove from the heat and strain. Add the vanilla extract and lime peel, and let cool.

Whisk in the cognac and bitters. Refrigerate for at least 2 hours before serving.

Puerto Rican Coconut Eggnog

Coquito

In Puerto Rico, as Christmas Eve approaches, groups of carolers playing the *güiro* (a percussion instrument made from a gourd), the *cuatro* (a four-stringed guitar), and maracas visit friends and neighbors, asking for food and drink. They are usually greeted with *coquito*, a frothy coconut drink spiked with rum. Here is my Puerto Rican cousin Elbita's recipe, with a couple of touches of my own.

MAKES 8 CUPS (SIXTEEN 4-OUNCE SERVINGS)

One   12-ounce can evaporated milk
  2   large egg yolks
One   15-ounce can unsweetened coconut milk
One   14-ounce can sweetened condensed milk
  1   cup white rum
  ¼   teaspoon ground cinnamon
      Pinch of salt

▶ Beat together the evaporated milk and egg yolks in a medium bowl. Strain into a 3-quart pot and simmer over medium heat until slightly thickened, about 5 minutes. Remove from the heat and let cool.

Transfer the egg yolk mixture to a blender, and blend in batches. Add the remaining ingredients,

blending at high speed until frothy. Pour into a pitcher and refrigerate until chilled before serving.

COCKTAILS

Daiquiri

No! The daiquiri was not invented by Hemingway, nor were mojitos. He and his characters certainly consumed lots of them in watering holes like the Bar Florida, known as Floridita, and the Bodeguita del Medio, in Old Havana. They became powerful symbols for some of his most beguiling characters, like Thomas Hudson, in *Islands in the Stream*, who filled his emptiness with glass after glass of Constante's double-frozen daiquiris with no sugar. But this emblematic Cuban drink, the essence of the tropics, had much earthier origins. It comes from a beach called Daiquirí in Oriente Province. There are various stories of its invention; I like this one from a 1928 book titled *When It's Cocktail Time in Cuba*, by Hollywood scriptwriter Basil Woon. He recounts how the daiquiri was born at the Venus Bar in Santiago de Cuba. According to Woon, Jennings Cox, the superintendent of the local mine, used to meet a group of cronies at the Venus every morning and knock back a few rounds of a Bacardi-fueled creation based on planter's punch, minus a few usual touches. One morning, Cox supposedly said, "Boys, we've been drinking this delicious little drink for a while, but we've never named it. Let's christen it now!" After a bit of debate, they baptized it "daiquiri," after their place of work.

SERVES 1

½ cup crushed ice
   Juice of 1 large lime (about 2 tablespoons)
1 tablespoon sugar
1½ ounces white rum (preferably Bacardi)

▶ Place the ice in a cocktail shaker, add the rest of the ingredients, shake for about 20 seconds, and strain into a fluted champagne glass.

Cuban Bush Daiquiri

Daiquirí Mambí

My parents' longtime friends Luis Felipe and Pupy Ross, both born and raised in Santiago de Cuba, taught me to make this gutsier version of our city's famous drink, sweetened with brown sugar. The *mambí* were guerrilla-like freedom fighters who fought against Spain during the wars of independence in the nineteenth century. Since the archetypal *mambí* was of peasant extraction, like *azúcar parda*, the Cuban brown sugar, and fought in the countryside, the term has come to be synonymous with the *manigua*, the Cuban bush or countryside. In Santiago, the *daiquirí mambí* was always drunk on the rocks, and that's how I serve it at my restaurant Cucharamama, where it is a favorite.

SERVES 1

2 ounces Bacardi dark aged rum or Bacardi select rum
1 tablespoon dark brown sugar or dark Muscovado sugar
   Juice of ½ large lime (about 1 tablespoon)
3 drops Angostura bitters
3 ice cubes

▶ Combine all the ingredients in a cocktail shaker and shake for 30 seconds. Serve in a rock glass.

Mojito

I believe that the mojito and the bourbon-based mint julep of the American South are more than kissing cousins, but for most Cubans, mojitos are a totally Cuban creation.

SERVES 1

6 mint leaves, plus 2 to 3 sprigs for garnish
1½ teaspoons sugar (1 tablespoon if you are Cuban)
2 ounces white rum (preferably Bacardi)
   Juice of 1 large lime (about 2 tablespoons)
3 to 4 ice cubes
   About 1 ounce chilled club soda or Sprite
   Dash of sweet vermouth (optional)

▶ Place the mint leaves and sugar in a cocktail shaker. Lightly crush (muddle) the mint with the back of a spoon, then rub a little of the mint around the rim of an 8-ounce glass. Add the rum, lime juice, and ice cubes to the cocktail shaker and shake for 20 seconds. Pour into the prepared glass. Fill with club soda or Sprite and stir in the vermouth, if desired. Serve garnished with the mint sprigs.

Nicaraguan Guava-Citrus Cocktail

Macuá

Cuba has the daiquiri and mojito; Mexico the margarita; Peru and Chile the pisco sour. But Nicaragua had no national cocktail of its own until 2006, when Flor de Caña, the country's leading rum producer, sponsored a contest to invent one. The winner was a doctor from the town of Granada, who came up with this refreshing blend of guava and citrus juices with rum, named "*macuá*" for a Central American bird.

1½ ounces white rum, preferably Flor de Caña
1 ounce guava juice (canned)
1 ounce freshly squeezed orange juice
½ ounce freshly squeezed lime juice
⅓ ounce Simple Syrup (page 356)

▶ Place all ingredients in a cocktail shaker with ice cubes. Shake well and pour into a tall cocktail glass. Serve garnished with a wedge of guava or an orange slice.

Simple Syrup for Cocktails

Jarabe de Goma

Traditional cocktail recipes call for a sugar syrup instead of granulated sugar. In Peru and Chile, the syrup is called *jarabe de goma*.

MAKES 3 CUPS

2 cups sugar
1 cup water

▶ Place the sugar and water in a small saucepan and bring to a boil over high heat, stirring to dissolve the sugar. Remove from the heat and let cool.

Store in a tightly covered container, refrigerated, until ready to use. It will keep for 2 to 3 weeks.

Cucharamama Peruvian-Style Pisco Sour

The pisco sour, a frothy mix of pisco, Latin America's oldest grape brandy, with lime juice, egg whites, sugar, and Angostura bitters, is the national drink of both Peru and Chile. There is no family gathering, celebration, or special occasion when this tangy, delicious drink is not served. This Peruvian-style pisco sour is the one I serve at my restaurant Cucharamama. I use a mixture of two different piscos.

SERVES 1

Juice of 1 large lime (about 2 tablespoons)
1 tablespoon sugar, or to taste
3 ounces Peruvian pisco (preferably a mixture of *pisco puro* or *quebranta* and aromatic *pisco italia*)
1 tablespoon egg white (fresh or pasteurized; lightly beat it before measuring)
¼ cup lightly crushed ice
Dash of Angostura bitters

▶ Place the lime juice and sugar in a blender and pulse to dissolve the sugar. Add the pisco, egg white, and ice and blend at high speed until frothy. Pour into an old-fashioned or rock glass. Splash the bitters into the center of the drink and serve immediately.

Malabar Pisco Sour

Every Peruvian restaurant and bar takes pride in its pisco sour, but none takes it as seriously as Malabar, a family-owned restaurant in Lima's posh San Isidro neighborhood, known for the cutting-edge "new Peruvian" cuisine of Pedro Miguel Schiaffino, one of the country's most talented chefs. Here you can have a terrific *piqueo* (selection of snacks) washed down with a pisco sour made with one of the excellent house piscos, La Botija (Bodega Tabernero) and Las Dunas (Bodega Viejo Tonel), or with your choice from a broad selection of other brands in various styles (Quebranta, Acholado, Italia, Torontel). The lengthy pisco and pisco cocktail list, which also offers ten pisco cocktails and pisco tastings by the shot glass, is a veritable encyclopedia on the subject with historical notes researched by José Antonio, the chef's father. Here is my take on Malabar's pisco sour.

SERVES 1

Juice of 1 large lime (about 2 tablespoons)

2 tablespoons Simple Syrup for Cocktails (page 356)

3 ounces Peruvian pisco (preferably a nonaromatic *pisco puro*)

1 tablespoon egg white (fresh or pasteurized; lightly beat it before measuring)

¼ cup lightly crushed ice

Dash of Angostura bitters

▶ Place all the ingredients except the bitters in a cocktail shaker and shake vigorously to create a froth. Pour into a rock glass. Add the bitters and serve immediately.

Hotel Schuester's Pisco Sour

My Chilean-born friend Oscar Baeza is a well-known cardiovascular surgeon who is also deft at making pisco sours. As newlyweds, Oscar and his wife, Maria Eugenia, loved pisco sour made from a closely guarded formula and served at *las onces* (elevenses, pronounced "lah-HON-ceeh") in Chile in the lounge of the venerable Hotel Schuester in Valdivia.

Years later, when they went back to Valdivia with me, we dined at a lovely beachfront restaurant in Corral, not far from the downtown area. We ordered pisco sours, and Oscar instantly recognized the special taste of Hotel Schuester's version. Sure enough, the owner of the restaurant confirmed his hunch; he had befriended the octogenarian bartender of the Schuester and been let in on the secret. After much cajoling, he gave us the recipe.

SERVES 1

1 small lime, cut into 6 wedges

Grated zest of ½ medium orange

3 tablespoons sugar

2 ounces Chilean pisco (preferably Pisco Control or Altos del Carmen)

1 cup small ice cubes

▶ Place all the ingredients in a blender and blend for 2 minutes on high. Strain into a pitcher and keep cool in the refrigerator until ready to serve.

Algarrobina Cocktail

Cóctel de Algarrobina

The traditional version of this Peruvian cocktail calls for egg yolks, but I find that the *algarrobina* syrup and canned milks add enough creaminess.

SERVES 1

2 ounces *pisco quebranta*

2 tablespoons *algarrobina* syrup (sold in Peruvian and other Latin markets; see box on page 358)

2 tablespoons sweetened condensed milk

¼ cup evaporated milk

4–5 ice cubes, crushed

Pinch of ground cinnamon

▶ Place all the ingredients except the cinnamon in a blender and blend at high speed until frothy. Serve in an old-fashioned glass, sprinkled with the cinnamon.

ALGARROBINA SYRUP

On a noontime walk not far from the town of San Pedro de Lloc in northern Peru, I found refuge from the sweltering sun in an *algarrobo* grove. In this desolate landscape, where the wind swept the coastal sand against rocky hills to form gigantic dunes, these lovely trees provided the only splashes of green. A New World native of the Leguminosae family, the coastal *algarrobo* (*Prosopis pallida*) is similar in shape to the acacia and prospers in many arid regions of Latin America. I picked a couple of its long, yellowish pods and had a taste of the sticky pulp that covered the hard beans within. They were pleasantly sweet, with the subtle, tangy bitterness I have come to appreciate in *algarrobina* syrup (known in Spanish as *jarabe de algarrobina*).

A trademark of northern Peru, this sweet, aromatic syrup, which is the color of tar and the consistency of molasses, has a touch of acidity and a beany quality that reminds me of hoisin sauce. Used in cocktails and desserts, it is an assertive ingredient, and its distinctive flavor lingers in your mouth.

I first tasted it in a popular Peruvian pisco cocktail that is a cross between a milk punch and a brandy Alexander. In typical Latin fashion, it mixes condensed and evaporated milks with eggs and the *algarrobina* syrup. The syrup lends backbone that cuts though the sweetness and blends seamlessly with the pisco. I fell in love with this ingredient, and began developing *algarrobina* flans, puddings, and ice creams for my restaurant Cucharamama.

The *algarrobina* sold in Peruvian and other Latin markets in the United States is incorrectly labeled carob syrup. The two share some similarities, but carob is the pod of an Old World Legume of a different genus.

Algarrobo seeds have been found in archaeological sites dating from the Moche period (A.D. 200–800) along with the seed remains of other edible plants like peppers, beans, corn, and squash. Today, in parts of Peru such as Piura, close to the Ecuadorian border, *algarrobo* is a regional industry. The pods, produced twice a year, are harvested once they have fallen to the ground, then boiled in water and pressed; the resulting liquid is strained and condensed through evaporation to make the syrup. The pods are also dried and ground into a flour (*harina de algarrobina*) that is used for desserts or toasted to make a substitute for coffee.

A relative of the North American mesquite, the Peruvian *algarrobo* makes excellent charcoal, and in rural regions where most people depend on wood or charcoal for cooking, *algarrobo* groves are being cut down for fuel, contributing to soil erosion and habitat destruction. I heard the sound of trees being cut down while I rested in that grove. A Peruvian friend who is a conservationist predicted that despite strict government regulations, the indiscriminate lumbering of the *algarrobo* will continue. I felt a profound sadness, for solutions are not simple in this case. The *algarrobo* is a useful plant that protects the environment, providing food and shelter for people and animals in a land where wind erosion extracts a heavy toll. But the traditional cooking of this part of Peru also owes part of its terrific flavor to the aroma of the *algarrobo* wood and charcoal. Without it, the food will not taste the same.

Perhaps the solution is in conservation and propagation, in reaching a balance that will allow cooks to enjoy the *algarrobo* in all its goodness. ◆

Bar Queirolo *Chilcano*

On a visit to the venerable Bar Queirolo in Pueblo Nuevo, a working-class neighborhood in Lima, I saw a group of old men playing cards and drinking highballs. A large bottle of pisco sat on their table, and the men took turns mixing their own drinks. It was Sunday morning, just before lunch, and they were having a grand time. I approached them and asked what they were drinking. They not only gave me the recipe but mixed a drink for me. It was a *chilcano*, a refreshing mix of pisco, lime juice, and ginger ale. It was terrific with the bar's hearty pork sandwich (*sanduche de butifarra*).

SERVES 1

      Ice cubes
2–3 ounces pisco (preferably *pisco puro*)
      A squeeze of fresh lime juice, or to taste
One 12-ounce can ginger ale
      A few drops of Angostura bitters

▶ Put a few ice cubes in a tall highball glass and pour in the pisco and lime juice. Fill the glass with ginger ale, add Angostura bitters to taste, and stir. Serve immediately.

Variation: In Bolivia, a similar drink, called *chuflay*, is made using *singani*, a pisco-like local brandy based on muscat grapes. Until very recently, it was difficult to find *singani* in the United States, but now brands such as San Pedro de Oro, Rujero de Colección Privada, and Casa Real de Etiqueta Negra are available in select liquor stores and through mail order. To make a *chuflay*, substitute *singani* for the pisco, and omit the bitters and lime juice. Garnish with a wedge of lime.

The Captain (Peruvian Pisco Manhattan)

El Capitán

Several years ago, my friend Arturo Rubio, the owner of La Huaca Pucllana, one of Lima's most attractive restaurants, came to the United Nations Delegates Dining Room with his then-chef Pedro Miguel Schiaffino to do one of those marathon culinary feats for thousands that usually kick in with a more private press luncheon held in the kitchen. The food was terrific, but the atmosphere was understandably somewhat tense because a Korean national had just opened fire outside the building. Luckily for those of us present at the luncheon, we had already had a few calming glasses of "el Capitán," a Peruvian cocktail reminiscent of a Manhattan, made with pisco and a mixture of sweet and dry vermouth.

SERVES 1

3 ounces pisco (preferably *pisco puro*)
1 ounce vermouth (sweet and dry mixed in equal parts)
   A few drops of Angostura bitters
   A maraschino cherry

▶ Place all ingredients except the cherry in a cocktail shaker with a few ice cubes. Cover and shake vigorously; strain into a Martini glass and garnish with the cherry. Alternatively, pour into a rock glass, garnish, and serve.

Caipirinha

Loosely translated, *caipirinha* means little country girl. It is also the name of Brazil's most famous drink, a potent cocktail made from the sugarcane liquor known as *cachaça*. In Brazilian restaurants and bars, *caipirinhas* are made to order. Using a spoon, the bartender crushes a lime, cut into small pieces, with sugar in a short, stocky glass, then adds ice cubes and fills it with the powerful liquor, also known as *pinga*.

SERVES 1

- ½ lime, cut lengthwise
- 2 tablespoons sugar
- 2 ounces *cachaça*
- ¼ cup lightly crushed ice
- Sugar to coat the rim of the glass (optional)

▶ Cut the lime half lengthwise into 2 pieces. Trim off the stem end and the membrane separating the sections. Cut crosswise into 8 pieces. Place the lime and sugar in a cocktail shaker. With a pestle or a wooden spoon, crush (muddle) the lime and sugar to release the lime juices and the aromatic oils from the rind, about 1 minute. Add the *cachaça* and ice and shake to mix, about 10 seconds. Pour into an old-fashioned or rock glass, and serve immediately.

Fruit *Caipirinhas*

I have a weakness for classic cocktails and rarely succumb to the allure of a mango mojito or a strawberry daiquiri. But when it comes to *caipirinhas*, I break my own rule, as I could happily live on the many delicious versions Brazilians make with tropical fruits such as *cajú* (cashew apple), *siriguelas* (purple or yellow *mombin*), and *cupuaçu*, a relative of cacao.

Cachaça, the Brazilian sugarcane liquor at the heart of the *caipirinha*, has an extraordinary affinity with the complex flavors and aromas of these tropical beauties. On a recent trip to Salvador, in time for the Feast of Saint Anthony, I made a point to visit the saint's fair at the Largo de Santo Antônio to have a fruit *caipirinha* at a small kiosk. The fruits could not have been fresher and the bartender was generous with both fruit and liquor.

Unlike most tropical cocktails where only the fruit juice is used, fruit *caipirinhas* are made with the whole fruit, which is crushed in a cocktail shaker or similar container with a pestle. Ideal for this purpose are fruits like the cashew apple that do not become a paste in the process. There is nothing more delicious than drinking your *caipirinha* and then sucking on the fresh fruit that has soaked in the liquor.

Back at the apartment I was renting, I tried my hand at different combinations of flavors with fresh fruit I had bought at the São Joaquim market in the lower city and several aged *cachaças* that I found as delicious as any aged rum. My genial driver, Cacique, a great mixologist, gave me a few pointers.

Cashew Apple *Caipirinha*

Caipirinha de Cajú

Although it is associated with Asian cuisine and is a major cash crop in southeastern Africa, the cashew is native to the Orinoco and Amazon Basins. The low-growing, umbrella-shaped tree has gnarled branches and glossy leathery green leaves. Depending on the season, you may see strange, multicolored fruits that end in hard kidney-shaped shells hanging from the branches. The true fruits are the nuts encased in those shells. The larger "cashew apples" to which they are attached are technically "false fruits," but are used as fruit throughout Latin America.

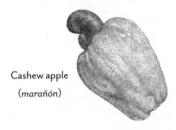

Cashew apple
(*marañón*)

The sixteenth-century European explorers who found cashew trees growing on the banks of the Marañón River in the Peruvian Amazon named the fruit *marañón* or *jocote marañón*. From its birthplace in these humid, forested lowlands, the tree traveled to other parts of the Americas and across the sea with the Portuguese as far as India and Mozambique. The "false" fruit is juicy but does not dissolve into a pulp when crushed. It has a lovely aroma and an astringent quality that I find appealing. Fresh cashew apples are not available here, but you can buy frozen cashew apples in Hispanic markets. You do not need to thaw them to use in *caipirinhas*. Before using the cashew apple, cut off the nut and discard it. Do not bite into it, as it is highly caustic and can burn your lips badly.

SERVES 1

   ¼ lime
 One 1-ounce piece of cashew apple
 2–3 teaspoons sugar
   2 ounces *cachaça*
   ¼ cup lightly crushed ice

▶ Cut the lime and apple piece into small pieces. Place the lime, cashew apple, and sugar in a cocktail shaker. With the back of a wooden spoon, crush (muddle) the fruit to release the juices, about 1 minute. Add the *cachaça* and ice and shake to mix, about 10 seconds. Pour into an old-fashioned or rock glass and serve immediately.

Purple or Yellow *Mombin Caipirinha (Caipirinha de Siriguela)*

In the Hispanic Caribbean, the purple or yellow *mombin* is known as *ciruela*. In Brazil, it is *siriguela*. Shaped like a small plum, the fruit has yellow flesh with a pleasant acidity.

Follow the directions above for Cashew Apple *Caipirinha*, substituting 3 to 4 purple or yellow *mombins* for the cashew apple.

Tamarind *Caipirinha (Caipirinha de Tamarindo)*

Tamarind, a distant relative of the carob tree, is an Old World plant native to India that became naturalized in the New World tropics. We now think of tamarind as our very own, and the trees grow in backyards together with other imports such as mangoes and native tropical fruits like papayas. The mature fruits of the tamarind tree are brown pods with a crumbly skin. The pulp is tart but very pleasant. Tamarind is eaten as a fruit and its pulp is mixed with sugar to make juices and candies. In Latin America, most tamarinds are puckery tart, but in recent years, I have seen sweeter tamarinds in Latin markets. You might need to reduce the sugar in the recipe or add more lime if your tamarinds are on the sweet side.

Follow the directions above for Cashew Apple *Caipirinha*, substituting 3 tamarinds for the cashew apple. Break open the skin and remove the pulp, which is encased in long fibrous filaments. Cut into 1-inch pieces and proceed with the recipe, being sure to crush the pulp thoroughly.

Passion Fruit *Batida*

Batida de Maracujá

Batidas are Brazilian milk shakes spiked with potent *cachaça*. They come in many flavors and are particularly delicious made with tropical fruits like passion fruit.

MAKES 3 CUPS (SIX 4-OUNCE SERVINGS)

¾ cup passion fruit juice

6 ounces Brazilian *cachaça* or white rum, or to taste

½ cup sweetened condensed milk, or to taste

1½ cups crushed ice

▶ Place all the ingredients in a blender and blend at high speed until smooth and frothy. Serve ice cold in rock glasses.

AGAVE-BASED DRINKS: *PULQUE*, TEQUILA, AND MEZCAL

A lover of dry, sunny days and cold nights, the agave plant prospers in the arid lands of Mexico. Like the camel, this sturdy succulent—with more than 136 species in Mexico alone—can live with little water. The plant stores whatever moisture its roots can find in succulent spiky, thorny leaves that shoot out toward the sun and in its pineapple-like heart, the *cabeza* or *piña*, where it turns into nourishing sap, the sweet promise of beloved drinks like *pulque*, mezcal, and tequila.

The agave is a generous plant. From its thick leaves, farmers get fiber for clothing and ropes, as well as a thin paper-like membrane called *mixiote* that is used to wrap foods to be cooked *barbacoa*-style in a pit oven. Upon reaching maturity, a flowering stem called *quiote* will grow from the agave's center. It is a last grand gesture, a dying wish, for the plant will die and shrivel once the last flowers have scattered their seeds to the wind. Farmers sometimes harvest the *quiote* before the blossoms are open and roast it, cut into pieces like hearts of palm, in pit ovens. The closed buds are also good to eat, and Mexicans pickle or panfry them with spices to eat with fresh tortillas.

But in agave lands, it is more likely that the *quiote* will never have a chance to develop. Since pre-Columbian times, Mexicans have tapped agave's sweet juice by cutting off the emerging flowering stalk and carving out a cavity, *cajete*, in the plant's swollen center. Then they scrape the tough fibers around it with a spoon-like tool to help the agave's juices flow into the *cajete*. The agave farmers siphon off the juices daily, sometimes twice a day, with an elongated gourd that is perforated at either end.

In ancient Mexico, the sweet agave sap was used as a sweetener for nourishing chocolate drinks and corn-enriched *atoles*, but it was more often fermented into *octli*, a sacred alcoholic drink reserved for the old or given to warriors before they were sacrificed. In the beautiful illustrated codices of pre-Columbian Mexico, the agave is depicted as the goddess Mayahuel, a fertile earth mother with four hundred breasts filled with sap to feed her many children.

The Spaniards who conquered Mexico in the sixteenth century called the sweet agave sap *aguamiel*, "honey water," and the milky fermented drink *pulque* or *vino de la tierra*, "local wine." With the Spanish conquest, *pulque* lost its sacred trappings since it was no longer a restricted drink. Unlike other native beverages that fell into oblivion, *pulque* became popular with non-Indian Mexicans and foreigners alike, who liked to drink it at lunch. And in less than a century, the *pulque* hacienda became a common sight in the highlands of Mexico. The heart of the operation was the *tinacal*, where the *aguamiel* was fermented in large cowhide containers and then transferred to barrels for shipment.

Juan de Viera, a Pueblan Jesuit writing in 1777, reported that 300,000 pesos' worth of *pulque* were consumed yearly in Mexico City. *Pulquerías* and *tepacherías* sold *pulque* plain or flavored with various fruit juices (in which case it was called *tepache*), served with some form of free lunch. Today little *pulque* is produced outside the states of Hidalgo and Tlaxcala, but it is enjoying something of a revival. It is now sold in cans in supermarkets, and it is also being used in creative new ways by contemporary chefs like Patricia Quintana, who prepares a delicate *pulque* sauce for fish at her innovative Mexico City restaurant Izote.

With the introduction of distillation techniques by the Spaniards, two similar but distinct new liquors produced from different species of agave, mezcal and tequila, began to compete with *pulque*. Unlike *pulque*, which is fermented fresh *aguamiel*, mezcal and tequila are distilled clear liquors that come from the sap or honey extracted from the roasted or steamed *piña*, the heart of the agave plant, which looks like a large pineapple.

For tequila, the *piñas* of only blue agave (*Agave tequilana Weber*) are roasted or steamed in large conventional ovens. The cooked *piñas*, which can weigh from 80 to 300 pounds, are crushed in special mills (usually horse-drawn mills for artisanal mezcal) to extract their juices. Fermentation, which is usually accelerated by the addition of yeast, turns the sugar in the juices into ethyl alcohol, which is then distilled in copper or stainless steel stills into the hard liquor. Tequila often goes through a double and even a triple distillation to rid it of any impurities. When cane sugar is added to the fermenting juices (*mosto*), the tequila is labeled as *mixto* (mixed), a lower-quality liquor that is sold at lower prices. Premium tequilas are made with 100 percent agave, with no added sugars. Companies like Herradura pride themselves in producing only premium tequila.

Tequila-like liquors are produced in countries around the world from Venezuela to Japan, but only beverages made with 100 percent agave produced in particular districts within four Mexican estates—Michoacán, Guanajuato, Tamaulipas, and Nayarit—and in all of Jalisco have the legal right to be called tequila.

A Mexican document from 1621 refers to the making of *vino de mezcal*, "mezcal wine." Since *mezcal* was also a common name for the heart of the agave plant, from which the sap is extracted, there is no way of knowing if this is a reference to a liquor distilled from the true blue agave. The word *tequila* comes from the name of a small town and valley not far from Guadalajara, the largest producer of this potent liquor in Mexico today. Large-scale tequila distilling began at the end of the eighteenth century; Cuervo, probably the oldest continuous producer, was given a license to manufacture tequila in 1795.

The Mexican Wars of Independence (1820–1821) did much to popularize the patriotic consumption of tequila rather than wine, which was considered a Spanish drink, but then it fell temporarily out of favor under the government of Porfirio Díaz, whose Francophile proclivities encouraged a taste for imported wines and liquors among the Mexican upper classes. The populist Mexican revolution of 1910, however, succeeded in enthroning tequila as Mexico's national drink.

Fresh from its distillation, tequila is a clear liquid. In this state, it is known as *blanco* (white or silver). Aging it in wooden barrels changes its color, flavor, and aroma and turns it into *reposado* (rested) or *añejo* (aged) tequila. Which one to choose is a matter of taste. The longer the tequila remains in a wooden barrel, the closer it will come to a brandy or cognac, its color darkening to a golden amber. I like to sip these fine tequilas from a cognac glass or the traditional *caballito* (literally, little horse), a small shot glass that is narrower at the base. *Blanco* tequilas have an assertive agave flavor that is not muted by contact with wood.

Mezcal has more surprises and a more individual character. To start with, it is made from a broader genetic spectrum of agaves. More than 130 agave species grow in Mexico, all preferring different habitats and often different altitudes. About a dozen, both wild and cultivated, are still used for mezcal, each contributing its own flavors and volatile components. Though mezcal-making still goes on in several parts of Mexico, it is particularly associated with Oaxaca state, where a colorful range of *mezcales* are distilled by small artisanal producers from some chosen agave species or a combination of several. Indeed, the craft is growing, and single-village bottlings by renowned local producers are starting to win a following outside of Mexico, joining the growing ranks of single-origin foods, from wine to chocolate, that are capturing consumers' imaginations. The names of species like *Agave espadin* (the most widely used in Oaxaca, said to have been the ancestor of blue agave), *A. salmiana* (a tall, spiny kind known as *maguey manso*), and *A. tobala* (also called *maguey mezcalero*, a wild mountain version that grows in beautiful blue-green rosettes) are beginning to become known to connoisseurs.

What sets mezcal apart is the process of roasting the *piñas*. Both mezcal and tequila employ a technique based on the pre-Hispanic art of steaming or steam-roasting in underground earth ovens lined with stones, the same method still used for versions of clambakes (Chilean *curanto*) or true barbecues in different parts of Latin America (see page 700). But mezcal remains closer to the ancient technology. Like the Yucatecan *pib*, mezcal ovens are first heated with burnt oak wood or charcoal before the agave hearts are heaped in the center and the huge pit (some 12 feet across) is covered with a number of organic insulators ranging from agave or banana leaves to palm fiber mats and finally heaped with earth. The *piñas* are left to cook in the smoky steam of the sealed pit for a period of three to five days. After they are taken from the oven and left to start fermenting in the open air, they are still intensely infused with smoke. The rest of the process—crushing on millstones, fermenting for up to a month in wooden vats, distillation (normally once), and aging in oak casks to create lighter or darker shades of color and edgier or more mellow flavor—only slightly softens the characteristic smoky bite that mezcal drinkers find irresistible.

No two versions are exactly alike. Amazingly, a few makers still cling to the ancient custom of throwing chicken or turkey breasts into the pit with the *piñas* for more complex fermentation—something still found in some Peruvian versions of the fermented sprouted-corn drink *chicha de jora* (page 95)—or add handfuls of favorite herbs and fruits. The glory of the finest tequilas is to be smooth and rounded. The glory of the most admired *mezcales*—like some single-malt Scotch whiskies—is to keep a rough edge of smoke and earth, telling of their preindustrial origins. ◆

Gloria's Margarita

Margarita de Gloria

There are many versions of the creation of the popular tequila drink known as the margarita. Some say it was born in Acapulco. Others trace its origins to a spot in Ciudad Juárez called the Kentucky Bar, a 1920s–vintage bar with dark wooden panels and pictures of visiting celebrities like Marilyn Monroe and Arthur Miller plastered on the walls.

Whatever the origin, this tart citrusy drink has become the unofficial national drink of Mexico, its fame spanning the globe.

Many years ago Gloria Soto, a Mexican-American friend, gave me a formula for margaritas with equal amounts of lime juice, tequila, and Triple Sec. At the time I thought it was perfect. Later I found I wanted the tequila and citrus to stand out more. So the formula has wandered far from the innocent first version, but I still call it "Gloria's Margarita."

SERVES 1

1½–2 ounces white tequila, preferably Herradura or El Tesoro
   1 ounce Triple Sec or Cointreau
      Juice of 2 limes (about 4 tablespoons)
   2 teaspoons sugar
   1 cup small ice cubes

▶ Place all ingredients in a blender and blend to a smooth frothy slush. Serve in a salt-rimmed margarita glass or a rocks glass.

Margarita on the Rocks

Margarita en las Rocas

This is the version of margarita preferred by purists who don't care for the distractions of the frozen slush version. You can play with the choice of tequila (use an *añejo* or *reposado* for mellower flavor, or try other brands), experiment with the milder Triple Sec or more distinctly orangey Cointreau, and adjust the amounts of lime juice and syrup to your taste.

SERVES 1

1½ ounces tequila, preferably Herradura Silver
 ½ ounce Triple Sec or Cointreau
   1 ounce freshly squeezed lime juice
 ½ ounce Simple Syrup (page 356), or to taste

▶ Place all ingredients in a cocktail shaker with ice cubes. Shake and pour into a short rocks glass rimmed with coarse salt.

Ecuadorian Hot Toddy

Canelazo de Naranjilla

Canelazo is the name of an Ecuadorian hot toddy that I fondly remember from my first visit to the highland town of Cuenca. On my first night in the city, I walked to a small, quaint restaurant in the middle of the old town and sat on an inviting candlelit patio. It was freezing outside, but no one but me seemed to mind. The first thing the waiter offered me was an *abreboca* (a "mouth opener"). It turned out to be not the expected complimentary appetizer but a squat little tumbler of something warm and reviving, in which I recognized the jolt of *aguardiente* (the generic name of every regional Latin cane liquor). In the chill of the night, it tasted heavenly, sweet and aromatic, warming my hands and my throat. I had another.

It was one of my first clues to the fact that in the Ecuadorian Andes, much about food and drink revolves around the need to keep warm. Though temperatures dip considerably during the night year-round, most houses and public spaces have no heating. After dinner, families will drink warm, thick, rich *coladas*, which contain grains or fruits or both, or indulge in delicious warm alcoholic drinks made with *aguardiente*.

During popular festivals, like Cuenca's anniversary on April 12, *canelazos* are sold by the same people who sell *empanadas de viento* (puffy cheese empanadas), ears of roasted corn (*choclo*), or morsels of fried pork (*fritada*). In country districts, there used to be a folk custom of leaving a few drops in the glass and throwing them on the floor. I was told the story of the nonagenarian Juan Solís, born in Solano in the province of Cañar, who would politely carry out this point of etiquette, then wipe his mouth with the back of his hand, adjust his hat, and inquire, "*Hay otrito?*" ("Got another little one?").

Canelazo is made by preparing a hot sugar syrup flavored with the tart Andean fruit called *naranjilla* or *lulo*, or with cinnamon, and combining it in large shot glasses with *aguardiente*. Sometimes people use both *naranjilla* and cinnamon. There is also a lighter version of *canelazo* called *gloriado*, which includes only a few drops of *aguardiente*. You might ask why Ecuadorians add the water in two stages. Well, they claim, this is the way to get more flavor and color from the cinnamon and to keep the thickness of the syrup under control. I see no need to argue.

Cook's Note: Both the whole *naranjillas* and *naranjilla* puree are sold frozen in the United States. If using the whole fruit, defrost it in warm water, then make a cross-shaped cut in one of the fruits and squeeze out the pulp. Mash lightly with a fork. If you can't find *naranjilla*, you can substitute passion fruit puree.

MAKES SIX 4-OUNCE SERVINGS

For the Syrup
½ cup thawed frozen or fresh *naranjilla* puree or passion fruit puree
2½ cups water

½ cup sugar
4 Ceylon cinnamon sticks (*canela*)

1 cup *aguardiente* (preferably Ecuadorian Zhumir, Colombian Cristal, or Guatemalan El Venado)

▶ To make the syrup, place the puree in a 3-quart saucepan, add 2 cups of the water, the sugar, and the cinnamon, and bring to a boil over medium heat. Lower the heat and simmer, covered, for 15 minutes.

Uncover, add the remaining ½ cup water, and bring back to a simmer until reduced to about 1 cup, another 15 minutes.

Strain the syrup and keep warm.

Ask your guests how they want their drinks, mild or strong. Pour the *aguardiente* into 4-ounce tequila shot glasses or rock glasses and fill with the syrup.

Don Juan's Hot Hibiscus Punch
Ponche Caliente de Don Juan Tenorio

It is always cold at the end of October around Lake Pátzcuaro, and I still remember how good it felt to clutch a mug of this hot deep-red punch close to my chest while watching the play *Don Juan Tenorio* in the dark cloister of the 500-year-old Franciscan church of Tzintzuntzan, not far from the town's cemeteries. This Spanish play, a tradition of the Days of the Dead vigil on October 31, tells the story of Don Juan, the rascally Spanish nobleman and unrepentant womanizer, who receives just punishment for his many crimes when he encounters the souls from purgatory (*ánimas*). The play's most exciting moment, when the souls come out of their tombs, takes place precisely at midnight, when Mexicans believe the souls of their dead come to visit the living.

I serve my own version of this drink on Halloween. I named it after Don Juan Tenorio, of course.

What gives this punch its deep red color is *flor de jamaica* (see page 339). The main flavors come from an assortment of fruits. Here you can be flexible. I use whatever fruit is in season, sometimes even sliced star fruit, or carambola, which comes to the market from Florida starting in November.

Cook's Note: *Tejocote* is a round, yellow fruit with a greenish tinge native to Mexico and Guatemala, a member of the Rosaceae family. It is known in English as Mexican hawthorn. It is an essential ingredient of the hot punch consumed in parts of Mexico during the Days of the Dead.

SERVES 16

    6   quarts water
    3   ounces (about 3¼ cups) *flor de jamaica*
    1   pound brown loaf sugar (preferably *piloncillo* or *panela*), broken up into small pieces, or 3 cups packed dark brown sugar
    4   Ceylon cinnamon sticks (*canela*) or cassia cinnamon sticks
    1   teaspoon whole cloves
    1   teaspoon allspice berries
        Generous ½ cup pitted prunes, quartered
   ¾   cup dark raisins
    3   ripe guavas, tops and bottoms sliced off, cut into wedges, or 6 canned guava shells in syrup, drained and cut into wedges
    1   crisp sweet-tart red apple such as Honeycrisp, peeled, cored, and cut into ¼-inch dice

    6   ounces ripe pineapple, peeled, cored, and cut into ¼-inch dice (about 1 cup)
    1   orange, cut into ¼-inch pieces
    1   small lime, cut into ¼-inch pieces
    6   ounces *tejocotes* (available in Mexican markets; optional)
    8   tamarinds, shelled and cut crosswise in half
Three   6-inch pieces sugarcane, unpeeled or peeled, rinsed and cut lengthwise into 6 sticks each, for garnish

▶ Place the water in a large pot, add the *flor de jamaica*, sugar, cinnamon, cloves, and allspice berries, and bring to a boil over medium heat. Lower the heat and simmer for 20 minutes, stirring occasionally.

Strain the liquid, discarding the solids, and return it to the pot. Add the remaining ingredients (except the canned guava, if using) and bring to a simmer, then reduce the heat and simmer gently for about 45 minutes, or until the fruits are soft. If using canned guava, stir in now.

Serve hot in mugs or stocky glasses, garnished with the sugarcane sticks. Or chill the punch in the refrigerator before serving. Or spike it with about 1 cup dark rum or tequila for a fabulous tropical fruit punch.

Uruguayan White Wine Sangría

Clericot

During the summer, Uruguayans and their Argentinean neighbors flock to the beaches of Punta del Este for family reunions and outdoor grilling. The Uruguayan temperate-climate fruits like peaches and apples are at the height of their season, and they go into this traditional sangría. Sometimes I use a red wine like a potent Uruguayan Tannat.

MAKES ELEVEN 8-OUNCE SERVINGS

- 2 (750 ml) bottles white or red wine, preferably a fruity Chardonnay or citrusy Sauvignon Blanc, or a potent Uruguayan Tannat
- 4 large, juicy peaches, not peeled, pitted and cut into ½-inch dice
- 1 medium orange, cut into ½-inch pieces
- 1 Golden Delicious apple, peeled, cored, and cut into ½-inch dice
- 1½ cups ripe strawberries, hulled and quartered
- 1 medium lime, cut into ¼-inch pieces
- ½ cup sugar, or to taste

▶ Mix all the ingredients together in a pitcher, stirring to dissolve the sugar. Chill before serving.

White Wine Sangría with Fresh Peaches

Clery de Duraznos

In Chile, the traditional sangría, or *clery*, uses white wine, and ripe cherimoyas. I make this refreshing variation, which I find very similar to a wonderful white wine sangría I once tasted in southern Spain called *limonada cordobesa*.

MAKES SIX 8-OUNCE SERVINGS

- 1 (750 ml) bottle Chilean Chardonnay or Sauvignon Blanc
- ¼ cup sugar
- 1 Ceylon cinnamon stick (*canela*)
- 2 ripe peaches, not peeled, pitted and cut into wedges
- 6 sprigs mint, for garnish

▶ Combine the wine, sugar, and cinnamon stick in a large glass pitcher, and stir well to dissolve the sugar. Add the peaches. Refrigerate for at least 24 hours before serving.

Serve garnished with mint sprigs.

CHAPTER 9

LITTLE LATIN DISHES

Latin Americans are great noshers, nibbling on savory and sweet snacks from morning till evening. Lunch is our most substantial meal of the day, but we like to eat a snack or two on our coffee breaks or on our way home. Our urge to nibble does not stop after dinner, and often we see the light of the day at a local market after a night of partying, looking for a bowl of soup, a cebiche, or the little salad Bolivians from Cochabamba call *soltero* (the bachelor) to give us back our strength.

The names of the little dishes that people eat without any particular order or ceremony throughout the day are as numerous as there are countries in Latin America. Mexicans call these snacks *botanas* or *antojitos*, but they are *bocas* in Nicaragua and Costa Rica, *saladitos* in Cuba, *cuchifritos* in Puerto Rico, *salgadinhos* and *quitutes* in Brazil, and *piqueos* in Peru.

THE *MERIENDA*

In the afternoon, before dinner (which in some Latin countries like Argentina is usually late, as in Spain), we have a repast called the *merienda*, a soothing, relaxed preamble that cements family relationships and connects us with our friends. When I was growing up in the 1950s, my maternal aunts always prepared something special for my brothers and me, sweet treats like rice pudding, a type of French toast called *torreja* (which they made by the dozen and perched on top of the refrigerator to keep us from eating them all), or a thin Key lime pie (*pastel de limón*) topped with baked meringue. They also fed us savory foods like chicken salad or small beef empanadas, and we could always count on buttered Cuban bread with steaming *café con leche*.

The Cuban bakeries of old were popular places to grab something to eat in the afternoon, such as crescent-shaped flaky pastries filled with guava paste and cream cheese (*cangrejitos de guayaba y queso*) or ham croquettes. And friends would often meet at a *cafetería* to eat tea sandwiches on white bread, or a *medianoche* (a layered sandwich of roast pork, ham, Swiss cheese, and a pickle) on a soft egg roll, or a croquette platter with slices of ham and cheese and a cup of *café con leche* or a tropical fruit milk shake. Cuban *cafeterías* and bakeries in the United States continued these wonderful traditions.

In Chile, the *merienda* is called *las once* and is similar to the British high tea, with tiny sandwiches, small pastries, and usually black tea served with formality, using the family's best tea service and china. I have heard time and again in Chile that the term *las once* (the elevens) refers to the eleven letters of the word *aguardiente* (a young spirit distilled from sugarcane juice or grapes), indicating that someone was drinking something more substantial than tea at *las once*. But in fact the term is the Spanish translation of the British "elevenses," a morning tea taken at 11:00 A.M., probably the time when Chilean men traditionally got together for a snack and a shot of *aguardiente*.

My Chilean friend María Eugenia Baeza explains that *las once* is a socially ingrained ritual that enables women to treat their friends and relatives at a neutral hour between lunch and dinner with foods that are easy to prepare at home but that can also be bought at a local bakery. When most women stayed at home, this little ritual could take place on any day of the week. Now that so many Chilean women work out of the house, Sunday afternoon is the preferred time.

In Argentina, the strongly caffeinated local brew called *mate* (page 346) anchors the afternoon meal. Argentineans sip *mate* with a single silver straw from a gourd that they pass around to all the guests as a symbol of intimacy while they eat *facturas*, little cakes and pastries, and sometimes empanadas, bought at bakeries.

Years ago while staying with my friend Raquel Torres, an anthropologist and chef, at her ranch house on the outskirts of Xalapa, I became addicted to the Mexican *merienda*. I worked briefly at Raquel's restaurant, the Churrería del Recuerdo, helping cooks prepare for the busy afternoon shift while I learned about Veracruzan cooking. The best part of the job was watching people eat their *merienda*. By six, the place was packed with Mexicans eagerly gulping down layered *tortas* (sandwiches) on soft buns called *pambazos*, deep-fried corn tortillas (*tostadas*) smeared with refried beans (page 273) and heaped with savory toppings, and lusty *tamales rancheros* made of a silky strained corn dough filled with pork morsels seasoned with licorice-scented *hoja santa*. These were all washed down with nonalcoholic drinks, mostly fruit-based *aguas frescas*, the milky coconut drink called *horchata*, and hot chocolate frothed with the clever wooden device called a *molinillo*.

PARTY FOOD

Other little Latin dishes are party food: the endless assortment of canapés (*petites bouches*) that are served at any Chilean reception; the cold cuts and salami (*picadera*) Dominicans eat at the beginning of each party, big or small; and the fried tidbits such as corn-flour *empanaditas*, the cigar-shaped cheese

sticks wrapped in dough (*tequeños*), and cold cuts passed around with rum cocktails or whiskey at any Venezuelan party.

In Guadalajara, I was treated to a taco party (*taquisa*), the likes of which I had never experienced. My hosts, a well-to-do Mexican family, bridged social boundaries by bringing street-food vendors to their home and patio to cook for us. The *cocineras* (female cooks) they had hired from their favorite *taquería* (taco stand) re-created their place of business in the middle of the carefully tended garden. Organized in an assembly line, the youngest ones took lumps of corn *masa* and deftly hand-shaped them into tortillas. The older ones cooked them on portable gas-fueled griddles, replenishing baskets and bowls with fresh tortillas and tangy sauces. All the while, a group of mariachis, selected from the throng of musicians who peddled their services near the Libertad market, belted out lively *rancheras* and mournful love songs.

There were at least ten different chile salsas and fillings to accompany the freshly made corn tortillas. Shredded marinated and baked goat (*birria*), melted cheese with Spanish chorizo and strips of fire-roasted poblano peppers, and many more delicious treats were all set out in colorful bowls on flower-decked tables. Each guest made his or her own taco with a favorite combination of filling and sauce. It was wonderful to see how greedily these elegantly attired, bejeweled Mexicans gulped them down, accompanied by shots of tequila and ice-cold local beer.

In Nicaragua, a similar type of party is called a *caballo bayo* (literally, spotted horse), but it is more rigidly choreographed around a set of nine dishes served with warm tortillas to make tacos. On one platter, you will find lightly crushed pork cracklings made from the skin; on another, crumbled blood sausage sautéed with onion and pepper. Another platter, this one of shredded pork, sits next to a bowl of refried red beans. There are also bowls of guacamole, a red chile salsa, and a green tomatillo salsa with green peppers, cilantro, and Nicaraguan congo pepper, a *Capsicum chinense* relative of the habanero chile, for heat. To complete the ensemble, there is cow's-milk cheese (*queso blanco*) and a bowl of cultured cream (*crema fresca*). As in the *taquisa*, guests are invited to make their own tacos, and many of them combine the meat, sausage, and cracklings with a small dollop of each of the other ingredients for a complete taste sensation.

The *taquisa* and the *caballo bayo* are terrific party concepts that you can adapt for serving a variety of dishes from this book, not just Mexican or Nicaraguan. Here are some suggestions for fillings or toppings: Pork Cracklings in the Style of Minas Gerais (page 84); Veracruzan Refried Bean Dip (page 277) or Refried Ayocote Beans (page 273); Costa Rican Chayote, Fresh Corn, and Beef Hash (page 230) or Nicaraguan Ground Beef and Baby Corn (page 696); shredded *cochinita pibil* (page 725); Green Tomatillo-Chile Salsa (page 114); Tomato and Serrano Chile Salsa (page 114); "Finger Sauce" (page 116); grated *cotija* cheese (page 95); and Mexican or Venezuelan Ripened Cream (page 148) or Central American Ripened Cream (page 147).

Deck the table with tropical blooms or leaves or interesting Latin objects such as baskets, pottery, ceramics. Present the food in colorful plates and bowls arranged around baskets of hot freshly made corn tortillas, brittle yuca bread, Venezuelan or Colombian corn *arepas*, or any breads of your choice. Mix margaritas and rum cocktails like El Macuá, Nicaragua's newly minted national cocktail (a mixture of guava juice and Nicaraguan rum *flor de caña*), and bring out the mariachi band, salsa music. This is a party for all the senses.

THE FIRST COURSE

We call the appetizers we serve at the beginning of a formal sit-down meal *entradas*, *entremeses*, or *aperitivos*. Whether or not a family begins a meal with a formal first course is a matter of both social and economic class and national preferences. Hispanic Caribbean cookbook authors, from Ana Dolores Gómez, the doyenne of Cuban cooking, to Lidia Bornia, of the Dominican Republic (an elegant lady who cooked like an angel), were middle- and upper-class women deeply influenced by European cooking. Their books, which became bibles for generations of cook, gave recipes for fancy appetizers and instructions on how to set an elegant table, as well as all manners of table etiquette, with recipes for traditional *criollo* foods. A formal Hispanic Caribbean sit-down dinner of the 1950s inspired by these books would begin with a shrimp cocktail or seafood in mayonnaise, or a half avocado or a tomato stuffed with seafood dressed with mayonnaise. In many households, these touches are still very much alive. But for everyday meals, a plate of soup has always ushered in the meal, or if it is a big soup like a *sancocho* or an *ajiaco*, it is a meal in itself.

In South America, particularly in Peru, where the legacy of the colonial period is still evident in upper-class households, formal sit-down dinners always begin with a first course. But the boundary between street foods and home-cooked foods was always tenuous, as even the wealthiest families had a preference for native *criollo* foods over European imports, and today the distinction has all but disappeared. The quintessential cebiche of Peru, for example, began as a popular street food, the domain of humble restaurants called *cebicherías*. Now *cebicherías* are fashionable and top chefs regard cebiche as a food worthy of their attention. At a formal lunch in Lima, cebiche can be a first course lovingly served on fine china. So popular has cebiche become in recent years that you can count on finding a full cebiche table at any wedding, side by side with the sushi station.

The popular *papas a la huancaína*, boiled potato slices drenched in a creamy hot pepper, walnut, and cheese sauce—a dish that you can eat at a roadside food stand or while sitting on a stool at a market—also comes to the table as a first course. Another favorite Peruvian first course is the *causa*, a potato puree seasoned with Andean hot peppers, lime juice, and oil, often layered with various fillings as a terrine.

In Chilean middle- and upper-class homes, where meals for company have traditionally been formal, a first course is de rigueur. My friend María Eugenia Baeza might start a meal with a half avocado filled with seafood such as Patagonian king crab (*centollo*), abalone (*loco*), or goose barnacles (*picorocos*) with mayonnaise; beef empanadas (which are also eaten as snacks at all hours of the day); a gratin of pink clams (*machas*); or sea urchin roe served in fine glass bowls with a spicy green *pebre* sauce. This would be followed by a consommé of beef, turkey, or chicken; and a main course, perhaps a châteaubriand of beef tenderloin accompanied by potatoes and a vegetable; and a salad of onion and tomatoes.

An Argentinean meal often begins with a pasta dish such as potato gnocchi. In Venezuela, where an Italian influence is also strong, the chef Nestor Acuña, who worked for many years at Ercole, a restaurant in Puerto Ordaz on the Orinoco River, makes both yuca gnocchi and a delicious black bean pasta nestled on two pepper sauces as a first course.

As innovative young chefs modernize Latin American cooking, the first course has become the showcase for their creative talents. Young Lima chefs, in particular, have become masters of the little-dish tradition, turning the Peruvian *piqueo* into a wonderful adventure for the palate. For cocktail parties, Marilú Madueño from La Huaca Pucllana serves cebiches and *causas* in bite-sized spoons for ease of serving and visual effect. Gastón Acurio, the chef-owner of La Mar and the celebrated Astrid y Gastón, serves miniature versions of the traditional potato *causa* colored green, orange, or red with natural seasonings such as cilantro and *rocoto* peppers and topped with brightly flavored seafood or anything he loves. For him, the humble *causa* lends itself to endless interpretations.

I am a believer in small flavorful dishes that keep my palate intrigued and engaged, a friend of anything fried and crunchy, a tapas lover. So I would not dream of having a sit-down dinner without a first course of sorts, even if I plan to follow it with a substantial and hearty one-pot meal or a typical all-on-one-plate *criollo* extravaganza. But I am flexible as to where to start the meal. There is nothing that gives me more pleasure than to invite people into the kitchen while I fry some yuca fingers or any other tidbit that is best eaten fresh from the pot as a tapa.

Today North Americans have fallen under the spell of Spain's tapas culture. What many people do not know is that the movement started in 1983 at a restaurant called the Ballroom in New York City, with the first full-fledged tapas bar in the

Big-Bellied Argentinean Beef Empanadas *(page 422)*, served with Red Chimichurri *(page 133)*

My Fresh Corn Tamales Cuban Style
(page 455) with "Finger Sauce"
(page 116)

Puerto Rican *Pasteles* (*page 474*) with
Ajilimójili (*page 143*)

Ecuadorian Shrimp Cebiche with Peanuts in the Style of Jipijapa (*page 493*), garnished with peanut butter; roasted, salted peanuts; and plantain chips

Huanchaco Fish Cebiche *(page 487)* with
Ecuadorian Toasted Corn *(page 154)*

Chicken and Vegetable
Sancocho (page 503)

Havana-Style Black
Bean Soup (*page 507*),
ready to be served,
with steamed white
rice (*page 294*)

Brazilian *Feijoada* (*page 512*), served with orange
slices; Kale in the Style of Minas Gerais (*page 516*);
Cacique's Spicy *Malagueta* Pepper Table Sauce
(*page 144*); *farinha*; black beans; and the meats

country. It was owned by the late Felipe Rojas-Lombardi, a Peruvian-born chef who introduced Americans to the convivial eating style that is part of everyday life in Spain—savory dishes, some as simple as anchovies in vinegar, others as complex as a paella, presented on little plates at a bar counter to be savored with wine at all hours of the day. Though he trained with James Beard and was a lover of European food, Felipe always gave his tapas layers of flavor that revealed his Peruvian roots. Typically he would marinate most meats with a paste of garlic and spices such as cumin, a favorite seasoning in Peru. His cooking sauces were spicy, redolent of cilantro and colored gold with achiote-infused oil.

Although Spanish purists often found his Peruvian-inspired tapas too baroque and intense, most people, including myself, were converts after one taste of his boldly seasoned little dishes. I will never forget Felipe's suckling pig. Like any good Peruvian cook, he basted the skin with achiote-infused olive oil or lard (something Spaniards would never do). The skin was beautiful, with a tempting rich copper patina. Though crunchy, it melted in my mouth like a delicate cracker.

Even before Felipe's untimely death in 1991, it seemed as if the tapas concept would disappear. In the eighties, the only other restaurant in Manhattan that could be called a true tapas bar was El Internacional, created by Montse Guillén and her companion, food artist Antoni Miralda. It was wildly successful and very Spanish, but it closed after a few years. But sparked by the emerging popularity of Spain as a new frontier in cooking, the tapas concept is back in full swing today. Americans have finally been lured by these little dishes full of flavor and often prefer them to a full meal.

This chapter is the first of four focusing on various categories of small dishes, also including empanadas, tamales, and cebiches. Think of this ensemble as a buffet table for the senses, dazzling with variety, vibrant flavor, and inspiration. Here are dishes that fit the modern way of eating in small portions, foods that can be flexibly adapted as formal first courses, as snacks, as party food—and enough of them can make a meal.

Jicama Sticks with Chile and Lime

Botana de Jícama con Chile y Limón

In Querétaro, Mexico, next to many old churches you will find women selling crunchy jicama *botanas*. I never cease to be amazed at their art. They can turn the humblest vegetable or fruit into a magnificent still life, cutting the burly jicamas into perfect long strips and seasoning them lightly with citrus fruit and a sprinkling of hot pepper. Inspired by these Mexican *botanas*, I like to arrange long strips of jicama in tequila shot glasses and bring them to the table as an amuse-bouche.

Jicama

Jicama is a vine of the legume family that grows a large edible root shaped like a turnip. Beneath the tan skin, the root flesh has a crunchy texture, not unlike that of water chestnuts. Neutral-flavored with a touch of sweetness that offsets its subtle starchy quality, jicama absorbs the heat of the chile and the tang of the citrus juice to make for a crisp and refreshing starter.

Cook's Note: Some jicamas, especially large ones, tend to be fibrous. Look for a medium-size jicama with dense and crunchy flesh.

What to Drink: A shot of an aged tequila, such as Padrón, Herradura Natural, or Corazón, or a Margarita on the Rocks (page 365)

SERVES 6

- 1 pound jicama, peeled
  Juice of 2 limes (about ¼ cup)
  Juice of ½ bitter orange (about 1 tablespoon)
- 1 tablespoon distilled white vinegar
- ¼ teaspoon ground dried chile, cayenne, or red pepper flakes
- ¼ teaspoon salt
- ⅛ teaspoon freshly ground black pepper
- 1 teaspoon finely chopped cilantro, optional
- 1 teaspoon sugar (only if the jicama is very fresh and firm)

▶ Cut the jicama lengthwise into ½-inch-thick slices, then cut the slices into ½-inch-wide sticks. Place them in a medium bowl and toss with the rest of the ingredients. Arrange in small 2-ounce tequila shot glasses, standing up like breadsticks, and moisten with the juices of the marinade.

Spicy Prickly Pear Cocktail

Cóctel de Tunas al Chile Piquín

The Mexican prickly pear, or *tuna*, is the fruit of a cactus of the *Opuntia* genus. It is mildly sweet with strong vegetable notes that I find refreshing. At the Mercado Libertad in Guadalajara, women vendors entice passersby with plastic glasses filled with rounds of the tempting fruit. But I like my *tunas* prepared to order. The vendor plunges them in a bucket of water to clean, then peels and slices them in a jiffy and finishes with a squirt of lime and a sprinkling of ground chile.

Prickly pear (*tuna*)

Tuna, the Spanish name of the fruit, comes, surprisingly, from the Taíno (Arawak) language of the Hispanic Caribbean islands, where the Spaniards first found prickly pears. *Nopal* is the Nahuatl name for the cactus paddle, the edible branch of the plant. According to early Spanish chronicles of the conquest of New Spain (Mexico), the Spanish were enchanted with the light-colored yellow-green *tunas*, which they found refreshing and similar in flavor to pears or grapes.

My favorites, however, are the red ones, because they are so gorgeous, like miniature melons when peeled. At home, I dress them up by serving them in lovely hand-blown margarita glasses from Tlaquepaque, a market town in Guadalajara.

Cook's Note: If you ever find yourself picking prickly pear in the wild, be extremely careful, for the fruit is completely covered with minute, almost invisible thorns. Fortunately, the fruits available in our markets have practically no thorns.

What to Drink: A shot of an aged tequila, such as Padrón, Herradura Natural, or Corazón, or a Margarita on the Rocks (page 365)

SERVES 6

 12 prickly pears, preferably red (about 5½ ounces)
    Juice of 4 large limes (about ½ cup)
  1 teaspoon salt
  1 teaspoon sugar
  ½ teaspoon ground dried *piquín* chiles or cayenne
    Sprigs of *yerbabuena* (similar to spearmint) or other mint, for garnish

▶ Rinse the prickly pears under cold running water. Peel them, removing all of the skin to reveal the flesh. Cut into ¼-inch-thick rounds. Place in a bowl and toss with the remaining ingredients (except the *yerbabuena*). Cover and refrigerate until chilled.

Serve as a relish alongside roast chicken or fish, or serve as an appetizer in margarita glasses garnished with sprigs of *yerbabuena*.

GREEN CUISINE

As June approaches, mango trees in south Florida hang heavy with hard green fruit. For all mango lovers, the elliptical spheres dotting the lush canopies are a promise of the juicy harvest ahead. For people of the tropics, from the Caribbean to South America to Southeast Asia to India, they are a present-tense pleasure as well.

Unripe tropical fruits such as mango and papaya found their way onto the table through a combination of need, thrift, and culinary experimentation. What is certain is that the practice spans the globe.

"Each person born in the tropics has a story to tell about green fruits," says Noris Ledesma, a Colombian horticulturist working in the tropical fruit program at Fairchild Tropical Botanic Garden in Coral Gables, Florida. "As mango season approaches, I become a child again and crave green mangoes seasoned with salt. An old man in a large straw hat used to sell them in small plastic bags in front of my school. They were *criollo* mangoes, probably seedlings of Tommy Atkins, and they were so delicious," she recalls, smacking her lips with delight. "In Colombia, green mango with salt is a popular snack eaten in small towns and at the marketplace," adds Ledesma, who is a mango sleuth. "It is not the kind of fruit experience you would have in a large town like Bogotá."

Thoughts of green tropical fruits take me back to the small backyard of my parents' home in southwest Miami-Dade County, where the newest generation of my family has learned to savor them. Even before she could speak, my niece Chachi Espinosa would sit with my father under our tamarind tree and chew on the tart leaves or suck on the immature pods in quiet concentration until her mouth puckered. In summer, she would be the first to scout the yard for fallen green mangoes, and she would munch on salt-laced slices of the crisp, sour fruit with as much relish as she devoured sweet, juicy ripe mangoes.

All Latin Americans have a long, though fairly simple, tradition of eating and cooking with green fruits. For us, any green mango will do for the snacks we love so much. But I have learned through trial and error that the Asian mango varieties grown in Florida to be eaten exclusively at their green stage have much better texture and flavor than varieties that are meant to be eaten when fully ripe. One of my favorite cultivars is Nam Doc Mai, which has crisp, juicy flesh, mild acidity, and a pleasant aroma. ◆

Mexican-Style Green Mango with Chile and Lime

Botana de Mango Verde con Chile y Limón

In Mexico, raw green mango seasoned with lime juice, salt, and chile powder is a favorite street food. The mango is either cut into slices or carved like a flower and served on a stick like a giant lollipop.

In my version, I add a bit of sugar to enhance the mango's flavor if it is very green, much as Thai and Vietnamese cooks serve green mangoes and papayas with sweet-sour dipping sauces.

Cook's Note: Any mango is fine for this snack, but you will get the best results with Nam Doc Mai or other Asian green mangoes. Keitt, a big, juicy, Florida-bred mango with a bite reminiscent of a Granny Smith apple, is also a good choice.

What to Drink: A shot of an aged tequila, such as Padrón, Herradura Natural, or Corazón, a Margarita on the Rocks (page 365), or Mexican beer like Pacífico Clara

SERVES 4

- 1 green or half-ripe mango, preferably Nam Doc Mai or other Asian mango or Keitt
- 2 teaspoons sugar
- 1 teaspoon pure chile powder or ground cayenne, or to taste
- 1 teaspoon salt, or to taste
- 3 tablespoons fresh lime juice, or to taste

▶ Peel the mango. Cut the flesh away from each flat side in thick slices, cutting as close to the pit as possible. Cut the slices into long ½-inch-wide

sticks. Place in small bowl and toss with the sugar, chile, salt, and lime juice. Serve chilled at room temperature, arranged in shot glasses, standing up like breadsticks.

Potatoes in *Huancaína* Sauce

Papas a la Huancaína

I had spent several hours shopping and interviewing vendors at a neighborhood Lima market when I noticed a small counter with a few stools and a woman making a sauce in a blender as if she were working in her own kitchen. It was *huancaína* sauce, a Peruvian classic.

I sat on one of the stools and watched her prepare my food. She put walnuts, fresh cheese, yellow Andean peppers (*ajíes amarillos*), evaporated milk, and saltine crackers in the blender, and out came a creamy sauce for potatoes, which she poured liberally over sliced boiled potatoes nestled on a lettuce leaf.

She garnished my plate with purple olives and quartered hardboiled eggs and handed it to me. Although delicious, I preferred the *huancaína* sauce my Peruvian friend the chef Felipe Rojas-Lombardi had taught me to make, a cheesier, spicier version without evaporated milk or crackers.

In Peru, these potatoes are a popular starter and snack. You can pour the sauce over cold or warm potatoes, whole or sliced. I also like to make a seasoned potato puree with lime juice, ground pepper, and some oil, and shape it into small balls, as Felipe often did (see variation, page 379).

Historians of Peruvian food say this dish was born in the highland town of Huancayo, a place famous for its potatoes, at the time a railroad line was being built in the area. Street vendors plied their food to the hungry railroad workers. They soon came to favor a woman who sold a dish of cold potatoes drenched in a sauce made with fresh cheese and the chubby *rocoto* pepper. They called her *huancaína*, the woman from Huancayo, and her potatoes were dubbed *papas a la huancaína*. The version that has become popular today all over Peru no longer calls for *rocoto* chiles but instead uses dried *mirasol* or fresh yellow chiles.

Cook's Note: If the sauce has been refrigerated, bring it to room temperature and, if necessary, thin it with evaporated milk or whole milk to a pourable consistency.

What to Drink: Cucharamama Peruvian-Style Pisco Sour (page 356), Bar Queirolo *Chilcano* (page 359), Peruvian Purple Corn Punch (page 338), or Pilsen Callao

SERVES 4

- 4   medium russet potatoes (about 1½ pounds)
- 1   tablespoon salt
     Peruvian Walnut–*Mirasol* Pepper Sauce (*huancaína*, page 128)
- 16 Peruvian purple olives or Kalamata olives, for garnish
- 2   large hard-boiled eggs, quartered, for garnish
- 8   ounces fresh cow's milk cheese (*queso blanco*), cut into 3-inch slices, for garnish

▶ Place the potatoes in a medium saucepan, add 2 quarts water and the salt, and bring to a boil. Reduce the heat slightly and cook until tender, about 20 minutes. Drain.

When the potatoes are cool enough to handle, peel them and cut into ¼-inch slices. Place on individual appetizer plates or a serving platter and

blanket with the sauce. Serve garnished with the olives, hard-boiled eggs, and fresh cheese.

Variation: Alternatively, pass the still-warm peeled potatoes through a ricer into a bowl. Season with 1 teaspoon fresh lime juice, 1 to 2 teaspoons ground dried *mirasol* peppers (page 54), ½ teaspoon salt, and 2 tablespoons achiote-infused oil (page 89). Stir to combine thoroughly. Shape the seasoned potato puree into small balls about the size of a Ping-Pong ball. Place on a platter with a bowl of the Peruvian Walnut–*Mirasol* Pepper Sauce, and serve garnished with the olives, hard-boiled eggs, and cheese.

Potatoes in Peruvian Peanut–*Mirasol* Pepper Sauce

Ocopa Arequipeña

Huancayo and Arequipa, two highland Peruvian towns, both claim this classic Peruvian starter as their own. The name *ocopa* comes from the Quechua word *oqopa*, which means ground pepper, and the hot dried *mirasol* pepper is an essential element of the creamy sauce. Enriched with peanuts and flavored with the assertive herb *huacatay*, it is spooned generously over boiled potatoes, quartered or left whole.

There are many variations of *ocopa*. One incorporates the heads of river langoustines caught in Andean streams and uses their bodies as a garnish. Another thickens the sauce with walnuts rather than peanuts, and sometimes the sauce is thickened with bread crumbs or crackers, particularly sweet animal crackers.

Cook's Notes: If the sauce has been refrigerated, bring it to room temperature and, if necessary, thin it with evaporated milk or whole milk to a pourable consistency.

What to Drink: Cucharamama Peruvian-Style Pisco Sour (page 356), Peruvian Purple Corn Punch (page 338), or Cuzqueña beer

SERVES 4

    4   medium russet potatoes (about 1½ pounds)
    1   tablespoon salt
        Peruvian Peanut–*Mirasol* Pepper Sauce (page 127)
   16   Peruvian purple olives or Kalamata olives, for garnish
    2   large hard-boiled eggs, quartered, for garnish
    8   ounces fresh cow's-milk cheese, cut into 3-inch slices, for garnish

▶ Place the potatoes in a medium saucepan, add 2 quarts water and the salt, and bring to a boil. Reduce the heat slightly and cook until tender, about 20 minutes. Drain.

When the potatoes are cool enough to handle, peel and quarter them, or leave whole. Place on individual appetizer plates or on a serving platter and blanket with the sauce. Serve garnished with the olives, hard-boiled eggs, and fresh cheese.

Puerto Rican Corn and Cheese Sticks

Surullitos de Maíz

Puerto Rican cooks have a way with frying. As you drive around the island, you'll come upon women frying food in small kiosks on the roadside. I admire their independence and skill, their ability to turn the simplest ingredients into something delicious with an economy of means and a minimum of fuss. To set up a stand, all they need are sturdy grates, a wood fire, and a large blackened cauldron. Thinking about the simplicity of their setup keeps me sane when equipment breaks down in my restaurant kitchens.

The *surullito* (or *surullo*, also spelled *sorullo*) is just one of many delicious fritters made of starchy vegetables—plantains, yuca, or *malanga*—that you are likely to find at these roadside stands. In the early colonial period, large *surullos* made of corn or wheat flour and steamed like tamales in plantain leaves or corn husks served as a filling breakfast.

Though based on a Taíno (Arawak) corn preparation, *surullos* derive their name from the old Spanish word *zurullo*, meaning a lump of dough. Berta Cabanillas, a Puerto Rican food historian, writes that it was black women, most probably freed slaves from the coastal plantations, who first fried *surullos* instead of steaming them. They sold these fried corn sticks at makeshift stands called *friquitines*, the ancestors of today's roadside kiosks, together with salt cod fritters (*bacalaítos*), fried green plantains (*tostones*), and empanadas.

Today, *surullitos* can be found in home kitchens and in fancy restaurants as well. They come in all sizes, but I prefer small cigar-shaped ones, like those I tasted in La Parguera, a lovely fishing village on Puerto Rico's southwest coast. A Dutch cheese like Gouda or Edam, two Puerto Rican favorites, is a must. I like to add a bit of Parmesan for a sharper, cheesier flavor and cayenne for bite. In Puerto Rico, *surullitos* are served with a dipping sauce of mayonnaise and ketchup. At home, I make a dipping mayonnaise flavored with *ají dulce* chile, the island's classic seasoning.

What to Drink: Ice-cold beer, such as Puerto Rican Medalla Light or Mexican Corona or Pacífico Clara; or a rum cocktail, such as piña colada

MAKES 40 FRITTERS

A heaping ⅓ cup (2½ ounces) grated Gouda or Edam cheese
A heaping ¼ cup (1½ ounces) grated Parmesan cheese
1½ cups water
1 teaspoon salt
¼ teaspoon sugar
¼ teaspoon ground cayenne
2 tablespoons extra-virgin olive oil
1½ cups (about 11 ounces) fine yellow cornmeal
2 cups corn oil for deep frying
Puerto Rican–Style *Ají Dulce* Sauce (page 143), for serving

▶ Combine the cheeses in a small bowl and set aside.

Combine the water, salt, sugar, cayenne, and olive oil in a medium saucepan and bring to a rolling boil over high heat. Remove from the heat, add the cornmeal and cheese, and stir with a wooden spoon to make a thick dough that comes away from the sides of the pan. Let cool slightly.

When the dough is cool enough to handle, scoop out a tablespoonful and roll it into a ball between the palms of your hands, then roll the ball into a cigar-shaped cylinder with tapered ends. Place on a plate, and repeat with the rest of the dough. Cover with a damp cloth to keep the fritters from drying out.

Heat the corn oil to 350°F in a heavy saucepan. Add 5 or 6 *surullitos* at a time and fry until crunchy and golden, about 3½ minutes. Lift out with a slotted spoon and drain on paper towels. Serve at once with the *ají dulce*.

Brazilian Salt Cod and Potato Balls

Bolinhos de Bacalhao

These crunchy salt cod and potato balls, a type of croquette, can be found everywhere in Brazil. They are as Portuguese as the big meat and vegetable soup *cozido*. *Bolinhos* are served at cocktail parties with *caipirinhas*, and one can eat them as a street food or seated at a sidewalk café or restaurant.

The Confeitaria Colombo in downtown Rio, an amazing fin-de-siècle coffee house-cum-pastry shop, makes very good *bolinhos*. They are kept in a glass case under hot lights together with other tidbits (called *salgadinhos*), waiting for the throng of store clerks and office workers to descend upon them when they take their midday or late afternoon breaks. However, since I love *bolinhos* straight from the pan, I am more likely to eat them in restaurants, where I am sure they will be made to order. For years the venerable Rio restaurant A Cabaça

Grande (The Big Gourd—the old establishment on the Rua do Ouvidor, close to the stock exchange, not the restaurant's other branches) made them best. The restaurant served these addictive tidbits for ninety years, and the cooks were masters of the art. The golden brown *bolinhos*, the size of Ping-Pong balls, came to the table hot, crunchy, and with the right balance of cod and potatoes. You knew the *bolinhos* were good the minute you bit into them. They were heavy on the cod, which was as expensive then as it is these days. There are several classic versions of *bolinhos*. I prefer to make a mixture of the cod and potatoes without a batter, and then coat the *bolinhos* with bread crumbs before frying.

What to Drink: *Caipirinhas* (page 360) or Brazilian beer, such as Skol, Antarctica, or Brahma

MAKES ABOUT 24 *BOLINHOS*

For the Salt Cod

    12 ounces salt cod fillets (see page 613), preferably Canadian
     1 quart whole milk

For the Cooking Sauce

     2 medium russet potatoes (about 12 ounces)
     ½ teaspoon salt, or to taste
     2 tablespoons extra-virgin olive oil
     4 garlic cloves, finely minced
   One large yellow onion (about 12 ounces), finely chopped (about 2 cups)
     ¼ cup tomato sauce or finely chopped tomatoes
     ¼ cup finely chopped flat-leaf parsley
     ¼ teaspoon ground cayenne (optional)

For Frying the *Bolinhos*

     1 large egg, lightly beaten
     1 tablespoon whole milk
     1 cup fine bread crumbs or Cuban cracker meal (available in Hispanic markets), for coating
     3 cups light olive oil or corn oil, for deep-frying
        Lime wedges, for serving

Preparing the Cod ▶ Place the salt cod in a large bowl, cover with cold water, and soak in the refrigerator for at least 12 hours, changing the water 3 times. If using Norwegian salt cod with skin and bones, soak for 24 hours, changing water often.

Drain the cod, place in another bowl, and cover with the milk. Refrigerate, covered for at least 6 hours.

Drain the cod. Pull it into very small, fine shreds with your hands, and reserve. (If using Norwegian cod, remove the skin and bones.) You should have about 2 cups shredded fish. Set aside.

Making the Cooking Sauce ▶ Peel and quarter the potatoes. Place in a 4-quart pot, add 2 quarts water and salt to taste, and bring to a boil. Reduce the heat slightly and cook until soft, 15 to 18 minutes.

Drain the potatoes and mash into a coarse puree.

Heat the olive oil in a medium skillet over medium-high heat. Add the garlic and sauté until barely golden, about 20 seconds. Add the onion and cook until soft, about 5 minutes. Add the tomato sauce or chopped tomatoes, parsley, and cayenne pepper and cook, stirring, for 3 minutes. Add the cod and cook, stirring, for 3 minutes or until heated through. Transfer the cod mixture to a bowl, add the mashed potatoes, beaten egg, and milk, and mix well. Taste for seasoning and add more salt and cayenne pepper if needed. Let cool, then cover and refrigerate for at least 1 hour to firm up the mixture and make the balls easier to shape.

Shaping and Frying the *Bolinhos* ▶ Shape the cod mixture into balls the size of a Ping-Pong ball. Spread the bread crumbs or cracker meal on a plate. Dip the cod balls in the egg, then roll them in the crumbs to coat evenly and arrange on a platter. Refrigerate the balls, covered with plastic wrap, for a couple of hours.

Heat the oil to 360–375°F in a large heavy saucepan. Using a slotted spoon, drop the balls, a few at a time, into the hot oil and turn occasionally until they are golden brown all around. As they are done, lift out onto paper towels to drain.

Serving the *Bolinhos* ▶ Serve piping hot, with lime wedges. At A Cabaça Grande, I have seen customers cutting open their *bolinhos* with a fork and drizzling olive oil into the moist interior. I think that's overkill. I like mine with just a squirt of lime juice. In the United States, people expect a sauce with any fritters. With these, slightly salty cod treats I love *allioli* (page 135), but any garlicky or hot sauce would do. Try, for instance, a Brazilian Hot Pepper and Lime Sauce (page 144), the table sauce used for *feijoadas* (page 514), or the spicy "Finger Sauce" (page 116).

Puerto Rican Salt Cod Fritters

Bacalaítos

Say "*bacalaíto*" to a Puerto Rican, and his or her mouth will water. What makes the simple fritters special is good-quality salt cod and a batter with the right ratio of liquid to flour, yielding fritters crispy on the outside and supple inside.

My relatives on the Puerto Rican side of the family are expert *bacalaíto* makers. When I stayed in the one-room cabin of my cousin's father-in-law, Virgilio Brunet, in La Parguera, a small fishing village not far from Cabo Rojo, the smell of *bacalaítos* he fried early woke me up every morning. Most days we ate breakfast outdoors on the veranda, facing the calm waters of the Caribbean—He seasoned the *bacalaítos* with a bit of garlic and chopped parsley, sandwiched them between fat slices of bread, and served them alongside hot chocolate or *café con leche*. My cousin Marino Menéndez, a Cuban who is married to Elbita, Virgilio's daughter, likes to add some beer to the batter, which adds flavor and lightness to the fritters.

Cook's Note: When scooping batter for savory fritters, dip the spoon into vinegar first; this will keep the batter from sticking to the spoon. I learned this trick from the nineteenth-century *Diccionario del cocinero mexicano, The Dictionary of the Mexican Cook.*

What to Drink: Cold beer, such as Puerto Rican Medalla Light or Mexican Corona or Pacífico Clara, or any rum cocktail.

MAKES 30 LARGE OR 60 SMALL FRITTERS

8 ounces salt cod fillets (see page 613), preferably Canadian

1¾ cups all-purpose flour

1 cup water

½ cup Pilsener beer

1 large egg

1 teaspoon baking powder

1 medium yellow onion (about 8 ounces), finely chopped (about 1¼ cups)

2 tablespoons finely chopped flat-leaf parsley

½ teaspoon salt, or to taste

¼ teaspoon freshly ground black pepper

4 cups corn oil, for deep-frying

About 1 cup distilled white vinegar, for the spoon

Preparing the Salt Cod ▶ Place the cod in a bowl and cover with cold water. If using Canadian salt cod fillets, soak for 12 hours, changing the water 2 or 3 times. If using Norwegian cod with bones and skin, soak for 24 hours, changing the water often.

Drain the cod. Place in a saucepan, add 1 quart water, bring to boil. Boil for 2 to 3 minutes. Drain. Finely shred the cod and place in a bowl. (For Norwegian cod, remove the skin and bones.) You should have about 1½ cups shredded fish.

Making the Batter ▶ In a medium bowl, combine the flour, water, beer, egg, and baking powder and beat with a whisk to blend well. Add the onion, parsley, salt, and cod and stir to combine.

Shaping and Frying the Fritters ▶ Heat the oil to 375°F in a large heavy saucepan. Place the vinegar in a small bowl next to the batter. Working in batches, dip a stainless steel soup spoon into the vinegar, then scoop out a spoonful of the batter and slide it into the hot oil; or use a dessert spoon to make smaller

fritters. Fry the *bacalaítos* until golden brown, about 1 minute and 40 seconds for larger fritters, 1½ minutes for smaller ones. Drain on paper towels.

Serving: Arrange the *bacalaítos* on a serving platter or a basket with a bowl of *allioli* (page 135) and serve piping hot.

Variation: For *accras de morue*, the cod fritters of Martinique and Guadaloupe, season the batter with 1 Scotch bonnet or habanero chile, seeded and finely chopped, along with 3 to 4 scallions, white and pale green parts, finely chopped.

Salvador's Black-Eyed Pea Fritters

Acarajé

On every street corner of Salvador, the capital of the Brazilian state of Bahia, where the writer Jorge Amado lived for many years, you find turbaned matrons dressed in billowing white dresses fringed with lace seated next to large cauldrons bubbling with bright orange *dendê* oil. They are frying oval black-eyed pea fritters, which come out of the hot oil crunchy and golden brown. The women cut them open and fill them with a golden shrimp and nut cream called *vatapá* and a chunky salsa called *molho de acarajé*.

Though the basic recipe is fairly standard, I began to detect subtle differences in texture and flavor when tasting fritters from various vendors. I preferred the *acarajés* of a woman named Cira, who has a roadside kiosk in the beach town of Itapuá, about twenty minutes from Salvador. She has a large following, and with good reason. Her oil is pristine, the fritters are flavorful and fresh at all times, her *vatapá* is creamy, and the sauce is perfectly seasoned.

In Salvador, street vendors and restaurants such as the excellent Bargaçao make *acarajés* as large as duck eggs. They are filling and can double as lunch. For appetizers at home, I generally prefer smaller fritters, but the larger size I use here is a compromise between tradition and my own taste, both to bring the recipe close to the original and so that the fritters can be filled with enough *vatapá*. For cocktail parties, I fry teaspoon-sized *acarajés* and serve them with a simple sauce.

In Bahia, *acarajés* are fried in bright-orange *dendê* oil. Here in the United States, I use a mixture of corn oil and *dendê* oil.

Do not expect light and airy fritters—*acarajés* are dense, and that's how Brazilians like them. You will soon be addicted to them like any Bahian.

What to Drink: *Caipirinhas* (page 360) or Brazilian beer, such as Skol, Antarctica, or Brahma

MAKES 28 *ACARAJÉS*

For the Fritters

- 1 pound dried black-eyed peas
- 2 teaspoons salt, or to taste
- 1 teaspoon freshly ground black pepper
- 1 large yellow onion (about 12 ounces), grated

For the Sauce (*Molho*)

- 3 ounces dried small shrimp, preferably smoked (available in Asian and Latin markets)
- 6 pickled *malagueta* peppers, drained
- 4 scallions, white and 3 inches of green parts, chopped

- 2½ cups *dendê* oil (sold in Latin and West African markets)

For Frying

- 2 cups corn oil

For the Filling

About 1¾ cups Bahian Dried Shrimp and Nut Cream (*vatapá*, page 620)

For Serving

Fourteen 10-inch squares of banana leaf, singed according to the instructions on page 447 (optional)

Preparing the Black-Eyed Peas ▶ There are two ways to get rid of the skin of the black-eyed peas.

Manual method: Place the peas in a bowl and cover generously with water. Let soak overnight in the refrigerator. The next day, with the peas still in the bowl, rub them between the palms of your hands to release the skins, changing the water frequently.

Processor method: Drain the peas. Place them in a food processor or blender, cover with water, and pulse 12 times to help dislodge the skins of the peas. (Do this in batches if using a blender.) Do not over-process—you want the peas to remain whole. Then place the peas in a large bowl, cover generously with water, and rub the peas between your palms to help release the skins. Tip the bowl and carefully drain the water to separate the skins from the peas. You should get 4 cups after cleaning.

Making the Fritter Mixture ▶ Place the peas, salt, and pepper in a food processor and process to a coarse puree. The paste should have some texture, but you should not see large bits of peas. Place in a bowl and mix with the grated onion. Set aside.

Making the Sauce (*Molho*) ▶ Soak the dried shrimp in 2 cups water for 15 minutes. Drain.

Place the shrimp in a food processor or blender with the *malagueta* peppers and pulse into a coarsely textured meal.

Heat ½ cup *dendê* oil in a small skillet over medium heat. Stir in the scallions and sauté for 2 minutes. Add the ground shrimp and cook for 3 more minutes. Remove from the heat.

Frying the Fritters ▶ Heat the corn oil and the remaining 2 cups *dendê* oil to 300°F in a deep skillet. Scoop up a heaping soup spoon of the fritter mixture and slide it into the oil with the help of another spoon. Turn over with a slotted spoon as soon as the fritter sets, to brown evenly. The oil temperature must remain constant at 300°F; if you try to expedite the frying process by raising the heat, the fritters will have a nice golden brown color outside and be raw inside. Cook in small batches, turning occasionally, for 5 to 6 minutes, depending on how brown you want your fritters. Drain on paper towels.

Filling and Serving the Fritters ▶ *Vatapá* is normally eaten at room temperature, but I like to warm it a little before using it as filling. While they are still warm, with a serrated knife cut a slit down each fritter, as with a sandwich roll—do not cut all the way through. Fill each one with 1 tablespoon *vatapá*.

To serve the *acarajés* the traditional way, line each appetizer plate with a banana leaf square and arrange the stuffed fritters on the leaves. Or simply arrange them on the plates. Top each with a scant teaspoon of the shrimp *molho*.

Variations: You can be creative when filling *acarajés*: Cuban-Style Shrimp in *Enchilado* Sauce (page 624), Bogotá Cheese Cooking Sauce (page 52), and salt cod hash (page 412) are all good choices instead of the *vatapá*. And instead of the Brazilian sauce (*molho*), you might substitute a Mexican salsa (pages 113–16) or a Venezuelan *ají de leche* (page 122).

Yuca Fingers with Cilantro Sauce Presilla

Yuquita Frita con Salsa de Cilantro a la Presilla

I never imagined that my yuca fries with cilantro sauce would become as popular as they have. The result of my curious exploration of Latin tubers and dipping sauces in the early 1980s, the pairing is now served in Cuban restaurants all over the United States.

In Cuba, cooks fry yuca in large chunks, which is fine for a side dish. But when I started playing with yuca as an appetizer for my parties at home, I came up with French fry–sized yuca fingers, more delicate and attractive and also easier to handle, like the yuca fries I had seen in other Latin American countries. I wanted a dipping sauce other than the traditional Cuban *mojo*, and under the spell of a trip to India, where I had been smitten with a particularly delicious cilantro chutney in Meerut, a town near Delhi, I came up with the creamy cilantro sauce on page 136.

When I put the two ideas together, some Cuban friends who had never used cilantro in large amounts fell in love with the sauce and kept asking for the recipe. Soon thereafter, food writer Suzanne Hamlin tasted the fries and published the recipe in the *Daily News* in 1983. Her article launched my professional food career. We had been introduced by Paula Wolfert, who had discovered me preparing *surullitos*, the Puerto Rican fritters, in Felipe Rojas-Lombardi's New York restaurant, the Ballroom. (Funny that my life took such a dramatic turn from teaching to cooking because of a couple of Latin fritters.) Later I put the yuca fries with cilantro sauce on the menu of Victor's Café, also in Manhattan, and it was quickly embraced by other cooks, who now think of it as a traditional Cuban combination.

What to Drink: Mojito (page 355), daiquiri on the rocks (page 354), or a floral Susana Balbo Crios Torrontes from Mendoza, Argentina

SERVES 6 TO 8

> 3 pounds fresh yuca, peeled and cut into 5-inch chunks, or 2 pounds frozen yuca
> Corn oil or light olive oil, for deep-frying
> Salt
> Creamy Cilantro Sauce Presilla (page 136)

▶ Boil the yuca according to the instructions on page 167 until soft but not falling apart. Drain in a colander and let cool. Cut the yuca lengthwise into 3- to 5-inch-long fingers about an inch thick, like French fries. Line a baking sheet with waxed paper and arrange the yuca fingers on it in a single layer. Cover loosely with plastic wrap or waxed paper and refrigerate until chilled and firm, preferably overnight. (The yuca fingers can be refrigerated for 2 to 3 days before frying.)

Heat the oil to 350°F in a large saucepan or deep skillet over medium heat. Working in batches, add the yuca fingers a few at a time to the hot oil and turn until lightly golden on all sides. Drain on

paper towels and sprinkle with salt. Serve at once with the sauce.

King Kong *Patacones* with Everything

Patacones "King Kong" con Todo

When my nephew Adrián was six years old, he named these very large thin fried green plantain rounds King Kong *tostones*. They could also be called "the revenge of the tortilla press." The idea of using a tortilla press to flatten fried green plantains, what we know in Cuba as *tostones*, came to me on a trip to Barranquilla, a city on the Caribbean coast of Colombia. As I was driving into town, I saw a storefront restaurant with a sign that read PATACONES CON TODO, Fried Green Plantains with Everything. It piqued my curiosity, and I went in to investigate.

When I walked into the place, I saw people eating thin *patacones* as large as a dinner plate as if they were pizzas, topped with onions, sausages, cheese, or ham. If you know plantains, you can tell that even if you cut them into very large rounds, you can't get them to be as broad and as perfectly round as a plate with a regular plantain press (*tostonera*). The owner was not very friendly and he said bluntly that he would not show me how he did it—it was his trade secret!

My Barranquilla friends apologized profusely, explaining that this man was not from the coast but from the interior. (Every Latin country has its regional feuds.) I just laughed. But I do know tortillas and that marvelous piece of equipment called a tortilla press, the best Mexican invention since the *metate* and the *molcajete*. When I came back home

I tried flattening my *tostones* with a tortilla press. It worked, though I could not get them as wide as a plate. You can use almost anything you like for a topping, including many of the recipes in this book.

What to Drink: Club Colombia or other beer

SERVES 6

- 2 large green plantains (about 13 ounces each)
- 4 cups corn oil, for deep-frying
- 1 cup water
- 1 teaspoon salt

▶ Peel the plantains according to the instructions on page 181. Cut into 2-inch-long pieces.

Heat the corn oil to 350°F in a large saucepan. Meanwhile, combine the water and salt in a small bowl and stir to dissolve the salt. Add the plantains to the oil and fry until they float. Lift them from the oil with a slotted spoon, quickly dip them in the water, and immediately remove.

Cut two rounds of plastic wrap and line a tortilla press. Place a plantain round in the center of the press and flatten it to 5 inches in diameter.

Raise the heat to 375°F. One or two at a time, return the plantains to the hot oil and fry until golden brown all around, about a minute. Drain on paper towels.

Place each plantain round on an appetizer plate and top with a few generous spoonfuls of the topping of your choice and a spoonful of a spicy relish. Serve immediately.

Serving: You can take *todo* as literally as you want. Or more modestly, a savory hash flavored with a *sofrito*-type sauce works well with the fried plantains. Try

Costa Rican Chayote, Fresh Corn, and Beef Hash (page 230), Cuban Ground Beef Hash (page 695), or the tuna or salt cod hash used as filling for Galician Empanadas (page 411). For a tangy touch, finish with a spoonful of a spicy relish like Peruvian Onion and Yellow Pepper Slaw/Relish (page 150) or Yucatecan Red Onions Pickled in Bitter Orange Juice (page 149).

Bolivian Boiled Corn, Potatoes, and Fava Beans with Fried Cheese and Hot Sauce

Plato Paceño

One of Bolivia's favorite street foods is a plate of boiled Andean corn, mealy potatoes, and fresh fava beans served with a side of fried cheese and a dollop of a hot fresh salsa called *llajwa*. The result is a marvelous combination of contrasting colors, textures, and flavors that Bolivians consume with relish at La Paz's famous January fair (Feria de las Alasitas) and during Holy Week and Carnival. Peeling the fava beans is left to the diner, but nobody minds. I love preparing *plato paceño* for a leisurely Sunday brunch, served with grilled chicken or ribs. The cheese is a firm fresh cow's milk variety that keeps its shape when cooked.

What to Drink: Bolivian Paceña beer, Cucharamama Peruvian-Style Pisco Sour (page 356), or Bolivian *chuflay* (page 359)

6 ears frozen white Andean corn, thawed, or fresh
yellow corn
Salt

6 medium russet potatoes (about 2 pounds),
scrubbed

3 pounds fresh fava beans, shelled (about 3 cups)
Corn oil, for frying

1 pound fresh cheese, preferably *queso blanco para
freír*, cut into twelve 1-inch-thick slices
Spicy Bolivian Table Sauce (page 117)

▶ If using frozen corn, rinse it. If using fresh corn, husk the corn and remove the silks; reserve the husks from 2 ears. Set aside.

If using fresh corn, line a large cooking pot with the reserved husks; they will add delicious flavor. Pour 3 quarts water into the pot, add salt to taste, and bring to a boil over high heat. Add the potatoes and cook for 15 minutes. Add the corn and cook for 5 minutes (Andean corn might take a bit longer). Add the fava beans and cook for 1 to 2 minutes. Drain the vegetables and transfer to a platter. Set aside, covered, to keep warm.

Heat about ½ inch of oil in a 9- or 10-inch nonstick skillet. Add the cheese, 2 slices at a time, and fry, turning once, until light brown and slightly blistered, about 1 minute on each side. Drain on paper towels and keep in a warm oven.

To serve, distribute the fava beans evenly among six plates and place 1 ear of corn, 1 potato, and 2 slices of fried cheese next to each portion. Top the potato with a couple of tablespoons of sauce, and serve piping hot. Each diner peels his or her own beans.

Peruvian Grilled Beef Heart Kebabs "El Condorito"

Anticuchos "El Condorito"

When my North American friends ask me what to eat in Peru, I always urge them to try the beef heart kebabs called *anticuchos*. At sundown, you'll find street vendors everywhere cooking *anticuchos* on charcoal grills and basting them with a flavorful, puckery marinade. There are people who will not go near *anticuchos*—my husband, for instance. But he is missing a fabulous treat. *Anticuchos* are spectacular. The heart is the most intensely beefy meat you can hope to eat. And the rich Peruvian *adobo* that is used to marinate it only intensifies that marvelous lean beefiness.

I have tasted good *anticuchos* near El Puente de Los Suspiros (the Bridge of Sighs) in Lima's Barranco district, but I found the very best in Cusco. In a ramshackle, chaotic part of town near the market, next to another bridge, the Puente Grau, there was a little restaurant of sorts that specialized in *anticuchos*. The "heart" of the place was Berta Bárcena, a matron who started the business a generation ago, selling *anticuchos* in the market. Her food became so popular that her husband and son decided to build her a little restaurant. Over the years hundreds of visitors, the poor and the rich, the foreign and the local, even Alberto Fujimori when he was president, paid a visit to El Condorito (The Little Condor).

The name of the restaurant was a tribute to a popular comic-strip character, El Condorito, a condor who looks like the cricket in *Pinocchio*. All over the restaurant were murals depicting the antics of this endearing, mischievous character. They were especially amusing considering that one of the owners, a son, Edward Bárcena, looked like the *condorito*—he knew it, too.

Cook's Notes: Latin butchers sell heart in all its anatomically correct glory, with arteries and membranes intact, but they will clean it for you if you ask. At Bandera, my local market in Union City, New Jersey, hearts come conveniently cleaned and packed, ready to make *anticuchos*. But just in case you are handed a plastic pouch with a large, uncleaned heart, use a sharp knife to cut the heart in half lengthwise and remove the arteries and connective membrane, then trim away the excess fat.

In Peru, cooks use special skewers made of split bamboo that are broader and sturdier than the typical bamboo skewers we use. When I come across them in my Latin market, I buy them by the hundreds in case I can't find them again. If you can't get these, use flat metal skewers.

Both Peruvians and Bolivians claim to have the best *anticuchos*. The truth is that each country makes excellent *anticuchos*, but each has a style of its own. Peruvian *anticuchos* are chunky, marinated in a vinegary *panca* pepper *adobo*, and cooked on bamboo skewers. In Bolivia, the hearts are cut thinner, most often marinated with lime juice and dried *mirasol* pepper, grilled on metal skewers, and served with a spicy peanut sauce.

What to Drink: Cold *Cuzqueña* beer or Cucharamama Peruvian-Style Pisco Sour (page 356)

SERVES 6

- 1 beef heart (about 2½ pounds), cleaned
- 6 dried *panca* peppers, stemmed and seeded, or 2 tablespoons ground *panca* peppers (page 54)
- 1 head garlic, cloves separated, peeled, and mashed into a paste with a mortar and pestle, or finely chopped and mashed
- ¼ cup red wine vinegar
- ¼ cup achiote-infused corn oil (page 89)
- 1 teaspoon ground cumin
- 1 teaspoon salt
- 1 teaspoon freshly ground black pepper
- 2 tablespoons achiote-infused oil or freshly rendered lard (page 82) or bacon drippings, for basting

Preparing the Heart ▶ Rinse the heart under cold water and pat it dry with paper towels. Cut into 1- to 2-inch kebabs and place in a bowl. Set aside.

If using dried chiles, soak in 3 cups hot water until soft; or place in a small saucepan with 3 cups water and simmer over medium heat until soft. Drain, reserving ¼ cup of the cooking liquid.

Place the soaked peppers and the reserved cooking liquid or the ground chiles in a blender or food processor, add the rest of the ingredients except the basting oil, and process to a thick puree. Add the puree to the bowl of kebabs and toss to coat evenly. Cover with plastic wrap and marinate in the refrigerator for at least several hours, or, preferably, overnight.

Prepare a hot fire on a charcoal or gas grill.

Drain the kebabs, reserving the marinade. Thread the kebabs on skewers, allowing 4 to 5 for a 7-inch skewer. Set aside while you prepare the basting sauce.

Place the marinade in a small saucepan, add the achiote-infused oil, lard, or drippings, and bring to a simmer. Simmer for a few minutes, stirring. Remove from the heat. Have a brush ready (or a bunch of scallions tied together as a brush).

Place the skewers on the grill. Cook, basting

often with the oil, for 2 to 3 minutes on each side for medium-rare, 4 to 5 minutes per side for more well done. But heart is a very lean meat that should not be overcooked. Serve hot.

Serving: Serve as an appetizer with a spoonful of Peruvian Onion and Yellow Pepper Slaw/Relish (page 150) or Fava Bean, Corn, and Fresh Cheese Salad/Relish (page 268). Or serve with Bolivian Peanut Sauce (page 130).

Variations: You can use the same marinade for grilling other cuts of beef or other red meats, poultry, fish, or shellfish. For a shrimp version, use 24 medium shrimp, shelled and deveined, and marinate for only 15 minutes or so. Grill, turning once, for 3 to 5 minutes, or until firm but still juicy. For chicken *anticuchos*, use about 1 pound skinless, boneless chicken breasts, cut into cubes or long strips. Grill until cooked through but still juicy, about 15 minutes.

Martini's Shrimp in Garlic Sauce with Guajillo Chile

Camarones al Ajillo con Chile Guajillo al Estilo de Martini

One night in 1996, I ate with a group of other food writers at a restaurant called Martini's in the border town of Juárez. We were sitting at a long table and laughing and acting boisterously, as one would behave in a cantina, but Martini's was no dive. Solicitous old waiters dressed in white jackets solemnly boned our fish table-side. The menu was straight from the fifties, long and ambitious, with plenty of dishes in béchamel sauce; even escargots were offered.

My shrimp was particularly good, circulating so briskly around the table that I had to order seconds. It was brought to the table sizzling in a reddish garlicky sauce garnished with thinly sliced guajillo chiles. The flavors were sharp, clean, and not as spicy as you might expect from a mountain of guajillo. Here is my interpretation of Martini's shrimp. It could be a main course with Mexican rice, but I prefer serving it as a first course in earthenware *cazuelitas*, because it reminds me of the classic Spanish shrimp with garlic sauce, *camarones al ajillo*.

What to Drink: Mexican beer like Carta Blanca or Negra Modelo or a zesty Chilean Montes Sauvignon Blanc Reserva Casablanca Valley

SERVES 4

- 1 pound medium shrimp, shelled and deveined
  Salt
- 1 teaspoon fresh lime juice
- 4 dried guajillo chiles
- ¼ cup extra-virgin olive oil
- 1 large head of garlic, cloves separated, peeled, and finely chopped
- 1 teaspoon hot *pimentón* (Spanish smoked paprika)
- ¼ cup dry sherry
  Lime wedges, for garnish

▶ Place the shrimp in a bowl and season with salt to taste and the lime juice. Set aside.

Stem and seed the chiles, trying to keep them whole. Heat a *comal* or heavy skillet and roast the chiles over medium-high heat for about 2 minutes on each side. Transfer to a cutting board and slice crosswise into very thin rounds.

Heat the oil in a large skillet over medium heat. Add half of the garlic and sauté until light gold, about 30 seconds. Add the paprika and chiles and cook, stirring, for 2 minutes. Add the shrimp and sauté for 2 minutes, until barely cooked. Stir in the sherry and salt to taste and sauté for 1 more minute. Stir in the remaining garlic and cook for a few seconds.

Serve hot with crusty bread and the lime wedges.

Mussels in the Style of Chilca

Choros a la Chilcana

Chilca is a small fishing village south of Lima that was once a summer retreat for the city's aristocracy. The fishermen there used to make simple seafood dishes cooked in a powerful fish broth that is now popular all over Peru. Here the mussels are cooked in that broth and served at room temperature as an appetizer, topped with a spicy mixture of corn and chopped onions—a tasty and pretty idea. There are many variations of this simple dish using all kinds of seafood, from mussels to fish to shrimp.

What to Drink: Bar Queirolo *Chilcano* (page 359) or a grassy, lively Chilean Montes Sauvignon Blanc Leyda Valley

SERVES 6

- 2 pounds mussels, well scrubbed
- 1 cup All-Purpose Fish Broth (page 540) or bottled clam juice
- 1 medium red onion (about 8 ounces), finely chopped (about 1 cup)
- 1 frozen Andean yellow pepper (*ají amarillo*), thawed, 1 medium-hot pepper such as a Hungarian yellow pepper, or 2 jalapeños, seeded, deveined, and finely chopped
  Juice of 1 lime
- 1 tablespoon ground dried *mirasol* pepper (page 54) or cayenne
- 1 teaspoon salt
- ½ cup Andean giant white corn kernels or sweet corn kernels, cooked
- 2 tablespoons finely chopped flat-leaf parsley, plus a few sprigs for garnish

▶ Place the mussels and broth or clam juice in a large deep skillet, cover, and bring to a boil over medium heat. Stir, lower the heat to medium-low, and simmer for about 5 minutes or until the mussels have opened. Lift them out of the pan with a slotted spoon as they open, to keep them from overcooking, and place in a bowl. Scoop out about ½ cup of the broth.

When the mussels are cool enough to handle, remove one half-shell from each, and arrange the mussels on a large decorative platter.

In a small bowl, combine all the remaining ingredients except the parsley sprigs. Place a teaspoon of the mixture on top of each mussel. To moisten the topping, sprinkle with the reserved mussel broth. Garnish with parsley sprigs. Delicious! Watch out for those who will pick out the Andean corn.

Octopus with Peruvian Purple Olive Sauce

Pulpo al Olivo

On the menu of every Peruvian restaurant you will find a first course of octopus served with a creamy mayonnaise flavored with meaty Peruvian purple olives (*aceitunas de botija*). This lovely sauce is credited to the late Rosita Yimura, a Peruvian cook of Japanese descent.

Although Rosita's sauce does not call for hot pepper, I suggest adding a dried *panca* pepper. It gives a delicious flavor and subtle heat to the sauce. Traditionally the octopus is garnished with slivered onions and purple olives.

What to Drink: Pisco sour (pages 356 and 357), Bar Queirolo *Chilcano* (page 359), The Captain (page 359), or Pilsen Callao beer

SERVES 4 TO 6

One 3-pound octopus
  1 dried *panca* pepper, seeded (optional)
 19 Peruvian purple olives or Kalamata olives (about 5 ounces), drained and pitted
 ¼ cup mayonnaise, homemade (page 135) or store-bought
  1 teaspoon fresh lime juice
 ¼ teaspoon salt

▶ Rinse the octopus under cold running water. Bring 5 quarts water to a boil in an 8-quart pot over high heat. Holding the octopus by a tentacle, plunge it in and out of the boiling water 3 times (traditional cooks swear that this ritual tenderizes the meat). Add the octopus to the pot, cover, and cook at a rolling boil until fork-tender: The timing can vary dramatically according to the quality of the octopus: Start checking for doneness after 30 minutes; it may take as long as 1 or to 1½ hours. Lift the octopus out onto a platter. Some cooks like to remove the purplish skin; I never do. The skin is tasty and gives character to the octopus. With a small sharp knife, cut all around the head to detach it. With a knife or scissors, cut the tentacles into ½-inch slices. Place the tentacles on a large serving platter and cover with plastic wrap.

If using the *panca* pepper, place in a small saucepan with 2 cups water and bring to a boil over medium heat. Boil until tender, about 10 minutes. Alternatively, soak in 2 cups hot water for 20 minutes, until soft. Drain.

Combine the *panca* pepper, olives, mayonnaise, lime juice, and salt in a blender or food processor and process to a smooth puree.

To serve, pour the olive sauce over the octopus.

Serving: Garnish with Peruvian Onion and Yellow Pepper Slaw/Relish (page 150); Fava Bean, Corn, and Fresh Cheese Salad/Relish (page 268); cilantro leaves; or Peruvian purple olives or Kalamata olives, pitted and thinly slivered.

Michoacán-Style Small Pork Tacos "El Paraíso"

Taquitos de Carnitas "El Paraíso"

The Mexican state of Michoacán is famous for its *carnitas*, morsels of pork so tender they melt in your mouth. The *carnitas* are cut from a large, succulent piece of pork that has cooked slowly in its own fat in a covered pot. Some of the best *carnitas* I have tasted were sold by street vendors in the town of Quiroga and in a small café in Pátzcuaro, called El Paraíso.

El Paraíso used to be *carnitas* paradise. The *carnitas* were served only twice a day, once in the morning and once in the afternoon, and then the normally quiet café filled with hungry people. One approached the counter where a huge piece of pork was being cut into manageable pieces. "How many *taquitos*, señora, ten, fifteen?" you would be asked. "What kind of sauce, señora, *verde* or *pico de gallo*?" The *carnitas* were wrapped in small, fresh, supple tortillas and spiced up with a dollop of tangy sauce. Like many Mexican *botanas*, they were irresistible. At El Paraíso, *carnitas* were so good that one *taquito* was never enough. One morning, my husband and I ate twenty each—a bit less than the people around us.

What to Drink: Margarita on the Rocks (page 365), dark Negra Modelo beer, or a Robledo Pinot Noir from Carneros

MAKES 20 TAQUITOS

One 3-pound piece boneless fatty pork shoulder, cut in half
1 pound fresh pork belly (*barrigada*) with layers of meat and fat attached
2 teaspoons salt
½ cup bitter orange juice, or equal parts lime juice and orange juice
20 freshly made corn tortillas (page 579), about 4–5 inches in diameter, or store-bought corn tortillas trimmed into 4- to 5-inch rounds using a saucer as a template

▶ Season the meats all over with the salt. Place in a heavy medium pot, add 2 cups water and the orange juice, and bring to a boil over medium-high heat. Lower the heat and simmer, covered, until the meat is fork-tender and the liquid has almost evaporated, about 2 hours; turn the meat every 20 minutes so that it cooks evenly.

Increase the heat and turn the meat to brown it on all sides. Transfer to a cutting board.

Cut the pork into small pieces, mixing the pieces of shoulder and the belly, and make tacos with corn tortillas. Accompany with a *salsa cruda* like *pico de gallo* (page 113), or a chunky tomatillo sauce (page 114).

Ecuadorian-Style Spareribs with "Dirty *Mote*"

Fritada Ecuatoriana con Mote Sucio y Agua de Manos

The *fritada* is an Ecuadorian institution. Go to any market from Quito to Cuenca and your nose will guide you to the *fritada* section. You will see women busy scooping out golden morsels of pork and ribs from large cauldrons and piling them on enameled plates along with huge mounds of piping-hot *mote* (Andean hominy) and the golden potato patties called *llapingachos* (see the following recipe). To be authentic, the *fritada* must be served with *mote* sautéed in the flavorful fat released by the spareribs as they cooked. Because the *mote* gets dark and speckled with bits of dark meat and fat, it is called *mote sucio* (dirty mote). The whole is topped with a simple *salsa cruda* made with shredded lettuce, onions, and chopped tomatoes. It is absolutely delicious. People call it *agua de manos* (literally "hand water") because vendors briefly refresh the onion and lettuce in cold water using their hands.

What makes it even more appealing to me is the cooking method. Once the meat is marinated, it cooks with no fuss in its own juices.

What to Drink: Ecuadorian Pilsener or Biela beer, Zafra's One-Lime Limeade (page 346), or Montes Cherub Rose of Syrah from Marchigue, Chile

SERVES 6

4½ pounds meaty spareribs, cut into 3-by-2-inch sections (you can have the butcher do this)
Salt
1 tablespoon ground cumin
1 teaspoon freshly ground black pepper
12 garlic cloves, peeled and coarsely mashed with a mortar and pestle or finely chopped and mashed
1 tablespoon red wine vinegar
6 cups cooked Andean Hominy (page 251)

For the Salsa

2 ripe large tomatoes (about 7 ounces each), coarsely chopped
1 medium red onion (about 8 ounces), cut lengthwise in half and finely sliced
½ head iceberg lettuce, finely shredded
1 tablespoon fresh lime juice

▶ Place the ribs in a large bowl or baking dish. Rub with 1 tablespoon salt and the cumin, pepper, garlic, and vinegar. Refrigerate, covered with plastic wrap, for at least 2 hours or up to 24 hours, to intensify the flavor.

Place the ribs in a heavy pot, cover, and simmer over medium-low heat until tender, 1 to 1½ hours; check often for doneness and to make sure they don't scorch (add a little bit of water if necessary). Uncover the pot and increase the heat to brown the meat, about 15 more minutes. Transfer the ribs to a serving platter, leaving the fat in the pot, and set aside in a warm place. Stir the hominy into the pot and sauté, stirring, over medium heat, for about 5 minutes, just enough to heat it through and to let it absorb the flavor of the fat. Remove from the heat.

While the ribs cook, mix all the ingredients for the salsa in a small bowl.

Divide the ribs among serving plates, with an abundant side of *mote sucio*. Top the ribs with a spoonful of the salsa. *Fritada* is classically served with the following *llapingachos*.

Ecuadorian Potato and Cheese Patties with Peanut Sauce

Llapingachos con Ají de Maní

Whenever you find *fritada* (preceding recipe) in an Ecuadorian market, you will also find the golden potato and cheese patties called *llapingachos*. (The name is a hybrid of the Quechua *llapin* and the Castilian *chato*, both meaning flat.) What makes this combination so appealing is not only the rich and succulent meat but the marvelous layering of flavors and textures, particularly the garlicky taste of the pork against the neutral creaminess of the potato.

My favorite *llapingachos* are from Cuenca in southern Ecuador, a beautiful town perched above the lively Tomebamba River that was once inhabited by the native Cañari people. Like its namesake in Spain, Cuenca boasts colonial houses with enclosed wooden balconies that overhang the cliff, affording a view of the river below.

Its romantic charm aside, Cuenca is an active market town that draws people from the southern sierra. On market days, Indian women in bowler hats and men in business suits alike line up to buy *llapingachos*. Standing behind smoky griddles, robust mestizo women paint the patties an appealing golden hue with achiote-infused lard and flip them with their bare hands, oblivious of the heat. When the patties are crusty on both sides, they slide them onto a waiting plate and top them with a relish of shredded lettuce, julienned red onions, and diced tomatoes that's refreshed quickly in cold water and seasoned with lime juice to taste. (I have adapted the idea as a relish for the *fritada*.) In some parts of Ecuador, *llapingachos* are also served with a creamy peanut sauce, which enhances the nutty taste of the mealy Ecuadorian potatoes.

When I first visited Cuenca, I would go daily to the central market for breakfast or lunch just to eat *llapingachos*. As I stood in a corner, plate in hand, I knew that if I ever owned a restaurant, I would have to serve this marvelous example of potato creativity from the Andes.

And, sure enough, *llapingachos* have been on the menu since the day I opened Zafra. I serve them as an appetizer topped with the peanut sauce and red onion relish or together with kale, rice, and beans in a vegetarian "blue plate." For breakfast and brunch, I pair *llapingachos* with sautéed chorizo, eggs, and toasted Cuban bread. With a steamy cup of *café con leche*, there is nothing better.

Cook's Note: True to their name, the *llapingachos* served in markets all over Ecuador are *chatos*, flat. They are also large and uneven, oozing melted cheese and reddish achiote oil. At Zafra, I serve the Cuencan home kitchen's more refined version: smaller, less oily patties that keep their shape when cooked and look much prettier on the plate. *Llapingachos* can be assembled a few hours or up to a day ahead, and refrigerated until cooking time.

What to Drink: A fresh Bodegas Aldial Naia from Rueda, Spain, or a Bodega Lurton Pinot Gris from Mendoza, Argentina

MAKES 12 PATTIES (SERVES 4)

4 medium russet potatoes (about 1½ pounds), peeled and quartered

1 tablespoon plus ¼ teaspoon salt

6 scallions, white part only, finely minced

3 ounces soft, crumbly fresh cow's-milk cheese, preferably an Ecuadorian *queso fresco*, or Monterey Jack cheese, coarsely grated (about ⅔ cup)

½ teaspoon freshly ground black pepper

¼ cup achiote-infused corn oil (page 89), for frying

1⅔ cups Ecuadorian Peanut and Milk Sauce (page 128)

▶ Place the potatoes in a medium pot, add 2 quarts water and 1 tablespoon salt, and bring to a boil. Reduce the heat and simmer until soft, about 15 minutes. Drain. Pass the hot potatoes through a potato ricer or a food mill into a bowl. Let cool slightly. When the puree is still warm to the touch, add the scallions, cheese, remaining ¼ teaspoon salt, and pepper, and mix well. Shape the puree into 12 balls, using about 2 heaping tablespoons of puree for each, and flatten into patties 3 inches across and ½ inch thick. Place on a baking sheet lined with parchment paper and refrigerate, loosely covered with plastic wrap, for at least 20 minutes before cooking, or they will stick to the pan and fall apart. (The patties can be refrigerated for several hours.)

Heat a 10-inch nonstick or well-seasoned skillet over medium heat. Brush the skillet lightly with achiote oil. Place 3 or 4 patties in the skillet, brush the top of each with achiote oil, and cook for 3 minutes, or until a crust forms on the bottom. With a narrow spatula, flip the patties over and brown them on the other side for about 3 minutes. Transfer to a platter and cover loosely to keep warm. Repeat with the remaining patties.

Serve hot with the peanut sauce. The mixture of shredded lettuce, onion, and tomatoes suggested in the *fritada* recipe is a wonderful addition.

Spicy Baked Corn and Cheese Patties

Arepitas de Queso Sazonadas

Arepas are the corn-flour griddle cakes Venezuelan and Colombians eat like bread with all their meals or as a snack. Here I have turned them into cocktail appetizers by adding a flavorful fresh cheese, herbs, and minced peppers to the dough and making the *arepas* smaller.

Cook's Note: There are several excellent brands of precooked white corn flour (*harina de maíz blanco precocida*) for *arepas*. I prefer the Venezuelan brand P.A.N., which comes in 2-pound packages. For more information, see page 253.

What to Drink: Cuban *daiquirí mambí* (page 355)

MAKES 24 *AREPITAS*

- 1 cup (about 6 ounces) precooked white corn flour for *arepas* (see Cook's Note)
- ½ teaspoon salt, or to taste
- 1 tablespoon grated brown loaf sugar (preferably *papelón*, *panela*, or *piloncillo*) or Demerara sugar
- 1 cup warm water
- 1 tablespoon light olive oil
- 8 ounces fresh cow's milk cheese (*queso blanco*), finely grated (about 2 cups)
- 15–20 (about 4 ounces) small Caribbean sweet peppers (*ajíes dulces*) or 2 cubanelle peppers, seeded and finely chopped
- 3 tablespoons finely chopped cilantro
- 1 tablespoon finely chopped chives
- 1 small red bell pepper (about 5 ounces), cored, seeded, deveined, and finely chopped (about 1 cup)
- 1 jalapeño, seeded and finely chopped

▶ Preheat the oven to 375°F. Lightly butter a baking sheet.

Mix the corn flour, salt, and sugar in a medium bowl. Pour in the warm water and olive oil and mix with a fork until well blended. Kneading with your hands, gradually add the cheese and the rest of the ingredients until you have a smooth dough.

Roll 1 tablespoon of dough (about 1 ounce) into a ball between your palms, then flatten the ball between your hands into a circle 2 inches in diameter and place on the prepared baking sheet. Repeat with the rest of the dough.

Bake for 10 minutes. Turn the *arepitas* and bake

for another 10 minutes, or until golden. The *arepitas* can also be grilled or barbecued wrapped in plantain leaves. Serve hot.

Serving: Pair with Venezuelan Chunky Avocado Sauce (page 137) or Caracan Black Bean Cream Soup (page 528).

Venezuelan Fresh Corn Griddle Cakes

Cachapas Venezolanas

Venezuelan *cachapas* made from coarsely ground fresh corn are sold by roadside vendors and in the restaurants called *areperas*, which unsurprisingly specialize in *arepas* (page 583). They are usually cooked on griddles also called *cachapas*, and served with Venezuela's rich, soft fresh cow's milk cheese.

Venezuelan corn is starchy, and the pureed corn needs only to be heated to set into cakes; cooks don't need to mix the corn with anything else as we do here, where the corn is more watery. But Venezuelan precooked corn flour comes to the rescue: just a little bit, about ¼ cup per pound of corn, will keep the corn patties together without changing the flavor or texture of the *cachapas*. Mexican instant corn *masa* mix can also add body to the corn mix, but the flavor will be slightly alkaline because it is made with nixtamalized corn.

Cook's Note: A Venezuelan friend of mine, chef Miriam Córdoba, always uses frozen corn to make *cachapas* here in the United States because she feels that it has a higher starch content than fresh. She might be right, but I like the sweetness of the fresh corn, with a little corn flour for body.

MAKES EIGHT 3-INCH *CACHAPAS* (SERVES 4)

3⅓ cups fresh corn kernels (from 4 large ears)
¼ cup heavy cream
1 tablespoon sugar
½ teaspoon salt
¼ cup precooked corn flour for *arepas*, preferably P.A.N. brand
2 tablespoons butter, melted
8 slices *queso blanco* or mozzarella *de bufala*, optional

▶ Place the corn kernels, cream, sugar, and salt in a food processor or blender and grind to a coarse paste. Pour into a bowl and stir in the corn flour.

Heat a 12-inch nonstick or well-seasoned skillet over medium heat. Brush lightly with some of the melted butter. Pour in ¼ cup of the corn mixture and, with a spatula, spread to a circle 3 inches in diameter. Cook 2 or 3 at a time for 3 minutes or until golden brown on the first side, then flip over with a spatula and keep cooking for another 3 minutes, or until golden brown like a pancake. Stack the cooked cakes on a warm platter as you cook the remaining batter. Serve topped with slices of fresh cheese or mozzarella de *bufala*.

Variations: At my restaurant Cucharamama, we serve a spoonful of salmon roe presented in a small wooden spoon propped over each *cachapa* and a dollop of Venezuelan Ripened Cream (page 148), beside it. The salty salmon roe is a marvelous counterpoint to the sweetness of the corn, and the ripened cream brings it all together.

Cali-Style Baked Fresh Corn Cakes

Arepas de Choclo al Estilo de Cali

On my way from Guanares to Valencia in Venezuela, I spotted a woman baking *cachapas* in an adobe oven by the side of the highway. Street vendors grilling *cachapas* are a common sight in Venezuela, but this one was special. I had seen women baking something similar in Cali, Colombia, called *arepas de choclo*, but never in Venezuela. I stopped the car—not a big sacrifice, braking for *cachapas*.

The woman poured the soft corn dough into small cast-aluminum *calderos* and baked until golden. Then she split the *cachapas* open and filled them with Venezuelan *queso de mano*, a soft fresh cheese. And soon the mystery was solved. The baker was not Venezuelan but an immigrant from Cali.

Back home, I set out to replicate the Cali-style *arepas de choclo*. At my local Latin American hardware store, I was able to by a bunch of small, slightly tapered, cast-aluminum *calderos*, each about 5 inches across the top. I made the *arepas de choclo* by pouring a small amount of batter into each, then unmolding them after baking. They were wider and flatter than the *cachapas* of my roadside discovery, so instead of splitting them open, I adapted the original by using the cheese for a topping. They have become a favorite at my restaurant Cucharamama, where we bake them in our wood-burning oven to give the cakes a crunchy golden brown crust.

As a substitute for Latin American *calderos*, you can use 10-ounce Pyrex custard cups. Be sure to grease them well with butter or oil.

MAKES 12 CAKES

6   cups fresh corn kernels (from about 6 large ears)
½   cup heavy cream
1½ teaspoons salt
¼   cup sugar
½   cup precooked corn flour for *arepas*, preferably P.A.N. brand
2   tablespoons butter, melted, or corn oil
    Fresh cow's milk (*queso blanco*) cheese

▶ Preheat the oven to 450°F.

Working in 3 batches, combine all ingredients except the butter in a blender or food processor and puree until smooth, transferring each batch to a bowl. Mix well.

Brush the bottoms and sides of 12 *calderos* or custard cups (see headnote) with ½ teaspoon melted butter or corn oil. Pour ½ cup of the corn mix into each *caldero* or custard cup.

Place them on a baking sheet and bake until the tops of the *arepas* are golden brown, about 20 minutes. Unmold and serve hot, topped with a slice of fresh cheese.

Rinconada's Delicious *Garnachas*

Garnachas Deliciosas

Mexican *garnachas*, a specialty of Veracruz, are crisp fried tortillas smothered in a savory chile sauce and a number of other tasty toppings. I think the most delicious examples can be found in Rinconada, a small town along the main road that once joined the port of Veracruz with Xalapa, the capital city of the state. The old highway divides the town in two, and on each side of the road resourceful women have opened up food stands where they cook and sell *garnachas*. I know of people in Xalapa who plan their trips to Veracruz strategically so that they can stop for breakfast or lunch in Rinconada.

On numerous outings from Xalapa to the coast, I would pass by hundreds of stands, and eventually I came to favor the *garnachas* of a woman named Máxima Medina, who owns a stand called Antojitos Carolina (Carolina's Snacks). She and I became quite friendly, and after much cajoling, she decided to share her recipe. I learned that Máxima uses what is almost a *mole* sauce instead of a simple *garnacha* sauce. She boils the ground-up paste of tomatoes, chiles, and spices rather than frying it, which is more typical of local *moles*.

Garnachas are made to order, and one can choose the toppings. I liked Máxima's sauce so much that I kept ordering *garnachas* topped only with the rich sauce, some cheese, and onions. Here I am giving you the whole treat, with refried beans, shredded beef, and potatoes, another example of the skillful way Mexicans build layers of flavor in a humble dish. Think of this recipe as a guide, not as gospel—in the end, you might want to simplify the whole thing and go, as I do, for the sauce.

Working Ahead ▶ The sauce and the meat can be prepared at least a couple days ahead and kept refrigerated, well covered with plastic wrap.

What to Drink: Mexican beer like Corona, Robledo Family Winery Merlot from Carneros, California, or nonalcoholic *tepache* (page 338) or Yucatecan *horchata* (page 345)

MAKES 18 TO 20 *GARNACHAS*

For the Sauce

- 8 dried guajillo chiles, stemmed and seeded
- 4 dried chipotle chiles, stemmed and seeded
- 10 ripe medium plum tomatoes (about 2 pounds)
- 1 large white onion (about 12 ounces), unpeeled
- 8 garlic cloves, unpeeled
- 1 teaspoon black peppercorns
- 1 teaspoon anise seeds
- 1 Ceylon cinnamon stick (*canela*)

For the Meat

- 8 ounces flank steak
- 1 large white onion (about 12 ounces), peeled and cut in half
- 1 teaspoon salt

For the Tortillas

- 2 cups (about 9 ounces) instant corn *masa* mix, preferably Maseca
- 1¼ cups water
- 2 cups corn oil or melted lard
- 1¼ cups Veracruzan Refried Bean Dip (page 277), warm
- 2 large russet potatoes (about 12 ounces), peeled, boiled, and coarsely mashed with a fork while still warm
- 6 ounces hard cow's-milk cheese such as Mexican *cotija* cheese or ricotta salata, coarsely grated (about 1⅓ cups)
- 1 medium white onion (about 8 ounces), finely chopped (about 1 cup)

Making the Sauce ▶ Slit open the dried chiles with a sharp knife and remove the seeds.

Heat a large *comal*, heavy skillet, or griddle over medium-high heat. Add the chiles and roast for 40 seconds on each side. Transfer to a bowl, cover with 1 quart warm water, and let soak until softened, about 20 minutes.

Meanwhile, place the tomatoes, onion, and garlic on the hot *comal* and roast, turning occasionally with tongs, until lightly charred on all sides, about 8 minutes. Set aside.

Add the spices to the hot *comal* and roast, stirring, until fragrant, about 1 minute. Transfer the spices to an electric spice mill or coffee grinder. and grind to a powder. Set aside.

Peel the onion and garlic. Drain the softened chiles, reserving 1 cup of the liquid.

Combine all of the roasted ingredients in a blender or food processor, add the reserved 1 cup of soaking liquid, and process to a fine puree. Force the puree through a mesh strainer, pushing on the solids with a wooden spoon, into a medium saucepan. Bring just to a boil, and boil gently for about 15 minutes, stirring frequently, until lightly thickened. Remove from the heat; you should have about 2 cups.

Cooking the Meat ▶ Place the steak, onion, and salt in a medium pot, add 2 quarts water, and bring to a boil over high heat. Lower the heat and simmer, covered, until tender, about 1 hour.

Lift the meat out of the pot and onto a plate. When it is cool enough to handle, shred into very thin strands about 2 inches long. Keep the meat refrigerated, tightly covered with plastic wrap, until ready to use. Reheat before serving.

Preparing the Tortillas ▶ Place the masa mix and water in a bowl and mix and knead with your hands to form a pliable dough, adding a little more water if the *masa* feels too dry. Shape into 18 or 19 balls (about 1 ounce each). Cut 18 or 19 5-inch rounds of plastic wrap to keep the tortillas from drying after pressing. Place each ball in a tortilla press lined with 2 additional rounds of plastic and press into rounds of about 3½ inches in diameter. Peel away from the plastic used for pressing, place on a fresh round of plastic, and cover with another round. Continue with the remaining balls of dough, stacking the tortillas as they are pressed with a layer of plastic under and over each tortilla. Keep them between the plastic rounds until ready to use. Do not let rest for too long, since the *masa* might become dry.

Frying the Tortillas ▶ Heat the corn oil or lard in a heavy medium pot until it reaches 375°F. Peel off a tortilla and transfer to the palm of your right hand. Slide gently into the hot oil; it will puff up and float. Fry for 15 seconds on each side. Remove immediately from the oil with a slotted spoon or a wire skimmer and drain on paper towels. Repeat with the remaining tortillas.

Assembling the *Garnachas* ▶ Spread 1 tablespoon of the refried beans on each tortilla, leaving a ¼-inch border all around it. Spread 1 tablespoon of the sauce over the beans. Scatter some shredded meat over the beans and finish with a generous teaspoon of the potatoes, 1 tablespoon grated cheese, and 1 teaspoon chopped onion. Serve immediately.

Corn *Pupusas* Filled with Cheese

Pupusas de Queso Champa del Comal

Pupusas are thick, spongy corn tortillas that can be stuffed with various fillings before cooking. They are a specialty of El Salvador, where people consume them with a passion at all hours of the day but particularly in the evening accompanied with tangy relishes. Not far from the city of San Salvador is the Planes del Rendero, a park atop a hill. Its claim to fame is the so-called Puerta del Diablo, Hell's Gate, and the best *pupusas* in town. All along the steep road to the park there are *champas*, roadside shacks where women sell *pupusas*. My favorite, La Champa del Comal, is the only one where

Chipilín

pupusas are cooked on a traditional clay griddle (*comal*) over an open fire, which makes them even more delicious, because the smoke flavors the *pupusas*. Others use metal griddles that require cooks to grease them. When cooking a *pupusa* on a hot clay *comal*, you do not use any fat to keep it from sticking to the pan, but you need to know exactly on what part of the *comal* to place it. It has to be on a section that is not too hot, not too cold, or the *pupusa* will stick, and when you try lifting it onto a plate it will fall apart.

Pupusas come with a variety of fillings, staples like beans and *chicharrones* (not the pork cracklings of other countries but fried morsels of fatty pork ground to a paste), dried shrimp, squash blossoms, and wild greens like *chipilín* and the fragrant blossom *loroco*.

This is a basic recipe that will give you a good handle on the art of *pupusa* making.

Cook's Note: One of the important things I learned from the street *pupusa* makers in San Salvador and Izalco, a historic town famous for *comal*-baked *pupusas*, is that *pupusas* have to be moist and succulent, not dry like Mexican tortillas. For that your dough must be supple and on the wet side. If you feel that the dough has too much water, let it rest undisturbed for a few minutes, because doughs made with corn flour will invariably absorb lots of liquid. Just make sure that you can easily shape the dough

into balls without too much of the *masa* sticking to your fingers. Otherwise, knead in a bit of flour until you get the right consistency.

What to Drink: Salvadorian Pilsener, Regia Extra, or Guatemalan Famosa beer; Costa Rican Hibiscus Wine (page 339), or Rice *Horchata* (page 345)

MAKES 18 *PUPUSAS*

For the Tortillas

3¼ cups instant corn *masa* mix (about 16 ounces), preferably Maseca brand

4 cups water

For the Filling

8 ounces crumbled Salvadorian hard cheese (available in Latin markets as *queso duro*) or ricotta salata

8 ounces fresh mozzarella (about 2 cups), shredded

¼ cup water, or more as needed

½ cup corn oil or melted freshly rendered lard (page 82)

Making the Tortillas ▶ Place the *masa* mix and water in a large bowl, mix well, and knead with your hands to form a soft, pliable dough. Let rest to allow excess water to be absorbed. Shape into 18 balls (about 1¼ ounces each) and place on a baking sheet, covered with a damp kitchen towel, to keep them from drying out.

Preparing the Filling ▶ Place the two cheeses in a small bowl and add the water. Knead with your hands to soften and mix together. Shape into 18 balls of equal size and place on a baking sheet along with the balls of dough.

Filling the *Pupusas* ▶ Savvy Salvadorians pat down the tortillas by hand, and it is my preferred method. Place a ball of dough on the palm of your left hand and press lightly with your fingertips. Hold between your palm and fingers and make a well or cup in the center by pressing with your fingertips. The cup should be deep and wide enough to hold the ball of cheese comfortably. Press the cheese into the cup. Close the dough around it, and again shape into a ball. Flatten lightly with your fingertips and place between two thick squares of plastic film 5 to 6 inches across. Using your fingertips, flatten each *pupusa* into an even 4¼- to 4½-inch circle. Make 2 or 3 at a time and keep covered with a damp kitchen towel while you work.

Cooking the *Pupusas* ▶ Grease a metal *comal* or a heavy skillet or griddle at least 10 inches in diameter and heat over medium heat. Add 2 or 3 *pupusas* at a time to the pan. Brush lightly with some oil. Cook about 6 minutes on each side, slightly less if you want your *pupusas* more moist. Make sure the *pupusas* do not stick to the pan and brush with more oil as needed. Lift out with a spatula and place on a platter. Keep warm.

Serving: Serve hot with *curtido*, a Salvadorian *Pupusa* Relish (page 151).

**Variation: *Pupusas* with Cheese and *Loroco*
(*Pupusas de Queso y Loroco*)**
I would say that cheese and *loroco* is my favorite filling for *pupusas*. You will never find a more felicitous combination. *Loroco* is a wild Central American plant with tiny flowers that are picked as buds, smelling and tasting just like ripe cheese. The buds are highly prized by Salvadorians and Guatemalans, who also

use them to fill tamales. On my first visit to El Salvador, I arrived in *loroco* season, and I went temporarily insane, eating *pupusas* with *loroco* everywhere I went.

I buy *loroco* frozen or pickled in brine in my local Latin market. It is not as flavorful as the fresh, but it comes close. Using the recipe above, add 1 tablespoon of *loroco*, fresh or frozen (thawed) or from a jar (drained) to the cheese filling of each *pupusa* and cook as instructed above.

Loroco buds

Variation: You can also fill the *pupusas* with refried beans and cheese. Use any of the refried bean recipes on pages 273, 276, or 277. Just add a tablespoon or so of beans to the cheese filling and cook as indicated in the recipe.

Costa Rican Small Corn Tortillas with Assorted Toppings

Gallitos Surtidos

On our way down from a hike to the Poás volcano in Costa Rica, my husband and I stopped for lunch in a pretty restaurant, Los Chubascos, where we caught our breath and rested our eyes, which were irritated from the volcanic gases. Outside, thick sheets of rain fell with a fury, but we felt protected in a cocoon of warmth.

Los Chubascos is a rustic country house with dining rooms that open onto a garden full of trumpet lilies and amaryllis. Its menu is an anthology of typical Costa Rican dishes. I asked for the house special, *el casado* (the married man), a combination of yellow rice, beef, and ripe plantain with a simple salad of cabbage and carrots. My husband, who preferred something lighter, ordered assorted *gallitos*. The delightful little corn tortillas came smothered with different toppings, including shredded beef, beans, chayote, and a potato hash. They were all delicious, and I found myself stealing them from his plate, until he gave up, passed me the plate, and asked for another order.

At home, I make *gallitos* often, and my toppings are usually leftovers, not necessarily from Costa Rican dishes. I serve *gallitos* at the kitchen counter, where my guests gravitate before sitting at the table.

What to Drink: Costa Rican beer, such as Cerveza Imperial

MAKES 30 *GALLITOS*

For the Tortillas

1 cup (about 4½ ounces) instant *masa* mix for tortillas, preferably Maseca

¾ cup water

Suggested Toppings

Costa Rican Chayote, Fresh Corn, and Beef Hash (page 230)

Veracruzan Refried Bean Dip (page 277)

Cuban *ropa vieja* (page 714)

Yucatecan *frijoles colados* (page 276)

▶ Place the *masa* mix and water in a bowl and mix together to form a pliable dough. Knead briefly. Let rest for a few minutes, covered with a damp cloth.

Divide the *masa* into 30 small balls. Using a tortilla press lined with 2 plastic rounds, press each ball into a tortilla of about 2½ inches in diameter. (I like my *gallitos* very small.) Unless you can work rapidly, it is best to protect the tortillas from drying out by stacking them between layers of plastic wrap as suggested in the recipe for Rinconada's Delicious *Garnachas* (page 399). You will need 30 rounds of plastic.

Heat a *comal*, heavy skillet, or griddle over medium-high heat. Peel each tortilla from the plastic round onto the palm of your right hand and slide it gently onto the *comal*. Flip over with a spatula when the edges begin to dry. Cook until you see it covered with soft brown spots. Flip over again and cook for a few seconds; encourage the tortilla to puff by tapping it gently. Place in a cloth-lined basket and cook the remaining *gallitos*, stacking them in the basket and covering them with a napkin to keep warm.

To serve, place 4 or 5 *gallitos* at a time on the warm *comal*, griddle, or skillet, and top each with 1 to 2 tablespoons of your favorite topping, which should be warm or at room temperature. Heat through, but be careful not to burn the *gallitos*, especially if using a *comal*.

Serving: Serve 4 to 6 assorted *gallitos* per person, with 2 or 3 types of relish. I like Guatemala Radish Salad (page 556), Yucatecan Red Onions Pickled in Bitter Orange Juice (page 149), Salvadorian *Pupusa* Relish (page 151), and *Arracacha* Salad (page 215). I also like to add a dollop of a spicy salsa to each *gallito*, such as Green Tomatillo-Chile Salsa (page 114) or Salvadorian *Salsa Cruda* (page 121). Also bring some grated cheese to the table. You can fold the *gallitos* into tacos and eat them with your hands.

EMPANADAS

Empanadas are the ultimate portable meal, a filled dough package that you can eat with your hands. Small and half-moon shaped or as large as a pizza, baked or fried, flaky or breadlike, empanadas offer a secret world of flavor. Between the crusts lies a filling that may surprise you with unexpected touches. It's this sense of anticipation that heightens the pleasure of eating an empanada, that elevates this humble food into something special.

The word *empanada* comes from a medieval Spanish word, *empanar*, which means to bread (as in coating in crumbs) or to serve something on bread or within a bread crust. But the empanada probably existed long before the medieval period. A possible ancestor is the Roman *placenta*, a sort of pie in a round, cakelike shape, sometimes brought to temples as a ritual offering. A second-century B.C. *placenta* recipe recorded by Cato the Elder in his treatise *De agricultura* involves a filling of fresh sheep's cheese and honey layered with oiled sheets of dough (possibly like large lasagna noodles made with a sturdy semolina dough) with everything finally wrapped in a crust made from fine wheat flour and baked on a bed of bay leaves in the Roman beehive oven. To me the wrapping technique sounds like a forerunner of the large Galician empanadas. Another possible precursor to the empanada was the medieval custom of using a trencher, a thick piece of stale bread, as a plate. Who could fail to notice that, drenched with the juices of the foods, the bread tasted really good?

In Spain, references first crop up in twelfth-century art and literature. There is a famous sculpture in the Pórtico de la Gloria of the Cathedral of Santiago de Compostela in Galicia, Spain, a jewel of European Romanesque art, depicting a glutton condemned to eat a round empanada. Historians joke that the empanada must have been made of a spiny fish like sardines, a Galician favorite, so the bones could pierce his gullet. In a poem in the thirteenth-century Castilian collection of miracle stories called the *Cantigas de Santa María* (Canticles of Holy Mary), robbers ambush a group of pilgrims heading to a shrine of the Virgin and rob them of their empanadas.

I have also come across recipes for empanadas in both thirteenth-century Islamic Spanish cookbooks and Spanish recipe collections of the fourteenth and fifteenth centuries. The *Libro de cozina* (Book of Cooking, 1529), a Spanish version of the Catalan *Libre del coch* by Ruperto de Nola (1520), groups empanadas in the section on foods for Lent, which is especially fitting because most are fish empanadas.

Spaniards brought empanadas to the New World. They kept some of their traditional recipes and adapted others to new ingredients wherever they settled. In Mexico, for example, there are empanadas made with wheat flour (some modeled after earlier Spanish recipes) and others made with the corn dough used by pre-Columbian Mexicans for tortillas. The Mexican *quesadilla* is nothing but a half-moon empanada made with a corn-flour dough and filled with cheese.

No matter where you go in Latin America, the essence of the empanada remains the same. What changes are the ingredients from which the dough is made (wheat, corn, yuca, or plantain flour), its texture, and its shape—it may be round or football-shaped, folded over into a half-moon or like an envelope, thick-crusted or thin and brittle.

Another variable is whether the empanada is fried or baked in the oven. For the most part, this is ruled by climate. In temperate Chile and Argentina, oven empanadas (*empanadas de horno*) are more prevalent, baked in Spanish-style beehive adobe ovens. In the Caribbean and Mexico, empanadas are more often fried or cooked on the griddle-like *comal*. In the Hispanic Caribbean, large Galician-style baked empanadas are often made in bakeries. These are the thick, breadlike kind brought by Spaniards from Galicia, the empanada capital of Spain, and cooked to this day by their descendants throughout the Americas.

Traditional fillings generally combine sweet and sour notes, indicating a link with colonial cooking and with recipes from medieval and Renaissance Spain. From Mexico to Patagonia, you find the same flavorful triad of olives, raisins, and hard-boiled eggs mixed with highly seasoned, finely chopped meat or fish.

The distinction between chopping and grinding meats is an important one for many South American cooks. Most claim the meat stays juicier when chopped by hand. Onion is usually a crucial seasoning—especially in Argentina, where cooks fill their empanadas with equal amounts of meat and onions, so that the onion and meat juices mingle during cooking. Chileans also add a good measure of onion to their fillings to make them juicier. A favorite of mine is the Chilean *calduda* empanada. *Calduda* means souplike, and this delicious onion-laden empanada lives up to its name, dripping juice all over when you bite into it.

In Latin America, empanadas are sometimes eaten with drinks before a sit-down dinner, particularly in Chile and Argentina. More often, though, they are consumed as snacks at different times of the day, bought at small cafeterias or bakeries or from street food vendors (who may even deliver their empanadas to offices and shops).

In Chile and Argentina, there is still a strong tradition of homemade empanadas, but as more women are working outside the home, there has been an upsurge in the number of bakeries that specialize in empanadas. On weekdays, you will always find people waiting in line to buy them to take home for a light late-afternoon meal. On weekends, the lines get longer, for empanadas are something of a ritual for weekend meals. Walk into any Chilean home for a Sunday lunch or dinner and you will be greeted by someone holding a tray of golden empanadas and someone else offering you a frothy pisco sour. In Argentina, when you are invited to a barbecue (*asado*), you know you are going to eat beef empanadas first, with a glass of red wine.

In Bolivia, every day is punctuated by empanadas: by nine in the morning people are buying *empanadas salteñas* (small, gilded empanadas shaped like footballs) to have with juice or soda or *café con leche*. In the afternoons, the children and adults who come streaming out of schools and offices stand on the street eating *salteñas*, dripping juice all over their shirts.

The two most popular, the *salteña* and the *tucumana*, are inspired by empanadas from two provinces in the northeast of Argentina that border on Bolivia, Salta and Tucumán. But in Bolivia these empanadas, simply seasoned with some cumin and paprika, have become something much more complex and delicious, exploding with flavor. The *salteña* is the sweetest empanada I have ever tasted—both the dough and filling are sweetened. But there is balance in the ensemble, because the filling is also spicy with lots of Andean hot peppers. Great attention is paid to the look of the *salteña*. Cooks brush the empanada with beaten egg yolk and achiote oil so that they will bake to a shiny saffron color.

Making Argentinean empanadas is a fastidious art, carefully practiced by women who seal the seams with delicate and beautiful folds (*repulgo*). Chilean empanadas, too, are a beautiful sight to behold, emerging from the oven like parchment envelopes, edges burnished, dark spots shining on the smooth ivory surface. You know instantly that biting into one will be like eating bread fresh from the oven. For the most part, classic Chilean empanadas are filled with a hand-chopped beef hash called *pino*, a name that comes from the language of the Mapuche Indians and means something small and thin, like pine needles. Occasionally they have a touch of *merkén*, the fabulous paprika ground from hot *cacho de cabra* peppers, which makes them absolutely divine.

The empanada is the ultimate master of disguise, adjusting to climate and taste. Its basis is very simple—wheat flour, water, and fat, or any starchy vegetable dough—and can be adapted in many ways. The dough can be rolled paper-thin so that the empanada will puff up when fried; leavened with yeast, mixed with lard, and kneaded like bread to obtain the crumbly texture of a good piecrust; or made from puff pastry for flaky layers. The possibilities for the filling are also endless. You can play with leftovers or cross over to other cuisines, using something as indulgent as foie gras. Whatever you do, always remember the wisdom of the empanada's medieval sweet-and-sour foundation, the combination of smooth and crunchy textures. It's a basic grammar that satisfies all parts of your palate.

In this chapter, I have gathered recipes that illustrate the major categories of Latin empanadas, from the large two-crust pies brought by Galician immigrants, with their yeast dough and generous fillings, to New World interpretations of the concept, crunchy half-moon turnovers made out of dough from corn or starchy vegetables such as plantain.

Here you'll find basic dough recipes for baked and fried empanadas, filling suggestions, and recipes for savory pies ideal for entertaining. I hope you not only take from the recipes formulas or ideas that you can incorporate into the way you cook and eat, but also acquire a newfound respect for the Latin art of the empanada, a way of life for millions of people in the Americas.

THE EMPANADA FILLING

Fillings for traditional savory Latin American empanadas are somewhat predictable: meats, fish, or vegetables flavored with regional variations of the ubiquitous cooking sauce (*sofrito*) and enriched with olives, raisins, and hard-boiled eggs. Though Latins do make seafood, chicken, and vegetable empanadas, in the case of Chilean, Argentinean, and Cuban empanadas, I decided to concentrate on the classic beef fillings that are everyone's favorites.

Be aware that when it comes to classic beef empanadas, people do not often deviate from their regional preferences. Using black olives instead of green, adding a little too much cumin or not enough, or including a spoonful of tomato sauce when it is not called for—all of these will be noticed and criticized. But don't let the empanada border patrol keep you from experimenting with fillings. When I make empanadas at home, as when I make tamales, I fill them with whatever I like or intrigues me—duck pâté or foie gras, Cabrales cheese from Spain mellowed by onion confit, roast or braised duck, a spicy venison hash from Yucatán. After all, one of the major reasons people in Latin America make empanadas is to provide new uses for leftovers.

When improvising, however, do remember that the choice of dough is crucial to the enjoyment of the filling. When a filling is rich in olive oil, I pair it with my spongy olive oil dough for two-crust Galician empanadas, which I like to roll as thin as possible. Whatever your choice, always let the filling cool before assembling the empanada.

A NOTE ABOUT FROZEN EMPANADA DOUGH

There is no doubt that empanadas made from scratch are delicious, but there are times when you crave empanadas yet don't feel like making them. In Latin America, you can always buy empanadas in shops, but for many of us here in the United States the only alternative is to start with ready-made frozen empanada disks (*discos* or *tapas de empanada*). When I began working on this book, I could find only frozen disks for Cuban fried empanadas in my local Hispanic markets, but now there are more than a dozen brands, some with a flaky dough meant for oven baking. Even Goya has frozen disks for both fried and flaky oven empanadas (*tapas hojaldradas*). One new development is that most of these come separated by wax paper or plastic wrap, which makes for easier handling and keeping.

I have found a few brands that suit me. La Salteña brand makes a flaky dough that works very well for some types of Argentinean oven empanadas.

Both La Fé and Goya sell empanada disks for frying that will produce the crunchy, blistered empanada casing that is traditional in the Hispanic Caribbean. Try a few brands to compare their merits.

WORKING AHEAD

For the vast majority of empanadas, both baked and fried, both the dough and filling can be made ahead. Most fillings can be made at least 1 day ahead and refrigerated. The doughs can be wrapped in plastic wrap and refrigerated for up to 1 day. They can also be frozen, tightly wrapped, up to 3 months. If you like, roll out the dough and cut into disks according to the recipe instructions, then stack between sheets of parchment paper, wrap tightly, and freeze for up to 3 months. Let thaw at room temperature until the dough circles are flexible but still slightly cool to the touch. If the dough is allowed to get warm, it will absorb the juices from the filling and become soggy or greasy.

If using store-bought frozen empanada disks, defrost overnight in the refrigerator or for 2 to 3 hours at room temperature.

Assembled unbaked empanadas can be refrigerated for 2 days or frozen for up to 3 months. Freeze until firm on a baking sheet lined with wax paper, then transfer to freezer containers or bags. Defrost at room temperature until the dough feels flexible but is still cool to the touch, and bake according to the recipe instructions.

GALICIAN EMPANADAS

EMPANADAS GALLEGAS

Of all the regions of Spain, Galicia had the greatest influence in the Americas in the postindependence period at the end of the nineteenth century. So sizable was the Galician migration to the New World that Latin Americans slipped into the habit of referring to any Spanish immigrants as *gallegos*. The *gallegos* came by the thousands. Most were fleeing poverty, escaping lives spent tilling the soil of farms too small to support them or the dangers of the cold, turbulent Galician sea. For the young and eager, the verdant hills of Galicia were confining. Across the Atlantic lay warmer lands filled with promise.

One way immigrant Galicians kept their ties to their homeland alive was through food. No matter how creolized the household might become, two classic Galician dishes were often prepared on Sundays or special occasions. One was a kale-and-white-bean broth called *caldo gallego*. The other was the Galician empanada, a large, double-crusted pie made with a breadlike dough and any of a delicious array of fillings that is served cut into slices or squares. No *criolla* wife of a *gallego* would fail to try to master the art of the empanada to please her husband.

While the tradition of the Galician empanada remained intact throughout the Americas, it also lent itself to many reinterpretations. Chileans and Argentineans kept the breadlike dough but folded it over the filling to form a half-moon, like an Italian calzone. Under the influence of *criollo* cooking, the empanadas became plumper in the Hispanic Caribbean, with all kinds of fillings generously flavored with tomato *sofritos*.

In the tapas bars of Galicia, the large empanadas are made early in the morning and left out on the bar or counter to seduce customers. These thin-crusted empanadas are normally served at room temperature, although an occasional customer might want them hot. I have seen similar empanadas, sold whole or in square portions, in bakeries and pastry shops in Cuba, Puerto Rico, and Venezuela, and in Union City, New Jersey, and Miami. (Bakery empanadas are usually rectangular because it is easier to cut them that way.) They are made with a thick, soft, spongy breadlike crust, and the usual fillings are chicken, chorizo, tuna, or salt cod cooked in a tomato sauce. Because they are always sold lukewarm or cold, I take them home to reheat in the oven.

Although the basic principles are always the same, no two recipes for Galician empanada dough are alike. Some are simple, made without eggs and with olive oil. Others are richer, calling for eggs, milk, broth, and lard, butter, or sometimes beef fat, or a combination. The way in which ingredients are blended into the flour also varies. Some cooks like to dissolve the yeast, salt, and sugar in the liquid together with the eggs and the fat; this mixture is set near the stove for a few minutes to warm before it is added to the flour. Others prefer to proof the yeast in just a little of the liquid and follow the more conventional method of mixing the other dry ingredients with the flour and then adding the liquids.

Then there are differences in the thickness of the crust. Some prefer their empanada crust thin and delicate; others like it thick, like focaccia. Regardless of the technique, cooks strive for dough that will bake into flavorful crusts that are soft and light when the empanada cools. *Crisp* is not an adjective traditionally associated with *empanadas gallegas*, and Galician cooks cover empanadas with a cloth the minute they come out of the oven, to soften the crust. But I confess to being a New World iconoclast. I like my empanadas hot and crisp. If they have gotten cold or soggy, you will always catch me putting them back in the oven.

Shaping and Baking Galician Empanadas

To bake their empanadas, Galicians use pans called *empanadeiras*, which are like pizza pans with raised rims about 1 inch high; they can be round or rectangular. You can use whatever is on hand—a round pizza pan or a rectangular baking sheet—the shape doesn't really matter. In fact, you can always create a free-form empanada and bake it on a baking sheet. But be sure to use a heavy-gauge pan—avoid flimsy ones. My favorite pans for empanadas are paella pans. They are shallow with a low rim, just like an *empanadeira*. I use a 13-inch copper paella pan for my deluxe party-size empanada, large enough for 15 to 20 people. For smaller dinner parties of 6 to 8 people, I use a paella pan 11 inches in diameter.

No matter what pan you use, coat it with about 1 teaspoon olive oil, butter, or lard, or sprinkle it lightly with semolina flour, as if making pizza. For round empanadas, divide the dough in half. Working from the center outward, roll each half into a circle as directed in the recipe. Place one round on the prepared pan and spread the filling over it evenly, leaving a ½- to 1-inch border. Place the second round over the filling and press the edges together with your thumb and forefinger. If the edges are thick and heavy, trim away a little of the dough. If you are making a free-form empanada on a baking sheet, gently roll the edges upward, then seal by pinching between your thumb and forefin-ger to make a scalloped edge. In either case, make several 1-inch slashes on the top with a sharp knife or prick with a fork to let steam escape. If you want a shiny glaze, brush the top very lightly with beaten egg yolk or about a tablespoon of olive oil. I always bake empanadas on the center rack of the oven.

Galician Empanada with Tuna or Salt Cod Hash

Empanada Gallega de Bacalao o Atún

My favorite filling for Galician empanadas is a tuna or salt cod hash flavored with plenty of fire-roasted red bell peppers. Because the olive oil dough is light yet breadlike and has the unassertive flavor of pizza crust, it is an ideal envelope for the substantial filling. When you eat it, it will remind you of a soft focaccia sandwich.

Cook's Notes: If you prefer a richer crust flavored with butter or lard, use a dough from one of the recipes on pages 418–24.

The filling, in both the tuna and salt cod versions, is a versatile savory hash (*salpicón*) in its own right. Eat it hot with rice like a *picadillo*, or fold it inside tortillas and romaine lettuce leaves (perhaps along with a few avocado slices) for a great soft taco filling.

Working Ahead ▶ The filling can be made a day ahead and refrigerated. When making this empanada for company, bake it early in the afternoon. Let cool completely and wrap it in foil or plastic. Just before serving, unwrap it and let warm and crisp for about 5 minutes in a preheated 400°F oven.

What to Drink: A Conde de Albarei (an Alvariño from the Rías Baixas), a mellow and fruity red such as Seis de Azul y Garanza (a blend of Cabernet and Merlot from Navarra), or a peppery red from Ribera del Duero like Señorío de Valdehermoso

SERVES 6 TO 8

For the Dough

- 2 teaspoons active dry yeast
- 1 cup warm (about 110°F) water
- 3½ cups (about 1 pound 2 ounces) bread flour, plus more if needed
- 2½ teaspoons salt
- 2½ teaspoons sugar
- ¼ cup dry white wine or dry sherry
- ¼ cup plus 1 tablespoon extra-virgin olive oil

For the Filling

- Three 5-ounce cans solid white tuna packed in water or *Bonito del norte* (Spanish tuna packed in oil), or 1½ pounds salt cod (*bacalao*), soaked and drained according to the instructions on page 613
- ¼ cup extra-virgin olive oil, plus 1 tablespoon to grease pan
- 5 large garlic cloves, finely chopped
- 2 large yellow onions (about 1 pound 8 ounces), finely chopped (about 4 cups)
- 2 medium red bell peppers (about 1 pound), roasted (see page 67), peeled, cored, seeded, and cut into ¼-inch-wide strips
- 1 teaspoon ground cumin
- 1 teaspoon dried oregano
- ½ teaspoon *pimentón* (Spanish smoked paprika, hot or sweet)
- 1 teaspoon salt
- 1 teaspoon freshly ground black pepper
- ¼ teaspoon ground cayenne or crushed red pepper flakes
- ⅓ cup dry white wine
- ⅓ cup dark raisins
- ⅓ cup pitted green olives (about 18), halved crosswise
- 1 tablespoon finely chopped parsley

- 1 tablespoon extra-virgin olive oil, or 1 large egg yolk, lightly beaten with 1 tablespoon water for egg wash (optional)

Making the Dough ▶ Dissolve the yeast in ¼ cup warm water in a small bowl. Let sit for 10 minutes.

Combine the flour, salt, and sugar in a large bowl. Make a well in the center of the flour and pour in the dissolved yeast. Start incorporating the flour with your fingertips. Then gradually add the remaining ¾ cup water, the wine, and ¼ cup olive oil and knead the dough in the bowl until it comes together in a ball. If it feels sticky, work in a little more flour.

Transfer the dough to a work surface (this dough does not need a floured surface, but have a little flour at hand in case it gets sticky) and knead vigorously for 10 minutes, or until it feels smooth. Shape into a ball. Rub the remaining 1 tablespoon oil all over the dough and place in a large bowl. Cover with plastic wrap and let rise in a warm (about 80°F), draft-free place for 1 hour, or until it is doubled in size.

Making the Filling ▶ Drain and finely flake the tuna or finely shred the soaked drained cod.

Heat the oil in a 12-inch skillet over medium heat. Add the garlic and cook until golden, about 40 seconds. Add the onions and cook until soft, about 7 minutes. Add the bell pepper strips, cumin, oregano, *pimentón*, salt, black pepper, and cayenne and cook, stirring, for 3 minutes, to let the flavors meld. Stir in the wine, raisins, and olives. Add the fish and cook for 5 minutes, stirring occasionally. The mixture should be slightly juicy but not liquid. Remove from the heat and let cool. Add the parsley; adjust seasoning with salt and pepper. You should have about 4 heaping cups filling.

Preheat the oven to 400°F.

Assembling the Empanada ▶ Punch down the risen dough, transfer to a lightly floured work surface, and knead for 2 to 3 minutes to relax it. Divide the dough in half. Shape each half into a ball. Flatten and stretch each ball with your hands and a rolling pin into an even circle 13 inches in diameter and ¼ inch thick.

Lightly grease a 12-inch pizza pan or paella pan or a large baking sheet with olive oil. Place a round of dough in or on the pan. If using a pizza or paella pan, trim the edges with a sharp paring knife, leaving about ½ inch between the dough and the edge of the pan. Place the filling in the center of the dough and spread evenly with the back of a spoon or a spatula to ½ inch from the edges of the dough. Top with the second round of dough and press the edges together. If necessary, trim the edges slightly—you don't want a thick doughy rim. Gently roll the edges upward, then seal by pinching the dough between your thumb and forefinger to make a scalloped edge. Make 1-inch slashes in the top of the empanada with a sharp knife or prick with a fork to let steam escape. If you want a shiny glaze, brush the top very lightly with the olive oil or the beaten egg yolk (but I find that the top browns very nicely by itself).

Baking the Empanada ▶ Bake for 35 to 45 minutes, rotating the pan after 20 minutes. After 35 minutes, check to make sure the bottom is not burning: Lift an edge of the empanada from the pan, using a long spatula, to check the color of the bottom. Tap the bottom quickly with your fingertips; it should sound hollow, like a loaf of bread. Return to the oven for another few minutes if necessary.

To serve, slide onto a large cutting board, or lift with two broad spatulas to prevent it from splitting. Cut into wedges and serve hot.

Galician Empanada with Chorizo

Empanada Gallega de Chorizo

The filling for this empanada is equally at home in Galicia, Spain, or anywhere in Latin America. Sautéing flavorful paprika-laced Spanish chorizo in extra-virgin olive oil releases its deep orange color and imparts a special smokiness to the classic *sofrito*. I also give some extra texture to the filling by cutting the onion and peppers into strips instead of chopping them.

Working Ahead ▶ The filling can be made a day ahead and refrigerated. When making this empanada for company, bake it early in the afternoon. Let cool completely and wrap in foil or plastic wrap. Just before serving, unwrap and let it warm and crisp for about 5 minutes in a preheated 400°F oven.

What to Drink: A lively tempranillo like Sierra Cantabria Colección Privada or a more substantial San Vicente tempranillo, made from a variety called *tempranillo peludo*, both from Rioja, Spain

SERVES 6 TO 8

For the Dough

  1 recipe dough for Galician Empanada with Tuna or Salt Cod Hash (page 412)

For the Filling

- 2 teaspoons extra-virgin olive oil
- 1 pound Spanish chorizos (two 10-inch or six 3½-inch chorizos), cut into ¼-inch slices
- 4 large garlic cloves, finely chopped
- 1 large yellow onion (about 12 ounces), cut lengthwise in half and thinly sliced
- 2 large red bell peppers (about 9 ounces each), cored, seeded, deveined, and cut into ¼-inch-wide strips
  Pinch of dried oregano
- ½ teaspoon salt, or to taste
- ½ teaspoon crushed red pepper flakes or ground cayenne
- 1 bay leaf
- ¼ cup dry white wine

- 1 tablespoon extra-virgin olive oil or 1 large egg yolk, lightly beaten with 1 tablespoon water, for egg wash (optional)

▶ Make the dough and set aside to rise as directed on page 413.

Making the Filling ▶ Heat the oil in a heavy 12-inch skillet over high heat. Add the chorizo and cook, stirring, for 2 minutes, or until it begins to render its fat. Lower the heat to medium, stir in the garlic, and cook until golden, about 40 seconds. Add the onion and bell peppers and cook, stirring occasionally, for 7 minutes, or until the onion is translucent. Add the oregano, salt, red pepper, and bay leaf, and cook, stirring, for 1 minute. Pour in the wine and cook for 1 more minute. Remove from the heat and let cool before proceeding. Remove the bay leaf and adjust the seasoning with salt and pepper. You will have about 4 cups of filling.

Preheat the oven to 400°F.

Assembling the Empanada ▶ Punch down the risen dough, transfer to a lightly floured work surface, and knead for 5 minutes to relax it. Cut the dough in half. Shape each half into a ball. Flatten and stretch each with your hands and a rolling pin into an even circle 13 inches in diameter and ¼ inch thick.

Lightly grease a 12-inch pizza pan or paella pan, or a large baking sheet with olive oil. Place a round of dough on the pan. If using a pizza or paella pan, trim the edges with a sharp paring knife, leaving about ½ inch between the dough and the edge of the pan. Place the filling in the center of the round and spread evenly with the back of a spoon or a spatula to ½ inch from the edges of the dough. Top with the second round of dough and press the edges together. If necessary, trim the edges slightly—you don't want a thick doughy rim. Gently roll the edges upward, then seal by pinching the dough between your thumb and forefinger to make a scalloped edge. Make 1-inch slashes in the top crust with a sharp knife or prick with a fork, to let steam escape. Brush the top very lightly with the olive oil or the beaten egg yolk, if desired.

Baking the Empanada ▶ Place on the center rack of the oven. Bake for 35 to 45 minutes, rotating the pan after 20 minutes. After 30 minutes, lift an edge of the empanada, using a long spatula, to check that the bottom is not overbrowning. Tap the bottom quickly with your fingertips; it should sound hollow, like a loaf of bread. Return to the oven for another few minutes if necessary.

To serve, slide onto a large cutting board, or lift with two broad spatulas to prevent it from splitting. Cut into wedges and serve hot.

SAVORY DOUBLE-CRUST PIES

Venezuelan Chicken Pot Pie

Pastel de Polvorosa Venezolano

Latin Americans have many wonderful recipes for savory double-crust pies. While they are not empanadas per se, they call for a dough to enclose a filling like an empanada and are often eaten in the same way.

At an elegant Venezuelan dinner, you are likely to be served a creamy soup made from the Andean tuber *arracacha*, followed by the chicken pie called *pastel de polvorosa*. The recipe harks back to the colonial period, and the name of the dish translates literally as "the pie with the crust that crumbles into dust." The crust is so tender and flaky that it practically melts in your mouth at first bite.

It took me some time to come up with a crust recipe that would live up to *pastel de polvorosa*'s reputation as the flakiest of all Latin American savory pies. But I finally got it, and now it has become one of my favorite crusts for pot pies with delicate fillings and appetizer-size oven empanadas.

Cook's Note: Look for one of the shortenings without trans fats, such as Crisco All-Vegetable shortening.

What to Drink: Viña Aquitania Chardonnay Sol de Sol from Traiguén, Chile

MAKES 1 PIE, SERVES 4 TO 6

For the Dough

- 3½ cups (about 1 pound 2 ounces) all-purpose flour
- 1¼ teaspoons salt
- ⅓ cup plus 1 tablespoon confectioners' sugar
- 1½ cups butter or vegetable shortening
- 1 large egg yolk, beaten with 1 tablespoon cold water

For the Chicken

- 3 teaspoons salt
- 6 garlic cloves, mashed to a paste with mortar and pestle
- One 3½-pound chicken, cut up into 8 serving pieces (see page 659), or 3½ pounds chicken thighs
- 1 large green bell pepper (about 8 ounces), halved and seeded
- 1 medium yellow onion (about 8 ounces), halved
- 1 leek, trimmed, cleaned, and split in half, 1–2 inches of green part included (about 5 ounces)
- 4 cilantro sprigs
- 1 teaspoon black peppercorns
- 3 quarts water

For the Cooking Sauce (*Ahogado*)

- ¼ cup extra-virgin olive oil
- 6 garlic cloves, finely chopped
- 1 medium yellow onion (8 ounces), finely chopped (1 cup)
- 1 leek, trimmed, cleaned, and finely chopped, 1 inch of green part included (⅓ cup)
- 1 medium red bell pepper (about 8 ounces), seeded and finely chopped (1 cup)
- 12 Caribbean sweet peppers (*ajíes dulces*) or 1 cubanelle pepper, finely chopped (¾ cup)
- 6 scallions, trimmed and finely chopped, 1 inch of green part included (⅓ cup)

8   ripe medium plum tomatoes (about 1½ pounds)
    cored, peeled, seeded, and finely chopped (3
    cups) or one 16-ounce can plum tomatoes,
    drained and coarsely chopped

4   tablespoons (2 ounces) grated brown loaf sugar
    (preferably *papelón* or *panela*), Muscovado sugar,
    or dark brown sugar

2   teaspoons sweet *pimentón* (Spanish smoked
    paprika)

1   teaspoon ground cayenne pepper

½   teaspoon freshly ground black pepper

2   tablespoons drained capers, finely chopped

¼   cup port or Moscatel wine

3   tablespoons cider vinegar

3   tablespoons Worcestershire sauce

¼   cup sweet gherkins, finely chopped

1   tablespoon prepared yellow mustard

1   tablespoon salt, or to taste

1   large egg, beaten with a pinch of salt, for egg
    wash

Making the Dough ▶ In a large bowl, mix together the flour, salt, and sugar. Work in the butter or shortening with your fingertips or a pastry blender until the mixture resembles cornmeal. Make a well in the center, add the egg mixture, and stir just until a rough dough forms; don't overwork.

Turn the dough out onto a lightly floured work surface and knead lightly to combine. Roll the dough into a cylinder, then cut in half and shape into 2 disks. Wrap in plastic wrap and refrigerate for at least 1 hour or up to 24 hours to rest and firm up.

Cooking the Chicken ▶ Place 1 teaspoon of the salt and the mashed garlic in a small bowl and mix well

with a spoon. Rub the chicken with this mixture and place the pieces in an 8-quart nonreactive pot; let rest for 1 hour. Add the green bell pepper, onion, leek, cilantro, peppercorns, water, and the remaining 2 teaspoons salt. Bring to a boil, skim any impurities that rise to the top of the broth, lower the heat, and simmer, covered, for 30 to 35 minutes. Transfer the chicken pieces to a bowl and strain, reserving 1 cup of the broth. When the chicken is cool enough to handle, skin and bone it. Cut the meat into ¼-inch pieces and set aside. You should have about 3 cups.

For the Cooking Sauce (*Ahogado*) ▶ Heat the oil in a 12-inch skillet or sauté pan or a 4-quart pot over medium heat. Add the garlic and sauté until light gold, about 40 seconds. Add the onion, leek, red bell pepper, *ajíes dulces*, and scallions and sauté, stirring occasionally, until softened, approximately 7 minutes. Stir in the tomatoes and cook for 8 minutes, until soft. Add the brown sugar, paprika, cayenne pepper, and black pepper. Cook, stirring, until the sugar dissolves. Add the capers, wine, vinegar, Worcestershire sauce, gherkins, mustard, and salt. Stir to mix and add the reserved chicken and broth. Let it heat through for 2 to 3 minutes while stirring. Remove from the heat and let cool to room temperature. Taste for salt and pepper. If not using immediately, transfer to a large bowl and refrigerate overnight, lightly covered with plastic wrap.

Assembling the Pie ▶ Preheat the oven to 350°F. Place one half of the dough on a lightly floured surface and pound lightly with a rolling pin to flatten it. Place between two sheets of wax paper or parchment and roll into a round 11 inches in diameter and ⅛ inch thick.

Transfer the round of dough to a 10-by-2-inch round baking dish or a 10-inch tart pan with a removable bottom. With your fingertips, press it gently onto the bottom and up the sides. Trim any excess dough with a small sharp knife. Pour in the filling and spread evenly with a spatula.

Roll the second half of the dough into an 11-inch round. Place it over the filling. Trim any excess dough and press the edges between your thumb and forefinger to seal. Crimp to make a decorative trim. Lightly brush the top of the pie with the egg wash. Using a sharp knife, cut ventilation slits about ½ inch long in the top crust.

Baking the Pie ▶ Place on the center rack of the oven. Bake for 35 minutes, or until golden. Let cool for 5 to 10 minutes before serving.

Variation: Helena Ibarra's *Polvorosa* Pot Pies
My friend Helena Ibarra, an innovative Venezuelan chef trained in France who finds the bottom crust of the traditional Venezuelan *pastel de polvorosa* soggy, solves this problem by making individual pot pies topped with a very thin crust that melts in your mouth.

You will need six 4½-inch round baking dishes or 10-ounce ramekins.

MAKES SIX 4½-INCH POT PIES

> 1 recipe dough, filling, and egg wash from Venezuelan Chicken Pot Pie (page 416)

▶ Preheat the oven to 350°F. Pound the dough flat on a lightly floured surface and roll out to a circle ⅛ inch thick. Using a 5-inch round cutter, or any suitable template, cut out six 5-inch circles.

Place 1 cup of the filling in each of the six bak-ing dishes or ramekins. Place a disk of dough over each and pinch the edges in a decorative fashion. Press against the edges to seal. Lightly brush the top of each pie with the egg wash. With a sharp knife, cut ventilation slits about ½ inch long in the crusts. Place on a baking sheet and bake for 25 minutes, or until the tops are golden. Let cool for 5 to 10 minutes before serving.

FOLDED BAKED EMPANADAS

Chilean Beef Empanadas
Empanadas Chilenas de Horno

From the yellowing recipe notebook of Luisa Nogués Duvanced, a marvelous Chilean cook and dear friend who died a few years ago, comes this wonderful recipe for Chilean baked empanadas. Next to the recipe's heading is a note saying, "*Muy buena.*" And very good they are—indeed, better than good. Hot from the oven, the crust seems like thin-crusted bread, a delicate envelope for the juicy filling, made by hand-chopping beef and cooking it with lots of yellow onions. (In Chile, most baked empanadas are rectangles. If the empanadas are spicy, they are usually shaped into a triangle to indicate their smoldering contents.)

María Eugenia Baeza, Luisa's daughter, always made these wonderful empanadas when we visited her sprawling horse farm in Hillsborough, New

Jersey. There was nothing better than a hot Chilean empanada washed down with a pisco sour made fresh by her husband, Oscar Baeza. They moved back to Chile, but the memory of their friendship and their empanadas still warms my heart. And when I visit the Baezas in their seafront home near Valparaíso, I want nothing more than to sit on their porch, looking out at the ocean while eating Luisa's delicious empanadas.

Cook's Note: This dough recipe will produce the light, breadlike crust Chileans like for their oven empanadas. If you are using shortening, I recommend Crisco All-Vegetable shortening; for a crispier, flakier crust, use only lard. You can also substitute frozen empanada disks. Look for Goya's puff pastry disks for oven empanadas. They do not bake truly flaky, like puff pastry, but more like a smooth, dry bread crust, which is appropriate for these empanadas.

Working Ahead ▶ See page 410.

What to Drink: Hotel Schuester's Pisco Sour (page 357), a lively Viña Montes Alpha Syrah from the Colchagua Valley, a fruity, medium-bodied La Misión Carménère, or, for a celebration, Montes Purple Angel, a stupendous Carménère from Colchagua Valley in Chile

MAKES 12 MEDIUM EMPANADAS (SERVES 6)

For the Filling

- 8 ounces lean beef, such as boneless beef shin or top sirloin, or ground sirloin or chuck
- 2 tablespoons extra-virgin olive oil
- 6 medium garlic cloves, finely chopped
- 1 large yellow onion (about 12 ounces), finely chopped (about 2 cups)
- 1 teaspoon salt
- 1 teaspoon *pimentón* (Spanish smoked paprika, hot or sweet) or *Merkén* from Chillán (page 74)
- ½ teaspoon ground cayenne
- 1 teaspoon ground cumin
- 12 black olives (Chilean, Peruvian, or Kalamata), pitted and cut into slivers
- ⅓ cup dark raisins
- 3 hard-boiled eggs, quartered

For the Dough (see Cook's Note)

- 4 cups (about 1 pound 5 ounces) all-purpose flour
- 2 teaspoons baking powder
- 1 cup vegetable shortening or freshly rendered lard (page 82), or a mixture
- ⅔ cup cold water
- ⅓ cup whole milk, plus a little extra
- 2 teaspoons salt

Making the Filling ▶ Unless you are using ground meat, cut the meat into ¼-inch-thick slices, then cut into ¼-inch-wide strips and chop into ⅛-inch dice. Set aside.

Heat the olive oil in a 12-inch skillet over medium heat, add the garlic, and sauté until light gold, about 40 seconds. Add the onion, salt, *pimentón*, cayenne, and cumin and cook, stirring occasionally, until the onion is softened, about 7 minutes. Add the beef, cover, and cook for 5 minutes. Transfer the filling to a bowl, cool, and let stand until you are ready to make the empanadas. The filling can be refrigerated, covered, overnight.

Making the Dough ▶ In a large bowl, combine the flour and baking powder. Cut the shortening or lard into small bits. Working quickly, cut the fat into the dry ingredients with your fingertips or a pastry blender until the mixture resembles coarse cornmeal.

In a small bowl, combine the water, milk, and salt. Gradually pour the liquid into the flour mixture, stirring, until the dough can be gathered into a ball. Transfer to a work surface.

Preheat the oven to 350°F.

Assembling the Empanadas ▶ Cut the dough into 12 equal pieces. With a rolling pin, flatten each into a very thin circle 7 inches in diameter and about ⅛ inch thick. Roll out one or two at a time.

Place a scant ¼ cup filling in the center of a dough round. Garnish with a few olive slivers, a few raisins, and a wedge of hard-boiled egg. Moisten the edges of the dough with milk, fold the dough over the filling to make a half-moon, and seal by pressing the edges with your fingertips. Make a shallow fold (about ¼ inch) along the rounded side to create a straight edge. Then fold in the left and right sides to create straight edges, so you have a rectangle of about 5 by 2 inches. Place on a baking sheet and repeat with the remaining dough rounds and filling.

Baking the Empanadas ▶ Place on the center rack of the oven and bake until the crusts are golden and the bottoms sound hollow when tapped, about 25 minutes.

Serving: Serve with Chilean "Goat's Horn" *Pebre* (page 131).

ASSEMBLING CHILEAN EMPANADAS

1. Place a scant ¼ cup filling in the center of a dough round.

2. Moisten the edges of the dough with milk, and then fold the dough over the filling to make a half-moon.

3. Make a shallow fold along the rounded side to create a straight edge.

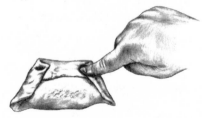

4. Fold in the left and right sides to create straight edges, so you have a rectangle of about 5 by 2 inches.

ARGENTINEAN EMPANADAS

MAKING AUTHENTIC ARGENTINEAN EMPANADAS

RENDERING BEEF SUET

Most Latin American meat markets sell beef fat. This is not the delicate lacy deposits around the kidneys but scraps of fat with some meat attached, which you will need to cut away before using. As a rule of thumb, you need about 5 pounds of scraps of beef fat to obtain 3 cups suet. It should be cut into chunks no more than 2 inches long and wide.

With a sharp knife, cut away all pieces of meat and tissue from the fat. Place it in a large heavy pot, set over very low heat, and cook for 5 hours, covered. It will smell like roast beef cooking, and you don't have to watch it. Remove from the heat and let cool to room temperature. Strain the fat into a plastic container or large glass container. (Argentineans use the cracklings to flavor bread.) Covered tightly and refrigerated, it will keep for 3 months.

THE DECORATIVE BORDER (*REPULGO*)

To make the *repulgo*, place a filled half-moon on the palm of one hand, with the straight edge perpendicular to you (or place it on the table if that's easier), and start at either end; I like to start with the side near me. With the thumb and index finger of your other hand, make a small triangular pleat, between ¼ and ⅓ inch deep, then fold it over toward the right and pinch. Repeat this folding and pinching all the way around the edge of the empanada, making the last pleat like a little folded tab.

THE SECRET IS IN THE ONION

When making empanadas with Renée Carmona, a cook from San Juan in Argentina's northwest, and later with traditional older cooks in Mendoza, the country's foremost wine region near the Andes, I learned that onions are fundamental for Argentinean empanadas. Cooks do not sauté the onions but instead boil them until soft, to keep the filling of the empanada very juicy. This goes against the common practice of browning onions for extra flavor, but it certainly works for traditional Argentinean empanadas like Matilde's Classic Beef Empanadas (page 424).

THE FLOUR

Traditional Argentinean cooks prefer to use an extra-soft low-gluten flour like the Italian-style Blanca Rosa 000 brand for their flaky empanadas. Or they may use an Italian Tipo 00 or a self-rising flour. ◆

MAKING THE DECORATIVE BORDER (*REPULGO*) FOR ARGENTINEAN EMPANADAS

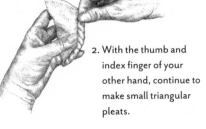

1. Hold an empanada disk in one hand, and start making a triangular pleat at one end.

2. With the thumb and index finger of your other hand, continue to make small triangular pleats.

3. Repeat this folding and pinching all the way around the edge of the empanada.

Big-Bellied Argentinean Beef Empanadas

Empanadas Panzudas de Carne

I like empanadas with flavorful beef fillings and more seasonings than some of the spartan versions I have encountered. After much experimentation, my Argentinean-born assistant Natalia Machado and I came up with *panzudas* (paunchy or big-bellied) empanadas bursting with vibrant flavors. They are a delight when fresh from the oven, plump and golden, begging to be eaten with a dollop of tangy chimichurri. Because we blended the garnishes—hard-boiled eggs, olives, and scallions—with the filling, they are easy to assemble. Before taking a bite, break off one end of the empanada and let the steam escape. Natalia's father, Amílcar, taught her to break open both ends of a hot empanada and blow through one end to cool it a little.

Cook's Notes: The best Argentinean empanadas are made with hand-chopped beef, but you can use ground beef; be sure to buy ground top sirloin or chuck.

If you'd rather not make the dough from scratch, you can use 12 store-bought empanada disks. La Salteña empanada disks come in two styles: a flaky, buttery kind and a drier, less flaky type labeled *criollas para horno*, which are the ones you want here.

Working Ahead ▶ See page 410.

What to Drink: A Susana Balbo Malbec or Tikal Patriota, a blend of Bonarda and Malbec, both from Mendoza, Argentina

For the Dough (see Cook's Notes)

- 6 cups (about 2 pounds) extra-fine flour (preferably Argentinean Blanca Rosa 000) or cake flour
- 2 teaspoons salt
- 2 teaspoons sugar
- 1 cup freshly rendered suet (see box, page 421) or freshly rendered lard (page 82)
- 2 extra-large eggs
- 1¼ cups cold water, or as needed

For the Filling and Glaze

- 1 pound lean beef, such as boneless shin or top sirloin, or ground sirloin or chuck
- ¼ cup extra-virgin olive oil
- 3 large garlic cloves, finely chopped
- 2 large yellow onions (about 10–12 ounces each), finely chopped (about 4 cups)
- 4 scallions, white and 3 inches of green parts, finely chopped
- 1 medium red bell pepper (about 6 ounces), cored, seeded, deveined, and finely chopped (about 1 cup)
- 1 tablespoon salt, or to taste
- 2 teaspoons freshly ground black pepper
- 1 teaspoon Argentinean ground hot red pepper (*ají molido*) or ground cayenne
- 1 teaspoon hot *pimentón* (Spanish smoked paprika)
- 2 teaspoons ground cumin
- 2 teaspoons dried oregano
- 3 hard-boiled eggs, coarsely chopped
- 24 Manzanilla olives, pitted and quartered (about 1 cup)
- 2 large eggs, beaten with 2 tablespoons cold water, for glaze

Making the Dough ▶ Place the flour, salt, and sugar in a large bowl. Make a well in the center, place the suet or lard in the well, and work it into the dry ingredients with your fingertips or a pastry blender.

In a small bowl, whisk together the eggs and water. Add the mixture to the flour a little at a time, mixing to form a dough. If the dough feels too dry to hold together, add a little more water a tablespoon at a time. Transfer the dough to a work surface and knead vigorously for 5 minutes, or until smooth. Divide in half. Roll each half into a 12-inch-long log. Wrap in plastic wrap and refrigerate for at least 1 hour, or preferably up to 24 hours.

Making the Filling ▶ Unless you are using ground meat, cut the meat into ¼-inch-thick slices, then cut into ¼-inch-wide strips and chop into ⅛-inch dice. Set aside.

Heat the oil in a 12-inch skillet over medium heat. Add the garlic and sauté until golden, about 40 seconds. Stir in the onions, scallions, bell pepper, salt, black pepper, hot red pepper, paprika, cumin, and oregano and cook until the onions are soft, about 7 minutes. Add the meat and cook, stirring to break it up, for 4 to 5 minutes, until cooked but still juicy. Transfer to a container about 12 inches square and 2 inches high, smooth the surface of the filling with a spatula, and let cool. Spread the chopped eggs and olives evenly over the meat (so when you scoop out a portion of the filling, it will have equal amounts of eggs and olives). Cover with plastic wrap and refrigerate until chilled.

Preheat the oven to 375°F.

Assembling the Empanadas ▶ Unwrap the dough and cut each log into twelve 1-inch sections. Roll out and fill one at a time, keeping the unused dough covered with a kitchen towel. Knead one piece briefly with the heel of your hand. With a rolling pin, roll out a round ⅛ inch to 1/16 inch thick. Using a large round cookie cutter, or any suitable template, cut the dough into a 5-inch circle. (If using the defrosted frozen empanada disks, trim them into neat 5-inch circles.) Holding the disk in the palm of one hand, place 2 generous tablespoons of filling in the center, then fold the two edges of the disk together, as if you were making a taco. Pinch the middle of the edges together, then seal the empanada using the decorative pleating called *repulgo* (see box, page 421). Place on a baking sheet. Fill and seal the remaining empanadas.

Baking the Empanadas ▶ Brush lightly with the egg wash. Bake for 25 to 30 minutes, until the crusts are golden and the empanadas sound hollow when tapped on the bottom. Let cool slightly, and serve warm.

Serving: Serve as an appetizer or as a light lunch, with a bowl of Argentinean Chimichurri (page 132) and a green salad or Chilean Tomato Salad (page 549).

Matilde's Classic Beef Empanadas

Empanadas de Carne de Matilde

One fall afternoon in 2005, I sat on the porch of a handsome Mendoza country home with Nicolás Catena, one of Argentina's most respected winemakers, and his wife, Elena. He poured me a glass of his Catena Alta Cabernet Sauvignon, and Elena handed me an empanada still steaming from the wood-burning oven. It was stuffed with a savory beef filling laden with onions, and it dripped hot juice all over my hands when I took my first bite. This, everyone agreed, is the sign of a good empanada.

Elena explained that the recipe came from their old head cook, Matilde Herrera, who had lived in Mendoza all her life. Somewhat smaller than the empanadas I had eaten in Buenos Aires and other provincial capitals, these had a light flaky crust and moist interior that made me want to learn the recipe.

The following day I watched the cooks prepare a batch. They made a smooth dough with a mixture of extra-fine flour, self-rising flour, and cornstarch bound with beef suet, oil, and butter. They rolled out the dough with a rolling pin, brushed it with butter, and dusted it with cornstarch, then folded it like puff pastry and passed it through a pasta machine. (I have opted for simply rolling the dough.) Then they started the juicy filling by boiling lots of onions until soft before adding them to the beef.

Cook's Notes: If you prefer, you can use 30 La Salteña frozen dough disks for flaky empanadas (*hojaldradas*) instead of making the dough.

I noticed that the cooks did not use any raisins in the filling, which I assumed was a regional quirk, but Elena Catena explained that they had simply forgotten to add them. I liked my empanada just fine without raisins and left them out of this recipe. If you want to add them, however, use 3 to 4 raisins per empanada.

Working Ahead ▶ See page 410.

What to Drink: Catena Alta Cabernet Sauvignon from Mendoza, Argentina

MAKES 30 EMPANADAS

For the Dough (see Cook's Notes)
- 2 cups water
- 2 tablespoons salt
- 5½ cups extra-fine flour, preferably Argentinean Blanca Rosa 000, or cake flour
- 1 cup self-rising cake flour
- 1 cup cornstarch, plus about ½ cup for dusting
- 4 teaspoons powdered milk
- 1 teaspoon baking powder
- ¼ cup freshly rendered suet (see box, page 421) or lard (page 82), melted
- 4 tablespoons butter

For the Filling, Assembly, and Glaze
- 8 ounces boneless beef shin or top sirloin chuck, or ground beef
- 1 tablespoon plus 1 teaspoon salt
- 2 medium white onions (about 1 pound), peeled and finely chopped (about 2 cups)
- 6 tablespoons butter
- 2 tablespoons corn oil

1½ teaspoons freshly rendered suet (see box, page 421) or lard (page 82)

1½ teaspoons dried oregano

1½ teaspoons sugar

1½ teaspoons all-purpose flour

1 teaspoon freshly ground black pepper

½–¾ teaspoon Argentinean ground hot red pepper (*ají molido*) or crushed red pepper flakes

30 green or black olives, drained and pitted

4 hard-boiled eggs, cut into 8 wedges each

2 large eggs, beaten with ½ teaspoon water, for glaze

Making the Dough ▶ Place the water and salt in a small bowl and stir to dissolve the salt. Set aside.

Combine both flours, 1 cup of the cornstarch, the powdered milk, and baking powder in a large bowl. Add the suet and butter and cut them into the flour mixture until it resembles fine meal. Stir in half of the salted water, then mix, adding more salted water little by little, until a rough dough forms.

Transfer to a lightly floured surface and knead until smooth. Wrap in plastic wrap and refrigerate for 1 hour.

Making the Filling ▶ Unless you are using ground meat, cut the beef into slices, then cut into long strips and mince. Or grind with a meat grinder to a coarse consistency. Set aside.

In a medium pot, bring 2 quarts water and 1 tablespoon salt to a boil over medium heat. Reduce the heat to low, add the onions, and cook, stirring occasionally, until soft, about 15 minutes. Drain.

Return the onions to the pot, add the meat, 2 tablespoons of the butter, oil, suet, oregano,

sugar, flour, both peppers, and the remaining 1 teaspoon salt, and cook over medium heat, stirring often, until the meat is cooked through but has not browned; it must remain juicy. Taste for salt and pepper. Transfer to a bowl and let cool.

Cover the filling with plastic wrap and refrigerate for at least 2 hours, or as long as overnight.

Assembling the Empanadas ▶ Position a rack in the upper third of the oven and preheat the oven to 400°F.

Melt the remaining 4 tablespoons butter; set aside.

Check the filling for seasoning, and add salt if needed. Place the olives and eggs on a plate and set aside.

Divide the dough into 10 equal pieces. Roll one piece on a clean, lightly floured surface into a 7-by-11-inch rectangle. Brush with butter and dust with cornstarch. Fold the dough lengthwise in half and roll out to a ¹⁄₁₆-inch thickness. Using a 4¼-inch round cutter, or any suitable template, cut out 3 disks; discard the scraps. Lightly dust disks with cornstarch, stack, cover with plastic, and set aside. Repeat with remaining dough, butter, and cornstarch.

Lay one dough disk on a work surface and place 1 tablespoon filling in the center. Top with 1 olive and 1 egg wedge. Fold the disk over into a half-moon shape, pinch the middle of the edges together, and seal the empanada using the decorative pleat called *repulgo* (see box, page 421). Place on a baking sheet. Repeat the process with the remaining disks, filling, olives, and eggs, placing the empanadas on two baking sheets at least ½ inch apart. Brush with the egg wash.

Baking the Empanadas ▶ Bake for 25 to 30 minutes, switching the position of the two baking sheets after about 12 minutes, until the empanadas are golden and hollow-sounding when tapped on the bottom. Serve hot.

Serving: In Argentina, these empanadas are not served with any sauce, but I like to bring them to the table with a bowl of Argentinean Chimichurri (page 132).

FRIED EMPANADAS

Cuban Fried Beef Empanadas

Empanadillas Cubanas de Picadillo

In Cuba, fried empanadas are known as *empanadillas*. They can be found in any Cuban-American *cafetería*—golden brown half-moons with blistered skins and crimped edges shining under the light bulbs that keep them warm. At the *cafetería* or bakery or at home, they are eaten with a cup of espresso or *café con leche*, or perhaps a refreshing milk shake (*batido*) or Coca-Cola. For a large party, they are made smaller, daintier, and more delicate, meant to be devoured in just a couple of bites. You could fill the *empanadillas* with chicken, fish, salt cod or tuna hash, cream cheese with guava paste, or whatever tickles your fancy, but for Cubans this *picadillo* (beef hash), is the favorite filling.

Cook's Notes: Goya and La Fé introduced frozen disks of dough for Cuban *empanadillas* a few decades ago, and few cooks now make them from scratch. I give a recipe for the dough, but you can substitute 24 frozen empanada disks for frying, preferably La Salteña, La Fé, or Goya.

Eggs and baking powder are common in many Cuban recipes for the dough, but they make it dense and spongy and I omit them. I like my empanada dough to be thin and delicate.

Working Ahead ▶ See page 410.

What to Drink: A light Latin beer like Hatuey, Corona, or Presidente, or a Cuban rum cocktail like mojito (page 355) or daiquiri (page 354)

MAKES 24 EMPANADILLAS

For the Dough (see Cook's Notes)
- 4 cups (about 1 pound 4 ounces) all-purpose flour
- 2 tablespoons sugar
- 2 teaspoons salt
- 6 tablespoons (about 3 ounces) freshly rendered lard (page 82)
- 1 cup cold water
- 4 tablespoons dry white wine

For the *Picadillo* Filling
- 2 tablespoons extra-virgin olive oil
- 6 large garlic cloves, finely chopped
- 1 large yellow onion (about 11 ounces), finely chopped (about 1¼ cups)
- 1 medium red bell pepper (about 6 ounces), cored, seeded, deveined, and finely chopped (about 1 cup)

1 small green bell pepper (about 4 ounces), cored, seeded, deveined, and finely chopped (about ½ cup)

5 Caribbean sweet peppers (*ajíes dulces*) or 1 cubanelle pepper, seeded and finely chopped

8 ounces ground beef (chuck or top round)

2 bay leaves

1 teaspoon dried oregano

3 medium plum tomatoes (about 9 ounces), peeled, seeded, and finely chopped (about 1 cup)

⅓ cup dark raisins

12 pimiento-stuffed olives, thinly sliced

2½ tablespoons finely chopped parsley

½ cup dry white wine

2 tablespoons tomato puree

1 teaspoon salt

4 cups corn oil for deep-frying

Making the Dough ▶ Combine the flour, sugar, and salt in a large bowl. Add the lard and cut it into the flour with your fingertips or with a pastry blender until it has the consistency of coarse cornmeal. Make a well in the center, add the water and wine, and mix with your hands until a dough forms; do not overwork.

Transfer the dough to a work surface and divide it in half. Shape each half into a 12-inch-long log. Wrap in plastic wrap and refrigerate for at least 1 hour, or up to 24 hours.

Making the Filling ▶ Heat the oil in a medium skillet over medium heat. Add the garlic and cook until golden, about 40 seconds. Add the onion and cook, stirring occasionally, until soft, about 7 minutes. Add all the peppers and cook for 2 minutes. Stir in

the beef and cook, stirring occasionally, until lightly browned, 4 to 5 minutes.

Add the bay leaves and oregano, stir, and cook for 1 minute. Add the tomatoes and cook until softened, about 5 minutes. Stir in the raisins, olives, and parsley. Add the wine, tomato puree, and salt, stir, reduce the heat to low, and cook, covered, for 20 minutes, or until the meat has absorbed most of the liquid. Taste for salt. Remove the bay leaves, transfer to a bowl, and let cool to room temperature. You should have about 4 cups. The filling can be refrigerated, covered, for up to 3 days.

Assembling the *Empanadillas* ▶ Cut each log of dough into twelve 1-inch pieces. Using a rolling pin, roll out one piece of dough about ⅛ inch thick. Using a large round cutter, or using a plate as a guide, cut the dough into a 4½-inch circle. If using the defrosted disks, roll out ⅛ inch thick and trim into neat 4¼-inch circles. Place 2 tablespoons

CUBAN EMPANADILLAS

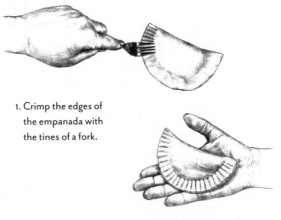

1. Crimp the edges of the empanada with the tines of a fork.

2. A Cuban empanada ready for frying.

filling in the center of each circle, fold the dough over the filling to make a half-moon, and pinch the edges to seal. Crimp the edges with the tines of a fork.

Frying the *Empanadillas* ▶ Heat the oil to 375°F in a large heavy pot or a deep skillet. Working in batches, add the *empanadillas*, no more than 2 or 3 at a time, to the hot oil, and cook until they are golden and blistered; do not overbrown. Drain on paper towels and keep warm in the oven.

Serving: Serve hot with "Finger Sauce" (page 116), Antillean Three-Pepper Sauce (page 117), or Chilean "Goat's Horn" *Pebre* (page 131).

Variations: Instead of the beef hash, use one of the following: the filling for *Cuitlacoche* and Jalapeño Quesadillas (page 246); the tuna or salt cod filling for Galician Empanadas (page 411); Cuban-Style Shrimp in *Enchilado* Sauce (page 624, coarsely chop the shrimp); Chicken Fricassee Cuban Style (page 662, bone the chicken and cut into small pieces). You could also bake the *empanadas*: Use La Salteña's frozen flaky empanada disks or the dough for Big-Bellied Argentinean Beef Empanadas (page 422) or Matilde's Classic Beef Empanadas (page 424); and bake at 375°F for 25 to 30 minutes.

Argentinean-Style Blue Cheese and Caramelized Onion Fried Empanadas

Empanadas Argentinas de Queso Azul y Cebolla Caramelizada Fritas

This filling is an Argentinean favorite, a delicious alternative to the predictable meat-filled empanada. I like to pair it with the Cuban dough for fried *empanadillas* because the dough's sweetness and subtle dry wine undertaste are a perfect complement to the salty cheese filling.

Working Ahead ▶ See page 410.

MAKES 24 EMPANADAS

For the Filling

- 2 tablespoons extra-virgin olive oil
- 2 medium yellow onions (about 8 ounces each), thinly slivered lengthwise
- 2 teaspoons sugar
- 2 teaspoons freshly ground black pepper
- 1 pound blue cheese, preferably Cabrales or Roquefort (an Argentinean favorite), crumbled

- 1 recipe dough for Cuban Fried Beef Empanadas (page 426), made with 3 tablespoons sugar, chilled; or 24 frozen empanada disks for frying (La Salteña, La Fé, or Goya)
- 4 cups corn oil for deep-frying

Making the Filling ▶ Heat the oil in a small skillet over medium heat. Add the onion and sauté for 5 minutes, or until golden. Add the sugar and pepper and cook, stirring, until the onions are caramelized, about 5 minutes. Remove from the heat, let cool, and add the crumbled cheese. You should have about 4 cups filling

Assembling the Empanadas ▶ If using the empanada dough, follow the recipe through the stage of cutting each log into twelve 1-inch pieces. Using a rolling pin, roll out one piece of dough about ⅛ inch thick. Using a large round cutter, or using a plate as a guide, cut the dough into 4½-inch circles. If using the defrosted disks, roll out to ⅛ inch thickness and trim into neat 4¼-inch circles. Place 2 tablespoons filling in the center of each circle, fold the dough over to make a half-moon, and pinch the edges to seal. Crimp the edges with the tines of a fork. Assemble all the empanadas and place on a cookie sheet lined with wax paper before frying.

Frying the Empanadas ▶ Heat the oil to 375°F in a large heavy pot or a deep skillet. Working in batches, add the empanadas to the hot oil, no more than 2 or 3 at a time, and cook until they are golden and blistered; do not overbrown. Drain on paper towels.

"Hot Air" Cheese Empanadas from Cuenca

Empanadas de Viento Cuencanas

These light empanadas are a popular street food in Cuenca, Ecuador, where they are sold outside the town's magnificent churches. After Sunday night mass, you can always find women sitting on little stools stirring large cauldrons bubbling with oil over small aluminum coal braziers. On their knees they hold wooden boards, where they roll the dough paper-thin and fill it with cheese or mashed bananas. It's an amazing feat—handling fire and board at the same time while people wait in line. At home, these puffy, blistery empanadas are made on weekends and for family reunions.

The first time people eat these empanadas, they are in for a surprise. Because the empanadas puff up when fried, they look as if they are brimming with filling, but in reality, they are filled with *viento* (air). The cheese melts into the crunchy dough, as the empanadas cook, leaving a pocket of hot air.

Cook's Note: If rolled thin enough, the dough will produce light empanadas that puff like a blowfish and turn around in the hot oil. Be sure to roll out the dough very thin, about ¹⁄₁₆ inch thick.

What to Drink: These empanadas are always accompanied with *tinto*, a cup of black coffee.

MAKES 24 EMPANADAS

For the Dough

4⅔ cups (about 1½ pounds), all-purpose flour, plus
       up to ½ cup more if needed

   4   tablespoons freshly rendered lard (page 82),
       melted and cooled slightly

1½–1¾ cups ice water

   2   teaspoons salt

   ½   teaspoon sugar

   4   tablespoons fresh lime juice

For the Filling

12   ounces fresh Latin American cow's milk cheese,
     crumbled, preferably a soft Ecuadorian cheese
     like Queso Fresco San Francisco from Azuay or
     Santa Cruz Queso Ecuador Crema from Cuenca
     (2¼ cups)

4   cups corn oil for deep-frying
    Sugar for sprinkling

Making the Dough ▶ Place the flour in a bowl and add the lard. Mix with your fingertips or a pastry blender to the consistency of coarse cornmeal.

In a small bowl, mix the water, salt, sugar, and lime juice. Pour into the flour little by little, mixing with your fingertips or a fork. Transfer to a lightly floured work surface and knead until a soft dough comes together. If the dough is too wet and sticks to your fingers, work in a little more flour; if it is too dry, add a few drops of water. Knead the dough vigorously, slapping it against the work surface, until smooth and elastic, about 5 minutes. Shape into a ball, cover with a cloth or plastic wrap, and let rest for 20 minutes.

Making the Empanadas ▶ Lightly flour the work surface. Divide the dough into 3 pieces. Keep the unused pieces covered with a kitchen towel. Roll each piece of dough into a very thin circle, about ¹⁄₁₆ inch thick. Using a large round cutter, or using a plate as a guide, cut the dough into 4½-inch circles.

When ready to fill the empanadas, turn the circles over. (The side against the work surface is always moister, so you will not need any water to seal the empanadas.) Place 1 tablespoon crumbled cheese on each circle. Fold over into a half-moon and make the decorative pleat called *repulgo* (see page 421), or pinch the edges with your fingertips to seal and crimp with the tines of a fork.

Frying the Empanadas ▶ Heat the oil to 375°F over medium heat in a medium pot or large deep skillet. Working in batches, drop the empanadas into the hot oil, no more than 2 or 3 at a time. In about 3 minutes they will float, puff up, and turn over by themselves. When they are golden, another few seconds, remove from the hot oil and drain on paper towels. Sprinkle with sugar and serve hot.

Variations: Ecuadorians also like to fill their *empanadas de viento* with a mixture of cheese and mashed ripe bananas. In a medium bowl, combine 2 ripe bananas, mashed, and 8 ounces fresh cow's-milk cheese (see suggestions above), crumbled, 2 tablespoons *aguardiente*, preferably Zhumir (see Cook's Notes page 457) or grappa, ½ teaspoon anise seeds, ¼ cup sugar, and 2 teaspoons ground cinnamon. Crush the mixture with a fork and fill each empanada with a heaping tablespoon.

SOUTH AMERICAN EMPANADAS WITH CRACKED CORN OR PLANTAIN DOUGH

Wheat flour crusts proclaim the Spanish origin of Latin American empanadas. But over the centuries, cooks here also invented pastry envelopes based on such tropical plants as corn and plantains. Empanadas using cracked corn (*maíz trillado*, page 445) are a favorite in Colombia and Venezuela. They are also popular in Ecuador as *empanadas de morocho*, but the harder strains of highland corn used there create a different texture. Not long ago, women cracked the corn at home in large mortars, soaked it for several hours (sometimes days) to soften it, and then ground it to a paste in a plate corn mill (see illustration on page 33)—a painstaking chore that was rewarded by enough *masa* for the hundreds of empanadas served at feasts and holidays.

Nowadays, most cooks resort to dehydrated precooked corn flour, which is also used to make *arepas*. But there is a world of difference between using precooked flour and making a fresh dough from home-ground corn. The fresh dough does not dry out and crack, as often happens with the precooked corn flour, and it has a substantially better flavor. You will need to plan ahead, because the corn should be soaked overnight, or for at least 6 hours, to soften, before being ground into a smooth paste with a corn mill. The result, a pliable dough that is easy to handle and tastes like corn, is well worth the effort.

The plate corn mill is indispensable for anyone who seriously wants to work with corn doughs.

(This includes Mexican doughs made from nixtamalized corn. The hand-ground version remains far better than anything made with the many commercial products from commercially preground dried nixtamal.) Thousands of South American cooks still insist on buying inexpensive hand mills and grinding soaked cracked corn themselves for *arepa* and empanada doughs. The principal brands are Corona and Universal, both sold in many Latin American stores; ask for a *molino de granos de maíz*. The mill is a heavy tinned cast-iron device that clamps onto the edge of a counter or table; a hand crank forces the mass of soaked corn from a hopper between two adjustable ridged metal plates. It produces a better consistency than a food processor or any other electrical appliance.

If you instead opt for the convenience of dough made from instant dehydrated corn flour, there is one paramount thing to remember when working with the dough: keep it moist. This is easier if you work fast. Always cover it with a damp towel while you work to prevent it from drying. The filled empanadas should also be covered with a damp cloth while waiting to be fried.

Here are recipes for both doughs, which can be used interchangeably. Note the use of brown loaf sugar, which adds both sweetness and complexity. You can subtly vary the ratio of sugar to corn depending on your individual preference and the particular flavors of the fillings. I suggest experimenting with anything between 1 and 3 tablespoons sugar per pound of dough. I prefer the higher amount, especially when working with salty fillings. I enjoy the sweet-and-salt interplay.

Fresh Corn Dough for Colombian and Venezuelan Empanadas

MAKES ABOUT 2 POUNDS, ENOUGH FOR 14 TO 16 MEDIUM-SIZED EMPANADAS

14 ounces (about 1¾ cups) dried yellow or white cracked corn (available at Hispanic markets)

2 teaspoons salt, or to taste

2–6 tablespoons finely grated brown loaf sugar (preferably *panela* or *papelón*), Muscovado sugar, or packed dark brown sugar

2 teaspoons achiote-infused corn oil (page 89) or to taste, optional (only if using white corn)

▶ Place the corn in a colander and rinse under cold running water. Place in a large bowl and cover with 2 quarts water. Let soak for at least 6 hours, or overnight.

Drain the corn and place in a 6-quart pot. Add 10 cups cold water and bring to a boil over high heat. Lower the heat to medium and simmer, covered, until the corn is al dente, 40–45 minutes. Do not overcook; if the corn is allowed to cook until soft it will absorb too much water. (Overlong cooking and excess water will throw the yield off; also, the dough will take longer to fry and absorb more fat.) Drain at once in a colander. Place in a bowl and rinse with cold water until the water runs clear. Drain in a colander again.

Grind the corn to a coarse dough with a plate mill (see page 431). You will need to help the grain through the hopper by pushing with a heavy wooden or stone pestle, or a stout wooden spoon.

Place the ground corn in a large bowl and add the salt, sugar, and oil, if using. Mix well with your hands. Cover the dough with a damp cloth or wrap in plastic wrap. The dough is best used as soon as it is made, for the corn tends to dry out and to ferment quickly.

Instant Corn Dough for Colombian and Venezuelan Empanadas

MAKES ABOUT 2 POUNDS, ENOUGH FOR 14 TO 16 MEDIUM-SIZED EMPANADAS

2 cups warm water

2–6 tablespoons finely grated brown loaf sugar (preferably *papelón*), Muscovado sugar, or packed dark brown sugar

2 teaspoons salt

2 cups (about 10 ounces) white or yellow precooked corn flour for *arepas*, preferably P.A.N. brand

2 teaspoons achiote-infused corn oil (page 89) or to taste, optional (only if using white corn)

▶ Place the warm water in a large bowl, add the sugar and salt, and stir to dissolve. Gradually stir in the corn flour, mixing well. Add the achiote oil, if using, and knead until smooth, about 5 minutes. Cover with a damp kitchen towel or wrap in plastic wrap. The dough must be used as soon as it is made, or it will dry out too much to work with.

Valle del Cauca White Corn Empanadas with Potatoes and Peanuts

Empanadas de Pipián Vallecaucana

The cooks of Valle del Cauca, Colombia, make crunchy empanadas out of dried white corn, a local staple. They are filled with a chopped potato and peanut mixture—the same filling used for the area's legendary tamales—bound together with a tasty cooking sauce. The combination is lovely. Like all empanadas made with corn dough, these are best eaten very hot, fresh out of the cooking oil.

Cook's Note: Make the dough just before you are ready to shape and cook the empanadas. Keep the dough and the finished empanadas covered with damp kitchen towels while you work.

Working Ahead ▶ If making the fresh corn dough, soak the corn the night before. You can prepare the filling a few hours ahead and refrigerate it, well covered with plastic wrap.

What to Drink: Tropical fruit juice or a cup of hot *tinto* (Colombian coffee)

MAKES 28 TO 32 EMPANADAS

For the Filling

- 1 large russet potato (about 8 ounces), peeled and cut into ¼-inch dice
- ¼ cup achiote-infused corn oil (page 89)
- 3 large garlic cloves, finely chopped
- 1 medium white onion (about 8 ounces), finely chopped (about 1 cup)
- 4 scallions, white and 3 to 4 inches green parts, finely chopped (about ½ cup)
- 1 small red bell pepper (about 4 ounces), cored, seeded, deveined, and finely chopped (about ½ cup)
- 3 medium plum tomatoes (about 9 ounces), peeled, seeded, and finely chopped (about 1 cup)
- ½ teaspoon ground cumin
- 1 teaspoon salt, or to taste
- ½ cup roasted unsalted peanuts, coarsely chopped
- 2 hard-boiled eggs, coarsely chopped (optional)

For the Dough

Double recipe (about 4 pounds) Fresh Corn Dough or Instant Corn Dough for Colombian and Venezuelan Empanadas (page 432), made with only 1 tablespoon sugar per pound

4 cups corn oil, for deep-frying

Making the Filling ▶ Place the diced potato in a medium saucepan, add 1 quart water, and bring to a boil over high heat. Reduce the heat slightly and cook until barely tender, about 15 minutes. Drain and set aside.

Heat the oil in a medium skillet over medium heat until it ripples. Add the garlic and sauté for 40 seconds. Add the onion and scallions and sauté until soft, about 5 minutes. Add the bell pepper, tomatoes, cumin, and salt, stir to combine, and cook until the vegetables are soft, about 5 minutes. Add the peanuts, hard-boiled eggs, if using, and reserved potatoes; stir to combine, and cook just to blend the flavors. Taste for salt. Remove from the heat and let cool completely. You should have about 3½ cups filling.

Assembling the Empanadas ▶ Place the dough in a bowl. Divide into 28 to 32 equal-sized pieces (about 2 ounces each) and shape each one into a ball. Keep the unused dough covered with a damp cloth as you work. You will need two pieces of sturdy plastic; I suggest a zip-top bag cut into two pieces. Place one ball of dough between the sheets of plastic. With a rolling pin, gently roll out the dough into a circle a little more than 5 inches across. Peel away the top sheet of plastic. Use a large cookie cutter or any suitable template to cut a 5-inch round. Save any scraps of dough and reroll them later. Place 1½ tablespoons filling in the center. Lift up an edge of the plastic wrap and fold the dough over the filling. Press the edges together with your fingertips, making a border of about ⅓ to ½ inch and gently indenting the edges with your fingers at ½-inch intervals. (The dough is forgiving and can easily be patched if it breaks.) Remove the empanada from the plastic and place on a baking sheet or work surface. Cover with a damp kitchen towel and repeat with the remaining dough and filling.

Frying the Empanadas ▶ Heat the corn oil to 375°F in a deep heavy pot or deep skillet. Working in batches of no more than 3 or 4 at a time, drop the empanadas into the hot oil and fry, turning once, until golden on both sides, about 2 minutes altogether. Lift out with a slotted spoon and drain on paper towels.

Serving: Serve with Colombian Hot Peanut Sauce (page 126).

Venezuelan Corn Empanadas with Shredded Beef, Black Beans, and Fresh Cheese

Empanaditas de Pabellón

I had been touring a cacao plantation in the Paria peninsula a few hours after a substantial breakfast composed of shark *empanaditas* (*empanadas de cazón*), fruit juices, and hot chocolate, when I heard my friend, Venezuelan cacao expert Lilian Reyes, musing aloud about the traditional Venezuelan *pabellón*, a one-plate meal of shredded beef with black beans and rice topped with grated cheese. "Ayyy! How delicious it would be to eat a little bit of all that in a crunchy corn empanada," she said out of the blue, as she examined a sick cacao tree.

I immediately started writing the recipe in my head, imagining the flavors of black beans and cheese mingling and contrasting with the sweet corn dough. When I got home from Venezuela, I put Lilian's craving to the test. I began by cooking flank steak with all the ingredients that would be used for beef to be served as part of the classic *pabellón*. I took those other two indispensable partners, cooked black beans and grated Latin American hard cheese. (The one I ended up with was a very flavorful Salvadorian cheese with a lively goaty edge that is surprising in a cow's milk cheese.) I put dabs of all three inside a corn empanada crust. It was as good as Lilian had imagined. Of course, I couldn't fit in the rice, but you can dream about it, aloud, of course.

Cook's Notes: Make the dough just before you are ready to shape and cook the empanadas. Keep the dough and the finished empanadas covered with damp kitchen towels while you work.

You can cook the beans as directed for Mexican-Style Boiled Black Beans (page 271), or for a more truly Venezuelan flavor follow the recipe for Caracan Black Bean Cream Soup (page 528) through the final cooking stage before pureeing.

Working Ahead ▶ If making the fresh corn dough, soak the corn the night before. You can prepare the filling ahead and refrigerate it, well covered with plastic wrap.

What to Drink: Venezuelan Polar beer, or a Colombian beer such as Aguila or Club Colombia

MAKES 28 TO 32 EMPANADAS

For the Meat

- 1 pound flank steak, in one piece
- 1 small yellow onion (about 5 ounces), peeled
- 1 small red bell pepper (about 4 ounces), halved and seeded
- 1 teaspoon black peppercorns
- 1 teaspoon cumin seeds
- 1 teaspoon dried oregano
- 2 teaspoons wine vinegar
- 1 teaspoon salt

For the Cooking Sauce

- ¼ cup achiote-infused corn oil (page 89)
- ½ teaspoon salt, or to taste
- 6 garlic cloves, finely chopped

- 1 medium yellow onion (6–7 ounces), finely chopped (about 1 cup)
- 1 medium red bell pepper (about 8 ounces), cored, seeded, deveined, and finely chopped (about 1 cup)
- 1 teaspoon freshly ground black pepper
- ¼ teaspoon dried oregano
- ¼ teaspoon ground cumin
- 2 teaspoons Worcestershire sauce

For the Dough

Double recipe (4 pounds) Fresh Corn Dough or Instant Corn Dough for Colombian or Venezuelan Empanadas (page 432)

For the Beans

- 1 cup cooked black beans (see Cook's Notes), drained, or 1 cup canned Cuban-style beans, preferably Goya brand, drained

For the Cheese

- 1 cup (3½ ounces) grated hard cow's-milk cheese, preferably Salvadorian *queso duro* La Ricura, or ricotta salata

- 4 cups corn oil, for deep-frying

Precooking the Meat ▶ Place the meat in a heavy 6-quart pot, cover with 2 quarts water, and add the onion, bell pepper, peppercorns, cumin seeds, oregano, vinegar, and salt. Bring to a boil over high heat. Lower the heat to medium and cook, covered, for 1 hour, or until the meat is tender. Lift the meat onto a plate. Strain the broth through a fine-mesh sieve and reserve; discard the solids. Place the meat on a work surface, pound with a mallet to loosen the fibers, and pull the meat into very thin shreds.

Sautéing the Meat ▶ Heat the oil in a medium sauté pan or skillet over high heat. When the oil begins to smoke, add the meat and fry until golden brown, stirring frequently, about 6 minutes or until very crisp. Season with the salt. Add the garlic and sauté until golden, about 40 seconds. Add the onion, bell pepper, black pepper, oregano, and cumin and cook, stirring, for 7 minutes. Stir in 1 cup of the reserved broth (save the rest for another purpose) and add the Worcestershire sauce. Reduce the heat to very low and cook for 10 minutes longer, covered. Let cool to room temperature; it can be refrigerated, covered, for up to 2 days.

Assembling the Empanadas ▶ Divide the dough into 28 to 32 equal-sized pieces (about 2 ounces each) and shape each one into a ball. Keep the unused dough covered with a damp cloth as you work. You will need two pieces of sturdy plastic; I suggest a zip-top bag cut into two pieces. Place one ball of dough between the sheets of plastic. With a rolling pin, gently roll out the dough into a circle a little more than 5 inches across. Peel away the top sheet of plastic. Use a large cookie cutter or any suitable template to cut a 5-inch round. Save any scraps of dough and reroll them later. Place 2 teaspoons of the beans in the center of each round. Top with 2 teaspoons of the meat mixture and 2 teaspoons grated cheese. Lift up an edge of the plastic and fold the dough over the filling to make a half-moon. Press the edges together with your fingertips, making a border of about ⅓ to ½ inch and gently indenting the edges with your fingers at ½-inch intervals. (The dough can easily be patched

if it breaks.) Remove the empanada from the plastic and place on a baking sheet or work surface. Cover with a damp kitchen towel and repeat with the remaining dough and filling.

Frying the Empanadas ▶ Heat the corn oil to 375°F in a deep heavy pot or deep skillet. Working in batches, add the empanadas, no more than 3 or 4 at a time, and fry, turning once, until golden on both sides, about 2 minutes. Lift out to drain on paper towels.

Serving: You need only a few slices of ripe avocado, or Venezuelan Chunky Avocado Sauce (page 137), Venezuelan Ripened Cream (page 148) or crème fraiche, or Spicy Milk Sauce from Ciudad Bolívar (page 122) to turn the *empanaditas* into a complete meal.

Plantain Empanadas with Shrimp in *Merkén Adobo*

Empanadas de Verde con Camarones al Adobo de Merkén

Green plantains are used for essentially everything in coastal Ecuador, including empanadas. Plantain dough empanadas are ubiquitous, invariably filled with Ecuadorian fresh cheese that melts deliciously inside a hot fried empanada. During my apprenticeship cooking at the Ballroom in New York under Felipe Rojas-Lombardi, I happily experimented with plantain doughs that I would use to make empanadas from anything I found on hand that day, from duck to caponata. Later I devised this empanada with a filling of shrimp cooked in an *adobo* laced with *merkén*, the sexy Chilean mix of smoked paprika and other spices. Still, I have never lost my fondness for the simple cheese version, which I present here as a variation.

What to Drink: Catena Alta Chardonnay from Mendoza, Argentina

MAKES 18 TO 24 EMPANADAS

For the Dough

4½ large green plantains (about 4 pounds), peeled according to the instructions on page 181

2 teaspoons salt

1 garlic clove, mashed to a paste with a mortar and pestle or finely chopped and mashed

1 teaspoon lime juice

For the Filling

12 large garlic cloves

1 tablespoon store-bought *merkén*, homemade *Merkén* from Chillán (page 74), or 2 teaspoons hot *pimentón* (Spanish smoked paprika)

1 teaspoon salt, or to taste

6 scallions, white and 3–4 inches of green parts, finely chopped (½ cup)

1 small yellow onion (about 5 ounces), finely chopped (¾ cup)

¼ heaping tablespoon finely chopped cilantro

¼ cup plus 1 tablespoon extra-virgin olive oil

2 tablespoons red wine vinegar

1 pound medium-sized shrimp (16–20 per pound), peeled, deveined, and cut into ½-inch pieces

4 cups corn oil or light olive oil for deep-frying

Making the Dough ▶ Cut 3 of the green plantains into 3 pieces each. Place in a 6- to 8-quart pot, cover with water, and add 1 teaspoon of the salt. Bring to a rolling boil over high heat and cook until the plantains are fork-tender, about 20 minutes. Drain.

Place the plantains in a large bowl and mash with a fork. Peel the remaining whole and half plantain and grate them finely on a box grater. Add to the cooked plantain mash with the garlic, lime juice, and remaining 1 teaspoon salt, and pass the mixture through a food mill into a large mixing bowl. Work the mixture together with your hands into a dough and knead for 5 minutes, until all ingredients are thoroughly integrated. Gather the dough into a ball and wrap in plastic wrap. (This dough is more pliable while still warm).

Making the Filling ▶ Using a large mortar and pestle or a small food processor, mash the garlic and *merkén* to a paste. Add 1 teaspoon salt, the scallions, onion, cilantro, ¼ cup olive oil, and vinegar and stir to blend. You will have about 1½ cups *adobo*.

Place the shrimp in a bowl. Add the *adobo* and toss to coat. Let sit for 20 minutes.

Heat the remaining 1 tablespoon olive oil over medium heat in a 12-inch skillet. Add the shrimp and *adobo* and sauté, stirring, for 3 minutes. Taste for salt and add more if needed. Set aside to cool to room temperature. Drain any excess cooking juices. You should have about 2 cups filling and ½ cup juice. The filling can be covered and refrigerated for up to 24 hours. (Reserve the juice, which can be used to give a seafood kick to sauces; it is fantastic blended into *Mirasol* Mayonnaise, page 136.)

Shaping the Empanadas ▶ Divide the plantain dough into 18 equal-sized pieces (about 2 ounces each) and shape each one into a ball. Keep the unused dough covered with a damp cloth as you work. You will need two pieces of sturdy plastic; I suggest a zip-top bag cut into two pieces. Place one ball of dough between the sheets of plastic. With a rolling pin, gently roll out the dough into a circle a little more than 4½ inches across. Peel away the top sheet of plastic. Use a large cookie cutter or any suitable template to cut a 4½-inch round; save any scraps of dough and reroll them later. Place 1 heaping tablespoon of filling slightly off-center on each round. Lift up an edge of the plastic and fold the dough over the filling to make a half-moon. Press the edges together with your fingertips, making a border of about ⅓ to ½ inch and gently indenting the edges with your fingers at ½-inch intervals. (The dough can easily be patched if it breaks.) Remove the empanada from the plastic and place on a baking sheet or work surface. Cover with a damp kitchen towel and repeat with the remaining dough and filling.

Frying the Empanadas ▶ Heat the oil to 375°F in a deep heavy pot or deep skillet. Working in batches, add the empanadas, no more than 2 or 3 at a time, and fry for 3 minutes on each side or until golden. Lift out and place on a paper towel to drain, then place in a warm oven until ready to serve. Serve hot.

Serving: Serve with a bowl of spicy Chilean "Goat's Horn" *Pebre* (page 131), Colombian Hot Peanut Sauce (page 126), or *Mirasol* Mayonnaise (page 136) enriched with some of the shrimp *adobo* juices.

Variation: Ecuadorian Green Plantain Empanadas with Cheese (*Empanadas de Verde con Queso*) Follow the preceding plantain dough recipe, and use about 10 ounces fresh cow's milk cheese, preferably a soft Ecuadorian cheese, grated or crumbled (about 2 cups) as filling. Fill each empanada with approximately 2 heaping tablespoons cheese; assemble and fry as directed above.

CHAPTER 11

THE TAMAL FAMILY

Nestled in a protective bundle of leaves, a tamal emerges from its steam bath fragrant with earthy aromas that awaken the appetite. You unwrap the warm, moist leaves with a feeling of anticipation, uncovering a succulent *masa* (dough) made of grated corn or another starchy vegetable. A first bite does not reveal all that lies within, for the *masa* may enclose a chunk of gooey, salty cheese or a juicy filling of braised meat seasoned with briny olives, bits of chopped hard-boiled eggs, and sweet raisins.

The idea of cooking food inside leaves predates the making of pottery. Native Americans discovered that if they wrapped *masa* in corn husks or other leaves and placed the packets on the dying embers of a fire, the food inside would cook without burning. Later generations placed the leafy bundles in pots on wooden trivets or stacks of corncobs and steamed them over boiling water—the cooking method used to this day.

What began as a Native American staple evolved into the quintessential *criollo* Latin American food. From Juárez to Patagonia, every Latin culture has many versions of tamales, gift-wrapped packages enclosing centuries of culinary wisdom.

The first record of tamales comes from the Spaniards who encountered them in Cuba on Columbus's first voyage, in 1492. Though yuca was the main staple of the Taíno (Arawak), the Indians also harvested corn twice a year. They ground the kernels on large stone or wooden graters and cooked the resulting dough wrapped in green corn husks over embers. The Spaniards were unimpressed.

In Mexico, however, they were amazed to find the Aztecs cooking an enormous variety of tamales. The sixteenth-century Spanish chronicler Bernardino de Sahagún describes tamales that were white and almost round, "*como pella*" (like balls), and others that were red and sun-dried. He writes that the Aztecs filled tamales with beans or chiles for everyday eating, but in the kitchens of the warrior and merchant classes, cooks filled them with elaborate mixtures of meat, fish, turkey, maguey worms, tufts of corn silk, amaranth seeds, and/or wild cherries, and decorated the tops with whimsical patterns. So prized were tamales that they were considered food for the gods. The *Codex Borbónico*, a lavishly illustrated sixteenth-century Aztec manuscript, shows women taking baskets of them to temples as offerings.

The word *tamal* comes from Nahuatl, the language of the Aztecs, who used it to mean any corn dough cooked in corn husks. Other tribes, of course, spoke different languages, and local names for tamales have survived throughout Mexico, but to the Spaniards they were all tamales. Spanish cooks embraced the concept and the word and brought tamales to areas of the New World where they were previously unknown, which is how we find tamales made with local staples such as yuca in coastal Ecuador and rice in Andean Colombia and Amazonian Peru.

A BEAUTIFUL FEAST FOOD

Ancient Aztec women spent two or three days making tamales for wedding feasts, and it still takes that long to make them for a crowd. Because they are labor-intensive, tamales were traditionally reserved for birthdays, weddings, Christmas, and other holidays or celebrations, when there would be many willing hands available. For me, tamales conjure up the summer carnival in my hometown, the aroma of damp earth from the boiled corn husks and the garlicky fragrance of the spicy crab fricassee called *enchilado* mixed with the musky scent of sweat and beer as people listened to music and danced. I remember clouds of smoke rising from huge cauldrons and people opening the steaming golden packages and eating their tamales with rice and red kidney beans (*congrí oriental*) and fried green plantains (*tostones*).

In Venezuela, large tamales called *hallacas* are Christmas foods that involve an elaborate, time-consuming choreography, with half a dozen garnishes neatly arranged on the work table. Dried white corn, dyed with achiote-infused lard or oil to make it a beautiful orange-gold color, is used for the dough. In Mexico, achiote-colored tamales are a specialty of Mérida, in the Yucatán, for the Days of the Dead. Called *muk-bil pollos* (popularly spelled *mucbipollos*) they are like huge corn pies wrapped in plantain leaves, with a moist chicken filling. Yucatecan women assemble their tamales at home and take them to their local bakeries or to a *pib* master, who buries them in a fire-heated underground pit to cook in the steam that emanates from the earth itself, a technique that goes back to Maya times.

The *mucbipollo* belongs to a special tamal family, the *tamalón*, or big tamal. In some regions of Latin America, especially Mexico, you'll find tamales so huge they can feed an army. The *zacahuiles* of Hidalgo and the Huasteca region in northern Veracruz can measure 6 feet long and require a wheelbarrow to transport them to the wood oven. These big tamales not only are full meals but come conveniently fitted with their own serving dishes, an aromatic wrapping of plantain leaves.

The *zacahuil* of the Huasteca and Hidalgo has nothing to do with the *sacahuil* of Papantla, Vera-cruz, which is closer to a cornmeal porridge. There cooks dissolve nixtamalized (lime-treated) corn *masa* in water or broth and put it in an earthenware pot with a whole leg of pork. The *sacahuil* cooks overnight at low heat in a wood-burning oven and is served for breakfast or midday in restaurants and markets in the Papantla area.

TAMAL TIME

Tamales can be eaten as a snack, as a side dish, or as a meal. In the Colombian highlands, tamales and *hallacas* are often enjoyed in the afternoon with hot chocolate. In Mexico, eating tamales is a way of life and they are enjoyed at all hours of the day, but particularly for the late afternoon *merienda* with hot chocolate.

Some years ago, I was given free access to Raquel Torres's Churrería del Recuerdo in Xalapa, Mexico. From her cooks, I learned to make delicate pink and green sweet tamales and drinks (*horchatas*) of many flavors, to beat chocolate with a wooden mill (*molinillo*), and to assemble three types of sandwiches (*tortas*) at once while flipping tortillas on a griddle for the *merienda*. I managed to steal a moment to spy on the moves of Josefa, the woman in charge of the *tamales rancheros* and the chocolate. What I remember most is Josefa's strong hands as she strained a huge pot of liquidy *masa* and then stirred it with fresh lard for a long time until it set and looked shiny. Straining and cooking the tamal *masa* seemed an awesome chore, but having been often disappointed with tamales simply made with ordinary *masa* and lard, I soon realized the wisdom of this time-consuming technique. It renders silky and succulent tamales every time.

This chapter will introduce you to the various forms tamales take, organized by the type of *masa*, or dough. It begins with creamy tamales from Cuba, Ecuador, and Chile made with fresh corn. Then it moves on to the gutsier Mexican tamales made from lime-treated dried corn *masa* or commercially prepared nixtamalized corn flour, both with a mys-terious aroma of rain falling on hot pavement. Next are the silky tamales of the Colombian Andes, made from a *masa* of strained corn, and the substantial Peruvian tamales made with *mote pelado*, the starchy Andean hominy. Finally comes a sumptuous Puerto Rican *pastel* made from an earthy blend of green bananas, plantains, and the tuber *malanga*, a won-derful example of a tamal made with a vegetable dough.

A SELECTED TAMAL GLOSSARY

FRESH CORN TAMALES

Ayaca: Also spelled *hallaca* or *hayaca*, this term is used in Santiago, on the southern coast of eastern Cuba.

Pamonha: Sweetened and enriched with coconut milk, this Brazilian tamal is eaten with relish on the feast of Saint Anthony of Padua in June.

Humita: Also spelled *huminta*, this Qechua Indian word is used in the Andean regions of Peru, Ecuador, Chile, and northwestern Argentina for a fresh corn tamal known since pre-Columbian times. In Argentina, when it is made without a wrapping, it is called *humita al plato*.

Uchepo: This marvelous tamal from Michoacán State in Mexico comes from the steamer still slightly soft and not set, quivering with milky juiciness. It may be either sweet or savory.

Yoltamal: This Nicaraguan name derives from the Nahuatl word for fresh corn, *tlaolin*.

NIXTAMALIZED CORN TAMALES

These tamales are made from dried corn boiled with mineral lime to make removing the hulls easy (the pro-cess is called nixtamalization; see page 444). The hulled corn is then ground to a dough (*masa*) according to vari-ous recipes.

Corunda: This thick, triangular tamal wrapped in the narrow leaves of the corn plant is from the Mexican state of Michocán; its name derives from the native Tarascan word *kurunda*.

Mucbipollo: Stuffed with red *adobo*-flavored chicken and wrapped in plantain leaves, this huge tamal is served on the Days of the Dead in the Yucatán. As it is baked in an underground oven (*pib*), the golden brown dough becomes crusty and aromatic, and there is a gentle syn-ergy between the dough and the plantain wrapper.

Nacatamal: This Nicaraguan national dish is so laden with good things—rice, pork, bacon, chickpeas, pota-toes, olives, raisins, and prunes—that you can serve it as a complete meal. The name is Nahuatl, a word for meat, *nacatl*. Technically speaking, the *nacatamal* belongs to the refined family of the strained tamal.

CRACKED CORN TAMALES

Bollo Limpio: This loaf-like corn dough and cheese tamal comes from Colombia's Caribbean coast; *bollo* is Spanish for small bread and *limpio* means clean, because there's no filling.

Hallaca: A Christmas tradition in Venezuela, *hallacas* are made from a dough of cracked white corn that's subtly sweetened with brown loaf sugar (*papelón*), with a filling of seasoned pork and chicken, capers, olives, and raisins. Each *hallaca* is fastidiously tied like a roast with several precisely cut layers of plantain leaves. A final layer, *la faja*, keeps it watertight during boiling.

VEGETABLE TAMALES

Abará: Wrapped in a plantain leaf and steamed, rather than fried like its twin, the fritter *acarajé*, this Brazilian tamal is made from ground black-eyed peas mixed with *dendê*, an oil extracted from an African palm that adds bright orange color and a distinctive smoky flavor.

Bacán: From Baracoa in eastern Cuba, this cylindrical tamal is made from bananas or plantain flavored with a cooking sauce enriched with coconut milk.

Bollo de Yuca: This small tamal from Colombia's Caribbean coast is made with grated raw yuca.

Juanes: This unusual tamal is a must in Iquitos, Peru, on the feast day of San Juan (Saint John) in late June, an occasion for unabashed drinking and eating. Made from locally grown rice and filled mostly with chicken, it is shaped like a huge beggar's purse, meant to resemble the head of Saint John the Baptist, who was decapitated on the orders of King Herod. ◆

THE LAYERS OF THE TAMAL

The Dough or Batter (*Masa*)

What matters most for the Latin cook is the dough (which is sometimes like a thick batter). A perfect balance of corn or other vegetable base, liquid, and fat yields a perfect tamal—a moist, silken, cohesive bundle that melts in your mouth with every bite.

FRESH CORN TAMALES

Known in every Latin country, fresh corn tamales are a seasonal treat enjoyed only at the beginning of the corn season, when the tender kernels are filled with milky juice. To replicate them in a U.S. kitchen requires adjustments, because most Latin American corn is far starchier and mealier than its sweeter North American counterpart. So to prevent my fresh corn tamales from falling apart after steaming, I cook down the grated sweet corn kernels into a dense mass that resembles polenta or add cornmeal to the dough (about 1 cup for every 7 cups grated kernels). It's best to start with the freshest corn possible. Grate it on a box grater—a day ahead if you can, for it will thicken overnight in the refrigerator as the sugars turn to starch, making the finished dough firmer and easier to handle.

I cannot unreservedly recommend frozen North American corn kernels as a substitute for freshly grated corn in tamal fillings, but realize that many cooks will welcome them for saving time and labor. If you are obliged to substitute, a general rule of thumb is that 1 pound frozen corn kernels yields roughly 6 cups thawed. To obtain the equivalent of the 7 cups grated kernels called for in My Fresh Corn Tamales Cuban Style (page 455), thaw about 1 pound 4 ounces frozen kernels.

NIXTAMALIZED CORN TAMALES

One confusing bit of tamal terminology is "fresh *masa*." It is not, as the name suggests, dough made from fresh corn but instead dough freshly made from dried flint corn that has been nixtamalized: nixtamalization is the process of boiling dried corn in a lime solution to remove the hulls from the kernels.

Fresh *masa* makes moist, flavorful tamales. For centuries, women have ground this treated corn into a thick paste on a three-legged *metate*, a platform made of rough volcanic stone, or in a hand-cranked rotary grinder. Traditional cooks usually sift the coarse-ground damp flour to make it finer before kneading it into *masa* for tamales. Nowadays in Latin America, you can find mills in every neighborhood or marketplace that sell their own fresh *masa* or will custom-grind and knead batches of dough for their customers, using their nixtamalized corn and following their specifications for fine or coarse grinding.

In the United States, you can buy fresh *masa* from tortilla factories and some mail-order sources. If you wish to grind your own nixtamalized corn, the only satisfactory grinder I have found is a Corona cast-aluminum plate mill from Colombia. Even so, it will never grind it to the smooth consistency of dough ground in Mexican homes with a *metate* or in an industrial mill.

The alternative for most people in the United States is an instant nixtamalized corn *masa* mix, sold under several labels, the most popular being the Maseca brand and Quaker's Masa Harina. The term *masa harina* is loosely applied to all such products, but it is a trademark of the Quaker Oats Company.

Maseca and *masa harina* both look like fine corn flour. They are made from fresh *masa* that has been dehydrated and ground to a powder. These products are a convenient, quick way to make dough for tamales and tortillas. But tamales made with *masa harina* will be dense and dry unless adequate quantities of liquid and lard are added. Mexicans like to use equal parts of lard and *masa harina*; I find that 8 ounces lard for each pound of *masa harina* works. The amount can be reduced if you use rich chicken or meat broth instead of water. I get acceptable results when I add from 2 to 4 cups of liquid (water or broth), sometimes a bit more, per pound of *masa harina*. But for the Play-Doh-like *masa*, easily smeared over corn husks, that Mexicans like, you need to beat in at least ½ pound lard per pound of instant corn *masa* mix and reduce the liquid.

CRACKED CORN TAMALES

As an alternative to nixtamalization, which imparts a faint mineral taste, cooks in Colombia and Venezuela have traditionally removed the hulls from dried corn kernels by pounding them in a large wooden mortar called a *pilón*. In rural communities, women still perform this painstaking and laborious task, but for the most part, it has been industrialized. In Venezuela, corn is stored in large silos and sent to gigantic hydraulic *pilones* for hulling and cracking. The corn is winnowed, precooked with steam, and pressed into thin flakes that are cooled and ground to the desired texture for *arepas* and tamales or *hallacas*. Cracked corn (sometimes sold as *maíz trillado*) as well as cornmeal of varying fineness can be found in any Hispanic market.

The best tamales are made with cracked white corn boiled and kneaded into a dough at home. The best brands for this purpose are Maíz Trillado Blanco La Venezolana (a Venezuelan brand) or Goya. You will need a Corona plate corn mill to grind the soaked and boiled corn. When time is of the essence, use precooked white corn flour. I recommend the Venezuelan brand P.A.N. The problem with most tamales made from precooked corn flour is dryness. For simple tamales with very little filling, I solve the problem by adding more water or broth than recipes generally call for. The result is quite a runny dough, which is a bit difficult to work with, but the payoff is a softer, more succulent result. Adding steamed and pureed *calabaza* (West Indian pumpkin) to the *masa*, as many traditional cooks do, makes it softer and more flavorful as well.

STRAINED *MASA* TAMALES

This is a very special tamal family that crosses borders. The *masa* becomes soft and silky because it is first dissolved in water or in broth, then strained and cooked down on the stovetop until it has the consistency of a delicate polenta. Then it is folded in corn husks or plantain, banana, or other leaves to be steamed or boiled. In Mexico, tamales made with this method include *vaporcitos* and the *tamal colado* of the Yucatán and *tamal ranchero* of Veracruz. In Central America, the most striking example of this category is the baroque Nicaraguan *nacatamal*. In Colombia, both the *tamal de resplandor* and the *tamal de pipián* from the Valle del Cauca region are made with a *masa añeja*, aged dough, that is dissolved in water, strained, and cooked until it resembles polenta, turning into a silky dough by further cooking wrapped in plantain or banana leaves.

VEGETABLE TAMALES

Starchy vegetables like plantains and bananas and tubers such as yuca and *malanga* are ideal for making tamal doughs. In Puerto Rico, the *pastel*, a beloved Christmas food, is made primarily with a mixture of green bananas, plantains, and *malanga* (which Puerto Ricans call *yautía*). In eastern Cuba, a similar tamal shaped into a cylinder is called *bacán*; it is flavored with a savory cooking sauce calling for coconut milk. The Caribbean *calabaza*, a firm-fleshed winter squash, is also added to *pasteles* and tamal doughs to lighten them.

In towns such as Santa Marta, Valledupar, and Mompox in the Magdalena state of Colombia, cooks make a type of tamal called *bollo de yuca* with grated raw yuca. When the balls emerge from the steamer, they have been transformed into shimmering, translucent art objects. The *bollo* has the glassy, gemlike look of a Japanese rice-flour dessert, exotic and stylized. The texture is glutinous and pleasantly chewy, the flavor dewy sweet yet earthy, like yuca itself.

The Wrappers

At first glance, a tamal is a simple package tied with kitchen string. But when you open it, you realize that the wrapper does more than merely contain the dough; it infuses it with a distinctive flavor. For centuries, leaves such as licorice-scented *hoja santa*, *chaya* (a small tropical bush), and avocado have been used to wrap tamales. In Veracruz, the lush leaves of the San Martín caballero or *planta de los cinco dedos* (five-finger plant, for its five well-defined leaflets) are used for a triangular sourdough tamal called *xoco*.

In Central and South America, the leaves of the *bijao* plant, which resemble those of the plantain, are still used as a wrapper, and in Ecuador and parts of Colombia, cooks prize the broad, flexible green leaves of the *achira*, a relative of our ornamental cannas. Most popular of all are the leaves of banana plants and plantains, introduced to the Americas by the Spanish in 1516, and the husks of the indigenous corn ear. In parts of Michoacán, in Mexico, the long slender leaves of the corn plant are used for wrapping the triangular tamales called *corundas*. The husks, used both fresh and dried, are the more common wrapping.

Styles of tying—with kitchen twine or strips of corn husks—vary too. Mexicans often leave the ends of the husks unfolded and tie them like candy wrappers. Guatemalans make a very small tamal called a *chuchito*, tying the dried husk like a pouch. In the Peruvian Amazon, the same pouch method is used for the gigantic banana-wrapped rice *juanes*. Boiled tamales, such as Puerto Rican *pasteles*, are tied with special knots to keep the water from seeping in and diluting the *masa*. For the same reason, Puerto Rican, Venezuelan, and some Colombian cooks tie pairs of tamales with their seams facing in to make a watertight *atao* (bundle).

FRESH CORN HUSK WRAPPERS

In Latin America, fresh corn tamales are often wrapped in fresh green corn husks. Each one is about 9 inches wide and 10 inches long, large enough to accommodate about a cup of *masa*. In the United States, ears of fresh corn are smaller, so 2 or 3 husks are generally needed to wrap one tamal.

Cut off the husks at the base of the cob, just above the stem; one large ear of corn will yield about six husks. Trim the tips if they have darkened. If the husks are narrow, overlap two or three on their long sides to make one wrapper. If you are preparing the *masa* a day ahead, you can prepare the husks then too. Layer them between damp paper towels so they will not dry out, seal in a plastic bag, and store in the crisper section of the refrigerator.

DRIED CORN HUSK WRAPPERS

Dried corn husks imported from Mexico are available in Hispanic markets, usually in 8-ounce packages. Try several brands, looking for the widest and cleanest husks, with no visible dirt or tiny insects. Once you have prepared your dough, lay the dried husks flat in a wide bowl of warm water and let them soak 5 to 10 minutes, until supple. (This process will also remove any hidden debris.) Pat them dry with paper towels before using.

COLORED DRIED CORN HUSKS

Dyeing dried corn husks with natural edible coloring makes for a festive presentation. Use Brazil wood for red, achiote for orange-gold, and dried hibiscus flowers (*flor de jamaica*, see page 339) for purple. While the husks are soaking, combine 2 ounces of the coloring agent with 1 quart water in a saucepan and bring to a boil. Weight them if necessary to keep them submerged. Lower the heat and simmer 5 minutes. Strain the infusion into a 9-by-13-inch pan and add your just-soaked husks. Let them infuse for about 30 minutes, then transfer them to baking sheets to dry.

PLANTAIN OR BANANA LEAF WRAPPERS

Frozen plantain and banana leaves, usually imported from the Philippines, Costa Rica, or the Dominican Republic, are sold in Latin markets in 1-pound packages, each usually containing 7 to 9 folded pieces about 4½ to 6 feet long and 10 to 12 inches wide (this varies according to brand.) To prepare them, defrost them in the refrigerator overnight or, if you're in a hurry, in warm water for about 20 minutes. Wipe both sides clean with a damp cloth and pat dry with paper towels. Working on a cutting board, use a ruler and knife to measure and cut the leaves into squares or rectangles according to your recipe.

To release the natural oils in the leaves, which will allow their flavor to permeate the dough during cooking, singe the squares by running each side over a gas flame or an electric burner set on high for a few seconds. You will notice that the leaf immediately becomes supple and its outer side shinier. If any leaves are torn, just overlap a couple of them when wrapping the dough. To store the prepared pieces, wrap in stacks of about a dozen in a damp kitchen towel and refrigerate. They will keep for up to 3 weeks; wipe them clean once a week and wrap again in a damp towel. Before using, wipe the leaves clean again.

ALUMINUM FOIL WRAPPERS

When Latin cooks are working with a runny *masa* or don't have husks or leaves on hand, they resort to foil pouches. Simply cut the foil (preferably not heavy-duty) into pieces of the appropriate size.

Wrapping Methods

I can usually tell where a tamal comes from by the way it is wrapped and tied. The chosen method is a crucial signature that distinguishes tamales from different regions and countries. Here I describe four general methods to wrap tamales, which I refer to in the following recipes. In a few cases, I also offer variations and alternative methods unique to the area the tamales are from. Latin cooks are fiercely possessive about their national techniques for wrapping and tying.

THE ONE-CORN-HUSK WRAP

Lay the prepared fresh or dried husk on a work surface or the palm of your hand. Place the *masa*

WRAPPING *CHUMALES* (PAGE 457)

1. Place about ⅓ cup *masa* in the center of the husk.

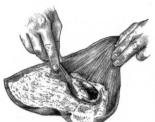

2. Spread the *masa* to within about 3 inches of the tip and 1 inch of the other three sides.

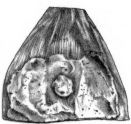

3. Place about 1 tablespoon of the cheese filling in the center of the husk.

4. Fold the left-hand side toward the center.

5. Fold down the tip about 2 inches.

6. Fold the right-hand side toward the center, slightly overlapping the other side.

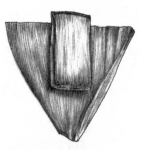

7. To close the packet, place the tamal on a prepared husk with the open end pointing toward the tip and the closed end extending just slightly beyond the wide edge.

8. Fold one long side of the husk toward the center.

9. Fold over the other long side, slightly overlapping.

10. Fold up the tip and tie with kitchen twine or thin strips of corn husk.

in the center and spread it to within about 2 inches of the tip and 1 inch of the other three sides. Bring together the two long sides, overlapping them to enclose the *masa*. Fold the package nearly in half by bringing the tip of the husk over the seam in the center of the tamal. You can also fold the tip of the husk in the opposite direction, over the seamless side of the husk. Tie a strip of husk or a piece of kitchen string over the tip to hold it in place. The wide end of the husk is usually left open. If the recipe calls for both ends to be folded over, tie a strip of husk or string around the other end too. Tamales with one open end are often arranged in the steamer standing on the folded end so they prop each other up.

THE CANOE (TWO-HUSK) WRAP

In countries where the corn husks are smaller, cooks use 2 husks, fresh or dried, to wrap each tamal. If using dried corn husks imported from Mexico or Central America, arrange 2 husks with the wide ends together, overlapping by about 2 inches, to form a canoe shape with tapered ends. (If using fresh husks from corn grown in the United States, you may need 4 husks, as they are narrower. Overlap 2 pairs of husks along one of their long sides, then overlap the pairs at the wider ends to form the canoe shape.)

You can work with either the side or tip of the "canoe" facing you. Spread the *masa* down the center into a rectangle according to the recipe. Bring one long side of one of the husks over the *masa*, and then the other side of the same husk, overlapping them by 1 inch or so. Fold the tip of the husk over the center seam. Repeat with the

THE CANOE (TWO-HUSK) WRAP FOR A CUBAN TAMAL

1. Overlap 2 husks along their wide ends, to form a canoe shape. Spread the *masa* down the center according to the recipe.

2. Bring one long side of one husk over the *masa*.

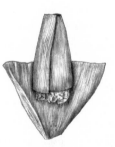

3. Bring the other long side of the same husk over the *masa*, overlapping the sides.

4. Fold the tip of the husk over the center seam.

5. Bring one long side of the second husk over the package.

6. Repeat with the other long side, then fold the bottom tip over the center seam.

7. Tie in a simple bow using kitchen twine.

other husk. Cut a 30- to 36-inch piece of kitchen twine for each tamal and tie the tamal like a gift. This is how Cuban tamales are wrapped and tied.

Another way to wrap tamales using the canoe shape is a Mexican method I call the "candy wrap." Instead of folding the tips over, tie each one closed with a small piece of string 1½ to 2 inches from the tip. Shred the tips of the husks with your fingers or cut them into thin matchstick strips with scissors for a decorative effect.

THE *PASTEL* WRAP

The simplest method to wrap most plantain or banana leaf tamales is to place a prepared leaf square on a work surface with the veins perpendicular to you. Place the required amount of *masa* in the center and spread into a round or oval extending to within about 1 inch of the top and bottom edges. Place the required amount of filling in the center of the *masa*. Fold down the top edge a little more than halfway, pressing lightly, then unfold. Fold up and press the bottom edge in the same way; unfold. The *masa* will now completely enclose the filling.

Now fold down the top half again a little more than halfway toward you. Hold it in place while you bring up the bottom edge to make a seam about ½ inch from the folded side. Holding the seam closed, fold back the open right and left ends of the packet into flaps slightly overlapping under the seamless side.

For another wrapping that produces prettier gift-like packets, start by placing and spreading the *masa* on the leaf as described above. Place the filling in the center of the *masa*. Fold the top edge of the leaf all the way to the bottom edge. Hold the two edges closed and fold them back to within 1 inch of the top. Flatten the seam neatly all the way along the packet. Again fold down the joined edges along the whole length of the packet, this time making a narrow fold about 1 inch wide and smoothing it neatly. Turn the packet over with the seamless side facing up; fold the open ends into slightly overlapping flaps.

THE ALUMINUM FOIL POUCH

When Latin American cooks are working with a runny *masa* or don't have husks or leaves on hand, they resort to foil pouches. Cut the foil (preferably not heavy-duty) into squares or rectangles of the appropriate size, usually 8 by 8 inches. Take a square and fold it into thirds like a business letter with a seam along one long edge. Fold the seamed edge back over itself by 1 inch to crimp the seam shut. Turn the package over and make three narrow ½-inch folds in succession along one of the short ends to seal it shut. The unsealed end is now the mouth of a pouch. To fill, open the unsealed end and spoon or pour in the *masa*. Seal it like the other end with three narrow folds. The finished package should be about 2½ by 5 inches. (To infuse the dough with the aroma of corn husks, some cooks place a small section of husk in the foil pouch before filling.)

THE *PASTEL* WRAP

1. Top a prepared plantain or banana leaf with *masa* and spread to within an inch of the edges. Place the required amount of filling in the center of the *masa*.

2. Fold down the top edge a little more than halfway, pressing lightly, so the dough begins to cover the filling. Unfold.

3. Fold up and press the bottom edge the same way; unfold again.

4. The *masa* will now completely enclose the filling.

5. Fold down the top half again a little more than halfway toward you.

6. Hold the top half in place when you bring up the bottom edge to make a seam about ½ inch from the folded side.

7. Holding the seam closed, fold back the open right and left ends of the packet into flaps slightly overlapping under the seamless side.

8. For tying the *pastel*, fold a piece of string in half and place the string crosswise under the center of the tamal, with the loose ends toward you.

9. Keeping the loose ends together, pull the string around the *pastel* to center the loop on the top of the tamal.

10. Separate the loose ends of the string and pull them in opposite directions toward the short ends of the tamal.

11. As you separate the string, use it to spread the two loops of string wrapped around the tamal toward the short ends. To divide the package into six sections, make the two sections in the middle wider than the other sections. Pull the string down tightly over the short ends.

12. Turn the tamal over and tie the string with a half-knot at the center of the tamal.

13. Turn the tamal over again and make another knot.

14. Finish with a half-bow, which will make it easy to fish the tamal out of the pot.

HOW TO FASHION A TAMAL STEAMER (*TAMALERA*)

In Mexico, simple tamal steamers of many sizes (*tamaleras*) can be bought in any market. Many come with a rack on the bottom to elevate the tamales above the water. A kettle-type vegetable steamer also works well; you can also use the small folding steamer baskets that have short legs and fit into a large pot.

Alternatively, for a batch of 12 tamales, you can use a 12-inch stainless steel colander or pasta insert set over a large, deep pot. Pour about 2 inches of water into the pot and bring to a boil. Line the colander with four 12-inch squares of plantain leaf or 6 to 8 corn husks, to infuse the steam and the tamales with aroma and flavor. Arrange the tamales in the colander according to the recipe instructions and set the colander over the pot, making sure that the bottom is at least 2 inches above the boiling water. Cover the pot with a lid or seal completely with foil. ◆

Tamal steamer

COOKING AND SERVING TAMALES

You might be surprised to know that steaming tamales is not a universal practice in Latin America. With the exception of Mexico, some Central American countries, and highland Ecuador, most Latin Americans boil their tamales in abundant water. They use whatever pot they have on hand, such as a wide cast-aluminum *caldero* or a clay pot big enough to hold a large amount of water and tamales at a rolling boil. But I find that no matter how careful you are wrapping and tying your tamales, some water gets into the tamal, diluting the flavor of the dough. Steaming is my preferred method. The tamales are both more flavorful and easier to remove from the pot. (If you do elect to boil your tamales, the cooking time is the same as for steaming.) To steam tamales, pour water into the steamer pot, place the steamer basket in the pot, and arrange the tamales in the basket. Cover the pot and bring the water to a boil, then lower the heat to a simmer and steam the tamales until they are set. The timing depends on the size and composition of the tamales, but most take about 1 hour. Be sure to check the water level in the pot from time to time and replenish with boiling water as necessary.

I learned a trick I call the "penny alarm" in Xalapa, Veracruz. Place a couple of pennies in the bottom of the pot with the water. They will rattle merrily as the water boils. If the water evaporates, then the end of the rattling sound will alert you. Keep a kettle of simmering water next to your pot to replenish the hot water if necessary.

To test for doneness, remove one tamal from the steamer after 45 minutes. With a knife or scissors, cut the string and open the tamal. If it is made with dried corn, the masa will separate cleanly from the leaf when done. If it is made with fresh corn, it should be set and feel moist to the touch. If the *masa* is runny, rewrap and tie the tamal and return it to the pot for another 5 to 15 minutes. Let the finished tamales rest for 5 minutes before serving.

On formal occasions (or when I have cooked the tamales in foil), I like to open them in the kitchen. Then I garnish them with a crimson-colored onion relish or top them with a contrasting sauce. For more casual gatherings, I pile the still-wrapped tamales on a beautiful tray or in a basket and let my guests open them. If the wrappers look a bit unappetizing from the prolonged steaming, I unwrap the tamales and transfer each one to a cleaned corn husk, sometimes dyed by the method described on page 447, or a cleaned plantain-leaf square. I usually tie one end of the husk or leaf about 2 inches from the tip and snip the tip into decorative shreds.

Cooked tamales can be refrigerated for a couple of days and reheated in the microwave for about 2 minutes wrapped in moist paper towels. Once cooled, they can also be frozen, well wrapped, for up to 3 months. Thaw before reheating in the microwave, or steam, still frozen, for 15 to 20 minutes.

TAMAL LINGO

Each country has certain names for the various components of the tamal. It may seem confusing, but it all adds to their mystery and appeal. No wonder that in popular slang, *tamal* means mess or confusion. When you get into big trouble, you say, "I got myself into a huge *tamal*." And when a woman is unshapely or poorly dressed, we say she "looks like a *tamal*."

Adorno: Garnishes for the tamal filling, such as olives, raisins, hard-boiled eggs, and pimiento strips.

Atao: A bundle formed by tying together two tamales with the seams facing each other; this term is commonly used in the Valle del Cauca region of Colombia.

Cabuya: Strips of corn husks, plantain leaves, or *bejucos* (vines), used to tie tamales.

Cagüinga: A flat spoon used to stir strained *masa*, such as that for the *tamales de resplandor* in the Valle del Cauca region of Colombia.

Condumio: In Ecuador, the filling of the tamal. This is a medieval Spanish word that may stem from the Latin *condomium*, accessories; in seventeenth-century Spanish, *condumio* were the things you ate with bread.

Chala: In some Andean countries, the corn husk used to wrap *humitas* (as in the Argentinean *humitas en chala*).

The word comes from the Quechua *cchala*, meaning green or dry corn husk.

Guiso de Jigote: The stewed meat filling of Valle del Cauca tamales. Like *condumio*, *jigote* (also spelled *gigote*), has a medieval pedigree—it comes from the French *gigot*, leg of lamb, and in Spanish it came to mean meat finely chopped after stewing; in Cuba and other parts of the Americas, *jigote* is a soup made with finely chopped meat.

Masa: Any type of dough used in making tamales.

Naiboa: A Taíno (Arawak) word used in Gibara, Cuba, for the starch of fresh corn used in some tamales.

Panca: In Peru, dried corn husk.

Relleno: Generic Spanish term for tamal filling.

Tamalera: Steamer for tamales.

Tusa de Maíz: In Cuba and Ecuador, corn husk.

Zhungo: A Quechua word meaning the heart (the germ tip) of the large Andean corn kernel. When making hominy (*maíz pelado*) for tamales, the germ tip, as well as the nail-shaped callous dent above, is often removed. Highland Ecuadorians often call the filling of anything—breads and empanadas, as well as tamales—*zhungo*. ◆

FRESH CORN TAMALES

Fresh Corn Tamales from Michoacán

Uchepos

In October, at the end of the rainy season in Lake Pátzcuaro, Mexico, when the cool air ripples the emerald-green fields and the marigolds show their ruffled orange crests, the farmers say, "*El maíz se agüero* (The corn has turned blond)." This is the moment, when the corn is fully grown, with golden tassels of silk, and the kernels are at their most tender, that the corn harvest begins. This is the best time to eat the fresh corn tamales called *uchepos*.

To celebrate this joyful occasion, families prepare corn feasts, called *elotadas*, in the fields. The women grill the tender ears of corn on a *comal* over wood fires or boil corn on the cob. At home, everyone is busy making fresh corn tamales. Bite into one, and you're hooked by the fresh corn taste, pure as dew-cold grass.

My friend Francisca, who lives in Uricho, a lakeside community, grinds the tender corn to a paste on a three-legged *metate* and wraps the dough in large green corn husks. Her *uchepos* emerge from the steamer slightly soft and unset. Around the lake, *uchepos* are light and fresh, smoothed with a bit of oil. They may be savory, served with thick cream, or sweet, dabbed with a trace of cinnamon and sugar and served with tangy tomatillo sauce.

In the restaurants of Pátzcuaro and Morelia,

the capital of Michoacán, *uchepos* are a more elaborate affair: older corn is blended with cream and butter, so the dough is richer and sets into firm rectangles. On the side you'll find garlicky morsels of pork, a bright tomato sauce, and a dollop of thick Mexican *crema*. It's a perfect ensemble of tastes: the spiciness of the pork, the sharp acidity of the tomato sauce, and the sweet corn *uchepos*.

Cook's Notes: In Mexico, one husk is large enough to wrap one *uchepo*. Because the corn in the United States is smaller, you will need to buy a half-dozen extra ears of corn, since you'll have to use 2 or 3 overlapping husks to wrap each tamal.

I do not recommend using frozen corn kernels for *uchepos*.

What to Drink: If serving the tamales as an appetizer or main course, a flavorful light Mexican beer such as Corona; when eating tamales with thick *crema*, hot chocolate (pages 339 and 340) or Don Juan's Hot Hibiscus Punch (page 366)

MAKES 32 TAMALES

For the *Masa*

- 5 large ears corn, such as Silver Queen or Butter and Sugar
- 4 tablespoons (½ stick) butter, at room temperature
- 2 tablespoons Mexican *crema* (page 148) or crème fraîche
- 5 teaspoons sugar
- 2 teaspoons salt, or to taste

For the Wrappers

- 32 fresh, flexible corn husks (from the 5 ears of corn used above, plus husks from 5 or 6 extra ears, as needed)

Making the *Masa* ▶ Husk the corn, reserving the husks. Grate the corn on the finest side of a box grater. Or cut off the kernels, place in a food processor or blender, and process until the corn is almost smooth but still has some texture. Add the remaining ingredients and process to blend, about 1 minute. You should have 3½ to 4 cups *masa*.

Wrapping the Tamales ▶ Spread 1 corn husk open on a work surface and overlap with another 2 to 4 corn husks if they are small. Hold them flat with one hand, spoon 2 tablespoons of the *masa* onto the center, and spread it into a 3-inch-long rectangle. Fold the sides of the husks over the *masa*, slightly overlapping. Then fold back the tips of the husks to close the *uchepos*. Do not tie. Repeat with the remaining husks and *masa*.

Cooking the Tamales ▶ In Morelia and Pátzcuaro, I have seen large batches of these tamales steamed standing up. I prefer to steam them lying down flat in the steamer basket. Steam as described on page 452 for 1½ to 1¾ hours. Serve hot.

Serving: In restaurants, these tamales are served with pork morsels (*carnitas*, page 494) and Mexican *crema* (page 148). You can also serve them with refried beans (pages 273, 276, or 277), crème fraîche, and a dollop of a contrasting spicy fresh sauce such as *pico de gallo* (page 113).

Variation: At her restaurant La Terraza, in Morelia, Michoacán, Livier Ruíz makes a seductive main course from cooked *uchepos*. She layers the (unwrapped) tamales with grated cheese and *crema* in a baking dish and bakes them until the tops are golden.

My Fresh Corn Tamales Cuban Style

Mis Tamales Cubanos de Maíz Tierno

My version of the *tamal cubano* is a marriage of the rustic and the refined. It is a creation that has more to do with the Cuban tamal of my imagination than with any fresh corn tamal I have eaten in Cuba or at any restaurant in the Cuban communities in the United States.

My crossover recipe compensates for the juiciness of sweet North American corn by adding some fine cornmeal to the dough. The vivid flavors of the *sofrito*—the smokiness of the bacon, the heat of the red pepper, the slightly bitter taste of the cumin—are a perfect counterpoint to the soft, sweet corn base.

If you would like to enrich the *masa* with a meat filling, try Cuban Ground Beef Hash (page 695), Chicken Fricassee Cuban Style (page 662), or morsels of ham or cooked pork, allowing about 1 heaping tablespoon per tamal. Like creamy polenta served in corn husks, these tamales pair beautifully with a variety of foods.

Cook's Note: Grating the corn by hand yields just the right creamy consistency. You can cut off the kernels with a knife and puree them, but this faster method renders a more watery puree. The grated or pureed corn can be prepared a day ahead and refrigerated.

What to Drink: Serve with ice-cold beer like Hatuey or Mexican Corona; if serving as an appetizer, a Cuban *mojito* (page 355) or a daiquiri (page 354), or a floral Susana Balbo Crios Torrontes

For the Corn

14–16 large ears corn with large kernels (9 inches when husked) or 24 medium ears (7 to 8 inches when husked) or 1 pound 4 ounces frozen corn kernels, thawed, if using a grater; or

12 large ears or 28 medium ears or 4 pounds frozen corn kernels, thawed, if using a food processor or blender

For the Cooking Sauce

2 tablespoons achiote-infused extra-virgin olive oil (page 89)

8 ounces slab bacon, finely diced

8 garlic cloves, minced

1 medium yellow onion (about 8 ounces), finely chopped (about 1½ cups)

4 canned plum tomatoes, drained and coarsely chopped

1 teaspoon ground cumin

1–3 teaspoons crushed red pepper flakes (optional)

1 tablespoon coarse salt, or to taste

For the *Masa*

½ cup milk or heavy cream

2 tablespoons butter

1 cup (5⅓ ounces) fine yellow cornmeal

For the Wrappers

60 dried corn husks or 30 11-by-10-inch aluminum foil rectangles

Kitchen twine

Grating the Corn ▶ Husk the corn. Using the finest side of a box grater, grate the kernels from the cobs. Measure 7 cups and set aside.

Pureeing the Corn Using a Processor or Blender ▶ If using fresh corn, husk the corn and cut the kernels from the cobs with a sharp knife. Working in batches, puree the fresh or thawed frozen kernels in a food processor or blender until smooth. Measure 7 cups and set aside.

Making the Cooking Sauce ▶ In a heavy 3-quart Dutch oven or cast-aluminum *caldero*, heat the oil over medium heat until it sizzles. Add the bacon and sauté until golden brown. Add the garlic and sauté just until light golden, about 20 seconds. Add the onion and sauté for 5 minutes, until barely soft. Add the tomatoes, cumin, red pepper flakes, if using, and salt and cook for 5 minutes, stirring.

Making the *Masa* ▶ Stir the corn, milk or cream, and butter into the sauce. Add the cornmeal in a thin stream, stirring constantly until smooth. Cook for 2 to 3 minutes, stirring, until slightly thickened. Transfer the *masa* to a bowl and let cool before assembling the tamales.

If using dried corn husks, soak as directed on page 447.

Wrapping the Tamales ▶ If using corn husks, follow the instructions for the canoe wrap (page 449), using ⅓ cup *masa* for each tamal. If using aluminum foil, follow the instructions for the foil pouch method (page 450).

Cooking the Tamales ▶ Steam as described on page 452 for 1 hour. Serve hot.

Serving: In Cuba, tamales are served as a side dish for roast pork (page 721), goat stew, or spicy shrimp or land crab in *enchilado* sauce (pages 624 and 640).

To serve as an appetizer, I top the tamales with cubes of bacon in *adobo* sauce (page 723) or boned duck from a Peruvian *seco* (page 757), topped with a spoonful of *ajilimójili* sauce (page 143) or "Finger Sauce" (page 116) and garnished with Peruvian Onion and Yellow Pepper Slaw/Relish (page 150) or Yucatecan Red Onions Pickled in Bitter Orange Juice (page 149).

Variations: For breakfast, panfry day-old tamales (unwrapped) in olive oil until golden brown on both sides. For lunch or supper, cut the tamales into cubes and toss with greens for a tamal salad.

Ecuadorian Fresh Corn Tamales Spiked with *Aguardiente*

Chumales

These delectable anise-scented tamales from southern Ecuador are a once-a-year treat. When I drove through the town of Cuenca close to Mother's Day, at the beginning of the corn harvest, I saw signs hanging from the doorways of grocery stores and *cafeterías* announcing the arrival of these lovely fresh corn tamales: "*Hay chumales con café* (We have *chumales* served with coffee)." Inside, I saw people hunched over wooden tables, devouring them with spoons.

Since Andean corn is dense and very starchy even when young and fresh, the dough is kneaded with eggs, butter, sugar, and anise, whose sharp licorice taste tames the rough, mealy edge of the corn. When you bite into the sweet aromatic dough, you might think you are eating dessert—until you encounter the filling of salty fresh cheese and chopped scallions.

In Quechua, *chuma* means "in a drunken stupor," and the Cuenca people call these fresh corn tamales *chumales* because they are spiked with *aguardiente*, the potent sugarcane liquor. In other parts of the Andean region, tamales made with tender young corn (*choclo*) are known by their Quechua name, *humitas*.

Cook's Notes: *Aguardiente* (literally, firewater or burning water) is the crude, intensely alcoholic spirit that results from the distillation of sugarcane sap. Zhumir is Ecuador's favorite brand. You might not be able to find it in all Hispanic liquor stores, but you can be sure to find the more popular anise-scented Colombian brand, Cristal. If using Cristal, omit the anise seeds from the recipe.

Frozen corn from Ecuador and Peru, with its colossal kernels, can be found in Hispanic markets catering to a South American clientele. If it is unavailable in your area, the tamales will still be delicious with North American sweet corn. If using North American corn, you will also need precooked white corn flour to approximate the proper texture. In this country, I have had good results using frozen sweet corn kernels.

At home, people eat *chumales* both fresh from the steamer and—when there are leftovers—for breakfast the next morning, removed from the wrappers and pan-fried.

What to Drink: *Chumales* are typically accompanied by black coffee, *café tinto*. I also like them with Ecuadorian Purple Colada (page 342), Colombian Fruit and Corn Punch (page 343), and Ecuadorian Hot Toddy (page 365).

MAKES 14 TO 16 TAMALES

For the Corn

7 cups frozen (5 cups thawed) Ecuadorian or Peruvian corn kernels, thawed, or ten 5½-inch-long ears Ecuadorian or Peruvian frozen corn, unthawed, or 6 cups fresh corn kernels (from 6–8 large ears) from U.S. sweet corn, or 6 cups frozen U.S. corn kernels, thawed

1 cup (about 6 ounces) precooked white corn flour, (preferably P.A.N. brand), if using fresh corn

For Flavoring the *Masa*

4 tablespoons (½ stick) butter, melted

2½ tablespoons freshly rendered lard (page 82)

2 large eggs, separated

½ cup sugar, or to taste

1 tablespoon salt

1 tablespoon anise seeds

¼ cup *aguardiente* (preferably Ecuadorian Zhumir)

1 teaspoon baking powder

For the Filling

6 ounces lightly salted crumbly fresh white cheese, preferably Ecuadorian Queso Fresco San Francisco from Azuay or Santa Cruz Queso Ecuador Crema from Cuenca

3 scallions, white and 4 inches of green parts, finely chopped (about ½ cup)

1 tablespoon achiote-infused corn oil (page 89), plain corn oil, or lard

For the Wrappers

32 dried corn husks

Kitchen twine or additional corn husks for making ties

Preparing the Corn ▶ If using frozen ears of Andean corn, remove the kernels while still frozen by pushing downward on the kernels with your thumb. Thaw the kernels; reserve 2 corn cobs for steaming. Working in batches, transfer whichever kind of kernels you are using to a food processor or blender and puree until very smooth, 3 to 4 minutes. You should have about 4 cups pureed corn. Return all the corn to the processor or blender.

Making the *Masa* ▶ Add the butter, lard, egg yolks, sugar, salt, anise, *aguardiente*, baking powder, and corn flour (if using fresh corn) to the corn puree and process for about 2 minutes, until smooth. Transfer the *masa* to a medium bowl.

In a medium bowl, beat the egg whites with an electric mixer until stiff but not dry. Gently fold the whites into the *masa* with a rubber spatula just until incorporated. You should have about 5½ cups.

Making the Filling ▶ In a small bowl, crumble the cheese with a fork. Stir in the scallions and oil.

Wrapping the Tamales ▶ Soak the corn husks as directed on page 447 and pat dry. Place 16 soaked and dried husks on a work surface, tips pointing away from you. Place about ⅓ cup *masa* in the center of each and spread it to within about 3 inches of the tip and 1 inch of the other three sides. Place about 1 tablespoon of the cheese filling in the center of the husk, lightly pressing it with the back of a spoon. Fold the left-hand side toward the center, then fold down the tip about 2 inches. Fold the right-hand side toward the center, slightly overlapping the other side.

You will now have a tamal open at the wide end. Cooks sometimes steam *chumales* by propping them upright in the steamer open end facing up. But careful Ecuadorian cooks prefer to make closed packets as follows: Have ready 16 more soaked and dried husks. Place them with the tips facing you. Place a tamal on the husk with the open end pointing toward the tip and the closed end extending just slightly beyond the wide edge. Fold one long side of the husk toward the center. Fold over the other long side, slightly overlapping. Fold up the tip and tie with kitchen twine or thin strips of corn husk. Repeat with the remaining *chumales*. You will now have 16 neat, watertight packets. (See the illustrations on page 448.)

Cooking the Tamales ▶ If you have them, place the reserved cobs of Andean corn in the center of the steamer basket. Arrange the tamales around and over the cobs. Steam fresh corn tamales as described on page 452 for 45 minutes to 1 hour, the Andean corn tamales for about 30 minutes longer.

Serving: I like to serve *chumales* as a side dish with rich lamb or beef stews or as a snack, with a dollop of Mexican *crema* (page 148) or a dash of Ecuadorian Spicy Onion and Tamarillo Salsa (page 138). Or pan-fry the leftovers for breakfast as suggested in the Cook's Notes.

Chilean Fresh Corn Tamales Flavored with Basil

Humitas Chilenas

Chilean fresh corn tamales are strictly a summer treat, which is fine with me. Anything as fresh and delicious as this should be anticipated, the way one looks forward to vine-ripened tomatoes. *Humitas* are tied in the middle with a bow, giving them an hourglass shape with a darling little waist. Their flavor is straightforward, fragrant with basil and the clean smell of the green husks.

Cook's Notes: Chilean corn is a bit starchier than ours. My Mapuche friend Sofia Chanilao told me firmly not to thicken the *masa* with corn flour, but I found it did not set as well as hers when made with North American sweet corn. By cooking down the ground corn, I finally achieved soft yet properly set golden rectangles.

By all means use fresh corn husks to capture their fragrance. But be aware that you will have to use up to twice the quantity you would for dried. See directions on page 449.

What to Drink: Hotel Schuester's Pisco Sour (page 357), a Cousiño-Macul Riesling from the Maipo Valley, Chile, or Viña Esmeralda, a blend of Moscatel and Gewürztraminer from Penedès, Spain

MAKES 20 TO 22 TAMALES

For the Corn

14–16 large ears yellow corn, 9 inches when husked, or 24 medium ears, 7–8 inches when husked; or substitute 1 pound 4 ounces frozen corn kernels, thawed

For the *Masa*

¼ cup freshly rendered lard (page 82) or 4 tablespoons (½ stick) butter

2 medium yellow onions (about 8 ounces each), finely chopped

2 banana peppers or 1 jalapeño, seeded and finely chopped

1 tablespoon salt

2 tablespoons finely chopped basil

For the Wrappers

40 dried corn husks

Kitchen twine

Preparing the Corn ▶ Grate the corn on the finest side of a box grater. You should have 7 cups. Set aside.

Making the *Masa* ▶ Heat the lard or butter in a 12-inch skillet over medium heat until melted. Add the onions and the peppers and sauté for about 5 minutes. Stir in the grated corn and the salt. Cook, stirring, until the mixture resembles a thick polenta, about 20 minutes if the corn is young and watery; older, starchier corn will thicken in 5 to 10 minutes. Stir in the basil. Remove from the heat and let the *masa* cool to room temperature.

Soak the corn husks as directed on page 447.

Wrapping the Tamales ▶ Follow the directions for the canoe wrap (page 449), using ⅓ cup *masa* for each tamal and tying each in the middle with a strip of corn husk or kitchen string to give it an hourglass shape.

Cooking the Tamales ▶ Steam as described on page 452 for 45 minutes to 1 hour.

Serving: Serve the tamales with a simple Chilean salad of onion and juicy vine-ripened tomatoes (page 549). Top them with diced avocado if you wish.

TAMALES MADE FROM NIXTAMALIZED CORN

Guatemalan White Corn Cheese Tamales

Tamalitos Blancos de Queso Guatemaltecos

These simple cheese tamales are eaten like bread in many parts of Guatemala and are also cooked together with rich stews such as *suban ic'k* (page 751). You can make them with commercial nixtamalized *masa* dried and ground to a flour (see page 248). They are better still if you can obtain fresh *masa* from a small tortilla factory or a mail-order source.

MAKES ABOUT 24 *TAMALITOS*

For Tamales with Fresh *Masa*

- ¾ cup (about 6 ounces) lard, preferably freshly rendered (page 82)
- 2 teaspoons salt
- 1 pound 3 ounces (about 6 cups) fresh *masa*
- 8 ounces fresh cow's-milk cheese, preferably a Latin fresh cheese such as Cacique or Tropical brand *queso fresco*, finely grated (about 1¼ cups)
- 1½ cups chicken broth, homemade (page 538) or store-bought, or water

For Tamales with Instant Corn *Masa* Mix

- ¾ cup (about 6 ounces) lard, preferably freshly rendered (page 82)
- 2 teaspoons salt, if using unsalted broth or water
- 1⅓ cups nixtamalized corn flour, preferably Maseca brand

3 ounces fresh cow's milk cheese, preferably a Latin *queso fresco* such as Cacigne or Tropical brand, finely grated (about ⅔ cup)

2 cups chicken broth, homemade (page 538) or store-bought, or water

For the Wrappers

48 dried corn husks
   Kitchen twine

Making Tamales with Fresh *Masa* ▶ Place the lard and salt in the bowl of a standing mixer fitted with the paddle attachment and beat at medium speed until light and fluffy, 3 to 5 minutes, stopping from time to time to scrape the sides of the bowl. (You can also do this by hand with a wooden spoon.) Add the *masa* and cheese and beat until well blended. Gradually pour in the liquid and beat for about 5 minutes more, until the *masa* is very soft but spreadable.

Making Tamales with Instant Corn *Masa Mix* ▶ Place the lard and salt, if using in the bowl of a standing mixer fitted with a dough hook and beat at medium speed until fluffy, about 3 minutes. (Or mix by hand with a wooden spoon.) Beat in the *masa* mix and cheese, then continue beating while gradually adding the broth. Beat for 10 minutes. This is more of a batter than a dough.

Soak the corn husks as described on page 447.

Wrapping the Tamales ▶ Follow the instructions for the canoe wrap (page 449), using 3 tablespoons dough for each and spreading it into a 5-by-3-inch rectangle.

Cooking the Tamales ▶ Steam as directed on page 452 for 1 hour and 15 minutes.

Squash and Dried Shrimp Tamales with Vanilla in the New Style of Papantla

Tamales Papantecos de Calabaza y Camarón con Vainilla

A surprise awaits you inside these Veracruzan tamales from Papantla, a small town on the Gulf Coast of Mexico: a filling of golden *calabaza* (the meaty West Indian pumpkin), cuddled within soft corn *masa*. What I like most about this specialty of the Totonacapan (the land of the Totonac Indians), in northeastern Veracruz, is the sophisticated seasoning. Briny dried shrimp and aromatic spices including vanilla, a traditional Totonac Indian crop, serve as point and counterpoint to the sweet squash.

The people of Papantla favor light, silky *masas*, some, like this, as soft as a runny polenta. Celina Ibáñez López, who gave me this recipe, mixes nixtamalized corn flour with lard and plenty of broth or water, then uses the blender to turn the loose, lumpy mixture into a pourable batter.

Celina belongs to an organization of older women called Alegría de Vivir (Joy of Living), Papantla's chapter of INSEN (Mexico's National Institute for the Elderly), who are intent in reviving vanilla's use in cooking. When the women cook, an aromatic cloud of fresh vanilla lingers over every traditional dish they prepare, from soups to salsas to desserts. The traditional recipe for these tamales does not call for vanilla, and you can omit it, but I suggest you try this version.

Cook's Note: Dried shrimp are available in Hispanic and Asian markets.

Working Ahead ▶ You may make the filling and prepare the plantain leaves the day before.

What to Drink: Vino Piedra de Sol Chardonnay, from Baja California; a fruity Finca La Anita Tocai Friulano from Mendoza, Argentina; Gloria's Margarita (page 364); or nonalcoholic drinks such as Rice *Horchata* (page 345) and Hot Chocolate *"Agasajo"* (page 339)

MAKES 14 TAMALES

4 pounds *calabaza* (West Indian pumpkin) or Hubbard or kabocha squash

For the Filling

2 ounces small dried shrimp

12 medium plum tomatoes (about 2 pounds), peeled, seeded, and coarsely chopped, or 4 cups drained and chopped canned plum tomatoes

1 medium white onion (about 8 ounces), coarsely chopped

3 garlic cloves

2 tablespoons coarsely chopped cilantro

¼ teaspoon dried thyme

¼ teaspoon dried oregano

⅛ teaspoon ground cloves

1 teaspoon freshly ground black pepper

⅓ cup extra-virgin olive oil

2 small bay leaves

½ cup green olives, pitted and coarsely chopped

¼ cup capers, drained

Salt to taste

2 plump vanilla beans, preferably Mexican, coarsely ground in a mini-processor, or 1 tablespoon pure vanilla extract, preferably Mexican

For the *Masa*

⅔ cup (5 ounces) freshly rendered lard (page 82)

2 teaspoons salt, or to taste

2 cups instant corn *masa* mix, preferably Maseca brand

4 cups chicken broth, homemade (page 538) or store-bought, or water

For the Wrappers

Fourteen 12-inch plantain leaf squares (about three 1-pound packages), prepared according to the instructions on page 447

Fourteen 42-inch-long pieces of kitchen twine

Preparing the Squash ▶ Cut the squash into 4-inch chunks. Remove the seeds but leave the skin on. Place in a 6-quart pot, add 4 quarts water and salt to taste, and bring to a boil over high heat. Lower the heat to medium and simmer until the squash is soft, about 20 minutes. Drain.

When the squash is cool enough to handle, peel and puree in a food processor or mash with a fork. Set aside.

Making the Filling ▶ Place the dried shrimp, tomatoes, onion, garlic, cilantro, thyme, oregano, cloves, and pepper in a food processor or blender and puree.

Heat the oil in a 12-inch skillet over medium heat until it ripples. Add the pureed seasonings and the bay leaves and cook, stirring occasionally, for about 10 minutes, or until the fat separates from the solids and starts sizzling again. Add the pumpkin puree and cook, stirring, for about 10 minutes, or until the puree separates cleanly from the bottom of the skillet. Stir in the olives and capers, then add salt to taste. Remove the skillet from the heat and stir in the vanilla until well combined. Allow the filling to cool to room temperature.

Making the *Masa* ▶ *To mix by hand* (my preferred method for this kind of runny batter), place the lard and salt in a large bowl and beat with a wooden spoon until light and fluffy, 10 to 15 minutes. Gradually beat in the *masa* mix. When the batter looks smooth and well combined, gradually add the broth or water and continue beating until the batter looks like lumpy oatmeal. The fat will separate from the liquid, forming small lumps. Working in 2 or 3 batches, process the batter in a blender until it is smooth, about 5 minutes.

To use an electric mixer, place the lard and salt in the bowl of a standing mixer fitted with the paddle attachment and beat at medium speed until light and fluffy, about 2 minutes. Add the *masa* mix and beat until well combined. With the mixer on low speed, gradually add the broth or water, then increase the speed to medium and beat for 5 minutes. Stop the mixer from time to time to scrape down the sides of the bowl. If the fat separates from the *masa*, process in the blender as directed above.

Pour the batter into a large measuring cup or other container with a spout.

Wrapping the Tamales ▶ Place a plantain leaf square on a work surface with the veins perpendicular to you. Pour about ½ cup *masa* onto the center of the leaf. Place about ⅓ generous cup pumpkin filling in the center of the dough. Wrap the tamal following the directions and illustrations for the *pastel* wrap (pages 450 and 451); Mexicans do not bother to tie their tamales, but it is easier to remove them from the pot if you do. Continue making tamales with the remaining ingredients.

Cooking the Tamales ▶ Steam as directed on page 452 for about 1 hour and 15 minutes.

Serving: Serve with Totonac Vanilla and Prunes in *Aguardiente* (page 804) and Mexican Rice (page 302) or as an appetizer with a dollop of Chipotle and Vanilla Table Sauce (page 119).

SOUTH AMERICAN TAMALES MADE WITH CRACKED CORN

Venezuelan Christmas *Hallacas* Caracas Style

Hallacas Venezolanas al Estilo de Caracas

There is no Christmas in Venezuela without these delicious, steaming golden packages of corn, which share the holiday plate with roast pork, chicken salad, and another favorite, *pan de jamón*, a bread filled with ham. Together with the Nicaraguan *nacatamal* and the Yucatecan *mucbipollo*, this is one of the most baroque tamales of Latin America, but rather than inspiring terror for the labor it entails, it is a reason for rejoicing, for bringing family and friends together in a feast of cooking and eating. As with many Venezuelan dishes, making *hallacas* is an almost sacred tradition.

This is one case where I feel obliged to describe a special wrapping technique in great detail because it is strongly associated with a place. Every region of Venezuela has its own way of not only cooking but "packaging" Christmas *hallacas*. In Caracas, tradition-minded cooks would never dream of presenting them without exactly the right gift-wrapped effect, using plantain leaves and kitchen twine. Once the classical garnishes like capers, onion rings, and quarters of hard-boiled eggs are carefully arranged over the rich *guiso* (stew) of pork and chicken simmered in a vividly seasoned sauce atop a layer of sweetened cracked-corn *masa*, each *hallaca* is fashioned into a dainty leaf-wrapped square and done up with a single length of kitchen twine so as to appear sectioned into twelve neat rectangular panels. (It may be encased in an extra plantain-leaf section called the *faja*, or belt, to protect the contents during cooking.) A favorite technique is to tie up two of the neatly wrapped packets together, seam sides facing each other, to create an *atao* (bundle) with the same paneled effect.

Recipes for Venezuelan *hallacas* are generous. People seldom make fewer than fifty because they can freeze what is not eaten on the day of the feast. The next day, they also make a simpler type of *hallaca* with leftover filling, *masa*, and garnishes, which I find as tasty as its artfully constructed mother dish. The jazzier "son" is more improvisatory, with all the ingredients mixed together, so that you get a burst of intense, melded flavors and textures in every mouthful.

This is a somewhat pared-down recipe that I put together after cooking with many extraordinary Venezuelan cooks who are also busy professional women. It follows traditional guidelines but offers some shortcuts.

Cook's Note: To hard-boil eggs, place the eggs in a saucepan, cover with cold water, and bring just to a boil over high heat. Remove from the heat, cover the pan, and set aside for 15 minutes. Drain the eggs and rinse under cold water to stop the cooking. Cover with cold water and let sit for 5 minutes. Drain, place in a covered container, and refrigerate.

Working Ahead ▶ This recipe might seem daunting, but organization and division of labor are the keys for a pleasurable experience. The *hallacas* should be prepared over 2 days, as directed below, with the help of family and friends.

What to Drink: Beer, preferably Venezuelan Polar Beer, or a crisp Venezuelan Pomar chardonnay

MAKES 20 *HALLACAS*

  1 cup achiote-infused lard or mild olive oil
     (page 89)

For the *Masa*

  1 recipe Cracked Corn Dough for *Hallacas* (page 469) or Corn Flour and *Calabaza* Dough for *Hallacas* (page 468)

For the Chicken

  ¼ cup fresh lime juice
  6 garlic cloves, mashed to a paste with a mortar and pestle or finely chopped and mashed
  1 tablespoon salt
One 3½-pound chicken, cut into 8 serving pieces (see page 659), or 3½ pounds chicken thighs
  1 medium yellow onion (about 8 ounces), halved
  1 medium green bell pepper (about 6 ounces), halved, cored, seeded, and deveined
  1 leek, white and pale green parts, split in half

4 cilantro sprigs
1 teaspoon black peppercorns
3 quarts water

For the Meats

1 pound boneless pork shoulder
½ teaspoon salt
½ teaspoon freshly ground black pepper
8 ounces slab bacon, rind removed
1 small yellow onion (5 ounces), halved
1 small green bell pepper (4–5 ounces), halved, cored, seeded, and deveined

For the Cooking Sauce

1 large head garlic, cloves separated, peeled, and finely chopped
1 medium yellow onion (8 ounces), finely chopped
1 leek, white and 1 inch of green parts, finely chopped
6 scallions, white and 1 inch of green parts, finely chopped
1 medium red bell pepper (about 6 ounces), cored, seeded, deveined, and finely chopped
12 Caribbean sweet peppers (*ajíes dulces*) or 1 cubanelle pepper, finely chopped
8 ripe medium plum tomatoes (about 1½ pounds), cored, peeled, seeded, and finely chopped, or one 16-ounce can plum tomatoes, drained and coarsely chopped
¼ cup grated brown loaf sugar (*papelón* or *panela*) or packed light brown sugar
2 teaspoons sweet paprika, preferably *pimentón* (Spanish smoked paprika)
1 teaspoon ground cayenne
½ teaspoon freshly ground black pepper
2 tablespoons drained capers, finely chopped
¼ cup port or moscatel wine

3 tablespoons cider vinegar
3 tablespoons Worcestershire sauce
¼ cup sweet gherkins, finely chopped
1 tablespoon prepared yellow mustard
1 tablespoon salt, or to taste
¼ cup precooked white corn flour, preferably P.A.N. brand
2 cups chicken broth (reserved from cooking the chicken)

For the Garnishes

5 large eggs
1 large red bell pepper (8 ounces), fire-roasted (see page 67), peeled, cored, seeded, and cut into ¼-inch-wide strips
3 very small yellow onions (5 ounces total), cut into ¼-inch rounds and separated into rings
40 pimiento-stuffed olives
½ cup dark raisins
1 cup capers, drained
¼ cup slivered almonds
¼ cup sweet gherkins, chopped

For the Wrappers

Forty 12-inch plantain leaf squares (four 1-pound packages), prepared as directed on page 447
Twenty 5½-by-15-inch plantain leaf rectangles (two 1-pound packages), prepared as directed on page 447 (optional)
Forty 90-inch pieces of kitchen string

DAY ONE

Prepare the achiote-infused lard or oil and keep in a covered container until ready to use. You will need it for the cooking sauce and to brush over the plantain squares. (You can store what is left in the refrigerator for other uses.)

If preparing the cracked corn dough from scratch, soak the corn overnight.

The filling consists of the chicken, the meats, and the cooking sauce. While the chicken marinates, prepare the meats. When the meats are done, go back to the chicken, then prepare the seasonings.

Preparing the Chicken ▶ Place the lime juice, mashed garlic, and 1 teaspoon of the salt in a small bowl and mix well with a fork. Rub the chicken with the garlic mixture, place in an 8-quart non-reactive pot, and let it marinate for 1 hour. Set aside.

Preparing the Meats ▶ Rub the pork with the salt and pepper. Place in a 4-quart pot and add the bacon, onion, bell pepper, and 2 cups water. Bring to a boil, then lower the heat and simmer for 8 minutes. Transfer the bacon to a plate and cook the pork for 10 minutes more.

Drain the pork, discarding the cooking water, and transfer to a plate to cool.

Cut the bacon into 2-by-¼-inch strips and refrigerate, covered. Cut the pork into ¼-inch pieces and set aside.

Cooking the Chicken ▶ Add the onion, bell pepper, leek, cilantro, peppercorns, water, and the remaining 2 teaspoons salt to the pot with the chicken. Bring to a boil, then lower the heat and simmer, covered, for 30 minutes.

Transfer the chicken pieces to a bowl; strain and reserve 2 cups of the broth. When the chicken is cool enough to handle, skin and bone it. Cut the meat into ¼-inch pieces and set aside.

Preparing the Cooking Sauce ▶ Heat ¼ cup of the achiote-infused lard or oil in a deep 12-inch skillet or a 4-quart pot over medium heat. Add the garlic and sauté until light gold, about 20 seconds. Add the onion and sauté, stirring, until soft, about 5 minutes. Add the leek, scallions, and peppers and sauté, stirring, for 5 minutes. Stir in the tomatoes and cook for 8 minutes, or until soft. Add the brown sugar, paprika, cayenne, and black pepper and cook, stirring, until the sugar dissolves. Add the capers, wine, vinegar, Worcestershire sauce, gherkins, mustard, and salt and stir to mix.

Finishing the Filling ▶ Add the chicken and pork to the sauce. Dissolve the corn flour in the reserved chicken broth, then stir into the pan and cook, stirring, for 5 minutes. Transfer to a large bowl and let cool to room temperature, then refrigerate overnight, tightly covered with plastic wrap.

Preparing the Garnishes ▶ You can prepare all of the garnishes ahead: Cook the eggs; roast the pepper and cut into strips; slice the onions; and chop the gherkins. Measure all the other ingredients. Place all the garnishes in separate containers. Set the raisins and almonds aside at room temperature and refrigerate the remaining garnishes, covered.

DAY TWO

Making the *Masa* ▶ Prepare the dough of your choice, cover with plastic wrap or a wet kitchen towel, and set aside.

Assembling and Wrapping the *Hallacas* ▶ Organize your work space for an assembly-line operation. Cut the hard-cooked eggs lengthwise into quarters. Set aside on a plate. Set out all the remaining garnishes. Place the reserved bacon strips on a plate and divide into 20 portions. Pour ¼ cup of the achiote-infused lard or olive oil into a bowl and set out with a pastry brush. Towel-dry each plantain leaf, and keep them stacked and covered with a towel next to the lard or oil and the dough. Set out the filling and kitchen twine. Also set out a plastic bag like the ones for carrying groceries and a flat object like a small cutting board. They will be useful for rubbing the plantain-leaf squares with lard or oil, and later for spreading the *masa* evenly while keeping your hands relatively free of gunk.

Place 2 plantain leaf squares next to each other with the shiny veined side up and the veins perpendicular to you. Brush lightly with the lard or oil. Scoop up a scant ¼ cup of *masa* and roll it into a ball. Place on the center of the left-hand leaf. Rub a little lard or oil over one side of the plastic bag and place it over the ball of *masa*. Now use the cutting board to press out the *masa* into a 6-inch circle. Spread 3 heaping tablespoons of the filling on the center of the circle, leaving a ½-inch border all around. Top with 1 egg quarter, 1 or 2 pepper strips, 2 onion rings, 2 olives, 6 raisins, 4 capers, a few almond slivers, a pinch of gherkins, and a portion of bacon. Scoop up another ¼ cup *masa* and roll into a ball.

Place on the center of the right-hand leaf and press into a 6-inch circle as before. Slide your hand under the right-hand leaf and flip it over onto the left-hand leaf. Pinch the top and bottom edges together. Now run your fingers around the circumference of the filled *masa* rounds, under the top leaf, to feel their contours. With your fingertips, press the 6-inch circle into a square with roughly 4½-inch sides. This will leave a border of about 3¾ inches on all sides. Pinch the right-hand edges together and fold over toward the center of the *hallaca*. Repeat with the left-hand edges so that the edges meet in the center of the *hallaca*. Fold the top and bottom edges to form a 4½-inch square package.

Caracan cooks take the tying of the filled *hallacas* very seriously. Part of the reason is that *hallacas* are most often boiled, not steamed, and it is necessary to make the packets as watertight as possible. This is also the reason that people in Venezuela almost always envelop *hallacas* in an extra piece of plantain leaf, the *faja* (belt), which I recommend but don't absolutely require. To make the *faja* for each *hallaca*, take one of the 5½-by-15-inch rectangles of plantain leaf listed as optional parts of the wrapping. Place it on a work surface with the veins perpendicular to you. Place a *hallaca* on the center of the leaf, seam side down. Fold over one side as far as it will go. Fold over the other side so that the end is level with the edge of the packet.

The tying process is the same whether or not you have used the *faja*. Feel free to use any gift-tying technique that works for you, as long as the packet is tied into 12 or more equal panels. But for the traditional Caracas flourish, proceed as follows: Take a 75-inch length of twine and run it crosswise under the center of the packet, bringing the ends together. Make a hitch over the center and bring the two loose ends toward the short sides of the packet, at right angles from the original direction. Turn it over and make another right-hand hitch, about ¾ of the way toward one short side. Turn over again and make another right-hand hitch, this time about ¾ of the way toward a long side. Turn over once more and finish by tying a bow, with one loop longer than the other (to make it easier to fish out of the pot later), about ¾ of the way toward the remaining short side.

Cooking the *Hallacas* ▶ Using 2 pots if necessary, steam as directed on page 452 for 1 to 1½ hours. (Venezuelan cooks usually boil them, but steaming is my preference.)

Serving: In Venezuela, the *hallacas* are served on Christmas Eve with chicken salad, roast pork, and a slice of Venezuelan Christmas Ham Bread (page 598). You can also serve *hallacas* as a main course for lunch or dinner, accompanied by a tomato and avocado salad and Fried Green Plantains (page 182). For a jolt of heat, there is nothing as good as Spicy Milk Sauce from Ciudad Bolívar (page 122).

Corn Flour and *Calabaza* Dough for *Hallacas*

When time is of the essence, make this simple dough for Venezuelan and Colombian *hallacas*. The squash does wonders for it, softening the gritty edge of the cracked cornmeal and giving the *masa* a subtly sweet flavor and a light consistency.

Working Ahead ▶ You can cook and puree the squash and prepare the achiote-infused lard the day before.

MAKES 5 POUNDS DOUGH

For the Pumpkin
  1 pound *calabaza* (West Indian pumpkin) or Hubbard or kabocha squash, peeled, seeded, and cut into 1-inch chunks
  1 tablespoon light brown sugar
  1 teaspoon salt

For the *Masa*
  1¾ pounds precooked white corn flour (preferably P.A.N. brand)
  ½ cup achiote-infused lard (page 89)
  1 cup plain lard (7 ounces), preferably freshly rendered (page 82), melted, or mild olive oil
  6 cups chicken broth, homemade (page 538) or store-bought
  2 tablespoons grated brown loaf sugar (*papelón* or *panela*), Demerara sugar, or light brown sugar
  2 teaspoons salt

Preparing the Squash ▶ Place the squash in a 3-quart saucepan, add 1½ quarts water and the sugar and salt, and bring to a boil over high heat.

Lower the heat to medium and simmer until the squash is soft, about 15 minutes. Drain.

Puree the squash in a food processor or blender. Set aside.

Making the Dough ▶ Place the corn flour in a large bowl, add the achiote-infused lard, and knead until uniformly colored. Add the melted lard and knead until smooth and homogeneous. Add the broth 1 cup at a time, kneading well after each addition. Add the pumpkin puree, the sugar and salt, and knead until smooth, about fifteen minutes more. Cover the bowl with plastic wrap and allow the *masa* to rest briefly before using (no more than 30 minutes, or it will dry out).

Cracked Corn Dough for *Hallacas*

Masa de Maíz Trillado

Classic Venezuelan *hallacas* are made with a dough of cracked white corn. The corn is soaked and then traditionally ground into a paste with a Corona plate mill, but I use the grinder attachment of my KitchenAid standing mixer with good results. This recipe makes about 5 pounds *masa*, but the weight will vary according to how long it takes to cook the soaked corn. The longer the corn is cooked, the heavier it will become, having absorbed more water.

Working Ahead ▶ You must soak the corn overnight.

MAKES ABOUT 5 POUNDS

1¾ pounds dried cracked white corn (such as Venezuelan Maíz Trillado Blanco La Venezolana or Goya brand)

½ cup achiote-infused lard or mild olive oil (page 89)

1 cup plain lard, preferably freshly rendered (page 82), or mild olive oil

2 cups chicken broth, homemade (page 538) or store-bought

3 tablespoons grated brown loaf sugar (*papelón* or *panela*), Demerara sugar, or light brown sugar

2½ teaspoons salt

▶ Pick over, wash, and drain the corn. Place in a large bowl, cover with 2 quarts water, and let soak overnight at room temperature.

Drain the corn and combine with 2 quarts fresh water in a 5 to 6-quart pot. Bring to a boil, then lower the heat to medium and cook for 30 to 40 minutes. The kernels should be soft but a bit al dente; do not overcook. Drain the corn in a colander, rinse with cold water and let cool.

Using a plate corn mill or the grinding attachment of a standing mixer, grind the corn into a large bowl. Add the achiote-infused lard and knead well by hand. Add the plain lard and continue kneading for about 5 minutes more.

Pass the ground corn through the plate corn mill or grinding attachment again to make the *masa* smoother and more uniformly colored, and return to the bowl. Pour in the broth, sugar, and salt and continue kneading until smooth, 5 to 8 minutes. If not using immediately, refrigerate tightly covered with plastic wrap. This dough should be used as soon as possible, because corn tends to ferment rapidly.

Colombian Tamales with Potato and Peanut Hash

Tamales de Pipián

Eating this silky tamal with total concentration, savoring each morsel, a Colombian friend said, "I do not want my tamal to end." I understood completely. A specialty of the Valle del Cauca region filled with *pipián*, an earthy, crunchy potato hash enriched with ground peanuts, it is one of the tastiest tamales I have eaten.

The tamales and empanadas from the Valle del Cauca are considered a delicacy, and for good reason. They are made with a dough that turns to silk and melts in your mouth. The *masa* is called *añeja*, which means aged, because the cracked corn (*maíz trillado* or *maíz pilado*) is soaked for 5 days before it is milled. The ground corn *masa* is dissolved in water and then strained to make a soft gruel that is allowed to rest so the solids form a sediment in the bottom of the pot. The water is carefully poured off, and the soft residue is cooked in a heavy pot, stirred constantly with a *cagüinga* (flat wooden paddle) to prevent sticking, until it feels like a thick polenta that pulls away from the pot. I have streamlined the aging process, reducing the soaking of the corn to just one day or overnight.

Cook's Note: This recipe calls for roasted unsalted peanuts. You can buy them already roasted or roast raw peanuts yourself as follows: Heat a medium skillet over medium heat. Add the peanuts and roast, stirring constantly, until they are light brown and beginning to smell nutty. Transfer to a plate to cool.

Working Ahead ▶ You can make the *masa*, cook the filling, and prepare the plantain leaves a day ahead.

What to Drink: Colombian beer such as Club Colombia or Aguila

MAKES 12 TAMALES

For the *Masa*

- 2 pounds dried cracked white hominy corn (such as Venezuelan Maíz Trillado Blanco La Venezolana or Goya brand)
- 6 cups chicken broth, homemade (page 538) or store-bought, or water
- 5 tablespoons achiote-infused lard or mild olive oil (page 89)
- 1 tablespoon grated brown loaf sugar (*papelón* or *panela*) or light brown sugar
- 1 tablespoon salt, or to taste (less if using canned chicken broth)

For the Filling

- 1 pound russet potatoes, peeled and cut into ¼-inch dice
  Salt
- 3 tablespoons corn oil
- 1 large white onion (about 10 ounces), finely chopped
- 4 scallions, white and pale green parts, finely chopped
- 1 medium red bell pepper (about 6 ounces), cored, seeded, deveined, and finely chopped
- 4 ripe medium plum tomatoes (about 12 ounces), peeled, seeded, and finely chopped, or 4 canned plum tomatoes, seeded and finely chopped

⅛ teaspoon ground cinnamon

2 hard-boiled large eggs, coarsely chopped

½ cup roasted unsalted peanuts (see Cook's Note), coarsely ground

For the Wrappers

Twelve 12-inch plantain leaf squares (about two 1-pound packages), prepared as directed on page 447

Twelve 42-inch pieces of kitchen twine

Making the *Masa* ▶ Pick over, wash, and drain the corn. Place in a 12-quart pot and cover with 4 quarts water. Soak the corn for about 24 hours, changing the water twice to prevent fermentation.

Drain the corn and return it to the pot. Add 4 quarts fresh water and bring to a boil, then reduce the heat to medium and cook until the corn is soft, about 45 minutes. Drain and let cool. Using a Corona plate mill or the grinding attachment of a standing mixer, grind the corn into a large bowl. Add the broth or water and mix well with a wooden spoon. It will have the consistency of a thin batter. Let rest for 15 minutes.

Rub the mixture between the palms of your clean hands to remove any large lumps. Strain it through a fine mesh strainer into a heavy pot, pushing with the back of a ladle or wooden spoon to force it through. Place over medium-low heat, add the lard or oil, the sugar, and salt, and cook, stirring often with a wooden spoon, until the dough is as thick as polenta and comes away from the bottom of the pot, about 1½ hours. Transfer to a large bowl and let cool.

Making the Filling ▶ Place the potatoes, salt to taste, and 1 quart water in a medium saucepan and bring to a boil over medium heat. Cook until barely tender, about 10 minutes. Drain and set aside.

Heat the oil in a 12-inch skillet over medium heat. Add the onion and scallions and sauté until light gold, about 3 minutes. Add the red pepper and cook for 3 to 5 minutes. Add the tomatoes, cinnamon, and ½ teaspoon salt and cook for 5 minutes, stirring occasionally. Stir in the potatoes, eggs, and peanuts. Taste for salt. Let cool before using.

Wrapping the Tamales ▶ Place a plantain leaf square on a work surface with the ridges perpendicular to you. Scoop up a scant 1½ cups *masa* and place it on the center of the leaf. Spread into a 6-inch square. Spoon 3 tablespoons filling down the center of the *masa*. Wrap the tamal following the directions and illustrations for the *pastel* wrap (pages 450 and 451). Repeat with the remaining wrappers, *masa*, and filling. (You will have extra filling; save it to serve with the cooked tamales.)

Cooking the Tamales ▶ Steam as directed on page 452 for about 1 hour.

Serving: I like to serve the tamales on fresh plantain leaf squares topped with a spoonful of the reserved filling and a dollop of Colombian Hot Sauce (page 124). A spoonful of the creamy Bogotá Cheese Cooking Sauce (page 52) is also delicious with these tamales.

TAMALES MADE WITH ANDEAN HOMINY (*MOTE PELADO*)

Chicken Tamales from Lima

Tamales Limeños de Maíz Blanco

On a visit to Lima many years ago, I almost suffered a corn overdose. When I stepped from the plane, my friend Ana María Rojas-Lombardi and one of her brothers were waiting for me outside customs, holding huge ears of boiled Andean corn like flower bouquets. As we drove though Lima at the crack of dawn in her beat-up Volkswagen Beetle, I munched on an ear of corn with one hand while holding my suitcase in the other.

Little did I realize my corn immersion had just begun. We arrived at Ana María's house to find the table set for breakfast with large white corn tamales filled with pork, raisins, and olives and tender green *tamalitos* (small tamales) made by her husband, who is from the north of the country, together with a special home-cured ham and marvelous fresh cheese.

We had not even finished breakfast when we heard the voice of a man calling out, "*Vendo tamales, tamales calientes* (I sell tamales, hot tamales)." We rushed to the street and found a tall young black man selling special tamales from the coast, with another type of filling. When I was halfway through my coastal tamales, Ana María hurried us to a nearby bakery, where a couple stood behind huge baskets filled with tamales, sprigs of *ruda* (rue) adorning the man's basket for good luck. Their tamales were astounding, large, bountiful with sauce and filling, so terrific that I could not stop eating them even after everything else I had already eaten.

In Peru, the seasoning for tamales is full-bodied and complex, a mixture of pungent Andean dried peppers, cumin, and lots of cilantro. The *masa* is made with the local hominy, *mote pelado*, and has a distinctive, crunchy texture from the addition of ground sesame seeds and peanuts. Sautéed onions, bay leaf, garlic, smoky cumin, and briny black olives add sharp accents of flavor. This recipe is a composite of the many tamales I enjoyed in Lima. When I first made this recipe years ago, I had to use sweet North American corn because Andean hominy was not yet available in our markets. The texture was softer and more supple and the flavor sweeter than anything I had eaten in Lima, but the tamales were delicious. I have written the recipe to accommodate either type of corn.

Cook's Note: You will need a Corona plate corn mill or a standing mixer with a grinding attachment to grind the Andean corn.

Working Ahead ▶ If using dried corn, you will need to soak it for 24 hours. You can also make the filling (straining and reserving the broth) and prepare the seasoning ingredients for the *masa*, the garnishes, and plantain leaves the day before.

What to Drink: Cucharamama Peruvian-Style Pisco Sour (page 356), Bar Queirolo *Chilcano* (page 359), or Peruvian Pilsen Callao beer

For the Corn

Two 14-ounce packages dried skinned Andean corn
for *mote* (see page 251), 7 cups sweet corn
kernels (from about 14 large or 24 medium ears),
or 6 cups frozen sweet corn kernels, thawed

For the Filling

One 3½-pound chicken, skinned and cut into 8 serving
pieces (see page 659), or 3½ pounds chicken
thighs, skin removed

2 quarts water

1 large yellow onion (about 10–12 ounces), halved

1 bay leaf

2 tablespoons corn oil or mild olive oil

1 large head garlic, cloves separated, peeled, and
mashed to a paste with a mortar and pestle or
finely chopped and mashed

1 teaspoon ground cumin

1 teaspoon salt

For the Seasonings

¼ cup sesame seeds

7 ounces roasted, unsalted peanuts (see Cook's
Note, page 470), coarsely ground

2 tablespoons ground dried *panca* pepper (page 54)

2 tablespoons ground dried *mirasol* pepper (page 54)

1¼ teaspoons salt

1¼ cups achiote-infused lard (page 89)

For the Garnishes

3 hard-boiled large eggs, quartered

15 roasted, unsalted peanuts

15 Peruvian purple olives or Kalamata olives,
preferably halved and pitted

For the Wrappers

Fifteen 12-inch plantain leaf squares (about two 1-pound
packages), prepared as directed on page 447

Fifteen 42-inch pieces of kitchen twine

Preparing the Corn ▶ If using Andean corn, pick
over, wash, and drain it. Place in a 6- to 8-quart
pot, add 4 quarts water, and let soak for 24 hours,
changing the water twice.

Making the Filling ▶ Place the chicken pieces,
water, onion, and bay leaf in a 6-quart pot and
bring to a boil. Lower the heat and simmer until
the chicken is barely tender, about 20 minutes.

Remove the chicken from the pot and cut into
2-inch pieces. Strain the broth and set aside to cool.

Heat the oil in a 12-inch skillet over medium
heat. Add the garlic, cumin, and salt and cook for
just a few seconds. Stir in the chicken and cook for
about 5 minutes. Add ¼ cup of the reserved broth
and cook for 1 more minute. Remove from the heat
and set aside to cool.

Making the *Masa* ▶ If using Andean corn, drain it
and cut out the germ tip and nail-shaped "heart"
from each kernel. Return the corn to the pot, add 2
quarts fresh water, and bring to a boil over medium
heat. Boil for 30 minutes. Drain and allow to cool.

Meanwhile, toast the sesame seeds in a small,
dry skillet over medium heat just until they begin to
pop and change color, stirring constantly to prevent
burning. Transfer to a plate to cool.

Using a plate corn mill or the grinding
attachment of a standing mixer, grind the drained
corn into a large bowl. Or, if using fresh or thawed
frozen sweet corn, grind it to a paste in a food pro-

cessor in batches and transfer to a large bowl. Add the sesame seeds, peanuts, ground dried peppers, salt, achiote-infused lard, and the reserved broth and knead by hand to mix all the ingredients. Cover and set aside.

Wrapping the Tamales ▶ Set out all the garnishes. Place one plantain leaf square on a work surface with the veins perpendicular to you. Scoop up ½ cup *masa* and place it on the center of the leaf. Spread into a 6-inch square, leaving a 3-inch margin on all sides. Top with 3 pieces of chicken and then with 1 egg quarter, 1 peanut, and 1 olive. Wrap and tie the tamal following the directions and illustrations for the *pastel* wrap (pages 450 and 451). Repeat with the remaining wrappers and ingredients.

Cooking the Tamales ▶ Steam as directed on page 452 for 2 hours if using Andean corn, 1 hour if using sweet corn.

Serving: Serve with Peruvian Onion and Yellow Pepper Relish (page 150), or Spicy Milk Sauce from Ciudad Bolívar (page 122). If you have any leftovers, use them in a salad.

TAMALES MADE WITH STARCHY VEGETABLE DOUGH

Puerto Rican *Pasteles*

Pasteles Puertorriqueños

The Christmas season in Puerto Rico is blessed with balmy weather and clear skies. There is nothing like dining under the shade of a gourd tree on Christmas Eve, savoring every morsel of the earthy tamales called *pasteles* and *adobo*-flavored pork while looking at the sea.

Puerto Rican women get together with their families to prepare *pasteles* by the hundred, freezing them until needed for Christmas Eve, Christmas Day, family reunions, the Fiesta de Reyes, and the religious season called *octavas* that follows the Feast of the Epiphany.

It is the blend of the tiny pepper *ají dulce* and broad-leaf *culantro* in the fragrant *sofrito* (cooking sauce) that gives an unmistakable Puerto Rican identity to these earthy tamales. A dash of vinegar lends the *sofrito* just the right amount of tang against the mild dough of *malanga* and plantain tinted orange-yellow with achiote-infused lard.

I learned to make these in the traditional kitchen of the Puerto Rican side of my family. While one person took care of trimming the plantain leaves, others were busy grating the vegetables and making the *sofrito*. There the vegetables are grated by hand, though you can find machines designed specially for this purpose in any market or use a food processor. Puerto Ricans are extremely fussy about the wrapping—it has to be perfect and watertight because *pasteles* are normally boiled. But I prefer to steam them.

Working Ahead ▶ You can make the seasoning base (*recado*) and the *sofrito* and prepare the plantain leaves the day before.

MAKES 25 PASTELES

For the Seasoning Base (*Recado*)

- 6 large tomatoes (about 3 pounds), coarsely chopped
- 1 medium green bell pepper (about 6 ounces), cored, seeded, deveined, and coarsely chopped
- 1 medium yellow onion (about 8 ounces), coarsely chopped
- 8 garlic cloves, peeled
- 20 Caribbean sweet peppers (*ajíes dulces*), seeded and cut in half
- ½ cup tomato sauce, homemade (page 48) or store-bought
- ¼ cup coarsely chopped cilantro
- 2 broad-leaf *culantro* leaves
- 1½ tablespoons cider vinegar
- 1 teaspoon dried oregano

For the Cooking Sauce (*Sofrito*)

- ¼ cup achiote-infused extra-virgin olive oil (page 89)
- 8 ounces slab bacon, rind removed, cut into ¼-inch dice
- 1½ pounds boneless pork shoulder or butt, cut into ½-inch dice
- ¼ cup chicken broth, homemade (page 538) or store-bought

For the *Masa*

- ⅓ cup whole milk
- 1½ pounds *malanga*, peeled and cut into 1-inch cubes
- 1½ pounds green bananas, peeled and thickly sliced
- ½ green plantain, peeled (see page 181) and thickly sliced
- 8 ounces *calabaza* (West Indian pumpkin) or Hubbard or kabocha squash, peeled, seeded, and cut into 1-inch cubes
- ¼ cup achiote-infused olive oil
- ½ to 1 teaspoon salt, or to taste

For the Wrappers

Twenty-five 12-inch plantain leaf squares (4 to 5 packages), prepared as directed on page 447
- ¼ cup achiote-infused olive oil
Twenty-five 42-inch pieces of kitchen twine

For the Garnishes

- ⅓ cup dark raisins
- One 15-ounce can chickpeas, drained and rinsed, or 2 cups cooked chickpeas
- 2 medium red bell peppers (about 6 ounces), roasted (see page 67), peeled, cored, seeded, and cut into ¼-inch-wide strips
- 50 pimiento-stuffed olives, cut in half

Making the *Recado* ▶ Place all the ingredients in a blender or food processor and puree. Set aside.

Making the *Sofrito* ▶ Heat the oil in a 12-inch skillet over medium heat. Add the bacon and brown for 2 to 3 minutes. Add the pork and cook, stirring, until it begins to release its fat, about 15 minutes.

Stir in the *recado*, reduce the heat to low, and cook, covered, for about 50 minutes, or until the pork is tender when pierced with the tip of a sharp knife. Add some chicken broth if the sauce thickens too much during cooking. When the meat is done, transfer it to a plate with a slotted spoon. Set the sauce aside.

Making the *Masa* ▶ Working in 2 or 3 batches, puree the milk, *malanga*, green bananas, green plantain, and *calabaza* in a blender or food processor and pour into a large bowl. Add the oil and salt and mix well to color the *masa* evenly. Stir in the reserved sauce. Taste for seasoning and set aside.

Wrapping the Tamales ▶ Place one plantain leaf square on a work surface with the veins perpendicular to you. Brush generously with achiote oil. Place 3 heaping tablespoons of *masa* in the center of the leaf and spread into a 6-inch square, leaving a 3-inch margin on all sides. Place 3 tablespoons of the diced pork on top, forming a rectangle. Garnish with 4 raisins, 4 chickpeas, a strip of red pepper, and 4 olive halves. Tie the tamal following the instructions and illustrations for the *pastel* wrap (pages 450 and 451). Repeat with the remaining wrappers and ingredients.

Cooking the Tamales ▶ Using two steamers (or working in batches), steam as directed on page 452 for about 1 hour.

Serving: I adore these tamales, enjoying them warm or cold, without sauce or embellishment. For company, though, I find that most people like them with a little sauce. *Ajilimójili* (page 143), Spicy Milk Sauce from Ciudad Bolívar (page 122), or Central American Ripened Cream (page 147) are all good choices.

CEBICHES

Something wonderful happens when you add an acidic ingredient such as lime juice, bitter orange juice, or vinegar to seafood. The moist, translucent flesh changes color and turns opaque. Scientists may tell you about proteins coagulating, but those who love cebiche know that this is one of the most exciting ways there is to "cook" and flavor food.

Long a popular first course served in humble beachfront restaurants or sold as an early morning pick-me-up at markets along the coasts of Latin America from Mexico to Peru, primarily on the Pacific Coast, cebiche may be the most popular Latin cooking technique to have crossed over to North America. But the origins of the "cooking" or "curing" method, and even the etymology of the name, remain obscure.

FROM *CEBO* TO *SIBECH*

Some historians look beyond Latin America—to Spain, Asia, or the Philippines—for the origins of the technique. Some say that the idea of "cooking" fish in citrus juice came across the Pacific with the galleons that controlled Spain's Asian trade through the port of Acapulco. In the Philippines, for example, there is *kinilaw*, mostly seafood "cured" in vinegar and other souring agents, which may either precede or be an offshoot of cebiche. Others look closer to home, exploring the possibility that the ancient Peruvians of the northern coast used the tart and perfumed juice of a fruit now called *tumbo* or *curuba* (*Passiflora mollissima*) to prepare fish and seafood.

But just as the same myths live in the collective memory of people as different as Eskimos and northern Europeans, "cooking" foods in an acidic medium surely has had more than one point of origin. Even if someone came up with a date and a name claiming to pinpoint the origin of cebiche outside of the Americas, I would never dismiss other possible connections—the idea of someone from the flourishing pre-Inca states of the northern Pacific coast of Peru, the Moche or their descendants the Chimu, flavoring raw mussels, clams, or fish with hot pepper and then adding a squeeze of tart fruit juice for extra flavor. I have seen passion fruit and *tumbo* seeds excavated by archaeologists from Moche sites dating from A.D. 200 to 800, side by side with hot pepper seeds and the remains of shellfish and fish bones. The natives of Peru were no strangers to vinegary brews. Their fermented corn *chicha*, which is also acidic, can coagulate the proteins of any fish or seafood just like lime or bitter orange juice.

But even if no acidic juice ever came close to a pre-Columbian cebiche, the native people of the Peruvian coast often seasoned raw seafood with briny seaweed and hot peppers, two important ingredients in some of the contemporary cebiches in the area. On a visit to the archaeological site of El Brujo on the north coast, about one hour from Trujillo, I saw the women of the fishing village of Huaca Prieta wade into the frigid waters of the Pacific—fully dressed to keep warm—to catch crustaceans, small fish, and crabs with their bare hands to sell at the market in neighboring Cartavio. As I walked back to the car, I noticed a woman cooking outside her little house. On the ground was a plastic bucket filled with tiny purple crabs, the lacy seaweed called *mococho*, and biting *ají limo*, the area's favorite hot pepper. The woman invited me to take a bite, and I grabbed a crab and a piece of seaweed. I recognized the unmistakable acidic, garlicky tang of a cebiche, the lime and garlic marking the great cultural divide brought about by the Spanish conquest.

The fact is that today's cebiches are "cooked" not with anything of local origin, but with citrus juice from Old World trees brought by the Spaniards. This seems to indicate that the Spanish colonists either embraced an existing Peruvian cooking technique, transforming it by using ingredients familiar to them, such as bitter orange and lime juice, or they came up with this cooking method on their own, independently of anything they had learned in Peru.

Anyone who marinates food in Latin America is bound to notice what acids do to seafood—they change its color and texture, firming up the flesh. We marinate everything, and we inherited this wonderful practice from medieval Spanish cooking. Look at the *Libre de Sent Soví*, a fourteenth-century Catalan cookbook, and you will find lime, orange, and vinegar marinades for fish and seafood. Doesn't it make sense to see the way the first Spanish settlers marinated their foods as one possible inspiration for the contemporary Latin cebiche?

But what puzzles me is that I can't find any direct reference to the term *cebiche* in any of the chronicles of the conquest of Peru in the sixteenth century, when cebiches seem to have been first created. The people who wrote those chronicles, even the Peruvian-born El Inca Garcilaso, tended to focus on the cuisine of the landlocked highlands, where the first capitals created by the Spaniards in the Andean region were located. Furthermore, the word is conspicuously absent in colonial cookbooks from Peru and elsewhere in the Americas. In these books, you will find plenty of *escabeches* but not a single reference to the term *cebiche* until the early nineteenth century, when a popular song dedicated to *chicha*, the fermented corn brew, lists cebiche (still the preferred spelling) among the country's national dishes. The song appeared in 1820, a year before Peru gained its independence from Spain. It was a kind of cultural independence song, proclaiming the virtues of *criollo* Peruvian foods over Spanish foods, which represented the colonial yoke. The song also reveals the traditional way of eating cebiche, with a large glass of *chicha*. Today, in many areas of Peru *chicha* and beer are the drinks of choice for cebiche. Along the north coast, *chicha* is the preferred choice.

Perhaps some of the legends surrounding the word *cebiche* can give us clues as to the origins of the term. In Peru, you hear that cebiche was created by a group of fishermen lost at sea who were forced to eat raw fish marinated with some limes they had conveniently stashed aboard. I prefer to imagine the fishermen having a great time, cutting off little bits of *anchovetas* (anchovies), as if for *cebo* (bait), and sprinkling them with lime and a bit of salt as a midday snack. Have you seen Peruvian and Chilean fishermen at work? They like to slurp oysters and clams, sea urchins and *huelpos* raw. Why not some raw fish with lime juice? But what is telling about this story is the idea that the fish for the cebiche was compared with *cebo*, bait. Perhaps the word *cebiche* was born of a creative compromise between the Spanish word *cebo* and the term *escabeche*—after all, *escabeches* are also foods cooked in an acidic medium.

In medieval Spanish, the word *cebo* also meant food—not just for fish, but for people. The word came from the Latin *cibus* (food), and it was first documented in the Castilian poems of the twelfth-century poet Gonzalo de Berceo: "And he blessed his *cebo*, when he wanted to eat." This is my own grain of salt, or squeeze of lime juice, to add to the ongoing debate. Another interesting hypothesis has been formulated by the Peruvian historian Juan José Vega, who believes that *sebiche* (the spelling he uses) is a Spanish deformation of the Arabic word *sibech*, which means acidic food (the term is related to the Arabic word for *escabeche*). Professor Vega further claims that it was the female Moorish slaves (*las moriscas*) brought by the Spaniards to Peru as cooks and servants in the early sixteenth century who first added citrus juice to the pre-Columbian preparation of raw seafood seasoned with hot pepper and seaweed.

The first Peruvian cebiches were made with the juice of Seville (bitter) oranges, the first citrus to be introduced to the New World. Until a few decades ago, the most popular fish for the cebiche was not the pristine white-fleshed sole or corvina (see page 605) that is favored today, but oily fish like bonito and smallish fish like the Peruvian anchovy and *pejerrey* (Peruvian silverside) that can be used as bait.

Another tradition embedded in the culture of cebiche is the time of day it is eaten. In northern Peru and in some other parts of the country, cebiche is a morning meal. Fish is classified as a "cold" food that can be dangerous if eaten at night. This stems from Spanish medieval and early Renaissance beliefs about food and health that go back to the ancient world, particularly the Greco-Roman theory of humors, which took firm root in Peru during the colonial period.

But in *La mesa Peruana, el libro de las familias* (The Peruvian Table, the Book of Families), a late nineteenth-century cookbook published in Arequipa, the author instructs readers to prepare a fish or crayfish cebiche (which he spells *seviche*) in the morning to eat in the afternoon. "Overcooking" the cebiche this way was common practice in Peru until a few years ago. (Today, the new chefs consider that an abomination.) The recipe calls for bitter oranges or the lime known as *limón sutil*. The name *sutil* is a deformation of the Spanish word *ceutí*, meaning from Ceuta in North Africa, where these limes were thought to have originated. The recipe ends with instructions on garnishes: "Never serve cebiche by itself," writes the author, but with some toasted corn (*cancha* or *tostado*) and boiled hominy (*mote*) or chunks of boiled corn (*choclo*). To this day, toasted corn and chunks of fresh corn are served with cebiche all over Peru, in combination with other starchy vegetables, like boiled sweet potato or yuca.

Whatever the origins of the word and the ingenious cooking method, cebiche is delicious, whichever way you spell it: cebiche, ceviche, sebiche, seviche. To me, a simple Peruvian fish cebiche is perfection—the fish cooked in the juice of bitter oranges, as was traditional, or with limes, as it is done today, flavored with thinly slivered red onions and hot peppers such as *rocoto*, fresh Andean yellow pepper (*ají amarillo*), biting *ají mochero*, or tiny *ají limo*, the whole given a touch of freshness with finely chopped cilantro. This is the cebiche against which I judge all others.

LIMA, CEBICHE CENTRAL

The nineteenth-century cookbook *La mesa Peruana* (The Peruvian Table) called cebiche a national dish (and spelled it "ceviche"), and with reason. From the highlands to the coast and across the Andes to the Peruvian Amazon, every Peruvian loves cebiche. But there is no doubt that Lima is the cebiche capital of the country.

In any market and on every beach, you will find vendors selling all types of cebiche, from black clam (*conchas negras*) to succulent corvina. After a night of partying and drinking, it is common for men to end up in the market eating cebiches—it's considered a hangover cure. On every corner, there are *cebicherías*, restaurants that specialize in seafood, where you can eat your cebiche for lunch (few people eat cebiche at dinner) without worrying about health hazards.

Lima cebiches range from homey to refined, from dirt cheap to very expensive. On one of my first visits to Lima, a group of friends took me to Estrella Náutica, a restaurant on the city's beachfront boulevard, the *costanera*. It was late at night and we sat near a window to hear the sea crashing against the stilts on which this whimsical restaurant is built—right in the ocean. An assortment of cebiches was brought to the table in a giant clamshell. They looked lovely and were well seasoned.

Now I am more likely to meet friends at the popular La Mar, Gastón Acurio's inventive *cebichería* with branches in Latin America and the United States. I also love eating cebiches at popular *cebicherías* like Punta Sal (now with five locations), where owner Adolfo Perret Bermúdez serves cebi-

ches and *tiraditos* seasoned with the assertive flavors of his home region, Piura, in northern Peru.

Some Peruvians assert that *tiraditos*, slices of raw fish closely resembling sashimi that are seasoned like cebiche, have nothing to do with the Japanese, that the concept was brought to Lima by immigrants from the northern coast. This is possible, but the Japanese who emigrated to Peru throughout the twentieth century gave *tiradito* its current form, inspired by sashimi.

I have eaten creative cebiches, some made with vegetables, chicken, or duck, cold and warm, at homes and small restaurants all over Peru. A few years ago I went to El Callao, Lima's port, looking for a small restaurant called La Cabaña de Maquila, the birthplace of a much-imitated cebiche flavored with milk and cheese. El Callao is a fascinating city dotted with beautiful old mansions that show the ravages of time and *huariques* (popular restaurants) where you can eat very well. Maquila looked like a beach shack, but Arturo García Calderón, the owner and creator of the elusive recipe, a tall, rugged man in his sixties, could not have been nicer. He took me into his tiny kitchen and demonstrated the recipe. He cut up a luscious piece of sole into bite-size pieces, placed it in a bowl with the expected slivered red onion, some parsley, lime juice, and grated Parmesan cheese, and then proceeded to open a can of evaporated milk, which he poured slowly into the cebiche while beating vigorously to make a creamy emulsion.

The recipe, which Arturo first served in 1984, has spawned countless imitators, but I had witnessed the real thing, and felt good sitting at a table in Maquila, eating Arturo's creation and looking out at the ocean.

FROM SIMPLE CEBICHES TO BAROQUE SALADS

As you move north from Peru up the Pacific Coast, cebiches become more elaborate and are seasoned with more ingredients. In many cases, the fish or seafood is blanched, even cooked through first. The shrimp cebiche you can find in Guayaquil and other coastal towns comes in a bowl with a sweet-and-sour broth, flavored with ketchup, that you eat with a spoon. I am also very fond of the fruity cebiches of highland Ecuador. Some old cooks I met in Quito use the marvelous yellow *tomate de árbol*, a beautiful Andean fruit that is sold in the United States as tamarillo or tree tomato. The cebiche is accompanied by a number of side dishes served in bowls: a spicy salsa to which lupins (*chocho*) are added, toasted corn (*tostado*), and popcorn. Coastal cebiches are usually accompanied by long plantain chips (*chifles*).

In Central America and coastal Mexico, cebiches are exceedingly popular, coming to the table dressed to the nines with chopped tomatoes and avocado. In Panama, where prepared cebiche is sold in huge plastic jars in every market, a corvina cebiche is often tossed with fruits and vegetables like the peach palm fruit (called there *pixbae*), pineapple, mango, and even apples, or mixed with mayonnaise to make a kind of salad.

In the last ten years, cebiche has increased in popularity throughout Latin America. Perhaps motivated by the success of cebiche in the United States—anything Latin that makes it in the United States then becomes a great hit in Latin America—it is no longer relegated to humble *cebicherías* and market stalls. Now people are making more cebiches at home, eating them at all hours of the day, and serving them at party buffets.

In this chapter, I give you a brief introduction to the expanding world of cebiche, but I have limited my selection to fish and seafood cebiches. I have concentrated on South American Pacific coast recipes, particularly those from Peru, which I consider the cradle of cebiche (until further notice), and its neighbor Ecuador, which has its own unique cebiche culture, to illustrate important regional variations.

MAKING GREAT CEBICHE

PURGING ONIONS (*EL DESFLEMADO*)

Ecuadorians, and to a somewhat lesser extent Peruvians, are fussy about the treatment of onions for cebiche and raw table salsas. They love raw onions but not their harsh bite. To make them less aggressive, cooks often use a simple method known by the old chemical or alchemical term *desflemado*. The technique is simple: In a bowl, toss the sliced onion with salt, allowing 1 tablespoon salt per cup of onions. Cover with hot tap water and let sit for 5 minutes. Drain in a colander and rinse well under cold running water; pat dry before using. With this "purging," onions will not dominate the whole (or give you heartburn) but rather blend in beautifully with other ingredients.

ADDING BITE

Cebiches get their heat from fresh hot peppers. In Peru, the favorite peppers are Andean *ajíes*, like the ruby red and chubby *rocoto*, the bright orange *ají amarillo* (also called *ají escabeche*), and small multicolored, intensely perfumed peppers of the *Capsicum chinense* family, such as *ají limo*, *ají montaña*, and *ají mochero*. These are all favorites in the north of the country, and in my opinion, they give the best flavor and aroma to cebiche.

Ají limo is available fresh from specialty farms at the end of the growing season, and frozen or jarred in brine in Latin markets catering to Peruvians. To use, crush the fresh, thawed, or drained pepper lightly before adding it to the cebiche, to better control the dispersion of the heat; do not chop. Both the scorching-hot habanero and the Scotch bonnet pepper, which share a potent herbal aroma, can be used interchangeably with *ají limo*. The Brazilian *pimenta de cheiro* and the *cumari* pepper, available jarred or fresh in farmers' markets, have a similar herbal, musky aroma. If you must, use any hot pepper with bite, such as jalapeño and serrano, but I suggest you seek out hot peppers with great aroma.

ADDING UMAMI

In many parts of Peru, cooks enhance the flavor of their cebiches by adding a pinch of a seasoning powder called *aji-no-moto* to the lime juice. This is actually monosodium glutamate, which was popularized by the Chinese and Japanese communities of Lima. Pedro Miguel Schiaffino, a young Lima chef, uses instead a concentrated broth made with seaweed or tuna flakes.

Another natural way to add umami to cebiche is to season it with a savory, milky broth composed of seasoned fish juices combined with fish broth; it is called *leche de tigre*, tiger's milk. This is one of the secrets of the tasty cebiches of the northern coast. Cooks first prepare a concentrated broth by boiling fish bones with some garlic and onion. Then they season the fish trimmings with salt, lime juice, and hot pepper and grind them in a blender with some of the broth. They strain the resulting mixture through a sieve to extract the fish juices. Some people spike the tiger's milk with pisco and drink it as an aphrodisiac and restorative, but most use it to flavor to cebiche; see pages 485 and 486.

TEN TIPS

1. Above all, use only the freshest ingredients. Ask your fishmonger for sashimi-grade fish.
2. Select firm-fleshed fish that will not fall apart when marinated in an acidic medium. There is no limitation on the type of ocean fish you can use, as long as it is very fresh. In Peru, cebiches have been made traditionally with both oily and white-fleshed fish. Among my favorite white-fleshed fish for cebiches are sole, grouper, flounder, halibut, and red snapper. Oily fish such as mackerel and small fish like smelts are also delicious.
3. Use a very sharp knife and a clean cutting board to make all your cebiches and *tiraditos*.
4. Some cooks recommend soaking the fish in salted cold water first to firm up the flesh.
5. If you like, use the fish bones and trimmings to make the broth called tiger's milk, which is traditionally added to the cebiche of the north Peruvian coast to enhance flavor (see pages 485 and 486).
6. Squeeze the limes only a few minutes before making the cebiche.
7. To tone down the acidity of the lime juice, add some ice cubes; remove before the ice melts completely, or it will water down the flavor.
8. To control the heat of the cebiche, do not chop the hot pepper. Add it seeded but whole, or split in half, to the lime juice. Then remove it, if you wish, once you have obtained the desired degree of heat.
9. Do not overmarinate the fish; it will become tough. Let the fish stand in the cebiche marinade just long enough for it to lose its translucency.
10. Serve the cebiche accompanied by boiled sweet and starchy vegetables such as corn, sweet potato, and yuca. These traditional garnishes help tone down the acidity of the lime. ◆

Simple Tiger's Milk for Peruvian Cebiches

Leche de Tigre Simple

Sex and cebiche go together; that's what Peruvians think. To keep those juices flowing, Peruvian men like to spike the tart and spicy liquid of their beloved cebiches with aromatic Peruvian pisco and drink it as a cocktail. Long ago I had a taste of one such cocktail called *leche de pantera* (panther's milk), a brew the color of *café con leche*, in Piura. I later learned that it was made with the juices of a black clam cebiche. I also tasted a lighter-colored cocktail called *leche de tigre* (tiger's milk) made with fish cebiche juices and a strong dose of pisco, and I found another such brew called *leche de monja* (nun's milk). Having survived an elementary school run by very stern Spanish and Cuban nuns, that was a drink I could not bring myself to try.

In Peruvian restaurants, particularly in Lima, tiger's milk has now become synonymous with a cebiche-enhancing broth that takes the place of the popular *aji-no-moto* (monosodium glutamate) to give umami to the dish. It is also served in shot glasses as an amuse-bouche at elegant Peruvian restaurants. At its simplest and most practical, it calls for a fish broth made with fish bones and blended with some leftover fish to make a milky broth that is added to the cebiche after the fish or seafood has been "cooked" or "cured" in the lime juice. It tones down the acidity of the lime and gives depth to the cebiche.

MAKES 1 CUP

For the Broth

1 pound fish bones and some fleshy trimmings
1 quart water
1 medium red onion (about 8 ounces), halved
1 celery stick, coarsely chopped
3 whole garlic cloves
3–4 cilantro sprigs
Salt to taste

For Finishing the Dish

Fish trimmings, coarsely chopped (about ½ cup)
1 teaspoon lime juice
Salt to taste

Making the Broth ▶ Place the fish bones and trimmings in a medium pot with the water and add the onion, celery, garlic, cilantro, and salt. Bring to a boil over medium heat. Lower the heat and simmer for about 40 minutes to obtain a well flavored broth. Strain and reserve 1 cup of the broth. Use the rest of the broth for another use or make more tiger's milk as needed.

Making the Tiger's Milk ▶ Place the broth, chopped fish trimmings, lime juice, and salt in a blender and process lightly, making sure not to liquefy all the fish. Strain and place in a small bowl. Refrigerate, covered with plastic film, until ready to use in your cebiche.

Variation: Huaca Pucllana's Tiger's Milk
The Huaca Pucllana is one of my favorite Lima restaurants, where I go to be pampered by its owner, Arturo Rubio, and to eat the pristine and very elegant cebiches of chef Marilú Madueño. The Huaca's tiger's milk is a well-seasoned broth with all the classic flavors of a Lima cebiche: *rocoto*, fresh yellow

Andean pepper, *ají limo*, celery, ginger, red onion, and lime juice, processed in a blender with fish trimmings until barely liquefied, and strained. More than a flavor enhancer, it is the flavor base of the restaurant's cebiches and is prepared in large quantities.

Scallop Cebiche in *Tumbo* Juice

Cebiche de Conchitas en Jugo de Tumbo

One theory about the origin of cebiche is that ancient Peruvians from the coast used the tart juice of a fruit called *tumbo*, a relative of passion fruit, to "cook" raw seafood. When I first read about this idea I decided to try it at home—I could get *tumbo* juice frozen in my local market.

Before committing a couple of pounds of expensive scallops to the experiment, I started discreetly, filling two bowls with *tumbo* juice and putting a piece of sea bass in one bowl and a scallop in the other. I found that the fish took too long to become opaque and did not benefit much in flavor from the fruit juice, but with scallops, it was another matter altogether. After 30 minutes, they lost their translucent quality and tasted sweet and tender. After an hour, they were perfect.

What to Drink: Viña Esmeralda, a blend of Moscatel and Gewürztraminer from Penedès, Spain

SERVES 6

- 1 large red onion (12 ounces), finely slivered lengthwise
  Salt
- 1 pound bay or sea scallops, quartered if large

- 2 garlic cloves, finely chopped
- 16 ounces frozen *tumbo* juice (sold as *curuba* pulp in most Hispanic markets), thawed, or 2 cups passion fruit juice
- 3 scallions, white and 3 inches of green parts, finely chopped
- 2 tablespoons finely chopped cilantro
- 1 tablespoon ground *mirasol* pepper (page 54)

▶ Purge the onion with salt according to the instructions on page 139. Drain. Combine the onion, scallops, 1 teaspoon salt, garlic, *tumbo* juice, scallions, cilantro, and ground pepper in a bowl and let stand, refrigerated, for 1 to 2 hours. This cebiche will keep well in the refrigerator, covered, for up to 2 days. Serve in small bowls.

Grouper Cebiche with Tiger's Milk in the Style of Northern Peru

Cebiche de Mero Norteño con Leche de Tigre

The provinces of northern Peru—Piura, Trujillo, Lambayeque—are known for their good food and assertive seasonings. One can tell a northern Peruvian cebiche a mile away. The fish is seldom cut neatly but is rather sliced into irregular strips, the onions are always tossed with the seafood, and the cebiche is usually garnished with chunks of boiled corn, sweet potato, and yuca. In some communities, such as Moche, a small town near Trujillo, cebiche is served with a side dish of toasted Andean corn. What gives heat to the cebiches of both Moche and Trujillo is *ají mochero*, a bitingly hot pepper that looks like a small, more tapered jalapeño, and slices of red *rocoto*, a chubby Andean pepper.

What to Drink: Peruvian beers, such as Pilsen Callao, Cusqueña, or Cristal

SERVES 6

For the Vegetable Sides

1 pound (trimmed weight) fresh or frozen yuca, cut into 3-inch sections, boiled according to the instructions on page 167, drained, and kept warm

2 medium Caribbean sweet potatoes (*boniatos*) or orange-fleshed North American sweet potatoes (about 1¾ pounds), peeled, cut into 1- to 2-inch slices, boiled according to the instructions on page 171, drained, and kept warm

For the Cebiche

1 medium red onion (8 ounces), thinly slivered lengthwise
  Salt

1½ pounds skinless grouper fillets
  Juice of 8 limes (about 1 cup)

1 tablespoon finely chopped cilantro

1 *ají mochero*, habanero, or Scotch bonnet pepper, seeded and lightly crushed

¼ cup Simple Tiger's Milk (page 485)

For the Garnishes

1 cup Ecuadorian Toasted Corn (page 154)

½ fresh-frozen red *rocoto* pepper or 2 red jalapeños, seeded and sliced into thin rings

Preparing the Vegetable Sides ▶ Cut the boiled yuca into serving pieces. Leave the sweet potato in

slices, as is traditional in the north of Peru, or cut into 1- to 2-inch cubes. Keep warm until ready to serve.

Preparing the Cebiche ▶ Purge the onion with salt according to the instructions on page 139. Drain and set aside.

Cut the fish into irregular strips about 1½ inches long. Then cut into ½-inch-wide chunks no more than ½ inch thick and place in a medium bowl. Cover with cold water and stir in 1 tablespoon salt. Let stand for 15 minutes. Drain and rinse in a colander under running cold water. Pat dry and put in a bowl.

In a small bowl, mix the onion, lime juice, cilantro, *ají mochero* or other hot pepper, and ¾ teaspoon salt. Add a couple of ice cubes to cool and tone down the acidity of the lime; remove before they melt completely. Pour the liquid over the fish and toss to mix. Let stand until the fish begins to look opaque. Then immediately pour the tiger's milk over the cebiche.

To serve, mound the cebiche on a serving platter and garnish with the yuca and sweet potatoes and toasted corn. Spoon into individual soup plates with the vegetable garnish.

Huanchaco Fish Cebiche

Cebiche de Pescado al Estilo de Huanchaco

Margot Verna Isla and her sister María Jesús run the lovely Restaurante El Caribe with great energy and charm. This homey storefront restaurant in the beach town of Huanchaco in northern Peru is a seafood haven and my favorite place in town to eat cebiche. The sisters like to work with white-fleshed

Pacific fish like corvina, the succulent *ojo de uva*, and grouper.

El Caribe's cebiche is minimalist: just enough red onion for crunch, a barely discernible trace of cilantro for fragrance, the right amount of lime juice for balanced acidity, and a couple of crushed *limo* peppers for heat. Crushing rather than chopping this fiery pepper releases its heat more gently into the lime and fish juices. This way the hot peppers are also easier to remove if you prefer your cebiche on the milder side.

This is the emblematic cebiche combination throughout Peru's Libertad department. Like most northern Peruvian cebiches, the dish is not complete without its starchy sides of piping-hot boiled yuca, sweet potato, and Andean white corn, along with a small bowl of toasted corn (*cancha* or *tostado*) at the table. You are supposed to bundle a little bit of everything onto your fork and eat it together for a symphony of contrasting flavors and textures—the crunch of the toasted corn, the sweetness of the potatoes, the mealy quality of the Andean corn, and the juicy acidity of the lime mingling with the briny taste of the fish.

Working Ahead ▶ Since the fish should not steep in the lime juice for more than a few minutes, it is important to prepare the vegetables ahead and keep them warm until it is time to serve the cebiche. The toasted corn can be made 1 or 2 days ahead and kept in a tightly sealed container. The fish should not look completely opaque at the time of serving but remain a bit translucent.

What to Drink: Peruvian beer, such as Pilsen Callao

SERVES 6

For the Vegetable Sides

1 pound (trimmed weight) yuca, cut into 3-inch sections, boiled according to the instructions on page 167, drained, and kept warm

2 medium Caribbean sweet potatoes (*boniatos*) or North American sweet potatoes (about 1¾ pounds), peeled, cut into 2-inch slices, and boiled according to the instructions on page 171, drained, and kept warm

1 large ear frozen Andean corn, thawed and cut into 1-inch pinwheels, boiled according to instructions on page 561, drained, and kept warm

1 cup Ecuadorian Toasted Corn (page 154)

For the Cebiche

2 pounds skinless grouper or sole fillets

2 teaspoons salt, or to taste

¾ cup fresh lime juice (from 6–7 limes)

4 garlic cloves, mashed to a paste with a mortar and pestle or finely chopped and mashed

1 small red onion (about 6 ounces), finely slivered lengthwise

2 fresh or frozen *limo*, habanero, or Scotch bonnet peppers (preferably yellow), seeded, deveined, and lightly crushed

1 tablespoon finely chopped cilantro

Preparing the Vegetable Sides ▶ Cut the yuca into serving pieces. Leave the sweet potatoes in slices, as is traditional in the north of Peru, or cut into 1- to 2-inch cubes. Keep warm until ready to serve.

Preparing the Cebiche ▶ Place the fish in a colander and rinse under cold running water. Drain and pat dry. Cut each fillet lengthwise in half, then cut across on an angle into ¼- to ½-inch pieces. Place in a medium bowl.

Toss the fish with the salt and let stand for 5 minutes.

Add the lime juice, garlic, onion, hot peppers, and cilantro to the fish and toss together. (In Lima, cooks often add a couple of ice cubes to the cebiche both to cool the juices and to tone down the acidity of the lime).

Serving: Serve immediately in individual soup plates with the yuca, sweet potato, Andean corn, and some toasted corn.

Marisa Guiulfo's Lima Fish Cebiche

Cebiche Limeño de Marisa Guiulfo

Lima's cebiches are tamer than those in the north. In more elegant restaurants and in many homes, they are served with the slivered red onions on top of the fish, a frilly side of toasted corn kernels, and a few slices of *rocoto* pepper as a garnish. That's how I ate it at the beach home of Marisa Guiulfo, Lima's premier caterer and restaurateur.

Marisa had invited me to spend the weekend at her house in Pucusana, a fishing village near Lima, where she cooked almost nonstop for a stream of visitors. The cebiche looked lovely on a large white oval platter. While she was putting it together, I noticed the wisdom of using corn kernels and cubed sweet potatoes as garnish for ease of serving. She was feeding a hungry crowd!

What to Drink: Peruvian-Style Pisco Sour (page 356)

SERVES 6

For the Vegetable Sides

- 1 cup frozen Andean corn kernels (available in Latin markets), boiled according to the directions on page 561
- 2 medium orange-fleshed sweet potatoes (about 1 pound), peeled, cut into 1-inch cubes, and boiled according to the directions on page 171
- 1 cup Ecuadorian Toasted Corn (page 154)

For the Cebiche

- 2 pounds skinless sole, flounder, grouper, red snapper, or halibut fillets
- 2 teaspoons salt
- 4 garlic cloves, finely chopped
- 1 large red onion (about 12 ounces), finely slivered lengthwise
  Juice of 8 limes (about 1 cup)
- 1 fresh-frozen Andean yellow pepper (*ají amarillo*), cut into thin slivers
- 1 tablespoon finely chopped cilantro

For the Garnish

- 1 small fresh or frozen *rocoto* pepper, seeded and cut into thin rings, or 2 red jalapeños, thinly sliced
  Cilantro leaves

Preparing the Vegetable Sides ▶ Drain the boiled corn and sweet potatoes and place on separate plates. Place the toasted corn in a decorative bowl.

Preparing the Cebiche ▶ Cut the fillets into ¾-inch cubes. Place in a bowl and toss with the salt and garlic. Let stand for at least 10 minutes.

In a small bowl, mix together the onion, lime juice, hot pepper, and cilantro. Add 2 to 3 ice cubes to cool the liquid and to tone down the acidity of the lime juice. Taste and add more ice if needed, but remove the ice cubes before they melt completely.

Pour the lime juice and onions over the fish, and let stand for 10 minutes, or until the fish is opaque.

Serving: Transfer the fish to a deep serving platter or shallow bowl. Place the boiled corn kernels on one side of the cebiche and the diced sweet potatoes on the opposite side. Top with the pepper slices and a couple of cilantro leaves.

Sole *Tiradito*

Tiradito de Lenguado

Eduardo Peschiera is a busy man. When I met him he was traveling back and forth between his native Lima and Santiago de Chile, in which cities he owned three successful Peruvian restaurants, all beautiful and called El Otro Sitio (The Other Place). I ate in all of them, but my favorite remains the original, housed in a colonial mansion that stands near one of the most poetic corners of Lima, El Puente de los Suspiros, the Bridge of Sighs. Several years ago, I tasted a lovely *tiradito* there, fresh and delicious, lovingly presented in pristine china and garnished with huge kernels of mealy white Andean corn.

Tiradito comes from the Spanish word *tira*, strip. To make *tiradito*, the fish is cut into thin slices, almost like sashimi.

SERVES 6

- 1 pound sole fillets
- 1 fresh-frozen Andean yellow pepper (*ají amarillo*), cut into thin slivers

- 1 tablespoon finely chopped cilantro
- 3 garlic cloves, finely chopped
  Juice of 4 limes (about ½ cup)
- 2 tablespoons pisco, preferably Pisco Italia
- ½ teaspoon salt
- 2 ice cubes

▶ Cut the fillets into 1-inch-wide by 1-inch-thick pieces. Cut straight down against the grain into ½-inch-thick slices. Fan the fish slices on a large platter and top with the slivered pepper and chopped cilantro. Mix the garlic, lime juice, pisco, salt, and ice cubes in a small bowl and pour over the fish. Serve immediately.

Mackerel *Tiradito* with Bitter Orange Juice, Chilean Paprika Oil, and Fava Beans

Tiradito de Caballa con Naranja Agria, Color Chilena, y Habas

Here is my own version of *tiradito*, thin strips of the freshest mackerel colored with paprika-infused olive oil and garnished with fava beans.

Cook's Note: For this dish, use Boston mackerel (*Scomber japonicus*, available in Japanese or Korean markets), not Spanish mackerel.

SERVES 6

- 1 pound sashimi-grade Boston mackerel fillets
- ¼ cup fresh bitter orange juice or equal parts lime juice and orange juice
  Salt and freshly grated white pepper to taste

2 pounds fresh fava beans, shelled (about 2 cups), cooked according to the directions on page 268, and peeled

¼ cup plus 2 tablespoons Chilean Paprika-Infused Oil (page 91)

1 tablespoon Chilean Hot Pepper Sauce (page 131)

2 whole garlic cloves, peeled

3 tablespoons finely chopped cilantro

▶ Cut the fillets crosswise into 3-inch-wide by 1-inch-thick pieces. Cut against the grain into ¼-inch-thick slices.

In a medium bowl, combine the citrus juice, salt, and pepper. Add the fish and marinate, about 2 minutes. Drain.

Mound the fava beans in the center of a large serving platter and arrange the fish around them.

In a small skillet, heat the oil and the hot pepper sauce. Add the garlic and sauté until golden, about 20 seconds. Strain the oil mixture, discarding the garlic, and pour over the fish and fava beans. Sprinkle with the chopped cilantro. Serve immediately.

Coque Ossio's Flounder *Tiradito* with Yellow Pepper Cream

Tiradito a la Crema de Ají Amarillo al Estilo de Coque Ossio

Chef Coque Ossio comes from a family of great cooks. His mother, Marisa Guiulfo, Lima's preeminent caterer, is an inspired cook with a million terrific ideas for entertaining at home. Marinating the cebiche with a creamy sauce spiked with the fresh

Andean yellow pepper (*ají amarillo*) is a contemporary twist on the classic cebiche theme that has become exceedingly popular in Lima. The idea for using the *ají amarillo* this way comes from Humberto Sato, the Japanese chef of Costanera 700, a restaurant that made history in Lima (it has since been relocated to Miraflores). Sato processes the peppers with some broth in a blender and adds them to a base of red onions, sliced *ají limo*, celery, a bit of sugar, *aji-no-moto*, and the fish. Coque has given it his own twist.

What to Drink: Cucharamama Peruvian-Style Pisco Sour (page 356) or Pilsen Callao beer

SERVES 4

¼ cup fresh Key lime juice or Persian lime juice

½ teaspoon salt, plus more to taste

6 garlic cloves, finely chopped

1 *ají limo* (available pickled in Hispanic markets), rinsed, seeded, deveined, and finely chopped, or 1 fresh jalapeño or serrano, seeded, deveined, and finely chopped

1 tablespoon Andean yellow pepper paste (sold in Latin American markets as *pasta de ají amarillo*) or 1 fresh-frozen Andean yellow pepper (*ají amarillo*), seeded and ground to a paste with 2 tablespoons water in a small processor

1 tablespoon finely chopped cilantro
Freshly ground white pepper, to taste

1 pound skinless flounder fillets

1 cup frozen Andean corn kernels, boiled according to the directions on page 561, drained, and kept warm, for garnish.

▶ In a small bowl, whisk together the lime juice, salt, garlic, chopped pepper, yellow pepper paste, cilantro, and white pepper. If using immediately, add a few cubes of ice to cool the mixture and tone down the acidity of the lime juice; remove the ice cubes before they melt completely. If not, cover and refrigerate. Cut the fillets into 1-inch-wide, 1-inch-thick pieces. Cut against the grain into ½-inch-thick slices.

Fan the slices on a large platter and season with salt to taste. Pour the lime juice mixture over the fish and serve at once, garnished with the corn.

Ecuadorian Highland Cebiche with Tree Tomato

Ceviche Ecuatoriano Serrano con Tomate de Árbol

I adore the highland cebiches of Ecuador, which are enriched with the pureed Andean yellow tamarillos (tree tomatoes). I learned how to make it from two elderly sisters from Quito, Berta and Elisa Peña, who warned me not to use red tamarillos, because they come from Colombia. The best seafood for these kinds of cebiche are shrimp and corvina.

SERVES 6

- 1 large red onion (12 ounces), finely slivered lengthwise
- 2 teaspoons salt, plus more to taste
- 3 cilantro sprigs
- 1 pound medium shrimp with shells
- 6 yellow tamarillos
- 4 garlic cloves, finely chopped
- 1 fresh or frozen Ecuadorian hot red pepper (*ají colorado*; see page 60), or 1 fresh cayenne or jalapeño, preferably red, seeded and finely chopped

Juice of 4 limes (about ½ cup)
- ¼ cup finely chopped cilantro

▶ Purge the onion with salt according to the instructions on page 139. Drain and set aside.

Place 5 cups water, 2 teaspoons salt, and the cilantro in a large saucepan and bring to a boil over medium-high heat. Add the shrimp and cook for 1 minute. Drain and let cool, then peel and devein.

Place the tamarillos in a medium saucepan and add water to cover. Bring to a boil, then reduce the heat and simmer for 10 minutes, or until soft. Drain and let cool. Peel the tamarillos, place in a blender or food processor, and puree. Strain to remove the seeds.

Place the shrimp in a bowl, add the onion, tamarillo puree, and remaining ingredients, and toss well. Add salt to taste and toss again.

Serving: Ecuadorian cebiches are saucy, so serve in a bowl. If you want the full *serrano* (highland) experience, set out small bowls with the classic garnishes of Ecuadorian Toasted Corn (page 154), Boiled Lupins (page 283), and Ecuadorian Popcorn (page 155) for guests to scatter over each helping.

Ecuadorian Soupy Coastal Shrimp Cebiche

Ceviche Ecuatoriano de Camarones de la Costa

The people of coastal Ecuador prepare a shrimp cebiche so liquidy that it is often eaten with a soup spoon. The shrimp are blanched in a seasoned broth that is later added to the cebiche base of onions, hot pepper, and cilantro. Adding a touch of ketchup and often mustard at the table is traditional.

SERVES 6

1 large red onion (12 ounces), finely slivered lengthwise
  Salt
3 cilantro sprigs
½ small white onion (8 ounces), halved
1 pound medium shrimp with shells
1 fresh or frozen Ecuadorian hot red pepper (*ají colorado*; see page 60) or 1 fresh cayenne pepper or jalapeño, preferably red, finely chopped (optional)
½ cup fresh lime juice (from about 4 limes)
½ cup fresh orange juice
2 tablespoons finely chopped cilantro

▶ Purge the red onion with 1 tablespoon salt according to the instructions on page 139. Drain and set aside.

Place 5 cups water, 2 teaspoons salt, and the cilantro and white onion in a large saucepan and bring to a boil over medium-high heat. Add the shrimp and cook for 1 minute. Drain, reserving 1 cup of the cooking liquid, and let cool.

Peel and devein the shrimp.

Place the drained red onion in a bowl and toss with 1 teaspoon salt, the hot pepper, and the citrus juices. Add the shrimp and toss to mix. Add the reserved cooking liquid and the chopped cilantro. Refrigerate until well chilled.

Serving: This cebiche is downright soupy, so serve in bowls with spoons for people to eat the juices. Also, encourage guests to add dollops of ketchup and mustard to the cebiche and stir well before eating. Set out small bowls of Ecuadorian Popcorn (page 155) and Plantain Chips (page 181) for each guest.

Ecuadorian Shrimp Cebiche with Peanuts in the Style of Jipijapa

Ceviche de Camarones con Maní al Estilo de Jipijapa

This is my version of a delicious cebiche I tasted in Jipijapa, an old colonial town in the province of Manabí. What makes it different from other tomato-enriched cebiches from coastal Ecuador is the addition of a dollop of peanut butter right before serving. The fresh tomato sauce seasoned with lime and orange juice is soupy and delicious. Ecuadorian cebiches are not overly spicy, as people prefer to add the hot pepper to their food at the table. I sometimes use red serranos or jalapeños, but I also love the stronger heat and aroma imparted by peppers of the habanero or Scotch bonnet type, which do occur in the Andes.

MAKES 6 APPETIZER PORTIONS

For the Shrimp

- 1 pound medium shrimp, with shells and heads
- ½ large red onion (about 6 ounces), peeled
  A few sprigs of cilantro
- 2 teaspoons coarse sea salt
- 1 teaspoon black peppercorns
- 6 cups water

For the Onion Relish

- 1 large red onion (about 12 ounces), thinly slivered lengthwise
- 1 tablespoon salt
- 1–2 red serrano peppers, jalapeños, or Scotch bonnet peppers, stemmed and thinly sliced crosswise
  Juice of 4 large limes, about ½ cup
- 1 garlic clove, mashed to a paste
- 2 tablespoons finely chopped cilantro or more to taste

For the Tomato Cebiche Sauce

- 2 pounds very red vine-ripened medium tomatoes, cored and coarsely chopped
  Juice of 4 large oranges, about 1¼ cups
- 3 tablespoons ketchup
- 2 teaspoons salt, or to taste

For the Peanut Butter

- 4 ounces (about 1 cup) lightly roasted unsalted shelled peanuts (see Cook's Note, page 470)

Additional Garnishes

Dijon or yellow mustard
Fresh cilantro
Coarsely chopped roasted peanuts
Long or round Plantain Chips (page 181)

Preparing the Shrimp ▶ Rinse the shrimp, then peel and devein. Place the shells and heads in a medium pot with the onion, cilantro, salt, and peppercorns. Cover with the water and bring to a boil over medium heat. Cook for 5 to 10 minutes. Remove the shells and solids with a slotted spoon and add the shrimp. Cook for barely 1 minute, remove to a medium bowl, and let cool. Reserve ¼ cup of the liquid and set aside.

Preparing the Onion Relish ▶ Purge the onion with the salt, according to the directions on page 139. Add the hot pepper, lime juice, garlic, and cilantro and toss to combine. Add the shrimp and mix well. Let rest for about 10 minutes.

Preparing the Tomato Cebiche Sauce ▶ Place the tomatoes in a blender or food processor and process into a smooth puree (makes about 3 cups). Push through a medium-mesh strainer into a bowl. Combine with the orange juice, ketchup, and reserved shrimp broth and season with salt. Pour over the shrimp and stir to combine. Refrigerate until lightly chilled.

Preparing the Peanut Butter ▶ While the cebiche chills, prepare the fresh peanut butter. Place the peanuts in a small food processor and process at high speed until chunky. Scoop out into a serving bowl.

Serving: Divide the shrimp and a generous amount of sauce among 6 wide bowls or soup plates. Right before serving, place a dollop of peanut butter and a bit of mustard (if desired) over the shrimp. Garnish with fresh cilantro and some chopped peanuts and bring to the table with a bowl of Plantain Chips (page 181). Let your guests crumble some of the chips over the cebiche. This dish is normally eaten with a spoon, as the sauce is very soupy.

Black Clam Cebiche

Cebiche de Conchas Negras

When shucked, these hefty Pacific Ocean clams (*Anadara tuberculosa*) are a shockingly carnal sight—moist, quivering clams stained red and oozing black ink, like flesh parting open. What makes them even more dramatic is that there is no merciful transition between the raw and the cooked. You must take them as they are, in all their fleshy and savage glory. If you can push past the initial jolt, though, you will be rewarded with a delicate, intensely flavored clam, a favorite ingredient for cebiches all along the warm Pacific from El Salvador to northern Peru.

Cook's Notes: If you can't find black clams, you can use large hard-shell clams and add some squid ink to the liquid of the cebiche to stain it with the dark color characteristic of the *concha negra* juices.

> Before shucking the clams, place them in a large bowl, cover with water, and let stand for at least 20 minutes prior to opening. The sand will settle at the bottom of the bowl.

SERVES 4

- 1 medium red onion (8 ounces), thinly slivered lengthwise
  Salt
- 12 *conchas negras*, or large hard-shell clams, like quahogs, shucked, juices reserved
  About ½ cup fresh lime juice (from 4 limes)
- 1 *ají limo*, habanero or Scotch bonnet pepper, lightly crushed
- 2 tablespoons finely chopped cilantro

▶ Purge the onion with 1 tablespoon salt following the instructions on page 139. Drain.

Mix the onion, clams, lime juice, pepper, cilantro, 1 teaspoon salt, and reserved clam juices in a bowl. Let stand for 15 minutes before serving.

Sea Urchin Roe with Chilean *Pebre*

Lenguas de Erizo en Pebre a la Chilena

Chile's windswept coast yields many sensuous though hard-won treasures, like sea urchin roe, shielded from prying hands by bristling needles. In winter, the roe swells up, becoming succulent and sweet. That's when Chileans rush to Santiago's Mercado Central to savor the treat that they call "tongues" (*lenguas*) rather than "roe" (*huevas*). The Mercado Central, the Sistine Chapel of Pacific seafood, is a beautiful ornate Beaux Arts cast-iron and glass structure. Under the huge dome and clustered around a central courtyard are elegant restaurants that compete for space with seafood and fruit vendors.

The pioneer of the restaurant scene there is Donde Augusto, owned by a seasoned fishmonger and his wife. I once visited the kitchen and was stunned to see a handful of cooks cleaning what seemed to be a mountain of live sea urchins. The first time I ate there, my Chilean friend Miro Popiç taught me not to chew the roe but to savor it in my mouth, allowing its intense marine flavor and strange rose-petal fragrance to expand for a few seconds before I gulped it down. I love to season the roe at the table with a squeeze of one of the tiny limes from Pica (a relative of the Key lime) or with a spoonful of the restaurant's lovely cilantro *pebre* (a sauce similar to chimichurri) just seconds before popping it into my mouth.

What to Drink: At Donde Augusto, Miro Popiç taught me that the best drink to accompany the roe is a cheap, oxidized wine called Las Encinas that tastes like dry sherry. A Spanish amontillado sherry, such as Alvear Amontillado from Montilla-Moriles, is also delicious.

SERVES 4

Roe from 12 large sea urchins (ask your fishmonger to prepare the roe)
2 cups Chilean "Goat's Horn" *Pebre* (page 131) or Patagonian *Pebre* Sauce with *Merkén* (page 132)

▶ Place the roe in a small bowl and pass it around with the *pebre*, allowing your guests to serve themselves. Eating sea urchins is a very personal experience.

LA OLLA: Soups and Hearty Potages

If I were to conjure up Latin American cooking in a single image, it would be a woman standing over a simmering soup pot and stirring. The scene could be anywhere: outdoors under cooling palm fronds, at a roadside stand, near a potato field in the Bolivian highlands, or in a modern urban kitchen. Latin American cooking is womanly, slow, and round like the *olla*, the soup pot that is always being stirred.

In Latin America, soup is as predictable as the sunrise—which for many people is greeted with a bowl of soup. To warm themselves up on chilly mornings, the people of Bucaramanga in the Colombian Andes savor *chingua*, a comforting milk and potato soup garnished with poached eggs, dunking pieces of corn *arepas* into the ivory broth while sipping their coffee. In the barren Bolivian *altiplano* early in the morning, amid wheat and potato fields, you see farmers huddled around a pot of soup that might contain slowly simmering potatoes and *mote* (Andean hominy), flavored with a piece of freeze-dried lamb (*chalona*). This spartan breakfast will sustain them until the noonday meal (also soup) or perhaps even until sunset. Chileans consider nothing as restorative the morning after a night of partying as a bowl of concentrated fish broth. The men flock to the local markets at the crack of down and gulp down the steamy broth, standing up as if they were drinking a cup of espresso.

All over Latin America, the noon meal, the most important one of the day, has traditionally included soup. It can be as basic as a clear chicken broth seasoned with cilantro and epazote, as Mexicans like it; a chicken noodle soup; or a one-pot soup brimming with meats and starchy vegetables. In urban households throughout the highlands of Ecuador, a potato and cheese soup colored gold with achiote often anchors the noon meal. People eat the soup with rice and a little salad, as if they were eating a stew. Sometimes the soup itself provides different courses, when its various components are served in separate plates. I call these "pregnant soups," because they magically materialize in several dishes. These bountiful soups can be the center of a meal or the focus of holiday entertaining. How often have my Latin friends asked me, "Would you like to join us for lunch this weekend to eat a big soup?" It's an invitation I never decline, whether the dish in question is Cuban *ajiaco*, Uruguayan or Yucatecan *puchero*, Brazilian *feijoada*, or Andean *locro*.

Each of the soups of Latin America is distinguished by the ingredients specific to the region where it is served. Hispanic Caribbean soups feature tropical tubers like yuca and *malanga* and sturdy vegetables such as plantains and pumpkin. In the Andean highlands, from Colombia to Chile, potatoes (both fresh and freeze-dried) rule, along with corn in different forms and other grains. And wherever a rice culture has taken root in the Americas, you will find lavish soups featuring rice. Some are as thick as a risotto. The Puerto Rican *asopao*, for example, calls for just a bit more broth than some of the island's popular rice and chicken dishes. The Peruvian *aguadito* is a more liquid version of a similar idea, seasoned with Andean yellow pepper (*ají amarillo*), either fresh or dried, and a variety of meats and seafood.

In Chile and other coastal areas, people favor seafood soups. Some are concentrated clear broths made with fish heads like the Chilean *caldos criatureros* (broths said to make you have children); others are like chowders, enriched with coconut milk and thickened with plantains, peanuts, yuca, or potatoes, such as the *sangos* and *biches* of Ecuador. You are likely to find coconut milk soups anywhere in the tropical Americas where Africans settled, from the Caribbean coast of Honduras to the Pacific coast of Ecuador. I am partial to the conch chowder of Honduras, in which coconut milk provides a silky matrix for ivory morsels of conch and a rich array of tropical vegetables from plantain to chayote.

When I travel to Chile, I rush from the airport to the central market of Santiago de Chile—never mind jet lag—to eat *caldillo de congrio*, the country's famous fish and potato soup, a rich concoction of firm, succulent conger eel steaks simmered in a broth seasoned with a simple base of garlic, onions, and tomatoes. I love to sit at the pristine white-tablecloth-covered tables on one side of the market, surrounded by fruits and vegetables, freshly butchered meats, and live seafood. A solicitous waiter who responds, "*Sí, reina,* (Yes, queen)" to every question comes to the table with a black earthenware bowl from Pomaire filled to the brim with the steamy soup.

Bean soups are another constant throughout Latin America. In Mexico, these soups run on the lighter side. Peasant women on a ranch near Tzintzuntzan in Pátzcuaro, for instance, season their bean soups simply with some lard and epazote, and the beans swim in their cooking liquid. In the Hispanic Caribbean, as well as in Venezuela, Ecuador, and Peru, bean soups, sometimes called *potajes* (potages) or *menestras*, are rich and stewlike and often involve one or more tubers and vegetables. Latin cooks are very fussy about the quality of the beans, choosing only those that will remain whole and creamy after cooking. The stewed beans could be eaten like soup by themselves, but they are more likely to be served over or alongside white or yellow rice with a meat,

fish, or chicken dish. When used this way, I think of these soups as bean sauces that give flavor to the rice.

In this chapter, you will find the whole panoply of soups we Latins bring to our tables at different hours of the day: the big classic soups that are the centerpieces of a special meal, such as Cuban *ajiaco* and the *sancocho*—baroque stick-to-the-ribs concoctions that call for everything but the kitchen sink and send you off to siesta-land; nourishing bean soups that range from the lighter soups of Mexico to the thick and hearty potages of the Hispanic Caribbean; creamy vegetable soups that are delicious, elegant starters for an evening meal; cheese and nut-enriched Andean soups; hearty seafood soups and chowders; and light soups that entice the palate with the clean, vibrant flavors and aroma of Seville orange, cilantro, and epazote. And, finally, there are essential broths that can serve as flavor backbones for any cooking.

THE BIG SOUP: BUILDING LAYERS OF FLAVOR IN THE POT

When the Spaniards arrived in the Americas, they carried memories of hearty soups and eternally bubbling cauldrons. An illuminated page of *Las cantigas de Santa María* (*The Canticles of Holy Mary*), a virtual encyclopedia of thirteenth-century Spanish life and thought, depicts a Castilian woman spinning wool with a hand spindle and distaff while a simmering pot hangs over a fire. I can imagine her preparing a simple vegetable or bean soup flavored with a ham bone or a big soup, a gargantuan mix of legumes, vegetables, and many types of meat.

This big Iberian soup may have gotten its odd name, *olla podrida*, or rotten pot, from a long simmering process that often brought with it the strong smell of cabbage and turnips. But since in Spain the word *podrido* also signifies excess, as in being "filthy rich," I prefer to think that the soup was so named because it was rich with everything edible that grew from the earth, flew, crawled, or ran.

At lavish medieval banquets, a huge roasted boar was often brought to the aristocratic table with pomp and ceremony, celebrating the victory of the lord as hunter over nature and beast, the size of the roast a sign of his prestige and power for all to see. Yet medieval Spanish documents indicate that a well-filled *olla* was just as much a sign of conspicuous wealth, because it was dense with layer upon layer of ingredients. Images of soup pots even adorned the coats of arms and tombs of some Spanish nobles.

When the Spaniards arrived in the New World in the fifteenth century, they found people who loved one-pot meals as much as they did. In Cuba and Hispaniola, they observed Taíno (Arawak) Indians cooking a big soup called *ajiaco* in clay pots set over a wood fire. This was a mélange of tubers like yuca, *malanga*, and sweet potato, vegetables like squash and corn, and the meats of wild animals like the *jutía*, a small rodent native to Cuba, seasoned with fermented yuca juice, hot pepper, and achiote seeds for color.

The Spaniards embraced the Indian *ajiaco* because it resembled their own *olla podrida*. Both dishes simmered a long time, their flavors and texture changing as the cook added new ingredients to the pot. As Spanish settlers in the Hispanic Caribbean started bringing cows, pigs, chickens, vegetables like onion and garlic, and seasonings like saffron to the New World, these elements made it into the *ajiaco* pot. By the turn of the nineteenth century, the hybrid Castilian-Spanish *ajiaco* was regarded as the quintessential *criollo* dish. And everywhere the Spaniards settled in the Americas, they adapted the big soups, adding their own ingredients to the *locros* and *chupes* of Ecuador, the *lawas* of Bolivia, and the *pozoles* of Mexico.

Equally fond of soups and stews were the Africans who were brought as slaves from the sixteenth century on to work on sugarcane and cacao plantations. In the big iron pots supplied by slave owners, the Africans cooked bean soups, sometimes enriched with pork and dried beef. The Cuban and Brazilian okra stews also originated in the one-pot cookery of slave plantations, cooked as was customary in Africa with various meats and green leafy vegetables.

To this day, each region of Latin America has its own favorite big soup born of the historic mingling of Native Americans, Spaniards, and Africans: Cuba has the *ajiaco*; Puerto Rico, the Dominican Republic, and coastal Colombia and Venezuela have the *sancocho*; Brazil has the *feijoada*; and the Andes have the *locro*. There are practical reasons for this. Wild animals make for tougher meat that needs to be simmered for a long time; the legumes have more minerals than in the United States and must be soaked and cooked for many hours. It makes sense to cook them together and let their flavors mingle in the pot. In highland places such as Bolivia, the round soup pot holds heat beautifully, and cooking foods together means conserving scarce fuel.

Regardless of the historical and practical reasons for the big soup, I've often thought that Latin Americans came up with it as another way to blend and mix their foods, their favorite way of eating a meal—layer upon layer of different textures and flavors in one delicious spoonful.

AJIACOS AND SANCOCHOS

My Grandmother's Ajiaco

Ajiaco Cubano

The Cuban *ajiaco* is a peasant dish, a big soup chockfull of starchy vegetables and several meats that sticks to your ribs and leaves you ready for a long siesta. Yet it has a surprisingly mellow flavor and subtle sweetness, along with a smoky undertaste that anchors all the flavors.

Members of my father's family, whose roots stretch to the Oriente Province bush, are great *ajiaco* makers. For special occasions, my grandmother Paquita would make a huge batch for her nine children and countless grandchildren. I remember this tiny, stocky woman with worn hands stirring a huge pot. Her *ajiaco* was like none I have since tasted, because it was always made with a special ingredient: smoked dried beef (*tasajo*) or smoked pork. My grandmother preferred the taste of the dried meats smoked in the stone oven in her family farm in Jauco, a remote region in northern Oriente.

The word *ajiaco* is probably of Taíno (Arawak) origin, from *axi* or *ají*, the word for pepper. By the

turn of the last century, *ajiaco* was regarded as the quintessential *criollo* dish of Cuba, but by then its Taíno origins and probable heat had been forgotten. José Triay, in his *Nuevo manual del cocinero criollo* (*The New Manual of the Creole Cook*), a popular Cuban cookbook written in 1903, asserted that *ajiaco* was a "natural" offshoot of the Spanish *cocido*, that is, of the *olla podrida*.

I make *ajiaco* when I am homesick or I want to entertain a crowd in authentic Cuban style. I usually bring a Canary Islands green sauce to the table, a touch Paquita would perhaps have approved.

Cook's Note: In Cuba, dried salted beef was imported from Montevideo, Uruguay. This meat, *tasajo*, is still sold in Hispanic markets, where it comes enveloped in a film of yellow fat. It is strong-tasting and heavily salted for preservation; it must be desalted and reconstituted by soaking before using. You can also use Brazilian dried beef, either *carne seca* or the sun-dried *carne de sol*.

What to Drink: Bacardi Hatuey or Mexican Corona beer, or Luca Chardonnay from Mendoza, Argentina

SERVES 12 AS A MAIN COURSE

For the Meats

- 8 ounces *tasajo* (dried beef) or Brazilian dried beef (*carne seca* or *carne de sol*), cut into 6 pieces
- 2 smoked pork chops, each chopped into 3 pieces (ask your butcher to do this)
- 6 quarts water
- 8 ounces flank steak or brisket, cut into 2 or 3 pieces
- 1 pound boneless pork neck meat (ask for *aguja* at Hispanic meat markets) or shoulder
- 8 ounces boneless pork chops, cut into 2 or 3 pieces each

One 3½-pound chicken, skinned and cut into 8 pieces (see page 659) or 3½ pounds chicken thighs, skin removed

4 broad-leaf *culantro* leaves or 8 cilantro sprigs

10 Caribbean sweet peppers (*ajíes dulces*) or 1 cubanelle pepper, seeded and coarsely chopped

2 cups Light Tomato Sauce (page 48) or store-bought tomato sauce

1 teaspoon ground cumin

½ teaspoon dried oregano

1 teaspoon salt

For the Vegetables

1 green plantain, peeled (see page 181) and cut into ½-inch slices

1 pound *malanga*, peeled and cut into 1-inch slices

1½ pounds white yams, peeled (see page 175) and cut into 1-inch sections

2 half-ripe plantains (see pages 179–80), peeled and cut into ½-inch slices

1 ripe plantain, peeled and cut into ½-inch slices

1 cup Canary Islands Cilantro *Mojo* (page 141), optional

Soaking the Dried Beef ▶ Place the dried beef in a bowl and cover with water. Let soak for at least 12 hours, or overnight, changing the water twice.

You can also prepare the vegetables and leave in cold water in the refrigerator overnight.

Cooking the Meats ▶ Drain the dried beef. Add the beef, smoked pork chops, and water to a large (at least 12-quart) heavy pot and bring to a boil over high heat, then reduce the heat to low and simmer gently, covered, for 30 minutes.

Add the flank steak or brisket, pork neck meat, and pork chops and simmer gently, covered, until the meats are almost tender, about 1 hour.

Add the chicken, *culantro*, peppers, tomato sauce, cumin, oregano, and salt and simmer, covered, for 10 minutes.

Cooking the Vegetables ▶ Add the green plantain and *malanga* and simmer, covered, for 10 minutes. Add the yams and the remaining plantains and simmer, covered, until soft, about 20 minutes.

To thicken the soup, scoop out a few chunks of *malanga* and yam and mash with a fork. Stir back into the pot and simmer, stirring, until the broth thickens slightly, about 10 minutes. Taste for salt and add a little if desired. Remove from the heat.

To serve, bring the *ajiaco* to the table in a soup tureen. Distribute the meats and vegetables among large soup plates and ladle the broth over them. Pass the *mojo* separately, if desired.

Chicken and Vegetable *Sancocho*

Sancocho de Pollo

The Spanish word *sancocho* comes from the verb *sancochar*, which, in turn, comes from the Latin *semicoctus*, or half-cooked. In the Americas, *sancochar* came to mean cooking by slow simmering until the meats fall off the bones and the vegetables practically melt into the broth.

Today there are *sancochos* in many parts of the Americas. The ones from the Hispanic Caribbean are reminiscent of the Canary Islands *sancocho*, a big soup that came to Hispaniola (now Haiti and the Dominican Republic) and Puerto Rico with settlers from those islands.

I like to make a lighter, less complicated *sancho* than the original, which sometimes is as elaborate as the *ajiaco*. With Avocado and Onion Salad (page 547) and Cuban Bread (page 591) or Yuca Bread (page 573), it is a substantial main-course lunch.

What to Drink: Dominican Presidente beer

SERVES 6

3	tablespoons achiote-infused olive oil (page 89)
1	cubanelle pepper, seeded and coarsely chopped
12	sweet Caribbean peppers (*ajíes dulces*), coarsely chopped (optional)
1	medium yellow onion (about 8 ounces), coarsely chopped
4	garlic cloves, crushed
1½	teaspoons ground cumin
1	bay leaf
1	cup crushed canned tomatoes
1	teaspoon dried oregano, crumbled
3	broad-leaf *culantro* leaves or 8 cilantro sprigs
1½	teaspoons salt, or to taste
6	chicken thighs (about 2½ pounds), skin removed
8–9	cups chicken broth, homemade (page 538) or store-bought, or water
4	medium carrots (about 1 pound), peeled and cut on the bias into 1-inch slices
4	large *boniatos* (Caribbean sweet potatoes; about 1 pound each), peeled and cut into 4 chunks each
3	medium ears corn, husked and cut into 2-inch rounds
	Freshly ground black pepper
1	West Indian avocado or 2 Hass avocados, peeled, pitted, and diced, for garnish (optional)

▶ Heat the oil in a 12-quart pot over medium heat until it sizzles. Add the cubanelle and Caribbean peppers, onion, garlic, cumin, and bay leaf and sauté until the vegetables are soft, about 8 minutes.

Stir in the tomatoes and cook for 1 minute. Add the oregano, *culantro* or cilantro, and salt. Then add the chicken and pour in the broth or water, and bring to a boil over high heat. Reduce the heat to medium-low and simmer gently for 15 minutes.

Add the carrots and boniatos and simmer gently, covered, over low heat, until the chicken is fork-tender, about 45 minutes; skim the fat occasionally.

Add the corn and cook until tender, about 15 minutes. Season with salt and pepper, if necessary, and remove from the heat.

Serving: Serve in soup bowls, garnished with the diced avocado, if desired, and a dollop of Antillean Three-Pepper Sauce (page 117) or Puerto Rican *ajilimójili* (page 143).

Orinoco Big Fish *Sancocho*

Sancocho de Pescado del Orinoco

Years ago, on the Feast of the Virgin at the end of July, I maneuvered an old boat from the Angostura Bridge to the riverfront fish market in Ciudad Bolívar, on the Orinoco River. Somewhat to my amazement, I managed to bring the boat safely to the pier and felt, for the first time in days, that all was well with the world. It was now time to relax and have lunch, and I chose a restaurant called Ña María, right by the water, where I had been twice before. I sat outdoors and ordered the house specialty, a lovely, aromatic fish soup called *sancocho de morocoto*, brimming with chunks of river fish and tropical tubers. The owners, Ana Farfán and her mother, María, an affable Guayanese with a ready smile and arms covered with shiny gold bracelets, a sign of her success, sat down to chat.

I felt as much at ease as if I were visiting old friends, and the earthy, musky taste of that great soup was dear and familiar. At the time of my visit, river fish were abundant, even though the summer rains were late to come. My *sancocho* was made with *morocoto*, a tasty fish with big teeth to chomp on fruits and flowers of the flooded jungle. But a few weeks after my return home, I called María to ask her a question about the soup, and she explained that now she was using grouper because river fish had become practically impossible to find. "The rains never came," she explained.

Here is María's recipe, with no embellishments of my own (though I often use fish broth instead of water), but using grouper instead of *morocoto*.

SERVES 6

For the Fish

Six 4-ounce grouper steaks
½ teaspoon salt
4 quarts water

For the Seasonings

4 garlic cloves, finely chopped
1 medium yellow onion (8 ounces), finely chopped
1 bunch scallions, white and pale green parts, finely chopped
1 tablespoon finely chopped cilantro
3 broad-leaf *culantro* leaves
12 Caribbean sweet peppers (*ajíes dulces*), seeded and finely chopped
1 small green bell pepper (4 ounces), cored, seeded, and finely chopped

2 celery stalks with leaves, finely chopped
1 fat leek, white and pale green parts, washed, split lengthwise, and finely chopped
1 tablespoon finely chopped flat-leaf parsley

For the Vegetables

1 pound yuca, peeled and cut into 1-inch chunks
1 pound taro, peeled and cut into 1-inch chunks
1 pound *malanga*, peeled and cut into 1-inch chunks
1 pound Caribbean pumpkin (*calabaza*) or Hubbard, butternut, or acorn squash, peeled, seeded, and cut into 1-inch chunks
1 pound white yams, peeled (see page 175) and cut into 2-inch chunks
1 green plantain, peeled (see page 181) and cut into 1-inch sections
1 half-ripe plantain (see pages 179–80), peeled and cut into 1-inch sections

To Finish

1 teaspoon achiote-infused corn or extra-virgin olive oil (page 89)
4 garlic cloves, finely chopped
3 cups Spicy Milk Sauce from Ciudad Bolívar (page 122), optional

Preparing the Broth ▶ Season the grouper steaks with the salt and set aside.

Pour the water into a 6-quart pot and add all the seasonings. Bring to a boil over high heat, reduce the heat to medium–low, and simmer for 10 minutes.

Cooking the Vegetables ▶ Add the yuca, taro, and *malanga* and simmer for 10 minutes. Add the squash, yams, and plantains and simmer until all the vegetables are tender, about 15 minutes.

Finishing the Soup ▶ Add the fish steaks and simmer until the fish is cooked through, about 5 minutes.

Just before serving, heat the achiote-infused oil in a small skillet over medium heat. Add the garlic and sauté until golden, about 40 seconds. Add to the pot and stir to mix. Remove from the heat.

Transfer the fish to a plate. Distribute the vegetables among bowls, top each with a fish steak, and ladle the broth over the fish. Place the sauce in a bowl and pass around, if you want a touch of heat.

Serving: Accompany with yuca bread, homemade (page 573) or store-bought.

BEAN SOUPS

Black Bean Soup with Epazote and Chipotle

Caldo de Frijoles Negros

The late Sara Hervis was one of the best cooks I knew in Las Tuxtlas, the forested region in Veracruz State in Mexico. Because of her knowledge of medicinal herbs and plants and her way with forest animals, her friends thought Sara was a bit of a *bruja* (witch)—a good, wise one, I might add. I found Sara's approach to cooking so in tune with her natural surroundings it was almost mystical. From Sara, I learned to season soups with generous bunches of cilantro or epazote, not just a few sprigs. In her

restaurant, the simmering broths and beans always had a top layer of herbs so lush that they seemed to be growing out of the pot. What amazes me is that when used this way, epazote never overwhelms the soup, despite its powerful aroma when raw.

SERVES 6 TO 8

For the Beans

- 1 pound (about 2 cups) dried black beans, picked over and rinsed
- 2½ quarts water
- 1 medium white onion (about 8 ounces), peeled and halved
- 1 large bunch epazote

For the Chipotle Puree

- 2 tablespoons safflower oil
- 20 small or 11 medium dried chipotles (about 1 ounce)
- 3 garlic cloves, coarsely chopped

For the Seasonings

- 2 tablespoons lard, preferably freshly rendered (page 82), or safflower oil
- 1 medium white onion (8 ounces), finely chopped
- 2¼ teaspoons salt, or to taste

Cooking the Beans ▶ Place the beans with the water, onion, and epazote in a 6-quart heavy pot and bring to a boil over high heat. Lower the heat to medium and simmer, partially covered, about 1½ hours, or until the beans are soft.

Preparing the Chipotle Puree ▶ Heat the oil in a medium skillet over medium heat. Add the chipotles and roast, turning with tongs, until fragrant, about 1 minute. Transfer to a small saucepan, cover with 3 cups water, and bring to a boil over medium heat. Cook until softened, about 10 minutes. Drain, reserving ¼ cup of the cooking liquid.

Place the chiles, reserved cooking liquid, and garlic in a food processor or blender and process to a puree.

Seasoning the Soup ▶ In a medium skillet, heat the lard or oil until sizzling. Add the onion and sauté until golden, about 8 minutes. Stir in the chipotle puree and salt and remove from the heat.

When the beans are tender, discard the onion and epazote. Stir in the puree. Taste for salt and add more if needed. Simmer until lightly thickened, about 15 minutes. Serve piping hot in earthenware bowls.

Havana-Style Black Bean Soup

Sopa de Frijoles Negros Habanera

I was studying medieval history at the University of Valladolid in Spain, and my family in Miami had sent me a few pounds of dried black beans, not easy to find in Spain. I decided to surprise some good friends from Havana and make black bean soup, one of the great dishes of their hometown. To my bewildered embarrassment, they congratulated me on the lovely red kidney bean soup in the style of my home territory, Oriente. Then they proceeded to set me straight: "Never, never, never, do you use tomatoes in a Havana black bean soup." And never, never, never did I forget the lesson, though I later learned that one of Havana's cherished old black bean recipes, *frijoles negros a la Voldés-Fauli*, calls for a tomato *sofrito*. But to some people, like my friends,

the no-tomato Havana-style black bean soup is a classic you do not tinker with.

The soup sometimes gets some of its deep flavor from ham hocks or bacon, but many Cubans prefer to make simpler, but equally flavorful, vegetarian versions. In two recipes that appear in classic 1950s cookbooks, attributed to prominent families from Havana, the beans get their flavor from the traditional aromatic cumin-and-oregano-scented *sofrito* cooked with olive oil and roasted peppers (canned peppers in the originals). I have adapted the idea, using freshly roasted peppers and an extra drizzle of olive oil added at the table to enhance the natural earthiness of the beans and give the soup a silky and aromatic finish. *Ají dulce*, the tiny Caribbean pepper that Cubans call *ají cachucha*, is a key ingredient of the vegetarian black bean soup from Havana and the western provinces of Cuba. Adding the roasted pepper is optional in Havana.

Cubans call their bean soups *potajes* (potages), meaning something more substantial than a plain soup. When they eat black beans as a soup, in a bowl by itself, they normally add a generous spoonful or two of steamed white rice. But more often they ladle the soup over the white rice or serve it by the side of the rice. If you want to garnish the soup, I recommend a dollop each of homemade Mexican or Central American *crema* (page 148 or 147) and "Finger Sauce" (page 116), which are nontraditional touches, or some chopped white onion and parsley.

Cook's Notes: If you want to double the recipe to feed 12—the ideal amount for a Cuban Christmas Eve party with roast pork and a side of white rice—cook the beans in an 8-quart pot with 4 quarts water, adding more water if necessary as the beans cook. The soup should be brothy yet creamy. Cooking beans is not an exact science; you must check the water often.

Some Cubans prefer their soup without visible traces of the onion and green pepper used in the cooking sauce. If you belong to the "invisible seasoning club," puree the cooking sauce with ¼ cup of the beans and ¼ cup broth (or up to ⅓ cup if necessary) and return to the pot to let the broth thicken.

Working Ahead ▶ The soup tastes even better the day after it's made. Let it cool, then refrigerate, tightly covered. When reheating, do it at a very gentle simmer. The soup can also be frozen for up to 3 months (which is why I always at least double the recipe).

What to Drink: A dry sherry or amontillado, such as Alvear Amontillado from Montilla-Moriles, Spain, or any sherrylike Jura white, such as vin jaune

SERVES 4 TO 6

For the Beans

- 1 pound (about 2 cups) dried black beans, picked over and rinsed
- 3 quarts water
- 1 small yellow onion (6 ounces), peeled
- 1 small green bell pepper (4 ounces), cored and seeded
- 1 bay leaf

For the Cooking Sauce

- ¼ cup extra-virgin olive oil
- 4 large garlic cloves, finely minced
- 1 small yellow onion (about 6 ounces), minced
- 1 medium to large green bell pepper (about 8 ounces), cored, seeded, and minced
- 10 Caribbean sweet peppers (*ajíes dulces*) or 1 cubanelle pepper, seeded and finely chopped
- 1 bay leaf

- 2 teaspoons ground cumin
- 2 teaspoons dried oregano

To Finish the Soup

- 1 tablespoon red wine vinegar
- 1½–2 teaspoons salt, or to taste
- ½ teaspoon freshly ground black pepper, or to taste
- 1 large red bell pepper, fire-roasted (see page 67), peeled, seeded and finely chopped (optional)
- 2 teaspoons sugar

Cooking the Beans ▶ Place the beans, water, onion, green pepper, and bay leaf in a 6-quart heavy pot and bring to a boil over high heat. Lower the heat to medium and simmer until the beans are tender, 1½ to 2 hours. Discard the onion, pepper, and bay leaf and lower the heat. Ladle out about ⅓ cup of the beans to a bowl and mash with the back of the ladle or a spoon into a coarse puree; reserve. Keep the soup at a simmer while you make the *sofrito*.

Making the Cooking Sauce ▶ Heat the oil in a medium heavy skillet over medium-high heat. Add the garlic and sauté until light golden, about 20 seconds. Add the onion, green pepper, Caribbean peppers, and bay leaf and sauté for 5 minutes, or until the vegetables are soft. Add the cumin and oregano and cook, stirring, for 1 minute. Stir in the mashed black beans and cook for 1 minute. Remove from the heat.

Finishing the Soup ▶ Add the bean-enriched cooking sauce to the pot of beans, then stir in the vinegar, salt, pepper, and sugar. Taste and correct the seasoning if necessary; the soup should be aromatic, with sweet, tangy notes. Place the pot over medium-low heat, add the chopped roasted peppers, if using, and simmer until the soup is creamy, 30 to 45 minutes. Remove the bay leaf before serving.

Serving: Bring a cruet of olive oil to the table and invite your guests to drizzle it over the soup.

Puerto Rican Stewed Red Kidney Beans

Habichuelas Coloradas Guisadas

Puerto Ricans use a lovely verb to refer to the cooking of beans, *guisar*, which means to braise and also to stew, not simply boil. It really conveys the building of flavors in this deceptively simple dish. The sautéed mixture of salt pork belly, ham, and garlic, a meaty flavor-enhancing *sofrito*, is given extra flavor through the addition of a *recado* (page 58), a puree of seasonings and aromatics.

Working Ahead ▶ You can prepare the soup a day ahead and store, once cooled, tightly covered in the refrigerator. Reheat at a very gentle simmer. The soup can also be frozen up to 3 months.

SERVES 6 TO 8

For the Beans

- 1 pound (about 2 cups) dried red kidney beans or pink beans, picked over and rinsed
- 4 quarts water
- 2 broad-leaf *culantro* leaves or 4 cilantro sprigs
- 4 Caribbean sweet peppers (*ajíes dulces*)
- 1 cubanelle pepper, halved and seeded
- 1 small yellow onion (4 ounces), halved

For the Cooking Sauce (*Sofrito*)

- 2 tablespoons achiote-infused lard or corn oil or mild olive oil (page 89)
- 3 ounces salt pork belly or pancetta, cut into small dice
- 4 ounces Virginia ham, diced
- 4 large garlic cloves, finely chopped
- 1 cup Charito's Puerto Rican Seasoning Mix (page 58)
- 2 teaspoons salt
  Freshly ground black pepper to taste

▶ Place the beans in a large bowl, cover with the water, and soak overnight.

Cooking the Beans ▶ Place the beans and their soaking water in a heavy 6-quart pot, add the *culantro* or cilantro, peppers, and onion, and bring to a boil over high heat. Lower the heat to medium, cover, and simmer until the beans are tender, about 1½ hours.

Preparing the Cooking Sauce ▶ Heat the lard or oil in a medium skillet over medium heat until rippling. Add the diced salt pork and sauté until golden brown, about 5 minutes. Add the ham and cook until golden, about 2 minutes. Add the garlic and cook, stirring, until golden, about 40 seconds. Stir in the seasoning mix and cook for 10 minutes, stirring occasionally. Remove from the heat.

Finishing the Beans ▶ When the beans are soft, stir in the cooking sauce. Simmer for another 20 minutes.

Serving: Like most Hispanic Caribbean bean dishes, this can be served on its own in soup bowls or ladled over white rice. If serving by itself, garnish with avocado slices and, if desired, a dollop of Puerto Rican-Style *Ají Dulce* Sauce (page 143).

Salvadorian Red Silk Bean and Short Rib Soup-Stew

Sopa Salvadoreña de Frijoles de Seda con Costillas

Salvadorian silk beans are mealy and flavorful. When cooked with beef short ribs and topped at the table with grated aged cheese and a fresh Salvadorian hot sauce, *chirmol*, they are truly divine.

Cook's Note: Silk beans are available in many Latin markets. If you can't find them, use kidney beans or small red beans and reduce the cooking time by a third to a half.

SERVES 8

For the Beans

1 pound dried (about 2 cups) Salvadorian red silk beans (*frijoles rojos de seda salvadoreño*), small red beans, or red kidney beans, picked over and rinsed

4 quarts water

1 pound beef short ribs, cut into 2½-inch pieces

For the Seasonings and Vegetables

3 tablespoons corn oil

4 garlic cloves

1 tablespoon finely chopped flat-leaf parsley

1 tablespoon finely chopped cilantro

2 green plantains, peeled (see page 181) and cut into 1-inch rounds

9 ounces Caribbean pumpkin (*calabaza*), peeled and cut into 1-inch dice (about 2 cups)

1 light or dark green chayote (about 9 ounces), pitted, peeled, and cut into 1-inch dice

About ¼ medium green cabbage, cut into 1-inch-wide strips (about 2 cups)

1 tablespoon salt

¼ cup grated Salvadorian aged cheese, Mexican *cotija*, or ricotta salata, for serving

3½ cups Salvadorian *Salsa Cruda* (page 121), for serving

▶ Place the beans in a large bowl, add the water, and soak overnight.

Cooking the Beans ▶ Pour the beans and the soaking liquid into an 8-quart heavy pot and bring to a boil over high heat. Lower the heat to medium and simmer, partially covered, for about 2 hours.

Add the ribs and continue cooking, covered, for about 1½ hours, or until the beans and the meat are tender. For kidney or common red beans, cook for 1½ hours total. Remove the ribs from the pot and place on a plate. Keep the beans at a low simmer while you prepare the seasoning.

Seasoning and Finishing the Beans ▶ When the beans are nearly done, heat the oil in a 12-inch skillet over medium heat until rippling. Add the ribs and brown on all sides, about 10 minutes. Remove and set aside.

Add the garlic to the oil remaining in the pan and sauté until golden, about 40 seconds. Add the ribs, garlic, parsley, and cilantro to the beans. Then add the plantains, pumpkin, and chayote and simmer for 20 minutes, or until the vegetables are just tender. Stir in the cabbage and salt and cook until tender, about 10 minutes.

Serve in soup bowls, and pass the grated cheese and hot sauce.

Stewed Peruvian Canary Beans

Menestra de Frijoles Canarios

Canary beans are native to South America. In northern Peru, peasants call them *frijoles parados*, standing beans, because they grow as freestanding bush beans instead of having to be trained on poles. They have a lovely soft canary yellow color, hence their name, and a distinctive mealy texture that Peruvians adore.

In Lambayeque and Piura, two large cities in northern Peru, these are the beans of choice for this thick, potage-like *menestra*, which is ladled over white rice, to eat with the rich cilantro-flavored meat or poultry stews known as *secos*. Cooks from this region use leftover beans from the *menestra* to make a tasty *tacu tacu*, a fried bean and rice combination that is served shaped into a tapered cylinder.

The word *menestra*, like the Italian *minestra*, goes back to the Latin *ministere* (to serve), but the two took on different modern meanings. Today *minestra* can refer to a broad variety of Italian soups, thick or thin. At one time in Spain, *menestra* meant something like "rations" and referred to a kind of potage-porridge made of dried legumes that was traditionally doled out in jails and barracks. Nowadays the word signifies a braised medley of vegetables flavored with chopped ham. But across the ocean in Ecuador and northern Peru, it still carries the old meaning, a thick stewlike dish of dried beans or lentils.

SERVES 6 TO 8

For the Beans

- 1 pound dried Canary beans, picked over and rinsed
- 1 medium red onion (8 ounces), peeled
- 3 quarts water

For the Cooking Sauce

- 5 dried *mirasol* peppers, stemmed and seeded
- 2 cups water
- ¼ cup extra-virgin olive oil
- 4 garlic cloves, finely minced
- 1 medium red onion (8 ounces), finely chopped
- 1 teaspoon ground cumin
- 2 teaspoons salt
- 1 tablespoon finely chopped cilantro, for garnish

Cooking the Beans ▶ Place the beans and onion in a heavy 6-quart pot, add the water, and bring to a boil over high heat. Reduce the heat to medium and cook, partially covered, until tender, about 2 hours. Remove the onion. Depending on the beans, the cooking may take longer, even close to 3 hours; check the water level from time to time, and add more as needed.

Preparing the Cooking Sauce ▶ Place the dried *mirasol* peppers in a small saucepan, add the 2 cups water, and bring to a boil over high heat. Lower the heat to medium and simmer until soft, about 20 minutes. Drain, reserving the cooking liquid.

Place the peppers and ¼ cup of the reserved cooking liquid in a blender or food processor and process into a smooth puree.

Heat the olive oil in a medium skillet over medium heat until rippling. Add the garlic and sauté until golden, about 40 seconds. Add the onion and cook, stirring, for 3 minutes. Stir in the cumin and salt, pour in the pepper puree, and cook, stirring, for 2 minutes. Remove from the heat.

Finishing the Soup ▶ Add the sautéed mixture to the beans along with the remaining cooking liquid, stir well to mix, and simmer, covered, for 20 more minutes.

To serve, ladle into soup bowls and garnish with the cilantro.

Brazilian *Feijoada*

Feijoada Completa

Feijoada completa is the ultimate tropical bean soup-stew: a massive mound of fresh, smoked, and salted meats cooked with beans (most often black but sometimes a type of pinto bean), dished up with classic accompaniments including rice, sautéed kale, a pungent table sauce, and *farinha*, the beloved Brazilian yuca meal. A complete *feijoada* with all the fixings is a descendant of the great Iberian one-pot boiled dinners belonging to the family of the *olla podrida*. If it weren't for the New World hot sauce and *farofa* and the beans replacing the Old World chickpeas, you could imagine Sancho Panza doing justice to this epic assemblage of good things.

The *feijoada* is also part of the heritage of Brazilian slave-plantation cooking. We can guess that bean soup-stews made with less meat and few (or none) of the modern *feijoada* trimmings were often fed to sugar and cacao workers. In fact, comparatively plain versions of *feijoada* are still popular—I say "comparatively," because it's a richly hearty dish

no matter what—and if you decide to omit some of the many meats in the ingredients list, you will be doing exactly what many Brazilians do.

I ate one of the best *feijoadas* of Brazil in Pelourinho, the historic district of the city of Salvador. My taxi driver, Cacique, had mentioned a place called Coco Ban Ban, next to the Largo de Pelourinho, as the best place in town to eat *feijoada*. I was expecting a small restaurant, but what I found was a group of tables placed perilously on the street, a few inches from the traffic.

This makeshift café belongs to an enterprising Bahian. A couple of his cooks prepare the *feijoada* at home, and he brings the food to town every Saturday, with cooks and pots in tow, and sets up shop under the stairs of a dilapidated building. His customers are people like me who like adventurous eating and regulars who come with their own containers to take the *feijoada* home. The man never stops. He shuttles full bowls back and forth, brings extra portions of meat and sausages when someone asks for more, pops open bottles of beer, all while the women scoop out ladlefuls of beans and meats into shallow clay bowls that keep the food piping hot. The rice comes separately to the table, and everyone ladles a few spoonfuls over the beans and meat with a dollop of the spicy sauce (*molho*). It was a magnificent *feijoada*, perfectly seasoned and salted, meaty and succulent—unforgettable.

If you do make full-scale *feijoada* with all the trimmings, you will be tasting the marriage that took place in Brazilian bourgeois kitchens between the plantation dish, which was served in soup bowls like the Caribbean *ajiaco* or *sancocho*, and the Portuguese *cozido*, which was cooked in one pot but served in two courses: the rich broth first, the array of meats second. The *feijoada*'s soupy aspect comes from the pot of beans to which all the meats are added in order depending on their cooking time. The beans and the meats are served at the same time but separately: a tureen for the beans, a groaning platter for the handsomely sliced meats, moistened with a little of the cooking liquid. These are surrounded by other bowls or dishes with the hot sauce, *farinha*, thinly sliced sweet oranges, sautéed kale, and rice. In true Latin fashion, all the guests immediately start crowding and mingling these elements on their plates. People generally ladle the beans over a large helping of rice while heaping some or all of the meats next to the kale, and then apply the other condiments with a liberal hand to balance the flavors. The sweetness of the orange, the acidity and stinging heat of the *molho*, and the slight herbal astringency of the kale help to offset the heaviness of the meats, while the starchy *farinha* both cuts the fat and binds it all together.

A *feijoada completa* is at least a two-day undertaking, possibly more if shopping for special ingredients turns into several different expeditions. For the sake of your guests, you should remember that it is best eaten at leisure—great leisure. Trying to crowd it into a short dinner hour will only leave everyone gasping for air. In short, make the *feijoada completa* into a festive event.

Though lengthy to prepare, a *feijoada completa* is not in any way tricky or complex. The most difficult part may well be assembling the meats. Brazilian butcher shops will probably have all or nearly all of them; other Latin butchers or Latin supermarkets will almost certainly have some of them, perhaps even cut up into suitably sized chunks or slices. Here is the complete roster:

Carne seca **or** *carne de sol*: Air-dried or sun-dried salted beef, this has a distinctive cured flavor and chewy texture. You can substitute the somewhat different-tasting Hispanic *tasajo* or a chunk of smoked dried beef from a good country butcher. It must be soaked and parboiled before cooking.

Salted pig's feet and tail: These add gelatinous body and a little salt—there is no substitute. Ask the butcher to cut into several pieces; they must be soaked before cooking.

Smoked pork: Smoked pork, preferably ribs or chops imparts a pleasant smokiness to the beans and other meats. Chops cut from smoked pork loins are often available from German butchers.

Slab bacon: This lends both smokiness and richness. The bacon acquires a luscious melting texture in cooking.

Smoked ham hocks: These reinforce the smoky flavors of the *feijoada*, and they become tenderly meaty in cooking. Ask the butcher to cut them into several pieces.

Smoked beef tongue: A *feijoada* without a display of beautifully carved tongue surrounded by all the other meats is unthinkable to Brazilians. Smoked beef tongue is available in Brazilian meat markets and can be ordered from specialty butchers (German, kosher, and Eastern European).

Fresh pig's feet: These add extra gelatin and succulence. They are available at many ethnic butchers (Chinese, for example). Ask the butcher to cut them up into several pieces.

Pig's ears: Brazilians, like Chinese, love the crunchy texture of pig's ears. These are also very gelatinous. Ask the butcher to cut these in two.

Beef chuck: The most flavorful boneless beef cut for soup-stews.

Linguiça: These are cured Portuguese sausages that resemble Spanish chorizo.

When you visit a Latin market, your shopping list should also include pickled *malagueta* peppers or *pimenta de cheiro* for the *molho* (hot sauce), as well as *farinha* (yuca flour) to serve in any of several possible ways as an indispensable table condiment. And don't forget the *cachaça* for the *caipirinhas* (page 360) and Brazilian beer like Skol, Brahma or Antarctica.

This recipe is based on the version of *feijoada completa* that my friend Nair, a savvy old Brazilian woman, used to cook at my home several times a year for parties. Once all the salted meats had been soaked overnight and we were ready to begin, Nair would move around my kitchen as gracefully as a virtuoso dancer. I watched, hypnotized, as she sliced pound after pound of kale into perfectly uniform shreds, added each of the meats to the pot of beans in its appointed order, and prepared the whole battery of classic accompaniments without missing a beat. When the *feijoada* was ready to serve, the table looked majestic—the meats lovingly sliced, the beans ensconced in a china tureen, the oranges invitingly arranged. A pitcher of *caipirinhas* was chilling in the refrigerator, and Nair, at the end of our labor, seemed as fresh as if she had spent the day relaxing.

Not all of us will be able to carry out the multiple tasks for a *feijoada* without some help. But if you organize the work into a manageable order, you might even have fun in the process.

SERVES 12 TO 14

For the Meats

- 2 pounds salted pig's feet, cut into several pieces
- 1 pound salted pig's tail, cut into several pieces
- 1 pound Brazilian *carne seca* or *carne de sol* (dried beef), in 1 piece
- 1½ pounds meaty smoked pork chops, cut into 2 to 3 pieces each
- 1 pound smoked slab bacon, cut into 2 pieces
- 2 pounds meaty smoked ham hocks (3 medium hocks), cut into several pieces each
- One 3-pound smoked beef tongue
- 1 pound beef chuck, cut into 2 pieces
- 1 fresh pig's foot, cut into several pieces
- 2 pig's ears, cut in half
- 1 pound Portuguese-style *linguiça* or Spanish-style chorizo

For the Beans

- 1½ pounds (about 3 cups) dried black beans, picked over and rinsed
- 6 quarts water
- 1 head garlic, halved crosswise
- 3 bay leaves

For the Cooking Sauce

- 3 tablespoons extra-virgin olive oil
- 1 small head garlic, separated into cloves, peeled, and finely chopped
- 1 medium yellow onion (8 ounces), finely chopped

For the Sides and Condiments

3½ cups Brazilian *farinha crua* or *farinha torrada* (uncooked or roasted yuca flour; see page 152) or a double recipe of either Simple Buttered *Farofa* (page 153) or Scrambled Egg *Farofa* (page 153)

A double recipe of Brazilian Hot Pepper and Lime Sauce (page 145)

3 recipes of kale in the style of Minas Gerais (recipe follows)

A double recipe of Brazilian-Style Simple Pilaf (page 298)

6 oranges, peel and pith removed, cut into slices

Soaking the Salted Meats ▶ The day before you plan to make the *feijoada*, rinse the salted pig's feet and salted pig's tail under cold running water. Place them and the dried beef in a large deep bowl (or in separate bowls). Add cold water to cover by several inches and let soak for at least 12 hours, changing the water 3 times. When you are ready to proceed, drain the soaked meats.

Blanching or Precooking the Meats ▶ Bring 6 quarts water to a boil in a large pot. Working with one or two of the meats at a time, add the salted pig's feet and tail, smoked chops, slab bacon, and ham hocks and cook each for 10 minutes. Transfer to a platter.

Discard the cooking liquid and rinse out the pot. Add the dried beef, smoked tongue, and 6 quarts water and bring to a boil. Adjust the heat to a simmer and cook, covered, for 1 hour. Transfer to a platter and discard the cooking liquid.

Cooking the Beans ▶ Place the beans in a very large (at least 12 quarts) Dutch oven or wide pot, add the water, garlic, and bay leaves, and bring to a boil over high heat. Reduce the heat to medium and cook, partly covered, until the beans are slightly softened but still a little chalky in the middle, about 1 hour.

Assembling the *Feijoada* ▶ Add the beef chuck to the beans, then add the fresh pig's foot and pig's ears, dried beef, tongue, salted pig's feet and tail, smoked pork, bacon, and ham hocks and bring to a boil over medium-high heat.

Preparing the Cooking Sauce (*Refogado*) ▶ Heat the oil until rippling in a medium skillet over medium heat. Add the garlic and sauté until golden, about 40 seconds. Add the onion and sauté for 2 to 3 minutes.

Add the mixture to the pot of meats and beans, stir to combine, and adjust the heat to maintain a gentle simmer. The meats should now cook until tender but not overdone. Check frequently and transfer each one to another large pot as it is done. Cover, to keep it from drying out.

After the *feijoada* has cooked for about 1 hour, ladle out 1 cup of the beans into a bowl and mash thoroughly with the back of a spoon. Stir back into the pot, add the *linguiça*, and cook until the bean liquid is slightly thickened and all the meats are tender, about 20 minutes.

Preparing the Sides ▶ While the meats and beans are cooking, prepare the *farinha* or *farofa*, *molho*, kale, and rice, timing the rice to be done at the same time as the *feijoada*. Slice the oranges and arrange in an overlapping pattern on a plate.

To serve, transfer the meats to a cutting board or platter and ladle the beans into a soup tureen or deep bowl; cover to keep warm. Carve or cut up the meats as follows: Remove the skin from the tongue with a small sharp knife. Trim away the thick "roots" and discard. Carve the tongue into thin slices and arrange in the center of a large serving platter (use two if necessary). Slice the bacon into thin slices or cubes. Cut the pig's ears into thin julienne. Bone the ham hocks and cut the meat into small pieces. Cut the chops, chuck, *carne seca*, and *linguiça* into large bite-sized chunks. Arrange all of these with the remaining pig parts as handsomely as possible around the tongue. Moisten the meat with some beef broth. Let the guests help themselves first to rice, topped with the beans, then to the meats and other accompaniments.

Kale in the Style of Minas Gerais

Couve a Mineira

Kale, known as *berza* in Spanish and *couve* in Portuguese, is a favorite in northeastern Spain, Portugal, and Brazil. In Brazil this sturdy, assertive green takes center stage. You will always find finely shredded *couve* as part of the tasty entourage of the baroque *feijoada completa* or adding a touch of freshness and a pleasant bitter edge to the hearty blue plates of the state of Minas Gerais.

SERVES 6

    4 bunches flat-leafed kale (about 2 pounds each)
    1 tablespoon freshly rendered lard (page 82) or
       light olive oil
    8 ounces smoked slab bacon, cut in small dice
   12 garlic cloves, peeled and thinly sliced crosswise
    1 teaspoon salt, or to taste

▶ Chop off the stems of the kale and reserve for other uses. Wash and pat dry the leaves with a kitchen towel. Working in batches of 2 or 3 leaves, stack the leaves and roll tightly. With a sharp knife shave across into very thin strands. By the time you are finished, the mound of *couve* will look gigantic. But you will not be able to feed an army. *Couve* will reduce dramatically once it is sautéed. Heat the lard in a large heavy-bottomed skillet over medium heat. Add the smoked bacon and sauté, stirring, until it is golden brown and has released some fat. Stir in the garlic and cook briefly until light gold, about 20 seconds. Add the kale in batches and cook, stirring, just until coated and slightly softened. Season with the salt. Do not overcook; kale should keep its deep green color and delightful crunchy texture.

Serving: This simple kale dish is one of the traditional accompaniments of the *feijoada completa* (page 512) and classic *mineiro* dishes such as *canjiquinha* (page 254) and *tutu à mineira* (page 277).

Variations: Curly-leafed kale also makes a good basis for the dish. At home for everyday use, I often do not bother to cut the kale (either the flat-leafed or curly type), so thinly. I also like to sauté the greens in only extra-virgin olive oil, omitting the pork. To turn it into a tasty salad, just add a couple tablespoons of a good vinegar and some freshly ground black pepper.

GRAIN SOUPS

Grains like corn, wheat, and barley are multifaceted staples that Latin Americans use in numerous dishes from breads to porridges to soups. In the Andes, dried corn that has been treated with lime to remove the hulls (*mote pelado*) is cooked in robust soups such as Ecuadorian *motepata*, which is thickened with squash seeds. Ecuadorians also make soups with barley or wheat thickened with potatoes and fresh cheese. In Ecuador, Bolivia, and Chile, soups and other dishes are made with wheat that has been boiled in a lime solution to hull it (*trigo pelado* or *mote de trigo*). Mexicans use a similar process to hull dried corn for *pozole* (hominy); the kernels are then boiled until they become tender and open up like rosettes.

Pozole is both the main ingredient and the name of a traditional Mexican soup with many regional variations. There are *pozoles* rich in meats—chicken along with parts of the pig, like trotters and head, that are flavorful and gelatinous—and simpler *pozoles* made with just one ingredient, such as chicken. Some versions, the so-called white *pozoles* have a clear broth, but many versions are seasoned with bright red chiles, *pozole rojo* or *colorado*. An important part of many *pozoles* is table condiments, usually chopped radishes, finely chopped onions, shredded lettuce or cabbage, and Mexican oregano, which are set out for people to stir into their soup to taste.

I braved a furious summer rainstorm to eat my first Mexican *pozole* at a celebrated restaurant named La Chata in Jalisco, Guadalajara, because my friend Lourdes Verea had sworn that it was the very best place for *pozole* in the city. It was a Macondo kind of rain, relentless and pounding—streams of water coursed from a central courtyard though the dining area and between our feet. By the time our waiter managed to weave his way from the kitchen to our table bearing the *pozole* and its accompaniments, we were shivering with cold, but we soon forgot our wet clothes and the flood. We just propped our feet on the chairs and warmed ourselves with the fragrant steam wafting from our bowls. It was red *pozole*, redolent of Mexican oregano and filled with succulent chicken and pork, the gelatinous morsels of pig's feet and head melting in our mouths, the hominy fully opened like flowers, the steamy liquid tamed by the coolness of lime juice and fresh radishes.

After that I looked for *pozole* wherever I traveled in Mexico. I tasted a simple but practical *pozole* made with leftover cooked meats at the home of Lourdes's mother in Guadalajara, and a chicken *pozole* in Oaxaca that I came to adore, with its concentrated broth of sharp *puya* and guajillo chiles. In Tzintzuntzan, a small town on the shores of Lake Pátzcuaro, I found people eating red *pozole* with a variety of meats and little embellishments at the all-night street fair for the Days of the Dead, from October 31 to November 2. *Pozole* kept them warm during long vigils at the town's two cemeteries.

While I was in Tzintzuntzan working on an illustrated book about the embroiderers of Lake Pátzcuaro, I met an old woman named Pomposa Rendón who told me about a duck *pozole* once typical of the area. "At this time of the year, there used to be many ducks," she said. "Everybody made duck *pozole* because these are days of vigil, the Vigil of the Little Angels. Many men would hunt the ducks and share them among themselves. Now they are gone—

there are no more ducks, "she said with sadness. "We used to see flocks of them fly there, over the marsh."

In my many trips to the area, I had never spotted a single duck nor tasted tamales or *pozole* made with duck. But I had seen a large mural depicting a duck hunt in the lake at Mexico City's anthropology museum. Only older women like Pomposa could recall the duck *realadas* (as the hunts were called) and the lovely food made with the hunters' bounty. I like to imagine the taste of that extinct *pozole*, and I often make duck *pozole* as a variation of recipes that call for chicken.

But first impressions are always powerful, and I still think of *pozole* and the Jalisco rain. To me there is no better way to enjoy the soup's concentrated warmth than on a stormy day when the rain falls like spears.

Oaxacan Chicken *Pozole*

Pozole de Pollo

This is a simple but very tasty *pozole* that I like to serve to friends and family for dinner on the Day of the Epiphany (January 6) before cutting the ring-shaped cake called *torta de reyes* (kings' cake), a Mexican tradition that I have made my own. When I serve *pozole* for company, I start dinner with a very light appetizer (*botana*). I want my guests to come to my *pozole* truly hungry, and I expect them to come back for seconds and even thirds. That is the true meaning of the Mexican expression *pozolear*—to eat *pozole* until you are truly satisfied.

What to Drink: Dos Equis Ambar Mexican beer

SERVES 6

For the Chicken

One   3½-pound chicken

For the Chile Sauce

3   dried guajillo chiles (about ¾ ounce)

13   dried *puya* chiles (about 1½ ounces)

3   cups water

3   garlic cloves

½   small white onion (about 6 ounces)

3   medium plum tomatoes (about 8 ounces), quartered

1   teaspoon dried oregano, preferably Mexican

1   teaspoon ground cumin

2   tablespoons corn oil

2   chicken bouillon cubes, crushed

For the Hominy

1½   pounds Basic Mexican *Pozole* (page 250) or three 15-ounce cans white hominy (use any Mexican brand or Goya), drained

1   tablespoon dried oregano, preferably Mexican

For the Garnish

2   bunches radishes (about 1 pound), trimmed and cut into ¼-inch dice

1   medium red or white onion (about 8 ounces), cut into ¼-inch dice

1   medium green cabbage (about 1¼ pounds), finely shredded

Dried oregano, preferably Mexican

Warm corn tortillas, preferably homemade (page 579), for serving

Preparing the Chicken ▶ Cut the chicken into 10 pieces according to the instructions on page 659. Remove the skin and set aside.

Preparing the Sauce ▶ Stem, seed, and rinse the chiles according to the instructions on page 744. Drain the chiles, place them in a medium saucepan with the 3 cups water, and bring to a boil over medium heat. Boil until soft, about 15 minutes.

Transfer the chiles, with the cooking water, to a blender or food processor, add the onion, tomatoes, oregano, and cumin, and process to a smooth puree. Strain through a medium-mesh strainer into a bowl and set aside.

In a medium saucepan, heat the oil until rippling. Add the strained sauce and cook, stirring, for about 6 minutes. Add the crushed chicken bouillon cubes and cook, stirring, for 3 more minutes. Set aside.

Finishing the *Pozole* ▶ Place the chicken in an 8-quart pot, add 3½ quarts water and the chile sauce, and bring to a boil over medium heat. Reduce the heat slightly and simmer for about 30 minutes.

Add the hominy and oregano and simmer until the bird is tender, about 20 more minutes. Remove the chicken from the pot, take the meat off the bones, and cut into bite-sized pieces. Return to the pot and heat through.

Ladle the *pozole* into a soup tureen and bring to the table with the garnishes served in bowls. Warm corn tortillas complete the feast.

Variation: You can use duck pieces instead of chicken. Simmer until tender, about 1½ hours, before adding the hominy. Finish the *pozole* as directed.

Andean Hominy and Pumpkin Seed Soup

Motepata

During most of the year, Cuenca is a quiet Andean town, the temple of Ecuadorian belles lettres, a bastion of civility. But during the three days of carnival before Shrove Tuesday, it turns into a madhouse, where revelers are given carte blanche to soak anyone who crosses their path. Bakers come out of their shops armed with big kneading tubs full of water. Little ladies who otherwise would not dare to offend anyone reach out from their balconies and gleefully hurl buckets of water onto any passersby.

Those who prefer to stay dry plan ahead and stock up to avoid last-minute trips to the market. They stay at home, eating home-baked bread and *motepata*, a succulent soup of *mote* (hominy) thickened with pumpkin seeds that is never missing during carnival. In Spanish, the name sounds as if cow's hooves, *patas*, were involved, but this is just a coincidence. The word is actually derived from the Quechua word for a kindred dish called *motepatashca*, in which *mote* is cooked down almost to a mush. *Motepata* is creamy because of the addition of milk and ground pumpkin seeds.

Cook's Note: Normally the *mote* for Andean hominy is soaked overnight before cooking. But if you don't have time to do this, you can streamline the process in a pressure cooker. Place 1 pound Andean corn for *mote* and 2½ quarts water in the pressure cooker, lock the lid, and heat over high heat. When the valve begins to whistle, lower the heat to medium and cook for 1½ hours. Drain.

For the Hominy

Andean Hominy (page 251; see Cook's Note above for streamlined pressure-cooker method)

For the Meat

1 pound pork shoulder or boneless butt, cut into 2-inch pieces, or meaty boneless pork chops
2 quarts water
1 tablespoon salt
1 teaspoon freshly ground black pepper

For the Cooking Sauce

3 tablespoons achiote-infused corn oil (page 89)
3 garlic cloves, finely chopped
½ small white onion, finely chopped
½ small red onion, finely chopped
½ teaspoon ground cumin
1 teaspoon salt
½ teaspoon freshly ground black pepper

For the Thickener

1½ cups whole milk
⅓ cup hulled pumpkin seeds (about 1½ ounces), roasted
1 teaspoon dried oregano

Preparing the Hominy ▶ Prepare the *mote* by either the traditional or the pressure-cooker method. Set aside.

Cooking the Meats ▶ Place the pork, water, salt, and pepper in a medium pot and cook, covered, over medium heat until fork-tender, about 1¼ hours

if using pork shoulder or butt, 45 minutes if using pork chops.

Preparing the Cooking Sauce ▶ Heat the oil in a 12-inch skillet over medium heat until rippling. Add the garlic and sauté until golden, about 20 seconds. Add the onion and cook, stirring, until soft, about 5 minutes. Stir in the cumin, salt, and pepper and cook for 1 more minute. Remove from the heat.

When the meat is tender, stir the sauce into the pot and add the hominy. Bring to a gentle simmer.

Meanwhile, place the milk and pumpkin seeds in a blender or food processor and process until smooth.

Finishing the Soup ▶ Stir the pumpkin seed mixture into the pot, bring to a simmer, and cook, covered, for 20 to 25 minutes, until the soup thickens lightly. Sprinkle with the oregano just before serving. Serve in soup bowls, with Cuenca's White Sandwich Rolls (page 589).

Bolivian Corn and Fava Bean Soup

Lawa de Choclo y Habas

In Bolivia, soups are categorized according to their thickness. A light soup with many ingredients is a *chupe*. A thicker soup is a *lawa*, and a porridgelike soup in which the ingredients are ground to a paste is a *ch'aque*. This version of a *lawa* is my adaptation of a recipe by cookbook author Nelly de Jordán, a native of Cochabamba.

10 cups beef broth, homemade (page 540) or store-bought

1 small white onion (about 6 ounces), finely chopped

2 large plum tomatoes (about 6 ounces), peeled, seeded, and finely chopped (about ½ cup)

¼ cup minced flat-leaf parsley

½ teaspoon ground cumin

¼ teaspoon dried oregano

1 teaspoon salt

⅛ teaspoon freshly ground black pepper

4 cups (about 1 pound) fresh or frozen Andean corn or fresh sweet corn kernels

1 tablespoon ground *panca* peppers

4 medium russet potatoes (about 1½ pounds), peeled and quartered

3 pounds fresh fava beans, shelled (about 3 cups), cooked and drained according to the instructions on page 268

▶ Combine the broth, onion, tomatoes, parsley, cumin, oregano, salt, and pepper in an 8-quart pot and bring to a boil over high heat. Reduce the heat to medium to maintain a gentle simmer.

Combine the corn and *panca* pepper in a food processor or blender and process to a coarse paste. Gradually add to the pot, stirring with a wooden spoon, then add the potatoes. Cook until the potatoes are done, about 20 minutes.

Add the fava beans and cook for 5 more minutes. Remove from the heat.

Serving: Ladle into a soup tureen and bring to the table with a bowl of Spicy Bolivian Table Sauce (page 117).

Chicken and Sweet Cornmeal Stew in the Style of Chol Chol

Cazuela de Ave con Chuchoca de Chol Chol

All over Chile, people eat *cazuelas* of poultry, meats, and vegetables. *Cazuela* is a word we are more likely to associate with a clay pot, but in Chile the basic meaning is something like "stewing pot" and, by extension, the stew or soup made in it.

This *cazuela* is made with chicken and the broth is thickened with *chuchoca*, cornmeal made from sweet corn (see page 236) that has been blanched and dried when fresh to retain its sweetness, a specialty of the Mapuche Indians of Patagonia. You can easily make *chuchoca* following the basic recipe on page 244.

I learned this chicken dish in Chol Chol, a town in southern Chile not far from Temuco, the land of the Patagonian Mapuche. Like many simple Latin stews and soups, it is raised to special heights when served with a lively table sauce—in this case a Chilean *pebre* with the local smoked paprika (*merkén*). If you have pottery bowls to match the earthy character of the dish, they will add to your pleasure. I love the Chilean black pottery from Pomaire; a similar pottery from Colombia is available in the United States.

SERVES 4 TO 6

6 chicken thighs (about 3 pounds), skin removed

2 quarts water

1 garlic clove, finely chopped

1 small yellow onion (about 6 ounces), finely chopped

½ red bell pepper, cored, seeded, and cut into ¼-inch-wide strips

1 medium carrot (about 4 ounces), peeled and cut into 3-by-¼-inch sticks

1 teaspoon dried oregano

1 teaspoon store-bought *merkén* or homemade Coriander-Flavored *Merkén* from Temuco (page 76) or *pimentón* (Spanish smoked paprika, hot or sweet)

1 teaspoon salt

8 ounces green beans, ends trimmed and cut into 3 pieces each

2 medium ears corn, husked and cut into 1-inch rounds

8 ounces Caribbean squash (*calabaza*), or kabocha or butternut squash, peeled, seeded, and cut into 2-inch chunks

¾ cup Chilean Sweet Yellow Cornmeal (page 244)

▶ Place the chicken, water, garlic, onion, bell pepper, carrot, oregano, *merkén* or paprika, and salt in a medium pot and bring to a boil over high heat. Lower the heat to medium and simmer, covered, for 15 minutes.

Add the beans, corn, and squash to the pot and cook until tender, about 15 minutes.

Gradually add the cornmeal in a fine stream, stirring to prevent lumps. Cook, covered, for 10 minutes, or until the stew thickens lightly. Add more water if it becomes too thick; it should have body but not become a porridge. Remove from the heat.

Serving: Serve hot, passing around a bowl of Patagonian *Pebre* Sauce with *Merkén* (page 132).

THICK AND CREAMY SOUPS

Quito's Potato and Cheese Soup

Locro de Quito

The name *locro* comes from the Quechua word *lucru*, a thick soup of potatoes and vegetables. There are several versions of *locro* in Andean Ecuador, some featuring ingredients like broccoli rabe, cabbage, and *zambo*, a type of squash, but the simplest and most popular is made with mealy potatoes.

The mother of my friend Inés Mantilla made this satisfying *locro* for me in Quito. Having spent time in the southern highlands, where *locro* is also a staple soup, I quickly saw the relationship. They are all substantial vegetarian meals in a bowl based on potatoes, milk, and cheese. In parts of the southern highlands, like Azuay, the soup is enriched with a soft cheese. You can now find this cheese in Latin markets catering to Ecuadorians, but you could substitute Monterey Jack. In my memory, the cheese used in the Quito soup was stronger tasting, probably closest to a French feta.

SERVES 6

2 teaspoons achiote-infused corn oil (page 89)

1 tablespoon salted butter

2 garlic cloves, finely chopped

½ small red onion, finely chopped (about ¼ cup)

¼ teaspoon ground cumin

2 teaspoons salt

¼ teaspoon freshly ground black pepper

1½ quarts water

2½ pounds russet potatoes (5 large), peeled and cut into 2-inch chunks

1½ cups whole milk

4 ounces crumbled French feta cheese, a soft, crumbly Ecuadorian cheese (such as San Fernando Queso Fresco from Azuay), or Monterey Jack cheese

4 scallions, white and pale green parts, finely chopped (about 1 cup)

▶ Heat the oil and butter in a medium pot over medium heat. Add the garlic and sauté until barely golden, about 40 seconds. Add the onion, cumin, salt, and pepper and sauté until the onion softens, about 5 minutes. Add the water and potatoes and bring to a boil. Reduce the heat and simmer until the potatoes are half-cooked, about 10 minutes.

Add the milk and cook for 5 more minutes. Add the crumbled cheese and cook for 5 more minutes, or until the potatoes are tender. Ladle into bowls and serve piping hot.

TRIPE

Honeycomb tripe, one of the world's greatest delicacies, comes from the honeycombed lining of a cow's second stomach, and it is appreciated by cooks and connoisseurs from France, where *tripes à la mode de Caen* has something close to a cult status, to China, where it is robust street fare. Spanish cooks often prepare it with a cow's foot (or calf's or pig's foot), which, like the tripe, benefits from prolonged slow cooking and develops a similar succulent quality as the gelatin in it too is gradually released.

Honeycomb tripe

The taste for stews and soups with tripe (or tripe and cow's foot) crossed the Atlantic long ago. People in the Americas generally call tripe (and tripe dishes) *mondongo* (especially in the Hispanic Caribbean) or sometimes *guatita* (Ecuador and Chile), and cook it with classic Caribbean or Andean seasonings.

BUYING

Please note that honeycomb tripe is not the same as other kinds of innards that may be labeled "tripe." You can recognize it by its ivory color and the network of ridges and folds that give it its name. In this country, it is generally sold partly cooked, which can create problems judging the cooking time.

CLEANING AND PREPARING

Whether precooked or not, honeycomb tripe needs to be well cleaned before cooking. I never trust the job to have been thoroughly done by the butcher (incompletely cleaned tripe will fill your kitchen with a horrible stench as it boils). Cuban peasants used to soak it in water along with fresh basil, *albahaca mondonguera*—so called because it was picked just for the purpose of taking the offensive smell out of tripe. I scrub it with lime or lemon juice. ◆

Argentinean Vegetable and Tripe Soup

Buseca de Mondongo

La Boca, a Buenos Aires neighborhood not far from the Rio de la Plata, was once home to Italian immigrants speaking an argot called Lunfardo. They made a version of *busecca*, a Milanese tripe and borlotti bean stew with their own ingredients, which became an Argentinean favorite with the hispanicized spelling *buseca*. In Milan, the stew is usually ladled over bread slices and sprinkled with grated cheese. In Argentina, it is flavored with paprika and served over rice.

Cook's Note: To cook the tripe, you can use a pressure cooker, which will not only save time but also produce tender, flavorful results with a tough customer like tripe. Place the tripe, water, onion, garlic, and bay leaves in the pressure cooker and bring to full pressure over high heat. Lower the heat to medium and cook for 30 minutes. Remove from the heat and let the pressure release. Test for doneness; if the tripe is still tough, reseal the pot and repeat the process, cooking for 10 more minutes.

Working Ahead ▶ The tripe can be cooked 2 or 3 days ahead and stored in the refrigerator, tightly covered. The soup can also be kept refrigerated, tightly covered, for a couple of days. It reheats very well.

SERVES 6

For the Tripe

- 1½ pounds honeycomb tripe
- 1 lemon, halved
- 4½ quarts water
- 1 large yellow onion (12 ounces), halved
- 1 large head garlic, halved crosswise
- 2 bay leaves

For the Soup

- 2 tablespoons corn oil
- 6 garlic cloves, finely chopped
- 1 medium yellow onion (8 ounces), finely chopped
- 1 medium red bell pepper (6 ounces), cored, seeded, and finely chopped
- 1 large carrot (5 ounces), peeled and cut into ¼-inch rounds
- 4 medium plum tomatoes (12 ounces), cored, seeded, and coarsely chopped
- 1 pound russet potatoes, peeled and cut into 1-inch dice
- 2 Spanish-style chorizos (about 3½ ounces), cut into ¼-inch slices
- One 16-ounce can chickpeas, drained
- One 15-ounce can kidney beans, drained
- 1 tablespoon *pimentón* (Spanish smoked paprika, hot or sweet)
- 2 teaspoons salt
- ¼ teaspoon dried oregano

Cleaning the Tripe ▶ Put the tripe in the sink and squeeze the lemon over it. Use the lemon halves to scrub the tripe thoroughly. Rinse under warm running water, squeezing and scrubbing, then give it a good sniff. If there is any strong odor left, go on rinsing and scrubbing until it smells perfectly clean.

Cooking the Tripe ▶ Place the tripe in a large pot or Dutch oven, add the water, onion, garlic, and bay leaves, and bring to a boil over high heat. At once reduce the heat to medium and simmer, covered, until the tripe is tender, about two hours.

Drain the tripe, reserving 4 cups of the cooking liquid. Let cool, then cut the tripe into 2-by-¼-inch strips. Reserve.

Preparing the Soup ▶ In a large, heavy pot, heat the oil over medium heat until rippling. Add the garlic and sauté until golden, about 40 seconds. Add the onion, bell pepper, and carrot and cook for 5 minutes. Add the tomatoes and cook for 5 minutes.

Add the tripe, potatoes, chorizos, chickpeas, and kidney beans, then stir in the smoked paprika, salt, and oregano. Let cook for a minute, and taste for seasoning; adjust as needed. Lower the heat to medium and cook, covered, until the vegetables are tender, about 15 minutes. Remove from the heat.

Serve in soup bowls with white rice or crusty Italian bread.

White Bean and Tomato Cream Soup with Chilean Smoked Paprika

Crema de Frijoles Blancos y Tomate con Merkén

My white bean and tomato cream soup takes the elements of a hearty rustic soup and turns them into something subtly different. Spanish friends say it reminds them of a northern Spanish *fabada*, a cousin to cassoulet. For my Chilean friends, the combination of basil, paprika, and beans brings back memories of summer meals with the cranberry bean stew that they call *porotos granados*.

My take on the idea is pureed and strained soup, its parts melding into a refined and harmonious whole without surrendering the integrity of the original ingredients. Smooth and silky but with all the muscle and substance of a big one-dish meal, the soup has layers of complementary and contrasting flavor and texture. Every spoonful carries the earthiness of the white beans, the tart edge of the Cuban tomato *sofrito*, and the powerful heat and smokiness of Spanish *pimentón*. A spoonful of Latin American brown loaf sugar reduces the acidity of the tomato and intensifies its fresh, fruity flavor. Basil enhances the smoky flavor of the paprika with its clove-like perfume.

I serve the soup in delicate soup plates, repeating the accents of basil and paprika in the garnish. If you want, add freshly made croutons, still hot from the pan and dusted lightly with the same smoked paprika, to give it the soup another layer of texture.

Cook's Note: The beans and the *sofrito* can be cooked the day before and refrigerated.

SERVES 6 TO 8

For the Beans

- 1 pound (about 2 cups) small dried white beans, picked over and rinsed
- 4 quarts water
- 1 medium yellow onion (about 8 ounces), halved
- 1 medium green bell pepper (about 8 ounces), halved, cored, seeded, and deveined
- 2 bay leaves

For the Cooking Sauce

- 3 tablespoons extra-virgin olive oil
- 5 ounces slab bacon, cut into ¼-inch dice (about ¾ cup)
- 12 garlic cloves, finely chopped
- 1 large yellow onion (about 10 ounces), finely chopped (abut 1½ cups)
- 1 medium green bell pepper (about 8 ounces), cored, seeded, deveined, and finely chopped (about ½ cup)
- 1 large red bell pepper (about 10 ounces), cored, seeded, deveined and finely chopped (about 1⅓ cups)
- 12 Caribbean sweet peppers (*ajíes dulces*) or 1 cubanelle pepper, seeded and finely chopped (about ¼ cup)
- 2 bay leaves
- 2 teaspoons hot *pimentón* (Spanish smoked paprika) or *Merkén de Chillán* (page 74)
- ½ teaspoon ground cumin
- 1 cup tomato sauce, homemade (page 48) or store-bought
- 2 tablespoons grated brown loaf sugar (*panela* or *piloncillo*), dark Muscovado sugar, or dark brown sugar
- 2½ teaspoons salt, or to taste
- 4 basil leaves

For the Soup

- 2 tablespoons extra-virgin olive oil or butter
- 2 cups chicken broth, homemade (page 538) or store-bought
- ¼ cup heavy cream
  Salt

- 8 large whole basil leaves, for garnish

Cooking the Beans ▶ Place the beans, water, onion, green pepper, and bay leaves in an 8-quart pot and bring to a boil over high heat. Lower the heat and simmer, uncovered, until the beans are very tender but still retain their shape, about 1½ hours. Remove and discard the vegetables and bay leaves; reserve the beans in their cooking liquid.

Making the Cooking Sauce (*Sofrito*) ▶ Heat the oil in a large, heavy skillet over medium heat. Add the bacon and sauté for about 4 minutes, until golden brown. Add the garlic and sauté until light golden, about 20 seconds. Add the onion and cook until soft, about 5 minutes. Add all the peppers, the bay leaves, paprika, and cumin and cook, stirring, for 3 minutes. Add the tomato sauce, sugar, and salt and cook for 5 minutes. Remove the bay leaves and stir in the basil leaves. Set aside.

Making the Soup ▶ Working in batches, puree the beans in a blender or food processor with the cooking liquid and the *sofrito*. With a wooden spoon, force the puree through a fine-mesh strainer into a bowl.

Heat the olive oil or butter in a large saucepan over medium heat. Pour in the puree, stir, and bring to a low boil. Stir in the chicken broth and cream and simmer for 1 minute. Season with salt. Keep the soup warm over low heat while you prepare the garnish.

Making the Basil Chiffonade ▶ Stack the basil leaves, roll up tightly lengthwise, and cut crosswise into very fine strips with a sharp knife.

Ladle the soup into bowls and garnish with the basil.

Smoky Pureed Pumpkin and Cacao Soup

Crema de Calabaza y Cacao

People who have tasted this soup always ask me what country it comes from. My answer is the Latin kitchen I have created in New Jersey at my Weehawken home and at my restaurant Zafra. Anyone who eats my food often knows that one of my favorite flavor combinations is *calabaza*, the firm, meaty Caribbean pumpkin, smoky chipotle chile, and chocolate—in this case, a combination of cacao nibs and premium dark chocolate.

Cook's Note: Cacao nibs, the kernels of roasted and shelled cacao beans, add a fascinating, deep level of flavor and aroma to savory food. They come already roasted and they can be sprinkled on salads or stirred into soups and stews. Cacao nibs are the raw material for chocolate. They will melt in hot liquid, just like chocolate. For more even melting, I prefer to grind them to a powder in a spice mill or blend them in a food processor or blender with a cooking sauce, such as the *sofrito* here. In this soup, the nibs are discernible only as minuscule dark specks that might pass for black pepper.

SERVES 6 TO 8

For the Squash
- 2 pounds *calabaza* (Caribbean pumpkin) or kabocha or Hubbard squash

For the Cooking Sauce
- 4 medium plum tomatoes (about 12 ounces)
- ½ small white onion (about 3½ ounces), not peeled
- 4 garlic cloves, not peeled
- 1 canned chipotle chile in *adobo*
- ⅛ teaspoon ground allspice
- ⅛ teaspoon ground cinnamon
- ⅛ teaspoon anise seeds
- 1 ounce cacao nibs
- 1 tablespoon extra-virgin olive oil
- 1 tablespoon grated brown loaf sugar (*panela* or *piloncillo*) or Demerara sugar
- 8 cups chicken broth, homemade (page 538) or store-bought
- 1 ounce dark chocolate, preferably Pacari Esmeraldas 60% or Manabí 65%, coarsely chopped

For the Garnish
- 1 cup diced manchego cheese (about 3 ounces)
- 1 cup Mexican *crema* (page 148) or crème fraîche Maya Cacao and Chile Balls (page 76), optional

Preparing the Squash ▶ Peel and seed the squash and cut into 1-inch pieces. Place in a bowl and set aside.

Preparing the Cooking Sauce ▶ Heat a *comal*, griddle, or heavy skillet over medium heat. Add the tomatoes, onion, and garlic and roast, turning occasionally with tongs, until the tomatoes are blistered and the onion and garlic are charred in spots, about 10 minutes. Remove to a plate. Scrape off the charred bits from the tomatoes, and peel the onion and garlic.

Place the tomatoes, onion, and garlic in a food processor, add the chipotle chile, allspice, cinnamon, anise seeds, and cacao nibs, and process to a smooth puree.

Heat the oil in a medium heavy pot over medium heat until sizzling. Add the puree (watch out for splatters), stir in the brown sugar, and cook, stirring, for 5 minutes. Add the squash, then pour in the broth and let come to a boil. Reduce the heat to low and simmer, covered, until the squash is tender, about 15 minutes. Remove from the heat. Working in batches, puree the soup in a blender or food processor. With a wooden spoon, force the puree through a fine-mesh strainer into a large saucepan and bring to a boil over medium heat. Stir in the chocolate and cook, stirring until it melts, about 3 minutes. Remove from the heat.

Serving: Ladle into bowls and serve garnished with the diced cheese and cream. If desired, pass the cacao-chile balls with a small cheese grater and invite your guests to grate a pinch over the soup. For a touch of freshness, add a dollop of "Finger Sauce" (page 116) or Tomato and Serrano Chile Salsa (page 114).

Caracan Black Bean Cream Soup

Puré de Caraotas Negras Mantuano

In Venezuela, the heritage of the colonial sugar trade lingers in the cuisine. My friend José Rafael Lovers, a distinguished Venezuelan food historian, says that during the colonial period, evidence of a sweet tooth—though common to all social classes—was especially pronounced in the *cocina mantuana*, the cooking of the plantation-owning upper classes (whose womenfolk could afford to wear fine *mantos*, shawls, hence their name, *mantuanas*). The quality of the brown loaf sugar (*papelón*) in Venezuela is suaver and more delicate than any other, and Venezuelan black bean soup is distinguished from other Latin American counterparts by its mellifluous sweetness. The sweeter the soup, the more steeped is the cook in Venezuelan tradition.

Working Ahead ▶ Both the beans and the cooking sauce can be prepared at least 1 day ahead. The pureed soup also keeps well for a couple of days.

SERVES 4 TO 5 (MAKES 6 CUPS)

For the Beans
- 1 pound (about 2 cups) black beans, picked over and rinsed
- 3½ quarts water
- 1 medium yellow onion (8 ounces)
- 1 large green bell pepper (8 ounces), halved, cored, seeded, and deveined
- 5 ounces, or to taste, brown loaf sugar (*papelón* or *panela*), grated (about ¾ cup) or cut into small pieces, or Muscovado sugar, or dark brown sugar

For the Cooking Sauce
- 2 tablespoons corn oil or light olive oil
- 5 ounces slab bacon, cut into ¼-inch dice
- 8 garlic cloves, mashed to a paste with a mortar and pestle or finely chopped and mashed
- 1 medium yellow onion (about 8 ounces), grated
- 2½ teaspoons salt, or to taste
- 1 teaspoon freshly ground black pepper

For the Soup

- 2 tablespoons extra-virgin olive oil
- 4 garlic cloves, mashed to a pulp with a mortar and pestle or finely chopped and mashed

Cooking the Beans ▶ Place the beans, water, onion, and green pepper in a 6-quart pot and bring to a boil over medium heat. Cook, partially covered, until the beans are tender but still retain their shape, 1½ to 2 hours.

Preparing the Cooking Sauce ▶ Heat the oil in a medium skillet over medium heat until rippling. Add the bacon and sauté until lightly browned and crisp, about 5 minutes. With a slotted spoon, transfer the bacon to paper towels to drain.

Add the garlic to the fat remaining in the pan and sauté until lightly golden, about 40 seconds. Add the grated onion, salt, and pepper, and cook over low heat until soft, about 5 minutes. Remove from the heat.

Making the Soup ▶ Add the brown sugar to the beans and stir to dissolve. Stir in the cooking sauce. Taste for seasoning and add more salt if needed. Lower the heat, cover the pot, and cook for 30 to 45 minutes.

Just before the soup is done, heat the olive oil in a small skillet over medium heat until it ripples. Add the garlic and sauté until light golden, about 40 seconds. Stir into the soup. Remove from the heat.

Working in batches, puree the soup in a blender or food processor. With the back of a wooden spoon or ladle, force the puree through a fine-mesh strainer into another saucepan. Reheat just to a simmer.

Serving: Serve hot in soup bowls, garnished with the reserved bacon and, if you like, Venezuelan Ripened Milk (page 146) or crème fraîche.

FISH AND SHELLFISH SOUPS

Chilean Conger Eel Soup
Caldillo de Congrio

Caldillo de congrio, a rich conger eel soup, is Chile's most famous fish soup. Celebrated by the poet Pablo Neruda in his "*Oda al Caldillo de Congrio*" (Ode to the Conger Eel Soup), it is a dish you can't miss when you travel to Chile.

My friend Miro Popiç, a Chilean-born wine writer and food journalist, makes a sublime *caldillo de congrio* that fills you with warmth and appreciation for the simple things of life. But it is only one version of a dish that every Chilean has a strong opinion about. The one glorified by Pablo Neruda, for example, is based on shrimp and conger eel and finished with "a swirl of cream." Miro's recipe leaves out the cream (for myself, I love its wonderful caress) and shrimp and adds potatoes and carrots, which are very traditional.

Conger eel is not well known in the United States, and you may have trouble finding it. It is a meaty, white-fleshed Pacific ocean fish quite different in flavor and texture from the common American eel. Some consider it among the finest of all fish, and the French love it in bouillabaisse. If you cannot find it at a specialty fish purveyor, substitute a firm-fleshed white fish like grouper or halibut. When I first tested this recipe, I used Chilean sea bass, also known as Patagonian toothfish, which I like for its gelatinous flesh, but it is now an endangered species, and I have stopped using it. I use grouper or halibut instead.

For the Fish

6   Chilean conger eel steaks or grouper or halibut steaks (about 5 pounds)
Salt and freshly ground black pepper

For the Cooking Sauce

3   tablespoons extra-virgin olive oil

3   garlic cloves, finely chopped

1   medium white onion (8 ounces), finely slivered lengthwise

One   16-ounce can plum tomatoes, drained and crushed

1¼   teaspoons salt, or to taste

For the Soup

6   cups fish broth, homemade (page 540) or store-bought

4   medium red potatoes (about 1 pound), cut into ½-inch-thick slices

2   large carrots (about 12 ounces), peeled and cut into ½-inch slices on a diagonal

½   cup chopped cilantro or flat-leaf parsley

For Serving

2   tablespoons extra-virgin olive oil, for garnish

1   tablespoon coarsely chopped cilantro or flat-leaf parsley, for garnish

Seasoning the Fish ▶ Season the eel steaks with salt and pepper to taste. Set aside on a plate.

Making the Cooking Sauce ▶ Heat the oil in an 8-quart heavy pot over medium-high heat until rippling. Add the garlic and sauté until barely golden, about 20 seconds. Add the onion and cook until soft, about 5 minutes. Add the tomatoes and salt and cook, stirring, for 3 minutes.

Making the Soup ▶ Add the fish broth, potatoes, carrots, and cilantro or parsley to the cooking sauce. Taste for seasoning and add more salt and pepper if needed. Cook until the vegetables are tender, about 20 minutes. Taste and correct the seasoning if necessary.

Add the fish and simmer until it is just cooked through—it should be opaque at the bone—about 5 minutes. Remove from the heat.

Serving: Ladle into soup bowls, preferably earthenware. Drizzle with the olive oil and garnish with the cilantro or parsley. If a touch of heat is desired, season with Chilean "Goat's Horn" *Pebre* (page 131).

Creamy Ecuadorian Corn, Plantain, and Shrimp Soup

Sango de Camarones

The *sangos* of Ecuador (from the Quechua word *sankhu*, for a porridgelike soup) are savory soups thickened with starchy ingredients such as fresh corn, quinoa, and plantains. (Do not confuse them with Peruvian *sangos*, which belong to the family of egg-based colonial desserts.) This adaptation of a flavorful chowder from the coastal province of Manabí is one of my favorite seafood soups for company.

I now make this with American sweet corn, which gives the soup a sweetness that is not in the original. I balance the sweetness of the corn with a nontraditional *salsa cruda* inspired by Ecuadorian *Ají* (page 123), which would be another wonderful table condiment for the soup.

Cook's Notes: In Ecuador, this soup would be made with the fantastically fresh white shrimp caught along the coast. People buy them whole with the heads on and use the heads and shells to make the broth. If you cannot find an Asian or other fish market that sells shrimp with the heads still attached, use a well-flavored fish broth, or just use the shells for the broth. The shrimp can be added to the soup whole or coarsely chopped. The latter makes for easier eating.

Working Ahead ▶ The soup, without the shrimp, can be made a day ahead and stored in the refrigerator tightly covered, reheat before serving and cook the shrimp as directed. You can peel the shrimp ahead and refrigerate, but don't marinate them until the following day.

SERVES 6 TO 8

For the Shrimp

- 2 pounds medium shrimp, preferably Ecuadorian, in the shell and with heads on
- 4 garlic cloves, finely chopped
- 1 scallion, white and pale green parts, finely chopped
- 2 tablespoons fresh lime juice
- 1 teaspoon salt

For the Soup

- 6 cups fish broth, homemade (page 540) or store-bought (see Cook's Notes), or water
- 2 cups fresh corn kernels (from about 3 ears), or thawed frozen kernels
- 2 cups whole milk
- 2 green plantains, peeled (see page 181) and finely grated

For the Cooking Sauce

- 2 tablespoons achiote-infused corn oil or mild extra-virgin olive oil (page 89)
- 2 garlic cloves, finely chopped

- 1 large red onion (about 12 ounces), finely chopped
- 1 small red bell pepper (about 6 ounces), cored, seeded, deveined, and finely chopped
- 3 ripe medium plum tomatoes (about 9 ounces), peeled and coarsely chopped
- 1 teaspoon ground cumin
- 3 cilantro sprigs
  Salt
- ¼ teaspoon ground cayenne (optional)

For the Corn Salsa (*Ají de Choclo*)

- 1 cup sweet corn or Andean corn kernels, cooked in boiling water until tender
- 3 medium plum tomatoes (about 9 ounces), peeled, seeded, and finely chopped
- 2 scallions, white and pale green parts, finely chopped
- 1 fresh-frozen Ecuadorian hot red pepper (*ají rojo*, available in some Latin markets), thawed, or any hot red pepper
  Juice of 1 lime
- 2 tablespoons finely chopped cilantro
  Salt and freshly ground black pepper

Marinating the Shrimp ▶ Peel and devein the shrimp. Reserve the heads (if any) and shells for the broth. In a bowl large enough to hold the shrimp, whisk together the garlic, scallion, lime juice, and salt. Add the shrimp and toss to coat. Set aside to marinate for 1 hour in the refrigerator.

Making the Broth and Thickener ▶ Place the broth or water in a medium saucepan and add the shrimp heads and shells. Bring to a gentle simmer and cook for about 10 minutes. Strain into a bowl, discarding the solids. Set aside.

Place the corn and milk in a blender or food processor and process to a smooth paste. With a wooden spoon, force the corn mixture through a medium-mesh strainer into a bowl. Stir in the grated plantain. Set aside.

Making the Cooking Sauce ▶ Heat the oil in a 4-quart heavy pot over medium heat. Add the garlic and sauté until gold, about 40 seconds. Add the onion and bell pepper and cook until soft, about 5 minutes. Stir in the tomatoes and cumin and cook for 3 minutes. Add the pureed corn and plantain mixture, fish broth, cilantro, salt to taste, and cayenne, if using. Simmer, stirring occasionally, until the mixture thickens to the consistency of a cream soup, about 15 minutes.

Preparing the Corn Salsa ▶ Combine the corn, tomatoes, scallions, and hot pepper in a small bowl. Stir in the lime juice and cilantro. Season with salt and pepper to taste. Set aside.

Finishing the Soup ▶ Working in batches, puree the soup in a blender or food processor and return to the saucepan. Bring just to a boil. Taste for seasoning and add salt or cayenne pepper (if using) as needed. Add the reserved shrimp (whole or cut up in bite-sized pieces) and cook until pink, about 3 minutes.

Ladle the soup into individual bowls. Top each serving with a tablespoon of the fresh corn salsa and sprinkle with chopped cilantro leaves. Bring any extra salsa in a bowl to the table for guests.

Peruvian Shrimp *Chupe*

Chupe de Camarones

Judith Lombardi de Rojas was one of the best cooks I ever met in Peru. For decades, she collected her recipes, beautifully written, in composition notebooks now yellowing and worn with use. She shared this recipe with me while I was visiting her in Lima.

Chupes are among the oldest dishes of the Andean region. The name is from the Quechua *chupi*, meaning a soup with many ingredients. In colonial Peru, the main meal of the day for working-class people was the afternoon *comida (lunch)*, which usually featured *chupe* or another main-dish soup, but today these fortifying dishes are enjoyed by Peruvians anywhere on the social ladder. Some people consider *chupes* to be chowders because they contain milk, but I think they are a category unto themselves. In addition to fish or shellfish, such as crayfish from Andean streams, and vegetables such as *caiguas* in the highlands (see page 232), they usually contain Peruvian fresh cheese, for which I often substitute French feta. The eggs are traditionally poached in the soup, but I like to poach them separately, to keep their shape and prevent overcooking.

Cook's Note: To poach eggs, I cook them one at a time in a small saucepan filled with 1½ quarts water and set over medium to medium-low heat; the water should be barely bubbling. Stir in 3 tablespoons distilled white vinegar. One at a time, break each egg into a saucer. Make a vortex in the center of the pan by swirling the handle of a wooden spoon in it, and slip the egg into the vortex. Cook for 3 minutes, then lift out with a slotted spoon and place in a bowl of cold water. The eggs will keep, refrigerated, for 1 to 2 days. Let warm to room temperature before adding to the soup.

SERVES 6

For the Cooking Sauce

- 5 dried *mirasol* peppers, stemmed and seeded
- 5 dried *panca* peppers or 3 ancho chiles, stemmed and seeded

3 cups water

3 tablespoons extra-virgin olive oil

4 garlic cloves, finely minced

1 large red onion (about 12 ounces), finely chopped

1 teaspoon ground cumin

1 teaspoon dried oregano

For the Soup

10 cups chicken broth or fish broth, homemade (page 538 or 540) or store-bought

2 ears of frozen Andean corn or fresh white corn, cut into 1½-inch sections

4 small russet potatoes (about 1 pound 4 ounces), peeled and cut into 1-inch cubes

1 pound fresh fava beans, shelled (about 1 cup)

4 ounces green cabbage, roughly chopped

3 pounds meaty kabocha or butternut squash, peeled, seeded, and cut into 1-inch cubes

2 fat carrots, peeled and cut into ¼-inch slices (about 1⅓ cups)

¼ cup long-grain white rice

4 sprigs mint, plus 6 sprigs for garnish

1 cup whole milk

3 ounces French feta cheese, crumbled (about ½ cup)

1½ pounds medium shrimp (16 to 20 per pound), preferably Ecuadorian, peeled and deveined

6 poached eggs (see Cook's Note)

Making the Cooking Sauce ▶ Place the peppers in a medium saucepan, cover with the water, and bring to a simmer over medium heat. Simmer until soft, about 20 minutes. Drain, reserving ¼ cup of the cooking liquid.

Place the peppers and reserved liquid in a blender or food processor and puree until smooth. Set aside.

Heat the oil in an 8-quart pot over medium heat. Add the garlic and sauté until golden, about 40 seconds. Add the onion and sauté until soft, about 5 minutes. Add the cumin, oregano, and pepper puree and cook for 3 minutes, stirring.

Making the Soup ▶ Add the broth and bring to a boil over medium heat. Add all the vegetables, the rice, and the mint and simmer until the vegetables are tender, about 25 minutes.

Stir in the milk and crumbled cheese and cook for another 2 to 3 minutes. Add the shrimp and cook until pink, about 2 minutes. Remove from the heat.

To serve, distribute the shrimp among the serving bowls, reserving 6 or 12 for garnish. Ladle the soup over the shrimp and place a poached egg on each serving. Garnish with the reserved shrimp and mint sprigs.

Manabí's Rich Fish Soup

Biche de Pescado Manabita

The coastal Ecuadorian region of Manabí, cooled by the Humboldt Current, is one of the loveliest and most pleasant parts of the country, with little of the sweltering humidity of its neighbor Colombia to the north. The area is a mixture of coastal desert and lush forested mountains that are home to Ecuador's iconic Nacional cacao. It is also dotted with plantations of the prized Panama hat palm (*toquilla*). Despite the name, the industry is centered in Ecuador, and Manabí is more closely associated with hats (the famous *superfinos* of Montecristi) than cooking. But among Ecuadorians, it has a reputation as the home of the tastiest seafood. All along the Pacific coast here you will find small fishing villages where you can stop to eat, knowing that you will be well fed even in the humblest beach shack. There you are certain to find a fish soup that shows the imprint of indigenous Indian cooking: plantains, peanuts, yuca, and corn, enhanced with Spanish flavoring techniques.

SERVES 6 TO 8

For the Fish

6 garlic cloves, mashed to a paste with a mortar and pestle or finely chopped and mashed

1 teaspoon salt

¼ teaspoon freshly ground black pepper

¼ teaspoon ground cumin

2 teaspoons fresh lime juice

1½ pounds skinless firm-fleshed white fish fillets, such as drumfish, croaker, or grouper, cut into 2-inch pieces

For the Cooking Sauce

2 tablespoons achiote-infused corn oil (page 89)

6 garlic cloves, finely chopped

1 medium white onion (about 8 ounces), finely chopped

1 medium green or red bell pepper (about 6 ounces), cored, seeded, and finely chopped

½ teaspoon finely chopped oregano

½ teaspoon ground cumin

2 teaspoons salt

1 teaspoon freshly ground black pepper

For the Soup

3 medium ears corn, husked

8 ounces (1 cup) roasted unsalted peanuts

1 cup whole milk

10 cups fish broth, homemade (page 540) or store-bought

1 pound yuca, peeled and cut into 1-inch dice

1 ripe plantain, peeled and cut into 1-inch dice

¼ cup finely chopped cilantro

Marinating the Fish ▶ In a medium bowl, mix the garlic, salt, pepper, cumin, and lime juice. Add the fish and toss to coat. Refrigerate for 20 to 25 minutes.

Making the Cooking Sauce ▶ Heat the oil in a medium pot over medium-high heat until it ripples. Add the garlic and sauté until golden, about 40 seconds. Add the onion and bell pepper and sauté, stirring, for 3 minutes, until soft. Add the oregano, cumin, salt, and pepper. Cook, stirring, for 2 minutes. Remove from the heat and set aside.

Making the Soup ▶ Scrape the kernels from 2 of the ears of corn. Cut the third into ½-inch rounds. Set aside. Puree the peanuts with the milk in a blender. Set aside.

Add the broth to the cooking sauce and bring to a boil, stirring. Reduce the heat to medium and add the corn kernels and sliced rounds, then stir in the yuca and plantain and simmer, covered, for 15 minutes. Add the pureed peanut mixture and cook for 5 minutes, or until the broth thickens lightly. Add the fish and cilantro and simmer just until the fish is cooked through, about 5 minutes. Remove from the heat.

Serving: Distribute the fish and vegetables evenly among the soup bowls and top with the broth. Pass a bowl of salsa for guests to add their own: with this soup, I like Ecuadorian Peanut and Milk Sauce (page 128) or Ecuadorian Pumpkin Seed Sauce (page 129).

Andean Hominy and Pumpkin Seed Soup (*page 519*)

Xalapa's Smoky Oyster Mushroom Soup *(page 537)*

Puerto Rican Pan-Fried Yellowtail Snapper *(page 631)*, served with
Mojitos *(page 355)*, Fried Green Plantains *(page 182)*, and
Simple Cuban *Mojo* for Boiled Root Vegetables *(page 140)*

Clam, Pork, and White Bean Stew with Smoked Paprika and Garlic Sauce (*page 643*)

Grilled "Leaping Frog" Chicken
(*page 665*)

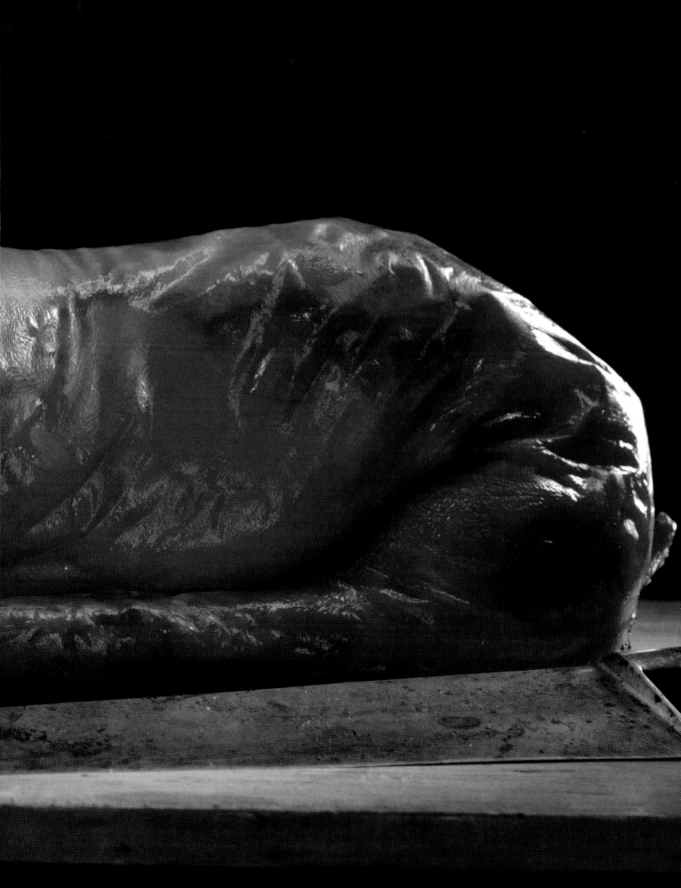

Roast Suckling Pig *(page 735)*

Grilled Skirt Steak (*page 704*) with Argentinean Chimichurri "La Porteña" (*page 132*) and Peruvian Warm Purple Potato and Squash Salad with Olive Oil and Paprika Dressing (*page 205*)

LIGHT AND FLAVORFUL SOUPS

Chipotle Chicken Soup with Vegetables

Chilate de Pollo

Like most people around the world, Mexicans think of chicken soup as a restorative, but they also regard it as a hangover cure, particularly if it is very spicy. No wonder it is often served for lunch (sometimes breakfast) the day after a party. In Oaxaca, spicy chicken soups are called *chilates*, which literally means chile waters. My version calls for smoky chipotles in *adobo* sauce and a trio of vegetables: potatoes, carrots, and chayotes.

Cook's Note: I like to use a free-range chicken. It holds up sturdily when served. Chicken bouillon cubes are the secret weapon of many Mexican and Latin American cooks, as much a part of Latin cooking as free-range organic chickens.

SERVES 6 TO 8

For the Chicken
One 3½-pound chicken, preferably a free-range organic bird, skinned and cut into 10 serving pieces according to the directions on page 659 (backbone included)
1 tablespoon salt
2 quarts water

2 medium carrots (about 12 ounces), peeled and cut into ½-inch dice
3 medium red potatoes (about 1 pound), cut into 1-inch dice
3 medium light green or white chayotes (about 1¼ pounds), peeled, seeded, and cut into 1-inch dice

For the Chile Sauce
3 canned chipotle chiles in *adobo*, with some of their sauce
3 garlic cloves
½ small white onion (about 3 ounces)
1 ripe medium plum tomato (about 3 ounces), quartered
1 teaspoon black peppercorns
¼ teaspoon ground cumin
½ cup water
2 tablespoons corn oil
2 chicken bouillon cubes, preferably Knorr

For the Garnish
2 limes, cut into wedges
1 medium white onion (about 8 ounces), finely chopped
¼ cup finely chopped cilantro

Cooking the Chicken ▶ Place the chicken, salt, and water in a 6-quart pot and bring to a boil over high heat. Lower the heat to medium and simmer, uncovered, until the chicken is about half cooked. This will vary between 15 to 30 minutes for different free-range birds. The usual commercial birds will take about 10 minutes. Add the vegetables and cook until they are almost tender, about 15 minutes.

Preparing the Sauce ▶ Place the chiles, garlic, onion, tomato, peppercorns, cumin, and water in a blender or food processor and process to a smooth puree. Strain through a medium sieve into a bowl, pushing the sauce through with a wooden spoon.

Heat the oil in a medium skillet over medium-high heat until it sizzles. Add the sauce and sauté, stirring, for about 5 minutes. Add the bouillon cubes and stir until dissolved, about 5 minutes.

Finishing the Soup ▶ Stir the sauce into the soup and simmer for 10 minutes. Ladle into bowls and garnish with the lime wedges and chopped onion and cilantro.

Yucatecan *Lima* Soup

Sopa de Lima Yucateca

In Mérida, Mexico, where I first tasted this wonderful *sopa de lima*, the soup is made with a local citrus fruit. Smaller than an orange, with a yellowish lime-green color and a very smooth skin, *lima* (*Citrus limetta*) has a sweet, refreshing taste and a pronounced aroma. As a child, I loved to eat it in wedges because it was mild and sweet with very little acidity. The *lima* is added only very late in the cooking and removed when it has contributed its aroma. In this country, I use Seville (bitter) oranges because of their equally fragrant skin. Once in a while I have been able to find *limas* in my local markets, but now I am hooked on the flavor of the soup with the bitter orange.

Cook's Note: This soup is based on a delicate but very richly spiced chicken broth called *salpimentado*; you save some of the chicken used for cooking the broth and shred it to be used in the finished dish. I have come to love *salpimentado* so much that I often make up a double or triple batch and freeze some to use in other dishes where I want a really special broth.

Working Ahead ▶ You can prepare the *salpimentado* a couple of days in advance and refrigerate it, tightly covered. Or you can freeze the soup for up to 3 months. If you have made a large batch ahead of time and frozen it, you will need 8 cups broth for the soup. In that case, instead of dedicating another whole chicken to the cause, you can poach a small skinless chicken breast in the thawed broth (allow about 15 minutes over medium heat), then cool it enough to pull the meat into thin shreds.

SERVES 6 TO 8

For the Broth (*Salpimentado*)

- 1 head garlic, separated into cloves but not peeled
- 1 medium white onion (8 ounces), not peeled
- One 3½-pound chicken, cut into 8 pieces (see page 659)
- 4 quarts water
- 2 Ceylon cinnamon sticks (*canela*)
- 1 teaspoon allspice berries
- 8 cloves
- ¼ teaspoon anise seeds
- 1 teaspoon ground cumin
- 1 teaspoon dried oregano
- 2 broad-leaf *culantro* leaves or 4 cilantro sprigs

For the Soup

- 1 habanero chile
- 2 tablespoons corn oil
- 1 medium white onion (8 ounces), finely chopped
- 2 medium plum tomatoes (about 6 ounces), finely chopped
- 2 teaspoons salt, or to taste

2 *limas* or 1 bitter orange, seeded and cut into thin slices

4 corn tortillas, for garnish

¼ cup corn oil, for frying

Making the Broth ▶ Heat a *comal*, griddle, or heavy skillet over medium heat until a drop of water sizzles on contact. Add the garlic and onion and roast, turning occasionally, until darkened on all sides, about 8 minutes. Remove and let cool. Meanwhile, roast the habanero for the soup, turning with tongs, until lightly charred, about 1 minute. Set aside.

Peel the roasted garlic and onion.

Place the chicken in a large pot and add the water, garlic and onion, cinnamon, allspice, cloves, anise seeds, cumin, oregano, and *culantro* or cilantro. Bring to a boil over high heat, reduce the heat to medium, and cook, covered, until the broth is reduced by half, about 1½ hours.

Transfer the chicken to a plate and strain the broth. Rinse out the pot and return the broth to it.

When the chicken is cool enough to handle, pull the breast meat into fine shreds. Save the rest of the chicken for another purpose.

Seed and finely chop the roasted chile, or crush it lightly, depending on how much heat you want. Set aside.

Making the Soup ▶ In a small skillet, heat the oil until rippling over medium heat. Add the onion and sauté until soft, 3 to 4 minutes. Add the tomatoes and cook for 3 minutes. Stir in the roasted chile and salt.

Scrape the mixture into the broth and add the *lima* or orange and the shredded chicken breast. Bring to a boil, then adjust the heat to maintain a simmer and cook for 10 minutes. Remove the *lima* or orange slices. If using a crushed habanero, remove it from the pot.

Cut the tortillas into ¼-inch-wide strips. In a large skillet, heat the oil until it ripples. Add the tortilla strips in batches and fry, stirring and tossing to coat evenly, until golden. Lift out onto paper towels to drain.

To serve, ladle the soup into bowls and serve garnished with the fried tortilla strips.

Xalapa's Smoky Oyster Mushroom Soup

Sopa de Hongos Ostra Ahumada

The area around Xalapa, the capital of Veracruz State in southeastern Mexico, is prime mushroom-hunting territory, and my friend Raquel Torres, of the now-defunct restaurant Churrería del Recuerdo in Xalapa, is the queen of mushrooms. She cooks them in every imaginable way, always managing to keep the full flavor. This soup is one of her triumphs. The chipotle chiles give it a rich smokiness and the *epazote* contributes a pungent herbal quality; neither overwhelms the whole.

Cook's Note: Pureed chipotles are a versatile seasoning—so useful, in fact, that I often make up a large batch and keep it in the refrigerator ready to use like tomato sauce. It will keep well for up to a month. (Sometimes I use chicken broth instead of water as the soaking liquid; this shortens the keeping time to a week.) For 1 cup, use 1 ounce chipotles (about 20 small or 11 medium), ¼ cup water or broth, and 3 garlic cloves.

For the Chipotle Puree

  2–3 dried chipotle chiles, stemmed and seeded
    1 garlic clove

For the Soup

    2 tablespoons extra-virgin olive oil
    1 large white onion (about 12 ounces), finely chopped (about 2 cups)
  ⅛ teaspoon dried thyme
    1 bay leaf
  12 ounces oyster mushrooms, trimmed, washed, patted dry, and cut into 2-inch pieces
    8 cups chicken broth, homemade (recipe follows) or store-bought
    1 bunch epazote, tied together with kitchen string

Making the Chipotle Puree ▶ Heat a *comal*, griddle, or heavy skillet over medium heat. Add the chiles and roast, turning occasionally, until lightly charred on all sides, about 2 minutes. Remove to a small bowl, cover with warm water, and let soak until softened, about 15 minutes.

    Transfer the chiles and a spoonful or two of the soaking liquid to a mini–food processor, add the garlic, and process to a puree. Set aside.

Making the Soup ▶ In a large saucepan, heat the oil over medium heat until it ripples. Add the onion and sauté until soft, about 4 minutes. Stir in the chile puree, thyme, and bay leaf. Add the mushrooms and cook, stirring, for 1 minute. Add the broth and epazote and bring to a boil. Reduce the heat to low and simmer, covered, for 10 minutes. Remove the epazote. Skim the fat from the top for a milder-flavored soup or leave it to keep more of the chipotle heat.

    Ladle into bowls and serve at once.

COOKING BROTHS

In Latin America, broth is not the primary building block of a dish as it is in French cooking. We often use water and build layers of flavor with other techniques, such as adding a cooking sauce or marinating meats before cooking. When we do use broths, they are simple, flavorful concoctions. Perhaps because of my professional training, I prefer to add broth rather than water to a stew or a soup. These are some of the basic, multipurpose broths I use.

Simple Chicken Broth

Caldo de Pollo Simple

This is an easy yet flavorful chicken broth that can be used in numerous dishes, even those made with seafood.

MAKES ABOUT 2 QUARTS

    6 garlic cloves
    1 medium white onion (8 ounces), halved
 One 3½-pound chicken, cut into 8 pieces (see page 659)
    4 quarts water
    1 medium red or green bell pepper (8 ounces), cored, seeded, and halved
    2 fat carrots (about 1 pound), peeled and cut into 2-inch pieces
    3 medium plum tomatoes (9 ounces), quartered
    1 teaspoon allspice berries
  ½ teaspoon dried oregano
  ¼ teaspoon ground cumin

2 broad-leaf *culantro* leaves or 4 cilantro sprigs (optional if using for a dish that calls for cilantro)

▶ Heat a *comal*, griddle, or heavy skillet over medium heat until a drop of water sizzles on contact. Add the garlic and onion and roast, turning occasionally, until blotched on all sides, about 5 minutes.

Place the chicken in a medium pot and add the water, roasted garlic and onion, bell pepper, carrots, tomatoes, allspice, oregano, cumin, and *culantro* or cilantro. Bring to a boil over high heat, then reduce the heat and simmer, covered, until the broth is reduced by half, about 1½ hours. Strain through a fine-mesh sieve.

Let cool, then refrigerate tightly covered, or freeze.

Storing: Freeze in 1-quart containers for easier use. The broth will keep well for up to 3 months.

Amber Chicken Broth

Caldo de Pollo de Jorge Kawas

My friend Jorge Kawas, a talented chef from Tela, Honduras, taught me to make this simple but deeply flavorful amber-colored chicken broth. When Jorge came to visit or to work with me, he knew that I would ask him to make it. I like to freeze it and keep it on hand to cook just about anything that calls for broth (even fish). This can be substituted for my simple chicken broth in any recipe.

Cook's Note: I buy 2 whole 3½-pound chickens and bone them at home. That way I can use the bones for this recipe and the meat for another recipe.

MAKES ABOUT 2 QUARTS

3½–4 pounds raw chicken bones, with some meat left on (see Cook's Note)
2 medium yellow onions (1 pound), halved, not peeled
2 medium carrots (8 ounces)
2 celery stalks, coarsely chopped
1 ripe medium tomato (or 2 medium plum tomatoes; about 6 ounces), halved
1 bouquet garni—1 leek, trimmed, halved lengthwise, and rinsed; 3 sprigs thyme; and 1 sprig basil, tied together with kitchen string
4 quarts water
1 tablespoon plus 1 teaspoon salt

▶ Preheat the oven to 375°F.

Place the chicken bones in a roasting pan lined with aluminum foil and roast, turning occasionally, until well browned, about 45 minutes. Set aside.

Heat a *comal*, griddle, or medium heavy skillet over medium-high heat. Place the onion halves in the skillet cut side down, reduce the heat to medium, and cook until the cut surface is charred, about 10 minutes.

Transfer the charred onions to a large stockpot and add the carrots, celery, chicken bones, tomato, bouquet garni, and water. Bring to a boil over medium heat. Reduce the heat to a simmer and skim the fat and scum off the top. Add the salt, skim again, and simmer for 1½ hours.

Strain the broth and let cool, then refrigerate or freeze, tightly covered.

Storing: Freeze in 1-quart containers for easier use. The broth will keep, well refrigerated, for up to 1 week, and up to 3 months in the freezer.

Simple Beef Broth

Caldo de Costillas Simple

For beef soup and simple broths such as this one, short ribs always deliver good flavor; flank steak is also good for broth. In Cuba, when we use flank steak, the broth is drunk as a consommé and the meat is shredded for a braised dish called *ropa vieja* (literally, old clothes; page 714).

MAKES 2½ QUARTS

2 pounds beef short ribs or trimmed flank steak, cut into 2 or 3 pieces

4 quarts water

1 bunch cilantro (or flat-leaf parsley for dishes that do not call for cilantro)

1 teaspoon black peppercorns

1 medium red onion (8 ounces), halved

▶ Place the short ribs or flank steak in a large pot, add the water, cilantro, peppercorns, and onion, and bring to a rolling boil over high heat, skimming occasionally. Reduce the heat and simmer, partially covered, for 1½ hours, or until the meat is fork-tender.

Remove from the heat and transfer the meat to a platter. Strain the broth and let cool, then refrigerate. Remove the top layer of fat before using.

When the meat is cool enough to handle, separate the rib meat from the bones, discarding fat and gristle, and finely chop with a sharp knife; or shred the flank steak. Reserve for another use.

Storing: Freeze in 1-quart containers for easier use. The broth will keep, well refrigerated, for up to 1 week, and up to 3 months in the freezer.

All-Purpose Fish Broth

Caldo de Pescado

The head and bones of a white-fleshed fish like red snapper, grouper, or sea bass make a rich broth when teamed with aromatic vegetables such as onions, carrots, celery, and parsley stems. I don't use cilantro for this recipe because it can overpower the broth. Add any fish trimmings you may have if you happen to be making another fish dish.

MAKES ABOUT 4 QUARTS

Head(s) and bones from 1 or 2 large white-fleshed fish

1 medium yellow onion (about 8 ounces), cut into 1-inch dice

2 celery stalks, coarsely chopped

1 medium carrot (about 4 ounces), peeled and cut into ¼-inch slices

2 leeks, trimmed, split lengthwise, and rinsed Stems from 1 bunch flat-leaf parsley

4 quarts water Juice of ½ lemon

▶ Rinse the fish head(s) and bones under cold running water. Remove the gills and rinse again.

Place all the ingredients in a large pot and slowly bring to a boil over medium heat. Reduce the heat to low and simmer for 20 to 25 minutes.

Let cool, then strain through a fine-mesh sieve. Refrigerate or freeze, tightly covered.

Storing: The broth will keep in the refrigerator for up to 3 days or in the freezer for up to 3 months.

CHAPTER 14

SALADS

IN THIS CHAPTER

Latin Americans tend not to serve salad as a separate course. Even in countries with a strong European tradition, such as Argentina, Uruguay, and Chile, a salad is usually eaten with other foods, as a side dish.

There are, of course, exceptions. At many upscale restaurants, innovative chefs have transformed salads into complex dishes that can be offered as a first course. Take, for example, Emmanuel Piqueras Villaran's Peruvian mixed salad with a confit of alpaca (a relative of the llama), served with *ollucos* (an Andean tuber) and a vinaigrette of Andean herbs, or Patricia Quintana's tomato salad with cilantro vinaigrette, topped with a piece of goat's-milk cheese wrapped in a licorice-scented *hoja santa* leaf and accompanied by onion confit. As Latin Americans become more familiar with North American–style menus and there is less time for the traditional two-hour midday meal, eating a salad as a main course during lunch has become popular among working men and women in large cities throughout Latin America. (Eating salad as a form of dieting has also contributed to this change.)

Specialties resembling salads are also traditionally eaten by themselves as a quick meal. They mostly belong to the big family of eat-on-the-go street foods that Latins buy from vendors and devour on the spot. Good examples are the Mexican cactus paddle salad, the snack of salty green mangoes spiced with chiles and a squirt of lime that Mexicans adore, the midmorning pick-me-up of lupins with onion relish and toasted corn eaten in parts of Andean Ecuador, and *solteros*, a blend of Andean corn, cheese, and fava beans that Bolivian men eat as an antidote for hangovers.

But the fact remains that Latins still usually eat salad as a side dish. The traditional instinct is to pile up everything on one plate. Salads, big and little, are thought to be an integral part of this ensemble. At our first meal at an American restaurant in Orlando, Florida, scarcely a year after our arrival in the United States, my husband and I were startled when the waitress brought us a green salad as a first course. We could not conceive of eating it alone—entrenched habits are hard to shed—so we put it aside and waited for the main course to arrive, then made room for it on the plate with our steaks. The usual combination of meat, rice, beans, and a starchy vegetable so popular in my native Cuba and in other parts of tropical Latin America is likely to be rounded off with a little salad. If you have eaten in a Hispanic Caribbean restaurant, you can probably visualize what the plate looks like—perhaps a piece of beef, with a mound of rice, a pool of beans, some fried or boiled vegetables, and a side of thinly sliced tomatoes tossed with shredded lettuce, everything topped with raw onion rings. Even if the ingredients are not cut into small pieces, these "little salads" fulfill the function of a table condiment by adding a touch of freshness and acidity to the whole. I like to call them "salsa salads."

For these simple salads, the most elemental ingredients will do—ripe tomatoes bursting with juice, onions, some shredded cabbage, a little parsley, a couple of lettuce leaves, a single succulent slice of avocado. Nothing is needed to flavor these raw ingredients beyond a sprinkling of olive oil, vinegar, salt, and perhaps black pepper added at the table, before the diners get to work scrambling everything up for maximum flavor impact. But they add color and freshness and somehow make the plate more complete.

The word *ensalada* can also refer to certain hearty composed dishes that blend several vegetables or fruits or combine meats or seafood with vegetables. My friend Mary Kawas in Tela, Honduras, makes a fresh conch and vegetable salad and dresses it with homemade mayonnaise. She sets it out on the table with the rest of the dishes that make up the meal, and her family and guests serve themselves. No matter that the salad is every bit as filling as the other dishes that constitute the meal. Cubans and Puerto Ricans have the same proclivity to want too much of a good thing. They prepare substantial salt cod and vegetable salads that are complete meals in themselves, but they seldom serve them alone. In the Ecuadorian highlands, cooks make warm potato and cabbage or broccoli rabe salads that are inevitably accompanied by other filling foods, such as rice and meat.

The salad kings of Latin America are the Argentineans, Uruguayans, and Brazilians. Their gargantuan feasts of grilled or spit-roasted meats are always eaten with an array of salads that are not meant to balance heavy-duty menus with a little light relief—rather, they are supposed to match the Rabelaisian spirit of the event. These baroque salads, often laden with potatoes, seem to play the function of starchy side dishes, the way rice and beans do in other parts of Latin America.

Uruguayan and Argentinean salads range from simple tomato-onion combinations to filling versions of *salade russe* (*ensalada rusa*), with potatoes, carrots, string beans, chopped hard-boiled eggs, and peas bound by an eggy mayonnaise. In Argentina, you are likely to find a larger selection of salads than of meats at the big grilling places (*parrilladas*), and when they reach the table, they are as outsized as the slabs of meat sizzling on the grill. As for the theatrical Brazilian *rodizios* (restaurants with a fixed-price meat menu), where waiters walk around brandishing meat-filled skewers the size of fencing swords, the excess extends to the lavishly choreographed buffets displaying more than twenty kinds of salad, from hearts of palm as big as small tree trunks to corn and bean salads, from artichokes in vinaigrette to tropical fruit salads with quail eggs. I once suspected that these riotous vegetarian displays were a ploy to dull your appetite and keep you from overindulging on the fixed-price meat menu, but no! People pile mountains of these salads on their plate, and even go back for seconds, yet they are left with enough appetite to enjoy round after round of meat from the grill.

No account of Latin American salads could fail to mention the elaborate ones served on special occasions and holidays. I happily remember the Cuban chicken and potato salad that was traditional for birthday parties. The birthday cake was not served as a separate dessert course, but on the same plate as the salad, along with miniature ham croquettes and tiny crescent-shaped savory pastries. Later I learned that a somewhat similar chicken salad is traditional for birthday dinners in coastal Colombia, though the accompaniment there would be coconut rice. Every time I tell the story of our birthday chicken salads, my American friends cringe in disbelief. They become even more incredulous when I tell them that we never took a bite of the cake by itself. The forks and spoons that we took to our mouths carried bits of everything—the cake, the salad, the croquettes, the savory pastries filled with beef hash (*picadillo*) or guava paste. We thought the mix was delicious. I still do!

The visual effect of a salad reserved for celebration is very important. In our family, the main ingredients of the birthday chicken salad were beautifully diced, and touches of red and green (usually from canned pimientos and asparagus) were arranged with care. Color is an essential element of these festive salads. A notable example, the Mexican Christmas Eve salad, belongs to a family of salads rooted in colonial cooking traditions that feature an assortment of meticulously diced vegetables and fruits dyed a lovely red with beet juices.

By the nineteenth century, most Latin American cookbooks had sections dedicated to salads that often show great care in preparation as well as creativity. In a Cuban cookbook published in 1891, the author instructs readers to soak hearts of lettuce for six hours to get rid of a "certain bitterness that is common to lettuce grown in warm climates," and to add a bit of sugar to the olive oil and vinegar dressing. The Mexican *Nuevo cocinero americano en forma de diccionario* (The New American Cook in Dictionary Form), published in 1893, gives more than eighty-five recipes ranging from simple lettuce and leafy greens dressed with oil and vinegar to more complex vegetable, fruit, legume, seafood, and game salads, often seasoned with chiles and garnished with nuts, olives, raisins, pomegranate seeds, or capers, or a combination. As a sign that cooks were paying more attention to the presentation of food, the book notes that leafy greens such as escarole and romaine lettuce are often decorated with edible rose, borage, and orange blossoms. These *ensaladas floridas* (flower salads) would be at home today on any upscale restaurant menu.

In this chapter you will find a sampling of Latin American salads, from the crunchy chopped tomato and onion "salsa salads" with their vivid notes of acidity and freshness to more elaborate feast-day creations. In between come my own salads, the ones I serve in my pan-Latin kitchen and restaurants: salads big and small that reflect my understanding of what a tasty salad should be, the spirit of the places that inspired them, and the part a salad should play on the contemporary Latin table. While my dressings are on the simple side—just enough olive oil for satiny smoothness, a judicious touch of vinegar or citrus juice for a kick of tartness—I like to play with Latin herbs and spices, adding hot peppers here and there to bring out flavors, or a touch of one of our wonderful brown loaf sugars to tame the harshness of the vinegar.

These salads are versatile dishes that can be eaten in the traditional sense as salads or as appetizers and side dishes for the meat, fish, and poultry dishes offered throughout the book.

AVOCADOS

By the time the Spanish came to the New World, the avocado species (*Persea americana*) had several major branches. In the sixteenth century, the Spanish Franciscan friar Motolinía could already describe some clearly differentiated types in New Spain (Mexico). There was one, he wrote, with a flavor like pine nuts and enough fat to furnish oil for cooking or lamp fuel; a tiny kind not much bigger than an olive; one like an outsized pear, which he considered the best fruit of New Spain; and a still larger one, like a small pumpkin, that belonged to the *tierras bien calientes* (very hot regions).

Later observers, surveying these and the avocados of the Caribbean islands, eventually classed all avocados into three main races (the botanical word for varieties) and gave them names that are unfortunately more convenient than precise.

MEXICAN (*PERSEA AMERICANA* VAR. *DRYMIFOLIA*)

The so-called Mexican avocado is suited to the cooler parts of Mexico (it flourishes in highland terrain) and is often extravagantly rich in the oil that made the Spanish again and again compare avocados to butter or even beef suet. The fruits are usually small to medium, with waxy thin or pebbly skin that ranges from green to black.

GUATEMALAN (*P. AMERICANA* VAR. *GUATEMALENSIS*)

Guatemalan avocados exhibit a range of traits but tend to be more tolerant of heat than the Mexican variety. Most are roundish and usually small to medium in size, though some varieties can grow larger. Their skin is rough and thick.

WEST INDIAN (*P. AMERICANA* VAR. *AMERICANA LOWLAND*)

The West Indian kind (which was first found in the Caribbean islands but was never exclusive to the region) thrives in humid, sweltering conditions unsuited to the others. It can reach enormous size (3 to 4 pounds) and has only a fraction of the oil content of a Mexican-type avocado. Most have thin, shiny, leathery green skin.

AVOCADOS IN U.S. MARKETS

The avocados in U.S. markets today are mostly crosses of either the Mexican or the West Indian type with Guatemalan stock, but markets generically identify them as either Florida or California avocados.

CALIFORNIA AVOCADOS

California avocados are usually Mexican-Guatemalan crosses with varietal names such as Fuerte, Bacon, Gwen, Reed, Pinkerton, Zutano, and the star of stars: Hass. They are smaller, more pear-shaped, and much higher in fat than the ones with strong West Indian ancestry. In California, avocados grow from Mendocino to the Mexican border (the largest growing area is San Diego's North County), and they are shipped to markets all over the country at different times throughout the year. The rough-black-skinned round Reed is available all summer long. By early fall, you are likely to find Zutano, a medium-sized shiny green avocado that people often confuse with Fuerte, a Mexican varietal with creamy greenish flesh. Late fall to spring is the season for both Fuerte and Bacon, a medium-sized green-skinned hybrid with buttery yellow-green flesh. All year round, you can count on the trusted Hass. Purchased as a seedling by an American postman named Rudolph Hass in the late 1920s, the Guatemalan Hass eventually came to supplant Fuerte as America's most widely consumed avocado. The Hass is easy to spot; look for a small fruit with a rough, pebbly skin that turns from dark green to purplish black when ripe. When properly ripened, the golden flesh has a delicious nutty taste and buttery consistency that make it ideal for guacamole and "salsa salads." Hass and other Mexican or Guatemalan avocados need to be consumed as soon as they ripen because they rapidly spoil or develop brown spots.

Hass avocado

FLORIDA AVOCADOS

Florida avocados have more West Indian parentage than California types. They are big, rounded, green, and shiny, with firm and comparatively lean flesh. Although there are more than fifty kinds of avocados growing in Florida—the most popular cultivars being Hall, Pollock, Simmonds, and Monroe—sellers just generically call them West Indian or Florida avocados without going into more detail. Because West Indian avocados do poorly in cool weather, most are grown in warmer, subtropical south Florida, particularly in the Redlands of Homestead, a small town southwest of Miami. The Florida avocado's growing season stretches from June to March, but the fruit is most plentiful between August and December. Because of their large size, low fat content, and high water content, Florida avocados are not suitable for dips and creamy sauces. They are at their best in refreshing salads.

SELECTING AND RIPENING AVOCADOS

Unlike other tropical fruits, avocados do not ripen on the tree. Stubbornly, they remain firm until gravity or a gust of wind makes them fall to the ground. Home gardeners wait eagerly until this happens, but commercial growers pick avocados from the tree when they have reached their optimum size, shipping them to markets still hard as rocks. Latin grocers often go to the trouble of selecting avocados according to their degree of ripeness, and in some markets you will always find a few perfectly ripe avocados for use the same day stashed next to the register.

To make sure an avocado is ripe, press the fruit gently with your fingers. The skin should yield slightly, and there should be no sunken spots. Weigh the fruit in your hand and shake it a little. If it feels light for its size, or if you hear the pit rattling inside, the fruit is overripe and the flesh will be discolored by mold.

If buying an unripe avocado, choose a fruit that feels heavy for its size and is free of scratches or blemishes. Let stand at room temperature until it yields slightly to soft pressure, or store in a paper bag together with a fruit that emits ethylene gas, such as an apple or a banana, for faster ripening. Avocados ripen best at room temperature; do not refrigerate until they are perfectly ripe. Once they are ripened, they will keep well in the refrigerator for 2 or 3 days.

PEELING AN AVOCADO

The most efficient way to prepare an avocado is to cut the unpeeled fruit lengthwise in half, working around the pit, and gently twist the two halves back and forth to dislodge them. In a perfectly ripe avocado, the pit will cling to one half. Slide the tip of a knife or a spoon under the pit to pry it out. (If not using immediately, do not remove the pit; it will keep the flesh around it from darkening.) To peel and cut into even slices, place each avocado half cut side down on a work surface and slice it lengthwise into 1- to 2-inch-wide wedges. Peel each segment by hand or with a paring knife. If you are preparing guacamole or a dip, it is easier to halve and pit the avocado, then spoon out the flesh. Avocados will discolor when in contact with the air. If not using immediately, sprinkle the cut flesh with a little vinegar or lime or lemon juice to retard oxidation, or cover tightly with plastic wrap.

Avocados do not freeze well. Although some cooks add lime juice to the pulp and freeze it for several months, I find that the frozen pulp becomes too watery when defrosted. There is nothing more pleasurable than a fresh avocado. ◆

Avocado and Onion Salad

Ensalada de Aguacate y Cebolla

There is something endlessly seductive about the bland creaminess of a slice of avocado. Though Brazilians regard avocado as a fruit and eat it sprinkled with sugar, as many Iberian conquistadores did, the most common use in Latin America is in salads seasoned with oil and vinegar or lime juice, or as a garnish for soups, stews, or main dishes. In the Caribbean and Andean traditions, a beautiful salad of West Indian avocado such as this is an indispensable complement to soups and stews, rice dishes, and roasted meats, especially pork.

I am very fond of the rich, buttery avocados from California, but I have to say that people who criticize the West Indian ones because they are less creamy are missing something. Nothing beats a ripe, fatty avocado for guacamole, but the West Indian type really tastes more like a vegetable in its own right. It has an elusive sweetness and delicately sensual quality that is exactly what I want for a salad of sliced avocados, where I am looking for a refreshing partner for a simple vinaigrette. Try it and you will understand.

SERVES 4

- 1 large Florida (West Indian) avocado
- 3 garlic cloves, finely chopped
- ¼ cup extra-virgin olive oil
- 2 tablespoons fresh lime juice
- 1 teaspoon salt, or to taste
- ¼ teaspoon freshly ground black pepper
- 1 small white onion (5 ounces), thinly slivered lengthwise

▶ Cut the avocado lengthwise in half around the pit and remove the pit. Place the avocado halves cut side down on the work surface and slice lengthwise into 1-inch-wide wedges. Peel each segment by hand or with a paring knife and arrange on a platter. Place the garlic, olive oil, lime juice, salt, and pepper in a small bowl and whisk to combine. Taste for salt.

Scatter the onion over the avocado slices, pour on the dressing, and serve immediately.

Cuban Avocado, Watercress, and Pineapple Salad

Ensalada de Aguacate, Berro, y Piña

Watercress is the green of choice in Cuba, its peppery taste a perfect foil for the avocado and the sweet pineapple in this classic Cuban salad. I serve it with shrimp in a spicy tomato sauce called *enchilado de camarones*. In Cuba, the pineapple is never roasted,

but this technique adds another dimension of flavor I find very appealing.

SERVES 6 TO 8

- 2 bunches watercress
- One 2½-pound pineapple, peeled, cored, and cut into four 1-inch-thick slices
- 1 tablespoon sugar
- 3 garlic cloves, finely chopped
- ¼ cup extra-virgin olive oil
- 2 tablespoons cider vinegar or fresh lime juice
- ⅛ teaspoon ground cumin
- 1 teaspoon salt
- ¼ teaspoon freshly ground black pepper
- 1 large Florida (West Indian) avocado or 2 Hass avocados
- 1 small red onion (5 ounces) thinly slivered lengthwise

Preparing the Watercress ▶ Place the watercress in a colander and rinse under cold running water to remove any grit or sand. Discard any yellowing leaves and remove the tough stems; for this salad, you want only the leaves and tender stems. Pat dry with paper towels and refrigerate while you prepare the rest of the salad.

Broiling the Pineapple ▶ Preheat the broiler. Place the pineapple slices on a baking pan and sprinkle the sugar evenly on top of them. Broil about 4 inches from the heat source, turning once, for 10 minutes on each side, until lightly golden brown. Let cool, then cut into 1-inch cubes. Set aside.

Preparing the Dressing ▶ Place the garlic, olive oil, vinegar or lime juice, cumin, salt, and pepper in a small bowl and whisk to combine. Taste for seasoning. Set aside.

Peeling the Avocado ▶ Cut the avocado(s) lengthwise in half around the pit and remove the pit. Place the avocado halves cut side down on the work surface and slice lengthwise into 1-inch-wide wedges. Peel each segment by hand or with a paring knife, and cut into 1-inch cubes.

Assembling the Salad ▶ Place the watercress in a medium bowl and toss with half the dressing. Arrange on a large platter.

Add the pineapple and avocado to the same bowl and toss with the rest of the dressing. Mound the pineapple and avocado over the bed of watercress. Garnish with the slivers of red onion and serve immediately.

Chilean Tomato Salad

Ensalada Chilena

This is the simplest and one of the oldest of Latin salads, found in Uruguay, the Hispanic Caribbean, and anywhere the Spaniards introduced the tomato dishes developed in Spain in the eighteenth century. In Chile this is the quintessential salad, the one most passionately enjoyed. Don't make it unless you have really ripe, juicy tomatoes.

Cook's Note: In many parts of Latin America, tomatoes are seldom peeled and seeded for salads, but María Eugenia Baeza, the Chilean cook who gave me this recipe, insists that peeling is essential.

SERVES 6

12 very ripe medium plum tomatoes or 4 very ripe medium globe tomatoes (about 2 pounds)

1 large white or yellow onion (12 ounces), cut lengthwise in half and then into thin slivers

1 small hot pepper (preferably the Chilean *ají cristal*, available pickled in Hispanic markets), seeded and finely chopped

1 tablespoon finely chopped flat-leaf parsley or cilantro

½ cup extra-virgin olive oil

¼ cup red wine vinegar

2 large garlic cloves, finely chopped

1 teaspoon salt

½ teaspoon freshly ground black pepper

▶ Cut an X in the bottom of each tomato. Plunge into a pot of boiling water for 30 seconds. Remove and peel. Halve the tomatoes and seed them. Cut lengthwise into wedges or into cubes. Place the tomatoes in a bowl and toss with the onion, hot pepper, and parsley or cilantro.

In a small bowl, whisk together the oil, vinegar, garlic, salt, and pepper. Pour over the tomatoes and toss to mix. Serve immediately.

Shrimp and Hearts of Palm Salad

Ensalada de Camarones y Palmitos

Despite their lustrous, creamy appearance, hearts of palm do not have a creamy texture. Rather, they have long smooth fibers, like bamboo shoots, with a slight bite that is welcome in salads such as this simple but attractive combination with shrimp and tomatoes. Their lovely shiny white color contrasts with the rosy, succulent shrimp.

Serve at room temperature or chilled, as a light lunch or with rice for a more filling main course.

1   bay leaf

8   allspice berries

2½   teaspoons salt

8   ounces medium shrimp, preferably Ecuadorian
     (16–20 per pound)

1   small red onion (5 ounces), finely chopped
     (about 1 cup)

2   ripe large tomatoes (about 1 pound), seeded and
     cut into ¼-inch cubes

4   ounces canned hearts of palm, drained and cut
     into ¼-inch rounds

¼   cup extra-virgin olive oil

1   tablespoon cider vinegar

1   tablespoon orange juice

½   habanero or Scotch bonnet pepper, seeded and
     finely chopped

▶ Place 1 quart water, the bay leaf, allspice, and 2 teaspoons salt in a medium saucepan and bring to a boil over high heat. Add the shrimp and cook for 3 minutes. Drain thoroughly.

When the shrimp are cool, shell and devein them. Place in a bowl with the onion, tomatoes, and hearts of palm.

Whisk the oil, vinegar, orange juice, remaining ½ teaspoon salt, and chile together in a small bowl. Pour over the shrimp and vegetables and toss to coat. Serve at room temperature or chilled.

Leftover salad will keep in the refrigerator for a couple of days covered with plastic wrap.

KING OF HEARTS: THE PALMITO

Throughout tropical America, one of the most prized vegetables for salads is really a tree shoot, *palmito*, or heart of palm. It is harvested by trimming palm trees to expose the delicate ivory inner core that forms a slender column running down into the trunk from the terminal bud at the top of the tree.

Hearts of palm

Though it is sometimes possible to buy fresh *palmitos* in this country, they normally come in jars or cans, cut into lengths like white candles and packed in a citric acid solution. They have a pleasant, slightly fibrous texture and a delicate herbal flavor like asparagus and artichokes.

The heart of palm is a versatile vegetable. It is lovely in salads, but it can also be braised, added to stews, cooked in rice dishes, or topped with a creamy cheese sauce and broiled until golden.

Traditional restaurants and steak houses in Argentina always offer hearts of palm split lengthwise, cut into chunks, and drenched in a pink sauce that tastes like American bottled Russian dressing. Called *salsa golf*, it is not a 1950s American creation but the invention of Argentinean men horsing around in the 1920s. Reportedly the sauce was the brainchild of the Nobel Prize laureate Luis F. Lenoir. Legend has it that when Lenoir was in medical school, he and his friends spent their leisure hours at the Golf Club of Playa Grande on the River Plate. One morning, as they were eating shrimp and *langostinos* dressed with mayonnaise—

which is the favorite salad dressing in Argentina after oil and vinegar—Lenoir asked friends, "Aren't you all bored with the same old mayonnaise on the *langostinos* day in and day out?" He then asked the waiter to bring him all the sauces and condiments in the kitchen for a tableside mix-and-match experiment. Everyone voted for the mix of mayonnaise, ketchup, egg, mustard, and heavy cream, which was christened *salsa golf* then and there. The club started serving the sauce with hearts of palm and it became a popular classic, enjoyed all over Argentina and wherever there are Argentineans. The name and the sauce are reminders of the strong British influence on upper-class life in Argentina.

The growing demand for *palmitos*, considered a delicacy in many parts of the world, has led to the over-harvesting of numerous palm species with single stems in several Latin American countries. Despite strict laws restricting indiscriminate exploitation, *palmito* harvesters (*palmiteiros*) are wreaking havoc with the *juçara* palm (*Euterpe edulis*) in the Brazilian Atlantic forest. The spiny *jauarí* palm (*Astrocaryum jauari*) along the Rio Negro, and the *huasai* palm (*Euterpe precatoria*) in Peru. Even in the Dominican Republic, where *palmitos* are not a staple, people are cutting down majestic royal palms to harvest their coveted hearts. In the Petén, the thickly forested region of Guatemala that is adjacent to Belize, there are nearly a dozen varieties of palm trees that are being systematically cut down to extract *palmitos* for Western consumption.

Environmentalists realize that the only way to curtail the extinction of these edible palms is to develop alternatives. The *açai* (*Euterpe oleracea*), a tropical palm that bears dark purple fruits that are delicious in juices and sorbets, has multiple stems that can be judiciously harvested for *palmitos* without killing the tree. I am always careful to choose brands that get their *palmitos* from ecologically sustainable plantations in Brazil or Costa Rica. ◆

São João's Hearts of Palm and Mango Salad with Lime Dressing

Ensalada de Palmito com Mango "São João"

Whenever I am lucky enough to find juicy, perfectly ripe mangoes and Brazilian hearts of palm, I make this salad. It is a perfect study in complementary colors, textures, and flavor that can make a light meal by itself. It takes me back to happy moments in São João, a beautiful farm in Brazil owned by the historian Antonio Bueno. Though only about twenty-two miles from São Paulo, one of the largest cities of the Western Hemisphere, São João is a window on the once-wild Brazilian interior, now mostly despoiled through overdevelopment. Antonio is a direct descendant of Bartolomeu Bueno da Silva (known as Anhangüera), the most notorious of the seventeenth-century *bandeirantes*, the roving Portuguese or mixed-race soldiers of fortune from São Paulo who extended the frontiers of the colony in their search for Indian slaves and gold. Antonio's wife, Catarina Cardoso Bueno, is the daughter of a famous cartographer and explorer. Their house is painted in classic *bandeirante* colors, whitewashed with blue-trimmed windows, and built in typical *bandeirante* style, with the two front rooms (originally a chapel and a guest bedroom) completely walled off from the main quarters. Today, instead of wilderness, a thick growth of bamboo groves and orchard trees laden with fruit surrounds the cleared farmland of São João, tilled by a Japanese tenant farmer who grows yuca, pumpkin, and greens.

We sat in a clearing by the pool, drinking caipirinhas made with tropical fruits from the farm (my favorite was flavored with the perfumed subtly astringent cashew apple), until we were called back to the house for a buffet lunch under the shade of a gigantic jackfruit tree. Among the most memorable dishes of that meal was this delightful salad garnished with quail eggs, which are very popular in Brazil.

SERVES 6 TO 8

- ½ cup extra-virgin olive oil
- ¼ cup fresh lime juice
  Salt and freshly ground black pepper
- 3 ripe mangoes (about 2½ pounds)
- One 15-ounce can hearts of palm, drained
- 16 quail eggs or 8 small eggs, hard-boiled

▶ Whisk the oil, lime juice, and salt and pepper to taste in a small bowl. Set aside.

Peel the mangoes. Cut off the flesh in 4 thick lengthwise slices, going close to the pit; you will have 2 wide slices and 2 narrow ones. Cut each slice on an angle into 1-inch slices. Set aside.

Cut the hearts of palm crosswise in half on a slight angle. Set aside.

Peel the eggs. Cut quail eggs lengthwise in half, or quarter regular eggs. To assemble the salad, alternate the slices of mango and heart of palm in a decorative pattern on a large platter. Top with the eggs and either pour the dressing over the salad or pass in a sauce boat.

Panamanian Green Papaya Salad

Ensalada de Papaya Panameña

Green papayas come to market as hard as a rock. Asians use them raw in salads, but Latin Americans boil them first. In both Panama and Colombia, you find green papaya salads seasoned with a simple olive oil dressing. Here I like to bring out the sweetness of the fruit by adding a little grated brown loaf sugar.

SERVES 6

- 1 very large firm green or 2 smaller green papayas (about 4 pounds total)
- 1 tablespoon salt
- ½ cup extra-virgin olive oil
- ¼ cup cider vinegar
- 1 tablespoon grated brown loaf sugar, Demerara sugar, or light brown sugar
  Salt and freshly ground black pepper
- 1 tablespoon finely chopped mint or cilantro

▶ Cut the papaya(s) lengthwise in half. Scoop out and discard the seeds. Peel and cut into ½-inch cubes. Place in a bowl, cover with water, and let stand for 2 to 3 hours, changing the water 2 or 3 times to remove some of the astringent sap.

Drain the papaya and place in a medium pot. Add 4 quarts water and the salt and bring to a boil over high heat. Lower the heat to medium and simmer until the papaya is fork-tender but not mushy, about 20 minutes. Drain and let cool.

In a medium serving bowl, whisk together the oil, vinegar, sugar, and salt and pepper to taste. Add the papaya chunks to the vinaigrette and toss to coat well. Taste and correct the seasoning if necessary. Scatter the mint or cilantro over the top.

Storing: The salad will keep for several days in the refrigerator, tightly covered with plastic wrap; in that case, add the mint or cilantro just before serving

Cuban Birthday Party Chicken Salad

Ensalada de Pollo de Cumpleaños

As predictable a fixture of the Cuban birthday feast as a *piñata*—at least during my childhood—was a special salad made with chicken, potatoes, and apples. Most people we knew made the salad with shredded boiled chicken and mayonnaise from a jar. But not our family! My aunt Belén was the official salad maker. Even as a child, I knew her version was a masterpiece of layered flavors. Like all Cuban cooks of her generation, she did garnish the salad with the ubiquitous canned peas, pimientos, and asparagus, but otherwise the difference was like night and day. Belén marinated the chicken in a garlicky allspice-flavored *adobo* and braised it in a flavorful cooking sauce based on a tomato and wine *sofrito*. She was careful to cut the chicken into even cubes, and she gave the salad a rich final patina of *allioli* (garlic mayonnaise), which she had learned from the Catalan side of our family.

What to Drink: Bacardi, Hatuey beer, or daiquiris (pages 354 and 355)

SERVES 8

- 2 pounds red potatoes, peeled, cut into ½-inch dice, and kept in cold water until cooking time to prevent discoloration
- 1 tablespoon salt, plus more to taste
- 1 recipe Chicken Fricassee Cuban Style (page 662)
- 4 Granny Smith apples, peeled, cored, diced, and kept in cold acidulated water (1 tablespoon lemon juice per 3 cups water) until cooking time to prevent discoloration
- 30 pimiento-stuffed green olives, halved
- 2 tablespoons capers, drained
- 1 cup cooked fresh or frozen peas (or drained tiny canned peas)
- 2 large red bell peppers (1 pound), fire-roasted (see page 67), peeled, seeded, and cut into ¼-inch-wide strips
- 2 cups Garlic Mayonnaise (page 135)
  Juice of ½ lime (about 1 tablespoon)
  Freshly ground black pepper
- 8 ounces lightly blanched fresh asparagus tips, for garnish
- 1 tablespoon minced flat-leaf parsley, for garnish

▶ Place the potatoes, 1 tablespoon salt, and 1½ quarts water in a medium saucepan and bring to a boil over high heat. Boil until the potatoes are tender but not falling apart, about 15 minutes. Drain and allow to cool.

Remove the chicken from the sauce; reserve some of the sauce. Bone and skin the chicken and cut the meat into 1½-inch cubes; you should have about 3 cups. Place in a large bowl and toss with the reserved sauce. Cover with plastic wrap and refrigerate until ready to use.

At least 2 hours before serving, add the reserved potatoes, apples, olives, capers, peas, roasted peppers, mayonnaise, lime juice, and salt and pepper to taste to the chicken and toss well to combine. Refrigerate until well chilled. Garnish the salad with the asparagus and parsley and serve chilled.

Storing: The salad will keep well in the refrigerator for 2 days, tightly covered with plastic wrap.

Octopus Salad "Mina Cote"
Ensalada de Pulpo de Mina Cote

The warm waters of La Parguera, a fishing cove on the southern coast of Puerto Rico, teem with octopus, which lurk in the rocky bottom close to shore. At night, they come out of hiding to feed on mollusks, crabs, and lobster, and fishermen usually lure them to the surface by dangling a crab or a piece of lobster over the water.

With such a diet, it is no surprise that the octopus meat is as delicious and succulent as that of a lobster. I like to braise it in a savory wine sauce enriched with a tomato *sofrito* or just boil it and season it with olive oil and paprika, in the style of Galicia. I am also fond of boiled octopus in salads dressed simply with homemade mayonnaise or an olive oil vinaigrette, like the unforgettable salad I tasted at La Parguera. That salad was prepared with care by Mina Cote, a lithe fisherwoman who lives year-round in a houseboat.

On a starry night, Mina Cote invited me and some friends on a fishing outing. Expertly, she steered her flat-bottomed boat (*yola*) through the lush mangrove keys while sea birds flew shrieking into the dark. As we approached the Key of the White Birds, an islet on the edge of the deepest part of the cove, Mina turned off the engine and stood up, pointing to the water. "This is where I saw a blinding light and a mother ship coming up from the water," she announced.

Over a robust dinner of rice with green pigeon peas and a fabulous salad made with the small octopus she had caught the night before, Mina related her experiences. One had occurred while she was fishing near the spot we'd just come from. On another occasion, she explained, "I was busy in the kitchen scaling fish when I turned around and saw four luminous revolving spheres hovering near the door as if they were watching me." And just the day before, "as I walked through the marshes looking for wild cucumbers for this octopus salad, I saw the lights following me again."

"Mina, what a coincidence," I mumbled between bites of the fantastic octopus salad, "every time you met the aliens you were fishing or hunting for ingredients or cooking. I think maybe the aliens came here looking for out-of-this-world food."

Mina told me that this is an Italian-style salad, but the flavors that come through most vividly are distinctly Puerto Rican: the musky taste of the tiny bonnet-shaped sweet pepper called *ají dulce*, and the pungency of *culantro*, the New World herb with broad serrated leaves that tastes very much like cilantro. Serve the salad with Puerto Rican Rice and Green Pigeon Peas (page 312) or any rice and bean combination.

What to Drink: A fresh and spicy Susana Balbo Crios Rosé de Malbec from Mendoza

One 2-pound octopus

 1 cubanelle pepper, seeded and finely chopped

12 Caribbean sweet peppers (*ajíes dulces*), seeded and finely chopped

 1 medium white onion (about 8 ounces), finely chopped (about 1½ cups)

 6 scallions, white and 3 inches of green parts, finely chopped

 4 broad-leaf *culantro* leaves, finely chopped, or 1 tablespoon chopped cilantro

 1 tablespoon dried oregano

 1 cup extra-virgin olive oil

½ cup cider vinegar

 3 sweet gherkins, cut into ¼-inch slices

▶ Bring 5 quarts water to a boil in a large pot over high heat. Holding the octopus by one of its tentacles, plunge it in and out of the boiling water 3 times. (Years ago I was told by a Galician friend that this little ritual scares the octopus, which makes it become more tender.) Put the octopus back into the pot, this time for good, and cook at a rolling boil until fork-tender, from 45 minutes to 1 hour. Lift it out of the pot and let cool.

There are two ways to go about preparing the octopus for the salad: Some cooks like to retain the octopus's purplish skin; others remove it. The skin is tasty and gives character to the octopus, but it may bother some people. Cut off the head of the octopus and discard. With a knife or scissors, cut the tentacles on an angle into ¼- to ½-inch-wide slices. Set aside.

In a large bowl, combine the chopped peppers, onion, scallions, and *culantro* or cilantro. Add the oregano, oil, vinegar, and gherkins and stir well.

Add the octopus to the vinaigrette and toss to distribute all the ingredients evenly. Let sit at room temperature for 2 hours before serving, or refrigerate overnight tightly covered with plastic wrap. Serve chilled.

Storing: The salad will keep well for 2 to 3 days in the refrigerator.

Variation: For a tasty mixed seafood salad, add 1 pound cooked shrimp.

Yucatecan Fruit Salad with Bitter Orange–*Chile Piquín* Dressing

Xec

I first tasted this unusual, piquant fruit salad at the stylish palm-thatched home of Perla Coll Meyer in Cholul, a small town a few miles from Mérida in the Yucatán. Perla was born in Argentina of Sephardic Jewish parents and has traveled the world with her biologist husband. When I met them, the Meyers had lived in Cholul for several years. Their home, a study in sustainability, was surrounded by their own food supplies—a populous chicken coop, vegetables in the garden, trees full of fruit. The ingredients for the salad came entirely from the garden and orchard: sweet papaya, several kinds of citrus, and jicama, tossed with the classic Yucatecan seasonings of bitter orange juice, hot chile, and a little cilantro.

When I make *xec* (pronounced "check") in the United States with fruit that may not come up to the standard of Perla's orchard, I often add a touch of honey or sugar to bring out the sweetness and balance the tart edge of the bitter orange and the pungency of the chile. In Cholul, this salad would be served as an appetizer or a dessert. I've also found it good as a relish for grilled chicken or fish.

SERVES 6 TO 8

¼ cup bitter orange juice or ¼ cup regular orange juice plus 1 tablespoon fresh lime juice

1 tablespoon wildflower honey

½ teaspoon finely ground lightly toasted *piquín* chiles (see page 744) or cayenne

½ teaspoon salt, or to taste

1 very ripe large papaya (about 2 pounds), preferably an orange-fleshed variety, peeled, seeded, and cut into ½-inch dice

1 large jicama, peeled and cut into ¼-inch dice

3 oranges, peeled and separated into segments

3 mandarins or tangerines, peeled and separated into segments

1 grapefruit, preferably pink, peeled and separated into segments

1 tablespoon finely chopped cilantro

▶ Whisk together the orange juice, honey, ground chile or cayenne, and salt in a small bowl. Mix all the fruits in a glass bowl and toss well. Add the cilantro, pour the dressing over the fruits, and toss well. This salad is best served at once, but you can keep it for a couple of hours at room temperature or in the refrigerator.

Guatemalan Radish Salad
Chojín

The hybrid cuisine of Guatemala City and Antigua, the centers of Spanish power in Guatemala, came to be known as *cocina chapina*. Typical of this cuisine is this radish salad. Perfumed with fresh mint and bitter orange juice and spiced with fresh hot *chiltepe* chile (*chile piquín*), it usually accompanies grilled meats and *frijoles volteados* (refried beans shaped into a log). In this recipe, I call for the more readily available serrano chile. Pork cracklings are a traditional part of the salad in Guatemala, and I've listed them as an option here, but I like it better without them—I do not want to distract my senses from the wonderful fragrance of the fresh radishes.

Confusingly enough, in the Pacific lowlands of Guatemala the name *chojín* is applied to a meat stew laden with tropical vegetables.

SERVES 6

4 bunches radishes (approximately 1½ pounds)

⅓ cup bitter orange juice, or equal parts lime juice and orange juice

1 small white onion (5 ounces), finely chopped (about 1 cup)

⅓ cup finely chopped mint leaves

1 serrano chile, seeded and finely chopped

4 ounces pork cracklings, homemade (page 82), or store-bought, coarsely chopped, or 2 slices bacon, cooked until crisp and crumbled (optional)
   Salt to taste

▶ Trim the stems and roots of the radishes. Rinse and dry well. Coarsely chop with a large sharp knife, or use a food processor; do not overprocess.

Place the radishes in a bowl and toss with the rest of the ingredients. Cover and refrigerate until well chilled, then serve.

Storing: The salad will keep well in the refrigerator, tightly covered, for 2 to 3 days.

Nicaraguan Yuca and Cabbage Salad with Pork Cracklings

Vigorón

Vigorón, a boiled yuca and cabbage salad garnished with pork cracklings, is a specialty of Granada, a charming colonial town on the shore of Lake Nicaragua, the largest freshwater lake in Central America. Take a stroll around the town's central plaza, as I did a few years ago, and you will find a frilly pergola under which *vigorón* is served from morning till late afternoon—the yuca still warm, the freshly shredded cabbage crunchy, the cracklings properly brittle and golden.

This combination of ingredients is very old, but the name *vigorón* was coined in Granada about a hundred years ago by an enterprising woman who was selling food door to door. The city was hosting a group of athletes who were training for a big baseball game, and the astute vendor touted the salad as *vigorón*, an "invigorating," nutritious blend sure to turn any man or child into a champion athlete. From then on, that was its name. You can find the salad in home kitchens and on restaurant menus all over the country, but those in the know make the pilgrimage to Granada to enjoy the town's best *vigorón* under the trees on the plaza.

SERVES 6

2 pounds yuca, peeled according to the instructions on page 166
2 teaspoons salt
 Juice of 1 lime (about 2 tablespoons)
3 cups finely shredded green cabbage (about ⅓ of a small head)
4 medium plum tomatoes (about 12 ounces), cut into ½-inch dice
1 medium white onion (about 8 ounces), cut into thin rings or halved lengthwise and cut into thin slivers
2 tablespoons distilled white vinegar
6 cabbage leaves, for garnish
4 ounces pork cracklings (page 82), for garnish (about 1 cup)

▶ Place the yuca and 1 teaspoon salt in a large saucepan, add 1½ quarts water and the lime juice, and bring to a boil over high heat. Lower the heat to medium and boil gently for about 25 minutes, or until the yuca is tender but not falling apart. Drain and let cool slightly.

Remove the central vein from the yuca and cut into 2-inch chunks. Set aside.

In another large saucepan, bring 1 quart water to a boil. Add the cabbage and blanch for just 1 minute. Immediately turn the cabbage out into a colander to drain. Pat dry with paper towels and set aside.

Combine the tomatoes, onion, vinegar, and remaining 1 teaspoon salt in a small bowl.

Place the yuca and cabbage in a bowl, add the tomato mixture, and toss to mix.

Arrange the cabbage leaves on individual serving plates. Spoon the salad onto the leaves, and scatter the pork cracklings over the top.

Calabaza and Grilled Pineapple Salad with Brown Sugar Vinaigrette and Cacao Nibs

Ensalada de Calabaza y Piña a la Brasa con Vinagreta Aromática y Cacao

An aromatic olive oil vinaigrette lightly sweetened with brown loaf sugar and punctuated by crunchy pumpkin seeds and cacao nibs (the shelled kernels of roasted cacao beans) adds depth and tangy flavor to this salad of West Indian pumpkin and grilled pineapple. The aroma of the grill permeates the fruit like a heady seasoning, giving it a succulent, almost meaty quality.

SERVES 6 TO 8

For the Pineapple
- 1 ripe pineapple (about 4 pounds), peeled, cored, and cut into 1-inch slabs
- ¼ cup Simple Brown Loaf Sugar Syrup (page 101)

For the *Calabaza*
- 2 pounds *calabaza* (West Indian pumpkin) or Hubbard or kabocha squash, peeled, seeded, and cut into 1-inch dice
- 2 bay leaves
- 1 Ceylon cinnamon stick (*canela*)
- 2 teaspoons salt
- 10 allspice berries

For the Vinaigrette
- 4 garlic cloves, mashed to a paste with a mortar and pestle or finely chopped and mashed
- ¼ cup cider vinegar
- ¼ cup extra-virgin olive oil
- ¼ teaspoon ground allspice
- ½ teaspoon salt
- 2 tablespoons Simple Brown Loaf Sugar Syrup

For the Garnish
- ⅓ cup hulled green pumpkin seeds (about 2 ounces), lightly roasted
- 1 tablespoon cacao nibs
  Hot *pimentón* (Spanish smoked paprika)
  Extra-virgin olive oil

Cooking the Pineapple ▶ Prepare a hot fire in a grill or preheat the broiler.

To grill, place the pineapple slabs on the grill and cook, turning once, for 10 minutes on each side. Brush with the syrup and cook for 5 more minutes until lightly blackened.

To broil, place the pineapple on a baking sheet and brush with some of the syrup. Broil about 4 inches from the heat source for 8 minutes, then turn over and brush again with the syrup. Broil for 8 more minutes.

Cut the pineapple into 1-inch cubes and set aside.

Preparing the *Calabaza* ▶ Place the pumpkin in a 4-quart pot, add 2 quarts water, the bay leaves, cinnamon, salt, and allspice berries, and bring to a boil over medium heat. Cook until the pumpkin is fork-tender, about 15 minutes. Drain and set aside.

Making the Vinaigrette ▶ Place the garlic, vinegar, olive oil, allspice, salt, and syrup in a small bowl and whisk to combine.

Assembling the Salad ▶ Place the pumpkin and pineapple in a large bowl and toss with the vinaigrette and roasted pumpkin seeds. Mound on a serving platter and sprinkle with the cacao nibs and *pimentón* to taste. Drizzle with extra-virgin olive oil and serve.

Puerto Rican Salt Cod Salad

Serenata

Serenata is the poetic Puerto Rican name for a salad of salt cod and the starchy vegetables that people in the Hispanic Caribbean call *viandas*. The usual way of serving this generous dish is to toss the shredded cod with a garlicky dressing and place it on a platter surrounded by the just-cooked *viandas*. My version is based on that of my Puerto Rican cousin Elbita in San Juan. I have tasted this dish all over Puerto Rico, but her "serenade" is music to my palate. Serve as a main-course salad or appetizer.

What to Drink: Sauvignon Blanc Casa Marín "Cypress Vineyard" from San Antonio Valley, Chile

SERVES 6 AS A MAIN COURSE, 8 AS AN APPETIZER

For the Salt Cod

- 1½ pounds salt cod, soaked according to the instructions on page 613 and drained
- 1 medium white onion (8 ounces), finely slivered lengthwise
- 8 medium plum tomatoes (about 1½ pounds), peeled, seeded, and quartered
- 4 ounces green cabbage (about ¼ small cabbage), finely shredded and blanched for 30 seconds
- 2 medium red bell peppers (about 1 pound), fire-roasted (see page 67), peeled, cored, seeded, and cut into ¼-inch-wide strips

For the Dressing

- 12 small Caribbean sweet peppers (*ajíes dulces*) or 2 cubanelle peppers, cut into 2 or 3 pieces
- 3 garlic cloves
- 1 teaspoon ground cumin
- ½ teaspoon freshly ground black pepper
- ¾ cup extra-virgin olive oil
- ½ cup distilled white vinegar

For the Vegetables

- 2 *malangas* (about 1 pound), peeled and cut into 1-inch chunks
- 2 green bananas (about 1 pound), peeled and cut into 1-inch sections
- 2 Caribbean sweet potatoes (*boniatos*; about 1 pound), peeled and cut into 1-inch rounds
- 1 tablespoon salt
- 2 ripe plantains (about 1 pound), peeled and cut into 1-inch rounds

- 1 West Indian avocado, halved, pitted, peeled, and cut lengthwise into 1-inch slices, for garnish

Preparing the Salt Cod ▶ Finely shred the cod with your fingers. Place in a bowl and toss with the onion, tomatoes, cabbage, and roasted peppers. Set aside.

Making the Dressing ▶ Place the peppers, garlic, cumin, black pepper, olive oil, and vinegar in a blender or food processor and blend until smooth. You should have about 1⅓ cups. Set aside.

Cooking the Vegetables ▶ Place the *malangas*, green bananas, and sweet potatoes in a large heavy pot, add water to cover by 2 inches and the salt, and bring to a boil over high heat. Cook for 10 minutes. Add the ripe plantains and boil for 10 more minutes. Drain and cover to keep warm.

Assembling the Salad ▶ Pour the dressing over the fish mixture and toss to coat well. Mound on a large serving platter and surround with the hot vegetables. Serve garnished with the avocado slices.

Variation: For an extra touch of flavor, I like to drizzle the salad with Puerto Rican *ajilimójili* (page 143). It is also delicious to drizzle warm Cuban *mojo* (page 140) over the vegetables.

Cactus Paddle Salad from Querétaro

Ensalada de Nopalitos Queretana

This salad is one of the signature marketplace offerings in the Mexican colonial city of Querétaro. The women who sell it spend hours trimming off the sharp thorns that cover the leathery green *nopalitos*. They prepare the salad by cutting the *nopalitos* into small pieces, boiling them in water with some lime or lemon juice to get rid of the sticky juice, and tossing them with chopped avocado, tomato, and cilantro in a dressing laced with *manzano* chiles (the Mexican name for the chubby, fiery hot pepper called *rocoto* in the Andes and sold frozen under that name in Latin markets).

SERVES 6 TO 8

- 8 plump, unbruised *nopalitos* (cactus paddles)
  Juice of ½ lime (about 1 tablespoon)
- 2 teaspoons salt, or to taste
- ½ cup extra-virgin olive oil
- ⅓ cup distilled white vinegar
- 3 garlic cloves, finely chopped
- 1 fresh or frozen *rocoto* pepper (see headnote), seeded and finely chopped, ½ habanero, seeded,

  deveined, and finely chopped, or 1–2 jalapeños, deveined, seeded, and finely chopped
  Freshly ground black pepper
- 3 Hass avocados, halved, pitted, peeled, and diced
- 6 plum tomatoes (about 1 pound), peeled, seeded, and diced
- ½ cup finely chopped cilantro
- 6–8 lettuce leaves, for serving

Cactus paddle (*nopalito*)

▶ To prepare the *nopalitos*, hold each one by the stem, inspect it carefully for any thorns, and shave them off with a sharp knife held at an angle. Cut each paddle into long 1-inch-wide strips, starting 2 inches from the base of the paddle, then cut the strips into 1-inch cubes. Discard the base.

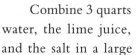

Cleaning a cactus paddle

Combine 3 quarts water, the lime juice, and the salt in a large saucepan and bring to a boil over medium heat. Drop in the cactus paddles and cook, uncovered, until they have released their viscous juice and are tender but still have a little bite (you don't want them mushy). Drain in a colander, rinse under cold running water, and drain again. Set aside.

In a small bowl, whisk together the oil, vinegar, garlic, hot pepper, and salt and pepper to taste.

In a salad bowl, toss the cactus paddles with the avocados, tomatoes, and cilantro. Add the dressing and toss to mix well. Arrange the lettuce leaves on salad plates and top with the salad.

Variation: For a more substantial meal, add any kind of fresh *queso blanco*, diced.

Spicy Andean Corn and Cheese Salad

Soltero Cochabambino

I first tasted this wonderful perfumed Andean corn and cheese salad in La Paz, far away from Cochabamba, its reputed place of origin. It was my first meal in Bolivia, and I was being very careful with what I ate—the altitude had given me a mild case of mountain sickness, and I was not about to indulge in wild eating as I usually do when I encounter new foods.

I was staying at the Hotel La Paz, which has a well-known restaurant on the top floor with a full view of spectacular Mount Illimani. I approached the salad bar and was drawn to a colorful salad with huge kernels of corn. It was love at first bite. The combination of the substantial mealy kernels and the creamy cheese was stupendous, the whole perfumed by *quillquiña*, a green herb with tiny elongated leaves, more aromatic than any other Andean herb I had tasted.

In Cochabamba, I discovered that *soltero* is also eaten during midmorning, the so-called *sajra hora*, or hour of the devil. My friends in Cochabamba tell me that this salad is called *soltero*—"the bachelor"—because it is often eaten by young single men early in the morning after a night of drinking.

Back home, I could not find *quillquiña*, so I first tried the salad with cilantro. Though still I loved the salad, I missed the perfumed *quillquiña*. Now that I grow this herb in my backyard, I can truly enjoy my Cochabamba *soltero*. The more widely available *papaloquelite*, a deeply aromatic Mexican herb, is a good substitute.

Serve as a salad, side dish, or appetizer.

SERVES 6 AS A MAIN COURSE, 8 AS AN APPETIZER

- 1 pound corn kernels (preferably from frozen Andean corn, available in Latin markets)
- 12 small plum tomatoes (about 2 pounds), seeded and cubed
- 1 pound soft, crumbly fresh cheese (such as *queso fresco* or *queso blanco*), homemade *cuajada* (page 104), or French feta cheese, crumbled or cubed
- 1 medium red onion (8 ounces), finely slivered lengthwise
- 1 yellow Andean pepper (*ají amarillo*), fresh or frozen, or 1–2 jalapeños, seeded, deveined, and finely chopped
- 2 tablespoons finely chopped flat-leaf parsley
- 1 tablespoon finely chopped *quillquiña* or *papaloquelite* (see headnote) or cilantro
- 1 teaspoon freshly ground black pepper

▶ Bring a large saucepan of salted water to a boil over medium heat. Add the corn kernels and cook for 15 minutes. Drain and let cool.

Combine the corn and all the remaining ingredients in a large bowl and mix well. Let stand for at least 30 minutes before serving, to allow the flavors to mingle.

Andean Fava Bean and Fresh Pork Rind Salad

Soltero con Cuchicara "La Chola"

The *picantería* La Chola is a Cusco institution. When I first visited it in its original location back in the 1990s, it was a small, sparsely furnished restaurant with long communal wooden tables painted a deep turquoise and banquettes covered in tan goat's skin. On a board hanging on the wall, below the poster of a sultry nude blonde, were listed the seductive day's specials, beginning with everyone's favorite, the *soltero de cuchicara*.

The *soltero* is an Andean salad that can be found in both southern Peru and Bolivia, with subtle differences. In Cochabamba, Bolivia, it is made with corn, tomatoes, and cheese, perfumed with *quillquiña*, a marvelous Andean herb (see page 73). In Arequipa and Cusco, Peru, it is a fava bean and cheese salad, sometimes enriched with boiled pork belly rind or a local seaweed called *cochayuyo*. The pork rind, with its crunchy yet gelatinous texture, is the perfect counterpoint to the mealy fava beans and the creamy cheese.

This is a substantial salad, colorful and balanced, that can be served as an appetizer or a complete meal.

SERVES 12 AS AN APPETIZER, 6 TO 8 AS A MAIN COURSE

For the Pork Rind
- 13 ounces fresh pork belly rind (order from a Hispanic, Italian, German, Hungarian, or Chinese meat market)
- 1 teaspoon salt

For the Vegetables
- 1 pound corn kernels (preferably from frozen Andean corn, available in Latin markets)
- 2 pounds fresh fava beans, shelled (about 2 cups), or frozen shelled fava beans
- 8 medium plum tomatoes (about 1½ pounds), peeled, seeded, and cut into ½-inch dice
- 12 Peruvian purple olives or Kalamata olives, pitted and cut into slivers
- 1 medium red onion (about 8 ounces), finely slivered lengthwise
- 8 ounces French feta cheese, cut into ½-inch dice (about 2 cups)
- 2 tablespoons finely chopped *quillquiña* (see page 73), *papaloquelite* (see page 73), or cilantro
- 1 fresh or frozen *rocoto* pepper (see page 61), seeded and finely chopped, or 1 to 2 jalapeños, preferably red, seeded and finely chopped

For the Dressing
- ⅓ cup extra-virgin olive oil
- ⅓ cup distilled white vinegar
- Juice of 1 lime
- ⅛ teaspoon ground cumin
- 1 teaspoon salt
- ½ teaspoon freshly ground black pepper

Preparing the Pork Rind ▶ Cut the rind into 9-inch squares. Place in a large pot, add 3 quarts water and the salt, and bring to a boil. Reduce the heat and simmer for about 40 minutes until soft. Drain.

Cut the rind into 2½-inch long, ½-inch-wide strips. Set aside.

Cooking the Vegetables ▶ Place the corn in a medium pot, add 1 quart water, and bring to a boil.

Lower the heat and cook for 10 to 15 minutes; drain and set aside.

While the corn cooks, boil the fava beans according to the instructions on page 268. Let cool, then peel. Set aside.

Making the Dressing ▶ Place the oil, vinegar, lime juice, cumin, salt, and pepper in a large bowl and whisk to mix.

Assembling the Salad ▶ Add the corn, fava beans, tomatoes, olives, onion, cheese, herb, and hot pepper to the dressing and toss well.

Serve right away or at room temperature. Garnish with pork rind.

Warm Ecuadorian Cabbage and Fresh Cheese Salad

Ensalada de Col y Quesillo

In Ecuador, *ensalada* often refers to dishes featuring vegetables such as cabbage briefly cooked in the typical mixture of onion and garlic sautéed in golden achiote-infused oil (*rehogado*, the local equivalent of *sofrito*), then tossed with an unripened fresh cheese. These can be served as the main course of a simple meal, accompanied by white rice.

SERVES 4 TO 6

For the Cooking Sauce

2 tablespoons achiote-infused corn oil (page 89)
5 garlic cloves, finely chopped

1 medium white onion (8 ounces), finely chopped (about 1½ cups)
1 teaspoon ground cumin
1¼ teaspoons salt, or to taste
½ teaspoon freshly ground black pepper, or to taste

For the Salad

6 medium russet potatoes (about 2 pounds), peeled and cut into 1-inch dice
2 cups water
½ small green cabbage (about 8 ounces), finely shredded
½ cup whole milk
6 ounces soft, crumbly fresh cheese (*queso fresco* or *queso blanco*), French feta cheese, or homemade *cuajada* (page 104), crumbled or diced (about 1½ cups)
¼ teaspoon dried oregano

Making the Cooking Sauce ▶ Heat the oil in a 12-inch heavy-bottomed skillet over medium heat. Add the garlic and sauté until pale golden, about 30 seconds. Add the onion and sauté for 5 minutes, or until translucent. Stir in the cumin, salt, and pepper.

Preparing the Salad ▶ Add the potatoes to the cooking sauce and sauté for 1 minute. Add the water and simmer, covered, over low heat for 12 minutes.

Add the cabbage, cover, and cook for 3 minutes, until soft. Add the milk and cheese and cook, stirring, for 2 minutes. Add the oregano and stir to mix well. Taste for seasoning. Remove from the heat and serve hot or warm, by itself or with a side of rice.

Warm Ecuadorian Broccoli Rabe and Potato Salad

Ensalada de Nabo

In highland Ecuador, cooks strip the slightly bitter leaves of broccoli rabe from the stalks and combine them with potatoes for a lovely warm salad. It makes a good main dish for people on a budget, or it can be served as an accompaniment to a meat dish and white rice.

While we are very concerned about cooking our vegetables al dente and keeping our potatoes from disintegrating, Ecuadorians expect exactly the opposite. In this dish, the potatoes are supposed to be almost crumbly and the broccoli rabe very soft—that's the charm of this simple salad.

SERVES 4 TO 6

1 tablespoon achiote-infused corn oil (page 89)
4 garlic cloves, finely chopped
1 small white onion (about 3 ounces), finely chopped
½ teaspoon ground cumin
1½ teaspoons salt
¼ teaspoon freshly ground black pepper
2 cups water
6 medium russet potatoes (about 2 pounds), peeled and cut into 1-inch dice
1 large bunch (about 1 pound) broccoli rabe
1 tablespoon extra-virgin olive oil
1 tablespoon distilled white vinegar

▶ Heat the oil in a medium pot or a large deep skillet over medium heat. Add the garlic and sauté until golden, about 40 seconds. Add the onion and cook until light golden, about 4 minutes. Stir in the cumin, salt, and pepper, add the potatoes, and cook, stirring, for 2 minutes. Add the water and simmer, covered, for 15 minutes.

Meanwhile, pluck the leaves from the stalks of the broccoli rabe (save the stems and flowerets for another use). Cut the leaves crosswise into ½-inch-wide strips. In a small saucepan, bring 3 cups water to a boil over medium heat. Add the leaves and cook, covered, for 8 minutes; drain well. Let cool slightly, then squeeze with your hands to get out as much water as possible.

When the potatoes are soft and ready to disintegrate, lift them out of the pot with a slotted spoon and place in a bowl. Return the pot to the heat and let the liquid reduce to about ½ cup over medium-high heat. Stir in the oil and vinegar, and remove from the heat. Add the greens to the potatoes, pour the oil mixture over the vegetables, and toss to mix. Serve warm.

CHAPTER 15

BREADS

IN THIS CHAPTER

I have always viewed the art of the baker with reverence and fear. But I stopped being intimidated when I saw how the Garífuna women of La Ensenada, a small town on the Caribbean coast of Honduras, bake their favorite coconut rolls over a wood fire. The Garífuna are descendants of shipwrecked African slaves who intermarried with Carib Indians on the island of Saint Vincent in the seventeenth century. In 1797, the British expelled them to Roatán, an island off the coast of Honduras, from which they migrated to various parts of the Caribbean coast of Central America, including La Ensenada.

In this small village, the men fish and the women grow staples like yuca and bake coconut bread for a living. A few years ago, my Palestinian friend Mary Kawas, who lives in nearby Tela, took me there to buy the bread for a late breakfast. We found one of the women baking outdoors under the shade of tall coconut trees. Like most Garífunas I had met in Honduras, she was languorous and easygoing, her talk marked by familiar, affectionate flourishes, such as calling everyone "Mama" or "Papa." "What are you cooking today?" I asked her. "*Un poco de todo, Mama* (A little bit of everything, *Mama*)," she answered sweetly, with a broad smile, handing us a couple of coconut rolls so hot they almost burned our hands. We sat on a tree trunk and ate them with delight while the gentle waves of the Caribbean lapped just feet away. We bought all the bread the woman had baked for a few dollars, and I knew I would have to come back to learn how to make it.

The next morning, I woke at the crack of dawn and drove from San Pedro de Sula, Honduras's second-largest city, to La Ensenada at record speed. The women there had told me they like to start working on their bread very early in the morning, when the breeze from the Caribbean still cools their palm-thatched huts. When I arrived, I found that they had already hacked open dozens of coconuts with machetes to gather the meat and extract the creamy milk, and they were piling up the empty shells to make the fire. Inside a small hut, a kind of beach shack where they sell their bread and other foods, a woman had begun to mix flour, coconut milk, coconut oil, and sugar in large, deep wooden troughs (*artesas*). She kneaded the dough briefly with relaxed long strokes, as if washing cloth on a river stone, and shaped it into a couple dozen rounds that resembled kaiser rolls, which she set to rise in a large metal washbasin. By then the lively coconut-shell and wood fire burned between three stones. She propped the basin over the stones and covered it with a piece of corrugated metal. Every so often she checked on the rolls and changed their position according to their degree of doneness. At the end of baking, they were golden with dark brown spots and had a delicious coconut fragrance that mingled with the marine scent of the nearby beach. People from nearby Tela go to the hamlet just to buy the rolls for lunch, and by noon almost all of the bread was gone.

I thought I had the recipe etched in my mind—it seemed simple enough. Back at home, however, my first attempts using my modern oven yielded rolls with a nice golden crust and a faint coconut flavor that didn't taste very much like the crusty, smoky rolls I had eaten in La Ensenada. So I decided to attempt to re-create the original bread, cooking it outdoors, even going so far as to use a worn-out metal washbasin and a piece of corrugated tin to cover the rolls. My first two tries failed miserably, but the third and fourth attempts—this time using my Weber kettle grill—resulted in bread that was very close to the original as I remembered it.

Was all the trouble worth it? I doubt that

anyone in America would want to burn their lawn to bake a dozen coconut rolls, but my failures and frustration helped me to remember the very primitive, challenging conditions under which many Latin Americans produce very tasty bread today.

Though all varieties of breads are now produced industrially in the large cities of Latin America, from native American breads like corn tortillas to French-style baguettes, much of the bread that comes to Latin American tables is still artisanally made, in the true sense of the word. Cooks make flatbreads on stovetop griddles. They bake simple yeast bread in makeshift ovens fueled by wood fires, or in backyard adobe ovens. The recipes, passed down for generations, are usually very old and involve fascinating stories of loss, survival, and gain.

Despite the plethora of different names—*casabe, mbeiú, tlayuda, chipa, timbal, pan amasado, pandebono, telera, tekiana, pan de gloria, chapalele, semita, pupusa*—Latin American breads can be divided into two straightforward categories: unleavened flatbreads, made mostly with corn, yuca, potatoes, or wheat, and a greater variety of yeasted wheat breads. This latter category is a hodgepodge of baking styles and cultural influences. In different countries, old breads that came to the Americas in the early days of Spanish colonization coexist with more modern breads descended from the Catalan *pan de flama*; with European breads like the French baguette and the Italian ciabatta; with wheat flatbreads like pita popularized by Lebanese, Syrian, and Palestinian immigrants; and with American-style commercial white sandwich bread, *pan de miga* or *pan de molde* (a must for party sandwiches). There are also many sweet yeast breads, deliciously scented with anise seeds, cloves, or cinnamon, developed in convent kitchens during the colonial period. These have endured through the centuries with little change, though nowadays they may be prepared with commercial yeast and artificial coloring.

FLATBREADS

The great majority of Latin American flatbreads hark back to pre-Columbian times and are in fact among the oldest food staples of the Americas. The Mesoamerican corn tortillas, the South American corn cakes called *arepas*, and the Caribbean and tropical forest yuca breads *casabe* and *beijú* (also called *mbeiú* in Paraguay), have survived to this day practically unchanged because the first wave of Spanish and Portuguese conquistadores and subsequent generations of European settlers embraced them. These native American breads not only satiated their hunger but also fit the European definition of what a bread is and the role it plays in a meal.

The people from the Iberian Peninsula, true to their Roman Mediterranean heritage, choreographed their meals around bread. They dunked bread into soup, used bread as a plate, and at times lived on bread alone. For many of the indigenous populations of the New World, native breads played that same central role. The keystone of the Mesoamerican diet was dried corn treated with lime and turned into thin flat cakes that were cooked on griddles over wood fires. The Spanish first named this native bread *pan de maíz* (corn bread) and then later *tortilla*, because its shape resembled a type of Spanish wheat bread cooked in the ashes of the hearth called *tortilla al rescoldo*, which they brought to many parts of the Americas, including Chile.

From the accounts of Bernardino de Sahagún, the sixteenth-century Dominican friar who wrote extensively about Aztec culture as it existed at the time of the Spanish conquest, it is evident that these early tortillas were far from simple and that they were consumed by all classes. He explains that there were several types of tortilla for the common people as well as special tortillas consumed by the Aztec nobility. There were everyday tortillas that were "very white and very thin, and broad, and very soft," "very white and large, and coarse," or "dark and very good eating"; layered tortillas that were very delicate; and tortillas made from fresh corn kernels and small ears of corn.

Bernal Díaz del Castillo's epic chronicle of the conquest of Mexico by Hernán Cortés in the sixteenth century, *Historia verdadera de la conquista de la Nueva España* (The True History of the Conquest of New Spain), conveys the importance of corn tortillas for the Spanish conquistadores. They had to depend on the generosity of their Mexican allies to supply them with dried corn and on tortilla-making women to replace the first cache of New World bread they had brought from Cuba—*casabe*.

Casabe, the flat yuca bread made by the Taíno Indians of the Caribbean, had at first seemed hard and strange to the conquerors. But when they realized they could dip it into a soup or stew, use it as a plate or even as a spoon, or eat it by itself, they adopted *casabe* as bread, at least in times of need. *Casabe* kept Columbus and his men alive during their early explorations and on their journeys back to Spain. *Casabe* made in the Cuban town of Trinidad fed Hernán Cortés and his men on their Mexican expeditions. But every Spaniard who tasted *casabe* and wrote about it agreed that it was coarse and wholly inferior to the fine wheat bread from Castile.

With the Spanish conquest of "New Spain" (Mexico) came wheat, which grew plentifully in temperate regions of the country like the valleys of Mexico, Puebla, and El Bajío. Flour mills were established there as early as 1525, and soon steady supplies of wheat flour from New Spain reached the Spanish settlements in the Hispanic Caribbean.

As soon as a reliable supply of wheat bread became available, *casabe* dropped in the Spanish food hierarchy. Letters to the Spanish Crown by official colonial overseers and Dominican and Franciscan friars refer to abuses committed by Spanish land-owners on the island of Hispaniola, such as feeding their Indian workers on nothing but *casabe* softened in water boiled with hot peppers. A royal decree dated 1511 addresses such complaints and orders landowners to supply their Indians with a daily ration of one pound of beef or fish, one and a half pounds of *casabe*, and five pounds of tubers, "each with its hot pepper." Later, under the plantation system fueled by African slave labor, *casabe* became the bread of slaves, as well as the urban poor, peasants, and sailors. *Casabe* was the first foodstuff to be produced in industrial-size facilities in Cuba; ironically, the indigenous population had been practically eradicated by then.

Casabe still has a place in the cuisines of the Hispanic Caribbean, especially in the countryside and in black communities, even though leavened wheat bread baked in Spanish-style bakeries became the bread of choice. In South American countries such as Venezuela, wheat grew so bountifully by the end of the sixteenth century that it was exported to other Spanish colonies. Yet the taste for *casabe* has remained strong until the present, in large part because native populations survived the onslaught of the Spanish conquest in the more remote Orinoco

Basin and in the Venezuelan Amazon. The tastiest Venezuelan *casabe* comes from the Orinoco, where one often finds large rounds of it stacked as high as a man in local markets. Miniature *casabe* rounds can be bought in Venezuelan supermarkets. People serve them as *pasapalos* (appetizers), garnished with salmon roe, cheeses, and all sorts of toppings, even at posh receptions. This sometimes comes as a surprise in a country that also loves wheat bread and has a wonderful European-style and *criollo* baking tradition.

Though the Orinoco Basin is prime *casabe* territory, the Warao Indians who live in the spidery river delta in Venezuela prepare a similar bread made from starch extracted from the *moriche* palm (*Mauritia flexuosa*). It is the primary staple of their diet, more important to them than the nourishing fish of the Orinoco. The extraction of the starch is an elaborate process that includes rituals and chanting. Yet during the rainy season, because they can't cut the palms when the *moriche* groves are flooded, the Warao have come to rely on the leavened wheat flour sold by traders from Trinidad or the nearby town of Tucupita. They use it to make a flatbread called *domplina*, from the English word *dumpling*.

While the people of Venezuela and the Hispanic Caribbean use only the coarse yuca flour to make *casabe*, many of the native tribes of Brazil use a mixture of this flour and the finer yuca starch, or just the starch, to make a bread called *beijú*, which is more delicate and fragile than *casabe*. At Belém's fabulous Ver-o-Peso market, one can buy *beijú* shaped into thin pure white scrolls. In Brazilian cities like Salvador and São Paulo, *beijú* is often mixed with grated coconut and condensed milk to make a popular snack. A rich yuca starch and cheese bread named *mbeiú* (also known as *mbeiyú*) is made in a skillet in Paraguay.

The Andean region does not have an important native bread tradition in the same way as Central America or the Orinoco and Amazon regions, where yuca bread still reigns supreme. Sixteenth-century Spanish chroniclers describe how the Indians of Peru made breadlike corn cakes called *tanta* ("bread" in the Quechua language), *humintas* or *humitas* (tamales made with fresh corn), and a corn dough called *sanco* that they fashioned into loaves. But the chronicler El Garcilaso, one of the most reliable sources for this early period, writes that the Indians rarely ate bread made out of corn except on feast days. It seems that Andean people met their carbohydrate needs instead with staples like corn prepared in the form of *mote* (hominy) or *chicha* (a fermented drink), toasted as *cancha*, and made into porridges, as well as with potatoes in all sorts of dishes.

WHEAT BREADS

The Spaniards introduced wheat throughout the Andes at different points during the sixteenth century, but it took a while for the supply to be plentiful enough to be made into bread. According to sixteenth-century chronicler Garcilaso, though fields of wheat were growing near Cusco in 1547, there was no wheat bread yet in the city. Spanish bread-making techniques eventually took root in the Andes, but wheat bread did not replace the native staples as the main source of carbohydrates.

Latacunga, a town in the highlands of Ecuador, is famous for a wheat bread called *allulla*. After an early morning drive from Quito with my Ecuadorian friend Inés Mantilla, the thought of bread fresh from the oven with a cup of coffee seemed inviting, and we stopped to buy *allullas* from the first street vendor we saw. It was not love at first bite. I thought the *allullas* must be at least a week old because they were so hard. Inés assured me they were not. "*Allullas*," she explained, "are left in the oven after they are baked to dry like crackers." In Ecuador, this bread, the simple rolls called *pan blanco*, and a plethora of delicious sweet breads, are primarily eaten as snacks or for sandwiches.

In Chile, however, where the Spaniards found the Mapuche Indians making a kind of bread from a corn paste called *mültrum*, Spanish-style breads like *pan amasado* and the unleavened cinder-baked *tortillas al rescoldo* became daily bread, particularly in rural areas, where they are still baked in Roman-style beehive adobe ovens brought by the Spaniards. These breads, made with what professional bakers describe as "straight" or "direct" doughs, are best eaten when fresh from the oven; when they cool, they have the texture of cardboard. In Chilean Patagonia, they coexist with *mültrum*, which is still made in some Mapuche communities, but mostly with wheat flour instead of corn.

In Mexico, after the Spanish arrived, tortillas began being made with wheat, especially in the north of the country. But no matter how many Spanish-style bakeries sprang up there or how much wheat was grown, the tortilla made with nixtamalized corn still reigned supreme—even though it was regarded by the upper classes as the food of the enslaved and the conquered. The endurance of the corn tortilla in its many regional forms can be partly explained by its versatility and ease of preparation, compared to a huge *casabe* round or a yeast bread. Though the process of treating the dried corn

with lime to hull it can be time-consuming, it is something that a woman can do in her own home. Once the dough is ready, making tortillas takes only minutes, and they can be baked on top of the stove.

In Mexico, pre-Columbian and European bread-making traditions were able to exist side by side because they fulfilled different purposes. Throughout Mexico, corn tortillas are used as bread at a meal and as bases for countless little dishes (*antojitos* or *botanas*). Savory breads, both the French types known as *teleras*, *flautas*, or *rehiletes* and the more compact Spanish loaves, are generally preferred for European-style sandwiches. For the most part, these are consumed in urban areas. But sweet breads account for the overwhelming majority of breads found in any Mexican bakery. They are eaten as snacks, especially for breakfast and for the afternoon *merienda*, to accompany hot chocolate, juices, *aguas frescas*, or coffee, or during important religious holidays.

Sweet breads such as *rosca de reyes* (a ring-shaped coffee cake) and *pan de muerto* (Days of the Dead bread) are directly descended from Spanish religious practices and are feast-day fare in Mexico and other parts of Latin America. Highland Ecuadorians, for example, celebrate the Days of the Dead with *guaguas de pan*, sweet loaves shaped like swaddled infants and frosted in bright colors. The Latin American sweet bread tradition was born in convent kitchens. In Cuenca, a town in the Andean highlands of Ecuador, the names of the breads—Christ's knees (*rodillas de Cristo*) or nun's bread (*pan de monja*)—and the smells of anise, cloves, and cinnamon wafting from local bakeries still conjure up a nunnery's kitchen.

Cuenca is known for the quality and variety of its breads, most of them produced in wood-fueled adobe ovens resembling those used by the early bakers attracted by the first mill, built in 1542. Another place that has an impressive variety of breads, surprisingly, is Bolivia. As in Ecuador and Peru, hard wheat grew plentifully in the cool highlands, and peasants threshing wheat in the golden fields are a familiar sight in the windswept *altiplano*. In La Paz, next to sacks of fresh and freeze-dried potatoes—the staples of the cuisine—are baskets brimming with rust-colored French-style rolls called *marraqueta*, bow-tie *kaukita*, and *sarnitas*, round buns speckled with cheese, similar to the Ecuadorian *tukianas* or *rodillas de Cristo*. These are the bakery breads of the *mestizo* and the urban populations of Bolivia, but rural cooks also bake *sarnitas* in their wood-burning ovens.

Despite some disappearing traditions, the story of bread in Latin America is one of survival and gain rather than loss. The ancient traditions were never really stamped out. Instead, we find well-defined niches of adaptation and survival for both Native American and European-style breads.

This chapter begins with the important family of unleavened flatbreads that are at the heart of Latin American regional cuisines: *casabe*, the brittle native bread of the Hispanic Caribbean and the Orinoco Basin made with yuca flour, and several South American flatbreads made with yuca starch, including the Paraguayan *mbeiú* and *chipa*, the Colombian *pandebono*, and the addictive Brazilian cheese roll, *pâo de queijo*. We then move on to flatbreads made with corn dough, such as Mexican corn tortillas and the *arepas* of Venezuela and Colombia, and whole wheat tortillas, a specialty of the Lake Pátzcuaro area in Michoacán. Although there are hundreds of wonderful leavened breads in Latin America, here I focus on just a few of my favorites, like Cuban bread, the indispensable foil for a Cuban sandwich; the Venezuelan Christmas ham bread (*pan de jamón*); and sweet breads such as Ecuadorian *rodillas de Cristo*, to illustrate some of the important categories of our European-influenced bread-making tradition.

CINDER-BAKED CHILEAN FLATBREAD
Tortilla al Rescoldo

My Chilean friends the Baezas used to talk to me endlessly about *tortilla al rescoldo*, a cinder-baked flatbread they would eat near Santiago. I knew it was one of the oldest Spanish breads to have taken root in the Americas, and listening to them, I could imagine its smell as it emerged from an adobe hearth, lightly charred and covered with ashes. It sounded like something I'd love making in my own fireplace on a cold winter's night and eating at leisure while sipping wine and listening to Chilean love songs.

My romantic dreams were shattered, however, when I first visited Chile. On a trip to Pomaire, the village that supplies the country with black earthenware pottery, I saw a street vendor peddling ash-covered *tortillas al rescoldo*. I was overjoyed. The breads were large and round, with a thin ashy coating that looked just like what I had expected for so long. The man was delighted when I asked to see his oven and learn his baking secrets. As we walked uphill to his house, I could smell bread baking in wood-burning ovens all around us. What a perfect preamble, I thought, to the *tortilla* of my dreams. What I found was artisanal bread, as most home breads could be called, but with none of the primitive grace and romance I had envisioned. There in his large kitchen were a conventional bread oven and trays full of raw breads ready to be baked. "But where is the hearth?" I cried, thinking that perhaps there was an outdoor oven. "No, señora, these tortillas are baked in a gas oven," he replied. "But how do you get them so ashy?" Proudly, he showed me a large metal salt shaker full of ashes. "I go around town and pick up wood ashes from all the restaurants. A good idea, huh?"

Sadder but wiser, I continued my quest during two successive trips to Chile. Every time I saw a sign for *torti-llas al rescoldo* along the road, I eagerly stopped the car, to hear that the baking was done only on weekends. Finally, in southern Chile, I saw an elderly Mapuche woman selling *tortillas al rescoldo* on the roadside. I stopped, this time with very little hope. I examined her breads, bought one, bit into it, and closed my eyes. I had found it! This was the *tortilla* of my dreams, still warm from the oven, with that unmistakable flavor and aroma that can come only from dying embers and ash, not from a salt shaker. ◆

UNLEAVENED BREADS MADE WITH YUCA, CORN, OR WHEAT

Yuca Bread

Casabe

Casabe is the native bread of tropical America, a large, brittle yuca flatbread that retains the musky sweetness of the root. It is still eaten today by millions of people from the Hispanic Caribbean to the steamy jungles of the Orinoco and Amazon Basins. I learned to love it from my father, who eats it drizzled with olive oil and smeared with garlic for breakfast and crumbles it into soups as if it were a cracker.

In the United States, one can find packaged *casabe* from the Dominican Republic in Latin markets. The large rounds come quartered and are usually sold three to a package. I find the quality uneven; some loaves are crunchy, others tough. When I have the time, I prefer to prepare my own.

I traveled all the way to the Orinoco to learn how to make *casabe*. It is one of the most fascinating and satisfying cooking processes I know. When I make *casabe*, I feel as if my kitchen has grown roots that stretch to pre-Columbian America. The basics of the recipe have not changed much from the days before Columbus's landfall in Hispaniola. The yuca still needs to be grated and forcefully squeezed to rid it of its juices, sieved to turn the squeezed pulp into a dry flour, and finally baked on a hot flat surface.

The native peoples of the Orinoco and Amazon Basins make *casabe* using ingenious tools of amazing beauty, such as the *cibucán* (called *tipiri* in the Orinoco Basin), a squeezer fashioned out of palm leaves; ornate wooden graters studded with quartz teeth (*rallos*); sieves shaped like flexible flat baskets; and huge clay griddles called *budares*. These are among the most striking handcrafted objects to come out of the Americas, and I have collected many of them. But when I began experimenting with my own kitchen equipment, I was happy to discover that the food processor worked just fine for grinding the yuca, that a square of cheesecloth was just what I needed to squeeze the grated pulp, and that a Mexican *comal* or plain heavy skillet was perfect for baking the bread.

Homemade *casabe* is beautiful. Its pitted surface looks like a parched landscape. You can see patches of brown and spidery veins, like the dried-out beds of desert streams. It is also delicious, crunchy like a cracker, and versatile. Because it is unsalted and somewhat bland, like matzo, it is a *tabula rasa* for all kinds of tasty toppings.

Cook's Note: In tropical America, *casabe* is made with bitter yuca, a variety laden with cyanide. Cooks wash the pulp and then squeeze it dry to get rid of this toxin. Bitter yuca is not available in the United States, so you don't need to worry about being poisoned. I use the sweet yuca from my local market with satisfactory results.

MAKES SIX 10-INCH ROUNDS

5 pounds yuca (about 4 pounds 3 ounces when peeled)

Peeling and Grating the Yuca ▶ Peel the yuca according to the instructions on page 152. Cut it into 1-inch chunks and, working in small batches, process to a smooth paste in a food processor, about 4 minutes per batch. Or grate the yuca on the fine side of a box grater; in that case, cut the peeled roots crosswise in half before grating them. You should have about 6½ cups.

Preparing the Yuca Flour ▶ Cut a 16-inch square of tightly woven cheesecloth. Working in 1-cup batches, roll up the grated yuca in the cheesecloth, tie the ends tightly, and wring out as much juice as you can into a bowl or into the sink. (The smaller the batch, the easier on your hands.) When you have wrung out the last drop, combine all the yuca in a bowl. It will now be dry enough to crumble with your fingertips. Rub it between your palms to pulverize it evenly.

Sift through a coarse sieve or strainer. The flour will have the texture of a very coarse cornmeal or grated Parmesan cheese. You should have about 6 cups (slightly less than 2 pounds).

Making the *Casabe* ▶ Heat a 10-inch *comal*, griddle, or heavy skillet over medium heat. Working quickly, scatter 1 cup of the yuca flour into the pan, spreading with a wide spatula to form an even circle about 10 inches in diameter; do not worry if the edges are not completely even. When you first spread the yuca flour in the pan, it seems impossible that it will harden into a cohesive flat pancake—but it will! Cook, pressing down with the spatula occasionally, until you see the edges beginning to brown and detach from the pan, 7 to 8 minutes. Carefully turn over with the spatula. Because the bread is only 10 inches in diameter, not a couple of feet like the ones you find in South America, it is not going to fall apart in the process. Continue cooking until the bread is light gold on the underside. Transfer to a baking sheet; repeat with the remaining flour to make a total of 6 breads.

Drying the *Casabe* ▶ If you were a Yanomami Indian, you would throw the loaves onto the roof of your *shabono* (hut) to dry, but, thankfully, here in America we have ovens. Put the *casabe* in a 200°F oven for 15 minutes, and it will dry perfectly. That way the bread will be crunchier, not chewy, and it will last longer.

Serving: I like to serve *casabe* in beautiful baskets lined with shiny plantain leaves. It looks spectacular! Just before serving, brush the bread with a mixture of minced garlic and the best extra-virgin olive oil you can find—a peppery Spanish olive oil from Murcia or a brash first-pressed oil from California will work beautifully. Slide into a preheated 375°F oven for 5 minutes to warm. If you wish, sprinkle the warm bread with freshly grated Parmigiano-Reggiano and a little finely chopped oregano and parsley. You can also serve *casabe* with a dipping sauce like Venezuelan *suero* (page 146) or Central American *crema* (page 147). Cut into bite-sized pieces and topped with salt cod or beef hash, salmon roe or smoked salmon and crème fraîche, it makes a delicious appetizer.

Variation: I also bake *casabe* in the oven. Spread 3 cups of the yuca flour evenly over a 13-by-18-inch baking sheet or 14-inch pizza pan. Place the pan on the bottom of a preheated 400°F oven and bake for 10 minutes, until the yuca flour solidifies. Remove from the oven and turn over, using another baking sheet to prevent the bread from falling apart. Bake for another 8 minutes. These large breads have a tendency to buckle a little; if you want to keep them flat, place another baking sheet on top to press each one down as it bakes. Repeat with the remaining yuca flour. Makes 2 large breads.

Storing: *Casabe* will keep amazingly well for several months at room temperature tightly wrapped in plastic wrap or in a dry place in a paper bag.

Yuca and Fresh Cheese Pancake

Mbeiú Paraguayo

In the Paraguayan countryside, the daily bread is a simple yuca starch flatbread made in a skillet. In urban households, richer versions with plenty of cheese are a side dish for roasts and a favorite snack. Children love it, and eat it in wedges like pizza. When my friend Cecilia Caballero was teaching me to make *mbeiú* (often spelled *mbeiyú*) at her family compound in Villetas, Paraguay, word spread and the family's children, a troop of about twenty, descended upon us to devour the *mbeiú*.

The traditional recipe I learned in Villetas makes a bread about the size of a small pizza. It is thin like a pancake, somewhat crisp, approaching an Italian *frico*, but a bit denser and softer. I have tried it at home using a 13-inch nonstick skillet, which worked beautifully. But a pancake that size can be a bit difficult to flip, so here is a recipe for two pancakes made one after the other in a medium-sized skillet. If you want to make a big one, invert it onto a plate like a frittata and then slide it back into the skillet.

MAKES 2 PANCAKES (SERVES 8 TO 10)

⅓ cup (about 3 ounces) lard, preferably freshly rendered (page 82)

3 large egg yolks

8 ounces Muenster cheese, grated (about 2 cups)

½ cup whole milk

1 cup (about 6 ounces) yuca starch (sold as *almidón de yuca* in Hispanic markets and *polvilho azedo* in Brazilian markets)

¾ teaspoon salt
   Melted butter, for cooking
   Coarse sea salt, to taste (optional)

▶ Place the lard in the bowl of a standing mixer and beat with the paddle attachment at high speed until fluffy, about 6 minutes. Add the egg yolks and beat until pale in color, about 3 minutes. Add the cheese, milk, yuca starch, and salt and beat at low speed for about 1 minute to blend thoroughly.

Brush a 10- to 11-inch skillet, preferably non-stick, very lightly with melted butter and set over medium heat. Pour half the batter into the skillet and spread evenly with the back of a metal spoon dipped in lukewarm water. Cook until the bread is golden on the bottom and the edges are beginning to brown, 7 to 10 minutes. Flip the bread over like a pancake (or invert it onto a plate and slide it back into the skillet). Cook on the other side for 3 to 5 more minutes, until golden brown and crisp. Keep warm in a low oven while you repeat with the remaining batter.

Serve hot, cut into wedges, sprinkled, if you wish, with coarse sea salt.

Paraguayan *Chipa*

Chipa Paraguaya de Almidón

"*Chipas, se venden chipas, chipas calientes, chipas baratas!*" (*Chipas*, we sell *chipas*, hot *chipas*, inexpensive *chipas!*) is the cry of the Paraguayan vendors strolling the streets and even the sports stadium of Asunción during soccer games. They carry large baskets full of warm *chipas*, the crumbly unleavened rolls made with cheese and corn or yuca starch that serve as bread all over this landlocked South American country and also in neighboring northeastern Argentina. Paraguayan families consume *chipas* especially on weekends and during Holy Week. In fact, some families eat nothing but *chipas* on Holy Thursday and Good Friday.

One morning I met a *chipa* vendor in Asunción who invited me to visit her home bakery in the town of Barrero Grande. Everyone I met in Asunción rhapsodized about the *chipas* of this town, about two hours by car from the city. I reached Barrero early in the morning. As I drove uphill to the woman's house, I smelled *chipas* baking in wood-fired ovens all over town and saw women balancing flat baskets of *chipas* covered with white cloth on their heads. They were on their way to the side of the busy highway, where they set up shop, enticing passersby to stop for a hot *chipa* and a cup of *mate cocido* (boiled *mate* or a convenient teabag version).

In Paraguay, there are dozens of *chipas*, some enriched with wheat flour, *chipa piru*; others flavored with anise; others, like *chipa so'o*, filled with ground beef, in the manner of *empanadas*. A tasty variation is the *chipa guazu*, or big *chipa*, which is something like fresh corn bread.

One constant ingredient is the fresh cheese known as *queso paraguay* or *queso del país*—literally, the cheese of the country. It's a soft, buttery cheese very similar in taste and texture to the Muenster cheese made by Mennonite cheesemakers from the Chaco region. To my knowledge, it is not available in this country. But Paraguayans living in the United States make do with soft cheeses like Muenster or Italian Fontina for *chipas* and the corn bread named *sopa paraguaya*.

Regardless of what goes into them, everybody agrees that the best *chipas* are those baked in *tatacuás*, the igloo-like adobe ovens introduced by the Spaniards. *Tatacuá* is a descriptive Guaraní word meaning "hole" or "place of fire." Though I liked the *chipas* of Barrero Grande, I much preferred the *tatacuá*-baked *chipas* at the home of my sister-in-law's relatives, the Castillo family, who live in the town of Villeta on the River Paraguay. This is my adaptation of their recipe.

MAKES 20 *CHIPAS*

- 6½ ounces (about 1 scant cup) freshly rendered lard (page 82) or unsalted butter
- 5 large egg yolks
- ¾ pounds Muenster or Italian Fontina, grated (about 3 cups)
- 1 pound (about 4 cups) yuca starch (sold as *almidón de yuca* in Hispanic markets and *polvilho azedo* in Brazilian stores)
- ½ cup whole milk
- 1½ teaspoons anise seeds
- 1 teaspoon salt

▶ Preheat the oven to 450°F. Beat the lard or butter in the bowl of a standing mixer with the paddle attachment at medium speed until light and fluffy, about 10 minutes. Add the egg yolks one at a time, beating for 5 minutes after each addition. Add the cheese and half the yuca starch, then the milk and remaining starch. Beat in the anise seeds and salt. Mix for 5 minutes.

Divide the dough into 20 equal-sized balls. Either roll each ball into a 4-inch cylinder and pinch the ends together to form a doughnut shape, or pat each ball slightly between your palms and flatten into a 3-inch round to make a flat roll. Place at least 1 inch apart on a nonstick or greased and floured baking sheet and bake for 15 minutes, until golden.

Serving: Serve hot from the oven with hot Argentinean-style *mate* (see pages 332, 346, and 348) or cold Paraguayan *tereré* (page 347).

Minas Gerais Yuca and Cheese Rolls

Pão de Queijo Mineiro

After only a few days in São Paulo, Rio, or Minas, you begin to crave *pão de queijo*. These golden cheese puffs are positively addictive. In the morning, you have them for breakfast. Before lunch, you rush to a *cafetería* very fittingly called Casa de Pão de Queijo (House of the Cheese Bread), with branches all over Brazil, to have them piping hot, filled with creamy cheese. Mmmm! They taste heavenly with a *café com leite* made with smooth Illy coffee. At the everything-on-a-skewer *rodízio*, where you devour the whole cattle ranch, you first munch on tiny cheese rolls and then ask the waiter for seconds.

Pão de queijo is not your average cheese bread. These golden rolls are made with the starch of the poisonous bitter yuca, which in Brazil is called *polvilho azedo*, and they look like cheese *gougères*. When you cut one open, fresh from the oven, you see translucent starchy strands stretching between the two halves of your roll. Because they are laden with sharp *queijo mineiro*, an aged cow's-milk cheese that tastes a bit like Parmesan, it is the cheese that envelops your taste buds first. But then there is the wonderful sweet flavor, the seductive glutinous texture that can come only from yuca.

Mineiros claim *pão de queijo* as their own. After all, they are not only the greatest cheesemakers of Brazil, but also the country's most notorious noshers. Every Mineiro family I have met, from Belo Horizonte to Tiradentes, seems to have not one but several ways of making these rolls. Some scald the *polvilho* with boiling water or milk. Others mix all the ingredients at room temperature. To turn yuca starch into rolls that will puff up in the oven, the dough must have lots of fat. Mineiros use lard, butter, or vegetable oil. I have experimented with all three and found that the most flavorful rolls are made with either vegetable oil or butter and milk, not water. Here is one of my favorite recipes.

Working Ahead ▶ *Pão de queijo* freezes very well. Bake for 15 minutes, until half done. Let cool and place in a freezer bag. Close tightly and freeze. To serve, bake at 375°F for 15 minutes without defrosting and serve hot.

MAKES ABOUT 24 SMALL ROLLS

- 2½ cups (about 10 ounces) yuca starch, sold as *polvilho azedo* in Brazilian stores and *almidón de yuca* in Hispanic markets
- 1 cup whole milk
- 4 tablespoons (½ stick) butter
- 1 teaspoon salt
- 2 large eggs, lightly beaten
- 1 cup finely grated Parmigiano-Reggiano or Argentinean Sardo cheese (about 4 ounces) Vegetable oil, for moistening your hands and coating the baking sheets

Making the Dough ▶ Place the yuca starch in a medium bowl. Combine the milk, butter, and salt in a saucepan and bring to a boil over medium heat. Stir to dissolve the butter. Pour the boiling milk over the starch and beat with a wooden spoon to combine. The dough will feel dense and will stiffen into a ball. Let cool for 15 minutes. Meanwhile, lightly grease two baking sheets with vegetable oil.

Shaping and Baking the Rolls ▶ Preheat the oven to 450°F. When the dough is cool, add the eggs

and cheese. Combine with the spoon or your hands, being careful not to overmix. The more you handle or beat the dough, the more difficult it is to shape. Oil the palms of your hands lightly and pull off a 1-ounce portion of the dough. Shape into a ball as best you can. It does not have to be perfect. Place the ball on an oiled baking sheet, and repeat with the rest of the dough.

Lower the oven temperature to 375°F. Place the rolls on the middle rack and bake for about 25 minutes. If you want the rolls to be more golden, with a crunchy outside and a spongy interior, bake for an additional 5 minutes.

Serving: Serve hot with coffee, fruit juices, milk shakes, or cocktails such as *caipirinhas* (page 360) and *batidas* (page 362).

Colombian Yuca, Corn, and Cheese Rolls

Pandebono

My favorite Colombian bread is *pandebono*, a soft, lightly sweet roll that is a specialty of the Valle del Cauca region of the country. For years I have been buying this bread at my local Colombian bakeries, always trying to get a recipe that would remind me of the delicious *pandebonos* I ate in Cali. But no baker was willing to part with his or her formula. Once a Colombian cook I know offered to teach me her well-guarded recipe, but I discovered that her "big" secret was using a box of ready-mix.

It was only after learning to make a similar bread from Venezuela, *almojábanas andinas*, that I understood the basic principles of the Colombian recipe and could tackle the bread on my own. I tried several variations and decided to settle for one made with a mixture of yuca starch and corn flour for *arepas*. In Colombia, cooks use a combination of a fresh soft cheese called *cuajada* and *queso añejo*, a sharp aged cheese. Several Latin American companies sell soft fresh cheeses resembling *cuajada* in the United States. The closest substitute for the Colombian aged cheese is Mexican *cotija*. During baking, the cheeses melt, forming golden freckles on the surface of the bread.

MAKES 20 SMALL ROLLS

- 2½ cups warm water
- 2 cups (about 14 ounces) precooked white corn flour for *arepas*, preferably P.A.N. brand
- 1 cup (about 4 ounces) yuca starch (sold as *almidón de yuca* in Hispanic markets and *polvilho azedo* in Brazilian stores)
- 1 tablespoon unsalted butter, softened
- 2 tablespoons sugar
- 2 large egg yolks
- 8 ounces fresh cheese, preferably *cuajada* (page 104), crumbled (about 1 cup)
- 12 ounces aged cheese, preferably Mexican *cotija*, crumbled or grated (about 3 cups)

▶ Preheat the oven to 350°F and butter a baking sheet. Place the warm water in a large bowl. Pour in the corn flour in a thin stream while mixing with the other hand, then knead with both hands until the dough no longer sticks to your fingers. This makes about 1 cup. Let rest for 5 minutes, covered with a kitchen towel. Add the yuca starch, butter, sugar, egg yolks, and cheeses and mix with a wooden spoon to make a soft dough.

Using your hands, shape the dough into twenty 2-ounce balls. Flatten each ball lightly with the heel of your hand and place on the baking sheet, leaving about 1 inch between the rolls. Bake for 25 minutes, until the rolls turn golden with brown spots.

Serving: Serve hot or at room temperature. They are best eaten warm with hot chocolate (page 339 or 340) or *café con leche* (page 351).

Storing: The rolls will last 2 days stored in zip-top bags at room temperature.

Mexican Corn Tortillas

Tortillas de Maíz

In Mexico, there are many types of corn tortillas, varying in width, thickness, color, and texture according to region and each cook's preference. This recipe is for all-purpose Mexican corn tortillas of the kind most Mexicans call *tortillas blancas* (white tortillas), and it is my attempt to simplify an ancient bread that is enormously complex.

Tortillas are made from a dough (*masa*) prepared from dried corn that has been nixtamalized—that is, cooked with slaked lime (*cal*, short for calcium hydroxide) before being ground and kneaded. Traditional cooks in many parts of Mexico still shape the tortillas by hand, rhythmically patting and turning a ball of dough until it becomes a thin, flat, perfectly supple round. In most modern homes, however, tortilla dough is made with instantized flour from dehydrated corn *masa* and shaped with a tortilla press. This is the procedure I present here. Much as I would like to give directions for making the *masa* and tortillas from scratch, I find that it is impossible to achieve a fine enough dough without commercial-scale equipment.

A well-made tortilla is speckled with nice toasted spots, not burned. It puffs up during cooking, and it feels light and airy, not dense and heavy. Even though this recipe has only two ingredients, it is still a complex process. Like riding a bike, once you learn how to make it, it's easy to repeat. I mastered the making of good tortillas only when I took the time to observe what Mexican and Central American cooks were doing, learning their judgment calls when kneading the *masa* and imitating the movement of their wrists and then practicing the recipe until I got it right.

In Mexico, tortillas are cooked on a large metal or clay griddle called a *comal*. The process of making tortillas is dynamic and involves a constant stream of rolling, pressing, and flipping. The *comal* (especially the clay kind) has warmer and cooler spots, and the *tortillera* (tortilla maker) knows when to move the tortilla from one to the other.

The most important variable is the heat. Some cookbook authors recommend using two skillets, with higher and lower temperatures. But I have had consistent success with a single metal *comal* or a heavy-bottomed skillet set over constant moderate heat. To test whether the griddle is the correct temperature, hold your hand 2 inches above its surface. See how long you can hold it there without pulling it away. If you can hold it there between 15 and 20 seconds, the heat is probably right.

Another important lesson is to be able to read the *masa*. An experienced *tortillera* will notice the changing textures of the dough as it cooks, from the moment it first hits the *comal*. After about 20 seconds a part of one of the edges of the tortilla will begin to dry, pulling away from the *comal*. When it has curled up just enough, she makes the first flip, using her fingertips. Throughout the cooking, there is lots of movement as the cook lifts the tortilla and peeks underneath to check how it's browning.

USING THE TORTILLA PRESS

Tortilla presses can be made of tinned or uncoated cast iron, cast aluminum, hard plastic, or wood. The metal ones are easiest to use. Whichever you use, it is important to get to know the characteristics of your particular press. Some tend to press the *masa* too thin at the hinge side, some at the handle side. To

Tortilla press

make tortillas, line the tortilla press with two pieces of plastic slightly larger than the diameter of the tortilla. Any kind of plastic will do, but I have found that a heavy-duty zip-top bag works best. Cut the bag into two equal pieces. The plastic should be clear enough that you can spot broken or thin edges, cracks, or holes and repair them. Thin or cracked edges can be fixed by folding the damaged edge of the dough over and patting it gently.

Once you have your ingredients and materials, practice making a few tortillas with your press. With most presses you will find it necessary to press the tortilla twice or more, rotating or flipping it between pressings to even out the surface.

USING A *COMAL*

The traditional Mexican kitchen always has at least two *comales*, one for making tortillas and one for roasting seasoning ingredients such as dried chiles, tomatoes, onion, and garlic. A good *comal* for making tortillas is no less than 10 inches across and must be properly cured. In Mexico they are often made of clay, which requires curing with a paste of lime after every use. For cooks in this country I recommend the more durable cast iron. To cure a new cast-iron *comal*, wash it with hot water, using a gentle scouring pad. Dry the pan immediately with a lint-free cloth. Cover the surface of the pan with a thin layer of oil and a generous amount of coarse salt. Heat over a medium flame or place in a hot oven for 15 minutes. Wipe the surface clean with paper towels.

If the *comal* is not hot enough or too hot, your first tortilla may stick to it. Scrape it away as soon as possible and wipe off the burned bits. The first tortilla may have a bald spot. But if your *comal* is used only to make tortillas, it will never need to be washed. Wipe it clean with a clean cloth. If you wash it, you will have to season it again.

While a *comal* is a most useful piece of equipment to make tortillas, a well-seasoned heavy-bottomed skillet or griddle will also do a good job.

MAKES 15 CORN TORTILLAS

3½ cups (about 12 ounces) instant corn *masa* mix for tortillas, preferably Maseca brand

2¼ cups hot tap water

Preparing the *Masa* ▶ Place the *masa* mix in a large bowl. Slowly add the water while kneading the dough. Once all the water has been incorporated, continue to knead until the dough is smooth, 3 to 5 minutes. The *masa* should be very soft but not sticky, just about the consistency of Play-Doh. If it is too dry, work in a bit more water. If it is too wet, continue kneading until it dries out a bit or knead in additional *masa* mix. Instant *masa* dries out very quickly and will continue to do so as you make the tortillas. Once it is at the right consistency, keep it covered with a damp kitchen towel at all times.

Shaping and Cooking the Tortillas ▶ Heat a *comal*, griddle, or heavy skillet over medium heat. Pinch off about 2 ounces *masa* and roll into a ball about 1¾ inches in diameter. Flatten it slightly between your palms to make a 2½-inch round. Place in the center of the open tortilla press between two sheets of plastic. Press the lever gently but firmly to flatten the dough. Flip the tortilla (still in the plastic) and press again into an even 6- to 6½-inch round. Place the tortilla (still between the 2 sheets of plastic) in your left hand (if you are right-handed). Peel the plastic from the top of the tortilla. Invert the tortilla onto your right hand, primarily onto your finger-tips. Peel off the second sheet of plastic. Keeping your hand palm side up, release the tortilla with a sweeping motion and let it fall gently and flatly on the surface of the *comal*.

Cook the tortilla just until one of the edges begins to appear dry, 15 to 25 seconds. If you overcook the tortilla at this step, it will not cook properly. Flip the tortilla and cook on the second side just until it is speckled with brown spots, 1 to 2 minutes, rotating it once. Flip the tortilla again. Almost instantly it will puff up like a balloon. If it doesn't, tap the edges or top gently with your fingers or the flat of a spatula. Once it is puffed and just beginning to brown on the bottom, flip the tortilla again and place it on a cooler part of the *comal*, toward an edge. Let the tortilla continue cooking slowly there until most of it appears semitranslucent when held up to the light, 30 to 60 seconds.

Stack the cooked tortillas in a basket lined with a large napkin that you can fold over the top. This will keep the tortillas warm and enable them to continue steaming, which keeps them soft and pliable.

Storing: You can store cooked tortillas in the refrigerator, well wrapped, until ready to use. To reheat, place them one at a time on a hot *comal*, griddle, or heavy skillet or wrap a stack in a damp towel and place in the microwave for a few seconds.

Lake Pátzcuaro Whole Wheat Tortillas

Tortillas de Harina Integral del Lago Pátzcuaro

Wheat and corn grow tall and plentiful on the shores of Lake Pátzcuaro in Mexico's Michoacán state, and they also coexist in harmony in the adobe kitchen of my friend Francisca de La Luz Cortés, who lives in Uricho, a lakeside community. Francisca's husband is a farmer who tills the soil in a large cornfield on the outskirts of town and a smaller *milpa* that stretches to the rim of the lake behind their house. Three days a week Francisca walks a few miles to the town of Erongarícuaro, carrying a basket full of corn and whole wheat tortillas to sell. They don't last long. I know of people in Erongarícuaro who buy everything she makes.

To make her whole wheat tortillas, she first flattens them on the *metate* (page 34) and then hand-shapes them. Her hands fly, patting them between her palms, then stretching them wide and thin. Before you know it, a large tortilla with not a crevice or fold in sight is cooking flat on the *comal*.

When I visit her, we eat these fresh from the *comal* with scrambled eggs and melted bits of smoked cheese. I kneel on a straw *petate* next to a wood fire to scramble the eggs in an iron frying pan set on three stones while Francisca stands next to her propped-up *comal*. The tortillas don't have a moment to cool. We fill them with the piping hot egg mixture and roll them up like large tacos. They are fantastic!

Working Ahead ▶ When making these tortillas ahead of time, stack them and store in a zip-top bag. When ready to eat, heat the whole stack for 1 minute in the microwave or one by one on the *comal*. Wheat tortillas freeze well for at least 3 months.

MAKES 16 TORTILLAS

2 cups (about 9 ounces) whole wheat flour
2 cups (about 9¼ ounces) bread flour
1½ teaspoons salt
¼ cup corn oil
1¼ cups water

Preparing the Dough ▶ Combine the flours and the salt in a large bowl. Add the oil and rub it into the flour with your fingertips or between your palms until thoroughly blended. Then add the water, a little at a time. Begin by mixing it in with your fingers and follow by kneading. Gather the dough into a ball and transfer to your work surface. Knead it until completely blended and smooth, about 3 minutes. Divide the dough into sixteen 2-ounce balls. Flatten them slightly and let them rest on a plate or a baking sheet, covered with plastic wrap, for 30 minutes.

Shaping and Cooking the Tortillas ▶ Heat a *comal*, griddle, or heavy skillet over medium to medium-high heat. With a rolling pin, roll 1 disk of dough to a very thin (less than ⅛ inch) 7- to 8-inch tortilla. Place the tortilla on the palm of one hand or drape it over the back of your hand. Pinch and pull the edges with the other hand, stretching evenly. Francisca's *comal* is huge, but mine is 10 inches wide, so that's as far as I like to stretch my tortillas.

Gently lay the tortilla on the *comal*, trying to keep it as flat as possible, which is sometimes difficult. After 15 seconds, turn it over with a metal spatula or your fingers. It will look as if much of the dough is completely raw; that's just fine. Cook the tortilla until it gets a few browned spots underneath, about 40 seconds. Flip the tortilla over again. It will puff up in sections like a corn tortilla. Cook the puffed tortilla for about 20 seconds, until the underside is spotted with brown, and then flip it again and finish with 10 to 20 seconds on the other side.

As each tortilla cooks, roll out and stretch the next one. As you remove the tortillas from the *comal*, stack them in a basket lined with a cloth napkin to keep warm.

Serving: Anything that tastes good with a corn tortilla will also be delicious with these whole wheat tortillas. I particularly like them with scrambled eggs and smoky cheese (you can use Idiazábal, a smoky cheese from the Basque country) for breakfast, or with a sharp manchego.

SOUTH AMERICAN CORN FLATBREADS (*AREPAS*)

Arepas are to Colombians and Venezuelans what corn tortillas are to Mexicans and Central Americans: their daily bread, their basic staple. Like tortillas, *arepas* are simple, elemental round cakes tasting mostly of dried corn. But unlike the corn tortillas of Mexico, these earthy South American flatbreads are made with a dough of white corn whose skin has been removed by pounding with mortar and pestle, not by being softened with strong alkali. Because of this essential difference, *arepas* do not taste as assertive as corn tortillas. At their most basic, *arepas* have an appealing, comforting blandness.

When the conquistadores explored northern South America, they found the natives of western Venezuela and the Colombian Andes baking their *arepas* on clay griddles not unlike the Mesoamerican *comales*. Hunger and the absence of wheat made them embrace this native bread. In time, as Spaniards moved freely from one end of the Americas to the other, they carried the concept of the *arepa* to other regions, where it was interpreted freely and often transformed. In Piura in northern Peru, there are sweet corn cakes called *arepas*. In Ecuador, small pastries are known by that name. But the true homeland of the *arepa* remains Colombia and Venezuela. In these countries, eating *arepas* borders on an obsession. In Venezuela in particular, *arepas* are eaten at all times of the day: early in the morning instead of toast, as a midmorning snack with a variety of fillings, for dinner as bread, and late at night or at dawn as a restorative sandwich after a night of partying.

It is not difficult to tell a plain Venezuelan *arepa* from a Colombian one. For the most part, Colombian *arepas*, particularly the ones from Antioquia in the interior of the country, which are sometimes made with yellow corn, are large and on the flat side. Although there are thin-as-cracker *arepas* in Lara Estate and very large, flat ones made with nixtamalized corn in Coro, traditional Venezuelan *arepas* for everyday eating are plump, almost rounded, with distinctive brown spots on their top. This marking, called *concha*, is the proof that one has at least tried to do part of the cooking according to tradition on a *budare*, a clay or metal griddle.

Colombians eat *arepas* with little ceremony. Venezuelans, on the other hand, are very particular. For large *arepas*, the preferred method is to steady the hot *arepa* in one hand, protected by a napkin, while cutting open a pitalike pocket with a knife. They cut just enough to be able to hollow out the soft hot interior. In *areperas* (establishments specializing in *arepas*), the inside is often discarded, but at home people eagerly mix it with butter or shredded cheese and devour it by itself or put it back into the shell. It is not unlike hominy grits. The hollowed-out shell is turned into a kind of sandwich, buttered on the inside and filled with anything from crumbled fresh cheese or shredded Gouda to black beans or hard-boiled quail eggs with Thousand Island dressing to shredded stewed meat to chicken salad. An *arepa* filled with chicken salad and avocado is called *reina pepiada*. For breakfast, a little butter, some cheese, and a dollop of cultured cream on your *arepa* will do nicely with your fried eggs.

Basic Dough for *Arepas*

Masa para Arepas

Traditionally, the making of *arepas* and tamales in Colombia and Venezuela was announced by the sound of women pounding corn kernels in large wooden mortars called *pilones*. It's a painstaking job requiring much stamina.

In rural areas, women still crack and peel their corn in the *pilón*, but the process has been industrialized, in much the same way that nixtamalization is now done industrially in most parts of Mexico and Central America. The industrial product is sold as precooked corn flour or cornmeal for *arepas* (*harina de maíz precocida para arepas*; see page 253).

Making *arepas* with this product is a breeze—all you do is mix the right proportion of water and flour and knead it until you have a homogeneous dough (*masa*). I have been making *arepas* in this fashion for many years, but once I tasted *arepas* made with cracked corn (*maíz pilado*) at the Caracas home of Venezuelan food historian José Rafael Lovera, I have never been completely satisfied with the instant version. Since then I have tried to find time to make the dough with brands of cracked corn (Goya, La Venezolana) available in the United States.

Preparing your own *masa* is not at all difficult. You only need dried cracked white corn (see page 445) and elbow grease to grind the corn in a corn mill. Then you knead the dough until smooth with any other ingredient called for in the individual recipe. The *masa* will remain moist for much longer than nixtamalized corn flour, which tends to dry very quickly. That alone is a powerful reason for trying to make fresh *masa* for *arepas* at least once.

MAKES ABOUT 2 POUNDS *MASA*

- 1 pound (about 2½ cups) cracked white corn (see headnote)
- 1¼ teaspoons salt

▶ Place the corn in a large bowl and rinse in several changes of water until it runs clear. Cover with 2 quarts water and soak for 1 day, changing the water twice. Rinse again, drain, and place in a large pot with 4½ quarts water and the salt. Simmer for 30 minutes over medium heat until al dente. Drain well and grind to a paste with a corn plate mill (see page 33) or the grinding attachment of a standing mixer. Use the dough as soon as possible after grinding, because it goes sour quickly. Refrigerate, well covered, if holding for longer than 1 day.

Arepas in the Style of Caracas

Arepas Caraqueñas

I have been watching Venezuelans make *arepas* for years, and it always surprises me to find so many minute variations on a recipe that calls for just two or three ingredients. Every cook I know claims that the order of using the ingredients—whether the precooked corn flour is added to the warm water or vice versa—or how long the dough is kneaded affects the outcome. I have tried many versions and found that the key variable is the right proportion of water to corn flour. When working with instant corn flour, be sure to add enough water to hydrate it. Then the dough should be allowed to rest for a few minutes. Only then can you be certain that you have added the right amount of liquid. A *masa* that feels too wet right after kneading can dry out quickly after a few minutes. If the dough feels dry to the touch, work in more water, a little at a time, until it feels right. If it feels too wet, knead in some more corn flour.

This is the recipe of my Venezuelan friend Nelly Guinand de Galavís, who taught me to eat *arepas* like a Caracan, scooping out the soft interior and eating it by itself, like grits; buttering the *arepa*, stuffing it with grated Gouda cheese, and finally smearing it with tart ripened cream.

MAKES SIXTEEN 1-OUNCE OR FOUR 4-OUNCE *AREPAS*

Using Fresh *Masa*

½ recipe Basic Dough for *Arepas* (page 584)

1 teaspoon salt

1 tablespoon sugar

Using Precooked Corn Flour for *Arepas*

2½ cups warm water

1 teaspoon salt

1 tablespoon sugar

2 cups (about 14 ounces) precooked white corn flour for *arepas*, preferably P.A.N. brand

Corn oil, for cooking

Preparing Fresh *Masa* ▶ Place the *masa* in a bowl with the salt and sugar and knead until smooth. Cover with a damp kitchen towel and let rest until ready to shape.

Preparing Precooked Corn Flour ▶ Place the warm water in a bowl, add the salt and sugar, and stir to dissolve. Pour in the flour in a thin stream while mixing with the other hand. Then knead with both hands until the dough no longer sticks to your fingers. Let rest for 5 minutes, covered with a kitchen towel.

Shaping and Cooking the *Arepas* ▶ Preheat the oven to 375°F. Divide the dough into 16 portions (about 1 ounce each) or 4 portions (about 4 ounces each). Roll each portion into a ball. To keep the dough from sticking to your fingers, wet your hands slightly with cold water from time to time as you work. If making small *arepas*, flatten the balls lightly but leave them somewhat convex. For larger *arepas*, flatten the portions into 4-inch rounds. Cover with a kitchen towel to keep the dough from drying out as you work.

Heat a large *comal*, griddle, or heavy skillet over medium heat and grease lightly with corn oil. Place the *arepas* on the griddle at least 1 inch apart; work in batches as necessary. Bake until there is a golden, crusty patch on the bottom, about 4 minutes. Turn and bake the other side in the same way.

Place the *arepas* on a baking sheet, at least 1 inch apart, and bake for 20 to 25 minutes for small *arepas*; 35 minutes for the larger ones. They will sound slightly hollow when tapped.

Serving: The *arepas* should be filled and devoured while hot.

Variation: Deep-Fried *Arepa* Fingers (*Panochas*)

In the household of the Guinand Cuervo family in Cumarebo, a town in Falcón state in Venezuela, breakfast often consists of deep-fried *arepas* called *panochas*. The family eats them as they do *arepas*, hollowing out the interior and filling the shell with grated aged cheese from Churuguara. To make, use 1 recipe *Arepas* in the Style of Caracas and 3 cups corn oil for frying. Prepare the dough and divide it into 8 equal portions. Wet your hands lightly and roll each portion into an oval shape about 3½ inches long, 2 inches wide, and 1 inch thick. In a deep, heavy medium skillet, heat the corn oil to 350°F. Add the *panochas*, about 3 at a time. When they bob to the surface, in about 12 minutes, tap them lightly with a spoon to help them puff evenly. Turn and cook for 3 more minutes, tapping as before, until golden brown. Lift out with a slotted spoon and drain on paper towels. Makes 8 servings.

To serve, cut crosswise in half. Scoop out the soft inside, butter the shell, and fill as you wish with crumbled fresh cheese, Venezuelan Pan-Fried Shredded Beef (page 715), or the beans from Caracan Black Bean Cream Soup (page 528) and a dollop of a ripened cream called *nata coriana*. This is more acidic than the *suero* on page 146, which is a specialty of another part of Venezuela. To come close to the *nata coriana*, mix some sour cream and a few tablespoons of heavy cream to make a cream with the consistency of crème fraîche.

All-Purpose Venezuelan *Arepas*

Arepas Venezolanas para Todo

Like most Venezuelans, my friend chef Miriam Córdoba can make *arepas* with her eyes closed. Ask her about measurements and she will tell you she works by the *ojo por ciento*, that is, the "eye percent." Miriam does not sweeten her *arepas*, as some cooks do, but she does add a little oil to make the dough smoother. I use her recipe when I want a plain *arepa* dough that can be used to make Colombian *pandebono* (page 578), empanadas, or *almojábanas andinas* (an Andean bread).

MAKES 13 *AREPAS*

> 2 cups (about 11 ounces) precooked white corn flour for *arepas*, preferably P.A.N. brand
> 1¼ teaspoons salt
> 2½ cups water
> 1 teaspoon corn oil, plus 1 tablespoon for brushing the pan

▶ Heat the oven to 350°F.

Combine the corn flour and salt in a large bowl. Drizzle the water and 1 teaspoon oil over the surface of the corn flour and shake the bowl back and forth to mingle the ingredients. Set this mixture aside for 1 minute, until the water is completely absorbed.

Knead the dough until smooth and let it rest another 5 minutes. Knead the dough again until it doesn't stick to the bowl or your fingers. Cover with a wet cloth and let rest for about 1 minute.

Divide the dough into thirteen 2-ounce balls. Flatten them lightly with the heel of your hand into 3-inch-wide patties.

Heat a *comal*, griddle, or heavy 10-inch skillet over medium-high heat. Lightly brush the pan with some oil. Place the *arepas*, 4 at a time, on the pan and cook for 3 minutes on each side, until a golden crust forms in the center. Repeat with the remaining *arepas*, then transfer to the oven and bake for 15 minutes, or until the *arepas* sound hollow when tapped at the bottom.

Serving: Serve at once with butter or Venezuelan Ripened Milk (page 146).

Anise-Scented Sweet *Arepas*

Arepitas Dulces Fritas

In Mérida in the Venezuelan Andes and on the neighboring plains of Barinas, I tasted crunchy sweet anise-perfumed *arepas* that are deep-fried, like fritters. Clara Alarcón, the cook of the Carmelite convent in Mérida, made them for me while Fray Carlos Jiménez, a good friend, brewed drip coffee using a cloth filter. The combination of the hot mild coffee and the crunchy *arepas* on a cold Andean morning was just perfect.

MAKES 20 SMALL *AREPAS*

- 1 recipe dough for All-Purpose Venezuelan *Arepas* (page 586)
- 6 tablespoons (about 1¼ ounces) grated brown loaf sugar (*papelón* or *piloncillo*) or light brown sugar
- 2 teaspoons anise seeds
- 2 ounces grated fresh cheese, preferably a soft *queso blanco* or *queso fresco* (about ¼ cup)
- ¼ teaspoon salt
- 3 cups corn oil, for frying

▶ Place the dough and all the remaining ingredients except the oil in a bowl and knead until the dough no longer sticks to your fingers. Divide into twenty 1-ounce balls and flatten each into a 3-inch round with the heel of your hand.

Heat the oil to 350°F in a heavy medium pot. Add the balls to the hot oil, 2 at a time. First they will sink to the bottom. When they resurface, turn and fry for another 3 minutes, or until golden brown. Using a slotted spoon, lift onto paper towels to drain.

Serving: Eat hot with Venezuelan Ripened Milk (page 146). I like to serve them for brunch along with white rice, beans, and Venezuelan Pan-Fried Shredded Beef for *Pabellón Criollo* (page 715).

Colombian Grilled Corn and Cheese *Arepas*

Arepas de Queso Asadas

My favorite Colombian *arepa* is a grilled version made with lots of cheese from the town of Barranquilla, on the Caribbean coast. It is one of the street foods eaten during the town's famous carnival. For four days in February, Barranquilla explodes with the frenzied sound of a thousand and one dancing groups called *comparsas* and *cumbias*. Carnival is ushered in with the Battle of the Flowers, when hundreds of floats decorated with fresh flowers parade through the congested streets. Their aroma mixes in with the smell of Cristal brand anise-flavored *aguardiente*, sweat, and the traditional assortment of fried foods, called *fritanga*.

For weeks before the carnival, enterprising

cooks set up makeshift street kitchens in front of their houses to cook Barranquilla's favorite foods: big pork cracklings, fried *bocachico* (a spiny river fish), and *arepas* of all sizes and flavors. Cooks work in an assembly line, shaping homemade white corn dough into *arepas*. They are like Botero, the painter, when it comes to their *arepas*: they like them on the plump side, especially if they are meant to be grilled. They know these simple but tasty breads dry out easily, and they want them moist and succulent to serve as containers, or even plates, for gargantuan portions of other hearty foods.

My friend Rita Ruíz, who is from Barranquilla, told me that the secret of these *arepas* is the cheese. The more cheese you add, the better the *arepa*. And she is right. That's why I never skimp on the cheese. At home I cook these *arepas* under the broiler. My family loves them for breakfast and the afternoon *merienda*, and I love them at all times.

MAKES 11 LARGE *AREPAS*

- 3 cups (about 1 pound) precooked white corn flour for *arepas*, preferably P.A.N. brand
- 2 tablespoons sugar
- 3 cups warm water
- 5 tablespoons unsalted butter, melted
- 1½ pounds soft fresh cheese such as a Colombian-type *queso blanco* or *queso fresco*, coarsely grated (about 4 cups, well packed)
- 8 ounces aged cow's-milk cheese, preferably Mexican *cotija*, grated (about 2 cups)
- 1½ teaspoons salt

Making the Dough ▶ Combine the corn flour and sugar in a large bowl. Add the water gradually, mixing with your fingers. Work in 4 tablespoons butter. Knead to a soft dough. Work in the cheese, 1 cup

at a time, while kneading. Add 1 to 2 tablespoons more water if the mixture seems too dry. Taste the dough (some cheeses are very salty), then add the salt if needed, ½ teaspoon at a time or to taste, while kneading. Continue kneading until the dough feels soft and smooth, with no lumps. Set aside for at least 15 minutes, covered with a damp cloth.

Shaping and Cooking the *Arepas* ▶ Divide the dough into 11 portions, roughly 5 ounces or ½ cup each. Roll the portions into balls between your palms and cover with a kitchen towel as they are shaped. Flatten each ball into a thick 3½-inch round. Place on a tray and cover with a kitchen towel.

Line the broiler with aluminum foil and preheat. Brush the foil lightly with the remaining 1 tablespoon butter. Arrange the *arepas* on the foil and broil about 4 inches from the heat source for about 10 minutes on each side, until both sides are golden brown and unevenly spotted.

Serving: In Colombia, cheese *arepas* are street food or are made at home for breakfast or a light early supper and served with *café con leche* (page 351), tropical juices, or perhaps a piece of leftover meat. They are also a wonderful side dish for braised game birds.

LEAVENED BREADS

Cuenca's White Sandwich Rolls

Pan Blanco Cuencano

The people of Cuenca, in the Ecuadorian highlands, love to eat roast pork sandwiches in small anise-scented rolls called *pan blanco*, or white bread, which belong to a large family of soft, lightly sweet, all-purpose Latin American breads made without prefermentation or chilling of the dough. They are best eaten fresh from the oven, though in Cuenca people often store them in clay jars to keep them fresh longer.

MAKES 12 SMALL ROLLS

- 2 cups whole milk, plus more for brushing the loaves
- 1 tablespoon anise seeds
- 1¼ teaspoons active dry yeast
- 4 cups bread flour (about 1¼ pounds)
- 2 tablespoons sugar
- 2 teaspoons salt
- 2 tablespoons freshly rendered lard (page 82) or butter, melted

Preparing the Dough ▶ In a small saucepan, bring the milk to a simmer over medium heat with the anise seeds. Reduce the heat to low and simmer gently for 1 minute, stirring. Cool to 110°F and strain, discarding the seeds. Sprinkle in the yeast. Let sit until the yeast bubbles, about 15 minutes, and whisk lightly.

Sift together the flour, sugar, and salt. Pour the yeast mixture into a large mixing bowl together with the melted lard or butter. Add the sifted flour mixture gradually while working it in with the tips of your fingers.

Gather the dough into a ball and turn out onto a work surface. Knead vigorously for 20 minutes. Lightly grease a bowl with oil or butter. Turn the dough in the bowl to coat the surface and let sit, covered with plastic wrap, at room temperature until it has doubled in size and springs back a little when poked with a finger, about 2 hours. Lightly grease 2 baking sheets.

Shaping the Rolls ▶ Turn the dough out onto a work surface. Shape it into a log and cut it into 12 equal pieces with a sharp knife. Cup a piece in one hand and lightly roll into a ball on the work surface, then repeat with the remaining pieces. With a rolling pin or the heel of your hand, flatten the balls into 3-inch rounds. Place them on the baking sheets and let rise again for 1 hour, loosely covered with plastic wrap.

Baking the Rolls ▶ Preheat the oven to 400°F and place an empty baking pan on the floor of the oven. Brush the rolls lightly with milk to ensure a soft crust. Bring 2 cups water to a boil and pour into the hot pan to create a cloud of steam. Immediately slide the rolls onto the lower or middle rack of the oven. Using a spray bottle, spray the walls of the oven with water twice, at 30-second intervals. After the second spray, wait 10 minutes before rotating the baking sheets to ensure even baking. Continue baking for 10 more minutes, until the rolls are lightly golden. Let cool to room temperature before serving.

Storing: In Cuenca, the rolls are stored in a tightly covered clay pot to keep fresh. Here you can use zip-top plastic bags.

Cuenca Pork Sandwich

To make Cuenca's popular pork sandwich (*sandwich de pernil*), split the bread open and fill with thinly sliced pork or shredded *fritada* (page 394). Top with a couple of spoonfuls of Ecuadorian Spicy Onion and Tamarillo Salsa (page 138).

Chilean White Rolls

Pan Amasado Chileno

When you drive through Chile, you see small roadside bakeries signs reading "*Hay pan amasado*" (We have white rolls). These lightly flattened rolls are one of the oldest Spanish-style breads in Chile. They are dense and chewy and are delicious when freshly made in a wood-burning oven and smeared with tangy Chilean salsas.

Pan amasado means "kneaded bread." This probably refers to the fact that the dough is stiff and requires vigorous kneading. I learned this recipe from Sofía Chanilao, a Mapuche woman who was born in Chol Chol, a small village in Patagonia.

MAKES 12 SMALL ROLLS

1¾	cups warm (110°F) water
2¼	teaspoons active dry yeast
1	tablespoon sugar
1	tablespoon salt
5¼	cups bread flour (about 1⅝ pounds)
6	tablespoons freshly rendered lard (page 82)

Preparing the Dough ▶ In a small bowl, combine the water and yeast. Let sit until bubbly, about 10 minutes, and whisk lightly. Add the sugar and salt and stir to combine. Place the flour in a large bowl, make a well in the center, and pour in the yeast mixture. Using a wooden spoon or your fingers, work the flour into the yeast mixture until it is nearly integrated. Add the lard and work it in until the mixture begins to come together. Add a few more tablespoons water if needed. Turn the dough out onto a work surface and knead vigorously for 20 minutes. You may want to use a machine with a dough hook for the last few minutes.

Shape the dough into a ball and place in a lightly greased bowl; turn to coat evenly. Cover with plastic wrap and set in a draft-free place at room temperature until doubled in size, about 1 to 1½ hours.

Butter a baking sheet.

Shaping the Rolls ▶ Punch the dough down with your fist and turn out onto a work surface. Divide into twelve 2-ounce pieces and shape the pieces into balls, covering them with plastic wrap as you make them. With a rolling pin or the heel of your hand, flatten each ball to a 3-inch round and place on the baking sheet. Prick the top of each roll with a fork and let rise, covered with plastic wrap, for another 30 minutes.

Baking the Rolls ▶ Preheat the oven to 400°F and place an empty baking pan on the floor of the oven. Just before baking, bring 2 cups water to a boil. Pour the water into the hot pan to create a cloud of steam. Immediately slide the rolls onto the lower or middle rack of the oven. Using a spray bottle, spray the walls of the oven twice at 30-second intervals. After the second spray, wait 10 minutes before rotating the baking sheet, to ensure even baking. Continue baking for 15 minutes more, until lightly golden.

Serving: Serve as dinner or sandwich rolls for any Chilean meal, with Chilean "Goat's Horn" *Pebre* (page 131).

Cuban Bread

Pan Cubano de Manteca

My memories of Cuban bread aren't about dough rising under towels on the kitchen counter or Grandmother greeting us with golden loaves fresh from the oven. For me, Cuban bread conjures up a visit to the bakery.

Cuba does not really have a home bread-making tradition. Even *casabe*, the native yuca bread of the Taíno Indians, came to be made in industrial-sized establishments to meet the needs of the Spanish fleet. But I certainly never felt deprived: Cuban bakeries were and are wonderful institutions that greet you with the smells of freshly brewed coffee and pastries and savories. Lined up on trays are beautiful, whitish loaves that are long and elliptical. They have a soft crunch, with an interior that is a foamy cloud that melts in your mouth. These are not neat breads: break them open and a million crumbs scatter everywhere. What a convenient way to feed the chickens!

Cuban bread is made with a sponge method. Part of the flour, water, and yeast are worked together to form a soft dough that is allowed to ferment for 6–8 hours or overnight. This ensures a more flavorful dough. The following day the rest of the ingredients are added and the dough is first shaped and allowed to rise.

The secret to perfect Cuban bread is prolonged kneading. In Cuban bakeries, the dough is passed twenty times through the rolling cylinders of a machine called the *sobadora*, which ensures a perfectly smooth, flawless crust. You can tell immediately whether the bread has been *sobado*, rolled, or not. Many small bakeries cannot afford the classic *sobadora*, and the crusts of their bread always look lumpy and full of wrinkles. A perfect, eggshell-smooth crust is the sign of a good *sobadura* (rolling) and an authentic Cuban bread.

I know a few of the secrets of Cuban baking because I was taught by an excellent baker, my old friend Luis López. The founder of one of the most successful Cuban bakeries in New Jersey, Luis gave me only very general explanations of how to make Cuban bread for almost twenty years. Perhaps he feared competition. But just before he retired and moved to Miami, he let me in on all the little details that matter. For weeks I kept up calling him with questions: Why has this happened? What do I do now? After failing many times, I finally got it right. One of my big breakthroughs was to use my pasta machine to mimic the effect of Luis's *sobadora*. That day I called Luis and teased him: "Now I am ready to open my own Cuban bakery, Luis," I said. He answered, laughing, "You go ahead and open it. I am going to Miami."

This recipe is for the bread we call *pan de manteca* because it is enriched with lard. Cubans call a long loaf of bread *barra* or *flauta de pan*.

Cook's Note: Cuban bread is closely related to French bread and is made with similar techniques. You need to produce steam in your oven to build a shiny, light crust. Use a roasting pan full of boiling water and a mister bottle to spray the oven walls during the first half of the baking time. The baking temperatures are not a misprint. Although unusual, they are just right for perfect Cuban bread. You can knead the dough by hand or in a pasta machine, but the machine is best, because the finished bread is closer in texture to authentic Cuban bread. Treat the dough like pasta, folding it in half after each pass through the machine.

Working Ahead ▶ Allow 6 to 8 hours, preferably overnight, to make the sponge.

MAKES FOUR 8-OUNCE LOAVES

Day One: For the Sponge

1 cup warm (110°F) water
¼ ounce cake yeast
3 cups bread flour (about 1 pound)

Day Two: For the Dough

¼ cup lukewarm (110°F) water
1 tablespoon sugar
1 tablespoon salt
3 tablespoons melted lard (about 1¼ ounces), preferably freshly rendered (page 82)
1 cup bread flour (about 5½ ounces)

Making the Sponge ▶ Place the water in a large bowl. Add the yeast and stir with a fork to dissolve. Add the flour and mix to form a soft dough. Cover with plastic wrap and let rise for 6 to 8 hours or overnight in a draft-free place at room temperature.

Making the Dough ▶ Place the water in a small bowl, add the sugar and salt, and stir with a fork to dissolve. Add to the sponge along with the lard, and mix with a wooden spoon to form a loose dough. Gradually add the flour to form a firm dough.

Transfer the dough to a floured work surface and knead vigorously by hand for 20 to 30 minutes. After each kneading, turn the dough slightly counterclockwise and knead again until the dough is very smooth and elastic.

Alternatively, you can "knead" the dough in a pasta machine. For this method, smooth the dough with a rolling pin, fold it onto itself as if you were making puff pastry, and smooth again. Divide the dough into 4 equal portions and pass each piece through the widest opening of the pasta machine 20 times, folding the dough in half after each completed roll. If the dough is sticky, lightly flour your hands and sprinkle some flour on the dough. Use sparingly; too much flour can toughen the dough.

Shaping the Bread ▶ Lightly butter a baking sheet. If you have kneaded the dough by hand, cut into 4 equal portions.

Roll one portion in your hand to form a ball. Flatten with your hand and then continue flattening it with a rolling pin into a 10-by-10-inch rectangle. Starting with the side opposite you, form a log by rolling the dough tightly toward you. Taper the ends of the log, tucking in the layers. Pinch along the seam to seal. Roll and shape the remaining 3 pieces of dough.

Place the loaves on the baking sheet. Place a coffee cup at each corner of the baking sheet and stretch a layer of plastic wrap over them to keep the bread from forming a crust. Allow the loaves to rise at room temperature until doubled in size, about 1 hour.

Baking the Bread ▶ Preheat the oven to 380°F for at least 1 hour. Set one rack in the center and place a deep roasting pan on the floor of the oven.

Have on hand a spray bottle. Meanwhile, boil about 3 quarts of water. When you are ready to put the bread in the oven, pour the boiling water into the hot roasting pan. Lower the oven temperature to 360°F. Immediately place the baking sheet on the center rack. Working quickly, spray the oven walls with water and close the door. Spray the oven walls 3 more times during the first 10 minutes of baking. Work quickly each time and open the oven door just enough to have room to spray. The idea is to create moist heat without disturbing the rising of the bread.

Bake the loaves for a total of 18 to 20 minutes, or until they are light golden and sound hollow when tapped on the bottom. When done, transfer the loaves to a cake rack to cool.

Serving: To serve at the table, cut a loaf on the bias into slices, place them on a baking sheet, and briefly reheat in a 350°F oven. Serve with butter, extra-virgin olive oil, or pieces of an excellent dark chocolate.

Cuban Sandwich

Because of its smooth, soft crust, which becomes deliciously crunchy when toasted in the oven, broiler, or sandwich press, Cuban bread is ideal for sandwiches. To prepare an authentic Cuban sandwich, cut a loaf in half lengthwise and place it on the kitchen counter. Spread one side generously with softened butter. Spread yellow or Dijon mustard on the other side. Arrange Swiss cheese, cut into thin slices, on the buttered half and top with about 4 ounces thinly sliced ham and two pickle slices. Distribute a few slices (about 4 ounces) of marinated roast pork (such as Santiago de Cuba's Roast Pork Marinated in a Garlicky Allspice-Cumin *Adobo*, page 721) on the side smeared with mustard. Place the open sandwich under the broiler for 1 or 2 minutes, being careful not to burn it. If you have a sandwich or panini press, press the sandwich flat until the crust is golden and crunchy and the cheese is melted. Otherwise, heat it in a 375°F oven. Serve immediately with long Plantain Chips (page 181). I often cut Cuban sandwiches into 1½- to 2-inch sections to serve as tapas at cocktail parties. I call these *cubanitos* (little Cubans).

Garífuna Coconut Bread

Pan de Coco Garífuna

Though made with staples and the most primitive of baking utensils, this bread is remarkable—dense and a bit chewy, with a seductive smoky coconut taste that cannot be duplicated in the fanciest baker's oven. You can bake it in your oven and get nice-tasting rolls. But only outdoors can you come close to the original Garífuna coconut bread. I have cooked the bread in a washbasin over a wood fire and experimented with my Weber barbecue grill. To my delight, the grill works very well, so that is what I recommend here.

Cook's Note: My friend Jim Koper, who is an amateur baker of great skill, tried the recipe on his gas grill with very good results. He describes the bread as primal in its simplicity, with the aroma of a well-made pizza, a delicious flavor, and a moist, chewy texture. "It was like candy," he said. "Whenever there was a piece around, my guests tore off chunks and ate them without even thinking about it."

MAKES NINE 4-OUNCE ROLLS

4 cups all-purpose flour (about 1¼ pounds)

1 cup Creamy ("First") Coconut Milk (page 50) or unsweetened canned coconut milk

½ cup warm (110°F) water

3 tablespoons sugar

1 tablespoon coconut oil, preferably freshly rendered (page 82), or unsalted butter

2¼ teaspoons active dry yeast

1 tablespoon salt

Making the Dough ▶ Place the flour in a large bowl and make a well in the center. In a small bowl, whisk together the coconut milk, water, sugar, and coconut oil. Stir in the yeast and 2 tablespoons flour. Let stand until the mixture begins to bubble lightly, about 10 minutes. Whisk lightly and pour into the flour. Begin mixing with your fingertips; sprinkle in the salt and work the dough until all the ingredients are well incorporated. If it seems dry, work in 1 or 2 tablespoons water.

Gather the dough into a ball and turn onto a lightly floured work surface. Knead until smooth and silky, about 15 minutes. Shape into a ball and place in a lightly oiled bowl; turn to coat evenly. Cover with plastic wrap and place in a warm draft-free space. Let the dough rise until doubled in size, about 2 hours. Punch down the dough. Knead again briefly and let rise for 1 more hour, covered with plastic wrap.

Shaping and Baking the Rolls ▶ Oil a baking sheet. Divide the dough into nine 4-ounce pieces, roll into balls, place on the baking sheet, and flatten gently with a rolling pin or the heel of your hand into 3-inch rounds. Cover with plastic wrap and let rise for 30 minutes.

A kettle barbecue grill fitted with a lid will do a beautiful job as an oven. Spread about 3 inches of hardwood charcoal on the bottom rack of the kettle (mix with coconut shells if you have any). Light the fire at the sides and in the center.

While the fire burns, place the risen rolls in 1 or 2 large oiled cast-iron skillets and cover with plastic wrap. Let rise again, about 20 minutes.

When the high flames subside, the coals look ashy, and an oven thermometer placed in the center of the grill reads between 400°F and 425°F, remove the plastic wrap and place the skillet or skillets on the grill. (If your grill is too small to hold 2 skillets, bake in 2 batches.) Using a spray bottle, lightly spray the rolls with water. Close the grill lid and bake the rolls for about 12 minutes. Open the lid just long enough to lift each roll and place it facedown, to produce the dark spots that characterize Garífuna coconut bread. Continue baking for 5 to 8 minutes. Prop the rolls on the edge of the skillet and bake for another 5 minutes. Be vigilant, and move the rolls with tongs if they seem to be burning. Using tongs, place the baked rolls on a wire rack.

Serving: This bread is best eaten as soon as it is cool enough to handle. I like it for Sunday brunch with a tropical fruit jam, or Peruvian Purple Corn and Fruit Compote (page 826), or a dollop of *dulce de leche* (page 809). Serve with *café con leche* (page 351), or Hot Chocolate *"Agasajo"* (page 339).

Christ's Knees

*Tukianas, o Rodillas de Cristo
(Enquesilladas)*

This Ecuadorian bread created in the convents of Cuenca gets its name from the bright cross-shaped marks on the crust, which come from achiote-dyed cheese and are said to symbolize the open wounds on Christ's knees on his way to Calvary. A similar bread can be found in Bolivia, where it is called by the unpleasant name *sarnitas* (little scabs). The cheese crust gives a distinctive look and an even better flavor to these simple rolls. The people of Cuenca enjoy them with a cup of coffee in the early afternoon.

MAKES 12 SMALL ROLLS

- ¼ cup sugar
- 1½ cups warm (110°F) water, plus 1 tablespoon for the crust
- 3 tablespoons freshly rendered lard (page 82) or butter
- 1¼ teaspoons active dry yeast
- 4 cups bread flour (about 1¼ pounds)
- 1 tablespoon salt
- 2 ounces Monterey Jack cheese, coarsely grated (about ½ cup)
- 1 tablespoon achiote-infused corn oil (page 89)

Preparing the Dough ▶ Combine the sugar and 1½ cups warm water in a small saucepan, add the lard or butter, and gently heat, stirring to dissolve the sugar, just until it melts. Let the mixture cool to 110°F. Whisk in the yeast and let sit until bubbly, about 10 minutes, then whisk lightly.

Place the flour and salt in a large mixing bowl and combine. Make a well in the center and pour in the yeast mixture; mix with a fork until combined. Gather the dough into a ball, turn onto a work surface, and knead vigorously until smooth, about 10 minutes. Place in a lightly oiled bowl, turn to coat evenly, and cover with plastic wrap. Let rise until doubled in bulk, about 1½ hours.

Shaping the Rolls ▶ Turn out the dough onto a lightly floured work surface. Knead vigorously for 3 minutes and form into a ball. Shape the dough into a 14-inch-long log and cut it into twelve pieces with a sharp knife. Cup each piece in one hand and roll against the work surface to shape into a ball.

Butter a baking sheet. In a small bowl, combine the grated cheese and achiote oil. Mix to a rough paste with the remaining 1 tablespoon warm water. Flatten each roll lightly with the palm of your hand and cut a shallow cross in the center with scissors. Push about 1 teaspoon of the cheese mixture into the cut. Place the rolls on the baking sheet, cover loosely with a moist kitchen towel, and let rise for 1 hour.

Baking the Rolls ▶ Preheat the oven to 400°F. Using a spray bottle, spray the oven walls with water. Quickly slide the rolls into the oven and reduce the heat to 350°F. Repeat the spraying twice at 30-second intervals. Bake the rolls, turning the pan halfway through cooking, until they develop a golden crust, about 20 minutes.

Serving: Serve warm with coffee or as dinner rolls.

Glory Bread (Cuban Coiled Egg Rolls)

Pan de Gloria

When I was going to high school in Santiago de Cuba, chronic shortages of public transportation forced me to walk for miles to catch a bus. My friends and I discovered that the only sure way to find room on the overcrowded buses was to walk downtown to the bus depot. The long trek under the unrelenting sun was not much fun, but the bakery near the bus stop was a consolation. Into the late sixties, it managed to produce some very good pastries and breads. The best of all, *pan de gloria*, were soft coiled rolls modeled after the *ensaimadas* of Majorca. They were generously glazed with sugar syrup and sprinkled with confectioners' sugar.

I have never found *pan de gloria* that tasted quite like those of my bus-waiting days. And frankly, I never felt the urge to bake these rolls at home until very recently. After a few tries, I came close to the balance of saltiness and sweetness I remember.

MAKES 16 LARGE ROLLS

2	cups whole milk
¼	teaspoon active dry yeast or ⅓ ounce cake yeast
5	large eggs
1¼	scant cups sugar
6½	cups (about 2 pounds) bread flour
1	tablespoon salt
3	ounces freshly rendered lard (page 82), melted
¾	cup water
	Confectioners' sugar, for dusting

Preparing the Dough ▶ In a small saucepan, gently heat the milk to 110°F over medium heat. Remove from the heat and add the yeast, eggs, and about 3 tablespoons sugar. Stir to mix and let rest until bubbly, about 15 minutes.

Place the flour in a large bowl. Make a well in the center and pour in the milk mixture. With your fingers, mix roughly to form a dough. Work in the salt, turn the dough out onto a lightly floured work surface, and knead for about 20 minutes, until the dough is smooth and elastic. Place in an oiled bowl, turn to coat evenly, and cover with plastic wrap. Let rest at room temperature in a draft-free place until doubled in bulk, about 2 hours.

Punch down the dough, knead briefly, and shape into a ball. Return to the bowl to rise again for another hour, covered with plastic wrap or a clean, lightly moistened kitchen towel.

Shaping the Rolls ▶ When the dough is doubled in bulk, punch it down and turn it out onto a work surface. Divide into sixteen pieces and roll each piece into a ball. With a rolling pin, roll out each ball into a 7-by-7-inch square and brush lightly with the melted lard. Starting from the far side, roll the dough toward you to form a cylinder. Pinch the ends shut and roll with your palms into an 18-inch rope. Coil loosely into a spiral, tuck in the end, and pinch to fasten.

Place the rolls on 2 baking sheets, allowing at least 2 inches between them. Let rise, covered with plastic wrap, until doubled in size, about 1 hour.

Preparing the Syrup ▶ While the dough rises, make a syrup by combining 1 cup sugar and the water in a small saucepan. Bring to a boil over medium heat and simmer for 5 minutes, stirring, to dissolve the sugar. Set aside.

Baking the Rolls ▶ Preheat the oven to 380°F and place an empty baking pan on the floor of the oven. Just before baking, bring 2 cups water to a boil. Pour into the hot pan to create a cloud of steam. Immediately slide the rolls onto the lower or middle rack of the oven. Using a spray bottle, spray the walls with water twice, at 30-second intervals. Bake the rolls for 20 minutes, rotating the sheets halfway through baking. Remove the rolls from the oven, brush with the syrup, and sprinkle with the confectioners' sugar.

Serving: *Pan de gloria* is best fresh from the oven with a cup of hot chocolate (pages 339, 340, and 342) or *café con leche* (page 351).

Nicaraguan Cheese Rolls

Pupusas o Picos

These big triangular rolls speckled with grated cheese and glistening with a sugar glaze can be found in every Nicaraguan bakery under the name *picos* or *pupusas*. The latter, confusingly, is also the name of the popular Salvadorian filled tortillas. But since *pupusa* means "stuffed" or "plump" and these rolls are plumped with a cheese filling, the name suits them.

Nicaraguans, like most Latin Americans, love sweet breads. They eat these rolls as a snack or for breakfast accompanied by a glass of *tiste*, a popular drink made with toasted corn and cacao.

MAKES 6 LARGE ROLLS

For the Dough

1¼ cups warm (110°F) water

1 tablespoon sugar

2¼ teaspoons active dry yeast

½ cup butter, melted and cooled to room temperature

4 large egg yolks

1½ teaspoons salt

4½ cups bread flour (about 1 pound 6 ounces), plus more for kneading

For the Filling

6¼ ounces hard Salvadorian *queso añejo*, Mexican *cotija* cheese, or ricotta salata, coarsely grated (about 1 cup)

For the Glaze

1 cup sugar

¾ cup water

1 teaspoon fresh lime juice

1 Ceylon cinnamon stick (*canela*)

5 whole cloves

5 allspice berries

Preparing the Dough ▶ In a bowl, combine the water with the sugar and yeast. Stir to dissolve. Stir in the butter, egg yolks, and salt. Let sit for 10 minutes or until lightly bubbly.

Place the flour in a large bowl. Make a well in the center and pour in the yeast mixture. Mix with a fork to form a loose dough, then work with your hands to form a ball. Turn the dough out onto a lightly floured work surface and knead vigorously for 10 minutes, working in up to ¼ cup more flour if the dough feels too wet. Knead until smooth and silky. Alternatively, place the dough in a standing mixer with a paddle attachment and beat for 4 minutes.

Shape the dough into a ball, place in a lightly greased bowl, turn to coat evenly, and cover with plastic wrap. Let rise in a draft-free place at room temperature until doubled in bulk, about 1 hour.

Shaping and Filling the Rolls ▶ Butter a baking sheet.

Punch down the dough, transfer to a work surface, and knead for 5 minutes. Divide the dough into six portions and roll each into a ball. Flatten lightly with a rolling pin and roll out into an 8-inch round. Scatter 2 tablespoons of the grated cheese in the center of each round. Now fold in about a third of the dough to make one side of a triangle. Fold symmetrically from the other side, overlapping slightly, then fold up the last third to enclose. Place the rolls seam side up on the baking sheet, cover loosely with a moist kitchen towel, and let rise for 45 minutes.

Preparing the Glaze ▶ While the rolls rise, make a glaze by combining the sugar, water, lime juice, cinnamon, cloves, and allspice in a small saucepan. Bring to a boil over medium heat and simmer for 5 minutes, stirring to dissolve the sugar. Strain out the spices and set aside.

Baking the Rolls ▶ Preheat the oven to 375°F and place an empty baking pan on the floor of the oven. Sprinkle each roll with 2 teaspoons grated cheese. Just before baking, bring 2 cups water to a boil. Pour into the hot pan to create a cloud of steam. Immediately slide the rolls onto the lower or middle rack of the oven. Using a spray bottle, spray the walls with water twice, at 30-second intervals. Bake

the rolls until golden, about 25 minutes, turning the sheet halfway through baking. When the rolls are done, place on a wire rack and brush generously with the glaze while still hot.

Serving: Eat at once for breakfast or as a midafternoon pick-me-up with coffee or tropical fruit juice.

Storing: The rolls will keep well stored in a plastic bag at room temperature for 2 or 3 days.

Venezuelan Christmas Ham Bread

Pan de Jamón Venezolano de Miro Popiç

On Christmas eve, Venezuelans eat a particular combination of foods on a single plate: their beloved and baroque *hallacas* (page 463), a chicken salad made with a stewing hen (*ensalada de gallina*); roast pork; and a slice of *pan de jamón*, a luscious bread filled with ham, raisins, and olives.

I had always assumed that this bread was an old colonial recipe, but my friend Miro Popiç, a food critic in Caracas who once made a living baking this Christmas bread from his home, explained my error. After reviewing newspaper archives for a book he wrote called *El libro del pan de jamón* (The Ham Bread Book), Miro concluded that the bread was first made at the beginning of the twentieth century in a Caracas bakery, most probably the Panadería Ramella. During this period bakeries had started preparing baked ham (*jamón planchado*) for the Christmas feasts with imported Ferris ham (a well-known U.S. brand), and bakers began to use the leftovers to fill loaves of bread, an idea that was eagerly received by the people of Caracas. In 1906, the Montauban & Cia bakery in Caracas published an ad in *El Constitucional* newspaper listing *pan de jamón* as one of their Christmas specialties. The next year other bakeries followed suit. By the 1920s, competing bakeries were adding olives, raisins, and even capers for extra appeal.

I learned to make *pan de jamón* in Miro's kitchen in El Hatillo. The loaves were monumental, filled to the brim with ham, bacon, raisins, and olives. Miro brushed them with a brown loaf syrup that burnished the crust and gave it a delicious sweetness to contrast with the saltiness of the filling. I use less yeast than Miro does, but I follow his recipe for the filling and glaze.

This moist and succulent bread is terrific for brunch or buffets; a slice makes a very nice first course.

What to Drink: Miro Popiç suggests a voluptuous and fruity Montes Alpha Syrah from Chile, a young, fresh Bodega Pomar *tempranillo* from Venezuela, or a Bodegas Luis Alegre Crianza *tempranillo* from Rioja, Spain. You can also serve the bread with the Venezuelan Christmas drink *Ponche Crema* (page 353).

MAKES 1 LARGE LOAF (SERVES 12)

For the Dough

- ¼ cup warm (110°F) water
- ¾ teaspoon active dry yeast
- 2 tablespoons sugar
- 1 cup milk
- 1½ teaspoons salt
- 2 tablespoons butter
- 4½ cups bread flour (about 1 pound 6 ounces)
- 3 large eggs, lightly beaten

For the Filling

- 1 tablespoon unsalted butter, melted
- 1 pound good-quality ham, such as York, honey, or sugar-cured, thinly sliced
- 8 thick slices (about 5 ounces) smoked bacon
- 25 pitted Spanish manzanilla olives, thinly sliced
- ¾ cup (about 3 ounces) dark raisins
- 2 tablespoons capers, drained

For the Glaze

- 4 ounces (about ½ cup) grated brown loaf sugar (*papelón* or *panela*), Muscovado sugar, or dark brown sugar
- ¼ cup water

Preparing the Dough ▶ Place the water in a small bowl and add the yeast and ½ teaspoon sugar. Stir to dissolve and set aside for 10 minutes.

Pour the milk into a saucepan and warm over low heat. Add the remaining sugar and the salt and butter and heat, stirring, until the butter melts.

Pour the flour into a large mixing bowl and make a well in the center. Pour in the yeast and milk mixtures and the eggs. Mix together with clean hands to form a ball. Turn onto a lightly floured surface and knead vigorously for 15 minutes. The dough should feel smooth and elastic. Place in a lightly oiled large bowl. Cover with plastic wrap, set in a warm, draft-free place, and let rise until doubled in bulk, about 1½ hours.

Shaping and Filling the Bread ▶ Lightly grease and flour a baking sheet.

Punch the dough down with your fist. Turn onto a floured work surface and knead for about 5 minutes. With a rolling pin, roll out the dough into a 16-by-16-inch square and lightly brush with the melted butter. Layer the ham slices on top, slightly overlapping, leaving a 1-inch border. Place the bacon slices over the ham, spacing them evenly. Sprinkle the olives, raisins, and capers as evenly as possible over the ham and bacon. Fold 1 inch of each side of the dough over the filling and roll the dough away from you like a jelly roll. Taper the ends and flatten the seam. Place the bread on the baking sheet, seam side down. Cover with a kitchen towel soaked in warm water and well wrung out and let rise for about 30 minutes. Prick the top of the loaf with a fork.

Preparing the Glaze ▶ While the loaf rises, place the brown sugar and water in a small saucepan and heat over medium heat until the sugar is melted. Simmer, stirring occasionally, for about 5 minutes. Reserve.

Baking the Bread ▶ Preheat the oven to 350°F and place an empty baking pan on the floor of the oven.

Just before baking, bring 2 cups water to a boil. Pour into the hot pan to create a cloud of steam. Immediately slide the bread onto the lower or middle rack of the oven. Using a spray bottle, spray the walls with water twice, at 30-second intervals. Bake the bread for about 1 hour, turning the sheet halfway through baking. After 45 minutes, brush lightly with the glaze to give the crust a lovely golden brown color and sweetness. Bake for about 15 minutes longer. Remove from the oven and let rest for at least 10 minutes before slicing.

Serving: Serve as an appetizer, or as a side for Venezuelan Christmas *Hallacas* (page 463). Or combine with Cuban Birthday Party Chicken Salad (page 553), and a few slices of Pork Tenderloin with Passion Fruit–Pink Peppercorn Sauce (page 718) for a festive Venezuelan-inspired Christmas meal

FISH
AND
SEAFOOD

Latin America is thick with lore about the sea. In every fishing village, men who earn their living in small boats, with line, tackle, and net, gather around the hearth to share mysterious tales of sirens and ships. Once, over a cup of *mate*, I heard fishermen from the island of Chiloé talk about the Pincoya, a blond siren they believe lives on Chile's southern coast of stark fjords and pounding surf. The fishermen say that fish and seafood are gifts of the Pincoya. When they see her dancing on the beach with arms stretched out toward the ocean, it will be a good fishing day; if she dances with her back to the sea, they know there will be no fishing. The Pincoya hovers as a watchful spirit who will take away her bounty if the ocean is not respected.

I find such tales heartening. I take them as a sign that in a country such as Chile, where huge fleets, salmon and turbot farms, and a thriving seafood export market make fishing a major industry, some of the mystique and romance that come only from intimate contact with the sea survives. Along Latin America's varied coastlines, lakes, and rivers, the livelihood, culture, and rituals of millions of people still depend on the tides, the movement of fish, the cycles of rain and drought marked by shifting ocean currents.

Water and fish are life-givers, symbols of plenty that are celebrated in religious and communal feasts from Mexico to Patagonia. For the Corpus Christi, a festival celebrated in early June around Lake Pátzcuaro in central Mexico, the fishermen of Ojo del Agua feed the whole town of Tzintzuntzan. The lively procession starts near the lake as townspeople and fishermen hold a large net and pretend to catch a man wearing a huge papier-mâché fish head. Women carry big baskets filled with fried lake fish, which will feed the crowd in the sixteenth-century monastery complex of San Francisco (St. Francis of Assisi).

On June 24, fishing communities across the Americas celebrate the eve of the great feast of St. John the Baptist. In Ocumare de la Costa, a small coastal town on Venezuela's Caribbean coast, the celebrations are particularly spectacular. Dressed in bright red—the color of St. John—people from nearby fishing communities move toward the pier in a great, pulsing procession, dancing to hypnotic drumbeats, carrying images of St. John, and waving red and yellow banners as they drink *chicha* or *aguardiente*. When they reach the sea, throngs jump in, wading toward the boats that are carrying the images to Ocumare. In this great explosion of fireworks and color, they celebrate the sea and its purifying power.

Fishing villages such as Ocumare dot Latin America's extensive coastlines. The Pacific coast stretches from Baja California nearly to Antarctica, and the Atlantic coastline meanders south, warmed by the Gulf of Mexico, waking up in the Caribbean's azure waters, turning swampy in Nicaragua, fierce in Costa Rica, and shining and tame again near Panama's San Blas Islands, the land of the Kuna Indians. From Cartagena in Colombia to the Paria Peninsula in Venezuela, the coast varies from flatlands to high mountains to low hills until it reaches the flat delta of the Orinoco. South of Venezuela, Brazil's northeastern coast is dry, but it becomes lush near Rio de Janeiro and flattens as it reaches the River Plate delta by Buenos Aires. Very few fishing villages appear along the rough, inhospitable coast that stretches to the southern tip of Patagonia.

Working on this chapter gave me the opportunity to cook and eat next to the water all over Latin America—two of the greatest pleasures life has to offer. During my work I sailed up and down the Orinoco and Amazon rivers. On the shores of

Lake Titicaca, in Bolivia, I watched Aymara Indian women scale enormous rainbow trout. Back at sea level on the northern coast of Peru, I stood in awe of the fishermen who went out to sea on flimsy reed boats (*caballitos de totora*) as their Moche ancestors had done in pre-Columbian times.

THE CARIBBEAN

At La Parguera (the Snapper Cove), a village not far from Cabo Rojo, in Puerto Rico, I stayed at a humble house on stilts owned by Virgilio Brunet to watch artisanal fishermen work and to get recipes. Related by marriage to a branch of my family that left Cuba for Puerto Rico in the 1970s, the Brunets have always been my window to island family life and cooking. For forty years, Virgilio and his wife had been coming to this small fishing village, building a tiny shack in the shallows of a mangrove key and gradually turning it into a modest, comfortable retirement retreat. For years, friends and family from San Juan descended on the cabin every weekend like a swarm of locusts, sleeping in bunk beds or on the bare floor to enjoy the unique experience of having a mangrove key as a backyard. I especially loved our after-breakfast excursions to Cayo Caracoles, one of the mangrove islets fringing the cove. There we swam in crystal-clear waters, watching schools of fish pass and finding an occasional conch on the sandy bottom.

Such paradises don't stay undiscovered for long. The abundant snapper for which La Parguera was named have been depleted by indiscriminate fishing, and the conchs have moved to deeper water. Motor-

boats and sailboats now disturb La Parguera's weekend peace, and nearby Phosphorescent Bay, teeming with microorganisms that beam colors on moonless nights, attracts thousands of tourists every year.

But from Monday to Friday, La Parguera belongs to the families who have been in the area all their lives. Most live in small, colorful cabins built on stilts in the coastal marshes or near the mangrove islets; some prefer houseboats. La Parguera is a gregarious, outgoing place where neighbors come visiting by boat, sharing loads of freshly caught fish. From the verandas of most cabins, you can see small mangrove snappers, "Irish pompanos" (or "striped *mojarras*"), blowfish, and trunkfish swimming between the stilts.

The trunkfish, known as *chapín* in Puerto Rico, is an odd fish shaped like a triangular box covered with hard plates. I think of it as the little Sherman tank of the Caribbean. But its meat is white and firm, with a lobster-like flavor. It is similar to monkfish, but it must be carefully separated from its skin, which is highly toxic. Puerto Ricans marinate the meat in lime juice and garlic and sauté it in a tasty *sofrito* made with garlic, peppers, and chopped onions to make a wonderful filling for empanadas.

Of the many varieties of deep-water fish I have tasted at La Parguera, I am partial to the rosy *chillo* (silk snapper), with flesh as delicate and subtle as that of red snapper, and the sleek *colirrubia* (yellowtail snapper), which Virgilio pan-fries to perfection. Pan-fried yellowtail deserves to be eaten slowly, morsel by morsel. I take time to separate the bones from the meltingly sweet flesh, and pick every ounce of succulent meat from the head. Dangling my feet lazily over the water or stretched out in a hammock, I savor the heavenly experience of eating

Virgilio's *colirrubia*, especially on a Monday, when nothing as pleasurable as this is supposed to happen.

The *rancherías* of Venezuela's Paria Peninsula, fishing villages nestled in lagoons and protected coves and keys, are among my other favorite spots. Venezuelan fishermen seldom venture out too far into the open sea. Sometimes they set their nets close to shore and the women and children splash in the shallow waters, scaring the fish so they do not swim away. The men dry and mend their nets while the women clean the catch and then turn the fish into stews or big soups or simply marinate and fry them.

In Paria, as on the neighboring Margarita Island, baby shark (*cazón*) is a delicacy. Its firm meat is sautéed in rich cooking sauces to fill empanadas made of dried cracked corn dough. On Margarita, *chucho* or spotted whip ray (*Aetobatus narinari*) is a favorite. Fishermen dry it in the sun, and the meat is eaten like cod in dishes such as a layered savory pie with cheese, béchamel sauce, and fried ripe plantains called *pastel de chucho*.

About a hundred miles from La Guaira, the port of Caracas, is a glorious necklace of islands known as Los Roques, some with funny names like Krarky, Krasky, Espenky, Noronky, Rasky, and Mosquitoky. The suffix *ky*, also spelled *qui*, is a corruption of the English word *key*, demonstrating how Venezuelan fishermen have for centuries lived side by side with those from Dutch Curaçao, Aruba, and Bonaire. These islands are so barren that you can't even plant a garden, but the compensation lies in the shallow lagoon waters, which teem with delicious fish like yellowtail, *carite* (king mackerel), grouper, red snapper, and succulent spiny lobster. But even with this bounty, the lives of the Roqueños are spartan. When out to sea, the fishermen usually eat only a cold polenta called *funche*.

THE PACIFIC

While the Caribbean beckons with its warmth, the cold, dramatic Pacific stirs admiration but also fear. The fishing grounds from humid Chocó in Colombia to the southern tip of Patagonia are among the world's most abundant. No wonder the people of this region are great fish and seafood lovers.

One of the region's most popular fish is the *corvina*, a catchall term for croakers and drumfish belonging to the Sciaenidae family. Two species, the Peruvian *corvina* and the Chilean *corvina*, are particularly abundant from Ecuador south to Chile and crop up on most restaurant menus. Archaeologists studying pre-Columbian fishing settlements believe the white-fleshed Peruvian *corvina* and some closely related drums were favored by the elite, while smaller, oily fish like anchovies and sardines seem to have been more important for commoners. This ancient dichotomy finds an echo in the contemporary Peruvian diet.

Warm waters are not typically the richest in seafood, and the abundance of marine resources so close to the equator is the gift of the great Humboldt Current, which carries cold water from the Antarctic region northward, keeping the climate of western South America temperate and dry. In northern Peru, the Humboldt Current bends out to sea, joining the Equatorial Current flowing westward across the Pacific and cooling the waters around the Galápagos Islands. Here the combined action of the cold current and wind patterns provokes a phenomenon known as upwelling, which brings colder water rich in nutrients from the depths of the ocean to the surface. This in turn activates the development of phytoplankton, which sustain all kinds of marine life and are at the base of the ocean's food chain.

The Pacific was as crucial as the Andes Mountains in the rise of some of South America's seminal civilizations, including the Moche, who flourished in northern Peru between A.D. 200 and 800. At El Brujo, a Moche site near the city of Trujillo, I viewed chambers and platforms of an adobe pyramid being excavated by a team of Peruvian archaeologists. Brilliant murals included an enthralling seascape in vivid shades of blue, terracotta, yellow, and black, showing skates swimming beneath crested waves in the same waters I could see from the top of the pyramid. A vivid polychrome fresco recently discovered on a platform above the burial chamber of the Lady of Cao (a Moche chieftain or shaman discovered in 2005) shows the stylized fish called *life*, a type of catfish that lives in Andean streams and irrigation canals and is a prized food to this day. Another polychrome frieze shows Moche fishermen taking to the sea in the same kayak-sized *caballitos de totora* (little reed boats) I had seen in daily use in the nearby village of Huanchaco. They are made from a very light, buoyant local species of reed and float so high in the water that you can ride on their backs without getting wet. And it appears that the nets towed by the *caballitos* are made in the same manner and from the same kind of native cotton thread as the ones in the wall paintings.

The fishermen in the Moche murals plied the Pacific some 1500 years ago, but the story of Peruvian fishing is at least 4600 years old. Fishing was an integral part of the economy in the oldest city of the Americas, Caral, 120 miles north of Lima and 15 miles inland, in the Supe River valley. The pyramids there have been dated to 2600 B.C.—the age of the earliest Egyptian pyramids—and were built by a civilization that left no evidence of weapons or warlike activities, a unique attribute among mother cities. The people apparently lived on squash, beans, and other crops—and on a lucrative trade in cotton nets, which they exchanged for fish and mollusks from the coast.

Today the fishermen of Huanchaco are still using an ancient technology that respects the fragile interface between shore and desert. They tap into the high water table of this boundary zone to create the necessary *totorales* (reed beds) for building the *caballitos* (incidentally making ideal refuges for shorebirds). The boats and nets are made for one-man fishing, which doesn't deplete the environment. And yet the environment is being depleted daily, for reasons beyond the artisanal fishermen's control. Every day in Huanchaco I saw the reed boats come back after hours in the frigid waters with meager catches of a few croakers like *suco* and the drumfish *lorna*. When one fisherman brought back a small red cusk eel, he told me he had not seen another in months. Diners in local restaurants eat cebiches made with *corvina* shipped to the Huanchaco market from Piura, near the Ecuadorian border.

Hardship is nothing new to Peruvian fishermen. Since humans first came into the region, they have been at the mercy of periodic natural disasters triggered by the weather fluctuations known as El Niño (the little boy) and La Niña (the little girl). La Niña cools the air and water of the Pacific, nourishing marine life but causing drought all along the coast. El Niño is exactly the reverse. It brings warm water and air from the western Pacific, causing heavy rains along the coast, which nourishes the desert valleys of Peru and northern Chile but decreases the surfacing of sea nutrients, with catastrophic effects on marine life and fishing.

These natural fluctuations are magnified by climate change, overpopulation, and pollution and by the depletion of small fish like the *anchoveta*, a key link of the marine food chain. Creeping urbanization has encroached on the reed beds, which are shrinking. How long can village fishermen maintain their threatened way of life? As it is, tourists who pay cash for the thrill of watching the fearless riders on their *caballitos* account for much of their income. For me, the joys of discovering the seafood traditions of South America's Pacific coast have been tempered with sorrow for what is vanishing before our eyes—the living links with the ancient Pacific civilizations.

While the Pacific is gray in Peru and all along the desert coast of northern Chile, it explodes with brilliant ultramarine fury near Valparaíso and in Chile's misty southern coasts, where legend tells of the Caleuche, a lit-up ship of wizards that appears on foggy nights. In Isla Negra, near Valparaíso, Pablo Neruda had a fanciful beach home, now a museum, from which I could see the inky tendrils of *cochayuyo* (an edible seaweed) spread over the blue rocks. Fishermen sun-dry the *cochayuyo* until they resemble tan leather belts, and tie them into sturdy packets that smell like the sea.

Back in Valparaíso, I stopped at a lovely restaurant up in the hills to take in a full view of the towering Aconcagua, the highest peak of the Andes, while eating my favorite Chilean seafood dish, *machas a la parmesana*: Pacific pink clams on the half shell, broiled with Parmesan cheese. Another favorite is the classic soup *caldillo de congrio* (page 529), made with the fascinating cusk eel. It tastes best at the central market of Santiago, where you will find several species of *congrio*. Despite the local name, these creatures are not congers. They belong to a completely different family (Ophidiidae) and appear for sale as *congrio negro*, *dorado*, or *colorado* (black, pink, or red cusk eel). These fish can reach a great length and weight and are terrific in soups and braises.

Among the glories of Chilean shellfish are the big local *erizos* (sea urchins), whose succulent orange roe is eaten raw with the green parsley or cilantro sauce called *pebre*; the abalone, or *loco*, which Chileans eat with mayonnaise; and the *picoroco*, a strange crustacean with a hard birdlike beak and succulent flesh protected by a shell that resembles a crenellated rock. The first time I saw a *picoroco*, I was amazed. The creature emits a burbling sound and looks like a bird caught up inside the rock. You must break open the shell to extract the crustacean inside, but the white flesh is as sweet as lobster.

Picorocos and abalones are among the many kinds of seafood cooked in the Chilean version of a clambake, called *curanto*. All kinds of seafood are cooked together with chicken, smoked pork, sausages, ham, and seasoned potato patties. On the island of Chiloé and all over southern Chile, these ingredients are cooked in layers in an earthen pit lined with hot stones. The layers are separated by the gigantic leaves of a plant named *pangüe*. In the *curanto*, the sea merges with the earth—the two poles that define life in Chile, a country squeezed between the mighty Andes and the rough Pacific Ocean.

Just as famous as the Patagonian *curanto* is the coveted but highly controversial Patagonian toothfish, which was not really known by most people in Chile or elsewhere until the 1990s. This member of the Nototheniidae family is better known in this country as Chilean sea bass, and it is now endangered. I had never seen it in Chile but got to taste it in 1997 in the Buenos Aires restaurant of Galician chef Ramiro González Pardo, who served it to me as *merluza negra* (black hake). González Pardo, who made a big deal about it, explained that the fish, caught in the Argentine Patagonia, had been recently commercialized in the country. (In fact, the first Argentinean fishery engaged in fishing it started operating in 1988.) I found it delicious and recognized it as Chilean sea bass when I tasted it later in the United States. In Chile it is also called *bacalao de profundidad* (deep water cod). Succulent, with flesh that melts in your mouth because of its high fat content, the Patagonian toothfish lives at great depths in waters around Antarctica. Its history, from being an almost unknown species in the 1970s, to being the "in" fish of the 1990s, to having the current status of an endangered species because of indiscriminate overfishing, is a cautionary tale.

FRESHWATER BOUNTY

The rivers and lakes of the Americas are as diverse as its coastlines. Lake Pátzcuaro of Michoacán in Mexico is idyllic, surrounded by green fields of alfalfa and corn and high mountains, once active volcanoes. Not long ago, the main attraction for visitors to the area was the fishermen, who paddled small boats from one corner of the lake to the other to catch the delicate white fish that they simply called *pescado blanco* with small nets shaped like the wings of a butterfly. Lake Nicaragua, the largest lake of Central America, is what remains of a saltwater sea, now cut off from the Pacific. While strolling along the shore near Granada, I stopped to gaze across the lake, trying unsuccessfully to catch a glimpse of the other shore, and spotted the gray dorsal fins of

a couple of sharks, living proof of the lake's ancient history.

Lake Nicaragua, surrounded by active volcanoes, and Lake Titicaca, on the roof of the world in Bolivia, with its deep cobalt waters that seem to fuse with the sky, are awe-inspiring. But nothing compares to the sheer grandeur of the great rivers of South America, the Orinoco in Venezuela and the Amazon in Brazil.

The Orinoco begins as an insignificant stream high in the Parima Mountains near the Brazilian-Venezuelan border and flows down through 1,320 miles of Venezuelan territory. In its journey toward the Atlantic, the river is nourished by glacier streams from the snowcapped mountains of the Venezuelan and Colombian Andes, the murky rivers that flow through the interminable western plains, and the mysterious black-water rivers born in the Guayana highlands, the oldest rock formations on earth.

This enormous body of water empties into one of the world's largest deltas, a maze of tributary channels (*caños*) that cut through mangrove swamps, *moriche* palm groves, and alluvial flatlands. In this largely unexplored water world live the Warao Indians of Venezuela—in their language, "the people who paddle," the people of the canoe. It is in canoes, their only means of transportation in the complex network of water roads that crisscross the delta, that the Warao spend most of their lives—literally from birth to death, since they are buried in their canoes.

The river is a great geographic and cultural divide, the frontier between the tamed land of *criollos* and immigrants and what is left of the great Venezuelan wilds. The region is a grand theater where the problems that plague Latin America's remaining natural resources are played out with startling clarity: the disappearance of many native species;

the poisoning of rivers with mercury by miners; the clash and melding of different cultures; and the loss of forest lands. Yet you can still visit native villages where you find both ancient foods and the vigorous cuisines produced by cultural collisions.

A few years ago, I found myself renting a boat and heading for the Orinoco delta on a writing assignment for *Gourmet* magazine. A photographer and I, together with my Venezuelan friend Silvino Reyes, had been invited to stay with a group of scientists, mostly marine biologists, at the La Salle camp (officially Fundación La Salle de Ciencias Naturales, Programa Warao Punta Pescador), a cluster of interconnected palm-thatched huts on stilts built in the traditional Warao style. The scientists' aim was to study the river fauna and help the Waraos sell their fish at a fair price to outside markets, avoiding exploitation by Venezuelan and Trinidadian opportunists who swap staples such as leavened flour and hard liquor for the valuable river fish.

I was amazed at the variety and size of the fish the Warao caught in the waters around our camp. Every day I saw the fishermen of the village return from a night of fishing loaded with *morocotos* (which look like oversized piranhas, with silvery scales that turn reddish brown on the belly and short, tightly pursed mouths) and huge catfish (which look positively Jurassic—some are silvery or golden, others dark gray with pink stripes or spotted like waterbound jaguars). I found the catfish surprisingly flavorful, particularly the *bagre dorado* (golden catfish), with none of that muddy taste one expects from a bottom feeder. The marine biologists explained that the Orinoco catfish are not sluggish but are vigorous swimmers with a varied diet.

As immense and bountiful as it is, the Orinoco has just a fraction of the grandeur, richness, and sheer immensity of the Amazon River, which stretches for 4,000 miles from its source almost 17,000 feet high in the Peruvian Andes to its delta opening on the Atlantic. At some points the river is 7 miles wide, and during floods it can widen to 35 miles, looking more like a sea. No wonder the Portuguese explorers dubbed it O Rio Mar, the River Sea.

The Amazon and its tributaries are home to the most diverse freshwater life in the Americas: hundreds of species of catfish, mollusks, playful pink dolphins, porpoises, stingrays, slow-moving manatees, turtles, caimans, eels, otters. It is said that the rivers of Amazonia contain more species than the Atlantic Ocean.

Many of the river fish are enormous, such as the hefty *pirarucú*, called *paiche* in Peru, weighing up to 200 pounds, with tough, bright red skin and scales harder than nails. There is the largest catfish in the world, the *piraíba*, capable of swallowing a small child; the *tapaquí* (a relative of the *morocoto*), a dark green fish fitted with strong teeth to eat the rubber tree fruits that fall to the water during the flood season; and menacing *piranhas*, good in soups despite their deadly reputation.

Amazonian river fish is eaten both salted and fresh, in simple, rustic preparations, sometimes grilled whole, cut into steaks wrapped in plantain leaves, or cooked in nourishing soups thickened with vegetables and tubers. In Peru, the *tambaquí*, also known as *gamitana*, is cooked in a loose gruel of grated plantains, seasoned with an *aderezo* (*sofrito*) made with garlic, onion, and cilantro, and garnished with plantain dumplings. *Shirumbi*, another popular river soup, often combines the coveted *paiche*, salted or fresh, with yuca. Another river favorite is *rumu api*, a thick yuca porridge flavored with lots of cilantro and bits of salted *paiche*. For many river people in the Peruvian Amazon, early breakfast consists of *challwa-ishpa*, a dish made with the viscera of small fish fried in pork lard and accompanied by boiled yuca and baked plantains.

THE LATIN WAY WITH FISH

Even in remote areas like the Orinoco and Amazon River Basins, Latin Americans cook fish with the techniques they apply to other foods. They might begin by seasoning it with a marinade or a dry rub of garlic, salt, and pepper, or perhaps a simple squeeze of lime, often adding more flavor with a *sofrito* in its many local variations. In Veracruz, they bake snook and pompano wrapped in *acuyo* (*hoja santa*), a beautiful broad licorice-scented leaf. In other parts of Mexico, fish is doused with rich, powerful chile sauces. In Cuba, shrimp and lobster are cooked in savory tomato sauces called *enchilados*, though they have no chiles, only green bell peppers. On the Pacific coast of northern Ecuador, as well as on the coasts of Colombia, Venezuela, and Brazil, delicious fish and seafood stews are enriched with silky coconut milk and tubers like yuca.

By and large, though, the favorite fish dishes are simply seasoned. Even in countries such as Mexico and Peru, where the cuisines are highly complex, the cooking of fish remains a relatively straightforward affair.

Escabeche

Escabeche extends the life of a piece of fried or sautéed fish, meat, or vegetable by pickling it in a blend of vinegar and abundant olive oil flavored with a tasty cooking sauce. As a child I watched in astonishment as my aunts ladled thick sawfish (*sierra*) steaks swimming in a tart *escabeche* sauce into a wide earthenware *cazuela* and let the fish rest there—unrefrigerated—at room temperature in their savory pickling bath for a few days. Years later, the practical implications of this preservation technique dawned on me while I was helping my parents secure their Miami home against Hurricane Andrew. I was probably one of the few people in our local supermarket buying olive oil and vinegar by the gallon. The night of the storm I cooked three different types of *escabeche*, which proved a godsend when we lost electricity, and, of course refrigeration, for several days.

The Romans were no strangers to preserving fish in vinegar and oil—Apicius gives a recipe for fried fish preserved in vinegar in *De re coquinaria* (late fourth century). But *escabeche* probably came into Spain with the Muslims. The word comes from the Arabic *iskedeg*, which in turn is a popular form of the Persian word *sikbaj*. A thirteenth-century Baghdadi recipe for *sikbaj* instructs cooks to fry fish in sesame oil with coriander seeds and then pour vinegar colored with saffron over it.

Like the Romans before them, the cooks of Moorish Andalusia used vinegar and olive oil in creative combinations, perfuming their fish and vegetable *escabeches* with fascinating blends of herbs and spices. As portions of Al-Andalus passed gradually into Christian hands between the thirteenth and fifteenth centuries, the techniques endured. Following the rules of medieval Spanish cooking, which always strove for balance between sweet and sour, Spanish *escabeches* on the eve of the Spanish conquest of the Americas were often flavored with a mixture of honey and spices. In the fourteenth-century *Libre de Sent Soví*, there is a recipe called "How to Make *Escabeche* with Fried Fish and Almond Milk," in which the author advises readers to add salt to the *escabeche* in addition to a touch of sweet and sour.

Escabeche survives to this day in Spain but has gradually returned to the essentials—garlic, onion, and bay leaf for the cooking sauce, oil and vinegar for preservation. In the Americas, *escabeches* run from simple concoctions to more complex recipes that reveal their venerable medieval Islamic roots. For instance, a fish *escabeche* from the port city of Veracruz is similar to Hispanic Caribbean *escabeches*, relying on the basic Spanish flavoring triad of onions, garlic, and bay leaf. Farther inland, in Xalapa, the state's capital, a sea bass *escabeche* explodes with the aromas of thyme, marjoram, cloves, black pepper, cumin, and cinnamon. Also from Xalapa comes the *escabeche colorado* (red e*scabeche*), an artful blend of Mediterranean spices and herbs—cilantro, oregano, cinnamon, and cloves—and New World ancho peppers, which tint the olive oil and vinegar matrix with their deep red color.

Frying

Frying is one of the most popular ways of preparing all kinds of fish all over Latin America. Peruvians love to eat huge mounds of crunchy fish and seafood, usually sprinkled with lime juice and hot sauce, often with a side of fried yuca. From the Puerto Rican fisherman in La Parguera who fries his yellowtail in sizzling oil in a worn-out frying pan to the black matrons in Cartagena on the Colombian Caribbean who fry their snapper in recycled oil, we all adore fried fish. There is nothing more inviting than a fried whole fish, its skin crispy golden, the flesh moist and succulent, finished with a squeeze of lime juice.

Cooking with Dried Shrimp and Salt-Dried Fish

Despite the abundance of fresh fish and seafood, the people of Latin America also love to cook with salted dried fish and shrimp. In the northeast of Brazil, particularly in the state of Bahia, which has a sizable black population, dried smoked shrimp is a staple. On a trip to Morro de São Paulo, a few hours south from Salvador da Bahia, I saw people smoking small shrimp over wood and charcoal fires and setting them to dry further under the sun. This was the same shrimp that I found heaped in bright orange mounds in markets all over the state. The shrimp are small, but not tiny like the dried shrimp you often find in Chinese markets. Shoppers prefer them lightly moist, and you can even eat them without cooking as a snack. Cooks use them lavishly in sauces (*molhos*) for the black-eyed pea fritter *acarajé* and to flavor all kinds of dishes, from black-eyed pea salad and okra stews to the creamy *vatapá*.

When it comes to dried fish, Latin Americans use both local and imported varieties. Salvadorians observe Holy Week by eating salt-fish fritters called *tortas de pescado*, made with Pacific ocean fish such as *boca colorado*, a stunning bright red snapper. In Piura in northern Peru, cooks dry the banded guitarfish, known there as *pez guitarra*, and use it like salt cod. On Christmas Eve, Mexicans observe fast-day restrictions and eat a succulent dish of salt cod. For Easter, Ecuadorians make *fanesca*, a baroque soup that calls for salt cod and a dozen varieties of grain. In La Parguera, Virgilio Brunet wakes up his family and friends with crunchy salt cod fritters (*bacalaítos*) sandwiched in crusty bread and served with *café con leche*.

Substantial and filling as a piece of pork, flaking easily like any fish, ivory-colored and as versatile as chicken breast, with a smell as potent and distinct as that of cauliflower, salt cod belongs to a special category of foods, including truffles, caviar, well-ripened cheeses, and cruciferous vegetables such as cabbage and cauliflower—foods whose flavor and aroma beguile because they border on the dangerous. The taste of salt cod grows on you until you begin to crave its savory sensation of umami.

It is an accident of history and geography that some of the great salt cod eaters of the world, the peoples of the Iberian Peninsula, the Mediterranean, and Latin America, have never been familiar with cod as a fresh fish. The Basque fisherman who secretly ventured out to the Grand Banks, the frigid and shallow waters off Newfoundland and Labrador, centuries before John Cabot explored this area in 1497, gave this fish an immortality of sorts. Far away from home, their only chance to stay at sea for long periods of time was to gut and split their catch and salt it heavily before drying it. Because they always carried loads of salt aboard their ships, they could wait to get back to Spain to dry the fish in the open air. Cured in this fashion, Atlantic cod became one of the most important food commodities of the preindustrial era, a nutritious source of protein that could be transported to every market without fear of spoilage.

By the sixteenth century, Spanish texts refer to salt cod as *bacalao*. The origin of the name is shrouded in mystery, though some claim it comes from the Latin word *baculum* (cane), because salt cod was hung on hooks from cane-shaped rods at the marketplace. Wherever the name originated, *bacalao* was a godsend for Spaniards and other Catholic Europeans. Packed with flavor, salt cod dishes added a welcome variety to the restrictive menus of Holy Friday, Lent, and Advent. And as Spain, Portugal, England, and France developed plantation economies based on slave labor in the Americas, salt cod that was rejected at home because of poor quality was shipped across the Atlantic to feed the slaves cheaply. Gradually everyone in the Americas—slaves and peasants, the urban poor and the rich—became hooked on cod. Though its popularity has faded elsewhere, the people of Portugal, Spain, and Latin America remain fiercely loyal to this relic from a more pious, prerefrigeration time.

This chapter just scratches the surface of Latin America's rich seafood traditions. Each country boasts terrific recipes using fish and seafood that are familiar to us and available in North American markets and many more dishes made with ingredients only found locally, such as the great catfish of South America or the *pescado blanco* of Mexico's Lake Pátzcuaro in Michoacán and Lake Chapala in Jalisco. Making a selection from this vast reservoir of culinary knowledge was not easy, but I have tried to make this chapter approachable by offering recipes that can be duplicated easily with fresh fish or seafood found in our markets.

The chapter is organized by main ingredient—salt cod and dried shrimp, fresh shrimp, red snapper, yellowtail, squid, pompano, blue crab, tuna, and clams, among other Latin favorites—rather than by specific preparations. Within each category, you will find dishes using basic techniques such as pan-frying, braising, and stewing. Many more fish and seafood recipes are distributed in other chapters of the book. In the soup chapter, for instance, you will find some tasty seafood soups from Ecuador, Peru, and Chile. There are also fish and seafood recipes in the salad, empanada, and appetizer chapters. And you will find some of the most popular ways of cooking fish and seafood in Latin America in the cebiche chapter. Most of my recipes serve six, and I have included several calling for whole fish. For sautéing and frying fish, I recommend using nonstick skillets and sauté pans, or very well-seasoned cast-iron pans. For whole fish, I like to use a 13-inch nonstick skillet or a large braising pan that is wide and not too deep.

SALT COD

BACALAO

It is hard to believe that something as hard as a wooden plank and odd-looking as an ancient fossil can provide the raw material of some of the most mouthwatering dishes in Latin America. But show a piece of dried salt cod to Latin cooks and immediately they will start planning dishes from crunchy fritters to succulent casseroles. And how do these cooks manage to turn this creature into the Prince Charming of Hispanic cuisine? Not by kissing it, but by plunging it into a big bucket of cold water and soaking it to remove some of the salt. After 6 to 12 (or more) hours, with several changes of water, the creamy flesh of the fish will regain its moisture and be ready to cook. In Brazil, the water soaking is followed by an additional soaking in milk, which is believed to remove more of the salty taste.

Most Latin American recipes call for *bacalao* to be shredded after soaking and before being added

to a dish. Here you must realize that the origin of the fish will affect the handling and the yield. Most salt cod from Canada is sold skinless and boneless; it has a relatively moist texture, requires fairly short soaking to reconstitute, and involves little waste. But in Hispanic markets, you are also likely to find salt cod with bones and skin, labeled *bacalao noruego* (Norwegian cod) or "Spanish" or "Portuguese" cod (prepared the same way). You need patience to clean this kind of fish and will get a smaller yield once you have discarded the bones, cartilage, and tough bits of skin. But the flavor is deeper.

Most Latin American recipes suggest briefly boiling salt cod after soaking. This does make it easier to remove the skin and bones from Norwegian-type *bacalao*. I personally prefer to shred it raw to keep more of its flavor and to prevent it from getting mushy and overcooked later. But in each recipe, I follow the preferred method of individual cooks.

Brazilian Salt Cod and Potato Casserole

Bacalhoada

As the pastry chef of a well-known French restaurant in New York sat at my table at the end of dinner, a couple sitting nearby joined in our conversation. They were Brazilian. In perfect French and accentless English, the wife, Gina Nogueira, made admiring comments about the chef's chocolate desserts and then began to tell us about her favorite Brazilian recipes.

As a result of that chance encounter, the Nogueiras and I became friends and I ended up visiting them at their home in São Paulo. Since they love to cook for visitors and their extended family, helping Gina cook gave me a firsthand look at a very eclectic but traditional Brazilian kitchen. In her pantry Gina keeps a variety of cooking fats for different uses: *dendê* oil for Bahian dishes, safflower oil for everyday cooking, and Portuguese and Spanish extra-virgin olive oil for fish dishes, especially salt cod, a fish for which Gina feels a passion that borders on reverence.

This is one of Gina's tastiest recipes for salt cod: reconstituted salt cod, potatoes, and onions layered in an earthenware casserole, drenched in a generous amount of olive oil, and baked until the potatoes are tender. *Bacalhoada* is the quintessential Portuguese-Brazilian salt cod dish.

Cook's Note: For this dish Gina follows the Brazilian practice of soaking the cod in milk after it has been reconstituted in water.

What to Drink: A lively and citrusy Montes Classic Series Sauvignon Blanc from Casablanca Valley in Chile

SERVES 6

For the Cod

5 pounds salt cod with skin and bones or 4 pounds boneless, skinless salt cod fillets
1 gallon whole milk

For the *Bacalhoada*

2 pounds red-skinned potatoes, peeled and cut into ¼-inch slices
2 teaspoons salt, plus more to taste
6 ripe globe tomatoes (about 2 pounds), cut into ½-inch slices
2 large white onions (about 1½ pounds), cut into ⅛-inch slices

1 cup extra-virgin olive oil
Freshly ground black pepper to taste

Reconstituting the Cod ▶ Place the salt cod in a large bowl and cover with cold water. Soak for 12 hours, changing the water two or three times. Taste the cod often; if it is too salty, continue soaking for up to 12 hours longer. Discard the soaking water and cover the cod with the milk. Let rest, covered with plastic wrap, in the refrigerator for at least 6 hours. Discard the milk (or reserve to use in a chowder); rinse the cod in cold water and set aside.

Assembling the *Bacalhoada* ▶ In a large pot, bring 2 quarts water to a boil over high heat. Reduce the heat to medium-low, add the fish, and simmer until the flesh flakes easily, 3 to 4 minutes. Do not overcook. Drain and let cool. Shred the cod, discarding any skin and bones. You will have about 4 pounds of cleaned cod flesh.

Put the potatoes in a large pot with 2 quarts water and 2 teaspoons salt. Bring to a boil over high heat. Lower the heat to medium and simmer until the potatoes are barely cooked, about 10 minutes. Drain and set aside.

Preheat the oven to 350°F. Oil a deep, round 12-inch baking dish, preferably an earthenware *cazuela*. Place a third of the potatoes on the bottom of the *cazuela* and top with a layer of tomatoes, then a layer of onions, and finally a layer of salt cod. Sprinkle each layer with olive oil and salt and pepper to taste. Repeat the layers until you have used all the ingredients. Pour the remaining olive oil over the final layer and bake the *bacalhoada* for 35 minutes, or until the vegetables are cooked.

Serving: Serve with rice and an avocado salad.

Mexican-Style Salt Cod Casserole for Christmas Eve

Bacalao a la Vizcaína para Nochebuena

One of the glories of the cuisine of the Basque country in northern Spain is *bacalao a la vizcaína*, salt cod braised in a sauce of sautéed onion, garlic, and the pulp of dried peppers called *ñoras* or *pimientos choriceros*, all thickened with bread. These ingredients are ground with mortar and pestle, then strained and added to an earthenware *cazuela* to cook slowly with the cod. In the hands of Mexican cooks, this Basque classic became a rich stew of shredded cod cooked in a spicy tomato sauce, with many regional variations. In coastal Veracruz, the shredded cod is mixed with potatoes. In other parts of Mexico, *bacalao a la vizcaína* is a simple but deeply flavored hash enriched with olives and capers and occasionally garnished with fiery jalapeños *en escabeche*. To season the cod, many cooks sauté raw garlic, onion, and tomatoes in olive oil. Others follow a more traditional Mexican technique of roasting these ingredients, then grinding them in the *molcajete* or pureeing them in a blender.

This recipe is a composite of ideas. I prefer to roast and puree the flavoring ingredients before sautéing them, which helps intensify their flavor. I also enjoy layering sliced potatoes and cod in a casserole, which comes in handy when entertaining. The dish can be assembled ahead of time without fuss—even the day before the party—and reheated in the oven for 20 minutes or so before serving. Since this is a very mild dish by Mexican standards, I feel that a mixture of warm jalapeños or serranos *en escabeche* and sautéed onion rings ladled over the cod gives it texture and a pleasing jolt of heat.

What to Drink: Adobe Guadalupe Kerubiel from Guadalupe Valley in Baja California

SERVES 8 TO 12

3 pounds boneless, skinless salt cod fillets

12 ripe medium plum tomatoes (about 2 pounds)

2 large white onions (about 12 ounces each), 1 left whole, 1 peeled and cut into thick rings

8 garlic cloves, peeled

6 medium russet potatoes (about 2 pounds), peeled and cut into ¼-inch slices

5 tablespoons extra-virgin olive oil

12 pickled jalapeños or serranos, homemade (page 151) or store-bought, sliced into rounds
Salt

4 large red bell peppers (about 2 pounds), fire-roasted (see page 67), peeled, cored, seeded, and cut into ½-inch-thick strips

½ cup finely chopped flat-leaf parsley, plus more for garnish

24 pimiento-stuffed green olives

¼ cup capers, drained

Preparing the Cod ▶ Place the cod in a large bowl and cover with cold water. Soak for 6 to 12 hours, depending on the saltiness of the fish, changing the water two or three times. Bring 2 quarts water to a boil in a large pot over high heat. Lower the heat to medium and add the cod fillets. Simmer until the fish flakes easily, about 3 minutes—do not overcook. Drain the cod in a colander, reserving the cooking water, and let cool. Shred the cod into small irregular pieces and reserve.

Making the Braise ▶ Heat a *comal*, griddle, or heavy skillet over medium-high heat. Add the tomatoes and whole onion and roast, turning occasionally with tongs, until lightly charred on all sides, about

10 minutes. When cool enough to handle, peel the onion and cut it into 4 wedges. Place in a blender or food processor with the tomatoes and garlic and process into a coarse puree.

While the vegetables are roasting, bring the reserved cod cooking liquid back to a boil over high heat. Add the potato slices, lower the heat, and simmer until the potatoes are barely tender but still whole, 12 to 15 minutes. Drain, reserving 1 cup of liquid; set aside.

Heat 3 tablespoons olive oil in a 12-inch sauté pan. Stir in the onion rings and cook over medium heat, stirring, until barely golden, about 10 minutes. Lift out with a slotted spoon and place in a small bowl with the pickled chiles. Season with salt to taste, toss well, and set aside, covered, in a warm place.

Add the remaining 2 tablespoons oil to the pan and heat over medium heat. Add the onion-tomato puree and simmer for about 20 minutes, stirring often. Stir in the fish, roasted peppers, parsley, olives, and capers. Add 1 cup reserved cooking liquid and 1 teaspoon salt, or to taste. Mix gently and simmer for 5 more minutes.

Assembling the Casserole ▶ Preheat the oven to 350°F. Lightly oil a 12-inch *cazuela* or a 13-by-9-inch glass baking dish. Line with the reserved potato rounds. Spoon half of the cod mixture over the potatoes. Top with another layer of potatoes, and finish with the remaining salt cod. Bake for about 20 minutes.

Serving: To serve, garnish with the pickled chile and onion mixture. Sprinkle with chopped parsley and serve with white rice or Mexican Rice (page 302).

Salt Cod Solé

Bacalao a la Catalana Solé

Catalan-born José Ignacio Solé Gil, who immigrated to my hometown, Santiago de Cuba, in the 1920s, liked to cook this sweet-and-sour salt cod stew enriched with cubed potatoes, raisins, and olives for his family. The only people he taught the recipe to were his Cuban-born children, Pepito Solé and Nena (Virginia) Bacardi Solé.

I ate this dish many times, first in Cuba and later in the United States, when Pepito and his children moved here. But no one wanted to part with the recipe. I asked for it over and over, and every time I was given the run-around. Luckily, in every family there is a kitchen spy. Shortly before her death, my cousin Elsa Infante, Pepito's sister-in-law, sent me some old family recipes. In the yellowing pages of a notebook written in Elsa's elegant hand was a recipe that read "Catalan bacalao from Virginia's grandfather—it is marvelous."

Like José Ignacio and his children, I make this dish for special occasions when I want to feed a crowd, serving it Cuban style, with rice and fried green bananas. It is also one of my favorite fillings for empanadas and empanadillas.

What to Drink: A full-bodied Catalan Alvaro Palacios "Les Terrasses"

SERVES 8 TO 12

For the Salt Cod

3¼ pounds salt cod with skin and bones

For the Potatoes

4 large red potatoes (about 2 pounds), peeled and cut into ¼-inch dice

2 teaspoons salt

For the Cooking Sauce

6 tablespoons extra-virgin olive oil

2 heads garlic, separated into cloves, peeled, and mashed to a paste with a mortar and pestle or finely chopped and mashed

1 large yellow onion (12 ounces), finely chopped (about 3 cups)

1 medium green bell pepper (8 ounces), cored, seeded, deveined, and finely chopped

Two 28-ounce cans whole plum tomatoes, lightly crushed

1 tablespoon sugar

1 cup slivered almonds

1 cup dark raisins

1 cup prunes, pitted and coarsely chopped

1 cup pimiento-stuffed green olives, sliced

Two 14-ounce cans roasted Spanish sweet red pimientos, drained and cut into ½-inch strips

1 cup fresh or thawed frozen green peas

For the Garnish

8 slices Cuban or Italian bread, ¼ inch thick, toasted

6 hard-boiled eggs, sliced

Preparing the Cod ▶ Cut the salt cod into 4-inch chunks. Place in a large bowl and cover with cold water. Let soak for 24 hours, changing the water several times. Taste a little piece before proceeding; the salt cod should be a bit salty, not bland. Drain the cod and pull it into 1-inch shreds, discarding the skin and bones. Set aside.

Preparing the Potatoes ▶ Place the potatoes in a medium pot with 4 cups water and bring to a boil over medium-high heat. Cook until soft but whole, about 15 minutes. Drain and set aside.

Making the Braise ▶ Heat 4 tablespoons of the oil in a 14-inch earthenware *cazuela* or a wide heavy-bottomed pan over medium-high heat. Add the garlic and sauté until light gold, about 30 seconds. Add the onion and cook until soft, about 4 minutes. Add the green bell pepper and cook for 2 more minutes, stirring. Add the crushed tomatoes and the sugar. Cook, stirring, for 10 minutes. Add the almonds, raisins, prunes, and olives. Cook for 5 more minutes. Then add the cod and cook, stirring occasionally, until the liquid is nearly evaporated, about 10 minutes. Add the cooked potatoes, roasted peppers, and peas and cook for 5 minutes to heat through. Drizzle with the remaining olive oil.

Serving: Garnish with the toasted bread and hard-boiled eggs and serve with any rice dish.

LATIN HOLY WEEK: SALT COD SEASON

In the popular imagination of this country, we Latins are a passionate and exuberant lot, a people of boisterous fiestas and hearty feasting, sultry music and seductive dance. But Holy Week (*Semana Santa*) is a time when we focus on a passion of an entirely different sort and on the deep resonance that pain and tragedy have in our collective souls. Rather than emphasizing the joy of Easter, with its promise of rebirth and the springtime symbolism of fluffy bunnies and painted eggs, Latin Americans embrace the somber pathos of Christ's Passion. Throughout the region, the preceding week moves in a crescendo toward Good Friday, the tragic act in the two-thousand-year-old Christian saga of suffering and deliverance.

The Cubans of my childhood flocked to their local churches on Holy Thursday to view the images of the crucified Christ and the Virgin of Sorrows that were to be taken out on procession the next day. The dim sanctuaries, the scent of incense, and the flickering candles that cast ghostly shadows on the effigies created a mournful atmosphere that stirred my emotions.

From Antigua in Guatemala to Ayacucho in Peru, great processions symbolizing the stations of the cross inch their way through cobbled streets and ancient plazas on Good Friday. One of the most vivid is in Antigua, where a theatrical reenactment of Christ's final moments includes some townspeople dressed like Roman soldiers and others, robed in purple, carrying heavy litters bearing exquisite life-sized images of the crucified Christ and his mother. As in Seville and other parts of Spain where these acts of collective piety originated, the mood is solemn but the pageantry is magnificent.

The same can be said of the season's culinary traditions, which derive from the spirit of abstinence surrounding Lent, the forty days leading up to Easter, and particularly Good Friday, when Catholics have traditionally refrained from eating meat. This is a season for *humitas* (fresh corn tamales) and for *malarrabia*, the tasty mash of boiled plantains and cheese eaten for lunch on Good Friday in Piura, Peru. It is a time for salt cod to shine, as in the baroque *fanesca*, a Lenten chowder from Ecuador.

On the same day, Salvadorians eat fritters called *tortas de pescado* made with salted fish like the flavorful *boca colorado*, a stunning bright red Pacific snapper that comes to market as dry as a plank. The giant, spongy *tortas* are prepared with large pieces of dried fish and a batter of nixtamalized corn flour. Once fried to a golden brown, they are soaked and softened in a rich broth made with the heads of the salt fish and served in soup bowls with broth and a side dish of white rice.

Between processions and prayers, vigils and heart-wrenching dramatizations of the Passion, families spend more time outdoors and in churches than at home during Holy Week, but this does not mean cooks lavish any less care on their food. In Ecuador, for example, copious amounts of time are spent soaking the dry legumes, desalting the cod, peeling astronomical amounts of fresh-cooked fava beans, and preparing Andean hominy for *fanesca*. The painstaking preparation yields a soup so exquisite and subtle that it turns the dour days of fasting into a time of holy feasting. ◆

Ecuadorian Salt Cod and Vegetable Chowder

Fanesca

For a soup with so many ingredients, *fanesca* is amazingly subtle, with the salt cod serving as an accent for a plethora of vegetables, grains, and legumes. Though inextricably connected with Holy Week, it is also a harvest soup in the Andean highlands, where the Easter season coincides with the arrival of tender grains and legumes in markets. In Ecuador, I have eaten *fanesca* garnished with tiny dumplings, fried ripe plantain rounds, avocado slices, and hard-boiled eggs. The soup keeps well in the refrigerator for a couple of days, though it tastes best straight from the pot.

SERVES 8 GENEROUSLY

- 1 pound boneless, skinless salt cod fillets

For the Cooking Sauce

- ¼ cup achiote-infused vegetable oil (page 89)
- 5 large garlic cloves, finely chopped
- 4 scallions, white and 3 inches of green parts, finely chopped
- 1 teaspoon ground cumin

For the Soup

- 2 quarts water
- 1¼ pounds *queso blanco* or French sheep's milk feta cheese, cut into ¾-inch dice
- ¼ cup brown lentils
- 1 pound carrots, cut into ½-inch pieces
- 4 ears fresh corn, shucked
- ½ pound snow peas or green beans, cut into ½-inch pieces
- 1 pound zucchini, cut into ½-inch pieces
- 1 pound Caribbean pumpkin (*calabaza*) or kabocha or butternut squash, peeled, seeded, and cut into 1-inch pieces
- 1 pound green cabbage, coarsely chopped
- One 10-ounce package frozen baby lima beans, not thawed
- One 10-ounce package frozen baby peas, not thawed
- ½ cup cooked *mote* (Andean Hominy, page 251) or drained canned Mexican-style hominy
- 5 cups warm (110°F) whole milk
- 2 tablespoons butter
- 2½ cups cooked beans (canned or homemade; a combination of chickpeas, cranberry, Canary, pinto, small kidney, and/or small white beans)
- One 4-inch piece canned heart of palm, sliced into ¼-inch rounds

For the Garnish

- Hard-boiled eggs, quartered
- Avocado slices

Preparing the Salt Cod ▶ Rinse the cod under cold running water. Place in a large bowl and cover with water. Let soak for about 6 hours, changing the water three or four times. Taste for salt and soak up to another 6 hours if it is too salty. Drain, cut into 1- to 2-inch pieces, and reserve.

Preparing the Cooking Sauce ▶ Heat the oil in a heavy 8–quart pot over medium heat. When the oil ripples, add the garlic and sauté until golden, about 40 seconds. Add the scallions and cumin and sauté, stirring, for about 2 minutes.

Preparing the Soup ▶ Add the water to the pot and bring to a boil over medium heat. Add ⅔ of the cheese and stir until it melts. Add the lentils and carrots, lower the heat, and simmer until the lentils are tender, 20 minutes or as needed. Cut 2 of the ears of corn into 1-inch rounds. Cut the kernels from the remaining ears, discarding the cobs. Add the corn, snow peas, zucchini, pumpkin, cabbage, lima beans, peas, hominy, milk, and butter to the pot and simmer 10 minutes. Add the cooked beans and the heart of palm and simmer, stirring occasionally, about 5 minutes. Add the salt cod and simmer 2 minutes.

Serving: Remove the corn rounds from the soup and cut into ½-inch pieces. Stir the remaining cheese into the soup. Ladle into bowls or soup plates and top each portion with a piece of fish. Garnish with hard-boiled egg and avocado.

SHRIMP

Dried Shrimp and Nut Cream
Vatapá

Vatapá is one of the emblematic dishes of the city of Salvador in the state of Bahia in Brazil: a smooth cream rich with coconut milk, thickened with bread and cashew nuts, golden with *dendê* oil, and given backbone with dried smoked shrimp. It is a dish hard to define and classify. In theory it is a dried shrimp stew and can be the main dish of a meal, but one also finds it as a side dish with *xinxim de galhina* (page 666), another stew, or as the filling for the crunchy black-eyed pea fritters called *acarajé*. The techniques it uses recall both the Mexican *moles* and the creamy nut-and-bread-thickened dishes of medieval Portugal and Spain, only with a strong African touch.

This is my interpretation of a *vatapá* recipe that has been handed down from mother to daughter in the household of Eduzvita Delinha, a proud *bahiana* who is also a priestess of Orisha Oxosi, the Yoruba patron of the forest and healing. At Eduzvita's home, *vatapá* is always eaten at room temperature.

Cook's Note: For best results, use the smoked dried shrimp available in Brazilian markets.

SERVES 12 AS A SIDE DISH, 8 AS A MAIN COURSE

For the Thickeners

One 10-ounce loaf stale Cuban or French bread, cut into small dice

2 cups Creamy ("First") Coconut Milk (page 50) or unsweetened canned coconut milk

2   cups water or All-Purpose Fish Broth (page 540)

⅓   cup (about 2 ounces) unsalted roasted cashews

For the Cooking Sauce

2   scallions, white and light green parts, coarsely chopped

1   large yellow onion (about 12 ounces), peeled and quartered

2   plum tomatoes (about 6 ounces), peeled, seeded, and coarsely chopped

1   tablespoon freshly grated ginger

2   cilantro sprigs

½   pound dried shrimp

⅓   cup *dendê* oil

Pureeing the Thickeners ▶ Place the bread, coconut milk, and water or broth in a large bowl and let soak for 15 minutes. Transfer to a blender or food processor with the cashews and process to a smooth paste. Transfer back to the bowl.

Making the Cooking Sauce ▶ Place the scallions, onion, tomatoes, ginger, cilantro, and dried shrimp in a food processor or blender; process into a smooth puree.

Heat the oil in a large, heavy saucepan over medium heat. Stir in the shrimp mixture and cook, stirring, for 6 minutes.

Making the *Vatapá* ▶ Add the bread mixture and continue cooking over medium heat for 30 minutes, stirring continuously with a large wooden spoon. The mixture becomes thick, like polenta. When it comes away smoothly from the bottom and sides of the pot, pour it into a serving bowl. The *vatapá* is supposed to thicken nicely and smoothly in its serving platter. When it jells, *bahianos* say it is *dormido* (asleep).

Serving: Serve warm or at room temperature as a side dish for Bahian stews like the following *moqueca*, use to fill *acarajé* (page 384), or serve warm as a main dish with white rice.

Shrimp in Coconut Sauce in the Style of Bahia

Moqueca de Camarâo

Moquecas are seafood braises cooked in *moquequeiras* (round-bottomed earthenware pots sold in every market), enriched with coconut milk and powerful *dendê* oil. This shrimp *moqueca* has the layered quality that's the trademark of Bahian cooking. Because the shrimp cooks too fast to absorb the flavors of the cooking sauce, it is always marinated first in a simple mixture of garlic, lime, and salt. The onion and sweet peppers are cut into rings in traditional Bahian style. Halving the fiery chile and adding it briefly will give you a measure of control over the heat level. For an authentic Bahian touch, add a spoonful of *dendê* oil at the end of cooking to intensify the color and balance the flavor.

Cook's Note: If not using *dendê* oil, you can cook the vegetables in achiote-infused olive oil (page 89) to lend color to the dish.

What to Drink: Susana Balbo Crios Torrontes, from Mendoza, or the equally floral Alamos Viognier (Bodega Catena Zapata) from Mendoza

SERVES 6

For the Shrimp

2 pounds medium shrimp (16–20 per pound), peeled and deveined

3 garlic cloves, mashed to a paste with a mortar and pestle or finely chopped and mashed
Juice of 1 lime

½ teaspoon salt

For the Cooking Sauce

2 tablespoons extra-virgin olive oil

1 medium yellow onion (8 ounces), cut into thin rings

6 scallions, white and green parts, finely chopped

½ medium red bell pepper (3 ounces), cored, seeded, deveined, and cut into thin rings

½ medium green bell pepper (3 ounces), cored, seeded, deveined, and cut into thin rings

6 plum tomatoes (about 1 pound), peeled and cut into thin rounds

¼ cup store-bought tomato sauce

½ cup Creamy ("First") Coconut Milk (page 50) or unsweetened canned coconut milk

1 Brazilian *pimenta de cheiro*, Scotch bonnet pepper, or habanero pepper, cut in half and seeded

1 teaspoon salt

1 tablespoon *dendê* oil (optional)

1 tablespoon finely chopped cilantro

The Shrimp ▶ Place the shrimp in a large bowl and toss with the garlic, lime juice, and salt. Let sit for no more than 30 minutes.

The Cooking Sauce ▶ Heat the oil in a 12-inch skillet over medium-high heat until it ripples. Add the onion, scallions, and bell peppers and cook, stirring, 3 to 4 minutes. Add the tomatoes and cook until soft, about 5 minutes. Reduce the heat to medium-low, stir in the tomato sauce, coconut milk, hot pepper, and salt, and simmer, uncovered, until the sauce thickens slightly, about 8 minutes. Taste the sauce and remove the hot pepper when the sauce is spicy enough for you.

Add the shrimp and increase the heat to medium-high. Cook, stirring, until the shrimp are pink and opaque, about 3 minutes. Stir in the *dendê* oil, if using, and cilantro. Taste for seasoning.

Serving: Serve hot with Brazilian-Style Simple Pilaf (page 298) and a spoonful of *vatapá* (page 620).

Mexican Shrimp and Poblano Aspic

Aspic de Camarones María Dolores Torres Yzábal

I got this recipe from María Dolores Torres Yzábal, one of Mexico's most celebrated cooks. María Dolores's private universe was the side of Mexico that often gets hidden in the boisterous vibrancy of the markets and street life. She lived in the posh Chapultepec section of Mexico City, and her home was as elegant as her cooking, with marvelous still lifes of fruits and fish by Chucho Herrera hanging in all the rooms, and delicate linen tablecloths and heirloom porcelain plates on her dinner table.

María Dolores was born and raised in Sonora, "where the stews end and the roasts begin," she explained, in a family that believed in ceremony at the dining table. For decades, María Dolores's mother kept a detailed handwritten log of all the dinner parties she held, together with precious recipes such as this refined aspic. María Dolores continued her mother's tradition, and this recipe comes from that marvelous evolving collection.

The thought of gelatin might conjure up images of quivering Jell-O or outmoded and tasteless aspics. Not so in Mexico, where cooks have found myriad ways to work with unflavored gelatin. In this recipe, the technique is European but the flavors are unmistakably Mexican—deep, full, and assertive. This dish is both pretty and practical, the aspic a translucent setting for rows of rosy pink shrimp. When serving, I cut the aspic into even squares, trying to leave the shrimp intact for visual appeal. This dish is ideal for a summer luncheon or buffet party.

What to Drink: Robledo Family Sauvignon Blanc "Seven Brothers," Pinot Blanc or Pinot Grigio from Lake County, California

SERVES 6

For the Shrimp

1 garlic clove, peeled
1 bay leaf
½ teaspoon black peppercorns
2 slices lime
1 pound medium shrimp (16–20 per pound), in the shell

For the Aspic

1 envelope unflavored gelatin
¼ cup cold water
1 cup hot water
½ teaspoon salt
2 tablespoons Mexican-style chile sauce, homemade (pages 114–16) or store-bought

3 poblano chiles, fire-roasted (page 67), peeled, and finely diced
¼ cup finely diced red bell pepper
1 tablespoon finely chopped chives
2 tablespoons finely chopped cilantro
Juice of ½ lime

Cooking the Shrimp ▶ In a medium pot, bring to a boil 1 quart water with the garlic, bay leaf, peppercorns, and slices of lime. Add the shrimp and cook until opaque and firm, 3 to 5 minutes. Drain the shrimp, cool, peel, and devein. Set aside.

Making the Aspic ▶ Place the gelatin and cold water in a medium bowl and let soften for about 5 minutes. Add the hot water and stir to dissolve. Then add the salt, chile sauce, poblano chiles, bell pepper, chives, cilantro, and lime juice.

Assembling the Aspic ▶ Lightly oil the bottom and sides of a 9-by-9-inch glass dish. Line the dish with plastic wrap and lightly oil the wrap as well. Pour in a thin layer of aspic, trying to keep it clear of pepper or chive bits, and refrigerate until lightly set.

Arrange all the shrimp in one layer over the set gelatin, leaving a little space between them. Refrigerate again to allow to set completely.

Gradually add the remaining aspic with the chiles and peppers. Allow each layer to set before adding the next. Leave the finished aspic to set completely in the refrigerator for at least 2 hours before unmolding.

Serving: Unmold onto a decorative plate. Serve with Mexican *crema* (page 148) or crème fraîche seasoned with salt.

Cuban-Style Shrimp in *Enchilado* Sauce

Camarones Enchilados a la Cubana

The word *enchilar* means to cook foods in a chile sauce. In Cuba, where hot peppers were tamed into oblivion by bourgeois and Spanish tastes, there are seafood dishes known as *enchilados*, but the pepper is always sweet bell pepper. Only in areas with a strong black presence, such as Santiago de Cuba and other parts of the former Oriente Province, do you find *enchilados* spiced with cayenne pepper or a native hot pepper grown in somebody's backyard (for instance, the hot *ají guaguao*, in much use during the colonial period). But mild or spicy, seafood *enchilado* is a feast food all over Cuba, a dish Cubans think about when planning a meal for special company.

What to Drink: Susana Balbo Crios Rosé de Malbec or Hatuey or Corona beer

SERVES 6

For the Shrimp

- 2 pounds medium shrimp (16–20 per pound), shelled and deveined, with tails on
- 8 garlic cloves, 4 mashed to a paste with a mortar and pestle or finely chopped and mashed, 4 finely chopped
- 1 teaspoon salt
  Juice of ½ lime (about 1 tablespoon)

For the Sauce

- 3 tablespoons extra-virgin olive oil
- 1 medium yellow onion (8 ounces), finely chopped
- 2 medium green bell peppers (12 ounces), cored, seeded, deveined, and finely chopped
- 1 jalapeño or ½ habanero chile, seeded and finely chopped
- 1 teaspoon ground cumin
- 1 teaspoon dried oregano
- ⅛ teaspoon ground allspice
- 1 cup tomato sauce, homemade (page 48) or store-bought
- ¼ cup dry white wine (preferably Latin American *vino seco*), dry sherry, or lager beer
- 2 tablespoons ketchup
- 1 tablespoon Worcestershire sauce
- 1 teaspoon salt, or to taste
- 1 teaspoon freshly ground black pepper
- ¼ cup finely chopped flat-leaf parsley or cilantro

Preparing the Shrimp ▶ Place the shrimp in a large bowl. Rub them all over with the mashed garlic, 1 teaspoon salt, and the lime juice. Let sit for at least 30 minutes, covered with plastic wrap.

Preparing the Enchilado Sauce ▶ Heat the oil in a 12-inch skillet over medium-high heat. Add the chopped garlic and sauté until golden, about 40 seconds. Add the onion and bell peppers and cook, stirring, for about 8 minutes. Stir in the chile, cumin, oregano, and allspice. Pour in the tomato sauce, wine, ketchup, and Worcestershire sauce and add the salt, black pepper, and parsley or cilantro. Stir to mix and simmer, covered, until the sauce thickens lightly, about 10 minutes. Add the shrimp and continue to simmer for another 3 minutes.

Serving: Serve with white rice or Moors and Christians (page 310), Fried Green Plantains (page 182), and Cuban Avocado, Watercress, and Pineapple Salad (page 548).

FISH

Aunt Carolina's Roasted Red Snapper in Green Sauce

El Pargo en Salsa Verde de la Tía Carolina

Along with *arroz con pollo*, a large whole red snapper roasted in a thick and aromatic green sauce over a bed of potatoes was the quintessential Sunday lunch treat at my family's house in Santiago de Cuba back in the 1950s. Red snapper was available year-round, but the tastiest, largest fish were plentiful in October and November. When cold winds ruffled the open sea, huge schools of red snapper were pushed close to shore—a phenomenon known as the *arribazón* (the teeming). At the first sign of red snapper weather, my uncle Oscar would set out in his flimsy *chalana* (small boat) with a group of friends and fish for a couple of nights, bringing home huge red snappers that were given out to our extended family and friends.

The largest, most handsome fish would be reserved for roasting, one of Aunt Carolina's specialties. Her red snapper in *salsa verde* was extraordinary—juicy, succulent, balanced, full of flavor, the potatoes at the bottom of the pan drenched in the fish juices. We never expected less than perfection from Carolina, an Amazon of the kitchen, who made it her life's work to tame in her pot all the wild things her unruly fisherman-hunter husband brought to her kitchen.

What to Drink: Laura Catena's Luca Chardonnay or Catena Alta Chardonnay from Mendoza, Argentina

SERVES 6

For the Red Snapper

One 5-pound red snapper, scaled, cleaned, and gutted

12 garlic cloves, mashed to a paste with a mortar and pestle or finely chopped and mashed

1 teaspoon salt

2 tablespoons bitter orange juice or equal parts lime juice and orange juice

1 large yellow onion (12 ounces), cut into thick slices

For the Green Sauce

1 large bunch flat-leaf parsley, rinsed

1 bunch cilantro, rinsed, or 1 additional bunch parsley

1 medium yellow onion (8 ounces), peeled and quartered

1 head garlic, separated into cloves and peeled

2 hard-boiled egg yolks

¼ cup toasted blanched almonds

1 jalapeño, seeded (optional)

¼ cup capers, drained

¼ cup pitted green olives

1 cup dry sherry

1 tablespoon cider vinegar

1 teaspoon salt

½ cup extra-virgin olive oil

1 cup chicken broth, homemade (page 538) or store-bought, or All-Purpose Fish Broth (page 540)

For Roasting

6 medium russet potatoes (about 2 pounds), peeled, cut into ¼-inch slices, and parboiled

2 tablespoons extra-virgin olive oil

1 teaspoon salt

½ teaspoon freshly ground black pepper

Marinating the Fish ▶ Place the fish in a large baking pan. In a small bowl, combine the garlic, salt, and bitter orange juice. Rub the fish inside and out with this seasoning paste. Cover with the onion slices and let rest, covered with plastic wrap, for at least 2 hours.

Making the Green Sauce ▶ Preheat the oven to 400°F.

Place all the sauce ingredients except the olive oil and broth in a blender or food processor and process into a smooth puree.

Heat the oil in a medium skillet or sauté pan over medium heat. Stir in half of the puree. Cook, stirring, until thickened and fragrant, about 10 minutes. Add the chicken or fish broth and cook, stirring, for 2 more minutes. Set aside.

Roasting the Fish ▶ Place a layer of parboiled potato slices on an oiled baking dish or baking sheet large enough to hold the whole fish. Cover with the onions used in the fish marinade. Pour the cooked green sauce over the onions and potatoes. Place the fish on this bed of vegetables and sprinkle with olive oil and salt and pepper. Bake for 45 minutes. Pour the uncooked green sauce over the fish and return it to the oven for 10 or 15 minutes. Check for doneness by inserting a fork in the thick part of the flesh; if the flesh is white and flakes easily, the fish is done.

Serving: Bring the fish to the table whole on a large serving platter, surrounded by the potatoes and onions. Serve with white rice, Havana-Style Black Bean Soup (page 507), Fried Green Plantains (page 182), and Avocado and Onion Salad (page 547).

Red Snapper in the Style of Veracruz

Huachinango a la Veracruzana

Serenaded by troubadours playing guitars and singing the songs of Agustín Lara, I enjoyed a fascinating meal at Doña Lala's restaurant in colorful Tlacotalpan, a coastal town in the Mexican state of Veracruz. There Doña Lala introduced me to her childhood friend Doña Luz del Carmen Valenzuela de Rojas, an accomplished cook and the owner of the restaurant La Bilbaína. We were happy to discover that many of our favorite recipes were similar, with that Spanish touch that is characteristic of both the Hispanic Caribbean and Veracruz. Here is Doña Luz's version of *huachinango*; see Veracruz Tomato Sauce for Fish (page 48) for another version of this beautiful sauce. This famous dish is enriched with olives and capers, a combination of flavors that is as familiar in Havana and Panama City as it is in Veracruz.

What to Drink: A Casa de Piedra Tempranillo and Cabernet Sauvignon blend from Ensenada, Baja California

SERVES 6

One 8-pound red snapper, scaled, cleaned, and gutted
About ¾ cup extra-virgin olive oil
Juice of 1 lime (about 2 tablespoons)
Salt
12 jalapeños, seeded, deveined, and cut into thin strips

1 large white onion (12 ounces), finely chopped

6 garlic cloves, finely chopped

1 bay leaf

Three 28-ounce cans whole plum tomatoes, drained and coarsely chopped, or 16 medium plum tomatoes (about 3 pounds), coarsely chopped

1 cup green manzanilla olives, pitted and sliced

½ cup capers, drained

▶ Rinse the fish and pat it dry. Rub inside and out with a mixture of 3 tablespoons olive oil, lime juice, and salt and set aside.

Heat ⅓ cup olive oil in a large saucepan. Add the jalapeños, onion, garlic, and bay leaf and sauté, stirring, until the onion becomes translucent, about 5 minutes. Add the chopped tomatoes, olives, and capers. Cook, stirring frequently, until the sauce thickens, about 15 minutes.

▶ Preheat the oven to 350°F. Oil a baking dish or baking sheet large enough to hold the fish.

Pour half the sauce over the bottom of the dish. Place the fish on top, cover with the remaining sauce, and drizzle with the remaining ¼ cup olive oil. Place the dish on the middle rack of the oven and bake for 45 minutes or until the fish is cooked through.

Serving: Serve with white rice or Mexican Rice (page 302) and a green salad.

Broiled Salmon Trout with Green Sauce

Trucha Asalmonada en Salsa Verde

Years ago, I befriended Mexican chef Livier Ortiz, who gave me a couple of private cooking lessons at her restaurant La Terraza in Morelia, the capital of the state of Michoacán in central Mexico. On the menu was farm-raised salmon trout blanketed with a very Spanish green sauce, a kind of thick pesto made of olive oil, parsley, and garlic. She wanted the sauce to be very Spanish and refrained from adding a single hot pepper. But when I tested the recipe at home, I sneaked in a couple of serranos to give it a Mexican kick.

What to Drink: A Robledo Family Pinot Blanc from Lake County, California

SERVES 6

For the Fish

6 salmon trout or brook trout (about 1 pound each), butterflied

Salt and freshly ground black pepper

For the Green Sauce

1½ cups packed finely chopped flat-leaf parsley

6 garlic cloves, peeled

2 serrano chiles, seeded and coarsely chopped (optional)

½ teaspoon dried oregano

1 cup extra-virgin olive oil

⅓ cup distilled white vinegar

⅓ cup dry white wine

1 tablespoon Worcestershire sauce

Preparing the Fish ▶ Rinse the fish and pat dry. Season with salt and pepper to taste and let rest for about 10 minutes

Preparing the Sauce ▶ Place the chopped parsley, garlic, serranos (if using), oregano, olive oil, vinegar, wine, and Worcestershire sauce in the bowl of a food processor or blender and process into a smooth puree. Pour a couple of spoonfuls of the sauce over the inside of the fish and spread with the back of the spoon.

Preheat the broiler and line a baking pan with aluminum foil. Place the trout on the pan, skin side down, and broil about 6 inches from the heat source until cooked through but not dry. Pour the rest of the green sauce into a sauceboat and bring to the table with the trout.

Serving: Serve with a side of Mexican Rice (page 302).

Fish Fillets in Tropical Juice *Adobo* Cooked in Plantain Leaves

Maito de Pescado Sazonado con Adobo de Jugo de Frutas y Asado en Hojas de Plátano

This recipe is my adaptation of a wonderful cooking method I learned in Santa Rita and Archidona, two communities in the Napo River region of the Ecuadorian Amazon. Locally called *maito*, it consists of river fish, chicken, or the meat of any local wild animal steamed or grilled in a bundle of the fragrant leaves of the *bijao* plant. *Bijao* leaves are used much like those of plantain or banana, but are more convenient since they are only a fraction of the size. *Maitos* are flavored with the acidic local *chonta chicha* brewed from peach-palm fruit (page 193), and usually served with white rice, boiled yuca, and an onion and tomato relish (*ají*). Since it will be hard to get hold of *chonta chicha* in the United States, I have chosen to use *naranjilla*, another Amazonian fruit, for my source of acidity. My preferred cooking method is grilling, which results in a lovely smoky flavor. The fillets are also excellent steamed or broiled.

Cook's Note: The fruit I use in the marinade is *naranjilla*, which looks like a small greenish orange with fuzzy skin. (In Colombia it is known as *lulo*.) This relative of the tomato is native to the Ecuadorian Amazon. At times I find the fresh fruit in my Hispanic market, but the juice, which is light olive green and very aromatic, is available frozen year-round. (Thaw before using in any recipe.) What makes *naranjilla* interesting is not only its penetrating aroma but its elusive aftertaste, a musky bitterness that adds backbone to any marinade. The only fruit that compares in aroma is passion fruit, but I have reduced the amount if you are using that instead, because it is very acidic.

What to Drink: A white wine with floral notes, such as Susana Balbo Crios Torrontes from Mendoza, Argentina

SERVES 6

For the Fish

   6 striped bass, sea bass, or red snapper skinless fillets (about 5 ounces each)

  ½ teaspoon salt

  ½ teaspoon freshly ground black pepper

For the Marinade

⅓ cup *naranjilla* juice, thawed and strained, or
¼ cup passion fruit juice, strained

6 garlic cloves, finely chopped

6 scallions, white and 3 inches of green parts, finely
chopped

1 Scotch bonnet or habanero chile, seeded and
finely chopped

¼ cup finely chopped cilantro

1 tablespoon extra-virgin olive oil

For the Wrap

6 plantain leaves, cut into 14-by-10-inch pieces and
prepared according to the instructions on page 423

1 cup *Naranjilla* Mayonnaise (recipe follows), for
serving

Marinating the Fish ▶ Place the fish fillets in a large bowl and season with the salt and pepper. Combine the *naranjilla* or passion fruit juice with the garlic, scallions, hot pepper, cilantro, and olive oil. Stir to mix well. Pour this mixture over the fish fillets and rub all over. Let sit for about 15 minutes.

Wrapping the Fish ▶ Place a plantain-leaf rectangle on a work surface with a short side facing you. Place a fish fillet in the middle of the leaf and fold both long sides over it. Now make a 2-inch fold from the top, bringing it over the seam. Repeat with the bottom side. Now you have a small package shaped like a tamal. Tie the fish tamal with string like a gift package finished with a dainty bow. Repeat until you have used all the fish.

Cooking the Fish ▶ **To grill**, place the packages on a hot grill and cook for 6 minutes on each side.

To steam, place the packages in the basket of a steamer and steam over simmering water for 8 minutes. The fish will be perfectly cooked and very juicy.

To broil, place the packages 3 inches from the heat source and broil for 4 minutes on each side. The plantain leaves will char, imparting a delicious flavor to the fish.

Serving: Open the plantain packages and top the fish with a dollop of *Naranjilla* Mayonnaise. I like to serve them with Sweet Ripe Plantain Puree (page 185) or Spiced *Arracacha* Puree (page 216). Or use the more authentic accompaniments mentioned above.

Naranjilla Mayonnaise

Mayonesa de Naranjilla

Now that the Amazonian fruit called *naranjilla* or *lulo* reaches us fresh from Ecuador and Colombia, I have taken to cooking with it, sometimes expanding its uses in unorthodox ways. This flavored mayonnaise is a great table sauce with any type of steamed fish, chicken, or shellfish. Plantain leaves (page 423) make the best steaming wrappers.

Cook's Note: To extract the juice of the *naranjilla*, use 4 fresh or frozen (thawed) *naranjillas*. Cut each in half and squeeze as you would lemons. you could also cut a shallow cross on the blossom end of the fruit and squeeze it. The whole pulp will slide out easily. Pass it through a mesh strainer, pushing with a wooden spoon to extract as much juice as possible. You should have about ½ cup of juice.

MAKES ABOUT 1½ CUPS

1 cup Garlic Mayonnaise (page 135) or store-bought mayonnaise

½ cup pureed *naranjilla*, from fresh or frozen fruit

12 fresh sweet Caribbean peppers (*ajíes dulces*) or 1 fresh cubanelle pepper, seeded

6 garlic cloves (if using store-bought mayonnaise)

¼ teaspoon ground cumin

1 teaspoon salt, or to taste

▶ Place all ingredients in a blender or food processor and process into a smooth sauce. Keeps well for up to 3 days, tightly covered, in the refrigerator.

Braised Fish in Coconut Milk in the Style of Bahia

Moqueca de Peixe

In Salvador, the capital of the state of Bahia, the *moqueca de peixe* is a sight to behold. It comes to the table still bubbling in its earthenware cooking pot and garnished brightly with rounds of ripe tomato and onions. Though beautiful, I find this traditional method makes for overcooked fish. I much prefer to start the sauce first, enrich it with coconut milk, and then add the fish, cooking it only until it flakes easily and no longer.

SERVES 6

For the Fish

2 pounds grouper or red snapper skinless fillets
Juice of 1 medium lime (about 2 tablespoons)

1½ *pimentas de cheiro* or Scotch bonnet or habanero chiles, seeded and finely minced

4 garlic cloves, mashed to a paste with a mortar and pestle or finely chopped and mashed
Salt

For the Sauce

¼ cup extra-virgin olive oil

4 garlic cloves, finely chopped

1 medium yellow onion (about 8 ounces), cut into thin slices

1 small green bell pepper (about 4 ounces), cored, seeded, deveined, and cut into thin slices

1 small red bell pepper (about 4 ounces), cored, seeded, deveined, and cut into thin slices

4 ripe medium globe tomatoes (about 1¼ pounds), cut into rounds

1 cup Creamy ("First") Coconut Milk (page 50) or unsweetened canned coconut milk
Salt to taste

1 cup All-Purpose Fish Broth (page 540)

2 tablespoons *dendê* oil

4 tablespoons finely chopped cilantro, for garnish

Preparing the Fish ▶ Rinse the fish and pat dry. Place in a bowl and season with the lime juice, hot pepper, garlic, and salt to taste.

Making the Sauce ▶ Heat the olive oil in a 12-inch skillet over low heat. Sauté the garlic, onion, green pepper, and red pepper until they are soft, about 10 minutes. Add the tomatoes and sauté for 2 more minutes. Stir and pour in the coconut milk and the fish broth, and add salt to taste. Stir and simmer over low heat for 10 minutes or until the sauce thickens. Add the seasoned fish and the *dendê* oil and cook for 2 to 3 minutes more, or until the fish is cooked through. Check for seasoning and garnish with the cilantro.

Puerto Rican Pan-Fried Yellowtail Snapper

La Colirrubia Frita de Virgilio Brunet

My Puerto Rican friend Virgilio Brunet had a special wooden table in the back of his house at La Parguera exclusively for gutting and scaling fish. He dressed fish that weighed less than 3 pounds very simply, always leaving the head on, for he thought this the best part of the fish. There is nothing as tasty as pan-fried yellowtail. Virgilio marinated the fish, dipped it in seasoned flour, and pan-fried it until golden brown in whatever fat he found at hand: lard, corn oil, or olive oil.

Cook's Note: The yellowtail of the Caribbean is not the same fish that appears in Japanese sushi bars, a kind of jack related to tuna and pompano that the Japanese call *buri* or *hamachi*. It is a tropical snapper (*Ocyurus chrysurus*) known in the Caribbean as *colirrubia* or *chillo*, a beautiful fish that rarely exceeds 5 pounds. It is easy to spot in any fish market, for it sports a prominent yellow stripe that runs from the mouth to the tail, broadening as it passes the dorsal fins; the yellowtail lives up to its name because of its deeply forked yellow caudal fin.

What to Drink: A bright, citrusy Quinta de Consuelo Alvariño from the Rias Baixas in Galicia, Spain

SERVES 2

---

5 garlic cloves, peeled
   Salt and freshly ground black pepper
   Juice of 2 medium limes (about ¼ cup)
1 whole yellowtail snapper (about 1 pound), scaled, cleaned, and gutted
¼ cup all-purpose flour
¼ cup extra-virgin olive oil
   Lime slices, for garnish

▶ In a mortar with a pestle, mash the garlic with ½ teaspoon salt and ½ teaspoon pepper. Add the lime juice and stir. Rub the fish with this marinade and let rest for at least 1 hour.

When you are ready to fry, combine the flour and ¼ teaspoon pepper on a shallow platter. Coat the fish lightly in the flour and shake to remove the excess.

Heat the oil to about 350°F in a 12-inch skillet or sauté pan, preferably nonstick. Add the fish and cook until golden brown, about 3 minutes on each side. Remove to a platter with a large skimmer or slotted spatula.

Serving: Serve garnished with lime slices alongside a mound of white rice doused with a ladleful of Puerto Rican Stewed Red Kidney Beans (page 509), a side of Fried Green Plantains (page 182), and a tomato and onion salad.

Variation: Virgilio had another delicious recipe for yellowtail snapper. He marinated the fish, either whole or in fillets, in the traditional Puerto Rican *adobo*, as directed above, but tossed the fish with slices of green cubanelle peppers, slivered onions, chunky slices of red tomato, and 2 tablespoons olive oil. After coating the fish in flour, he fried it in a heavy cast-iron skillet until golden and then added the vegetables and a bit of water to the pan. He covered the pan and let the fish simmer for 10 minutes. The result is fish with a slightly crunchy crust and tender, moist flesh that has absorbed the tart flavor of the lime and tomatoes and the pungency of the garlic. The thin sauce with chunks of pulpy tomato and peppers that remains is spooned over the fish.

Fish *Escabeche* "La Bilbaína"

Escabeche de Pescado "La Bilbaína"

When the witty and keen-eyed Scottish wife of the Spanish ambassador to Mexico arrived in Veracruz in 1839, she was feted by all the best local families. Then Madame Calderón de la Barca (Frances Erskine Inglis) began to see a pattern. Many of the dishes, she reported in her letters, had been "Veracrucified"—that is, drenched in garlic and olive oil. Nothing is more typical of this style of cooking than fish *escabeche*. In Mexico, it is commonly stored in large glass jars, or *cuñetes*, that give it the name *pescado al cuñete*.

Doña Luz del Carmen Valenzuela de Rojas, the genial chef-owner of the decades-old La Bilbaína restaurant in Veracruz, shared this classic Mexican *escabeche* with me. Any firm-fleshed fish steak will do well, but in Veracruz and throughout Latin America, sawfish and swordfish are the favorites.

What to Drink: A full bodied Mexican beer like Dos Equis Amber Lager

SERVES 6

1 cup extra-virgin olive oil

Six ½-inch-thick steaks (7–8 ounces each) of any firm-fleshed fish, such as swordfish, tuna, or shark

2 large white onions (1½ pounds), cut into thick rings

6 garlic cloves, thinly sliced

16 jalapeños, seeded, deveined, and cut into thin slivers

3 bay leaves

20 black peppercorns

1 cup distilled white vinegar

▶ Heat ½ cup oil in a 12-inch sauté pan or skillet, preferably nonstick, over medium heat. Add the fish steaks to the pan, 2 at a time, and sauté on both sides until golden, about 2½ minutes per side. Lift out of the pan with a slotted spatula and transfer to a deep earthenware, glass, porcelain, or enameled serving dish large enough to accommodate all the fish in a single layer. Set aside.

In the same oil, sauté the onions, garlic, jalapeños, bay leaves, and peppercorns until the onions are soft, about 5 minutes. Stir in the vinegar, bring to a simmer, and simmer for about 5 minutes. Pour everything over the fish and top with the remaining ½ cup oil.

Serving and Storing: If the *escabeche* is to be eaten on the same day, keep at room temperature for at least 4 hours before serving. If not, cover with plastic wrap and refrigerate until ready to use. It will keep well for 1 week. Always bring the *escabeche* back to room temperature or warm it gently before serving.

Salted Mackerel in *Escabeche* Sauce with Yellow Potato Puree in the Style of Moche

Causa en Lapa al Estilo de Moche

A satiny yellow potato puree kneaded with some fish broth and served in a hollowed-out gourd called a *lapa*, topped with salted mackerel in a bright *escabeche* sauce, this is a classic Holy Week dish in the town of Moche in northern Peru. It is a harmonious combination that surprises with its complexity and good taste. I consider it one of the glories of Peruvian cooking.

I first tasted it on Good Friday at a small outdoor restaurant next to the Pyramid of the Sun. Dora Asmat, the chef-owner, made the dish for me the old-fashioned way, kneading the potato puree by hand in the *lapa* while enriching it with oil and fish broth until it glistened. The fish was salted *caballa*, a kind of Pacific mackerel, a favorite in the Libertad department. Dora buys it fresh, splits it open, and salts it herself, leaving it to rest for two or three days in the refrigerator. The process intensifies the flavor but leaves the fish moist. The fish is simply boiled and then dressed at serving time with an *escabeche* sauce garnished with strips of yellow Andean peppers, Peruvian purple olives, and hard-boiled eggs.

I use achiote-infused oil to obtain the yellow hue Dora likes for the sauce. This oil also comes in handy to color the puree yellow. Though you could use Yukon Gold potatoes, the texture of Russet Burbank comes closer to that of Peruvian yellow potatoes.

Cook's Notes: Salted Pacific mackerel (*Scomber japonicus*) similar to the *caballa* that Dora Asmat used for this dish—lightly salted, without sugar or strong seasonings—is imported to Korean and Japanese markets in North America. Keep it in the refrigerator for up to 3 days after purchase and refresh by briefly placing in cold water and rinsing before proceeding with the recipe. Taste the fish when you remove it from the refrigerator, and if the flavor is too salty, let it soak in cold water for about 2 hours, changing the water a couple of times.

If you are unable to find Japanese or Korean salted Pacific mackerel, you can cure Pacific or Atlantic mackerel at home as follows: Choose a whole scaled, cleaned, and gutted fish of about 1¼ pounds. Rinse thoroughly and pat dry with paper towels. Cut 2 diagonal slashes on either side. Rub 1 tablespoon coarse salt over the fish outside and inside, pushing it well into the slashes. Wrap the fish in several thicknesses of paper towel, place it on a rack set over a deep plate or shallow bowl, and refrigerate for 2 to 3 days. Unwrap the fish and rinse off any clinging salt. Taste to judge the level of salt, and soak the fish in several changes of fresh cold water until it is to your taste. Remember, however, that the potato puree will partly cancel out the salt fish flavor, so don't soak until it is completely bland.

What to Drink: A grassy, crisp Montes Classic Series Sauvignon Blanc from Casablanca Valley, Chile

SERVES 4 AS A MAIN COURSE, 6 AS AN APPETIZER

For the Fish

- 1 medium salted mackerel (about 1 pound 3 ounces)
- ½ medium red onion (4 ounces), peeled
- 3–4 cilantro sprigs

For the *Escabeche* Sauce

- 4 fresh-frozen yellow Andean peppers (*ajíes amarillos*), stemmed, seeded, deveined, and coarsely chopped
- 1 tablespoon dried ground *panca* pepper, homemade (page 54) or store-bought, or 2 whole dried *panca* peppers
- ⅓ cup vegetable oil or mild extra-virgin olive oil
- 1 tablespoon achiote-infused vegetable or mild extra-virgin olive oil (page 89)
- 6 garlic cloves, mashed to a paste with a mortar and pestle or finely chopped and mashed
- 1 large red onion (about 12 ounces), cut into ½-inch-thick lengthwise slivers
- 2 tablespoons red wine vinegar, or to taste Salt
- 12 Peruvian purple olives or Kalamata olives

For the Potato Puree

- 6 medium russet potatoes (about 2 pounds), unpeeled
- 1 tablespoon salt, plus more if needed
- ½ cup reserved fish broth, or as needed
- ½ cup achiote-infused vegetable oil or mild extra-virgin olive oil (page 89)

For the Garnish

- ½ recipe Boiled Yuca (page 167)
- 2 hard-boiled eggs, quartered
- 2 limes, preferably small Key limes, halved

Preparing the Fish ▶ Place the salted mackerel in a medium bowl and cover with water. Let rest for 5 to 6 minutes and rinse under cold running water. Cut into 4 serving pieces and place in a medium saucepan with 1½ quarts water and the onion and cilantro sprigs. Bring to a boil over medium heat and simmer until the fish is cooked, 8 to 10 minutes. Set aside the fish in its cooking broth.

Preparing the *Escabeche* Sauce ▶ Place the yellow peppers in a blender with 2 tablespoons water and process into a smooth puree. Scrape into a bowl and clean the blender.

If you are using whole dried *panca* peppers, soak them in 1 cup hot water until soft or boil for 10 to 15 minutes until soft. Drain, reserving ¼ cup liquid. Place in a blender with the reserved liquid and process into a smooth puree; set aside.

Heat the two oils in a medium skillet or saucepan over medium-high heat. Add the garlic and sauté until golden, about 20 seconds. Stir in the reserved fresh pepper puree and cook, stirring, about 2 minutes. Add the ground dried *panca* pepper or the dried pepper puree and cook for 1 more minute, stirring. Add the onion and sauté for 3 to 4 minutes, then add the vinegar and salt to taste and check the seasoning. Lower the heat to medium-low and add ¼ cup of the fish broth. Stir in the olives and turn off the heat. Keep in a warm place.

Preparing the Potato Puree ▶ While the *escabeche* is cooking, place the potatoes in a medium saucepan with enough water to cover and the salt. Bring to a boil over medium-high heat and cook until just tender, about 20 minutes. Drain. When cool enough to handle, peel and pass through a potato ricer into a bowl (or a gourd, if you are lucky enough to have one). Knead with clean hands or a potato masher while adding small amounts of fish broth and oil. Taste for salt and season accordingly. The puree is ready when it is totally smooth and glistening.

Assembling the Dish ▶ Lift the fish out of the warm broth and pick out the bones. Remove the skin if you wish. Place a mound of puree on each serving plate (a shallow bowl is appropriate) and flatten it lightly with the back of a spoon. Place a piece of fish on the puree and top with a generous serving of the *escabeche*. Garnish with the yuca, eggs, and lime. This dish can be served warm or at room temperature.

"Sweated" Fish in the Style of Huanchaco

Sudado de Pescado

This is the favorite way of preparing fish throughout the Libertad department in northern Peru: a simple braise seasoned with red onions, garlic, and the bright orange–yellow pepper known as *ají escabeche* (sold here as *ají amarillo*). Walk to any house along the coast on a weekday and you will find cooks preparing this dish with whatever fish is in season. This version comes from two sources, the wife of a fisherman I met in the village of Huanchaquito and the Isla sisters, who own Restaurante El Caribe in Huanchaco. The fisherman's wife likes to use small whole fish caught by her husband, and the Isla sisters prefer thick white fillets of a Pacific fish called *ojo de uva*, with lovely firm white flesh. Grouper is my choice for this recipe, since it is easy to find in our markets.

What to Drink: Peruvian Pilsen Callao or Cuzqueña beer

SERVES 4

For the Fish
- 2 pounds grouper or any firm white-fleshed fish, filleted or whole
- 1 teaspoon salt
  Juice of 1 medium lime (about 2 tablespoons)
- 1 teaspoon freshly ground black pepper
- 1 tablespoon finely chopped cilantro

For the Cooking Sauce
- 8 fresh-frozen yellow Andean peppers (*ajíes amarillos*)
- ¼ cup vegetable oil or mild extra-virgin olive oil
- 4 large garlic cloves, mashed to a paste with a mortar and pestle or finely chopped and mashed
  Salt
- 1 medium red onion (8 ounces), cut into ½-inch-thick lengthwise slivers
- 2 medium plum tomatoes (about 6 ounces), halved, seeded, and coarsely chopped
- 1 teaspoon dried oregano, lightly toasted

For the Garnish
- 2 limes, cut in half

Preparing the Fish ▶ Rinse the fish under running cold water and pat dry. If using whole fish, cut into 4 serving pieces. Place in a bowl and season with the salt and lime juice, black pepper, and cilantro; let rest while preparing the cooking sauce.

Making the Cooking Sauce ▶ Place the Andean peppers in a colander and rinse under cold running water. Stem, seed, and devein them. Coarsely chop

4 of the peppers; cut the remaining 4 into strips and set aside.

Place the chopped peppers in a blender with 2 tablespoons water and process into a smooth puree; set aside.

Heat the oil in a 12-inch sauté pan over medium-high heat. Add the garlic and sauté until golden, about 40 seconds. Add the pepper puree and salt to taste and sauté for 2 minutes. Add the onion and cook, stirring, until soft, about 5 minutes. Stir in the oregano and add the fish and the marinade.

Finishing the Dish ▶ Pour in ⅓ cup hot water and place the reserved pepper strips and the tomatoes over the fish. (You can adjust the amount of water to your taste.) Lower the heat to medium and continue cooking, covered, for 10 minutes.

Serving: Garnish with lime halves and serve immediately, with white rice and Boiled Yuca (page 167).

Pompano Cooked in *Hoja Santa*

Pámpano en Acuyo

In Veracruz, Mexico, several types of fish are wrapped before being cooked in the broad heart-shaped leaf called *hoja santa* or, locally, *acuyo*. I learned several recipes using *acuyo* from Doña Luz del Carmen Valenzuela de Rojas, the chef-owner of Bilbaína Restaurant in Veracruz City. The starring dishes at her wedding feast over fifty years ago

in the river town of Tlacotalpan were huge *róbalos* (snook) prepared this way. Pompano, another regional favorite, tastes just as good wrapped in the fragrant leaves.

A whole pompano wrapped in *acuyo* leaves and fresh from the oven is a wonderful sight to behold. If you bring it to the table in a large baking dish and unwrap it with great pomp and ceremony, it will make any dinner special.

SERVES 4 TO 6

4–6 fresh or dried *hoja santa* leaves (see Cook's Note, page 783)
  1 whole Gulf Coast pompano (about 4 pounds), scaled, cleaned, and gutted
     Salt and freshly ground black pepper
  1 medium white onion (8 ounces), quartered
  3 garlic cloves, peeled and quartered
  2 jalapeños, seeded and deveined
  1 bunch cilantro, coarsely chopped
  1 bunch flat-leaf parsley, coarsely chopped
  2 canned chipotles *en adobo*
  ¼ cup extra-virgin olive oil
  2 teaspoons fresh lime juice
  ⅓ cup All-Purpose Fish Broth (page 540) or chicken broth, homemade (page 538) or store-bought

▶ If using dried *hoja santa* leaves, place in a small bowl and cover with water. Let sit until the leaves are flexible and rehydrated, about 5 minutes. Drain and set aside on paper towels.

Preheat the oven to 375°F. Place the fish on a plate and season with salt and pepper to taste.

Combine the onion, garlic, jalapeños, cilantro, parsley, chipotles, olive oil, lime juice, broth, and salt to taste in a blender or food processor and process into a smooth puree. Pour 1 cup of the puree over the fish and rub it in. Let sit for at least 15 minutes.

Place half of the *hoja santa* leaves in the bottom of a baking dish large enough to hold the fish. Place the fish on them. Place the remaining leaves over the fish. Tuck the edges around the fish to wrap it; cover with the rest of the puree. Place on the middle rack of the oven and bake for 20 minutes. (Open the leaves for a peek at the fish. It should be opaque and flaky.)

Serving: Unwrap the fish at the table and serve with Mexican Rice (page 302) and freshly made corn tortillas (page 579).

Tuna and White Beans Peruvian Style

Atún con Frijoles Blancos a la Peruana

Tuna is as versatile as pork, and has a similar affinity for white beans and assertive seasonings such as a cooking sauce (*aderezo*) flavored with golden dried *mirasol* peppers. You only need crusty bread and a lively red wine to turn this robust white bean casserole into a complete meal.

Cook's Note: For a shortcut, use a 15-ounce can of white beans, drained.

What to Drink: A Spanish tempranillo such as Sierra Cantabria Crianza

SERVES 6

For the Beans

- 8 ounces dried Great Northern beans (about 1 cup)
- 1 large yellow onion (12 ounces)

For the Tuna

- 2 garlic cloves, mashed to a paste with a mortar and pestle or finely chopped and mashed
- 2 teaspoons ground dried *mirasol* pepper, homemade (page 54) or store-bought, or ½ teaspoon ground cayenne
   Juice of ½ medium lime (about 1 tablespoon)
- 1 teaspoon extra-virgin olive oil
- 1 teaspoon salt
- 1 teaspoon ground cumin
- 1 pound fresh tuna steak

For the Cooking Sauce

- 6 dried *mirasol* peppers, stemmed and seeded
- 2 tablespoons extra-virgin olive oil
- 4 garlic cloves, finely chopped
- 1 small red onion (4 ounces), finely chopped
- 1 teaspoon ground cumin
- 1 teaspoon salt
- 2 tablespoons finely chopped cilantro
- ¼ cup cider vinegar

Cooking the Beans ▶ Place the beans and onion in a large stockpot with 3 quarts water and bring to a boil over high heat. Lower the heat and simmer, covered, adding more water if the beans dry out. Cook only until the beans are tender but retain their shape, 1 to 1½ hours. Discard the onion. Drain the beans and reserve. Makes about 3½ cups.

Seasoning the Tuna ▶ In a medium bowl, whisk together the garlic, ground *mirasol* or cayenne pep–

per, lime juice, olive oil, salt, and cumin. Add the tuna and toss to coat evenly. Let rest for at least 15 minutes.

Preparing the Cooking Sauce ▶ Place the *mirasol* peppers and 3 cups water in a small saucepan. Bring to a boil over medium heat and cook until soft, 15 to 20 minutes. Drain, reserving ½ cup of the cooking liquid. Place the peppers in a blender or food processor with the reserved cooking liquid and process to a smooth puree.

Heat the oil in a 12-inch sauté pan or skillet. Add the garlic and sauté until golden, about 40 seconds. Add the red onion, *mirasol* pepper puree, cumin, and salt. Cook for 3 minutes, stirring, until the onion is translucent. Stir in the cilantro and vinegar and cook for 2 more minutes.

Finishing the Dish ▶ Add the tuna to the cooking sauce and cook briefly, depending on how rare you like it. Stir in the reserved beans and cook just until heated through, about 5 minutes.

Serving and Storing: Serve warm, not hot, as a main course for a light meal. The dish will keep, well covered, in the refrigerator for a couple of days.

CALAMARI

Quinoa and Broccoli Rabe–Stuffed Calamari with *Panca* Pepper and Pisco Sauce

Calamares Rellenos de Quinua y Nabo en Salsa de Ají Panca y Pisco

Stuffed calamari is a favorite all over Latin America. Pork sausages are a popular stuffing, but sometimes I prefer a combination of quinoa and broccoli rabe, two Andean favorites, for a more delicate contrast. Peruvian pisco does wonders for the cooking sauce spiced with *panca* peppers. It has a smooth flavor and lovely grape aroma that reminds me of a good dry French vermouth.

SERVES 4 TO 6

1 pound small squid

For the Filling
　Salt
1 cup quinoa (about 8 ounces), well rinsed and drained (see page 258)
3 ounces broccoli rabe, coarsely chopped
2 tablespoons extra-virgin olive oil
6 garlic cloves, finely chopped
1 small red onion (5 ounces), finely chopped
2 ounces smoked pork chop, smoked ham, or slab bacon, finely chopped
1 teaspoon freshly ground black pepper

For the Cooking Sauce

6 dried *panca* peppers

2 tablespoons extra-virgin olive oil

7 garlic cloves, finely chopped

1 small red onion (5 ounces), finely chopped

4 medium plum tomatoes (about 12 ounces), peeled, seeded, and finely chopped

1 teaspoon ground cumin

1 teaspoon hot *pimentón* (Spanish smoked paprika)

¼ cup Peruvian pisco, preferably Pisco Italia

1 cup water or chicken broth, homemade (page 538) or store-bought

Cleaning the Squid ▶ Place the squid in a large bowl. Rinse under cold running water. Pull or cut the tentacles and head from each body and set them aside for another purpose or discard. Pull the transparent pen or quill bones from the bodies and discard. Clean the interior of the squid by rinsing each one under cold running water. Remove the thin spotted pinkish skin that covers the body and cut off the lateral fins. Set aside.

Making the Filling ▶ In a medium saucepan, bring 2 quarts water to a boil with salt over high heat. Add the quinoa and lower the heat to medium. Simmer for about 10 minutes, or until just barely cooked. The quinoa is done when all the grains have turned translucent. Remove from the heat and drain well in a colander.

In a clean medium saucepan, bring 2 quarts water to a boil over high heat. Add the broccoli rabe, reduce the heat to medium-high, and cook for 2 minutes. Immediately remove with a slotted spoon or strainer and plunge into a bowl of ice water. Drain and chop finely.

Heat the oil in a 12-inch sauté pan. Add the garlic and sauté until golden, about 40 seconds. Add the onion and smoked pork, ham, or bacon and cook for 3 minutes. Season with the pepper and salt to taste. Add the broccoli rabe and the cooked quinoa. You should have 3½ cups. Set aside.

Making the Sauce ▶ Place the *panca* peppers and 1 quart water in a medium saucepan and bring to a boil over medium heat. Cook until soft, about 15 minutes. Drain, reserving ½ cup of the cooking liquid. Place the peppers and reserved liquid in a blender or food processor and process to a puree.

Preheat the oven to 300°F. Heat the oil in a 12-inch sauté pan over medium heat. Add the garlic and sauté until golden, about 40 seconds. Add the onion and cook until soft, about 5 minutes. Add the tomatoes, cumin, and *pimentón* and cook, stirring, for 5 more minutes. Stir in the pisco and cook, stirring, for 2 minutes. Add the water or broth and let simmer, covered, until the sauce thickens lightly, about 10 minutes. Set aside.

Assembling the Dish ▶ Spoon some filling into each squid body, making sure not to overfill. Close with a toothpick.

Pour the sauce into a 13-by-9-inch baking pan. Arrange the stuffed squid over the sauce and bake for 15 minutes, until tender. Do not overcook.

Serving: Halve each squid on the bias. Pour the sauce onto a serving platter and arrange the squid on top. Serve with a salad.

SHELLFISH

Cuban-Style Crabs in Spicy *Enchilado* Sauce

Cangrejos Enchilados

In Cuba, land crabs (*cangrejos de tierra*) begin a death march in mid-July, crawling from the mangrove swamps onto busy roads, where they are crushed by passing cars. When I lived in Santiago de Cuba, *cangrejos enchilados* was one of the most popular Carnival dishes of my hometown, heralding the fun and the orgiastic eating that were to come.

Between July and August men and women combed the mangroves after sundown, carrying torches or flashlights to startle the crabs, wooden sticks, and large burlap bags. The feisty crabs would seize the hunters' sticks, and into the bags they went.

The first time I accompanied my father and uncle Oscar on one of these nocturnal forays, my father assigned me the job of holding the sack of crabs, but one huge crab escaped and started crawling up my hand. Shrieking, I dropped the bag. My father dropped his torch, and I fled into the darkness. After half an hour of shouting back and forth, my father and uncle finally emerged, and to this day, my father and I argue about what really happened: He says I acted hysterically. I accuse him of having too many Hatuey beers with my uncle and dropping the light. One thing I did learn: I refuse to be the one left holding a bag full of live crabs.

Back home the crabs were placed in wire cages where they were fed with corn and tubers for a whole week. This purged the possible toxins that Caribbean crabs sometimes ingest from eating the fruits or leaves of the manzanillo tree. Come cooking time, my father would boil water in a large cauldron set on a handy charcoal hibachi-style grill (*anafre*) in the backyard. My brother Marco pleaded to save them, while the rest of us laughed and salivated in anticipation. The crabs were plunged in boiling water and cooked until they turned a beautiful red color, then scrubbed with a large bristle brush, eviscerated, and quartered.

The way my father cooked and served the crabs was the same as in the kiosks that lined the heart of the carnival celebrations. He ordered the women of the house to cut up all the ingredients for a huge *sofrito*—onions, fresh tomatoes, green peppers, parsley, and enough garlic to wipe out an army. No water went into the cooking—just Hatuey beer. The table was covered with newspaper, and a river stone or wooden mallet placed at every setting. The crabs sat in their huge cauldron next to a large platter of ripe fried plantains, and another filled with a mound of fluffy white rice. We loved eating with messy hands, cracking the claws with the stones to suck out the moist sweet flesh, and then dredging our rice in the sauce.

Cook's Note: Caribbean land crabs are not sold in the United States. But when Dungeness crabs are in season, I make *cangrejos enchilados* the way my father taught me. I find that these large Pacific crabs look and taste like the ones we used to eat in Santiago. This recipe cries out for good company, a backyard, and, of course, ice-cold beer.

SERVES 6

For the Sauce (*Sofrito*)

½ cup extra-virgin olive oil

1 head garlic, separated into cloves, peeled, and finely chopped

1 large yellow onion (about 12 ounces), peeled and finely chopped

2 medium green bell peppers (about 1 pound), cored, seeded, deveined, and finely chopped

2 medium red bell peppers (about 1 pound), cored, seeded, deveined, and finely chopped

1 teaspoon ground allspice

½ teaspoon ground cumin

½ teaspoon ground oregano

½ teaspoon dried thyme

32 medium plum tomatoes (about 6 pounds), peeled, seeded, and finely chopped, or three 32-ounce cans good-quality canned plum tomatoes, peeled, drained of juice, and finely chopped

½ cup tomato puree

2 cups beer

1 tablespoon salt, or to taste

1 tablespoon freshly ground black pepper

1 Scotch bonnet or habanero chile, seeded and finely chopped

2 dozen Dungeness crabs, cleaned and quartered

1 bunch flat-leaf parsley, finely chopped

▶ Heat the olive oil over medium-high heat in a wide, deep pot or *caldero*. Add the garlic and sauté until golden, about 40 seconds. Add the onion and cook until golden, stirring occasionally, about 8 minutes. Add the bell peppers, allspice, cumin, oregano, and thyme and cook, stirring, for 2 minutes. Stir in the plum tomatoes and the tomato puree. Cook for 8 minutes, stirring. Add the beer, salt, black pepper, and Scotch bonnet or habanero chile, lower the heat, and simmer for 3 to 4 minutes. Add the crabs and parsley and continue to simmer, stirring, for 10 minutes.

Serving: Serve the crabs in a decorative deep platter with sides of white rice, Fried Ripe Plantains (page 183), and plenty of cold beer. If serving outdoors, cover a picnic table with newspapers or plantain leaves and give your guests a river stone or beach pebble to use for cracking the claws.

Cracked Crab Sautéed with Andean Yellow Pepper, Seaweed, and Scrambled Eggs

Reventado de Cangrejo

From Huanchaco to Pacasmayo, in the northern fringe of the Libertad department in Peru, the purple stone crab is cooked in cebiches and other popular dishes like "cracked" crab. The moniker fits, since cooks crack the crab with a stone before cooking it so that it can best absorb the flavor of the sauce, a delicious combination of garlic, red onion, and pureed Andean yellow pepper accented with some cumin and lime juice. What makes the sauce special is the addition of *mococho*, a lacy seaweed in hues of green and purple that gives it a deep briny marine taste. Finishing the dish with beaten eggs might seem odd, but the eggs have a way of binding the sauce and seaweed to the crab as they cook. The whole might look a little messy, but suck on the crab and you will realize that this combination is pure magic.

Cook's Note: My version of *reventado de cangrejo* is inspired by the recipes of three wonderful northern Peruvian cooks: Maria Jesús Viera Isla (Restaurante El Caribe); América Sánchez Pérez, from Magdalena de Cao; and Maximina Villegas, from the fishing village of Huaca Prieta. They all consider *mococho* essential for this dish. I have bought it frozen in Latin American markets and found it to be of excellent quality. The label reads *yuyo*, which is the generic Quechua name for all seaweed in Peru.

What to Drink: Peruvian beer, Pilsen Callao or Cuzqueña

SERVES 4 TO 6

12   large Peruvian purple stone crabs or blue, Dungeness, or Buey crabs (available in Spanish seafood markets)

4   yellow Andean peppers (*ajíes amarillos*), fresh or frozen

3   ounces frozen Peruvian seaweed

½   cup vegetable oil or light olive oil

12   medium garlic cloves, finely mashed with a mortar and pestle or finely chopped and mashed

1   large red onion (about 12 ounces), finely chopped (about 2 cups)

1   teaspoon salt, or to taste

½   teaspoon freshly ground black pepper

Juice of 1 lime (about 2 tablespoons)

3 or 4   large eggs, lightly beaten

Preparing the Crabs ▶ Place each crab on a kitchen towel. Using a sharp paring knife or your fingertips, lift up the crab's apron, pull it back, and break it. Put your thumb under the shell and push it up to separate it from the body. Reserve 4 to 6 shells and discard the rest. Remove the grayish gills at both sides of the apron and discard. Cut each crab in half and rinse under cold water. With a mallet, lightly crush the body, claws, and legs; set aside.

Preparing the Andean Peppers ▶ If using frozen peppers, thaw at room temperature or place in a colander and rinse under lukewarm water. Stem, seed, devein, and chop coarsely. Place in a blender with 2 tablespoons water and process into a fine puree. You should have about ⅓ cup. Set aside.

Preparing the Seaweed ▶ Place the seaweed in a bowl and cover with water to defrost. Drain and pat dry. Cut into 3-inch segments and set aside.

Cooking the Crabs ▶ Heat the oil in a large skillet or lidded 12-inch sauté pan over medium-high heat. Add the garlic and sauté until golden, about 40 seconds. Add the onion and sauté until golden, about 10 minutes. Stir in the pepper puree, salt, and black pepper and cook for 2 more minutes. Add the crab, the reserved shells, and the lime juice and cook, stirring to coat the crab with the cooking sauce, for 1 to 2 minutes. Pour in ½ cup warm water, stir, and cover. Let the crab simmer for 8 to 10 minutes, or until the crab is cooked and has had time to absorb the flavors of the sauce. Uncover and add the seaweed and the beaten eggs. Cook, stirring, until the eggs are set but still soft.

Serving: Bring to the table piping hot on a large platter, propping the shells over the crab bodies for a more colorful effect. Accompany with white rice and Stewed Peruvian Canary Beans (page 511).

Clam, Pork, and White Bean Stew with Smoked Paprika and Garlic Sauce

Cazuela de Almejas, Cerdo, y Frijoles Blancos con Salsita de Pimentón Ahumado

Like a red dress that transforms a plain woman into a siren, a sultry sauce of smoked paprika, olive oil, garlic, and vinegar turns this soothing, homespun stew into something irresistibly alluring. The moment you add it, you will find your hand reaching for a spoon and your mouth begging for a bite. I like to serve the stew in deep earthenware bowls with a crusty bread.

What to Drink: A dry, spicy rosé with backbone, like Montes Cherub Rose de Syrah from Archangel Estate in Marchigüe, Chile

SERVES 6 TO 8

For the Beans
- 8 ounces Great Northern beans (about 1 cup)
- 1 medium yellow onion (8 ounces), peeled and quartered
- 2 bay leaves

For the Stew
- 4 dozen Manila clams, scrubbed and rinsed
- 2 tablespoons extra-virgin olive oil
- 6 garlic cloves, finely chopped
- 1 medium yellow onion (8 ounces), finely chopped (about 1 cup)
- 2 teaspoons hot *pimentón* (Spanish smoked paprika)
- 1 teaspoon ground cumin
- 6 medium plum tomatoes (about 1 pound), peeled, seeded, and finely chopped
- 2 celery stalks, finely chopped
- 2 medium carrots (8 ounces), peeled and cut into ¼-inch dice
- 1 pound boneless pork shoulder or butt, cut into 1-inch dice
- ¼ cup dry white wine
- 1 teaspoon cider vinegar
- 1¼ teaspoons salt
- 1 pound green cabbage, coarsely shredded
- 8 ounces Caribbean pumpkin (*calabaza*) or kabocha or Hubbard squash, peeled, seeded, and cut into ½-inch dice
- ¼ cup finely chopped flat-leaf parsley

For the Sauce
- ¼ cup extra-virgin olive oil
- 6 garlic cloves, peeled and minced
- 1 tablespoon sweet *pimentón* (Spanish smoked paprika)
- 1 tablespoon cider vinegar
- ½ cup chicken broth, homemade (page 538) or store-bought
- ¼ teaspoon salt

Cooking the Beans ▶ Put the beans, onion, and bay leaves in a heavy pot, add enough cold water to cover by 1 inch, and simmer over low heat, adding up to 8 more cups of cold water to cover the beans as they dry out. Never allow the beans to boil. It takes a long time to cook the beans by this Catalan method, but they will come out tender and perfect in shape. Drain and reserve.

Opening the Clams ▶ Place 1 cup water in a large skillet. Bring to a boil. Lower the heat, add the clams, and remove them to a bowl with tongs as they open. Strain the broth and set aside for another use.

Making the Stew ▶ In a large, heavy pot, heat the oil over medium-high heat. Sauté the garlic until golden, about 40 seconds. Add the onion and cook until translucent, about 8 minutes. Stir in the paprika and cumin and cook 1 minute. Add the tomatoes, celery, and carrot, and cook 5 minutes. Add the pork, wine, vinegar, and salt, lower the heat, and simmer, covered, 30 minutes. Add the cabbage, squash, and parsley and cook until the vegetables are soft but still whole, 15 to 20 minutes.

Making the Sauce ▶ While the stew simmers, heat the oil and sauté the garlic for about 40 seconds. Add the paprika and cook, stirring, 1 minute. Stir in the vinegar, broth, and salt. Cook 2 minutes and remove from the heat.

Finishing the Stew ▶ Add the beans and opened clams with their juice to the stewed pork and vegetables. Stir in the sauce and cook over medium heat until the stew is hot, 5 to 6 minutes.

Serving: Serve immediately with crusty bread. A side of white rice is a good accompaniment.

CURANTO: THE CHILEAN EARTH POT

A few years ago, my friend Miro Popiç made arrangements for me to go to the island of Chiloé, off of southern Chile, where a great *curanto* (clambake) awaited me. Unfortunately, a huge Antarctic storm swept southern Chile during my trip, closing airports and seaports, and I was not able to reach the island.

Finally I made it to Valdivia, where I rented a tiny island in the Valdivia River for a day to make the *curanto* of my dreams with a group of fishermen from the larger neighboring island, Mancera. I wanted to do a feast for my Chilean friends Oscar and Maria Eugenia Baeza, who had met me there, and some of Oscar's friends from his days as a medical student at the University of Valdivia. Cooking on an island that thrusts up from the waters like a steep mesa was surreal—digging the pit in the sand; marinating the meats (chicken and pork); making *chapaleles* (potato patties); and lighting the fire with the fishermen and their wives. While we worked, I loved listening to the *curanto* master, Eleuterio Bravo Rivera, tell the story of how he survived the monstrous 1960 tidal wave by riding its crest in his fishing boat.

A *curanto* is actually shorter to do than an American-style clambake. The fishermen dug a shallow 2-foot hole in the ground and filled it with firewood.

Then they placed flat rocks on top and arranged them like roof shingles, with a few branches protruding for lighting the fire. Once the fire became very intense, the stones collapsed into the hole and created a hot lining to bake the food.

The meats and chicken had been marinated and precooked in huge cauldrons over a wood fire in the kitchen, giving them a head start on the fast-cooking seafood. The men also prepared patties made from grated potatoes, which they squeezed in cheesecloth to eliminate excess water. Then came the astonishing variety of fresh mollusks with their forbidding, encrusted shells: clams, *cholgas* (mussels, some as big as a shoe), and burbling *picorocos*. All the ingredients were set down in precise layers separated by *pangüe* leaves, which resembled gigantic acanthus leaves. The earth oven was sealed with burlap and thick rounds of sod. After an hour, the men peeled the layers back. Great plumes of steam wafted into the air, bearing an intense marine smell. I felt I had been transported to an earlier Patagonia, immersed in the cold Pacific and reveling in its fresh, deep flavors. ◆

Chilean Clambake in a Pot

Pulmai

During the summer, on those rare occasions when the sun shines full-force in southern Chile, the people of Valdivia make *curantos* in their backyards and on the nearby beaches. But when a cold rain pours incessantly over this lovely town on the shores of the Valdivia River, the *curanto* is brought indoors, where it is sealed in a pot and becomes a *pulmai*.

This recipe is an adaptation of the wonderful *pulmai* cooked by my Valdivian friend Mabel Corti. Her *pulmai* is a no-nonsense, homespun concoction with no hard-to-find ingredients like *picorocos*, but it is every bit as flavorful as a full-blown *curanto*.

What to Drink: A full-bodied sunny Viña Aquitania Sol de Sol from Traiguén, Chile

SERVES 6

¼ cup extra-virgin olive oil
1 large yellow onion (12 ounces), finely chopped
2 Chilean *cacho de cabra* peppers or dried New Mexican or guajillo chiles, stemmed, seeded, and lightly crushed
2 pounds smoked pork chops
2 pounds pork loin, cut into 2-inch chunks and seasoned with salt and pepper
6 pounds mussels, bearded and scrubbed
2 pounds littleneck clams, scrubbed
2 pounds steamer clams or razor clams, scrubbed
2 pounds Spanish chorizo
6 medium russet potatoes (about 2 pounds)
1 bottle Chilean Sauvignon Blanc
Chilean "Goat's Horn" *Pebre* (page 131), for serving

Browning the Meats ▶ Heat the oil in a large stockpot over medium heat. Add the onion and dried peppers and cook, stirring, for 2 to 3 minutes, until the onions are translucent. Add the pork chops and sear briefly, about 3 minutes per side. Then add the pieces of pork loin and sear for 6 to 7 minutes, until they are brown on all sides.

Assembling the *Pulmai* ▶ Once the meats are browned, arrange the other ingredients in layers over them. First add the mussels, then the clams. Place the sausage over the seafood and top with the whole, unpeeled potatoes. Pour the bottle of wine into the pot. Place a clean cloth over the ingredients. Cover the pot with a heavy lid and secure it with a weight so the steam cannot escape. Bring to a boil. Then lower the heat to medium-low and simmer for about 1 hour. Taste for seasoning. Check the potatoes. When they are done, remove the *pulmai* from the fire.

Serving: In Valdivia, the ingredients of *pulmai* are brought to the table in separate plates so that people can serve themselves. The broth is ladled separately into small soup bowls. As they eat, people spoon the *pebre* over the shellfish and meats. I like to serve *pulmai* as a big soup. I first drain the pot of its broth, since I often make *pulmai* in a stockpot fitted with a spigot. (You can siphon off most of the broth into a small pan using a bulb baster.) Then I arrange the seafood, meats, and potatoes in individual soup plates, pour in the broth, and invite my guests to spoon some of the *pebre* on top.

POULTRY

My family raised chickens and other birds in Cuba, so it was only natural that I would start a little flock as soon as I could here in the United States. In 1975, my husband and I had just moved to Miami and were renting a tiny efficiency apartment in a garage in the southwestern section of the city when my uncle Oscar brought us a scrawny chicken as a gift. He had rescued it from a poultry market and had no idea of its sex or breed. Our landlords, who were from my home region, Oriente, had nothing but encouragement when I asked their permission to raise the animal. She ended up being a lovely and very prolific Leghorn hen—a Mediterranean breed that became the quintessential all-purpose bird in America—and she laid large white eggs all over the backyard.

I named her Clodomira, and every night she slept perched on a wire fence by our front door, leaning on a Chianti bottle covered with straw. Clodo was more like a dog than a bird. She would come quickly when I called her name, strutting happily and jumping up and down like a puppy to catch whatever treat I was holding in my hand for her. One stormy night we found Clodo soaking wet next to her Chianti bottle. We felt so sorry for her that we had to bring her inside. We dried her with a hair dryer and let her sleep perched on the edge of the kitchen sink. That night we truly bonded. She lived a good life. I had sheltered her as a pet and shed tears the day I had to leave her behind with my landlords when I moved to New York. I visited her every time I went back to Miami, until one day I learned she had been sent to a greener henhouse in the sky by a marauding raccoon.

With Clodo I broke an important family tradition. In Cuba, we loved our chickens dearly, but they all ended in the cooking pot sooner or later. I would rather have died than eat my hen. (That's the problem with naming a chicken.) Later, when I moved to New Jersey, I became a more serious chicken keeper, yet I still raised the birds to obtain their eggs and to study their behavior, not for their meat. I moved on to exotic bantam breeds, like the Chinese silkies, with their black skin and soft feathers resembling rabbit fur; the smart and agile Araucanas from Chile, tailless little birds, with tufts of feathers hanging from their ears, that laid lovely blue eggs; and the flighty Penedesencas, a large Catalan breed that laid large chocolate brown eggs like the Marans of France. My Catalan great-grandfather was from Villafranca de Penedès, the town where this breed originated, and remembered them well.

In Latin America, keeping chickens and other types of poultry, such as ducks and turkeys, was and still is as natural as growing fruit trees. Thinking back to the quality and freshness of our eggs and the flavorsome meat of the birds raised in our backyard, I realize how lucky we were. I can't think of more luxurious foods. No wonder that we loved to eat eggs for lunch or dinner with rice and ripe plantains, and that poultry held such a special place in our diet. In Cuba, chicken was kept for special days; for our beloved Sunday lunch, we often ate rice and chicken (*arroz con pollo*); turkey was a treat reserved for Christmas Day and New Year's Eve. This reverence for poultry is shared by other Latin American countries. In Mexico, for example, turkey is feast food, served at weddings, baptisms, and Christmas, but a bountiful chicken soup flavored with chiles is as much a cause of celebration the day after the party as the party food itself.

THE NATIVE BIRDS OF THE AMERICAS MEET THE OLD WORLD CHICKEN

The Spanish conquistadores considered the birds of the New World to be a marvel of nature for their abundance and variety. Flocks of shorebirds signaled the way to land for ships approaching the coast. In the South American grasslands, local birds that the Spanish dubbed "partridges" were so numerous and tame that horseback riders could simply lasso them from their saddles, with a rope tied to the end of a stake like a fishing line.

As the Spaniards explored the lands they would come to call New Spain, they discovered that the Aztecs kept a variety of birds in different stages of domestication. Spanish soldiers entering abandoned towns found turkeys, pheasants, and partridges that the Aztecs had kept in cages. These and other exotic birds like parrots and eagles were sold for food at the spectacular market of Tlatelolco in Mexico. In the emperor Moctezuma's capital, Tenochtitlán, Cortés found the imperial household raising dozens of kinds of waterfowl taken from the surrounding lakes and waterways. Even today what is left of Lake Texcoco is a magnet for migratory waterfowl from all over Mexico, and plans to build new airport runways over their habitat have had environmentalists up in arms since the late 1990s.

People still hunt for wild birds in Latin America, but most of what they eat today is domesticated Old World poultry brought by the Spanish in the sixteenth and seventeenth centuries. The only lasting American contributions to European tables were turkeys and Muscovy ducks.

The turkey (*Meleagris gallipavo*) was the most important domesticated animal of Central America and the one native bird that truly captured the Spaniards' attention. They called the female "the hen of the land" (*gallina de la tierra*) and the tom "bearded rooster" (*gallo de papada*) for their resemblance to European domestic chickens. Bernal Díaz del Castillo, a soldier in Cortés's army and the most famous historian of the conquest of Mexico, often wrote about the large hens the Indians brought as tribute to the Spaniards (causing some confusion among later researchers, who wondered whether chickens could have existed here before Columbus). The conquistador was in effect referring to female and male turkeys.

During the sixteenth century, the Spaniards took turkeys back to the Old World, where they became an instant hit. Europeans began breeding them and incorporating them into their diets, but they greatly misunderstood their origin. The English thought the birds came from Turkey and called the bird "Turkey fowl." The French thought they came from either India or the West Indies and called them *coq d'Inde* (Indian rooster), which was eventually shortened to *dinde*. In Spain, the large bird was mistakenly considered a relative of the peacock and hence named *pavo de Indias* (peacock of the Indies), ultimately shortened to *pavo*. The bird has other names in different parts of Latin America:—*guajolote* in Mexico (from the Nahuatl *uexolotl*), *guanajo* in Cuba, and *chompipe* in Nicaragua and Guatemala.

But it was the Spanish who took the turkey home, bestowed on it rich medieval treatments for chicken and other birds, and brought it back to the New World like a prodigal son. Their synthesis of medieval spices and marinades with native braising sauces such as the Aztec *chilmoles* or *chirmoles* (based on tomatillos, tomatoes, chiles, and pumpkin seeds) brought out the sweetness of the meat. In Latin America today, turkey gets the royal treatment. Turkey in *mole* sauce is a classic wedding and Christmas dish in Mexico. In Guatemala, cooks make great turkey soups for village feasts. In Cuba, turkey often beats out the classic pork for Christmas and New Year's dinners. In Panama, marinated turkey is a filling for special wedding sandwiches.

While turkey reigned supreme in Mexico and Central America, the most important domesticated bird in the Caribbean islands and South America was the Muscovy duck (*Cairina moschata*). As a domesticated species these ducks go back several millennia in South America, and duck is still one of the specialties of the north Peruvian coast, where cooks prepare it in various guises. Scientists consider both the New World Muscovy duck and the Old World wild mallard (*Anas platyrhyncos*) to be the ancestors of all domestic ducks. In pre-Columbian times, wild ducks had a wider geographic range than they do today, ranging from coastal Mexico through Central America to South America, but they were especially important on the Caribbean islands.

At home in Cuba, my father used to raise the same kind of big black, white, or splashed colored ducks that Dr. Chanca, the scientist on Columbus's second voyage, reported seeing kept by the Taínos (Arawaks) in Hispaniola. Our native ducks—*patos criollos*, as they are known in the Caribbean—were handsome birds; especially the males, with their warty red carbuncles, characteristic knobs at the base of the bills, and piercing steely eyes. It was hard not to notice them. They would spend the day flying from one end of the yard to the other, being chased by our pig and our brave Brahma rooster. My father loved to paint them. I remember an extraordinary oil painting he did of a sweet white female and a majestic black drake. Unfortunately, we had to leave it behind when we left Cuba.

The males were my father's favorites and therefore were saved from the cooking pot. But on the rare occasion when he would cook one of his drakes, we rejoiced. The meat of free-range Muscovies is lean and muscular, and my father always braised the duck in a large cast-aluminum pot with plenty of onions, garlic, peppers, and green olives and lots of beer or wine. The duck cooked for a long time, until it practically fell apart. I never knew which I liked better, the duck or the sauce.

When the Spaniards brought chickens to the Americas in the sixteenth century, the native birds were demoted to a secondary position. Even in Mexico, where turkey is still feast food, chicken became the refined visitor that arrived for special days. As in the United States a few generations back, all over Latin America chicken became the food of leisurely Sunday lunches, the meat of choice offered to special guests. This honored position was earned, not accidental. It is the result of the chicken's ingrained versatility, the deep, vigorous flavor of the breeds introduced in the New World, and the way in which they were fed and raised.

Scientists believe that chickens were first domesticated in Southeast Asia about six thousand years ago, not because of their meat or eggs but for sport. Agile and slender and fitted with spectacular long tails, they were used primarily for cockfighting. It was the Greeks and then the Romans who raised these birds for their meat and eggs, disseminating them throughout the Mediterranean basin and Europe. Although archaeologists have found evidence that Polynesians may have introduced Asian breeds to Chile before Columbus, it was the Spaniards who first brought Mediterranean breeds like the White-Faced Spanish, a large chicken with a smooth white face and prominent earlobes, and several types of fighting birds. Asian breeds followed because of commercial contacts between the Philippines and Mexico, and later Peru. The same happened in Brazil as a result of the active trade between Portugal and Asia. This might explain the presence of Asian traits in many South American breeds: naked necks, blue or brown eggs, blue- or black-tinted skin, a pea-shaped comb, feathered shanks, and tufts. The Araucana chicken, which Martha Stewart made famous because she loves their blue eggs, is a cross between two breeds of Asian chickens raised by the Mapuche Indians of southern Chile, the *collonca* and the *quettro*, and was created by a veterinarian in Valparaíso. The Araucana was first imported in the United States and bred successfully in 1930. Today, this breed is better known in this country and Europe than in Chile, and dedicated aficionados strive to preserve them.

In general, the early chicken breeds of Latin America are hybrids of mixed Asian or European and Asian stock. The famous Cuban Cubalaya, a slender fighting cock with shiny black feathers and a long tail, prized for its meat and egg production, is a cross between a European hen and a Philippine fighting cock. During the nineteenth century, Mediterranean breeds like the Blue Andalusian and the Catalana del Prat, much prized for its succulent meat, became popular in Latin America. Later, chicken breeds developed in the United States were even more prized, as they were designed to produce handsome birds with abundant meat and reliable egg production. In every Latin backyard you could find Rhode Island Reds, Plymouth Rocks, and varieties of the Leghorn strutting about with our older breeds.

I still remember our fierce Brahma. We bought him as a chick from the stand of an American poultry feed producer at an agricultural fair in Santiago de Cuba. He was sold to us as an Indian River chick, a fluffy ball colored pink with aniline dye. I later found out that he was really a Brahma, an Asian cross between a Cochin and a Malay that became immensely popular in New England during the nineteenth century. The rooster grew fat and tall, to become the king and guardian of our backyard. We loved him but were terrified of his sharp spurs; he was a menace. Once he attacked my grandmother Paquita, pushed her to the ground, and pecked furiously at her head. He drew blood, and that was the last day of his reign of terror. He ended his days as a stew.

Birds like our rooster had mature, tasty meat that was highly regarded for slow-cooked dishes like soups and stews because it kept developing more flavor the longer you cooked it. This was also true of the laying hens that people would keep to a ripe old age, killing them only when they stopped producing. Today, city dwellers go to great lengths to find the perfect free-range chicken in the live poultry markets, a muscular animal with rich and substantial meat that flourishes in slow-cooked dishes like soups, fricassees, *secos*, and *estofados*. The Hispanic Caribbean big soup, *sancocho*, tastes best with a hen that has had a long, full life. After hours of cooking, it will still hold up sturdily when served. Other Latin chicken classics, like the Central American sweet-and-sour stew called *gallo en chicha* and the Venezuelan "rooster in a pot" (*olleta de gallo*), call for a large old hen or a rooster. An older hen is also the bird of choice for soup (*caldo de gallina*), especially if it is meant for the sick. But for deep-frying, stir-frying, or roasting, and for making chicken salads or subtle delicate soups, Latins like a younger, more tender bird.

In many parts of Latin America, a melanotic (black-skinned) hen is preferred to all others. Like the Chinese, who attribute curative and magical powers to the meat and bones of their black-skinned silkie bantams, Latin Americans believe that the broth from a black-skinned hen is so nutritious that it can literally raise the dead. Having tasted a silkie hen in soup, I can recommend it.

However, the poultry that Latin Americans now eat on a daily basis is almost identical to that found in North American markets. From Juárez to Patagonia, chicken reigns supreme, followed in popularity by turkey, duck, quail, guinea hen, squab, and pigeon. Pheasants are special treats for those who hunt. Goose is consumed in the temperate countries of South America, especially among people of Germanic ancestry.

Some Old World birds that were introduced to Latin America are probably more familiar to cooks there than they are here in the United States. Guinea fowl, thought to have originated in West Africa, were brought to the Caribbean during the centuries of the active slave trade. They are still thriving on the land. I remember them roaming free in Cuba and Puerto Rico, the delicate mottled dark gray and white feathers of a whole flock fluttering against a sea of swaying golden-yellow summer grass as they noisily fled to some nearby guava trees. My uncle Oscar hunted wild guinea fowl on his farm, Sevilla; they were bony birds with firm, very dark flesh that called for prolonged gentle stewing

Latin Americans are also fond of pigeons (we eat both the young squabs and the less tender mature pigeons) and of birds known in Spanish as *codorniz* (quail). The quail we grew up eating are similar to the wild birds found throughout the United States. American quail is a game bird of the type loosely called "partridge." It is not related to European quail, but American settlers thought it resembled the quail back home and called it by the same name. In the United States, the birds are further identified by regional names: bobwhite in the East, partridge in the South, blue quail in the Southwest, as well as California quail, mountain quail, and Montezuma quail.

For farm raising, the preferred bird, however, is usually the Japanese coturnix or pharaoh quail, introduced in the United States around 1870 and now also widely popular throughout Latin America. Supermarket quail is farm-raised, and the meat is more delicately flavored than that of its wild brethren, but it can be cooked like a game bird—roasted, broiled, or fried when young and cooked with moist heat when older. Quail is the rare bird that tastes best when cooked almost rare, but nothing gives me more pleasure than braised or stewed quail, juicy and tender. It is delicious with a side of crusty cheese *arepas*, traditional rice and beans, wild mushroom risotto . . . almost any starchy dish that will soak up the juices.

I hope you will take my recipes as a chance to experiment with birds you haven't tried before and to discover unexpected character in ones you thought you knew. Here you find recipes from all regions of Latin America: braises full of flavor; recipes for pot roasting that keep birds moister and more succulent than when baked in the oven; delightful Dominican-style chicken "cracklings" that will make you a convert of marinating before frying; an opulent Peruvian-style roast turkey marinated with golden *mirasol* peppers and pisco that will add surprise to your holiday table; and everyday recipes that illustrate the Latin American way to create excitement from the simplest ingredients.

WHERE AND WHAT TO BUY

When I was growing up, people everywhere in Latin America either raised or could easily buy poultry that was all the things a natural food enthusiast could desire: organic, free-range, cage-free, antibiotic-free, and the rest of the things that U.S. consumers started hearing about only as a result of the organic and animal-rights movement. Our chickens and turkeys had a flavor that many people in this country will never be lucky enough to experience. The Latin American fondness for keeping poultry meant that cooks would walk into the backyard and pick a bird of the desired size, age, and even sex. Whether it was a tiny 2-pound turkey or a big rooster for dishes requiring a lot of strong-flavored meat, you had plenty of choice.

Unfortunately, Latin markets in this country don't offer that kind of variety in the poultry department. Over the years, the changes I've seen have not all been for the better. As they get bigger and cater to a more mixed—and affluent—population, the *supermercados* often become Americanized, with the same narrow choices of mass-produced poultry you find in any Anglo supermarket. If you don't want to settle for mediocrity and want to find the poultry that will make your recipes taste truly Latin American, learn to look beyond the mass-produced chickens and turkeys in the supermarkets.

One option is to visit a live poultry market catering to an ethnic clientele. Do some looking at farmers' markets, specialty stores, gourmet butchers, and Chinese markets. I especially like shopping for chicken at the Chinese markets, where chickens are commonly sold with the head and feet on (which add to the flavor and richness of soup) and even the

rare black-skinned hens of the Chinese silkie breed are often for sale. If you want to approximate the flavor of a traditional Latin American hen soup or stew, use a tender Chinese silkie hen. You might be startled and slightly put off by the black skin, but the flavor is extraordinary.

Another option is to find out what brands of organic, free-range poultry your local supermarket carries—you might be surprised.

Chicken

If you are new to shopping for poultry beyond "family packs" of breasts or thighs, these are the major categories of chickens used by Latin cooks, in order of size and age:

POUSSIN (*POLLO TIERNO*)

Very young chicken, usually under 2 pounds, used for roasting or for special, delicate soups.

BROILER-FRYER (*POLLO* FOR SMALLER ONES, *POLLÓN/POLLONA* FOR LARGER ONES)

Small young chicken, about 7 weeks old and usually 3 to 4½ pounds; the chicken parts in supermarkets come from cut-up broiler-fryers. They are suitable for frying, roasting, and broiling; they can be used for soups and stews but are not ideal for these recipes unless they have been allowed to range freely. Large Cornish game hens (about 2 pounds) can substitute for the hard-to-find small broiler-fryers. They have become very popular in Latin American markets.

ROASTER (*POLLO GRANDE, POLLO PARA ASAR*)

Medium to large chicken, about 3 to 5 months old and 5 to 7 pounds. They are meatier than broiler-fryers and suitable for most uses, though only free-range birds will give optimum flavor in soups and stews. This is the bird of choice when Latins want to roast a chicken for a large family.

CAPON (CAPÓN)

Castrated male chicken, usually 6 to 8 months old. They are generally found at 7 to 9 pounds and are thought to be the finest roasting bird because of the flavorful but tender meat. Throughout Latin America, a Catalana del Prat capon, a Spanish breed, is reserved for special occasions and served instead of turkey.

FOWL OR HEN (GALLINA)

A female beyond laying age. On small farms, they might reach 3 years or older before being put in the stew pot. In most live poultry markets they are not likely to be older than 1½ years. The usual size is 5 to 6 pounds. Latin Americans use them primarily for soups and stews.

COCK OR ROOSTER (GALLO)

The biggest and toughest of chickens, an intact male. They are hard to find except at live poultry markets or (rarely) ethnic markets, and there is no general commercial standard of age or size. Latins prize the dark, lean, slightly gamy meat for some traditional soups and stews. Every Latin country has particular recipes designed for rooster.

Turkey (*Pavo, Guajolote, Guanajo, Chunto, Chompipe*)

Latin Americans have traditionally liked both chickens and turkeys with more flavor and character than U.S. commercial birds, which are bred for maximum tenderness and huge amounts of breast meat. In many Latin countries, turkey is usually braised, not roasted, whole or cut up. And a turkey of 5 to 10 pounds is nothing unusual. It's really great for

Latin cooks to be able to buy turkey parts, which are available year round in our markets. Legs, thighs, and wings are excellent for the braises and soups that are classic Latin American turkey dishes. When you do buy a whole turkey for roasting, consider looking for an heirloom variety from a small farmer. Sometimes these are not as large as the white turkeys that were developed for the Thanksgiving/Christmas season in the United States in the past forty or fifty years, but they certainly have much better flavor and texture.

Duck (*Pato, Pato Criollo*)

From my years living in the United States, I have learned to cook and love the rich, fatty ducks that derive from the Pekin breed, usually called Long Island ducklings. Because these are the most familiar to U.S. cooks, I have included several recipes based on them. The Long Island birds are not always interchangeable with the New World Muscovy ducks, which grow much larger (growers often market them at a younger age to match the 4 or 5 pounds of Long Island ducklings). But mature Muscovy ducks—especially the males, which can be twice the size of the females—can be as heavy as a small turkey. They are also much leaner and meatier than Long Island ducks. But if you pick birds of comparable size, you can cook one by methods suitable for the other, allowing for the big difference in fat content. (Removing the skin of a Long Island duck is one way to compensate.) Remember that the preferred Latin American method is braising a cut-up bird, not roasting a whole one. The breast will usually be done in about 10 minutes, before the other parts (remove it to a warm place and return it to the pot for a few minutes before serving).

In markets that carry both kinds of duck, Latins will always choose Muscovies. They will never ask for rare breast meat, which I happen to like (I pan-fry or broil the breast separately in dishes like duck cebiche, remove it and carve it when rare, then add it to the pot with the braised parts just a few minutes before turning off the heat).

As lovers of American foie gras may know, the Moulard duck is a sterile cross of the Muscovy and Pekin breeds. Force-fed to produce an enlarged, tender, and richly flavored liver, Moulards are sometimes marketed for their own sake and can be cooked like Muscovy ducks.

Guinea Fowl (*Gallina de Guinea, Guinea,* Spanish *Pintada*)

This African bird is too dry and lean for some North American tastes, but it responds magically to the usual Latin American moist-heat cooking methods. You will usually find birds of 2 to 3 pounds, though the so-called guinea squab (not related to the young pigeons also known as squab) may be under a pound. Because of their extreme leanness, they are wonderful for braising in mixtures that have plenty of lard, olive oil, bacon, or other fat. (I don't think I've had guinea fowl cooked any other way in Latin America.) The hens are tenderer than the drakes. Guineas are always available at live poultry markets; specialty butchers and some gourmet shops will order them for you.

Squab (*Pichón, Pichón Tierno*)

This is the name for young, just-fledged pigeons that have not learned to fly. Several kinds of pigeons have reached the New World from the Old, and others belong to different genera that are native to the Americas. Squabs are a wonderful choice for both braises and soups because the meat is dark,

firm, and well flavored but tender enough to please lovers of the less muscular poultry varieties. They are usually about a month old and weigh less than a pound. Older pigeons, like the doves sought by both North American and Latin hunters, can weigh more and need the classic braising methods.

Quail (*Codorniz, Codorna* in Brazil)

Once the Spaniards got to the New World, they started applying their own names to everything in sight. Things got even more confused when the Old World birds were imported to the Western Hemisphere. Today people who can't get squabs will often look for *codorniz* (the true Old World quail, *Coturnix coturnix*) or some of the similar-sized quail-like birds of the Americas. European quail is often used as a substitute for squab and cooked in the same ways (braised, except for the very small young quails, which can be broiled, fried, or briefly roasted). Quails, or birds of either American or European parentage called quails, are always sold in Latin American live poultry markets. Latins prefer to braise them and hardly ever eat them on the rare side. They are a favorite ingredient for *escabeches* in South America.

A NOTE ON COOKING TIMES

When I began work on this book, I assumed that few people would be able or willing to look for any kind of chicken other than the mass-produced broiler-fryers and roasters in every supermarket. But since then the range of options has broadened quite a lot, as concern over factory-raised poultry has mounted. This is wonderful, but it is important to remind cooks of the many variables in nonstandardized poultry. Timing is a particular problem. Even mass-produced chickens and turkeys can present timing problems, though the usual difficulty in that case is that the breast is done before the dark meat. This is why I usually prefer to cook cut-up pieces rather than whole birds and either buy all legs and thighs or remove the breast about 10 minutes before the rest of the pieces are done.

A 3½-pound supermarket broiler-fryer chicken may have a significantly different cooking time from a 3½-pound free-range chicken, and the various free-range birds may differ just as drastically from each other. Since there is no perfect formula, I've decided to give timings based on a conventional supermarket chicken, with the recommendation that if you substitute any of the superior free-range ones now available, you start testing for doneness at the time given in the recipe and keep testing every 5 to 10 minutes until it is done to your taste.

A NOTE ABOUT ROASTING CHICKEN

Few Latin cooks I know follow the traditional U.S. technique of trussing a chicken and roasting it on a rack. Latin American cooks do not mind if the skin gets a bit soggy in parts, and they are perfectly happy to put a chicken right down in a roasting pan with no rack, so that it will be in contact with its own pan juices and melted fat. I think that by now it will come as no surprise that I prefer braising to roasting, both for chicken and turkey parts and for whole birds. People who want a nice crisp roasted chicken usually buy the spit-roasted chickens that are all the rage in Latin America, sold by restaurant chains in almost every country. They have also become ubiquitous in Latin neighborhoods in the United States. My favorites are the ones in Peru, because they are marinated in a mixture of garlic and Andean pepper before being roasted over a wood fire.

CHICKEN

Deep-Fried Chicken "Cracklings"

Chicharrón de Pollo

Dominicans love chicken that has been cut into small pieces, marinated, and deep-fried until the skin is as crunchy as a pork crackling (*chicharrón*), as the title of the recipe suggests. I think the Dominicans learned this dish from the Chinese storefront restaurants (*fondas*) that are so popular in their country. These small restaurants serve Cantonese food together with Latin staples like rice and beans, and people flock to them for their tasty food and low prices.

The first wave of Dominican restaurants in the United States, particularly in upper Manhattan, Queens, and the Bronx, generally included *chicharrón de pollo* on their menus. For other Latin immigrants, who had a taste for similar crunchy deep-fried dishes, the chicken was familiar and endearing. Nowadays many uprooted Latins make *chicharrones de pollo*, each adding their special touch to the seasoning. This Dominican version seduces with a crispy skin that encloses juicy, tender morsels of chicken, bone and all, seasoned with a garlicky marinade made with bitter orange, cumin, and a touch of soy sauce, which provides the perfect saltiness and depth of flavor. In my experience, you are better off doubling the recipe. Once you start munching on this chicken, your hand will keep reaching for more.

Working Ahead ▶ Cut the chicken into serving pieces and marinate a day before. Keep tightly covered in the refrigerator until ready to use.

What to Drink: Presidente beer from the Dominican Republic or a citrusy Sauvignon Blanc like a Montes Reserva from the Curico Valley, Chile

SERVES 4 TO 6

3½ pounds chicken, either whole or cut up

For the *Adobo*

6 garlic cloves, mashed to a paste with a mortar and pestle or finely chopped and mashed

½ cup bitter orange juice or equal parts lime juice and orange juice

¼ cup soy sauce

1 tablespoon cider vinegar or distilled white vinegar

1 teaspoon salt, or to taste

1 teaspoon ground cumin

1 teaspoon freshly ground black pepper

For the Seasoned Flour

2 cups all-purpose flour

2 teaspoons paprika, preferably sweet *pimentón* (Spanish smoked paprika)

2 teaspoons salt

1 teaspoon freshly ground black pepper

4 cups corn oil, for frying

Lime wedges, for garnish

Cutting up the Chicken ▶ A Hispanic Caribbean or Chinese butcher will cut up a whole chicken especially for this dish. You could also ask your regular butcher to cut it into 10 pieces and then cut it into 24 bite-sized pieces yourself (see page 659). Reserve the back for soup, and be sure to leave the skin as intact as possible for the best crispness. Place in a large shallow bowl.

Marinating the Chicken ▶ In a small bowl, combine the garlic with the orange juice, soy sauce, vinegar, salt, cumin, and pepper. Pour the mixture over the chicken pieces and toss to coat evenly. Refrigerate, well covered with plastic wrap, for at least 6 hours and a maximum of 12 hours.

Frying the Chicken ▶ Scrape the marinade from the chicken pieces; discard. In a deep plate or wide shallow bowl, combine the flour with the paprika, salt, and pepper. Dredge the chicken pieces in the mixture, shaking off as much excess flour as possible. (I do this in a large colander.)

Heat the oil in a heavy medium saucepan over medium-high heat until a thermometer registers 350°F. Add the chicken pieces in 3 batches and fry until crisp and golden brown, 6 to 7 minutes per batch. With tongs, lift the chicken out onto paper towels to drain.

Serving: Serve at once, very hot, with lime wedges, white rice, and Puerto Rican Stewed Red Kidney Beans (page 509).

CUTTING A CHICKEN INTO SERVING PIECES

FOR 8 PIECES

PREPARE THE CHICKEN

Rinse the chicken inside and out with cold water. Pat completely dry with paper towels. Trim excess fat and skin from the bottom opening.

REMOVE THE LEGS AND THIGHS

Place the chicken breast side up on the work surface. Pull one leg away from the body and, with a sharp knife, cut through the skin between the leg and the breast until you hit the joint. Hold the chicken with one hand and bend the leg away from the body with the other, pressing your fingertips into the back of the joint until you pop the ball out of the socket. Continue cutting through the joint with the knife to separate the leg and thigh from the body.

Place the leg and thigh piece, skin side down, on the work surface. Pull the skin back slightly to reveal the thin line of fat that marks the joint. Cut exactly along that line, through the joint, to separate the drumstick from the thigh. Repeat with the other leg.

REMOVE THE WINGS

Turn the chicken breast side down. Hold a wing away from the breast and cut carefully around the base of the wing to reveal the joint. Cut between the bones of the wing joint, then through the skin at the base of the wing, cutting as little as possible of the breast meat. Repeat with the other wing. Remove tips by cutting through the wings at the first joint. Discard the wing tips or save for broth.

REMOVE THE BREAST PIECES

Turn the chicken breast side up. Lift the breast to open the cavity and reveal the ribs. Cut through the ribs on both sides toward the neck, opening the bird as you go and staying as close to the backbone as possible. Cut through the shoulder joint to separate the breast from the back completely. Trim the small rib bones from the underside of the breast. Save the back and ribs for broth or add to a braise or soup for more flavor and body. At home in Latin America, we always add the back to any moist-cooked chicken dish.

Place the breast skin side up on the work surface, with the thickest part of the breast away from you. To divide the breast in half, place the middle of the knife in the V at the top of the breast and cut through the breastbone, pressing firmly.

FOR 10 PIECES

Prepare the chicken as when cutting into 8 pieces. Place the breast halves on the work surface, skin side up. Using a sharp chef's knife or a cleaver, cut each diagonally into 2 equal serving pieces.

FOR 24 PIECES

Prepare the chicken as when cutting into 8 pieces. Place the breast halves on the work surface, skin side up. Using a sharp chef's knife or a cleaver, cut each diagonally into 6 equal serving pieces. Break each wing at the joint and cut through the skin and joint. Place the thighs on the work surface, skin side down. Cut each into 2 equal serving pieces by placing a heavy knife or cleaver in the center of the thigh and hitting it firmly with a wooden mallet until it cuts through. Halve each of the drumsticks in the same manner, cutting away from the center of the bone, through the meatier end. ◆

Quinoa-Crusted Chicken Fingers

Chicharrón Novoandino de Pollo
con Costra de Quinua

In this dish, quinoa plays the part of bread crumbs, only it is infinitely crunchier and more nutritious. I learned this inventive dish from Cucho la Rosa, one of Peru's first practitioners of the pioneering *cocina novoandina* (New Andean Cuisine). These are favorite chicken appetizers at my restaurant Cucharamama, where we season the chicken with Cuban *adobo*. The meat is flavorful and all you need to give it added zest is a squeeze of lime, but our customers are so used to our little table sauces that we came out with a Chino-Latino mixture to please them: a mixture of garlic, Andean *panca* peppers, soy sauce, and a touch of wild oak honey from Cataluña in Spain.

Working Ahead ▶ The chicken can be seasoned and coated with quinoa and allowed to rest in the refrigerator overnight before frying.

MAKES ABOUT 20 PIECES

For the Chicken

- 2 boneless, skinless chicken breasts (about 2 pounds), cut into 3-by-1-inch strips

For the Marinade

- ½ cup fresh orange juice (from 1 large orange)
- ½ cup fresh lime juice (from 4 limes)
- 6 garlic cloves, mashed to a paste with a mortar and pestle or finely chopped and mashed
- 1 teaspoon dried oregano
- 1 teaspoon ground cumin
- 1 teaspoon salt
- ½ teaspoon freshly ground black pepper

For the Quinoa Crust

- 3 cups Simple Boiled Quinoa (page 258)
- ½ cup all-purpose flour
- 4 eggs, lightly beaten

For Frying

- 3 cups corn oil, for frying

Marinating the Chicken ▶ In a medium bowl, combine the orange juice, lime juice, garlic, oregano, cumin, salt, and pepper. Add the chicken strips, toss well, and let rest for an hour.

Coating the Chicken with Quinoa ▶ Spread the quinoa on a baking sheet and place the flour in a medium bowl. Wipe the excess marinade from the chicken pieces and dip them into the flour, shaking to remove the excess. Add the chicken pieces to the beaten eggs and coat well. Roll the chicken pieces in the quinoa to coat well, place on a baking sheet, and cover with plastic wrap. Refrigerate if not frying immediately.

Frying the Chicken ▶ Heat the oil to 350°F in a medium saucepan or deep skillet. Add the chicken in 3 or 4 batches and fry, turning with tongs until lightly golden on all sides, about 3 minutes per batch. Lift out from the oil with a slotted spoon and drain for 1 minute on paper towels. Serve as an appetizer.

Guatemalan Chicken Soup-Stew with Tomatillos

Pollo en Joc'on

In Quiche Maya, *joc'on* refers generically to a cooking sauce. But in this classic Guatemalan dish, the *joc'on* is a slightly tart green herbal tomatillo sauce used to season poached chicken pieces. The color comes from tomatillos, cilantro, and parsley. Some cooks like to throw in lettuce leaves to accentuate the green; I like to add green bell peppers.

Cook's Note: In some regions of Guatemala, *joc'on* also includes vegetables like chayote. Feel free to enrich this basic recipe with the vegetables of your choice. All *joc'on* recipes call for a thickener for the sauce—bread or prepared corn *masa* or flour. I use 2 tablespoons of nixtamalized corn flour because it adds a nutty taste to the sauce. The simplest versions call for grinding the seasoning vegetables to a paste without roasting or sautéing them first. I find that sautéing them in some oil gives more concentrated flavor to the sauce.

Working Ahead ▶ The soup-stew can be made up to 1 day ahead to the point where you add the thickener. Keep refrigerated, tightly covered with plastic wrap. Bring to a gentle boil over medium heat and thicken as directed in the recipe.

What to Drink: Guatemalan Gallo beer or an herbal Veramonte Sauvignon Blanc from Chile's Casablanca Valley

SERVES 6

For the Chicken

One 4-pound chicken, cut into 8 pieces, backbone included (see page 659)

3 teaspoons salt

For the Sauce (*Joc'on*)

3 tablespoons corn oil or mild extra-virgin olive oil

3 garlic cloves, finely chopped

1 medium white onion (8 ounces), finely chopped (about 1 cup)

1 large green bell pepper (8 ounces), cored, seeded, deveined, and finely chopped (about ¾ cup)

12 ounces tomatillos (about 8 medium), husked and coarsely chopped

1 teaspoon freshly ground black pepper

½ cup coarsely chopped cilantro

½ cup coarsely chopped flat-leaf parsley

2 tablespoons precooked corn *masa* mix, preferably Maseca brand, or 1 slice stale white bread, crust removed and finely crumbled

Cooking the Chicken ▶ Place the chicken in a 4-quart pot with 2 quarts water and 2 teaspoons salt. Bring to a boil over medium heat and simmer, covered, until tender, about 20 minutes. Strain the cooking broth; separately reserve the cooked chicken and 3¼ cups broth (save the rest for another purpose).

Making the Sauce (*Joc'on*) ▶ In a 12-inch sauté pan or medium saucepan, heat the oil over medium heat. Add the garlic and sauté until lightly golden, about 30 seconds. Add the onion and bell pepper; sauté, stirring, for about 3 minutes. Add the tomatillos, the remaining 1 teaspoon salt, and the black pepper and sauté, stirring, for about 3 minutes. Stir in 1 cup of the reserved chicken broth. Pour the mixture into a blender or food processor, add the cilantro and parsley, and process to a coarsely textured puree; you should have about 3¼ cups.

Return the puree to the saucepan, stir in 2 cups cooking broth, and add the reserved chicken. Bring to a gentle boil over medium-low heat and simmer, covered, until tender, about 20 minutes.

To thicken the sauce, in a small bowl stir the *masa* mix into the remaining ¼ cup cooking broth, or soften the bread with some of the broth. Stir into the hot stew and cook, stirring, until the sauce thickens, about 5 minutes.

Serving: Serve at once with plain white rice and Fried Ripe Plantains (page 183).

Chicken Fricassee Cuban Style

Fricasé de Pollo Cubano

In Cuba, the name *fricasé* refers to a family of stews usually composed of meats, vegetables, and lots of potatoes and enriched with a garlicky tomato cooking sauce. As in most Spanish-inspired stews, the dish is finished with olives, capers, and raisins.

This recipe is a classic everyday Cuban version that is served with rice and beans, a side of fried plantains (green or ripe), and a salad. Cuban cooks like to use chicken prepared *fricasé* style as a filling for savory pies, empanadas, and croquettes.

Cook's Note: You are likely to find this dish as a daily special in Cuban restaurants in the United States. Most restaurant versions are made with a light tomato sauce. I like my *fricasé* sauce to be thicker and darker, with

more beer and broth than tomato sauce, which I find too acidic. I only make it more tomato-y if I have homemade tomato sauce.

Working Ahead ▶ This dish can be made a day ahead and reheated in the microwave or on the stove when ready to eat.

What to Drink: Hatuey beer, or a Rioja Tempranillo like Sierra Cantabria Colección Privada, or the lively Ribera del Duero Tinta del País Prado Rey Roble

SERVES 4 TO 6

One 3½-pound chicken, cut into 8 serving pieces (see page 659)

For the Seasoning Paste

8 garlic cloves, mashed to a paste with a mortar and pestle or finely chopped and mashed

2 tablespoons fresh lime juice

1 teaspoon ground cumin

1 teaspoon salt

½ teaspoon freshly ground black pepper

For the Cooking Sauce

3 tablespoons extra-virgin olive oil

6 garlic cloves, finely chopped

1 medium yellow onion (about 8 ounces), finely chopped

1 medium green bell pepper (about 8 ounces), cored, seeded, deveined, and finely chopped

1 medium red bell pepper (about 6 ounces), cored, seeded, deveined, and finely chopped

½ cup tomato sauce, homemade (page 48) or store-bought

½ cup lager beer or dry white wine

20 pimiento-stuffed olives

¼ cup capers, drained

¼ cup dark raisins

2 bay leaves

1 tablespoon chopped flat-leaf parsley

1 teaspoon ground cumin

1 teaspoon salt

1 teaspoon freshly ground black pepper

6 large Red Bliss potatoes (about 2 pounds), peeled and quartered

1½ cups chicken broth, homemade (page 538) or store-bought

Seasoning the Chicken ▶ In a small bowl, combine the garlic with the lime juice, cumin, salt, and black pepper. Rub the mixture all over the chicken and refrigerate, tightly covered with plastic wrap, for at least 2 hours or a maximum of 12 hours.

Cooking the Chicken ▶ In a wide, heavy 12-inch skillet or sauté pan, heat the oil to rippling over medium-high heat. Scrape as much of the marinade from the chicken as possible and reserve. Add the chicken to the pan and sauté, turning occasionally, for about 12 minutes, or until evenly browned. Lift onto a plate with a slotted spoon.

In the remaining oil, sauté the garlic until golden, about 40 seconds. Add the onion and sauté until translucent, about 3 minutes; stir in the bell peppers and sauté for another 3 minutes. Pour in the tomato sauce, reserved marinade, and beer and cook for 5 minutes, stirring. Add the olives, capers, raisins, bay leaves, parsley, cumin, salt, and black pepper. Add the chicken pieces, potatoes, and broth. Lower the heat to medium-low and simmer, covered, for about 20 minutes, or until the chicken and potatoes are tender. Remove the bay leaves.

Serving: Serve hot with a side of white rice or any rice and bean combination, like Moors and Christians (page 310); Havana-Style Black Bean Soup (page 507); Fried Green or Ripe Plantains (page 182 or 183); and Avocado and Onion Salad (page 547).

Central American Sweet-and-Sour Chicken Stew

Gallo en Chicha

In this Salvadorian and Guatemalan dish, the fermented pineapple beverage called *chicha* both flavors and tenderizes the meat of a seasoned rooster. This is a lovely sauce with fruity overtones and a pleasant acidity that does wonders for any kind of poultry. It's the same sweet-and-sour interplay found in other colonial Latin American recipes, such as *olleta de gallo*, a Venezuelan rooster stew.

Cook's Note: For best results, you should look for a chicken with more character than the usual roaster-fryers. A fowl for soup is a good choice if you cannot find a live poultry market carrying hens and roosters. But even a more tender chicken will taste great in this recipe if it is a free-range, organically grown bird.

Working Ahead ▶ Pineapple *chicha* is simple to prepare, but you need to do it 2 or 3 days ahead of time to let it ferment properly. If you have no time to make *chicha*, substitute a mixture of ½ cup cider vinegar, 1 cup grated brown loaf sugar, and ¼ cup beer. Stir well to mix.

What to Drink: Susana Balbo Crios Rosé de Malbec or a floral Crios Torrontes from Mendoza, Argentina

SERVES 6 TO 8

For the Chicken

- 1 large fowl or rooster (about 5 pounds) or a 4-pound organic roaster-fryer, cut into 8 pieces (see page 659)
- 1 teaspoon salt, plus more to taste
- 1 teaspoon freshly ground black pepper

For the Cooking Sauce

- 8 ripe medium plum tomatoes (about 1½ pounds)
- 1 large yellow onion (about 12 ounces), unpeeled
- 1 medium red bell pepper (about 6 ounces)
- ½ cup Salvadorian Spice Mix (page 45)
- ¼ cup achiote-infused corn oil (page 89)
- 8 garlic cloves, mashed to a paste with a mortar and pestle or finely chopped and mashed
- 2 cups chicken broth, homemade (page 538) or store-bought, plus more if needed
- ¼ cup grated brown loaf sugar (preferably *panela* or Salvadorian *dulce de tapa*), Muscovado sugar, or packed dark brown sugar
- 1 cup Fermented Pineapple Drink (*chicha*; page 337)
- ½ cup pitted prunes, cut in half
- ¼ cup whole pimiento-stuffed olives
- ¼ cup capers, drained
- ½ cup cocktail onions (optional)

Preparing the Chicken ▶ Rinse the chicken under cold water and pat dry. Place in a bowl and season with salt and pepper. Set aside.

Preparing the Cooking Sauce ▶ Heat a *comal*, griddle, or heavy skillet over medium-high heat. Add the tomatoes, onion, and red bell pepper and roast, turning occasionally with tongs, until lightly charred all over, 8 to 10 minutes. Lift onto a plate. When the vegetables are cool enough to handle, peel the onion and rub off any charred bits of tomato skin. Peel and seed the pepper, cut it into strips, and set aside. Place the roasted onion and tomatoes in a food processor or blender with the Salvadorian spice mix and process to a coarse puree. Set aside.

In a heavy 8-quart pot, heat the oil over medium heat to rippling. Add the chicken and sauté, turning occasionally, until evenly golden, about 8 minutes. Lift onto a plate with a slotted spoon. Add the garlic to the pan and sauté until golden, about 40 seconds. Add the reserved onion and tomato puree and cook, stirring, for about 5 minutes. Return the chicken to the pot and add the broth, sugar, *chicha*, and salt to taste. Reduce the heat to medium-low and simmer, covered, until the chicken is tender. This might take close to 2 hours with a rooster; if you decide to use a supermarket roaster-fryer, it will be done in 45 minutes to 1 hour. Stir the pot occasionally and check the amount of liquid; add a little extra broth if it seems to be evaporating too fast. It should be on the soupy side.

When the chicken is nearly tender, add the prunes, olives, and capers and continue cooking until the chicken is tender.

Serving: Serve in soup bowls, garnished with the reserved fire-roasted peppers and, if you like, cocktail onions, as is done in Guatemala. The classic accompaniment is white rice, but I also like it with Garífuna Rice and Beans with Coconut Milk (page 311).

Grilled "Leaping Frog" Chicken

Pollo Rana a la Parrilla

Argentineans often cut chicken for grilling in a funny shape that reminds me of a leaping frog. Cut in this fashion, the breast and legs cook fairly evenly. This is my favorite way of grilling or broiling chicken for lunch or for a family barbecue. My seasoning is a mixture of my cumin-allspice-scented Cuban *adobo* and typical Argentinean flavorings like *ají molido* (mildly hot ground pepper, available in Latin American stores), oregano, and fresh lemon. Once you experience how moist and flavorful every part of the chicken is after grilling or broiling, you will be hooked.

SERVES 4

One 4-pound chicken, cut "frog style" (see below and page 666)

For the Marinade (*Adobo*)

8 garlic cloves

3 teaspoons Argentinean ground hot pepper (*ají molido*), crushed red pepper flakes, or hot *pimentón* (Spanish smoked paprika)

1 tablespoon sea salt

1 teaspoon freshly ground black pepper

1 tablespoon dried oregano

1 tablespoon ground cumin

¼ teaspoon ground allspice

2 tablespoons extra-virgin olive oil, plus more for basting

1 lemon, cut into ¼-inch slices

Preparing the Chicken ▶ Rinse the chicken with cold water. Pat completely dry with paper towels. Trim excess fat and skin from the opening. Place the chicken breast side up on the work surface. Pull one leg away from the body of the chicken and, with a sharp knife, cut through the skin between the leg and the breast until you hit a joint. Do not cut through the joint. With your fingers behind the joint, bend the leg back until the joint pops. Repeat with the other leg. Lift the breast to open the cavity and reveal the small ribs. Cut through the rib bones (starting from the thigh) on both sides of the breast up to, but not through, the shoulder joints. Turn the chicken so that it lies skin side up on the work surface. Press firmly in the center of the breast with the heel of your hand to crack the breastbone, flattening the breast to the same thickness as the legs and back.

Preparing the Adobo ▶ Using a mortar and pestle, mash the garlic to a paste with the *ají molido*, salt, black pepper, oregano, cumin, and allspice. Add the olive oil and stir to mix.

Seasoning the Chicken ▶ Using the lemon slices, scoop up some of the seasoning mixture and rub it all over the chicken. Using your fingers or a small paring knife, loosen the skin around the breast and thighs and insert the lemon slices and remaining mixture to intensify the flavors. Cover the chicken with plastic wrap and refrigerate, preferably overnight, before grilling or broiling. When ready to proceed, scrape the excess marinade from the chicken and place it in a bowl with some olive oil for basting.

To Grill ▶ Prepare the grill with hardwood charcoal and start the fire. When the flames have subsided but some of the coals are still fiery red, place the chicken on the grill and cook for 5 minutes on each side. Move the chicken to a cooler section of the grill and wait until the coals become ashy. Baste with the reserved marinade-oil mixture and grill until tender and browned on both sides, about 20 minutes, turning occasionally with tongs. If you have a grill fitted with a lid, leave the cover on, with the smoke vent slightly open.

To Broil ▶ Place the chicken on a baking sheet and slide it into a preheated broiler about 4 inches from the heat source. Broil for 20 minutes on each side, starting with the skin side down. Baste with the reserved marinade-oil mixture and finish broiling for an additional 5 minutes, skin side up, until the chicken is golden brown.

Serving: Transfer the chicken to a cutting board and cut into serving pieces. Slice the breast and drizzle with some of the pan juices if broiling. Serve with Guatemalan Red Cabbage Relish (page 150) and a starchy side.

PREPARING A CHICKEN "FROG STYLE"

1. Pull one leg away from the body of the chicken and with a sharp knife cut the skin between the leg and the breast until you hit a joint (do not cut through the joint).

2. With your fingers behind the joint, bend the leg back until the joint pops. Repeat with the other leg.

3. Cut through the rib bones (starting from the thigh) on both sides of the breast up to, but not through, the shoulder joints. Open the chicken, skin side up.

4. Press on the breast-bone to crack and flatten with the heel of your hand.

5. The chicken, flattened.

Spicy Bahian Chicken and Shrimp Stew

Xinxim de Galinha

The combination of seafood and chicken is not uncommon in Latin America. In this terrific stew from Bahia, where Africa meets Portugal with ease and gusto, the shrimp becomes a seasoning for the poultry. As in so many Bahian dishes, the sauce can be fiery, heated by the scorching *pimenta de cheiro*, a relative of the Scotch bonnet pepper and the habanero chile, and is colored a reddish orange with *dendê* oil. Also typical of Bahian stews is the way the peanuts and cashews give body and flavor to the sauce. Bahians love to serve this dish with their loose white rice.

What to Drink: Fresh *caipirinhas* (page 360) or Susana Balbo Crios Torrontes or Crios Rosé de Malbec, both from Mendoza, Argentina

For the Chicken Marinade

One 4-pound chicken, cut into 8 serving pieces (see page 659)

4 garlic cloves, finely chopped

Juice of ½ lime (about 1 tablespoon)

2 teaspoons salt

1 teaspoon freshly ground black pepper

For the Shrimp Marinade

1 pound large shrimp (about 20), peeled and deveined, with tails on

4 garlic cloves, finely chopped

Juice of ½ lime (about 1 tablespoon)

1 teaspoon salt

1 teaspoon freshly ground black pepper

For the Cooking Sauce

2 tablespoons peanut oil

3 garlic cloves, finely chopped

One 1-inch piece of ginger, finely chopped (about 1 tablespoon)

1 large yellow onion (about 12 ounces), finely chopped

2 *pimentas de cheiro* (jarred in brine and drained), finely chopped, or 1 Scotch bonnet or habanero chile, seeded and finely chopped

1 medium green bell pepper (about 6 ounces), cored, seeded, and finely chopped

8 ripe medium plum tomatoes (about 1½ pounds), coarsely chopped

¼ cup finely chopped cilantro

1 bay leaf

1½ teaspoons salt

1 cup chicken broth, homemade (page 538) or store-bought

For Finishing the Stew

¼ cup unsalted roasted peanuts

¼ cup unsalted roasted cashews

1 tablespoon *dendê* oil or achiote-infused oil (page 89)

Marinating the Chicken ▶ Place the chicken in a large bowl. In a small bowl, mix the garlic, lime juice, salt, and pepper. Rub the chicken with this marinade and let rest for at least 30 minutes.

Marinating the Shrimp ▶ Place the shrimp in a large bowl. In a small bowl, mix the garlic, lime juice, salt, and pepper. Pour over the shrimp and toss well. Let rest for 30 minutes.

Cooking the Chicken ▶ Scrape the marinade from the chicken and reserve.

Heat the peanut oil in a heavy 12-inch sauté pan or skillet over medium heat. Add the chicken and sauté until golden brown on all sides, about 12 minutes. Transfer to a plate.

Add the garlic and ginger to the pan and sauté until golden, about 20 seconds. Add the onion and peppers and sauté until soft, about 3 minutes. Add the tomatoes and cook for 5 more minutes. Add the cilantro, bay leaf, and salt; stir to combine. Put the chicken back in the pan; add the chicken broth. Bring to a gentle boil, lower the heat to medium, and simmer, covered, until the chicken is tender, about 30 minutes.

Finishing the Stew ▶ Add the nuts and cook for 5 minutes. Add the shrimp and *dendê* oil and cook for 3 more minutes. Remove the bay leaf.

Serving: Serve hot with Brazilian-Style Simple Pilaf (page 298) or Baked Rice with Hearts of Palm (page 309).

Braised Chicken in Coconut Sauce in the Style of Cartagena

Pollo en Salsa de Coco al Estilo de Cartagena

I learned this dish when staying with friends in Cartagena, an old colonial city on the Caribbean coast of Colombia. As in neighboring Barranquilla, the cooks of Cartagena are fond of cooking with coconut milk, an ingredient as common in coastal Colombia as tomato sauce in the islands of the Hispanic Caribbean. Coconut milk is what gives a silky texture and nutty flavor to the region's famous coconut rice and a number of braised dishes, like this chicken.

As is traditional in this part of Colombia, the ingredients of the *sofrito* (locally called *ahogao* or *hogao*) are all grated by hand. The resulting sauce has a coarse texture. It is up to you whether or not to strain it to obtain a finer texture. This is a saucy dish best served with rice.

Working Ahead ▶ If using fresh coconut milk, prepare it the day before.

What to Drink: Floral and aromatic white wines enhance the inherent sweetness of the coconut milk sauce. I recommend Susana Balbo Crios Torrontes and Tocai Friulano Finca la Anita from Mendoza, Argentina; Torres Viña Esmeralda from Penedès, Spain; or Cousiño Macul Riesling, from Maipo Valley, Chile.

SERVES 4

For the Chicken Marinade

- 8 large garlic cloves, peeled
- 1 tablespoon salt
- ½ teaspoon freshly ground black pepper
- 2 teaspoons ground cumin
- 1 teaspoon dried oregano
  Juice from 1 large lime (about 2 tablespoons)
- 1 tablespoon Worcestershire sauce
- 3½ pounds chicken parts, preferably drumsticks and thighs

For the Cooking Sauce

- 8 medium plum tomatoes (about 1½ pounds), cut crosswise in half
- 1 large yellow onion (about 12 ounces), peeled and cut crosswise in half
- 1 medium red bell pepper (about 6 ounces), cored, seeded, and quartered
- 1 medium green bell pepper (about 6 ounces), cored, seeded, and quartered
- 1 large carrot (about 5 ounces), peeled
- 2 tablespoons extra-virgin olive oil
- 2 bay leaves
- 1¾ cups Creamy ("First") Coconut Milk (page 50) or one 15-ounce can unsweetened coconut milk
- 1 teaspoon salt

Marinating the Chicken ▶ Place the garlic cloves in a mortar with the salt, pepper, cumin, and oregano. Mash to a coarse paste. Stir in the lime juice and Worcestershire sauce. Place the chicken pieces in a large bowl and toss with the marinade. Let sit for at least 2 hours at room temperature, or cover tightly with plastic wrap and refrigerate for a maximum of 6 hours.

Preparing the Dish ▶ Using the coarse side of a box grater, shred the tomatoes, onion, red and green bell peppers, and carrot, placing each in a separate bowl. To shred the tomatoes and onion, hold each half and press the cut side against the shredder. (You will be left with the tomato skin.) Set aside.

Scrape as much marinade from the chicken as possible. Reserve.

Heat the oil in a 3½-quart cast aluminum *caldero* or saucepan over medium-high heat. Add the chicken pieces and sauté, turning with tongs, until brown on all sides, about 8 minutes. With a slotted spoon, remove the chicken from the pan and set aside. Add the reserved marinade and sauté until golden, about 30 seconds. Add the onion and sauté until soft, about 3 minutes. Add the peppers and cook, stirring, for 3 minutes. Add the carrot and cook until soft, about 5 minutes. Add the tomatoes and bay leaves and cook, stirring, until the tomatoes turn light orange and the sauce starts to thicken, about 5 minutes. Add the reserved chicken and cook, stirring, for about 2 minutes to coat well. Stir in the coconut milk and salt and bring to a gentle boil. Lower the heat to medium-low and simmer, covered, until the chicken is fork-tender, 20 to 25 minutes. Remove the bay leaves. For a finer sauce, remove the chicken to a serving dish and force the sauce through a medium-mesh strainer, then pour the sauce over the chicken.

Serving: Serve hot with plain rice such as Ecuadorian-Style Rice (page 295) or Fried Coconut Rice with Raisins from Cartagena (page 300).

Colombian "Sweated" Chicken Stew

Pollo Sudado

What the busy port city of Barranquilla lacks in beauty, it makes up for with the warmth of its people and delicious food like *sancocho*, a hearty soup brimming with tubers, and *pollo sudado*, chicken braised or "sweated" in its own juices. This is an everyday dish that I got to know best through the Lapeira sisters, three Barranquilla natives who worked for me as kitchen assistants and spoiled me with their home cooking. Now retired, they helped me test this recipe. They savored it with approval, even though, following a recipe in Patricia McCausland-Gallo's *Secrets of Colombian Cooking,* I had added mustard and Worcestershire sauce—something the sisters never do. We ate it Barranquilla style, with white rice, avocado salad, and *patacones*, the local cousin of Cuban *tostones*.

Cook's Note: The tiny yellow potatoes are called *papas criollas* (local potatoes) in Colombia; starchy Russet Burbanks do just as well. Though seemingly out of place, the mustard and Worcestershire sauce are favorite Colombian ingredients.

What to Drink: In true Barranquilla fashion, this dish should be paired with a fresh tropical fruit juice; guava juice is an excellent choice. For company, I would add a Spanish Vega Sindoa Chardonnay from Navarra, Spain.

SERVES 4 TO 6

For the Chicken

- 12 chicken thighs
- 1 medium onion (about 8 ounces), finely chopped (about 1 cup)
- 2 tablespoons extra-virgin olive oil
- 2 tablespoons yellow mustard
- 2 garlic cloves, finely chopped
- 2 teaspoons salt
- ¼ teaspoon freshly ground black pepper

For the Cooking Sauce

- 1 tablespoon extra-virgin olive oil
- 2 medium yellow onions (about 8 ounces each), thinly sliced
- 8 ripe medium tomatoes (about 1½ pounds), coarsely chopped
- 2 tablespoons finely chopped cilantro
- 2 tablespoons finely chopped flat-leaf parsley
- 2 teaspoons Worcestershire sauce
- 1 teaspoon salt
- 1 teaspoon ground achiote (page 89), *bijol* (page 89), or turmeric
- 1 chicken bouillon cube, lightly crushed
- 1½ pounds whole small yellow potatoes (about 12), unpeeled, or 3 medium russet potatoes, peeled and quartered

Seasoning the Chicken ▶ Place the chicken thighs, onion, oil, mustard, garlic, salt, and pepper in a large bowl. Mix well and set aside for 30 minutes.

Preparing the Cooking Sauce ▶ Heat the oil in a 12-inch sauté pan or *caldero* over medium heat. Add the sliced onions and sauté, stirring occasionally, until they are soft and beginning to color, about 4 minutes. Add the tomatoes, cilantro,

parsley, Worcestershire sauce, salt, achiote, and bouillon cube and sauté for about 4 minutes, stirring constantly.

Finishing the Dish ▶ Add the seasoned chicken and ½ cup water. Cover and simmer for 20 minutes. Add the potatoes and simmer until they are tender, about 20 more minutes.

Serving: Transfer to a deep serving platter and serve with white rice, Fried Green Plantains (page 182), and Avocado and Onion Salad (page 547).

Cuban-Style Pot-Roasted Chicken

Pollo Asado en Cazuela a la Cubana

Juicier than oven-roasted chicken, this is the chicken that all Cubans crave: moist, succulent, with pan drippings that carry the taste of the garlic and citrus *adobo* that is the hallmark of Cuban cooking. The secret is slow cooking in our beloved cast aluminum *calderos* (see page 33), but any heavy-bottomed pot with a tight lid will do. All you need for a perfect meal is a side of rice or a starchy tropical vegetable puree to sop up the juices.

Working Ahead ▶ As with most Cuban meat and poultry dishes, you can prepare the marinade and season the chicken the day before. Store, tightly covered with plastic wrap, in the refrigerator for a maximum of 12 hours.

What to Drink: Bacardi Hatuey or Mexican Bohemia beer, or a fresh, citrusy Luca Chardonnay from Mendoza, Argentina

SERVES 4 TO 6

One whole 4-pound chicken

1 head garlic, separated into cloves, peeled, and mashed to a paste with a mortar and pestle or finely chopped and mashed

⅓ cup bitter orange juice or equal parts lime juice and orange juice

2 teaspoons salt

½ teaspoon freshly ground black pepper

2 tablespoons extra-virgin olive oil

1 large yellow onion (about 12 ounces), cut into ½-inch slices

1 large green bell pepper (about 8 ounces), cored, seeded, deveined, and cut into ½-inch slices

1 cup dry white wine

1 bay leaf

Marinating the Chicken ▶ Rinse the chicken and pat dry, inside and out. In a small bowl, mix together the garlic, orange juice, salt, and pepper. Rub the chicken with this marinade and let rest for at least 1 hour.

Cooking the Chicken ▶ Heat the oil over medium-high heat in a deep, heavy 8-quart pot or Dutch oven. Scrape the marinade from the chicken and reserve.

Add the chicken to the pot and sauté until golden brown on all sides, about 6 minutes. Remove the chicken from the pot and set aside. Add the reserved marinade and cook until lightly golden, about 40 seconds. Add the onion and pep-per and sauté until the onion is golden but the rings are still whole, about 4 minutes. Return the chicken to the pot, add the wine and bay leaf, and bring to a boil over medium heat. Cover, reduce the heat to very low, and braise for 40 minutes. Uncover the pot and raise the heat to medium-high. Continue cooking until the liquid evaporates and the chicken starts to fry in the remaining fat, about 10 more minutes.

Serving: Cut the chicken into serving pieces and accompany with white rice, Moors and Christians (page 310), or Silky White Yam Puree (page 177) and Cuban Avocado, Watercress, and Pineapple Salad (page 548).

Creamy Peruvian Chicken Stew

Ají de Gallina

This creamy golden stew, one of the most popular chicken dishes of Peru, is a direct descendant of the milk- and bread-enriched casseroles of colonial Latin America. Traditional cooks render the fat of chicken skin to add flavor to the dish, but I much prefer olive oil. In Peru, the dish comes to the table dressed to the nines with a garnish of juicy black olives, boiled potatoes, and hard-boiled eggs. The usual accompaniment is white rice.

What to Drink: Pisco sour (page 356), Rosé de Tacama, a fresh rosé from Peru's Ica Valley, or a Robledo Family Pinot Blanc from Lake County, California

SERVES 6

2 slices (about 2 ounces) white bread, crusts removed

1½ cups whole milk

One 3½-pound chicken, cut into 8 serving pieces (see page 659)

2 tablespoons extra-virgin olive oil

6 garlic cloves, finely chopped

1 large yellow onion (about 12 ounces), finely chopped

1 tablespoon Peruvian *Ají Mirasol* Cooking Sauce (page 53)

½ teaspoon ground dried *mirasol* pepper, homemade (page 54) or store-bought

½ teaspoon salt

½ teaspoon freshly ground black pepper

½ teaspoon dried oregano

2 ounces French sheep's milk feta cheese, crumbled (about ½ cup)

2 ounces Parmigiano-Reggiano cheese, grated (about ¼ cup)

¼ cup shelled walnuts, coarsely chopped

3 hard-boiled eggs, cut in eighths, for garnish

1 small yellow onion, thinly sliced, for garnish

12 Peruvian purple or Kalamata olives, for garnish

▶ Soak the bread in ½ cup milk and process in a blender or food processor to a smooth puree; set aside.

In a wide 4-quart pot, bring 2½ quarts water to a boil over high heat. Lower the heat to medium and add the chicken. Simmer until tender, about 40 minutes. Let cool in the pot. Lift out of the broth; remove and discard the skin and bones. Pull the meat into bite-size pieces; set aside. Strain the broth and reserve 1½ cups.

In a large heavy pan, heat the oil over medium-high heat. Add the garlic and sauté until golden, about 40 seconds. Add the onion and cook until transparent, about 4 minutes. Add the *ají mirasol* sauce, ground *mirasol* pepper, salt, pepper, and oregano and cook for 2 more minutes. Add the bread puree and cook, stirring, for 1 minute. Add the remaining 1 cup milk and the reserved broth while stirring constantly. Cook, stirring, for 10 minutes. Add the chicken, feta and Parmesan cheese, and chopped walnuts. Cook for 2 more minutes, stirring gently.

Serve hot, garnished with the hard-boiled egg, onion, and olives.

Mendoza Boned Stuffed Roast Chicken with a Mustard-Coriander Crust

Pollo Relleno Mendocino "Dominio del Plata"

While staying at the home of winemakers Susana Balbo and her then husband Pedro Marchevsky in the Andean town of Mendoza, Argentina, my husband and I felt pampered. Susana is an exquisite cook, lavishing care on every meal and setting a beautiful table with embroidered linen made by her mother. No wonder the couple hardly ever ate out. During the harvest they had all their meals at a large wooden table set beside a huge picture window overlooking the holding tanks at the winery.

Though her cooking is eclectic, Susana relishes the traditional foods of Mendoza and Salta Province, where she spent several years after graduating as an oenologist from the University of Cuyo in 1981. Knowing of my interest in traditional foods, she treated us to a string of superb regional classics. Our favorite was this partly deboned roast chicken, somewhat resembling a galantine. It had a savory brown crust of mustard speckled with aromatic coriander seeds and was stuffed to capacity with ham, cheese, and fire-roasted peppers, a totally retro combination that Argentineans love. These not only offer a colorful contrast to the chicken's ivory flesh but also flavor it and keep it moist.

Cook's Notes: For this recipe, it is important to use a firm cheese like Gouda or Edam, two Latin American favorites, that will soften but not dissolve during baking.

You will need a trussing needle and thread for sewing up the chicken.

Working Ahead ▶ Bone and marinate the chicken the day before cooking. Also fire-roast the red bell peppers, seed and cut them into strips, and keep refrigerated, wrapped in plastic wrap, until ready to use.

What to Drink: Susana Balbo Crios Rosé de Malbec

SERVES 6

For the Chicken

One 6-pound roasting chicken
6 garlic cloves, finely chopped
  Juice of 1 or 2 lemons (about 3 tablespoons), or to taste
1 teaspoon salt
1 teaspoon freshly ground pepper, preferably a combination of black, green, white, and pink peppercorns
  Lightly crushed rosemary leaves, fresh or dried, to taste

For the Stuffing

1 pound Gouda or Edam cheese (see Cook's Notes), cut into neat 3-by-2-by-1-inch pieces or 1-inch-thick slices
2 large red bell peppers (about 1 pound), fire-roasted (see page 67), cored, seeded, and cut into ½-inch strips
1 pound baked ham, thinly sliced

For the Crust

  Salt
¼ cup Dijon-style mustard
4 garlic cloves, finely chopped
  Lemon juice, to taste
2 tablespoons coriander seeds, lightly bruised

Boning the Chicken ▶ Place the chicken breast side up. Lift up the neck skin to locate the wishbone. Using a boning knife or sharp paring knife, run the knife along either side, pushing it downward to release the wishbone. Pull the wishbone out. Flip the chicken over breast side down. Holding the knife at an angle, run it down the whole length of the backbone, working the flesh away from the bone all around the frame. When you get to the legs, locate the joints on each side and cut to separate them from the main body without cutting through the skin. Find the wing ball joints and cut to separate them as well. Working on one side at a time, continue scraping the flesh away from the frame to release it completely. Remove the frame and open the chicken like a book, skin side down. Cut the wing tips off. Cut around the wing joints and then scrape away the meat to remove the bones; repeat this process with the leg bones, making sure to release the knee joints before scraping the flesh from the bones. Rinse and pat dry. Rub the flesh with the garlic, lemon juice, salt, pepper, and rosemary, inserting the seasonings under the skin wherever possible. Place on a large platter or baking sheet and let rest for at least 30 minutes.

Stuffing the Chicken ▶ Wrap the pieces of cheese and 2 or 3 red pepper strips in a couple of ham slices to form little packages. Arrange all over the cut side of the chicken, inside the breast pocket, layered between the tenderloin and the breast meat, and inside the skin next to the breast. Alternatively, arrange slices of ham and cheese and roast pepper strips in layers over the cut side and inside the breast pocket. Place a cheese package in each of the legs and wings to maintain the shape of the bird. Bring the edges of the skin together to close the chicken, trying to keep its original shape, and sew with basting thread.

Finishing the Dish ▶ Preheat the oven to 400°F. Turn the chicken breast side up. Rub with salt. In a small bowl, combine the mustard, garlic, and lemon juice. Rub all over the chicken, then sprinkle the coriander seeds over it. Let rest for 10 to 15 minutes.

Place the chicken in a large, deep roasting pan and roast, uncovered, for 1½ hours, or until the breast juices run clear when pierced with a fork. Let rest for 10 minutes before carving.

Serving: Carve into thick slices and serve with a tomato and lettuce salad or mashed potatoes.

TURKEY

Alta Verapaz Turkey Stew

Sac-ic de Chunto o Chompipe

In the mountains of Alta Verapaz, in Guatemala, this hearty, fragrant soup-stew is a feast dish. It would be made with a turkey less than half the size of our huge birds; in this country I always use turkey wings or legs. The broth is served in earthenware bowls with a piece of turkey accompanied by cheese-enriched tamales and seasoned with a fresh grating of the favorite local condiment, a cacao-chile mixture shaped into balls and dried.

What to Drink: A fragrant pineapple *chicha* (page 337) or Guatemalan Gallo beer

SERVES 6 TO 8

For the Turkey

- 5 pounds turkey wings or legs
- 2 leeks, trimmed and thoroughly cleaned
- 1 medium white onion (8 ounces), peeled and cut in half
- 1 bunch scallions, white and tender green parts
- 1 bunch cilantro
- 1 bunch fresh mint
- 1 teaspoon allspice berries
- 1 whole head garlic, cut crosswise in half

For the Cooking Sauce

- 12 medium plum tomatoes (about 2½ pounds)
- 1 pound medium tomatillos, husked
- 1 medium red bell pepper (8 ounces)
- 1 large white onion (12 ounces), unpeeled
- 1 whole head garlic
- 1 teaspoon allspice berries
- 1 teaspoon black peppercorns
- One 1-inch Ceylon cinnamon stick (*canela*)
- 1 teaspoon cumin seeds
- 3 teaspoons salt
- 1 teaspoon ground achiote (page 89)
- 1 cup finely chopped cilantro
- ½ cup finely chopped fresh mint
- 2 tablespoons corn *masa* mix for tortillas, preferably Maseca brand
- ¼ cup cold water

Mint sprigs, for garnish
Maya Cacao and Chile Balls (page 76), for serving

Preparing the Turkey ▶ Cut the turkey parts into 10 or so serving pieces. Wash the pieces and wipe clean with paper towels. Place in a large stockpot or large deep saucepan and add 3 quarts water and the leeks, onion, scallions, cilantro, mint, allspice, and garlic. Bring to a boil over medium-high heat, then lower the heat to medium-low and simmer, covered, skimming occasionally, until the turkey is tender, about 1½ hours. Remove the turkey pieces. Strain the cooking broth through a fine-mesh sieve and discard the solids. Return the turkey and strained broth to the pot.

Making the Cooking Sauce ▶ Heat a dry *comal*, griddle, or heavy skillet over medium-high heat. Working in batches, add the tomatoes, tomatillos, bell pepper, onion, and garlic and roast, turning occasionally, until lightly blistered, about 10 minutes. When cool enough to handle, rub away any blackened skin from the tomatoes and pepper. Peel the onion, and garlic and set aside.

Add the allspice, peppercorns, cinnamon, and cumin seeds to the *comal* or griddle, reduce the heat to medium-low, and roast lightly for 1 minute, or until fragrant. Transfer to a platter, let cool slightly, and grind to a fine powder in a spice mill or coffee grinder.

Place the roasted vegetables and spices in a food processor or blender with the salt and achiote and process to a puree. Stir into the turkey broth with the chopped cilantro and mint.

Dissolve the *masa* mix in the cold water. Stir into the broth and simmer, stirring, until the broth has thickened to the consistency of a light cream soup.

Serving: Serve at once, garnished with sprigs of mint. It is traditionally partnered with Guatemalan White Corn Cheese Tamales (page 460). You can also serve it with a side of white rice or Mexican Corn Tortillas (page 579). Bring the cacao-chile balls to the table in a bowl and pass around with a small cheese grater, so everyone can grate some over the stew to taste.

Turkey Meatballs in Yucatecan Black Sauce

Albóndigas de Pavo en Relleno Negro

Yucatecan cuisine revels in the chthonic. Cooks bury foods in underground ovens to steam them with the flavors of the earth. Black sauces anoint turkey dishes, and black is the color of the region's most exciting condiment, an extravagantly aromatic seasoning paste known as *recado negro* (black *recado*). Its dark hue comes from small dried red chiles (known simply as *chiles secos*) that are roasted on a *comal* or burned with alcohol until they are mercilessly carbonized. Little remains of the chile flavor with this treatment except a subtle taste of smoked paprika and some residual heat, but this is the only way to get the *recado* truly black.

I learned to prepare the *recado* in Cholol, a town not far from Mérida, and that experience took care of my skepticism about eating charcoal. A friend needed to make a large batch of *recado* to season *pavo en relleno negro* (turkey in black stuffing), one of the most popular turkey dishes in the Yucatán. After igniting several pounds of *chiles secos* with alcohol in her backyard (which sent me running for cover) and reducing them to charred bits, she ground them to a black paste with half a dozen charred seasoning vegetables and toasted spices. She deftly used some of the paste to season the stuffing of the turkey, a mixture of pork and hard-boiled eggs that she shaped into a large ball, and dissolved the rest in a flavorful chicken broth. Once the turkey was stuffed and sewn, she plunged it into a pot brimming with the seasoned broth. The pot was then wrapped in banana leaves and handed to a local man who specialized in roasting in a *pib*, an underground oven that works as a big steamer. The man buried the pot in the *pib* and steamed it for several hours. The turkey was tender and succulent, but I was more interested in the stuffing and the sauce, which were extraordinary. No wonder the stuffing is often cooked separately; people enjoy it more than the turkey.

When I got back home, I began to explore the enormous possibilities of this world-class seasoning paste. This is one of the fruits of my experiments, turkey meatballs cooked in a pitch-black *recado negro* that you cannot stop eating. They are easier to cook and serve than a whole turkey, and they combine the idea of the turkey and its stuffing in a single savory mouthful.

Cook's Note: You can use any good chicken broth in this recipe, but the *salpimentado* that is the base of Yucatecan *Lima* Soup (page 536) is guaranteed to raise good to fantastic. Yucatecan *chiles secos* are not available in the United States, but I've had good results with ancho chiles, which are readily available in most Hispanic markets. To approximate the flavor of the Yucatecan chiles, I like to add a pinch of smoked paprika to the sauce.

Working Ahead ▶ The recipe looks difficult because of its many steps, but this is a dish that should be done in stages. The *recado negro* can be prepared 2 to 3 weeks ahead of time and kept refrigerated. The turkey meatballs and the aromatic Yucatecan chicken broth can be assembled the day before.

What to Drink: A silky yet robust red with notes of dried fruits and chocolate, like Les Eres Vinyes Velles from Priorat, Catalonia, or a complex Susana Balbo Malbec from Mendoza, Argentina

For the *Recado Negro*

- 8 ancho chiles (about 4 ounces), stemmed
- 1 cup *salpimentado* (page 536) or any flavorful chicken broth, homemade (page 538) or store-bought
- 1 medium white onion (8 ounces), unpeeled
- 1 head garlic, unpeeled
- 5 medium plum tomatoes (about 1 pound)
- 1 tablespoon black peppercorns
- 1 tablespoon allspice berries
- 1 tablespoon cumin seeds
- One 3-inch Ceylon cinnamon stick (*canela*)
- 5 whole cloves
- 1 tablespoon dried oregano
- 2 teaspoons dried epazote or 3 fresh epazote sprigs
- ½ teaspoon *pimentón* (Spanish smoked paprika, hot or sweet)
- 2 tablespoons ground achiote (page 89)

For the Black Sauce

- 4½ cups *salpimentado* or any flavorful chicken broth, homemade or store-bought
- 1½ cups *recado negro*
- ¼ cup corn *masa* mix, preferably Maseca brand
- ¼ cup cold water or broth

For the Turkey Meatballs

- 2½ pounds ground turkey
- ½ cup *recado negro*
- ¼ teaspoon ground Ceylon cinnamon (*canela*)
- 1 small day-old French roll or 2 slices stale bread
- ½ cup *salpimentado* or any other flavorful chicken broth, homemade or store-bought
- 3 hard-boiled eggs, cut into eighths
- 2 tablespoons mild extra-virgin olive oil

Making the *Recado Negro* ▶ Heat a dry *comal*, griddle, or heavy skillet over high heat. Add the chiles and roast, turning occasionally with tongs, until deeply charred, about 4 minutes. (Open your kitchen door and windows, because the caustic fumes of the burning chiles can irritate your eyes.) Place the blackened chiles in a bowl, cover with the broth, and soak, turning occasionally with a spoon, for about 10 minutes, until softened.

While the chiles soak, place the onion, garlic, and tomatoes on the *comal* or griddle over high heat and roast, turning occasionally with tongs, until charred all over, about 10 minutes. When they are cool enough to handle, peel the garlic and onion and quarter the tomatoes. Lightly toast the peppercorns, allspice, cumin, cinnamon, cloves, and oregano. Let cool slightly and grind in a spice mill or a coffee grinder.

If using dried epazote, soak in ¼ cup warm water to soften, about 5 minutes, and drain. Place the ground spices, roasted vegetables, chiles with their soaking broth, paprika, ground achiote, and epazote in a blender or food processor and process to a fine puree. You should have about 3½ cups. It will keep well, stored tightly covered in the refrigerator, for 2 to 3 weeks.

Making the Black Sauce ▶ In a mixing bowl, combine the broth with the 1½ cups *recado negro*. Strain through a medium-mesh sieve, pushing with the back of a spoon to force through as much as possible. Pour into a medium saucepan and bring to a gentle boil over medium heat. In a small bowl, mix the *masa* mix to a paste with the water or broth. Whisk into the sauce and simmer, stirring frequently, for 15 minutes, or until the sauce is slightly thickened. Set aside while you make the meatballs.

Making the Meatballs ▶ In a medium bowl, combine the ground turkey with the ½ cup *recado negro* and the cinnamon. Toast the bread to a very dark brown, break it into very small pieces, and puree in a blender or food processor with the broth. Add to the turkey mixture, combine thoroughly, and refrigerate, covered with plastic wrap, for at least 20 minutes (this makes the meatballs easier to shape).

Scoop out 3 heaping tablespoons of the turkey mixture (about 2 ounces) and shape into a ball. Flatten it between the palms of your hands and place a wedge of hard-boiled egg in the center. Shape neatly into a ball around the egg. Repeat, using all the ground turkey and egg pieces.

In a 12-inch sauté pan, heat the oil over medium-high heat until sizzling. Add the meatballs and sauté, turning, for 1 to 2 minutes. Pour the black sauce over the meatballs and simmer for 15 minutes.

Serving: Serve with Yucatecan Saffron Rice (page 301), Yucatecan Refried Beans (page 276), Mexican Corn Tortillas (page 579), and a spoonful of Yucatecan Red Onions Pickled in Bitter Orange Juice (page 149).

A LATIN AMERICAN THANKSGIVING MENU

My first Thanksgiving dinner in the United States was in 1970; my family had been in Miami only four months, staying with relatives. I was in no mood to celebrate. The pain of leaving behind my beloved aunts, grandmother, and boyfriend was compounded by the seeming unfriendliness of our new neighborhood. Still, the golden turkeys of television commercials and magazine ads beckoned, reminding me of our traditional New Year's feasts back in Cuba. More poignantly, the story of the Pilgrims began to resonate in my mind as a symbol of hope in the face of our own tribulations.

Like most newcomers to this country, we turned Thanksgiving into a hybrid feast. Accustomed to selecting a muscular turkey from our own backyard flock, we succumbed to the easy charm of a plump-breasted Butterball turkey from the supermarket, which we dutifully defrosted and marinated Cuban style with plenty of garlic and bitter orange juice. Instead of braising the turkey in a large cauldron, as we had often done back home, we roasted it in the oven. We served it with *congrí*, the rice and red kidney bean dish traditional to Santiago de Cuba, plus canned yams and cranberry sauce—concessions to what we considered true Thanksgiving fare that also satisfied our Cuban penchant for mixing sweet and sour flavors.

Teary-eyed, we toasted our good fortune and those we had left behind with Spanish cider, a Cuban Christmas tradition. I felt a surge of gratitude for the roof over my head, and for the first time since our arrival, I lightened up with a real sense of optimism. That same night, as we cleared the table, we got news that the man who is now my husband had managed to swim across Guantánamo Bay to the U.S. naval base and freedom.

Since that day, Thanksgiving has symbolized crossover and arrival for my husband and me. Wherever we happen to be, we gather with family or friends (or both) for a heartfelt feast. The canned stuff has been replaced by fresh sweet potatoes and cranberries, but our menu continues to be a paean to the best of two worlds, with foods rooted in history and tradition.

I usually gravitate toward the Cuban *adobo* of my hometown and family, with its emphatic aroma of cumin, oregano, and allspice, but I have come to love other Latin ways of seasoning turkey. I have grown fond of the vibrant mixture of golden *mirasol* peppers, garlic, and cumin in Peruvian cooking sauces and marinades.

A quicker alternative, though no less tasty, is a succulent casserole of marinated dark turkey meat cut into bite-sized pieces and braised with tropical vegetables in the oven. This is not only a time-saving idea (the meats and the vegetables cook together) but a nod to the Latin American tradition of cooking turkey parts.

To round out the meal, I like to serve foods that conjure up the bounty of the season, like a small version of *arepas* (page 583) and a *Calabaza* and Grilled Pineapple Salad (page 559). Rice is never absent, and I usu-ally use heart of palm, a native American vegetable, in Baked Rice with Hearts of Palm (page 309). And in addition to cranberry sauce, I often serve Peruvian Purple Corn and Fruit Compote (page 826).

For me, the beauty of the holiday table lies in the merging of ingredients and traditions, in the homey casseroles and the sweet-and-sour pairings of the traditional American Thanksgiving presented in fresh guises. For my family, this is the quintessential crossover feast, the yearly marker of who we were, who we have become, where we have been, and where we are going. ◆

Roast Turkey in Andean Pepper and Pisco *Adobo* with Roast Plantains and Sweet Potatoes

Pavo en Adobo de Ají Mirasol y Pisco con Plátanos y Camotes Asados

A golden Peruvian *adobo* of Andean *mirasol* peppers, garlic, and cumin gives roast turkey a delicious boost of flavor and a lovely copper patina. This is one of my favorite recipes for turkey.

Working Ahead ▶ Prepare the hot pepper marinade and season the turkey a day before; keep refrigerated, tightly covered with plastic wrap, until ready to roast.

What to Drink: Crios Syrah-Bonarda or Tikal Bonarda from Mendoza, Argentina

SERVES 8 TO 10

For the Turkey

One 15- to 20-pound fresh turkey, preferably organic
1 tablespoon salt

For the *Adobo*

12 dried *mirasol* peppers, stemmed and seeded
3 heads garlic, separated into cloves and peeled
1 cup bitter orange juice or equal parts lime juice and orange juice
1 tablespoon ground cumin
1 teaspoon ground allspice
¼ cup coarsely chopped cilantro
½ cup achiote-infused extra-virgin olive oil (page 89)
¼ cup pisco, preferably *pisco italia*
1 cup chicken broth, homemade (page 538) or store-bought

6 half-ripe plantains, unpeeled (about 3 pounds), cut into 3 pieces each
6 sweet potatoes, quartered
2 teaspoons cornstarch
¼ cup cold water

Preparing the Turkey ▶ Wipe the turkey clean with paper towels and rub with 1 tablespoon salt. Set aside.

Making the *Adobo* ▶ Bring 2 quarts water to a boil in a medium saucepan. Add the dried peppers and simmer until soft and plump, about 15 minutes. Drain the peppers and place in a blender or food processor with the garlic, bitter orange juice, cumin, allspice, cilantro, oil, and pisco. Process to a coarse puree. Rub the mixture all over the turkey, inside and out. Place on a large nonreactive platter or pan, cover with plastic wrap, and refrigerate overnight.

Roasting the Turkey ▶ Preheat the oven to 350°F. Transfer the turkey to a large, deep ovenproof pot of at least 12-quart capacity, preferably a Latin *caldero* (page 33). Add the broth, cover with aluminum foil, and roast on the floor of the oven for 2½ hours. Remove the foil and arrange the plantains and sweet potatoes around the turkey; replace the foil and roast for another 30 minutes. Remove the foil and roast for 1 more hour, basting frequently with the pan juices.

Making the Gravy ▶ Remove the turkey to a carving board or platter. Pour the pan juices into a small saucepan and bring to a boil over medium heat. In a small bowl, mix the cornstarch to a paste with the water. Stir the mixture into the juices and cook, stirring, until the gravy thickens. Pour into a sauceboat and bring to the table with the turkey.

Serving: Serve the carved turkey with the roasted plantains and sweet potatoes, Sautéed Quinoa with Swiss Chard (page 258), and Spicy Bolivian Table Sauce (page 117).

DUCK AND OTHER BIRDS

Grilled Duck Breast with Tamarillo and Pink Peppercorn Sauce

Pechuga de Pato a la Parrilla con Salsa de Tomate de Árbol y Bayas Rosadas

I adore pan-seared duck breast, with its crisp skin, and find that it blossoms with fruit sauces that are not cloyingly sweet but rich with personality. (This is one case where I prefer Long Island duck to the more muscular Muscovy.) My favorite fruit for this purpose is the elegant Andean tamarillo (tree tomato). Tamarillos are beautiful, with an aerodynamic egg shape and smooth skin in gorgeous shades of red or yellow. They are also intensely flavorful, with the acidity of a good ripe tomato and a kind of bittersweet backbone that places them in a special category between fruit and vegetable. I use them in many recipes in place of tomatoes, and love them in shrimp cebiches, in spicy sauces for calamari, poached like pears for dessert, in marmalades, in marinades for pork and chicken, in cocktails and juices, and in sauces for duck.

I am smitten with the mustard-yellow flesh of yellow tamarillo and the deep crimson flesh of the red ones. I use both. Combined with the aromatic pink peppercorns that grow wild in Venezuela and other parts of Latin America, they make a superb foil for grilled and broiled game dishes, especially duck and venison.

Cook's Note: It seems that the quickest way for a Latin American fruit to cross into North American markets is to be picked up by savvy farmers from New Zealand. The fresh tamarillos one buys in North American markets are a long-standing specialty in New Zealand, and *tamarillo* is a name that the New Zealand growers invented for marketing purposes—a cross between *tomato* and *tomatillo*. In Latin America the fruit is mostly known as *tomate de árbol* (tree tomato). The red variety grows chiefly in Colombia and cold parts of Venezuela. In the Colonia Tovar, a wooded mountain community not far from Caracas, descendants of German immigrants raise it in beautifully tended gardens and farms. Ecuadorians prefer the golden-fleshed tamarillo.

What to Drink: An opulent Susana Balbo or Catena Zapata Malbec from Mendoza, Argentina

SERVES 6

For the Duck

6 boneless Long Island duck breasts (about 8 ounces each), with skin
Salt and freshly ground black pepper
¼ teaspoon dried thyme
6 garlic cloves, mashed to a paste with a mortar and pestle or finely chopped and mashed
1 tablespoon fresh lime juice

For the Tamarillo Sauce

12 golden or red tamarillos, fresh or frozen
4 ounces brown loaf sugar, preferably *papelón* or *panela,* grated (about 1 cup), or Muscovado sugar or packed dark brown sugar
1 tablespoon pink peppercorns, plus more for garnish
⅛ teaspoon dried thyme
5 allspice berries

1 whole clove
½ Ceylon cinnamon stick (*canela*)

1 cup fresh orange juice
Fresh mint, for garnish

Seasoning the Duck Breasts ▶ Rinse the duck breasts and pat them dry. Score shallow cross-hatches in the skin with a small sharp knife. In a small bowl, mix salt and pepper to taste; add the thyme, garlic, and lime juice and mix. Rub the mixture all over the duck. Let sit for at least 1 hour.

Preparing the Tamarillo Sauce ▶ If using fresh tamarillos, plunge them into 2 cups boiling water, cook for 1 minute, drain, and peel. If using frozen ones, simmer in water until soft, about 10 minutes, drain, and peel. Place in a food processor or blender and process to a fine puree.

Pour the tamarillo puree into a medium saucepan and add the sugar, pink peppercorns, thyme, allspice, clove, cinnamon, and orange juice. Bring to a gentle boil over medium heat and simmer until the sauce has thickened slightly, 15 to 20 minutes. Strain and set aside.

Cooking the Duck Breasts ▶ Heat a large, heavy dry skillet over medium-high heat. Scrape the seasoning from the duck breasts. Add the duck to the pan, skin side down, and cook until the skin is brown and crisp. Turn and cook for 1 minute longer. Remove to a cutting board and slice at an angle.

Serving: Ladle some of the tamarillo sauce onto each of 6 dinner plates and arrange the sliced duck over it. Serve garnished with pink peppercorns and sprigs of mint. The dish goes well with Spiced *Arracacha* Puree (page

216) or Simple Peach Palm Fruit Puree (page 194). It is also delicious with Sautéed Quinoa with Swiss Chard (page 258) or Mountain Quinoa (page 260).

Peruvian Braised Duck "Cebiche"

Cebiche de Pato

Peruvians make duck and chicken braises that they call cebiches. They are not technically cebiches, since they are cooked to perfection, but the meat is braised in a spicy cooking sauce enlivened with citrus juice, just like a cebiche. I like to serve this dish lukewarm or at room temperature. You can use Long Island duck if you are unable to find Muscovy.

SERVES 6

For the *Mirasol* Pepper Paste
- 2 ounces dried *mirasol* peppers (about 8 peppers), seeded

For the Marinade
- 6 garlic cloves, mashed to a paste with a mortar and pestle or finely chopped and mashed
- ½ cup fresh orange juice
- ½ cup fresh lime juice (from about 4 limes)
- 1 teaspoon dried oregano
- 1 teaspoon ground cumin
- 1 teaspoon salt
- ½ teaspoon freshly ground black pepper
- One 4-pound Muscovy duck, cut into 12 serving pieces (see Cutting a Chicken into Serving Pieces, page 659)

For Braising
- ¼ cup extra-virgin olive oil
- 6 garlic cloves, finely chopped
- 1 small red onion (6 ounces), finely chopped
- ¼ cup pisco, preferably *pisco italia* or *acholado*
- ¼ cup chicken broth, homemade (page 538) or store-bought
- ¼ cup fresh orange juice
- ¼ cup fresh lime juice (from about 2 limes)
- 1 medium red onion (about 8 ounces), finely slivered lengthwise

- 2 tablespoons finely chopped cilantro, for garnish

Making the *Mirasol* Pepper Paste ▶ Place the *mirasol* peppers in a small saucepan and cover with 2 cups water. Bring to a boil over medium heat and cook until soft, 10 to 15 minutes. Drain and let cool. In a food processor or blender, process the peppers into a smooth puree. Set aside.

Marinating the Duck ▶ In a large bowl, mix the garlic, orange and lime juices, 1 tablespoon of the *mirasol* pepper paste, oregano, cumin, salt, and black pepper. Add the duck and toss to coat well; let rest for at least 2 hours, covered with plastic wrap.

Braising the Duck ▶ Scrape the excess marinade from the duck pieces; reserve. Heat the oil in a large 12-inch sauté pan or deep skillet over medium heat, add the duck pieces, and sauté without browning for 3 minutes on each side. Lift from the pan and set aside.

Add the garlic to the pan and sauté until golden, about 40 seconds. Add the onion and cook until translucent, about 3 minutes. Add the remaining *mirasol* pepper paste and cook, stirring, for 2 more minutes. Add the reserved marinade, pisco, and broth and bring to a boil. Add the duck pieces, lower the heat, cover, and cook until tender, about 45 minutes.

Remove the duck to a hot serving dish. Add the orange juice, lime juice, and slivered onion to the pot and cook, stirring, for 10 seconds.

Serving: Pour the hot sauce over the duck pieces. Sprinkle with chopped cilantro and serve with Boiled Yuca (page 167) and boiled potato chunks.

Braised Muscovy Duck with Prunes and Olives

Pato Criollo Asado en Cazuela con Ciruelas y Aceitunas

This was one of my father's favorite ways of roasting our beautiful backyard *patos criollos*—Muscovy ducks—in a blackened cast-aluminum *caldero*, flavored with dried prunes, briny olives, and sweet wine. This lovely combination of flavors, enhanced by the aroma of allspice and cumin and the bittersweet tang of Seville orange juice, brings out the sweetness and richness of the duck. This belongs to the family of braises where the main ingredient ends by browning in its own fat, leaving behind deeply concentrated pan juices.

What to Drink: Vértice Vinho Tinto from Portugal or Ben Marco Malbec from Mendoza

SERVES 4

For the Marinade

- 1 head garlic, separated into cloves, peeled, and mashed to a pulp with a mortar and pestle
- 1½ teaspoons salt
- 1 teaspoon freshly ground black pepper
- ½ teaspoon ground cumin
- ½ teaspoon ground allspice
- ⅓ cup bitter orange juice (from 2 oranges) or equal parts lime juice and orange juice
- One 3½- to 4-pound young Muscovy duck, cut into 8 serving pieces (see Cutting a Chicken into Serving Pieces, page 659), or 8 legs and thighs

For the Cooking Sauce

- 2 tablespoons extra-virgin olive oil
- 1 large yellow onion (about 12 ounces), cut into ½-inch slices
- 2 large green bell peppers (about 1 pound), cored, seeded, deveined, and cut into ½-inch slices
- 1 cup ruby port
- 1 cup pitted prunes, cut in half
- 1 cup pimiento-stuffed olives

Marinating the Duck ▶ In a large bowl, combine the garlic, salt, black pepper, cumin, allspice, and orange juice. Toss the duck pieces with this marinade and let rest for at least 1 hour.

Cooking the Duck ▶ Scrape the marinade from the duck pieces and reserve. Heat the oil in a large, heavy skillet or sauté pan over medium-high heat. Add the duck and sauté until brown, about 8 minutes on each side. Lift out of the pot and set aside. Drain the fat from the pan, reserving ¼ cup.

Add the reserved marinade and sauté about 40 seconds. Add the onion and bell peppers and cook until soft, about 4 minutes. Put the duck pieces back in the pan, add the port, and bring to a gentle boil; reduce the heat to medium-low, cover, and cook for 25 minutes. Add the prunes and olives and continue cooking until the duck is tender, about 1 hour and 20 minutes. Uncover the pot, raise the heat to medium-high, and cook until the liquid evaporates and the duck starts to fry in the remaining fat, about 5 more minutes.

Serving: Serve with Moors and Christians (page 310), Colombian-Style Rice with Caribbean Pumpkin (page 303), or a plantain puree (pages 185–87) and Guatemalan Radish Salad (page 556).

Quail in Almond Sauce

Codornices en Salsa de Almendra

The aromatic almond sauces of Spanish medieval cooking flourished in the New World and became a standard fixture of colonial kitchens everywhere. In this Mexican recipe, a rich almond sauce is elegantly paired with quail.

What to Drink: Bodegas Aldial Naia Verdejo from Rueda, Spain, or a Piedra de Sol Blanco, a Chardonnay from the Casa de Piedra winery in the Guadalupe Valley in Baja California

SERVES 6

2 tablespoons extra-virgin olive oil
6 quail (3–4 ounces each), cleaned
4 ounces slab bacon, finely diced
5 garlic cloves, finely chopped
1 medium white onion (8 ounces), peeled and thinly slivered lengthwise
2 bay leaves
Salt to taste
1 teaspoon freshly ground black pepper, plus more to taste
1 teaspoon ground cumin
¼ teaspoon ground cloves
¼ teaspoon ground allspice
1 cup dry sherry
3 cups chicken broth, homemade (page 538) or store-bought
About 2 ounces blanched almonds, lightly toasted
1 hard-boiled egg yolk
¼ cup pomegranate seeds, for garnish (optional)

▶ In a 12-inch sauté pan or skillet, heat the olive oil over medium heat. Add the quail and brown, turning occasionally, for 3 minutes. Remove the quail from the pan and set aside.

Add the bacon and sauté until golden and slightly crisp, about 8 minutes. Add the garlic and onion and sauté until the onion is translucent, about 5 minutes. Add the bay leaves, salt, and spices and cook until they are fragrant, about 1 minute. Stir in the sherry and chicken broth. Add the quail and simmer for 10 minutes.

Meanwhile, grind the almonds and egg yolk to a coarse paste in a food processor. Stir the mixture into the sauce and cook, stirring, for 10 minutes, until the quail is tender and the sauce is rich and thick. Thin the sauce with some broth or water if it becomes too thick. Remove the quail from the pan and set aside, and remove the bay leaves from the sauce.

Serving: Ladle the sauce onto a large serving platter and arrange the quail on it. In colonial times, a sauce like this would have been garnished with hard-boiled eggs, but I like the contrasting touch of pomegranate seeds instead. Serve with a silky plantain puree (pages 185–87) or Colombian-Style Rice with Caribbean Pumpkin (page 303).

Quail Escabeche "La Serena"
Codornices en Escabeche

When the Popiç family arrived in La Serena, a small coastal town north of Santiago de Chile, they made a commitment to their new country but vowed to preserve many of their Croatian customs, like producing their own olive oil. In the early 1940s, Irma Popiç, the family's matron, wrote down her favorite recipes in a little notebook, which she passed down to her son Miro, my friend. As I read the yellowing pages, I felt as if I were watching Irma carefully hoarding food for the long winter and making use of the abundant game of coastal Chile. Miro recalls how the hunting season at La Serena began on the first Sunday of March; Irma pickled the quail his father, Roko, brought home, using the aromatic olive oil her husband had pressed himself. She stored the quail *escabeche* in large sterilized glass containers for use during the winter, and the family ate it cold as an appetizer or as a main dish accompanied by rustic bread.

What to Drink: A citrusy and grassy Arboleda Sauvignon Blanc from the cool Leyda Valley, Chile

SERVES 6

6 quail (3–4 ounces each), cleaned
    Salt and freshly ground black pepper
½ cup extra-virgin olive oil
1 medium white onion (8 ounces), thinly slivered lengthwise
5 garlic cloves, finely chopped
8 large carrots (about 2½ pounds), trimmed, peeled, and cut into 3-by-¼-inch slivers
3 bay leaves
20 black peppercorns
1 teaspoon ground cumin
1 cup distilled white vinegar
⅓ cup dry white wine

Preparing the Quail ▶ Rub the quail with salt and pepper to taste. Heat ¼ cup of the olive oil in a large, heavy skillet or sauté pan over medium-high heat. Add the quail to the pan, 2 at a time, and sauté until golden on all sides, about 8 minutes total. Transfer the quail to a deep serving platter and set aside.

Preparing the *Escabeche* Sauce ▶ Add the onion, garlic, carrots, bay leaves, peppercorns, and cumin to the skillet and sauté in the same oil until the onion softens, about 5 minutes. Lower the heat to medium-low. Stir in the vinegar and the wine, season with salt and pepper to taste, and cook for 5 minutes. Pour the sautéed vegetables over the quail and top with the remaining oil.

Serving and Storing: If the *escabeche* is to be eaten on the same day, leave it at room temperature for at least 1 hour before serving. Otherwise, store in the refrigerator, covered with plastic wrap, until ready to use. Bring to room temperature or warm gently before serving. Serve as an appetizer. For a main course, double the recipe.

Cañas Quail and White Bean Stew

Codornices con Frijoles Caballeros

This recipe comes from my Ferrer relatives, cacao and coffee farmers who live in the mountains of eastern Cuba on the edge of the Jauco River. Like most small farmers in this deeply forested region, they eat what they grow and hunt. Though their chicken coops are well populated, they prefer wild birds such as squab and quail. I first tasted this stew with squabs and fresh shell beans. It was a magnificent combination. When I duplicated the dish at home back in the United States, I tried it once with quail and dried white beans and loved the result. This is a hearty one-pot meal that can be served at a party or buffet. I like to serve it simply, with Cuban Bread (page 591).

Cook's Notes: Traditionally the recipe is prepared with squabs, but quail are not only more readily available in U.S. markets but also more economical. For fresh quail, check local Hispanic markets or live poultry markets, where you can order them and have them prepared to your specifications. It is best to call ahead to place the order.

    When searing the quail, do not crowd the pan. It is best to sear the birds in batches to achieve a rich golden brown crust. Just before searing, remove as much of the marinade as possible; otherwise the crushed garlic will burn in the hot oil. Also make certain to use the skillet in which you sear the quail to prepare the cooking sauce. The browned bits from the bottom of the pan will add great flavor.

What to Drink: A complex, full-bodied Toro red wine like Numanthia Termes, from Spain

SERVES 6 TO 8

For the Beans

- 1 pound dried white beans, such as Great Northern beans
- 1 medium yellow onion (about 8 ounces), peeled

For the Quail

- 6 garlic cloves
- 1 teaspoon salt
- Juice from ½ lime (about 1 tablespoon)
- 1 teaspoon extra-virgin olive oil
- 1 teaspoon ground cumin
- 12 small quail, halved (about 2 pounds total)

For the Cooking Sauce

- ¼ cup achiote-infused corn oil (page 89)
- 4 garlic cloves, finely chopped
- 1 medium yellow onion (8 ounces), finely chopped
- 1 tablespoon chives, finely chopped
- 4 plum tomatoes (about 12 ounces), peeled, seeded, and finely chopped
- 1 teaspoon ground cumin (optional)
- 4 fresh broad-leaf *culantro* leaves, finely chopped
- 1 tablespoon finely chopped cilantro
- 1 teaspoon fresh oregano leaves
- 2 teaspoons salt

Cooking the Beans ▶ Pick over beans for stones and rinse in cold running water. Soak the beans overnight in 3½ quarts water. (The beans will absorb a good deal of the water while soaking.) Transfer the beans and water to a large *caldero* or a heavy ovenproof pot; add the onion. Cover and bring to a boil. Lower the heat and cook, covered, over medium-low heat until tender, 1 to 1½ hours.

Marinating the Quail ▶ In a mortar, mash the garlic and salt to a paste with the pestle. Add the lime juice, olive oil, and cumin and stir to mix. Place the quail in a medium bowl and rub with this paste. Cover and marinate at least 30 minutes or refrigerate, covered with plastic wrap, overnight.

Cooking the Quail ▶ Remove the quail from the marinade, scraping away as much of the garlic as possible, and reserve the marinade.

Heat the achiote oil in a large skillet over medium-high heat, add the quail in batches, and cook until seared a rich golden brown on both sides, 5 to 7 minutes. Transfer the quail to a plate and set aside.

Reduce the heat to medium. Add the garlic and sauté until golden, about 20 seconds. Add the onion and chives and cook, stirring occasionally, until the onion is soft, 2 to 3 minutes. Add the tomatoes, cumin, *culantro*, cilantro, oregano, and salt. Simmer, stirring occasionally, until the mixture is dry and concentrated, about 10 minutes.

Finishing the Stew ▶ When the beans are tender, heat the oven to 350°F. Remove 1 heaping cup of the beans with a little of the broth from the pot and place in a small bowl. Mash the beans to a smooth paste with a fork or the back of a spoon. (Alternatively, use a handheld blender to pulse the beans 3 to 4 times, until creamy.) Stir the paste back into the beans. Add the reserved marinade, the seared quail, and the tomato mixture and stir to combine. Cover and transfer to the oven. Braise until the quail are completely tender and the beans are smooth and creamy, about 1 hour. Taste and adjust the seasoning with salt and pepper.

Guinea Hen Braised with Puerto Rican *Recado*

Guineas Guisadas

Guinea fowl were introduced to the Caribbean from Africa as part of the broad exchange of plants and animals that took place during the centuries of the slave trade. We always ate wild guinea fowl hunted by Uncle Oscar on his farm. They were bony animals with firm, very dark flesh that begged for prolonged cooking. My aunt Carolina was an expert. She would make large batches in a cauldron set over a charcoal fire outside her kitchen, stirring the pot with a big spoon and taking sips of the allspice-perfumed sauce from time to time to check the seasoning. We would eat the birds with boiled white yams and were allowed to suck the bones and make a mess with the drippings.

Much later, in Puerto Rico, I relived the long-forgotten taste of guinea hen when my relatives greeted me with guinea hen cooked outdoors in a cauldron. They also cook it in luscious braises flavored with *sofrito*. But the sauce has the unique savor of a Puerto Rican *recado*, rich with cilantro, broadleaf *culantro*, and the tiny sweet pepper *ají dulce*.

Cook's Note: Guinea fowl are available in Hispanic and Italian live poultry markets. They are called *gallinas de guinea* in Cuba and just *guineas* in Puerto Rico.

What to Drink: Martínez de la Cuesta Crianza, a lively Rioja tempranillo

SERVES 6 TO 8

For the Guinea Hens

> 2 guinea hens (about 3½ pounds each), each cut into 8 pieces (see Cutting a Chicken into Serving Pieces, page 659)
>
> 2 cups Charito's Puerto Rican Seasoning Mix (page 58)

For the Cooking sauce (*Sofrito*)

> 3 tablespoons achiote-infused extra-virgin olive oil (page 89)
>
> ¼ pound slab bacon, finely chopped
>
> 1 head garlic, separated into cloves and peeled
>
> 1¾ cups lager beer
>
> 1¼ cups chicken broth, homemade (page 538) or store-bought
>
> 2 bay leaves
>
> 1 cup pimiento-stuffed olives
>
> ⅓ cup capers, drained
>
> ½ teaspoon ground cayenne
>
> ½ teaspoon sweet *pimentón* (Spanish smoked paprika)
>
> ½ teaspoon salt
>
> ½ teaspoon freshly ground black pepper

Marinating the Guinea Hens ▶ Lightly rinse the pieces of guinea hen under cold running water and pat dry. Rub all over with ⅔ cup of the seasoning mix. Refrigerate, tightly covered with plastic wrap, and let rest for at least 4 hours or a maximum of 12 hours.

Preparing the Stew ▶ In a heavy 8-quart pot, heat the oil over medium-high heat until it ripples. Scrape the marinade from the guinea hen pieces and reserve. Add the guinea hen pieces to the oil in 2 batches and brown on all sides, turning with tongs, for about 8 minutes per batch. Remove from the pan and keep warm.

In the remaining oil, sauté the bacon until golden brown, about 5 minutes. Add the garlic and sauté until lightly golden, about 30 seconds. Stir in the remaining seasoning mix, including that scraped from the marinated hens, and sauté until the oil begins to separate, about 5 minutes. Return the hens to the pan and add the beer, broth, bay leaves, olives, and capers. Stir in the cayenne, paprika, salt, and black pepper and simmer, covered, over medium-low heat until the meat is tender, about 1 hour. Remove the bay leaves.

Serving: Serve with Puerto Rican Rice and Green Pigeon Peas (page 312) or Plantain-Eggplant Puree from Barranquilla (page 192).

MEAT

I went to Huexca, a town in Morelos state, Mexico, to spend a week in the home of Juan Castillo as he and his family prepared a feast for the fifteenth birthday of his niece Marisol. Juan is a farmer, and he had fattened a bullock in a small corral in the backyard of his house, using all his skill to make it plump and tasty. The bullock was to be killed and prepared barbecue style for the upcoming party.

During the week leading up to the party, I ate every meal with Juan and his family and saw some meat on the table just once—a few thin slices of fried pork, which we all shared almost as a condiment for refried beans and tortillas. Our meals were simple and satisfying: refried or soupy beans with a dollop of homemade cultured cream and a tablespoon of a hot green salsa made with garlicky *guaje* seeds, chicken soup flavored with guajillo chiles, scrambled eggs in a savory broth. What a contrast to the carnivorous feast that followed!

The day before the event, Juan and a couple of relatives hauled the struggling bullock onto a pickup truck at first light and headed for the slaughterhouse in nearby Cuautla. By noon they were back in Huexca with the meat, ready to begin the cooking. Waiting for them was Octavio, a caterer of sorts and the town's barbecue specialist. I found a quiet spot next to a tree and watched Octavio and his assistants work on the bullock in his front yard. They cut the meat into large pieces and smeared it with a crimson vinegary seasoning paste made of half a dozen kinds of chiles and an equal number of Mediterranean spices. Then they scrubbed the stomach, tripe, and hooves and proceeded to clean and stuff the stomach with a mixture of organ meats that they had already chopped and seasoned separately.

In one corner of the yard were three huge drums perched on portable gas burners and holding a little water. In each sat a large pot containing a mixture of rice, vegetables, and legumes, topped with a large rack. The men added the hooves to the pots and stacked the meat on the rack, including the stuffed stomach, which looked like a giant balloon. They then sealed the drums with sheets of heavy plastic. The meat steamed for eight long hours, its juices dripping into the pots and mixing with the vegetables and legumes to make a delicious soup. While the meat cooked, Octavio and his crew butchered and fried the meat of two 200-pound pigs in huge cauldrons.

On the day of the party, while Marisol was receiving the traditional blessing at the local church, Octavio and his men showed up with the three drums full of meat and what seemed like tons of fried pork. Quickly they set to work, helped by a few women, shredding the steamed beef and cutting the fried pork into more manageable bits. By the time Marisol and her guests were back from church, the meats had been plated with a side of reddish rice and refried red beans; the plastic plates threatened to break in half with the weight of so much meat. The family later claimed that one thousand people attended the feast. They were probably not exaggerating, because all through the night I saw hundreds of guests getting second helpings, and platters filled to the brim with beef and pork circulated briskly at every table.

At the end of the meal, a select few were given plastic cups filled with the broth that had simmered inside the drums enriched with the meat drippings. It was as delicious as the meat, and I saw men tilting their heads back and closing their eyes with pleasure as they gulped it down.

My visit to the Castillo family captured two sides of eating in Mexico: a daily diet based on a few vegetable staples such as beans and corn and the occasional meat, followed by a Rabelaisian,

European-style banquet centered on meat—meat, mind you, seasoned with chiles and served, as in most of tropical Latin America, with mountains of beans and rice.

All through my stay in Morelos and nearby Puebla, as I feasted on meat and drove through golden fields where cattle grazed and men in cowboy hats milked their cows in the shadow of the Popocatépetl volcano, I kept thinking of Hernán Cortés's perilous march to Tenochtitlán, the capital of the Aztec empire. He crossed this land in the summer of 1519, experiencing both fierce battles and successful alliances with local rulers. We know of his journey through Bernal Díaz del Castillo, a soldier who accompanied Cortés, whose famous chronicle *Historia verdadera de la conquista de la Nueva España* (*The True History of the Conquest of New Spain*) describes the foods they encountered and the Spaniards' ingenuity in getting the Indians to feed them.

Aboard their ships, Cortés and his men had survived on the salt pork and native American yuca bread (*casabe*) they had purchased in Cuba. In Veracruz, as their supplies dwindled, they were forced to embrace the foods of the land, dining on Mexican hairless dogs or turkeys, which they called *gallinas* (hens). In 1519 there were no other domesticated animals, but cattle, pigs, goats, and sheep were already being brought to the islands of the Caribbean, and not much later they arrived in Mexico. From there they spread throughout Central and South America, transforming the landscape wherever they set hoof.

The new animals were welcomed by the natives, who quickly integrated meat into their soups and stews. This is not to say that the indigenous people had been complete strangers to animal protein before the Spanish arrived. From deer in Central America to penguins in northern Peru, from monkeys and capybaras in the Amazon to Muscovy ducks, turkeys, and hairless dogs in Mexico to guinea pigs, llamas, and other camelids in the Andes, local meats added variety to diets that otherwise centered on a few staple plants: corn, beans, potatoes, or yuca.

Assimilation in the kitchen was abetted by the remarkable speed with which Old World domesticated animals began to multiply all over the Americas. Just a few years after the introduction of Iberian pigs to Hispaniola during Columbus's second voyage in 1493, the island was overrun with thousands of wild pigs. The Spaniards hunted them with bows and arrows and cooked them on grills, as the Taíno (Arawak) Indians did. Although Puerto Rico was not colonized by the Spaniards until 1508, Captain García Alonso Cansino had released pigs and goats from cages on his ship onto the island five years before. By the time the Spaniards finally landed to settle in 1508, these animals had multiplied, ensuring a familiar source of protein for the new settlers.

The promiscuous pig wheedled its way onto every hearth. The first meat sold at a market in Lima was pork. Because pigs were easy to raise and the meat and lard were cheap and plentiful, pork showed up smoked as bacon, salted as fatback, and fresh. When the meat was not used for roasting, it was ground to make sausages or used as a filling for empanadas and tamales, melted into lard, and fried for the market-vendor *fritadas* of the Ecuadorian Andes. In the Hispanic Caribbean, where pigs were more abundant than piety, the last day of Advent, which according to the dictates of the Church should be celebrated with fish, is marked with a golden pork roast.

Although the feast food in most Latin American countries is roast pork—a large leg or a whole pig—beef is king in both the temperate regions of

South America and the cattle ranching plains of Venezuela and Colombia. In tropical regions, the only cattle are the descendants of the cattle brought by the Spaniards, zebus from India, or crosses of European stock and zebus, used more for milk than for their somewhat stringy meat. A lot of the beef dishes here are braised, not roasted.

Lovers of steaks and roasts looking for some of the world's major beef breeds (Aberdeen Angus, Hereford, and Shorthorn) must go to Argentina or Uruguay. Though Argentina is home to a sizable population of cattle directly descended from the Iberian strains brought by the Spaniards, now known collectively as *ganado criollo* (home-grown cattle), British cattle, which made powerful inroads in the nineteenth century, are now preferred by many breeders for the higher fat content of their meat. Argentinean *criollo* cattle are less fatty and more muscular and have larger bones.

Cattle also found hospitable terrain on the plains of Hispaniola, Cuba, Venezuela, and Colombia, and in the south of Brazil. In Central American countries with large Indian populations, such as Mexico, Honduras, Guatemala, and El Salvador, and even in more European Costa Rica, beef shares a privileged spot with corn, beans, and avocado. Even in the Hispanic Caribbean, where the typical plate is divided between rice, beans, tubers, fried plantains, and any kind of meat, beef is a prized source of protein.

In Uruguay and Argentina, beef sits on a throne, unrivaled. Beef is the meat of choice for everyday eating and for feasting. It is the central element of any meal, usually accompanied by potatoes or a salad. When Argentinean and Uruguayan bricklayers stop for lunch, they huddle together at a quiet spot on the worksite and build a fire for a beef barbecue. When middle-class Argentinean

and Uruguayan families get together on a Sunday or holiday, it is to enjoy a lavish beef barbecue feast called an *asado*.

Sheep were more at home in flat lands with colder climates, such as the Bolivian *altiplano* and Patagonia, where they could be moved seasonally from pasture to pasture, as was common in Spain. In Chile, the fishermen who make a living selling the most spectacular seafood in the Americas would rather eat Patagonian lamb (*cordero magallánico*) than anything else. And who can blame them? This free-range lamb ranks among the most flavorful in the world.

Sheep need large expanses of land to graze, but goats, which can live just about anywhere, took well to mountainous and arid terrains in Latin America. Goat meat became the backbone of the cuisine of the Indians of the Guajira Peninsula, the desert between Colombia and Venezuela, whose feast food is a dish of goat's blood and entrails called *friche*. Goats are also common in northern Peru, where one of the most popular dishes is a cilantro-rich stew called *seco*, made from baby goat. Goat is a staple in Lara state in Venezuela and in the northern regions of Mexico, where it is called *borrego*. In Guadalajara, the most famous of all *borrego* dishes is *birria*, goat marinated in a penetrating chile sauce and steamed in a pit oven; the cooked meat is shredded and eaten with corn tortillas.

All Latin Americans like the smoky flavor of meat cooked on the grill, but for everyday cooking, the most commonly used techniques are pan-frying, braising, and stewing. Roasting is usually reserved for feast foods such as a large cut of pork or a whole pig. As in other parts of the world, braising and stewing are more common preparations for tough cuts and one-pot meals. For stewing, Latins like flavorful cuts that require long, slow cooking, such as eye of round, bottom round, flank, and shin. The meats are often seasoned before cooking with each country's traditional marinade or rub, sautéed, and simmered for a long time in a rich cooking sauce of onions, peppers, tomatoes, and a few other vegetables.

In Colombia and Venezuela, most meats are first browned with the local brown loaf sugar (*panela* or *papelón*) to intensify the color and add sweetness to the sauce. In most of Latin America, especially Mexico and Central America, meats and poultry undergo a double cooking process much like that used with dried beans: boiling followed by shredding and braising or frying. This method transforms tough and less expensive meats into tender, flavorful dishes. In Cuba, skirt or flank steak is boiled, shredded, and braised with a savory *sofrito* and wine to make *ropa vieja* (old clothes), an old Spanish dish with many Latin American versions. The *pabellón criollo*, the favorite blue plate of Venezuela, is a very similar dish of boiled, shredded, and pan-browned flank steak served with black beans, rice, and fried ripe plantains.

Because fresh meat spoiled quickly in hot climates before refrigeration, people in all of Latin America learned drying and curing methods that are still valued today for the special flavor they give to meats. Some of our cured meats, like ham, sausages, and dried beef, are familiar to everyone; others are an acquired taste. In the pre-Columbian Andes, llama and alpaca meat was freeze-dried in the cold dry air to produce a leathery, strong-smelling meat called *charqui*. The same method today produces both *charqui* and a version made with lamb called *chalona*, which is reconstituted and added to soups in tiny amounts, more as a flavoring than as a meat.

In Argentina and Uruguay, before the modern beef industry developed, cattle were mostly used for

hides and to make a tough, salty beef jerky called *tasajo*, which was exported to Cuba and the Caribbean as slave rations. (It was seldom eaten where it was produced, and still isn't one of the local foods.) Probably many Cubans first heard of Uruguay through the famous *tasajo de Montevideo*, which was exported as far away as Spain. People still cook it by the same method used in the islands: soaking it in water to remove the salt, then boiling, shredding, and finally cooking it with sautéed onions, peppers, and tomatoes.

In Mexico and Peru, a similar ancient method is used to produce a slightly chewy but savory dried beef called *cecina*, made by slicing and pounding the meat into thin sheets, rubbing it all over with a chile-laced seasoning mixture, and hanging it up to cure and dry at the same time. It does not become as desiccated as *tasajo* or *chalona*, so it can be pan-fried without having to be soaked.

The North American idea of steaks and roasts doesn't exist in Latin America. With few exceptions, you will not find carefully aged prime cuts that can be cut with a fork and taste perfect with no seasoning except salt and pepper. Our way with meat is different. Our pork is richer and more flavorful. Our beef has character. We might serve a thin, chewy steak very well done—some of my friends would say cooked to the shoe-sole stage—but deftly seasoned and accompanied by a retinue of vegetables or rice or both, together with a little salad. We are masters of rubs and marinades. Often we eat meat in thrifty dishes that pair a little meat with a lot of vegetables and/or starches. Even in Argentina, Uruguay, and the south of Brazil, where beef is ubiquitous and some people hardly feel they've eaten unless they have barbecued beef every single day, what you find when you go to a typical *parrillada* (place serving grilled meat) is not an all-steak menu but an extravaganza involving every part of the animal, from skirt to tripe to kidneys. The customers expect to sample just about everything from nose to tail.

Everywhere in Latin America, the names of cuts of meat are different (people from one country have a terrible time buying meat in another), and what's more, the cuts don't match the standard North American cuts at all. Latin Americans who move to this country all complain about the problem of getting meat to use in their favorite dishes. Cookbooks often just add to the confusion. You may see *matambre* translated as "flank steak," but it's really a thin layer of meat above the flank, which is cut off by butchers and used in the famous rolled stuffed dish called *matambre*.

In the following recipes, I have tried to concentrate on cuts available in most U.S. butcher shops and supermarkets. My selection draws generously on the wide Latin repertoire of dishes calling for inexpensive ground meat and braising cuts. Here and there, where a difficult-to-duplicate dish is too important to be left out, I have suggested close equivalents.

BEEF AND VEAL

Cuban Ground Beef Hash

Picadillo Cubano de Mi Casa

Picadillo, a seasoned ground beef hash, is popular all over Latin America. There are numerous local variations, but in Cuba it has a much-loved combination of olives and raisins that harks back to medieval Andalusia. My homespun recipe is the kind of family-style dish that I never hesitate to serve for special company. People are always surprised by its complex blend of flavors and textures and keep piling more on their plates.

Havana's ladies of the night used to gain their strength back after a night of battle with a plateful of picadillo topped with a couple of fried eggs. In Cuba today, these women are called *jineteras* (women on horseback), though they might now end their shift in a hotel restaurant as guests of the many foreigners who use their services. I have named this ever-popular dish on my restaurant Zafra's lunch menu after them. Every Cuban who reads the menu smiles knowingly.

The traditional accompaniments for Cuban picadillo are white rice and fried ripe plantains. Purists don't add beans to the mix, but I think that a ladleful of black beans over the rice makes the combination taste even better. Picadillo is also the traditional filling for *empanadillas* (page 426) and stuffed potatoes.

Cokok's Note: The traditional Cuban picadillo is not spicy and is always flavored with parsley, but I feel it tastes best with a touch of heat from jalapeños or ground cayenne or hot pepper. I also like my picadillo with cilantro, but feel free to choose whichever herb you prefer.

What to Drink: Bodegas Juan Gil Wrongo Dongo, a lively Monastrell from Jumilla, Spain

SERVES 4 TO 6

2 tablespoons extra-virgin olive oil

10 large garlic cloves, finely chopped

1 medium yellow onion (about 8 ounces) , finely chopped (about 1 cup)

1 medium red bell pepper (about 6 ounces), cored, seeded, deveined, and finely chopped (about 1 cup)

1 medium green bell pepper (about 6 ounces), cored, seeded, deveined, and finely chopped (about ¾ cup)

10 Caribbean sweet peppers (*ajíes dulces*) or 1 cubanelle pepper, seeded and finely chopped

1 pound ground beef (chuck or top round)

2 bay leaves

2 teaspoons dried oregano

1 teaspoon ground cumin

½ teaspoon ground allspice

6 medium plum tomatoes (about 1 pound), peeled, seeded, and finely chopped

1 jalapeño, seeded and finely chopped, or 1 teaspoon ground cayenne or crushed red pepper flakes (optional)

⅓ cup dark raisins (about 2 ounces)

12 pimiento-stuffed olives, thinly sliced

1 teaspoon salt

2½ tablespoons finely chopped cilantro

½ cup dry white wine, preferably Latin American *vino seco*

4 tablespoons tomato puree

▶ Heat the oil in a medium skillet over medium heat. Add the garlic and cook until golden, about 20 seconds. Add the onion and cook until soft, 4 to 5 minutes. Add the red, green, and Caribbean peppers and cook for 2 more minutes. Stir in the beef and cook, stirring occasionally, until lightly browned, about 15 minutes. Add the bay leaves, oregano, cumin, and allspice, stir to combine, and cook for 1 minute. Add the tomatoes and the jalapeño or cayenne, if using, and

cook until the tomatoes have softened, about 5 minutes. Add the raisins, olives, salt, and cilantro. Pour in the wine and tomato puree, stir, and reduce the heat to low. Remove the bay leaves and taste for seasoning, adding more salt or a pinch of cumin or allspice if necessary. Cook, covered, for 20 minutes, until the meat has absorbed the juices and is plump.

Serving: Serve with white rice topped with a ladleful of Havana-Style Black Bean Soup (page 507), Fried Ripe Plantains (page 183), or *jinetera* style, with two fried eggs on top of the picadillo.

Nicaraguan Ground Beef and Baby Corn

Carne Molida con Elotes Tiernos Nicaragüense

Strolling through the market of Masaya, a small town in Nicaragua, I saw a woman bending over a large sizzling pot. I stood next to her and followed her every move as she made this tasty beef hash with fresh baby corn. Tiny ears of corn are a seasonal treat in Nicaragua and are eaten whole as a vegetable.

What to Drink: Altos de Luzón Monastrell from Jumilla, Spain

SERVES 4 TO 6

3 tablespoons corn oil or mild extra-virgin olive oil

6 garlic cloves, finely chopped

1 medium yellow onion (about 8 ounces), finely chopped (about 1 cup)

1 small red bell pepper (about 4 ounces), cored, seeded, and finely chopped (about ¾ cup)

1 pound ground beef (chuck or sirloin)

1 teaspoon dried oregano

3 medium plum tomatoes (about 9 ounces), peeled, seeded, and finely chopped

24 ears baby corn, fresh, frozen, or canned

1 teaspoon salt

▶ Heat the oil in a 12-inch sauté pan or skillet over medium heat. Add the garlic and sauté until golden, about 20 seconds. Add the onion and sauté, stirring, for 2 minutes. Add the red pepper and sauté for 2 more minutes. Stir in the meat and cook for 15 minutes, until browned. Add the oregano and cook for 1 minute, then add the tomatoes and cook for 5 more minutes. Finish by adding the baby corn. Season with the salt, stir, taste for flavor, and cover. Simmer over low heat for 20 minutes.

Serving: Serve with white rice.

Paraguayan Meatballs in Broth

Soo Apuá Yuquysí (Albóndigas en Caldo)

Paraguay's flat terrain and grassy savannas are ideal for cattle ranching. Not surprisingly, beef is a staple of the Paraguayan diet, cropping up in many guises: broiled, stewed, and in soups. I first tasted this dish in Valletas, a small town on the Paraguay River. I have always loved meatballs, but usually in rich tomato sauces, so I was surprised to find myself asking for a second helping of this simple dish of meatballs cooked in a light vegetable broth. The meatballs were supple and punctuated by the aromatic tang of oregano, Paraguay's favorite cooking herb.

What to Drink: A mellow Felipe Rutini Merlot from Mendoza, Argentina

SERVES 6

For the Broth

2 tablespoons peanut oil

3 large garlic cloves, finely chopped

1 medium yellow onion (about 8 ounces), finely chopped (about 1½ cups)

1 large green bell pepper (about 8 ounces), cored, seeded, deveined, and finely chopped (about 1½ cups)

5 medium plum tomatoes (about 1 pound), seeded and finely chopped

2 medium carrots (about 12 ounces), peeled and finely chopped

4 cilantro sprigs

2 teaspoons salt

¼ cup long-grain rice

For the Meatballs

1 pound ground beef (chuck or sirloin)

3 large garlic cloves, mashed to a paste with a mortar and pestle or finely chopped and mashed

1 small yellow onion (about 5 ounces), shredded on a box grater

1 small green bell pepper (about 4 ounces), cored, seeded, and shredded on a box grater

2 teaspoons dried oregano

1 teaspoon ground cumin

1 teaspoon salt

1 large egg, lightly beaten

½ cup fine yellow cornmeal

Making the Broth ▶ Heat the oil over medium heat in a wide 4-quart pot. Add the garlic and sauté until golden, about 40 seconds. Add the onion and sauté until soft, about 4 minutes. Add the green pepper and cook for 3 more minutes, stirring constantly. Add the tomatoes and cook until soft, about 5 minutes. Add the carrot and cook for 1 minute. Add 2½ quarts water, the cilantro sprigs, and the salt and bring to a boil over high heat. Reduce the heat to medium-low and simmer for 10 minutes. Add the rice and cook for 10 more minutes, until the rice is just slightly hard in the center.

Making the Meatballs ▶ While the broth simmers, prepare the meatballs. In a large bowl, mix together the meat, garlic, onion, green pepper, oregano, cumin, salt, and egg until all the ingredients are well combined. Add the cornmeal in 2 batches and mix lightly with your hands. Divide the meat into about twenty-eight balls.

Finishing the Soup ▶ Drop the meatballs into the broth and simmer over medium heat, covered, until the rice is soft and the meatballs are cooked through, about 15 minutes. Serve immediately.

Beef *Barbacoa* in the Style of Huexca

Barbacoa de Toro

This is an adaptation of the large *barbacoa* prepared for the *quinceañera* of Marisol Pérez (see page 302). It is also a practical interpretation of the traditional pit barbecue known as *barbacoa* (or *barbacoa de hoyo*) in Mexico (see page 724). For that, cooks wrap marinated meats in *mixiote*, the thin, parchment-paper-like outer layer of the succulent leaves of the agave plant, and steam them in a stone-lined pit. This is a version of a pre-Columbian cooking method found throughout Latin America.

All over Mexico, cooks have managed to bring the concept of the pit *barbacoa* to their home kitchens. A popular method is to build a contraption that works as a steamer within a larger pot. A pot containing water, vegetables, and legumes is placed within a larger pot, and a steamer basket is propped on top. The meat, already marinated in a heady chile sauce and wrapped in a protective cover of plantain leaves, corn husks, or aluminum foil, is stacked in the steamer. The meat cooks in the fragrant steam that comes from the smaller pot, and its juices drip back into that pot, flavoring the broth.

My home method works very well. I use a large stockpot and a deep wire colander, because my steamer does not fit. I make my broth simply, with legumes and vegetables, but you can add 1 or 2 cow's feet if you like, for more gelatin. The rice thickens the broth, but it disintegrates after 3½ hours of cooking, so it is really optional. If you want less spiciness, take out some of the *puya* chiles and increase the number of guajillos.

Cook's Note: In some Latin markets catering to Argentineans or Uruguayans you can get the so-called *tira de asado*, short ribs cross-cut in long strips according to your specifications. They are very convenient: at home you just cut them between the bone into pieces of the desired width.

Working Ahead ▶ The *adobo* can be prepared 2 or 3 days ahead and the meat can be seasoned 1 day ahead. The cooked meat keeps for several days, well covered in plastic wrap, in the refrigerator. Add some broth to the meat before reheating, to moisten it.

What to Drink: A silky, full-bodied Robledo Family Cabernet Sauvignon from Napa Valley, California

SERVES 8

For the *Adobo*

10 dried guajillo chiles (about 2 ounces), stemmed and seeded

5 dried pasilla chiles (about 1 ounce), stemmed and seeded

3 dried ancho chiles (about 1 ounce), stemmed and seeded

4 dried New Mexican chiles (about ½ ounce), stemmed and seeded

6 dried *costeño* chiles (about ½ ounce), stemmed and seeded

6 dried *puya* chiles (about ½ ounce), stemmed and seeded

1 tablespoon cumin seeds

1 teaspoon allspice berries

1 teaspoon ground cloves

1 teaspoon dried marjoram

1 teaspoon dried thyme

One 3-inch Ceylon cinnamon stick (*canela*)

2 heads garlic, separated into cloves and peeled

1 tablespoon salt

3 tablespoons red wine vinegar

For the Meat

5 pounds flank steak, trimmed and cut across into 5-inch long pieces

2½ pounds cross-cut short ribs, cut into 3-by-6-inch pieces (see Cook's Note)

1 tablespoon salt

For the *Barbacoa* Broth

4½ quarts water

8 ounces dried chickpeas (about 1½ cups)

5 ounces green cabbage (about ¼ of a small head of cabbage)

2 medium carrots (about 8 ounces), cut into 1-inch pieces

1 cup long-grain rice, rinsed and drained (optional)

One 3-ounce package corn husks (about 15), rinsed and patted dry

Making the *Adobo* ▶ Place all the chiles in a medium saucepan and cover with water. With your hands, swish them around to dislodge any dirt clinging to them. Pour out the water, holding your hand over the peppers so they don't wash away. Place the chiles back in the pan with 2½ cups water, bring to a boil over medium-high heat, and cook for 3 minutes. Drain, reserving the cooking liquid, and set aside.

Heat a *comal*, griddle, or heavy skillet over medium-high heat. Add the cumin seeds, allspice berries, cloves, marjoram, thyme, and cinnamon and roast, stirring, until fragrant, about 40 seconds. Let cool and grind in a coffee or spice grinder into a fine powder. Set aside.

Working in batches as necessary, place the chiles, garlic, ground spices, salt, reserved liquid, and vinegar in a blender or food processor and process to a fine puree. Force through a fine-mesh strainer, pushing against the mesh with the back of a spoon. Set aside. Makes about 4½ cups.

Preparing the Meat ▶ Place the meat in a large bowl. Season with the salt and rub the *adobo* all over it. Cover with plastic wrap and let rest in the refrigerator for a minimum of 6 hours and a maximum of 24 hours.

Preparing the Broth and *Barbacoa* ▶ Place 2 cups water in a 12-quart stockpot about 12 inches in diameter. Place a 3-quart pot inside the larger pot, and add to the smaller pot the rest of the water, the chickpeas, cabbage, carrots, and rice, if using. Place a colander 10 to 11 inches in diameter on top of the smaller pot. Line with a layer of corn husks. Arrange the flank steak and ribs in layers in the colander and cover with the rest of the corn husks. Place a clean kitchen towel over the husks and cover the larger pot tightly. Cook over medium heat until the meat is fork-tender, about 3 hours. While cooking, the contents of the smaller pot will spill into the larger stockpot.

When the meat is fork-tender, lower the heat to low. Using oven mitts or potholders, uncover the pot and lift out the colander (be careful, and avert your face to avoid being burned by the cloud of steam). Set aside. Lift out the smaller pot and pour its contents into the larger pot. Keep the broth warm over low heat. When the meat is cool enough to handle, shred it finely or cut into serving pieces.

Serving: Mound the meat on a serving platter and moisten with one or two ladlefuls of broth. Pour the rest of the broth and vegetables into a soup tureen and bring to the table with the meat. Serve the broth separately, in small bowls or glasses, or ladle into soup plates and then add some of the meat.

At Marisol's party, the shredded beef was served alongside pork morsels, refried beans, and Mexican Rice (page 302). People ate the meat rolled up in hot tortillas with a dollop of fresh salsa and some of the refried beans.

Grilling

There is no single word to describe the range of outdoor cooking done in Latin America. Grilling as we know it in the United States, with foods cooked on the grill over a charcoal fire, is just one of the many ways in which Latins cook foods outside the kitchen.

Grilling in the great *llanos* of northern South America, in the pampas or in southern Brazil, is an experience that hinges on man's relationship with cattle and the transience of life in a vast open space. On the plains of Colombia, Venezuela, and the pampas, gigantic iron rods (*espetones*), doubling as skewers for large pieces of beef, pork, lamb, or goat, circle a smoldering fire. The rods are planted at an angle and moved at various stages of the cooking to control exposure to the source of heat. The rods are as important for the plainsmen as their riding gear, and just as easy to carry. When the gauchos are hungry, a steer can be slaughtered at a moment's notice and cooked over a smoldering fire. The meat is cut with a knife while still on the cooking rods and eaten with the same knife.

Today, though, most plainsmen cook on flat grills or *parrillas*. The *parrillas* of the pampas can be quite complex. Some can be raised or lowered to control the cooking, although in my experience, the meat has a tendency to be overcooked anyway. With a grill, one chars the outside of the meat for a crisp, chewy texture and a smoked flavor.

Outdoor cooking also reflects the division of labor between the sexes. Usually men huddle around the grill, strategizing, building, digging, coming up with complicated techniques. It is part of a manly ritual, part engineering, part cooking. In the meantime, the women retreat to the kitchen in boredom to prepare the marinade or the side dishes typical of the region: rice and beans, empanadas, tortillas, or salad. The men are left to turn plans into action and tend to the barbecue while drinking rum, beer, or *chicha*—also an obvious part of the manly ritual.

In Latin America, though, the planning and fretting is more ritualistic than driven by practical concerns. For those who cook outdoors, there are no major hurdles. In *parrilla* lands, everyone has a built-in *parrilla*, or enough green wood to make one, or rods, or hardwood charcoal, or a spot in the backyard where a *pib* can be dug and the right kind of stones to line it. Real technical problems arise only when Latins try to duplicate the barbecues they grew up with in the northern zones of the United States, where it snows, and even in Miami, where manicured gardens are covered with a meticulous carpet of groomed grass that nobody wants to burn.

To make their beloved *asados*, my Argentinean friends commission craftsmen to make elaborate grills or *parrillas* fitted with chains and pulleys to adjust the distance of the grill from the fire. Some are built into walls—very serious pieces of equipment. Others are smart and whimsical, made of an odd mix of parts, including bicycle chains. I am particularly taken with the one used by my friend Techa Sapiach: a cut-out barrel painted fire-engine red set on wheels, like a Weber, with a movable grilling rack and a lovely chimney sticking out of the barrel.

Grilling also lends itself to commercial adaptations, which can be found all over Latin America. The Mercado del Puerto, a marketplace in Montevideo, is my favorite place to eat grilled meats. Dozens of establishments offer the traditional Uruguayan grilled mix of sausages and *achuras* (tripe, sweetbreads, kidneys) followed by short ribs (*tira de asado*), skirt steak (*entraña*), and flank steak (*vacío*). You sit at a counter and watch the drama of the grill unfold in front of your eyes. The movable grills are expertly tilted by sweaty cooks to control timing, so red bell peppers get the smoky treatment along with the meats.

In Argentina, the *parrillas* are urban versions of the rough and manly experience of grilling meats in the countryside. In Buenos Aires, the older traditional *parrilladas* are somber and dark-paneled. The newer ones on Puerto Madero, a strip of elegant office buildings and gentrified restaurants along a section of the city's busy port, are frillier and more contemporary-looking, perhaps in imitation of the lively steakhouses of Brazil.

The Brazilian *rodizio* is part medieval banquet, part *pampa parrilla*. It started in temperate Rio do Sul, home of the Brazilian gaucho, a somewhat scruffier cousin of the more sophisticated Argentinean gaucho. When *rodizio* was transported to São Paulo and Rio, it became gentrified. At first I shunned it, as the idea of gorging on a endless stream of grilled meats seemed revolting. But then I let myself be guided by a couple of savvy *paulistanos* who took me to their favorite *rodizio*, the Barbacoa Grill. I loved it. The place was beautifully put together, airy and elegant. The salad bar boasted close to forty fresh salads, which ranged from huge succulent *palmitos* (hearts of palm) to lovely artichoke hearts, and the meats were magnificent. In a regular *churrascaría*, one orders one cut of meat and concentrates on its flavor. In the *rodizio*, all parts of the animal are brought to you by solicitous waiters, who will carve just a tiny slice of *picanha* (a special section of rump), a slice of udder or *fraldinha* (a particular cut of bottom sirloin), or perhaps a sliver of the zebu's hump (*cupim*), which is a lovely, well-marbled meat. In all, at the baroque and theatrical *rodizio* you can sample all parts of an entire steer and compare their flavors and textures.

River Plate Grill

Asado al Estilo del Río de la Plata

A few years ago, on a cool spring day when tiny leaves and purple flowers had just begun to sprout on my wisteria, an Uruguayan friend volunteered to do a South American mixed grill (*asado*) in my backyard. Following his precise instructions, I bought wood charcoal and picked up a selection of meats from an Uruguayan butcher. When the butcher handed me the package, it was as heavy as lead. Inside were *chunchulines* (tripe), *ubre* (udder), sweetbreads, a whole kidney, beef ribs cut into strips, *entraña* (skirt steak), Argentine pork, and even bull's testicles.

All afternoon, I proudly arranged the charcoal in my shiny Weber kettle grill and readied such necessities as boiled potatoes and string beans for a potato salad and Argentine and Uruguayan red wines for the guests.

When my friend arrived and took a look at my grill, he laughed and asked, "Are you crazy?" I suggested setting the grate from the grill over a pit I had once dug for roasting pigs. He laughed again and set to work. First he took the grate out of the kettle grill and propped it over a few bricks beside my wisteria. He built a large fire next to it, and when the embers were bright, he began arranging them between the brick supports. It was a slow, meticulous process performed with enormous concentration.

He only trusted me to mind the coals for a minute while he ransacked my kitchen for iron hooks, which he used to hang the skirt steak from the wisteria vine. When the flames made a steady heat, he began grilling the meats, adding each at its own time, brushing them only with a brine. Barbecue on the pampas, I mused, is not about digging holes in the ground but about surface grilling on the flat open spaces, about total concentration and absolute, manly control of the meat and the fire.

My friend soon banished me to the kitchen with precise instructions for making an Uruguayan chimichurri. He crouched in the dark, lit only by flashing embers, enveloped in the smoke that curled up into the rapidly wilting wisteria leaves. He was a man alone, tense and absorbed, oblivious of the friends who sat nearby in comfortable chairs, chatting and sipping wine. Like clockwork, he shouted for me as each cut of meat was ready, and I rushed to his side, serving platter in hand, to catch the pieces of the cow puzzle he was assembling. It was like the theater of the grill I had once witnessed at a fancy Argentine *estancia*, but this stage, my Jersey backyard, paradoxically seemed more savage and earthy—a lonely pampa dominated by a lonely gaucho.

Then I understood. The man who guards the fire and choreographs the grilling is the one who defines the experience. The meat was a bit overdone for my taste, lacking the tang I have come to love from marinating. But it had the pungent, smoky aroma of the live wood fire. I have had wonderful *asados* in many places, but this one was truly unforgettable. Now, each spring, when my wisteria begins to show its color, I imagine *churrasco* hanging from its gnarled branches.

What to Drink: Uruguayan White Wine Sangría (page 368) and red wine, preferably a full-bodied Malbec or Bonarda from Mendoza

SERVES 12

For the Sausages

6 Argentinean or Uruguayan pork sausages for grilling (*chorizos parrilleros*)

6 blood sausages

Olive oil, for brushing

For the Innards

1 pound small-intestine pig's tripe (*chunchulines*, often called chitlins in the U.S.)

2 pounds sweetbreads

¼ cup fresh lime juice

2 teaspoons salt

Olive oil, for brushing

Lime wedges

For the Meat

2 whole flank steaks (about 3½ pounds each)

2 whole skirt steaks (about 1½ pounds each)

6 pounds short ribs, cut into 5-by-2-inch strips (see Cook's Note, page 698)

3 rib-eye steaks

Coarse salt, preferably Argentinean Dos Anclas

Olive oil, for brushing

Uruguayan Chimichurri (page 133), for brushing

Preparing the Fire ▶ The ideal grill for a Uruguayan *asado* has movable racks, but any large flat grill will do the job. Light a wood charcoal fire and spread the coals evenly.

Grilling the Sausages ▶ When the flames subside and the coals are fiery red, place the sausages on the grill and brush lightly with the oil. Grill, turning occasionally, until they are golden brown and thoroughly cooked, about 15 minutes. Transfer to a cutting board and cut into thick slices. Serve to your guests with a glass of red wine and some crusty bread.

Preparing and Grilling the Innards ▶ Rinse all the innards thoroughly under cold running water. Place in a bowl and season with the lime juice and salt. Place on the grill, brush lightly with the oil, and cook until crisp and golden, about 10 minutes. Serve to your guests with the lime wedges and more wine.

Preparing and Grilling the Meat ▶ Place all the meats in a large bowl and season with coarse salt to taste. Place on the grill and brush with either olive oil or some chimichurri sauce (this is an unorthodox practice that I find very effective).

The meats will cook at different rates because of their varying thickness and degrees of tenderness. The ribs and flank steak will take 10 to 12 minutes on each side (always place the ribs on the grill meat side down), and the skirt steak and the rib-eye will take 5 to 8 minutes on each side for a juicy medium-rare.

Serving: Cut the meat into serving portions. Set on the table with several salads, a bowl of chimichurri sauce, and the sangría and red wine. Fire-Grilled Provolone (page 703) is a good accompaniment.

Fire-Grilled Provolone

Provolonetta a la Parrilla

Thick slices of provolone cheese, grilled and served with a dollop of chimichurri sauce, are just one of the many grilled appetizers that usher in the great feast that is the Argentinean barbecue. When cheese began to be made in the pampas, it was usually of very poor quality. Travelers commented on how the gauchos grilled it, which improved its taste.

SERVES 4 TO 6

- 1 tablespoon corn oil
- 1 pound provolone cheese, cut into ½-inch-thick slices
- 1 cup Uruguayan Chimichurri (page 133)

▶ Prepare the grill. When the coals turn ashy, brush the grill with the corn oil. Place the cheese on the grill and cook for 2 to 3 minutes on each side. Remove from the grill with a spatula and top with 1 teaspoon chimichurri. Serve as an appetizer or as a side for the meats of the River Plate Grill (page 702).

Grilled Skirt Steak with Argentinean Chimichurri

Entraña con Chimichurri Argentino

Skirt steak, commonly known by the generic name of *churrasco*, is a long, thin, and deeply flavorful strip of meat with well-defined open fibers cut from the diaphragm muscle of the cow, just below the ribs. Popularized by Argentinean and Hispanic Caribbean restaurants in the United States, it is by far the most requested cut of meat in any Latin restaurant today. While Argentineans simply salt it and grill it and then lavishly smother it with chimichurri sauce at the table, Hispanic Caribbean cooks like to marinate it with some of the sauce before pan-frying it, broiling it, or cooking it on the barbecue grill or *a la plancha* (on the griddle).

Cook's Note: Latin American butcher shops sell long skirt steaks that can be as long as 27 inches and weigh close to 2 pounds. Halve and trim each steak to a manageable size before cooking. I like my skirt steak long (about 14 inches) and on the generous side, ranging between 14 ounces and 1 pound.

SERVES 4

- 4 skirt steaks (about 1 pound each), trimmed Coarse salt
- 1 recipe Red Chimichurri (page 133)

▶ Light a grill or preheat a broiler on medium-high heat. Season the steaks with salt and brush with some of the chimichurri sauce. Grill or broil the steaks about 4 inches from the source of heat for 4 to 5 minutes on each side, or until medium rare. Let stand for 5 minutes before serving. If you wish, thinly slice the steaks across the grain at an angle before serving.

Serving: Bring to the table with a bowl of Red Chimichurri (page 133) or Chilean "Goat's Horn" *Pebre* (page 131). Serve with rice and beans or with Peruvian Warm Purple Potato and Squash Salad (page 205).

Salvadorian Grilled Sirloin Tip Steak

Filetes de Punta de Puyaso al Carbón

In both Guatemala and El Salvador, sirloin tip or *punta de puyaso* is used for grilling. Salvadorians like to marinate their beef in heavy *adobos* rich in mustard, Worcestershire sauce, and the seasoning mix called *relajo*. In El Salvador, meats are usually cut thin, but some of my Salvadorian friends in the United States like to grill thick steaks as Americans do, and marinate them in their favorite *adobos*.

SERVES 6

For the *Adobo*

- 3 tablespoons grated brown loaf sugar (*panela* or *piloncillo*), Muscovado sugar, or dark brown sugar
- 2 tablespoons butter
- ¼ cup cider vinegar
- 1 tablespoon Worcestershire sauce
- 1 tablespoon ground Salvadorian Spice Mix (page 45)
- 1 tablespoon yellow mustard or good Dijon mustard
- 1 teaspoon salt
- 1 teaspoon freshly ground black pepper
- ¼ cup water

Six 1-inch-thick sirloin tip steaks (about 12 ounces each)

▶ Place all the ingredients except the meat in a small saucepan and bring to a boil. Lower the heat and simmer until the sugar is dissolved; let cool.

Place the meat in a medium bowl, pour the marinade over it, and let rest for 2 to 3 hours, covered with plastic wrap.

Prepare a grill with wood charcoal and light the fire. When the embers are ashy, place the steaks on the grill and cook for 8 minutes on each side.

Serving: Serve with a mixed salad.

Stir-Fried Beef and Potatoes Peruvian Style

Lomito Saltado

Between 1849 and 1869, thousands of Chinese indentured workers arrived in Peru to serve eight-year contracts in guano fields and sugarcane plantations. They had crossed the Pacific to escape hunger and poverty in their native Canton, only to find that in Peru their lot did not improve much. Only at the end of their contracts were they able to fulfill their dreams; many moved to Lima and other large cities, where they opened small markets and restaurants. Because their contracts had been drawn with great precision, specifying just what foods they must be supplied with, they were never without basic Chinese staples such as rice, tea, and soy sauce.

The Peruvian Chinese restaurants, first called *fondas* and *cenas* and later, in the 1920s, *chifas* (from the Cantonese term *chow fan*), became immensely popular and presented a wonderful hybrid style that melded Chinese cooking techniques like stir-frying with the native Andean hot peppers and potatoes as well as Old World spices. This dish, with its delightful mingling of ingredients from three continents, is a wonderful example of the *chifa* influence.

Cook's Note: The key to the success of this dish is to rapidly stir-fry the beef in smoking-hot oil to infuse it with the smoky fragrance that Chinese cooks call *wok hay* (breath of the wok).

What to Drink: Tikal Patriota, a seductive blend of Bonarda and Malbec, the two emblematic grapes of Mendoza, Argentina, with lively cherry notes with hints of red meat and chocolate

For the Potatoes

- 6 medium russet potatoes (about 2 pounds)
- 2 cups corn oil
- 1 teaspoon salt

For the Meat

- 2 pounds beef tenderloin, trimmed and cut into ½-inch-thick slices
- 1 tablespoon soy sauce
- 1 teaspoon freshly ground black pepper
- 1 teaspoon ground cumin
- 2–4 tablespoons corn oil or mild extra-virgin olive oil

For the Vegetables

- 3 large garlic cloves, finely chopped
- 2 medium red onions (about 1 pound), thickly slivered lengthwise
- 3 fresh-frozen yellow Andean peppers (*ajíes amarillos*), jalapeños, or any yellow hot peppers, thawed, stemmed, seeded, and cut into fine slivers
- 5 ripe medium plum tomatoes (about 1 pound), peeled and cut lengthwise into wedges
- ¼ cup dry red wine
- ¼ cup beef broth, homemade (page 540) or store-bought
- 3 tablespoons soy sauce, or to taste
- 2 tablespoons finely chopped cilantro

For the Potatoes ▶ Peel the potatoes and cut them lengthwise into ½-inch-thick sticks. Place in a large bowl and cover with cold water. Let sit for at least 20 minutes. Drain and pat dry.

Heat the oil in a 2-quart pot over medium heat until it is about 350°F. Working in 3 batches, drop the potatoes into the hot oil and deep-fry, stirring, until golden brown, about 4 minutes per batch. Remove with a slotted spoon and let drain on paper towels. Season with the salt and set aside.

For the Meat ▶ Place the meat in a large bowl and toss with the soy sauce, black pepper, and cumin. Heat 2 tablespoons oil over high heat in a 12-inch sauté pan or 14-inch wok. Working in 2 or 3 batches, add the meat and rapidly stir-fry until golden brown, about 5 minutes. Add more oil to the pan if necessary. Remove with a slotted spoon and set aside.

For the Vegetables ▶ Reduce the heat to medium, add the garlic, and sauté until golden, about 20 seconds. Add the onions and sauté for 2 minutes. Add the peppers and sauté for 1 more minute. Remove with a slotted spoon and set aside. Add the tomatoes to the pan and cook, stirring, for 2 minutes.

To Finish ▶ Increase the heat to medium-high and add the meat and the reserved vegetables. Stir in the red wine, beef broth, and 3 tablespoons soy sauce. Cook, stirring, for 2 minutes, then add the cilantro and stir well. Just before serving, add the potatoes to the pan. Stir gently to mix, being careful not to break the potatoes. Serve immediately, with white rice.

Drunken Braised Meat and Potatoes

Carne Borracha

Though I have yet to meet a spice I don't like, I also enjoy making simple, almost minimalist braises of beef simmered in wine. In this cherished family recipe, a minimum of ingredients—onion, garlic, bay leaf, and a generous amount of wine—come together to flavor beef shin, one of my favorite cuts of meat for braising or stewing. The meat flourishes with slow cooking, becoming even more tender and gelatinous with the addition of wine, which not only adds flavor but also acts as a tenderizer. Starchy potatoes, added when the meat is almost done, absorb some of the concentrated sauce, leaving just enough to keep the meat moist.

What to Drink: A Rioja tempranillo like Sierra Cantabria Colección Privada

SERVES 6

- 4 tablespoons extra-virgin olive oil
- 2 pounds beef shin, cut into 2-inch chunks
- 4 garlic cloves, peeled and sliced
- 1 medium yellow onion (8 ounces), peeled and quartered
- 1 bay leaf
- 2½ cups dry white wine or Latin American *vino seco*
- 6 medium russet potatoes (about 2 pounds), peeled and cut into 2-inch cubes
- 1½ teaspoons salt
- ½ teaspoon freshly ground black pepper
- 1 medium red bell pepper (about 8 ounces), fire-roasted (see page 67), cored, seeded, and cut into 2-inch strips

▶ Heat the oil over medium-high heat in a heavy pot large enough to hold the meat without crowding it. Add the meat and cook, stirring occasionally, to brown evenly, 10 to 12 minutes. Add the garlic, onion, and bay leaf and cook, stirring, for 2 minutes. Pour in the wine and bring to a simmer over medium heat. Reduce the heat to low and cover tightly. Let simmer until very tender, about 1¼ hours. Add the potatoes, salt, and black pepper and cook, covered, until the potatoes are tender, 15 to 18 more minutes. Just before serving, stir in the fire-roasted pepper and cook until heated through, about 1 minute.

Serving: Serve hot, as a complete meal, or with a side of white or yellow rice or any rice and bean dish for an authentic tropical combination. As with most braised dishes, this is even better the day after cooking. Refrigerate, covered, overnight, and reheat just before serving, thinning the sauce with just a little broth or water.

Pot-Roasted Stuffed Eye of Round Cartagena Style

Posta Mechada Cartagenera

In the hands of skillful and patient Latin cooks, inexpensive but tough cuts of meat like the eye of round become tender and delicious. My favorite way to prepare this cut is to stuff it with carrots and prunes and a few strips of smoked bacon.

This recipe brings together some of the techniques I learned in coastal Colombia and particularly in Cartagena, where eye of round (*posta*) is a favorite. The Lapeira sisters from Barranquilla taught me to season the meat with grated vegetables like onions, tomatoes, and Italian frying peppers. (On the Caribbean coast of Colombia the vegetables that season marinade mixtures are traditionally grated with a box grater, never in a blender.) The idea of coating the meat in flavorful brown sugar before browning comes from another great Cartagena cook, Marcela Lorduy Benedetti. I am just crazy about this sugar, which gives the roast a deep golden color and a sublime sweetness with character.

Cook's Notes: Eye of round is known by different names throughout Latin America, and even for us Latins this can be bewildering. Cubans call it *boliche* or *carne para mechar* (meat for stuffing or larding). In coastal Colombia it is known as *posta* and *bollo*, in Bogotá as *bola,* and in the Valle del Cauca and Bucaramanga as *muchacho*. In Venezuela, eye of round is *muchacho redondo*: imagine a stuffed round boy, a *muchacho redondo relleno*.

In Latin America, eye of round is normally cooked in a cast-aluminum *caldero*. I own *calderos* of all sizes, and they are wonderful to cook with. But for dishes using acid foods like tomatoes, I prefer a nonreactive pot. My favorite is a large tin-lined French copper *rondeau*, about 13 inches in diameter and with straight sides about 5 inches high. The heavy bottom allows me to braise the meat slowly without scorching while using little liquid, and the pot is wide enough to heat the cooked meat slices in a single layer before serving. A heavy Dutch oven is a practical alternative. If you don't have a pot that will hold a 12-inch cut of meat, cut the eye of round into two 6-inch pieces.

Working Ahead ▶ You can roast the meat a day ahead and store it, tightly wrapped in plastic wrap, in the refrigerator. Slice and reheat with the sauce before serving.

What to Drink: Tikal Amorío, an expressive Malbec from Mendoza, Argentina, with notes of black cherry that harmonize with the fruitiness of the brown loaf sugar

SERVES 8

One 4-pound eye of round, about 12 inches long

For the Stuffing

- 1 large, thick carrot (about 8 ounces), cut lengthwise into quarters, or 2 thinner carrots (about 4 ounces each), peeled and halved
- 20 pimiento-stuffed olives
- 12 pitted prunes
- 4 ounces slab bacon, cut into long ½-inch strips
- ¼ cup capers, drained

For the Marinade

- 1 large yellow onion (about 12 ounces), peeled
- 3 medium plum tomatoes (about 9 ounces)
- 6 garlic cloves, mashed to a paste in a mortar and pestle or finely chopped and mashed
- 1 cubanelle pepper, stemmed and seeded
- 1 teaspoon ground allspice
  Salt and freshly ground black pepper

For Cooking the Meat

- 4 ounces grated brown loaf sugar (preferably Colombian *panela*), or 1 cup Muscovado sugar or packed dark brown sugar
- 2 tablespoons corn oil or mild extra-virgin olive oil
- ½ cup dry sherry
- 1 tablespoon bitter orange juice or sweet orange juice
- 1 cup beef broth, homemade (page 540) or store-bought
  Salt and freshly ground black papper

Stuffing the Meat ▶ Ask your butcher to prepare the eye of round for stuffing by making a wide lengthwise incision through the center of the meat from one end to the other. If your butcher is not accommodating, do it yourself: With a long carving knife, pierce the meat at one end and then at the other end. Rotate the blade like a screwdriver to open up a long tunnel wide enough to hold the filling; repeat from the other end.

Fill the incision with the carrot, olives, prunes, bacon, and capers, pushing the ingredients in to fill the complete length of the roast. This is not a neat process. But even if the stuffing is not arranged as evenly and artfully as you would like, the result will still be colorful and, most important, delicious.

Marinating the Meat ▶ Place the stuffed meat in a long, shallow stainless steel pan. Cut the onion in half, and grate into a bowl against the shredding side of a box grater. Do the same with the tomatoes. (You will end up holding only the skin.) Repeat with the pepper. (If you find this process awkward, finely chop all of these ingredients in the food processor.) Combine these ingredients in the bowl with the garlic, allspice, 2 teaspoons salt, and 1 teaspoon pepper. Rub the mixture all over the meat. Cover with plastic wrap and let sit in the refrigerator for a minimum of 6 hours and a maximum of 12 hours.

Cooking the Meat ▶ Scrape all the marinade from the meat; set aside. Rub the meat with the sugar.

Heat the oil over medium heat in a heavy pot at least 13 inches wide, with a tight-fitting lid. Add the meat and brown on all sides, about 10 minutes. Add the sherry, orange juice, broth, reserved marinade, and salt and pepper to taste. Cover and cook over medium-low heat until tender, 2 ½ to 3 hours.

When the meat is cooked, lift it onto a platter with a slotted spatula and let rest for at least 20 minutes or until completely cool before slicing.

While the meat cools, place the sauce in a blender or food processor and process to a puree. Strain the pureed sauce through a fine-mesh sieve into a small bowl, pushing the solids against the mesh with the back of a wooden spoon or ladle. You should have about 2¼ cups sauce.

Cut the roast into ½-inch slices. Pour half of the sauce back into the cooking pot. Place the meat slices over it, preferably in a single layer. Pour the rest of the sauce over the meat to moisten it. Heat over low heat for 10 minutes or until warmed through. Alternatively, arrange the meat and half the sauce on a baking dish large enough to accommodate the slices in a single layer and heat in a preheated 350°F oven until warmed through.

Serving: Lift the meat onto a large serving platter with a slotted spoon. Pour the remaining sauce into a sauceboat or spoon over the meat. Traditional accompaniments for eye of round in Colombia are white rice or Fried Coconut Rice (page 300), Drunken Stewed Plantains (page 190), and Avocado and Onion Salad (page 547).

Argentinean Veal Stew with Peaches

Carbonada Criolla con Duraznos

Most Latin cookbooks associate *carbonada* with Argentina. But in reality this stew is a regional South American dish, with versions in Chile and Peru and roots that hark back to medieval Europe or Moorish Spain. One of the culinary meanings of the word *carbonada* in sixteenth-century Spain was slices of meat sautéed with seasonings and braised or stewed in some broth. In other parts of Europe, such as Belgium, a similar dish called *carbonnade flamande* was flavored with beer. In the New World, the Spanish colonists enriched their veal or beef *carbonadas* with New World vegetables.

Carbonadas are popular in Chile and Peru, where they are mostly simple, hearty meat stews with potatoes and various vegetables, sometimes also rice. They are something far grander in Argentina, where everyone regards *carbonada criolla* as the nation's quintessential marriage of Spanish and New World cooking. The dish is frequently enlivened with peaches, lending a sweet-and-sour brightness that suggests the Arabic and Persian strains of medieval Spanish cuisine, and of course it is made with European techniques. Pair these elements with the marvelous vegetables that the Spanish encountered in South America—potatoes, sweet potatoes, corn, tomatoes, and big meaty squashes—and you have a *criollo* extravaganza.

Different regions have their own versions, adding yuca (to make the Brazilian *carbonada con mandioca*), more kinds of fruit (for *carbonada con frutas*), or rice. The most spectacular is *carbonada en zapallo*, from central Argentina, essentially a *carbonada criolla* finished and served in a hollowed-out pumpkin shell.

Carbonada proved elusive in Buenos Aires (though regional dishes like this are still alive and well in homes). I was lucky enough to find it on the menu of one of the few Buenos Aires restaurants that serves regional specialties. The chef, who looked like a Guaraní Indian, was from Entre Ríos, the humid region adjacent to Paraguay. But he had learned this dish from one of the cooks who came from Salta, in the northwest of the country, where *carbonada criolla* is a specialty.

What to Drink: Susana Balbo Crios Rosé de Malbec from Mendoza, Argentina, or Montes Cherub Rosé de Syrah from Colchagua Valley, Chile

SERVES 6 TO 8

For the Meat

- 3 pounds veal shoulder, cut into 1½-inch cubes
- 2 teaspoons salt
- 1 teaspoon freshly ground black pepper
- 1 tablespoon sugar

For the Cooking Sauce

- 2 tablespoons corn oil, plus more if needed
- 1 large yellow onion (about 12 ounces), finely chopped (about 2 cups)
- 1 large red bell pepper (about 8 ounces), cored, seeded, deveined, and finely chopped (about 1 cup)
- 3 large plum tomatoes (10–11 ounces), peeled and seeded
- 1 tablespoon sugar
- 1 tablespoon *pimentón* (Spanish smoked paprika, hot or sweet)
- ½ teaspoon dried rosemary

½ teaspoon dried thyme

½ cup dry white wine

2 medium carrots (about 12 ounces), peeled and cut into 1-inch chunks

2 cups beef or chicken broth, preferably homemade (page 540 or 538)

1 pound meaty Caribbean pumpkin (*calabaza*) or kabocha, Hubbard, or butternut squash, peeled, seeded, and cut into 2-inch cubes

6 slightly underripe peaches (about 2 pounds), peeled, pitted, and quartered

3 russet potatoes (about 1 pound), peeled and cut into 1½-inch cubes

3 ears yellow corn, cut into 1-inch sections

¼ cup dark raisins

Seasoning the Meat ▶ Place the meat in a bowl and season with 1 teaspoon salt and the pepper. To help the meat to brown to a lovely golden color, add the sugar. The sugar will caramelize in cooking, adding a nice color and flavor to the meat.

Making the Cooking Sauce ▶ Heat the oil over medium-high heat in a large, 8-quart heavy pot with a tight-fitting lid. Add the meat and brown, stirring occasionally, for 15 to 20 minutes. Lift out the meat with a slotted spoon and set aside.

If no fat is left, add another tablespoon to the pan. Add the onion and sauté until golden, about 5 minutes. Add the bell pepper and cook until soft, stirring, for 3 minutes. Add the tomatoes and continue cooking for 3 minutes. Add the sugar, paprika, rosemary, and thyme and cook, stirring. Pour in the wine and simmer until nearly evaporated.

Return the meat to the pot; add the carrots and broth and the remaining 1 teaspoon salt. Reduce the heat to low and cook, covered, until

the meat is not quite fork-tender, about 1 hour. Add the pumpkin, peaches, potatoes, corn, and raisins. Cook, covered, for another 15 minutes, or until the vegetables and fruit are done. Serve in soup plates with crusty bread.

Piedad's Oxtail Stew

El Rabo Encendido de Piedad

Piedad Robertson, who was my English teacher at college in Miami and later became the president of Santa Monica College in California, is one of the most well-rounded cooks I know, as confident tackling a difficult French sauce as when preparing a mean Cuban-style oxtail stew. This recipe is inspired by hers. It is a rich and robust stew, with meat falling off the bone in a sauce that has the same intense but clean taste as a ragout—only with some heat, for this is one of the few Cuban dishes that calls for hot pepper. I learned from Piedad to value humble but tasty dishes such as this stew and make them the centerpiece of any special meal. I especially like to serve oxtail on a cold winter's night, ladling the meat into a wide soup plate alongside a mound of the savory green plantain puree we call *fufú*. You only need some white rice (there are those who would not eat the stew without a ladleful of white rice) and a peppery red wine for a stupendous meal.

Working Ahead ▶ I never serve oxtail stew the same day I cook it. I let it cool to room temperature, store it in a plastic container, and place it in the refrigerator overnight. The following day I remove the thick layer of fat that has formed on the surface and reheat the stew before serving. Removing the fat is easier if you store the sauce and the pieces of oxtail separately.

What to Drink: An opulent *tinta del país* from the Ribera del Duero, like Emilio Moro Malleolus

SERVES 6

For the Meat

- 1   cup all-purpose flour
- ½   teaspoon salt, or to taste
- ½   teaspoon freshly ground black pepper
- ¼   teaspoon dried oregano
- 6   pounds oxtail, trimmed of fat and cut into 2-inch pieces
- 6   tablespoons extra-virgin olive oil

For the Cooking Sauce

- 6   garlic cloves, finely chopped
- 1   large yellow onion (12 ounces), finely chopped (about 2 cups)
- ½   medium green bell pepper (4 ounces), cored, seeded, deveined, and finely chopped (about ¾ cup)
- 1   bay leaf
- ¼   teaspoon ground cumin
- ½   cup tomato puree
- ½   teaspoon salt, or to taste
- ½   teaspoon ground cayenne, or to taste
- 2   cups dry red wine, plus more if needed
- 1   cup beef broth, homemade (page 540) or store-bought, plus more if needed
- 3   tablespoons chopped flat-leaf parsley

Browning the Meat ▶ Mix the flour, salt, pepper, and oregano in a large bowl. Roll the oxtail pieces in this mixture, shake off the excess, and place on a platter.

Heat the oil in a large, wide, ovenproof pot with a lid over medium-high heat. Add the pieces of oxtail to the pan in 2 or 3 batches and brown evenly, turning occasionally, about 8 minutes per batch. Lift out with a slotted spoon onto a double layer of kitchen towels to drain.

Preparing the Cooking Sauce ▶ Preheat the oven to 350°F. Add the garlic to the pot and sauté until golden, about 40 seconds. Add the onion and green pepper and sauté until the onion is light gold, about 8 minutes. Add the bay leaf and cumin and sauté for 1 minute. Add the tomato puree, salt, and cayenne and cook, stirring, for 3 minutes. Taste for seasoning, and add more salt and cayenne as needed. Add the oxtail pieces to the sauce, pour in the wine and broth, add the parsley, and stir to mix. Cover the pot and bake until the meat practically falls off the bone and the sauce thickens, about 1½ to 2 hours. Check periodically, adding more broth or wine if the sauce seems too dry. Remove the bay leaf. Skim off as much fat as you can if you are serving the stew immediately. Otherwise, let it cool to room temperature and store it in the refrigerator, covered. Remove the fat the following day. Reheat gently before serving.

Serving and Storing: Serve in soup bowls with a ladleful of Cuban Green Plantain Mash with Garlic and Olive Oil (page 186) and some white rice. Oxtail stew will keep well refrigerated for 3 or 4 days. It will last well in the freezer for about 3 months.

Short Ribs in Black Sauce with Chocolate and Cacao

Costillas de Res en Salsa de Asado Negro

I grew up eating short ribs in soups. In Argentina and Uruguay they are often grilled, but I much prefer them braised to really enjoy their wonderfully rich and gelatinous texture. My favorite way to cook short ribs is to caramelize them with a mixture of olive oil and brown loaf sugar and then braise them in a flavorful concentrated sauce that looks almost black at the end of cooking. This is the basic technique for the Venezuelan eye-of-round braise called *asado negro* (black roast), which I have adapted to my taste and enriched with dark Venezuelan chocolate and cacao nibs for depth and a final bit of crunch.

What to Drink: Susana Balbo Malbec from Mendoza, Argentina

SERVES 6

For Seasoning the Ribs

- 4 garlic cloves, mashed to a pulp with a mortar and pestle or finely chopped and mashed
- ¼ teaspoon dried oregano
- ⅛ teaspoon ground allspice
- ¼ teaspoon salt
- ¼ teaspoon ground cayenne
- 6 large short ribs (8–9 ounces each)

For Searing the Ribs

- 3 tablespoons extra-virgin olive oil
- 1 cup all-purpose flour
- 1 cup grated brown loaf sugar (preferably *panela*), Muscovado sugar, or packed brown sugar

- 2 medium carrots (12 ounces), finely chopped
- 2 celery stalks, finely chopped
- 1 medium yellow onion (8 ounces), finely chopped (about 1½ cups)
- 6 garlic cloves, finely chopped
- 1 cup dry red wine
- 2 cups chicken broth, homemade (page 538) or store-bought
- 2 tablespoons tomato paste
- 1 teaspoon fresh or dried rosemary

- 1 ounce Venezuelan dark chocolate, preferably El Rey Gran Samán (70%), coarsely chopped
- 2 tablespoons cacao nibs
  Rosemary sprigs, for garnish

Seasoning the Ribs ▶ In a small bowl, combine the mashed garlic with the oregano, allspice, salt, and cayenne. Rub this mixture over the ribs and let sit for at least 2 hours.

Searing the Ribs ▶ Heat the oil over medium heat in a 12-inch skillet. Dredge the ribs in the flour, shaking off the excess. Add to the skillet and cook, turning occasionally, until golden, about 8 minutes. Add the brown sugar and continue cooking until the sugar melts and coats the ribs. Remove the ribs to a platter.

Add the carrots, celery, onion, and finely chopped garlic to the pan and sauté for 5 minutes. Add the red wine and cook for 3 minutes, then add the chicken broth, tomato paste, and rosemary. Return the ribs to the pan, reduce the heat to medium, and cook, covered, until the ribs are very tender, about 2 hours. Remove the ribs to a platter and let the sauce simmer, uncovered, 10 more minutes or until it thickens. Before serving, stir in the chocolate, let it melt, and scatter in the cacao nibs.

Serving: Ladle some of the sauce onto a large serving plate, arrange the ribs over the sauce, and garnish with sprigs of rosemary. These ribs are heavenly when paired with Sautéed Quinoa with Swiss Chard (page 258).

Cuban Braised Shredded Beef ("Old Clothes")

Ropa Vieja

Every Latin American country has a version of a classic Spanish dish known as *ropa vieja* (old clothes), a name that refers to the cooking process. A piece of meat first used to make soup is recycled, pulled into shreds like an old garment, and then braised in a savory sauce. In Cuba, *ropa vieja* is an everyday dish, as predictable in the weekly menu as the ubiquitous picadillo or *palomilla* steak.

Working Ahead ▶ This dish can be made 2 or 3 days ahead and kept refrigerated. You can also cook the meat and keep it refrigerated with the broth for 1 or 2 days before proceeding with the recipe.

What to Drink: Bodegas Juan Gil Wrongo Dongo, a fun Monastrell wine with a whimsical name to match *ropa vieja*

SERVES 6

For the Meat

- 2 pounds flank steak
- 1 medium yellow onion (8 ounces), peeled and halved
- 1 medium green bell pepper (6 ounces), halved, cored, and seeded
- 5 allspice berries
- 2 bay leaves
- 2 teaspoons salt

For the Cooking Sauce

- 3 tablespoons extra-virgin olive oil
- 8 garlic cloves, finely chopped
- 1 large yellow onion (12 ounces), slivered lengthwise
- 1 large red bell pepper (8 ounces), cored, seeded, and cut into ¼-inch strips
- 1 teaspoon ground cumin
- 1 teaspoon dried oregano
- ¼ teaspoon ground allspice
- 1 teaspoon crushed red pepper flakes (optional)
- One 14-ounce can plum tomatoes, crushed
- ½ cup dry red wine

Cooking the Meat ▶ Place the meat in a medium pot with 2 quarts water and the onion, bell pepper, allspice berries, bay leaves, and salt. Bring to a boil over high heat. Lower the heat to medium and simmer, covered, for 1 hour, or until tender. Lift the meat onto a platter. Strain the broth through a fine-mesh sieve, pushing on the solids with the back of a wooden spoon, and discard the solids. When the meat is cool enough to handle, pull it into ⅛-inch shreds. Reserve.

Making the Cooking Sauce ▶ Heat the oil in a 12-inch sauté pan over medium heat. Add the garlic and sauté until golden, about 40 seconds. Add the onion and bell pepper and sauté for 2 to 3 minutes. Add the cumin, oregano, allspice, and red pepper flakes, if using, and cook, stirring, for 1 minute. Stir in the crushed tomatoes and wine. Cook for 10 minutes, until slightly concentrated. Add the shredded beef and 1 cup of the reserved broth and simmer for 15 minutes.

Serving: Serve with white rice and Fried Ripe Plantains (page 183).

Venezuelan Pan-Fried Shredded Beef for *Pabellón Criollo*

Carne Frita para Pabellón

Venezuela's national dish is a blue plate of braised shredded beef, white rice, black beans, and fried ripe plantains. What makes it Venezuelan is not so much the combination of elements or that touch of Worcestershire sauce but the way the beef is shredded. Traditional Venezuelan cooks insist that the meat should be shredded as thin as flies' legs—not a very appetizing thought, but a metaphor that reminds the cook that this shredding business requires meticulous care.

What to Drink: Susana Balbo Crios Syrah-Bonarda from Mendoza, Argentina

SERVES 6

For the Meat

- 2 pounds flank steak
- 1 large yellow onion (12 ounces)
- 1 large red bell pepper (8 ounces), halved and seeded
- 1 tablespoon black peppercorns
- 1 teaspoon cumin seeds
- 1 teaspoon dried oregano
- 1 tablespoon red wine vinegar
  Salt to taste

For the Cooking Sauce

- ¾ cup achiote-infused corn oil (page 89)
- 1½ teaspoons salt, or to taste
- 8 garlic cloves, finely chopped
- 1 medium yellow onion (8 ounces), finely chopped (1½ cups)
- 1 large red bell pepper (8 ounces), cored, seeded, deveined, and cut into ¼-inch strips
- 1 teaspoon freshly ground black pepper
- ¼ teaspoon dried oregano
- ¼ teaspoon ground cumin
- 1 tablespoon Worcestershire sauce (optional) or 1 tablespoon good red wine vinegar

Precooking the Meat ▶ Cut the meat against the grain into several 2½- or 3-inch-long pieces. Place in a heavy 6-quart pot, cover with 2 quarts water, and add the onion, bell pepper, peppercorns, cumin seeds, oregano, vinegar, and salt to taste. Bring to a boil over high heat. Lower the heat to medium and cook, covered, for 2 hours, or until the meat is tender. Lift the meat onto a plate. Strain the broth through a fine-mesh sieve and reserve; discard the solids.

Place the meat on a work surface and pound with a mallet to loosen the fibers. Pull the meat into the thinnest possible shreds, preferably less than ⅟₁₆ inch thick. You should have about 4 cups.

Sautéing the Meat ▶ Heat the oil in a 12-inch sauté pan or skillet. (Do not use a small pan. You need surface space to crisp the beef evenly and to avoid clumps.) When the oil begins to smoke, add the meat and fry until golden brown, stirring frequently, 12 minutes or until very crisp. Season with the salt. Add the garlic and sauté until golden, about 40 seconds. Add the onion, bell pepper, black pepper, oregano, and cumin; cook, stirring, for 2 to 3 minutes. Return the meat to the skillet and continue cooking, stirring, for 2 minutes. Stir in 1 cup of the reserved broth (save the rest for another purpose) and add Worcestershire sauce or vinegar. Reduce the heat to very low and cook for 15 minutes longer.

Serving: Serve with plain white rice, Caracan Black Bean Cream Soup (page 528), Fried Ripe Plantains (page 183), and a dollop of Venezuelan Ripened Milk (page 146).

Tongue in Almond Sauce

Lengua en Nogada

Tongue cooked in an ivory almond sauce is a traditional dish in many parts of Latin America, such as Mexico and Chile, where it is called *lengua en nogada* or *pepitoria*. The preparation of the dish and the name *nogada* come straight from the medieval-inspired cooking of colonial Latin America. As with many colonial dishes, it comes to the table garnished with chopped hard-boiled eggs.

What to Drink: A floral Crios Torrontes from Mendoza, Argentina

SERVES 4 TO 6

For the Tongue
- 1½ pounds veal tongue
- 1 medium yellow onion (8 ounces), peeled
- 1 tablespoon black peppercorns

For the Sauce
- ¼ cup extra-virgin olive oil
- 1 cup all-purpose flour
- 1 medium yellow onion (8 ounces), finely chopped
- 1 bay leaf
- ¼ cup dry sherry or Latin American *vino seco*
- 3 cups cooking broth from tongue, or chicken broth, homemade (page 538) or store-bought
- 1 cup sliced blanched almonds, toasted and coarsely ground
- 1¼ teaspoons salt, or to taste

- 1 hard-boiled egg, coarsely chopped, for garnish

Cooking the Tongue ▶ Rinse the tongue in cold running water. Place in a heavy 8-quart pot with 4 quarts water, the onion, and the peppercorns. Bring to a boil, lower the heat to medium, and simmer, covered, until the tongue is soft, about 3 hours.

The cooking can also be done in a pressure cooker. Rinse the tongue in cold running water. Place in the pressure cooker with 4 quarts water, the onion, and the peppercorns and cook over high heat until the first loud hissing whistle of the pot's safety valve. Lower the heat to medium and cook for 45 minutes. Turn the heat off and let the pot cool before opening. The tongue should be fork-tender but whole.

Remove the tongue from the pot or pressure cooker, strain, and reserve 3 cups broth. Remove the skin. Cut the meat crosswise at an angle into ¼-inch slices. Set aside, covered with plastic wrap.

Preparing the Sauce ▶ Heat the oil over medium heat in a 12-inch sauté pan or skillet until it ripples. Lightly dredge the slices of tongue in most of the flour, reserving about 1 tablespoon. Add the tongue to the pan, 2 to 3 slices at a time, and brown on both sides, about 1 minute on each side. Lift out onto absorbent paper towels to drain.

In the oil remaining in the pan, sauté the

chopped onion with the reserved 1 tablespoon flour and the bay leaf for 3 minutes, stirring, until the onion is translucent. Stir in the sherry and cook for 5 minutes, until the liquid is nearly evaporated. Stir in the broth and cook for 3 to 4 minutes. Stir in the ground almonds and salt and cook, covered, on medium-low heat until the sauce thickens, about 5 minutes. Skim occasionally. Return the tongue to the pan and heat for a minute or two.

Serving: Divide the meat and sauce among serving plates and garnish with the chopped egg. Accompany with plain white rice.

PORK

Pork Meatballs in Sweet-and-Sour *Escabeche*

Albóndigas de Cerdo en Escabeche

I found this recipe in the nineteenth-century *Nuevo cocinero americano en forma de diccionario* (The New American Cook in Dictionary Form), a venerable encyclopedia of Mexican colonial cooking that enjoyed great popularity throughout the Americas. As in many other recipes for *escabeche* in colonial cookbooks, this one does not call for vinegar, just sweet wine. It seems that colonial cooks understood the term *escabeche* not only as foods preserved in a vinegary sauce but also as foods flavored with wine. I liked this recipe so much that I adapted it to my

taste, keeping the sweet undertone of the original and adding mellow balsamic vinegar to turn it into a sweet-and-sour dish.

What to Drink: Adobe Guadalupe Gabriel from Guadalupe Valley in Baja California

SERVES 6

For the Meatballs

- 1 pound pork shoulder, cut into 2-inch chunks
- 4 ounces ham (fully or partially cooked), coarsely chopped
- 1 large Spanish chorizo (about 7½ ounces), coarsely chopped
- ½ teaspoon freshly ground black pepper
- ¼ teaspoon ground cloves
- ¼ teaspoon ground cinnamon
- ¼ cup capers, drained and coarsely chopped
- ¼ cup dark raisins (about 1½ ounces)
- ½ cup blanched almonds (about 2 ounces), toasted and finely chopped
- 3 tablespoons extra-virgin olive oil

For the Sauce

- 2 tablespoons extra-virgin olive oil
- 2 tablespoons all-purpose flour
- ½ teaspoon freshly ground black pepper
- ¼ teaspoon ground cloves
- ¼ teaspoon ground cinnamon
- 2 bay leaves
- 2 cups good beef or chicken broth, homemade (page 540 or 538) or store-bought
- ½ cup balsamic vinegar
- ½ cup port or sweet sherry
  Salt
- 2 tablespoons toasted sesame seeds

Making the Meatballs ▶ Ask your butcher to finely grind the pork, ham, and chorizo together, or do it yourself with a clamp-on meat grinder or the grinding attachment of a standing mixer. Place the ground meat mixture in a large bowl and add the pepper, cloves, cinnamon, capers, raisins, and almonds. Mix well and shape into 32 to 36 meatballs.

Heat the oil in a 12-inch sauté pan or skillet, add the meatballs a handful at a time, and brown, turning, until evenly golden, about 8 minutes. Lift from the skillet with a slotted spoon and drain on paper towels.

Preparing the Sauce ▶ In a 12-inch sauté pan or skillet, heat the oil over medium heat. Stir in the flour and cook, stirring, until the flour is lightly browned, about 7 minutes. Add the pepper, cloves, cinnamon, bay leaves, broth, vinegar, wine, and salt to taste and bring to a boil. Add the meatballs, lower the heat, sprinkle with sesame seeds, and simmer, covered, for 20 minutes.

Serving and Storing: Serve with white rice or Mexican Rice (page 302). If not serving immediately, let cool, cover with plastic wrap, and store in the refrigerator. The dish will keep well for 3 or 4 days.

Pork Tenderloin with Passion Fruit–Pink Peppercorn Sauce

Lomo de Cochino en Salsa de Parchita con Bayas Rosadas

Several years ago I discovered that pink peppercorns grow wild around Caracas, where people walking past them on roadsides and in parks usually think they are pretty bushes. But the Venezuelan chef Helena Ibarra picks loads of the peppercorns every time they are in season. She bottles them in whimsical packages to give away and also uses them in her cooking. One of my favorite dishes from her ample repertoire is pork tenderloin marinated in an aromatic mixture featuring pink peppercorns and passion fruit juice and finished with a velvety, butter-enriched reduction of the pan juices.

What to Drink: Crios Rosé de Malbec from Mendoza, Argentina

SERVES 6 TO 8

- 3½ pounds boneless pork tenderloin
- 2 tablespoons pink peppercorns, plus a few more for garnish
- ½ cup passion fruit juice
- 3 tablespoons grated brown loaf sugar (*panela* or *papelón*), Muscovado sugar, or dark brown sugar
- ¼ cup dark rum
- 3 tablespoons soy sauce
- 3 tablespoons honey
- 3 tablespoons Worcestershire sauce
- 5 allspice berries, freshly ground
- 1 tablespoon dried rosemary
  Salt to taste
- 2 tablespoons unsalted butter, cut into small pieces

Rosemary sprigs, for garnish

▶ Wipe the meat clean with a damp cloth. If it has not been tied by the butcher, form it into a neat log and tie it with butcher's twine. Place the meat in a nonreactive roasting pan.

In a blender or food processor, combine the pink peppercorns and passion fruit juice with all the remaining ingredients except the butter and rosemary sprigs and process to a puree. You should have about 1¼ cups. Rub about ½ cup of the mixture all over the pork, reserving the rest. Let the meat sit for at least 4 hours at room temperature.

Preheat the oven to 350°F. Roast the meat on the center rack for 2½ hours, or until an instant-read thermometer inserted in the center registers 160°F. Lift the meat onto a carving board.

Place the pan over 2 burners and deglaze with the remaining marinade over low heat. Pour the deglazed pan juices into a small saucepan and bring to a bare simmer. Add the butter and swirl it into the sauce. Pour the sauce into a sauceboat and keep warm.

Serving: Carve the roast into ¼-inch-thick slices and serve garnished with sprigs of rosemary and pink peppercorns, with the sauce on the side. An ideal accompaniment is Spiced *Arracacha* Puree (page 216) or Simple Peach Palm Fruit Puree (page 194).

Jauco-Style Suckling Pig Broth and Fried Suckling Pig

Cochinito en Sopa y Frito al Estilo de Jauco

This fascinating recipe for fried suckling pig comes from the family of my paternal grandmother, Pascuala Ferrer, a large clan of cacao and coffee farmers who live deep in the mountains near the Jauco River in eastern Cuba. I tasted it when I arrived at my family's farm after almost thirty years away. That night we all sat around a huge cauldron of suckling pig soup and talked, warmed by the wood fire.

The dish was unusual. The men had cut the young pig into small pieces and plunged it in a bubbling cauldron with chives (a very common seasoning there), leeks, garlic, whole onions, broad-leaf *culantro*, and allspice berries. When the meat was tender, my cousin Mireya ladled the broth into tall glasses and we drank it as a soup. The morsels of meat remained in the cauldron; freshly rendered lard was added to the pot, and the morsels began to fry to a golden brown. The result was stupendous—pieces of pork delicately crunchy outside yet so tender and moist you could even eat the tiny bones.

Cook's Notes: You can find suckling pigs in many ethnic markets as well as in Italian and German butcher shops. Order a suckling pig, 9 to 12 pounds, and have the butcher cut it up in serving pieces (3- to 4-inch sections). Ask the butcher to include the feet and to cut the head into quarters.

To cook this dish in the authentic way, you will need a large, wide cooking pot, preferably a cast aluminum *caldero*. If you use a deeper and narrower pot, such as a stockpot, do not stir the ingredients unnecessarily, as this can bruise the meat.

Trim the gelatin-rich ears from the suckling pig and add to the soup, but discard the kidneys and the two quarters of the head that contain the brains and eyes. These organs spoil quickly and may cloud or taint the soup.

For a crystal-clear soup, there are a few things to watch out for. Most important, make sure your pig is very fresh. The fresher the pig, the clearer the soup and the whiter the meat. A very fresh pig also means there will be less foam to skim while the pork is simmering. Finally, do not cook the pork at a rolling boil, which clouds the broth; gently simmer it until fork-tender.

What to Drink: Montes Alpha Syrah from the Colchagua Valley in Chile

SERVES 12

For the Marinade

- 1 small suckling pig (9–12 pounds), cut into pieces (see Cook's Notes)
- 1 head garlic, separated into cloves and peeled
- 1 tablespoon salt
- 1 tablespoon fresh oregano leaves, plus more for garnish
   Juice of 2 bitter oranges (about ¼ cup)

For the Broth

- 10 quarts water
- 20 small Caribbean sweet peppers (*ajíes dulces*) or 4 cubanelle peppers
- 2 medium yellow onions (about 1 pound), peeled
- 2 leeks, white, pale green, and 4 inches of dark green parts, halved lengthwise and cut into 4-inch pieces
- 1 small bunch chives, coarsely chopped, plus whole chives for garnish
- 8 broad-leaf *culantro* leaves
- 6 cilantro sprigs
- 3 bay leaves
- 1 tablespoon allspice berries
- 1 tablespoon salt

   Chives, for serving
   Oregano sprigs, for serving
- 8–10 pounds freshly rendered lard (page 82), for deep-frying

Marinating the Pork ▶ Place the pork in a large bowl or a sealable plastic container. In a mortar, mash the garlic to a paste with the salt. Add the garlic paste, oregano, and orange juice to the pieces of meat. Stir to combine and coat. Cover and marinate, refrigerated, at least 2 hours or overnight.

Making the Broth ▶ In a wide 22-quart *caldero* (about 17 inches in diameter and 5 inches deep) or other large, wide pot, combine the water with the remaining broth ingredients. Cover and bring to a boil over high heat. Add the pork and its marinade, reduce the heat, and simmer, skimming occasionally, until the pork is fork-tender and the broth is flavorful, about 2 hours.

Remove the pork from the broth and set aside. Strain the broth through a fine-mesh sieve, pressing against the mesh with the back of a wooden spoon, and discard the solids. Taste for salt. Place sprigs of chives and oregano in stocky serving glasses. Ladle the broth into the glasses and serve at once.

Frying the Pork ▶ Wash and dry the *caldero*. Pat the pork dry with paper towels, removing any remnants of the marinade. (It is important for the pork to be clean and dry so it will not spatter when added to the hot lard.) Add the lard to the *caldero* and heat over high heat until it reaches 375°F on a deep-frying thermometer.

Using a slotted spoon or tongs and working in

batches, add the pork to the lard. (It is important not to crowd the pan, in order to maintain the correct temperature for frying.) Fry over medium-high heat until the skin is crisp and deep golden brown, 5 to 10 minutes.

Serving: Remove to a platter and serve with Fried Green Plantains (page 182) and a rice and beans dish.

Santiago de Cuba's Roast Pork Marinated in a Garlicky Allspice-Cumin *Adobo*

Cerdo Brujo

This heirloom family recipe has the distinctive allspice aroma of the cooking of my hometown, Santiago de Cuba, the only part of Cuba where this complex spice is used in a pork marinade. The combination of cumin and allspice is especially characteristic of my family's cooking. Originally a Christmas dish, *cerdo brujo* is now one of the most popular dishes at my restaurant Zafra, where we celebrate Christmas every day.

What to Drink: Luca Pinot Noir from Mendoza, Argentina, or Robledo Family Pinot Noir from Los Carneros, California

SERVES 8

For the *Adobo*

- 1   head garlic, separated into cloves and peeled
- 1   tablespoon salt
- 2   teaspoons black peppercorns
- 2   teaspoons ground cumin
- 2   teaspoons allspice berries or ground allspice

- ¾   cup bitter orange juice (from about 6 oranges) or equal parts lime juice and orange juice
- 1   cup sweet orange juice diluted with about ¼ cup water

For the Pork

One   8- to 9-pound leg of pork, with skin
- 1   teaspoon salt

- ¼   cup sweet sherry or port wine, for deglazing

Making the *Adobo* ▶ Place the garlic, salt, peppercorns, cumin, and allspice in a large mortar and pound to a paste with a pestle. Stir in the bitter orange juice. (You can also puree these ingredients in a blender or food processor.) Set aside.

Preparing the Pork ▶ Trim the skin from the inner part of the leg only. Wipe the meat clean with a damp cloth. Make several deep incisions all over the skinned portion and rub with the salt. Let rest for a few minutes. Rub the marinade all over the pork, pushing it into the gashes and between the meat and the skin. Cover with plastic wrap and refrigerate for 2 to 3 hours or a maximum of 12 hours. Wipe the marinade from the skin with a clean cloth.

Roasting the Pork ▶ Preheat the oven to 400°F. Place the pork in a roasting pan and bake uncovered, skin side up, for 3 to 4 hours. Check the roast often. As the pan juices evaporate, replenish them with a little of the diluted sweet orange juice. The pork is done when the skin is crackling and the juices run clear when the meat is pierced at the thickest part of the leg (about 160°F on a meat thermometer).

Finishing the Dish ▶ Remove the pork from the oven and lift it onto a cutting board, holding the bone with a cloth. With a sharp knife, remove the crisp skin and cut it into small serving pieces. Place them on a cookie sheet and set in the turned-off oven, uncovered (if you cover the crackling, it steams and gets soggy).

To deglaze the pan juices, place the roasting pan on the stove over medium heat and add the sherry, scraping up the browned bits with a wooden spoon.

Carve the pork and return to the roasting pan with the pan juices to keep the meat moist and flavorful. Pork dries out easily, so if you must hold it for more than 30 minutes, cover the pan with aluminum foil and return it to a warm oven.

Serving: Be sure to include some of the crisp skin and deglazed juices with each serving. Serve with rice and Havana-Style Black Bean Soup (page 507) or Puerto Rican Stewed Red Kidney Beans (page 509) and Venezuelan Yuca *Mojo* (page 142).

Peruvian-Style Roasted Leg of Pork Marinated in *Adobo Tacneño*

Chancho Asado al Estilo de Tacna

When it comes to marinades for a roast leg of pork, I like this Peruvian *adobo* from Tacna as much as the fragrant one from my hometown in eastern Cuba. The dried *mirasol* peppers give a fabulous golden color and spicy edge to the Mediterranean seasonings in the *adobo*, which is rubbed all over the leg of pork and allowed to marinate overnight. The result is heavenly—a mildly spicy but deeply flavorful roast that stays in your memory.

What to Drink: Montes Cherub Rosé de Syrah from Colchagua Valley, Chile

SERVES 8

For the Pork

6 dried *mirasol* peppers (about 1¾ ounces), stemmed and seeded

One 8-pound leg of pork or shoulder butt, bone-in and skin-on

1 teaspoon salt

For the *Adobo*

2 heads garlic, separated into cloves and peeled

1 tablespoon ground cumin

1 teaspoon dried oregano

1 teaspoon freshly ground black pepper

½ teaspoon turmeric

¼ cup red wine vinegar

2 teaspoons salt

Preparing the Pork ▶ Place the peppers in a small saucepan with 2 cups water and boil until tender, about 15 minutes. Drain, reserving ¼ cup liquid, and set aside.

Wipe the leg of pork clean with a damp cloth. With a sharp knife, make several deep incisions all over the meat. Rub with the salt. Let sit for 10 to 15 minutes while you make the marinade.

Making the *Adobo* ▶ In a blender or food processor, process the garlic to a puree with the *mirasol* peppers, cumin, oregano, pepper, turmeric, vinegar, salt, and reserved cooking liquid. Rub the mixture all over the meat, pushing it into the incision. Cover with plastic wrap and refrigerate for a minimum of 6 hours and a maximum of 24.

Roasting the Pork ▶ Preheat the oven to 350°F. Place the pork in a roasting pan, skin side up. Roast, uncovered, for 4 hours, or until the juices run clear when the thickest part of the leg is pierced.

Serving: Serve hot with plain white rice and Stewed Peruvian Canary Beans (page 511) or Canary Bean and Rice Log (page 275). Or slice thin and use for sandwiches.

Slab Bacon or Pork Belly in Guava–Bitter Orange *Adobo*

Tocino Entreverado o Barrigada en Adobo de Guayaba y Naranja Agria

This is my favorite way of cooking slab bacon or pork belly, in a rich and fruity Andean pepper and guava *adobo* with a citrusy backbone. I make this recipe with many variations, sometimes adding Spanish oloroso sherry or Catalan wild oak honey. In every incarnation, it is simply terrific as a partner for fried eggs or fresh corn tamales.

Working Ahead ▶ The hot pepper *adobo* can be made 2 or 3 days ahead, and the meat can be seasoned 2 days in advance and kept refrigerated, covered with plastic wrap.

What to Drink: Ben Marco Malbec from Mendoza, Argentina

SERVES 6 TO 8

- 4 pounds meaty slab bacon or pork belly, in 1 piece

For the Adobo

- 18 dried *panca* peppers (about 4 ounces), or equal parts dried *mirasol* and *panca* peppers, or a combination of dried ancho and guajillo chiles, stemmed and seeded
- 1 tablespoon extra-virgin olive oil
- 8 large garlic cloves
- 2 teaspoons ground cumin
- 1 teaspoon dried oregano
- ½ teaspoon hot *pimentón* (Spanish smoked paprika)
- ¼ teaspoon anise seeds
- ½ cup fresh orange juice
- ½ cup fresh bitter orange juice or ¼ cup lime juice
- 2 tablespoons guava preserve or 1 tablespoon Catalan wild oak honey
- ¼ cup oloroso sherry
- ½ cup grated brown loaf sugar (*piloncillo* or *panela*) or Muscovado sugar, or to taste
- 1 teaspoon salt, or to taste

For the Glaze

- ¼ cup guava preserve, or to taste
- ¼ cup grated brown loaf sugar, or to taste

For the Garnish

Cacao nibs (optional)

Preparing the Bacon ▶ Rinse the bacon or pork and pat dry. Score a grid pattern on the skin side without cutting through the skin.

Making the *Adobo* ▶ Heat a *comal*, griddle, or heavy skillet over medium heat. Add the dried peppers, in batches, and toast lightly, 3 to 4 seconds on each side. Lift out of the pan, place in a medium bowl, and cover with warm water to soften, or simmer with water in a saucepan for about 15 minutes until soft. When the peppers are soft, place in a blender or food processor with the olive oil, garlic, cumin, oregano, paprika, anise, citrus juices, 2 tablespoons guava preserve, the sherry, ½ cup sugar, and the salt and process into a smooth paste.

Place the meat in a 2-inch-deep baking pan that can hold it comfortably. Pour the *adobo* over the meat and rub thoroughly all over. Cover with plastic wrap and let marinate for at least 6 hours or overnight.

Roasting the Meat ▶ Preheat the oven to 350°F. When ready to roast, unwrap the meat and add about ¼ cup water to the pan. Cover tightly with aluminum foil and bake on the middle rack until golden brown and glistening, about 1 hour. For a moist look, prepare a glaze by mixing some of the pan juices with the remaining ¼ cup sugar and ¼ cup guava preserve. Brush the glaze over the meat and continue baking for 20 more minutes, until the meat is golden brown and fork-tender.

Serving: Transfer the meat to a large cutting board and carve into slices. Garnish with cacao nibs, if you wish. Serve with fried eggs or fresh corn tamales (pages 454–59) presented in their own husks.

Pit Cooking

Cooking outdoors in Latin America can be a day-long special event that embraces any number of culinary techniques. In regions with enduring Indian traditions, pit cooking—cooking in the ground—is popular. What is cooked and how it has been marinated, as well as the dishes that are served with the pit-cooked foods and the rituals that accompany the eating, will vary from region to region, but the cooking is always done in a hole dug in the ground and lined with hot stones, which acts as oven. The food is kept moist by a cloud of steam drawn from the earth and warmed by the heat of the stones.

In some parts of Mexico this method is called the *barbacoa*; in the Yucatán the *pib*; in Bolivia, the *watia*; in Peru, the *pachamanca*; and in the south of Chile, from Temuco down to the island of Chiloé, the *curanto*. What gets cooked also varies according to region. In southern Chile it is surf and turf, a feast with lots of fabulous Pacific Ocean shellfish as well as smoked pork, sausages, chicken, vegetables, and potato patties called *chapaleles* and *milcaos*. In Peru, the *pachamanca* is a celebration of *pachamama*, Mother Earth: marinated meats, large ears of corn, fava beans, potatoes, and the delicate fresh Andean corn tamales called *humitas*. The *pachamanca*, the harvest feast of Andean farmers, is an ancient ritual that dates back to pre-Columbian times, a riotous celebration that stands in marked contrast to the people's normally austere diet. It has also become a commercial phenomenon; in Lima everyone leaves on weekends and feast days for the nearby highland towns that specialize in *pachamancas*.

There are many ways of preparing the pit for a *pachamanca*, and here Peruvians show their ingenuity. In Tarma, a town in the central Andes, men dig a wide, deep pit and build a wood fire within. Then they fit a sheet of corrugated metal over the pit, held up by iron rods. Heavy roundish river stones are arranged over it, and another fire is built on the stones. The fires burn for several hours, and in the meantime, the men marinate huge chunks of goat or pork in an *aderezo*, a marinade made by the women using the bright orange-yellow pepper *ají amarillo*, tons of garlic, and the assertive herb *huacatay*. The women also make *humitas* from gigantic fresh white corn from the Andes.

When the fires have burned down, the men remove the metal sheet. With huge tongs, they carefully arrange the hot stones on the floor of the pit. Now, a kind of rough-hewn still life is created: A pot of sauce is propped in the center, surrounded by the vivid hues of meats, bumpy two-color potatoes, the dark green fava bean pods, and the apple green of the *humitas*. Huge quantities of herbs are stuffed between the blue-white stones, infusing the foods with their strong aromas. Over all this are arranged planks of wood, several wet burlap bags, and then a plastic tarpaulin, which seals in the steam. There is nothing dainty about a *pachamanca*: when the food emerges, it is doled out in hefty portions.

It is possible to duplicate the *pachamanca* in your own home, but it is a laborious process that requires skill and dedication. Even in Peru, you find people bringing the *pachamanca* indoors to be cooked on the stovetop or the oven. All the ingredients of the *pachamanca* are slowly cooked together in a large, tightly closed pot.

In the Yucatán, weddings, birthdays, and other important family gatherings involve *cochinita pibil*, the most famous of all barbecued dishes in Mexico. *Cochinita* is usually bought from people who specialize in *pib* cooking. Every town has several *pib* masters who earn a very comfortable living making *cochinita pibil* and a number of other *pib* dishes, such as turkey in *recado negro* or red beans with *chicharrones*. Whether it is bought or made at home, food cooked deep in an earth pit is always delicious.

Yucatecan *Pib*-Roasted Pork

Cochinita Pibil

One of my favorite sources for information about Maya life and food in Yucatán is the *Book of Chilam Balam of Chumayel*, which is full of riddles that are witty but often macabre. A father asks, "My son, bring me the bones of your father, those that you buried three years ago—I want to see them." "As you wish, O father," replies the son. "What he is being asked," explains the text, is for "yuca that has been cooked underground as food for the Chief Halach Uinic." If the text had not explained, I would have assumed that the riddle referred to the fact that yuca can remain in the ground for close to two years without spoiling. But there is no doubt; the text is laconic but clear. This is a reference to pit or *pib* cooking.

Before the coming of the Spaniards, the Maya must have cooked more than yuca in their *pibs*—for instance, whitetail deer, turkey, and tamales. They still do these. But the dish that we always associate with the *pib* is the postconquest *cochinita pibil*, a classic that fifty years ago could not be found outside Yucatán. Today *taquitos* of *cochinita pibil* can be found anywhere in Mexico, but the pork is cooked in a pot or the oven, not in the traditional *pib*.

I was in Yucatán early in 1995 with my friend Marilyn Tausend and had the rare opportunity to taste an authentic *cochinita pibil* and witness its ritualized preparation from beginning to end, at the house of a man named Silvio Campos in the town of Tixcocob. I was struck by the complexity of the process. Cooking in a *pib* is not for amateurs. It is a specialized occupation that involves several people and an inordinate number of man-hours. Silvio learned the art from his father. The family owns a large house with an ample backyard where pigs are raised, killed, and then cooked in the *pib* for several hours.

When I met Silvio, I kept staring at his immaculate white jacket, which had his name beautifully embroidered on its pocket. That's not the way *pib* masters normally dress. It made sense when I learned that Silvio had been invited to Chicago to practice his magic for none other than chef Rick Bayless. But no matter how spotless his jacket was, the flavor of his pork came from a burning hot, pitch-black hole in the ground.

The secret to a delicious *cochinita pibil* is not only the cooking method but the marinade, or *recado rojo*, a rich paste of achiote seeds and half a dozen spices that is smeared all over the pork before it is buried in the hot *pib*. Most Yucatecans buy a thick *recado rojo* from their local markets and freshen it at home by adding more spices and bitter orange juice to loosen it up a bit. With this rich, fragrant marinade on hand, you can season any meat and thus emulate the unique taste of Yucatecan *pib* foods. Nothing beats the taste of food cooked in a pit, but you can come close by wrapping seasoned pieces of meat in layers of plantain leaf and steam-roasting them in a tightly sealed roasting pan with some liquid in the oven to generate steam. But whatever you do, you must start your dish with a generous amount of *recado rojo*. The paste can be used to season any kind of meat, but it does wonders for fatty cuts of pork like shoulder and ribs.

What to Drink: Robledo Family Pinot Noir or Robledo Family Los Braceros, from California

SERVES 6

> 7 pounds meaty country-style spareribs
> 1 recipe Yucatecan Red Seasoning Paste for Pit-Roasted Pig (page 43)
> One 1-pound package plantain leaves
> 4 cups good chicken broth, homemade (page 538) or store-bought

▶ Rub the ribs with the seasoning paste and let rest for a couple of hours at room temperature. Preheat the oven to 425°F.

Wipe the plantain leaves clean with a damp kitchen towel and pat dry. Pass the leaves over the flame of a gas burner to toast. Flavorful oils will come to the surface, making the leaves look shiny.

Line an oval turkey roasting pan or any deep, heavy, ovenproof pot fitted with a lid with 3 overlapping layers of plantain leaves. Place the marinated ribs in the center of the leaves and fold the leaves over them to wrap like a package. Pour the broth gently down the side of the pot and cover tightly with the lid. Bake for 35 to 45 minutes. The broth will produce enough steam to cook the ribs.

Serving: Serve with Yucatecan Saffron Rice (page 301), Yucatecan Refried Beans (page 276), and Yucatecan Red Onions Pickled in Bitter Orange Juice (page 149).

Short Ribs in Black Sauce (*page 713*) and
Sautéed Quinoa with Swiss Chard
(*page 258*)

Young Goat Stew from Northern Peru
(*page 754*), and a serving of Young Goat
Stew with Stewed Peruvian Canary
Beans (*page 511*) and steamed white rice

Turkey in *Mole* Sauce
(*page 781*), served with freshly
made Mexican Corn Tortillas
(*page 579*) and Mexican
Rice (*page 302*)

Cuban Sandwiches (page 593) with
Mamey Sapote Milk Shake (*page 344*)

The *merienda* (CLOCKWISE FROM TOP LEFT): quince paste; fresh cheese; hot chocolate *"Agasajo" (page 339)*; Tamarillos in Syrup Ecuadorian Style *(page 824)*; honey; Colombian-Style Fresh Cheese with Brown Loaf Syrup *(page 823)*. Served with breads: Yuca Bread *(page 573)*; Colombian Grilled Corn and Cheese Arepas *(page 587)*; Colombian Yuca, Corn, and Cheese Rolls *(page 578)*; Christ's Knees *(page 595)*. PICTURED ON RIGHT: *molinillo*, a wooden utensil for frothing hot chocolate.

Valencia Orange and
Cheese Flan with
Orange Rum Sauce
(*page 828*)

Miami *Tres Leches* (page 844)

Cucharamama *Dulce de Leche*
Ice Cream *(page 852)* with
Peruvian *Alfajores (page 838)*

Home-Cured Boneless Peruvian Ham

Jamón del País

To take ham into your own hands, literally, follow this Peruvian recipe. Latin Americans love cured pork of all sorts, a taste inherited from Spain. But imported ham is costly, so Peruvians have created this homemade version packed with the flavors of their spicy *adobo* and slowly braised on the stovetop. This ham has no nitrates and is not dry-cured like a version made in the north of the country called *jamón del norte*, which calls for a similar *adobo*. The *mirasol* peppers and the smoked paprika preserve and cure the meat.

To cook the ham, there are two schools of thought. Some cooks like to cover the pork with water and allow it to poach over medium heat until done. Others add less water and brown the ham in the fat that remains in the pot when the liquid evaporates. Both methods work equally well.

Cook's Note: To intensify the flavor of the ham, leave it in its piquant marinade for 2 or 3 days in the refrigerator before rolling and tying it. Turn the meat over every 12 hours.

What to Drink: Peruvian Callao or Cuzqueña beer

SERVES 12

For the *Adobo*

- 12 dried *mirasol* peppers (about 3 ounces), stemmed and seeded
- ¼ cup red wine vinegar
- 2 large heads garlic, separated into cloves and peeled

- 1 tablespoon hot *pimentón* (Spanish smoked paprika) or *Merkén* from Chillán (page 74)
- 1 tablespoon dried oregano
- 1 tablespoon ground cumin
- 1 tablespoon ground achiote (page 89)
- 1½ tablespoons salt

For the Pork

- One 9-pound leg of pork or shoulder butt, bone-in and skin-on
- 2 large red onions (12 ounces each), peeled and halved
- 1 large red bell pepper (8 ounces), cored and seeded
- ¼ cup red wine vinegar
- 5 bay leaves
- 2 teaspoons salt, or to taste
- One 3-inch Ceylon cinnamon stick (*canela*)

Preparing the *Adobo* ▶ Soak the dried peppers in 1 quart hot water for 20 minutes or boil for 10 to 15 minutes, until softened. Drain, reserving 1 cup of the soaking liquid. Cool slightly. Transfer the peppers and reserved liquid to a food processor. Process to a smooth puree with ¼ cup vinegar and the garlic, paprika, oregano, cumin, ground achiote, and 1½ tablespoons salt. Makes about 2 cups.

Preparing the Pork ▶ You can ask the butcher to bone the meat or do it yourself: Work the rind away from the meat with a sharp knife, leaving as much of the fat intact as possible. Lay the pork on your work surface, fat side down. Make a straight deep cut to the bone and work the knife around the bone to detach the meat a little at a time. Set the bone aside. Cut into the thickest part of the pork almost all the way through, and open the two sides like a book. With a mallet or the bottom of a heavy saucepan, pound the meat to an even 1½ to 2 inches thick. Prick it all over with the point of the knife.

Transfer the pork to a nonreactive baking dish and spread the marinade over it. Cover with plastic wrap and refrigerate for at least 8 hours or overnight.

When you are ready to cook the meat, roll it into a cylinder, beginning with one of the short ends, tucking in any loose pieces of meat as you go. Tie with butcher's twine. Some cooks like to wrap the ham tightly in cheesecloth to compact the meat further while cooking and make it easier to slice when cooled.

Cooking the Meat ▶ Place the meat in a 12-quart Dutch oven or wide saucepan and add water just to cover, 4 to 5 quarts. Add the onions, bell pepper, vinegar, bay leaves, salt, cinnamon, and reserved pork bone. Bring to a boil over high heat, reduce the heat to medium-low, and simmer until the meat is tender when pierced with a knife, 4 to 5 hours (about 30 minutes per pound). When a thermometer inserted in the thickest part of the ham reads between 160°F and 180°F, the meat is done. Lift it out onto a carving board or platter and let sit until it reaches room temperature.

Serving: Slice the ham thin to make the popular sandwiches called *butifarras*. Stack it in Cuban Bread (page 591) and top it with tomato slices and Peruvian *salsa criolla* (page 150). Accompany with a Peruvian Warm Purple Potato and Squash Salad (page 205).

The broth (about 7 cups) can be used as the liquid in Peruvian hot pepper stews such as *adobo arequipeño* (page 747). When the broth is refrigerated, a layer of fat will settle on top. Scoop it out and use to cook Chicken Tamales from Lima (page 472).

Nanda's *Malta*-Mustard Spareribs

Costillitas al Horno con Malta y Mostaza al Estilo de Nanda

Using *malta* in cooking is a grown-up way to indulge in the flavors of childhood. In her adaptation of a cherished family recipe, my friend Nanda Machado combines *malta* with honey, garlic, cumin, and pungent Dijon mustard, a favorite flavoring for grilled meats in her native Argentina, to create a sultry sweet-and-sour sauce for meaty spareribs.

What to Drink: Dark Peruvian Cuzqueña beer or a fruity Budini Malbec from Mendoza, Argentina

SERVES 4 TO 6

For the Spareribs

  4 pounds meaty spareribs, in 1 piece
  1 teaspoon salt
  2 teaspoons freshly ground pepper
  1 cup Dijon mustard

For the *Malta* Sauce

  6 garlic cloves, mashed to a pulp with a mortar and pestle or finely chopped and mashed with the edge of a knife
Two 12-ounce bottles *malta* (Goya, Hatuey, and India brands are available in Latin markets)

2 tablespoons honey, preferably wildflower honey

2 teaspoons ground cumin

1 teaspoon salt

½ teaspoon pepper

Fresh rosemary or thyme sprigs, for garnish

Preparing the Spareribs ▶ Wipe the ribs clean and place in a large roasting pan. Rub with the salt and pepper and slather with the mustard, coating completely. Set aside for 30 minutes.

Preparing the *Malta* Sauce ▶ In a small bowl, whisk together the garlic, *malta*, honey, cumin, salt, and pepper. Pour over the ribs and set aside for at least 20 minutes.

Roasting the Spareribs ▶ Preheat the oven to 400°F. Place the roasting pan on the middle rack and roast the ribs until tender, about 2 hours (a bit more if you want the meat to fall off the bone). Halfway through roasting, baste the ribs with the pan juices.

Serving: Cut the ribs into individual portions. Place a pool of sauce on each plate and top with meat. Garnish with herb sprigs. Baked apples and pan-roasted potatoes and onions are good accompaniments.

New Venezuelan-Style Pork and Gouda Cheese

Nuevo Queso Gouda con Guiso de Cerdo

Dutch cheeses like Edam and Gouda made their way to Latin America when Spain, under the Hapsburgs, controlled parts of the Low Countries. In the early seventeenth century, the Dutch established their own commercial outposts and carried on a lively illegal trade with lands under Spanish control from Venezuela as far north as the Yucatán.

In those areas today, you will find recipes for *queso relleno* in which Gouda or Edam is hollowed out, filled with a savory stuffing of pork, seafood, or chicken, and steamed or baked until it softens. The typical Venezuelan filling is made with pork seasoned with *ají dulce* (Caribbean sweet pepper), Worcestershire sauce, and the sweet-and-sour counterpoint of brown loaf sugar, raisins, and olives. At home, I prepare a pared-down version similar to a gratin that I learned from the Venezuelan chef Edgar Leal. To serve it in individual portions, you need good-looking gratin dishes or ramekins of at least 1-cup capacity. You don't want the filling to overflow the bowl.

Cook's Note: I always try to get my hands on a raw-milk Gouda (such as Boerenkaas) or a blend of a young Gouda and an aged one. Gouda aged 3 or 4 years has superb flavor, with winy notes and nutty sweetness, and it makes a delicious crust when broiled. Gouda Parrano is also worth exploring. Relatively new to the U.S. market, this Dutch cheese has the creaminess of a traditional young Gouda and the nutty cooked-milk flavor of Parmigiano-Reggiano.

What to Drink: Dolium Reserva Malbec

SERVES 4 AS AN APPETIZER

For the Pork

- 1 pound boneless pork shoulder or leg
- 5 Caribbean sweet peppers (*ajíes dulces*), finely chopped
- 2 medium red bell peppers (6 ounces each), cored, seeded, deveined, and finely chopped (about 2 cups)
- 4 ripe medium plum tomatoes (about 12 ounces), peeled and shredded on a box grater
- 1 medium yellow onion (8 ounces), finely chopped (1½ cups)
- 2 scallions, white and some green parts, finely chopped
- 1 leek, white and light green parts, split lengthwise, rinsed, and finely chopped
- 4 garlic cloves, mashed to a pulp with a mortar and pestle or finely chopped and mashed
- 1 tablespoon Worcestershire sauce
- ½ teaspoon salt
- ½ teaspoon freshly ground pepper
- ¼ cup corn oil or canola oil
- 1 tablespoon unsalted butter
- 4 cups store-bought low-sodium chicken broth

For the Sauce

- 2 teaspoons corn oil or canola oil
- 3 ounces slab bacon, cut into ¼-inch dice
- 1 tablespoon tomato paste
- ½ cup dry red wine, preferably Cabernet Sauvignon
- 1 tablespoon Worcestershire sauce
- 15 green olives, pitted and sliced
- ½ cup dark raisins
- 1–2 tablespoons grated brown loaf sugar, preferably *panela*, or Muscovado or dark brown sugar
  Salt

- 8 ounces young Gouda or Gouda Parrano cheese, coarsely shredded
- 2 ounces aged Gouda cheese, finely grated

Seasoning the Pork ▶ Rinse the pork and pat dry. Place in a medium bowl and add the peppers, tomatoes, onion, scallions, leek, garlic, Worcestershire sauce, salt, and pepper. Rub all over the pork. Let rest for about 1 hour, tightly covered with plastic wrap.

Cooking the Pork ▶ Heat the oil and butter in a heavy medium saucepan at least 4 inches deep. Scrape the seasoning off the pork and set aside. Add the pork to the saucepan and brown on all sides. Add the seasoning and the chicken broth and bring to a boil over medium-high heat. Reduce the heat to medium and simmer until fork-tender, about 40 minutes. Remove from the heat and let cool. Strain the cooking liquid through a fine-mesh sieve into a bowl and reserve. Cut the pork into ¼-inch dice and set aside.

Preparing the Sauce ▶ Heat the oil in a medium saucepan over medium heat. Add the bacon and cook until golden brown, about 3 minutes. Discard all but 1 teaspoon fat from the pan. Add the tomato paste and cook for 1 minute, stirring. Stir in the red wine, reserved cooking liquid, Worcestershire sauce, diced meat, olives, raisins, and brown sugar. Taste and add salt if needed. Simmer until the sauce thickens a little, about 8 minutes.

Finishing the Dish ▶ Divide the pork into 4 portions (about ½ cup each) and place in individual ramekins or any decorative deep bowls you can heat under a broiler. Spoon the sauce over each portion and top with about 6 packed tablespoons of the shredded young Gouda and about 3 tablespoons of the grated aged Gouda. Place under the broiler, about 4 inches from the heat source, and broil until the cheeses melt and begin to turn light golden brown. Serve piping hot.

Roast Pig Cuban Style

Lechón Asado

In my house there is no gender typecasting—man barbecues, woman does empanadas. Years ago, my husband used to light the fire, but my dependence stopped when he taught me how to use a propane blowtorch. For me, grilling is a natural extension of the kitchen, and I treat it with the same practical reverence and proprietary zeal with which I claim control of cooking on my old Garland stove.

When it comes to roasting a pig outdoors, though, I need a man. Spit-roasting or grilling a pig Cuban style is a larger-than-life task, even if the pig is a miserly 35-pound piglet. This is a ritual that Cuban men are born to perform, because it challenges their resourcefulness. I am never short of masculine help when it comes to digging the hole or tending the fire, and there is a list of volunteers waiting to cook a pig in my backyard.

Years ago I discovered that in order to get my husband involved in the roasting of a pig I had to remain aloof, claiming weakness and ignorance. But left alone, he would soon lose interest, which spelled disaster. That's why I decided to bring Angel Alemán, a veteran pig roaster, to the rescue. Angel, who was a powerful seventy-one when he helped cook my pig, was raised in Jarahueca, a little rural town in Las Villas province. In Angel's part of Cuba, pigs were roasted Taíno style, on a makeshift grill made with green guava or *guamá* wood. The grill

was placed on *horquetas* (wooden pitchforks) over a pit dug in the ground. Everyone in Las Villas who had a yard and liked to roast pigs made their own wooden grills, which were discarded after use. Here in New Jersey, we had to be creative, since the only green wood belonged to cherished ornamentals that I was not willing to sacrifice.

The first day that Angel came to cook, he and my husband embarked on a detailed exploration of the backyard to find something they could use as a grill. They both knew that our local Home Depot had exactly what they needed, but each insisted on using something totally inappropriate, which they attempted to subdue for grilling. My husband grabbed a section of an old wrought-iron fence, a good idea if the fence had not been totally rusted. The old Cuban grabbed a piece of chainlink mesh, also rusty, and so tightly rolled up it would be practically impossible to unroll. Each claimed that in a few hours he could turn his find into a suitable grill. The two men seemed to be of the same tenacious, inventive species, *Homo cubanus*, but there was a substantial difference in their technical proclivities: my husband, the doctor, attempted to clean the rusty iron with a special metal scouring gun; Angel tried unsuccessfully to straighten the mesh wire with a huge hammer. As I predicted, the two of them ended up at Home Depot. They came home with a brand-new rolled-up piece of mesh wire. Angel had won! But I overheard him mumbling, "It's good to do this with people who have money."

The men politely continued to compete with each other until they agreed that only by joining forces would we be able to eat pork that evening. They managed to unroll the wire. They tied the loose ends to four sections of ½-inch galvanized iron pipes and made a grill that looked like a stiff stretcher for the pig. While they argued about whether to use bricks or four *horquetas* to support the grill, my nephew dug a trench about 3 feet long, 2 feet wide, and 1½ feet deep. I filled it with hardwood and lit the fire—with the blowtorch, naturally. That was my magical moment!

What follows is a recipe in two parts, one describing how to prepare and pit-roast the pig and another giving you step-by-step instructions for building what you need in your backyard. In addition to the equipment listed on pages 733–34, you will need a roll of heavy-gauge aluminum foil (for a makeshift tray to hold the pig while marinating) and two pieces of sheet aluminum 36 by 36 inches (have it cut to size at a hardware store). I suggest using a 35-pound pig, which has enough meat to make a succulent dish for a crowd but will not take 3 days to cook. The dish is best attempted in cool spring or fall weather, when the meat can be safely marinated outdoors.

Read through the entire recipe before you begin. Probably the trickiest part is turning the pig. This will take two strong people and a certain amount of coordination. I have given directions for making two grilling surfaces from wire mesh and pipes, so you can turn the pig by placing the second grill over it, inverting the whole thing, and lifting off the first grill.

What to Drink: Hatuey or Corona beer or Señorío de San Vicente, a *tempranillo peludo* from Rioja, Spain

Working Ahead ▶ You can marinate the pig at least 6 hours ahead.

SERVES 12

For the Pig

One 35-pound young pig
 4 tablespoons kosher salt

For the *Adobo*

 2 cups bitter orange juice (from about 12 oranges) or equal parts lime juice and orange juice
 5 large heads garlic, separated into cloves and peeled
 2 bay leaves, crushed
 1 tablespoon dried oregano
 1 tablespoon ground cumin
 1 tablespoon ground allspice
 1 tablespoon salt
 1 tablespoon freshly ground black pepper
 3 tablespoons freshly rendered lard (page 82)

Preparing the Pig ▶ Ask your butcher to butterfly the pig for you. For even roasting, the pig must be opened flat. Place it skin side up on the largest baking sheet you can find. If you must improvise, place your 2 largest baking sheets side by side and wrap aluminum foil around them to hold them together. Use more aluminum foil to mold a raised edge around all four sides. Line this makeshift platform with nonreactive plastic wrap such as Saran wrap. With a knife held at a slight angle, prick deep slits all over the pig's skin. Rub it all over with kosher salt. Turn the pig skin side down on the pan. Allow it to rest for at least 30 minutes before adding the *adobo*.

Making the *Adobo* ▶ Place ½ cup citrus juice in a blender or a food processor. Add all the remaining ingredients except the lard, and puree. Stir in the rest of the juice and blend well. Makes about 3⅓ cups.

Heat the lard in a small saucepan over high heat until rippling and pour in 1 cup *adobo*. It should sputter and sizzle vigorously. Immediately remove from the heat and reserve.

Marinating the Pig ▶ Rub the inside of the pig with the remaining 2⅓ cups *adobo*. Leave it to marinate at least 6 hours, and preferably overnight. This presents a problem, since it is too big for most refrigerators. Cubans leave the pig marinating overnight in a cold place in the house or even in the backyard if the weather is cool. I left mine to marinate on my porch, covered with plastic, when the outside temperature was 50°F.

Roasting the Pig ▶ Place the pig skin side up over one of the wire mesh *parrillas* that you have built, following the directions on page 734. Stretch out the legs and tie them loosely to the *parrilla* with galvanized wire so the wire can be easily cut with tinner's snips and removed when turning. When the coals are thoroughly heated and beginning to get ashy on the surface, place the *parrilla* over the pit. Cover the pig with 2 sheets of aluminum, each 36 by 36 inches.

The grilling requires constant attention. Every time you see the fire starting to die out, you must add more charcoal, shoveling it carefully under the *parrilla*. In all, a 35-pound pig will require about 40 pounds of old-fashioned hardwood charcoal. After about 2 hours, the pig will start smelling and looking roasted. This is the moment of truth, when the fat may literally hit the fire. Remove the sheets of aluminum and place your second mesh *parrilla* over the pig. Now you need to turn the whole heavy arrangement. This takes two people wearing thick heatproof mitts. Holding the long poles of the 2 *parrillas* together, lift from the fire, invert, and set back down on the fire. Remove the wire loops from the legs with your tinner's snips and lift off the first *parrilla*. At this point, brush the skin with about ½ cup of the lard-*adobo* mixture. Turn the pig over and brush the cavity with the rest of the mixture.

Put it back on the grill and replace the sheets of aluminum to cover. Continue to grill for another hour, then baste again. Turn the pig over once more, and baste with any remaining *adobo*. Roast for 1 more hour or until completely cooked.

Always keep cold beer at hand for the man who roasts the pig, and a first aid kit just in case he cuts or burns himself.

Cutting the Pork ▶ When the pig is cooked, transfer it to a cutting board or to the cleaned pan in which it was marinated, skin side up. Carve up the four legs first, then sections of the ribs. Give the ears and the tail to the man who cooked the pig.

Serving: Roast pork is served with very traditional foods: rice and beans, Boiled Yuca (page 167), Fried Green Plantains (page 182), Avocado and Onion Salad (page 547), and some *casabe* (page 573) to make it truly Cuban.

Roasting a Pig in Your Backyard

To Make the Grills (*Parrillas*)

   Tinner's cutting snips for metal

2 rolls of galvanized 2-by-3-inch wire mesh for fencing

4 ½-inch galvanized iron pipes (they are usually sold in 6-foot sections), with a blade for cutting if sawing the pipe yourself

1 roll of 14-gauge galvanized wire

4 cinder blocks or bricks to support the grill

To Make the Pit

   Pick and shovel

To Build a Fire

Twigs and small pieces of wood for kindling
1 cord of firewood (4 by 4 by 8 feet)
Two 20-pound bags of old-fashioned natural lump charcoal made with 100% hardwood

Making the Grill ▶ For each of the two *parrillas*: Using tinner's snips, cut the wire mesh into a rectangle 4 feet long by 2½ feet wide. Line up 2 of the 6-foot pipes along the edges of the long side of the mesh, centering the mesh so that you have about 12 inches of pipe to use as a handle at each end. Use loops of galvanized wire to fasten the pipes securely to the mesh or, even better, lace the pipes through the wire of the grid as if you were weaving and then secure them with loops of wire. With a metal saw, trim 2 more pipes to a length of 4 feet each. Line them up along the short sides of the mesh *parrilla* and fasten in the same way. The pipes and the mesh wire must be securely fastened together; otherwise your pig might fall into the pit.

Making the Pit and Lighting the Fire ▶ With a pick and shovel, dig a pit about 3 feet long by 2 feet wide and 1½ feet deep. Place the removed soil in a corner nearby and cover with a tarpaulin. (You will need it later to fill in the pit after the barbecue.) Line the pit with two layers of kindling and firewood. Light the fire (I use a propane blowtorch). When the wood is reduced to embers, spread 20 pounds of charcoal over the embers. When the flames subside and the charcoal begins to look ashy, get ready to place the grill, with the pig aboard, over the fire. The grill must be propped 1½ feet above the surface of the fire. If you can get hold of four strong forked sticks (*horcones*) of equal size, you are in luck. If not, prop the *parrilla* on cinder blocks or bricks.

COOKING A PIG IN THE CAJA CHINA

The Caja China is a Cuban-American invention patented in Miami to roast a whole pig without having to dig up a hole in your backyard for the traditional spit-roasted pork *lechón asado en púa*. Just as Cubans on the island have learned to keep old dinosaurs of cars going, Cubans in exile have created all kinds of contraptions for roasting a pig outdoors in all kinds of weather. The most remarkable of these is the brainchild of Roberto Guerra Sánchez, a tenacious immigrant now in his eighties from Las Martinas, a small town not far from Cabo San Antonio, the westernmost tip of Cuba. A simple rectangular plywood box lined with metal and topped with a tray-shaped metal lid to hold charcoal, the Caja China can roast anything from a whole pig to a turkey to golden, juicy perfection in half of the time that it takes in a conventional oven.

To me, everything about the Caja China is endearing: the rustic plywood finish, the funky Chinese characters on the box, and the curious name. I have heard that the Caja China was inspired by a similar contraption used in imperial China and later in Vietnam to torture and execute prisoners by roasting, and a few months ago someone told me that the box was invented in Havana's Chinatown. But Roberto Guerra assured me there is nothing Chinese about the Caja China except for the name. "Of all places, it all started in New Jersey," he began.

When Roberto Guerra told me his story, I felt like embracing him, for he represents the hard times and resourcefulness of the Cubans of my parents' generation, the ones who had to start from scratch and live hand to mouth until they made it. He and his family arrived in

Caja China

Miami in 1969 and relocated to Shelton, Connecticut. After several adventures, Roberto leased a small restaurant in Elizabeth, New Jersey, attached to a bar called El Bar de Víctor, which served broiled meats. Guerra had never seen a broiler in action, and he became fascinated with the way the food turned out golden and juicy.

Back in Miami, where he found a job in the construction business, Roberto often thought fondly of "those juicy steaks" in New Jersey, and he decided to create an outdoor roaster for pigs that would operate on the same principle, with the source of heat coming from above. After some experimenting, he produced the large box that is now his best-selling model. A smaller model for turkeys and chickens followed in 1990. Today,

Guerra reports steady sales of the Caja China throughout the United States and all over the world. "Only two countries in Latin America have not bought the Caja China yet, Paraguay and Uruguay," he says, "but they'll come around."

As for the funny name, Guerra explains that it was inspired by a jest. "You know how Cubans talk about difficult, painful things being a *tortura china* (a Chinese torture), right?" he said with a laugh. "How we say that a disease is so serious that not even *el médico chino* (the Chinese doctor) can cure it? I thought of all of that when trying to find a name for my invention. I thought it was good marketing, a name that would make you think." And he was right. For Cubans, anything ingenious is a *cosa de chinos* (Chinese thing), even if a *criollo* is the one who came up with the idea.

The Caja China can be ordered online from www .lacajachina.com. The company's website has all the information you need to successfully roast a large pig in record time. Roberto Guerra is not fond of elaborate *adobos*. He likes to brine his pigs by injecting them with a saline solution and add some *adobo* to the pork after it is roasted. I have cooked pigs in the Caja China following his instructions and also by seasoning the pig with my own *adobos*, and had good results with both. ◈

Roast Suckling Pig

Lechoncito Asado

Roast suckling pig is a fairly minor tradition in most of Latin America. The *lechón* that you usually find really is partly grown. I like them both. If you appreciate tender, melt-in-the mouth pork, then suckling pig is for you. Very young animals have not developed much fat; their meat is succulent and gelatinous, and they are easy to roast in a home oven. I even find them easier to roast than the Thanksgiving turkey. I like to place the pig on a bed of starchy vegetables that will absorb the pan juices. They are the perfect complement to the succulent yet delicate meat.

Cook's Notes: Season the pig at least 1 or 2 days ahead and wipe the skin clean before roasting. It is best to dry the skin completely. I often place a fan on my kitchen counter for this purpose, or use a hair dryer set on cool. Begin roasting at a high temperature but lower the temperature for the last hour of cooking.

What to Drink: Ben Marco Malbec or Ben Marco Expresivo from Mendoza, Argentina, or Asturian cider (if entertaining Latinos for Christmas Eve)

SERVES 8

For the Pig

- 1 small suckling pig (about 10 pounds)
- 4 teaspoons coarse salt
- 1 head garlic, separated into cloves and peeled
- 1 teaspoon cumin
- 1 teaspoon dried oregano
- 1 teaspoon freshly ground black pepper
  Juice of 5 bitter oranges, strained
  Juice of 2 sweet oranges, strained

For the Vegetables

- 2 large yellow onions (12 ounces each), peeled and quartered
- 3 Caribbean sweet potatoes (*boniatos*; about 2½ pounds), peeled and cut into 2-inch chunks
- 3 large carrots (about 1¼ pounds), peeled and cut at an angle into 2-inch pieces
- ¼ cup extra-virgin olive oil
- 1 teaspoon salt
- 2 teaspoons fresh rosemary leaves

- 2 pomegranates, quartered, for garnish
  Fresh rosemary sprigs, for garnish

Preparing the Pig ▶ Tell the butcher to butterfly the pig but leave the head intact. Rinse the pig under cold running water and pat thoroughly dry with a kitchen towel. Rub with 2 teaspoons salt and let rest on a baking sheet or roasting pan while preparing the marinade.

Crush the garlic and remaining 2 teaspoons salt to a paste with a mortar and pestle. Add the cumin, oregano, and black pepper and crush with the garlic. Stir in the juice of the bitter and sweet oranges.

Rub the *adobo* all over the pig and place in a large stainless steel bowl (reserve any remaining *adobo*). Cover with plastic wrap and refrigerate for a minimum of 24 hours and a maximum of 48 hours.

Roasting the Pig ▶ Preheat the oven to 400°F at least 1 hour in advance. Remove the pig from the bowl and stretch it out on a roasting pan or baking sheet, cut side down. Scrape all traces of the *adobo* from the skin and set aside with any previously reserved *adobo*. Wipe the skin dry with paper towels. Let rest for at least 30 minutes at room temperature to allow the skin to dry out completely.

Place the onions, sweet potatoes, and carrots in a roasting pan or on a baking sheet large enough to accommodate the pig. Toss with the olive oil, salt, rosemary, and reserved *adobo*. Prop the pig over the vegetables. Cover the tail and ears with aluminum foil to keep them from burning. Make a large ball of aluminum foil and place it under the pig's throat or snout to prop it up. Make a smaller ball, the size of a small apple, and place it in the pig's mouth to keep it open and make it easier to put an apple or a pepper in its mouth once it is roasted.

Slide the pan with the pig onto the lower rack of the oven and roast for 1 hour. Rotate the pan after 30 minutes for even browning. At the end of 1 hour, pour some hot water, chicken broth, or white wine into the pan to keep the vegetables from browning too much, and lower the temperature to 350°F. Roast for 1 more hour, until the skin is crisp and golden brown.

Remove the pig from the oven and remove the aluminum foil from the ears, tail, and mouth. Insert a lovely Scotch bonnet pepper or an apple in the mouth and show the pig to your guests, still on the baking sheet or on a serving platter surrounded by the roasted vegetables. Take it back to the kitchen to cut into serving pieces.

The idea is to assemble the carved pieces in such a way that the pig seems whole. Lift the pig onto a cutting board. Slice off its head with a kitchen knife and place at one end of a large serving platter. Separate the crisp skin from the pig's back and cut into large serving pieces. Cut the rest of the pig into 8 large pieces, trying to leave the legs in 1 or 2 pieces. Arrange artfully on the platter, following the outlines of the animal. Place the pieces of skin on top of the morsels of meat for easy serving. Surround with the roasted vegetables and garnish with the pomegranates and sprigs of rosemary.

Serving: Enjoy with Moors and Christians (page 310) and Cuban Avocado, Watercress, and Pineapple Salad (page 548).

GAME

Mendoza Braised Rabbit

Conejo a la Cazadora

The European gray rabbit introduced by the Spaniards to South America thrives in Mendoza's desert land, Argentina's premier wine region. Both wild and farmed rabbits are common staples and cooks like to braise them with onions and peppers and some wine, practically in their own juices. This version comes from winemaker Susana Balbo, who uses a combination of peppercorns to season most of her dishes. This is sold in Mendoza markets as a *potpourri de pimientas*, a potpourri of peppers. Pink peppercorns grow wild in Mendoza and are always used in conjunction with other peppers because people believe that they are toxic if consumed in quantity. Timing will vary according to the tenderness of the rabbit.

Cook's Note: For this recipe, Susana Balbo uses only young, tender farmed rabbits. When serving the dish for company, she usually removes the meat from the bones before cooking, in order to eliminate the sharp splinters that you get from chopping across the fragile bones. In the United States, rabbit is frequently sold already cut up into bone-in serving pieces, and this is what I suggest using. Freeing the meat from the bones, one piece at a time, is time-consuming but not difficult. If you are starting with a whole rabbit, follow the recipe directions.

What to Drink: Crios de Susana Balbo Torrontes

Two 2½- to 3-pound rabbits, thawed if frozen, cut into 6–8 serving pieces each

3½ teaspoons salt

1 teaspoon freshly ground black pepper

¼ cup extra-virgin olive oil

2 large yellow onions, finely chopped (about 4 cups)

6 garlic cloves, finely chopped

3 bay leaves

1 medium green bell pepper (6 ounces), cored, seeded, deveined, and cut into ¼-inch strips

1 medium yellow bell pepper (6 ounces), cored, seeded, deveined, and cut into ¼-inch strips

1 large red bell pepper (8 ounces), fire roasted (see page 67), cored, seeded, and cut into ¼-inch strips

4 carrots, cut into 3-inch batons

1 cup white wine (preferably the floral Crios de Susana Balbo Torrontes)

1 cup well-flavored chicken broth, homemade (page 538) or store-bought

1 teaspoon Argentinean ground hot pepper (*ají molido*), crushed red pepper flakes, or ground cayenne pepper, or to taste

1 teaspoon freshly ground pepper (a combination of white, green, black, and pink peppercorns)

2 teaspoons dried oregano

Cutting Whole Rabbits into Serving Pieces ▶ If you are using whole rabbits, begin by removing any innards that may have been included. Rinse the rabbits inside and out, and pat dry. With the tip of a boning knife or sharp paring knife, probe for the shoulder joints and detach the front legs from the body. Do the same with the thigh joints and hind legs. With a cleaver, chop lengthwise through the backbone to cut the saddle into two halves. Rinse off any splinters of bone and again pat dry.

Boning the Rabbit Pieces ▶ Inspect the rabbit pieces carefully to be sure no splinters of bone are clinging to them; if necessary, rinse them and pat dry. With a boning knife or sharp paring knife, free the meat from the bones as follows: Start by cutting a deep lengthwise incision along each front leg and each of the thigh or hind leg pieces. With the knife tip placed against the bone, work the blade back and forth to detach the meat along the length of the joint. Insert the knife tip between the meat and rib cage and work along the entire torso (or saddle and loin pieces, if they are already separated) to free the meat from the ribs and backbone. Discard the bones, or save for making stock.

Preparing and Cooking the Meat ▶ Season the meat with 1½ teaspoons salt and the pepper. Heat the oil in a 12-inch sauté pan or a wide heavy pot over medium high heat. Working in two batches, add the meat and brown on all sides for about 8 minutes. Transfer to a large plate and set aside. Lower the heat to medium and add the onion, garlic, and bay leaves. Cook, stirring, until the onion is translucent, about 5 minutes. Add the bell peppers and carrots and sauté for 3 minutes. Add the white wine and simmer for 5 minutes. Add the rabbit, broth, *ají molido*, pepper mix, oregano, and remaining 2 teaspoons salt. Taste and correct seasoning if needed. Cover and let simmer at medium low heat until the rabbit is tender, 45 minutes to 1 hour.

Spit-Roasted *Cuy* Cuenca Style
Cuy Asado al Estilo de Cuenca, Ecuador

The *cuy*, or guinea pig, has been considered a delicacy in Andean Ecuador, Bolivia, and Peru since pre-Columbian times. In rural areas, these adorable animals coexist in intimate proximity to humans. You can see them roaming around near the fire, feeding on alfalfa and being treated like chickens. But although loved as pets, that does not save them from the cooking pot or the grill.

I am particularly fond of spit-roasted *cuyes*. I first tasted them in Ecuador, at the Picantería Charito, a little storefront restaurant in the *ciudad baja* of Cuenca, in the Avenida Don Bosco, which can be dubbed Cuenca's *Cuy* Central. Rosario Crespo, the owner, a rosy-cheeked *mestiza* sporting shiny braids and a wide *pollera* (skirt), took the time to show me how she prepared her *cuyes* from beginning to end. She had plenty of competition, though. All along the avenue you could see open grills where women and children rotated golden *cuyes* that had been skewered on wooden sticks called *cangadores* over the hot embers.

At home, *cuyes* are spit-roasted on small grills about 1 foot high. The women of the house, who are always in charge of this task, sit on small stools about 8 inches high, rotating the *cuy* over the fire for at least one hour.

Cuy is a favorite feast-day food in the Ecuadorian highlands, and you can find it in any household, from the humblest farmer's table to the wealthiest one. Because they are small, the women gather around the fire to grill several *cuyes* at the same time. A Cuenca friend, the late Doña Aída Vázquez, was famous for her delicious *cuyes*. She had three or four *cangadores* secreted behind the kitchen door. She used them not only to spit-roast her *cuyes*, but to hit any unruly child of hers—it did not matter that they were already in their thirties.

People break rules of etiquette when eating *cuyes*. No matter how much you try to keep your composure at the table, you end up grabbing a little leg or a tiny ear with your hands. In Cuenca, people do not eat *cuyes*, they suck them. Every bit of the animal, including the head and the tiny feet, is sucked like candy to extract every last ounce of delicious meat and juice. You will never find leftover *cuy*.

After a *cuy* banquet, people drink a *draque* (spiced *aguardiente*) to prevent the *cuy* from kicking (*para que no patee el cuy*). The men, of course, always take this as an excuse to end the feast with several more rounds of *draque*.

Some people are taken aback by the sight of these tiny animals. They look at their little faces and tiny clawed feet and see glorified rodents. I don't see *cuyes* as mice, though, but as miniature pigs; their meat looks like the meat from the rib portion of a pig and is just as succulent and tasty.

You can find frozen Ecuadorian *cuyes* from Cuenca, already eviscerated and cleaned, in some Latin markets. I have bought them at Bandera in New Jersey, the largest Latin American supermarket in the northeast United States. You can also buy guinea pigs in some live poultry stores, but they are never as tasty as the ones from South America.

Cook's Notes: If you want spit-roasted *cuy*, find yourself a thick round stick of wood for a spit. You must be patient if choosing this method. You need to rotate the *cuy* over the hot embers while basting occasionally with achiote-infused lard or oil, which is what accounts for the marvelous golden skin of the Cuenca *cuyes*.

If you have no patience or can't find a stick for spit roasting, butterfly the *cuy* and flatten it. Then marinate and grill it as you would chicken.

SERVES 4

One 1–2 pound *cuy*, fresh or frozen and thawed
(imported *cuyes* ranging from 1 to 2 pounds are
small by Andean standards)

1 head of garlic, separated into cloves and peeled

1 teaspoon ground cumin

1 teaspoon salt

½ cup achiote-infused lard (page 89)

Seasoning the Cuy ▶ Rinse the *cuy* under cold running water. Pat dry with a kitchen towel and place in a bowl or a glass dish. Mash the garlic, cumin, and salt together with a mortar and pestle into a coarse paste. Rub the *cuy* all over with this paste, inside and out. Cover the bowl with plastic film and refrigerate overnight.

Preparing the Cuy for Spit-Roasting ▶ For spit-roasting you need a round stick of wood about 1 inch in diameter and at least 36 inches long to be able to hold the animal over the fire without burning your hands. You can get a wooden dowel cut to size in any lumber store, or if you want to recycle, use an old broomstick or the handle of a leaf rake. Scrape off the marinade from the skin of the *cuy* and impale it on the stick. It should fit fairly tightly; if the *cuy* slips around, secure the feet to the stick with a piece of wire.

Preparing the Grill ▶ When ready to cook, remove the grid from the grill and line with at least 3 inches of hardwood charcoal. Light your fire and wait until the flames subside and the charcoal is covered with an ashy film.

Spit-Roasting ▶ Hold the *cuy* about 1 foot above the burning charcoal and rotate slowly, about 10 seconds on each side. This is definitely a labor of love. You must hold the stick at that same distance from the fire from 1 to 1½ hours, according to the size of the *cuy*. Sit down on a bar stool and take turns with a friend or relative. When the skin starts to brown, brush with the achiote-infused lard. Continue roasting, and if you notice patches of skin that are not browning properly, brush with the lard. *Cuy* has a tendency to blister. People in Ecuador like to keep the blistering to a minimum by pricking the skin with a fork. The *cuy* is ready when it is completely golden brown like a roast suckling pig. When tapped, the skin must sound like a drum.

Serving: Cut off the head and reserve for the person who asks for it. It is considered a favorite treat. Cut the body across and then halve each section lengthwise. That makes four small servings. The traditional accompaniments for *cuy* are Ecuadorian Golden Potatoes (page 204), Andean Hominy (page 251), hard-boiled eggs, and a hot pepper *ají* (page 123).

Variation: Oven-Roasted Cuy (*Cuy al Horno*)
Susana Polo Eljuri, a wonderful Cuenca cook who makes *cuy* often, particularly when her chocolate-maker son Santiago Peralta comes to visit, gave me this simple recipe for oven-roasted *cuy*. She likes a plump young *cuy* with lots of fat around the belly and neck. Season the *cuy* as above and place it on an oiled roasting pan, belly side down. Cover the delicate feet and head with parchment paper or aluminum foil to keep them from burning. Roast at high heat, about 400°F, basting often with achiote-infused lard, until the skin is golden and sounds like a drum when tapped, about 1½ hours. At Susana's home, one fat *cuy* feeds two people.

CHAPTER 19

HOT PEPPER POTS:

Adobos, Secos, Saices, Picantes, Sajtas, Pepianes, and Moles

IN THIS CHAPTER

In my search to find the ways Latin Americans cook and eat, I discovered several families of stews and braises flavored with hot peppers. For a Cuban like me, a stew is always a rich, mellow dish of chicken or meat flavored with garlic, chopped onions, peppers, cumin, and tomatoes, simmered slowly with beer or wine until the meat is tender and the flavors meld. Hot pepper only came into my mother's stew as a final touch, just a pinch at the end of cooking to satisfy my father.

I still remember the first time I tasted a Peruvian *seco*. I simply could not believe that the basic underpinning of a sauce that I thought was a harmonious symphony of flavors, with fruity notes, salty pleasure, and silky texture, was a puree of hot Andean peppers. I was also struck by how long simmering mellowed the peppers. I could barely taste the raw pepper's flavor without recoiling from its burning bite; after slow cooking with all the familiar ingredients of my own childhood stews, it had surrendered its sting, and its heat had become a subtle background sensation.

Even before I understood their similarities, I embraced these magnificent pepper dishes with a passion, collecting them like trophies during my field trips to Latin America. Eventually I realized that they are not just dishes that happen to have some hot pepper in the sauce. They are all based on the same principles of flavoring, on time-tested techniques designed both to harness the pepper's heat and to intensify its color, flavor, and aroma. For this reason, I saw that it did not make sense to put them into chapters for poultry, meats, seafood, and so forth. People who live in the lands of hot pepper often do not think first of a particular ingredient, like beef or shrimp, when they are deciding what to have for dinner. What they are likely to debate

is the style of preparation—should they prepare an *adobo*, a *seco*, a *pepián*, or a *picante*? I realized that in order to convey the structure and kinship of these dishes, I would have to group them together in a chapter of their own.

What cooks in North America can learn from these Latin pepper pots is a freer, more flexible way of shopping for food and planning meals. A Mexican or Peruvian cook bent on cooking a hot pepper stew is not fazed if a specific main ingredient isn't available at the market or does not look good that day. She makes do with whatever meat or fish or vegetable catches her eye, since she knows that she has on hand the hot peppers and other seasonings for the sauce that will transform any main ingredient into an exciting and satisfying meal. In addition, she probably has pureed peppers or a cooking sauce base, or an all-but-complete sauce (for example, a Mexican *mole*), waiting in her pantry or refrigerator. Once you get the feel for making these, you too will be able to improvise and integrate the materials of Latin hot pepper pots into much of your daily cooking. Not only are these dishes delicious, but their sauces can be made ahead of time (some will last for months) and used to season other meals. These are generous dishes, basic enough for everyday eating and exciting enough to entertain a crowd with flair, and what is best, they will be blooming with flavor after one or two days in the refrigerator.

Some of the hot pepper pots of Latin America are already known to us in North America—for example, the *moles* of Mexico and *pepianes* of Central America. Less familiar but no less delicious are their cousins from the Andean regions. Peru and Bolivia in particular have a large variety of hot pepper stews that are known by at least half a dozen different names. The Peruvian stew called *adobo*, for instance, is a dish of Spanish parentage. Though some of its principles survive in modern Spanish cooking, the name is no longer used in Spain in this context, but in much of Latin America and as far away as the Philippines, *adobos* are still popular and are made with many of the original Spanish ingredients such as vinegar and black peppercorns, along with soy sauce.

Regardless of regional differences and names, in all of these preparations hot pepper is not a mere seasoning discreetly applied to the finished dish to give it heat but a central underpinning, a crucial ingredient that adds color, body, texture, and flavor as well as heat. Many of them feature combinations of different peppers, both hot and mild, to create various possible nuances, depending on the intrinsic sweetness, fruitiness, bitterness, herbal effect, and color of the individual peppers. Or the peppers may be used in combination with particular ingredients or clusters of ingredients for different flavor interactions—for example, the interplay between Andean hot peppers and huge amounts of cilantro in the classic *secos* of northern Peru.

These rich dishes enriched with hot peppers flow from the combination of old Spain and pre-Columbian America. More than any other category of Latin foods, these marvelous stews are edible history, revealing how complementary techniques and ingredients from two venerable but very different culinary traditions mingled during the early colonial period.

WORKING WITH DRIED HOT PEPPERS

It takes only a simple three-step dance to turn dried peppers into wonderful seasonings: cleaning and roasting; reconstituting; and grinding. These are the techniques cooks need to master to tackle most hot pepper stews, a process familiar in Mexico, Guatemala, Honduras, Nicaragua, and El Salvador, as well as parts of Andean South America. In Peru and Bolivia, traditional cooks prefer to toast dried *mirasol* or *panca* peppers very briefly over a flame or on a hot skillet before grinding them to a powder or adding them whole to soups and stews. Nowadays, most cooks do a much simpler two-step dance: the dried peppers are soaked in water to soften or boiled until plump and soft and then ground to a paste with a *batán* (see page 33) or in a blender.

First Step: Cleaning and Roasting

Before you roast dried peppers, examine them. They may be dusty, dirty, or bug-infested. If they look really messy, put them in a bowl and cover them with warm water. Let them soak for a few minutes, swishing them around to dislodge any dirt that might still cling to them, and then pour out the water, holding the peppers with one hand so they don't wash away. Once the peppers are clean, pat them dry thoroughly. If the peppers are in good condition, simply wipe them clean with a damp cloth. In either case, they must be completely dried before roasting. Then stem and seed the peppers if you wish. I call for seeding in some recipes to reduce the heat and create a smoother, silkier final texture. With broad peppers, seeding is easy: you

1. Stem the pepper.

2. Butterfly the pepper.

3. Remove the seeds.

4. Press against the pan with a
metal spatula for a few seconds.

5. Soak the roasted dried peppers in
warm water until they are reconstituted and look plump.

just pull out the stem and shake out the seeds. With thin peppers or peppers with a narrow stem end, stem them and then tear them open by sliding your index finger in lengthwise or slice them open with a sharp knife. Many cooks like to butterfly peppers before seeding.

For roasting, the best tool is a metal *comal* (see page 32). Its flat metal surface conducts heat evenly. You can also use a cast-iron or other heavy skillet or a griddle, or roast the peppers under the broiler. If roasting butterflied peppers, press the cut side against the *comal* with a metal spatula for a few seconds, flip the pepper over, and repeat. The peppers should be lightly toasted but not burned. Smooth and thin-skinned peppers like guajillo and *cascabel* can scorch easily. Wrinkled, meatier peppers like ancho and *mulato* might take longer to roast evenly at medium heat. When roasting small whole peppers, I find that I have more control if I handle them with tongs.

Second Step: Reconstituting

At some point in the making of most hot pepper stews (usually after roasting), most cooks cover the roasted peppers in warm water or in a mixture of water and vinegar or broth, or boil them briefly until they are plump. That way they are easier to grind into a smooth paste. I always reserve some of the soaking water, in case I need it to facilitate grinding or during cooking.

Third Step: Grinding

To grind the peppers, use a *molcajete* (see page 33), a blender, or a food processor. Mexican and Central American cooks love the coarse, rich texture of *molcajete*-ground peppers.

The three-step pepper dance is a dance of many partners. Mexicans and other Central Americans have learned that by roasting onions, garlic, and tomatoes; spices such as cloves and cinnamon; or nuts and seeds such as almonds, sesame seeds, and pumpkin seeds, they obtain a much more interesting and complex range of flavors and textures than if they were to sauté only raw ingredients.

ADOBOS

Aromatic seasoning pastes called *adobos*, featuring black pepper and other flavorings, including vinegar, were mainstays of Spanish cooking in medieval times. Spanish cooks undoubtedly rubbed these seasonings over meats to tenderize and preserve them. By the early Renaissance, recipes calling for the same vinegary seasoning as the basic flavoring of a stew called *adobo* appeared. It is obvious that Spanish cooks had begun to stretch the uses of the *adobo* as a flavoring. They probably had noticed that after hours of slow cooking over a wood fire, meat became infused with the mingled flavors of the peppery marinade and its own juices.

When the Spanish arrived in the New World, they found the people of Mexico, Central America, and the Andes making spicy, tangy stews that reminded them of their own *adobos*. Most of these dishes contained native peppers in combination with local flavorings and soured brews made from fermented fruits or corn. Native Americans would pound the peppers that grew around them—Mexican chiles and Andean *ajíes*—to a paste. Then they would smear the paste over their turkeys or guinea pigs and then scrape it off and use it as a cooking sauce for simmering the meat. It was not long before the Spaniards were using hot peppers in the same way. In turn the Indians learned to sauté the meats for a stew in some fat, as the Spaniards did, and to use vinegar and Mediterranean spices. All modern Latin American *adobos* result from the merging of these two traditions, with hot peppers replacing the black pepper used in Spain and with wine or cider vinegar replacing or used in combination with native American souring agents such as *chicha* (brewed sprouted corn).

To me, what makes the taste of Latin *adobos* so spectacular is the symbiosis between sauce and meat. Imagine succulent morsels of pork smeared with a paste of ground hot peppers, garlic, vinegar, and spices and allowed to sit until the meat is deeply infused with the rich flavors. Next, the pork is cooked gently in just enough liquid to keep it moist without weakening the concentrated quality of the flavorings. At the end the meat is fork-tender and succulent and the seasoning has been transformed into an intensely flavored sauce.

The two capitals of *adobo*-making in Latin America are Mexico and Peru. The majority of the *adobos* in this book are from Peru, just a few wonderful examples culled from the great cache of *adobo* recipes I collected on the north coast and in highland towns. They are on the whole extremely simple dishes marked by a few distinctive regional variations. The dish will usually be either brick red or orange-yellow, depending on whether the peppers are the dark-hued dried *ají panca* or the orange dried *ají mirasol*. The vinegar may be replaced with either beer or (especially in the north and the city of Cusco) the local sprouted-corn beer, *chicha de jora*. In some *adobos*, potatoes are added late in the cooking. The seasonings are often almost entirely Old World aside from the hot peppers, but some cooks add Andean herbs, such as the marigold-flavored *huacatay*. I have also included an *adobo* from Central America, where the name *adobo* can cover several different preparations, because it illustrates how native American tomatillos replace vinegar as the souring agent.

To make some of these recipes, you need a few special ingredients that can easily be obtained in Hispanic markets and specialty stores, such as dried Andean peppers and *chicha*, a delicious sweet-and-sour condiment that doubles as vinegar in most *adobos* (see page 95 if you want to make *chicha* yourself). Whenever possible I have suggested substitutions.

"El Estupendo" Pork Adobo from Arequipa

El Estupendo Adobo Arequipeño

When Peruvians want to eat the best *adobos*, they go straight to their local *picanterías*. No more than holes in the wall, with long communal wooden tables where working people consume huge portions of local dishes washed down with tall glasses of the fermented corn drink *chicha*, *picanterías* serve traditional, hearty fare bearing the distinct seasoning of each region of Peru.

The *picanterías* of Arequipa are famous for their stupendous *adobos*; hence the hyperbolic title of my recipe. Each region boasts the best *adobo*, but I usually find the differences to be small. The main variables are the amount of sauce (some cooks like their *adobos* soupy, others on the dry side, with little sauce), the type of hot pepper (*ají panca* or *ají mirasol*), the use of vinegar made from *chicha* versus store-bought vinegar, or the presence or absence of potatoes.

This *adobo* lives up to its name because it spells harmony: a pleasing balance of fruity and acidic tastes, flavors melded together seamlessly, the thick sauce just enough to spoon over a side dish of rice.

What to Drink: A bold Tikal Syrah-Bonarda from Mendoza, Argentina

SERVES 6 TO 8

For the Pork
- 3½ pounds boneless pork, preferably from the shoulder and with some fat, cut into 2½-inch cubes
- 1 teaspoon salt

For the Seasoning Paste (*Adobo*)
- 6 dried *panca* peppers (about 1¼ ounces) or dried guajillo chiles (about 1 ounce)
- 1 medium head garlic, separated into cloves and peeled
- 1 tablespoon salt
- 1 tablespoon ground cumin
- 2 teaspoons dried oregano
- 1 teaspoon ground allspice
- 1 teaspoon freshly ground black pepper
- 3 tablespoons cider vinegar, plus more if needed

For Finishing
- 2 tablespoons achiote-infused corn oil (page 89)
- 1 quart water
- 2 large red onions (about 1½ pounds), quartered
- 6 large russet, Yukon Gold, or Yellow Finn potatoes (about 2 pounds), peeled and quartered

Preparing the Meat ▶ Place the pork in a large bowl and rub all over with the salt. Set aside.

Preparing the Peppers ▶ Stem and seed the peppers according to the instructions on page 744. Add 3 cups fresh water and boil the peppers over medium heat until plump and softened, about 15 minutes.

Making the Seasoning Paste (*Adobo*) ▶ Drain the peppers and process to a puree in a food processor or blender with the garlic, salt, cumin, oregano, allspice, black pepper, and vinegar. Rub the mixture all over the pork cubes, cover tightly with plastic wrap, and let sit at room temperature for at least 2 hours or refrigerated for a maximum of 24 hours.

Cooking the *Adobo* ▶ In a heavy 12-inch sauté pan, heat the oil over medium heat until it ripples. Add the meat and cook, turning occasionally, until browned on all sides, about 10 minutes. Add the water and onions. Adjust the heat to medium-low and simmer, covered, until the meat is very tender and the liquid reduced by about half, 1 to 1½ hours. Correct the seasoning with salt and a splash of vinegar if needed. Add the potatoes and cook for 15 to 18 minutes, until they are tender.

Serving: Serve with plain white rice.

Lamb *Adobo* Tarma Style

Cordero en Adobo al Estilo de Tarma

Huacatay, an herb also known as black mint or Andean cilantro, is the dominant flavor of nearly all seasoning pastes and marinades in some highland towns of Peru, such as Tarma. I love making this *adobo* because I never cease to be amazed by the wonder of slow cooking with hot peppers. Just a bite of *huacatay* in its pure form is enough to numb your palate with the musky taste of marigolds. But when you mix it with fruity *mirasol* peppers and let it cook gently, this powerful condiment becomes a team player, providing an irresistible, almost mysterious backbone to the sauce.

Cook's Note: In Peru, this dish is usually made with young kid (*cabrito*), but I have found it also works well with lamb.

What to Drink: A spicy Montes Syrah from Apalta Valley in Chile

SERVES 6

For the Lamb

- 4 pounds boneless lean leg of lamb, cut into 2-inch cubes, or 5–6 meaty lamb shanks (about 5 pounds total)
- 1 teaspoon salt
- ½ teaspoon freshly ground black pepper

For the *Adobo*

- 6 dried *mirasol* peppers (about 1½ ounces)
- 1 tablespoon cider vinegar
- 1 large head garlic, separated into cloves and peeled
- 4 tablespoons frozen *huacatay*, thawed, or 1 tablespoon dried and ground *huacatay*
- 1 tablespoon ground allspice
- 1 teaspoon ground cumin
- 2 teaspoons salt
- 1 teaspoon freshly ground black pepper
- 2 tablespoons achiote-infused corn oil or extra-virgin olive oil (page 89)

- 1 cup dark beer, such as Peruvian Cuzqueña

Preparing the Lamb ▶ Place the lamb in a bowl and toss with the salt and pepper. Set aside.

Preparing the Peppers ▶ Stem and seed the peppers according to the instructions on page 744. Cover with 1 quart fresh water, bring to a boil over medium heat, and simmer until the peppers are plump and softened, about 15 minutes. Drain, reserving 1 cup of the cooking liquid.

Making the *Adobo* ▶ Place the peppers in a food processor or blender with the reserved cooking liquid, vinegar, garlic, *huacatay*, allspice, cumin, salt, and black pepper and process to a smooth puree. Rub the mixture all over the meat, cover tightly with plastic wrap, and let sit for at least 1 hour at room temperature, or refrigerate for a maximum of 24 hours.

Cooking the *Adobo* ▶ Scrape as much *adobo* from the meat as possible and set aside. In a heavy 12-inch sauté pan, heat the oil over medium heat until it ripples. Add the meat and cook, turning occasionally, until browned on all sides, about 10 minutes. Add the reserved *adobo* and beer. Taste the sauce for salt and add a pinch if needed. Lower the heat and simmer, covered, until the meat is fork-tender, about 1 hour for boneless meat, up to 1½ hours for lamb shanks. Check occasionally and add water or beer if the sauce is evaporating too fast. You should have enough sauce to keep the meat moist, with enough left over to spoon over rice.

Serving: Serve with white rice and Stewed Peruvian Canary beans (page 511).

Pork *Adobo* Cusco Style
Chancho en Adobo al Estilo de Cusco

Cusco, in southern Peru, competes with its lower-altitude neighbor Arequipa in the quality of its *adobos*. As in Arequipa, the bright red color and subtle heat of the Cusco *adobo* comes from dried *panca* peppers, but these are lightly toasted to give a delicious fruity flavor with a touch of smokiness to the thick, concentrated sauce. A touch of the fermented corn drink *chicha de jora* adds zest and a jolt of acidity.

What to Drink: La Misión Pinot Noir from Maipo Valley in Chile

SERVES 6

For the Pork

3 pounds boneless pork, preferably from the shoulder and with some fat, cut into 2-inch cubes

1 teaspoon salt

For the *Adobo*

6 dried *panca* peppers (about 1¼ ounces) or dried guajillo chiles (about 1 ounce)

¼ cup *chicha de jora*, homemade (page 95) or store-bought, or 2 tablespoons cider vinegar

1 medium head garlic, separated into cloves and peeled

2 teaspoons ground cumin

2 teaspoons dried oregano

2 teaspoons salt

3 tablespoons achiote-infused corn or extra-virgin olive oil (page 89)

Preparing the Pork ▶ Place the pork in a large bowl and rub all over with the salt. Set aside.

Preparing the Peppers ▶ Stem and seed the peppers according to the instructions on page 744. Heat a *comal*, griddle, or heavy skillet over medium heat. Add the peppers and lightly toast, turning over with tongs, until they release their aroma, about 20 seconds. Do not char or allow blisters to form.

Making the Adobo ▶ Place the peppers in a small saucepan with 1 quart fresh water and bring to a boil over medium heat. Lower the heat and simmer, uncovered, until the peppers are plump and softened, about 15 minutes. Drain, reserving 3 cups of the cooking liquid.

Place the peppers in a food processor or blender with the *chicha* or vinegar, garlic, cumin, oregano, and salt and process into a smooth puree. Place the pork in a bowl and rub all over with this mixture. Cover tightly with plastic wrap and let sit for at least 2 hours at room temperature, or refrigerate for a maximum of 24 hours.

Cooking the Adobo ▶ Scrape off as much *adobo* from the meat as possible and set aside. In a 12-inch sauté pan, heat the oil over medium heat until it ripples. Add the meat and brown on all sides, about 2 minutes per side. Stir in the reserved pepper cooking liquid and the reserved seasoning paste and bring to a gentle boil. Cover and simmer over medium-low heat until the sauce is thick and the meat is fork-tender, about 2 hours. Turn the meat every 30 minutes to ensure even cooking.

Serving: Serve with boiled potatoes and crusty bread.

Guatemalan Beef *Adobo*

Carne en Adobo Guatemalteco

In Guatemala, tomatoes and tomatillos are often the basis of the *recado* (essential cooking sauce). In this recipe, the *recado* doubles as a tangy marinade for beef stew, becoming the sauce for the dish. In typical Guatemalan fashion, cooks give the meat a head start by simmering it in some water until barely tender before adding the cooking sauce.

In a way, this Guatemalan recipe reminds me of a seventeenth-century Spanish version of the *adobo* from Diego Granado's *Manual del cocinero* (Cooks' Manual), where the meat is simmered with vinegar, aromatic spices, and tart fruits until tender. In the Guatemalan *adobo*, the tomatillos and tomatoes take the role of the vinegar and the sour fruits, mingling with the juices of the meat to form a light, tangy sauce you'll never tire of eating.

Cook's Note: A traditional ingredient of many Latin soups and stews, boneless beef shin is always available in Latin markets, where it is sold as *sapo* or *jarrete*. This is one of my favorite cuts of meat for stewing because it turns tender and velvety with slow cooking, practically melting into the stew and in your mouth. In non-Latin butcher shops, you are likely to find beef shin cut across the bone into thick hunks of about 1 pound 2 ounces (in the same manner as osso bucco, which is cut from veal shank or shin). Thick sections of cartilage (not fat), a collagen-rich connective tissue, practically divide the piece into neat sections. With long, slow cooking, the cartilage turns into a rich gelatin that gives the sauce body and a satiny sheen. The bone is another important flavoring, imparting a deep beefy taste to the stew. After about 2 hours of cooking over medium heat, it separates cleanly from the meat so you can remove it before serving. The only drawback to using bone-in beef shin is that it is fattier than boneless shin. The flavorful but fatty bone marrow melts, depositing a pool of bright orange (from the chiles) fat on the surface of the stew. To remove this, let the stew cool and store it in a plastic or glass container, tightly covered, in the refrigerator for at least 24 hours. The fat solidifies. When ready to serve, I scrape it off with a spoon and reheat the stew.

What to Drink: Borsao Crianza from Campo de Borja, Spain

SERVES 6

For the Beef

4½ pounds boneless beef shin, cut into 2-inch cubes, or 4 pieces bone-in beef shin (about 1 pound 2 ounces each)

1 large white onion (12 ounces), peeled

1 quart water

2 cups beef broth, homemade (page 540) or store-bought

For the Cooking Sauce (*Recado*)

2 dried pasilla peppers

1 pound tomatillos (about 12 medium), husks removed

4 medium plum tomatoes (about 12 ounces)

1 medium white onion (about 8 ounces), peeled and cut into 8 pieces

8 garlic cloves, peeled

2 teaspoons ground cumin

1 teaspoon freshly ground black pepper

1 teaspoon dried oregano

2½ teaspoons salt, or to taste

2 tablespoons lard, corn oil, or fruity extra-virgin olive oil

Preparing the Beef ▶ Place the beef shin in a 12-inch pot with the whole onion, the water, and the broth. Bring to a boil, lower the heat, cover, and simmer for 30 minutes. Remove and discard the onion.

Making the Cooking Sauce (*Recado*) ▶ While the meat simmers, pull the stems off the peppers, slit them lengthwise, and scrape out the seeds. Place the peppers, tomatillos, and tomatoes in a medium saucepan with 2 cups water and bring to a gentle boil over medium heat. Simmer until soft, about 10 minutes. Drain and place in a blender or food processor with the remaining onion, garlic, cumin, black pepper, oregano, and salt. Process to a thick puree. Strain well through a fine-mesh sieve, pushing against the solids with the back of a spoon. Discard the solids.

Cooking the Meat ▶ Heat the lard or oil in a medium skillet over medium heat. Stir in the meat and sauté for 10 minutes. Add the puree to the meat, stir, and cover. Simmer over medium heat, covered, until the meat is tender, 1½ to 2 hours. This dish should be saucy.

Serving: Serve with plain white rice and a salad.

Guatemalan Chile Stew with White Corn Cheese *Tamales*

Suban Ic

For this stunning dish, a specialty of San Martín Jilotepeque in Chimaltenango, Guatemala, simple white corn and cheese tamales and a rich and spicy Guatemalan chile stew made with chicken are steamed together, wrapped in plantain leaves. The Quiché Maya name of the stew, *suban ic* (also spelled *suban ic'k*), actually refers to the little tamales (*sub*), which are cooked in the chile sauce. The tamales can be made independently and served as a side dish for Guatemalan *pepianes* or *moles*.

I first heard of this dish from the late Ricardo Juárez Solera, a talented Guatemalan chef born in Antigua who once worked at the Rattlesnake Club in Denver. During a telephone interview for a Hispanic radio show in New York, he gave me the recipe in bold strokes. I later learned more details from Eugenia Escobar de Pérez, the chief of the department of tourism and hospitality of Inguat, the Guatemalan tourist office. Eugenia, who happens to be an extraordinary cook, was my guide in Guatemala. She took me to all the right kitchens and markets, helping me understand the complex layers of culture in her country.

Cook's Note: Traditional versions of this dish call for a combination of pork and chicken, but I prefer to use only chicken.

What to Drink: Guatemalan Dorada or Gallo beer

SERVES 8

One 3½-pound chicken, cut into 8 pieces (see page 659)
 3 dried guajillo chiles
 3 medium plum tomatoes (about 9 ounces)
 1 large white onion (about 12 ounces), peeled
 1 large head garlic, separated into cloves and peeled
 ¼ cup hulled pumpkin seeds (1¼ ounces)
 ¼ cup cider vinegar
 2 tablespoons ground achiote (page 89)
 1 tablespoon ground cumin
 1 teaspoon ground allspice
 1 tablespoon salt
 4 tablespoons corn oil

Six 32-inch-long plantain leaf pieces, plus more for serving
 Guatemalan White Corn Cheese Tamales (page 460)
 3 cups chicken broth, homemade (page 538) or store-bought, or water

▶ Rinse and pat dry the chicken pieces and place in a bowl. Stem and seed the chiles. Heat a *comal*, griddle, or skillet over medium heat. Add the chiles and roast, turning with tongs, for about 1 minute. Lift out and place in a saucepan with 2 cups lukewarm water. Let soak for 20 to 30 minutes. Drain.

While the chiles soak, place the tomatoes, onion, and garlic on the *comal* and roast until blistered and charred, about 10 minutes; remove from the heat. Add the pumpkin seeds to the pan and roast, stirring, until they pop. Place the chiles, vegetables, pumpkin seeds, vinegar, spices, and salt in a blender or food processor and process to a smooth puree.

Heat 2 tablespoons corn oil in a medium skillet over medium heat. Pour in the puree and cook, stirring, for 5 minutes. Let the mixture cool, then rub it all over the chicken pieces and let rest for a few hours, preferably overnight, in the refrigerator, well covered with plastic wrap.

Place the remaining 2 tablespoons oil in a large sauté pan over medium heat. Add the chicken, in batches if necessary, and brown on both sides, about 10 minutes.

Arrange 5 of the plantain leaf pieces in a crisscross pattern in a 14-inch carbon-steel wok placed on a wok ring. Mound the chicken pieces in the center. Surround with the tamales. Fold the leaves over the filling to cover. Place the remaining leaf piece over the covered package and tuck in the ends. Pour in the broth or water from the side of the wok. Cover with the wok lid and bring the liquid to a boil over high heat. Lower the heat to medium and cook for about 1 hour. If the chicken is not soft, check the liquid and add a little water. Cook for 15 to 20 minutes more, until the chicken is tender, checking the liquid periodically.

Serving: Line a serving platter with plantain leaves, softened according to the instructions on page 423. Mound the chicken on the leaves and surround with the tamales. The ideal table condiment is Maya Cacao and Chile Balls (page 76). Allow your guests to grate the balls themselves with a small cheese grater. Accompany with rice and Guatemalan *frijoles volteados* (page 274).

SECOS

If I were to name the most characteristic dishes of Peru, I would include the *secos* of the northern coast, a small family of stews flavored with dried or fresh Andean peppers and fresh herbs that are immediately recognized by their tangy, aromatic dark green sauce. Most *secos* are saucy; their name has nothing to do with the Spanish word for dry, *seco*. When the conquistadores first came to these parts, they noticed that the local Indian populations ate their hot pepper stews from large dried-out gourds called by the Quechua name *sheco*. The Spanish and their descendants kept the word to name their own adaptations. Over the centuries, *secos* acquired a rich mixture of Old and New World elements and are now distinguished by large amounts of cilantro, brought by the Spanish, which took over some of the roles of native cooking herbs like *huacatay*.

Piura-Style Chicken *Seco* with *Panca* Peppers and *Chicha de Jora*

Seco de Pollo Piurano

The towns of northern Peru, a barren coastal desert sandwiched between the Pacific and the peaks of the Andes, have a familiar Spanish feel. After all, Piura and Trujillo were the first towns founded by the Spaniards in Peru in the early sixteenth century. But the Andes are never far away. In Piura, close to the Ecuadorian border, the fermented corn drink *chicha*, *panca* peppers, and cilantro form the backbone of the flavorful *secos*. The combination is clever. The *chicha* adds a gentle sweet-and-sour touch to the sauce, which intensifies the fruitiness of the peppers. The peppers in turn color the sauce a rich brick red, but cilantro darkens it to a brown olive color, its grassy, penetrating taste playing against the heat of the peppers and the acidity of the *chicha*.

Cook's Note: Piura cooks always use a mature hen for their *secos*. I use a young chicken (3½ to 4 pounds), but if you have access to a live poultry shop, choose a 5-pound hen (see page 655) and plan on a longer cooking time (see page 656). If you have not tasted one before, I urge you to try it.

What to Drink: Catena Alta Chardonnay from Mendoza, Argentina

SERVES 6

One 3½-pound chicken, cut into 12 serving pieces (see page 659)

For the *Adobo*

- 1 head garlic, separated into cloves and peeled
- 1 tablespoon ground cumin
- 1 teaspoon salt
- ½ cup *chicha de jora*, homemade (page 95) or store-bought, or ¼ cup red wine vinegar and ½ cup light beer

For the *Seco*

- 4 tablespoons corn oil or fruity extra-virgin olive oil
- 1 large red onion (12 ounces), finely chopped (about 2 cups)
- 2 tablespoons ground dried *panca* pepper, homemade (page 54), or store-bought
- 1 teaspoon hot *pimentón* (Spanish smoked paprika)
- 1½ cups lager beer
- 1 cup packed finely chopped cilantro leaves

Cilantro sprigs, for garnish

Preparing the Chicken ▶ Remove and discard the skin from the chicken and place the pieces in a bowl.

Making the *Adobo* ▶ Place the garlic in a mortar with the cumin and salt and pound with energy into a coarse paste. Stir in the *chicha de jora* until well blended. Rub the paste all over the chicken. Cover tightly with plastic wrap and allow to rest a minimum of 1 hour at room temperature and no more than 24 hours in the refrigerator.

Making the *Seco* ▶ Heat the oil in a heavy 12-inch sauté pan over medium heat. Scrape the marinade from the chicken pieces and reserve. (If some of it remains, it doesn't matter.) Sauté the chicken in the oil, turning with tongs, until it is a light golden brown, about 8 minutes. Remove from the heat with a slotted spoon and set aside.

Add the onion to the remaining oil and sauté for 2 to 3 minutes, until golden. Stir in the ground *panca* pepper and *pimentón* and cook for a few seconds. Add the reserved marinade and cook, stirring, just until the garlic begins to brown. Add the chicken pieces and stir. Pour in the beer and stir well to mix. Cover the pan and simmer over medium heat for 15 minutes. Stir in the cilantro and cook for 10 minutes, covered. Serve on a deep serving platter garnished with the sprigs of fresh cilantro.

Serving: In Piura, *secos* are served with rice and a *menestra*, a potage of white beans (page 511) or a side dish of Boiled Yuca (page 167). I like to top *secos* with a few spoonfuls of a crunchy onion salsa from Piura called *sarza* (page 762).

Young Goat Stew from Northern Peru

Seco de Cabrito a la Norteña

Nicolás Suyón Carranza, the husband of my friend Ana María Rojas-Lombardi, comes from Chiclayo, in the north of Peru. He cooked this dish for her birthday on one of my visits, and I was instantly captivated. It has the typical flavors of the region (*chicha de jora*, *panca* peppers, and vinegar) and some of the qualities of other Peruvian *secos* and *adobos*, but it is less complicated to make. All you do is prepare a rich marinade, which then serves as the cooking sauce. You do not have to brown the meat or prepare a separate cooking sauce; the meat simply stews in the marinade and its own concentrated juices. Toward the end of the cooking, you add chunks of meaty pumpkin and a generous amount of minced cilantro, which miraculously smoothes any harsh acidity from the vinegar.

Cook's Note: Northern Peru is known for its excellent *cabrito*, or milk-fed kid, which is best eaten when the young animals are five to six months of age (between 15 and 20 pounds) and still unweaned, with pale rosy rather than red flesh. The meat is not cut into boneless pieces; the butchers chop up the whole carcass into bite-sized pieces, bone and all, if you request it. In this country, you can order milk-fed kid from specialty ethnic butchers (Latin American, Greek, West Indian, Middle Eastern or Pakistani halal, or Italian). They will usually sell you a whole or half kid. When I am not planning to serve this amount, I store the rest in the freezer. For a large party, I double or triple the recipe and make it in a large heavy-gauge stockpot. It is an ideal party dish—the more goat in the pot, the better it tastes. Do not try to substitute lamb, because lamb this country is much older than Peruvian *cabrito* and has the muttony flavor that lamb and kid start getting when the animals feed on grass. If you cannot get very young kid, use breast of veal, chopped across the rib into 2-inch sections.

What to Drink: Montes Alpha Syrah from Colchagua, Chile

SERVES 6 TO 8

For the Kid

6 pounds milk-fed kid, cut into 2-inch pieces (see Cook's Note)
1 tablespoon salt

For the Seasoning Paste

10 dried *panca* peppers (about 2 ounces)
6 large garlic cloves

¾ cup *chicha de jora*, homemade (page 95) or store-bought
¼ cup cider vinegar
3 teaspoons sweet *pimentón* (Spanish smoked paprika)
2 teaspoons freshly ground black pepper
3 bay leaves

2 pounds Caribbean pumpkin (*calabaza*) or meaty kabocha, Hubbard, or butternut squash, peeled, seeded, and cut into 1½-inch chunks
1 bunch cilantro, finely chopped (about 1½ cups)

Preparing the Meat ▶ Place the meat in a large (about 8-quart) Dutch oven or pot, add 2 teaspoons salt, and rub to coat evenly. Set aside.

Preparing the Peppers ▶ Stem and seed the peppers. Heat a *comal*, griddle, or heavy skillet over medium heat until a drop of water evaporates on contact. Add the peppers and toast, flattening slightly with a spatula, for about 30 seconds, turning once. Place the peppers in a small saucepan with 3 cups water and boil until they are plump and softened, about 10 minutes.

Making the Seasoning Paste ▶ Drain the peppers and place in a blender or food processor with the garlic, *chicha*, vinegar, *pimentón*, black pepper, and remaining 1 teaspoon salt. Process to a smooth paste. Add the paste to the meat and toss to coat evenly. Add the bay leaves and let marinate for 30 minutes.

Making the *Seco* ▶ Place the Dutch oven over medium heat, bring to a boil, and cook, covered, for about 1 hour, or until the meat is nearly tender. Add the pumpkin and 1 cup of the cilantro and cook until the pumpkin is tender, about 15 minutes longer. Just before serving, remove the bay leaves and stir in the rest of the cilantro.

Serving: Serve with plain white rice and Fava Bean, Corn, and Fresh Cheese Salad/Relish (page 268).

Breast of Veal Stew in the Style of Trujillo

Seco de Ternera Trujillano

Here is my adaptation of a traditional *seco* from Trujillo using breast of veal, a wonderful substitute for the traditional milk-fed kid. This dish is a prime example of layered flavoring. The meat is marinated in a paste of peppers, garlic, and cumin and then browned in some oil with more fresh seasonings. To give the dish a final layer of flavor, cooks add sweet-and-sour *chicha de jora* and a flavored cilantro puree to the sauce just minutes before finishing the cooking.

Cook's Note: Most butchers will gladly cut a breast of veal to your specifications. Traditionally this dish is made with fresh yellow Andean peppers (*ajíes amarillos*), known in Trujillo as *ajíes escabeches*, or with a combination of dried and fresh peppers. Here I use fresh-frozen yellow Andean peppers (be sure to allow time for defrosting). If you are not able to find fresh-frozen *ají amarillo*, use dried *ají mirasol* instead.

What to Drink: Viña Garcés Silva Sauvignon Blanc Amayna, from Leyda Valley, Chile

SERVES 6 TO 8

5 pounds bone-in breast of veal, chopped through the bone into 2-inch-square chunks

2 teaspoons salt

For the Seasoning Paste

8 dried *mirasol* peppers (about 2 ounces)

1 head garlic, separated into cloves and peeled

1 tablespoon ground cumin

1 tablespoon salt

½ cup *chicha de jora*, homemade (page 95) or store-bought, or ½ cup lager beer and 2 tablespoons cider vinegar

¼ cup Peruvian or Chilean pisco, grappa, or very dry vermouth (preferably Noilly Prat)

For the Cooking Sauce

2 fresh-frozen yellow Andean peppers (*ajíes amarillos*), thawed, stemmed, and seeded

3 tablespoons corn oil or fruity extra-virgin olive oil

4 garlic cloves, finely chopped

1 medium red onion (8 ounces), finely chopped (about 1½ cups)

6 scallions, white and light green parts, finely chopped

2 tablespoons cilantro, finely chopped

1½ quarts water

For the Cilantro Puree

½ bunch cilantro, coarsely chopped

½ medium red onion (4 ounces), coarsely chopped (about ¾ cup)

¼ cup *chicha de jora* or 2 tablespoons cider vinegar, for final seasoning

▶ Place the veal in a large bowl and rub with 2 teaspoons salt. Set aside.

Preparing the Seasoning Paste ▶ Stem and seed the peppers. Cover with 1 quart fresh water and boil over medium heat until the peppers are plump and softened, about 15 minutes. Drain and reserve 2 for future use.

Place 6 of the peppers in a food processor or blender with the garlic, cumin, 1 tablespoon salt, *chicha de jora*, and pisco. Process to a smooth puree. Rub the marinade all over the meat and let sit for a minimum of 2 hours at room temperature or for a maximum of 24 hours in the refrigerator, tightly covered with plastic wrap.

Making the Cooking Sauce ▶ Puree the thawed yellow Andean peppers with a little water in a food processor or blender. Simmer until the peppers are soft, 10 to 15 minutes. Drain; reserve ¼ cup cooking liquid. Place in a food processor or blender with the reserved liquid and process to a smooth puree.

Heat the oil in a 12-inch sauté pan over medium heat until it ripples. Sauté the garlic until golden, about 40 seconds. Add the onion and scallions and cook, stirring, until golden, about 5 minutes. Stir in the pureed yellow peppers and cook, stirring, for 1 minute. Add the cilantro and cook for 1 more minute. Add the meat and cook, stirring, for 5 minutes. Pour in the water, stir, lower the heat, cover, and cook until the meat is almost falling off the bone, about 1½ hours.

Preparing the Cilantro Puree ▶ Near the end of cooking, place the cilantro, red onion, and the 2 reserved reconstituted dried peppers in a blender or food processor. Process to a smooth puree.

Finishing the *Seco* ▶ When the meat is done, add the cilantro puree and the ¼ cup *chicha de jora* or

vinegar to the pot. Stir and simmer until the cilantro is heated through and integrated into the sauce, about 5 minutes.

Serving: Serve the *seco* with white rice, Boiled Yuca (page 167), and Stewed Peruvian Canary Beans (page 511).

Peruvian Duck and Cilantro Stew

Seco de Pato

With its firm, succulent flesh and beefy quality, Muscovy duck flourishes with long cooking in flavorful sauces, just as roosters and veteran hens are supposed to do. That's why Peruvians love duck in their spicy *secos*. I am always struck by the Old World spirit of this dish, with its intense cilantro fragrance, subtle notes of cumin, and perfect balance of sweet, sour, and salty.

What to Drink: Tikal Amorío Malbec from Mendoza, Argentina

SERVES 6

One Muscovy duck (about 6 pounds), cut into 8 serving pieces (see Cutting a Chicken into Serving Pieces, page 659), or 6 legs and thighs (about 7 pounds)

For the *Adobo*

 6 dried *mirasol* peppers (about 1½ ounces)
 1 head garlic, separated into cloves and peeled
 1 tablespoon ground cumin
 1 tablespoon salt
 ½ cup red wine vinegar

For the Cooking Sauce (*Aderezo*)

 2 tablespoons corn oil or fruity extra-virgin olive oil
 1 large red onion (12 ounces), finely chopped (about 2 cups)
 3 scallions, white and light green parts, finely chopped
 6 medium plum tomatoes (about 1 pound), seeded, peeled, and finely chopped
 1 cup coarsely chopped cilantro
 1 cup dark beer, plus more if needed
 1½ quarts water
 6 medium russet or Yukon Gold potatoes (about 2 pounds), peeled and quartered
 1 cup green peas, fresh or frozen

Preparing the Duck ▶ Wipe the duck clean and place in a large bowl.

Preparing the Peppers ▶ Stem and seed the peppers according to the directions on page 744. Cover with 1 quart fresh water and bring to a boil over medium heat. Lower the heat and simmer until soft and plump, about 15 minutes. Drain, reserving ¼ cup cooking liquid.

Making the *Adobo* ▶ Place the peppers in a blender or food processor with the reserved cooking liquid, garlic, cumin, salt, and vinegar and process to a smooth puree. Rub the puree all over the duck, cover tightly with plastic wrap, and let sit for 2 hours

at room temperature or no more than 24 hours in the refrigerator.

Browning the Duck ▶ Heat the oil in a 12-inch sauté pan over medium heat. Scrape the marinade from the duck pieces and reserve. Add the duck, skin side down, and cook until the skin browns, about 20 minutes. Remove to a plate and keep warm. Discard any excess fat, leaving only 3 tablespoons in the pan.

Making the Cooking Sauce ▶ Add the onion and scallions to the pan and cook, stirring, until the onion is golden, 5 to 6 minutes. Add the tomatoes and cook, stirring, for 3 minutes. Puree the cilantro with the beer in a blender or food processor. Stir into the pan and cook for 3 minutes. Pour in the water and stir to mix. Put the duck back into the pan, cover, and simmer over low heat until soft, about 45 minutes. Add the potatoes, cover, and simmer for 18 minutes. Then add the peas and continue cooking for 5 minutes. Add more beer if the sauce dries out.

Serving: Serve with white rice and Stewed Peruvian Canary Beans (page 511).

SAICES, PICANTES, AND SAJTAS

Peruvian *picantes* (literally "hot ones") are, as the name indicates, quite spicy, with a small amount of thick, concentrated sauce. They are often cooked with boiled potatoes, which act as a thickener, or may be bound with potato flour, cornstarch, or wheat flour.

The personality of these hot pepper pots changes slightly in neighboring Bolivia. There the main ingredient (seafood, poultry, guinea pig, or an Andean tuber such as *oca*) is braised in a thick cooking sauce based on ground dried peppers and seasoning vegetables like garlic and onions. Bolivians are also fond of *sajtas* (pronounced "SAKH-tas"), which seem to be close relatives of the Peruvian *picantes*. They too generally have a modest amount of concentrated and very hot sauce and are served with the classic Bolivian combination of fresh and freeze-dried potatoes. The Bolivian hot pepper *saice* contains ground *panca* pepper and is usually made with beef, either cut into small pieces or ground and braised in a thinnish cooking sauce that is soaked up by potatoes and peas.

Spicy Beef Stew in the Style of Tarija

Saice al Estilo de Tarija

Wildly popular all over Bolivia, *saice* (also written as *saisi* or *saise*) is a simple braised beef hash, an everyday dish that delights with its balanced yet vivid combination of flavors, the subtle background heat of fruity *panca* mingling with the tang of tomatoes and the sweetness of peas.

I have tasted *saice* in La Paz, high in the Bolivian *altiplano*, and in tropical Cochabamba, but I am partial to the *saice* of Tarija, a town in south-central Bolivia, with its lively kick of fermented *chicha de jora*. Though Tarijan cooks do not skimp on the hot peppers, they also enliven the *saice* at the table with a simple, spicy fresh table sauce called *sarza*,

made with the Andean pepper *locoto* (known as *rocoto* in Peru), which adds a jolt of heat and herbal freshness.

Cook's Note: Though you could use ground chuck to make *saice*, nothing beats the juiciness of hand-chopped meat. My favorite cut is top sirloin.

What to Drink: Bolivian Huari or Paceña beer

SERVES 6 TO 8

3 pounds top sirloin steak, bottom round, or chuck

For the Cooking Sauce (*Aderezo*)

3 tablespoons corn oil or fruity extra-virgin olive oil
6 garlic cloves, finely chopped
1 large white onion (12 ounces), finely chopped (about 2 cups)
2 teaspoons ground cumin
1 teaspoon salt
½ teaspoon freshly ground black pepper
4 dried *panca* peppers (about ¾ ounce), ground (page 54), or 3 tablespoons store-bought ground *panca* pepper
4 medium plum tomatoes (about 12 ounces), shredded on a box grater
1 cup beef broth, homemade (page 540) or store-bought
¼ cup *chicha de jora*, homemade (page 95) or store-bought, or ¼ cup lager beer and 2 tablespoons cider vinegar

For Finishing the Dish

5 large russet potatoes (about 1½ pounds), peeled and each cut into 6 pieces
8 ounces green peas, fresh or frozen
1 recipe *sarza* (page 762)

Preparing the Meat ▶ Cut the meat into long ¼-inch-thick slices. Cut each slice into ¼-inch strips, then chop into ½-inch dice. Set aside.

Making the Cooking Sauce ▶ Heat the oil in a 12-inch skillet or sauté pan over high heat. Add the garlic and sauté until golden, about 40 seconds. Add the onion and cook for 2 minutes. Add the cumin, salt, pepper, and ground *panca* peppers and cook, stirring, for 1 minute. Add the meat and cook, stirring, for 5 minutes. Stir in the tomatoes and cook for 4 minutes. Pour in the beef broth and *chicha de jora*, lower the heat, cover, and simmer for 40 to 45 minutes, until the meat is juicy and the sauce has darkened into a nice mahogany color. Stir in the potatoes, cover again, and simmer for 10 minutes. Add the peas, cover, and simmer for 5 more minutes.

Serving: Serve with plain white rice, accompanied by the *sarza*.

Shrimp in Spicy Peruvian Pepper Sauce

Picante de Camarones

My late friend Judith Lombardi de Rojas, one of the best cooks I met in Lima, prepared this delicious shrimp *picante* for me during my first visit to the city. It was love at first bite. The spicy, concentrated cheese sauce was thickened with crumbled potatoes, a perfect foil for mountain-fresh river crayfish. Even before I finished eating, I was asking for the recipe. Eventually Judith took me under her wing and gave me several cooking lessons I will never forget, teaching me to cook not one but many *picantes* with various types of seafood. This is still one of my favorites.

Cook's Notes: In Peru, the word *camarones* is applied to prawns and crayfish that live in Andean rivers. For this recipe I use ocean shrimp.

Judith found a mild French sheep's milk feta cheese to be the best substitute for the robust Peruvian *queso fresco*.

What to Drink: Luca Chardonnay from Mendoza, Argentina

SERVES 6 TO 8

For the Shrimp

- 2 pounds small shrimp (36–40 per pound), peeled and deveined
- 1 teaspoon salt

For the Cooking Sauce (*Aderezo*)

- 4 dried *panca* peppers (about ¾ ounce)
- 4 dried *mirasol* peppers (about ¾ ounce)
- ¼ cup extra-virgin olive oil
- 6 garlic cloves, finely chopped
- 1 large red onion (about 12 ounces), peeled and finely chopped (about 2 cups)
- 4 large russet, Yukon Gold, or Yellow Finn potatoes (about 1½ pounds), peeled and cut into ½-inch dice
- 1 teaspoon ground cumin
- ½ teaspoon salt
- 1 cup All-Purpose Fish Broth (page 540) or Simple Chicken Broth (page 538), or low-sodium store-bought broth
- ¼ cup Peruvian or Chilean pisco, grappa, or dry vermouth
- 1 tablespoon finely chopped cilantro leaves
- 4 ounces creamy French sheep's milk feta cheese, crumbled

Preparing the Shrimp ▶ Place the shrimp in a large bowl and rub with the salt. Set aside.

Preparing the Peppers ▶ Stem and seed the peppers. Cover with 1 quart fresh water and boil until plump and softened, about 15 minutes. Drain the peppers, place in a blender or food processor with ¼ cup of the cooking liquid, and process to a smooth puree. Set aside.

Making the Cooking Sauce (*Aderezo*) ▶ Heat the oil in a large skillet or sauté pan over medium heat. Add the garlic and sauté for 20 seconds. Add the onion and cook until soft and golden, about 10 minutes. Pour in the pepper puree and cook for 5 minutes, stirring. Add the potatoes, cumin, and salt and cook, stirring, until the ingredients are well integrated, about 1 minute. Add the broth and pisco and bring to a gentle boil. Lower the heat and simmer, covered, until the potatoes are soft, about 15 minutes. Add the shrimp and cook for 2 minutes. Add the cilantro and the crumbled cheese and stir to mix.

Serving: Serve with plain white rice and Peruvian Onion and Yellow Pepper Slaw/Relish (page 150).

Bolivian Chicken Stew with Fresh and Freeze-Dried Potatoes and *Rocoto* Pepper Salsa

Sajta de Pollo con Sarza

This popular Bolivian chicken dish gets its golden color and subtle heat from a garlicky seasoning paste made with ground dried *mirasol* peppers and cumin. Like many Bolivian stews, *sajta* is served with both fresh and freeze-dried potatoes and *sarza*, a spicy salsa of chopped tomatoes, freshly sliced onions, and hot *rocoto* peppers. The potato combination is a classic Bolivian accompaniment. Many times people have asked me, why go out of your way to use a potato that needs to be reconstituted when you could use fresh? The answer is that these potatoes carry the flavor of the Bolivian earth, a loamy aftertaste that adds depth and excitement to the dish. The potatoes are there not only as a garnish but as an integral part of the dish.

Cook's Note: For more on the freeze-dried potatoes called *chuño blanco* in Peru and *tunta* in Bolivia, see page 202. They normally come dried and uncooked in 1-pound packages. Overall they are on the small size, though in Andean markets you will find them in various sizes and qualities, the choicest ones being large and very white. When buying *chuño blanco*, look for packages with the largest light-colored whole potatoes.

If you can't find freeze-dried potatoes, substitute more fresh potatoes as suggested below.

Working Ahead ▶ Freeze-dried potatoes need to be reconstituted like salt cod to plump them up, then squeezed out to get rid of any residual bitterness. (Andean farmers normally select bitter varieties for freeze-drying.) It is best to soak them before boiling, so plan to do this 1 day ahead.

What to Drink: Paceña Bolivian beer or Casa Lapostolle Cuvee Alexandre Chardonnay from Casablanca Valley, Chile

SERVES 4 TO 6

For the Freeze-Dried Potatoes

1 pound white freeze-dried potatoes (if able to obtain; see Cook's Note)

For the Chicken

One 4-pound chicken, cut into 8 serving pieces (see page 659)

- 1 teaspoon salt
- 1 teaspoon freshly ground black pepper

For the Cooking Sauce

- 8 garlic cloves, peeled
- 4 tablespoons ground dried *mirasol* pepper, homemade (page 54) or store-bought
- 1 tablespoon ground cumin
- 1 teaspoon salt
- 1 teaspoon freshly ground black pepper
- 3 tablespoons corn oil
- 2 large white onions (12 ounces each), finely chopped (about 4 cups)
- 6 cups chicken broth, homemade (page 538) or store-bought
- 2 tablespoons finely chopped flat-leaf parsley

For the Fresh Potatoes

- 6 large russet, Idaho, or Yukon Gold potatoes (about 2 pounds), peeled (plus 2 more if not able to obtain freeze-dried potatoes)
- 1 teaspoon salt
- ½ pound fresh *queso blanco*, cut into 3-by-¼-inch slices

For the *Sarza*

- 1 fresh-frozen hot red Andean pepper (sold as *locoto* or *rocoto*) or Mexican *manzano* chile, or 2–3 serranos, stemmed, seeded (do not devein), and coarsely chopped
- 6 medium plum tomatoes (about 1¼ pounds), peeled, seeded, and coarsely chopped Leaves from 3 cilantro sprigs
- ¼ cup water
- 1 small white onion (4 ounces), finely slivered lengthwise
- 2 tablespoons finely shredded mint

Reconstituting the Freeze-Dried Potatoes ▶ Rinse the freeze-dried potatoes, if using, under running water. Place in a bowl and cover with 3 inches water. Let soak for a minimum of 8 hours and a maximum of 12 hours. When they have soaked, squeeze the potatoes between your hands and change the water. Let soak for a few minutes and drain. Squeeze the potatoes again. They might crumble a little, but they will still cook to a nice consistency. Set aside.

Preparing the Chicken ▶ Place the chicken in a medium bowl and season with salt and pepper.

Cooking the Freeze-Dried Potatoes ▶ If using the freeze-dried potatoes, place them in a medium pot with 2 quarts water and bring to a boil over medium-high heat. Lower the heat to medium and cook until tender, 30 to 45 minutes, checking the potatoes for doneness by piercing them with the tip of a small knife. (You'll find that they take longer to soften than fresh potatoes.) Drain.

Preparing the Cooking Sauce ▶ Using a mortar and pestle or a mini food processor, grind the garlic to a paste with the ground *mirasol* pepper, cumin, salt, and black pepper. Set aside.

Heat the oil in a heavy 6-quart pot over medium heat until it ripples. Add the onions and sauté until golden, about 8 minutes. Stir in the reserved seasoning paste and sauté, stirring, for about 2 minutes. Add the chicken pieces, broth, and parsley and bring to a boil over medium-high heat. Lower the heat to medium-low and simmer, covered, for 30 minutes, or until the chicken is tender.

Cooking the Fresh Potatoes ▶ While the chicken and freeze-dried potatoes are cooking, place the fresh potatoes in a medium pot with 2 quarts cold water and the salt and cook over medium heat for 20 minutes, or until tender. Remove from the heat and let the potatoes rest in the warm water until ready to serve. Drain at the last minute.

To prepare both kinds of potatoes for serving, cut them lengthwise two thirds of the way through and sandwich a slice of cheese between the two halves of each potato.

Preparing the Sarza ▶ Place the hot pepper in a blender or food processor with the tomatoes and cilantro leaves. Pulse to chop coarsely. Stir in the water to make a fluid salsa. If it becomes too thick as it sits, add more water. Pour into a bowl and stir in the onion and mint.

Serving: Place 1 or 2 pieces of chicken on each serving plate and arrange 1 or 2 stuffed freeze-dried potatoes and 1 or 2 stuffed fresh potatoes beside the chicken. Spoon some of the cooking broth over the chicken and top with *sarza*.

PEPIANES

Among the most complex of the hot pepper pots Spaniards encountered in the New World were the seed-enriched hot pepper pots that came to be called *pipianes* in Mexico and *pepianes* elsewhere in Central America. Like some of the Moorish-influenced stews of medieval Spain, they were thickened with ground nuts—or in this case pumpkin seeds, which served the same purpose as the almonds, walnuts, and hazelnuts of the Mediterranean. The *pepianes* described by early sixteenth-century eyewitnesses like Bernardino de Sahagún in Mexico were stews of fowl, shrimp, or fish, and the sauces they were

cooked in combined chiles and tomatillos with ground pumpkin seeds. These chile-enriched sauces were generically called *chilmolli* in Nahuatl, the language of the Aztecs, but the Spanish christened the ones made with pumpkin seeds *pepianes*, from *pepita*, their word for the seeds of fruits.

Making a Mexican or Central American *pepián* is not very different from making *mole*, but it is not as involved. For one thing, most *pepianes* call for far fewer ingredients than *moles*, and with few exceptions they are made with only one or two kinds of chiles. Otherwise, cooks use the same techniques: roasting and toasting the main ingredients and grinding them to a paste, frying this paste in lard, and diluting it with broth to form a thick sauce for chicken or other meat.

Pepianes come in many colors, green being the most popular; there are also red and yellow ones, and a deep black Guatemalan *pepián* not unlike the *mole negro* of Oaxaca. Normally, *pepianes* do not call for chocolate, but there's a popular version in Guatemala, the *pepián* from Sololá on Lake Atitlán, that does use chocolate and tastes practically like a *mole*.

Guatemalan Black Chicken *Pepián*

Pepián Negro de Pollo Guatemalteco

Pepianes are always thickened with seeds. In the case of this complex black version, the sauce gets most of its body from sesame seeds and pureed aromatic vegetables. These elements are collectively known as *recado*. In Guatemala we find different regional interpretations of the *pepián*: red, green, yellow. Most are stews that call for many vegetables, often including chayote (locally called *güisquil*).

Cook's Note: The intense black color of this *pepián* is caused by a piece of carbonized bread. If you fear that the charred bread will give a bitter taste to the sauce, don't worry. You will only be able to taste a subtle and pleasant smokiness.

What to Drink: A rich and supple Dolium Gran Reserva Malbec from Mendoza, Argentina

SERVES 6

For the Chicken

One 3½- to 4-pound chicken, cut into 8 pieces (see page 659), skin removed

3 quarts water

1 medium white onion (8 ounces), peeled and cut in half

½ medium head garlic, separated into cloves

2 teaspoons salt

For the Cooking Sauce

2 dried guajillo chiles (about ½ ounce)

2 dried pasilla chiles (about 1 ounce)

2 medium white onions (about 1 pound), unpeeled

6 garlic cloves, peeled

4 medium plum tomatoes (about 12 ounces)

6 slices from a baguette

2 ounces sesame seeds (about ½ cup)

2 tablespoons rice

6 allspice berries, ground to a powder

1 Ceylon cinnamon stick (*canela*), freshly ground (about 2 teaspoons)

½ cup dark raisins

¼ cup vegetable oil or mild extra-virgin olive oil

For the Vegetables

2 dark green or white chayotes (about 1½ pounds), peeled, pitted, and cut into long slices

3 medium carrots (about 12 ounces), peeled and cut into ¼-inch rounds

3 medium potatoes (about 1 pound), quartered
About 8 ounces green beans, trimmed and cut into thirds

Cooking the Chicken ▶ Place the chicken in a large pot with the water, onion, garlic, and salt and bring to a boil over medium heat. Lower the heat and simmer, covered, until tender, about 30 minutes. Remove the chicken and set aside. Strain the broth through a fine-mesh sieve and discard the onion and garlic. Return the broth and the chicken to the pot and set aside.

Preparing the Cooking Sauce ▶ Stem and seed the chiles. Heat a *comal*, griddle, or heavy skillet over medium heat until a drop of water evaporates on contact. Add the chiles and toast, flattening slightly with a spatula, for about 30 seconds, turning once. Place the chiles in a small saucepan, cover with 3 cups fresh water, and simmer over medium heat until the chiles are plump and softened, about 15 minutes. Drain, reserving ½ cup of the cooking liquid. Set aside.

Place the onions, garlic, and tomatoes on the *comal* or griddle and roast, turning occasionally, until blistered and charred on all sides, about 8 minutes. When they are cool enough to handle, peel the onion and garlic. Set aside.

Add the bread slices to the *comal* or griddle and toast until deeply charred and blackened. Remove from the griddle. Add the sesame seeds and toast, stirring, just until they pop. Quickly scoop them into a bowl. Scatter the rice on the griddle and toast, stirring, just until golden brown. Scoop into a bowl and cover with 1 cup water. Soak for 15 minutes, drain, and set aside.

In a blender or food processor, process all the roasted ingredients into a puree with the ground spices and raisins. In a deep skillet, heat the oil to rippling over medium heat. Stir in the puree and cook, stirring, for 8 minutes.

Finishing the *Pepián* ▶ Return the pot with the chicken and broth to the stove and bring to a boil over medium heat. Add the hot puree. Stir in the vegetables, lower the heat, and simmer gently until the vegetables are soft, 15 to 20 minutes.

Serving: Serve with rice and Guatemalan Red Cabbage Relish (page 150).

Guatemalan Red Chicken *Pepián*

Pepián Rojo de Pollo Guatemalteco

I'm not going to deceive you: preparing the seasoning ingredients for a red Guatemalan *pepián* takes time. That's why you cannot blame the busy Guatemalan cook for going to the grocery store to buy a packaged commercial *pepián* mix. But I won't pretend it is the same.

Because I love *pepianes* and make them often, I prepare a large batch of my own mix to keep on hand. This is not a shortcut, since everything has been prepared at home, but it gives me convenience without sacrificing quality or flavor. If you enjoy *pepianes* and plan to make them regularly, prepare my *pepián* mix. It will be worth your time, since you can stretch its uses; for instance, you can rub it on chicken, beef, or pork, or serve it as a condiment with other stews.

What to Drink: La Misión Carmenère from Maipo Valley, Chile

SERVES 6

For the Chicken

One 3½-pound chicken, cut into 8 pieces (see page 659)
 1 head garlic, separated into cloves, peeled, and mashed to a paste with a mortar and pestle or finely chopped and mashed
 1 tablespoon bitter orange juice or equal parts lime juice and orange juice
 ½ teaspoon salt
 ¼ teaspoon ground cumin

For the Cooking Sauce (*Recado*)

 3 medium plum tomatoes (about 9 ounces), cored and quartered
 3 tomatillos (about 4 ounces), husked and quartered
 1 small white onion (about 5 ounces), peeled and cut in half
 2 tablespoons achiote-infused vegetable or mild extra-virgin olive oil (page 89)
 2½ cups chicken broth, homemade (page 538) or store-bought
 ¼ cup Guatemalan Spice Blend for *Pepián* (recipe follows)
 1 teaspoon salt, or to taste

 2 tablespoons corn *masa* mix, preferably Maseca brand

Marinating the Chicken ▶ Place the chicken in a bowl. Rub with the garlic, juice, salt, and cumin. Cover tightly with plastic wrap and let rest for a minimum of 1 hour at room temperature or no more than 24 hours in the refrigerator.

Cooking the Chicken ▶ Place the tomatoes, tomatillos, and onion in a blender or food processor and puree. Scrape the marinade from the chicken and discard.

In a large skillet, heat the oil over medium heat. Add the chicken and brown, turning with tongs, for 10 to 15 minutes. Remove from the pan and set aside. Add the reserved tomato puree to the remaining oil and cook, stirring, for 10 minutes. Add the chicken pieces, 2 cups broth, *pepián* seasoning mix, and salt.

Dissolve the *masa* mix in the remaining ½ cup chicken broth and stir into the sauce to thicken. Simmer over medium-low heat until the chicken is tender, about 15 minutes.

Serving: Serve with rice and Guatemalan Red Cabbage Relish (page 150).

Guatemalan Spice Blend for *Pepián*

Polvo para Pepián

Commercial ground spice mixes are usually not ideal, having preservatives or other ingredients that compromise flavor. For the flavor of an authentic *pepián* without any additives, my solution is to grind together all the necessary dried ingredients in a large batch and store the resulting powder as a handy *pepián* base. It keeps for a long time, since it contains no liquid, and can shorten the preparation time for a *pepián* with no sacrifice of flavor.

MAKES ABOUT 3 CUPS

16–17 dried guajillo chiles (about 8 ounces)
  7 dried pasilla chiles (about 1½ ounces)
  ⅓ cup sesame seeds (about 2 ounces)
  ⅓ cup hulled pumpkin seeds (about 2 ounces)
  ⅓ cup whole blanched almonds (about 2 ounces)
  1 tablespoon allspice berries
  1 tablespoon whole black peppercorns
One 3-inch Ceylon cinnamon stick (*canela*)
  2 teaspoons whole cloves
  4 ounces cacao nibs (about ¾ cup)
  1 tablespoon salt

▶ Stem and seed the chiles. Heat a large *comal*, griddle, or heavy skillet over medium-high heat. Add the chiles in batches, starting with the guajillos, and roast, turning occasionally with tongs, for about 2 minutes. Remove and set aside on a plate. Toast the sesame seeds just until golden; instantly scrape into a small bowl and set aside. Add the pumpkin seeds and almonds and roast together until golden. Remove before they can scorch and set aside in a bowl. Reduce the heat to medium and add all the remaining ingredients except the cacao nibs and salt. Roast the spices briefly, about 2 minutes or until they release their aromas. Remove and let cool briefly in a small bowl. Adjust the heat under the pan to medium-low and roast the cacao nibs, stirring constantly, for about 2 minutes. Remove from the heat and let cool.

Chop the roasted peppers with a heavy knife or break them into smaller pieces with your hands. Place in a food processor, in two batches if necessary, and pulse to a coarse powder. Transfer to a bowl. Combine all the other roasted ingredients in the processor and pulse to a coarse powder. Add to the peppers along with the salt, and stir to mix well. Working in batches, grind everything to a fine powder in a spice or coffee mill.

Pass through a medium-mesh sieve to get rid of lumps, transfer the mix to a glass jar, and store, tightly capped, in a cool, dry place. It will keep for 2 to 3 months.

MOLES

The most elaborate of all the Latin American hot pepper pots sprang from pre-Columbian preparations that were transformed in colonial times with a whole panoply of new ingredients. Today these dishes bear the name *mole*, from *molli*, the Nahuatl word for sauce. *Moles* are better known to North American diners than any other member of the hot pepper pot family, but they are not necessarily better understood. They can be fairly simple or remarkably complex. The eighteenth-century *mole poblano* is an excellent example of the latter. It follows the broad idea of a *pepián* but with many baroque additions, such as the use of several nuts and seeds at once, a combination of different dried peppers, an elaborate array of Old World spices, and often chocolate. Yet if you analyze even this intricate dish, you can still discern the principles of the simpler stews from which it is descended.

Every history of Mexican cooking tells the story of how the country's most famous *mole*, *mole poblano*, was conceived in the Santa Rosa nunnery in Puebla de los Angeles. One day the nuns learned that their benefactor, the bishop Manuel Fernández de Santa Cruz, was coming to visit. Finding only a turkey in their courtyard, the flustered nuns ran around trying to figure out how to make a meal befitting a bishop with nothing but a turkey. One of the nuns, Sor Andrea de la Asunción, raided the pantry and was seized with a brilliant idea: she would boil the turkey and make a sauce for it using everything she could find, including chocolate.

Culinary gospel tells that the birth of this *mole* was an immaculate conception taking place in the virginal womb of the cloister kitchen. But on a closer look, this supposed virgin birth turns out to have come from a long line of parents, such as the pre-Columbian chile-thickened sauces described by Cortés and Bernardino de Sahagún and thickened chocolate drinks. Look even closer at the nuns' kitchen and you'll start to see the whole clan of ancestors—using nuts as a thickener, for example, which was a keynote of Spanish medieval cooking. Though *mole poblano* may be the only *mole* many Americans have heard of, each region of Mexico boasts its own terrific variation. My favorites come from Michoacán, Veracruz, and Oaxaca, the "land of the seven *moles*."

Mastering *Moles*

Moles have a reputation for being difficult and complex. Of course there are some that are neither. As for the most demanding ones, Mexicans understand that they are not for every day. In every part of Mexico certain *moles* are feast foods, the obligatory main course at any self-respecting wedding or birthday party. These are usually reserved for special occasions because of the sheer amount of time it takes to make them, particularly for a couple hundred guests. Imagine stemming and seeding pound after pound of dried chiles, with clouds of blinding smoke billowing forth as cooks griddle-roast or fry them, and roasting or frying and grinding astronomic quantities of nuts and spices! But making *moles* for a party is always a communal experience, shared by throngs of relatives and friends.

Tackling one of the big *moles* by yourself can scare novices and skilled cooks alike. But if you look closely at the process, you will see logic at work. Even the most complex *moles* are based on clusters of related ingredients that can be dealt with according to their nature and function, then combined in one great whole (because you will end up with a large quantity). Mexicans always make the big *moles* in big batches, even when it isn't done for two hundred guests; they prepare enough to last for weeks and use it a few cups or quarts at a time. My recipes are not banquet-scale, but they are not small; they are meant to produce enough sauce to season a 3½-pound chicken or a medium-size turkey. *Mole* pastes will keep for a long time in the refrigerator (Mexicans even keep them at room temperature) and can be used whenever you want in whatever amounts you prefer.

Deconstructing *Moles*

I have tried to distill the principles of *mole*-making to their essence. Of course, different *moles* follow different rules, but most of the ones in this book use the same general scenario.

Most *moles* are really puree-like sauces, but each of the ingredients contributes its own special nuances to the sauce and must be prepared so as to bring out its full flavor before it is added. All of the ingredients of the *mole* are processed in sequence, each at its own time. Usually the processing follows a predictable order: first you fry or roast, then you grind, and then you amalgamate. Finally, when all the ingredients have been combined in one heavy paste, you make the rich sauce still richer by frying it in hot fat, adjust the consistency by thinning it with some liquid (usually broth), and add some last-minute flavorings.

In Mexico, most ingredients are usually fried on their own first, so enormous quantities of lard go into the *mole* even before the final frying. But some schools of *mole*-making prefer to griddle-roast the main ingredients before pureeing, instead of frying them. I have generally followed this method.

The ingredients usually fall into nine categories. They do not have to be prepared in any rigid order, but the sequence I give is what I have found most helpful. The most elaborate sauces will contain all of these groups; the simpler ones may draw on only some. Knowing the function of each cluster of ingredients will allow you to be creative and to come out with simpler *moles* that use fewer ingredients but still cover all the bases of the gustatory palette.

1. **Dried chiles** (usually a combination of several different kinds). They may be omitted from some simple fresh *moles* but are always present in the complex ones. They add color, heat, and body to the sauce. They can be toasted (or fried), soaked, pureed, and strained as much as 1 week ahead. In some recipes, the seeds are used for extra heat. Traditional cooks puree the chiles separately from the other ingredients and start frying them in the hot fat before the rest of the sauce is added. I have had good results with this practice, but I do not think it is absolutely necessary.

2. **Spices.** These add many notes of elusive aroma and flavor to the complex whole. They may include black pepper, coriander seeds, cloves, cumin, allspice, anise, and cinnamon (always the soft-quilled true Ceylon cinnamon). Sometimes there is also a dried herb like oregano or thyme. These seasonings are dry-roasted to bring out their fragrance before being finely ground in a coffee mill or spice mill. They can be toasted and ground at least a week ahead (though they lose fragrance and freshness if prepared too far ahead).

3. *Nuts and seeds.* Like the spices, these are a link with the cooking of medieval Spain, especially sesame seeds and almonds. Some *moles* are made with walnuts, peanuts, or pumpkin seeds. They mellow out other flavors and contribute richness, and also act as thickeners. All are dry-roasted or fried before grinding, to develop a good toasty flavor. I don't like to do this ahead of time.

4. *Bread thickeners.* Many *moles* contain a small amount of toasted bread (either plain or egg-enriched rolls), sweet crackers, and/or corn tortillas, which help to thicken the sauce. In very dark *moles*, the bread or tortillas may be toasted to the point of charring, for color and a slightly bitter edge of flavor. Do this the same day you are making the *mole*.

5. *Basic seasoning vegetables*, such as onions, garlic, and tomatoes (sometimes tomatillos). These are like the flavor foundation of a classic *sofrito*, but instead of being sautéed, they are griddle-roasted to intensify their flavors. They also help give the sauce body. I don't like to roast these ingredients before the chiles and other ingredients, because they tend to gunk up the griddle. However, they can be prepared, pureed, and strained separately at least a couple of days ahead. Our cooks at Zafra actually prefer to puree the roasted tomatoes separately and add them to the *mole* paste only if it will be used within a week, because they make the paste more perishable.

6. *Dried or fresh fruits.* Most *moles* contain raisins or prunes, which give the sauce body, sweetness, and a little fruity acidity. Some may have cooked ripe plantains or apples, which add still more body and sweetness. In a few, such as *manchamanteles*, fresh apple and/or pineapple is added later in the cooking for a stronger sweet-and-sour effect. Ripe plantains and apples are usually fried before being added; some cooks fry raisins and prunes as well. I like to plump raisins in some of the chile soaking liquid before adding them to the other ingredients.

7. *Fat.* Mexicans traditionally used home-rendered lard for frying, but today many have switched over to commercial hydrogenated lard or vegetable oils. To my surprise, I have found that the next best thing to top-quality lard is a fruity extra-virgin olive oil, preferably one with a distinct green color. At Zafra we use a Catalan olive oil from Lérida, with a beautiful apple flavor that blends seamlessly with the fruity mole.

8. *Chocolate and sugar.* Some of the most important flavorings are added only at the last stage of cooking, when the *mole* paste is being fried. If chocolate is used, it is added at this late stage. So is sugar (plain white sugar, caramelized white sugar, or the rich Latin brown loaf sugar). These ingredients profoundly influence the depth, aroma, and consistency of the finished dish. Chocolate and loaf sugar can be chopped or grated ahead of time.

9. *Liquid.* After the main elements have been pureed and fried, the paste has to be diluted to a pourable consistency. In fact, the entire *mole* is commonly made ahead and stored in its thick, concentrated form, because it keeps best this way. The cook takes as much as she likes at a time and thins it with the appropriate amount of liquid for any meal. I generally dilute a very thick *mole* paste with an equal amount of liquid. Theoretically you can use water or already cooked broth, but in Mexico people plan the cooking so that the chosen meat or poultry will

be simmering in a light, simple broth that will be ready just when the paste needs thinning. Note that once any meat or poultry broth has been added, the thinned paste should be used within 1 or 2 days.

When you are lining up your ingredients, you should also line up your equipment. You will need a large, heavy griddle or skillet (or two smaller ones) for roasting onions, garlic, tomatoes, chiles, and other ingredients. The simple versatile Mexican clay *comal*, or a more practical steel one, is ideal if you can get one, but one or two cast-iron skillets or a large griddle will do fine. The actual grinding used to be done by hand using a *metate* (grinding platform) or large volcanic stone mortar. Nowadays you have a choice of blender or food processor. If using a food processor, make sure the liquid does not overflow. In either case, you may have to process the ingredients in several batches. You will also need a large saucepan, Latin American *caldero*, or Dutch oven heavy enough to simmer the *mole* without burning it, and with a good lid to keep the sauce from splattering all over. Finally, you need a mesh strainer. Most Mexican cooks I know like their *mole* sauce smooth and silky.

Finishing the *Mole*: When Does a *Mole* Become a Stew?

There are three general ways of finishing a *mole*. People usually boil some chicken, turkey, or pork in water with a few seasoning vegetables (though the meat can also be sautéed), and just before it is completely cooked they add it to the sauce, so the meat can simmer slowly and absorb the flavors of the sauce. In some simple *moles* calling for one or two

kinds of chile, the raw meat or poultry is cooked in the sauce (see the *mole verde* from Oaxaca, page 782). The finished sauce can also be poured over the cooked meat. In all cases, serving *moles* in the genuine Mexican style means ladling out oceans of sauce onto the plate. But this isn't the end of the many traditional or not-so-traditional uses. A little *mole* is often used to flavor empanadas or tamal fillings; tortillas may be dipped in *mole* to make *enmoladas*, just as they are dipped in chile sauces to make enchiladas. I like to add some to tamal doughs, vegetables, and rice dishes. I also use *moles* like European-style sauces; for example, crisp, golden, juicy grilled duck breasts with just a couple of spoonfuls of *mole poblano* belong in the stratosphere of culinary experiences. More and more crossover possibilities will occur to you as you work with these sublime sauces.

A Note on Chocolate for *Moles*

Contrary to the assumption of many American cooks, chocolate is not used in all *moles*. In fact, there are *moles* that can be described as light stews with no chocolate among the ingredients. It is, however, an important element in some of the most famous *moles*, particularly the velvety ones that grace holiday tables and are served on special occasions such as weddings and baptisms. Mexican cooks generally use the distinctive Mexican-style chocolate made by large manufacturers or small artisanal producers from cacao, sugar, cinnamon, and sometimes ground almonds. Cacao nibs are also used by some cooks. In my own cooking, I have come to prefer cacao nibs and premium chocolates with a high cacao content. (Most commercial Mexican chocolate brands have added coconut or palm oil, lots of sugar, artificial flavorings, and low percentages of cacao.) My usual choices are the bittersweet El Rey Bucare (58.5%), extra-bitter El Rey Gran Samán (70%), or Cluizel Los Ancones (67%) made with cacao from the Dominican Republic. For delicate *moles* with lots of sweetness I have started using Pacari Esmeraldas (60%) for its beautiful caramel and fruity notes, and the more floral Pacari Manabí (65%), both made with excellent Ecuadorian Nacional cacao (see page 341). If you want a taste of heirloom Mexican cacao from Chiapas, try Bonnat's Cacao Real del Xoconusco (75%) and Askinosie's Soconusco (75%). Since commercial Mexican chocolate is both easier to find and closer to Mexican practice, I list it in the following recipes. But I encourage you to experiment with premium chocolates as you become more at home with the nuances of *mole*.

The Famous *Mole Poblano* of Santa Rosa

El Famoso Mole Poblano de Santa Rosa

I have trouble accepting the standard story about the origin of *mole poblano*, in which the nuns of the Santa Rosa convent in Puebla rushed around frantically throwing together whatever they could find in the pantry in order to make dinner for an unexpected visiting bishop. If you know anything about nuns, you know that they do nothing by accident, particularly in the kitchen. When you look at this dish, it is no hodgepodge of ingredients but a sauce built on the classic principles of both Spanish and pre-Columbian Mesoamerican cooking. It brilliantly reflects the style of the colonial Mexican kitchen, as shown in recipe books from the seventeenth century on. The spices are almost purely Mediterranean, except for the carefully judged mixture of different dried chiles. The balance of sweet and savory also harks back to old Spain. The flavors and aromas remind me of some contemporary Moroccan dishes.

I have seen many recipes for *mole poblano*, and have tasted even more versions. In the end I decided to adapt a recipe from Salazar Monroy's 1945 *La típica cocina poblana y los guisos de sus religiosas* (The Typical Cooking of Puebla and the Dishes of Its Nuns), which purports to record the kitchen notes of the Dominican convent in which this famous *mole* first saw the light of day. Monroy's recipe yields eight times as much as mine, but I have kept the original proportions. We serve it often at my restaurant Zafra, where our Mexican-born cooks insist on making the sauce as refined as possible by passing the chiles and other ingredients through a fine-mesh sieve. It is a lot of work, but they swear that nothing less will serve to produce the perfect silky texture. You lose about a fifth to a quarter of the original volume this way; I sometimes use a medium-mesh sieve for a slightly larger yield, but I don't recommend skipping the straining.

Working Ahead ▶ Have all the ingredients measured, collected in related groups, and ready to assemble. Have ready a *comal*, griddle, or heavy skillet, preferably cast iron; a metal spatula and/or tongs; a food processor or blender; a medium saucepan; two large bowls; a spice or coffee grinder (preferably one that can handle nuts) or a small food processor; one or two large fine-mesh sieves or a chinois with a pusher; several sturdy wooden spoons; a large (6- to 7-quart) heavy lidded saucepan, preferably deeper than it is wide.

For the Dried Chiles

5 ounces dried pasilla chiles (about 19 chiles)

5 ounces dried ancho chiles (about 12 chiles)

4 ounces dried *mulato* chiles (about 11 chiles)

1 chipotle chile

For the Spices

One 1-inch Ceylon cinnamon stick (*canela*)

¼ teaspoon whole cloves

½ teaspoon anise seeds

2 teaspoons black peppercorns

1 teaspoon coriander seeds

½ teaspoon cumin seeds

For the Nuts and Seeds

⅓ cup whole almonds (about 1½ ounces)

2½ tablespoons sesame seeds (about ¼ ounce)

For the Bread Thickeners

1 slice from a baguette or 1 sandwich bread slice (about ¼ ounce)

Half of a store-bought corn tortilla

For the Seasoning Vegetables

2 medium plum tomatoes (about 6 ounces)

1 small white onion (about 5 ounces), unpeeled

6 garlic cloves, unpeeled

For the Fruit

½ cup dark raisins

For Frying

2 cups freshly rendered lard (page 82) or fruity extra-virgin olive oil

3 ounces grated brown loaf sugar, Muscovado sugar, or packed dark brown sugar (about ½ cup)

3½ ounces chocolate, preferably a dark premium chocolate with at least 50% cacao content, coarsely chopped

1 tablespoon salt, or to taste

Preparing the Chiles ▶ Stem and seed the chiles, reserving two tablespoons of the chile seeds (except those of the chipotle). Heat the *comal* or griddle over medium heat until a drop of water evaporates on contact. Working in 4 or 5 batches, add the chiles and roast, pressing with a spatula, until fragrant, less than 1 minute on each side (I like to roast each type of chile together for more even roasting). As they are done, lift them out into a large bowl. (Leave the griddle on the burner over low heat.) Cover with 5 cups hot water and let sit until softened, 20 to 30 minutes, or place in a medium saucepan with 5 cups water, bring to a boil, lower the heat to medium-low, and simmer, uncovered, until softened, about 10 minutes. Drain, reserving the soaking or cooking liquid.

Place the reserved chile seeds on the griddle and roast, stirring occasionally, until very dark. Set aside.

Working in batches, place the chiles in a blender or food processor with 1 cup (or as needed) of the reserved liquid and process to a smooth puree. Place in a bowl and set aside.

Preparing the Spices ▶ Place the cinnamon, cloves, anise seeds, peppercorns, and coriander and cumin seeds on the griddle and roast, stirring, until fragrant, about 2 minutes. Remove at once. Grind to a fine powder in a spice or coffee mill and set aside.

Preparing the Nuts and Seeds ▶ Place the almonds on the griddle and roast, stirring, until golden, about 2 minutes. Do not scorch. Set aside. Add the sesame seeds to the griddle, and roast, stirring constantly, until they start to pop, about 1 minute. Remove at once. Place the nuts and seeds in a small food processor or spice grinder, add the reserved roasted chile seeds, and process to a coarse powder. Set aside.

Preparing the Bread Thickeners ▶ Place the bread slice and tortilla half on the griddle and toast until the bread is golden on both sides and the tortilla is brittle, about 2 minutes. Set aside.

Preparing the Seasoning Vegetables ▶ Working in batches, place the tomatoes, onion, and garlic on the griddle and roast, turning occasionally, until the tomatoes and onion are blackened and the garlic is dark and soft to the touch, about 7 minutes. Remove from the griddle. When the vegetables are cool enough to handle, peel the onion and garlic, remove the most charred bits of the tomato skins, and set aside.

Preparing the Fruit ▶ Place the raisins in a small bowl and cover with ½ cup of the reserved chile liquid. Set aside.

Grinding the Prepared Ingredients ▶ Place the tomatoes, onion, and garlic in a food processor or blender with the ground spices, the nuts and seeds, the bread and tortilla, and the raisins and chile liquid (the liquid helps the action of the blades). Process to a fine paste. Scoop out into a bowl.

Frying the *Mole* ▶ Now you are ready to assemble the *mole*. Heat the lard or olive oil over medium heat until fragrant and pour in the chile puree. It will splatter vigorously, so be careful. Simmer, stirring frequently, for 20 minutes or until the fat begins to separate from the solids and sizzle. Stir in the vegetable puree and cook, stirring, to mix well, for about 25 minutes, until the fat again begins to separate from the solids and sizzle and the sauce thickens to the point where you can see the bottom of the pot as you move the spoon. Add the sugar and stir to dissolve. Add the chocolate and cook, stirring, until it is melted, about 2 minutes. Taste for sweetness and add more sugar if needed. Season with the salt. Force the puree through a fine-mesh sieve or chinois into a bowl, using a pestle or wooden spoon.

If you are planning to use this paste at once, see Finishing the *Mole*, page 770. Dilute it by stirring in an equal amount of good chicken broth until the *mole* is as heavy as tomato sauce. It isn't absolutely necessary, but the consistency will be much silkier if you again force the thinned mixture through a fine-mesh sieve by pushing with a wooden spoon.

Storing: If not using immediately, cool the *mole* paste to room temperature, transfer to several storage containers, and pour a thin film of melted lard or oil over the surface to help keep it from spoiling. Seal tightly and store in a cool place or the refrigerator. In Mexico, people keep it unrefrigerated for as long as several months, but here in the United States, I would recommend keeping it for no longer than 1 month.

Francisca's Wedding *Mole*

El Mole de Boda de Francisca

In the 1990s, I studied and collected embroideries from a group of Mexican women artisans who live in small towns around Lake Pátzcuaro in the state of Michoacán, for an illustrated book on life around the lake. One embroidered panel in particular always makes me hungry. It depicts a wedding with Tarascan men in hats and women wrapped in their striped shawls (*rebozos*), seated at a long banquet table after having danced their way from the best man's house to the groom's house. Near the table, women are stirring large clay pots over wood fires. I know what they are cooking. I have tasted it all around the lake on special feast days and weddings. It's a feast day *mole*, a richly colored sauce, not too sweet, with just the right kick of chile heat from a trio of chiles to bring the smooth, velvety paste alive.

Making *moles* for a wedding is a regional heritage and a bond that links generations of mothers, daughters, and sons. More than twenty-five years ago María López of Uricho, a village on the western shore of Lake Pátzcuaro, made a similar *mole* for the wedding of her daughter-in-law, my friend Francisca de la Luz Cortés. All her family as well as her neighbors came to help María in the cooking. When Francisca's son got engaged she began planning to repeat her mother-in-law's feat, again with the help of family and friends.

Several years ago, I gave Francisca a very wide, boldly patterned piece of fabric from IKEA. After she opened the package and admiringly spread it over her kitchen table, she embraced me tightly and exclaimed, "With this cloth, I will make the tablecloth for my son's wedding banquet." This recipe celebrates the bonding tradition of the *mole* in the rites of passage of generations of Michoacanos living in this beautiful lake region. I cannot help but imagine Francisca's mahogany-colored *mole* against that bright cloth, and the joy she must have shared with all those who gave of themselves for that feast of communion.

Cook's Note: In Michoacán, one of the chile types used would be a dark-hued dried poblano known as *chile Morelia negro*. The best substitutes in this country are *mulatos* or anchos.

Working Ahead ▶ See page 771.

MAKES ABOUT 6 CUPS FINELY STRAINED, UNDILUTED
MOLE SAUCE

For the Chiles
- 15 pasilla chiles (about 4 ounces)
- 10–11 dried *mulato* or ancho chiles (about 4 ounces)
- 12 guajillo chiles (about 4 ounces)

For the Fruit
- ½ cup dark raisins (about 3 ounces)
- 2 tablespoons freshly rendered lard (page 82) or mild and fruity extra-virgin olive oil
- 1 ripe medium plantain (about 8 ounces), peeled and cut into ½-inch rounds

For the Thickeners
- Two ¼-inch-thick slices from a French baguette, Cuban bread (page 591), or any white bread (about 2 ounces)
- 2 store-bought corn tortillas

For the Nuts and Seeds
- ½ cup whole blanched almonds (about 2 ounces)
- ⅓ cup walnut meats (about 2 ounces)
- 1 heaping tablespoon sesame seeds

For the Spices

1 teaspoon whole allspice berries

1 tablespoon black peppercorns

5 whole cloves

2 teaspoons whole cumin seeds

1 teaspoon Mexican oregano

1 teaspoon dried thyme

For the Seasoning Vegetables

5 medium plum tomatoes (about 1 pound)

1 medium white onion (about 8 ounces), unpeeled

12 garlic cloves, unpeeled

One 1-inch piece of ginger, peeled and coarsely chopped

For Frying

1½ cups freshly rendered lard (page 82) or store-brought lard, fruity extra-virgin olive oil, or corn oil

¼ cup brown loaf sugar (preferably *piloncillo*), grated

3 ounces chocolate (preferably a premium chocolate with a high cacao content, 50–70%, such as El Rey Bucare (58.5%), Pacari Esmeraldas (60%), or an artisanal Mexican-style chocolate for drinking, coarsely chopped

2 teaspoons salt, or to taste

Preparing the Chiles ▶ Stem and seed the chiles, reserving 2 tablespoons of the seeds to give more heat to the sauce. Heat a *comal*, heavy-bottomed cast-iron skillet, or griddle over medium heat. Working in two or three batches, roast the chiles lightly, turning them occasionally with tongs, allowing about 2 minutes per batch. Place the roasted chiles in a medium bowl. Cover with 3 quarts hot water to soften, about 30 minutes. Drain, reserving at least 2 cups of the chile soaking liquid to use as needed. Process the chiles in two batches in a blender or food processor, with about ½ cup, or more if needed, of the soaking liquid. Puree finely. Set aside.

Preparing the Fruit ▶ Place the raisins in a bowl and cover with ½ cup of the reserved chile soaking liquid to plump. Heat the lard or oil in a small skillet over medium heat. Add the plantain slices and fry until golden brown, turning twice for even cooking. Scoop out of the skillet with a slotted spoon and set aside.

Preparing the Thickeners ▶ Heat the *comal* over medium heat. Add the bread slices and toast for one minute on each side. Remove and set aside. Add the tortillas and char on both sides, about 2 minutes. Crumble and set aside.

Preparing the Nuts and Seeds ▶ Add the almonds and walnuts to the *comal* and roast, stirring with a wooden spoon, until fragrant, about 2 minutes. Remove and reserve in a bowl. Add the sesame seeds and roast until they pop and turn golden brown, about 1 minute. Quickly scoop them out into a bowl before they scorch and add them to the nuts.

Preparing the Spices ▶ Add the allspice berries, peppercorns, cloves, cumin seeds, oregano, and thyme to the *comal* and roast lightly, about 1 minute. Grind finely in a spice grinder or coffee grinder.

Preparing the Seasoning Vegetables ▶ Add the tomatoes, onion, and garlic to the *comal* and roast, turning with tongs, until blistered and partially charred, 8 to 10 minutes. Peel the garlic and the onion, leaving charred bits. Quarter the onion and the tomatoes. Reserve with the chopped ginger.

Pureeing the Ingredients ▶ Place the tomatoes, onion, and garlic in a blender or food processor with the raisins and their soaking liquid, fried plantains, reserved nuts, bread and tortillas, and spices and process to a coarse puree. Place in a bowl and set aside.

Frying the Ingredients ▶ Heat the lard or oil in a 12-inch sauté pan over medium heat until it ripples. Add the reserved chile puree and cook, stirring, for 10 minutes or until the fat begins to separate from the solids and starts to sizzle. Then add the vegetable puree and continue cooking while stirring for 15 more minutes, or until the fat again separates from the solids and begins to sizzle and you can clearly see the bottom of the pan when stirring. Add the sugar and stir to dissolve. Add the chocolate and stir to melt. Season with the salt. Force the puree through a fine-mesh sieve or chinois into a bowl, using a pestle or wooden spoon.

Storing: If not using immediately, cool the *mole* paste to room temperature, transfer to storage containers, and pour a thin film of melted lard or oil over the surface to help keep it from spoiling. Seal tightly and store in a cool place or the refrigerator.

Serving: See Finishing the *Mole* (page 770). Add enough chicken broth or other broth to the paste to thin it to the consistency of tomato sauce, about equal parts sauce to broth. Then add the cooked meats and heat throughout, or pour the sauce over the meats on a platter. Serve with Mexican Rice (page 302) and Mexican Corn Tortillas (page 579). This *mole* is also delicious for the enchiladas called *enmoladas* and as a seasoning for simple tacos. Try smearing hot corn tortillas with some *mole* sauce, top with grated cheese, and wrap like a taco.

Fruity One-Chile *Mole*
Mole Mulato

This simple fruity *mole* is my own invention, a good first *mole* for those who have never made one. Not only does it use fewer chiles than most (only the wonderful sweet *mulato*), but it calls for just a couple of spices instead of half a dozen.

When putting this *mole* together, I asked myself, what do I expect from a good *mole*? My answer is a balanced taste that blends spiciness, tartness, and fruitiness; just enough salt to bring out all the flavors; a background kick of heat to bring the creamy sauce to life; enough fat for unctuous smoothness; and evocative aromas. With these important qualities in mind, even a novice can quickly get the hang of selecting different chile types, nuts and seeds, fruits, and other seasonings to bring harmonious changes to the *mole* theme. For instance, using Ibarra chocolate or the traditional lard instead of olive oil will bring this particular *mole* closer to the Mexican taste, while varying the spices with a dash of oregano and clove or throwing in a few almonds or hazelnuts will add new dimensions. But first try it my way—it's one of the easiest *moles* I know.

Working Ahead ▶ See page 771.

MAKES ABOUT 2½ CUPS STRAINED AND UNDILUTED *MOLE* PASTE

For the Chiles
   6 *mulato* chiles (about 2¼ ounces)

For the Spices and Seeds
   1 teaspoon allspice berries

½ teaspoon anise seeds

1 tablespoon sesame seeds

For the Thickener

1 store-bought corn tortilla

For the Seasoning Vegetables

3 medium plum tomatoes (about 9 ounces)

1 medium white onion (about 8 ounces), unpeeled

3 garlic cloves, coarsely chopped

For the Fruit

1 cup pitted prunes (about 3¼ ounces)

For Frying and Finishing

1 cup fruity extra-virgin olive oil

2 ounces chocolate, preferably a premium chocolate with 50–70% cacao content such as El Rey Bucare or Pacari Esmeraldas, finely chopped, or an artisanal Mexican chocolate for drinking

1½ teaspoons salt, or to taste

Preparing the Chiles ▶ Stem and seed the chiles. Heat a *comal*, griddle, or heavy skillet until a drop of water sizzles on contact. Add the chiles and roast, pressing with a spatula, until fragrant, about 15 seconds on each side. As they are done, lift them out into a bowl. Pour 1 quart hot water over the chiles and let sit until softened, 20 to 30 minutes. Alternatively, place in a small saucepan with 1 quart water, bring to a boil, lower the heat to medium-low, and simmer, uncovered, until softened, about 10 minutes. Drain, reserving about ½ cup of the soaking or cooking liquid.

Preparing the Spices, Seeds, and Thickener ▶ Add the allspice berries and anise seeds to the griddle and

roast lightly for 30 seconds. Remove at once and set aside. Add the sesame seeds to the griddle and roast, stirring constantly, until they pop and turn golden, about 1 minute. Scoop into a bowl at once. Do not let them scorch. Grind all these ingredients to a powder in a spice or coffee mill and set aside. Add the tortilla to the griddle and toast until charred; crumble.

Preparing the Seasoning Vegetables ▶ Add the tomatoes and onion to the griddle and roast, turning occasionally with tongs, until lightly charred and blistered, about 8 minutes. Remove from the heat. When cool enough to handle, peel, leaving some bits of the charred skin, and cut into 2 to 3 pieces. Set aside.

Grinding the Prepared Ingredients ▶ Place the roasted chiles and ¼ cup of the reserved liquid in a food processor or a blender. Process to a smooth puree. Pour into a bowl and set aside. Place the spices, sesame seeds, tortilla, tomatoes, and onion in the blender or food processor with the garlic, prunes, and another ¼ cup of the reserved chile liquid; process to a smooth puree.

Frying the *Mole* ▶ Heat the oil over medium heat in a large pot until it ripples. Pour in the chile puree (guard against splatters) and simmer, stirring occasionally, for about 10 minutes or until the fat begins to separate from the solids and starts to sizzle. Add the vegetable puree and cook, stirring, for 15 to 20 minutes or until the fat again begins to separate from the solids and starts to sizzle and the sauce thickens to the point where you can see the bottom of the pot as you move the spoon. Add the chocolate and continue stirring until it is melted. Add the salt and taste for seasoning, adding a little more if necessary. Force the paste through a strainer or chinois into a bowl, using a pestle or a wooden spoon.

You now have enough *mole* paste to season up to 8 pounds of chicken, pork, duck, or turkey. If you are serving the *mole* at once, see Finishing the *Mole* (page 770). Add 3 to 4 cups of chicken broth to thin the paste to the consistency of tomato sauce. Then add the cooked or half-cooked poultry or meat to the sauce and let it simmer until it is heated through or completely cooked, or pour the sauce over the meat on a large platter.

Storing: If not using immediately, cool the *mole* paste to room temperature, transfer to several storage containers, and pour a thin film of melted lard or oil over the surface to help keep it from spoiling. Seal tightly and store in a cool place or the refrigerator.

Serving: If you are not using the *mole* at once in the liberally diluted Mexican fashion, experiment with it as a European-style sauce, diluted to your taste. Try as a sauce for Santiago de Cuba's Roast Pork (page 721) or Griddle-Fried Duck Breasts (page 781).

Lidia Aguilar's Black Oaxacan *Mole*

Mole Negro de Oaxaca

During my first visit to Oaxaca many years ago, I had the good fortune to meet the charming Inocencio Velazco and his wife, Lidia Aguilar, a fabulous cook, who invited me to join them for breakfast at their new hostel, La Posada de Chencho. Breakfast was robust and traditionally Oaxacan—tamales flavored with pitch-black *mole negro*, washed down with aromatic chocolate made from home-ground cacao. I thought the combination was heavenly. I spent the rest of the morning and subsequent days talking to Lidia about Oaxacan food and writing down some of her recipes, starting, of course, with the *mole negro*. I am so glad I did.

The *mole negro* of Oaxaca is as complex as a *mole poblano*, but much richer and deeper in flavor, with an intense fruitiness that lingers in your mouth and a subtle background heat that goes hand in hand with a smoky edge lent by charred chile seeds. Like the *recado negro* of Yucatán, this most famous of Oaxacan *moles* owes its color to the charred seeds of the chiles used to make it.

Cook's Notes: *Mole negro* is as carefully constructed as any other *mole*, but you need to plan for a particular hitch: burning the chile seeds, which is necessary to get the true *mole negro* flavor. It creates fumes that will leave you crying, coughing, and sneezing, irritate your eyes and throat, and leave a burning smell in your kitchen for hours. The first time I did it with my windows and doors closed, I understood why Aztec mothers punished mischievous children by holding them over burning chiles. If you can't do this process outdoors, as most people in Oaxaca do, make sure your windows and doors are wide open and the exhaust fan is at full blast. There is no shortcut for this. According to Lidia, "all that charcoal" makes *mole negro* "the most healthful and easily digestible of all the seven *moles* of Oaxaca."

An authentic *mole negro* requires a chile known in Oaxaca as *chilhuacle*, the Nahuatl word for "old chile." When green, it looks like a meatier and larger poblano. There are three kinds, black, red, and yellow.

The black has a triangular shape and smooth skin. It is still difficult to find in the United States. If you can't find *chilhuacles*, use sharp guajillos instead, as most Oaxacans do away from home.

Working Ahead ▶ See page 771.

What to Drink: An opulent Achaval Ferrer Finca Altamira Malbec from Mendoza, Argentina

MAKES ABOUT **6 CUPS** *MOLE* PASTE

For the Chiles

6 ounces dried *chilhuacle* or guajillo chiles (about 30 chiles)

2 ounces dried *mulato* chiles (about 5 chiles)

3 dried chipotle chiles

3 ounces dried Oaxacan pasilla chiles (about 8 chiles)

For the Spices

One 1-inch Ceylon cinnamon stick (*canela*)

1 teaspoon dried oregano

1 teaspoon black peppercorns

½ teaspoon whole cloves

For the Nuts and Seeds

4 tablespoons sesame seeds (about 1 ounce)

12 blanched almonds (¼ ounce)

For the Thickener

3 slices baguette

For the Seasoning Vegetables

3 medium plum tomatoes (about 9 ounces)

1 head garlic, unpeeled

1 medium white onion (8 ounces), unpeeled

For the Fruit

1 ripe plantain (about 8 ounces), peeled

¼ cup dark raisins

½ cup pitted prunes

For Frying

1 cup freshly rendered lard (page 82), store-bought lard, or fruity extra-virgin olive oil

For the Finishing Touches

3 ounces chocolate, preferably a premium chocolate with 50–70% cacao content (such as El Rey Bucare or Gran Samán), finely chopped, or an artisanal Mexican chocolate for drinking

1 tablespoon grated brown loaf sugar (preferably *piloncillo*), Muscovado sugar, or brown sugar

1 tablespoon salt, or to taste

Preparing the Chiles ▶ Stem and seed the chiles. Flatten them as much as possible. Set the seeds aside in a small bowl. Heat a *comal*, griddle, or heavy skillet over medium heat. When a drop of water sizzles on contact, place the chiles flat on the hot surface and press lightly with a spatula. Roast for 20 to 30 seconds on each side, until the chiles are blistered and wisps of fragrant smoke billow into the air. Place the chiles in a medium saucepan. Cover with 1 quart fresh water. Bring to a boil, lower the heat, and simmer until plump and soft, about 15 minutes. Drain, reserving the cooking water.

Place the chiles in a blender or food processor with 2 cups reserved cooking water and process to a smooth puree. Force through a fine-mesh sieve into a bowl, pushing against the mesh to get as much chile pulp as possible. Set aside.

Charring the Chile Seeds ▶ Scatter the reserved chile seeds over the *comal* or griddle and roast, stirring, until the seeds are completely charred but not reduced to ashes. Scoop out into a bowl and cover with water. Let soak for 30 minutes. Drain and set aside.

Preparing the Spices ▶ Add the cinnamon, oregano, peppercorns, and cloves to the *comal* or griddle and roast lightly, about 1 minute. Remove immediately and grind in a spice grinder or coffee grinder.

Preparing the Nuts and Seeds ▶ Place the sesame seeds on the *comal* or griddle and roast for about 2 minutes, stirring with a wooden spoon, until they pop and turn golden. Quickly scoop out into a bowl and reserve. Add the almonds and roast, stirring, for about 2 minutes. Add to the sesame seeds and set aside.

Preparing the Bread Thickener ▶ Toast the bread slices for 1 minute on each side. Remove and set aside.

Preparing the Seasoning Vegetables ▶ Place the tomatoes, garlic, and onion on the hot griddle and roast, turning with tongs, until blistered and partially charred, about 8 minutes. Remove. When they are cool enough to handle, peel the garlic and onion. Quarter the onion and tomatoes. Set aside.

Preparing the Plantain ▶ Cut the plantain into thin rounds. In a skillet, heat 2 tablespoons lard or olive oil over medium heat. Add the plantain slices and sauté until soft and golden, about 6 minutes. Remove and set aside.

Grinding the Ingredients ▶ Place the chile seeds, seasoning vegetables, bread, nuts and seeds, spices,

plantain, raisins, and prunes in a large bowl and mix with a spoon. Working in batches, place in a food processor or blender with the remaining chile cooking liquid and process to a puree. Force through a fine-mesh sieve or chinois into a bowl, pushing against the solids with a heavy pestle or the back of a spoon. Set aside.

Frying ▶ Heat the remaining lard in a deep, wide heavy pot or Dutch oven over medium heat until it ripples. Pour in the chile puree and cook, stirring, for 10 minutes, until the fat is sizzling. Stir in the vegetable and fruit puree and cook, stirring, for another 10 minutes. The fat should be beginning to separate and the sauce should be thick enough that you see the bottom of the pan as you move the spoon.

Adding the Finishing Touches ▶ Add the chocolate and stir to dissolve. Season with sugar and salt, stir, and taste for seasoning.

If you are using the *mole* right away, see Finishing the *Mole* (page 770). Place the amount you need in a pan and add broth to thin it to the consistency of tomato sauce. I like to use equal parts broth and *mole* paste. Bring the sauce to a gentle simmer and cook, stirring occasionally, for 15 minutes. Add the meat of your choice and heat it through in the *mole* sauce. If the sauce seems too thick, thin it by adding additional broth.

Serving: Serve with Mexican Rice (page 302) or plain white rice.

Storing: If not using the *mole* paste immediately, cool it to room temperature, transfer to several storage containers, and pour a thin film of melted lard or oil over the surface to help keep it from spoiling. Seal tightly and store it in a cool place or the refrigerator.

Turkey in *Mole* Sauce

Guajolote con Mole

How do you use a *mole* once you have made it? If you are Mexican, part of the answer is that while the sauce is under way, you are simmering some chicken, pork, or, most probably turkey, the undisputed king of the *mole* feast, in a large pot, to produce both the meat for the main course and enough broth to thin the *mole* to the desired consistency. Turkey becomes tender and mellow as it cooks slowly in a savory broth over a low fire, and its naturally sweet meat is enhanced by the fruitiness of the *mole* sauce.

What to Drink: A chocolatey Les Eres Vinyes Velles red from Priorat in Cataluña

SERVES 8 TO 10

One	8-pound turkey, cut into serving pieces, or 8 pounds turkey parts
3	quarts water
2	bay leaves
½	teaspoon black peppercorns
1	large onion (12 ounces), peeled and halved
1	head garlic, halved
	A few cilantro sprigs
2	teaspoons salt
4–5	cups undiluted *mole* paste, preferably The Famous *Mole Poblano* of Santa Rosa (page 771), Fruity One-Chile *Mole* (page 776), or Francisca's Wedding *Mole* (page 774)
4–5	cups cooking broth from the turkey

▶ Place the turkey in a large pot with the water, bay leaves, peppercorns, onion, garlic, cilantro, and salt. Stir and bring to a boil. Lower the heat and simmer until tender (40 to 45 minutes for a small turkey, an hour or more for parts from larger birds). Remove the turkey pieces from the broth, cover, and set aside. Strain the broth and reserve 4 to 5 cups.

Place the *mole* paste in a large pan. Add the turkey broth and thin to the desired consistency. (A mixture of 4 to 5 cups undiluted *mole* paste and 4 to 5 cups broth will produce enough sauce to season the turkey generously, with enough leftover sauce to spoon over rice.) Stir to mix. Bring to a gentle boil over medium heat. Add the turkey pieces and simmer until heated through. If the sauce seems too thick, thin it with a little more broth.

Serving: Serve with Mexican Rice (page 302) or plain white rice.

Griddle-Fried Duck Breasts with *Mole*

Pato a la Plancha con Mole

Turkey is the bird to go with when making most traditional *moles*, but duck is also an excellent choice. A fruity *mole* sauce does for grilled duck what hoisin sauce does for Peking duck, enhancing the succulent sweetness of the meat. I like to grill the duck breasts to produce crisp skin while leaving the meat juicy and almost rare.

What to Drink: A rich, expressive Susana Balbo Malbec from Mendoza, Argentina

SERVES 6

6 boneless duck breasts (about 8 ounces each)
  Salt and freshly ground black pepper
3 cups *mole* paste, preferably Fruity One-Chile
  Mole (page 776)
3 cups chicken broth, homemade (page 538) or
  store-bought
  Roasted sesame seeds, for garnish

▶ Pat the duck breasts dry and rub with salt and pepper to taste. Score a cross-hatch pattern on the skin with a sharp knife and let rest at room temperature, uncovered, to dry the skin, about 30 minutes.

Heat a 12-inch griddle or cast-iron skillet over high heat. Place the duck breasts on the griddle skin side down and let cook until the skin is crisp and most of the fat has been rendered, about 12 minutes. Turn to the other side and cook briefly, for 1 minute. Transfer to a cutting board and slice each breast on the bias in a fan shape.

Place the *mole* paste in a medium saucepan. Add the broth and stir. The sauce should have the consistency of tomato sauce; add more broth if necessary. Bring to a gentle simmer over medium-low heat.

To serve, ladle the sauce onto a decorative plate. Using a broad spatula, transfer the duck breasts to the plate and garnish with the sesame seeds.

Lidia Velazco's *Mole Verde*

Mole Verde de Lidia Velazco

Ask any Oaxacan about his or her favorite *mole*, and invariably the answer will be *mole negro* or *mole verde*. The latter, popularly known as just *verde* (green), is a perfumed, tangy stew with an appealing fresh green color and a background taste of licorice from the herb called *hoja santa*. It is made with braised meat or poultry and a few fresh vegetables, and differs from the most elaborate *moles* in that no dried chiles are used and that the main ingredients—tomatillos, garlic, and fresh green chiles—are not fried or griddle-roasted before pureeing. At the end of cooking, a mixture of pureed green herbs is stirred into the sauce to give it body, color, and fragrance. According to Lidia Velazco, *mole verde* needs to be eaten right away, before it changes color.

Cook's Note: If using dried *hoja santa*, place the leaves in a bowl with a little water (¼ to ½ cup) for 2 to 3 minutes, then puree in a blender or mini food processor. Strain the liquid through a fine-mesh strainer and add to the sauce; discard the leaves.

What to Drink: A citrusy, mineral Montes Limited Selection Sauvignon Blanc from the cool Leyda Valley, Chile

SERVES 6 TO 8

For the Chicken
One 3½-pound chicken, cut into 8 serving pieces (see page 659)
  2 teaspoons salt
  ½ teaspoon freshly ground black pepper
  3 tablespoons freshly rendered lard (page 82), store-bought lard, or fruity extra-virgin olive oil

For the *Mole* Sauce
  6 allspice berries
  5 whole cloves
  2 teaspoons cumin seeds
  15 large tomatillos (about 2 pounds), husked and cut in half

4 garlic cloves, peeled

2 jalapeños, seeded

1 baguette slice (1 ounce)

2½ cups chicken broth, homemade (page 538) or store-bought

3 medium chayotes (about 2 pounds), peeled, seeded, and cut into 1-inch dice

8 ounces green beans, cut in half

1 bunch flat-leaf parsley

½ bunch cilantro

4 sprigs fresh epazote

3 fresh or dried *hoja santa* leaves (see Cook's Note)

Preparing the Chicken ▶ Rub the chicken all over with the salt and pepper. In a 12-inch sauté pan, heat the lard over medium heat. Add the chicken pieces and brown on all sides, turning with tongs, about 10 minutes. Remove from the pan and reserve. Set the pan aside without washing.

Making the *Mole* ▶ Heat a *comal* or griddle over medium heat, add the allspice berries, cloves, and cumin seeds, and roast for 1 minute. Grind to a fine powder in a spice mill or coffee grinder.

Working in batches, process the tomatillos to a coarse puree with the garlic, jalapeños, and ground spices in a blender or food processor. Force through a medium-mesh sieve or strainer into a bowl, pushing with a pestle or wooden spoon.

Set the pan in which the chicken was browned over medium-high heat. When the fat ripples, pour in the tomatillo puree, watching out for splatters. Reduce the heat to medium and cook, stirring, over medium heat for 3 minutes.

Place the bread in a bowl and cover with 1½ cups broth. Place in a blender and puree.

Add the chicken to the tomatillo sauce, then stir in the pureed bread, chayote, and beans. Cook over moderate heat, covered, for 20 minutes.

While the chicken and vegetables cook, place the parsley and cilantro in a blender or food processor with ½ cup broth and process to a fine puree. Set aside. Place the epazote and *hoja santa* (or strained pureeing liquid) in the blender or food processor with the remaining ½ cup broth and process to a thin puree. Force through a medium-mesh sieve again, pushing vigorously.

When the chicken and vegetables are tender, stir the pureed herbs into the dish. Correct the seasoning, adding a pinch of salt if necessary, and serve immediately, before the wonderful intense green color of the sauce can darken.

Serving: Serve with Mexican Rice (page 302) or plain white rice.

Oaxaca's "Tablecloth Stainer" Fruit *Mole*

Manchamanteles

The celebrated sweet-and-sour, fruit-flavored "table-cloth stainer," one of the seven *moles* of Oaxaca, owes its marvelous brick red color to the dried chiles used to make it: ancho, guajillo, and—especially popular in Oaxaca—*costeño*. Its lovely color contributes to the surface orange fat that is to blame for the *mole's* reputation: just see what happens if you drop a speck on a white tablecloth.

Most versions call for a combination of pork and chicken. I prefer all pork, which I think goes magnificently with the delicious fruity sweetness of *manchamanteles*. Here I follow the combined advice of two good Mexican cooks, Lidia Aguilar of Oaxaca and Estela Zaragoza de Rodríguez of Guadalajara, with a few changes of my own.

What to Drink: Susana Balbo Crios Rosé de Malbec from Mendoza, Argentina

SERVES 6 TO 8

For the *Mole*

6 dried ancho chiles (about 2½ ounces)

6 dried guajillo chiles (about 1¼ ounces)

6 dried *costeño* chiles (about 1 ounce)

6 medium plum tomatoes (about 1¼ pounds)

8 garlic cloves, unpeeled

¼ cup blanched almonds (about 1¼ ounces)

¼ cup walnut meats (about 1¼ ounces)

¼ cup white sesame seeds (about 1 ounce)

1 Ceylon cinnamon stick (*canela*)

5 whole cloves

¼ teaspoon black peppercorns

¼ teaspoon dried oregano, crushed

½ cup dark raisins

5 tablespoons freshly rendered lard (page 82) or fruity extra-virgin olive oil

For the Meat

3 pounds boneless pork shoulder or butt, cut into 1½-inch cubes

3 teaspoons salt

1 teaspoon fresh lime juice

For Finishing

5 cups chicken broth, homemade (page 538) or store-bought

2 cups diced fresh pineapple (about 1 pound 6 ounces)

2 Golden Delicious apples, peeled and cut into 1-inch dice

Making the *Mole* ▶ Stem and seed the chiles. Heat a *comal*, griddle, or heavy skillet over medium heat. Working in several batches, add the chiles and roast lightly, pressing lightly with a spatula and allowing about 20 seconds per side. Remove as they are done and place in a medium saucepan. Cover with 2 quarts fresh water, bring to a boil, lower the heat, and simmer until the chiles are soft and plump, about 10 minutes. Drain, reserving 1 cup of the cooking liquid.

While the chiles are simmering, place the tomatoes and garlic on the hot *comal* and roast, turning occasionally, until lightly charred, about 8 minutes. Remove. When they are cool enough to handle, peel the garlic and remove any charred skin from the tomatoes. Set aside.

Add the almonds and walnuts and roast, stirring, for 2 minutes. Scoop out into a bowl. Add the sesame seeds and roast, stirring, until they pop and turn golden, about 2 minutes. Quickly scoop out into the bowl with the almonds and walnuts; set aside.

Add the cinnamon, cloves, and peppercorns to the *comal* and roast, stirring, until fragrant, about 1 minute. Remove and grind to a fine powder in a spice or coffee grinder.

Working in batches, place the chiles, tomatoes, garlic, nuts, sesame seeds, and spices in a blender or food processor with the oregano and raisins and process to a thick paste, using as much of the reserved chile cooking liquid as you need to facilitate processing.

Heat ¼ cup lard in a large deep skillet or 12-inch sauté pan over medium-high heat. Pour in the pureed mixture, guarding against splatters, and cook, stirring, for 5 minutes. Set aside.

Cooking the Meat ▶ Season the pork cubes with 2 teaspoons salt and the lime juice. In a 12-inch sauté pan or wide saucepan, heat the remaining 1 tablespoon lard over medium heat. Add the meat and cook, stirring, until evenly brown, about 15 minutes. Stir in the sauce and cook, stirring, for another 3 to 5 minutes.

Finishing the Dish ▶ Pour in the broth, stir well, and cook, covered, over medium heat until the meat is tender, about 1 hour and 15 minutes. Add a little more broth if the sauce becomes too thick. When the meat is almost tender, add the pineapple and apples and simmer, covered, for 30 more minutes. Test for salt and add a sprinkling if needed.

Serving: Serve with Mexican Rice (page 302) or plain white rice.

Guatemalan Ripe Plantain *Mole*

Mole de Plátanos Guatemalteco

Though Guatemala is the land of the *pepián*, *moles* sometimes make an appearance on special occasions. In Guatemala this rich *mole* would ordinarily be served at room temperature as a dessert, but I find it makes an excellent side dish with roast pork or grilled duck breasts. This is the *mole* I learned in San Antonio Suchitepequez, the capital of an important cacao-growing region in the Pacific Piedmont of Guatemala. Note that the chiles are not roasted or seeded.

What to Drink: Ben Marco Malbec from Mendoza, Argentina

SERVES 6

For the Plantains

- 4 ripe large plantains (about 3 pounds)
- 2 tablespoons freshly rendered lard (page 82) or extra-virgin olive oil

For the *Mole*

- 3 dried pasilla chiles (about 1¼ ounces)
- 5 ripe medium plum tomatoes (about 1 pound)
- 1½ cups pumpkin seeds (about 2 ounces)
- ¼ cup sesame seeds (about 1 ounce)
- 1 small sweet roll such as brioche, cut into slices (about 3 ounces)
- 2 Ceylon cinnamon sticks (*canela*)
- 1 teaspoon allspice berries
- 5 cloves
- 3 tablespoons achiote-infused corn oil or extra-virgin olive oil (page 89)
- 3 ounces chocolate, preferably a premium chocolate with 50–70% cacao content (such as El Rey's Bucare)
- 1 cup chicken broth, homemade (page 538) or store-bought
- ¼ cup sugar
- 1 teaspoon salt

Roasted white sesame seeds, for garnish

Preparing the Plantains ▶ Peel the plantains and cut into thin rounds. In a large skillet, heat 2 tablespoons lard or olive oil over medium heat. Add the plantain slices and sauté until soft and golden, about 6 minutes. Remove and set aside.

Making the *Mole* ▶ Place the chiles and tomatoes in a small saucepan with 1 quart water and bring to a boil over medium heat. Lower the heat and simmer until the chiles are soft and plump, about 15 minutes. Drain, reserving 1 cup cooking liquid.

Heat a *comal*, griddle, or heavy skillet over medium heat. Roast the pumpkin seeds and sesame seeds, stirring, until the pumpkin seeds puff up, about 1 minute. Scoop out into a bowl. Set aside.

Toast the bread on the hot *comal* until charred. Remove and set aside.

Add the cinnamon sticks, allspice berries, and cloves to the *comal* and roast lightly for 1 to 2 minutes. Remove and set aside.

Place the chiles, tomatoes, pumpkin seeds, bread, and spices with the reserved cup cooking liquid in a blender or food processor and process to a thick puree. Force through a fine-mesh sieve into a bowl, pressing firmly with the back of a spoon.

Heat the oil over medium heat in a heavy skillet or 12-inch sauté pan. Pour in the puree, watching out for splatters, and cook for 5 minutes. Add the chocolate and allow to melt, stirring. Thin the sauce with broth, stir in the sugar and salt, and let simmer for about 3 minutes. Add the cooked plantains to the sauce and heat through, about 3 or 4 minutes. Serve the *mole* on a decorative platter garnished with the reserved roasted sesame seeds.

CHAPTER 20

DULCE LATINO

IN THIS CHAPTER

What I see in Latin American sweets and desserts is the power of a soothing, reassuring stability that is also sensuous and magical. In most of our cooking we crave flavorful savory foods built in layers. We welcome the sting of hot peppers, the acidic touch of citrus juices and vinegar, the bite of raw onions in table condiments. We seek vivid contrasts between salty, sweet, bitter, acidic, and the savory sensation of *umami*. Dessert is meant to put a calming end to the sensory joyride that is the Latin meal. Assertive in our other cooking, we are subtle, often minimalist, when making sweets and desserts.

At restaurants and for special celebrations at home, we like to end a meal with dessert. We might be tempted to try a European-style dessert, but we consider a creamy custard to be the perfect finish. After an everyday meal, we welcome a bowl of rice pudding, a slice of cake dusted with some sugar, a piece of Spanish almond nougat during the Christmas season, or fruits cooked in syrup alongside some fresh cheese and crackers, and we are equally happy with a piece of fresh fruit.

Latins eat sweet things at all times, not only after a main meal. Our notorious habit of noshing on savories at all hours of the day is matched by an inveterate sweet tooth that keeps us searching for a piece of fruit or sweet nibbles from breakfast till way after dinner. We don't have to look far. Pastry shops (*pastelerías, dulcerías, confiterías*) and bakeries (*panaderías*) are showcases for the regional specialties that everybody loves and the European-style pastries that have been with us for centuries. These are welcoming places, often fitted with tables and chairs, where one can grab a cup of coffee or tea or a fruit milk shake (*batido*) or sit and have a midmorning pick-me-up, enjoy the afternoon *merienda* (teatime), or savor a late-night snack after the movies.

I have wonderful memories of the Cuban *dulcerías* and *panaderías* of my childhood, and Argentinean *confiterías* have the same upbeat spirit and energy. Many *confiterías* are pastry shops and cafés put together. Their counters are full of sweets and savories, from cookies to layered meringue-topped puff pastry cakes filled with *dulce de leche* (*torta rogel*), to ice creams like the tricolor *cassata helada* and the *bombón suizo* (iced whipped cream covered with chocolate), to sandwiches made with soft white bread filled with ham, chicken, or vegetables.

There is also a Latin American tradition of homemade confections and cakes. In fact, many women make a living selling these from their homes, but we also turn to our pastry shops for powdery cookies like *alfajores* (a specialty of Peru, Uruguay, and Argentina); sweet empanadas and flaky pastries (*pastelitos*) filled with guava (a Cuban treat); sweet breads; sweets that mark the religious feasts, such as sugar skulls for the Days of the Dead or the ring-shaped coffee cake called *torta de reyes* for the Epiphany (two Mexican traditions); and the frilly decorated cakes that are never missing at birthdays and weddings. On every street corner and in markets all over Latin America, vendors peddle artisanal confections such as nougats made with grated coconut, pumpkin seeds, cashews, and peanuts, as well as crunchy fritters, cookies, and candied fruits. Even stores that sell everything from souvenirs to guitars stock regional sweets.

In Trujillo, a large city in northern Peru, there are streets lined with all-purpose tourist shops that sell one main confection, *alfajores*, in many guises and sizes. Some are like small shortbread cookies filled with a kind of thick caramel made from the local brown loaf sugar (*chancaca*) or with *manjar blanco*, the Peruvian version of *dulce de leche*. Others, like the appropriately dubbed *alfajores* King Kong, a specialty of Lambayeque, are huge and multi-layered, each layer with a different filling: *manjar blanco*, pineapple or grated coconut cooked in syrup, peanut cream. Local lore has it that this gargantuan confection was created by a Lambayeque housewife in the 1930s and dubbed King Kong because it was huge like the gorilla in the movie, which was being shown at the time.

Mexico is a land of sweet wonders. In Morelia, the capital of the state of Michoacán, there is a block-long market under a stately arcade for sweets only, El Mercado de los Dulces. The closest thing to Candy Land, the market is richly stocked with local sweets beautifully arranged like still lifes at every counter. What I remember most from my visit are the fruit pastes (*ates*); the mounds of multicolored candied fruits (*frutas abrillantadas* or *glaseadas*) everywhere—*nopales*, prickly pears, pineapples, figs, limes; the stacks of *rompope* (holiday eggnog) bottles; and bees buzzing over the sweets. In fact, I suspect that Mexican vendors plant bees in their shops to call attention to their sweets. At the central market of Querétaro, a cloud of bees signals the stall selling glazed sweet potatoes, brown ovals covered with a dark, glistening, perfumed *piloncillo* (brown loaf sugar) syrup made from cone-shaped brown loaf sugar that are one of the most popular local sweets.

SPOONFULS OF HISTORY

The world of sweets is one place where the Columbian exchange of people and cultures ran almost entirely one way. New World ingredients such as chocolate and vanilla have become the very soul of desserts around the world. But in Latin America, they have not been used traditionally in desserts but rather in drinks, and there is scant record of any major tradition of eating sweets in the pre-Columbian world, even in the highly developed Aztec and Inca cultures.

The paucity of the sources does not mean that the people of Mesoamerica did not have sweeteners. Spanish chronicles describing the fabulous market of Tenochtitlán in Mexico on the eve of the conquest talk about "honey" obtained from many sources—cornstalks, agave (*maguey*), and *Opuntia* cactus (*nopal*), in addition to bees. We learn from contemporary sources (especially those chronicling Spanish settlements in the Yucatán) that the Indians were very advanced in the art of apiculture. But since the word *miel* could generally describe many syrups and sweet saps, it can be difficult to interpret these reports. It does seem clear that pre-Columbian Mexicans used various sweeteners with skill to preserve the seeds and flesh of squashes, and to make a paste with amaranth seeds similar to today's *alegrías*.

Besides these sweet treats, the one enduring pre-Columbian contribution to our Latin desserts is fruit. In parts of the Greater Antilles, Mexico, and Peru, the conquistadores were greeted by friendly delegations with gifts of local fruits that are still universal favorites. Like the Indians, the Spanish and Portuguese learned to eat these fruits raw or turn them into nourishing beverages, some with traces of drinks from Islamic Spain, leaving us a fantastic legacy of delicious fruit beverages. New immigrants to the United States soon seek their regional fruits in fresh or frozen form, so they can recreate traditional drinks and ice creams: passion fruit, tart and complex *naranjilla* (an Amazonian fruit that looks like a small orange), creamy cherimoyas, perfumed soursop (*guanábana*), luscious *mamey sapote*, astringent but divine cashew apples, and huge, flavorful Andean blackberries, among others.

Nonetheless, a total change came with the Spanish, for the heart of all Latin American sweets is sugar extracted from the cane that the Spaniards brought to Hispaniola after 1492. The principles of making sweets, the recipes, and even the sugarcane itself were brought by the Europeans. These became the grammar of a New World dessert tradition all over the Spanish- and Portuguese-speaking Americas.

Throughout the Americas, spiritual conquest went hand in hand with military and culinary conquest. As soon as the native peoples were subdued, the chaplains of the Spanish army—a handful of Franciscan friars—joined the small but formidable band of newly arrived monks from the peninsula. Their task, as they saw it, was to create monasteries, which were essentially headquarters for the conversion of the natives and the propagation of all aspects of Iberian culture. These monasteries, and the convents that followed, were designed to be self-sufficient and were equipped with vegetable and fruit gardens and cavernous stone-walled kitchens where monks and nuns cultivated the arts of cooking. They wanted to preserve the culinary traditions they had brought from Spain, a sign of their cultural identity, but inevitably they began to adapt them to changing circumstances and ingredients.

The friars developed a reputation as gifted cooks who knew how to turn both European and New World ingredients into tempting sweets. The English Dominican Thomas Gage, who traveled through Mexico in the seventeenth century, wrote of being regaled by fellow Dominicans with "a drink the Spaniards of the Indies call chocolate" and marveled at the enormous amounts of marmalade and fruit preserves they had prepared in their kitchens. Gage also mentioned that the bishopric of Oaxaca, where sugarcane grew and sugar mills abounded, produced the "best sweets of America."

Friars and monks helped established the material foundation for a new, sweet culture, but it was the nuns who planted Spanish confectionery traditions in the New World, through their role as educators of women. Nuns came to the Americas from many parts of Spain, but at first mainly from Andalusian convents. Throughout the centuries-long process known as the *reconquista*, long before 1492, the Iberian peninsula's Christian kingdoms had been expanding south into Islamic lands. Monasteries and convents were intended to spread Christian culture, including cooking, in territories that had recently been wrested from Islamic rule. But in fact they were also entry points for Muslim traditions. Convents in Andalusia, where Muslim women often worked as servants, were the repositories of numerous Islamic recipes for sweets, many of which survive to this day in both Spain and the Americas.

It took longer than might be expected for the nuns to actually cross the Atlantic. Resistance from influential church officials kept them out of Mexico and lack of resources delayed their arrival in Hispaniola in the first decades of the Spanish conquest. The historian Robert Ricard, who wrote an illuminating study on the mendicant orders in Mexico between 1523 and 1572 (*The Spiritual Conquest of Mexico*), explains that the first religious women to arrive in Mexico to take over the girls' schools created by the monks were technically not nuns. They were *beatas* (religious laywomen) of the Third Order of Saint Francis, brought from Spain to replace religious women not affiliated with cloistered orders who had come earlier, around 1534, to aid the friars. Since they were not cloistered nuns, they had a degree of mobility that did not sit well with the ecclesiastical authorities. In fact, most of them ended up taking jobs in the domestic sector. Every time the Franciscans and other friars wrote to Bishop Ramírez de Fuenleal, who presided over the powerful Audiencia de Mexico (the main arm of Spanish government authority), asking for *beatas*, he turned them down. Actually, every time the Spanish Crown suggested bringing in nuns, he said a firm no.

Fray Cipriano de Utrera, a Franciscan friar and historian of Hispaniola, recorded the moment when attitudes began to shift. In 1556, Agustín Campuzano, the prior of the local Dominican order, asked permission to bring a group of Andalusian Dominican nuns to Hispaniola. The idea was welcomed because "there were many young women on the island that would soon live in [their convent]." Since the Spanish colonization of the New World was clearly a continuation of the *reconquista*, convents were important for converting native people and educating the daughters of Spaniards born in the colonies.

Behind the enthusiastic response, though, was a practical consideration. A wealthy Spanish widow named María de Arana, who was planning to move back to Spain, had donated the money necessary to build the nuns a convent (Regina Angelorum) and a church. Establishing this one convent was not just a local matter, for over and over, once nuns had settled in one place, they spread out across the Americas. The nuns of the Regina Angelorum convent, for example, traveled to Cuba and to Trujillo in Peru to establish other convents. The first nuns of the Santa Clara convent in Caracas, Venezuela,

founded in 1617 by two generous local women, came originally from the Santa Clara convent in Santo Domingo. The first nuns of the Carmelite convent of Trujillo, founded in 1724, were from a sister convent in Quito. Such movement contributed to the dissemination of ideas and recipes.

And these transplants continue to this day. In 1992, four nuns from the celebrated Cistercian convent of Santa María la Real de las Huelgas in Burgos, Spain, were sent to the new Cistercian convent of Santa María de la Santísima Trinidad in Lurín, south of Lima. Among their duties is helping to cook marmalades and sweets, which the convent sells for income.

Sor Juana Inés de la Cruz, the wonderful seventeenth-century poet and writer, is the most famous of all Latin American nuns. She kept a mulatto slave who helped her cook in a kitchen in her own apartment at the monastery of Santa Paula of the Hieronymite order in Mexico City, where she spent most of her life. Sor Juana put together a number of recipes from the monastery's collection, mostly sweets of the type we identify as *dulces conventuales* (convent sweets), which clearly show the influence of Spanish cooking.

Sor Juana was obviously very fond of cooking and making desserts. In a celebrated letter addressed to her nemesis, Manuel Fernández de Santa Cruz, the bishop of Puebla, who had criticized her secular interests, she most famously wrote that "women can philosophize while cooking dinner" and that "Aristotle would have written more if he had prepared more meals."

No other colonial nun was as articulate as Sor Juana, but many nuns left clear evidence of their love and knowledge of sweets. Everywhere the sisters went, they took with them a general training in the art of making sweets, which in Spain and Portugal had been considered one of the refined and aristocratic areas of cooking. In New Spain, the nuns' initial mission was to educate native girls who had already been converted to Christianity by the friars. As more Spanish families settled in the colonies, however, the role of some of the richer convents changed very quickly. They became boarding schools for upper-class girls and young women, who brought with them retinues of female servants. The nuns maintained suitably maidenly surroundings for the young ladies and prepared them to be good wives and heads of households by teaching them cooking and dessert making. At the same time, these lessons were passed on to the native American, *mestizo*, and African servants, in their capacity as front-line cooks and kitchen help.

Teaching monasteries were rich because the parents of the aristocratic pupils always offered gifts of money to the nuns, but the Carmelites, who were cloistered and had vowed to maintain absolute poverty, were always in need of outside help. Like most convents under vows of poverty, they survived on donations. In hard times, the nuns—naturally helped by their servants—produced special sweets to sell to the public or to curry favor with influential public figures. Cloistered convents had a kind of rotating door or window (*portería* or *torno*) through which the nuns sold their famous sweets.

Puebla, in Mexico, distinguished itself for the culinary expertise of its convent kitchens. Credited with the creation of Mexican classics like *chile en nogada* (a stuffed poblano topped with a creamy almond sauce garnished with pomegranates) and *mole poblano*, the nuns of Puebla also enjoyed a well-deserved reputation as pastry chefs. In a letter written to his sister in Madrid on November 20, 1755, quoted in Carlo Zolla's *Elogio del dulce* (In Praise of Dessert), a wonderful book on the history of Mexican sweets, Guillermo Tortosa describes the nuns of a Puebla convent as "chubby, sweet white angels with heavenly hands." He goes on to give detailed information about the nuns' cooking abilities. They were busy preserving and candying peaches, guavas, pears, and quince. They prepared a thick caramelized goat's-milk sauce called *cajeta* as well as egg sponge and *mamón*, a type of genoise. Other desserts he described were traditional Spanish sweets such as *tocino del cielo* ("heaven's bacon," an egg-yolk custard). And some were Iberian desserts made with New World ingredients, cousins of the Brazilian egg and coconut custard *quindim*, fruits cooked in syrup.

Each convent had a specialty, which in many cases has survived to this day. The nuns of La Concepción in Mexico City prepared delicious sweet empanadas; the convent of La Encarnación in Lima was famous for its almond pastes; the Carmelites of Puebla were mistresses of the art of making *dulce de cielo* (an egg-laden custard). Another Pueblan convent, Santa Clara, was praised for marzipan made with a sweet potato paste mixed with unrefined sugar and molded into a small sweet potato shape. Many Latin American desserts still have suggestive religious names, like "nun's sighs" (*suspiros de monja*), "spiritual eggs" (*huevos espirituales*), and "little breaths of the most holy Mary" (*suspiritos de María santísima*).

To give the nuns their due, the more convents a country had, the more kinds of sweets its people enjoyed. Countries like Mexico and Peru, which were epicenters of viceroyal political power, had the greatest number of religious institutions and therefore richer and more complex sweet cuisines than the Caribbean islands, where organized religion played a lesser role.

SUGAR

Latin American desserts are very, very sweet. This penchant for sweetness goes back to the Moors, who planted sugarcane in the south of Spain during the eighth century and fostered a love for this luxury which was later shared by the Christian kingdoms. The medieval convents nurtured the art of cooking with sugar while it was still a prized treasure that only upper-class cooks could afford to use.

When sugarcane crossed the Atlantic with the conquistadores, it was first planted on Hispaniola. It then spread to all parts of tropical America, where it was planted alongside figs and peaches in monastic gardens. At first the native people of the Americas treated sugarcane as a fruit to be peeled and cut into sticks, something Latin children still eat. Once vast plantations and large sugar mills began to crop up throughout the Caribbean and Brazil, however, people rich and poor developed a taste for thick, dark molasses and the winey, intense taste of unrefined sugar. Used as homely everyday equivalents of the more expensive white stuff, they became the sugar of choice—a spice as well as a sweetener—for much Spanish-inspired Latin cooking.

Sugar had many advantages over other sweeteners, most importantly versatility. With white sugar, cooks could not only sweeten foods but make edible art. In Mexico today, sugar confection is a deeply entrenched craft. For the Days of the Dead, markets and street vendors sell sugar candy *calacas*—figures shaped like skulls and skeletons. The place to go for the best ones is the Feria del Alfeñique in Toluca, a lively sugar fair where renowned artisans such as Wenceslao Rivas Contreras try to top each other every year with elaborate *calacas*.

FAVORITES

Our desserts do not rely only on the shock of pure sweetness. Many convent confections are made with nuts cooked in syrup. Like so many elements of Spanish dessert making, these sweets were developed in Islamic Spain and later transplanted to convents.

Not as rooted in convent traditions but also showing a long-standing Spanish and Portuguese love affair with the combination of sweet and crunchy are the "fruits of the frying pan" (*frutas de sartén*), the fanciful name given to a varied clan of crisp deep-fried pastries sprinkled with sugar or doused in syrup. These also were an integral part of medieval Iberian and Islamic cooking.

Another Islamic survival in Latin America is fruit cooked in sugar syrup, either to sweeten the fruit for a silky, heady dessert or to preserve it as an intensely concentrated confection, jam, paste, or candy. With an abundance of sugarcane and a cornucopia of tropical fruits that could be plucked from backyard trees, plantation kitchens produced prodigious amounts of fruits cooked in syrup. From huge cauldrons simmering over wood or charcoal fires and stirred by slave hands emerged guava or coconut marmalade, green papayas, or bitter orange shells in syrup and many more stovetop desserts born of this mingling of traditions.

In the realm of modern Latin sweets, you never know whether you will find a very old Iberian dish in almost pure form or some inspired marriage of the hemispheres, like the Brazilian *quindim de yayá*, an egg yolk and coconut custard. Guavas or guava shells, native squashes, or cashew apples might take the place of peaches or quinces in some fruit desserts and pastes. Pumpkin seeds, cashews, coconut, peanuts, and even starchy plantains came to fill the place of Spanish almonds and other nuts in the Latin interpretation of nougats, marzipan, and other candies. Allspice, vanilla, and plants with unfamiliar names, like the cinnamon-scented Ecuadorian *ishpingo*, rapidly began scenting the same custards as the traditional cloves and cinnamon. The "fruits of the frying pan" received novel additions such as pumpkin or corn. When yuca and sweet potatoes weren't getting the deep-fried treatment, they were being used to make thick sweet creams and puddings that were creative departures from earlier desserts bound with rice or wheat flour.

Yet another Spanish and Portuguese legacy may be the most beloved dessert tradition of all in Latin America: the innumerable variations on the theme of sugar cooked with milk, egg yolks, or both to form a voluptuous mass almost like a custard or a cross between a custard and a syrup. The ones we crave the most are desserts made on top of the stove—long-simmering, deeply primal sweets. We dream of smooth rice puddings with just a trace of nubby texture from the almost-dissolved rice, often lightly punctuated by sweet-tart raisins, or the pan-Latin caramelized milk pudding/sauce called *dulce de leche*, made by cooking down milk and sugar to a satiny thickness. More complex milk-egg-sugar desserts include billowy *natillas*, which are almost airy custards, and sweetened egg-based creams flavored with cinnamon, anise, cloves, citrus zest, nutmeg, and ginger.

One newer ingredient was destined to make its mark on the map of Latin sweets. Sometimes mystifying to cooks of non-Latin background is the triumph of canned milk in many sweet desserts that hark back to Spanish ancestry.

Of course, fresh milk can be difficult to produce and keep safe in tropical countries, but what we really have here is an honest cultural preference dating back a hundred years, to the time when American companies started producing and shipping sweetened condensed milk and evaporated milk. Try to make the classic custardy sauces and flans of Latin America while sidestepping evaporated milk, condensed milk, or very often both at once, mixed with some fresh milk or cream, and you will be missing an important chapter in the story of our centuries-old fascination with sweetness.

NEW IMMIGRANTS, NEW DESSERTS

There are a few other ethnic footnotes to this essentially Spanish and Portuguese story. Immigrants from many parts of the world have brought their favorite desserts to Latin America or found particular commercial niches. The Italians have had enormous influence in Argentina and Peru since the nineteenth century. In Peru, Italian panettone is the traditional Christmas bread, and Argentinean bakeries and *confiterías*, which are often owned by people of Italian descent, make delicious Italian-style ice creams.

There is also a significant, widespread, and abiding African presence in the world of Latin sweets. In the massive kitchens of tropical plantations, or in any urban kitchen presided over by African matrons, a hybrid sweet cuisine came to be. But unlike the influence of Africans in other areas of cooking, it began as a matter of following and adopting the Spanish and Portuguese recipes and dessert techniques taught by their white masters. Later, emancipated slaves used the skills learned on plantations and in the homes of the rich to develop a unique repertoire of sweets.

Desserts made with coconut or seeds mixed with honey or dark sugarcane molasses are the legacy of black cooks. The *turrón de Doña Pepa*, a mixture of molasses, sesame seeds, and egg yolks flavored with anise seeds, was the specialty of a famous black nougat maker in Lima, who lent her nickname, Doña Pepa, to this delicious sweet. This nougat is the classic dessert in October during the feast of the Cristo Morado, the Purple Christ or the Lord of Miracles, and those who eat it are always reminded of the injustices perpetrated against black slaves in nineteenth-century Peru.

Also famous in Brazil are the desserts of black *bahianas*, hefty matrons who sell their sweets in markets and on street corners from traylike tables called *tabuleiras*: the *cocada branca*, made with grated coconut in white sugar syrup, and its sibling, the *cocada preta*, cooked with brown loaf sugar; *manuê* (a cornmeal cake); *pamonhas* (sweet fresh corn tamales); and *pe-de-moleque* (a kind of nut brittle).

Just as blacks were famous for specific sweets, in Cuba the Chinese were known for their ice creams and the sesame-sprinkled candies called *palanquetas*, made with toasted wheat and molasses—a little like the pre-Columbian sweets of amaranth seeds and honey that are the ancestors of the modern Mexican *alegrías*.

French pastry chefs came to Latin America during the eighteenth and nineteenth centuries and monopolized dessert courses on the banquet tables of a Francophile aristocracy. There was an altered social dimension as well. The traditional desserts had been loved and respected, but they had been unglamorously produced by women and small shopkeepers. They were paraded around town on trays balanced on the heads of black or native women. They belonged to convents, street vendors' carts, small artisanal pastry shops, and both wealthy and middle-class homes. The new French desserts carried another kind of prestige, both male and foreign. Charlottes, mousses, brioches, and Chantilly cream reigned supreme in aristocratic kitchens and chic commercial establishments presided over by French pastry chefs. When upper-class people wanted to entertain in style, the meal ended with a French dessert; the Spanish and *criollo* ones were left for everyday private meals. In 1840, when the countess of Merlin returned from France to her native Cuba, she found that all aristocratic families had a French chef on call. In her lively memoir *La Habana* she recalls her first meal in Havana and how she was served *suprème de volaille* (chicken breast, French style), which she indignantly rejected: "I have come here to eat *criollo* food," she protested.

The infatuation with things French outlasted Spanish rule. The menus of important state banquets given by the presidents of the nascent Latin American republics were usually written in French. In 1910, the centenary of Chile's independence from Spain was celebrated with a lavish state banquet attended by the presidents of Chile and Argentina. Following the *langouste à la bordelaise* and the *croustades Perigueux* came *croutes aux fruits* and *bombas Chantilly*, all accompanied by glasses of sparkling *viuda* (the widow), as Chileans of the time familiarly referred to Veuve Clicquot.

Admiration for French cooking remains undiminished in countries like Brazil without detracting from people's enjoyment of their own cuisine. My São Paulo friend Gina Nogueiras, who speaks French like a native, used to make an elaborate eight-course French meal crowned by a lovely *tarte tatin* for her son's birthday and follow it the next day with a traditional luncheon from the *sertão* (backwoods) of Bahia. It does not look as if the French presence will disappear from the Latin dessert table anytime soon. Underlying many of our most inspired modern desserts, even those made with native ingredients, are time-tested classic French techniques. It's like a sprinkling of colorful, even thought-provoking Gallicisms on a page of American Spanish or Portuguese.

THE LATIN DESSERT PANTRY

Most of our sweets, pastries, and desserts use only simple ingredients that can be bought in local supermarkets throughout the United States. But for some special Latin ingredients, such as brown loaf sugar and tropical fruits both fresh and frozen, you need to visit a Latin market or consult mail-order sources.

Here is a list of items that you need to have at the ready to make the recipes of this chapter. For more information on some ingredients mentioned here, see The Layers of Latin Flavor, pages 35–106.

Fresh Whole Milk and Canned Milk

Besides fresh whole milk (preferably not ultra-pasteurized), you need to stock whole, unsweetened evaporated milk and sweetened condensed milk. Latin American cooks prize them for their intense,

slightly caramelized flavor and richness and would not be without them. Nestlé Carnation, Eagle, and Magnolia brands are universally available in Latin countries (these companies even have factories there), and every cook is determinedly loyal to a particular brand. Carnation—*Clavel* in Spanish—has become a generic term for evaporated milk in Mexico.

Fresh Cream and Canned Cream

Fresh heavy and light cream go by the same name, *crema*, as the cultured cream that is a Mexican and Central American favorite. The fresh kind is seldom an essential ingredient in Latin desserts. One of its few uses is in combination with other milks for the triflelike cake called *tres leches*. In Panama, the canned evaporated cream made by Nestlé is popular in desserts like *sopa de gloria*. Made by heating cream to a high temperature to remove some of the water, it is thickened with carageenan and comes in light and heavy grades (*media* or just *crema*). Canned cream has a full-bodied, almost spoonable texture, pale tan color, and somewhat caramelized taste. Recipes for the Panamanian wedding cake *sopa de gloria* often call for many cans of cream, but it is understood that Nestlé cream is meant. My recipes specify whether canned or fresh cream is required.

Eggs

The ideal eggs for Latin American cooking are very fresh, with vivid yellow yolks, and come from free-range chickens. The label "organic" on some supermarket eggs (even the virtuous ones) does not guarantee that, so whenever possible, buy eggs from a small producer (at a farmers' market, for example) who has paid attention to the chickens and what they eat. From my own experience raising chickens, I know that birds fed fresh greens produce flavorful eggs with bright yellow yolks.

Sugar

Granulated white and confectioners' sugar are generously used in the Latin kitchen. But brown loaf sugar (*panela* in Colombia, *piloncillo* in Mexico, *chancaca* in Peru, Bolivia, and Chile) is closer to our culinary soul (see Stones of Honey, page 98). When we taste it, we taste a part of our colonial past. Brown loaf sugar is not interchangeable with U.S. commercial light or dark brown sugar—if you must, use these as substitutes, but be aware that you will be missing the rich and complex flavor of brown loaf sugar. In this country, brown sugar is just white sugar mixed with mass-produced molasses. The ones we love descend from an artisanal heritage. They lend a dough or syrup not just sweetness but sweetness with backbone, roundness, complexity, and character. *Piloncillo* and *panela* are widely available in Hispanic markets and will give any dish a level of authenticity that is impossible to attain with substitutions.

Brown loaf sugar must be grated or dissolved before use. Today, some Latin markets carry pre-grated *panela* from Colombia or *rapadura* from Brazil. I have used it successfully and it saves some labor without sacrificing flavor. Two alternatives for people without access to Latin markets are Demerara and Muscovado sugars from Mauritius, available in some specialty and health-food stores. Demerara is a mild, delicate brown sugar with coarse crystals, suitable in many Cuban recipes. The more intense flavor of Muscovado reminds me of loaf sugar from small, old fashioned *trapiches* (sugar mills) in the countryside. It harmonizes well with other deep, assertive flavors and complex spicing.

Flours and Starches

Harina is the Spanish word for every kind of flour, finely ground meal, and food starch, not just wheat flour, though that is the most important. Wheat was planted wherever it would grow in the early days of the conquest, and excellent wheat for flour is still harvested in Argentina and the Andean regions. Most of the flour used in pastries and desserts resembles U.S. all-purpose flour, which is what I call for in most of these recipes.

As bakers everywhere know, however, there are subtle or not-so-subtle differences between brands and even batches. My recipes will work well with any standard-brand, all-purpose flour, but there are a few recipes where cake flour, the "softest" flour in terms of low gluten content and fine texture, is specified. Until recently, cake flour was not widely available in Latin America, and cooks resorted to combining all-purpose flour and cornstarch (*maicena* or *fécula de maíz*), rice flour (*harina* or *fécula de arroz*), sweet potato flour (*harina de camote*), or freeze-dried potato starch (*harina de chuño*) in order to adjust gluten content for making cakes and cookies. This is still the norm in most places, so some of my recipes for cakes call for cornstarch in combination with wheat flour. You can also find an even finer and whiter soft wheat flour, freer of any dark bran particles, labeled "000." Latin markets carry Argentinean brands like Favorita and Blanca Flor 000, which are terrific for cookies like *alfajores*. They correspond to the Italian 00 flours found in some specialty markets; these are the best substitute.

Fats

Since the Spanish introduced butter and lard to the New World colonies, both have had their roles in different sweets and pastries. But it can be safely said that the most important fat for making desserts in Latin America was traditionally lard. Manufactured shortening and margarines later gained an important following, as in the United States, but I have always avoided them because I do not like their flavor. My recipes call for lard, butter, or combinations of lard and butter. The butter is salted, the most widely available type in Latin America, with the exception of Argentina, where unsalted butter for cooking is more prevalent. We are used to working with it in this form, and I like the subtle, uniform way in which the salt flavor permeates a dough. If you are a fan of unsalted butter, adjust the recipe by adding a larger pinch of salt.

Lard makes a very short, rich pastry or cookie dough. Homemade lard always should be strained before use, and unless the recipe calls for melted lard, it should also be chilled.

Coconut Meat and Coconut Milk

Prized throughout Latin America in all kinds of savory dishes, grated coconut meat and the thick, pure white milk extracted from it are also important dessert ingredients. I prefer to crack and grate fresh coconuts and make a new batch of coconut milk every time a recipe calls for it (see the detailed instructions on pages 50–51). I find the process grounds my cooking in an artisanal tradition that I admire and respect. But if the thought of doing this makes you hesitate to tackle a dessert you'd like to try, by all means use packaged unsweetened grated coconut and good unsweetened canned coconut milk. Some markets carry organic unsweetened grated coconut and fresh-tasting frozen grated coconut.

Unsweetened canned coconut milk imported from the American and Asian tropics is available in Latin markets and specialty stores. Many brands are stabilized with an emulsifier like carageenan or guar gum to keep them from separating into watery liquid and bits of pulp. Obviously, these seem richer than thinner-textured all-natural brands, but usually there is little difference in flavor. Some brands, however, contain preservatives that should be avoided by anyone sensitive to sulfites, so be sure to read labels. Some brands I have used with success are Goya, which is available in most Latin markets, and Thai Kitchen, Blue Mountain Country, and organic Native Forest, which are available at Whole Foods markets and specialty stores. Of the four, the all-natural Blue Mountain Country brand from Sri Lanka has the most coconuty taste, through it is a bit grayish.

Usually, Latin recipes calling for coconut milk make a distinction between the creamy, first-pressed coconut milk (see page 50) and the lighter milk of a second pressing (see page 51).

When using any type of canned coconut milk, it is important to stir it well before using in cooking, as solids and fats tend to separate even in the brands that contain emulsifiers or thickeners.

Fruits and Flowers

Our desserts use a large range of tropical fruit pulps, now widely available in Latin markets here in frozen form (usually sold in 14-ounce and 16-ounce bags). You can easily find mango, cherimoya, *guanábana*, guava, passion fruit, tamarind, Andean blackberries, *naranjillas* (also called *lulo*), and many others in the frozen food section. Today, rare Amazonian fruits like *açai* (the small deep purple fruit of a palm tree), *cupuaçu* (a cousin of cacao), and even cacao-fruit pulp are also available frozen from mail-order sources. Unless otherwise specified, defrost before using.

Lime, lemon, and orange juice lend a welcome tang to sweet syrups and sorbets, with freshly squeezed juice always preferable to frozen or bottled products. Use a zester, thin-bladed peeler, or nutmeg grater to remove or grate the outer layer of limes and oranges (the most popular citrus fruits) without digging into the bitter white pith when the fruit's aromatic zest is required.

Dried rosehips, rose petals, and orange blossoms are used in some Latin desserts. Extracts like rose and orange blossom water are good substitutes but need to be used with restraint, since they are stronger than the natural dried flowers.

Liqueurs, Spirits, and Fortified Wines

One of the legacies of colonial cooking in Latin America is the use of alcohol in sweet dishes. In Peru, pisco is widely used in custards and cakes like the egg-laden *huevos chimbos* and port is added to the meringue of the popular sweet *suspiro de limeña*. Not only is rum a common flavoring in Hispanic Caribbean cooking, but so is dry or sweet sherry, the salty oxidized cooking wine *vino seco*, and even Calvados, which is also used for flambeeing apples in Argentina. Brandy is often added to the dough for Argentinean *alfajores*, though I sometimes use Cointreau instead, for a hint of orange. The liqueurs, spirits, and wines most often called for in these recipes are port (preferably ruby), oloroso sherry, aged dark rum (preferably Bacardi, Guatemalan Zapata, Venezuelan Santa Teresa, Nicaraguan Flor de Caña, or the Puerto Rican Ron del Barrilito), Cointreau or a similar orange liqueur (Venezuelan Santa Teresa Rhum Orange, Triple Sec, or Bacardi O), and Peruvian Pisco Italia, which has a lovely muscatel grape aroma. In some recipes calling for an infusion of anise seeds, I give the option of substituting anisette.

Spices and Other Aromatic Flavorings

Latin American sweet cuisine is deeply aromatic, but if you look closely at the recipes in this chapter, you will notice that a few spices stand out. Buy spices in small quantities and keep them in tightly covered containers to maintain their freshness.

CINNAMON (*CANELA*)

I use both the hard quill cassia bark and the softer Ceylon cinnamon in my recipes. Both are called *canela* in Spanish, but in Latin America this name usually applies to true Ceylon cinnamon, which is available in Latin markets and spice stores. You also need ground cinnamon to sprinkle over desserts at serving time.

ANISE SEEDS

After *canela*, this is the most popular sweet flavoring of Latin America. Mexicans like to extract its flavor by boiling it in milk or water before adding other ingredients. *Miel de piloncillo*, a flavorful brown loaf syrup that usually accompanies sweet fritters like Mexican *hojuelas* and the ring-shaped *buñuelos*, is deeply scented with cinnamon and anise seeds. At first the anise seems excessive, but with cooking it mellows, leaving behind a certain bitterness that cuts through the sweetness of the syrup.

STAR ANISE

This star-shaped pod of Asian origin is often used interchangeably with anise seeds. I like to use them together, as they have slightly different scents. I normally add a handful of star anise pods to my custard and flan bases and let them steep for a few minutes. They never overwhelm the mix.

ALLSPICE

This marvelous New World dried berry has the combined aroma of other spices. It may be my favorite flavoring. I love combining it with star anise and anise seeds in custards, flans, and chocolate drinks. Just a few berries will give your sweets an ineffable aroma that is never overpowering.

VANILLA

Though the most flavorful vanilla comes from Mexico, it is not used as lavishly there or elsewhere in Latin America as it should be. Most people use extracts of poor quality and seldom venture to use the whole pod or its seeds. I am a vanilla lover and use it anytime I can. On trips to Papantla, Veracruz, a famous Mexican vanilla-growing region, I became a vanilla zealot. There I met a group of elderly women, many of them the wives and relatives of vanilla growers and curers, who use vanilla in every conceivable way and who are trying to revive its use in regional savory and sweet cooking. Whenever possible, use whole vanilla beans (preferably Mexican) and pure extracts from Madagascar and Mexican vanillas like the ones produced by Nielsen-Massey in the United States (available

in specialty stores). I also like the Mexican extract produced by Gaya in the town of Gutierrez Zamora in Veracruz, which has some sugar added.

MEXICAN VANILLA

Vanilla has been cultivated in Mexico since precolonial times, but details of its early history are scant and clouded in myth. The monumental *Historia de las cosas de la Nueva España* (*History of the Things of New Spain*), written by the learned Franciscan friar Bernardino de Sahagún around 1577, describes vanilla as a flavoring for cacao drinks—a remarkable association that still seduces us today. At the court of Moctezuma, where "many fine and delicate cacao drinks were concocted," he explains, a cacao drink was flavored with *vainilla tierna*, probably vanilla beans that were still plump and flexible. In pre-Columbian Mexico, vanilla pods were probably allowed to sun-dry while hanging from the plant until they turned dark brown and fragrant. That's why the Aztecs, who spoke the marvelously descriptive language Nahuatl, called vanilla *tlilxóchitl*, which means black flower.

Today, ninety percent of Mexico's vanilla is produced close to Papantla and elsewhere in the Totonacapan (land of the Totonacs) in Veracruz State. It was probably from this fertile part of the country that the imperialist highland Aztecs got their "black flowers." There was not a great supply: the vanilla plant, a kind of orchid, has a morphological condition that prevents it from pollinating itself. Left to the whims of nature, pollination is haphazard at best. It became possible to cultivate vanilla as a reliably productive crop only when someone figured how to hand-pollinate it in a systematic fashion. That happened in 1836, when, after many experiments and failures with vanilla plants taken from Mexico, the Belgian botanist Charles Morren solved the problem. Five years later, a freed slave named Edmond Albius on the French island of La Réunion invented a practical way of hand-pollinating with a slender wooden stick, and his method is still used today.

It took a long time for this breakthrough to reach Mexico. As late as 1860, an enlightened Papantla farmer named Francisco Fuentecilla Fuentes wrote a treatise on growing and curing vanilla which makes no mention of hand-pollination. Finally, in 1877, three colonists from Jicaltepec traveled to Paris and learned about hand-pollination at the Museum of Natural History. It is said that they did a brisk business teaching the technique to farmers in their area and farther north in Papantla, for ten pesos a lesson. Vanilla could now be grown for an expanding world market, and no longer depended on the goodwill of insects.

From the 1870s on, Papantla was a place where vanilla barons made great fortunes. Their beans won gold medals at expositions in Chicago and Paris, and they established flourishing offices in Philadelphia and New York City to sell their products. Papantla named itself "the city that perfumed the world," and photographers were called in to record streets blanketed with the fragrant beans and warehouses bursting with shiny, perfectly shaped vanilla bundles ready to be shipped.

However, the success of Mexican vanilla in the world market encouraged growers in other lands to increase their production, and synthetic vanillin, an artificial vanilla flavor first extracted from wood pulp in 1876, began to compete for use in mass-produced foods. In the Totonacapan, control of the crop was concentrated ever more tightly in the hands of a few families, many of them of European extraction. Peasant uprisings continuously undermined the prosperity of the region, and an increasingly lawless atmosphere in which theft and murder were not uncommon became a fixture of the harvest season. For fear of theft, many Totonac farmers rushed to cut their vanilla beans before they ripened properly on the vine. That practice resulted in poor-quality beans after curing, which helped erode the sterling reputation of Mexican vanilla in international markets. Finally, when unusually harsh spells of weather destroyed many vanilla fields in the 1960s and 1970s, local farmers turned to cattle ranching, to other crops, or to work in the growing oil fields. Vanilla, once a revered part of the life of the Totonacs, was now just another plant to fill in one corner of a farmer's field.

Of course, not all of the farmers in the Totonacapan abandoned their devotion to vanilla, and in 1998 the local Vanilla Council began actively seeking rigorous government quality control and a Denomination of Origin (*Denominacíon de Origen*) designation for Veracruzan vanilla. A certificate of origin and quality was to be granted to producers who met world standards of excellence in the size and shape of the pods; their color, texture, and flexibility; their percentage of moisture; and, most important, the complex bouquet of true vanillin and other factors that gives vanilla its characteristic flavor and aroma. In the years since, Mexican vanilla has regained its reputation in the world market.

In comparison with vanilla grown in Madagascar and Indonesia, which dominates the market, properly harvested and cured Mexican vanilla ranks very high in both flavor and aroma. If you obtain Mexican vanilla grown in Papantla, you will be seduced by the musky aroma of caramel or butterscotch and its elegant suavity. In tasting, you will detect a ripe acidity that reads as fruitiness—the rich, dark flavor of dried cherries, prunes, or raisins. When added to any sweet or savory dish, either as a bean or in extract form, this vanilla embraces all the other flavors in a subtle caress.

Homemade Mexican Vanilla Extract

Extracto de Vainilla Casero

Papantla vanilla master Heriberto Larios makes his own vanilla extract by steeping a handful of perfectly cured vanilla beans in fine brandy or rum. In less than fifteen days, the spirits are infused with the rich scent and attractive mahogany color of pure vanilla. Larios stresses the importance of storing this brew in a dark glass container, to prevent the extract from discoloring.

MAKES ABOUT 1 QUART (1 LITER)

- 10 Mexican vanilla beans, preferably from Papantla, split lengthwise
- 1 quart (1 liter) fine brandy or aged rum
- 1 teaspoon sugar (optional; sugar helps fix flavors)

▶ Place the vanilla beans in an amber-colored or other dark glass container or bottle with a lid. Combine the brandy and the sugar, if using, and stir until the sugar dissolves. Pour the liquid into the bottle, making sure to cover the vanilla beans. Close the lid tightly and store in a dark, cool place for 15 days or longer.

The extract will keep indefinitely. Keep replenishing the spirits and adding new vanilla beans as needed.

Totonac Vanilla and Prunes in *Aguardiente*

Vino de Vainilla y Ciruelas Pasas

Ask any Totonac Indian farmer about his favorite drink and he'll invariably answer, "*Vino.*" He is not talking about wine but about *aguardiente* (burning water), the raw and intensely alcoholic spirit that results from the distillation of sugarcane sap. *Aguardiente* is the first yield from the still, a brash rum wannabe that has not had the chance to age. For the Totonacs, *vino* is not only a celebratory drink but the basis for a number of herbal infusions, some consumed as medications, others drunk simply for pleasure.

The Totonacs like to infuse their powerful *vino* with lesser-grade vanilla (which they call *picadura* because it is usually chopped up into small pieces) and prunes. These ingredients mellow the *aguardiente* considerably, giving it a subtle grape flavor and turning it almost into a brandy. I love using this vanilla-infused liqueur to flavor all kinds of sweets, from bread pudding to fritters.

MAKES 5½ CUPS

5 Mexican vanilla beans, split lengthwise and coarsely chopped

2 cups prunes with pits

1 quart (1 liter) *aguardiente*, preferably Guatemalan El Venado

1 teaspoon sugar (optional)

▶ Combine the chopped vanilla and the prunes in a glass jar with a lid. Pour the *aguardiente* into a container with a spout and stir in the sugar, if using, until it dissolves. Pour the *aguardiente* over the prunes, making sure to cover the fruit completely, and close the jar tightly. Store in a cool, dark place for 15 days or longer. Serve in stocky shot glasses as an after-dinner drink or use in cooking. The prunes are as delicious as brandied cherries.

SYRUPS

Syrups are a must for dessert making in Latin America. Many are made with unrefined brown loaf sugars available in this country, like Colombian *panela* and Mexican *piloncillo*, but you can also use brown sugar or finer Indian Ocean granulated brown sugars like Demerara and Muscovado, which carry the aroma of the sugarcane juice from which they are made. I use these syrups to moisten a sponge cake fresh from the oven, as a base for many custards, to sweeten cocktails, and as dipping sauces for fritters. They take minutes to make and they keep well in the refrigerator for months.

Simple Citrus Syrup

Sirope Simple con Limón e Naranja

A simple syrup made with white sugar and scented with the zest of limes and oranges and natural vanilla belongs in every kitchen pantry. Not only can you use it to moisten a cake, but you can stir it into any drink in lieu of sugar, and even add a spoonful or two to savory dishes that require a touch of sweetness and aroma.

MAKES ABOUT 1 CUP

1 cup sugar

1 cup water

1 Ceylon cinnamon stick (*canela*)

Peel of 1 orange, cut into 2 or 3 pieces

Peel of 1 lime, cut into 2 or 3 pieces

½ orange

½ lime

1 vanilla bean, preferably Mexican, split lengthwise

▶ Place all the ingredients except the vanilla bean in a small saucepan. Scrape the black seeds of the vanilla bean into the saucepan and add the pod. Bring to a boil over medium heat while stirring to dissolve the sugar. Lower the heat and simmer gently for 5 minutes. Let cool. Strain; discard the solids and pour the syrup into a glass or plastic container. Tightly covered, it will keep well for 3 months in the refrigerator.

Light Brown Loaf Sugar Syrup

Sirope de Azúcar Parda Ligero

This tan-colored syrup is light yet packed with the deep, complex flavor and fruity acidity of Latin brown loaf sugar. I use it in place of simple white sugar syrup when I need a richer flavor.

MAKES 1½ CUPS

8 ounces grated brown loaf sugar (preferably *panela* or *piloncillo*), Demerara sugar, or light brown sugar
1 Ceylon cinnamon stick (*canela*)
Zest of 1 lime
Pinch of salt
1 cup water

▶ Place all the ingredients in a small saucepan. Bring to a boil over medium heat and let cook at a gentle boil, stirring frequently, until the syrup lightly coats the back of a spoon, about 8 minutes. Let cool; strain, and discard the solids. Store the syrup tightly covered in a glass or plastic container in the refrigerator. It will keep well for up to 3 months. Strain again when ready to use.

Fragrant Brown Loaf Sugar Syrup

Melado de Panela

This thick mahogany-colored syrup, rich with the aroma of citrus peel, sweet spices, and Spanish oloroso sherry, is best used as a sauce for ice creams and deep-fried fritters. I often add it to marinades to tame their garlicky edge, and I love to slather it over a duck or a large beef or pork roast for a golden crust.

MAKES 1½ CUPS

1 pound Latin grated brown loaf sugar (preferably *panela* or *piloncillo*), Muscovado sugar, or dark brown sugar
2½ cups water
½ cup sweet sherry, preferably Spanish oloroso or aged dark rum
2 Ceylon cinnamon sticks (*canela*)
15 allspice berries
8 whole cloves
2 star anise pods or 1 teaspoon anise seeds
Peel of 1 orange, cut into 2 or 3 segments
⅛ teaspoon salt

▶ Place all the ingredients in a heavy medium saucepan and bring to a boil over medium heat, stirring to dissolve the sugar. Reduce the heat to low and cook at a simmer until the liquid thickens to the texture of light molasses, about 15 minutes. Let cool. Strain into a glass or plastic container (discard the solids) and store tightly covered in the refrigerator for up to 3 months.

Peruvian Brown Loaf Sugar "Honey"

Miel de Chancaca

This heavy caramelized syrup is one of the favorite fillings for the cookies called *alfajores* (page 838). When ready to use, bring it to room temperature or warm a little before using as a filling.

MAKES ABOUT ½ CUP

- 8 ounces grated brown loaf sugar (preferably *chancaca* or *panela*), Muscovado sugar, or light brown sugar
- 1 cup water
  Peel of 1 orange or 1 lemon
- ½ teaspoon lime juice or distilled white vinegar

▶ Place the sugar, water, and citrus peel in a small saucepan and bring to a boil over medium heat, stirring to dissolve the sugar. Lower the heat to medium-low and continue simmering until the syrup reaches a temperature of 238°F on a candy thermometer. Stir in the lime juice or vinegar. Remove from the stove. Let cool and store in a tightly covered container. The syrup should have the consistency of thick honey. It will last for 3 months in the refrigerator.

Hibiscus Syrup

Sirope de Flor de Jamaica

I like to keep this deep red syrup in the refrigerator for a variety of uses. I stir it with rum and ice for a Caribbean punch. I drizzle it over vanilla ice cream. And I even paint it on a loin of pork for a shimmering red glaze almost at the end of roasting, or drizzle it over chocolate flan.

MAKES 1½ CUPS

- 4 ounces (about 4 cups) dried hibiscus flowers (*flor de jamaica*; see page 339)
- 2 cups sugar
- 2½ quarts water

- 2 Ceylon cinnamon sticks (*canela*)
- 5 allspice berries
- 5 whole cloves
- 1 star anise pod
  Peel of 1 orange

▶ Place all the ingredients in a medium saucepan and cook over medium heat for 30 minutes, stirring occasionally, until the syrup coats the back of a spoon. Strain through a fine-mesh sieve and pour the liquid back into the pot (discard the solids). Bring to a boil and simmer over medium-low heat until the liquid is reduced to the consistency of a thick syrup, about 20 minutes. Cool to room temperature and store refrigerated in a tightly covered glass or plastic container. The syrup keeps well for about 2 weeks.

STOVETOP DESSERTS

Creamy Rice Pudding

Arroz con Leche Cremoso

Ask Latin Americans about their national desserts, and they'll start the list with *arroz con leche* (rice pudding). This is the quintessential *dulce latino*. Every country has its version, with as many small variations as there are Latin cooks. You will find rice puddings as thick as mortar, others with the grains of rice still whole and as hard as flint, dancing in a bodiless milky fluid, and others dissolved to an unrecognizable paste. I believe that the rice in the pudding should be a suggestion. It must gently become one with the milk and the spices, turning smooth and creamy with just a trace of nubby texture—a bridge between the nourishing savory and the comforting sweet treat.

It is fundamental to cook the rice in water first, before adding the milk. If you attempt to bypass this important stage, the rice will never soften. Another crucial moment is to know when to stop cooking it. Never wait for the pudding to thicken in the pot. Take it off the fire while still fluid; it will become creamier as it cools.

This recipe calls for medium-short grain rice, which is perfect for this purpose since it absorbs much more liquid than long-grain rice. Here creaminess comes not only from the rice but from a can of condensed milk, as indispensable an ingredient in the Latin sweet kitchen as cinnamon.

Cook's Note: I tested this recipe with medium-short grain Montsia rice from Spain, which absorbs a great deal of liquid and becomes creamy and delicious with prolonged cooking. You might need to adjust the cooking time if using other types of short-grain rice.

SERVES 12 (MAKES ABOUT 9 CUPS)

- 1 cup medium-short grain rice (about 6½ ounces), preferably Spanish Montsia
- 2 quarts water
- 1 teaspoon salt
- 6 star anise pods or 1 tablespoon anise seeds
- 4 Ceylon cinnamon sticks (*canela*)
  Peel of 1 lime or lemon, cut into 2 or 3 pieces
- 3 cups whole milk
- Two 14-ounce cans sweetened condensed milk
- 1 tablespoon rosewater (optional)
- 1 tablespoon orange blossom water (optional)
- 1 tablespoon butter
  Ground cinnamon, for garnish

▶ Rinse the rice in cold water until the water runs clear. Place in a heavy 6-quart saucepan with the water and salt. Tie the spices and citrus peel in a piece of cheesecloth and add it to the pan. Bring to a boil over high heat, then lower the heat to medium and cook for 25 to 30 minutes, uncovered, or until the rice is very soft.

Stir in the whole and condensed milks. Reduce the heat to low and cook for 40 minutes, stirring occasionally, until creamy but still liquid. If you want to add an interesting dimension of aroma, stir in the rosewater and orange blossom water 10 minutes or so before removing from the heat. Add the butter and stir to melt. Remove the pan from the heat and pour immediately into a serving bowl. Dust lightly with ground cinnamon and let cool to room temperature.

Store, covered, in the refrigerator for 2 to 3 days.

Peruvian Rice Pudding with Brown Sugar and Coconut

Arroz Zambito

I first tasted this Peruvian rice pudding at Dulces Doña Carmen, an eighty-five-year-old pastry shop in Trujillo that had the look of an old family dining room. I was intrigued by the selection of regional desserts, and I ordered them all. The rice pudding was made with local long-grain rice and cooked in a rich aromatic syrup of *chancaca*, the Peruvian brown loaf sugar, flavored with grated coconut and raisins. Later I tasted the dish in Lima, but it was not as delicious as the Trujillo version. The trick, as I later found out, is to add enough syrup to keep the rice moist when it cools.

Zambo is the colonial name for the offspring of black and Indian parents, and *zambito* refers to the dessert's light caramel color. The name indicates that this dish was probably first created in the colonial period.

Cook's Note: For this recipe, use any long-grain rice except aromatic types like basmati.

SERVES 4 TO 6

- 1 cup long-grain rice (about 6¾ ounces)
- 7 cups water
- ⅛ teaspoon salt
- 8 ounces grated brown loaf sugar (preferably *chancaca* or *panela*), Muscovado sugar, or dark brown sugar (about 1½ cups)
- 1 tablespoon anise seeds
- 2 Ceylon cinnamon sticks (*canela*)
- ¼ cup grated fresh coconut (see page 50) or store-bought unsweetened grated coconut
- ¼ cup coarsely chopped walnuts
- ¼ cup dark raisins
- 2 tablespoons butter
  Ground cinnamon, for garnish

▶ Rinse the rice in cold water until the water runs clear. Place the rice in a heavy 3-quart pot with 6 cups water and the salt. Bring to a rolling boil over medium heat and cook, uncovered, for 5 minutes. When tiny craters form on the surface of the rice

and the water is almost absorbed, fluff with a fork, reduce the heat to the lowest possible setting, and cover tightly. Cook for 20 minutes, undisturbed.

In the meantime, place the sugar, anise, cinnamon, and remaining 1 cup water in a small pan and heat over medium heat. Stir to dissolve the sugar. Let steep for about 5 minutes, then strain and put back into the pan. Stir in the coconut, walnuts, and raisins and simmer until lightly thickened, about 20 minutes.

Uncover the rice, which should be soft and moist, and stir in the syrup. Let cook for about 10 minutes, stirring occasionally. Pour into a serving bowl and dust lightly with ground cinnamon.

Caramelized Milk Custard

Dulce de Leche

The people of Latin America have an inordinate fondness for this puddinglike sweet made from cooked-down milk and sugar. In this country, where it has become as popular in recent years as other Latin imports, it is best known as *dulce de leche*, its Argentinean and Uruguayan name. But every Latin American country has a particular name for this addictive sweet and a unique way of making it, which accounts for differences in color, flavor, and texture. In Peru and Chile it is called *manjar*, which literally means "appetizing food." In Colombia it is called *arequipe*, presumably after the town of Arequipa in Peru, and in Mexico it is called *cajeta*, after the boxes in which it was traditionally packed. The most famous *cajeta* in Mexico comes from the town of Celaya in the state of Guanajuato. The stores that line the streets sell it in several guises, including one with liquor (*cajeta envinada*) and some with fruits and vanilla.

But nobody in Latin America comes close to the all-embracing passion for *dulce de leche* of Argentineans and Uruguayans. They use this delicious satiny sweet in everything: rolled into crepes and cakes, stuffed between the powdery halves of the shortbread cookies called *alfajores*, and as a filling for every conceivable pastry. Go to any market in the River Plate region of Argentina and Uruguay and you can find dozens of brands of industrially processed *dulce de leche*. For pastries, cooks often use a thick, opaque version that contains additives and thickeners. I much prefer artisanal *dulce de leche* made in small batches. Though goat's milk is sometimes used, Argentinean and Uruguayan *dulce de leche* is primarily made with cow's milk, sugar, and bicarbonate of soda, which contributes to a deep caramel color.

You can now buy *dulce de leche* in North American supermarkets and find an even wider selection in Latin markets, but to enjoy the pure taste, try making it at home at least once. There's nothing more seductive than a pot of *dulce de leche* bubbling on the stove. You taste spoonful after spoonful of it, on the pretext of testing its consistency, and before you know it the sweet is half gone.

Cook's Notes: I learned some key tips for making *dulce de leche* from an old woman in the northeast of Argentina, a region where an old *criollo* cuisine lives on. She taught me to caramelize some of the sugar before adding the milk for a deep, rich dark color. Success also resides in paying attention to the changes in the milk and knowing when to stop cooking.

This is not a recipe that you can abandon while it is cooking. It requires not continuous stirring but vigi-

lance, especially at the end of cooking. Most people know by eye and feel the moment to take it off the heat, but I find that a candy thermometer is invaluable. To obtain a thick and creamy *dulce de leche*, cook it to 225°F, no more.

MAKES ABOUT 6 CUPS

- 2 pounds sugar (about 4¼ cups)
- 1 gallon (4 quarts) whole milk
- 1 vanilla bean, split lengthwise in half
- 1 teaspoon baking soda

▶ Heat a heavy 8-quart pot over medium heat for a couple of minutes. Add ¼ cup to ½ cup sugar (½ cup will give a very beautiful dark golden brown color like *café con leche*). Cook, stirring, until the sugar caramelizes to a golden color. Watching for spatters, quickly pour in the milk along with the remaining sugar, the vanilla bean, and the baking soda. Stir to mix. The milk will turn a light beige color.

Continue cooking over medium heat, stirring occasionally, for about 1½ hours. Then start checking the pan attentively while stirring more frequently. When the mixture starts bubbling steadily, begin checking the state of doneness by spooning some drops onto a plate to see whether they flow or stay in place, or use a candy thermometer. Make sure you wait a couple of seconds for your sample to cool a bit. If it solidifies some, or if it has reached 225°F on the thermometer, it is done.

Have ready a heatproof medium bowl placed over another bowl filled with cracked ice and a little water. When the *dulce de leche* has achieved the desired consistency, becoming a shiny, creamy custard that is still a bit liquid, pour it into the prepared bowl and let cool, undisturbed. It will thicken greatly when cool. Store, tightly covered, in a plastic or glass container at room temperature or in the refrigerator. It will last for months.

Variation: For Mexican *cajeta*, use a combination of cow's milk and goat's milk and do not cook past a temperature of 222°F, for a more fluid texture.

Peruvian Caramelized Milk

Manjar Blanco

The Peruvian version of *dulce de leche* is called *manjar blanco*, and true to its name, it is lighter in color than Argentinean and Uruguayan *dulce de leche* and Mexican *cajeta*. Traditional cooks make it by boiling down cow's milk mixed with sugar until it reaches the desired creamy consistency, but most people either buy it prepared or make it at home with a combination of sweetened condensed milk and evaporated milk. This is the recipe of Andrea Massaro, the pastry chef at Huaca Pucllana, one of my favorite restaurants in Lima.

MAKES 2 CUPS

Two 14-ounce cans sweetened condensed milk
One 12-ounce can evaporated milk
Pinch of salt

▶ Place the ingredients in a heavy medium saucepan and bring to a gentle simmer over medium heat. Lower the heat to low and cook, stirring occasionally, until the liquid is light brown, thick, and creamy, about 1 hour and 15 minutes. Pour into a bowl and let cool. Store in a tightly closed glass jar in the refrigerator. It will keep for 2 months.

Almond and Rosewater Gelatin

Gelatina de Almendra y Agua de Rosa

The inspiration for this recipe comes from two sources, the rose-scented milk recipes of India and Persia and the very Mexican tradition of milk gelatins enriched with almonds. Chopped pistachios and crushed dried or fresh roses make a beautiful, colorful garnish that contrasts with the light cream of the gelatin and gives it a sweet aromatic accent.

Cook's Note: Walk into any Mexican market and you will find dried rosebuds and petals sold in small packages as *rosa de castilla*, a generic term for the perfumed Gallic rose, one of the oldest cultivated roses in the southern Mediterranean, brought to the New World by Spanish settlers.

SERVES 8

6 cups whole milk
One ¼-ounce envelope unflavored gelatin
3 cups whole blanched almonds (about 1 pound)
1 cup sugar, or to taste
⅛ teaspoon salt
1 tablespoon rosewater
⅛ teaspoon almond extract
2 tablespoons unsprayed dried or fresh rosebuds or petals, for garnish
¼ cup green pistachios, coarsely chopped, for garnish

▶ Place 1 cup milk in a small saucepan and bring to a boil. Remove from the heat, add the gelatin, and stir until dissolved. Set aside.

Working in 2 batches, process the almonds, sugar, salt, and remaining 5 cups milk in a food processor or blender until smooth. Stir well and strain into a bowl. Stir in the rosewater, almond extract, and milk-gelatin mixture. Pour the mixture into an 8-inch-square glass dish or other mold and refrigerate until set, about 3 hours.

To serve, spoon the gelatin onto a delicate dessert platter and sprinkle with the rose petals or buds and chopped pistachios. Or bring the gelatin to the table in its mold, sprinkled with the flower and nut garnish.

Dominican Red Kidney Bean and Sweet Potato Cream

Habichuelas con Dulce

Beans of many colors are turned into rich and creamy stovetop desserts throughout Latin America, from the Dominican Republic to Peru. These puddings are earthy and distinct, with a sweetness that is never overpowering.

Beatriz Hernández from Bonao in the Dominican Republic is very particular about this traditional Dominican Lenten dessert. In Bonao it is customary to make large quantities to give away to favorite neighbors and friends. Belkis Hernández, who learned this recipe from Beatriz, his mother-in-law, recalls how she used to pass judgment on all the samples sent to her by her neighbors but was never truly satisfied with any of them. "This one is not well strained," she would say, frowning. "The sweet potato pieces are too big in this one." "This one smells too much of cloves." All the *habichuelas con dulce* Beatriz got as gifts ended up in a single pot, which she would hand over "very generously"

to a worker on her farm. He never suspected he was taking home a blend of rejects. I can understand Beatriz's fastidiousness and pride in her own cooking: her *habichuelas* are delicious.

Cook's Note: Select a heavy pot to cook the beans, and be gentle with the fire, patient with the stirring, and above all vigilant. Cast-iron pots lined with enamel and copper pots lined with tin or stainless steel are great conductors of heat. If cooking with these, keep the heat lower than with other pots. Be especially careful about stirring once you add the sweet potatoes and raisins. They tend to sink to the bottom of the pot and may stick to it.

SERVES 8 TO 12

- 1 pound small dried kidney beans
- 1½ cups whole milk
- One 14-ounce can sweetened condensed milk
- One 12-ounce can evaporated milk
- 1½ cups Creamy ("First") Coconut Milk (page 50) or one 13-ounce can unsweetened coconut milk
- 1 cup grated fresh coconut (from half a 1½-pound coconut; see page 50) or store-bought unsweetened grated coconut
- 1 medium sweet potato (about 8 ounces), peeled and cut into ½-inch dice
- ½–1 cup sugar
- 2 tablespoons butter
- 1 cup dark raisins
- 1 tablespoon vanilla extract
- 2 Ceylon cinnamon sticks (*canela*)
- 1 teaspoon salt
- 2 packages small Dominican crackers (*ciento en boca galleticas*, available in Hispanic markets; optional)

▶ Rinse and pick over the beans. Place in a large pot with 4 quarts water and cook until soft, about 2 hours. Drain the beans. Working in batches, blend the beans with the milks and grated coconut in a blender or food processor. Strain into a large, heavy saucepan, add the rest of the ingredients except the crackers, mix well, and cook over medium heat, stirring, for about 30 minutes, or until tender. Turn off the heat and remove the cinnamon sticks. Top with a handful of crackers, if using.

Variation: Kidney Bean and Sweet Potato Ice Cream
This creamy bean dessert also makes terrific ice cream. Place the finished mixture in an ice cream maker and process according to the manufacturer's instructions.

Brazilian Cracked Corn and Coconut Milk

Mungunzá de Engenho

This dessert was born in a sugarcane mill and first stirred by slave hands. Its ingredients are simple, yet it surprises with its richness and subtle flavor.

I adapted this recipe from one in Gilberto Freyre's *Açucar: una sociologia do doces com receitas de bolos e doces do Nordeste do Brasil* (Sugar: A Sociology of Dessert with Recipes for Cakes and Sweets from the Northeast of Brazil), a jewel of a book published in 1939. Freyre, a renowned Brazilian sociologist, belongs to a small and select cadre of Latin American researchers for whom food is a serious subject of study. This small, lively, and very personal volume is rich with information about the sweet history of Brazil, and it offers old recipes collected by Freyre in his native Pernambuco, a land of sugarcane fields and great plantations. Many of these recipes, like the one for *mungunzá*, do not list quantities, but it is easy to figure out the proportions. How can you go wrong with corn, coconut milk, and sugar?

Cook's Note: At the crack of dawn, working-class highland Ecuadorians go to the market to drink *morocho de leche*, a thick gruel of white corn cooked in milk, served hot from bubbling cauldrons stirred by powerful women known as *morocheras*. If you look at the list of ingredients and the cooking method, you will immediately see the similarity with the Bahian *mungunzá* (see the variation at the end of this recipe), except that the Ecuadorian version is made with cow's milk, not with coconut milk and grated coconut.

SERVES 6 TO 8

8 ounces cracked white corn (sold as *maíz trillado blanco* in Hispanic markets and *canjica de milho blanco* in Brazilian markets)

6 cups water

1¾ cups Creamy ("First") Coconut Milk (page 50) or one 13–15-ounce can unsweetened coconut milk

¾ cup sugar, or to taste

½ teaspoon salt

▶ Place the corn in a bowl and rinse in several changes of water until it runs clear. Drain, cover with cold water, and let soak overnight.

The following day, drain in a colander, place in a large saucepan with the 6 cups water and the coconut milk, and bring to a boil over high heat. Lower the heat to low and simmer, covered, 45 to 50 minutes, or until tender, stirring occasionally. Stir in the sugar and salt. Cook, uncovered, stirring occasionally, until the mixture thickens like rice pudding and the corn is soft and creamy. Total cooking time is about 1 hour and 10 minutes. Add a little hot milk if the mixture dries out.

Variation: *Mungunzá* **in the Style of Bahia**
Cook the corn in 6 cups milk, not water, with 5 whole cloves and 2 Ceylon cinnamon sticks (*canela*) tied in a cheesecloth bag. When soft, add 1 cup freshly grated coconut and cook, stirring occasionally, over medium-low heat until soft and creamy. Remove the spice bag before serving. This dish is a near cousin to the *morocho con leche* of Ecuador, though that contains no coconut.

Venezuelan Corn and Coconut Custard

Majarete Venezolano

Majarete, a rich spoon dessert made primarily with creamed and strained fresh corn, is a Hispanic Caribbean classic that dates back to the colonial period. In colonial times, cooks prepared the corn by pounding it with a pestle in a large mortar; hence the name, which comes from the Spanish verb *majar*, to pound.

Think of this Venezuelan version of *majarete* as a cross between a sweet tamal enriched with freshly extracted coconut milk and *dulce de leche*. The principle is just the same. The corn is ground to a paste, then soaked in water, milk, or coconut milk to soften it. The resulting gruel is carefully strained to get rid of the indigestible skin, then thickened by slow cooking until it jells. As with *dulce de leche*, the secret is in long, slow cooking with patient stirring. The result is an addictive creamy dessert. The Cuban *majarete* is normally yellow because it is sweetened with white sugar. But Venezuelans prefer the brown loaf sugar called *papelón*, their distinctive flavorful version of the Latin American *panela*. It gives a caramel tan to everything it touches.

SERVES 8 TO 12

- 3 cups grated fresh coconut (from three 1½-pound coconuts; see page 50)
- 6 cups fresh corn kernels (from 6 medium ears) or frozen kernels
- 1 cup brown loaf sugar (preferably *panela* or *papelón*), broken into small pieces, or Demerara sugar
- ½ teaspoon salt, or to taste
- 3 tablespoons cornstarch
  Ground cinnamon, for garnish

▶ Following the instructions on pages 50 and 51, use the grated coconut to make about 1½ cups Creamy ("First") Coconut Milk (using 1 cup warm water) and 4 cups Light ("Second") Coconut Milk (using 4 cups warm water).

Working in batches, place the corn kernels in a food processor or blender with ½ cup warm water. Grind to a paste and pour into a large bowl. Add the light coconut milk and mix. Strain the mixture, either by pouring it into a fine-mesh sieve and pushing with the back of a spoon to extract as much cream from the corn as possible or by squeezing it through cheesecloth. You should have close to 3 quarts.

Pour the mixture into a large heavy pot, stir in the sugar and salt, and bring to a boil over medium-high heat. Lower the heat to medium and simmer for 5 minutes. Meanwhile, mix the cornstarch with the reserved creamy coconut milk. Reduce the heat to low, add the cornstarch mixture, and simmer, stirring constantly, for 1 hour, or until the mixture thickens.

Pour the custard onto a shallow serving platter and allow to cool until it springs back when gently touched. Sprinkle with ground cinnamon and serve. I like to eat *majarete* at room temperature, but if you like, chill it in the refrigerator before serving.

Serving: Traditionally, *majarete* is eaten as an unaccompanied custard, an idea that that is somewhat alien to most Americans. Serve in individual custard cups or perhaps in goblets, accompanied with a dollop of whipped, unsweetened heavy cream. If you want to impress your guests with something very different and delicious, try using *majarete* to fill *alfajores* (page 837) or a layer cake such as Splendid *Majarete* Rum Torte (page 846). It is divine!

Brazilian Pumpkin Cream

Doce de Abobora

In Brazilian markets, which brim with produce fresh from the fields, pumpkins (*abobora*) are a gorgeous sight. The vendors cut them open for everyone to see, and they look like great orange suns. A silky Brazilian pumpkin custard is my favorite stovetop dessert to follow a *feijoada completa* (page 512). You can make this while waiting for the beans or the cured meats of the *feijoada* to finish cooking. To approach the authentic flavor of the Brazilian *abobora*, use Caribbean *calabaza* or kabocha squash.

Cook's Note: For this dessert, Brazilians use either white sugar or their light brown sugar, *rapadura*, which is interchangeable with commercial Demerara light brown sugar. Corn syrup is a common ingredient in Brazil and is added to desserts such as this and the egg yolk and coconut cake *quindim de yayá* (page 841) to give them shine.

SERVES 6 TO 8

2 pounds Caribbean pumpkin (*calabaza*) or kabocha squash, peeled, seeded, and cut into 1-inch pieces

5 whole cloves

¾ cup grated light brown loaf sugar (preferably *panela*), Demerara sugar, or light brown sugar

1 cup grated fresh coconut (from one ¾-pound coconut; see page 50) or store-bought unsweetened grated coconut
Pinch of salt

2 tablespoons light corn syrup
Ground cinnamon, for garnish

▶ Place the squash in a large saucepan with 4 quarts water and the cloves and bring to a boil over medium heat. Reduce the heat to low and cook, covered, for 45 minutes to 1 hour. When the squash is very soft, remove the cloves, drain, and mash to a paste with a potato masher or puree in a food processor until smooth.

In a medium saucepan, mix the sugar, coconut, and salt. Add to the pumpkin and cook over medium heat, stirring constantly. When the mixture begins to look glossy, add the corn syrup. Continue stirring until the mixture separates cleanly from the sides and bottom of the pan. Pour into a serving bowl and dust with a little cinnamon.

Peruvian Creamy Custard Topped with Port Meringue

Suspiro de Limeña

This layered dessert joins together two Peruvian favorites, a creamy egg custard based on the concept of *dulce de leche* and a meringue flavored with port wine. It is never missing from a Lima restaurant menu, but it can't be found in classic Peruvian cookbooks like Francisca Baylon's *Cocina y repostería* (On Cooking and Baking), published in several editions in the late 1940s and 1950s. This supports those who believe the dessert was created not long ago by the poet José Gálvez to honor the good cooking of his wife, Amparo Ayarez—hence the poetic name of this inspired dessert, "the sigh of a Lima woman."

At restaurants, *suspiro* is usually served in individual cups, with a layer of custard topped with carefully piped meringue. I much prefer to serve it in a pretty bowl, as I saw Marissa Guiulfo do at her beach house in Pucusana, a small fishing village not far from Lima. Marissa is one of Lima's best-known caterers, a woman of enormous ability in the kitchen who is also blessed with exquisite taste. Her *suspiro* looked dramatic and opulent.

SERVES 6

One 14-ounce can sweetened condensed milk
Two 12-ounce cans evaporated milk
Pinch of salt
6 large egg yolks, lightly beaten
¾ cups sugar
¼ cup ruby port
4 large egg whites

▶ Place the milks and salt in a medium saucepan and bring to a boil over medium heat. Lower the heat and cook, uncovered, at a gentle simmer until the mixture is creamy and coats the back of a spoon, about 45 minutes. Lower the heat to the lowest setting, add the egg yolks gradually, whisking, and cook for about 5 minutes. The mixture will thicken to the consistency of a custard. Remove from the heat and let cool.

Place the sugar and port in a medium skillet over medium-high heat and cook until the syrup is bubbly, about 8 minutes (240°F on a candy thermometer). Meanwhile, place the egg whites in the bowl of a standing mixer and beat at medium speed until soft peaks form. Increase the speed to high and pour the syrup into the egg whites in a stream. Beat until the meringue is firm and glossy, about 5 minutes.

Pour the custard into six 4-ounce ramekins and smooth it out with a spatula. Pipe the meringue on top with a wide fluted tip.

Malbec Meringue with Walnuts

Turrón de Malbec

A typical dessert from the province of Salta, where Argentinean winemaker Susana Balbo lived and worked for many years, this *turrón* is not the crumbly solid nut and sugar confection we have come to associate with Spain but a stiff Italian meringue sweetened with *arrope*, a honeylike syrup resulting from cooking down the juice of red or white grapes. When I visited Susana's Mendoza winery and home in 2005, she and I had the choice of two wonderful *arropes* for this recipe, but we opted to make our own with one of her husband's wines, Ben Marco Malbec. We absolutely loved the intense garnet color and the slightly tart flavor that the thick wine syrup lent to the meringue. Susana served it in a soufflé dish, running a spatula over the slightly coarse meringue to form soft peaks before sprinkling it with walnut halves for crunchy texture.

I no longer had doubts that this meringue would be a good dessert for Americans after I watched Chris Granger, the photographer who accompanied me on that trip, asking for seconds and thirds. I now make it at my restaurant on a regular basis as the icing for our popular South American *milhojas* cake, a tower of alternating thin puff pasty disks baked in our wood-burning oven smeared with *dulce de leche* and crushed walnuts.

Cook's Notes: Susana started with a bottle of wine (750 ml) and boiled it down to about 1½ cups; only then did she add the sugar. Then she cooked the mixture into a heavy syrup. The syrup should not caramelize, because it will lose its stunning garnet color. It should stick to the spoon and seem almost (but not quite) ready to reach the soft-ball stage.

SERVES 8 TO 10

- 1 bottle (750ml) Argentinean Malbec, preferably Ben Marco Malbec
- 1¾ cups sugar
- 4 large egg whites (about ½ cup), at room temperature
  Pinch of salt
- ½ cup walnut halves, for garnish

▶ Pour the wine into a medium heavy pot, bring to a simmer over medium heat, and cook until it is reduced by 1½ cups. Stir in the sugar and continue simmering until the mixture is barely starting to go from thread to soft-ball stage, between 230°F and 233°F on a candy thermometer. Remove from the heat.

While the syrup cooks, beat the egg whites with the salt at medium-high speed until they stand in soft peaks. Add the hot wine syrup in a thin stream while beating at high speed. Reduce the speed to medium and continue beating for about 5 minutes.

Transfer the meringue to a decorative bowl, make soft peaks with a spatula, and sprinkle with walnuts before serving.

Serving: You can use this wine meringue as a frosting for cakes, a sauce for fruit pies, or a topping for ice cream. At my restaurant Cucharamama, we use it to frost our signature mille-feuille cake (*milhojas*) filled with dulce de leche.

FRUITS AND VEGETABLES COOKED IN SYRUP

The satisfying mouthfeel and rich aroma of many Latin custards can also be found in stovetop fruit desserts such as guava shells, bitter orange shells, and figs cooked in sugar syrup, as well as in guava paste. In Brazil, at the *tabuleiros*, the lace-covered traylike tables where Bahian women sell their street food, there are always sweets made with grated coconut cooked in white sugar or brown sugar syrups, called respectively *cocada branca* and *cocada preta*.

Milk is never far away, though. Because these desserts are so intensely sweet, they are usually paired with a sharp, salty fresh cheese or cream cheese. In the Hispanic Caribbean, marmalades, fruits in syrup, and guava paste might be spread on a salted cracker, which neutralizes the concentrated sweetness and rounds off the gustatory experience. The combination of guava paste and fresh cheese from Minas Gerais or creamy *catupiry* cheese is so ubiquitous and beloved in Brazil that Brazilians call it Romeu e Julieta (Romeo and Juliet)—a fitting name for a pair that belongs together.

Fruits in syrup are usually made in large quantities when fruits are in season, because they keep for a long time. In Granada, Nicaragua, on the shores of Lake Nicaragua (the largest lake in Central America), a typical Lenten dessert called *curbasa* or *almíbar* consists of five fruits—the plumlike *jocote*, papaya, cashew apple, mango, and *mamey*—all cooked separately with white sugar and served together alongside corn *rosquillas*, a doughnut-shaped cookie made with corn *masa*, and fresh cheese or cream cheese.

Fruits in Syrup with Cheese

The combination of fruit in syrup and cheese is a an eternal favorite because cooks know that when there is no time to prepare an elaborate dessert, guests are just as happy with two or three guava or papaya shells (homemade or from a jar) with a little cheese and crackers. All the desserts in this section are terrific as a complement to Latin and Spanish cheeses and beloved classics like Parmigiano-Reggiano, whose sharpness contrasts beautifully with the sweetness of the fruit. Among my favorites cheeses to eat with a dollop of coconut sweet or a slice of rosy papaya in syrup are aged Manchegos, the meltingly rich Torta del Casar from Extremadura in Spain, and the smoked Idiazábal from the Basque country. I also love the creamy fresh Ecuadorian cheeses made from cow's milk that have started coming to our markets.

For entertaining, I like to assemble at least three interesting cheeses with three or four kinds of fruit cooked in syrup and at least one type of marmalade served in a pretty bowl, as well as slabs of guava or quince paste and a variety of Latin breads. I particularly like Cuban crackers, soft-crusted Cuban Bread (page 591), and even Yuca Bread (page 573). Cuban crackers are round and thick and come in different sizes. Their mealy texture and breadlike light saltiness is a perfect foil for the sweetness of the fruit and the sharpness of the cheese.

In a pinch, I don't hesitate to serve some of the excellent jarred fruits in syrup and marmalades available in Latin markets. Among my favorite are guava shells in syrup and Colombian *desamargados*, a combination of fruits that usually includes figs and half limes. I also like tamarillos (*tomates de árbol*) in syrup from Ecuador and the luscious papayas from

Chile (*Carica pubescens*). These do not have the soft, pulpy flesh of the Carica papaya but are rather firm and chewy. A good rule of thumb to follow when using store-bought fruits in syrup from Latin America is to add some lemon or lime juice to cut the sweetness.

Latin marmalades are a welcome departure from the traditional choices in U.S. markets. They are lovely with bread and cheese, and the guava preserve in particular is a terrific condiment for roast pork or grilled chicken or as the base for sweet-and-sour marinades.

In recent years, fruit preserves from Chile and Argentina have started to show up in the United States. Distribution is still limited to some key markets, like Miami, but you can obtain them through mail-order sources. Among my favorites are preserves made in southern Chile, a land where German immigrants have left their mark on the making of sweets.

Coconut and Pineapple in Syrup

Dulce de Coco y Piña

Wherever coconuts grow in Latin America, traditional cooks make simple desserts with the grated meat, sweetened and flavored with unrefined brown sugar or white sugar and just a touch of lime zest. In many countries, people eat these sticky sweets with soda crackers and salty fresh cheese to tone down their sweetness. I love their unmistakably coconuty character and earthy molasses flavor, but they are often too sweet for people who are not used to them.

This recipe reduces the sugar considerably, but not to the point of changing the texture of the dish radically. I tone down the sweetness by mixing the coconut with the acidic pineapple. Traditional coconut desserts sometimes swim in syrup; mine is moist but not drenched in syrup. If storing in the refrigerator, stir to moisten evenly, because the syrup sinks to the bottom of the container.

MAKES 8 CUPS

- 1 ripe pineapple (about 2¾ pounds), peeled
- 4 cups grated fresh coconut (from two 1½-pound coconuts; see page 50) or store-bought unsweetened grated coconut
- 1½ pounds grated light brown loaf sugar (preferably *panela* or *piloncillo*), Demerara sugar, or light brown sugar
- 2 cups water
  Grated zest of 1 lime
- 2 Ceylon cinnamon sticks (*canela*)

▶ Cut the pineapple into thick wedges, discarding the core, and shred into a bowl on the coarse side of a box grater. You should have about 3 cups. Add the coconut to the bowl.

Place the sugar in a medium heavy saucepan with the water, lime zest, and cinnamon sticks and cook over medium heat, stirring to dissolve the sugar. Cook for 5 to 10 minutes, until the syrup is slightly thickened. Add the grated pineapple and the coconut and let simmer gently over medium-low heat, uncovered, stirring frequently, for 15 minutes longer. Cool to room temperature and refrigerate.

Serving: Serve as a topping for ice creams or combined with cream cheese to fill layer cakes and sweet empanadas.

Coconut in Syrup in the Style of Bahia

Cocada Branca

Lush coconut palms grow abundantly all along the coast of the state of Bahia in the northeast of Brazil, framing sandy beaches and lining the shores of dark rivers that flow into the sea. Their fruit, hanging in luscious clusters from street vendors' carts and piled high in every market, is the foundation of Bahia's coastal cuisine. The coconut's sweet aroma and nutty nuances permeate most foods, from savories to sweets, like a banner of identity.

The tall *coqueiro-da-Bahia* (Bahian coconut), which bears green fruit, has been there at least since the sixteenth century, and may have arrived with the Portuguese by way of the Cape Verde Islands. (Some scientists even postulate it is a Bahian native.) It was the Portuguese who gave it the name *coco*, inspired, it's said, by the "eyes," which make the husked nut look like the face of a monkey (*coco*). Indigenous Brazilians mostly used the coconut at its green stage. It was the Africans, brought by the thousands to work as slaves in Bahia's cities and sugarcane fields, who fully explored its myriad possibilities.

By about six months of age, the coconut is filled with a sweet, thirst-slaking liquid and has a gelatinous meat that is good to eat with a spoon. Bahians hack off the young green fruit's fibrous top with a machete to turn it into an edible cup. When the coconut is fully mature, at about one year, the meat is thick and fatty, ready for cooking. At this stage, one of the "eyes" is punctured, the liquid is poured out, the shell is cracked with a machete or mallet, and the meat is grated or processed into coconut milk.

Grated coconut, fresh or packaged, is added to refined desserts of Portuguese origin like *quindim de yayá* (see page 841) and cooked in white or brown sugar syrups to make simple, rustic sweets called *cocadas*, like the one here. At the frilly, lace-covered tables of Bahian vendors selling *acarajés* (black-eyed pea fritters), you will always find plates of both *cocada branca* and its dark sibling, *cocada preta*, the former made with white sugar and the latter with Brazilian brown loaf sugar.

SERVES 8

- 4 cups sugar (about 1½ pounds)
- 1½ quarts water
- 4 whole cloves
- 2 Ceylon cinnamon sticks (*canela*)
- 4 cups grated fresh coconut (from two 1½-pound coconuts; see page 50) or store-bought unsweetened grated coconut

▶ Combine the sugar, water, cloves, and cinnamon in a medium saucepan and bring to a boil over medium-low heat. Add the coconut and continue cooking until thick, like a chunky marmalade. Remove the cinnamon and cloves and let cool at room temperature. Store in the refrigerator, covered with plastic wrap.

Serving: Serve as a topping for ice cream or to accompany sponge cake or simple custards.

Ecuadorian Squash in *Aguardiente*-Spiked Dark Syrup

Limeño con Miel de Panela y Zhumir

In many parts of Latin America, squashes are cooked in brown loaf sugar syrup until they caramelize without falling apart as might be expected with prolonged cooking. In parts of Mexico with a sugar-cane culture, such as Oaxaca and Michoacán and the Yucatán, this is a way of preserving the vegetable. Cooks soak squashes and fruits such as peaches in lime or ash water, cook them slowly in a molasses bath, and then set them out to dry until firm.

This Ecuadorian recipe for the large, meaty winter squash known as *limeño* is much simpler and produces lovely firm squash slices that can be eaten with their skin on. (In this country I use a whole kabocha squash.) Serving the squash with a ripened Central American cream is my own idea. The cream plays beautifully against the earthy molasses flavor of the brown loaf sugar.

Cook's Note: In Mexico, for the Days of the Dead feast, cooks soak squash in lime water and then cook it for 2 days with a mixture of Mexican brown loaf sugar, cinnamon, and fig leaves. In the Yucatán, cooks make holes in the squash and plunge it into the last cauldron of molten molasses in a traditional sugar mill (*tacha*) to make *calabaza en tacha*.

SERVES 6 TO 8

1 kabocha squash (about 3 pounds)
3 Ceylon cinnamon sticks (*canela*)
5 whole cloves
4 allspice berries
¼ cup *aguardiente*, preferably Zhumir (see Cook's Notes, page 457)
1½ pounds grated brown loaf sugar (*panela* or *piloncillo*), Muscovado sugar, or dark brown sugar
½ cup Central American Ripened Cream (page 147), plain sour cream, or crème fraîche, for garnish

▶ Cut the squash in half, scoop out the seeds, and cut the squash into 2-inch-wide slices. Arrange skin side down in a heavy pot wide enough to hold the slices in one layer. Cover with about 1½ quarts water, add the remaining ingredients, and bring to a boil over high heat. Reduce the heat to medium-low and simmer, covered, until the squash is tender yet firm, about 2 hours. You will be left with a syrupy sauce. Remove the spices. Serve with a dollop of *crema* for a sweet-and-sour contrast.

Zambo Squash and *Naranjilla* Dessert

Dulce de Zambo y Naranjilla

Naranjilla

Naranjilla (also known as *lulo* in Colombia) is a deeply perfumed Amazonian fruit (*Solanum quitoense*) with a tart flavor and subtle bitter aftertaste. Its tart edge mellows when you blend it with brown loaf sugar, and they both play to the herbal freshness of the squash and make it shine.

Zambo, available in the freezer section of many Latin supermarkets, has long filaments like the unrelated spaghetti squash. This is one of the more interesting and straightforward recipes for *zambo* I have found.

SERVES 4 TO 6

    3 pounds frozen *zambo*
One 14-ounce package frozen *naranjilla* juice or 2
        pounds frozen *naranjillas* (about 8 large fruits),
        thawed
    3 cups water
    1 pound light brown loaf sugar (preferably *panela*),
        grated or broken up, Demerara sugar, or light
        brown sugar
    2 Ceylon cinnamon sticks (*canela*)
    2 star anise pods
        Pinch of salt

▶ Peel the *zambo* and trim away the large seeds. Cut into thin slices.

If using whole *naranjillas*, peel by making a small cross on the bottom of the fruit and squeezing firmly from the other end over a small bowl. The pulp should pop out in one big piece. Place in a food processor or blender with 1 cup water and puree. Work the pulp through a fine-mesh sieve. The frozen juice needs no pureeing.

Place the sugar in a medium saucepan with the remaining 2 cups water, cinnamon sticks, star anise, and salt, and stir to dissolve over medium heat. Add the *naranjilla* juice and *zambo*, lower the heat to medium-low, and cook, stirring occasionally, until the *zambo* begins to break down into filaments. Push down with the back of a wooden spoon to accelerate this process. Simmer until the mixture is somewhat thickened and you can see the bottom of the pot as you stir, about 30 minutes.

Serving: In Ecuador, this dessert is served by itself in small bowls. I like to pair it with *queso blanco* and salty crackers or serve it over ice cream or as a filling for empanadas and pies. A dollop of this sweet to accompany Yuca Coconut Cake from Goias (page 848) or a simple Latin sponge cake (pages 842 and 843) is marvelous.

Guatemalan Stuffed Chayotes
Chancletas

In Guatemala, chayotes are called *güisquiles* and find numerous uses in the country's varied regional cuisines. Their tender flesh absorbs flavors beautifully in savory dishes like braises and stews and their subtle sweetness and herbal notes flourish in desserts like *chancletas*. Cooks boil the chayotes until tender, cut them in half, and scoop out the greenish ivory flesh to leave a natural shell for a sweet stuffing made by mashing the flesh and combining it with ingredients you might find in an aromatic bread pudding. Golden and luscious after baking, these sweet *chancletas* are delicious. But when I first tasted them and heard their name, I had to laugh. In Cuba, *chancletas* are inexpensive flip-flop sandals with a wooden sole and and a single black rubber strap. (I owned several pairs of those.) The loud *click-clack* sound the women make when walking the streets with them is the stuff of song and comedy, and women who are loud and brash are called "*chan-*

cleteras." So imagine my amusement to find such a delicate dish called *chancletas* in Guatemala. They are a refined treat, but they do look like *chancletas*.

SERVES 6

- 6 green or white chayotes
- 3 ounces dark raisins
- 1 ounce slivered almonds
- 6 egg yolks
- ¼ cup sweet sherry, preferably oloroso
- 2 teaspoons ground cinnamon
- 6 tablespoons sugar
    Pinch of salt, or to taste
- 2 sweet buns or 2 Garífuna Coconut Bread rolls (page 593), broken into crumbs, or ½ cup grated fresh coconut
- 4 tablespoons (½ stick) butter, cut into thick pats

▶ Rinse the chayotes and place in a saucepan with 2 quarts water. Bring to a boil and cook until tender, about 30 minutes. Drain the chayotes and cut lengthwise in half. With a spoon, scoop out the seeds and flesh, leaving a thin layer of flesh next to the skin (about ¼ inch). Discard the seeds and set aside the flesh and shells.

Preheat the oven to 350°F.

In a mixing bowl, mash the chayote flesh with a wooden spoon. Add the raisins, almonds, egg yolks, sherry, cinnamon, sugar, and salt. Mix to combine thoroughly. Fill the chayote shells with the mixture and top with the bread crumbs or grated coconut and the butter. Place the stuffed chayotes on a baking sheet, place on the middle rack of the oven, and bake until golden, about 30 minutes. Serve warm or at room temperature.

Colombian-Style Fresh Cheese with Brown Loaf Syrup

Cuajada con Melao de Panela

Thick slices of tender fresh cheese (*cuajada*) bathed in a thick syrup made with flavorful *panela* are a favorite dessert in the province of Cundinamarca in Colombia. Most people in Cundinamarca, and also in Costa Rica, where this dish is called *dulce de quesillo*, cook the cheese slices in boiling salted water. They then drain the cheese and bake it, covered with the syrup (*melao* in Colombia, *melado* elsewhere). This method, I think, destroys the cheese's natural freshness and light airy texture, turning it into something chewy and gummy. I like it fresh, lightly salted, and at room temperature. I just drizzle it with the hot syrup.

SERVES 6

- 2 cups Fragrant Brown Loaf Sugar Syrup (page 806)
- 1 pound Latin American–style fresh cow's-milk cheese, preferably homemade *cuajada* (page 104), cut into ½-inch slices

▶ Place the syrup in a saucepan over medium heat and heat until it is not quite simmering. Arrange the cheese on a serving platter and drizzle with the hot syrup. Serve immediately, with toasted bread or sweet rolls.

Tamarillos in Syrup Ecuadorian Style

Dulce de Ratones Ecuatorianos

These Ecuadorian *ratones* (mice), as people call them, are not rodents but tamarillos, which people cook in rich syrups with their stems attached so they resemble little mice. I prefer them to pears cooked in the same fashion. The egg-shaped fruits are tender and bittersweet, their curly stems a pleasure to behold and a good thing to hold if you decide to forgo the spoon or the fork.

Cook's Note: Tamarillos sometimes have bitter skins. Ecuadorians always blanch them in water and then peel them before proceeding with recipes.

SERVES 6

    12 red or yellow tamarillos, fresh or frozen
        (about 2¼ pounds)
     3 cups water
     1 cup sugar
     2 Ceylon cinnamon sticks (*canela*)
     3 star anise pods
     1 teaspoon anise seeds
     ½ teaspoon ground cloves
        Mint leaves, for garnish

▶ Place the tamarillos in a medium pot with 2½ quarts water, bring to a boil over medium heat, and cook for 10 minutes. Lift out from the water with a slotted spoon, and when they are cool enough to handle, peel them, keeping their stems (those are the mice's tails).

Mix the 3 cups water with the sugar and spices in a 6-quart pot, bring to a boil over medium heat, and simmer for 10 minutes. Add the tamarillos, lower the heat, and cook for 10 minutes. Cool and serve the fruits with some of the syrup, garnished with the mint leaves.

Cuban-Style Guava Shells in Syrup

Cascos de Guayaba

These are a favorite sweet throughout tropical America, particularly in the Hispanic Caribbean and Brazil. Though people who own guava trees have always made them in abundance, canned brands have existed for as long as I remember. They come in handy, because fresh guavas are hard to come by here in the United States. When I find them, however, I love to make these sweets. Guava has a most complex aroma, a floral scent that lingers in the air hours after cooking.

My cousin Elsita, who lives in Miami, has an eccentric guava tree that produces a mixture of very large and very small fruits. Every year in August and September, she collects hundreds of fruits, which she cooks in many ways. She makes jelly from the peels, marmalade from the pulp, and guava shells—everyone's favorite. This is her recipe.

SERVES 4

     6 ripe large guavas (about 7 ounces each)
     2 quarts water
     2 cups sugar
     1 Ceylon cinnamon stick (*canela*)
     2 teaspoons fresh lime juice
        Peel of 1 lime

► Peel the guavas, taking care not to leave sections of green skin. Cut each guava in half and scoop out the pulp. Reserve for another use.

Place the guava shells in a 3-quart pot with the water and bring to a boil over high heat. Reduce the heat to medium and simmer, covered, until the shells are soft but firm, about 45 minutes. Stir in the rest of the ingredients and simmer over low heat for about 1 hour and 15 minutes. Let cool to room temperature and pour into a serving bowl.

Serving: Serve with cream cheese or 2 or 3 slices of fresh *queso blanco*, manchego, or Parmigiano-Reggiano, and Cuban crackers.

Rosy Half-Ripe Papayas in Syrup

Dulce de Papaya Pintona de Amparo

On my first visit to the Boater's Grill, a restaurant in Cape Florida State Park in Key Biscayne, owner David González offered me a taste of this traditional Cuban dessert. Used to green papayas prepared in this fashion, I was enthralled by the unusual deep rosy hue (like sunrise over Cape Florida's lighthouse). David's mother-in-law, Amparo Rojas, a native of Pinar del Río, the westernmost region of Cuba, makes the restaurant's desserts and cooks the ripe papayas in more than their weight of sugar, without water or spices. The amount of sugar in this recipe might seem excessive, but it is needed to candy the papaya to a firm consistency.

Candied fruits should be eaten in small quantities, almost as a seasoning for salty crackers and a tangy

piece of *queso blanco*, another fresh cow's-milk cheese, or Philadelphia cream cheese—a true Latin favorite.

Cook's Note: Robert Wolke, a food scientist and author of *What Einstein Told His Cook*, explains that the concentrated syrup, which boils at a higher temperature than water, dehydrates the fruit, lending it a chewy bite and inhibiting bacterial growth.

SERVES ABOUT 12

4 pounds half-ripe or ripe papayas (1–2 papayas), peeled and seeded
9 cups sugar

► Cut each papaya into 4 to 6 long slices, then cut crosswise at an angle into 1½- to 2-inch pieces. Place in a large, heavy pot with the sugar and set the pot over very low heat, uncovered. Do not stir or disturb the sugar. At first it will seem as if nothing is going on, but after 30 minutes, you will see that the sugar touching the fruit has begun to melt into a simmering syrup. Over low heat, the fruit will be ready in about 2 ½ hours. (Once the sugar has completely dissolved, you can raise the heat to medium and accelerate the cooking; the fruit will be done in about another hour.) To test for doneness, remove a piece of fruit and let it cool to the touch. If the syrup sticks lightly to your fingers and the fruit is lightly firm to the touch, it is ready.

Remove the pan from the heat and let it cool to room temperature. Transfer to a bowl or glass jars and refrigerate, tightly covered. It will keep well for several weeks.

Serving: Serve with slices of *queso blanco*, cream cheese, farm Gouda, or chunks of Parmigiano-Reggiano.

Peruvian Purple Corn and Fruit Compote

Mazamorra Morada

Purple corn is the ingredient for two beloved Peruvian classics, the drink *chicha morada* (page 338) and a compote flavored with diced fruits, called *mazamorra morada*. I love them both and have found that *chicha* makes the perfect base for the dessert. This compote is deep purple, studded with fruit and scented with cinnamon and cloves.

Peruvians dust the compote with ground cinnamon and pair it with rice pudding for a contrast of colors and flavors. And that's the way I presented it in 2009 when I was invited to cook for Fiesta Latina, a lavish reception for 400 guests at the White House. I also like to serve the *mazamorra* as a side dish with Roast Turkey in Andean Pepper and Pisco *Adobo* (page 679). It is as delicious as cranberry sauce.

MAKES 8 CUPS

- 1 recipe Peruvian Purple Corn Punch (page 338; about 7½ cups)
- 1 cup dried pitted cherries (or dried cranberries)
- ½ cup pitted prunes (about 3 ounces), cut in half
- ¾ cup dried apricots (about 3 ounces), cut in half
- 1 piece fresh pineapple (about 9 ounces), cut into ¼-inch dice (about 2 cups)
- 1 medium red apple, cored, peeled, and cut into ¼-inch dice
- 1 medium Bartlett pear, peeled and cut into ¼-inch dice
- ⅓ cup Peruvian sweet potato starch (*harina de camote*) or cornstarch
- ⅓ cup water

▶ Place the purple corn punch in an 8-quart pot and bring to a boil over medium heat. Add the fruits and simmer over low heat until they are soft, about 30 minutes.

Dissolve the sweet potato starch or cornstarch in the water and stir to mix. Stir into the fruit mixture and simmer, stirring, until the mixture thickens into a light compote.

Pour the compote into a large bowl and let cool to room temperature. Cover with plastic wrap and chill until ready to serve.

Serving: Serve in small bowls or margarita glasses dusted with some cinnamon as a dessert, or as a sweet side for sponge cake or vanilla flan. Or serve with rice pudding: Place a layer of rice pudding at the bottom of a margarita or martini glass, top with *mazamorra morada*, and dust lightly with cinnamon.

FLANS AND PUDDINGS

Zafra's Hispanic Caribbean Flan

Flan o Quesillo de Zafra

When you are ready to sink your spoon into a slice of golden Hispanic Caribbean flan, stop for a moment and reprogram your mind and your taste buds. What you are about to taste is not a quivering, shivering, melt-in-the mouth crème caramel but a densely creamy dessert. In some countries, like the Dominican Republic and Venezuela, flan is called *quesillo*, an old Spanish word that translates as "little cheesecake."

The use of a vanilla bean is my own contribution to the classic flan recipe; most versions call for vanilla extract. What is traditional here is the use of evaporated and condensed milk. From Cuba to Venezuela, people like their flans creamy and dense, and that texture comes straight from a can.

I first ate flan enriched with canned condensed milk as a child at my aunt Eve Espinosa's house in Santiago de Cuba. I cleaned my plate and asked for seconds. I remember the occasion clearly because it was the first time I had asked for a recipe. I immediately made a mental note of the canned milk. Tía Eve's flan seemed creamier than the airy vanilla flan I had always enjoyed at the home of my maternal aunts. By the time I got my own kitchen years later, I was hooked on the creamy taste condensed milk gives to flan, but I enrich it further by steeping the milk with aromatic spices such as star anise, cinnamon, and vanilla bean, along with lime peel. This is probably the most popular dessert we serve at Zafra.

Cook's Note: Timing is of the essence when baking a creamy flan. Do not wait for the flan to be completely springy to the touch, because it will continue cooking after you take it out of the oven.

SERVES 8

- 1 cup sugar
- ¼ cup water
- ⅓ cup whole milk
- Two 12-ounce cans evaporated milk
- 1 vanilla bean or 1 teaspoon vanilla extract
- 1 Ceylon cinnamon stick (*canela*)
- 6 star anise pods
- Peel of 1 lime, cut into long strips
- 6 large egg yolks
- 2 whole eggs
- One 14-ounce can sweetened condensed milk
- Fresh mint, for garnish

▶ Have ready a baking pan at least 3 inches deep that is large enough to hold the flan mold comfortably.

Place the sugar and water in a small heavy saucepan, bring to a boil over medium-high heat, and cook until the liquid turns a light caramel color, carefully swirling the pan every few minutes to avoid crystallization, about 8 minutes. Pour the caramel into a mold, either a 9-by-2-inch round cake pan or an 8-by 4-inch loaf pan, and swirl to coat the bottom and sides. Let cool.

Place the whole milk and evaporated milk in a medium saucepan. Split the vanilla bean in half lengthwise, scrape the black seeds into the milk, and add the bean; or add the vanilla extract. Add the cinnamon, star anise, and lime peel and bring the milk barely to a boil over medium-high heat. Lower the heat and simmer gently for 2 to 3 minutes, then remove from the heat. Strain and discard the solids. Cover with plastic wrap and let cool.

Preheat the oven to 350°F. Place the egg yolks and whole eggs in a large mixing bowl and beat with a wire whisk while adding the condensed milk. Add the cooled steeped milk and stir gently until all the ingredients are well incorporated. Place the baking pan on the middle oven rack. Set the mold in the baking pan and pour in enough hot water to come halfway up the sides. Bake until just set, 1 hour to 1 hour and 10 minutes. Remove from the oven and let cool to room temperature. Chill in the refrigerator, in the pan, for at least 3 hours before serving. Unmold onto a decorative platter and garnish with sprigs of fresh mint.

Valencia Orange and Cheese Flan with Orange Rum Sauce

Flan de Queso y Naranja con Salsa de Naranja y Ron

This is a seductive flan with the texture of a creamy cheesecake and the aroma of fresh oranges and orange blossoms. I once made it for a friend who liked it so much I decided to serve it at my restaurants. The key flavoring is Venezuelan Santa Teresa Rhum Orange, an artful orange rum liqueur that gives the dessert flavor and depth. You can use other orange liqueurs, such as Cointreau or Grand Marnier, but try adding a tablespoon or two of a good aged rum as well. It does wonders for the flavor.

SERVES 8

2	cups sugar
¼	cup water
⅓	cup whole milk
Two	12-ounce cans evaporated milk
1	vanilla bean or 1 teaspoon vanilla extract
3	Ceylon cinnamon sticks (*canela*)
6	star anise pods
	Peel of ½ orange, cut into long strips
8	ounces cream cheese, preferably Philadelphia brand, softened
6	large egg yolks
2	whole eggs
One	14-ounce can sweetened condensed milk
½	cup orange-flavored liqueur, preferably Santa Teresa Rhum Orange or Cointreau
1	tablespoon orange blossom water
4	cups fresh orange juice (from 12–14 medium oranges)
	Peel of ½ orange, cut into thin slivers
	Orange slices, for garnish

▶ Have ready a baking pan at least 3 inches deep that is large enough to hold the flan mold comfortably.

Place 1 cup sugar and the water in a small heavy saucepan, bring to a boil over medium heat, and cook until the liquid turns a light caramel color. To avoid crystallization, do not stir, and brush the sides of the pan frequently with a pastry brush dipped in ice water. Pour into a mold, either a 9-by-2-inch round cake pan or an 8-by-4-inch loaf pan, and swirl at once to coat the bottom and sides. Let cool.

Place the whole milk and evaporated milk in a medium saucepan. Split the vanilla bean in half lengthwise, scrape the black seeds into the milk, and add the bean; or add the vanilla extract. Add the cinnamon, star anise, and orange peel and bring the milk barely to a boil over medium-high heat. Lower the heat and simmer gently for 2 to 3 minutes, then remove from the heat and let cool. Strain and discard the solids.

Preheat the oven to 350°F. Place the cream cheese, egg yolks, and eggs in a large mixing bowl and beat with a wooden spoon while adding the condensed milk until smooth and well integrated. Add the cooled steeped milk, ¼ cup liqueur, and the orange blossom water and stir gently until all the ingredients are well incorporated. Strain the mixture through a fine-mesh sieve into the caramelized mold. Place the baking pan on the middle oven rack. Set the mold in the baking pan and pour in enough hot water to come halfway up the sides. Bake until just until set, 1 hour to 1 hour and 10 minutes. Remove from the oven and let cool to room temperature.

While the flan is cooling, place the orange juice, the remaining 1 cup sugar, and the slivered orange peel in a medium saucepan and bring to a boil over medium heat. Lower the heat and simmer, uncovered, until the mixture is reduced almost by half. Stir in the remaining ¼ cup liqueur and continue simmering for 10 to 15 minutes, until the sauce coats the back of a spoon. Remove from the heat and let cool to room temperature on a wire rack. Refrigerate until ready to use.

Chill the flan in the refrigerator, in the pan, for at least 3 hours before serving. Unmold onto a decorative platter and garnish with orange slices. Pour the sauce into a decorative bowl and bring to the table with the flan.

Chocolate Flan

Flan de Chocolate

I have a passion for chocolate. But I must have an old soul lurking inside me. What makes my heart pound are not shiny towers of chocolate but sensuous chocolate drinks and stovetop desserts where chocolate is flavored with the same Old World spices that once made hot chocolate into the rage for polite society in Spain. This is one of my favorite creations, a richly spiced chocolate flan that I can imagine delighting the women who loved chocolate in the eighteenth century.

SERVES 8 TO 10

1½	cups sugar
¼	cup water
3	cups whole milk
1	14-ounce can sweetened condensed milk
¼	cup dark aged rum, preferably Bacardi or Guatemalan Zapata
4	star anise pods
5	cassia cinnamon sticks or 3 Ceylon cinnamon sticks (*canela*)
15–20	allspice berries
1	teaspoon anise seeds
1	teaspoon vanilla extract
4	cloves
	Pinch of salt
1	dried *chile de árbol*
8	ounces dark chocolate, preferably between 58 and 65% cacao (such as El Rey Bucare or Pacari Manabí), coarsely chopped
4	large egg yolks
2	whole eggs

▶ Have ready a baking pan at least 3 inches deep that is large enough to hold the flan mold comfortably.

Place 1 cup sugar and the water in a small heavy saucepan, bring to a boil over medium-high heat, and cook until the liquid turns a light caramel color, carefully swirling the pan every few minutes to avoid crystallization, about 8 minutes. Pour into a mold (a 9-by-2-inch round cake pan) and swirl at once to coat the bottom. Let cool.

Preheat the oven to 350°F. Place the whole milk and condensed milk in a saucepan with the rum, the remaining ½ cup sugar, and all the seasonings and bring barely to a boil over medium-high heat. Lower the heat and simmer gently for 2 to 3 minutes. Strain into a large bowl, add the chopped chocolate, and whisk to melt and blend. Cover with plastic wrap and let cool.

Place the egg yolks and eggs in a large mixing bowl and beat with a wire whisk. Pour the cooled chocolate mixture into the eggs and whisk to blend. Place the baking pan on the middle oven rack. Set the mold in the baking pan and pour in enough hot water to come halfway up the sides. Bake until just set, 1 hour to 1 hour and 10 minutes. Remove from the oven and let cool to room temperature on a wire rack. Chill in the refrigerator, in the pan, for at least 3 hours before serving. Unmold onto a decorative platter.

HOW *MAMEY* FOUND A HOME IN FLORIDA

A gigantic old *mamey* tree stands in Donald Pantín's lush one-acre backyard in Pinecrest, near Miami. From massive branches that shoot straight out, looking for the sun, grow football-shaped fruits with leathery skin the texture and color of sandpaper. Nothing about the stark exterior of the fruit prepares you for what is revealed when you cut one open: a long black seed, shiny as onyx, nestled in a custardy pulp the vivid color of wild salmon.

Miraculously, this tree has withstood the ravages of time, seasonal storms, and even Hurricane Andrew. The family calls it La Mamá, for this is literally the mother of the sweet and aromatic Pantín *mamey*, one of the tastiest tropical fruits today in Florida markets.

La Mamá is a relic of the time when Donald's father, Eugenio Pantín, born in La Coruña, Galicia, in Spain, began experimenting with tropical fruits on his five-acre farm in the Redlands, the tropical area south of Miami. Donald recalls how his father, a retired electrician newly arrived from Chicago, became a gentleman farmer with a passion for New World fruit trees of the Sapotaceae family—*mamey*, *sapodilla*, *canistel*, and *caimito*. Through trial and error, Eugenio mastered the technique of grafting, the only way to breed most fruit trees.

In the 1950s, a Cuban émigré named Josefina Jiménez gave Eugenio three *mamey* seeds she had smuggled into the United States in her brassiere. He planted the seeds and used the seedlings as rootstock to graft budwood from an old, proven *mamey* tree that grew near a fire station in Key West. The one survivor of Eugenio's experiment is the 60-foot tree that towers over Donald Pantín's sprawling ranch house. It was planted in 1953, the same year as Fidel Castro's attack on the Moncada barracks in Santiago de Cuba, the symbolic beginning of the revolution that would ultimately create an insatiable desire for *mamey* among the Cubans who fled to south Florida.

Because of the outstanding quality of La Mamá's fruit—a sweet, aromatic pulp with a bright salmon-red color and little fiber—the tree became the parent stock for Eugenio's *mamey* grove. Soon news of his superior fruit spread among connoisseurs, who came to know it as the "Key West *mamey*." Exiled Cubans longed for a steady supply of *mamey* and were willing to buy it at any price. (I remember paying $5 a pound in the 1980s.) Recognizing this eager market, Redland farmers rushed to grow the fruit. The intense demand led to such frequent thefts that many groves were protected with barbed wire and watchdogs, as if the trees held golden nuggets.

Mamey sapote with seed

It was in 1988, at the height of *mamey* fever, that I met Donald Pantín and his wife, Sara. Of course I was shown the majestic parent tree. "She is the mother of every single Pantín *mamey* grown in Florida," Donald said proudly. Today, 95 percent of the *mamey* grown on the 350 acres devoted to its cultivation in south Florida is the Pantín cultivar, in season from July through October. The rest includes such varieties as Pace, El Viejo, and the large Salvadorian Magaña, which come in season at different times of the year, creating an almost uninterrupted supply. ◆

Pantín *Mamey* Flan

Flan de Mamey Pantín

A single slice of perfectly ripe Pantín *mamey* from Florida is a luxury that I don't hesitate to serve as dessert at any elegant dinner. This delicate flan is another wonderful way to showcase the fruit's custardy pulp and musky aroma. I created it years ago and now serve it at Zafra when *mamey* is in season. The Pantín is ideal because it has little fiber, but I still strain the custard to be sure the flan is totally smooth.

The key to this flan is subtlety—even the caramel needs to be light. Vanilla (preferably the fresh bean), soft-quill Ceylon cinnamon (*canela*), and grated *mamey* seed enhance the aromatic quality of the fruit. (Crack open the hard outer shell of the seed with a mallet and grate the fleshy interior, which tastes like bitter almonds.)

This flan is also the perfect base for ice cream. Simply stir it or puree it in a blender after it has cooled and freeze it in an ice cream maker according to the manufacturer's instructions.

Cook's Note: *Mamey* usually comes to market as hard as a rock. To speed ripening, place it in a brown bag with bananas or apples at room temperature for a few days. When ripe, it will yield to the touch. If using half a *mamey*, cover the rest with plastic wrap and store it in the refrigerator.

SERVES 8

1 cup whole milk
One 12-ounce can evaporated milk
1 vanilla bean or 1 teaspoon vanilla extract
3 Ceylon cinnamon sticks (*canela*)
¼ *mamey* seed, grated, or ¼ teaspoon almond extract (see headnote)
About 3 cups fresh *mamey* pulp (from a 2- to 2½-pound ripe Pantín *mamey*) or two 14-ounce packages frozen pulp, thawed
4 large egg yolks
4 large eggs
One 14-ounce can sweetened condensed milk
1 cup sugar
½ cup water

▶ Place the whole milk and evaporated milk in a 3-quart saucepan. Split the vanilla bean in half lengthwise, scrape the seeds into the pan, and add the bean; or add the vanilla extract. Add the cinnamon and grated *mamey* seed or almond extract and barely bring to a boil over medium-high heat, stirring occasionally. Lower the heat to medium-low and simmer for about 5 minutes. Remove from the heat and let cool. Strain through an extra-fine-mesh sieve and set aside. If using fresh *mamey* pulp, place in a blender with 1 cup of the cooked milk mixture and process to a smooth puree.

Whisk together the egg yolks, whole eggs, and condensed milk in a large mixing bowl. Stir in the cooked mixture and the pureed fresh *mamey* or thawed *mamey* pulp. With a wooden spoon, push the mixture through an extra-fine-mesh sieve into a bowl. Set aside.

Preheat the oven to 350°F. Have ready a 9-inch round cake pan to serve as a mold, plus a baking pan at least 3 inches deep that is large enough to hold the other pan comfortably.

Place the sugar and water in a small saucepan and bring to a boil over medium-high heat, and cook until the liquid turns a light caramel color, carefully swirling the pan every few minutes to avoid crystallization, about 8 minutes. Working quickly, pour the caramel into the mold, tilting it to coat the interior evenly.

Place the baking pan on the middle oven rack. Set the mold in the pan and pour in enough hot water to come not quite halfway up the side. Bake for about 1 hour and 15 minutes. When done, the flan should feel a bit wiggly and soft to the touch, not at all dry or firm. Let it cool to room temperature on a wire rack. Refrigerate, covered with plastic wrap, for at least 3 hours before unmolding. To serve, cut into wedges and spoon some of the caramel over the flan.

Squash Bread Pudding with Prunes and Pisco

Pudín de Pan y Calabaza con Ciruelas y Pisco

Bread pudding spells comfort in any language. It is sustenance turned into luxury and a terrific dessert for large parties or holidays. My only rule of thumb when making bread pudding is to choose ingredients that evoke hominess and a feeling of well-being, and squash fills this job description perfectly. For Latins, squash is a staple plant, a year-round treat. In the Andean region, the type called *zapallo* is popular. Here in the United States, kabocha and butternut squash are good substitutes. This is a generous recipe that serves twelve or more, ideal for a buffet party, Christmas, or Thanksgiving. You can cut the recipe in half and bake it in an 8-by-8-inch pan. This pudding has a very custardy texture.

Cook's Note: Many Peruvian pisco brands are available in the United States I like *pisco italia* because it is very aromatic, but Ocucaje, Tacama, Barsol, Biondi, and Tabernero are also good.

Working Ahead ▶ The pudding can be made 1 day ahead and chilled, covered with plastic wrap.

SERVES 12

For the Prunes
- 1 cup pitted prunes (about 6 ounces), cut crosswise in half
- ½ cup pisco, preferably *pisco italia*

For the Squash
- 1½ pounds kabocha or butternut squash, peeled, seeded, and cut into 2-inch chunks, or one 16-ounce can solid-pack pumpkin puree
- 1 teaspoon salt

For the Custard
- 1 cup whole milk
- One 14-ounce can sweetened condensed milk
- Two 12-ounce cans evaporated milk
- ½ cup finely grated brown loaf sugar (preferably *panela*, *chancaca*, or *piloncillo*), Demerara sugar, or packed dark brown sugar
- 1 teaspoon anise seeds
- 5 whole cloves
- 2 Ceylon cinnamon sticks (*canela*)
- 8 allspice berries
- 6 tablespoons butter
- 1 teaspoon vanilla extract
- 6 egg yolks, lightly beaten
- 1 medium loaf 2-day-old Cuban, French, or Italian bread (about 8 ounces), cut into 1-inch cubes

For the Caramel

    1 cup granulated white sugar
    ¼ cup water

    Crème fraîche, for garnish

Preparing the Prunes ▶ Place the prunes in a small bowl and cover with the pisco. Let soak for at least 1 hour. Drain, reserving the pisco for another use.

Preparing the Squash ▶ If using fresh squash, place it in a medium saucepan with 2 quarts water and the salt, bring to a boil over medium heat, and simmer until soft, about 15 minutes. Drain, place in a food processor, and process into a smooth puree. You should have about 1⅔ cups puree.

Making the Custard ▶ Place the three milks in a medium saucepan with the brown loaf sugar, anise seeds, cloves, cinnamon, and allspice and bring to a gentle simmer over medium heat. Stir in the reserved squash puree, lower the heat to medium-low, and simmer for 8 to 10 minutes. Strain through a fine-mesh sieve, pushing against the solids with the back of a spoon, into a medium bowl. Add the butter and vanilla and stir until the butter is melted. Add the egg yolks and stir gently until well integrated. Add the cubed bread and let stand until the bread is soft and has absorbed the custard, about 20 minutes. Add the reserved soaked prunes.

Making the Caramel ▶ While the bread is soaking, place the white sugar and water in a small heavy saucepan, bring to a boil over medium-high heat, and cook until the liquid turns a light caramel color, carefully swirling the pan every few minutes to avoid crystallization, about 8 minutes. Pour into a mold

(a 9-by-13-inch baking dish) and swirl at once to coat the bottom and sides. Let cool. Preheat the oven to 350°F. Have ready a baking pan at least 3 inches deep, large enough to hold the caramelized mold.

Baking and Serving ▶ Pour the bread mixture into the caramel-coated mold. Place the larger pan on the middle oven rack. Set the mold in the pan and pour in enough hot water to come halfway up the sides. Bake until just set, 55 minutes to 1 hour. The pudding should be soft to the touch and slightly jiggly in the center when taken out of the oven. Unmold onto a serving platter and cut into squares while still warm or when cooled to room temperature, and serve with a generous dollop of crème fraîche.

CREPES

We usually associate crepes with France, but Galicians, who live in the northwestern corner of Spain, make a similar preparation called *filloas*, known since the Middle Ages. Galician *filloas* are carnival food. Cooks often add a bit of pork blood to the batter as seasoning, and they cook the crepes in pork fat. They are large and delicious, especially when fresh from the pan and sprinkled with sugar.

When people in Argentina, Uruguay, or Mexico mention crepes, they usually mean a *crepa* with a filling of caramelized milk or nestled in a pool of this creamy concoction. In Mexico, where it is prepared with *cajeta*, the crepe is usually folded like a napkin as for crêpes suzette and served atop a pool of liquidy *cajeta*. In South America the *dulce de leche* is a filling and the crepes (called *panqueques*, as in pancakes) are caramelized with some sugar under the broiler or with a salamander or torch.

Argentinean Crepes Filled with *Dulce de Leche*

Panqueques de Dulce de Leche

This is one of the most popular desserts in Argentina and the one sweet that is never missing on the menu of any Argentinean restaurant in the United States. *Dulce de leche* flourishes and tastes less sweet in a crepe that has a touch of saltiness. It's like eating *dulce de leche* with bread. Spread a couple of spoonfuls on a crepe, roll it, and then broil the crepes, using a bit of *dulce de leche* sprinkled with some sugar as a glaze.

Working Ahead ▶ You can prepare the crepes a day ahead and refrigerate them in a stack, separated with parchment paper and covered in plastic wrap. You can also freeze them for 2 to 3 months. Thaw at room temperature before using.

SERVES 6

- 1⅔ cups all-purpose flour
- 4 large eggs
- 2 cups whole milk
- 2 tablespoons melted butter, plus ⅓ cup softened butter
- 2 tablespoons sugar, plus more for dusting
- ½ teaspoon salt
- ½ teaspoon vanilla extract
  Pinch of ground cinnamon

1 cup *dulce de leche*, homemade (page 809) or store-bought

▶ Place the flour, eggs, milk, melted butter, sugar, salt, vanilla, and cinnamon in a blender and blend until smooth. Pass through a fine-mesh strainer into a large bowl and set aside for at least 1 hour before using.

Place a heavy 10-inch nonstick skillet over medium heat and brush with a little of the softened butter. When it foams, pour or ladle in about ¼ cup batter. Swirl the pan to coat the bottom with a thin layer of batter. Cook until the edges begin to curl, 50 to 55 seconds; lift up the bottom a little to check if it has begun to brown lightly in spots. Lift the crepe with your fingers and flip to cook on the other side. Cook until lightly golden, another 50 to 55 seconds. Slide onto a plate. Continue with the rest of the batter, adding butter to the pan as necessary, and stack the crepes on a platter. You should have about 12 crepes.

When all the crepes are cooked, place a crepe spotted side down on a work surface. Place 2 tablespoons *dulce de leche* in the center of the crepe and spread it out with the back of the spoon, leaving a 1-inch border on each side. Make a 1-inch fold on the left and then the right side of the crepe. Roll the side closest to you over the filling and continue rolling into a neat 5-inch package. Place the filled crepe seam side down on a small baking sheet. Continue filling the rest of the crepes.

To broil, smear the tops of the crepes lightly with *dulce de leche* and dust lightly with white sugar. Place the baking sheet under the broiler, about 4 inches from the heat source, and broil until the sugar caramelizes. Do not overcook. (My assistant Natalia Machado used to place a pointed-tip spatula on a gas burner and heat it until very hot to use as a burning iron for the crepes. Surprisingly, it worked, as she could easily run the red-hot blade all over the top surface of the crepes and burn all the sugar to a lovely caramel color. But then you have to warm the crepes first in the oven. That's why I use the broiler.)

Serve 2 crepes per person.

NOUGATS

Turrón (nougat), the traditional companion to marzipan on the Latin Christmas table, comes from the Spanish word *terrón*, which means "lump of earth." These confections arrive in November in Latin markets, and shopkeepers display them prominently along with marzipan near bottles of Asturian apple cider and the dried nuts and fruits of the season.

When I was a child in Cuba, my father bought our nougats at El Baturro, a Spanish deli and restaurant, and hid them until Christmas Eve. On that special night, my mother and her sisters prepared a lavish platter with assorted nougats and marzipan from Toledo, Spain, which came in lovely shapes. It was an easy way of taking care of dessert, freeing them to prepare the side dishes for the roasted pig.

My favorite was the crumbly Jijona nougat, named after a town in the province of Alicante, which is the source of most Spanish nougats. The eggy, toasted marzipan-like *turrón de yema* came second in my affections. There was also the hard and brittle Alicante nougat and the imperial torte, a large, thin round of almonds encased in white caramel covered with a thin wafer.

It is a testimony to the strength of Spanish traditions in the Americas that we still cherish these sweets and consider them to be our own. Like rice pudding, they were first created in Islamic Spain, the handiwork of refined cooks who loved the pleasures of the table and elevated the making of sweets to a fine art.

Here is my choice of nougats to serve twelve people as dessert on Christmas Eve or Christmas Day, arranged on a platter and offered with bowls of walnuts and hazelnuts. Cut each nougat into 12 pieces: 1 Jijona nougat (*turrón de jijona*); 1 Alicante nougat (*turrón de Alicante*); 1 toasted egg nougat (*turrón de yema tostado*); 1 imperial torte (*torta imperial*) broken into irregular pieces; and 1 box imperial almonds (*almendras imperiales*).

Doña Pepa's Anise-Scented Nougat

Turrón de Doña Pepa

This traditional nougat has a festive air. It reminds me of a large *alfajor*, with layers of pastry held together with a thick, honeylike syrup. I learned the recipe from my Peruvian friend the late Felipe Rojas-Lombardi, who learned it from his mother, Judith. I still remember Judith and her daughter Ana working with Felipe at his New York restaurant, the Ballroom, trying to come up with the tastiest yet easiest nougat recipe for his cookbook, *The Art of South American Cooking*. They settled on this one, which was beautiful as well as delicious.

There is no simple way to eat this sweet. It is built like a log cabin, with rows of pastry sticks, and it may crumble when you try to cut it. In the end you might like to do what I do and eat the nougat stick by stick.

SERVES 6

For the Dough

4¼ cups all-purpose flour

½ teaspoon salt

½ cup chilled freshly rendered lard (about 8 ounces; page 82) or ½ cup Crisco All-Vegetable shortening and ½ cup softened unsalted butter, cut into bits

6 large egg yolks

½ cup plus 2 teaspoons anisette or Sambuca

For the Syrup

1 cup fresh orange juice
 Juice of 1 lemon

12 ounces (about 1½ cups) grated brown loaf sugar, Muscovado sugar, or firmly packed dark brown sugar

½ cup granulated white sugar

For Decoration

½ teaspoon tiny multicolored candy sprinkles

1 teaspoon larger multicolored candy sprinkles

Making the Dough ▶ Sift 4 cups flour and the salt into a bowl. Add the lard or shortening and butter and quickly work the fat and flour with your fingertips or a pastry cutter until the mixture has the consistency of coarse cornmeal.

Place the egg yolks in a small bowl, add the anisette, and whisk until well mixed. Make a hollow in the center of the flour mixture, pour in the eggs, and work the mixture into a smooth dough with your hands. Divide into 36 equal portions and set aside.

Shaping and Baking ▶ Preheat the oven to 350°F and line a baking sheet with parchment paper. Sprinkle a little of the remaining flour on your work surface. Take 1 piece of dough and with the heel of your hand flatten it into a 5-by-2-inch rectangle. With lightly floured hands, push a long side of the rectangle toward the center, pressing against the work surface, rolling it into a 5-by-¼-inch stick. Repeat with the rest of the dough and place the sticks on the baking sheet. Bake on the middle rack of the oven for 45 minutes, or until the tips of the sticks are lightly golden. Remove from the oven, let cool for 2 to 3 minutes, and very carefully transfer to cooling racks.

Making the Syrup ▶ Combine the orange and lemon juices in a small saucepan with the brown and white sugars and simmer over very low heat, without stirring, for about 1 hour. Remove from the heat and let cool for 15 to 20 minutes, or until the syrup starts to thicken and a spoon makes a light track on the bottom of the pan.

Assembling the Pastry ▶ Place 12 pastry sticks in an even row, touching one another, on a small cutting board, marble slab, or flat serving platter. Spoon some of the syrup over the pastry to coat well. On top, arrange a row of 6 sticks close together at right angles to the first row, and then another row of 6 alongside it. Coat with more syrup. Place the remaining 12 sticks at right angles on top of the second layer. Spoon the remaining syrup over the entire structure to coat well. To finish, scatter the tiny colored sprinkles and then the larger ones on top. Let stand for several hours; then cut into individual portions with a sharp serrated knife and serve.

Storing: This sweet keeps well without refrigeration for a few days if stored in a cool place, covered with plastic wrap.

ALFAJORES

Latin America is home to several wonderful cookies made with simple ingredients. The oldest and most popular are related to Spanish cookies called *polvorones* and *mantecados*, two convent specialties.

My favorites are *alfajores*, the traditional cookies of Peru, Argentina, Uruguay, and Chile. The word *alfajor* comes from a Hispano-Arabic word meaning "stuffed"—perfectly descriptive of the contemporary *alfajor*, which is always filled, more often than not with *dulce de leche*.

Lemony Argentinean *Alfajor* Cookies Filled with *Dulce de Leche*

Alfajores de Maicena Argentinos

In Argentina, *alfajores* are sold everywhere, even at street kiosks, where children buy them to take to school. The kiosk *alfajores* are industrially produced. I much prefer the *alfajores* from bakeries and *confiterías*, which are more delicate and usually made with cornstarch, which contributes to their characteristic crumbly nature. These are filled with *dulce de leche* and finished in many guises, with a simple dusting of confectioners' sugar or covered with chocolate or fondant, and often rimmed with grated coconut.

Cook's Note: You can cut the dough into 1½- to 2-inch rounds to make petits fours.

Working Ahead ▶ You can prepare the *alfajor* dough the day before and keep it tightly covered in plastic wrap in the refrigerator. Prepare or buy the *dulce de leche* and grate the coconut (if using fresh) the day before.

MAKES 20 COOKIES

- 5 ounces butter (about 10 tablespoons), softened
- 6 large egg yolks
- ¾ cup (3½ ounces), confectioners' sugar, plus more for dusting
  Grated zest of 1 lemon
- 2 teaspoons Cointreau, Triple Sec, or Grand Marnier
- 1 teaspoon vanilla extract
- 2⅔ cups (about 10½ ounces) cornstarch
- 2 teaspoons baking powder
- ¼ teaspoon salt
- 1 cup *dulce de leche*, homemade (page 809) or store-bought, at room temperature
- ½ cup finely grated fresh coconut (page 50) or store-bought unsweetened grated coconut (optional)
- ¼ cup Simple Citrus Syrup (page 805; optional)

▶ Place the butter, egg yolks, sugar, lemon zest, liqueur, and vanilla in the bowl of a standing mixer and beat at high speed until creamy and fluffy, about 5 minutes. Transfer to a medium mixing bowl.

Sift together the cornstarch, baking powder, and salt. Add to the butter and egg yolk mixture and mix with a spoon. Shape into a ball, cover with plastic wrap, and refrigerate for at least 30 minutes to harden a bit.

Preheat the oven to 375°F. Unwrap the dough and cut into 2 equal portions. Keep the portion you are not using covered with plastic wrap. Place the other on a lightly floured surface and flatten with a rolling pin. Roll out the dough about ¼ inch thick and cut it into 2 ½-inch rounds with a cookie cutter. Repeat with the reserved dough.

Place the *alfajor* rounds on a buttered baking sheet and briefly bake on the middle rack of the oven—no more than 10 minutes; do not allow them to brown. Remove from the oven and let cool on a rack.

Place 2 or 3 teaspoons *dulce de leche* in the center of the flat, rough side of one *alfajor* and spread it toward the edges, leaving at least a ¼-inch space around it. Cover with another *alfajor* round, rough side down, and press gently to join the two cookies. Repeat with the remaining *dulce de leche* and cookies. If you wish, smear a bit of *dulce de leche* all around the edges of the *alfajores*. Place the grated coconut on a plate and, holding each *alfajor* on edge with your fingers, gently roll the edges in the coconut to coat. Argentineans dab a bit of syrup on the surface of each *alfajor* and dust it with confectioners' sugar.

Serving and Storing: Serve after a meal or with Argentinean *mate* (page 346) or Paraguayan *tereré* (page 348) for an afternoon snack. *Alfajores* keep very well for several weeks in a tightly covered container.

Peruvian *Alfajores*

Alfajores Peruanos

These are the simplest of Peruvian *alfajores*, traditionally made with a dough that has only a hint of salt. The recipe comes from the notebook of my late friend Judith Lombardi de Rojas, a skilled Lima cook. The touch of sugar is my addition, and I think it works.

Judith's *alfajores* are made with lard, which is the fat of choice for these cookies in Peru. Nowadays many cooks use margarine, which we are now learning is not an improvement on the original. Lard gives the dough a subtle pork taste that I find very appealing. It is a kind of savory backbone that cuts through the sweetness of the filling. In her recipe, Judith suggests a filling of either *manjar blanco* or *miel de chancaca*, a thick syrup made with the Peruvian brown loaf sugar *chancaca*. Colombian *panela*, which is widely available in this country, or brown sugar will do the job just as well.

Cook's Note: You can cut the dough into 1½- to 2-inch rounds to make bite-sized *alfajores*.

MAKES 12 *ALFAJORES*

- 1 pound pastry flour (preferably Argentinean or Uruguayan OOO flour, see page 799) or all-purpose flour, sifted (about 3⅓ cups)
- 2 tablespoons confectioners' sugar, plus more for dusting
- 1 teaspoon salt
- 8 ounces (about 1 cup plus 1 tablespoon) lard, freshly rendered (page 82) or store-bought, chilled
- 2–3 tablespoons lukewarm water
- 1 cup *manjar blanco* (page 811) or Peruvian Brown Loaf Sugar "Honey" (page 806)

▶ Place the flour in a large bowl and mix well with the sugar and salt. Add the lard and work with your fingertips as if preparing pie crust, until the dough resembles coarse meal. Add the water and continue kneading gently. Gather the dough into a ball and refrigerate for about 20 minutes, covered in plastic wrap.

Preheat the oven to 375°F. Unwrap the dough and cut into 2 equal portions. Keep the portion you are not using covered with plastic wrap. Place the other on a lightly floured surface and flatten with a rolling pin. Roll out the dough about ¼ inch thick and cut it into 3-inch rounds with a cookie cutter. Repeat with the reserved dough.

Place the *alfajor* rounds on a buttered baking sheet and briefly bake on the middle rack of the oven—no more than 10 minutes; do not allow them to brown. Remove from the oven and with a spatula place the cookies on a rack to cool.

Place 2 to 3 teaspoons *manjar blanco* or Peruvian brown loaf sugar honey in the center of the flat, rough side of 1 *alfajor* and spread it toward the edges, leaving at least ¼ inch space around it. Cover with another *alfajor* round, rough side down, and press gently to join the two cookies. Dust lightly with confectioners' sugar. Repeat with the remaining filling and *alfajores*.

Serving: Serve as dessert after a meal with coffee or as an afternoon snack.

CAKES, TRIFLES, AND TORTES

Egg and Pisco Sponge Cake
Huevos Chimbos o Tajadón

This simple egg cake bathed in liquor-flavored syrup must be one of the most popular convent desserts of Latin America, cropping up in several countries and making everybody believe it is their very own. In a 1925 Cuban cookbook, we find it as *huevos reales a la Isleña* (royal eggs in the style of the Canary Islands) and it is made with cane liquor.

The people of Maracaibo, Venezuela, call it *huevos chimbos* and make it in special molds christened *chimboteras*, spiking it with brandy. In both the Yucatán and Chiapas, Mexico, *huevos chimbos* is also known as *huevos reales*, and in Peru people know it as *huevos chimbos* or *tajadón* and flavor it with aromatic pisco.

When it comes to *huevos chimbos*, everyone has an opinion. Some cooks like to treat the cake informally, adding the syrup and serving the cake from the pan. Others unmold the cake, cut it into squares, and submerge them in warm syrup to plump. I prefer to add the syrup to the hot cake and then unmold it and cut it into serving pieces. *Huevos chimbos* is rich but delicate. It should be eaten in small portions, so you can savor every bite.

Cook's Note: I first made this dessert with my dear Lima friend the late Judith Lombardi de Rojas, who taught me one important lesson. She told me that for best results, the hot syrup must be added to the cake as soon as it comes out of the oven. None of the other recipes I have consulted mentions this, but after several tests I found that Judith was right.

SERVES 6

12 large egg yolks
⅛ teaspoon salt
1 teaspoon baking powder
1 tablespoon *pisco italia* or *acholado* (blended pisco)

For the Syrup
1 cup sugar
½ cup *pisco italia* or *acholado* (blended pisco)
½ cup water
2 Ceylon cinnamon sticks (*canela*)
1 teaspoon fresh lime juice

For the Garnish

¼ cup blanched slivered almonds

¼ cup dark raisins, soaked in ⅓ cup sweet sherry, port, or pisco for 30 minutes and drained

Preparing the Egg Batter ▶ Preheat the oven to 350°F. Choose a deep baking pan large enough to hold the first one. Place it on the middle oven rack and pour in 2 inches of hot water. Butter an 8-by-8-inch baking pan and line the bottom and sides with parchment paper. Lightly butter and flour the parchment.

Place the egg yolks in the bowl of a standing mixer and beat at high speed, gradually adding the salt, baking powder, and pisco, until the eggs are fluffy and have tripled in volume.

Baking the Cake ▶ Pour into the prepared mold and place it in the baking pan. Bake for 20 minutes, making sure not to open the door of the oven during the first 10 minutes of baking.

Making the Syrup ▶ While the cake bakes, place the sugar, pisco, water, cinnamon, and lime juice in a small saucepan and bring to a boil over medium heat. Add the almonds and the raisins. Stir, lower the heat to medium-low, and simmer for 10 minutes to thicken lightly.

When the cake is done, lift it from the water bath to a rack and immediately prick it evenly all over with a toothpick to facilitate the absorption of the syrup. Strain the hot syrup over the hot cake—you will see how it plumps up immediately. Discard the cinnamon but reserve the almonds and raisins in a small bowl or plate.

Unmolding and Cutting the Cake ▶ Let the cake cool for 15 minutes, then unmold it onto a small baking sheet or large platter. Cut into 12 equal squares. Transfer to a decorative platter and garnish each square with 3 raisins and 2 almond slivers. Spoon any extra syrup that seeps out of the cake over the top of each square to keep it moist.

Serving: Serve, allowing 2 pieces per person, after a meal or with coffee or sweet wine for the afternoon *merienda*.

Variation: Huaca Pucllana's *Huevos Chimbos*
For a larger batch of *huevos chimbos*, follow the proportions of Andrea Massaro, the pastry chef of Lima's Huaca Pucllana restaurant: 18 large egg yolks, 2 whole eggs, 1 teaspoon baking powder, 2 tablespoons pisco. Place the egg yolks and eggs in the bowl of a standing mixer and beat at high speed. Add the baking powder and pisco and continue beating until fluffy and tripled in size.

Grease a 9-by-13-inch ovenproof baking dish, line the bottom and sides with parchment paper, and butter and flour the parchment. Pour the batter into the dish and place in a larger baking pan with water, as above. Bake for 30 minutes.

Prepare a syrup with 2 cups sugar, 2 cups pisco, 1 cup water, and 1 cinnamon stick. Bring to a boil over medium heat, reduce the heat to medium-low, and add ½ cup blanched slivered almonds and ½ cup raisins. Simmer for 10 to 15 minutes.

Remove the cake from the oven and proceed as above. Cut the cooled cake into 2½- to 3-inch squares, transfer to a decorative platter sunny side up, and garnish with the raisins and almonds.

Small Golden Egg and Coconut Cakes from Bahia

Quindim de Yayá

These small cakes, a traditional sweet of the state of Bahia in Brazil, look like small suns glistening with a coating of sugar syrup. You dig your fork into the soft egg custard to find the crunch of a coconut layer at the bottom. I have eaten *quindims* all over Brazil, but the ones made by Azeni Julião Lima, the pastry instructor of Senac, a cooking school in Salvador de Bahia, are among the best. The professor explained to me that she had learned to make them at a local convent.

Quindim is a direct descendant of one of the most famous Portuguese egg desserts, *toucinho do céu*, which has a counterpart in Spain and all over Latin America called *tocino del cielo* (bacon from heaven). In typical Bahian fashion, the sweet is transformed by the addition of grated coconut, which floats to the top of the tiny mold, forming a tasty crust before you unmold and flip it.

Cook's Note: In Bahia, *quindim* is baked in 2-ounce molds. Tartlet molds will work well for this purpose.

MAKES 20 *QUINDIMS*

- 15 extra-large egg yolks
- 5 extra-large whole eggs
- 1 pound sugar (about 2½ cups), plus 2–3 cups more for coating the molds
- 2 tablespoons light corn syrup
- 1 tablespoon butter, melted, plus more for coating the molds
- Pinch of salt
- 4 ounces grated fresh coconut (page 50) or store-bought unsweetened grated coconut (about 1½ cups)

▶ Preheat the oven to 325°F. Combine the egg yolks and whole eggs in a medium bowl and mix gently with a whisk or wooden spoon. Add the rest of the ingredients and mix gently.

Brush 20 tartlet molds generously with melted butter. Place 2 to 3 cups sugar in a bowl and dip each mold into it, leaving about ⅛ teaspoon sugar on the bottom.

Place the filled molds in a large baking pan at least 1 inch deep. Pour the custard into the molds, up to the rims. Place on the middle rack of the oven and pour some hot water into the pan to come at least ¼ inch up the outside of the *quindim* molds. Bake for 1 hour and 10 minutes, carefully rotating the pan halfway through. Remove the pan from the oven and transfer the molds to a cooling tray or rack. Let cool to room temperature.

To unmold, press the edges of each mold and wiggle it a little to loosen the *quindim* from the bottom of the mold. Press down on one side, unmold into the palm of your hand, and slide the *quindim* onto a serving platter. Unmold the remaining *quindims*. If not serving immediately, cover the platter with plastic wrap, making sure not to touch the surface of the *quindims*, which should remain glistening like jewels.

Like most people in the Western world with European ancestry, Latin Americans are fond of cake and regard it as a celebratory dessert. Through the years our cake repertory has been enlarged by contributions from many immigrants and the abiding influence of the United States. Latin Americans now bake brownies and cheesecakes, eat Sara Lee pound cake, and decorate their cakes following the detailed instructions of the Wilton Cake Decorating Method.

There was a time, though, when the cakes that Latin cooks made for special occasions seldom resembled U.S. cakes. We had cakes brought by European immigrants, like the wedding cakes of Chile and Panama, which are fruitcakes, and the rich butter cakes made by bakers of German descent in parts of South America. But most traditional Latin cake batters loosely belong to the sponge-cake family and are direct descendants of a very old Spanish sponge cake that is often described as *pan de España* (bread of Spain) in Sephardic cookbooks.

The original Spanish sponge cake and its many Latin variations were meant to be rather light and porous, not overly moist or tender, because the baked cake was rarely eaten on its own. It was meant go into some triflelike presentation, or at least be paired with a syrup or a creamy custard sauce. The cake was a sturdy and usually rather simple backdrop for the other elements—layered fillings of tropical fruit purees or jams, *natillas* (the Latin version of crème patissière), *manjar blanco* (descended from the Spanish version of blancmange), or *dulce de leche*.

One of the most elaborate Latin cakes is the Peruvian *bola de oro*, a spectacular domed creation made with many layers of sponge cake smothered with *manjar blanco*, *dulce de leche*, and apricot jam. Once the layers are in place, cooks cover it with a thin layer of *maná*, a type of marzipan. The finished cake is often decorated with swirls of fondant and beautifully painted small fruits and flowers made from *maná*. This is the Peruvian cake for great occasions. In Lima, the best *bola de oro* makers are female artisan bakers who work from their homes.

While most European sponge cakes or biscuit recipes call for beating the egg yolks and whites separately, their Latin American cousins, *panetelas* and *bizcochuelos*, which are among our most traditional cakes, are often made by first beating the egg whites to stiff peaks and then incorporating the whole egg yolks one by one.

Recipes from Peru, Chile, and Venezuela often call for freeze-dried potato starch (*harina de chuño*), which is interchangeable with the kind you find in German and Jewish specialty stores. The potato starch plays the same role as cornstarch in cake recipes that use all-purpose flour rather than the softer, finer cake flour. In both cases the starch reduces the total amount of gluten that all-purpose flour contributes, making the cake lighter and more porous. ◆

Light Sponge Cake

Panetela Ligera

This is my recipe of choice to make the layered cakes Latins love so much, filled with custards and fruit creams and topped with a simple meringue or just dusted with powdered sugar. It makes a light, fine-textured cake with enough body to sustain a creamy filling.

This is a variation of the traditional Latin sponge cake recipe, which calls for beating the whole eggs and sugar together until tripled in size and then folding in the flour gradually by hand.

Cooks puzzled by the alternate traditional method of beating the stiff egg whites with the yolks and flour should find this method more to their liking. It is also easier to make than a European génoise, since you do everything in one bowl.

SERVES 8 TO 10

> 6 large eggs
> 1 cup sugar
> ⅛ teaspoon salt
> 1 teaspoon finely grated lime or orange zest
> 1½ teaspoons vanilla extract
> 1 cup all-purpose flour
> ¼ cup cornstarch

▶ Butter and flour two 9-by-2-inch round cake pans (or one 10-by-3-inch round cake pan if you want to split the cake into two or three layers). If you wish, butter the pans and line them with parchment paper, then butter and flour the parchment.

Beat the eggs, sugar, salt, citrus zest, and vanilla in the bowl of a standing mixer on high speed for 7 minutes, until the mixture is light, foamy, and tripled in volume and all the sugar has dissolved.

Preheat the oven to 350°F. Sift together the flour and cornstarch in a medium bowl. Gently sift half of this mixture into the beaten egg mixture and fold in with a balloon whisk or rubber spatula until barely blended. Sift in the rest of the flour mixture and continue folding until you can't see any more flour.

Pour the batter into the prepared pans and bake on the middle rack until the cake is lightly browned, springs back when gently touched, and separates from the sides of the pan, 30 to 35 minutes for 9-inch pans and 40 minutes for a 10-inch pan. Remove from the oven and let rest for about 10 minutes before turning out onto a rack to cool.

Serving: This is a delicious cake that you can eat by itself or with coffee or hot chocolate, or use as the basis for more elaborate recipes.

Perfect Sponge Cake for Latin Trifles

La Panetela Perfecta de Virginia

My sister-in-law, Virginia Valdor de Espinosa, once took a fabulous trip to Paris with the money she had earned by selling *tres leches* (page 844), a delicious and enormously popular trifle cake, to several Miami restaurants. This is her recipe: a foolproof Cuban *panetela* with a firm crumb and porous texture that will not crumble or turn into mush when included in a trifle. I have tried several *panetela* recipes for *tres leches*, using varying amounts of baking powder and different combinations of flour and starch, even cake flour, but I have given up. The finer and softer the cake, the less successful the *tres leches*. Virginia's firm, no-nonsense *panetela* wins hands down.

SERVES 8 TO 10

> 1 cup all-purpose flour
> 2 teaspoons baking powder
> 3 large eggs, separated
> 1 cup sugar
> ¼ cup whole milk

▶ Preheat the oven to 350°F. Grease and flour an 8-by-12-inch glass baking dish or a 9-by-2-inch round cake pan. Or, if you wish, butter the pans and line them with parchment paper, then butter and flour the parchment.

Sift the flour and baking powder together. Beat the egg whites in the bowl of a standing mixer at low speed until soft peaks form, about 2 minutes. Gradually add the sugar and beat another 7 to 8 minutes on medium speed, until the whites are glossy and the sugar is dissolved. Scrape down the sides of the bowl and beat in the yolks. Scrape down the bowl again, lower the speed to medium-low, and beat in the sifted flour and milk.

Pour the batter into the prepared pan and bake on the middle rack for 30 to 35 minutes, until the cake is lightly browned, springs back when gently touched, and begins to pull away from the sides of the pan. Run a knife around the edge of the cake and let cool in the pan for about 10 minutes before proceeding with any recipe.

Miami *Tres Leches*

Tres Leches de Miami

Tres leches is a trifle cake made by soaking a sturdy, porous *panetela*-style cake with three "milks": cream, condensed milk, and evaporated milk. The wildly enthusiastic acceptance of this simple concept by American diners and chefs has made me rethink my ideas of what constitutes a great dessert. Obviously Americans appreciate the same things that we admire in *tres leches*: ease of execution and simple, harmonious flavors that seduce.

How this cake became intrinsically linked with Nicaraguans in Miami is still subject to debate. I have not been able to find *tres leches* in any traditional Nicaraguan cookbook, nor did I ever eat it in Nicaragua, except in the homes of people with families in Miami. Several people claim paternity or maternity of this new classic. It is widely believed

that the dessert was born in somebody's home and then became a hit at the popular steakhouse Los Ranchos in southwest Miami. What is certain is that several Latin American countries as distant from each other as Mexico and Ecuador have similar versions of this dessert.

Cook's Note: Lately I have been making a variation of the classic *tres leches* by browning the meringue with a torch. I also like to use a sturdy Italian meringue that holds longer.

SERVES 8 TO 10

1 Perfect Sponge Cake for Latin Trifles (page 843), still just warm
1 cup heavy cream
One 12-ounce can evaporated milk
One 14-ounce can sweetened condensed milk
3 egg whites
1 cup light corn syrup

▶ While the sponge cake cools, mix together the cream, evaporated milk, and condensed milk. Prick the top of the cake all over at 1-inch intervals with a toothpick and slowly pour the milk mixture over the cake (prick more holes if needed). Be sure to include the edges and corners. The cake will absorb all the milk. Refrigerate for at least 1 hour before serving.

Place the egg whites in the bowl of a standing mixer and briefly beat at low speed, then increase the speed to medium and beat until soft peaks form. Slowly pour the corn syrup into the whites and continue beating for about 7 minutes, until stiff and glossy. Either spread the meringue over the cake or invert the cake onto a serving platter that can hold the milk sauce and spread or pipe the meringue over it. Cut the cake into slices or squares and serve cold.

Panamanian Glorious Wedding Trifle Cake

Sopa de Gloria Panameña

When you go to a Panamanian wedding reception, you will not see guests partaking of a multi-tiered wedding cake cut by the bride and groom. Instead, everybody will be digging into two traditional trifle cakes made by the bride's family: *sopa borracha* (layers of cake soaked in liquor) and the exquisitely presented *sopa de gloria*, artfully layered slices of cake drenched in a creamy custard. Of the two, *sopa de gloria* (served in heirloom silver trifle bowls) is the bigger star. The name literally means "soup of glory," "soup" having the old Spanish sense of bread or something breadlike that soaks up liquid.

This seven-layered version is a composite of two recipes. One, given to me by Marcela Wright's family after her daughter's wedding in Panama in 1994, calls for soaking slices of sponge cake (*bizcochuelo*) in a mixture of evaporated milk (called *leche crema* in Panama), condensed milk, and Nestle's canned cream made popular in the Canal Zone during the American tenure there. The mixture thickens to the right concentration and takes on a lovely caramelized flavor just by boiling down. Recently Elena Hernández, who owns a cooking school in Panama City, sent me a recipe minus the canned cream and intense reduction; it takes on a custardy richness by the addition of egg yolks. I have put together my own version, with the egg enrichment but also with an evaporated- and condensed-milk mixture slowly cooked down to bring out the caramel flavor.

Cook's Note: You will have some leftover custard that does not get absorbed in soaking. I like to strain and chill it and serve it as a sauce for the trifle. It can also be processed to semifreddo consistency in an ice cream machine and spooned over the trifle.

SERVES 10 TO 12

2	recipes Perfect Sponge Cake for Latin Trifles (page 843), baked in round 8-inch pans
Eight	12-ounce cans evaporated milk
Four	14-ounce cans sweetened condensed milk
3	Ceylon cinnamon sticks (*canela*)
½	teaspoon ground nutmeg
8	egg yolks
2	tablespoons vanilla extract
2	cups sliced blanched almonds, for garnish
	Ground cinnamon, for garnish
	Silver dragées, for garnish

▶ Unmold the sponge cakes and allow them to dry out, loosely wrapped in aluminum foil or paper bags, for 2 to 3 days.

In a heavy 8-quart pot, combine the evaporated milk and condensed milk with the cinnamon sticks and nutmeg and stir to mix with a wooden spoon. Bring to a boil over medium heat. Reduce the heat to very low and cook, stirring occasionally, for about 1½ hours, or until the mixture is a light tan color and tastes lightly caramelized. If you let it get darker, it will turn into a *dulce de leche*—too thick to be absorbed by the cake. Remove from the heat.

Place the egg yolks in the bowl of a standing mixer and beat until thick, fluffy, and pale yellow. Gradually whisk them into the milk mixture. Return to the heat and cook, stirring, over medium-low heat, until thickened into a light custard. Remove from the heat and strain into a large bowl; let cool, undisturbed. When the cream is cool, add the vanilla extract and stir to mix.

Have ready a large (3-quart) trifle dish. Cut

each sponge cake horizontally into ½-inch layers, then cut into 6 wedges. Dip several slices of cake into the bowl and let soak for a few minutes, until they thoroughly absorb the cream. Remove them and very gently squeeze out the excess cream by pressing them between two spatulas. Place in the serving dish. Repeat with the remaining cake, arranging the pieces in 7 layers. Top each layer with some almonds and dust lightly with ground cinnamon. Finish with an even layer of almonds, sprinkle lightly with cinnamon, and garnish with silver dragées. Refrigerate for 2 to 3 hours. To serve, spoon out the trifle onto plates. Pass a bowl of the chilled leftover custard mixture, plain or lightly frozen (see Cook's Note). It is very attractive served with fresh berries.

Splendid *Majarete* Rum Torte

Torta Esplendida de Majarete

After I have spent hours stirring the stovetop corn and coconut dessert called *majarete*, a voice inside tells me that all my hard labor deserves to be put to a higher purpose. In Latin countries, we love custards and spoon desserts for their comforting, predictable sameness and their nourishing warmth. But here in the United States, stovetop desserts are expected to offer grander attractions. Anything encased in a cookie tulip or hidden between the layers of a cake seems to get more attention than a simple bowl of custard, no matter how silken.

From the look of pleasure I saw on my friends' faces when they tasted this cake and discovered that the splendid filling was nothing more than our earthy corn and coconut custard classic, I knew I had finally done a sort of modern justice to my *majarete*.

Cook's Note: You can use store-bought grated coconut, but fresh is better. The fresh coconut flakes are juicy and flavorful and acquire caramel notes with toasting.

SERVES 8

- 1 Light Sponge Cake (page 842)
- 1 cup Fragrant Brown Loaf Sugar Syrup (page 806)
- 2 cups Venezuelan Corn and Coconut Custard (page 814)
- 1 cup grated fresh coconut (see page 50) or store-bought unsweetened grated coconut, toasted

▶ Cut the cake horizontally into 2 layers if you have baked it in a single pan. Sprinkle each layer with ½ cup syrup. Spread 1½ cups *majarete* over the bottom layer and cover with the top layer. Spread the top and sides with the remaining ½ cup *majarete*. Pat the toasted coconut evenly over the top and sides of the cake.

Venezuelan Ripe Plantain Torte

Torta Bejarana

Torta bejarana is a dense pudding moistened with liquor-scented syrup. Local lore has it that it was the creation of three sisters of African descent during the colonial period. I first tasted it in the home of a very distinguished Caracas family whose roots stretch back to that time. The cook, a marvelous octogenarian, explained that this was a nineteenth-century dessert that was no longer popular in Caracas. "No one bothers to cook it anymore," she sighed. That was my cue! I proceeded to eat every morsel with the concentration of a naturalist dissecting an endangered species. I had second and third helpings. I loved the sweetness of the ripe plantain and the brown loaf sugar and the crunchy toasted sesame seeds on the tip of my tongue. And I am glad that I paid attention.

A few months later, I came across the story of *torta bejarana* and the sisters who created it in *El Pan nuestro de cada día* (Our Daily Bread), written by Rafael Cartay, a food historian. Here is his version: The Bejarano sisters, Eduvigis, Belén, and Magalis, lived in nineteenth-century Caracas. Their desserts, which were sold door to door by young kids on commission, were the toast of the town. One of them in particular, a bread pudding made with plantains and cheese sprinkled with sesame seeds, made history. While the sisters' *torta* was eagerly accepted in Caracas's polite circles, their forays into those circles were the source of hot debate. For a society strictly divided along lines of color and status, it was inconceivable for a black woman to dress like an upper-class white woman. But one day the sisters bought beautiful fabrics from Spain, made stunning dresses, and sallied forth wearing them. This did not sit well with polite society, and a big fuss was made as to whether the Bejaranos should be allowed to dress this way. But the king of Spain, hearing of the sisters' predicament, intervened on their behalf with a special dispensation: "By this decree, let it be known that the Bejarano sisters are to be treated as if they were white."

SERVES 8 TO 10

- 3 ripe plantains (about 1¾ pounds)
- 3 cups fine dry breadcrumbs
- 6 ounces Venezuelan aged white cow's-milk cheese (*queso llanero*), Mexican *cotija*, or ricotta salata, grated (about 1 cup)
- ½ cup sesame seeds, lightly toasted
- 2 cups oloroso sherry or moscatel wine
- 6 tablespoons butter
- 1 teaspoon ground cinnamon
- ½ teaspoon ground cloves
- 1 pound grated brown loaf sugar (preferably *papelón* or *panela*), Muscovado sugar, or dark brown sugar
- 2½ cups water
- 2 Ceylon cinnamon sticks (*canela*)
- 15 allspice berries
- 8 whole cloves
- Whipped cream, for garnish

▶ Preheat the oven to 350°F. Boil or bake the plantains in their skins until soft, about 20 minutes. When they are cool enough to handle, peel and cut into small chunks. Place in the bowl of a standing mixer and add the breadcrumbs, cheese, ¼ cup sesame seeds, 1 cup sherry, butter, and the ground spices and beat at medium speed to mix thoroughly. Pour into a buttered 10-by-2-inch cake pan and bake until the torte is set but still soft to the touch, about 1 hour and 15 minutes.

Place the sugar in a medium saucepan with the water, cinnamon sticks, allspice, and cloves and bring to a gentle boil over medium heat. Cook, stirring, about 5 minutes. Add the remaining 1 cup sherry and cook a couple of minutes more. Set aside.

As soon as you remove the torte from the oven, prick it all over with a toothpick. Pour the syrup over the top a little at a time and wait until it has been absorbed before adding more. Let sit for a few minutes before unmolding.

Turn out the torte onto a decorative serving platter with a raised rim to hold the syrup. Sprinkle with the remaining ¼ cup sesame seeds and cut into wedges like a cake. Serve with a dollop of whipped cream (this is not traditional, but I believe it enhances the dish).

Yuca Coconut Cake from Goias

Mané Pelado

I first tasted this magnificent yuca cake, the creation of a street vendor named Maria Lourdes Ferrari Garcia, on a trip to São Paulo, Brazil, in the 1990s. I met Maria Lourdes at Trianon Park, a marvelous fin-de-siècle oasis in front of the Museum of Modern Art. As I strolled through the park, I was attracted to her table because it was so inviting, groaning with attractively decorated cakes and stovetop desserts. It was almost as if she had decided to set a beautiful afternoon tea table for friends. The frilly homemade touches, the graceful tablecloth— it was all there. Maria Lourdes, smiling behind her desserts and wearing a coquettish white apron fringed with lace, gave me a sample of everything, and I loved her *mané pelado*.

This recipe, a glorious, clever use of two tropical staples, yuca and coconut, is a specialty of the state of Goias. It's an amazingly light and airy dessert, more like a succulent pudding than a cake. The top is golden and crunchy like macaroons, the sides coconuty.

I left the park that day very pleased with myself. Maria Lourdes had given me detailed recipes! But when I got home and started checking my notes, I realized she had given me all the liquid measurements in *xicaras de chá*, or teacups. "What size are the teacups of Brazil?" I wondered, trying to remember. I finally found out: a *xicara de chá* is equivalent to ¾ cup.

SERVES 8 TO 10

- 2 cups whole milk
  Grated zest of 1 lemon
- 2 Ceylon cinnamon sticks (*canela*)
- 3 whole cloves
- 1 teaspoon vanilla extract
  Pinch of salt
- 3 pounds yuca, peeled (see page 166)
- 2 cups grated fresh coconut from one 1½-pound coconut; (see page 50) or store-bought unsweetened grated coconut
- 6 large eggs
- 2 cups sugar
- 3 tablespoons butter, melted
- 2 cups Creamy ("First") Coconut Milk (page 50) or canned unsweetened coconut milk
- 2 teaspoons baking powder
- 1 cup Simple Citrus Syrup (page 805), warm

▶ Preheat the oven to 300°F. Place the milk in a small saucepan with the lemon zest, cinnamon sticks, cloves, vanilla, and salt. Bring to a gentle boil over medium-low heat and let simmer for 5 minutes. Strain through a fine-mesh sieve and discard the solids. Set aside the milk.

Grate the yuca on the finest side of a box grater. Place in a bowl, add 1 cup grated coconut, mix thoroughly with a wooden spoon, and set aside.

Beat the eggs at high speed in the bowl of a standing mixer. Gradually add the sugar and the butter and continue beating until creamy and fluffy. Reduce the speed to low and add the spice-infused milk and the coconut milk. Add the yuca-coconut mixture and finally beat in the baking powder.

Line a 10-inch springform pan with aluminum foil and coat the foil with butter and flour. Pour in the batter and spread the remaining 1 cup grated coconut over the surface of the cake. Bake for 2 hours and 25 minutes to 3 hours, until the top of the cake is golden brown and set. Because of its density, the center takes a long time to cook, but even if it remains a bit soft after 3 hours, it will set when it cools.

Prick the top of the cake with a toothpick and pour the warm syrup over it a little at a time, waiting for the liquid to be absorbed before adding more. Let the cake cool in the pan. To remove from the pan, loosen the sides and lift out the pan bottom. Lift the cake from the bottom and keep the aluminum foil around it until ready to serve.

Serving: I love serving *mané* with a tropical fruit marmalade or with a dollop of *Zambo* Squash and *Naranjilla* Dessert (page 821).

Fresh Corn Torte from Veracruz

Torta de Elote Veracruzana

This moist fresh corn torte is a beloved dessert in Veracruz, Mexico. My Veracruzan friend Rosario Sanz Canal, a very accomplished cook, is particular about the crust. She likes it very brown, to contrast with the canary yellow interior, and eats the torte by itself, with no embellishments. I like to dust it lightly with a bit of confectioners' sugar mixed with a touch of cinnamon and serve it with a dollop of whipped cream.

SERVES 8 TO 12

- 4½ cups fresh corn kernels (from about 8 small ears), or frozen kernels
- 6 large eggs
- 1 stick butter (4 ounces), cut into several pieces
- One 14-ounce can sweetened condensed milk
     Pinch of salt

- 2 teaspoons baking powder
     Confectioners' sugar, for garnish
     Ground cinnamon, for garnish
     Whipped cream (optional), for garnish

▶ Preheat the oven to 375°F and butter and flour a nonstick 10-by-2-inch cake pan. Working in 2 batches, place all the ingredients except the garnishes in a blender or food processor and process into a creamy puree. Pour the corn mixture into the prepared pan and slide onto the middle rack of the oven. Bake for about 45 minutes, until a toothpick inserted in the center of the torte comes out clean and the torte is golden brown, Turn off the oven and let the torte rest for 5 more minutes. Remove and let cool, then unmold on a round serving platter. Just before serving, dust lightly with some confectioners' sugar and a bit of ground cinnamon. Cut into wedges and serve with a dollop of whipped cream, if you wish.

Papantla Coconut Vanilla Tamales

Tamalitos de Coco y Vainilla de Papantla

Coconut has found a home with vanilla in this spongy Veracruzan tamal. A blend of condensed and evaporated milks—the secret weapons of countless Latin cooks—softens the coarse texture of the grated coconut and turns it into a seductive, almost creamy custard steamed in a husk. The vanilla, both ground coarsely and chopped into tiny bits, takes the place of raisins, enlivening the comforting backdrop of the *masa* with flashes of fruity acidity and caramel notes.

1 pound 5 ounces corn *masa* mix, preferably Maseca brand

½ cup evaporated milk

⅓ cup sweetened condensed milk

1 teaspoon baking powder

2 sticks unsalted butter (8 ounces)

¼ cup freshly rendered lard (page 82)

1 cup plus 2 tablespoons sugar (8 ounces)

3 egg yolks

1 cup grated fresh coconut (see page 50) or store-bought unsweetened grated coconut

½ teaspoon salt

1 tablespoon vanilla extract, preferably Mexican

2 Mexican vanilla beans, 2 ground in a small processor or spice mill and 4 chopped into ⅛-inch bits (optional)

21 corn husks, softened in hot water and patted dry (see page 447)

Twenty-one 30-inch pieces of twine

▶ Place the *masa* mix in a large bowl together with the evaporated and condensed milks and the baking powder. Beat with a wooden spoon to blend for about 10 minutes. Set aside.

Place the butter and lard in the bowl of a standing mixer and beat with the dough hook until fluffy, about 5 minutes. Continue beating while adding the sugar gradually, stopping occasionally to scrape the sides of the bowl. Add the egg yolks one by one while beating at medium speed. Add the grated coconut gradually and keep beating for 5 more minutes. Pour this mixture into the milk-*masa* mixture. Add the salt, vanilla extract, ground vanilla, and chopped vanilla, if using, and beat to blend with a wooden spoon.

Lay a corn husk on the work surface and place ⅓ cup dough on the center of the husk. With an offset spatula, spread it into a rectangle 1¼ inches wide by 4 inches long. Bring the 2 long sides of the corn husk together to enclose the dough and fold the ends of the husk toward the center of the tamal, over the seam. Tie with kitchen twine like a simple package and finish with a bow. Repeat with the remaining husks and dough.

Prepare a steamer according to the instructions on page 452. Stack the tamales in the basket of the steamer and cover. Steam for 1 hour and 15 minutes.

Serving: Serve hot with a cup of steaming hot chocolate.

FROZEN DESSERTS

Andean children jump for joy when a storm descends from the mountains. While their parents fret about the crops, the youngsters run to the fields to gather hailstones, which are often the size of river stones, and dribble them with juice or syrup. An old family in Cuenca, Ecuador, told me that at the turn of the twentieth century, people brought snow from the Cajas Mountains to town with great fanfare to make *helados de paila*, a fruit sorbet churned by hand in huge kettles. People stood in long lines for a chance to taste the delicacy.

As a child I would run to the street when I heard the call of the ice-maker: "*Rallados, ricos rallados, de fresa y de limón, rallados!*" (Ices, delicious ices, of strawberry and lime, ices!) His cart contained a huge block of ice and a dozen bottles filled with mysterious colored syrups. I stood mesmerized as he shaved the ice with a planelike contraption, the *rallador*. Then he scooped out the ice, packed a mound into a paper cup, and drizzled it with sweet neon-colored syrup. Later, on a trip to Havana in the 1960s, I waited in line for almost three hours with hundreds of other people to eat at the famous Copelia ice cream parlor in the Vedado. I had a luscious *mamey sapote* ice cream that was worth the wait.

Modern ice cream parlors can be found everywhere in Latin America, but each country and region has its own specialties—deeply flavorful sorbets, custardy ice creams, grainy granitas, and shaved ices—that find their roots in Europe. Some of their names—*mantecados* (Cuba and Puerto Rico), *helados de paila* and *espumillas* (Ecuador), *nieves* (Mexico)—reveal their Old World origins. The wonderful ice cream traditions of Spain and Italy converged in Latin America and became richer with the fruits and vegetables of our lands.

You would be hard-pressed to find people with more fondness for ice cream than Latin Americans. The small town of Dolores Hildalgo in the colonial heartland of Mexico is famous not only for *El Grito* (the Cry), Father Hidalgo's proclamation of independence, but for its spectacular selection of ice creams. If you crave pork crackling ice cream, that's the place to find it. Equally unusual are the ice creams of the Heladería Coromoto, an ice cream parlor in Mérida in the Venezuelan Andes that boasts more than five hundred flavors. I was so rattled by the odd flavor combinations that I opted for a simple, clean-tasting, refreshing passion fruit ice cream.

Our generic word for ice cream, *helado*, has a broader connotation, meaning a multitude of frozen preparations. In fact, ice cream in the true sense of the term, a frozen dessert made with cream, is not the most popular preparation in Latin America. Most people prefer the velvety, seductive frozen treats made with a thick whole-milk-and-egg-based custard popularized by the French and Italians. In some countries, like Cuba and Puerto Rico, a custard-based frozen dessert is traditionally called *mantecado*, which refers to its unctuous texture.

With a variety of climatic zones concentrated in relatively small areas because of the mountainous topography, Latin Americans also have access to a plethora of fruits at all times of the year, and one of our favorite uses for fruit is in frozen desserts. South Americans have the greatest diversity. From the steamy tropical jungles of the Amazon and the Atlantic forests of Brazil come perfumed fruits with exotic-sounding names: *açai*, the purple fruit of a palm tree; *abiu* or *lúcuma*, with mealy, sweet, mustard-colored flesh; *buriti*, another palm fruit with a patterned leathery skin enclosing saffron-colored flesh; *jaboticaba*, round purple berries that grow by the thousand straight from the trunk of a beautiful tree; and my favorite, *cupuaçu*, a wild relative of the cacao tree—a large oval pod covered with a dusty brown skin enclosing a white mucilaginous flesh that tastes like litchis and can fill a room with its potent fragrance. The royal Annonaceae family grows from the Hispanic Caribbean to the warm valleys of the Andes, offering cherimoyas (sweetsops) and *guanábanas* (soursops), all marvelously perfumed and creamy. Everywhere in the Andes and particularly in temperate Chile and Argentina grow luscious apples and peaches, grapes and plums.

The omnivorous Latin palate for ice cream does not end with fruits. In Latin America, any vegetable or tuber is turned into ice cream. In Potosí, Bolivia's highest city, women wait for the cold June nights, when frost covers the rooftops, to put out boxes filled with a sweet creamy mixture made of sweet potato and the tuber called *oca,* to freeze it into an ice cream called *thaya.* The Brazilians, who have never thought of avocado as a salad vegetable, mash it to a paste and flavor it with sugar and lime juice to churn it into refreshing sorbets and ice creams. And then there are our traditional Latin custards and nourishing drinks, perfect ingredients for a broad range of frozen desserts.

Cucharamama *Dulce de Leche* Ice Cream

Helado de Dulce de Leche

This is the *dulce de leche* ice cream I serve at Cucharamama. It is a favorite there, and with reason. It is smooth, creamy, and not too sweet, and it has that marvelous depth of flavor that comes from the slow cooking of the custard. Many a customer has crossed the Hudson just to eat this ice cream.

MAKES ABOUT 2 QUARTS

1¼	cups *dulce de leche,* homemade (page 809) or store-bought (preferably Dulce de Leche Gandara, La Estancia, or Los Nieticos)
Two	12-ounce cans evaporated milk
1	cup whole milk
	Pinch of salt
8	large egg yolks
1	teaspoon vanilla extract
	Cacao nibs, for garnish

▶ Place the *dulce de leche,* evaporated milk, and whole milk in a medium saucepan with the salt and bring to a gentle boil while stirring. Reduce the heat to low and simmer until reduced by half, about 40 minutes.

Place the egg yolks in the bowl of a standing mixer and beat at medium speed until thick, fluffy, and pale yellow. Remove the milk from the heat and add the eggs gradually while beating with a wire whisk. Return to the burner, add the vanilla, and cook over medium-low heat until thickened into a light custard.

Pour the custard into a medium heatproof bowl set over a larger bowl filled with cracked ice and water to stop the cooking. When cool, pour the custard into the bowl of an ice cream maker and process according to the manufacturer's instructions for about 1 hour. Scoop into a stainless steel or plastic container and place in the freezer to harden.

Serving: Serve 3 scoops in a serving bowl and garnish with cacao nibs. Or serve a dollop of ice cream with warm Squash Bread Pudding with Prunes and Pisco (page 832), or scoop into serving bowls or margarita glasses garnished with Chilean Pumpkin Fritters (page 855) shaped like stars or birds. Pour a tablespoon of warm orange *chancaca* syrup (page 806) over the dessert just before serving. It is also delicious with a couple of Argentinean *alfajores* (page 837).

Mamey Sapote Sherbet

Helado de Mamey

This sherbet is so rich you would think it is made with cream and eggs, but no. The base is the same as for *Mamey Sapote* Milk Shake (page 344), just fruit pulp, milk, sugar, and some salt to bring out the flavor. The pulp of the beautiful *mamey sapote* is so dense that the ice cream thickens beautifully without crystallizing in less than 1 hour in an electric ice cream maker.

MAKES ABOUT 2 QUARTS

2½–3 pounds *mamey sapote* (1 medium *magaña sapote* or 2 Pantín *sapotes*)
4 cups whole milk
½ cup sugar, or to taste
¼ teaspoon salt

▶ Cut the *mamey sapote* open by slicing it in half lengthwise like an avocado. Scoop out the shiny black seed and reserve to flavor Spiced Venezuelan Hot Chocolate (page 340) or Pantín *Mamey* Flan (page 831). Cut each half into 2 or 3 lengthwise slices and peel off the skin. Cut the flesh into 1- to 2-inch chunks. You should have about 4 cups.

Working in 2 batches, place the fruit in a blender with the milk, sugar, and salt and blend until creamy. Pour into the bowl of an ice cream maker and process according to the manufacturer's instructions. Scoop into a stainless steel or plastic container and freeze to harden.

Andean Blackberry Ice

Helado de Paila de Moras de los Andes

In the northern highlands of Ecuador, a kind of sorbet called *helado de paila* (pot ice cream) is popular. Fruit purees or juices are mixed by hand with egg whites beaten to soft peaks in large copper tubs (*pailas*) sitting on ice. The most famous *helados de paila* are those made in Ibarra and in some convents north of Quito, and the nuns make good money selling their ices to local ice cream parlors. These *helados* can be addictive, because they are made with no artificial ingredients, just the sweetest and most exquisite fruits: soursops, passion fruits, *lúcumas*, Andean blackberries, and cherimoyas from the warm valley of Guayabamba.

You can try making *helados de paila* at home the old-fashioned way, beating the mixture by hand in a bowl over ice and coarse salt to freeze it, or you can churn the mixture in a modern ice cream maker. For this simple recipe, I use an Ecuadorian favorite, Andean blackberries, which are available frozen in Hispanic markets. These have a sweeter and richer flavor than U.S. blackberries, and the fruits are much larger. I do not recommend substituting domestic blackberries.

MAKES 5 CUPS

One 14-ounce package frozen Andean blackberries
1 cup sugar, or to taste
2 Ceylon cinnamon sticks (*canela*)
2 star anise pods
1 egg white

▶ Defrost the blackberries in their package, then pour into a blender or a food processor and puree. Strain through a fine-mesh sieve, pushing the fruit against the mesh with the back of a wooden spoon to extract as much juice as possible. You should have about 3 cups. Pour into a medium saucepan, add the sugar, cinnamon, and star anise, and bring to a boil over medium heat. Cook for 10 to 15 minutes, until lightly thickened. Remove from the heat, strain out the seeds and spices, and let cool.

While the syrup cools, beat the egg white in the bowl of a standing mixer until it forms stiff peaks. Set the bowl on the counter, pour the syrup gradually into the egg white, and fold with a spatula until mixed. Pour into an ice cream maker and process according to the manufacturer's until fully frozen. When the ice is ready, it will still be rather soft. Pour into a flat container such as an 8-by-8-inch glass baking dish, cover with plastic wrap and aluminum foil, and place in the freezer for 2 to 3 hours.

To Mix by Hand ▶ Have the fruit syrup and the beaten egg white ready in separate bowls. Fill a large bowl with ice cubes and stir in 2 tablespoons coarse salt. Set the bowl with the syrup over the ice and beat with a wooden spoon until ice crystals form. Add some of the egg white and beat to incorporate. Continue beating in the egg white a little at a time until you have used it all. When the mixture looks stiff and smooth, pour into an 8-by-8-inch glass baking dish and cover with plastic wrap and aluminum foil. Place in the freezer for at least 3 hours before serving.

Açai Sorbet

Sorbete de Açai

Cooking by color—that is, getting in the habit of selecting fruits and vegetables with saturated colors—is a smart way to ensure that we are consuming useful phytonutrients. Purple and blue foods like blackberries and *açai*, the fruit of a slender Amazonian palm tree, for example, are rich in anthocyanins, antioxidant compounds that contribute to cardiovascular health, among many other benefits.

This Amazon native has become the rage in health-food circles in the United States, and you can buy it as a frozen puree in specialty markets.

Like most Amazonian palms, the *açaizeiro* is a kind of jungle manna, providing wood and leaves for shelter as well as hearts of palm and edible fruits for forest-dwellers and their animals. The palm is multistemmed, which saves it from the ravages of heart-of-palm harvesters, and its round or egg-shaped purple fruits hang in large bunches. Though the *açaizeiro* produces fruit year-round, the peak of the harvest is in the dry months between July and October. When fully mature, *açai* looks almost black. It needs to be processed almost immediately, as the fruit ferments quickly even when refrigerated. Women soak the fruit in water to soften the pulp, then knead it by hand to separate the pulp from the dark seeds, which look like tiny coconuts. Then they strain the resulting purple paste, using tightly woven palm-frond sieves. The juice is made by dissolving the paste in water.

Frozen *açai* juice is widely available in packages of 14 ounces (roughly 2 cups). It has a complex grassy taste with a hint of chocolate and no trace of acidity or sweetness. I fell in love with it in Brazil, where people consume it in juices and desserts like sorbets and puddings, often thickened with tapioca and sweetened with condensed milk. At my restaurant I always add some lime juice to sweetened *açai* for a touch of tart freshness.

MAKES 1 QUART

- 2 cups frozen *açai* juice
- 2 tablespoons light corn syrup
- 1 cup Simple Citrus Syrup (page 805)
- ¼ cup fresh lime juice

Diced tropical fruits, such as mango, pineapple, and guava, for serving

2 tablespoons cacao nibs, for garnish

▶ Combine the *açai* juice, syrups, and lime juice in a bowl and stir to mix. Place in the bowl of an ice cream maker and process according to the manufacturer's instructions for about 1 hour. Scoop the sorbet out into a plastic or metal container and freeze to harden. The sorbet is at its best when freshly made. Serve over the diced tropical fruits, sprinkled with cacao nibs.

FRITTERS

For Latin Americans, the sizzling pan always beckons, even when it comes to dessert. There are a surprising number of fried desserts in Latin America, crunchy batter-fried sweets you fish out of the pan and dip in syrup, such as pumpkin and corn fritters, *almojábanas*, *sopaipillas*, *picarones*, *buñuelos*, and *hojuelas*. It's as if Latin Americans don't want to get too far from savories. These "fruits of the frying pan," as they were called in medieval and Renaissance cookbooks, were an integral part of Iberian cooking, and some date back to Islamic times.

Chilean Pumpkin Fritters

Sopaipillas Pasadas

Sopaipillas are one of my favorite sweet fritters, pillowy little melt-in-your-mouth cushions made from a dough of flour enriched with pumpkin. I learned this recipe from the late Luisa Nogues Duvanced, a refined Santiago cook and the mother of my friend María Eugenia Baeza. In other parts of Chile, *sopaipillas* are not so ethereal. In Patagonia, *sopaipillas* are made with flour alone and are thick, robust, and spongy, like Pueblo Indian fry bread. They are often consumed as bread. But Luisa Duvanced's *sopaipillas* are golden and featherlike, dissolving in your mouth before you know it, leaving behind only a trace of crunchy dough and the aroma of spicy brown loaf syrup. The secret is in how she rolled her dough: paper-thin.

When a Chilean asks if you want your *sopaipillas* "*pasadas*," expect your crisp gossamer-light fritter to be soaked in syrup until it turns into a soggy unrecognizable piece of dough, soft like a raviolo. I am true to the meaning of the word *pasar*—to pass by lightly—and simply coat my *sopaipillas* lightly with the boiling syrup. That way they have that wonderful balance between sweet and salty that I love so much and remain crunchy and delicious.

MAKES ABOUT 30 *SOPAIPILLAS*

10 ounces (about 2 cups) brown loaf sugar (preferably *panela*), cut into chunks, Muscovado sugar, or dark brown sugar

3¼ cups water

1 Ceylon cinnamon stick (*canela*)

½ orange, seeds removed

1 teaspoon cornstarch

2 cups all-purpose flour

1 cup pumpkin puree (preferably canned solid-pack pumpkin puree)

1½ tablespoons freshly rendered lard (page 82)

½ teaspoon baking powder

½ teaspoon salt

4 cups corn oil, for frying

▶ Place the sugar, 3 cups water, cinnamon, and orange half in a heavy medium saucepan and bring to a boil over medium-high heat, stirring to dissolve the sugar. Meanwhile, dissolve the cornstarch in the remaining ¼ cup water. When all the sugar is dissolved and the mixture is boiling, add the cornstarch and cook, stirring, for 2 minutes to thicken. Keep the syrup warm over very low heat while making the fritters.

Place the remaining ingredients except the oil in a bowl and knead into a soft dough that will not stick to your fingers. Form into a ball and turn onto a lightly floured work surface. Flatten the dough into a disk and roll it out ⅛ inch thick. Using a cookie cutter, cut into circles 4 inches in diameter and prick each one twice with the tines of a fork.

In a heavy medium saucepan or deep fryer, heat the oil to 370°F. Add the *sopaipillas* in batches, 3 or 4 at a time, and fry for about 30 seconds on each side, turning over with a slotted spoon. They will puff up like small cushions. Remove the fritters with a second slotted spoon and plunge them into the hot syrup. Turn them over to coat on both sides and immediately remove with the slotted spoon.

Serving: Place the *sopaipillas* on a nice serving platter and bring them to the table piping hot. They are delicious with *Dulce de Leche* Ice Cream (page 852). To use *sopaipillas* as a garnish, cut the dough into whimsical shapes with a cookie cutter. My favorite shapes are doves and stars, which look splendid crowning a luscious ice cream.

Christmas Fritters in the Style of Veracruz

Hojuelas con Miel de Piloncillo

On a visit to Chinchón, a historic town not far from Madrid, my friend Irma Alfonso and I stopped for lunch at the celebrated Mesón Cuevas del Vino, a cavernous restaurant in an old winery. For dessert, Irma suggested *miel sobre hojuelas*, a traditional sweet that can be loosely translated as honey over leaf-thin fried wafers. The fritters were crunchy and a bit salty, a perfect contrast to the aromatic honey.

The memory of that simple dessert resonated in my memory for years, becoming a craving. I learned that it was a very old Spanish recipe, perhaps born in convent kitchens, and I tasted it again in other Castilian towns and in Galicia, where it is called *orellas de carnaval* (carnival ears). I could clearly see the relationship between these Spanish originals and the *hojuelas* of Chile and Mexico, where the fritters are served with an aromatic syrup of unrefined brown sugar.

Veracruzan *hojuelas* are round and flat like flour tortillas, blistered like the dough of Cuban empanadas, and studded with tiny anise seeds. They are a Christmas treat that comes to the table after dinner with Spanish nougats, dried apples, pears, prunes, and lots of nuts.

This recipe is adapted from one by my friends the Sanz Canal sisters, Rosario and Crispina. They learned to make *hojuelas* from their grandmother. "In the old days, people used to go to the sugarcane mills to buy molasses for the *hojuelas*, but I much prefer the syrup, because it is flavored with anise," said Rosario, who faithfully cooks them for her family every Christmas. She pours the warm syrup into a coffee cup and breaks pieces of the fritters into it, a homey and comforting way to enjoy an old, familiar sweet.

Cook's Note: Rosario Sanz Canal's tips for success include kneading the dough until you can roll it easily without breaking, rolling it very thin, and frying it at a constant temperature, making sure not to overbrown the fritters. They should have a nice golden color. The amount of anise seeds may seem excessive, but surprisingly, the spice does not overwhelm the fritters.

MAKES 20 FRITTERS

- 1   cup whole milk
- ¼   cup granulated white sugar
- 6   tablespoons anise seeds
- 2   Ceylon cinnamon sticks (*canela*)
- 3⅓ cups all-purpose flour (about 1 pound)
- 1   teaspoon baking powder
- 2   large eggs, lightly beaten
- ⅓   cup freshly rendered lard (page 82), softened
- 4   tablespoons (½ stick) butter, softened and cut into small bits
- 1½ pounds brown loaf sugar (preferably *panela* or *piloncillo*), cut into chunks or grated, Muscovado sugar, or dark brown sugar (about 4 cups)
     Pinch of salt
- 4   cups water
- 4   cups corn oil

▶ Place the milk, granulated sugar, 2 tablespoons anise seeds, and cinnamon in a small saucepan and bring to a boil over medium heat, stirring to dissolve the sugar. Lower the heat to medium-low and simmer for 5 minutes. Remove the cinnamon and let the mixture cool slightly.

Place the flour and baking powder in a large bowl and mix well. Make a hole in the center and add the eggs. Work the eggs into the flour with your fingertips, gradually adding the milk mixture. Gradually add the lard and butter and continue mixing to form a wet dough.

Keep kneading for at least 15 minutes, until the dough is smooth and you can stretch a piece of it without breaking. Do not add more flour. Let the dough rest, covered with plastic wrap, for 1 hour. (The rest period is very important; don't rush it.)

While the dough rests, place the brown sugar, remaining 4 tablespoons anise seeds, salt, and water in a small saucepan and bring to a boil over high heat. Lower the heat to medium-low and simmer until the syrup thickens lightly, 30 to 40 minutes. Keep warm.

Take a lump of dough about the size of a walnut and roll it into a ball on a work surface. (The dough shouldn't stick, but if you wish, you may flour the work surface very lightly.) Flatten the ball with the palm of your hand and roll it with a rolling pin into a thin 7- to 7½-inch round—the thinner, the better. Let it rest for 5 minutes. If you have enough counter space, roll about half the dough and let it rest a few minutes before frying, or you can stack the rounds between sheets of waxed paper.

Heat the oil to 375°F in a deep 10-inch-wide saucepan or skillet. Add the fritters one by one to the hot oil and fry briefly, less than 1 minute on each side, until they are golden brown. Lift out with tongs and place on paper towels to drain. To serve, prop the fritters upright on a decorative serving platter or in a basket and bring to the table with the warm syrup in a pitcher.

Storing: Stored in a tightly closed container, the fritters will last for a week.

Peruvian Curled or Rosette Fritters

Ponderaciones

Fritters resembling the funnel cakes of the Pennsylvania Dutch are popular in Latin America and Spain. Known by many names, they are all crunchy and addictive, and pretty too, like large snowflakes. Unlike funnel cakes, which are made by piping batter into hot oil, most Latin fritters are made using flower-shaped frying irons lightly dipped in a flavorful batter. The Mexican frying irons have round heads with flower motifs, while the Peruvian ones have a wide spiral shape that produces curled ribbonlike fritters, eaten with *manjar blanco*, the Peruvian *dulce de leche*. Peruvian frying irons are hard to come by in the United States, but you will have no trouble finding Scandinavian rosettes, which are available in specialty cookware shops.

I love the batter of the Peruvian *ponderaciones*, airy with a touch of pisco. Stacked on a beautiful platter, they look festive and are ideal for a Christmas feast.

Cook's Note: To make sure that the batter dislodges easily from the frying iron, dip the iron lightly in the batter and twirl it gently in the hot oil.

MAKES ABOUT 24 FRITTERS

- 1 large whole egg
- 1 large egg yolk
- 1 tablespoon sugar
- 1¼ cups whole milk
- 1 tablespoon butter, melted
- 1 teaspoon ground anise seeds
- ½ teaspoon salt
- 2 tablespoons pisco or grappa
- 2 teaspoons vanilla extract
- 2 cups (about 10 ounces) all-purpose flour
- 4 cups corn oil, for frying
  Ground cinnamon, for garnish
  Confectioners' sugar, for garnish

▶ Place the whole egg, egg yolk, and sugar in a medium bowl and whisk to combine. Whisk in the milk, butter, anise, and salt. Add the pisco and vanilla. Whisk in the flour gradually until it is incorporated and the batter is smooth and free of lumps.

Place the oil in a medium saucepan and heat over medium heat until rippling. Dip the rosette iron into the hot oil and leave it there for about 30 seconds. Lift out and shake off the excess oil. Dip the rosette into the batter, making sure that only the surface of the iron touches it. Quickly dip the batter-coated rosette into the oil, swirling it around so the batter detaches from the iron. Fry the fritter until golden, about 1 minute on each side. Lift out with tongs and place on paper towels to drain. Repeat with the remaining dough. While hot, sprinkle with the cinammon and sugar.

Serving: Serve immediately, with a bowl of Peruvian *manjar blanco* (page 811), *dulce de leche* (page 809), or any of the brown loaf sugar syrups from this chapter (page 806).

ACKNOWLEDGMENTS

When you read this book, you will eat my life. *Gran Cocina Latina* is the travelogue of my expanding identity as a cook and a very personal account of how Latin American food became the core of my existence, trumping all my previous plans and unwittingly transforming me into a cook and restaurateur in the United States, the one country where all Latin cuisines have come to merge.

From the day Inés, my grandfather's cook, helped me stand on a stool to stir a pot of *congrí*, a mixture of rice and red kidney beans that had been cooking over a charcoal fire, it has been my fortune to have been mentored by wonderful Latin American home cooks across two continents. The teachings of the female cooks of my family, particularly my maternal aunts, Anita, Belén, Elena, and Carolina Parladé and my paternal grandmother, Pascuala Ferrer, made me a lover of the slow but detailed rhythms of the traditional Latin kitchen and prepared me to feel vicariously at home with similar cooks from Juarez to Patagonia. To all of them I am forever grateful.

This book is about crossovers, the taking of recipes from their home turf to a different environment to give them new life. True to my instinct as a historian, I tried to preserve vanishing traditions as faithfully as I could, but the cook in me also strove to bring accessible pleasure to the table. Helping me reach that important balance were my Latin friends in the U.S. and their families and friends in Latin America. With them I saw two sides of the same theme and learned how to re-create authentic Latin kitchens as diverse as those of Mexico, Ecuador, Venezuela, Peru, Honduras, Paraguay, and Chile in my own home kitchen in New Jersey. For being solid bridges of understanding, I acknowledge and thank the contribution of my friends María Eugenia and Oscar Baeza and their daughter Ana María Baeza from Chile; Mirza Salazar and the Solís and Ortiz families of

Cuenca, Ecuador; Cecilia Livingston, Berta Peña, and Inés Mantilla of Quito and Guayaquil, Ecuador; Nelly Guinand and Saúl Galavís of Barquisimeto and Caracas, Venezuela; Margarita Oviedo of Nicaragua; Lourdes Verea and her mother, Estela Zaragoza de Rodríguez, of Guadalajara, Mexico; sisters Rita Ruiz, Lourdes Castillo, Hilda García, and Claudia Canawuate of Barranquilla, Colombia; Jaime and Esther Gildinger, Fernando Botargues, and Natalia Machado and her mother, Nanda, all of Buenos Aires, Argentina; winemaker Laura Catena and her parents, Nicolás and Elena Catena, of Mendoza, Argentina; my Cuban-born sister-in-law Virginia Valdor and her Panamanian relatives Marcela Wright and family; my cousin Marino Menendez in Puerto Rico and his wife, Elbita, and father-in-law, Virgilio Brunet; Jorge Kawas and his mother, Mary Kawas, of Tela, Honduras; and the late Felipe Rojas-Lombardi, who gave me a chance to work and learn at The Ballroom, his creative restaurant in New York. His sister, Ana María Rojas, and his mother, Judith Lombardi de Rojas, two of the best Peruvian cooks I've known, became my Peruvian family and showed me the best of their country at a time before the age of superstar chefs.

In the course of my travels, I also met other wonderful people—restaurant chefs, home cooks, street-food vendors, chocolate makers, farmers, agronomists, scientists, food writers, even taxi drivers who cooked like three-star chefs. They opened their doors and hearts without reservations to an impossibly curious and prying stranger who taped their every word, photographed their every mood, and stuck a finger in every pot. Some of them have become dear friends, and our close connections through the years have helped me keep one foot firmly planted in the geographical Latin America and a finger on the pulse of the Latin culinary scene at all times. My profound gratitude to the following: the Velez family of Armeria, Colombia, and the Lapeira family of Barranquilla for generous hospitality and delicious food; Arlene Lutz of Costa Rica; Sinford Mejías for lessons on Garífuna Punta dancing and great recipes; Gloria Cuadras for receiving me at her lovely farm in Masaya, Nicaragua; Elena Hernández of Panama for opening windows to her country's cooking; Patricia MacCausland Gallo for sharing her secrets of Colombian cooking; chef Coco Pacheco of Santiago de Chile and Mabel Corti of Valdivia for showing me two stove-top versions of the fabled *curanto*; Sofia Chanilao of Chol-Chol for easing my way into the land of the Mapuche; Argentinean chefs Dolly Irigoyen, Francis Mallman, and Ramiro Pérez Pardo for inspired cooking, and food writer Elizabeth Checha for enlightened conversation; Juan McCloskey, Norma Caballero and the Caballero clan of Asunción, Paraguay, for their generous hospitality; Gina Nogueira and Antonio Bueno for special times in São Paulo; Dona Lucinha and her daughter Elisinha of Belo Horizonte for unforgettable lessons in the hearty cooking of Minas Gerais; Jurici Martins da Silva (aka Cacique), the best taxi driver cooking teacher of Salvador da Bahia, for showing me the heart and soul of his town.

In Xalapa, Veracruz, Raquel Torres has been a constant source of inspiration, and I thank her cooks at the Churrería del Recuerdo—Josefa Ramírez, Estela Pérez, Rosa Cadena, Olga Martínez, and Doña Estela—for patiently teaching me the inner workings of a busy Mexican restaurant. My heartfelt gratitude to the following Mexican cooks: the women embroiderers of Tzintzuntzan for their stories and recipes; Francisca de la Luz Cortés in Uricho; marvelous Carmen Barnard and Livier Ortíz in Morelia; Marylyn Tausend, for opening many doors; Silvio Campos, for making the best *pibil* of the Yucatán; Doña Lala for generous hospitality at her lovely restaurant in colorful Tlacotalpan; and to her friend Doña Luz del Carmen Valenzuela de Rojas, the owner of La Bilbaína restaurant in Veracruz, for wonderful recipes.

Everywhere I went in Venezuela doors opened and cooking pots sizzled. My thanks to Jorge Redmond, the president of Chocolates El Rey, for first introducing me to his country. In Caracas, Chilean-born food writer and peerless cook Miro Popiç became my guide to Venezuelan and Chilean foods. My gratitude to Miro, his wife, Yolanda, and his children, Maikel and Veronika, for becoming my Venezuelan family and offering me their lovely home at El Hatillo as my center of operations. Special thanks to agronomists Humberto and Lilian Reyes for many wonderful meals in cacao country and to my cacao business partners and friends Silvino Reyes and Ana Karina Flores for their warm hospitality. My thanks to Beatriz Escobar and her sister Consuelo, for many fantastic meals in the plains of Barinas and Guanare, and to brilliant Helena Ibarra, for giving me private lessons and feeding me with enormous flair and panache in Caracas. Special thanks to Ercole D'Addazio and his son Leo, for their contributions to Venezuelan cooking in Puerto Ordaz. My thanks and admiration to food historians Manuel Scannone, José Rafael Lovera, and José Cartay for their wisdom and detailed recipes.

In Ecuador, another South American country I have come to know intimately because of cacao, I met many accomplished cooks and food lovers who traveled with me to show me their country's varied cuisine. My thanks to Patricia León of Ciudad Cacau in Guayaquil, for sharing her decades-long experience with coastal cuisine, and the Cancedo family of Vinces, for showing me life and cooking in an old cacao plantation. In Quito I enjoyed the generous hospitality of Carla Barboto and Santiago Peralta, founders of Pacari Chocolate, and toured many cacao-growing regions with Santiago in search of iconic local foods and ingredients. Susana Polo Eljuri, Santiago's mother, is an accomplished Cuenca cook who gave me unforgettable lessons in southern Ecuadorian cooking and terrific recipes that I can't stop making. Though I never met her, I also learned much about the food of southern Ecuador from a legendary Cuenca cook named Eulalia Vintimilla, the author of the book *Secretos de la Cocina Cuencana* (Secrets of Cuenca Cooking). My thanks to Juan Vintimilla for talking to me about his late mother. My gratitude to talented chef Edgar León for his fantastic tastings of traditional Ecuadorian with a modern sensibility. My thanks also to Chef Sebastián Villavicencio, who is doing justice to Ecuadorian ingredients, and to Carlos Gallardo, president of the Ecuadorian Chef's Association, who is doing a marvelous and admirable job researching local culinary traditions.

Translating recipes from twenty Latin American countries to a U.S. kitchen was not an easy task, but it was possible for me because of the hard work and friendship of my long-time assistants Paloma Ramos Lestón and Mirza Salazar. Natalia Machado, an Argentinean chef who came to work with me on the final stages of the book, eventually became a sous chef at my restaurant Cucharamama during its first year. My gratitude to the friends who often came to the rescue and put long hours in the kitchen testing recipes: Rita Ruiz, Virginia Willis, Tamara Holt, Miriam Cordova, and the irrepressible and much-missed Shirley King.

My wide-eyed innocence about cookbook writing was soon shaken by my editor, Maria Guarnaschelli. Maria asked questions that had never occurred to me. Because of her, I had to look deeper and longer into every aspect of the great Latin American cuisines. Our relationship—often as dialectical as the *sic et non* arguments of medieval scholastics, often as tempestuous as an act of *Aida*—ultimately made this book stronger, and for that she will have my undying gratitude. Through it all Maria shared my belief in the book. An author could never hope to find a more formidable and brave champion. This book is ours.

My deep thanks to the W. W. Norton team. Melanie Tortoroli, Maria's assistant, had an amazing grasp of detail and an even and cheerful disposition that made working with her a pleasure. Anna Oler kept the book on schedule, while Susan Sanfrey patiently sifted through several versions of the manuscript, always asking the right questions, to make this lengthy book seem seamless.

Having my food captured on camera by the husband and wife team of Gentl and Hyers was a dream of mine. I admire their pictorial, Vermeer-like understanding of light and composition and thank them for their respect for the beauty of Latin food.

I have no words to thank my friend and fellow medievalist Anne Mendelson. Her knowledge of the subject matter and her keen eye for detail proved invaluable in copyediting the entire book. Her friendship and solidarity as well as her dedication to completing this monumental task with accuracy and elegance deserve my most profound respect and gratitude. Special thanks also to my friend Marc Aronson, a historian and prolific writer, and his wife, novelist Marina Budhos, for critiquing several versions of the manuscript and offering valuable comments.

To the people closest to me, my deep thanks for their support during the many years I invested in working on this book. To my father, my appreciation and love for caring about my progress. My thanks to my business partner, Clara Chaumont, for understanding what this book would mean for our lives and work. Finally, my deepest gratitude and unending love to my husband, Alejandro Presilla, for fully supporting my efforts during every stage of this project.

INDEX

For Index to Recipes in Spanish, see page 896.
For notes, bibliography, and sources, visit grancocinalatina.com.

INDEX TO RECIPES IN SPANISH

A NOTE ABOUT THE AUTHOR

MARICEL E. PRESILLA is the chef and co-owner of Zafra and Cucharamama, two Latin restaurants in Hoboken, New Jersey. She was named 2012 Best Chef in the Mid-Atlantic Region by the James Beard Foundation. She writes a weekly food column for the *Miami Herald* and has contributed articles to *Saveur*, *Food & Wine*, *Food Art*, and *Gourmet*. Maricel holds a doctorate in medieval Spanish history from New York University and lives in Weehawken, New Jersey.